LITERARY CRITICISM INDEX

by

Alan R. Weiner
Spencer Means

The Scarecrow Press, Inc.
Metuchen, N.J. and London
1984

Library of Congress Cataloging in Publication Data

Weiner, Alan R., 1938–
  Literary criticism index.

  Includes index.
  1. Literature--History and criticism--Indexes.
2. English literature--History and criticism--Indexes.
3. American literature--History and criticism--Indexes.
I. Means, Spencer. II. Title.
Z6511.W44 1984   016.809   84-1371
[PN523]
ISBN 0-8108-1694-6

RR 10-19-85

CONTENTS

PREFACE

There has long been a need for an index to the numerous bibliographies and checklists which provide quick and easy access to criticism of a specific work of literature. Using these bibliographies effectively frequently requires a knowledge of the work's genre, the period in which it was written, and/or the nationality of the author, as well as the criteria (and quirks) of individual compilers, who may treat a novel as a short story, a story as a novel, a verse drama as a poem, etc. Often the student cannot supply all the needed information, and a librarian, even one trained in literature, may have to consult reference works before deciding which tool is appropriate. Even if one bibliography is located, others which would also be useful may be missed. It is hoped that the <u>Literary Criticism Index</u> will increase the convenience and effectiveness of these useful bibliographic tools.

Works indexed include multiple-author bibliographies in which criticism of individual works is separately listed or in which annotations make it possible to determine exactly which work or works are being discussed. Bibliographies in which there is neither a breakdown by title nor annotations are excluded.

Certain bibliographies contain, in addition to individual author listings, general surveys of the literature with references to criticism scattered throughout the text. We have selected from these sources only those

references which clearly identify either general criticism of a specific author or criticism of an individual work.

Compilation of the _Literary Criticism Index_ was not without problems. Discrepancies in authorship of particular works were found in some bibliographies. Titles in translation varied from work to work. Diacritical marks were found in some sources but were omitted in others. Capitalization practices with respect to unemphatic prepositions, conjunctions, and articles, also varied.

The format used by some publishers, in which entire titles appear in upper-case, presented particular problems. This practice made it impossible to distinguish novels and dramas from brief works such as short stories and poems, a distinction the authors had chosen to make in this index. Moreover, variations from rules governing the use of capital letters in English and foreign language titles could not be determined.

Some bibliographies entered collaborative works under each author's name with occasional differences in works cited. It is suggested, therefore, that the researcher consult author and/or title indices in each of the bibliographies, if available, to be sure all pertinent information is obtained.

Since the main purpose of the _Literary Criticism Index_ is to aid librarians in identifying sources of literary criticism, we did very little to modify or correct references appearing in the bibliographies and checklists. The comparative nature of the indexing led, however, to the discovery of a number of obvious mistakes, and where possible these have been corrected through verification in national bibliographies and biographical dictionaries. Undoubtedly, some undetected errors have been perpetuated here. Of course, the authors accept full responsibility for their own errors.

It is hoped that the _Literary Criticism Index_ will fulfill a long-standing need and enable the librarian to save much time and effort in searching for criticial material. The authors gratefully accept suggestions

which would increase the value of future editions or supplements.

INTRODUCTION

Arrangement of the <u>Literary Criticism Index</u> is alphabetical by author with anonymous works preceding the alphabet. References to "General" criticism of a specific author are followed by references to criticism of the author's individual works, alphabetically arranged. Collaborative works follow the works of a single author in a new alphabetical sequence.

Each entry includes a symbol or symbols and page references directing the researcher to appropriate volumes containing citations to critical works. Consult the "Key to Symbols" for a complete bibliographic description of the source indexed.

Author Entries

Main entry is generally the name most often used by the author in the most complete form located. Alternate names are entered with "see" references. Transliterated foreign names are usually given in the form most commonly encountered, with "see" references where necessary. Birth and death dates are provided only to distinguish between authors having the same name.

Title Entries

For works not originally in English, English titles are preferred. The original title as well as alternate Eng-

lish titles are then given in brackets if they have been used in the bibliographies indexed. "See" references are provided from such titles in translation and variant titles only when they do not fall in alphabetical proximity to the preferred title. "See also" references are provided for those titles which appear in the bibliographies under more than one author.

Literary Forms

Quotation marks are used to designate short stories and poems. Titles of novels and plays do not appear in quotation marks.

KEY TO SYMBOLS

C AAF Margolies, Edward. <u>Afro-American Fiction, 1853-1976: A</u> <u>Guide to Information Sources.</u> Detroit: Gale Research Company, 1979.

C AAL Peavy, Charles D. <u>Afro-American Literature and Culture</u> <u>Since World War II: A Guide to Information Sources.</u> Detroit: Gale Research Company, 1979.

C AAPD French, William P. <u>Afro-American Poetry and Drama, 1760-</u> <u>1975: A Guide to Information Sources.</u> Detroit: Gale Research Company, 1979.

C AAW Turner, Darwin T. <u>Afro-American Writers.</u> New York: Appleton-Century-Crofts, 1970.

no AD Meserve, Walter J. <u>American Drama to 1900: A Guide to</u> <u>Information Sources.</u> Detroit: Gale Research Company, 1980.

ADC Eddleman, Floyd Eugene. <u>American Drama Criticism: In-</u> <u>terpretations 1890-1977.</u> 2nd Edition. Hamden, Conn.: Shoe String Press, 1979.

C AF Kirby, David K. <u>American Fiction to 1900: A Guide to</u> <u>Information Sources.</u> Detroit: Gale Research Company, 1975.

C Ai Aitken, William Russell. <u>Scottish Literature in English</u> <u>and Scots: A Guide to Information Sources.</u> Detroit: Gale Research Company, 1982.

no AL Andrews, Barry G. <u>Australian Literature to 1900: A</u> <u>Guide to Information Sources.</u> Detroit: Gale Research Company, 1980.

no ALL Koster, Donald N. <u>American Literature and Language: A</u> <u>Guide to Information Sources.</u> Detroit: Gale Research Company, 1982.

AN   Gerstenberger, Donna. The American Novel, 1789-1959: A Checklist of Twentieth-Century Criticism. Denver: Alan Swallow, 1961.

AP   Yannella, Donald. American Prose to 1820: A Guide to Information Sources. Detroit: Gale Research Company, 1979.

APC   Brier, Peter A. American Prose and Criticism, 1900-1950: A Guide to Information Sources. Detroit: Gale Research Company, 1981.

ASF   Weixlman, Joe. American Short-Fiction Criticism & Scholarship, 1959-1977: A Checklist. Chicago: Swallow Press, 1982.

Ba   Barker, Arthur E. The Seventeenth Century: Bacon Through Marvell. Arlington Heights, Illinois: AHM Publishing Corp., 1979.

BAF   Fairbanks, Carol. Black American Fiction: A Bibliography. Metuchen, N.J.: Scarecrow Press, 1978.

BALE   Lindfors, Bernth. Black African Literature in English: A Guide to Information Sources. Detroit: Gale Research Company, 1979.

BAP   Arata, Esther Spring. Black American Playwrights, 1800 to the Present: A Bibliography. Metuchen, N.J.: Scarecrow Press, 1976.

BAW   Rush, Theressa Gunnels. Black American Writers Past and Present: A Biographical and Bibliographical Dictionary. 2 Vols. Metuchen, N.J.: Scarecrow Press, 1975.

Be   Beasley, Jerry C. English Fiction, 1660-1800: A Guide to Information Sources. Detroit: Gale Research Company, 1978.

BN   Watt, Ian. The British Novel: Scott Through Hardy. Northbrook, Illinois: AHM Publishing Corp., 1973.

BN2   Wiley, Paul L. The British Novel: Conrad to the Present. Northbrook, Illinois: AHM Publishing Corp., 1973.

Bon   Bond, Donald F. The Age of Dryden. Northbrook, Illinois: AHM Publishing Corp., 1970.

Br   Breed, Paul F. Dramatic Criticism Index: A Bibliography of Commentaries on Playwrights from Ibsen to the Avant-Garde. Detroit: Gale Research Company, 1972.

n o   CFAE   Rosa, Alfred F. Contemporary Fiction in America and Eng-
              land, 1950-1970: A Guide to Information Sources. De-
              troit: Gale Research Company, 1976.

n o Cla   Clark, Harry Hayden. American Literature: Poe Through
              Garland. New York: Appleton-Century-Crofts, 1971.

✓ CN   Adelman, Irving. The Contemporary Novel: A Checklist   R EF
              of Critical Literature on the British and American Novel   Z
              Since 1945. Metuchen, N.J.: Scarecrow Press, 1972.   1 2 3 |
                                                                         o F 4 A 3 4

C Da   Davis, Richard Beale. American LIterature Through Bry-
              ant: 1585-1830. New York: Appleton-Century-Crofts,
              1969.   R 1 2 2 5
                                         2 D 3
                                                                         R E F
✓ DC1   Coleman, Arthur. Drama Criticism, Volume One: A Check-   Z
              list of Interpretation, Since 1940 of English and American 1 2 3 |
              Plays. Denver: Alan Swallow, 1966.   . 0 7
                                                                         C 6
                                                                         V |
✓ DC2   Coleman, Arthur. Drama Criticism, Volume Two: A Check-   R E F 1 2 3 |
              list of Interpretation Since 1940 of Classical and Con-   2 D 7 C 6
              tinental Plays. Chicago: Swallow Press, 1971.   . J. 2

n o Du   Dunn, Richard J. The English Novel: Twentieth Century
              Criticism: Volume I, Defoe Through Hardy. Chicago:
              Swallow Press, 1976.

C EC   Bond, Donald F. The Eighteenth Century. Northbrook,   2 2 0 1 3
              Illinois: AHM Publishing Corp., 1975.   . B 6 3

C ECL   Moyles, R. G. English-Canadian Literature to 1900: A
              Guide to Information Sources. Detroit: Gale Research
              Company, 1976.   R 1 3 7 5 . M 6 8

C ED   Penninger, F. Elaine. English Drama to 1660: A Guide
              to Information Sources. Detroit: Gale Research Com-
              pany, 1976.   R 2 2 0 1 4 . 0 7 P 4 6

✓ EDC   Palmer, Helen H. European Drama Criticism, 1900-1975.   R E F
              Hamden, Conn.: Shoe String Press, 1977.   2
                                                                        5 7 8 |
                                                                        . P 2
n o EDT   Conolly, Leonard W. English Drama and Theatre, 1800-   1 9 7 7
              1900: A Guide to Information Sources. Detroit: Gale
              Research Company, 1978.

✓ EN   Bell, Inglis F. The English Novel, 1578-1956: A Check- R E F
              list of Twentieth-Century Criticisms. Denver: Alan   2 2 0 1 4
              Swallow, 1958.   . F 5 B 4 4
                                                                       1 9 7 4

✓ ENE   Palmer, Helen H. English Novel Explication: Criticisms R E F
              to 1972. Hamden, Conn.: Shoe String Press, 1973.   2 2 0 1 4
                                                                       . F 5 P 2 6

xiv / Key to Symbols

ENES1   Abernethy, Peter L. English Novel Explication, Supplement I. Hamden, Conn.: Shoe String Press, 1976.

ENES2   Kloesel, Christian J. W. English Novel Explication, Supplement II. Hamden, Conn.: Shoe String Press, 1981.

EP   Anderson, Emily A. English Poetry, 1900-1950: A Guide to Information Sources. Detroit: Gale Research Company, 1982.

ERP   Harner, James L. English Renaissance Prose Fiction, 1500-1660: An Annotated Bibliography of Criticism. Boston: G. K. Hall, 1978.

Fi   Fitzgerald, Louise S. The Continental Novel: A Checklist of Criticism in English, 1967-1980. Metuchen, N.J.: Scarecrow Press, 1983.

Fog   Fogle, Richard Harter. Romantic Poets and Prose Writers. Northbrook, Illinois: AHM Publishing Corp., 1967.

Hen   Heninger, S. K. English Prose, Prose Fiction, and Criticism to 1660: A Guide to Information Sources. Detroit: Gale Research Company, 1975.

Ho   Holman, C. Hugh. The American Novel Through Henry James. 2nd Edition. Arlington Heights, Illinois: AHM Publishing Corp., 1979.

HR   Perry, Margaret. The Harlem Renaissance: An Annotated Bibliography and Commentary. New York: Garland Publishing, Inc., 1982.

ICBAP   Cline, Gloria Stark. An Index to Criticisms of British and American Poetry. Metuchen, N.J.: Scarecrow Press, 1973.

JW   Nadel, Ira Bruce. Jewish Writers of North America: A Guide to Information Sources. Detroit: Gale Research Company, 1981.

Ke   Kearney, E. I. The Continental Novel: A Checklist of Criticism in English, 1900-1966. Metuchen, N.J.: Scarecrow Press, 1968.

LCAB   Seidel, Alison P. Literary Criticism and Authors' Biographies: An Annotated Index. Metuchen, N.J.: Scarecrow Press, 1978.

Li   Link, Frederick M. English Drama, 1660-1800: A Guide to Information Sources. Detroit: Gale Research Company, 1976.

C   LJCD   Logan, Terence P. The Later Jacobean and Caroline Dramatists: A Survey and Bibliography of Recent Studies in English Renaissance Drama. Lincoln, Nebraska: University of Nebraska Press, 1978.

C   Log   Logan, Terence P. The Popular School: A Survey and Bibliography of Recent Studies in English Renaissance Drama. Lincoln, Nebraska: University of Nebraska Press, 1975.

C   Lon   Long, E. Hudson. American Drama from Its Beginnings to the Present. New York: Appleton-Century-Crofts, 1970.

Ma   Magill, Frank N. Magill's Bibliography of Literary Criticism: Selected Sources for the Study of More Than 2,500 Outstanding Works of Western Literature. Englewood Cliffs: Salem Press, 1979.

MAP   Day, A. Grove. Modern Australian Prose, 1901-1975: A Guide to Information Sources. Detroit: Gale Research Company, 1980.

MBA   Arata, Esther Spring. More Black American Playwrights: A Bibliography. Metuchen, N.J.: Scarecrow Press, 1978.

MBD   Carpenter, Charles A. Modern British Drama. Arlington Heights, Illinois: AHM Publishing Corp., 1979.

MD   Adelman, Irving. Modern Drama: A Checklist of Critical Literature on 20th Century Plays. Metuchen, N.J.: Scarecrow Press, 1967.

MDAE   Harris, Richard Hough. Modern Drama in America and England, 1950-1970: A Guide to Information Sources. Detroit: Gale Research Company, 1982.

Me   Mell, Donald C., Jr. English Poetry, 1660-1800: A Guide to Information Sources. Detroit: Gale Research Company, 1982.

Mi   Mikhail, E. H. English Drama, 1900-1950: A Guide to Information Sources. Detroit: Gale Research Company, 1977.

MP   Altieri, Charles F. Modern Poetry. Arlington Heights, Illinois: AHM Publishing Corp., 1979.

Ne   Nevius, Blake. The American Novel: Sinclair Lewis to the Present. New York: Appleton-Century-Crofts, 1970.

NI   Logan, Terence P. The New Intellectuals: A Survey and Bibliography of Recent Studies in English Renaissance Drama. Lincoln, Nebraska: University of Nebraska Press, 1977.

OMEP   Beale, Walter H. Old and Middle English Poetry: A Guide to Information Sources. Detroit: Gale Research Company, 1976.

PE   Kuntz, Joseph M. Poetry Explication: A Checklist of Interpretation Since 1925 of British and American Poems Past and Present. Boston: G. K. Hall, 1980.

Po   Pownall, David E. Articles on Twentieth Century Literature: An Annotated Bibliography, 1954 to 1970. New York: Kraus-Thomson Organization Limited, 1973.

PS   Logan, Terence P. The Predecessors of Shakespeare: A Survey and Bibliography of Recent Studies in English Renaissance Drama. Lincoln, Nebraska: University of Nebraska Press, 1973.

Re   Reiman, Donald H. English Romantic Poetry, 1800-1835: A Guide to Information Sources. Detroit: Gale Research Company, 1979.

Ri   Rice, Thomas Jackson. English Fiction, 1900-1950: General Bibliography and Individual Authors, Aldington to Huxley: A Guide to Information Sources. Detroit: Gale Research Company, 1979.

Ri2   Rice, Thomas Jackson. English Fiction, 1900-1950: Individual Authors, Joyce to Woolf: A Guide to Information Sources. Volume 2 of 2 Volume Set. Detroit: Gale Research Company, 1983.

SC   Lievsay, John L. The Sixteenth Century: Skelton Through Hooker. Northbrook, Illinois: AHM Publishing Corp., 1968.

Sch   Schlueter, Paul. The English Novel: Twentieth Century Criticism: Volume II, Twentieth Century Novelists. Chicago: Swallow Press, 1982.

SFC   Thurston, Jarvis. Short Fiction Criticism: A Checklist of Interpretation since 1925 of Stories and Novelettes (American, British, Continental), 1800-1958. Denver: Alan Swallow, 1960.

TA   Lauterbach, Edward S. The Transitional Age: British Literature, 1880-1920. Troy, N.Y.: Whitston, 1973.

TMAP   King, Kimball. <u>Ten Modern American Playwrights: An Annotated Bibliography.</u> New York: Garland Publishing, Inc., 1982.

TMBP   King, Kimball. <u>Twenty Modern British Playwrights: A Bibliography, 1956-1976.</u> New York: Garland Publishing, Inc., 1977.

TMIP   King, Kimball. <u>Ten Modern Irish Playwrights: A Comprehensive Annotated Bibliography.</u> New York: Garland Publishing, Inc., 1979.

TSD   Ribner, Irving. <u>Tudor and Stuart Drama.</u> Second Edition. Arlington Heights, Illinois: AHM Publishing Corp., 1978.

VP   Buckley, Jerome H. <u>Victorian Poets and Prose Writers.</u> 2nd Edition. Arlington Heights, Illinois: AHM Publishing Corp., 1977.

Wa   Walker, Warren S. <u>Twentieth-Century Short Story Explication: Interpretations 1900-1975, of Short Fiction Since 1800.</u> Third Edition. Hamden, Conn.: Shoe String Press, 1977.

WaS1   Walker, Warren S. <u>Twentieth-Century Short Story Explication. Supplement I to Third Edition.</u> Hamden, Conn.: Shoe String Press, 1980.

WIL   Allis, Jeannette B. <u>West Indian Literature: An Index to Criticism, 1930-1975.</u> Boston: G. K. Hall, 1981.

Wo   Woodress, James. <u>American Fiction, 1900-1950: A Guide to Information Sources.</u> Detroit: Gale Research Company, 1974.

ANONYMOUS
Abencerraje y de la hermosa
Jarifa, La historia del
Ke: 205
Abraham and Isaac DC1: 11
Adam DC1: 11
"Adam Lay I-bowdyn" PE: 2
"Advent" PE: 2
Agnes Tragedie Christienne
DC2: 1
"Almsgiving" OMEP: 113;
PE: 2
"Als I Lay up-on a Nith"
PE: 2
"Alysoun" PE: 2
"Amis and Amiloun" OMEP:
288
The Ancient, True, and Ad-
mirable History of Patient
Grisel ERP: 77
The Ancrene Riwle Hen: 16-
17
"Andreas" ICBAP: 1; OMEP:
75
Andromana; or, The Mer-
chant's Wife LJCD: 226-
227
Apollonius of Tyre Hen: 147
Arden of Feversham DC1:
11; ED: 201, 273; PS:
240-252
Arichandra DC2: 1
"Assembly of Ladies" ICBAP:
1; OMEP: 397
"At a Sprynge-wel under a
Thorn" PE: 2
"Athelston" OMEP: 284
Aucassin and Nicolette
Ma: 2178-2179
Auto de los Reyes Magos
see Los Reyes Magos
"The Awntyrs off Arthure at
the Terne Wathelyne"
OMEP: 271
"Azarias" OMEP: 113-114
A Banquet of Jests or Change
of Cheare ERP: 84
"The Bargain of Judas"
PE: 2
The Batchelars Banquet: Or

A Banquet for Batchelars
(Sometimes ascribed to
Thomas Dekker) ERP: 86
"Battle of Brunanburh" ICBAP:
1; OMEP: 61; PE: 2-3
"The Battle of Maldon" ICBAP:
1; OMEP: 61-62; PE: 3
Bay Psalm Book Da: 49
Beowulf ICBAP: 1-2; Ma:
2179-2180; OMEP: 64-70;
Po: 1301-1302
"Bevis of Hampton" Ma: 2180-
2181; OMEP: 284-285
"Bird with Four Feathers"
ICBAP: 2
The Birth of Merlin DC1: 11
Blanchardyn and Eglantine
see Caxton, William [trans.]
"Blodles and Bonles, Blod Has
Nou Bon" PE: 3
The Bloody Banquet DC1: 11
"Blow, Northerne Wynd" PE:
3
"The Body and the Soul"
OMEP: 224
Le Bone Florence of Rome
OMEP: 288
The Brome see Abraham and
Isaac
"Brussels Cross" OMEP: 137
The Buik of Alexander Ai: 29
"Bytuene Mersh and Aueril"
PE: 3
Caesar's Revenge DC1: 11-12
Il Capricco DC2: 1
"The Captain of Banditti: A
True Story" WaS1: 7
Captain Thomas Stukeley
Log: 162-166
Cardenio DC1: 12; ED: 200
"The Carle off Carlyle"
OMEP: 276
The Castle of Preservation
DC1: 12
The Cestus DC1: 12
Charlemagne; or The Distracted
Emperor Log: 181-183
"Charms" OMEP: 133
Chihamba, The White Spirit
DC2: 1

1

"The Child of Snow" ASF:
58-59
"Christ I," Lyric 4 PE: 3
"Christ I," Lyric 7 PE: 3
"Christ I," Lyric 9 PE: 3
"Christ and Satan" ICBAP:
2; OMEP: 95; PE: 4
Christ Led Up to Calvary
DC1: 12
"Christ Makith to Man a Fair
Present" PE: 4
"Clariodus" OMEP: 289
Claudius Tiberius Nero DC1:
12; NI: 317-318
"Cleanness" see "Purity"
Cloria and Narcissus ERP:
112
Clyomon and Clamydes DC1:
12
The Cobler of Caunterburie
ERP: 113-114
Comedia Thebayda see
Thebayda
Common Conditions DC1: 12
The Complaynt of Scotland
Ai: 38
The Concept Br: 1
Confrere de la Passion DC2:
1
The Contention between Lib-
erality and Prodigality
NI: 309-311
The Contention--Betwixt the
Houses of York and Lan-
caster DC1: 12; ED:
289-290
"The Corpus Christi Carol"
OMEP: 383; PE: 4
The Costly Whore LJCD: 213
"Crabbed Age and Youth"
PE: 4
"Cristes Milde Moder, Seynte
Marie" ["On God Ureisun
of Ure Lefde"] PE: 4
"Cursor Mundi" OMEP: 241-
242
The Cyprian Conqueror; or,
The Faithless Relict
LJCD: 227
"Dame Sirith and the Weeping
Bitch" PE: 4
"Daniel" DC2: 1; ICBAP:
2; OMEP: 96; PE: 4
"De Clerico et Puella" PE:
4
"Death and Liffe" OMEP:
369
"The Death of Edgar" PE: 4
Death of Lucretia see La Mort
de Lucresse
The Deceyte of Women ERP:
124
"Deor" OMEP: 80-81; PE: 4
"The Descent into Hell" ["Har-
rowing of Hell"] OMEP:
114-115; PE: 4
"The Desperate Negroe" ASF:
59
Dick of Devonshire LJCD:
218-219
"Distichs of Cato" OMEP: 234
"Dives at Pauper" Hen: 148
Dobson's Drie Bobs (Sometimes
ascribed to George Dobson)
ERP: 150-151; Hen: 170-
171
"Dream of the Rood" ICBAP:
2; OMEP: 104-105; PE: 5
Le Droit du Seigneur DC2: 1
Drowazagno DC2: 2
"Durham" OMEP: 137
"Edi Beo thu, Heuene Quene"
PE: 5
Edmond Ironside; or War Hath
Made All Friends DC1:
12-13; Log: 160-162
"Edward" PE: 5
Edward III DC1: 13; ED:
200; PS: 207-215
"Eglamour of Artois" OMEP:
289
Elche see Misterio d'Elig
Elckerlijc DC2: 2
"Emaré" OMEP: 296
The Epic of Gilgamesh Ma:
2181
"Erthe toc of erthe" PE: 5
Every Woman in Her Humour
NI: 319-320
Everyman DC1: 13; Ma:
2181-2182
"Exeter Book--Advent Lyric
VII" ICBAP: 2
"Exeter Book--Gnomic Verses"
ICBAP: 2
"Exeter Book--Riddle 60"
ICBAP: 2
"Exeter Book--Riming Poem"
ICBAP: 2
"Exeter Book--Wulf and Ead-
wacer" ICBAP: 2
Exeter Riddle 1, "Storm"

("Hwylc Is Haeleth a thaes
Horsc") PE: 5
Exeter Riddle 2, "Storm"
("Hwilum Ic Gewite") PE:
6
Exeter Riddle 3, "Storm"
("Hwilum Mec Min Frea")
PE: 6
Exeter Riddle 5, "Shield"
("Ic Eom Anhaga Iserne
Wund") PE: 6
Exeter Riddle 7, "The Swan"
("Hraegl Min Swigath")
PE: 6
Exeter Riddle 16, "The
Anchor" ("Oft Ic Sceal
With Waege Winnan") PE:
6
Exeter Riddle 20, "Sword"
("Ic Eom Wunderlicu Wiht,
on Gewin Scaepen")
OMEP: 130; PE: 6
Exeter Riddle 25, "Onion"
("Ic Eom Wunderlicu Wiht,
Wifum of Hyte") PE: 6
Exeter Riddle 39 ("Gewritu
Secgath thaet Seo Wiht
Sy") PE: 6
Exeter Riddle 45, "Dough"
("Ic on Wincle Gefraegn")
PE: 6
Exeter Riddle 47, "Book
Moth" or "Bookworm"
("Mothe Word Fraet")
PE: 6
Exeter Riddle 60 ("Ic Waes
Be Sonde") OMEP: 130;
PE: 6
Exeter Riddle 61 ("Oft Mec
Faeste Bileac") PE: 6
Exeter Riddle 72, "Ox" ("Ic
Waes Lytel") PE: 6
Exeter Riddle 74 ("Ic Waes
Faemne Geong") PE: 7
Exeter Riddle 75 ("Ic Swiftue
Geseah") PE: 7
Exeter Riddle 85, "Fish and
River" ("Nis Min Sele
Swige") PE: 7
Exeter Riddle 91 ("Min Heafod
Is...") PE: 7
Exeter Riddle 95 ("Ic Eom
Indryhten") PE: 7
"Exodus" ICBAP: 2; OMEP:
96-97; PE: 7
"The Eye and the Heart"

OMEP: 226
Fair Em PS: 216-218
The Fair Maid of Bristow Log:
214-216
The Fair Maid of the Exchange
Log: 120, 200-204
The Fairy Knight; or Oberon
the Second LJCD: 223-224
The Faithful Friends Log:
247-249
The Famous Historie of Fryer
Bacon, Also the Manner of
His Death ERP: 162
The Famous History of George
a Green, Pindar of the
Town of Wakefield [George
a Greene] ED: 202; ERP:
163-164
The Famous Victories of Henry
V DC1: 14; ED: 201;
PS: 169-176
Farce de Maistre Pierre Pathe-
lin see Pierre Pathelin
La Fausse Auberge DC2: 2
"Finnsburg Fragment" OMEP:
71
The First Part of the Reign of
Richard II: or Thomas of
Woodstock DC1: 14
"For Ou that Is So Feir ant
Brist" PE: 7
Fort Joyeuse de Pernet DC2:
2
"The Fortunes of Men" OMEP:
137; PE: 7
The Four Cardinal Virtues
DC1: 14
"Fowles in the Frith" ICBAP:
2; OMEP: 383; PE: 7
"Frankie and Johnny" PE: 7
Frederyke of Jennen ERP:
486-487
"Gabriel, Fram Evene-King"
PE: 7
Gammer Gurton's Needle
DC1: 14
"Genesis A" ICBAP: 3;
OMEP: 97-98
"Genesis B" OMEP: 98; PE:
7
George a Greene see The
Famous History of George
a Greene, Pindar of the
Town of Wakefield
"A Gest of Robyn Hode"
PE: 2

Gesta Romanorum Hen: 149
The Ghost; or, The Woman
    Wears the Breeches LJCD:
    225
"The Gifts of Men" OMEP:
    138; PE: 8
Gismond of Salerne see
    Wilmot, Robert
"Glade Us Maiden, Moder
    Milde" PE: 8
Gl' Ingannati DC2: 2
Glorious Resurrection of Our
    Lord DC2: 2
"Gnomic Verses" (Cotton
    Manuscript) ICBAP: 3
"Golagrus and Gawain" OMEP:
    271
"Gold and Al This Werdis
    Wyn" PE: 8
"Goosey-Goosey-Gander"
    PE: 8
Gorboduc see Norton, Thomas
"The Grand Old Duke of
    York" PE: 8
"The Grave" PE: 8
Le Gros Lot de Marseille
    DC2: 2
The Gude of Godlie Ballatis
    Ai: 39
"Guthlac" ICBAP: 3; OMEP:
    106-107
"Guy of Warwick" Ma: 2182;
    OMEP: 285-286
"Haile Be Thu, Mari, Maiden
    Bright" PE: 8
"Harrowing of Hell" see
    "The Descent into Hell"
"Havelock the Dane" ["Have-
    lock"] Ma: 2182-2183;
    OMEP: 286
"He Bare Him Vp, He Bare
    Hym Down" PE: 8
"He3e [sic] Louerd, Thou
    Here My Bone" PE: 8
"He Yaf Himself as Good
    Felowe" PE: 8
"Herodes, Thou Wikked Fo"
    PE: 8
"Heyl Be Thou, Marie, Milde
    Quene of Hevene" PE:
    8
Hickscorner DC1: 14
Hierarchomachia; or, The
    Anti-Bishop LJCD: 220
The Historie of the Damnable
    Life and Deserved Death

of Doctor John Faustus (Eng-
    lish trans. by P.F.) ERP:
    154-160
The History of Reynard the Fox
    see Caxton, William (Trans.)
"Homiletic Fragment I" (Vercelli
    Book) PE: 8
L'Homme, La Femme, Le Cure
    DC2: 3
How a Man May Choose a Good
    Wife from a Bad Log: 204-
    207
A Hundred Merry Tales ERP:
    104-105
"The Hunting of the Cheviot"
    PE: 8
"The Husband's Message"
    OMEP: 81-82; PE: 8-9
"I Am a Fol, I Can No God"
    PE: 9
"I Am Iesu, That Cum to Fith"
    PE: 9
"I Have Laborede Sore and Suf-
    fered Dey3th" PE: 9
"I Sayh Hym With Fless all Bi-
    sprad" PE: 9
"I Sing of a Myden" PE: 9
"I Wende to Dede" PE: 9
"Ich Am of Irlaunde" PE: 9
"Iesu Cristes Milde Moder"
    PE: 9
"Ihesu for Thy Holy Name"
    PE: 9
"In a Valey of this Restles
    Mynde" PE: 9
"Ipomadon" OMEP: 290
"Jacob and Joseph" PE: 9
Jagerin Diana see Die Ver-
    liebte Jagerin Diana
Jeu D'Adam see Mystere d'Adam
John of Bordeux see also
    Greene, Robert DC1: 14
"Johnie Armstrong" PE: 9
Joseph and His Brothers DC2:
    3
"Joseph and Sophia" ASF: 59
Joshua ED: 201
"Judas" ED: 201; PE: 10
"Judgment Day I" PE: 10
"Judgment Day II" OMEP:
    116; PE: 10
"Judith" ICBAP: 3; OMEP:
    76; PE: 10
Kaumudimahotsava DC2: 3
"Kemp Owyne" PE: 10
The Kidnapped Clergyman, or

Experience the Best Teach-
er ADC: 32
King Darius DC1: 14
"King Horn" Ma: 2184;
OMEP: 287
King Leir DC1: 14; ED:
201; PS: 219-226
A Knack to Know a Knave
DC1: 14-15; ED: 242-243;
PS: 281-287; TSD: 86
A Knack to Know an Honest
Man Log: 149-150
Kusein DC2: 3
"Kyng Alisaunder" OMEP:
282-283
The Lamentable Tragedy of
Locrine see Locrine
"The Land of Cockaygne"
OMEP: 217; PE: 10
A Larum for London; or The
Siege of Antwerp Log:
167-170
Lazarillo de Tormes Fi:
221-223; Ke: 206-208;
Ma: 2184-2186
"Lenten Ys Come With Loue
to Toune" PE: 10
"Ler to Louen as I Loue The"
PE: 10
"Leuedi Sainte Marie, Moder
and Meide" PE: 10
"Levedi, for Thare Blisse!
That Thu Heddest at the
Frume" PE: 10
"Libeaus Desconus" OMEP:
272-273
The Libel of English Policy
OMEP: 399
El libro del caballero Cifar
Fi: 223-224; Ke: 209
The Life and Death of Jack
Straw DC1: 15; PS:
252-258
"The Lion and the Unicorn"
PE: 10
Little Clay Cart see Sud-
raka, King
"Little Jack Horner" PE: 10
"Little Miss Muffet" (Mother
Goose) PE: 10
Locrine [The Lamentable
Tragedy of Locrine]
DC1: 15; ED: 200, 202;
PS: 258-272
"London Lickpenny" PE: 10
The London Prodigal Log:

220-224
Look About You Log: 171-174
"Lord Randall" PE: 10-11
"Louerd Thu Clepedest Me"
PE: 11
"Lovely Tear from Lovely Eye"
(or "Thu Sikest Sore")
PE: 11
Love's Changelings' Change
LJCD: 221
Lucretia DC2: 3
"Luf Es Lyf that Lastes Ay"
PE: 11
Lust's Dominion; or, the Las-
civious Queen DC1: 15;
Log: 48, 184-188
The Mabinogion Ma: 2186
The Mahabharata Ma: 2187
"Maiden in the Moor Lay"
["Maid of the Moor" or
"Moor Maiden"] OMEP:
383-384; PE: 11
The Maid's Metamorphosis NI:
305-308
Maistre Pierre Pathelin see
Pierre Pathelin
"Man in the Moon" PE: 11
Mankind DC1: 15
The Marriage of Wit and Science
DC1: 15
Mary of Nimmegen ERP: 246
"Maxims I" OMEP: 121; PE:
11
"Maxims II" OMEP: 121; PE:
11
"Menoloqium" OMEP: 138
Merry Devil of Edmonton
DC1: 15; Log: 209-213
Merry Tales, Witty Questions,
and Quick Answers ERP:
481-482
"Metaphysics of Bear Hunting"
ASF: 59
"Methingkit" PE: 11
"Metrical Epilogue to the
Pastoral Care" PE: 11
"Middelerd for Mon Wes Mad"
PE: 11
"The Middle Lomb Isprad o
Rode" PE: 11
Miracles de Nostre Dame DC2:
3
"Mirie It Is While Sumer Ilast"
PE: 11
The Miseries of Enforced Mar-
riage see Wilkins, George

Misogonus ED: 202
Misterio D'Elig DC2: 3
La Mort de Lucresse DC2: 3
"Le Morte Arthur" OMEP: 274-276
Mucedorus PS: 227-230
Mucedorus and Amadine DC1: 16
Mystere D'Adam DC2: 4
The Nature of the Four Elements DC1: 16
"Naueth My Saule Bute Fur and Ys" PE: 11
"Needy Knife-Grinder" (from the "Anti-Jacobin") ICBAP: 3
"The Negro" ASF: 59
Nero LJCD: 216
"New Morality" (from the "Anti-Jacobin") ICBAP: 3
The Nibelungenlied Ma: 2187-2188
Nice Wanton DC1: 16
Niemand und Jemand DC2: 4
Nobody and Somebody, with the True Chronicle History of Elydure Log: 226-229
"Nou Goth Sonne Under Wod" PE: 12
"Nou Sprinkes the Sprai" PE: 12
"Nou Sprinketh Rose ant Lylie Flour" PE: 12
"Nu this Fules Singet Hand Maket Hure Blisse" PE: 12
"Nutbrowne Mayde" PE: 12
"Ny Yh She Blostme Sprynge" PE: 12
"O Western Wind" PE: 12
Oberammergau DC2: 4
"Octavian" OMEP: 291
"Of a Rose, A Lovely Rose" PE: 12
Of Gentleness and Nobility see Rastell, John
"On God Ureisun of Ure Lefde" see "Cristes Milde Moder, Seynte Marie"
"On the Author" PE: 12
1 Jeronimo, with the Wars of Portugal Log: 216-220
I Richard II see Thomas

of Woodstock
"The Order of the World" OMEP: 138; PE: 12
"Owl and the Nightingale" ICBAP: 3; OMEP: 226-228
The Palmerin cycle Ke: 212-213
Palmerin D'Oliva see Munday, Anthony (translator)
"The Parlement of the Thre Ages" OMEP: 370; PE: 12
The Partial Law DC1: 16; LJCD: 217
La Pasion DC2: 4
"The Passionate Man's Pilgrimage" PE: 12
"Pastoral Care, Epilogue to" ICBAP: 3
Los Pastores DC2: 4-5
"Patience" ICBAP: 3; OMEP: 347; PE: 12-13
"Pearl" ICBAP: 3; OMEP: 348-351
Le Petit-Maistre de Campagne DC2: 5
Philander King of Thrace LJCD: 219
The Philosopher see Wit's Triumvirate
Philotus DC2: 5; NI: 315-317
"Phoenix" ICBAP: 3; OMEP: 108
"Physiologus" OMEP: 109
Pierce the Ploughman's Crede OMEP: 371
Pierre Pathelin DC2: 5
The Pinder of Wakefield ERP: 380-381
Planctus Mariae DC2: 5
Play of the Sacrament DC1: 16
Poem of the Cid Ma: 2188-2189
"Praise the Lord, Ye Heavens Adore Him" PE: 13
"A Prayer" PE: 2
"Preface to the Pastoral Care" OMEP: 139
"Pricke of Conscience" OMEP: 243
"Proverbs of Alfred" OMEP: 235
The Puritan, or The Widow of Watling Street ED: 200
"Purity" ["Cleanness"] OMEP:

351- 352
"Quanne Hic Se on Rode"
PE: 13
Queen of Lydia DC2: 6
Rabinal DC2: 6
The Rare Triumphs of Love
and Fortune PS: 162-164
Read and Wonder LJCD: 226
La Reina Penitente DC2: 6
"Resignation" OMEP: 117;
PE: 13
Revenge for Honor DC1: 16
The Revenger's Tragedy see
Tourneur, Cyril
Los Reyes Magos DC2: 6
"The Rhyming Poem" ["Riming
Poem"] OMEP: 139; PE:
13
"Riddles" OMEP: 129-130
Les Rivaux D'Eux-Memes
DC2: 6
"Roberd of Cisyle" OMEP:
291
"Rolliad" ICBAP: 3
"The Ruin" OMEP: 82; PE:
13
"St. Erkenwald" ICBAP: 3;
OMEP: 352-353; PE: 13
Salbenkramerspiel DC2: 6
Santa Dorothea DC2: 6
"Satire Against the Black-
smiths" PE: 13
"Seafarer: ICBAP: 4; OMEP:
82- 83, 85- 86; PE: 13-14
"The Search for the Lost Hus-
band" PE: 14
The Second Maiden's Tragedy
see Middleton, Thomas
The Second Report of Doctor
John Faustus ERP: 402
Selimus see Greene, Robert
"The Seven Sages of Rome"
OMEP: 217-218
"Shoot False Love I Care Not"
PE: 14
"Singular Recovery from
Death" ASF: 59
"Sir Degare" OMEP: 297-
298
"Sir Degrevant" OMEP:
292-293
Sir Gawain and the Green
Knight ICBAP: 4; Ma:
2189-2191; OMEP: 353-
357
"Sir Isumbras" OMEP: 293

"Sir Orfeo" OMEP: 299; PE:
14
"Sir Patrick Spens" PE: 14
"Sir Perceval of Galles" OMEP:
276- 277
"Sir Tristrem" OMEP: 277
"Sodenly Afraide/Half-Waking,
Half-slepyng" PE: 15
Soliman and Perseda PS:
231- 239
Solomon and Saturn OMEP:
140
"Somer Soneday" OMEP: 218
"Something Unaccountable"
ASF: 59
The Song of Roland Ma: 2191-
2192
"Song of the Husbandman"
PE: 15
"Soul and Body I" OMEP: 118
"Soul's Address to the Body"
ICBAP: 4
"Stod Ho There Neh" PE: 15
"Stond Wel, Moder, Vnder
Rode" PE: 15
"The Story of the Captain's
Wife, and An Aged Woman"
ASF: 59
"Suete Sone, Reu on Me, &
Brest Out of Thi Bondis"
PE: 15
"Summer Is Icumen In" PE:
15
"Sunset on Calvary" ICBAP:
4
"Swarte-Smekyd Smethes,
Smateryd wyth Smoke"
PE: 15
Swetnam the Woman-Hater Ar-
raigned by Women LJCD
210-212
"Taillah" ASF: 59
"Tale of an Incestuous
Daughter" OMEP: 218
Tales and Quick Answers
ERP: 481-482
"Tam Lin" PE: 15
The Taming of a Shrew DC1:
17; ED: 201, 290; PS:
194-205
Tarlton's News Out of Purga-
tory ERP: 484-485
Tchrimekundan DC2: 6
The Telltale LJCD: 224-225
"That Lovely Lady Sat and
Song" PE: 15

Thebayda DC2: 6
"Ther Is No Rose of Swych
Vertu" PE: 15
"Thirty Days Hath September"
PE: 15
Thomas Lord Cromwell see
The True Chronicle History
of Thomas Lord Cromwell
"Thomas of Ersseldoune"
OMEP: 414
Thomas of Woodstock [I Rich-
ard II] see also Wood-
stock DC1: 17; PS: 288-
301
"Thomas Rymer" PE: 16
The Thracian Wonder Log:
174-175
The Three Maries DC1: 17
"The Three Ravens" PE: 16
"Thureth" OMEP: 140
Tom Tyler and His Wife
DC1: 17
The Tragedies of Claudius
Tiberius Nero see
Claudius Tiberius Nero
The Tragedy of Alphonsus
Emperor of Germany Log:
153-157
The Tragical History of Guy
Earl of Warwick PS: 310-
311
The Trail of Treasure DC1:
18
The Travails of Three English
Brothers DC1: 17
The Trial of Chivalry Log:
198-200
Tristan and Isolde Ma: 2192-
2193
The Troublesome Reign of
King John (I & II) DC1:
18; ED: 201; PS: 177-189
The True Chronicle History
of Thomas Lord Cromwell
[Thomas Lord Cromwell]
ED: 200; Log: 190-194
The True Tragedy of Richard
Duke of York ED: 289-
290
The True Tragedy of Richard
III DC1: 18; PS: 272-
280
De Truwanten DC2: 6
"The Turke and Gowin"
OMEP: 278
"The Twa Corbies" PE: 16

The Two Noble Ladies and the
Converted Conjurer LJCD:
215
"Vainglory" OMEP: 118; PE:
16
Valentine and Orson Hen:
151
The Valiant Scot LJCD: 222
The Valiant Welshman; or, The
True Chronicle History of
the Life and Valiant Deeds
of Caradoc the Great Log:
245-246
Le Veillard Supplante DC2: 7
Die Verliebte Jagerin Diana
DC2: 7
La vida y hechos de Estebanillo
González see González,
Esteban
Virgilius ERP: 504-505
Vlomek Hry Divadelne Na
Umuceni Pane DC2: 7
"Vndo Thi Dore, My Spuse
Dere" PE: 16
"The Vox and the Wolf" OMEP:
219
"Waldere" OMEP: 71-72
"Wanderer" ICBAP: 4; OMEP:
83-86; PE: 16-17
"Wanne Mine Eyhnen Misten"
PE: 17
A Warning for Fair Women
DC1: 18; Log: 176-180
The Wars of Cyrus PS: 193
The Wasp LJCD: 220
"A Wayle Whyte ase Whalles
Bon" PE: 17
The Weakest Goeth to the Wall
DC1: 18; Log: 195-197
"Weep You No More, Sad Foun-
tains" PE: 17
"Wel, Qwa Sal Thir Hornes
Blau" ICBAP: 4; PE: 17
"Wen the Turuf Is Thi Tuur"
PE: 17
"Western Wind, When Wilt Thou
Blow" PE: 17-18
Westward for Smelts ERP:
508
"When Thi Hed Whaketh" PE:
18
When You See Me You Know
Me ED: 201
"Widsith" OMEP: 72
"The Wife of Usher's Well"
PE: 19

"Wife's Lament" (Exeter Book)
ICBAP: 4; OMEP: 87-88;
PE: 18-19
"William of Palerne" OMEP:
294
Wily Beguilded DC1: 18-19;
ED: 201; NI: 311-315
"The Wind of the Moor" PE:
19
The Wisdom of Doctor Dody-
poll NI: 303-305
The Wit of a Woman Log:
224-225
"With Faerstice" PE: 19
Wit's Triumvirate; or The
Philosopher DC1: 19;
LJCD: 221
"Wonder of Creation" PE: 19
Woodstock see also Thomas
of Woodstock DC1: 19
"Worldes Blisce, Haue God
Day" PE: 19
"Wulf and Eadwacer" OMEP:
88-89; PE: 19
"Wy Have Ye No Reuthe on
My Child?" PE: 19
"Wynnere and Wastoure"
OMEP: 371-372; PE: 19
"Wynter Wakeneth al My Care"
ICBAP: 4; PE: 19-20
The Yorkshire Tragedy
DC1: 19; ED: 200-201;
Log: 230-237
"Young Waters" ICBAP: 4;
PE: 20
"Ywain and Gawain" OMEP:
278
AE [pseud.] see RUSSELL,
George William
A., L. [translator]
The Seventh [Eighth] Books
of the Myrrour of Knight-
hood by Diego ORTUNEZ
DE CALAHORRA ERP: 69
ABAILARD, Pierre [Peter
ABELARD]
General LCAB: 1
ABBE, George
General Po: 1
ABBOTT, George
Ladies' Money ADC: 1
Sweet River ADC: 1
_____ and Leon ABRAHAMS
Heat Lightning ADC: 1
_____, Richard ADLER, and
Will HOLT

Music Is MBA: 1
_____ and Ann Preston BRIDGERS
Coquette ADC: 1
_____ and Philip DUNNING
Broadway ADC: 1
Lilly Turner ADC: 1
_____ and John Cecil HOLM
Three Men on a Horse ADC: 2
_____ and Frank LOESSER
Where's Charley? ADC: 2
_____ and George MARION Jr.
Beat the Band ADC: 2
_____ and Robert MERRILL
New Girl in Town ADC: 2
_____, Richard RODGERS, and
Lorenz HART
The Boys from Syracuse ADC:
3
_____, Betty SMITH, Arthur
SCHWARTZ, and Dorothy
FIELDS
A Tree Grows in Brooklyn
ADC: 3
ABDULLAH, Mohammed Ben
General BALE: 243
ABE, Kobo
The Woman in the Dunes Ma:
1
ABEL, Lionel
General MDAE: 47-48
Absalom Br: 1; DC1: 19;
MDAE: 47-48
The Death of Odysseus MDAE:
47
The Pretender DC1: 19;
MDAE: 48
Wives ADC: 3
ABELL, Kjeld
General Br: 1; MD: 19
Anna Sophie Hedvig EDC: 1
Days on a Cloud [Dage paa en
sky] Br: 1; EDC: 1
Den Blaa Pekingeser EDC: 1
Eva Serves Her Time as a
Child [Eva Aftjener Sin
Barnepligt] EDC: 1
Judith EDC: 1
Kameliadamen EDC: 1
The Melody That Got Lost
[Melodien Der Blev Vaek]
EDC: 1
The Scream EDC: 1
Silkeborg EDC: 1
Vetsera Blomster Ikke for
Enhver EDC: 2
ABELLIO, Raymond

General Po: 1
ABERCROMBIE, Lascelles
General Mi: 214; TA: 79
ABERNATHY, Robert
"Hostage of Tomorrow"
  WaS1: 1
ABISH, Walter
"Minds Meet" ASF: 42
ABOUT, Edmond
Germaine Ke: 15; Fi: 1;
  Po: 1851
Tolla Ke: 15
ABRAHAMS, Peter
General BALE: 244-247;
  Po: 1-2; WIL: 1
Mine Boy BALE: 245-246;
  LCAB: 1; WIL: 2
A Night of Their Own WIL:
  3
The Path of Thunder BALE:
  246; WIL: 1
Return to Goli BALE: 244;
  WIL: 2
Tell Freedom WIL: 2
This Island Now BALE:
  244-246; WIL: 3-4
Wild Conquest BALE: 245;
  WIL: 1-2
A Wreath for Udomo BALE:
  244-247; Br: 1; WIL:
  2-3
ABRAMHOFF, Sharyn
Carytids ADC: 3
ABRAMS, Thomas
"And When I Die Be Sure to
  Let Me Know" WaS1: 1
ABRUQUAH, Joseph Wilfred
General BALE: 247
ABSE, Dannie
General MDAE: 51
ACAZ, Mba
The Ambassadors MBA: 1
ACCIUS
Brutus DC2: 7
ACEVEDO Hernandez, Antonio
General Br: 1
ACHARD, Marcel
General Br: 2; MD: 19;
  Po: 2
La Belle Marinière Br: 2
Le Corsaire Br: 2
Domino Br: 2; MD: 19
La Femme en Blanc Br: 2
Jean de la Lune Br: 2
ACHEBE, Chinua
General BALE: 249-262;

CFAE: 25; LCAB: 1; Po:
  2-3
"Akeuke" WaS1: 1
Arrow of God BALE: 250, 252,
  254-260, 262
"Civil Peace" BALE: 251;
  WaS1: 1
"Dead Man's Path" WaS1: 1
"Girls at War" BALE: 251,
  261; WaS1: 1
"The Madman" WaS1: 1
A Man of the People BALE:
  255, 259, 262
"Marriage Is a Private Affair"
  WaS1: 1
No Longer at Ease BALE:
  251-252, 256-260, 262; Po:
  2
"The Sacrificial Egg" Wa: 1;
  WaS1: 1
Things Fall Apart BALE:
  249-254, 256-261; CFAE:
  25-26; LCAB: 1; Po: 3
"Uncle Ben's Choice" WaS1:
  1
"Vengeful Creditor" WaS1: 1
"The Voter" WaS1: 1
ACHONU, Oguike
General BALE: 262
ACHTERBERG, Gerrit
General Po: 3
ACKLAND, Rodney
General MDAE: 52
ACORN, Milton
General Po: 4
ACQUAYE, Saka
General BALE: 263
ADAM, Alfred
La Fugue de Caroline Br: 2
ADAMOV, Arthur
General Br: 3; LCAB: 1;
  MD: 19; Po: 4-5
All Against All [Tous Contre
  Tous] Br: 3; EDC: 2
As We Were [Comme Nous
  Avons Été] Br: 3
L'Aveu DC2: 7; EDC: 2
The Direction of the March
  [The Meaning of the Way;
  Le Sens de la Marche]
  Br: 4; EDC: 2
The Great and the Small
  Maneuver [La Grande et
  la Petite Manoeuvre] Br:
  4; EDC: 2; MD: 19
The Invasion [L'Invasion]

Br: 4; DC2: 7; EDC: 2;
MD: 19-20
The Meaning of the Way see
  The Direction of the March
Off Limits EDC: 2
Paolo Paoli Br: 4; EDC: 2;
  MD: 20
The Parody [Le Parodie]
  Br: 5; EDC: 3; MD: 20
Ping Pong [Le Ping-Pong]
  Br: 5; DC2: 7; EDC: 3;
  MD: 20
Printemps 71 see Spring 71
Le Professeur Taranne Br:
  5; EDC: 3; MD: 20
The Recoveries [Les Retrou-
  vailles] Br: 5
Le Sens de la Marche see
  The Direction of the March
Spring 71 [Printemps 71]
  Br: 5; EDC: 3; Po: 4
Tous Contre Tous see All
  Against All
ADAMS, Alger Le Roy [Philip
  B. KAYE]
  General BAF: 1; BAW: 20
  Taffy BAF: 1; BAW: 20
ADAMS, Andy
  General ASF: 42
  The Corporal Segundo" ASF:
  42
  "The Passing of Peg-Leg"
  ASF: 42
ADAMS, Arthur Henry
  General AL: 100-101
  The Wasters AL: 101
ADAMS, Clayton
  General BAF: 2; BAW: 20
ADAMS, Francis
  General AL: 104-105
  A Child of the Age AL: 105
ADAMS, Henry
  General ALL: 31-34; AN:
  7; APC: 52-54; Cla:
  10-12; Ho: 132-133;
  LCAB: 1; Po: 5-11
  Democracy AN: 7; Ho:
  132-133; Po: 10-11
  The Education of Henry
  Adams ALL: 32, 34;
  APC: 53; Cla: 10-12;
  Ma: 2-3; Po: 5, 11-14
  Esther Ho: 132-133; Po:
  6-7, 10-11, 14
  History of the United States
  ALL: 34; Po: 7, 14-15

Letters of Henry Adams
  LCAB: 1
Mont-Saint-Michel and Chartres
  ALL: 32-34; APC: 53-54;
  Cla: 10; Po: 5, 10, 14-15
Prayer to the Virgin of Chartres
  Po: 16
ADAMS, John
  General AP: 164-169; Da:
  61-62
  Autobiography Da: 61
  A Defense of the Constitutions
  of Government of the United
  States of America, 1787-
  1788 AP: 166-169
  Diary Da: 61
  Diary and Autobiography AP:
  165, 168
  Discourse on Davila AP: 166-
  167
  Thoughts on Government AP:
  167
ADAMS, John Quincy
  General AP: 171-172; Da:
  106
  Lectures on Rhetoric and Ora-
  tory AP: 172
ADAMS, Léonie
  General Po: 16
ADAMS, Levi
  General ECL; 107-108
ADAMS, Richard
  Watership Down ENES2: 1
ADAMS, Robert Simson
  "I Am No Prince of Darkness,
  Lord of Sorrow" PE: 1
ADAMS, Samuel Hopkins
  General AN: 8
  Revelry AN: 8
ADAMSON, Joy
  General LCAB: 1
ADDERLEY, Cannonball
  General MBA: 1
  Big Man--The Legend of John
  Henry MBA: 1
ADDISON, Joseph
  General EC: 46-48; LCAB:
  2; Li: 91-92
  The Campaign EC: 47
  Cato DC1: 19; EC: 47; Li:
  91; Ma: 4
  The Drummer DC1: 19; Li:
  92
  The Sir Roger de Coverly
  Papers Ma: 4-5
  The Spectator EC: 47-48;

Ma: 5-7
The Tatler Ma: 7-8
ADE, George
General APC: 24-26; ASF:
42-43; LCAB: 2; Lon: 55;
Po: 16-17
"Effie Whittlesy" ASF: 42
"The Two Mandolin Players
and the Willing Performer"
ASF: 42
ADELL, Ilung [William Adell
STEVENSON, III]
Sanford and Son MBA: 2
ADELUGBA, Dapo
General BALE: 263
ADLINGTON, William [translator]
The XI Bookes of the Golden
Asse with the Marriage
of Cupido and Psiches by
APULEIUS ERP: 74-75
ADY, André
General Po: 17-18
AELFRIC
Catholic Homilies Hen: 14
Lives of the Saints Hen:
14-15
AESCHYLUS
General LCAB: 2
Agamemnon see also Ores-
teia DC2: 7-12; EDC:
3-4; LCAB: 2; Ma: 9-10
Ajax DC2: 12
Choephoroi see also Ores-
teia; The Libation Bearers
DC2: 12-14
Danaid see also Egyptians;
Suppliants DC2: 14
Egyptians DC2: 14
Eumenides see also Oresteia
DC2: 14-16; EDC: 4-5
Glaukos Pontios DC2: 16
Libation Bearers see also
Choephoroi EDC: 5; Ma:
10
The Net-Haulers DC2: 16
Niobe DC2: 16
Oresteia see also Agamem-
non; Choephoroi; and
Eumenides DC2: 16-20;
EDC: 5-7; LCAB: 2;
Ma: 10-11; TMAP: 191
The Persians [Persae]
DC2: 20-21; EDC: 7-8;
Ma: 11-12
Prometheus Bound [Prome-
theia] DC2: 21-25;

EDC: 8-10; LCAB: 2;
Ma: 12-13
Seven Against Thebes [Septem
Contra Thebas] DC2: 25-
26; EDC: 10-11; Ma: 13-
14
The Suppliants [Supplices]
DC2: 26-27; EDC: 11;
Ma: 14
AESOP
Aesop's Fables Ma: 15
AFINOGENOV, Alexander Niko-
laevich
General Br: 5; MD: 20
Fear [Strakh] Br: 6; DC2:
28; MD: 20
Listen Professor [Mashenka]
MD: 20
On the Eve Br: 6
AGEE, James
General AN: 8; APC: 94-97;
ASF: 44; CFAE: 27-29;
CN: 21; LCAB: 2; Po:
18-19
"Bound for the Promised Land"
WaS1: 2
"Boys Will Be Brutes" ASF:
43; WaS1: 2
"Death in the Desert" ASF:
43; WaS1: 2
A Death in the Family APC:
96; CFAE: 28-29; CN:
21-22; Ma: 16-17; Po: 19-
20
"Dedication day" ASF: 43;
WaS1: 2
"Dream Sequence" ASF: 43
"The House" WaS1: 2
Let Us Now Praise Famous Men
APC: 95-97; Ma: 17; Po:
21
"The Morning Watch" APC:
94, 96; ASF: 43; CFAE:
29; CN: 22; Po: 21; Wa:
1; WaS1: 2
"A Mother's Tale" ASF: 43;
Wa: 1; WaS1: 2
"1928 Story" ASF: 43; Wa:
1
"Six Days at Sea" Wa: 1
"Sunday: Outskirts of Knox-
ville, Tenn." PE: 1
"They That Sow in Sorrow
Shall Reap" ASF: 43;
WaS1: 2
"The Waiter" Wa: 1

"The Waiting" ASF: 44
"A Walk Before Mass" ASF:
    44; Wa: 1; WaS1: 2
"Wall" WaS1: 2
AGNON, Shmuel Yosef
    General Po: 21-22
    "Agunot" Wa: 1; WaS1: 2
    "And the Crooked Shall Be
        Made Straight" Wa: 1
    "The Ascent of the Soul"
        Wa: 1
    "Ascents and Descents" Wa:
        2
    "At Hemdat's: Wa: 2
    "At the Death of Tsadik"
        Wa: 2
    "At the Entrance of the Day"
        Wa: 2
    "The Banished One" Wa: 2
    "Beneath the Tree" Wa: 2
    "The Betrothal Oath" ["Be-
        trothed"] Wa: 2
    "The Candles" Wa: 2
    En el corazón de los mares
        Po: 21
    "The Dead Child" Wa: 2
    "A Different Face" Wa: 2
    "A Different Talit" Wa: 2
    "The Doctor and His Divorcée"
        Wa: 2
    "The Document" Wa: 2
    "Edo and Enam" Po: 21;
        Wa: 2; WaS1: 2
    "Eternal Peace" Wa: 2
    "The Face and the Image"
        Wa: 2
    "Fathers and Sons" Wa: 3
    "Fernheim" Wa: 3
    "Forevermore" Wa: 3
    "Friendship" Wa: 3
    "From Dwelling to Dwelling"
        Wa: 3
    "From Heaven" Wa: 3
    "The Garment" Wa: 3
    "Hemdat" Wa: 3
    "The Home" Wa: 3
    "Honoring Father" Wa: 3
    "The House" Wa: 3; WaS1:
        2
    Huésped para una noche
        Po: 21
    "In the Forest and in the
        City" Wa: 3
    "In the Heart of the Seas"
        Wa: 3
    "In the Noontide of Her

    Day" Wa: 3
    Juramento de fidelidad Po: 21
    "The Kerchief" Wa: 3
    "The Kidnappers" Wa: 3
    "Kipurim" Wa: 3
    "Knots" Wa: 3
    "The Last Bus" Wa: 4; WaS1:
        2
    "Lawlessness" Wa: 4
    "The Legend of the Scribe"
        Wa: 4
    "The Letter" Wa: 4; WaS1:
        2
    "Like David They Fashioned
        Themselves Musical Instru-
        ments" Wa: 4
    "Metamorphosis" Wa: 4
    "Miriam's Well" Wa: 4
    "The Month of Tishre" Wa: 4
    "Nights" Wa: 4
    Nur wie ein Gast zur Nacht
        Po: 22
    "Offerings for the Dead" Wa:
        4
    "On One Rock" Wa: 4
    "On the Road" Wa: 4
    "On the Tora" Wa: 4
    "One Night" Wa: 4
    "The Orchestra" Wa: 4
    "Ovadia the Cripple" Wa: 4
    "The Paths of Righteousness"
        Wa: 4
    "The Sense of Smell" Wa: 5
    "Sheepfolds" Wa: 5
    "The Soil of Erets Yisrael"
        Wa: 5
    "The Song That Was Sung"
        Wa: 5
    "The Tale of a Goat" Wa: 5
    "Tehilah" Wa: 5
    "Thus Far" Wa: 5
    "To Father's House" Wa: 5
    "To the Doctor" Wa: 5
    "Twofold" Wa: 5
    "A Whole Loaf" SFC: 7; Wa:
        5; WaS1: 2
    "With Our Youth and With Our
        Aged" Wa: 5
AGUILAR, Gaspar
    Los Amigos Enojados DC2: 28
    La Venganza Honroso DC2:
        28
AGUILERA Malta, Demetrio
    General Br: 6
AGUIRRE, Isadora
    General Br: 6

AGUNWA, Clement
  General BALE: 264
AGUSTI, Ignacio
  General Po: 22
  Mariona Rebull Ke: 179
  El viudo rius Ke: 179
AGUSTINI, Delmira
  General Po: 22
AHLIN, Lars
  Bark and Leaves Fi: 400
  Cinnamon Girl Fi: 400
  "Coming Home to Be Nice"
    WaS1: 3
  The Great Amnesia Fi: 400
  If, About, Around Fi: 400
  My Death Is My Own Fi:
    400
  Night in the Market Tent
    Fi: 400
  "No Eyes Await Me" WaS1:
    3
  Normal Course Fi: 400
  Pious Murders Fi: 400
  "Squeezed" WaS1: 3
  A Stove of One's Own Fi:
    400
  Tabb with the Manifesto
    Fi: 400
  "The Wonderful Nightgown"
    WaS1: 3
AHMED, Iqbar
  "The Grandmother" Wa: 5
  "Time to Go" Wa: 5
AICHINGER, Ilse
  General Po: 22
  "The Bound Man" Po: 22;
    Wa: 6
  "Eliza, Eliza" Wa: 6
  "Spiegelgeschichte" Wa: 6
AIDOO, Ama Ata [Christina]
  General BALE: 265-266
  Dilemma of a Ghost BALE:
    265
  "Everything Counts" Wa: 6
  "A Gift from Somewhere"
    Wa: 6
  "In the Cutting of a Drink"
    Wa: 6
  "No Sweetness Here" Wa: 6
  "Something to Talk About on
    the Way to the Funeral"
    Wa: 6
  "Two Sisters" Wa: 6
AIG-IMOUKHUEDE, Frank
  General BALE, 266
AIKEN, Conrad

General ALL: 34; AN: 8;
    ASF: 45; ICBAP: 1;
    LCAB: 2; Ma: 18; Ne:
    15; Po: 22-24
  The Coming Forth by Day of
    Osiris Jones Po: 1971-1972
  "The Crystal" PE: 1
  "The Dark City" Wa: 6
  "Dead Leaf in May" ICBAP:
    1; PE: 1; Po: 24
  "Gehenna" ASF: 44; SFC:
    7
  "Impulse" ASF: 44; Wa: 6;
    WaS1: 3
  "The Last Visit" ASF: 44
  "Life Isn't a Short Story"
    ASF: 44; SFC: 7; Wa: 7
  "Mr. Arcularis" ASF: 44;
    Br: 6; Po: 24-25; SFC:
    7; Wa: 7
  "Morning Song from 'Senlin'"
    PE: 1
  "No, No, Go Not to Lethe"
    Wa: 7
  "The Professor's Escape" Wa:
    7
  Sheepfold Hill Po: 25
  "Silent Snow, Secret Snow"
    ASF: 45; Po: 25-26; SFC:
    7; Wa: 7
  "South End" PE: 1
  "Spider, Spider" ASF: 45;
    Wa: 7
  "Strange Moonlight" ASF: 45;
    Po: 26; SFC: 7; Wa: 7-8
  "Sursum Corda" PE: 1
  Ushant Po: 26
  The Voyage Between Po: 26-
    27
AIKEN, George L.
  Uncle Tom's Cabin ADC: 4
AINSWORTH, William Harrison
  General BN: 13; Du: 1
  Cardinal Pole ENES1: 1
  The Constable of the Tower
    ENES1: 1
  The Fall of Somerset ENES1:
    1
  Jack Sheppard Du: 1;
    ENES1: 1
  Old Saint Paul's ENES2: 1
  Rookwood Du: 1; ENES1: 1
  Tower Hill ENES1: 1
  The Tower of London ENES1:
    1; ENES2: 1
  Windsor Castle ENES1: 1

AJAJI, Afolabi
  Dream on Monkey Mountain
    BAP: 1
AJAMU
  The Brass Medallion MBA: 2
AKENSIDE, Mark
  General EC: 48-49; Me:
    103-105
  "A British Philippic" Me:
    105
  "Ode on the Winter Solstice"
    PE: 1
  "Ode to the Evening Star"
    Me: 104
  The Pleasures of the Imagina-
    tion EC: 48-49; Me:
    103-105
AKHMATOVA, Anna
  General Po: 27
AKINS, Zoë
  General MD: 20
  Daddy's Gone A-Hunting
    ADC: 4
  Déclassée ADC: 4
  The Furies ADC: 4
  Magical City ADC: 4
  The Moon-Flower ADC: 4;
    MD: 20
  Mrs. January and Mr. Ex
    ADC: 4-5; MD: 20
  O Evening Star ADC: 5
  The Old Maid ADC: 5
  A Royal Fandango ADC: 5
  Thou Desperate Pilot ADC:
    5; MD: 20
AKINSEMOYIN, Kunle
  General BALE: 267
AKPAN, Ntieyong Udo
  General BALE: 267
AKSAKOV, Sergey
  Family Chronicles Ke: 369
AKSENOV, Vasilij
  General Po: 27
  "Halfway to the Moon" Wa:
    8
  "It's Time" Wa: 8
  "Little Whale" Wa: 8
  "Oddball" Wa: 8
  "Oranges from Morocco" Wa:
    8
  "Papa, What Does It Spell?"
    Wa: 8
  Ticket to the Stars Ke:
    369
  "The Victory" Wa: 8
AKUTAGAWA, Ryunosūke

General Po: 28
  "The Fires" WaS1: 3
  "The Spider's Thread" Wa: 8
  "Ways of the Philippes" WaS1:
    3
AKYEA, E. Ofori
  General BALE: 267
ALAIN see CHARTIER, Emile
    Auguste
ALAIN-Fournier
  General Po: 1113-1115
  Colombe Blanchet Ke: 15
  Le Grand Meaulnes Fi: 1-2;
    Po: 1114-1115
  La Maison dans la foret Ke:
    15
  Miracles Ke: 15
  The Wanderer Ke: 15-16
ALARCON, Juan Ruiz de
  La Cueva de Salamanca DC2:
    28
  El Dueno de las Estrellas
    DC2: 28
  La Paredes Oyen [Walls Have
    Ears] DC2: 28
  La Verdad Sospechosa DC2:
    28
ALARCON, Pedro Antonio de
  El capitán Veneno Fi: 189;
    Ke: 179
  El escándalo Fi: 189; Ke:
    179
  El extranjero Ke: 179
  El final de Norma Fi: 189
  El niño de la bola Fi: 189;
    Ke: 179
  La pródiga Fi: 189; Ke:
    179
  The Three-Cornered Hat [El
    sombrero de tres picos]
    Fi: 189; Ke: 179; Ma: 19
  La ultima calaverada Fi: 189
ALAS, Leopoldo (Clarín)
  Antonio Azorin Fi: 190
  Doña Berta Fi: 190
  Una mediania Fi: 190
  La regenta Fi: 190; Ke:
    179-180
  Su unico hijo Fi: 190; Ke:
    180
  Supercheria Fi: 190
  Teresa DC2: 28
ALBA, Nanina
  General BAF: 2; BAW: 23
ALBEE, Edward
  General ALL: 34-36; Br:

6-8; LCAB: 2-3; Lon: 22-23; MD: 20-21; MDAE: 55-62; Po: 28-32; TMAP: 16-88

All Over ADC: 5; TMAP: 16, 40, 42-43, 49-50, 55, 59, 88-89; TMBP: 235

The American Dream ADC: 6; Br: 8-9; DC1: 20; Ma: 20-21; MD: 21; Po: 30, 32; TMAP: 16, 25, 31-32, 36, 39, 41-44, 46-47, 54, 56, 60, 63, 65-66, 68-71, 75, 82-84, 86, 89-91

The Ballad of the Sad Café ADC: 6-7; ALL: 35-36; Lon: 23; Ma: 21; MDAE: 56; Po: 32; TMAP: 20, 29, 36, 71, 91-92

Bartleby TMAP: 88, 90, 92

Box-Mao-Box ADC: 7; ALL: 35-36; Br: 9; MDAE: 57-58; TMAP: 26, 32, 42, 44-45, 62, 64, 79, 83,93-94; TMBP: 185

Counting the Ways ADC: 7-8; TMAP: 42, 94

The Death of Bessie Smith ADC: 8; Br: 10; Lon: 23; Ma: 21-22; MD: 21; MDAE: 62; Po: 32; TMAP: 25, 27, 30, 32, 36, 46, 56, 60, 67, 71, 74-75, 77-78, 88, 90, 94

A Delicate Balance ADC: 8-9; ALL: 34-36; Br: 10; Ma: 22-23; MDAE: 56, 58, 61; Po: 33; TMAP: 19-23, 26, 30-32, 44, 60, 64, 71, 73-74, 77, 81, 86, 89, 94-96; TMBP: 144

Everything in the Garden ADC: 9-10; Br: 10; MDAE: 56, 59; TMAP: 21-22, 25, 61, 74, 96-97

Fam and Yam Br: 11; TMAP: 88, 97

The Lady from Dubuque TMAP: 98

Listening ADC: 10; TMAP: 42, 98-99

Lolita TMAP: 53, 99-100

Malcolm ADC: 10; ALL: 35-36; Br: 11; MDAE: 56; Po: 29; TMAP: 65, 100-101

Quotations from Chairman Mao Tse-tung ADC: 10; ALL: 35-36; Br: 11; MDAE: 57-58, 60; TMAP: 26, 42, 79, 84, 93-94

The Sandbox ADC: 10; Br: 11; DC1: 20; Po: 29; TMAP: 27-28, 46-47, 56, 60, 65, 75, 88, 101

Schism TMAP: 78

Seascape ADC: 10-11; ALL: 36; TMAP: 19, 35, 42-43, 61, 70, 81-82, 101-102

Tiny Alice ADC: 11-12; ALL: 35-36; Br: 11-13; LCAB: 3; Ma: 23-24; MDAE: 57-61; Po: 28-29, 33-35; TMAP: 17, 18, 20, 23-25, 28-29, 31-34, 42-44, 46, 51-53, 57, 61, 63, 67-71, 73-74, 76-78, 81-82, 86, 102-105; TMBP: 224

Who's Afraid of Virginia Woolf? ADC: 12-16; ALL: 35-36; Br: 13-16; DC1: 20; LCAB: 3; Lon: 23; Ma: 24-25; MD: 21; MDAE: 55-61, 107-109; Po: 28-29, 35-40; TMAP: 16-21, 23-27, 29-37, 39-46, 48-49, 52-62, 64-73, 76, 78-79, 81-82, 85-88, 105-107

The Zoo Story ADC: 16-17; ALL: 34-36; Br: 16-17; DC1: 20-21; LCAB: 3; Lon: 23; Ma: 25-26; MD: 21; MDAE: 56, 59, 61-62; Po: 29-30, 40; TMAP: 16, 19, 21-22, 24-25, 27, 30, 32, 34-36, 40, 43-47, 50, 52, 54, 56-57, 59-60, 62, 64-71, 74-81, 83, 85, 86, 88, 91, 107-108, 161

ALBEE, George
"Fame Takes the J Car" Wa: 8

ALBERT, Allan
Corral ADC: 17

ALBERTI, Rafael
General Po: 41-42
El Adefesio Po: 43
Night and War in the Prado Museum Br: 17
Sobre los ángeles Po: 42-43

ALCALA Yáñez de Ribera,
   Jerónimo de
   El donador hablador   Ke: 180
ALCOTT, Amos Bronson
   General ALL: 36-37; LCAB:
   3
ALCOTT, Louisa May
   General ALL: 37; AN: 8-9;
   ASF: 46
   "Behind a Mask, or a Woman's
   Power" ASF: 45
   "An Hour" ASF: 45
   Little Women ALL: 37; AN:
   8; Ma: 27
   "M.L." ASF: 45
   "My Contraband" ASF: 46
   "Pauline's Passion and Punish-
   ment" ASF: 46
ALDANOV, Mark A.
   Devil's Bridge Ke: 369
   "For Thee the Best" Wa: 8
   The Ninth of Thermidor Ke:
   369
   "Punch Vodka" Wa: 8
   St. Helena Ke: 369
   "The Tenth Symphony" Wa:
   8
ALDECOA, Ignacio
   General Po: 43-44
   "Amadís" WaS1: 3
   "En el kilómetro 400" WaS1:
   3
   El fugor y la sangue Fi:
   191
   Great Sole Fi: 191
   Parte de una historia Fi:
   191
   "Santa Olaja de Acero"
   WaS1: 3
   "Solar del Paraiso" WaS1: 3
   With the East Wind Fi: 191
ALDINGTON, Richard
   General Po: 44; Ri: 89-92;
   Sch: 3
   All Men Are Enemies ENES2:
   1
   The Colonel's Daughter
   ENES2: 1; Ri: 89
   Death of a Hero ENE: 1;
   ENES2: 1; Ri: 89-92
   Rejected Guest ENES2: 1
   Roads to Glory ENES2: 1;
   Ri: 89
   The Romance of Casanova
   ENES2: 1
   Seven Against Reeves

   ENES2: 1
   Soft Answers ENES2: 1; Ri:
   91-92
   Very Heaven ENES1: 1;
   ENES2: 2
ALDISS, Brian Wilson
   General LCAB: 3
   An Age ENES2: 2
   "Ahead" see "The Failed
   Man"
   Barefoot in the Head ENES1:
   1; ENES2: 2
   The Dark Light-Years
   ENES2: 2
   "Dumb Show" WaS1: 4
   Earthworks ENES2: 2
   The Eighty Minute Hour
   ENES2: 2
   "The Failed Man" ["Ahead"]
   WaS1: 4
   Frankenstein Unbound
   ENES2: 2
   Greybeard ENES2: 2
   Hothouse ENES2: 2
   The Interpreter ENES2: 2
   The Malacia Tapestry
   ENES2: 2
   Non-Stop ENES2: 2
   The Primal Urge ENES2: 2
   Report on Probability A
   ENES2: 2
   A Soldier Erect ENES2: 2
ALDRICH, Bess Streeter
   General AN: 9
ALDRICH, Thomas Bailey
   General AN: 9; ASF: 46;
   C1a: 100
   "For Bravery on the Field
   of Battle" Wa: 9
   "Marjorie Daw" ASF: 46;
   Wa: 9
   "Shaw's Folly" Wa: 9
ALDRIDGE, Ira
   General AAPD: 297-298;
   BAP: 1-2; MBA: 2
   The Black Doctor BAP: 2
ALDRIDGE, James
   General Po: 44
ALDRIDGE, John W.
   General LCAB: 3
ALEGRIA, Ciro
   General Po: 44-45
   Broad and Alien Is the World
   Ma: 28
   "El cuarzo" Wa: 9
   "El lazo" WaS1: 4

"La madre" Wa: 9
"Muerte del cabo Cheo López"
Wa: 9
"La piedra y la cruz" Wa: 9
"El poeta que se volvió gus-
ano" WaS1: 4
"A qué lado de la cortina?"
WaS1: 4
ALEICHEM, Sholom [Sholom
RABINOWITZ]
General Po: 45
"Dreyfus in Kasrilevke"
Wa: 9
"The Enchanted Tailor"
WaS1: 4
"The Fiddler" WaS1: 4
"Gymnasia" WaS1: 4
"Home for Passover" WaS1:
4
"The Little Pot" WaS1: 4
"On Account of a Hat" WaS1:
4
"The Penknife" WaS1: 4
"The Purim Feast" WaS1: 4
ALEIXANDRE, Vicente
General Po: 45-46
ALEMAN, Mateo
Dorido and Clorinia Ke: 180
Guzmán de Alfarache Fi:
191-192; Ke: 180-181;
Ma: 29
Guzmán de Alfarache see
also Mabbe, James
[translator]
ALERAMO, Sibilla
A Woman at Bay Fi: 257
ALEXANDER, Lewis Grandison
General BAW: 24
ALEXANDER, Lorrimer
General WIL: 4
ALEXANDER, Ronald
Grand Prize ADC: 18
Holiday for Lovers ADC: 18
Nobody Loves an Albatross
ADC: 18
Time Out for Ginger ADC:
18
ALEXANDER, Sidney
"Part of the Act" Wa: 9
"The White Boat" SFC: 7;
Wa: 9
ALEXANDER, Sir William (1567?-
1640)
General Ai: 46; NI: 323-
324
[Supplement to] The Coun-

tesse of Pembrokes Arcadia
by Philip SIDNEY ERP:
75-76
ALEXANDER, William (1826-1894)
General Ai: 145
ALEXIS, Willibald
Schloss Avalon [Walladmor]
Ke: 256
The Werewolf Ke: 256
ALFIERI, Vittorio
Antigone DC2: 29
Mirra DC2: 29
ALFRED the Great [translator]
The Consolation of Philosophy
by BOETHIUS Hen: 202;
MOEP: 138
Historia Ecclesiastica Gentis
Anglorum by BEDE Hen:
201
Pastoral Care by POPE
GREGORY I Hen: 202
Soliloquies of ST. AUGUSTINE
Hen: 203
ALFRED, William
Agamemnon MDAE: 63
Hogan's Goat ADC: 18-19;
Br: 17-18
ALGER, Horatio, Jr.
General AN: 9-10; ASF: 47;
Ho: 133-134; LCAB: 3
"A Fancy of Hers" ASF: 46
"Five Hundred Dollars" ASF:
46
Jed, The Poor House Boy
AN: 9
"Little Floy" ASF: 46
"Lost and Found" ASF: 46
"A Race up the Hill" ASF:
46
"The Veiled Mirror" ASF: 47
ALGREN, Nelson
General AN: 10; ASF: 47;
CFAE: 31-32; CN: 22-23;
LCAB: 3; Ne: 15-16; Po:
46-47
"A Bottle of Milk for Mother"
ASF: 47; Wa: 9; WaS1: 4
"The Captain Has Bad Dreams"
WaS1: 5
"The Captain Is Impaled"
WaS1: 5
"Depend on Aunt Elly" WaS1:
5
"Design for Departure" ASF:
47
"The Face on the Barroom

Floor" WaS1: 5
"How the Devil Came Down
Division Street" ASF: 47;
Wa: 9; WaS1: 5
The Man With the Golden Arm
CN: 23; Ma: 30
Never Come Morning CN: 23;
Ma: 30
"So Help Me" ASF: 47;
WaS1: 5
Somebody in Boots CN: 24;
Ma: 31
A Walk on the Wild Side
CN: 24; Ma: 31; Po: 47
ALHAMISI, Ahmed Akenwale
[Ahmed Le Graham AL-
HAMISI]
General BAW: 24
ALI, Ahmed
"Our Lane" Wa: 10
ALI, Jamal
Black Joy MBA: 3
ALIFAIJO, Margaret
General BALE: 267
Alighieri, Dante see DANTE
ALIGHIERI
ALLAIS, Alphonse
General Po: 47
ALLAN, Glenn
"Boysi's Yaller Cha'iot" Wa:
10
ALLAN, Ted
General JW: 419
ALLEN, Charles [translator]
The Historie of Eurialus and
Lucretia by Enea Silvio
PICCOLOMINI ERP: 77
ALLEN, Ethan
General AP: 174-175; Da:
78
Essay on the Universal Pleni-
tude of Being AP: 175
A Narrative of Colonel Ethan
Allen's Captivity AP:
174-175
Reason the Only Oracle of
Man ... (often cited
as Oracles of Reason or
Oracle of Reason) AP:
174-175; Da: 78
ALLEN, Grant
General TA: 80-81
The British Barbarians
ENES2: 3
The Woman Who Did ENES2:
3

ALLEN, Hervey
General AN: 10
Action at Aquila AN: 10
Anthony Adverse AN: 10
The Forest and the Fort AN:
10
ALLEN, James Lane
General AF: 22-23; ALL:
38; AN: 10-11; ASF: 48;
LCAB: 3
Flute and Violin AF: 23
The Mettle of the Pasture
AF: 22
"Sister Dolorosa" ASF: 48
"Summer in Arcady" ASF: 48
"Two Gentlemen of Kentucky"
ASF: 48
ALLEN, Jay
Forty Carats ADC: 19
The Prime of Miss Jean Brodie
ADC: 19
ALLEN, John
General AP: 573
Oh, Say Can You See L.A.
ADC: 19
ALLEN, Junius Mordecai
General AAPD: 87; BAW:
25; LCAB: 4
Allen, Mrs. Lucy Ann [Terry]
see TERRY, Lucy Ann
ALLEN, Richard
General BAW: 26
ALLEN, Samuel [Paul VESEY]
General BAW: 29
Poems from Africa BAW: 29
ALLEN, Woody
General MDAE: 64-65
Don't Drink the Water ADC:
20
Play It Again, Sam ADC: 20
ALLESTREE, Richard
The Whole Duty of Man Hen:
40
ALLFREY, Phyllis Shand
General WIL: 4
The Orchid House WIL: 5
ALLISON, Hughes
The Trial of Dr. Beck [The
Trial] BAP: 2; Br: 18;
MBA: 3
ALLSTON, Washington
General LCAB: 4
ALMQVIST, Carl Jonas Love
"The Palace" WaS1: 5
The Queen's Jewelpiece
Fi: 400

"Skällnora Mill" WaS1: 5
"The Urn" WaS1: 5
ALONSO, Dámaso
General Po: 47-48
Hombre y Dios Po: 48
ALONZO, Cecil
Beaulah Johnson MBA: 3
Black Voices BAP: 2-3
Four Hundred Years Overdue
BAP: 3
ALOS, Concha
General Po: 48
Os habla Electra Fi: 192
ALSINA, Arturo
General Br: 18
ALSOP, Richard
General AP: 177
The Universal Receipt Book...
AP: 177
ALTAMIRA, Raphael
Reposo Fi: 181-182
ALTAMIRANO, Ignacio Manuel
General LCAB: 4
ALTENBERG, Peter
General Po: 48-49
ALUKO, Timothy Mofolorunso
General BALE: 268
Kinsman and Foreman BALE:
268
ALVAREZ Lleras, Antonio
General Br: 18
ALVAREZ Quintero, Joaquin
General Br: 18
_____ and Serafín
General MD: 21-22
Malvaloca MD: 22
ALVARO, Corrado
"Dorothea" Wa: 10
Gente in aspromonte Fi:
257
L'uomo nel labirinto Fi: 257
ALVERDES, Paul
"Kilian" Wa: 10
"Die letzte Pein" Wa: 10
ALYOSHIN, Samuel
Alone [Odna] Br: 18
At That Time in Seville
[Togda v Sevil'ye] Br:
18; DC2: 29
AMADI, Elechi
General BALE: 268-269
The Concubine BALE: 269
AMADO, Jorge
General Po: 49
Dona Flor and Her Two
Husbands Ma: 32

Home Is the Sailor Ma: 32
Shepherds of the Night Ma:
32
AMALI, Samson O. O.
General BALE: 269-270
AMANDO, Jorge
"The Two Deaths of Quincas
Wateryell" WaS1: 5
AMBESSER, Axel von
General Po: 49-50
Die Abrundige im Herrn Gers-
tenberg DC2: 29
AMBRUS, Zoltan
King Midas Ke: 369
You Will Be Alone Ke: 369
AMES, Richard
"The Folly of Love" PE: 1
AMIEL, Denys
Cafe-Tabac Br: 19
Le Couple Br: 19
La Femme en Fleur Br: 19
Mr. & Mrs. So-and-So
[Monsieur et Madame Un
Tel] Br: 19
Le Voyageur Br: 19
_____ and André OBEY
La Souriante Madame Beudet
Br: 19
AMIHAI, Yehuda
"The Battle for the Hill" Wa:
10
AMINI, Johari [Jewel C. LATI-
MORE]
Black Essence BAW: 31
Let's Go Somewhere BAW: 31
AMIS, Kingsley
General CFAE: 34-35; CN:
24-25; LCAB: 4; Po:
50-52; Sch: 4-5
The Alteration ENES2: 3
The Anti-Death League
CN: 25; ENE: 1; ENES1:
2; ENES2: 3
Girl, 20 ENES2: 3
The Green Man ENES2: 3;
Ma: 33
I Like It Here CFAE: 34;
CN: 25; ENE: 1; ENES1:
2; Po: 51-52
I Want it Now CN: 25;
ENES2: 3
Lucky Jim CFAE: 34; CN:
26; ENE: 1-2; ENES1:
2; ENES2: 3; LCAB: 4;
Ma: 33-34; Po: 52-53;
Sch: 5-6; TMBP: 93

My Enemy's Enemy ENE: 2
One Fat Englishman CN:
26-27; ENE: 2; ENES1:
2; ENES2: 3; Ma: 34-35;
Sch: 6
Take a Girl Like You CN:
27; ENE: 2; ENES1: 2;
ENES2: 4; Ma: 35-36;
Po: 51; Sch: 6
That Uncertain Feeling
CN: 27; ENE: 3; ENES1:
2; ENES2: 4; LCAB: 4;
Ma: 36-37; Po: 51
AMMONS, A. R.
General ICBAP: 1; MP: 16
"Corsons Inlet" PE: 1
"Hibernaculum" PE: 1
"I Went to the Summit"
PE: 1
"Periphery" PE: 2
"Play" PE: 2
Amor, José Blanco see BLANCO
AMOR, José
AMOR Ruibal, Angel
General Po: 53
AMORIM, Enrique
General LCAB: 4; Po: 53
AMOS, John
Truth and Soul MBA: 3
AMPHIS
Opora DC2: 29
ANACREON
General LCAB: 4
ANAND, Mulk Raj
"The Barber's Trade Union"
Wa: 10
"Birth" Wa: 10
"The Bridegroom" Wa: 10
"The Cobbler and the Machine"
Wa: 10
"A Cock and Bull Story"
Wa: 11
"The Conqueror" Wa: 11
"A Dark Night" Wa: 11
"Death of a Lady" Wa: 11
"Eagles and Pigeons" Wa: 11
"The Elixir of Life" Wa: 11
"The Gold Watch" Wa: 11
"A Kashmir Idyll" Wa: 11
"The Lost Child" Wa: 11
"The Maharaja and the
Tortoise" Wa: 11
"The Man Who Loved Monkeys
More Than Human Beings"
Wa: 11
"A Pair of Mustachios" Wa:

11
"Power of Darkness" Wa: 11
"The Price of Bananas" Wa:
11
"The Priest and the Pigeons"
Wa: 11
"The Prodigal Son" Wa: 11
"The Reflections on the Golden
Bowl" Wa: 12
"A Rumor" Wa: 12
"Silver Bangles" Wa: 12
"The Thief" Wa: 12
"Torrents of Wrath" Wa: 12
"The Tractor and the Corn
Goddess" Wa: 12
"A True Story" Wa: 12
ANDERSCH, Alfred
Die Rote Fi: 285
ANDERSEN, Hans Christian
"The Red Shoes" Wa: 12
"The Shadow" Wa: 12
ANDERSEN, Knud
The Brand of the Sea Ke:
346
ANDERSEN, Tryggve
Mot Kvaeld Fi: 401
ANDERSON, Alston
General BAF: 3
All God's Children BAF: 3
"Lover Man" BAF: 3; BAW:
32
ANDERSON, Colin
Magellan ENES2: 4
ANDERSON, Ethel
General MAP: 126
"Mrs. James Greene" MAP:
126
ANDERSON, Garland
General AAPD: 299; BAP:
3; BAW: 32
Appearances BAP: 3-4; Br:
19; MBA: 3-4
ANDERSON, Maxwell
General ALL: 38; Br: 19-24;
LCAB: 4; Lon: 24-25;
MD: 22-24; MDAE: 67;
Po: 53-54
Anne of the Thousand Days
ADC: 20; Br: 24; MD:
24
Bad Seed ADC: 20-21; Br:
24; Lon: 25; MD: 24
Barefoot in Athens ADC: 21;
Br: 24; Ma: 38; MD: 24;
MDAE: 67
Both Your Houses ADC: 21;

Br: 24-25; DC1: 21; Ma: 38; MD: 24

Candle in the Wind ADC: 21-22; Br: 25; MD: 24

Elizabeth the Queen ADC: 22; Br: 25; DC1: 21; Ma: 38-39; MD: 24

The Eve of Saint Mark ADC: 22; Br: 25; DC1: 21; MD: 24

The Feast of Ortolans ADC: 22; Br: 25; MD: 25

The Golden Six ADC: 22

Gypsy ADC: 23; Br: 26

High Tor ADC: 23; Br: 26; DC1: 21; Ma: 39; MD: 25

Joan of Lorraine ADC: 23; Br: 26; MD: 25

Journey to Jerusalem ADC: 23-24; Br: 26; DC1: 21

Key Largo ADC: 24; Br: 26; DC1: 21; Ma: 39-40; MD: 25

Mary of Scotland ADC: 24; Br: 27; DC1: 21; LCAB: 4; Lon: 24; Ma: 40; MD: 25; Po: 54

The Masque of Kings ADC: 24-25; Br: 27; Ma: 40-41; MD: 25

Night Over Taos ADC: 25; Br: 28; DC1: 22; Ma: 41; MD: 25; Po: 54

Outside Looking In ADC: 25; Br: 28; MD: 25-26

Saturday's Children ADC: 25; Br: 28

Sea Wife ADC: 25

Second Overture ADC: 25; Br: 28

The Star Wagon ADC: 25; Br: 28; DC1: 22; Ma: 41; MD: 26

Storm Operation ADC: 26; Br: 28; MD: 26

Truckline Café ADC: 26; MD: 26

Valley Forge ADC: 26; Br: 28-29; DC1: 22; Ma: 41-42; MD: 26

The White Desert Br: 29; DC1: 22; Lon: 25

The Wingless Victory ADC: 26-27; Br: 29; LCAB: 4; Ma: 42; MD: 26

Winterset ADC: 27-28; Br: 29-30; DC1: 22-23; Lon: 24-25; Ma: 42-43; MD: 26-27; Po: 54-55

_____ and Brendan GILL
The Day the Money Stopped ADC: 28

_____ and Harold HICKERSON
Gods of the Lightning ADC: 28; Br: 25-26; Ma: 39

_____ and Laurence STALLINGS
First Flight ADC: 28

What Price Glory? ADC: 28-29; Br: 29; DC1: 22; Lon: 25; Ma: 42; MD: 26

_____ and Kurt WEILL
Knickerbocker Holiday ADC: 29; Br: 27; MD: 25

Lost in the Stars ADC: 29-30; Br: 27; MD: 25; MDAE: 67

ANDERSON, Patrick
"The Unfinished Hotel" PE: 2

ANDERSON, Poul
"Goat Song" ASF: 48
"Sam Hall" ASF: 48

ANDERSON, Robert Woodruff
General Br: 31; MD: 27; MDAE: 69

All Summer Long ADC: 30; Br: 31; MD: 27

Come Marching Home MD: 27

The Days Between ADC: 30

I Never Sang for My Father ADC: 30; Br: 31

Silent Night, Lonely Night ADC: 30-31

Solitaire/Double Solitaire ADC: 31

Tea and Sympathy ADC: 31; Br: 31; Ma: 44; MD: 27; MDAE: 69

You Know I Can't Hear You When the Water's Running ADC: 31-32; Br: 31

ANDERSON, Sherwood
General ALL: 39-40; AN: 11-15; ASF: 55-57; LCAB: 4-5; Ne: 16-19; Po: 55-60; Wo: 39-41

"Adventure" ASF: 48; SFC: 7; Wa: 12; WaS1: 5

"Almost" Wa: 12

"An Awakening" ASF: 49; Wa: 13

Beyond Desire AN: 11

"The Book of the Grotesque"
ASF: 49; SFC: 8; Wa:
13; WaS1: 5

"Brother Death" ASF: 49;
SFC: 7; Wa: 13; WaS1:
6

"A Chicago Hamlet" ASF:
49; Wa: 13

"The Contract" Wa: 13

Dark Laughter AN: 11; Ma:
45

"Death" ASF: 49; Wa: 13;
WaS1: 6

"Death in the Woods" ASF:
49; Po: 60-61; SFC: 8;
Wa: 13-14; WaS1: 6

"Departure" ASF: 49; Wa:
14

"Drink" ASF: 50; Wa: 14

"The Dumb Man" ASF: 50

"The Egg" ASF: 50; Ne:
18; Po: 61; SFC: 8;
Wa: 14-15; WaS1: 6

"The Flood" SFC: 8; Wa:
15

"Godliness" ASF: 50; SFC:
8; Wa: 15; WaS1: 6

"Hands" ASF: 50; SFC: 9;
Wa: 15

" I Want to Know Why" ASF:
50; LCAB: 5; Po: 61-62;
SFC: 9; Wa: 15-16;
WaS1: 6; Wo: 41

"I'm a Fool" ASF: 51; SFC:
9; Wa: 16; WaS1: 6

Kit Brandon: A Portrait
AN: 11; Po: 62; Wo: 41

"Loneliness" ASF: 51; SFC:
9; Wa: 16-17; WaS1: 6

"A Man of Ideas" Wa: 17

"The Man Who Became a
Woman: ASF: 51; Po:
63; SFC: 9-10; Wa: 17;
WaS1: 6

Many Marriages AN: 11;
LCAB: 5; Po: 57

Marching Men AN: 11

"A Meeting South" ASF:
51

"Mother" Wa: 17

"The New Englander" ASF:
51; Wa: 17; WaS1: 6

"Nice Girl" Wa: 17

"An Ohio Pagan" ASF: 51

"Out of Nowhere into

Nothing" ASF: 51; SFC:
10: Wa: 17

"Paper Pills" ASF: 51; Wa:
17-18; WaS1: 6

"The Philosopher" ASF: 51;
Wa: 18

Poor White Ma: 45-46

"Queer" ASF: 51; Wa: 18

"Respectability" Wa: 18

"Responsibility" Wa: 18

"The Return" Wa: 18

"The Sad Horn-Blower" ASF:
52; Po: 63; Wa: 18

"Seeds" ASF: 52; SFC: 10;
Wa: 18

"Sophistication" ASF: 52;
SFC: 10; Wa: 18-19

A Story-Teller's Story Po:
59, 63

"The Strength of God" ASF:
52; WaS1: 6

"Surrender" SFC: 10; Wa:
19

"Tandy" Wa: 19; WaS1: 6

"The Teacher" ASF: 52;
SFC: 10; Wa: 19

"There She Is--She Is Taking
Her Bath" ASF: 52

"The Thinker" ASF: 52;
SFC: 10; Wa: 19

"The Triumph of the Modern"
ASF: 52; Wa: 19

"Unlighted Lamps" ASF: 52;
SFC: 10; Wa: 19; WaS1:
7

"The Untold Lie" ASF: 52;
SFC: 10-11; Wa: 19-20

"Unused" ASF: 52; SFC:
11; Wa: 20; WaS1: 7

Windy McPherson's Son AN:
11

Winesburg, Ohio AN: 11;
ASF: 52-55; LCAB: 5;
Ma: 46-47; Ne: 17-19;
Po: 63-67; Wo: 40-41

"The Yellow Gown" ASF: 55

ANDERSON, T. Diane
From Distant Rooms BAP: 4

ANDERSSON, Dan
David Ramm's Inheritance
Ke: 346
Three Homeless Ones Ke:
346

ANDRADE, Jorge
General Br: 31; Po: 411-
412

ANDRADE, Mario de
General Po: 67
ANDRES, Stefan
General Po: 68
"Hagia Moné" Wa: 20
"Die unglaubwürdige Reise des
Knaben" Wa: 20
"Die Vermummten" Wa: 20
"Wir sind Utopia" Wa: 20
ANDREW of Wyntoun
Original Chronicle OMEP:
406
ANDREWES, Lancelot
General Ba: 25; Hen: 30-31
ANDREWS, Bruce
"Bananas Are an Example"
PE: 2
ANDREWS, Regina M.
General BAP: 4; BAW: 34;
MBA: 4
Climbing Jacob's Ladder
MBA: 4
ANDREYEV, Leonid Nikolaevich
General Br: 31-32; MD:
27-28; Po: 67-68
"The Abyss" Wa: 20
Anathema Br: 32; EDC: 12;
MD: 28
"At the Window" Wa: 20
The Beautiful Sabine Women
[The Pretty Sabine Women;
Sabine Women] Br: 33;
EDC: 12; MD: 28
"Ben-Tobith" Wa: 20
Black Masks [Chyornye Maski]
Br: 32; DC2: 29; EDC:
12; Po: 68
"Christians" Wa: 20
The Curse of the Beast Ke:
369; Wa: 20
"Darkness" Wa: 20
"Deception" Wa: 20
Devil in the Wind Br: 32
"The Festival" Wa: 20
"The Foreigner" Wa: 21
"The Governor" Wa: 21
"Grand Slam" Wa: 21
He Who Gets Slapped [Tot,
Kto Poluchayet Rosh-
chechiny] Br: 32-33;
DC2: 29; EDC: 12;
MD: 28
"In the Fog" Wa: 21
"In the Springtime" Wa:
21
Judas Iscariot Fi: 415;

Ke: 369; Wa: 21
Katerina [Katherina Ivanovna]
Br: 33; EDC: 12-13; MD:
28
K Zvezdam see To the Stars
"Laughter" Wa: 21
"Lazarus" Wa: 21
The Life of Man [Zhizn' Chelo-
vieka] Br: 33; DC2:
29; EDC: 13; MD: 28
"The Life of Vasili Fiveisky"
Wa: 21
"Little Angel" Wa: 21
"The Marseillaise" Wa: 21
"My Memoirs" Wi: 21
The Ocean [Okean] EDC: 13;
MD: 28
"On the River" Wa: 21
"Once There Lived" Wa: 21
"Peter at the Dacha" Wa: 21
The Pretty Sabine Women see
The Beautiful Sabine Women
Professor Soritsyn MD: 28
The Red Laugh Fi: 415; Ke:
369-370; Wa: 21
Sabine Women see The Beauti-
ful Sabine Women
Samson in Chains [Samson v
Okovakh] EDC: 13
Samson Unchained MD: 28
Savva; or Fire Cures EDC:
13; MD: 28
"The Seven Who Were Hanged"
see The Story of Seven
Who Were Hanged
Shashka Zhegulev Ke: 370
"Silence" Wa: 22
Sorrows of Belgium MD: 28
"The Story of Sergei Petrovich"
Wa: 22
The Story of Seven Who Were
Hanged ["The Seven Who
Were Hanged"] Fi: 415;
Ke: 370; SFC: 11; Wa:
21-22
"The Thief" Wa: 22
Thou Shalt Not Kill MD: 28
"Thought" Wa: 22
"Thus It Was" Wa: 22
To the Stars [K Zvezdam]
EDC: 13; MD: 28
Tot, Kto Poluchayet Rosh-
chechiny see He Who
Gets Slapped
Tsar Hunger [Tsar Golod]
EDC: 13; MD: 28

"Vania" Wa: 22
"The Wall" Wa: 22
The Waltz of the Dogs MD:
    29
War's Burden Ke: 370
Zhizn' Chelovieka see The
    Life of Man
ANDRIAN, Leopold
    General Po: 68
ANDRIC, Ivo
    Bosnian Chronicle Ma: 48
    The Bridge on the Drina
        Fi: 415; Ke: 370; Ma:
        48
    Devil's Yard Fi: 415
    Travnik Chronicle Fi: 415;
        Ke: 370
ANDRZEJEWSKI, Jerzy
    Ashes and Diamond Fi: 415
ANGELOU, Maya
    General BAF: 4-5; BAW:
        35; MBA: 4
    Ajax MBA: 5
    And Still I Rise! MBA: 4-5
    Encounters MBA: 5
    Gather Together in My Name
        BAF: 5
    Georgia! Georgia! BAP: 5;
        MBA: 4-5
    I Know Why the Caged Bird
        Sings BAF: 4-5; BAW:
        35; Ma: 49
    Singin' and Swingin' and
        Gettin' Merry Like Christ-
        mas BAF: 5
ANGIRA-ROBERTS, Jared
    General BALE: 270
ANGOFF, Charles [Richard W.
        HINTON]
    General CFAE: 38; JW:
        175; Po: 68
d'ANGOULEME, Marguerite
    Heptameron Ke: 237
ANGUS, Marion
    General Ai: 202
ANIEBO, I. N. C.
    General BALE: 270
    The Anonymity of Sacrifice
        BALE: 270
ANNAND, James King
    General Ai: 284
Anodos see COLERIDGE, Mary
    Elizabeth
ANOUILH, Jean
    General Br: 33-36; LCAB
        5; MD: 29-30; Po:

69-71
L'Alouette see Lark
Antigone Br: 36-38; DC2:
    30-31; EDC: 13-14; LCAB:
    5; Ma: 50-51; MD: 30-31;
    Po: 70, 72-73
Ardele, or the Daisy [Ardèle,
    ou la Marguerite] Br: 38;
    DC2: 31; EDC: 14; Ma:
    51-52; MD: 31
Le Bal des Voleurs see
    Thieves' Carnival
Becket, or The Honor of God
    [Becket, ou L'Honneur de
    Dieu] Br: 38-39; DC2:
    32; EDC: 15; Ma: 52-53;
    MD: 31; Po: 73-74
Catch as Catch Can [La Foire
    d'Empoigne] Br: 42; EDC:
    15
The Cavern [La Grotte] Br:
    39-40; EDC: 15
Colombe [Mademoiselle Colombe]
    Br: 40; DC2: 32; EDC:
    15-16; Ma: 53-54; MD: 31;
    Po: 74
Dear Antoine [Cher Antoine]
    EDC: 16
Dinner with the Family [Le
    Rendez-vous de Senlis]
    Br: 40; DC2: 33; EDC:
    16; Ma: 54
Don't Awaken Madame [Ne
    Réveillez pas Madame]
    EDC: 16
The Ermine [L'Hermine] Br:
    41; DC2: 32; EDC: 16;
    Ma: 55; MD: 31
Eurydice [Legend of Lovers;
    Point of Departure] Br:
    41; DC2: 33; EDC: 16;
    Ma: 55-56; MD: 31; Po:
    70, 74-75
Fading Mansions see Romeo
    et Jeanette
The Fighting Cock [L'Hurlu-
    berlu, ou Le Réactionnaire
    Amoureux] Br: 42; EDC:
    16-17; Ma: 56-57; MD: 32
La Foire d'Empoigne see
    Catch as Catch Can
La Grotte see The Cavern
L'Hurluberlu, ou Le Réac-
    tionnaire Amoureux see
    The Fighting Cock
L'Invitation au Chateau see

Ring Around the Moon
Jezabel Br: 42; EDC: 17;
    MD: 32
Lark [L'Alouette] Br: 43;
    DC2: 32-33; EDC: 17;
    Ma: 57-58; MD: 30, 32;
    Po: 71-72
Legend of Lovers see Eury-
    dice
Léocadia see Time Remem-
    bered
Mademoiselle Colombe see
    Colombe
Medea [Médée] Br: 43-44;
    DC2: 33; EDC: 18;
    Ma: 58-59; MD: 32; Po:
    70, 75
Ne Réveillez pas Madame see
    Don't Awaken Madame
Ornifle, or The Draft [Orni-
    fle, ou Le Courant d'Air]
    Br: 44; EDC: 18; MD:
    32
Le Petit Bonheur Br: 44;
    MD: 32-33
Point of Departure see
    Eurydice
Poor Bitos, or The Masked
    Dinner [Pauvre Bitos, ou
    Le Diner des Têtes] Br:
    44-45; EDC: 18; Ma: 59;
    MD: 32
The Rehearsal [La Répétition,
    ou L'Amour Puni] Br: 45;
    DC2: 33; EDC: 18-19;
    Ma: 59-60; MD: 33
Le Rendez-vous de Senlis
    see Dinner with the Fam-
    ily
The Restless Heart [The Wild
    One; La Sauvage] Br:
    47; DC2: 34; EDC: 19;
    Ma: 60-61; MD: 33
Ring Around the Moon [L'In-
    vitation au Chateau] Br:
    45; DC2: 33-34; EDC:
    19; Ma: 61; MD: 32
Romeo et Jeanette [Fading
    Mansions] Br: 42;
    EDC: 19-20; MD: 33
La Sauvage see The Rest-
    less Heart
Thieves' Carnival [Le Bal
    des Voleurs] Br: 45-
    46; DC2: 32; EDC: 20;
    Ma: 61-62

Time Remembered [Léocadia]
    Br: 46; DC2: 33; EDC:
    20; Ma: 62; MD: 32
Traveller Without Luggage [Le
    Voyageur sans Bagage]
    Br: 46; DC2: 34; EDC:
    20; Ma: 62-63; MD: 33
Waltz of the Toreadors [La
    Valse des Toréadors] Br:
    46-47; DC2: 34; EDC: 21;
    Ma: 63-64; MD: 33
The Wild One see The Rest-
    less Heart
Y'Avait un Prisonnier Br: 48;
    MD: 33
ANOZIE, Sunday O.
    General BALE: 270
ANSKY, S. [Solomon RAPPOPORT]
    Dybbuk, or Between Two
        Worlds Br: 48; DC2: 34;
        EDC: 446-447; MD: 33
ANTHONY, Earl
    Charlie Still Can't Win No Wars
        on the Ground MBA: 5
    (Mis) Judgment MBA: 5
    The Pearl Maiden BAP: 5
ANTHONY, Michael
    General WIL: 5-6
    Cricket in the Road WIL: 8
    The Games Were Coming
        ENES2: 4; WIL: 6-7
    Green Days by the River
        ENES2: 4; WIL: 7-8
    Sandra Street and Other
        Stories WIL: 8
    The Year in San Fernando
        ENES2: 4; LCAB: 6;
        WIL: 7
ANTON, Robert
    General NI: 325
    Moriomachia ERP: 78
ANTONACCI, Greg
    Dance wi' Me, or the Fatal
        Twitch ADC: 32
    Dance with Me (a revision of
        his Dance wi' Me) ADC:
        32
Antoninus, Brother see EVER-
    SON, William
ANTROBUS, John
    General MDAE: 70
APOLLINAIRE, Guillaume
    General Br: 48; LCAB: 6;
        MD: 33-34; Po: 76-79
    Alcohols [Alcools] Po: 79-80
    Autumn Rhine Song [Rhénane

D'Automne] Po: 83

Breasts of Tiresias [Tiresias's
Breasts; Les Mamelles de
Tirésias] Br: 48-49;
DC2: 34; Po: 82

Les Collines see The Hills

Color of the Weather [Couleur
de Temps] Br: 49

Les Femmes see The Women

Les Fenêtres see The Win-
dows

The Heresiarch and Co.
[L'Hérésiarque et Cie]
Po: 81

The Hills [Les Collines] Po:
80

The House of the Dead [La
Maison des Morts] Po:
81-82

Le Larron see The Thief

Les Mamelles de Tirésias
see Breasts of Tiresias

The Mirabeau Bridge [Le Pont
Mirabeau] Po: 82

(O Ma Jeunesse Abandonée)
Po: 82

Pipe Po: 82

Rhénane D'Automne see
Autumn Rhine Song

Le Son du Cor Po: 83

The Thief [Le Larron] Po:
81

Tiresias's Breasts see
Breasts of Tiresias

The Windows [Les Fenêtres]
Po: 80

The Women [Les Femmes] Po:
80

Zone Po: 83

APOLLONIUS, Rhodius
Argonautica LCAB: 6

APPELFELD, A.
"Known" Wa: 22
"The Last Cover" Wa: 22
"On the Ground Floor" Wa:
22
"Reparation" Wa: 22

APRONTI, Jawa
"Funeral" BALE: 271

APULEIUS, Lucius
The Golden Ass see
ALDINGTON, William
[translator]
Metamorphoses, or The
Golden Ass Ma: 65-66
Summa Theologica Ma:

67-68

ARAGON, Alvaro Cubillo de
Los Desagravios de Christo
DC2: 34
El Senor de Noches Buenas
DC2: 35

ARAGON, Louis
General Po: 84-85
Les Communistes Fi: 2;
Ke: 16
Le Fou d'Elsa Po: 85
Holy Week [La Semaine Sainte]
Ke: 15; Po: 86
La Mise a mort Fi: 2
Mon coeur battait comme une
Voile dans ta Voix Po: 86
Nightwalker [Le Paysan de
Paris] Po: 86
The Passengers of Destiny
Ke: 16
A Peasant from Paris Fi: 2;
Ke: 16

ARANHA, Ray
The Estate ADC: 32; MBA:
5
My Sister, My Sister ADC:
32; BAP: 5-6; MBA: 5-6
The Prodigal Sister BAP: 6

ARANSON, Jack
Moby Dick ADC: 32

ARAYA, Enrique
General Po: 86-87
La Luna era mi tierra Po:
86-87

d'Arblay, Frances see BURNEY,
Fanny

ARBO, Sebastián Juan
Martin de Caretas Fi: 192

ARBUSOV, Aleksel Nikolaevich
The Irkutsk Story [Irkutskaja
Istorija] Br: 49; EDC:
21
The Promise [Moi Bednyi Narat]
EDC: 21

ARBUTHNOT, John
General Ai: 59; EC: 49
The Memoirs of Martinus
Scriblerus EC: 49

ARCHER, L. C.
Crosswise MBA: 6

ARCHER, William
General Ai: 164-165; TA:
82
Green Goddess EDC: 22

ARCHIBALD, William
The Cantilevered Terrace

ADC: 32
The Innocents ADC: 33;
Br: 49
Portrait of a Lady ADC: 33
ARDEN, Jane
General MDAE: 71
ARDEN, John
General Br: 49-50; MBD:
24-25; MD: 34; MDAE:
75-78; Po: 87-88; TMBP:
6-23
Armstrong's Last Goodnight
Br: 50-51; DC1: 23;
EDC: 22; MBD: 25;
MDAE: 76; TMBP: 8,
10, 14, 16, 18, 23-24
Ars Longa, Vita Brevis
Br: 51; Po: 87; TMBP:
7, 16
The Business of Good Govern-
ment Br: 51; Po: 87
Friday's Hiding Br: 51
The Happy Haven Br: 51-
52; DC1: 23; EDC: 22;
MBD: 24; MD: 34;
TMBP: 9, 11-12, 14, 19,
24, 262
Harold Muggins Is a Martyr
EDC: 22; MDAE: 78;
TMBP: 24
The Hero Rises Up EDC: 22;
MBD: 24; MDAE: 78;
TMBP: 21, 24
Ironhand MBD: 25; TMBP:
11, 24
Left-Handed Liberty Br:
52; EDC: 23; TMBP:
10-11, 14, 24
Live Like Pigs Br: 52;
EDC: 23; MD: 34;
TMBP: 10-12, 16, 24-25
Non-Stop Connolly Show
TMBP: 14-15, 25
Serjeant Musgrave's Dance
Br: 52-54; DC1: 23;
EDC: 23; MBD: 24-25;
MD: 34; MDAE: 75-77,
417, 513; Po: 88; TMBP:
7-20, 25, 159, 167, 171,
253
Soldier, Soldier Br: 54;
TMBP: 25
Squire Jonathan EDC: 24;
MBD: 25; MDAE: 77;
TMBP: 17, 25
The Waters of Babylon Br:

54; EDC: 24; MD: 34;
TMBP: 13, 16, 25
Wet Fish Br: 54; TMBP: 25
The Workhouse Donkey Br:
54-55; EDC: 24; MBD: 24;
MD: 34; TMBP: 8, 14,
25-26
_____ and Margaretta d'ARCY
The Ballygombeen Bequest
EDC: 24
The Island of the Mighty
EDC: 22, 24; TMBP: 13,
24
ARDREY, Robert
Shadow of Heroes Br: 55;
MDAE: 79-80
Sing Me No Lullaby ADC: 33
Thunder Rock ADC: 33-34;
Br: 55
AREMU, Aduke
Babylon II MBA: 6
ARENSBERG, Walter Conrad
General Po: 88
"Portrait" ICBAP: 5
"Sleeping Beauty" ICBAP: 5
"Voyáge a L'Infini" ICBAP:
5
ARENDT, Hannah
Eichmann in Jerusalem
LCAB: 6
ARENT, Arthur
Ethiopia Br: 55
One-Third of a Nation ADC:
34
Power ADC: 34
Triple-A Plowed Under Br:
55
ARETINO, Pietro
The Courtesan Ma: 69
ARGUEDAS, Jose Maria
General LCAB: 6
ARIOSTO, Ludovico
La Cassaria DC2: 35
Orlando Furioso Ma: 70
ARISTOPHANES
General LCAB: 6
Acharnians DC2: 35-36;
EDC: 24; Ma: 71
Batrachoi see The Frogs
The Birds [Ornithes] DC2:
36-37; EDC: 24-25; LCAB:
6; Ma: 71-72
The Clouds [Nubes; Nephelai]
DC2: 37-38; EDC: 25;
Ma: 72-73
Ecclesiazusae see Women in

Congress
The Frogs [Batrachoi] DC2:
38-40; EDC: 26; Ma:
73-74
The Knights [Hippes; Equites]
DC2: 40; EDC: 26-27
Lysistrata DC2: 40-41;
Ma: 74
Nephelai see The Clouds
Nubes see The Clouds
Ornithes see The Birds
Peace [Pax] DC2: 41; EDC:
27
Pluto [Plutus] DC2: 41-42;
EDC: 27
The Wasps [Vespae; Spekes]
DC2: 42-43; EDC: 27-28;
Ma: 75
Women in Congress [Ecclesia-
zusae] DC2: 38; EDC:
26
Women of Thesmophoria
[Thesmophoriazusae]
DC2: 42; EDC: 27; Ma:
74
ARISTOTLE
General LCAB: 6
The Poetics LCAB: 6-7;
Ma: 76-77
ARLAND, Marcel
General Po: 88-89
ARLEN, Michael
General Po: 89
"Ace of Cads" Wa: 22
"The Ancient Sin" Wa: 22
"The Black Archangel" Wa:
22
"The Cavalier of the Streets"
Wa: 23
"Consuelo" Wa: 23
"Farewell, These Charming
People" Wa: 23
"Gay Falson" Wa: 23
"The Gentleman from America"
Wa: 23
The Green Hat Po: 89
"The Luck of Captain Fortune"
Wa: 23
"The Prince of the Jews"
Wa: 23
"The Romance of Iris Poole"
Wa: 23
"Salute the Cavalier" Wa:
23
"The Smell in the Library"
Wa: 23

ARLT, Roberto
General Br: 55
ARMAH, Ayi Kwei
General BALE: 271-273;
LCAB: 7
The Beautyful Ones Are Not
Yet Born BALE: 271-273
Fragments BALE: 272-273
ARMATTOE, Raphael Ernest Grail
General BALE: 273-274
ARMIN, Robert
General NI: 325-327
Foole upon Foole: Or Six
Sortes of Sottes ERP:
79-81
A Nest of Ninnies see Foole
upon Foole: Or Six Sortes
of Sottes
d'ARNAUD, Baculard
Le Bal de Venise Fi: 2
Epreuves du sentiment Fi:
2-3
Nouvelles historiques Fi: 3
Theresa Fi: 3
ARNICHES BARRERA, Carlos
General Br: 55; Po: 89
La Señorita de Trevelez Br:
55
ARNIM, Achim von
Halle DC2: 43
"The Heirs" Wa: 23
"Juvenis" Wa: 23
Die Kronenwächter Fi: 285
"Liturgy" Wa: 23
Die Majoratsherren Fi: 285
"The Matchmaker" Wa: 23
"Mistris Lee" Wa: 23
Owen Tudor Fi: 285
Seltsames Begegnen und Wied-
ersehen Fi: 285
Der tolle Invalide auf dem
Fort Ratonneau Fi: 285;
Ke: 256; Wa: 23-24
ARNOLD, Matthew
General ICBAP: 5; LCAB:
7; Ma: 79-80; VP: 11-15
"Balder Dead" ICBAP: 5
"The Buried Life" PE: 20
"Cadmus and Harmonia"
ICBAP: 5
"Cromwell" PE: 20
Culture and Anarchy Ma: 78
"Dover Beach" ICBAP: 5;
LCAB: 7; PE: 20-21; VP:
11, 14
"A Dream" PE: 21

"Empedocles on Etna" ICBAP:
5; PE: 21-22; VP: 11, 13
"A Farewell" PE: 22
"The Forsaken Merman"
ICBAP: 5; PE: 22; VP:
13
"Fragment of an 'Antigone'"
PE: 22
"The Future" PE: 22
"Haworth Churchyard"
ICBAP: 5; PE: 22
"Human Life" PE: 22
"In Harmony with Nature"
PE: 22
"In Utrumque Paratus"
ICBAP: 6; PE: 22
"Isolation: To Marguerite"
PE: 22-23
"Last Glen" ICBAP: 6
"The Last Word" PE: 23
"Meeting" PE: 23
"Memorial Verses" PE: 23
"A Modern Sappho" PE: 23
"Morality" PE: 23
"Mycerinus" PE: 23
"The Neckan" PE: 23
"New Sirens" ICBAP: 6
On the Study of Celtic Liter-
ature LCAB: 7
"Palladium" PE: 23
"Parting" PE: 23
"Philomena" PE: 23
"Quiet Work" PE: 23
"Religious Isolation" PE: 23
"Requiescat" PE: 23
"Resignation" ICBAP: 6;
PE: 23
"Rugby Chapel" ICBAP: 6;
PE: 24
"The Scholar-Gipsy" ICBAP:
6; LCAB: 7; PE: 24;
VP: 12, 14
"Self-Dependence" PE: 24
"Shakespeare" ICBAP: 6;
PE: 25
"The Sick King in Bokhara"
PE: 25
"Sohrab and Rustum" ICBAP:
6
"Stanzas from the Grande
Chartreuse" ICBAP: 6;
PE: 25
"Stanzas in Memory of the
Author of 'Obermann'"
PE: 25
"The Strayed Reveller"

ICBAP: 6; PE: 25; VP:
13
"A Summer Night" PE: 25
"Switzerland" PE: 25
"Thyrsis" ICBAP: 6; PE:
26; VP: 12
"To Marguerite--Continued"
PE: 26
"Tristram and Iseult" ICBAP:
7; VP: 15
"Typho" ICBAP: 7
"The World and the Quietest"
ICBAP: 7; PE: 26
ARNOLD, William Delafield
Oakfield ENES1: 3; ENES2:
4
ARNOUX, Alexandre
General Br: 56
ARNOW, Harriette
General ASF: 59
"The Hunters" Wa: 24
"Marigolds and Mules" Wa:
24
"A Mess of Pork" Wa: 24
"Washerwoman's Day" Wa:
24
ARP, Bill
General SFC: 60
ARP, Hans
General LCAB: 7; Po: 89-
90
Er Nimmt Zwei Vögel Ab Po:
90
ARRABAL, Fernando
General Br: 56; Po: 90-91
The Architect and the Em-
peror [L'architecte et
l'empereur d'Assyrie]
Br: 56; Po: 90-91
The Automobile Graveyard
[Le Cimetière des Voitures]
Br: 56
Fando and Lis Br: 56
First Communion Br: 56
Le grand cérémonial Po: 90-
91
Le Labyrinthe Po: 90-91
Orison Br: 56
Picnic on the Battlefield Br:
56
The Two Executioners Br:
57
ARREOLA, Juan José
General Po: 91
"The Switchman" Wa: 24;
WaS1: 7

ARRICK, Larry
    Unlikely Heroes ADC: 34
ARRIGHI, Mel
    Castro Complex ADC: 34
    Ordinary Man ADC: 35
ARRIVI, Francisco
    General Br: 57
    Marie Soledad DC2: 43
ARTAUD, Antonin
    General Br: 57-58; MD:
        34-35; Po: 91-97
    Le Jet de Sang Br: 58
ARTHUR, Timothy Shay
    General AN: 15
ARTHUR, William Seymour
    No Idle Winds WIL: 8
ARTSYBASHEV, Michel Petrovich
    General Br: 58; MD: 35
    At the Brink Ke: 370
    Sanin Ke: 370
    The Woman That Stood Be-
        tween Ke: 370
ARVIN, Newton
    Longfellow LCAB: 7
ASALACHE, Khadambi
    General BALE: 274
ASANOV, N.
    The Secretary of the Party
        Bureau Ke: 370
ASARE, Bediako
    General BALE: 274
ASCH, Sholem
    General Br: 58; MD: 35
    The God of Vengeance [God
        of Revenge] Br: 58; DC2:
        43
    The Nazarene LCAB: 7
ASCHAM, Roger
    General Hen: 190; SC: 38
    The Schoolmaster Hen: 190;
        SC: 38
ASCHER, Isidore Gordon
    General JW: 138
ASHBERY, John Lawrence
    General ICBAP: 7; LCAB:
        7; MDAE: 81; MP: 17-18
    "As You Came from the Holy
        Land" PE: 26
    "The Chateau Hardware" PE:
        26
    The Heroes MDAE: 81
    "Illustration" ICBAP: 7
    "Leaving the Atocha Station"
        LCAB: 7-8; MP: 18;
        PE: 26
    "The Painter" PE: 26

"The Skaters" PE: 26
"The Tennis Court Oath" PE:
    26
"White Paper" ICBAP: 7
ASHBY, William Mobile
    General BAF: 6; BAW: 38
ASHFORD, Daisy
    General TA: 83
    The Young Visitors: or Mr.
        Salteena's Plan ENES1: 3;
        ENES2: 4; TA: 83
ASHLEY, Leonard R. N.
    "The Game" PE: 26
ASHLEY, Robert
    General SC: 38
ASHLEY, William
    General BAP: 6; BAW: 38
ASHMEAD, John
    General Po: 97-98
Ashton, Winifred see DANE,
    Clemence
ASHTON-WARNER, Sylvia
    Incense to Idols CN: 28
    Spinster CN: 28
ASIMOV, Isaac
    General ASF: 60-61; LCAB:
        8
    "Anniversary" Wa: 24
    "Author! Author!" Wa: 24
    "Belief" Wa: 24
    "The Bicentennial Man" ASF:
        60
    "Black Friar of the Flame"
        Wa: 24
    "Blind Alley" Wa: 24
    "Breeds There a Man" Wa: 24
    "The Callistan Menace" Wa:
        24
    "The Dead Past" Wa: 24
    "Death Sentence" Wa: 24
    "Dreaming Is a Private Thing"
        Wa: 25
    "The Dying Night" Wa: 25;
        WaS1: 7
    "Each an Explorer" Wa: 25
    "The Encyclopedists" Wa: 25
    "Escape" Wa: 25; WaS1: 7
    "Evidence" Wa: 25
    "The Evitable Conflict" ASF:
        60; Wa: 25; WaS1: 7
    "The Feeling of Power" Wa:
        25
    "Franchise" WaS1: 7
    "Galley Slave" ASF: 60; Wa:
        25
    "The General" Wa: 25

"Green Patches" Wa: 25
"Homo Sol" Wa: 25
"Hostess" Wa: 25
"Ideas Die Hard" Wa: 25
"I'm in Marsport Without Hilda"
  Wa: 25
"The Immortal Bard" Wa: 25
"In a Good Cause" Wa: 25
"The Key" ASF: 60; Wa:
  25
"The Last Question" Wa: 26
"Liar!" Wa: 26
"Marooned Off Vesta" Wa:
  26
"The Martian Way" Wa: 26
"The Mayors" Wa: 26
"The Merchant Princes" Wa:
  26
"Mirror Image" ASF: 60
"The Monkey's Finger" Wa:
  26
"Mother Earth" Wa: 26
"The Mule" Wa: 26
"Nightfall" ASF: 60; Wa:
  26; WaS1: 7
"Not Final!" Wa: 26
"Obituary" Wa: 26
"The Red Queen's Race" Wa:
  26
"The Resublimated Properties
  of Endochronic Thiotimoline"
  ASF: 60
"Risk" WaS1: 7
"Robbie" ASF: 60; WaS1:
  7
"Runaround" WaS1: 7
"Satisfaction Guaranteed"
  Wa: 26; WaS1: 8
"Sucker Bait" Wa: 26
"The Talking Stone" Wa: 26
"Trends" Wa: 26
"The Ugly Little Boy" Wa:
  26
"The Up-to-Date Sorcerer"
  Wa: 27
"Victory Unintentional" Wa:
  27
"What Is This Thing Called
  Love" Wa: 27
ASLANIAN, Mugerditch
  Ashken Satyan Ke: 370
ASPENSTROM, Karl Werner
  Ark DC2: 43
  Happy Brothers DC2: 43
  Noose DC2: 43
  Place is Wrapped in Smoke

  DC2: 43
  Poet and the Emperor DC2:
    44
  Shadows DC2: 44
  Unfinished Flyswatter DC2:
    44
ASSAGIOLI, Roberto
  General LCAB: 8
Assis, Joaquim Maria Machado de
    see MACHADO DE ASSIS,
    Joaquim Maria
ASTLEY, Thea
  General MAP: 128-129
  The Slow Natives MAP: 128
ASTLEY, William [Price Warung]
  General AL: 108-109
ASTURIAS, Miguel Angel
  General Br: 58; LCAB: 8;
    Po: 98-99
  "The Crystal Mask" Wa: 27
  Hombres de Maíz Po: 99
  "Juanantes, the Man Who Was
    Chained" Wa: 27
  "The Legend of the Singing
    Tablets" Wa: 27
  Leyendas de Guatemala Po:
    99
  "The Looking Glass of Lida
    Sal" Wa: 27
  The President [El Señor Presi-
    dente] Po: 100
  "Quincaju" Wa: 27
  "Torotumbo" Wa: 27
Asuncion Silva, Jose see
    SILVA, Jose Ascuncion
ATHERTON, Gertrude
  General AN: 15; ASF: 61
ATIENO-ODHIAMBO, E. S.
  General BALE: 274
ATKINS, Russell
  "Heretofore" BAW: 39
  "Maleficium" BAW: 39
ATKINSON, Percy
  "Votes for Men" WaS1: 8
ATTAWAY, William
  General AAW: 37; BAF:
    6-8; BAW: 39-40; LCAB:
    8
  Blood on the Forge BAF: 7
  Let Me Breathe Thunder
    BAF: 8
AUB, Max
  General Po: 100-101
AUBIN, Penelope
  The Life of Madam de Beau-
    mont ENES1: 3

AUBREY, John
  General Bon: 72
AUCHINCLOSS, Louis
  General CFAE: 42; CN: 28;
    LCAB: 8; Po: 101
  The Embezzler Ma: 81
  The Great World and Timothy
    Colt Ma: 81-82
  The House of Five Talents
    CN: 28; Ma: 82
  Portrait in Brownstone
    Ma: 82-83
  The Rector of Justin CN: 28;
    LCAB: 8; Ma: 83
  Romantic Egoists Ma: 83-84
  Tales of Manhattan Ma: 84
  Venus in Sparta CN: 28
AUDEN, Wystan Hugh
  General Br: 58-59; EP:
    50-63; ICBAP: 7; LCAB:
    8; Ma: 85-86; MBD: 26-
    27; MD: 35; MDAE: 83-
    84; Mi: 214-215; MP: 19-
    20; Po: 101-110
  "About the House" MP: 19;
    Po: 110
  "Address for a Prize-Day"
    PE: 27
  The Age of Anxiety EP: 51-
    52; Po: 111
  "The Alien" PE: 27
  "And the Age Ended, and the
    Last Deliverer Died" from
    "In Time of War" PE: 27
  "Another Time" PE: 27
  "As I Walked Out One Evening"
    PE: 27; Po: 111
  The Bassarids Po: 112
  "Bride in the 30's" ICBAP:
    7
  "Bucolics" EP: 54
  "Caliban to the Audience"
    PE: 27
  "Casino" PE: 27
  "A Change of Air" EP: 59;
    ICBAP: 7; LCAB: 8-9;
    Po: 112
  "Christmas 1940" ICBAP: 7
  "The Climbers" PE: 27
  "Crisis" PE: 27
  "The Cultural Presupposition"
    PE: 27
  "Dame Kind" PE: 27
  "The Dance of Death" Br:
    60; PE: 27
  "Dear, Though the Night Is

  Gone" PE: 27
  "The Decoys" from The Orators
    PE: 27
  "The Diaspora" PE: 27
  "Doom Is Dark and Deeper
    than any Sea-Dingle" PE:
    28
  "Dover 1937" ICBAP: 7
  The Duchess of Malfi see also
    WEBSTER, John MD: 35
  "The Fall of Rome" PE: 28
  "Family Ghosts" ["The Strings'
    Excitement"] PE: 28
  "Fish in the Unruffled Lakes"
    ICBAP: 7; PE: 28; Po:
    113
  "For the Time Being" EDC:
    28; EP: 50-51, 53, 57; PE:
    28; Po: 113
  "Foxtrot from a Play" PE: 28;
    Po: 113
  "Fugal-Chorus" PE: 28
  "Get There If You Can and See
    the Land You Once Were
    Proud to Own" (Poem 12 of
    Poems) PE: 28
  "Goodbye to the Mezzogiorno"
    EP: 58; Po: 114
  "Have a Good Time" PE: 28
  "A Healthy Spot" ICBAP: 7;
    PE: 28; Po: 114
  "Homage to Clio" PE: 28; Po:
    114
  "Horae Canonicae" PE: 28
  "In Memory of Sigmund Freud"
    ICBAP: 8
  "In Memory of W. B. Yeats
    (d. Jan., 1939)" ICBAP:
    8; LCAB: 9; PE: 29; Po:
    114
  "In Praise of Limestone" EP:
    54, 58; ICBAP: 8; MP: 20;
    PE: 29; Po: 115
  "In Sickness and in Health"
    ICBAP: 8
  "In Time of War," Sonnet 1
    PE: 29
  "Islands" EP: 58
  "It was Easter as I Walked in
    the Public Gardens" PE:
    29
  "It's No Use Raising a Shout"
    PE: 29; Po: 115
  "Kairos and Logos" PE: 29
  "Law Like Love" PE: 29
  "Lay Your Sleeping Head, My

Love" ICBAP: 8; PE: 29; Po: 115

"Letter to a Wound" PE: 29

"Malverns" ICBAP: 8

"Meiosis" PE: 29

"Memorial for the City" ICBAP: 8; PE: 30

"Mundus et Infans" ICBAP: 8; PE: 30; Po: 115-116

"Musee des Beaux Arts" ICBAP: 8; MP: 19; PE: 30; Po: 116

"New Year Letter" EP: 50-51, 53; MP: 19; PE: 30; Po: 116

"1929" ICBAP: 8; PE: 30

"Nones" PE: 30

"Now the Leaves Are Falling Fast" ICBAP: 8; PE: 30

"O What Is That Sound" PE: 31; Po: 117

"O Where Are You Going?" Po: 117

"O Who Can Ever Gaze His Fill" PE: 31

"Ode to My Pupils" PE: 30

On the Frontier Br: 60; DC1: 24

"One Evening" PE: 30

"...The One Whose Past It Is to Lean" (Poem III of Poems) PE: 30

"The Orators" EP: 52, 58; ICBAP: 8; PE: 30-31; Po: 117

"Our Hunting Fathers Told the Story" PE: 31

"Oxford" PE: 31

"Paid on Both Sides" Br: 60; EP: 56; Po: 118

"Paysage Moralisé" EP: 54; ICBAP: 8; PE: 31

"Petition" ICBAP: 9; PE: 31; Po: 118

"Pleasure Island" PE: 31

"Poem XX" PE: 31

"Prime" PE: 31

"The Questioner Who Sits So Sly" ICBAP: 9; PE: 31; Po: 118

"Reflections in a Forest" PE: 31

"The Sabbath" PE: 31

"Schoolchildren" PE: 31

"The Sea and the Mirror" EP: 50-51, 57: PE: 32;

Po: 118-119

"Secrets" PE: 32

"September 1, 1939" ICBAP: 9; LCAB: 9; PE: 32; Po: 119

"The Shield of Achilles" EP: 54, 58; PE: 32

"Sir, No Man's Enemy, Forgiving All" PE: 32

"Song for St. Cecilia's Day" ICBAP: 9; PE: 32; Po: 119

"Spain 1937" MP: 20; PE: 32

"The Strings' Excitement" see "Family Ghosts"

"Summer Night" ICBAP: 9

"Surgical Ward" ICBAP: 9

"Their Lonely Betters" PE: 32

"To T. S. Eliot on His Sixtieth Birthday" PE: 32

"Tonight at Seven Thirty" PE: 32

"Two Worlds" ICBAP: 9

"Venus Will Now Say a Few Words" PE: 32

"Victor Was a Little Baby" Po: 119

"The Wanderer" ICBAP: 9; PE: 33; Po: 119-120

"Which of You Waking Early and Watching Daybreak" PE: 33

"Which Side Am I Supposed to Be On?" (or "Ode to My Pupils") PE: 33

"Winds" EP: 58

"Woods" PE: 33

_____ and Christopher ISHERWOOD

The Ascent of F6 see also ISHERWOOD, Christopher Br: 59-60; DC1: 23-24; EDC: 28; MBD: 26; MD: 35; Po: 111-112

Cabaret EDC: 28

The Dog Beneath the Skin see also ISHERWOOD, Christopher Br: 60; DC1: 24; EDC: 28; MBD: 26; Po: 112-113

On the Frontier EDC: 29

_____ and Chester KALLMAN

The Bassarids MDAE: 84

The Magic Flute MDAE: 83

The Rake's Progress Br:
60; MDAE: 83-84
AUDIBERTI, Jacques
General Br: 61; MD: 36;
Po: 120-123
The Black Feast [La Fête
Noire] Br: 61; DC2:
44; MD: 36
L'empire et la Trappe Po:
123-124
The Evil Runs [Le Mal Court]
Br: 61; DC2: 44
Les Femmes du Boeuf DC2:
44
La Fête Noire see The Black
Feast
La Fournier Au Corps DC2:
44
The Hobby [La Hobereaute]
Br: 61; DC2: 44
The Landlady [La Logeuse]
Br: 61
Le Mal Court see The Evil
Runs
The Natives of Bordelais
[Les Naturels du Borde-
lais] Br: 61
L'Opéra du monde Po: 124
La Pucelle DC2: 44
Quoat-Quoat Br: 61; DC2:
44
Spoken Opera [Opéra Parlé]
Br: 62; MD: 36
AUDUBON, John James
The Birds of America LCAB:
9
AUGIER, Emile
Giboyer's Son DC2: 45
Impertinents [Les Effrontes]
DC2: 45
Son-in-Law of M. Poirer [Le
Gendre de M. Poirer]
DC2: 45
AUGIERAS, François
General Po: 124
AUGUSTINE, Saint
General LCAB: 9
The City of God Ma: 87
Confessions Ma: 87-88
Soliloquies see ALFRED the
Great [translator]
Augustinus, Aurelius, Saint
see AUGUSTINE, Saint
d'AULNOY, Marie Catherine
Histoire d'Hypolite, Comte
de Duglas Ke: 16

Auppergard, Louis see ROCHE,
Louis
AURELIUS ANTONIUS, Marcus
Meditations LCAB: 9
AUSTEN, Jane
General Du: 8-11; LCAB: 9
Emma Be: 180; Du: 1-3;
EN: 1-2; ENE: 3-5;
ENES1: 3-4; ENES2: 4-
6; LCAB: 10; Ma: 89-90
Lady Susan EN: 2; ENE: 5;
ENES1: 4; ENES2: 6
Love and Friendship ENE: 5;
ENES1: 4-5; ENES2: 6
Mansfield Park Du: 3-5; EN:
2-3; ENE: 5-7; ENES1:
5-6; ENES2: 6-8; LCAB:
10; Ma: 90-91
Northanger Abbey Be: 180;
Du: 5; EN: 3; ENE: 7-
8; ENES1: 6; ENES2: 8;
Ma: 92-93
Persuasion Du: 5-6; EN: 3-
4; ENE: 8; ENES1: 7;
ENES2: 9-10; Ma: 93-94
Pride and Prejudice Be: 180;
Du: 6-7; EN: 4-5; ENE:
8-9; ENES1: 8; ENES2:
10-11; LCAB: 10; Ma: 94-
96
Sandition EN: 5; ENES1: 9;
ENES2: 11; Ma: 96
Sense and Sensibility Du: 7-
8; EN: 5; ENE: 10;
ENES1: 9; ENES2: 11-12;
Ma: 96-98
The Watsons EN: 5; ENES1:
9; ENES2: 12
AUSTIN, Leo I.
Poems WIL: 8-9
AUSTIN, Mary [Hunter]
General AN: 15-16; ASF: 62
"The Bandit's Prayer" Wa: 27
"Papago Wedding" ASF: 62
"The Walking Woman" ASF:
62
"The Woman at the Eighteen-
Mile" ASF: 62
AUSTIN, William
"The Man with the Cloaks"
ASF: 62
"Peter Rugg, the Missing Man"
ASF: 62-63; Wa: 27
AVELLAN FERRES, Enrique
General Br: 62
AVERCHENCO, Arcadii

"The Young Man Who Flew
Past" SFC: 11; Wa: 27
AVISON, Margaret
General Po: 124-125
"Butterfly Bones; Or Sonnet
Against Sonnets" PE: 33
"Natural/Unnatural" PE: 33
"Prelude" PE: 33
AWOONOR, Kofi
General BAF: 8-9; BALE:
275-276; BAW: 41
This Earth, My Brother
BAF: 8-9; BALE: 275-
276; BAW: 42
AXELROD, George
General LCAB: 10; MDAE:
86
Goodbye Charlie ADC: 35;
LCAB: 10; MDAE: 86
The Seven Year Itch ADC:
35; Br: 62; LCAB: 10;
MDAE: 86
Will Success Spoil Rock Hunt-
er? ADC: 35; LCAB:
10
AYALA, Francisco
General Po: 125
The Bottom of the Glass Fi:
192
Dog's Death Fi: 192-193
El Inquisidor Po: 125
Muertes de Perro Po: 125-
126
El rapto Fi: 193
Ayala, Ramon Perez de see
PEREZ DE AYALA, Ramon
AYCKBOURN, Alan
General MDAE: 87-88;
TMBP: 29
Absurd Person Singular
TMBP: 29
How the Other Half Loves
TMBP: 29
Norman Conquests TMBP:
29, 73
Relatively Speaking TMBP:
29
AYME, Marcel
General Br: 62; MD: 36;
Po: 126-127
The Barkeep of Blemont Ke:
16
"Les Boeufs" Wa: 28
"Le Chien" Wa: 28
Clérambard Br: 62; MD:
36

La Convention Belzébir Br:
62
"Les Cygnes" Wa: 28
The Green Mare Ke: 17
Maison basse Ke: 17
"Le Mauvais Jars" Wa: 28
The Miraculous Barber Ke:
17
La Mouche Bleu MD: 36
The Second Face Ke: 17
The Secret Stream Ke: 17
Le Table aux creves Ke: 17
The Transient Hour Ke: 17
AYRTON, Michael
General Po: 127
AYTON, Sir Robert
General Ai: 46
AYTOUN, William Edmondstoune
General Ai: 140
AZANA, Manuel
General Po: 127
AZIKIWE, Nnamdi
General BALE: 276
AZORIN [José Martínez RUIZ]
General Br: 62-63, 571; MD:
36; Po: 2649-2654
Angelita DC2: 45; MD: 36-
37
Brandy, Mucho Brandy DC2:
45
El caballero inactual Fi: 193,
Ke: 182
Cervantes O La Casa Encantada
DC2: 45; MD: 37
Comedia del Arte MD: 37
Diario de un enfermo Ke: 182
Doña Inés Fi: 193; Po: 2654-
2655
Farsa Docente DC2: 45; MD:
37
La Fuerza del Amor MD: 37
La Guerrilla MD: 37
Lo invisible DC2: 46; MD:
37; Po: 2655
El libro de Levante Ke: 182;
Po: 2655
El licenciado Vidriera Po:
2655
Nuestro padre San Daniel Ke:
182
Old Spain DC2: 46
Pasión Po: 2655-2656
Pueblo Ke: 182
Salvadora de Olbena Fi: 192
"El secreto oriental" WaS1:
8

Tomas Rueda Fi: 193
"El topacio" WaS1: 8
La voluntad Fi: 193
_____ and MUÑOZ SECA,
    Pedro
El Clamor MD: 37
AZUELA, Mariano
    General LCAB: 10
    Los de abajo Po: 128
    The Fireflies Ma: 99
    The Underdogs Ma: 99-100
AZUONYE, Chukwuma
    General BALE: 276-277

                B

B., W. [translator]
    Certayne Conceyts & Jeasts,
        in The Philosophers Ban-
        quet by Michael SCOTT
        ERP: 82
BABAYEVSKI, S.
    Cavalier of the Golden Star
        Ke: 370-371
    Light Over the Land Ke:
        371
BABBITT, Irving
    General APC: 151-153;
        LCAB: 10; Po: 129
BABE, Thomas
    Kid Champion ADC: 35
    Rebel Women ADC: 35
BABEL, Isaac
    General LCAB: 10; Po: 129
    "After the Battle" Wa: 28
    "Argamak" Wa: 28
    "Awakening" Wa: 28
    "Bagrat Ogly and the Eyes
        of His Bull" Wa: 28
    "Childhood at Grandmother's"
        Wa: 28
    "The Church at Novograd"
        Wa: 28
    "Crossing into Poland"
        ["Perekhod Cherez
        Zbruch"] Po: 130; Wa:
        28
    "Dante St." Wa: 28
    "The Death of Dolgushov"
        Wa: 29
    "Di Grasso" SFC: 11; Wa:
        29
    "The End of St. Hypathius"
        Wa: 29

"Evening" Wa: 29
"The Father" Wa: 29
"First Love" Wa: 29
"Froim Grach" Wa: 29
"Gapa Guzhva" Wa: 29
"Gedali" Wa: 29
"Grishchuk" Wa: 29
"Guy de Maupassant" Wa: 29
"The History of My Dovecot"
    SFC: 11
"How It Was Done in Odessa"
    Wa: 29-30
"Ilia Isaacovich and Margarita
    Prokofievna" Wa: 30
"In St. Valentine's Church"
    Wa: 30
"In the Basement" Wa: 30
"An Inquiry" Wa: 30
"Inspiration" Wa: 30
"The Journey" Wa: 30
"Karl-Yankel" Wa: 30; WaS1:
    8
"The King" Wa: 30
"The Kiss" Wa: 30
"Kolyvushka" Wa: 30
Konarmia see Red Cavalry
"A Letter" Wa: 30
"Line and Color" Wa: 30
"Ljubka the Cossack" Wa: 30
"Mama, Rimma, and Alla" Wa:
    Wa: 30
"My First Goose" Wa: 31
"My First Literary Fee" Wa:
    31
"Oil" Wa: 31
"Old Shloime" Wa: 31
"Pan Apolek" SFC: 11; Wa:
    31
"Prischepa's Vengeance" SFC:
    11; Wa: 31
"The Quaker" Wa: 31
"The Rabbi" Wa: 31
"The Rabbi's Son" Wa: 31
Red Cavalry [Konarmia]
    Fi: 415-416; LCAB: 10;
    Ma: 101; Po: 129-130
"The Remount Officer" Wa:
    31
"The Road to Brody" Wa:
    31
"St. Valentine's Church" Wa:
    31
"Salt" Wa: 31
"Sashka the Christ" Wa: 31
"Shabos Nahamu" Wa: 31
"The Sin of Jesus" Wa: 32

"Squadron Commander Trunov" Wa: 32

"The S.S. Cow-Wheat" Wa: 32

Staraja Ploscad Po: 130

"The Story of a Horse" Wa: 32

"The Story of a Woman" Wa: 32

"The Story of My Dovecote" Wa: 32

"Sulak" Wa: 32

"Sunset" Wa: 32

"There Were Nine of Them" Wa: 32

"The Trial" Wa: 32

"With Old Man Makhno" Wa: 32

"You Were Taken In, Captain" Wa: 32

BACHELARD, Gaston
General Po: 130-131

BACHMANN, Ingeborg
General Br: 63; Po: 132
"Alles" Wa: 32
"Das dreissigste" Wa: 32
"Freies Geleit" Po: 132
Der Gute Gott von Manhattan Br: 63
Malina Fi: 285
"Ein Wildermuth" Wa: 32
Die Zikaden Br: 63

BACHSTROM, Johann Friedrich
Das Land der Inquiraner Fi: 285

BACKUS, Isaac
General AP: 574

BACON, Francis
General Ba: 27-30; Hen: 131-132; LCAB: 10-11; Ma: 102
Essays Ba: 30-31
The Historie of the Raigne of King Henry the Seventh Ba: 31; Hen: 53; Ma: 102-103
New Atlantis Ba: 31; Ma: 103-104

BACON, Peggy
General LCAB: 11

BAGCHI, Ganesh
General BALE: 277

BAGE, Robert
General Be: 54-55; LCAB: 11
Barham Downs ENES2: 12

The Fair Syrian ENES2: 12
Hermsprong, or Man As He Is Not ENES2: 12
James Wallace ENES2: 12
Man As He Is ENES1: 9; ENES2: 12
Mount Henneth ENES2: 13

BAGNOLD, Enid
General MDAE: 90
The Chalk Garden DC1: 24; EDC: 29; MD: 37; MDAE: 90
The Chinese Prime Minister EDC: 29
Gertie EDC: 29; MD: 37
Last Joke EDC: 29
Lottie Dundass EDC: 30
A Matter of Gravity EDC: 30
Poor Judas EDC: 30

BAHR, Hermann
General Br: 63; MD: 37; Po: 132
The Concert [Das Konzert] Br: 63; MD: 37
Dialog vom Marsyas Po: 132
Die Mutter DC2: 46; MD: 37

BAILEY, Philip James
"Life's More Than Breath and the Quick Round of Blood" (from Festus) PE: 33

BAILLIE, Joanna
General Ai: 99; EDT: 73-74
De Montfort: A Tragedy in Five Acts EDT: 74

BAKER, Elliott
A Fine Madness CFAE: 43; CN: 28
The Penny Wars ADC: 36

BAKER, Herbert
General LCAB: 11

BAKER, Karle W.
"Courage" PE: 33

BAKER, Thomas
The Fine Lady's Airs DC1: 24

BAKLANOV, Gregorii
An Inch of Ground Ke: 371

BAKUNIN, Mikhail Aleksandrovich
General LCAB: 11

BALDERSTON, John
General Po: 133
Farewell Performance ADC: 36
_____ and Hamilton DEANE
Dracula ADC: 36

_____ and J. E. HOARE
Red Planet ADC: 36
_____ and J. C. SQUIRE
Berkeley Square ADC: 36-
37; Po: 133
BALDWIN, James
General AAF: 76-77; AAL:
125, 133-139; AAPD: 340-
341; AAW: 37-40; ASF:
64; BAF: 10-17; BAP:
7-8; BAW: 46-48; Br:
63; CFAE: 47-52; CN:
29-31; LCAB: 11; MBA:
7; Ne: 19-20; Po: 133-
137
The Amen Corner AAPD:
341; ADC: 37; BAP: 8-
10; Br: 63; MBA: 7, 9
Another Country AAF: 77;
AAL: 135-138; BAF: 13,
16-17; CFAE: 48; CN:
31-32; LCAB: 11; Ma:
105; Po: 133, 137-138
Blues for Mister Charlie
AAL: 133, 138; AAPD:
340-341; ADC: 37-38;
BAP: 8-10; Br: 64;
MBA: 8-9; Po: 138
"Come Out of the Wilderness"
WaS1: 8
"Exodus" Wa: 33
The Fire Next Time AAL:
138
Giovanni's Room AAL: 136-
137; BAF: 11, 17-18; CN:
32-33; LCAB: 11; Ma:
105-106
Go Tell It on the Mountain
AAF: 76; AAL: 134, 136-
138; AAW: 38; BAF: 10-
13, 18: CFAE: 49; CN:
33-34; LCAB: 11; Ma:
106-107; Po: 133, 139
"Going to Meet the Man"
AAL: 138; AAW: 39; ASF:
63; BAF: 18; CFAE: 51;
Po: 139; Wa: 33; WaS1:
8
If Beale Street Could Talk
BAF: 18-19
"The Man Child" WaS1: 8
Nobody Knows My Name
AAL: 136
Notes of a Native Son AAL:
136; AAW: 40
"No Name in the Street"

BAW: 48
One Day When I Was Lost
BAP: 9; BAW: 48
"The Outing" AAL: 138; Wa:
33
"Previous Condition" AAL:
133; ASF: 63; Wa: 33;
WaS1: 8
"Sonny's Blues" AAL: 138;
ASF: 63; BAF: 13, 15-
16; Wa: 33; WaS1: 9
Tell Me How Long the Train's
Been Gone BAF: 19; CN:
34; Po: 139-140
"This Morning, This Evening,
So Soon" AAL: 137; ASF:
64; Po: 140; Wa: 33;
WaS1: 9
BALDWIN, Joseph Glover
General ASF: 64
"Samuel Hele, Esq." ASF:
64
"Simon Suggs, Jr., Esq."
ASF: 64
BALDWIN, William
A Marvelous Hystory Intitulede
Beware the Cat ERP: 83-
84
A Mirror for Magistrates SC:
38
A Treatise of Morale Philosophie
Hen: 190
BALE, John
General ED: 203-204; Hen:
98; SC: 39
King John DC1: 24; Ma:
108
Sir John Oldcastle DC1: 24
BALKE, Betty T.
"Apostle to Alpha" WaS1: 9
BALL, Hugo
Flametti Fi: 286
Tenderenda the Dreamer Fi:
286
BALL, John
General Po: 140
BALLANTYNE, Robert Michael
General Ai: 144; ECL: 110
The Coral Island ENES2: 13;
Po: 1309
BALLARD, James Graham
The Crystal World ENES1: 10
"The Drowned Giant" WaS1:
9
"The Impossible Man" Wa: 33
"The Terminal Beach" Wa: 33

"The Voices of Time" Wa: 34
BALZAC, Honoré de
General LCAB: 11-12
"Adieu" SFC: 11; Wa: 34;
WaS1: 9
Argow le pirate Ke: 17
The Bachelor's House Ke: 17
Béatrix Fi: 3; Ke: 17
Une Blonde Ke: 17
"Brother in Arms" Wa: 34
Le Centenaire Fi: 3; Ke:
17
César Birotteau Fi: 3; Ke:
17-18; Ma: 109
The Chouans Fi: 3; Ke:
18; Ma: 109-110
Christ in Flanders see Jesus
Christ in Flandres
Clotilde de Lusignan Fi: 3-4
Le Colonel Chabert Fi: 4;
Ke: 18; SFC: 12; Wa:
34
"Comedians Without Knowing
It" see "Involuntary
Comedians"
"A Commission in Lunacy"
["The Interdiction"] SFC:
12; Wa: 34
La Conquette de Plassans Fi:
4
"The Conscript" Wa: 34
The Country Doctor Ke: 18;
Ma: 110
Cousin Bette [La Cousine
Bette] Fi: 4; Ke: 18;
Ma: 110-111
Cousin Pons Ke: 18-19; Ma:
111
Le Curé de Tours see The
Vicar of Tours
Le Dangier d'estre trop
cocquebin Ke: 19
La Dernière fée Ke: 19
La Dernière Incarnation de
Vautrin Ke: 19
Dom Gigadas Ke: 19
"The Duchess of Langeais"
SFC: 12; Wa: 34
L'Ecole des Menages DC2:
46
The Elixir of Long Life Ke:
19
The Employees Ke: 19-20
"An Episode Under the Ter-
ror" SFC: 12; Wa: 34
Eugénie Grandet Fi: 4-5;

Ke: 20; Ma: 111-112
L'Excommunie Ke: 20
La Femme de trente ans Fi:
5
Father Goriot Ma: 112
Une Fille d'Eve Fi: 5
Gambara Fi: 5; Ke: 20;
SFC: 12; Wa: 34; WaS1:
9
Gaudissart Ke: 20; SFC:
12; Wa: 34
Gobseck Fi: 5; Ke: 20;
Wa: 35; WaS1: 9
"La Grande Breteche" SFC:
12; Wa: 35
"La Grenadière" SFC: 12;
Wa: 35
The History of the Thirteen
Ke: 20
Honorine Fi: 5
"The House of the Cat and
the Racket" SFC: 12; Wa
35
Human Comedy Fi: 5-7; Ke:
20-24; LCAB: 12; Ma:
113-114
"The Initiate" SFC: 13; Wa:
35
"The Interdiction" see "A
Commission in Lunacy"
"Involuntary Comedians"
["Comedians Without Know-
ing It"] SFC: 13; Wa:
35
L'Israélite Ke: 24
Jane la Pale Ke: 24
Jean Louis Fi: 7; Ke: 24
Jesus Christ in Flandres
Fi: 7; Ke: 24; SFC: 12;
Wa: 34; WaS1: 9
The Lily of the Valley Fi:
7-8; Ke: 24-25
Lost Illusions Fi: 8; Ke:
25; LCAB: 12; Ma: 114-
115
Louis Lambert Fi: 8; Ke:
25; SFC: 13; Wa: 35;
WaS1: 9
"Madame Firmiani" SFC: 13;
Wa: 35
"Maître Cornélius" see "Mas-
ter Cornelius"
"Les Marana" SFC: 13; Wa:
35
Marie Stuart Ke: 25
Massimilla Doni Fi: 8; SFC:

13; Wa: 35
"Master Cornelius" ["Maître
    Cornélius"] Ke: 25;
    SFC: 13; Wa: 35
Melmoth Converted Ke: 25;
    SFC: 13; Wa: 35
Mercadet DC2: 46
"The Message" SFC: 13;
    Wa: 36
La Muse du Département Fi:
    8
Oeuvres de jeunesse Ke: 25
"A Passion in the Desert"
    SFC: 14; Wa: 36; WaS1:
    10
The Peasants LCAB: 12
Le Père Goriot Fi: 8-9; Ke:
    26
Pierrette Fi: 9; Ke: 26
"The Provincial Muse" Wa:
    36
"The Purse" SFC: 13; Wa:
    36
The Quest of the Absolute
    Fi: 9; Ke: 26
La Rabouilleuse Fi: 9
"The Red Inn" SFC: 14;
    Wa: 36
Le Réquisitionnaire Ke: 26-
    27
Sarrasine Fi: 9-10
The Secrets of the Princess
    of Cadignan Ke: 27
The Splendors and Miseries
    of Courtesans Fi: 10; Ke:
    27
The Unknown Masterpiece
    Ke: 27; SFC: 14; Wa:
    36
Ursule Mirouët Ke: 27
El Verdugo Ke: 27; Wa: 36
Le Vicaire des Ardennes Fi:
    10; Ke: 27
The Vicar of Tours [Le Curé
    de Tours] Fi: 4; Ke:
    19; SFC: 14; Wa: 36
Vie et malheurs d'Horace de
    Saint-Aubin Ke: 27
La Vieille Fille Fi: 10
The Village Priest Ke: 27
The Wild Ass's Skin Fi: 10-
    11; Ke: 27-28; Ma: 115
BAMBARA, Toni Cade
General BAF: 20; BAW:
    49
Gorilla, My Love BAF: 20;

BAW: 49
BAN, Bank
Loyal Subject DC2: 46
BANCROFT, George
General Cla: 101
BANCROFT, Hubert Howe
General LCAB: 12
BANDEIRA, Manuel
General Po: 140-141
BANDELLO, Matteo
Certaine Tragicall Discourses
    see FENTON, Sir Geoffrey
    [translator]
BANERJEE, Tarashankar
"Boatman Tarini" Wa: 37
BANG, Herman
Haablose Slaegter Ke: 346
BANIM, John
General BN: 14
BANKS, John
General Li: 98
The Three Laws (I & II)
    DC1: 25
The Unhappy Favourite DC1:
    25; Li: 98
Virtue Betrayed Li: 98
BANNEKER, Benjamin
General LCAB: 12
BANVILLE, John
Birchwood ENES2: 13
Long Lankin ENES2: 13
Nightspawn ENES2: 13
Baraka, Imamu Amiri see
    JONES, Le Roi
BARALT, Luis A.
General Br: 64
Barba Jacob, Porfirio see
    OSORIO, Miguel Angel
BARBEY D'AUREVILLY, Jules
    Amédée
"A un dîner d'athées" WaS1:
    11
L'Amour impossible Fi: 11
La Bague d'Annibal Fi: 11
"Le bonheur dans le crime"
    Wa: 37; WaS1: 11
Le Cachet d'onyx Fi: 11;
    Wa: 37
Ce qui ne meurt pas Fi: 11
"Le dessous de cartes d'une
    partie de whist" WaS1: 11
L'Ensorcelée Fi: 11
Une Histoire sans nom Fi: 11
"Lea" Wa: 37
"Le plus bel amour de Don
    Juan" Wa: 37; WaS1: 11

Un Prêtre Marié Fi: 11
"Le rideau cramoisi" WaS1:
11
"La vengeance d'une femme"
WaS1: 11
Une vieille maîtresse Fi:
11-12; Ke: 28
BARBOUR, John
General Ai: 28; LCAB: 12
The Bruce Ai: 28; OMEP:
407
BARBUSSE, Henri
General Po: 141
Le Feu Fi: 12; Ke: 28
Barca, Pedro Calderon de la
see CALDERON DE LA
BARCA, Pedro
BARCLAY, Alexander
General SC: 39
The Ship of Fools SC: 39
"The Towre of Vertue and
Honoure" PE: 33
BARCLAY, John
Argenis ENE: 10
Euphomormionis Satyricon
ENE: 10
BAREA, Arturo
General Po: 141-142
The Forging of a Rebel Po:
141-142
BARFIELD, Owen
General Po: 142
BARGA, Corpus
General Po: 142
BARING, Maurice
General Mi: 216-217
BARING-GOULD, Sabine
General BN: 14
Mehalah BN: 14; ENES1:
10
BARKE, James
General Ai: 274
BARKENTIN, Marjorie and Pad-
raic COLUM
Ulysses in Nightgown ADC:
38
BARKER, Elliott
A Fine Madness Po: 142
BARKER, Eric
General Po: 142-143
BARKER, George
General MP: 22-23; Po:
143
Allegory of the Adolescent
and the Adult LCAB: 12
"The Amazons" PE: 33

"The Seagull, Spreadeagled,
Splayed on the Wind" PE:
34
"Sonnet to My Mother" PE:
34
Three Memorial Sonnets LCAB:
12
"To Father Gerard Manley Hop-
kins, S.J." PE: 34
BARKER, James Nelson
General AD: 70-72; Lon: 55
Marmion; or Flodden Field
AD: 70-71
Pocahontas; or the Indian
Princess AD: 70; DC1:
25; Lon: 55
Tears and Smiles AD: 71
The Tragedy of Superstition
AD: 70-72
BARKER, Jane
Exilius ENES1: 10
BARKER, William
General Hen: 211
BARKSTEAD, William
General NI: 327
BARLACH, Ernst
General Br: 64-65; MD: 37-
38; Po: 143
Der Arme Vetter see The
Poor Relation
The Blue Mr. Ball [Der Blaue
Boll] Br: 65; DC2: 46;
MD: 38; Po: 144
The Count of Ratzburg [Der
Graf von Ratzeburg] Br:
65
The Dead Day [Der Tote Tag]
Br: 65
Die Echten Sedemunds see
The Hundred Percenters
The Flood [The Deluge; Die
Sündflut] Br: 65; DC2:
47; MD: 38
The Foundling [Der Findling]
Br: 65-66
The Good Time [Der Gute
Zeit] Br: 66
Der Graf von Ratzeburg see
The Count of Ratzburg
The Hundred Percenters [The
Genuine Sedemunds; Die
Echten Sedemunds] Br:
66; DC2: 47
The Poor Relation [Der Arme
Vetter] Br: 66; DC2:
46; MD: 38; Po: 143

Die Sündflut see The Flood
Der Tote Tag see The Dead
Day
BARLAS, John [Evelyn DOUG-
LAS]
General TA: 84
BARLOW, Anna Marie
Glory! Hallelujah! ADC: 38
BARLOW, Joel
General AP: 179-183; Da:
62-63
"Advice to a Raven in Russia"
PE: 34
Advice to the Privileged Or-
ders in the Several States
of Europe AP: 179-181
The Columbiad Da: 62
"The Hasty Pudding" PE:
34
The Vision of Columbus Da:
63
BARNARD, John
Ashton's Memorial ENES2:
13
BARNARD, Marjorie
"Dry Spell" Wa: 37
"The Persimmon Tree" Wa:
37
"The Woman Who Did the
Right Thing" Wa: 37
BARNES, Barnabe
General Log: 250-251
BARNES, Djuna
General ASF: 67; MDAE:
91-92; Po: 144-145
"Aller et Retour" ASF: 66;
WaS1: 11
The Antiphon Br: 66; DC1:
25; MD: 38; MDAE: 91-
92, 191
"Beyond the End" see
"Spillway"
"A Boy Asks a Question of
a Lady" WaS1: 11
"Cassation" ASF: 66; WaS1:
11
"The Doctors" ASF: 66;
WaS1: 11
"Dusie" WaS1: 11
"The Grande Malade" ASF:
66; WaS1: 11
"Indian Summer" ASF: 66;
WaS1: 11
"Katrina Silverstaff" see
"The Doctors"
"Ladies Almanack" ASF: 66

"The Little Girl Continues" see
"The Grande Malade"
"A Little Girl Tells a Story to
a Lady" see "Cassation"
"Mother" WaS1: 11
"The Nigger" ASF: 66;
WaS1: 12
"A Night Among the Horses"
ASF: 66; WaS1: 12
Nightwood LCAB: 12; MDAE:
92; Po: 145
"No-Man's Mare" ASF: 66;
WaS1: 12
"The Passion" ASF: 66;
WaS1: 12
"The Perfect Murder" ASF:
66-67; WaS1: 12
"The Rabbit" ASF: 67;
WaS1: 12
"The Robin's House" ASF: 67
"Spillway" ASF: 67; WaS1: 12
BARNES, Margaret Ayer
General ASF: 67
"Arms and the Boy" Wa: 37
"The Dinner Party" Wa: 37
"Feather Beds" Wa: 38
"Perpetual Care" Wa: 38
BARNES, Peter
General MDAE: 93; TMBP:
33
Bewitched TMBP: 33
Leonardo's Last Supper
TMBP: 33
Noonday Demons TMBP: 33
Ruling Class MDAE: 93;
TMBP: 33
Sclerosis TMBP: 33
BARNES, William
General LCAB: 13
BARNFIELD, Richard
General SC: 40
Barnsley, Alan Gabriel see
FIELDING, Gabriel
BAROJA, Pío
General Po: 145-150
Agonías de nuestro tiempo
Fi: 193; Ke: 182
Aurora roja Ke: 182
Aventuras, inventos y mixtifi-
caciones de Silvestre Para-
dox Fi: 194
La Busca Po: 148
Caesar or Nothing Fi: 194;
Ke: 182; Ma: 116
Camino de perfección Po:
150

La dama errante Ke: 182
El escuadrón del Brigante
Fi: 194
El gran torbellino del mundo
Fi: 194; Ke: 182
Las inquietudes de Shanti
Andía Ke: 182; Po: 146
El mayorazgo de Labraz Ke:
182-183
Memorias de un hombre de
acción Fi: 194; Po: 150
El mundo es ansi Po: 146,
148
The Restlessness of Shanti
Andia Ma: 116
Las tragedias grotescas Ke:
183
The Tree of Knowledge Fi:
194; Ke: 182; Ma: 116
Vidas Sombrias Po: 151
The Way to Perfection Fi:
194
Zalacaín the Adventurer [Zala-
caín el aventurero] Ke:
183; Ma: 117; Po: 151
Baron Corvo see ROLFE,
Frederick
BARON, Robert
The Cyprian Academy ERP:
85
BARR, Robert ["Luke SHORT"]
General ECL: 114
BARRAULT, Jean Louis
General Po: 151
BARRES, Maurice
General Po: 151-153
Amori et Dolori Sacrum Ke:
28
Les Bastions de l'Est Ke:
28
Culte du moi Ke: 28; Po:
152
L'Ennemi des Lois Ke: 28
Un homme libre Po: 153
Le Roman de l'energie nation-
ale Ke: 28; Po: 152
BARRETT, Eaton Stannard
The Heroine ENES1: 10
BARRETT, Lindsay [Eseoghene]
General BAP: 20; BAW:
60; WIL: 9
Song for Mumu BAF: 26;
WIL: 9
BARRETT, Nathan
General BAW: 61
Bars of Adamant BAF: 26;

BAW: 61
BARRIE, Sir James Matthew
General Ai: 175-176; Br:
66-67; MBD: 27; MD: 38-
39; Mi: 217-218; Po: 153-
154; TA: 85
The Admirable Crichton Br:
67; DC1: 25; EDC: 30;
LCAB: 13; Ma: 118; MBD:
27; MD: 39
The Adored One Br: 67; MD:
39
Alice Sit-By-The-Fire Br: 68;
EDC: 30; Ma: 118
Auld Licht Idylls ENES1: 10;
Ma: 118
Barbara's Wedding EDC: 30
The Boy David Br: 68; DC1:
25; EDC: 30; Ma: 119;
MD: 39
Dear Brutus Br: 68; DC1:
25; EDC: 30-31; Ma: 119;
MD: 39-40
Farewell, Miss Julie Logan
ENES1: 10
A Kiss for Cinderella Br:
68; DC1: 25; EDC: 31;
Ma: 119
The Little Minister Br: 68;
ENES1: 10; Ma: 120: MD:
40
The Little White Bird ENES1:
10; Ma: 120
Margaret Ogilvy ENES1: 10
Mary Rose Br: 68; DC1:
25; EDC: 31; Ma: 120;
MD: 40
The New Word Br: 68; MD:
40
Peter and Wendy ENES1: 10;
Ma: 120
Peter Pan Br: 69; DC1:
26; EDC: 31-32; Ma:
121; MBD: 27; MD: 40;
Po: 154
Peter Pan in Kensington Gar-
dens ENES1: 10; ENES2:
13
Quality Street Br: 69; EDC:
32; Ma: 121; MD: 40-41
Richard Savage MD: 41
Rosalind EDC: 32
Rosy Rapture EDC: 32
Sentimental Tommy ENES1:
11; Ma: 121
Shall We Join the Ladies?

Br: 69; EDC: 32; MD: 41

Tommy and Grizel ENES1: 11; Ma: 122

The Twelve Pound Look Br: 69; DC1: 26; Ma: 122; MD: 41

Walker, London Br: 69; MD: 41

A Well-Remembered Voice DC1: 26

What Every Woman Knows Br: 69; DC1: 26; EDC: 32; Ma: 122; MD: 41

When a Man's Single ENES1: 11

A Window in Thrums ENES1: 11

BARRIOS, Eduardo
General Po: 154
"La antipatía" Wa: 38
Del Natural Po: 154
El Hermano Asno Po: 155
"Pages of a Poor Devil" Wa: 38
Vivir DC2: 47

BARRUCAUD, Victor
Chariot de Terre Cuite DC2: 47

BARRY, Bob
Murder Among Friends ADC: 39

BARRY, Julian
Lenny ADC: 39

BARRY, Lording
General NI: 327-328

BARRY, Philip
General BAP: 21; Br: 69-70; LCAB: 13; Lon: 25-26; MD: 41-42; MDAE: 94-95; Po: 155
The Animal Kingdom ADC: 39; Br: 70; MD: 42
Bright Star ADC: 39; Br: 71; MD: 42
Foolish Notion ADC: 39-40; Br: 71; DC1: 26; MD: 42
Here Come the Clowns ADC: 40; Br: 71; MD: 42-43
Holiday ADC: 40; Br: 71; DC1: 26
Hotel Universe ADC: 40; Br: 71-72; DC1: 26; Lon: 26; MD: 43
In a Garden ADC: 41; Br:

72; DC1: 26; MD: 43
John ADC: 41
The Joyous Season ADC: 41; Br: 72; DC1: 26; MD: 43
Liberty Jones ADC: 41
My Name Is Aquilon ADC: 41; MD: 43
Paris Bound ADC: 41; Br: 72; DC1: 26; MD: 43
The Philadelphia Story ADC: 41; Br: 72; DC1: 26; MD: 43
Spring Dance ADC: 42
Tomorrow and Tomorrow ADC: 42; Br: 73; DC1: 27; MD: 44
Without Love ADC: 42; Br: 73; MD: 44
You and I Br: 73; MD: 44
_____ and Elmer RICE
Cock Robin ADC: 42
_____ and Robert E. SHER-WOOD
Second Threshhold ADC: 42-43; Br: 72-73; DC1: 26; MD: 43; MDAE: 94-95

BARTH, John
General ASF: 70; CFAE: 55-57; CN: 34; LCAB: 13; Ne: 20-21; Po: 155-157
"Ambrose His Mark" ASF: 67; Wa: 38; WaS1: 12
"Anonymiad" ASF: 67-68; Wa: 38; WaS1: 12
"Autobiography: A Self-Recorded Fiction" ASF: 68; WaS1: 12
"Bellerophoniad" ASF: 68; Wa: 38; WaS1: 12
Chimera SFC: 68
"Dunyazadiad" ASF: 68; Wa: 38; WaS1: 12
"Echo" ASF: 68; Wa: 38; WaS1: 12
The End of the Road CN: 35; Ma: 123-124; Ne: 20; Po: 156-158
The Floating Opera CN: 35; Ma: 124-125; Ne: 20; Po: 158
"Frame-Tale" ASF: 68
Giles Goat-Boy CFAE: 56-57; CN: 35-36; LCAB: 13; Ma: 125-126; Ne: 20; Po: 156, 158-159

"Glossolalia" ASF: 68
"Life-Story" ASF: 68; WaS1: 13
"Lost in the Funhouse" ASF: 68-69; CN: 36; LCAB: 13; Po: 159; Wa: 38; WaS1: 13
"Menelaiad" ASF: 69; Wa: 38; WaS1: 13
"Night-Sea Journey" ASF: 69; Wa: 38-39; WaS1: 13
"Perseid" ASF: 70; Wa: 39; WaS1: 13
"Petition" ASF: 70; Wa: 39
The Sot-Weed Factor CFAE: 56; CN: 36; LCAB: 13; Ma: 126-127; Ne; 20; Po: 156, 159-160
"Title" ASF: 70
"Water Message" Wa: 39
BARTHELME, Donald
General ASF: 73; LCAB: 13; Ma: 128-129; Po: 160-161
"At the Tolstoy Museum" WaS1: 13
"The Balloon" ASF: 71; Wa: 39
"City Life" ASF: 71; Ma: 128; Wa: 39; WaS1: 13
"Daumier" ASF: 71; WaS1: 13
"The Dolt" ASF: 71
"Engineer-Private Paul Klee Misplaces an Aircraft Between Milbertscofen and Cambrai, March 1916" ASF: 71
"A Film" ASF: 72
"Game" Wa: 39
"The Glass Mountain" ASF: 72; WaS1: 13
"The Great Hug" ASF: 72
"The Indian Uprising" ASF: 72; Wa: 39
"Kierkegaard Unfair to Schlegel" ASF: 72
"Magellan" ASF: 72
"Me and Miss Mandible" Wa: 39
"On Angels" Wa: 39
Paraguay LCAB: 13
"The Party" ASF: 72; Wa: 39
"The Policemen's Ball" WaS1: 13

"Robert Kennedy Saved from Drowning" ASF: 72; Wa: 39; WaS1: 14
"The Sandman" ASF: 72; WaS1: 14
"Sentence" ASF: 72
"A Shower of Gold" ASF: 72
Snow White CFAE: 59; LCAB: 13; Ma: 129
"That Cosmopolitan Girl" ASF: 72
Unspeakable Practices, Unnatural Acts Ma: 130
"Views of My Father Weeping" ASF: 73; Wa: 39-40
"The Wound" ASF: 73
BARTHES, Roland
Sarrasine Fi: 12
S/Z Fi: 12
BARTRAM, John
General AP: 185-187; Da: 49
BARTRAM, William
General AP: 189-192; Da: 107-108
Travels Through North and South Carolina, Georgia, East and West Florida AP: 189-192
BART-WILLIAMS, Gaston
General BALE: 277
BARZINI, Luigi
General LCAB: 13
BASHEER, Vaikom Muhammad
"Birthday" Wa: 40
BASS, George
The Game BAP: 21
BASS, Kingsley B., Jr.
We Righteous Bombers BAP: 22; MBA: 24
BASSANI, Giorgio
General Po: 161
The Garden of the Finzi-Continis Fi: 258
BASSANO, Enrico
General Br: 73
BASSETT, Paul R.
War Zone ADC: 43
BASSHE, Emanuel Jo
General Br: 73
The Centuries Br: 74
Earth Br: 74; MBA: 24
Hoboken Blues MBA: 24
BASSING, Eileen
General LCAB: 14
BASSING, Robert

"Lullaby" ASF: 74
BASSO, Hamilton
General CN: 37; Po: 161-
162
In Their Own Image CN: 37
The Light Infantry Ball AN:
16
Sun in Capricorn AN: 16;
CN: 37
The View from Pompey's Head
CN: 37
BASTIEN, Eliot
General WIL: 9
Anancy Story WIL: 9
Bastos, Augusto Roa see
ROA BASTOS, Augusto
Antonio
BATAILLE, Georges
General Po: 162-164
L'Histoire de l'oeil Po: 164
La part maudite Po: 163
BATAILLE, Henry
General Br: 74
La Belle au Bois Dormant
DC2: 47
L'Homme a la Rose DC2: 47
Ton Sang DC2: 47
BATES, Arthenia J.
Seeds Beneath the Snow
BAF: 27
BATES, H. E.
General Po: 164
"The Small Portion" Wa: 40
Spella Ho ENES2: 13
BAUDELAIRE, Charles Pierre
General LCAB: 14
"Abel et Cain" Po: 4025
"La Fanfarlo" Wa: 40;
WaS1: 14
Flowers of Evil Ma: 131
BAÜER, Gérard
General Po: 164-165
BAUGH, Edward C.
General WIL: 9-10
BAUGHAN, Blanche Edith
"Pipi on the Prowl" Wa: 40
BAUM, Lyman Frank
General LCAB: 14
BAUM, Vicki
General Br: 74
Grand Hotel EDC: 32-33
_____ and Benjamin F.
GLAZER
Summer Night EDC: 33
Baus, Tamayo y see
TAMAYO Y BAUS,

Manuel
BAX, Clifford
General Mi: 218
BAXTER, James K.
The Spots of the Leopard Br:
74
BAXTER, Richard
General Hen: 38
BAYLIE, Simon
General LJCD: 228
BAYNTON, Barbara
General AL: 116
"The Chosen Vessel" Wa: 40
Bazan, Emilia Pardo see PARDO
BAZAN, Emilia, Condesa de
BAZIN, Hervé
"The Thousand-Franc Note"
Wa: 40
BEACH, Joseph Warren
The Glass Mountain Po: 165
BEACH, Lewis
Merry Andrew ADC: 43
A Square Peg ADC: 43
BEACONSFIELD, Benjamin Disraeli
Endymion EN: 5-6
Sybil EN: 6
BEALE, Mrs. O. A. S.
"Shadow in the House" ASF:
74
BEARDSLEY, Aubrey
General TA: 87
Venus and Tannhäuser
ENES2: 13
BEATTIE, James
General Ai: 73; EC: 50
"The Hermit" PE: 34
"Retirement" PE: 34
"Verses Occasioned by the
Death of the Revd Mr
Charles Churchill" PE: 34
BEAUMARCHAIS, Pierre Augustin
Caron
Barber of Seville DC2: 47-48;
EDC: 33
Les Deux Amis see Two
Friends
Eugenie DC2: 48; EDC: 33
The Guilty Mother [La Mere
Coupable] EDC: 33
Marriage of Figaro DC2: 48;
EDC: 33-34
Tarare DC2: 48
Two Friends [Les Deux Amis]
DC2: 48
BEAUMONT, Francis
"On the Tombs in Westminster

Abbey" PE: 34

_____ and John FLETCHER

General ED: 207-212; LJCD: 4-22, 51, 86-88; TSD: 36-39

Barnavelt see Sir John van Olden Barnavelt

The Beggar's Bush DC1: 71; EDC: 34; LJCD: 34-35, 117; Ma: 680

The Bloody Brother DC1: 72; LJCD: 35, 88, 118

Bonduca DC1: 27; EDC: 34; LJCD: 35-36; Ma: 677

The Captain DC1: 27; LJCD: 36

The Chances EDC: 34; LJCD: 36

The Coxcomb DC1: 27; EDC: 34; LJCD: 36-37; Ma: 134

Cupid's Revenge EDC: 34; LJCD: 37; Ma: 134-135

The Custom of the Country DC1: 27; EDC: 34; LJCD: 37-38

The Double Marriage DC1: 27; LJCD: 38, 117-118; TSD: 90

Elder Brother LJCD: 88, 118

The Fair Maid of the Inn DC1: 27; LJCD: 38-39, 88, 118

The Faithful Shepherdess DC1: 72; EDC: 34-35; LJCD: 31-32, 88; Ma: 677-678; TSD: 38

The False One LJCD: 39

Four Plays; or, Moral Representations, in One LJCD: 39-40

Henry VIII [The Famous History of the Life of King Henry VIII] LJCD: 40, 118; TSD: 38

The Honest Man's Fortune LJCD: 40

The Humorous Lieutenant EDC: 35; LJCD: 40-41

The Island Princess EDC: 35; LJCD: 41

A King and No King DC1: 27-28; EDC: 35; LJCD: 32-33; Ma: 135-136;

TSD: 38-39

The Knight of Malta DC1: 28; EDC: 35; LJCD: 41-42, 102-103

The Knight of the Burning Pestle DC1: 28; EDC: 35-36; LJCD: 22-25; Ma: 132-133; TSD: 37-38

The Laws of Candy LJCD: 42

The Little French Lawyer LJCD: 42

The Lovers' Progress [The Wandering Lovers] EDC: 36; LJCD: 42

Love's Cure; or the Martial Maid DC1: 28; EDC: 36; LJCD: 42-43

Love's Pilgrimage DC1: 28; LJCD: 43

The Loyal Subject see FLETCHER, John

The Mad Lover DC1: 28; EDC: 36; LJCD: 44, 118

The Maid in the Mill EDC: 36; LJCD: 44-45; TSD: 38

The Maid's Tragedy DC1: 28-29; ED: 208; EDC: 36; LJCD: 25-28, 88; Ma: 136-137; TSD: 38-39, 105

The Mask of the Inner Temple and Gray's Inn LJCD: 41

Monsieur Thomas LJCD: 45

The Nice Valour LJCD: 45, 89

The Night Walker LJCD: 45-46

The Noble Gentleman EDC: 36

Philaster DC1: 29; ED: 208; EDC: 36-37; LJCD: 28-31, 89; Ma: 137-138; TSD: 36-39

The Pilgrim see FLETCHER, John

The Prophetess EDC: 37; LJCD: 46, 89

The Queen of Corinth EDC: 37; LJCD: 46, 118

Rule a Wife and Have a Wife EDC: 37; LJCD: 46-47; Ma: 678; TSD: 37

The Scornful Lady DC1: 29; EDC: 37; Ma: 138-139

Sir John van Olden Barnavelt [Barnavelt] EDC: 34;

LJCD: 47; Ma: 680
Thierry and Theodoret see
    also FLETCHER, John
    and Philip MASSINGER
    EDC: 37; LJCD: 47, 89
Two Noble Kinsmen see also
    FLETCHER, John and
    William SHAKESPEARE
    ED: 208; EDC: 37-38;
    LJCD: 47
Valentinian DC1: 73; EDC:
    38; LJCD: 33-34, 89
A Very Woman LJCD: 47
The Wandering Lovers see
    The Lovers' Progress
A Wife for a Month EDC:
    38; LJCD: 48
The Wild Goose Chase DC1:
    73; EDC: 38; LJCD: 48
Wit at Several Weapons DC1:
    29; EDC: 38; LJCD: 49
Wit Without Money EDC: 38;
    LJCD: 49
The Woman Hater; or, The
    Hungry Courtier EDC:
    38; LJCD: 49-50, 89; Ma:
    133; TSD: 39, 87
The Woman's Prize DC1: 29;
    LJCD: 50; Ma: 678-679
Women Pleased LJCD: 50
BEAUMONT, Joseph
    "Psyche" ICBAP: 9
BEAUVOIR, Simone de
    General Po: 165-166
    All Men Are Mortal Fi: 12;
        Ke: 28
    All Said and Done Ma: 140
    The Blood of Others Fi:
        12; Ke: 29
    The Coming of Age Ma: 140
    La Femme rompue Fi: 12
    L'Invitée Fi: 12
    The Mandarins [Les Mandarins]
        Fi: 12-13; Ke: 29; Ma:
        141; Po: 166
    Memoirs of a Dutiful Daughter
        Ma: 141
    Pour une morale de l'am-
        biguïté Po: 167
    The Pretty Pictures Fi: 13
    The Second Sex Ma: 142
    She Came to Stay Ke: 29
BECHE, Louis
    "The Awful Duel on Utuana"
        Wa: 41
    "A Basket of Breadfruit"

Wa: 41
    "A Blackbirding Incident" Wa:
        41
    "The Chilean Bluejacket" Wa:
        41
    "A Dead Loss" Wa: 41
    "The Fate of the Alida" Wa:
        41
    "'Frank' the Trader" Wa: 41
    "Lufton's Guest" Wa: 41
    "Luliban of the Pool" Wa: 41
    "The Man Who Knew Every-
        thing" Wa: 41
    "Nerida, the Maid of Suwarrow"
        Wa: 41
    "Ninia" Wa: 41
    "Saunders and the Devil Fish"
        Wa: 41
    "A Tale of a Mask" Wa: 41
    "The Trader's Wife" Wa: 41
    "Yorke the Adventurer" Wa:
        41
BECHER, Johannes R.
    General Po: 167-168
    Schlacht um Berlin Po: 168
    Schritt der Jahrhundertmitte
        Po: 168
BECK, Beatrix
    General Po: 169
BECK, Robert [Iceberg Slim]
    General BAF: 28; BAW: 66
    Naked Soul of Iceberg Slim
        BAF: 28
BECK, Warren
    "Detour in the Dark" Wa: 42
BECKE, George Lewis
    General AL: 120
BECKER, Ernest
    General LCAB: 14
BECKER, Julius
    Last Supper DC2: 48
BECKER, Lucien
    General Po: 169
BECKETT, Samuel
    General Br: 74-78; CFAE:
        66-72; CN: 37-41; LCAB:
        14; MBD: 28-35; MD: 44-
        47; MDAE: 100-110; Po:
        169-200
    Act Without Words DC2: 48;
        EDC: 38; MD: 47
    Act Without Words I [Acte
        sans Paroles I] Br: 78
    Act Without Words II [Acte
        sans Paroles II] Br: 79
    All Strange Away Fi: 13

All That Fall [Tout Ceux Qui
  Tombent] Br: 79-80;
  DC2: 49; EDC: 38-39;
  MD: 47; MDAE: 100;
  Po: 174, 180-183
"Assumption" Wa: 42; WaS1:
  14
"The Calmative" ["Le Calmant"]
  Wa: 42; WaS1: 14
Cascando Br: 80; EDC: 39
"A Case in a Thousand" Wa:
  42
Cendres see Embers
Come and Go [Va et Vient]
  Br: 80-81; DC2: 49;
  EDC: 39
Comment C'est see How It
  Is
"Dante and the Lobster"
  Wa: 42; WaS1: 14
La Dernière Bande see
  Krapp's Last Tape
"Ding Dong" Wa: 42
"Draff" Wa: 42
Dream of Fair to Middling
  Women CN: 41; Fi: 13
Eh Joe Br: 81; EDC: 39
Eleutheria Br: 81; MDAE:
  103
Embers [Cendres] Br: 81-
  82; DC2: 49; EDC: 39-
  40; MBD: 28, 35; MDAE:
  100, 110; Po: 180
En Attendant Godot see
  Waiting for Godot
"The End" Wa: 42; WaS1:
  14
Endgame [End of the Party;
  Fin de Partie] Br: 82-
  84; DC2: 49-51; EDC:
  40-42; LCAB: 14-15; Ma:
  143; MBD, 28-31, 33-35;
  MD: 48-49; MDAE: 100-
  103, 105-110, 397; Po:
  181, 191-193
"Endless" see "Without"
Enough Fi: 13; Wa: 42;
  WaS1: 15
"The Expelled" Wa: 42;
  WaS1: 15
The Expulsion Ke: 29
Film Br: 84-85; DC2: 51;
  EDC: 42; MDAE: 106,
  108; Po: 191
Fin de Partie see End-
  game

"Fingal" Wa: 42
"First Love" WaS1: 15
"From an Abandoned Work"
  Wa: 42
Happy Days [Oh! Les Beaux
  Jours] Br: 85-86; DC2:
  51-52; EDC: 42-44; MBD:
  28-29, 31, 33, 35; MD: 49;
  MDAE: 102, 103, 105, 107-
  108; Po: 174, 193-194
How It Is [Comment C'est]
  CN: 41; ENE: 11; ENES1:
  11; ENES2: 14; Fi: 13-15;
  Ke: 29-30; LCAB: 15;
  Po: 169, 183; Wa: 43;
  WaS1: 15
Imagination Dead Imagine Fi:
  15; Po: 169; Wa: 43;
  WaS1: 15
L'innommable see The
  Unnamable
Krapp's Last Tape [La
  Dernière Bande] Br: 86-
  87; DC2: 52; EDC: 44-45;
  Fi: 15; Ma: 143-144; MBD:
  29-31, 34-35; MD: 50;
  MDAE: 102, 105, 109; Po:
  195; TMAP: 22; TMBP:
  142
Lessness Fi: 15; WaS1: 15
The Lost Ones EDC: 45;
  ENES1: 11; ENES2: 14;
  Fi: 15-16; Ma: 144; Wa:
  43; WaS1: 15
"Love and Lethe" Wa: 43
Malone Dies [Malone Meurt]
  see also Trilogy CFAE:
  68; CN: 41-42; ENE: 11-
  12; ENES1: 11-12; ENES2:
  14; Fi: 16-18; Ke: 30-31;
  LCAB: 15; Ma: 144-145;
  MDAE: 108; Po: 176,
  195, 197
Mercier et Camier ENES1:
  12; ENES2: 14; Fi: 18;
  Ke: 31; Ma: 145-146;
  MDAE: 104
Molloy see also Trilogy
  CFAE: 70-72; CN: 42-43;
  ENE: 12-13; ENES1: 12-
  14; ENES2: 15; Fi: 18-21;
  Ke: 31-32; Ma: 146-147;
  MDAE: 108; Po: 176, 195-
  197
More Pricks Than Kicks Fi:
  21

Mots et Musique see Words
and Music
Murphy CFAE: 66, 68; CN:
43; ENE: 13-14; ENES1:
14; ENES2: 15; Fi: 21-23;
Ke: 32; Po: 197
Not I EDC: 45
Oh! Les Beaux Jours see
Happy Days
"Ping" Wa: 43; WaS1: 15
Play Br: 87-88; DC2: 52;
EDC: 45-46; MBD: 28,
30, 32; MDAE: 106; Po:
198
"Premier Amour" Wa: 43
Proust Po: 198
"Residue" Wa: 43
"Texts for Nothing" ["Stories
and Texts for Nothing"]
Ma: 147-148; Wa: 43
Tout Ceux Qui Tombent see
All That Fall
Trilogy [Malone Dies; Molloy;
Unnamable] CN: 43-44
The Unnamable [L'innommable]
see also Trilogy CFAE:
70-71; CN: 44-45; ENE:
14; ENES1: 14-15; ENES2:
15-16; Fi: 23-25; Ke: 32-
33; Ma: 148-149; MDAE:
108; Po: 176, 194-195,
197
Va et Vient see Come and
Go
Waiting for Godot [En Atten-
dant Godot] Br: 88-97;
DC2: 52-57; EDC: 46-51;
LCAB: 14-15; Ma: 149-
150; MBD: 28-35; MD:
47-48; MDAE: 101-110,
471; Po: 170, 174, 181,
183-191; TMAP: 40, 63,
164; TMBP: 144, 151,
185, 224
"Walking On" Wa: 43
Watt CFAE: 68, 70, 72;
CN: 45-46; ENE: 15;
ENES1: 15-16; ENES2:
16; Fi: 25-27; Ke: 33-
34; MDAE: 419; Po:
198-200; TMBP: 177
"A Wet Night" Wa: 43;
WaS1: 15
"What a Misfortune" Wa:
43
"Without" ["Endless"] Wa:

43
Words and Music [Mots et Mu-
sique] Br: 97; EDC: 51-
52
"Yellow" Wa: 43
BECKFORD, William
General Be: 61-62; Du: 11-
12
Vathek Be: 61-62; Du: 11;
EN: 6; ENE: 15-16;
ENES1: 16; ENES2: 16-17
The Vision ENES1: 16;
ENES2: 17
BECKHAM, Barry
General BAF: 28; BAW: 67
My Main Mother BAF: 29;
BAW: 67
Runner Mack BAF: 29; BAW:
67
BECON, Thomas
General SC: 40
BECQUE, Henri Francois
General Br: 97
The Buffoons [Les Polichin-
elles] EDC: 52
Les Corbeaux see The Vul-
tures
L'Enfant Prodigue see The
Prodigal Son
Les Honnêtes Femmes see
Virtuous Women
The Merry-go-round [La Nav-
ette] EDC: 52
Michel Pauper EDC: 52
La Parisienne see The Woman
of Paris
Les Polichinelles see The
Buffoons
The Prodigal Son [L'Enfant
Prodigue] EDC: 52
Virtuous Women [Les Honnêtes
Femmes] EDC: 52
The Vultures [Les Corbeaux]
Br: 97; DC2: 57; EDC:
52
The Woman of Paris [La
Parisienne] Br: 97;
DC2: 57; EDC: 52
BEDDOES, Thomas Lovell
General Re: 190
Death's Jest Book DC1: 30
BEDE, The Venerable
"Death-Song" OMEP: 114;
PE: 34
Historia Ecclesiastica Gentis
Anglorum see ALFRED

the Great [translator]
BEDI, Rajindar Singh
"Lajwanti" Wa: 44
BEECHER, Henry Ward
General LCAB: 15
BEER, Johann
Simplizianischer Weltkucker
Ke: 256
Sommertage Ke: 256
Winternachte Ke: 256
BEER, Thomas
General AN: 16; LCAB: 15
Stephen Crane: A Study in
American Letters LCAB:
15
BEER-HOFMANN, Richard
General MD: 50
Count of Charolis DC2: 57
Der Tod Georgs Ke: 256
BEERBOHM, Max
General LCAB: 15; Ma:
151; Po: 200-201; Ri:
100-104, 106-107; TA: 89
"The Dreadful Dragon of Hay
Hill" Wa: 44
The Happy Hypocrite Ri:
105
"Hilary Maltby and Stephen
Braxton" Wa: 44
Seven Men Ma: 151
"Yai and the Moon" Wa: 44
Zuleika Dobson ENES1: 17;
ENES2: 17; Ma: 151-152;
Ri: 102, 105-106
BEERS, Lorna Doone
Prairie Fires LCAB: 15
BEHAN, Brendan
General Br: 97-98; MBD:
36; MD: 50; MDAE: 112-
113; Po: 201; Sch: 6;
TMIP: 10-29
The Big House TMIP: 24,
29
Borstal Boy ENES1: 17;
ENES2: 17; LCAB: 15;
Ma: 153; Po: 201; TMIP:
16, 18-19, 21, 23-24, 26,
29-30
Brendan Behan's Island
TMIP: 30
Brendan Behan's New York
TMIP: 30
Confessions of an Irish Rebel
TMIP: 30
A Garden Party TMIP: 24
An Giall MBD: 36; MDAE:

113; TMIP: 16, 28
Hold Your Hour and Have
Another TMIP: 30
The Hostage Br: 98; DC1:
30; EDC: 52-53; LCAB:
15; Ma: 153-154; MBD:
36; MD: 50; MDAE: 113;
Po: 201; TMIP: 10, 12-
24, 27-28, 30-32, 61
"Irish Folk Songs and Ballads"
TMIP: 32
Moving Out TMIP: 24
The Quare Fellow Br: 98;
DC1: 30; EDC: 53-54;
Ma: 154; MBD: 36; MD:
50; MDAE: 113; Po: 201;
TMIP: 10, 12, 14-18, 21-
24, 26-28, 32-33
The Scarperer ENES1: 17;
ENES2: 17; TMIP: 17, 33
_____ and Alan SIMPSON
Richard's Cork Leg EDC: 54;
TMIP: 14, 24, 26
BEHN, Aphra
General Be: 66-67; Li: 100
Abdelazer Li: 100
The False Count DC1: 30
The History of the Nun
ENES1: 17
Love Letters Between a Noble-
man and His Sister
ENES1: 17; ENES2: 17
The Lucky Chance--Or An
Alderman's Bargain DC1:
30
Oroonoko Be: 66-67; EN:
6; ENE: 16; ENES1: 17;
ENES2: 18; Ma: 155
The Round Heads; Or The
Good Old Cause DC1: 30
Sir Patient Fancy DC1: 30;
Ma: 155-156
Town-Fop: Or Sir Timothy
Tawdry DC1: 30
The Widow Ranter DC1: 30;
Li: 100
The Younger Brother DC1:
30
BEHRMAN, Samuel Nathaniel
General ALL: 40; Br: 99;
JW: 369-370; LCAB: 16;
Lon: 26-27; MD: 50-51;
MDAE: 116
Amphitryon 38 ADC: 43
Biography ADC: 43-44;
Br: 99; DC1: 31; MD:

51
Brief Moment ADC: 44; Br: 100
But for Whom, Charlie? ADC: 44; Br: 100
The Cold Wind and the Warm ADC: 44; MD: 51; MDAE: 116
Dunningan's Daughter ADC: 45; Br: 100; MD: 51
End of Summer ADC: 45; Br: 100; MD: 51
I Know My Love ADC: 45; Br: 100; MD: 51; MDAE: 116
Jacobowsky and the Colonel ADC: 45-46
Jane ADC: 46; MD: 51
Lord Pengo ADC: 46
Meteor ADC: 46; Br: 100
No Time for Comedy ADC: 47; Br: 100; DC1: 31; MD: 51
The Pirate ADC: 47; MD: 52
Rain from Heaven ADC: 47; Br: 100-101; DC1: 31; MD: 52
The Second Man ADC: 47-48; Br: 101; MD: 52
Serena Blandish ADC: 48
The Talley Method ADC: 48; Br: 101; MD: 52
Wine of Choice ADC: 48; Br: 101; DC1: 31; MD: 52
_____, Joshua LOGAN, and Harold ROME
Fanny ADC: 48-49
BEK, Alexander
The Life of Berezhkov Ke: 371; Po: 201-202
BELASCO, David
General AD: 75-78; JW: 374; Lon: 56; MD: 52
The Girl of the Golden West ADC: 49
The Heart of Maryland ADC: 49; Br: 101
Naughty Anthony ADC: 49
_____ and Henry Churchill De MILLE
Men and Women ADC: 49
_____ and John Luther LONG
The Darling of the Gods

ADC: 49
Madame Butterfly ADC: 49
BELDA, Joaquin
General Po: 202
BELING, Richard
A Sixth Booke to the Countesse of Pembrokes Arcadia ERP: 87
BELITT, Ben
"Double Poem" PE: 34
"Full Moon: The Gorge" PE: 34
"Xerox" PE: 34
BELKNAP, Jeremy
General AP: 193-194; Da: 108
The History of New Hampshire AP: 193; Da: 108
BELL, Adrian
Folly Field ENES2: 18
BELL, Charles
General Po: 202
BELL, James Madison
General AAPD: 56; AAW: 40; BAW: 68; LCAB: 16
BELL, Julian
General Po: 202
BELL, Martin
"Manicure" PE: 34
BELL, Vera
General WIL: 10
Ogog WIL: 10
BELLAMY, Edward
General AF: 26-28; ALL: 40-41; AN: 17; Cla: 102-103; Ho: 15; LCAB: 16
Equality AF: 26-28; ALL: 40; AN: 16
Looking Backward AF: 26-28; ALL: 40; AN: 16-17; Ho: 15, 142; Ma: 157-158
A Traveler from Altruria AF: 27
BELLEFOREST, François de
The History of Hamlet [Anonymous English translator] ERP: 254-255
BELLENDEN, John
General Ai: 38
BELLIDO, Jose-Maria
Football Br: 101
BELLOC, Hilaire
General Po: 202-203; TA: 90
Emmanuel Burden ENES1: 17

The Path to Rome Ma: 159
BELLOW, Saul
  General ALL: 41-42; AN:
    18; ASF: 75-76; CFAE:
    73-80; CN: 46-49; JW:
    181-182; LCAB: 16;
    MDAE: 118-119; Ne: 21-
    23; Po: 203-208
  "Address by Gooley Mac-
    Dowell to the Hasbeens
    Club of Chicago" ASF:
    74; Wa: 44
  The Adventures of Augie
    March ALL: 42; AN:
    17-18; CFAE: 76-77, 79-
    80; CN: 49-51; JW: 182;
    LCAB: 16; Ma: 160-161;
    Ne: 21-22; Po: 203, 207-
    209
  "By the Rock Wall" ASF: 74
  Dangling Man ALL: 42; AN:
    18; CFAE: 74; CN: 51-
    52; LCAB: 16; Ma: 161-
    162; Ne: 22-23; Po: 207
  "A Father-to-Be" ASF: 74;
    Wa: 44; WaS1: 15
  "The Gonzaga Manuscripts"
    ASF: 75; Wa: 44; WaS1:
    15
  Henderson the Rain King
    AN: 18; CFAE: 74-78;
    CN: 52-54; JW: 181-182;
    LCAB: 16; Ma: 162-163;
    Ne: 22; Po: 203, 207,
    209-211
  Herzog ALL: 41-42; CFAE:
    74-77, 79; CN: 54-56;
    JW: 181; LCAB: 17; Ma:
    163-165; Ne: 21-23; Po:
    204, 207, 211-213
  Humboldt's Gift ALL: 41;
    Ma: 165
  The Last Analysis ADC: 49-
    50; Br: 102; MDAE:
    118-119
  "Leaving the Yellow House"
    ASF: 75; Wa: 44; WaS1:
    16
  "Looking for Mr. Green"
    ASF: 75; Wa: 44-45;
    WaS1: 16
  Mr. Sammler's Planet ALL:
    41-42; JW: 181; Ma:
    165-166
  "Mosby's Memoirs" WaS1:
    16
  "The Old System" ASF: 75;
    Wa: 45
  Orange Soufflé [Under the
    Weather] ADC: 50
  Seize the Day ALL: 42; CFAE:
    80; CN: 56-58; LCAB: 17;
    Ma: 166-168; Ne: 22-23;
    Po: 207, 214; SFC: 14-15;
    Wa: 45-46; WaS1: 16
  "A Sermon by Doctor Pep"
    Wa: 46; WaS1: 16
  To Jerusalem and Back ALL:
    41
  "The Trip to Galena" ASF:
    75; Wa: 46
  "Two Morning Monologues"
    ASF: 75
  Under the Weather see
    Orange Soufflé
  The Victim CFAE: 75; CN:
    58-59; LCAB: 17; Ma:
    168-169; Ne: 21
BELYAYEV, Alexander
  The Leap Into Nothing Ke:
    371
BELYJ, Andrej
  "The Baptized Chinese" WaS1:
    16
  Four Symphonies Fi: 416
  Kotik Letaev Fi: 416-417
  Maski Fi: 417
  Moscow Fi: 417
  Petersburg Fi: 417-418; Ke:
    371; LCAB: 25; Po: 214
  The Second Symphony Ke:
    371
  The Silver Dove Fi: 418;
    Ke: 371
  Third Symphony: The Return
    Ke: 371
  Zapiski Chudaka Fi: 418
BENAVENTE, Jacinto
  General Br: 102-103; MD:
    52-53; Po: 215-216
  The Alien Nest EDC: 54
  Alma Triunfante see The
    Soul Triumphant
  The Angora Cat [La Gata de
    Angora] EDC: 54; MD:
    53
  Autumnal Roses [Rosas de
    Otoño] DC2: 58; EDC:
    55; MD: 54
  The Banquet of the Wild
    Beasts [La Comida de las
    Fieras] MD: 53

The Bonds of Interest [Los Intereses Creados] Br: 103; EDC: 54; Ma: 170-171; MD: 53

El Bufon de Hamlet DC2: 58

Campo de Armiño see Field of Ermine

La Ciudad Alegre y Confada see The Joyful and Confident

El Collar de Estrellas see The Necklace of Stars

La Comida de les Fieras see The Banquet of the Wild Beasts

Cuento de Amor DC2: 58

El Dragón de Fuego see The Fire Dragon

La Escuela de las Princesas see The School of Princesses

The Evil Done to Us [The Evil That We Do; El Mal Que Nos Hacen] EDC: 54; MD: 54

La Farándula see The Troupers

Los Favorites DC2: 58

Field of Ermine [Campo de Armiño] MD: 53

The Fire Dragon [El Dragón de Fuego] MD: 53

La Gata de Angora see The Angora Cat

Gente Conocido see People of Our Acquaintance

The Governor's Wife [La Gobernadora] Br: 103; MD: 53

The Graveyard of Dreams [La Losa de los Sueños] MD: 53

El Hombrecito see The Little Man

La Inmaculada de los Dolores see Our Lady of Sorrows

In the Clouds [Por las Nubes] MD: 54

La Infanzona Br: 103

Los Intereses Creados see The Bonds of Interest

The Joyful and Confident City [La Ciudad Alegre y Confada] MD: 53

The Law of the Children [La Ley de los Hijos] MD: 53

The Little Man [The Manikin; El Hombrecito] Br: 103; MD: 53

Lo Cursi see Vulgarity

La Losa de los Sueños see The Graveyard of Dreams

The Magic of an Hour EDC: 54

El Mal Que Nos Hacen see The Evil Done to Us

La Malquerida see Passion Flower

The Manikin see The Little Man

The Necklace of Stars [El Collar de Estrellas] MD: 53

La Noche del Sábado see A Witches' Sabbath

Noches de Verbena DC2: 58

Our Lady of Sorrows [La Inmaculada de los Dolores] MD: 53

Passion Flower [La Malquerida] Br: 103-104; DC2: 58; EDC: 55; Ma: 171; MD: 54; Po: 216

People of Our Acquaintance [People of Importance; Gente Conocido] EDC: 55; MD: 53

Por las Nubes see In the Clouds

Princess Bebe [La Princesa Bebé] Br: 104; EDC: 55; MD: 54

Rosas de Otoño see Autumnal Roses

Sacrifices [Sacrificios] MD: 54

Saturday Night EDC: 55; MD: 54

The School of Princesses [La Escuela de las Princesas] MD: 53

Señora Ama Br: 104; MD: 54

The Soul Triumphant [Alma Triunfante] EDC: 55; MD: 53

Titania DC2: 58

The Troupers [La Farándula] MD: 53

Vulgarity [Lo Cursi] Br: 104; EDC: 55; MD: 53

A Witches' Sabbath [La Noche

del Sábado] Br: 104

BENCHLEY, Nathaniel
"Deck the Halls" SFC: 15;
Wa: 47

BENCHLEY, Robert Charles
General APC: 39; LCAB:
17

BENDA, Julien
General Po: 216-217

BENDER, Hans
General Po: 217

BENEDETTI, Mario
General LCAB: 17
"As Always" Wa: 47
"The Iriate Family" Wa: 47
The Rest Is Jungle" Wa: 47
"Twilight Zone" Wa: 47

BENEFIELD, John Barry
General ASF: 77

BENEKE, Walter
Funeral Home Br: 104
El Paraiso de los Imprudentes
Br: 104

BENELLI, Sem
General MD: 54
Jest [La Cena delle Beffe]
MD: 54
Wings [Ali] MD: 54

BENER, Vüs'at O.
"The Homecoming" WaS1: 16

BENESOVA, Bozena
The Blow Ke: 372
Subterranean Fires Ke: 372
The Tragic Rainbow Ke:
372

BENET, Juan
General Po: 217

BENET, Stephen Vincent
General ALL: 42-43; ASF:
77; LCAB: 17; Po: 217-
218
"As It Was in the Beginning"
Wa: 47
"The Bishop's Beggar" Wa:
47
"By the Waters of Babylon"
Wa: 47; WaS1: 16
"A Death in the Country"
Wa: 47
"The Devil and Daniel Web-
ster" ASF: 77; Po:
218; SFC: 15; Wa: 47
"Freedom's a Hard-Bought
Thing" ASF: 77; Wa:
48
"Into Egypt" Wa: 48

"Jacob and the Indians" Wa:
48
John Brown's Body Ma: 172
"Johnny Pye and the Fool-
Killer" Wa: 48
"The Last of the Legions" Wa:
48
"Ode to Walt Whitman" PE:
35
"The Prodigal Children" Wa:
48
"Too Early Spring" Wa: 48

BENEZET, Anthony
General AP: 195

BENGAL, Ben
Plant in the Sun Br: 104

BENITEZ ROJO, Antonio
"El escudo de hojas secas"
WaS1: 16
"Estatuas sepultadas" WaS1:
17
"Primer balcon" WaS1: 17
"La tierra y el cielo" WaS1:
17

BENJAMIN, Rene
Il Faut Que Chacun Soit à Sa
Place Br: 104
Les Plaisirs du Hasard Br:
105

BENJAMIN, Walter
GENERAL Po: 218

BENN, Gottfried
General LCAB: 17; Po: 218-
221
"Gehirne" Wa: 48
"Nur Zwei Dinge" Po: 221
Der Ptolemaer Ke: 256

BENNETT, Alan
General MDAE: 120
God the Stone Breaker WIL:
10-11

BENNETT, Arnold
General BN2: 18-19; Br:
105; LCAB: 17; MD: 54-
55; Mi: 219-220; Po:
221-223; Ri: 123-137, 142-
143; Sch: 7-10; TA: 92
Accident ENES2: 18
Anna of the Five Towns BN2:
19; ENES1: 17; ENES2:
18; Ma: 173; Po: 223;
Ri: 125, 138
Body and Soul EDC: 55
Bright Island EDC: 55
Buried Alive ENES2: 18
The Card ENES2: 18; Ri:

125, 138

Clayhanger [The Clayhanger Trilogy] EN: 6; ENE: 16; ENES1: 18; ENES2: 18; Ma: 173-174; Po: 224; Ri: 123-126, 128-129, 135, 137-139; Sch: 10

"The Death of Simon Fuge" Wa: 48

Don Juan EDC: 55

A Dream of Destiny ENES2: 18; Ri: 139

The Glimpse ENES1: 18

Grand Babylon Hotel ENES2: 18

Great Adventure EDC: 55-56; Ri: 142

A Great Man ENES2: 18

Helen with the High Hand ENES2: 18

Hilda Lessways EN: 6-7; ENES1: 18; ENES2: 18; Po: 223; Ri: 123, 125, 135, 138-139; Sch: 10

Honeymoon EDC: 56

Imperial Palace ENES1: 18; ENES2: 19; Ri: 125, 139

Judith Br: 105; EDC: 56

Leonora ENES1: 18; ENES2: 19; Ri: 125

Lilian ENES2: 19; Ri: 134

The Lion's Share ENES2: 19

Lord Raingo BN2: 18; ENE: 16; ENES1: 18; ENES2: 19; Po: 224; Ri: 125-126, 132, 139

Love Match EDC: 56

A Man from the North ENES1: 18; ENES2: 19; Ri: 128, 139

"Matador of the Five Towns" Wa: 48

Milestones Ri: 142

Mr. Prohack ENES2: 19; Ri: 134

"The Muscovy Ducks" Wa: 48

The Old Wives' Tale EN: 7; ENE: 16; ENES1: 18; ENES2: 19; LCAB: 17; Ma: 174; Ri: 123-125, 127-128, 135, 137, 140-141; Sch: 10

The Pretty Lady BN2: 18; EN: 7; ENE: 16; ENES1: 18; ENES2: 19; Ri: 125,

132

The Price of Love ENES1: 18; ENES2: 19; Ri: 125

The Regent ENES2: 19

Return Journey EDC: 56

Riceyman Steps BN2: 18; EN: 7; ENE: 16; ENES1: 18; ENES2: 20; Ma: 175; Po: 224-225; Ri: 125-126, 141-142; Sch: 10

The Roll-Call ENES2: 20

Sacred and Profane Love EDC: 56; ENES1: 19; ENES2: 20

The Strange Vanguard ENES2: 20

These Twain EN: 8; ENES1: 19; ENES2: 20; Ri: 123, 126, 138-139; Sch: 10

The Title EDC: 56

Whom God Hath Joined ENES2: 20; Ri: 125

"The Woman Who Stole Everything" Wa: 48

_____ and Edward KNOBLOCK

London Life EDC: 56

Milestones EDC: 56; MD: 55

Mister Prohack EDC: 56

BENNETT, Hall

General BAF: 30

The Black Wine BAF: 30

Lord of Dark Places BAF: 30; BAW: 71

Seventh Heaven BAF: 30

Wait Until Evening BAF: 30

A Wilderness of Vines BAF: 30

BENNETT, Lerone, Jr.

General BAW: 72

BENNETT, Louise

General WIL: 11-12

Anancy Stories WIL: 12

Jamaica Labrish WIL: 12

Laugh with Louise WIL: 12

BENNETT, Michael, Cy COLE-MAN, and Dorothy FIELDS

Seesaw ADC: 50

BENSE, Max

General Po: 225

BENSON, Arthur Christopher

General Po: 225; TA: 93-94

BENSON, Mildred Wirt

General ASF: 77

BENSON, Robert Hugh

General TA: 95

BENSON, Sally

"The Overcoat" SFC: 15;
Wa: 48
The Young and Beautiful
ADC: 50
BENSON, Stella
"Story Coldly Told" Wa: 49
BENTLEY, Eric
Are You Now or Have You
Ever Been? ADC: 50-51
The Red White and Black
ADC: 51
BENTLEY, Norman K.
Drake's Mantle ENES2: 20
BERARD, Léon
General Po: 225
BERAUD, Antoine-Nicholas
La Corregidor DC2: 58
BERENGUER, Luis
General Po: 225
Marea escorada Po: 225
El mundo Juan Lobón Po:
225
BERESFORD, John Davys
General TA: 97
BEREZKO, Georgi
Greater Than the Atom Ke:
372
BERG, Gertrude and Leonard
SPIGELGASS
Dear Me, the Sky Is Falling
ADC: 51
BERGAMIN, José
General Po: 225-226
BERGELSON, David
"The Revolution and the Zuss-
mans" SFC: 15; Wa: 49
BERGENGRUEN, Werner
General Po: 226
Am Himmel wie auf Erden
Fi: 286; Ke: 257; Po:
226
"Die drei Falken" Wa: 49
Die Feuerprobe Ke: 256-257;
Po: 226; Wa: 49
The Fire Signal [Das Feuer-
zeichen] Ke: 257; Po:
226; Wa: 49
Das Hornunger Heimweh Ke:
257
Jungfräulichkeit Fi: 286;
Ke: 257
A Matter of Conscience Fi:
286; Ke: 257
"Der spanische Rosenstrock"
Wa: 49
Der Tod von Reval Ke: 257

Die Wunderbare Schreibmasch-
ine Fi: 286; Po: 226;
Wa: 49
BERGER, Gaston
General Po: 227
BERGER, Henning
Who Knows Ke: 346
BERGER, Thomas
General CFAE: 83
Crazy in Berlin Po: 227
Little Big Man CFAE: 83;
Ma: 176; Po: 227
Reinhart in Love Po: 227
de BERGERAC, Savinien Cyrano
General LCAB: 45
L'Autre monde Fi: 27
Voyage to the Moon LCAB:
45
BERGMAN, Hjalmar
General MD: 55; Po: 228
Death's Harlequin DC2: 58
Mr. Sleeman Is Coming [Herr
Sleeman Kommer] MD: 55
"Sardanapal" WaS1: 17
Swedenhielms MD: 55
BERGMAN, Ingmar
General MD: 55
BERGSTROM, Hjalmar
Karen Borneman MD: 55
BERKELEY, George
General EC: 50-51
BERKOWITZ, Isaac Dov
"At the Table" Wa: 49
"A Barbarian" Wa: 49
"The Chauffeur" Wa: 49
"Cucumbers" Wa: 49
"Cut Off" Wa: 49
"Faivke's Judgment Day" Wa:
50
"Grandchild" Wa: 50
"Guests" Wa: 50
"Moshkele Pig" Wa: 50
"Severed" Wa: 50
"The Uprooted" Wa: 50
"Yom Kipur Eve" Wa: 50
BERMANGE, Barry
General MDAE: 121
BERMUDEZ, J.
Nise Laureda DC2: 59
BERNANOS, Georges
General Br: 105; Po: 228-
230
A Crime [d'Un Crime] Fi:
27; Ke: 34; Po: 229
Dialogue of the Carmelites
[Dialogues des Carmelites]

Br: 105; Fi: 27; Po:
230

The Diary of a Country Priest
Fi: 27-28; Ke: 34; Po:
1370

Enfants humiliés Po: 229

L'Imposture Fi: 28; Ke: 35

Journal d'un curé de campagne
Po: 231

Joy Fi: 28; Ke: 35

Monsieur Ouine Fi: 28-29;
Ke: 35; Po: 229

Mouchette [Nouvelle histoire
de Mouchette] Fi: 29;
Po: 229, 231

Night Is Darkest Fi: 29

Under the Sun of Satan [Sous
le Soleil de Satan] Br:
105; Fi: 29; Ke: 35; Po:
229

BERNARD, Catherine
Eleonor d'Yvree Ke: 35

BERNARD, Ian
Chocolates ADC: 51

BERNARD, Jean-Jacques
General Br: 106; MD: 55
L'Ame en Peine see The
Unquiet Spirit
Denise Marette Br: 106
Le Feu Qui Reprend Mal
see Sulky Fire
Invitation to a Voyage
[Glamour; L'Invitation
au Voyage] Br: 106
Madeleine [Le Jardinier
d'Ispahan] Br: 106
Martine Br: 107; MD: 56
Nationale 6 Br: 107
Le Printemps des Autres
see The Springtime of
Others
A la Recherche des Coeurs
Br: 107
Le Secret d'Arvers Br: 107
The Springtime of Others
[Le Printemps des Autres]
Br: 107; MD: 56
Sulky Fire [Le Feu Qui Re-
prend Mal] Br: 107-108;
MD: 56
The Unquiet Spirit [L'Ame en
Peine] Br: 108; MD: 56

BERNARD, Kenneth
General MDAE: 122
Night Club and Other Plays
MDAE: 122

BERNARD, Richard
The Isle of Man ERP: 88

BERNARD, Thomas
Verstörung Po: 231

BERNARD, Tristan
General Po: 231

BERNARI, Carlo
Un foro nel parabrezza Fi:
258
Le radiose giornate Fi: 258

BERNASKOVA, Alena
The Road Is Open Ke: 372

BERNAUER, Rudolph and Carl
MEINHARD
Johannes Kreisler [Die Wun-
derlichen Geschichten des
Kappelmeisters Kreisler]
Br: 108

BERNE, Stanley
General ASF: 77

BERNEY, William and Howard
RICHARDSON
Dark of the Moon see also
RICHARDSON, Howard
and William BERNEY ADC:
51-52
Design for a Stained Glass Win-
dow ADC: 52
Protective Custody ADC: 52

BERNHARD, Thomas
Das Kalkwerk Fi: 286

BERNSTEIN, Henry
General Br: 108; MD: 56
L'Elevation MD: 56

BERNSTEIN, Leonard
Trouble in Tahiti ADC: 52

BERRIGAN, Daniel
The Trial of the Catonsville
Nine ADC: 52-53

BERRY, David
The Freedom Bird MBA: 24-
25
G. R. Point ADC: 53; MBA:
25

BERRY, John
"New Shoes" Wa: 50

BERRY, Wendell
General Ma: 177
"The Apple Tree" PE: 35
"The Return" PE: 35
"The White and Waking of the
House" PE: 35

BERRYMAN, John
General ALL: 43-44; ICBAP:
9; Ma: 181; MP: 24;
Po: 231-232

Berryman's Sonnets Ma: 178
"Delusions, etc." ALL: 43;
Ma: 178
"Desires of Men and Women"
PE: 35
"The Disciple" PE: 35
"The Dispossessed" PE: 35
"The Dream Songs" ALL: 43;
LCAB: 18
"Formal Elegy" PE: 35
"His Toy, His Dream, His
Rest" Ma: 179
"Homage to Mistress Brad-
street" ALL: 43; Ma:
179-180
"The Imaginary Jew" SFC:
15; Wa: 50
"Love and Fame" ALL: 43;
Ma: 180
77 Dream Songs Ma: 182-
183; Po: 232
"A Strut for Roethke" PE:
35
"Winter Landscape" ICBAP:
9; PE: 35; Po: 232
"World's Fair" PE: 35
BERTAUT, Jules
General Po: 232-233
BERTIN, Charles
Christophe Colomb Br: 108
BERTO, Guisseppe
General Po: 233
BERTRAN, Juan Bautista
General Po: 233
BERWINSKA, Krystyna
Rescue of Antigone [Ocalenie
Antygony] DC2: 59
BESANT, Walter
General BN: 15; TA: 98-99
The Alabaster Box ENES2:
20
All Sorts and Conditions of
Men ENES1: 19; ENES2:
20
Children of Gibeon ENES1:
19; ENES2: 20
BESIER, Rudolph
General Mi: 220
Barretts of Wimpole Street
EDC: 56-57; MD: 56
BESSETTE, Gérard
General Po: 233
BESTER, Alfred
General LCAB: 18
"The Push of a Finger" ASF:
78; WaS1: 17

BESTUZHEV-MARLINSKY, Alex-
ander [Alexander BESTU-
ZHEV]
"The Cuirassier" Wa: 50
"An Evening at a Bivouac"
Wa: 50
"The Frigate Hope" Wa: 50
"A Second Evening at a Bivou-
ac" Wa: 50
"The Terrible Divination" Wa:
50
"The Test" Wa: 51
"The Traitor" Wa: 51
BESUS, Roger
General Po: 233
Un Homme pour rien Ke: 35
Louis Brancourt Ke: 35
Le Refus Ke: 36
Le Scandale Ke: 36
Beti, Mongo see BIYIDI, Alex-
ander
BETJEMAN, John
General EP: 66-70; ICBAP:
9; LCAB: 18; Ma: 184;
MP: 25; Po: 234
Summoned by Bells EP: 67-
68, 70
BETTERTON, Thomas
General Li: 101-102
The Amorous Widow DC1: 31;
Li: 101
BETTI, Ugo
General Br: 108-109; MD:
56-57; Po: 234-235
Aqua Turbate see Troubled
Waters
The Burnt Flower Bed [L'Aiu-
ola Bruciata] Br: 109;
DC2: 59; EDC: 57
La Casa Sull' Acqua see The
House on the Water
Corruption at the Palace of
Justice [Corruzione al Pal-
azzo di Giustizia] Br: 109;
DC2: 59; EDC: 57
Crime on Goat Island [Delitto
all'Isola delle Capre] Br:
109; DC2: 59; EDC: 57
Frana Allo Scalo Nord see
Landslide at the North
Station
The Gambler [Il Giocatore]
EDC: 58; MD: 57
The House on the Water [La
Casa Sull' Acqua] EDC:
58

Inquiry [Ispesione] DC2: 59
L'Isola Meravigliosa see Wonderful Island
Landslide at the North Station [Frana Allo Scalo Nord] DC2: 59; EDC: 58
The Mistress [La Padrona] Br: 110; DC2: 60; MD: 57
A Night in the Rich Man's House [Notte in Casa del Ricco] EDC: 58
The Queen and the Rebels [La Regina e gli Insorti] Br: 110; DC2: 60; EDC: 58; MD: 57
Summertime EDC: 58
Time of Vengeance EDC: 58
Troubled Waters [Aqua Turbate] Br: 110; DC2: 60; EDC: 58; Po: 236
Wonderful Island [L'Isola Meravigliosa] EDC: 58

BETTIE, William
The Historie of Titana and Theseus ERP: 88

BETTS, Doris
General ASF: 78
"Beasts of the Southern Wild" WaS1: 17
"Clarissa and the Depths" Wa: 51
"The Mandarin" ASF: 78
"The Sympathetic Visitor" WaS1: 17
"The Ugliest Pilgrim" WaS1: 17

BEVAN, Donald and Edmund TRZCINSKI
Stalag 17 ADC: 53

Beyle, Marie Henri see STENDAHL

BHARATA
Natyasastra DC2: 60
Samavakara DC2: 60

BHASA
Balacarita DC2: 60
Dutavakya DC2: 60
Karbnabhara DC2: 61
Mrcchakitika DC2: 61
Naganandam DC2: 61
Urubhanga DC2: 61-62
Vow [Svapnavasavadattam] DC2: 61
Yajnaphalam DC2: 62

BHATTACHARYA, Bhabani
"Attainment" Wa: 51
"Bird's Feather" Wa: 51
"The Faltering Pendulum" Wa: 51
He Who Rides a Tiger Po: 236
"Steel Hawk" Wa: 51

BHAVABHUTI
Mahaviracarita DC2: 62

BIADULA, Zmitrok
Nightingale Ke: 372

BIBB, Eloise A. [Eloise Biff THOMPSON]
General AAPD: 56; BAW: 74

BICKERSTAFFE, Isaac
General Li: 103
Lionel and Clarissa DC1: 31
The Maid of the Mill DC1: 31

BIDPAI
The Morall Philosophie of Doni see NORTH, Thomas [translator]

BIELER, Manfred
Bonifaz oder der Matrose in der Flasche Fi: 286; Po: 236

BIENEK, Horst
Die Zelle Fi: 286

BIERCE, Ambrose
General AF: 31-34; ALL: 44-45; ASF: 80-81; Cla: 103-104; LCAB: 18; Po: 236
"The Affair at Coulter's Notch" ASF: 78; Wa: 51
"An Affair of Outposts" ASF: 78; Wa: 51
"A Baby Tramp" ASF: 78; Wa: 51
"The Boarded Window" WaS1: 17
"Chickamauga" ASF: 78; SFC: 16; Wa: 51
"The Coup de Grâce" ASF: 78; Wa: 51
"The Damned Thing" Wa: 52
"The Death of Halpin Frayser" ASF: 78; Wa: 52
"The Famous Gibson Bequest" ASF: 79; Wa: 52
"George Thurston" Wa: 52
"Haita the Shepherd" ASF: 79; Wa: 52
"A Horseman in the Sky" ASF: 79; SFC: 16; Wa:

52; WaS1: 17
In the Midst of Life LCAB:
18; Ma: 185
"Jupiter Doke, Brigadier-
General" ASF: 79; Wa:
52
"Killed at Resaca" ASF: 79;
Wa: 52
"The Man and the Snake"
ASF: 79; SFC: 16; Wa:
52
"The Mockingbird" ASF:
79; Wa: 52
"The Moonlit Road" Wa: 52
"Moxon's Master" ASF: 79;
SFC: 6; Wa: 52
"My Favorite Murder" ASF:
79; Wa: 52
"An Occurrence at Owl Creek
Bridge" ASF: 79; SFC:
16; Wa: 53; WaS1: 17
"Oil of Dog" ASF: 79; Wa:
53
"One Kind of Officer" ASF:
79; SFC: 16; Wa: 53
"One of the Missing" SFC:
16; Wa: 53
"One Officer, One Man"
ASF: 80; SFC: 16; Wa:
53
"Parker Adderson, Philosoph-
er" ASF: 80; Wa: 53
"A Resumed Identity" ASF:
80
"A Son of the Gods" ASF:
80; Wa: 53
"The Story of a Conscience"
Wa: 54
"The Suitable Surroundings"
ASF: 80
"A Tough Tussle" ASF: 80;
Wa: 54
"A Watcher by the Dead"
ASF: 80; Wa: 54
BIERMAN, Wolf
General Po: 237
BILLETDOUX, Francois
General Br: 110; Po: 237
Chin Chin [Tchin-Tchin]
Br: 110; DC2: 62; MD:
57; Po: 237
Il Faut Passer par les Nuages
Br: 110
Torpe's Hotel [Va Donc
Chez Törpe; Chez Torpe]
Br: 110; DC2: 62; MD:
57; Po: 237

BILLINGS, Josh
General ASF: 81
BILLY, André
General Po: 237
BINDING, Rudolf
"Angelucia" Wa: 54
"Der Opfergang" Wa: 54
"Unsterblichkeit" Wa: 54
"Die Waffenbrüder" Wa: 54
"Der Wingulf" Wa: 54
BINDLOSS, Harold
"The Two Priests of Konnoto"
Wa: 54
BINET-VALMER
Les Meteques Ke: 36
BINYON, Robert Laurence
General Mi: 221; TA: 99
"The Supper" PE: 35
BIRCK, Sixt
Joseph DC2: 62
BIRD, Robert Montgomery
General AD: 80-83; AN: 18-
19; ASF: 82; Ho: 134;
L Lon: 56
The Broker of Bogota AD:
81
The City Looking Glass AD:
82
The Gladiator AD: 81-82;
ADC: 53-54
News of the Night Lon: 56
Nick of the Woods AN: 18;
Ho: 134; Ma: 186
Oralloossa AD: 81; ADC:
54; Ho: 134
Pelopidas AD: 81
The Secret Records Lon: 56
BIRD, Stewart and Peter
ROBILOTTA
The Wobblies ADC: 54
BIRNKRANT, Samuel
A Whisper in God's Ear Br:
111
BISHOP, Denise Collette
A Hit on Wall St. ADC: 54
BISHOP, Elizabeth
General MP: 26; Po: 238
"At the Fishhouses" ICBAP:
10; PE: 35
"The Bight" PE: 36
"Cape Breton" PE: 36
"Chemin de Fer" ICBAP: 10
"The Colder the Air" PE: 36
"The Fish" PE: 36
"The Imaginary Iceberg" PE:
36
"Jeronimo's House" ICBAP:

10
"The Man-Moth" PE: 36
"The Map" PE: 36
"Monument" PE: 36
"Poem" PE: 36
"The Poem as Puzzle" ICBAP:
    10
"Quai d'Orleans" PE: 36
"Questions of Travel" PE:
    36-37
"The Sandpiper" PE: 37
BISHOP, John
    "The Saints" PE: 37
    The Trip Back Down ADC:
        54
BISHOP, John Peale
    General ASF: 82; LCAB:
        18; Po: 238-239
    Act of Darkness Po: 240
    "Ballet" ICBAP: 10; PE:
        37; Po: 240
    "Behavior of the Sun" PE:
        37
    "The Cellar" Wa: 54
    "The Corpse in the House"
        SFC: 16; Wa: 54
    "Divine Nativity" PE: 37
    "The Fireplace" Wa: 54
    "If Only: 1867-1900" ASF:
        82; SFC: 16; Wa: 55
    "A Man Who Thought" Wa:
        55
    "Many Thousands Gone" Wa:
        55
    "O Let Not Virtue Seek"
        PE: 37
    "Perspectives Are Precipices"
        PE: 37
    "Porphirio" Wa: 55
    "A Recollection" ICBAP: 10;
        PE: 37; Po: 240
    "Resurrection" Wa: 55
    "The Return" PE: 37
    "Southern Pines" PE: 37
    "Speaking of Poetry" PE:
        37
    "Toadstools Are Poison" Wa:
        55
    "The Tree" PE: 38
    "Twelfth Night" PE: 38
    "Young Death and Desire"
        Wa: 55
BISSELL, Richard
    General ASF: 82
BIYIDI, Alexander
    General LCAB: 19

BJORNEBOE, Jens
    Under en Hardere Himmel Fi:
        401
BJÖRNSON, Björnsterne
    General Br: 111; MD: 57-
        58
    Arne Fi: 401
    The Bankruptcy Br: 111
    Beyond Human Power [Beyond
        Our Strength] Br: 111;
        DC2: 62; Ma: 187; MD:
        58
    The Fisher Maiden Ke: 346
    Flags Are Flying in Town and
        Harbour Ke: 346
    A Gauntlet MD: 58
    Halte Hulda MD: 58
    In God's Way Ke: 346
    Maria Stuart MD: 58
    Married MD: 58
    Mother's Hands Ke: 346
    The New System Br: 111
    Paul Lange and Tora Parsberg
        Br: 111
BLACK, Jeanne Belcher
    The Pit MBA: 25
BLACK, Stephen
    The Pokey ADC: 54
BLACK, William
    General Ai: 152
BLACKMORE, Richard Doddridge
    General BN: 15
    Alice Lorraine ENES2: 20
    Christowell ENES2: 20
    Clara Vaughan ENES2: 21
    Cradock Nowell ENES2: 21
    Cripps, the Carrier ENES2:
        21
    Dariel ENES2: 21
    Erëma ENES2: 21
    Kit and Kitty ENES2: 21
    Lorna Doone BN: 15; ENE:
        17; ENES1: 19; ENES2:
        21
    The Maid of Sker ENES2:
        21
    Mary Anerley ENES2: 21
    Perlycross ENES2: 21
    Springhaven ENES2: 21
BLACKMORE, Sir Richard
    General EC: 51
    "Commendatory Verses on the
        Author of the Two Arthurs
        and the Satyre Against
        Wit" EC: 51
BLACKMUR, Richard Palmer

General APC: 156-157;
   LCAB: 19; Po: 240-241
"Judas Priest" PE: 38
"Missa Vocis" PE: 38
"The Spear" PE: 38
BLACKSHEAR, E. J.
   General BAW: 75
BLACKSON, Lorenzo Dow
   General BAF: 32; BAW:
   75-76
BLACKWELL, Don
   The Has Been MBA: 25
BLACKWOOD, Algernon
   General TA: 101
   "Ancient Sorceries" Wa: 55
   "The Damned" Wa: 55
   "The Willows" Wa: 55
Blair, Eric Arthur see ORWELL,
   George
BLAIR, Hugh
   General EC: 52
BLAIR, James
   General AP: 574
BLAIR, Robert
   "The Grave" Ai: 61; PE:
   38
BLAKE, Eubie
   General BAP: 23; MBA: 26
   The Blackbirds BAP: 23;
   MBA: 26
   Elsie BAP: 24
   Harlem on Parade BAP: 23
   Lew Leslie's Blackbirds
   BAP: 24
   Musical Melange BAP: 24
   The Sepia and Swing Revolu-
   tion BAP: 23-24
   _____, Flournoy MILLER, and
   Noble SISSLE
   Shuffle Along BAP: 24, 184;
   MBA: 26
   _____ and Noble SISSLE
   The Chocolate Dandies BAP:
   23-24, 184; MBA: 26, 179
BLAKE, George
   General Ai: 249
BLAKE, William
   General Fog: 9-12; ICBAP:
   10; LCAB: 19; Ma: 188-
   189; Me: 111-133
   "Ah, Sun-Flower" (Songs of
   Experience) ICBAP: 10;
   Me: 123, 126; PE: 38
   "Ahania" PE: 38
   "America" Fog: 14; PE:
   38

"The Angel" PE: 38
"The Argument" PE: 38
"Auguries of Innocence" Fog:
   12; ICBAP: 10; LCAB:
   19; Me: 123; PE: 38-39
"The Bard's Song" PE: 39
"Book of Thel" Fog: 15;
   ICBAP: 10; LCAB: 19;
   Me: 125, 127; PE: 39
"The Book of Urizen" Fog:
   15; Me: 127; PE: 39
"Chimney Sweeper" (Songs of
   Experience) ICBAP: 10;
   PE: 39
"The Chimney Sweeper" (Songs
   of Innocence) ICBAP: 10;
   Me: 127; PE: 39
"Clod and the Pebble" (Songs
   of Experience) Fog: 13;
   ICBAP: 11; Me: 124, 130;
   PE: 39-40
"A Cradle Song" PE: 40
"Crystal Cabinet" Fog: 12;
   ICBAP: 11; Me: 130; PE:
   40
"Divine Image" (Songs of Inno-
   cence) ICBAP: 11; PE:
   40
"Earth's Answer" Fog: 13;
   PE: 40
"The Echoing Green" PE: 40
"Europe" Fog: 14; PE: 40
"The Everlasting Gospel"
   Fog: 12; PE: 40
"The Fly" (Songs of Experi-
   ence) Fog: 14; ICBAP:
   11; Me: 123; PE: 40-41
"For the Sexes: The Gates of
   Paradise" PE: 41
"The Four Zoas; Night the
   Ninth" ICBAP: 11
"The Gates of Paradise"
   ICBAP: 11
"The Ghost of Abel" PE: 41
"Hear the Voice of the Bard"
   PE: 41
"Holy Thursday" (Songs of
   Experience) ICBAP: 11
"Holy Thursday" (Songs of In-
   nocence) ICBAP: 11;
   Me: 122; PE: 41
"How Sweet I Roam'd" PE:
   41
"The Human Abstract" Fog:
   12; PE: 41
"I Asked a Thief" PE: 41

"I Saw a Chapel All of Gold"
PE: 42

"Imitation of Pope: A Compliment to the Ladies"
ICBAP: 11; PE: 41

"In Englands Green & Pleasant Land" PE: 41

"Infant Sorrow" PE: 41

"Introduction" (Songs of Experience) PE: 42

"Introduction" (Songs of Innocence) PE: 42

"Jerusalem" Fog: 14; ICBAP: 11; Me: 116, 127

Job Fog: 15

"The Lamb" Me: 117; PE: 42

"The Lilly" PE: 42

"The Little Black Boy" PE: 42-43

"The Little Boy Lost" and "The Little Boy Found" PE: 43

"The Little Girl Found" Fog: 13-14; Me: 117; PE: 43

"Little Girl Lost" (Songs of Innocence) ICBAP: 11; Me: 117; PE: 43

"Little Vagabond" (Songs of Experience) ICBAP: 11; PE: 43

"London" (Songs of Experience) Fog: 13; ICBAP: 11; Me: 118-119; PE: 43-44

"Mad Song" PE: 44

"Marriage of Heaven and Hell" Fog: 12; ICBAP: 12; Me: 127, 131

"Memory" PE: 44

"Mental Traveller" Fog: 12-13; ICBAP: 12; LCAB: 19; Me: 128, 130-131; PE: 44

"Milton" Fog: 15; ICBAP: 12; Me: 132-133

"My Pretty Rose Tree" PE: 44

"My Spectre Around Me ... Night & Day" Me: 130; PE: 44

"Never Pain to Tell Thy Love" PE: 44

"Night the Eighth" PE: 45

"Night the First" PE: 45

"Night the Ninth" PE: 45

"Nurse's Song" (Songs of Innocence) PE: 45

"O Earth, O Earth, Return" PE: 45

"Poetical Sketches, 1783" Fog: 12; ICBAP: 12; Me: 122, 126, 131

"Poison Tree" ICBAP: 12; PE: 45

"A Pretty Epigram for the Entertainment of Those Who Have Paid Great Sums in the Venetian and Flemish Ooze" ICBAP: 12; PE: 45

Prophetic Books Fog: 14

"The Scoffers" PE: 45

"The Shepherd" PE: 45

"Sick Rose" (Songs of Experience) ICBAP: 12; PE: 45-46

"Song: How Sweet I Roam'd from Field to Field" PE: 46

"Song: My Silks and Fine Array" PE: 46

"A Song of Liberty" PE: 46

"The Song of Los" PE: 46

"Songs of Experience" Fog: 13; ICBAP: 12; Me: 120-122, 132

"Songs of Innocence" Fog: 13; ICBAP: 12; Me: 122, 132; PE: 46

Songs of Innocence and Experience Fog: 13

"Stanzas from Milton" PE: 46

Tiriel Fog: 15

"To Autumn" ICBAP: 12; PE: 48

"To Spring" ICBAP: 12; PE: 48

"To Summer" ICBAP: 12; PE: 48

"To the Accuser Who Is the God of the World" ["To the Accuser of This World"] ICBAP: 12; PE: 48

"To the Muses" PE: 48

"To Tirzah" PE: 48

"To Winter" ICBAP: 13; PE: 48

"The Tyger" (Songs of Experience) Fog: 15-16; ICBAP: 13; LCAB: 19; Me: 115, 123, 127, 129; PE: 46-48

"Vala (or "The Four Zoas")
Fog: 15; ICBAP: 13;
Me: 128-129, 132
"Visions of the Daughters of
Albion" Fog: 15; PE:
48
"William Bond" Me: 130;
PE: 49
BLANCHOT, Maurice
General Po: 241-243
Aminadab Fi: 29
L'Arrêt de Mort Fi: 29
L'Attente l'oubli Po: 243
Au moment voulu Fi: 29
Thomas l'obscur Po: 243
Le Tres-haut Fi: 29
BLANCO AMOR, José
General Po: 243-244
BLAND, Alden
General BAF: 32-33; BAW:
76
Behold--A Cry BAF: 33
Bland, Mrs. Hubert see
NESBIT, Edith
BLANKFORT, Michael and
Michael GOLD
Battle Hymn ADC: 121; Br:
112
BLASCO IBANEZ, Vicente
General Po: 244
A los pies de Venus Ke:
183
La araña negra Fi: 194
Arroz y tartana Ke: 183
La barraca Fi: 194; Ke:
183
La bodega Ke: 183
Cañas y barro Fi: 195; Ke:
183
La catedral Ke: 183-184
Los cuatro jinetes del Apo-
calipsis Ke: 184
Entre naranjos Ke: 184
Flor de Mayo Fi: 195; Ke:
184
La horda Ke: 184
El intruso Ke: 184
Los muertos mandan Ke:
184
El Papa del mar Ke: 184
Sónnica la cortesana Ke:
184
La tierra de todos Ke: 184
BLATTY, William Peter
General LCAB: 19
BLAUMANIS, Rudolfs

"Frost in Spring" Wa: 55
"Thunderstorm" Wa: 55
"Week" Wa: 56
BLAY, J. Benibengor
General BALE: 278
BLEIBTREU, Carl
Die Vielzuvielen Fi: 287
BLESSINGTON, Marguerite, Coun-
tess of
General BN: 15
BLEST GANA, Alberto
General LCAB: 19-20
BLISH, James Benjamin
A Case of Conscience
ENES1: 19
"Common Time" Wa: 56
"Surface Tension" Wa: 56
"A Work of Art" Wa: 56
BLITZSTEIN, Marc
General Br: 112
The Cradle Will Rock Br:
112; DC1: 31
Regina ADC: 54-55
Blixen, Karen see DINESEN,
Isak
BLIZINSKI, Josef
Shipwrecked [Rozbitki] DC2:
62
BLOCH, Jean-Richard
Le Dernier Empereur Br:
112
BLOCH, Robert
General LCAB: 20
"The Shambler from the Stars"
ASF: 82
BLOCK, Rudolph
"End of the Task" WaS1: 18
BLOHM, Bernice and Adelaide
BEAN
Bless the Child Br: 112
BLOK, Aleksandr Aleksandrovich
General Br: 112; MD: 58;
Po: 244-245
The King in the Square MD:
58
The Puppet Show MD: 58
The Rose and the Cross MD:
59
Roza i Krest DC2: 63
The Song of Fate MD: 59
The Stranger MD: 59
BLOOMSTEIN, Harry
Calling in Crazy ADC: 55
BLOT, Jean
General Po: 245
BLOY, Léon

General Po: 245-246
Le Désepéré Ke: 36
The Woman Who Was Poor
    Ke: 36
BLUE, Cecil A.
    General BAF: 33
    "The 'Flyer'" ASF: 82
BLUM, Edwin Harvey
    The Saving Grace Br: 112
BLUNDEN, Edmund Charles
    General Po: 246
    "A Summer's Fancy" PE: 49
    "Third Ypres" ICBAP: 13
    "Thomasine" PE: 49
    "'Transport Up' at Ypres"
        ICBAP: 13
BLUNT, Wilfred Scawen
    General TA: 102
    "Esther" ICBAP: 13
    "Love Sonnets of Proteus"
        ICBAP: 13
    "Natalia's Resurrection"
        ICBAP: 13
BLY, Robert
    General ICBAP: 13; Ma:
        190; MP: 27
    "Driving Toward the La Qui
        Parle River" PE: 49
    The Light Around the Body
        Ma: 190
    "Like the New Moon I Will
        Live My Life" PE: 49
    "Meeting the Man Who Wants
        Me" PE: 49
    "Night Journey in the Cook-
        ing Pot" PE: 49
    Silence in the Snowy Fields
        Ma: 191-192
    "The Teeth Mother Naked at
        Last" PE: 49
    "Watering the Horse" PE: 49
BOAKE, Barcroft
    General AL: 122-123
BOBRICK, Sam and Ron CLARK
    No Hard Feelings ADC:
        55
BOBROWSKI, Johannes
    General Po: 246-247
    Junger Herr am Fenster
        Po: 247
    Levins Mühle Fi: 287; Po:
        248
    Litauische Claviere Fi:
        287
BOBRUK, A.
    Mother and Son Ke: 372

BOCCACCIO, Giovanni
    General LCAB: 20
    L'Amorosa Fiammetta Ma: 195
    Andreuccio da Perugia Fi:
        258
    Corbaccio Fi: 258; Ke: 238
    Decameron Fi: 258-261; Ke:
        238-240; Ma: 193-194
    The Decameron (Anon. English
        trans. of 1620-1625) ERP:
        122-123
    Fiammetta Fi: 262
    Filocolo Fi: 262; Ke: 240
    Il Filostrato Ma: 194-195
    La Teseide Ma: 195-196
BODDY, Michael and Robert
    ELLIS
    The Legend of King O'Malley
        MAP: 385
BODEL, Jean
    Jeu de Saint Nicolas DC2: 63
BODET, Jaime Torres
    "Antonio Arnoux" Wa: 56
    "The Birth of Venus" Wa:
        56
    "Close-up of Mr. Lehar" Wa:
        56
    "Paralysis" Wa: 56
    "To Live Again" Wa: 56
BODKIN, Maud
    General LCAB: 20
BODUNRIN, A.
    General BALE: 278
Boehl von Faber, Cecilia see
    CABALLERO, Fernán
BOETHIUS, Anicius Manlius
    The Consolation of Philosophy
        see also ALFRED the
        Great [translator] Ma:
        197
BOETIE, Dugmore
    Familiarity Is the Kingdom of
        the Lost BALE: 278-
        279
BOGAN, Louise
    General Po: 248
    "Come, Break with Time"
        ICBAP: 13
    "Decoration" ICBAP: 14
    "The Dream" PE: 49
    "The Exhortation" PE: 49
    "Old Countryside" ICBAP:
        14
    "Roman Fountain" ICBAP: 14
    "Simple Autumnal" PE: 49
    "Solitary Observations..."

PE: 49
"Statue and the Birds"
   ICBAP: 14
BOGDANOV, A. A.
   Red Star Fi: 418
BOHANON, Mary
   Poems and Character Sketches
   BAW: 77
BOIARDO, Matteo Maria
   Orlando Innamorato Ma: 198
BOISROBERT, Francois de
   La Folle Gageure DC2: 63
   La Vraye Didon ou la Didon
   Chaste DC2: 64
BOISSONNAS, Edith
   General Po: 248
BOJER, Johan
   The Face of the World   Ke:
   347
   The Great Hunger Ke: 347
   The House and the Sea Ke:
   347
   The Last Viking Ke: 347
   Life Ke: 347
   The Power of a Lie Ke: 347
   The Prisoner Who Sang Ke:
   347
   Treacherous Ground Ke:
   347
BOKER, George Henry
   General AAL: 45; AD: 86-
   89; Lon: 27
   Anne Boleyn AD: 87
   The Bankrupt AD: 86; Lon:
   27
   The Betrothal AD: 86-87
   Calaynos AD: 87
   Francesca da Rimini AD:
   86-89; DC1: 31
   The World a Mask AD: 87
BOLAND, Bridget
   General MDAE: 123
   The Prisoner Br: 112; MDAE:
   123
BOLES, Paul Darcy
   General LCAB: 20
BOLES, Robert E.
   General AAW: 41; BAF:
   34; BAW: 77
   Curling BAF: 34; BAW:
   77
   "The Engagement Party"
   ASF: 82
   The People One Knows
   BAF: 34; BAW: 77
BOLINGBROKE, Henry St.

John, Viscount
General EC: 52-53
The Idea of a Patriot King
   EC: 52-53
BÖLL, Heinrich
   General Br: 113; Po: 248-
   251
   Acquainted with the Night
   Ke: 257; Ma: 199
   Ansichten eines Clowns Fi:
   287; Po: 251
   "The Balek Scales" Wa: 56
   Betrachungen über den Irisch-
   en Regen Po: 251
   Billiards at Half Past Nine
   Fi: 287-288; Ma: 199-200;
   Po: 249
   The Bread of Spring [Das
   Brot der Frühen Jahre]
   Fi: 288; Po: 251-252; Wa:
   56
   "Christmas Every Day" Wa:
   56
   The Clown Ma: 200
   Ende Einer Dienstfahrt Po:
   252
   Entfernung von der Truppe
   Po: 252
   Group Portrait with Lady Fi:
   288-289
   House Without Keeper Ke:
   257
   "In the Valley of the Thunder-
   ing Hooves" Wa: 57
   "Irisches Tagebuch" Wa: 57
   The Lost Honour of Katharina
   Blum Fi: 289
   "The Man with the Knives"
   Wa: 57
   "Murke's Collected Silences"
   Wa: 57; WaS1: 18
   "Nicht nur zur Weihnachtszeit"
   Wa: 57
   "Over the Bridge" Wa: 57
   "Der Tod der Elsa Baskoleit"
   Wa: 57
   The Train Was on Time Ke:
   257; Wa: 57
   "Traveler, If You Go to
   Spa---" Wa: 57
   Und Sagte Kein Einziges Wort
   Fi: 289; Po: 252
   Die Waage der Baleks Fi:
   289
   Es wird etwas geschehen
   Po: 252

Wo Warst Du, Adam? Fi:
289; Ke: 257
BOLT, Robert Oxton
General Br: 113; MBD: 37;
MD: 59; MDAE: 125-126;
Po: 253; TMBP: 38-42
The Critic and the Heart
TMBP: 42
Flowering Cherry Br: 113;
EDC: 58-59; MD: 59;
TMBP: 38, 41-42
Gentle Jack Br: 113; EDC:
59; TMBP: 38, 41-42
A Man for All Seasons Br:
114; DC1: 31; EDC: 59-
60; LCAB: 20; MBD: 37;
MD: 59; MDAE: 125-126;
Po: 253-254; TMAP: 171;
TMBP: 38-42
The Thwarting of Baron Bol-
ligrew Br: 114
The Tiger and the Horse Br:
115; EDC: 60; MD: 59;
TMBP: 38, 41-42
Vivat! Vivat Regina! EDC:
60; TMBP: 42
BOMBAL, Maria Luisa
"The Tree" Wa: 57
BOMPIANI, Valentino
General Br: 115
BONAVENTURA [F. W. J.
SCHELLING]
Die Nachtwachten Fi: 289-
290
BOND, Edward
General MBD: 37-38; MDAE:
128-129; Po: 254; TMBP:
46-51
Bingo TMBP: 50-52
Black Mass TMBP: 52
Early Morning TMBP: 46,
48-52
Lear MBD: 38; TMBP:
48-52
Narrow Road to the Deep
North MBD: 37-38;
MDAE: 128; TMBP: 46-
48, 50-53
The Pope's Wedding TMBP:
48-51
Saved MBD: 37-38; MDAE:
128-129; TMBP: 46, 48,
50-51, 53-54
The Sea TMBP: 50, 54
Spring Awakening TMBP:
54

BOND, Frederick Weldon
General BAP: 24
Family Affair BAP: 25
BOND, Horace Julian
General BAW: 78-79
Mother April's MBA: 26
BONDAREV, Yuri
The Shore Fi: 418
BONNEFOY, Yves
General LCAB: 20; Po:
254-255
"Du mouvement et de l'immobil-
ité de Douve" Po: 255
BONNER, Marita [Marita Bonner
OCCOMY]
The Purple Flower BAP: 25
BONNER, Sherwood [Katherine
S. B. McDOWELL]
General ASF: 83
"The Case of Eliza Bleylock"
WaS1: 18
"Coming Home to Roost" WaS1:
18
"The Gentlemen of Sarsar"
ASF: 82; Wa: 57; WaS1:
18
"Hieronymus Pop and the Baby"
WaS1: 18
"In Aunt Mely's Cabin" WaS1:
18
"Lame Jerry" Wa: 57; WaS1:
18
"On the Nine Mile" WaS1: 18
"The Revolution in the Life of
Mr. Balingall" WaS1: 18
"Sister Weeden's Prayer"
WaS1: 18
"The Valcours" WaS1: 18
"The Volcanic Interlude"
WaS1: 18
BONOME, Rodrigo
General Po: 255
BONTEMPS, Arna
General AAPD: 153; AAW:
41; BAF: 35-36; BAP:
25-26; BAW: 82-84; HR:
61-62; LCAB: 20
"American Negro Poetry"
BAW: 84
Any Place but Here BAW:
84
Black Thunder BAF: 36-37;
BAW: 84; LCAB: 20
"Boy Blue" ASF: 83; Wa:
57
"The Cure" Wa: 58

Drums at Dusk BAF: 37;
BAW: 84; LCAB: 20
God Sends Sunday BAF: 37;
BAW: 84; LCAB: 20
Golden Slippers BAW: 84
"Let the Church Roll On"
Wa: 58
The Old South BAF: 37
Sad Faced Boy BAW: 84
"A Summer Tragedy" ASF:
83; Wa: 58; WaS1: 18
They Seek a City BAW: 84
"3 Pennies for Luck" ASF:
83; Wa: 58
_____ and Countee CULLEN
The Saint Louis Woman
BAP: 26, 55; MBA: 27
BOOTH, Edward C.
The Tree of the Garden
ENES2: 21
BOOTH, Philip
General Ma: 201; Po: 255
BOOTHE, Clare
General MD: 59
Abide with Me ADC: 225
Child of the Morning ADC:
225
Kiss the Boys Goodbye
ADC: 225-226; Br: 390;
MD: 59
Margin for Error ADC: 226
The Women ADC: 226; Br:
391; DC1: 32; MD: 59
BOR, Matej
General Po: 255-256
BORCHARDT, Rudolf
General Po: 256
BORCHERT, Wolfgang
General Br: 115; MD: 60;
Po: 256
"Billbrook" Po: 256-257;
Wa: 58
"Die drei dunklen Könige"
Wa: 58
"Die Küchenuhr" Wa: 58
"Die lange lange Strasse
lang" Wa: 58
The Man Outside [Outside
the Door; Draussen vor
der Tür] Br: 115;
DC2: 64; MD: 60; Po:
257
"Mein bleicher Bruder" Wa:
58
"Nachts schlafen die Ratten
doch" Wa: 58

The Outsider Br: 115
BORDE, Andrew
The Merry Tales of the Mad
Men of Gottam ERP: 89-90
BORDES, Jean de
Maria Stuarta Tragoedia DC2:
64
BORDEU, Charles de
General Po: 257-258
BOREL, Pétrus
"Dina, la belle Juive" Wa:
58
"Don Andréa Vesalius l'ana-
tomiste" Wa: 58
Madame Putiphar Fi: 29
"Passereau l'écolier" Wa: 58
BORGEN, Johan
Blue Peak Fi: 401
"Chance" WaS1: 19
"Honeysuckle Vine" WaS1:
19
Jeg Fi: 401
"Legend" WaS1: 19
Little Lord Fi: 401
"Morning on Montparnasse"
WaS1: 19
My Arm, My Intestine Fi:
401
"Night and Day 1" WaS1:
19
"Ocean in Winter" WaS1: 19
The Red Mist Fi: 401
"She Willed It" WaS1: 19
"Star Song" WaS1: 19
"Trustworthy and Dutiful"
WaS1: 19
BORGES, Jorge Luis
General LCAB: 20; Po:
258-264
"Abenjácan the Bojarí, Dead
in His Labyrinth" ["Ibn
Hakkam al-Bokhari, Dead
in His Labyrinth"] Wa:
59; WaS1: 19
"The Aleph" ["El Aleph"]
Ma: 202; Po: 264-265; Wa:
59; WaS1: 19
"The Approach to Almotásim"
Ma: 202-203; Wa: 59
"Averroes' Search" Wa: 59;
WaS1: 19
"The Babylonian Lottery"
Ma: 203; Wa: 59-60;
WaS1: 20
"Biography of Tadeo Isidoro
Cruz" Wa: 60; WaS1:

20

"Brodie's Report" WaS1: 20

"The Child of His Friend"
Wa: 60

"The Circular Ruins" Wa:
60; WaS1: 20

"The Congress" Wa: 60-61

"The Dead Man" Wa: 61;
WaS1: 20

"Death and the Compass"
Ma: 203; Wa: 61; WaS1:
20

"Deutsches Requiem" Wa:
61; WaS1: 20

Doctor Brodie's Report Ma:
203-204

"The Dreadful Redeemer
Lazarus Morell" WaS1: 20

"The Duel" Wa: 61

"The Elder Lady" Wa: 61

"Emma Zunz" Ma: 204; Wa:
61-62; WaS1: 20

"The Encounter" WaS1: 20

"The End" Wa: 62; WaS1:
20

"The Enigma of Edward Fitzgerald" WaS1: 20

"El espantoso redentor Lazarus Morell" Wa: 62

"Examination of the Work of
Herbert Quain" Wa: 62;
WaS1: 20

"The Feast of the Monster"
Wa: 62

Fervor de Buenos Aires Po:
265

"Funes the Memorious" Ma:
204; Wa: 62; WaS1: 21

"The Garden of the Forking
Paths" Ma: 205; Wa: 62;
WaS1: 21

"The God's Script" see
"The Writing of the Lord"

"A Golem" Wa: 63

"The Gospel According to
Mark" Wa: 63

"Guayaquil" Wa: 63; WaS1:
21

"Hombre de la esquina rosada"
see "The Story of Rosendo
Juárez"

"The House of Asterion" Wa:
63; WaS1: 21

"Ibn Hakkam al-Bokhari,
Dead in His Labyrinth"
see "Abenjácan the Bo-
jari, Dead in His Labyrinth"

"The Immortal" Ma: 205; Wa:
63

"The Improbable Imposter Tom
Castro" WaS1: 21

"The Intruder" Wa: 63

El Jardin de senderos que se
bifurcan Po: 265

"Juan Muraña" Wa: 64; WaS1:
21

"The Library of Babel" Ma:
205-206; Wa: 64; WaS1:
21

"The Maker" Wa: 64; WaS1:
21

"The Man at the Pink Corner"
Wa: 64

"The Man on the Threshold"
Wa: 64

"The Other" WaS1: 21

"The Other Death" Wa: 64;
WaS1: 21

"The Parable of the Palace"
Wa: 64

"Pierre Menard, Author of
Quixote" Wa: 64; WaS1:
21

"The Plot" Wa: 64

"Political Legend" see "The
Story of Rosendo Juárez"

"The Restitution of the Key"
Wa: 64

"The Secret Miracle" Wa: 65;
WaS1: 21

"The Sect of the Thirty"
WaS1: 21

"The Shape of the Sword"
Wa: 65; WaS1: 21

"The Sorcerer Postponed"
WaS1: 21

"The South" Wa: 65; WaS1:
22

"The Story of Rosendo Juárez"
["Hombre de la esquina
rosada"] Wa: 63; WaS1:
22

El Sur Po: 265

"Theme of the Traitor and the
Hero" Ma: 206; Wa: 65;
WaS1: 22

"The Theologians" Wa: 65;
WaS1: 22

"Three Versions of Judas"
Wa: 65; WaS1: 22

"Tlön, Uqbar, Orbis Tertius"
Ma: 206-207; Wa: 65-66;

WaS1: 22
"The Unworthy Friend" Wa:
66
"Utopia of a Man Who Is
Tired" WaS1: 22
"La viuda Ching, pirata"
Wa: 66
"The Wait" Wa: 66
"The Writing of the Lord"
["The God's Script"] Ma:
207; Wa: 62-63
"The Zahir" Wa: 66; WaS1:
22
BORGESE, G. A.
Rube Ke: 240
BORNE, Alain
General Po: 266
BORROW, George Henry
General BN: 16; LCAB:
20-21
Lavengro ENE: 17;
ENES1: 19
BORSHCHAGOVSKY, Alexander
Where the Blacksmith Settles
Fi: 418-419
BORUFF, John
The Loud Red Patrick ADC:
56
BOSCO, Henri
General Po: 266
Malicroix Fi: 29-30; Po:
266
Sabinus Po: 266
Sanglier Po: 266
Bosis, Lauro de see DE
BOSIS, Lauro
BOSMAN, Henry Charles
"Kafir" Wa: 66
"The Rooinek" Wa: 66
BOSQUET, Alain
General Po: 266-267
BOSWELL, James
General Ai: 76-77; EC:
54-55; LCAB: 21
The Life of Samuel Johnson,
LL.D. EC: 54-55; LCAB:
21; Ma: 208-209
BOTTOMLEY, Gordon
General Mi: 222; Po:
267; TA: 103
The Acts of Saint Peter
Br: 115
BOUCHER, Anthony
General ASF: 83
BOUCHER, Jonathan
General AP: 198-199;

Da: 64
BOUCICAULT, Dion
General AD: 93-97; EDT:
91-92; Lon: 57
After Dark ADC: 56; EDT:
92
The Colleen Bawn ADC: 56;
EDT: 91
The Corsican Brothers EDT:
91-92
London Assurance ADC: 56
Mary Barton ADC: 56
The Octoroon AD: 93-95;
ADC: 56-57; DC1: 32;
EDT: 92; Lon: 57
The Shaughraun ADC: 57
The Streets of New York [The
Poor of New-York; The Poor
of Liverpool; The Streets
of London; The Poor of Lon-
don Streets; The Streets of
Philadelphia; The Streets of
Dublin; The Money Panic of
'57, etc.] ADC: 57
BOUDJEDRA, Rachid
Topologie ideale pour une
agression caracterisee Fi:
30
BOUHELIER, Saint-Georges de
General Br: 116
BOUILLY, Jean
Lenore [Beethoven's Fidelio]
DC2: 64
BOULANGER, Daniel
General Po: 267
BOULLE, Pierre
General Po: 267
BOURCHIER, John, Baron Bern-
ers
General ERP: 91, 94
The Ancient Historie of Huon
of Bordeaux ERP: 91-93
Arthur of Lytell Brytayne
ERP: 92-93
BOURDET, Denise
General Po: 268
BOURDET, Edouard
General Br: 116; MD: 60
The Captive [Le Prisonnière]
Br: 116; DC2: 64; MD:
60
BOURGET, Paul
General Po: 268
L'Apostat Ke: 36
The Disciple Fi: 30; Ke:
36

Un Divorce Ke: 36
L'Echéance Ke: 36
L'Emigré Ke: 36
L'Etape Fi: 30; Ke: 36
Le Fils Ke: 36-37
Le Geste du fils Ke: 37
L'Irreparable Ke: 37
Le Justicier Ke: 37
Le Luxe des autres Ke: 37
BOURJAILY, Vance
    General CFAE: 85; CN: 59;
        Po: 268
    Brill Among the Ruins Ma:
        210
    Confessions of a Spent Youth
        CN: 60; LCAB: 21; Ma:
        210
    The End of My Life AN: 19;
        CN: 60; Ma: 210-211
    The Hound of Earth CN:
        60
    The Violated AN: 19; CN:
        60; Ma: 211
BOURKE-WHITE, Margaret
    General LCAB: 21
BOURNE, Randolph
    General Po: 268
BOURNE, St. Claire
    General MBA: 27
BOUSONO, Carlos
    General Po: 268-269
BOUSQUET, Joë
    General Po: 269
BOVASSO, Julie
    Down by the River Where
        Waterlilies Are Disfigured
        Every day ADC: 57
    Gloria and Esperanza ADC:
        57
    Moon Dreamers ADC: 57
    The Nothing Kid ADC: 57
    Schubert's Last Serenade
        ADC: 57
    Standard Safety ADC: 57
BOWEN, Elizabeth
    General BN2: 19-20; CN:
        60-61; LCAB: 21; Po:
        269-270; Ri: 150-156;
        Sch: 11-12
    "Breakfast" Wa: 66
    "The Cat Jumps" Wa: 67
    "Coming Home" WaS1: 22
    "The Dancing Mistress"
        Wa: 67
    "Dead Mabelle" Wa: 67
    The Death of the Heart CN:

61-62; EN: 8; ENE: 17;
        ENES1: 19; ENES2: 21;
        LCAB: 21; Ma: 212-213;
        Po: 270-271; Ri: 151-156;
        Sch: 12-13
    "The Demon Lover" Ri: 157-
        158; Wa: 67; WaS1: 22
    "The Disinherited" SFC: 17;
        Wa: 67
    "The Easter Egg Party" Wa:
        67
    Eva Trout CN: 62; ENE: 17;
        ENES1: 20; ENES2: 22;
        Ri: 154: Sch: 13
    "Foothold" Wa: 67
    Friends and Relations CN:
        62; ENE: 18; ENES1: 20
    "The Good Girl" SFC: 17;
        Wa: 67
    "The Happy Autumn Fields"
        SFC: 17; Wa: 67; WaS1:
        22
    The Heat of the Day CN:
        62-63; EN: 8; ENE: 18;
        ENES1: 20; ENES2: 22;
        Ma: 213; Po: 271; Ri:
        151-156, 158
    "Her Table Spread" SFC: 17;
        Wa: 67
    The Hotel CN: 63; ENE: 18;
        ENES1: 20
    The House in Paris CN: 63;
        ENE: 18; ENES1: 20; Ma:
        213-214; Ri: 151, 153-155,
        158
    "In the Square" SFC: 17;
        Wa: 67
    "The Inherited Clock" Wa: 68
    "Ivy Gripped the Steps" Ri:
        158; SFC: 17; Wa: 68
    "The Jungle" Wa: 68
    The Last September CN: 63;
        ENE: 18; ENES1: 20;
        Ri: 154-156
    The Little Girls CN: 63-64;
        ENE: 18; ENES1: 20;
        LCAB: 21; Ri: 153, 156
    "Little Girl's Room" Wa: 68
    "A Love Story" Wa: 68
    "Making Arrangements" WaS1:
        22
    "The Man of the Family" Wa:
        68
    "Mrs. Moysey" Wa: 68
    "Mysterious Kôr" Wa: 68;
        WaS1: 22

"Queer Heart" Wa: 68
"Shoes: An International
Episode" Wa: 68
"Summer Night" Wa: 68;
WaS1: 22
"Tears, Idle Tears" Wa: 68
"Telling" Wa: 68
To the North CN: 64; ENE:
18; ENES1: 21; ENES2:
22
"A Walk in the Woods" WaS1:
23
"Woodby, John" WaS1: 23
"The Working Party" Wa:
68
A World of Love CN: 64;
ENE: 18-19; ENES1: 21;
Ri: 153-154, 158
BOWEN, John Griffith
General CFAE: 87; CN: 64;
MDAE: 131
After the Rain EDC: 60;
MBA: 27
Storyboard CN: 64
A World Elsewhere ENES1:
21
BOWERS, Edgar
General ICBAP: 14
"Adam's Song to Heaven"
PE: 49
"The Astronomers of Mont
Blanc" PE: 49
"Autumn Shade" PE: 49
"Dark Earth and Summer"
PE: 50
"Grove and Building" PE:
50
"Oedipus at Colonus" PE:
50
"A Song for Rising" PE: 50
"The Stoic" PE: 50
"Variations on an Elizabethan
Theme" PE: 50
BOWLES, Jane
General MDAE: 132
In the Summer House ADC:
57-58; MDAE: 132
BOWLES, Paul
General AN: 19; ASF: 84;
CFAE: 89-90; CN: 65;
Po: 271
"By the Water" Wa: 69
"The Delicate Prey" Wa:
69
"A Distant Episode" ASF:
84; Wa: 69

"A Friend of the World" Wa:
69
"He of the Assembly" Wa: 69
"The Hours After Noon" Wa:
69
Let It Come Down CN: 65;
Ma: 215
"Merkala Beach" see "The
Story of Lahcen and Idir"
"Pages from Cold Point" Wa:
69
The Sheltering Sky AN: 19;
CN: 65-66; Ma: 215-216
The Spider's House CN: 66
"The Story of Lahcen and Idir"
Wa: 69
"Tea on the Mountain" Wa:
69
"The Time of Friendship" Wa:
69
"Under the Sky" SFC: 17;
Wa: 69
"The Wind of Beni Midar" Wa:
69
BOWLES, William Lisle
"To the River Itchin" PE: 50
BOWRA, Sir Cecil Maurice
The Creative Experiment
LCAB: 21
Inspiration and Poetry LCAB:
21
BOYD, Francis A.
General BAW: 85; LCAB: 21
BOYD, James
General AN: 19; ASF: 84
"The Flat Town" ASF: 84
"Old Pines" ASF: 84
BOYD, John
General TMIP: 37
The Assassin TMIP: 37-38
The Flats TMIP: 37-38
BOYD, John
General BAW: 85; LCAB:
21
BOYD, Mark A.
"Fra Bank to Bank, Fra Wood
to Wood I Rin" PE: 50
BOYD, Martin
General MAP: 133-137; Po:
271-272
The Cardboard Crown MAP:
134, 137
A Difficult Young Man MAP:
134, 136-137
Lucinda Brayford MAP:
134-135, 137

The Montforts MAP: 134
When Blackbirds Sing MAP:
134
BOYER, Claude
Clotilde DC2: 64
Fils Suppose, Le DC2. 64
Oropaste DC2: 65
BOYESEN, Hjalmar Hjorth
General AN: 20; ASF: 84
"The Man Who Lost His Name"
ASF: 84
"Swart Among the Buckeyes"
ASF: 84
BOYLE, Kay
General ASF: 85; CFAE:
92; CN: 66; Po: 272
"Art Colony" Wa: 69
"The Astronomer's Wife"
ASF: 84; Wa: 69
Avalanche AN: 20; CN: 66
"The Bridegroom's Body"
ASF: 84; Wa: 69
"Count Lothar's Heart" Wa:
69
"The Crazy Hunter" ASF:
85; SFC: 17; Wa: 70
Death of a Man AN: 20
"Effigy of War" ASF: 85;
SFC: 17; Wa: 70
"Evening at Home" Wa: 70
"Keep Your Pity" SFC: 17;
Wa: 70
"Luck for the Road" Wa: 70
"Natives Don't Cry" SFC:
17; Wa: 70
"One of Ours" Wa: 70
"Rest Cure" ASF: 85; Wa:
70; WaS1: 23
"They Weren't Going to Die"
SFC: 17; Wa: 70
"The White Horses of Vienna"
ASF: 85; SFC: 17; Wa:
70
"Winter Night" Wa: 70
BOYLE, Patrick
"At Night All Cats Are
Grey" Wa: 70
Like Any Other Man ENES2:
22
"Meles Vulgaris" Wa: 70
Boyle, Roger see ORRERY,
Roger Boyle, Earl of
BOYLE, William
General Br: 116; Mi: 222
The Building Fund Br:
116

The Eloquent Dempsey Br: 116
The Mineral Workers Br: 116
BOZHENKO, Aleksandr Mikhailovich
General Po: 272
BRACCO, Roberto
General Br: 116-117; MD: 60
BRACE, Gerald Warner
General AN: 20; CN: 66
The Spire CN: 66
BRACKENRIDGE, Henry Marie
General AP: 201
BRACKENRIDGE, Hugh Henry
General AF: 36; ALL: 45-46;
AN: 20; AP: 203-204; ASF:
85; Da: 89-90; Ho: 134-
135
"The Cave of Vanhest" ASF:
85
Incidents of the Insurrection...
AP: 203-204
Modern Chivalry AF: 36; AN:
20; AP: 203-204; Da: 90;
Ho: 134-135, 157; Ma: 217
"Poem on Divine Revelation"
PE: 50
"The Trial of Mamachtaga"
ASF: 85
BRADBURY, Ray
General ASF: 86; LCAB: 22;
Po: 272-273
"And So Died Riabouchinska"
WaS1: 23
"And the Rock Cried Out"
ASF: 85
"The Anthem Sprinters" WaS1:
23
"The Beggar on O'Connell
Bridge" WaS1: 23
"The Cistern" WaS1: 23
"The Concrete Mixer" WaS1:
23
"The Crowd" WaS1: 23
"Dark They Were, and Golden
Eyed" WaS1: 23
"Death and the Maiden" WaS1:
23
"The Dwarf" WaS1: 23
"The Emissary" WaS1: 23
"The Exiles" ASF: 85; WaS1:
23
"Fever Dream" WaS1: 23
"The Fire Balloons" Wa: 70
"The Golden Apples of the
Sun" WaS1: 24
"The Great Wide World Over
There" WaS1: 24

"I See You Never" Wa: 71
"I Sing the Body Electric"
WaS1: 24
"Icarus Montgolfier" WaS1:
24
"The Illustrated Man" WaS1:
24
"Invisible Boy" WaS1: 24
"Jack-in-the-Box" WaS1: 24
"The Lake" WaS1: 24
"The Machineries of Joy"
WaS1: 24
"The Man in the Rorschach
Shirt" Wa: 71
"The Man Upstairs" WaS1:
24
The Martian Chronicles ADC:
58
"A Medicine for Melancholy"
WaS1: 24
"Night Call Collect" WaS1:
24
"Night Meeting" WaS1: 24
"No Particular Night or
Morning" WaS1: 24
"The One Who Waits" Wa:
71
"Pillar of Fire" WaS1: 24
"Powerhouse" WaS1: 24
"The Rocket Man" WaS1: 24
"The Scythe" WaS1: 25
"Skeleton" WaS1: 25
"Sun and Shadow" ASF: 86
"There Was an Old Woman"
WaS1: 25
"Uncle Einar" WaS1: 25
"The Watchful Poker Chip of
H. Matisse" WaS1: 25
"Way in the Middle of the
Air" WaS1: 25
"The Wind" WaS1: 25
"The Wonderful Ice Cream
Suit" WaS1: 25
"Zero Hour" WaS1: 25
BRADDON, Mary Elizabeth
General BN: 17
Lady Audley's Secret BN:
17
Mount Royal ENES2: 22
BRADFORD, William
General AP: 206-210; Da:
22
History of Plymouth Planta-
tion AP: 206-209; Da:
22; Ma: 218-219
BRADLEY, David

South Street BAF: 38
BRADSTREET, Anne
General ALL: 46; AP: 212-
213; Da: 23
"The Burning of Our House,
July 10th, 1666: PE: 50
"Contemplations" ICBAP: 14;
PE: 50
"Flesh and the Spirit" ICBAP:
14
"If Ever Two Were One, Then
Surely We" ICBAP: 14
"A Letter to Her Husband Ab-
sent Upon Public Employ-
ment" PE: 50
"Phoebus Make Haste, the
Day's Too Long..." PE: 50
"Upon a Fit of Sickness, Anno
1632" ICBAP: 14
"Upon the Burning of Our
House" ICBAP: 14
BRADY, Edwin James
General AL: 132-133
BRAINE, John
General CFAE: 93-94; CN:
66-67; Po: 273; Sch: 13
The Crying Game CN: 67;
ENES1: 21
The Jealous God CN: 67;
ENES1: 21
Life at the Top CN: 67;
ENES1: 21
Room at the Top CN: 67;
ENE: 19; ENES1: 21; Ma:
220
The Vodi (From the Hand of
the Hunter) CN: 67-68;
ENES1: 22
BRAITHWAITE, E.R.
General WIL: 13
Choice of Straws WIL: 15
Honorary White WIL: 15
A Kind of Homecoming WIL:
14-15
Paid Servant WIL: 14
Reluctant Neighbors WIL: 15
To Sir With Love WIL: 13-14
BRAITHWAITE, Edward Kamau
General WIL: 15-17
The Arrivants WIL: 19-20
Four Plays for Primary Schools
WIL: 17
Islands WIL: 19
Masks WIL: 18-19
Odale's Choice WIL: 17
Other Exiles WIL: 20

Rights of Passage WIL: 18
BRAITHWAITE, William Stanley
General AAPD: 90; AAW:
42; BAF: 38; BAW:
89-90
Lyrics of Life and Love BAW:
90
Selected Poems BAW: 90
BRAMSON, Karen
A Night Ke: 347
BRANCATI, Vitaliano
General Br: 117
Il bell Antonio Ke: 241
BRANCH, William Blackwell
General AAPD: 343; AAW:
42; BAP: 27; BAW: 92;
MBA: 27
In Splendid Error BAP: 27-
28; Br: 117; MBA: 27-28
A Medal for Willie ADC: 58;
BAP: 27-28; Br: 117;
MBA: 28
A Wreath for Udomo BAP:
27-28; BAW: 92; MBA:
28
BRAND, Dollar
General BALE: 279
BRANDANE, John [John Mac-
INTYRE]
General Ai: 206
BRANDÃO, Raul
"The Thief and His Little
Daughter" Wa: 71
BRANDES, Johann
Der Landevater DC2: 65
BRANDYS, Kazimierz
General Po: 273-274
BRANNER, Hans Christian
"Aegteskab" Wa: 71
Anguish Fi: 401; Ke: 347
"Anxiety" Wa: 71
"De blaa Undulater" Wa: 71
"Boheme" see "En halv Alen
Vand"
The Child Plays on the Beach
Fi: 401; Ke: 347
The Dream About a Woman
Fi: 401; Ke: 347
"Graenselandet" Wa: 71
"En halv Alen Vand"
["Boheme"] Wa: 71
"Ingeborg" Wa: 71
The Judge DC1: 32; Po:
274
"Kameliadamen" Wa: 71
The Mountains Fi: 401;

Ke: 348; Wa: 71
No Man Knows the Night Fi:
401
"Om lidt er vi borte" Wa: 71
"Pengemag" Wa: 71
The Riding Master Fi: 401;
Ke: 348
"Röde Heste i Sneen" Wa: 71
"Shagpiben" Wa: 72
The Siblings DC1: 32
"Sidst i August" Wa: 72
"Skibet" Wa: 72
"To Minutters Stilhed" Wa: 72
Toys Fi: 402
"De tre Musketerer" Wa: 72
BRANTLINGER, Patrick
"Cavalier and the Nun" ICBAP:
14
"The Scribes" ICBAP: 14
BRASHERS, Howard C.
"Crack, Crash Orange Flame"
WaS1: 25
BRASILLACH, Robert
General Po: 274
BRATHWAIT, Richard
General ERP: 96; Hen: 194
Panthalia: Or the Royal Ro-
mance ERP: 96
BRATHWAITE, L. Edward
General ICBAP: 15
BRATNY, Roman
General Po: 274
BRAUN, Richard E.
"Against Nature" PE: 51
BRAUN, Volker
Unvollendete Geschichte Fi:
290
BRAUTIGAN, Richard
General ASF: 86
"The Armored Car" Wa: 72
"The Betrayed Kingdom" Wa:
72
"Corporal" Wa: 72
"Forgiven" Wa: 72
"Homage to the San Francisco
YMCA" WaS1: 25
"1/3,1/3,1/3" Wa: 72
"The Post Offices of Eastern
Oregon" Wa: 72
"Revenge of the Lawn" Wa:
72
"A Short History of Oregon"
Wa: 72
"1692 Cotton Mather Newsreel"
Wa: 72
"The Wild Birds" Wa: 72

"The World War I Los Angeles Airplane" ASF: 86; Wa: 72; WaS1: 25

BRAWLEY, Benjamin
General BAF: 39; BAW: 95; ICBAP: 15; Po: 274-275

BRECHT, Bertolt
General Br: 117-122; LCAB: 22; MD: 61-64; Po: 275-295
Antigone [Die Antigone des Sophokles] DC2: 65; EDC: 60; Po: 295
Arturo Ui see The Resistable Rise of Arturo Ui
Der Aufhaltsame Aufstieg des Arturo Ui see The Resistable Rise of Arturo Ui
Aufsteig und Fall der Stadt Mahagonny see Rise and Fall of the City of Mahagonny
"Augsburger Kreideskreis" Wa: 73
Die Ausnahme und die Regel see The Exception and the Rule
Baal Br: 122; DC2: 65-66; EDC: 61; Ma: 221; MD: 64; Po: 296
Das Badener Lehrstueck vom Einverständnis see The Didactic Play of Baden: On Consent
Ballade vom Weib und dem Soldaten Po: 287
Behind the Wall DC2: 66
The Business Deals of Mr. Julius Caesar Fi: 290
The Caucasian Chalk Circle [Der Kaukasische Kreidekreis] Br: 123; DC2: 66-67; EDC: 61-63; LCAB: 22; Ma: 221-222; MD: 66; Po: 299-300
Children's Crusade [Kinderkreuzzug] Po: 300
Coriolan EDC: 63
The Days of the Commune EDC: 63
The Didactic Play of Baden: On Consent [Das Badener Lehrstueck vom Einverständnis] EDC: 63; MD: 65

Die Dreigroschenoper see The Threepenny Opera
Dreigroschenroman see The Threepenny Novel
Drums in the Night [Trommeln in der Nacht] Br: 124; EDC: 63; Po: 305
The Exception and the Rule [Die Ausnahme und die Regel] Br: 124; DC2: 65
Exiles' Dialogues [Fluchlingspräche] Br: 124
Fear and Misery of the Third Reich see Private Life of the Master Race
Frau Carrars Gewehre see Senora Carrar's Rifles
Furcht und Elend des Dritten Reich see Private Life of the Master Race
Galileo [The Life of Galileo; Das Leben des Galilei] Br: 124-125; DC2: 67-68; EDC: 64-65; LCAB: 22; Ma: 224-225; MD: 66; MDAE: 126; Po: 301-302
Gesang der punischen Soldaten Po: 287
The Good Woman of Setzuan [Der Gute Mensch von Sezuan] Br: 125; DC2: 68; EDC: 65-66; LCAB: 22; Ma: 223-224; MD: 65; Po: 298
Die Heilige Johanna der Schlachthöf see St. Joan of the Stockyards
Herr Puntilla und Sein Knecht Matti see Mr. Puntilla and His Hired Man Matti
In the Jungle of the Cities [In the Swamp of the Cities; Im Dickicht der Stadte] Br: 125; DC2: 69; EDC: 66-67; MD: 66; Po: 298
Der Jasager see The Yea-Sayer
Der Kaukasische Kreidekreis see The Caucasian Chalk Circle
Kinderkreuzzug see Children's Crusade
Kleines Organum für das Theater see Little Organon for the Theater
Das Leben des Galilei see Galileo

Legende Po: 302-303
Lehrstucke DC2: 69
The Life of Galileo see
  Galileo
Little Organon for the Theater
  [Kleines Organum für das
  Theater] Po: 300
Man's a Man [Mann Ist Mann]
  Br: 126; DC2: 69; EDC:
  67-68; Ma: 225-226; MD:
  66
Me-Ti: Buch der Wendungen
  Po: 303
The Measures Taken [Die
  Massnahme] Br: 126;
  EDC: 68; MD: 66
Mr. Puntilla and His Hired
  Man Matti [Herr Puntilla
  und Sein Knecht Matti]
  Br: 126; DC2: 70; EDC:
  68; MD: 66; Po: 298
The Mother [Die Mutter] Br:
  126-127; EDC: 68; MD:
  67; Po: 303
Mother Courage and Her Chil-
  dren [Mutter Courage und
  Ihre Kinder] Br: 127-
  128; DC2: 70-71; EDC:
  68-70; LCAB: 22; Ma:
  226-227; MBD: 33; MD:
  67; MDAE: 108; Po: 303-
  304
Nay-Sayer DC2: 71
Pauken und Trompeten see
  Trumpets and Drums
Private Life of the Master
  Race [Fear and Misery of
  the Third Reich; Furcht
  und Elend des Dritten
  Reich] Br: 128; DC2:
  71; EDC: 70; MD: 65
The Resistable Rise of Arturo
  Ui [Arturo Ui; Der Auf-
  haltsame Aufsteig des
  Arturo Ui] Br: 128; EDC:
  70-71; Ma: 227
Rise and Fall of the City of
  Mahagonny [Aufsteig und
  Fall der Stadt Mahagonny]
  Br: 128; DC2: 72; EDC:
  71
The Roundheads and the Peak-
  heads [Die Rundköpfe und
  die Spitzköpfe] Br: 129;
  DC2: 72; EDC: 71; MD:
  67; Po: 305

St. Joan of the Stockyards [Die
  Heilige Johanna der Schlach-
  thöf] Br: 129; DC2: 72;
  EDC: 71-72; Ma: 228; MD:
  65; Po: 298
Salzburg Dance-of-Death DC2:
  72
Schweyk in the Second World
  War [Schweyk im Zweiten
  Weltkrieg] DC2: 73; EDC:
  72; MD: 67
Senora Carrar's Rifles [Frau
  Carrars Gewehre] DC2: 73;
  EDC: 72
Seven Deadly Sins [Die Sieben
  Todsünden der Kleinbürger]
  DC2: 73; EDC: 72; Po:
  305
The Threepenny Novel [Drei-
  groschenroman] Fi: 290;
  Ke: 257-258; Po: 297
The Threepenny Opera [Die
  Dreigroschenoper] Br: 129;
  DC2: 73-74; EDC: 72; Ma:
  228-229; MD: 65; Po: 296-
  297
Trial of Joan of Arc at Rouen,
  1431 DC2: 74; EDC: 72
The Trial of Lucullus [Das Ver-
  hör des Lukullus] EDC: 72
Trommeln in der Nacht see
  Drums in the Night
Trumpets and Drums [Pauken
  und Trompeten] EDC: 73;
  MD: 68
Turandot, or The Congress of
  the Whitewashers [Turandot
  oder der Kongress der
  Weisswascher] EDC: 73;
  Po: 306
Das Verhör des Lukullus see
  The Trial of Lucullus
Warten auf Godot Po: 306
The Yea-Sayer [Der Jasager]
  Br: 129; DC2: 74
_____ and Lion FEUCHTWANGER
The Life of Edward the Second
  of England [Edward II; Leben
  Eduards des Zweiten] Br:
  126; DC2: 67; EDC: 63-64;
  MD: 66; Po: 302
Visions of Simone Machard [Die
  Gesichte der Simone Mach-
  ard] MD: 65
BREDEL, Willi
  Verwandte und Bekannte Ke:

258
BREGENDAHL, Marie
Highways and Wayside Inns
Ke: 348
BREIT, Harvey and Patricia
RINEHART
The Guide ADC: 58
BREMER, Fredrika
Grannarne Ke: 348
Nina Ke: 348
BREMOND, Henri
General Po: 306
BRENNAN, Christopher
General AL: 139-144; Po:
306-307
"Lilith" AL: 140
BRENTANO, Clemens
"Brave Kasperl and Beautiful
Annerl" Fi: 290; Wa:
73; WaS1: 25
Godwi Ke: 258; Ke: 290
"Lieblingslied der Geiziglen"
Wa: 73
Das Märchen von Gockel und
Hinkel Fi: 290
"Die mehreren Wehlmüller"
Wa: 73
Die Schachtel mit der Frieden-
spuppe Fi: 290
The Story of Just Caspar and
Fair Annie Ke: 258
BRENTON, Howard
General MDAE: 134
BRERETON, John Le Gay, Jr.
General AL: 147; Po: 307
BRESCIANI, Antonio
The Jew of Verona Ke: 241
BRETON, André
General Po: 307-314
L'Amour fou Fi: 30
Les Champs Magnétiques Po:
314
Nadja Fi: 30; Ke: 37; Po:
309, 314-315
Les Vases communicants Fi:
30-31
BRETON, Nicholas
General ERP: 99-100; Hen:
112; SC: 41
The Miseries of Mavillia
ERP: 98-99
"Passion of a Discontented
Mind" ICBAP: 15
A Poste with a Madde Packet
of Letters ERP: 100
The Strange Fortunes of Two

Excellent Princes ERP: 98-
99
BREUER, Bessie
"Home Is a Place" SFC: 18;
Wa: 73
BREUER, Miles J.
"Paradise and Iron" WaS1: 26
BREW, Kwesi
General BALE: 279
BREWER, Anthony
The Love-Sick King DC1: 32;
LJCD: 229
BREWER, George
Tide Rising Br: 129
BREWER, J. Mason
General AAW: 42
BREWER, Thomas
The Life and Death of the Mer-
ry Devil of Edmonton ERP:
101
BREWSTER, Anna Maria Hampton
General LCAB: 22
BREWSTER, Townsend
Please Don't Cry and Say No
ADC: 58
BREZA, Tadeusz
General Po: 315
BRIDGE, Ann
General Po: 315
BRIDGES, Robert Seymour
General EP: 73-76; LCAB:
22; Po: 316; TA: 104
"Eros" PE: 51
"Eros and Psyche" ICBAP: 15
"In the Summer House on the
Mound" PE: 51
"London Snow" PE: 51
"Low Barometer" PE: 51
"Nightingales" PE: 51
"Ode to Music" PE: 51
"On a Dead Child" PE: 51
"Testament of Beauty" EP:
73-74, 76; ICBAP: 15
BRIDIE, James Osborne Henry
[O.H. MAVOR]
General Ai: 236; Br: 130;
MBD: 38-39; MD: 68;
MDAE: 135-136; Mi: 223-
224
The Baikie Charivari, or, The
Seven Prophets Br: 130;
DC1: 32; MBD: 38; MD:
68; MDAE: 135-136
The Black Eye Br: 130; DC1:
32; MD: 68; Po: 2686
Daphne Laureola Br: 130;

DC1: 33; MD: 68
Gog and Magog Br: 130
Holy Isle Br: 130
Jonah and the Whale Br:
131
Mr. Bolfry Br: 131
The Queen's Comedy Br:
131; MDAE: 136
A Sleeping Clergyman Br:
131
The Sunlight Sonata Br:
131
Susannah and the Elders Br:
131
Tobias and the Angel Br:
131; MBD: 39; MD: 68
BRIEUX, Eugène
General Br: 132; MD: 68-
69
Les Bienfaiteurs see The
Philanthropists
Blanchette Br: 132
Damaged Goods [Les Avariés]
Br: 132; MD: 69
La Foi Br: 132
La Française Br: 132
Maternity [Maternité] Br:
132; MD: 69
The Philanthropists [Les
Bienfaiteurs] Br: 132
The Red Robe [La Robe
Rouge] MD: 69
The Three Daughters of Mon-
sieur Dupont [Les Trois
Filles de M. Dupont] Br:
132; MD: 69
BRIGHOUSE, Harold
General Mi: 224
BRIGHT, Timothy
General SC: 41
BRINNIN, John Malcolm
General Po: 316
"The Alps" PE: 51
"The Fortunate Isles" PE:
51
"Goodnight, When the Door
Swings" PE: 51
"Islands: A Song" PE: 51
"A Sail" PE: 52
"Second Sight" PE: 52
"Skin Diving in the Virgins"
PE: 52
"Views of the Favorite Col-
leges" PE: 52
"The Worm in the Whirling
Cross" PE: 52

BRISCOE, Sophia
The Fine Lady ENES2: 22
BRITTING, Georg
"Der Schneckenweg" Wa: 73
BRJUSOV, Valerij
General Po: 316
BROAD, Jay
Conflict of Interest ADC: 59
Killdeer ADC: 59
White Pelicans ADC: 59
BROCH, Hermann
General Po: 316-320
The Bewitchment Ke: 258
The Death of Virgil [Der Tod
des Vergil] Fi: 291; Ke:
258; Po: 322
The Guiltless [Die Schuldlosen;
Die Erzählung der Magd Zer-
line] Fi: 291; Ke: 258-
259; Po: 320-321
The Mountain Novel Fi: 291
The Sleepwalkers [Die Schlaf-
wandler] Fi: 291-292; Ke:
259; Po: 320-321
The Tempter [Der Versucher]
Fi: 292; Ke: 259; Po:
322-323
Tierkreis-Erzählungen Po:
321-322
Der Tod des Vergil see The
Death of Virgil
Die Unbekannte Grösse Fi:
292
BRODERICK, John
An Apology for Roses ENES2:
22
Don Juaneen ENES2: 22
The Fugitives ENES2: 22
The Pilgrimage ENES2: 22
The Waking of Willie Ryan
ENES2: 22
BRODKEY, Harold
"Sentimental Education" SFC:
18; Wa: 73
BRODSKY, Josip Anatolevich
General Po: 323
BROMBERG, Conrad
General Po: 323
The Defense of Taipei ADC:
59; Po: 323; TMBP: 144
Dream of a Blacklisted Actor
ADC: 59
Transfers ADC: 59
BROME, Alexander
"Leveller's Rant" ICBAP: 15
BROME, Richard

General ED: 213-214; LJCD: 174-179, 184-187, 191; TSD: 39-40

The Antipodes DC1: 33; LJCD: 179-181; TSD: 40

The Court Beggar LJCD: 182

A Jovial Crew LJCD: 181-182, 191

The Lovesick Court LJCD: 183

The Novella LJCD: 184

The Queen and Concubine LJCD: 183-184

The Sparagus Garden LJCD: 184

The Weeding of the Covent Garden LJCD: 182-183

_____ and Thomas HEYWOOD

The Late Lancashire Witches (See also: HEYWOOD, Thomas and Richard BROME) DC1: 33; LJCD: 191

BROMFIELD, Louis
General AN: 21; ASF: 87
The Farm LCAB: 22
Mr. Smith AN: 21
What Became of Anna Bolton? AN: 21

BRONK, Edwin
General ICBAP: 15

BRONNEN, Arnolt
General Br: 132
Parricide [Vatermord] Br: 132

BRONTÉ, Anne
General BN: 17-19; Du: 12-13
Agnes Grey Du: 12; ENE: 19; ENES2: 23; Ma: 230
The Tenant of Wildfell Hall Du: 12; ENE: 19; ENES1: 22; ENES2: 23; Ma: 230-231

BRONTÉ, Charlotte
General BN: 17-18, 20; Du: 16-18
Jane Eyre BN: 20-21; Du: 13-14; EN: 8; ENE: 19-21; ENES1: 22-23; ENES2: 23-24; LCAB: 22-23; Ma: 232-233; Po: 1896
The Professor Du: 15; EN: 8-9; ENE: 21; ENES1:

23; ENES2: 24-25; Ma: 233-234

"The Secret" WaS1: 26

Shirley BN: 21; Du: 15; EN: 9; ENE: 21-22; ENES1: 23; ENES2: 25; Ma: 234-235

Villette BN: 21; Du: 15-16; EN: 9; ENE: 22; ENES1: 23; ENES2: 25-26; LCAB: 23; Ma: 235-236; Po: 1896

BRONTÉ, Emily
General BN: 22; Du: 22-23; Ma: 237
"Cold in the Earth" PE: 52
"No Coward Soul Is Mine" PE: 52
Remembrance LCAB: 23
Wuthering Heights BN: 22-24; Du: 18-22; EN: 9-11; ENE: 22-26; ENES1: 24-25; ENES2: 26-28; LCAB: 23; Ma: 237-239

BROOKE, Emma Frances
A Superfluous Woman ENES2: 28

BROOKE [MOORE], Frances
General ECL: 116-117
The History of Emily Montague ECL: 117
The History of Lady Julia Mandeville [Lady Julia Mandeville] ECL: 117; ENES2: 28

BROOKE, Henry
General Be: 70-71
The Fool of Quality Be: 70; ENES1: 25; ENES2: 28

BROOKE, Rupert
General Ma: 240; Po: 323; TA: 105
"The Soldier" ICBAP: 15; PE: 52

BROOKE, Stopford Augustus
General TA: 106

BROOKE-ROSE, Christine
Between ENES2: 29
Thru ENES2: 29

BROOKS, Cleanth
General APC: 160-161; LCAB: 23; Po: 323-324

BROOKS, Gwendolyn
General AAL: 141-142; AAPD: 155-157; AAW: 43; BAF: 40-41; BAW: 100-102; ICBAP: 15; LCAB: 23;

Po: 324

"The Chicago Picasso" AAPD: 156; PE: 52

"The Children of the Poor" PE: 52

"In the Mecca" AAL: 142; Po: 324

"A Light and Diplomatic Bird" PE: 52

Maud Martha AAL: 142; BAF: 41

"The Third Sermon on the Warpland" PE: 52

"The Wall" AAPD: 156; PE: 52

"We Real Cool" PE: 52

BROOKS, John
General LCAB: 23

BROOKS, Van Wyck
General ALL: 46-47; APC: 164-166; LCAB: 23; Po: 324-325

The Flowering of New England LCAB: 23

Makers and Finders ALL: 46; Po: 325

BROOME, Barbara Cummings
Millie Brown MBA: 28

BROPHY, Brigid
General LCAB: 23-24

BROSZKIEWICZ, Jerzy
General Po: 325

The End of Book VI [Koniec Kniegi VI] Br: 133

The Historical Role of Quince [Dziejowa Rola Pigwy] Br: 133

I Come to Tell [Przychodze Opowiedziec] Br: 133

Scandal in Hellberg [Skandal W Helbergu] Br: 133

The Two Adventures of Lemuel Gulliver [Dwie Przygody Lemuela Gulliwera] Br: 133

BROUGHAM, John
General AD: 99-101

Columbus el Filibustero AD: 100-101

Much Ado About the Merchant of Venice AD: 100

Playing with Fire AD: 101

Po-ca-hon-tas AD: 100

BROWN, Alice
General ASF: 87

"At Sudleigh Fair" Wa: 73

"The Book of Love" Wa: 73

"A Day Off" Wa: 73

"Dooryards" Wa: 74

"The End of All Living" Wa: 74

"Farmer Eli's Vacation" ASF: 87; Wa: 74

"A Flower in April" Wa: 74

"Gardener Jim" Wa: 74

"Horn o' the Moon" Wa: 74

"A Last Assembling" Wa: 74

"A Meeting in the Market Place" Wa: 74

"Natalie Blayne" Wa: 74

"The Other Mrs. Dill" Wa: 74

"A Righteous Bargain" Wa: 74

"Rosamund in Heaven" Wa: 74

"A Sea Change" ASF: 87; Wa: 74

"A Second Marriage" ASF: 87; Wa: 74

"A Winter's Courting" Wa: 74

BROWN, Cecil M.
General BAF: 41-42; BAW: 103

The Gila Monster BAP: 29

"The Life and Loves of Mr. Jiveass Nigger" BAF: 41-42; BAW: 103

BROWN, Charles Brockden
General AF: 39-42; ALL: 47-48; AN: 22-24; AP: 216-217; Da: 90-91; Ho: 16-19, 142-143; LCAB: 24

Alcuin ALL: 47; AN: 21

Arthur Mervyn AF: 39-40; AN: 21; Ho: 16-18, 142; Ma: 241

Clara Howard AN: 21; Ho: 143

"Death of Cicero, a Fragment" SFC: 18; Wa: 75

Edgar Huntly AF: 39, 41; AN: 21-22; Ho: 17-18

"Insanity: A Fragment" ASF: 87

Jane Talbot AN: 22; Ho: 143

"A Lesson on Concealment" SFC: 18; Wa: 75

"The Man at Home" SFC: 18; Wa: 75

"Memoirs of Carwin the Biloquist" Wa: 75

Ormond AN: 22; Ho: 17-18, 142; Ma: 241-242

"Portrait of an Emigrant" ASF: 88

Stephen Calvert AF: 39
"The Story of Julius" ASF: 88
Thessalonica: A Roman Story SFC: 18
Wieland AF: 40-42; AN: 22; Ho: 17-19, 142; Ma: 242-243

BROWN, Charlotte Hawkins
General BAF: 42; BAW: 104

BROWN, Christy
Down All the Days ENES2: 29
A Shadow on Summer ENES2: 29

BROWN, Claude
General BAF: 43; BAW: 104
The Children of Ham BAF: 43
Manchild in the Promised Land BAF: 43-44

BROWN, Dee Alexander
Bury My Heart at Wounded Knee Ma: 244

BROWN, Frank London
General BAF: 44-45; BAW: 105-106
Trumbull Park BAF: 45; BAW: 106

BROWN, Frederic
General ASF: 88

BROWN, George Douglas [George DOUGLAS, George HOOD, Kennedy KING]
General Ai: 204-205; TA: 107
The House with the Green Shutters Ai: 205; ENES2: 29

BROWN, George Mackay
General Ai: 321
Greenvoe ENES2: 29

BROWN, Harry Peter M'Nab
"Fourth Elegy: The Poet Compared to an Unsuccessful General" PE: 52
A Sound of Hunting ADC: 59-60
A Walk in the Sun LCAB: 24

BROWN, Henry "Box"
General BAW: 106

BROWN, Heywood Campbell
General LCAB: 24

BROWN, James N.
General MBA: 28
The Barren Heritage MBA: 29

BROWN, John
General EC: 55

BROWN, Kenneth
General MDAE: 138-139; Po: 325
The Brig ADC: 60; Br: 133-134; DC1: 33; MDAE: 138-139; TMBP: 14

BROWN, Lennox John
General BAP: 30; MBA: 29
A Ballet Behind the Bridge ADC: 60; BAP: 30; MBA: 29
The Captive MBA: 29
Winti-Train MBA: 29

BROWN, Lloyd Louis
General BAF: 45
Iron City BAF: 45; BAW: 110

BROWN, Norman Oliver
Love's Body LCAB: 24

BROWN, Oliver Madox
Gabriel Denver ENES1: 26

BROWN, Oscar, Jr.
General BAP: 31; BAW: 111
Buck White BAP: 31; MBA: 29-30
In De Beginnin' MBA: 29
Joy BAP: 31
Kicks and Co. BAP: 31; MBA: 30

BROWN, Roscoe Lee
General MBA: 30
A Hand Is on the Gate BAP: 31

BROWN, Sterling A.
General AAPD: 92; AAW: 43; BAF: 46; BAW: 113; HR: 63-64
"Odyssey of Big Boy" ICBAP: 16

BROWN, Thomas
General Bon: 72

BROWN, Thomas E.
"My Garden" PE: 53

BROWN, Wayne
General WIL: 20
On the Coast WIL: 20-21

BROWN, William F.
General MBA: 30
The Girl in the Freudian Slip ADC: 60
The Wiz MBA: 30-33

BROWN, William Hill
General AF: 43-44; Ho:
135
Ira and Isabella AF: 44;
AN: 24; Ho: 135
The Power of Sympathy AF:
43-44; AN: 24; Ho: 135;
Ma: 245
BROWN, William Wells
General AAPD: 298; AAW:
43-44; BAF: 47-48; BAP:
32; BAW: 116-118; Ho:
135; LCAB: 24; MBA: 34
Clotel AAW: 43; BAF: 47-
48; Ho: 135
The Escape; or, A Leap for
Freedom BAP: 32-33;
MBA: 34
Experience, or How to Give
a Northern Man a Backbone
ADC: 60; BAP: 32
Browne, Charles Farrar see
WARD, Artemus
BROWNE, Sir Thomas
General Ba: 33-35; Hen:
137-138
Christian Morals Ba: 33
The Garden of Cyrus Ba:
33-34; Hen: 137-138
Hydriotaphia [Urn Burial]
Ba: 33-35; Hen: 137-138
Religio Medici Ba: 33-35
BROWNE, Theodore
General AAPD: 301; BAP:
33; BAW: 119; MBA: 34
Natural Man BAP: 33; Br:
134; MBA: 34
BROWNE, Thomas Alexander
General AL: 153-154
Robbery Under Arms AL:
153-154
BROWNE, William
General NI: 328
"Epitaph on the Countess
Dowager of Pembroke"
PE: 53
BROWNE, Wynyard
General MDAE: 140
Dark Summer Br: 134
A Question of Fact Br: 134
BROWNING, Alice C.
General MBA: 34-35
How's Your Sex Life MBA:
35
BROWNING, Elizabeth Barrett
General VP: 16-17

"Aurora Leigh" Ma: 246; VP:
17
"A Curse for a Nation" ICBAP:
16; PE: 53
Sonnet 6 from Sonnets from the
Portuguese PE: 53
Sonnet 22 from Sonnets from the
Portuguese PE: 53
Sonnet 43 from Sonnets from the
Portuguese PE: 53
Sonnets from the Portuguese
Ma: 246-247
BROWNING, Robert
General EDT: 102-108; ICBAP:
16; LCAB: 24; Ma: 248-249;
VP: 18-23
"Abt Vogler" ICBAP: 16; PE:
53
"Andrea Del Sarto" ICBAP:
16; PE: 53-54; VP: 19
"Any Wife to Any Husband"
PE: 54
"Balaustion's Adventure"
ICBAP: 16; PE: 54; VP:
22
"Bishop Blougram's Apology"
ICBAP: 16; PE: 54
"The Bishop Orders His Tomb
at St. Praxed's Church"
ICBAP: 16; PE: 54; VP:
22
A Blot in the Scutcheon DC1:
33; EDT: 103-106, 108
"Caliban Upon Setebos" ICBAP:
16-17; PE: 55; VP: 22
"Childe Roland to the Dark Tower
Cam" ICBAP: 17; PE: 55-
56; VP: 20, 23
"Christmas Eve" ICBAP: 17
"Cleon" ICBAP: 17; PE: 56;
VP: 21
"Clive" PE: 56
Colombe's Birthday EDT: 103,
106
"Count Gismond" ICBAP: 17;
PE: 56
"Cristina" PE: 56
"A Death in the Desert" PE:
56
"A Dialogue Between Apollo and
the Fates" Prologue, Parley-
ings PE: 56
"Dis Aliter Visum; or Le Byron
de Nos Jours" PE: 56
"Easter Day" ICBAP: 17
"The Englishman in Italy" PE:

57

"An Epistle Containing the Strange Medical Experience of Karshish, the Arab Physician" ICBAP: 17; PE: 57

"Evelyn Hope" ICBAP: 17; PE: 57

"Flute Music: With an Accompaniment" PE: 57

"Fra Lippo Lippi" ICBAP: 17; PE: 57-58; VP: 22

"The Glove" ICBAP: 17; PE: 58

"A Grammarian's Funeral" ICBAP: 17-18; PE: 58; VP: 18

"The Guardian Angel" PE: 58

"Holy-Cross Day" PE: 59

"Home-Thoughts, from the Sea" PE: 59

"How It Strikes a Contemporary" ICBAP: 18; PE: 59

"How They Brought the Good News from Ghent to Aix" PE: 59

"In a Balcony" DC1: 33; EDT: 102, 104, 107-108; ICBAP: 18; PE: 59

"In a Year" PE: 59

"The Inn Album" PE: 59

"The Italian in England" ICBAP: 18; PE: 59

"James Lee's Wife" ICBAP: 18

"James Lee's Wife" 1: "Speaks at the Window" PE: 59

"James Lee's Wife" 2: "By the Fireside" PE: 60

"James Lee's Wife" 3: "In the Doorway" PE: 60

"James Lee's Wife" 4: "Along the Beach" PE: 60

"James Lee's Wife" 5: "On the Cliff" PE: 60

"James Lee's Wife" 6: "Reading a Book Under a Cliff" PE: 60

"James Lee's Wife" 7: "Among the Rocks" PE: 60

"James Lee's Wife" 8: "Beside the Drawing Board" PE: 60

"James Lee's Wife" 9: "On Deck" PE: 60

"Johannes Agricola in Meditation" ICBAP: 18; PE: 61

"The King" PE: 61

King Victor and King Charles EDT: 106

"The Laboratory" PE: 61

"The Last Ride Together" ICBAP: 18; PE: 61

"Love Among the Ruins" PE: 61

Luria EDT: 102-104, 106

"Master Hugues of Saxe-Gotha" ICBAP: 18; PE: 61

"Meeting at Night" ICBAP: 18; PE: 61-62

"Men and Women" VP: 20

"Mr. Sludge, 'The Medium'" ICBAP: 18

"My Last Duchess" ICBAP: 18-19; LCAB: 24; PE: 62; VP: 18-20

"My Star" PE: 63

"Nationality in Drinks" ICBAP: 19; PE: 63

"Now" PE: 63

"One Word More" ICBAP: 19; PE: 63

"Paracelsus" EDT: 103, 105; ICBAP: 19; VP: 22

"Parleyings with Certain People of Importance in Their Day" PE: 63

"Parting at Morning" ICBAP: 19; PE: 63

"Pauline" ICBAP: 19

"Pictor Ignotus" ICBAP: 19; PE: 63

"Pied Piper of Hamelin" ICBAP: 19

"Pippa Passes" DC1: 33; EDT: 103, 105-107; ICBAP: 19; VP: 21

"Pippa's Song" ["The Year's at the Spring"] PE: 63, 67

"Popularity" PE: 63

"Porphyria's Lover" ICBAP: 19; PE: 63-64

"Prince Hohenstiel-Schwangau, Saviour of Society" ICBAP: 19

"Prospice" PE: 64

"Rabbi Ben Ezra" ICBAP: 19; LCAB: 24; PE: 64

"Red Cotton Night-Cap Country

or Turf and Towers"
ICBAP: 19
"Respectability" PE: 64
The Return of the Druses
EDT: 103-104, 106, 108
The Ring and the Book
ICBAP: 20; LCAB: 24;
Ma: 249-250; VP: 18-22
The Ring and the Book--Book
I ICBAP: 20
The Ring and the Book--Book
VI ICBAP: 20
The Ring and the Book--Book
VII ICBAP: 20
The Ring and the Book--
Books VIII and IX ICBAP:
20
"St. Martin's Summer" PE:
64
"La Saisiaz" PE: 61
"Saul" ICBAP: 20; PE: 64
"A Serenade at the Villa"
PE: 64
"Sibrandus Schafnaburgensis"
PE: 65
"Soliloquy of the Spanish
Cloister" ICBAP: 20;
PE: 65; VP: 22
"Sordello" ICBAP: 21; VP:
21-22
A Soul's Tragedy EDT:
104, 106
"The Statue and the Bust"
PE: 65
Strafford DC1: 33; EDT:
102-104, 106, 108
"Thamuris Marching" (Aris-
tophanes' Apology) PE:
66
"A Toccata of Galuppi's"
PE: 66
"Too Late" ICBAP: 21; PE:
66
"Transcendentalism" PE: 66
"Two in the Campagna"
ICBAP: 21; PE: 66
"Up at a Villa--Down in the
City" ICBAP: 21; PE:
66
"With Bernardde Mandeville"
PE: 67
"With Charles Avison"
(Parleyings with Certain
People of Importance)
PE: 66
"With Christopher Smart"

PE: 67
"With Daniel Bartoli" PE: 67
"With George Bubb Dodington"
PE: 67
"With Gerard de Lairesse" PE:
67
"With Francis Furini" PE: 67
BROWNSON, Orestes
General ALL: 48
BROWNSTEIN, Michael
"The Plot to Save the World"
Wa: 75
BRU, Hethin
"Alone on Lítla Dímun" Wa: 75
"Emanuel" Wa: 75
"Halgir" Wa: 75
"The Hermits" Wa: 75
"The Light" Wa: 75
"Sheep Fold" Wa: 75
"A Tall Tale" Wa: 75
"The White Church" Wa: 75
BRUCE, George
General Ai: 286
BRUCE, John Edward
General BAF: 48; BAW: 120
BRUCE, Michael
General Ai: 78
BRUCE, Richard
Sodhji MBA: 35
BRUCKNER, Ferdinand [Theodore
TAGGER]
General Br: 134; Po: 325-
326
The Criminals [Die Verbrecher]
Br: 134
Gloriana [Elizabeth von Eng-
land] Br: 134
Races [Die Rassen] Br: 134
Sickness of Youth [Krankheit
der Jugend] Br: 134-135;
MD: 69
BRUNNER, John
Age of Miracles ENES2: 29
The Jagged Orbit ENES2: 29
"Judas" Wa: 76
The Sheep Look Up ENES2:
29
The Shockwave Rider ENES2:
30
Stand on Zanzibar ENES2: 30
"The Windows of Heaven" Wa:
76
BRUNSON, Doris
General BAP: 34; BAW: 121
BRUSH, Katharine
"Birthday Party" Wa: 76

BRUSOV, Valery
"Republic of the Southern Cross" Wa: 76
BRUTUS, Dennis [John BRUIN, pseud.]
General BALE: 281-282
Letters to Martha and Other Poems from a South African Prison BALE: 282
BRUYN, Günter de
Preisverleihung Fi: 293
BRYANT, William Cullen
General ALL: 49-50; AP: 220-222; Da: 92-94; Ma: 251
The Death of Lincoln LCAB: 24
"The Evening Wind" PE: 67
"Green River" PE: 67
"Hymn to Death" PE: 67
"Inscription for the Entrance to a Wood" PE: 67
"The Prairies" Da: 93; Ma: 251-252; PE: 67
"The Song of the Sower" PE: 67
"Thanatopsis" Da: 92-94; ICBAP: 21; Ma: 252; PE: 68
"To a Waterfowl" Ma: 253; PE: 68
"Where Rolls the Oregon" Da: 94
BRYDEN, Bill
General Ai: 338
BRYMER, Robert
In These Days ENES2: 30
BRYNNER, Roc
Opium ADC: 61
BRZOZOWSKI, Stanislaw
Alone Among Men Ke: 372
Buchan, Anna see DOUGLAS, O.
BUCHAN, John
General Ai: 211; Po: 326; TA: 108
The Blanket of the Dark ENES2: 30
The Dancing Floor ENES2: 30
Greenmantle ENES2: 30
The Half-Hearted ENES2: 30
Huntingtower ENES2: 30
John Burnet of Barns ENES2: 30

John Macnab ENES2: 30
A Lost Lady of Old Years ENES2: 30
Midwinter ENES2: 30
Mr. Standfast ENES2: 30
The Power-House ENES2: 30
Prester John ENES2: 31
A Prince of the Captivity ENES2: 31
Salute to Adventurers ENES2: 31
Sick Heart River ENES2: 31
Sir Quixote of the Moors ENES2: 31
The Thirty-Nine Steps ENES1: 26; ENES2: 31
The Three Hostages ENES2: 31
BUCHANAN, George (1506-1582)
General Ai: 39-40; SC: 41
BUCHANAN, George (1904-)
Rose Forbes ENES2: 31
BUCHANAN, Robert William
General Ai: 151; EDT: 110
"The Ballad of Judas Iscariot" PE: 68
BÜCHNER, Georg
General Br: 135
Danton's Death [Danton's Tod] Br: 135-136; DC2: 74-75; EDC: 73-74
Lenz Fi: 293; Ke: 259; Wa: 76; WaS1: 26
Leonce and Lena Br: 136; DC2: 75; EDC: 75
Pietro Aretino EDC: 75
Woyzeck Br: 136; DC2: 75-76; EDC: 75-76; TMBP: 186
BUCHNER, Luise
Ein Dichter Fi: 293
BUCHWALD, Art
Sheep on the Runway ADC: 61
BUCK, Pearl S.
General AN: 24-25; ASF: 89; CN: 68; Po: 326-327; Wo: 45
Command the Morning CN: 68
A Desert Incident ADC: 61
Dragon Seed CN: 68; Ma: 254
"East Wind" ASF: 88
East Wind: West Wind CN: 68
"Enough for a Lifetime" Wa: 76

"The First Wife" Wa: 76
The Good Earth see also
   House of Earth Trilogy
   AN: 24; CN: 68-69; Ma:
   254; Po: 327; Wo: 45
A House Divided see also
   House of Earth Trilogy
   CN: 69
House of Earth Trilogy CN:
   69
Imperial Woman AN: 24
Kinfolk CN: 69
The Mother CN: 69
Other Gods CN: 69
The Patriot CN: 69
Pavilion of Women CN: 69
The Promise CN: 70
"The Rainy Day" Wa: 76
"Repatriated" Wa: 76
"The Revolutionist" Wa: 76
Sons see also House of
   Earth Trilogy CN: 70
This Proud Heart CN: 70
The Townsman CN: 70
BUCKLEY, F.R.
   "Gold-Mounted Guns" Wa: 77
BUCKLEY, Vincent
   General Po: 327
BUCKSTONE, John Baldwin
   General EDT: 112
BUDANTSEV, Sergei
   Rebellion Ke: 372
BUDRYS, Algis
   "Nobody Bothers Gus" Wa:
   77
BUECHLER, James
   "The Proud Suitor" Wa: 77
BUECHNER, Frederick
   General CFAE: 99
   The Final Beast Po: 327-328
   A Long Day's Dying AN: 25;
      CN: 70; LCAB: 25
   The Return of Ansel Gibbs
      CN: 70
BUENAVENTURA, Enrique
   General Br: 136
BUENO, Manuel
   General Po: 328
Buero Vallejo, Antonio see
   VALLEJO, Antonio Buero
Bugaev, Boris Nikolaevich
   see BELYJ, Andrej
BUKENYA, Augustine S.
   General BALE: 282
BUKOWSKI, Charles
   General Po: 331

BULATOVIC, Miodrag
   General Po: 331
   Godo je dosao Po: 331
BULGAKOV, Mikhail Afanas'evich
   General Po: 331-332
   Days of the Turbins Br: 137
   The Fatal Eggs Fi: 419; Ke:
      372
   The Heart of a Dog Fi: 419
   The Master and Margarita [Mas-
      ter i Margarita] Fi: 419-420;
      Po: 332
   Rokovye Iaitsa Fi: 420-421
   Sobach'e Serdtse Fi: 421
   Teatral'nyy Roman Fi: 421
   The White Guard Br: 137; Fi:
      421
BULGARIN, Faddei
   Ivan Vyzhigin Fi: 421
BULLINS, Ed
   General AAL: 145-146; AAPD:
      349-350; BAF: 49-50; BAP:
      37-38; BAW: 125; MBA:
      37-39; TMAP: 142-148
   Absurdities in Black MBA: 44
   Black Love Fable MBA: 39
   Black Quartet MBA: 44
   Clara's Ole Man ADC: 61;
      BAP: 38-40; MBA: 39, 44;
      TMAP: 149
   The Corner ADC: 61; MBA:
      39-40; TMAP: 147, 149
   Daddy ADC: 61; MBA: 44;
      TMAP: 149
   Death List MBA: 40, 44-45
   The Duplex AAL: 145; ADC:
      61-62; BAP: 39-40; MBA:
      40, 45; TMAP: 142, 145, 147,
      149
   The Electronic Nigger ADC:
      62; BAP: 39-40; MBA: 40,
      45; TMAP: 142, 145-146,
      149-150
   The Fabulous Miss Marie ADC:
      62; BAP: 39-40; MBA: 41,
      45; TMAP: 150
   Four Dynamite Plays MBA: 47
   Four One Act Plays: How Do
      You Do, A Minor Scene,
      Determinism, It Has No Choice
      BAP: 41
   The Gentleman Caller ADC:
      62; BAP: 40; MBA: 41, 45;
      TMAP: 150
   Goin' a Buffalo ADC: 62;
      BAP: 39-40; MBA: 41, 45;

TMAP: 147, 150-151

Home Boy ADC: 62; MBA: 45; TMAP: 151

House Party ADC: 62; BAP: 40; MBA: 41-42, 45; TMAP: 151

How Do You Do? BAP: 40; MBA: 42; TMAP: 151

The Hungered One AAL: 145; BAF: 50; BAP: 39; MBA: 42; TMAP: 145

I Am Lucy Terry ADC: 62; MBA: 42, 45; TMAP: 151

In New England Winter ADC: 62; BAP: 40-41; MBA: 42, 45; TMAP: 151

In the Wine Time ADC: 62-63; BAP: 39, 41; MBA: 42-43, 45-46; TMAP: 131, 147, 151-152

It Bees Dat Way ADC: 63

Jo Anne! ADC: 63; MBA: 43, 46; TMAP: 152

Michael (Man-Wo-man) TMAP: 152

The Mystery of Phillis Wheatley MBA: 43; TMAP: 152

The New Lafayette Theatre Presents MBA: 44, 47

Night of the Beast ADC: 63; MBA: 44

The Pig Pen ADC: 63; BAP: 41; MBA: 43, 46; TMAP: 152-153

The Psychic Pretenders MBA: 43

The Rally MBA: 43

The Reluctant Rapist BAF: 50

Sepia Star TMAP: 153

A Son, Come Home BAP: 39, 41; MBA: 43, 46; TMAP: 153

Street Sounds BAP: 41; MBA: 43; TMAP: 153

The Taking of Miss Janie ADC: 63; BAP: 39-41; MBA: 43-44, 46-47; TMAP: 153-154

The Theme Is Blackness: The Corner and Other Plays MBA: 44, 47

We Righteous Bombers AAPD: 350; BAP: 40-41

Who's Got His Own BAP: 41

BULLOCK, Clifton
Baby Chocolate and Other Stories BAF: 50

BULLOCK, Shan F.
Dan the Dollar ENES2: 31
The Loughsiders ENES2: 31
The Squireen ENES2: 31

BULWER-LYTTON, Edward George
General Du: 23-25; EDT: 115-116
Alice ENES2: 31
The Caxtons ENES2: 32
The Coming Race BN: 27; ENES1: 26; ENES2: 32
Devereux ENES2: 32
The Disowned ENES1: 26; ENES2: 32
The Duchess de la Valliere EDT: 116
Ernest Maltravers ENES2: 32
Eugene Aram ENE: 26; ENES1: 26; ENES2: 32
Falkland ENES2: 32
Godolphin ENES2: 32
Harold, the Last of the Saxon Kings ENES2: 32
"The Haunted and the Haunters; or, The House and the Brain" Wa: 77
Kenelm Chillingly ENES2: 32
The Lady of Lyons DC1: 119; EDT: 115-116
The Last Days of Pompeii ENE: 26; ENES2: 32
The Last of the Barons ENES2: 33
Lucretia ENES1: 26; ENES2: 33
My Novel ENES2: 33
Night and Morning ENES1: 26; ENES2: 33
The Parisians ENES2: 33
Paul Clifford ENES1: 26; ENES2: 33
Pelham ENES1: 26; ENES2: 33
Richelieu EDT: 116
Rienzi ENE: 26; ENES2: 33
A Strange Story ENE: 26; ENES1: 26; ENES2: 33
What Will He Do With It? ENES2: 33
Zanoni ENES1: 27; ENES2: 33

BULWER-LYTTON, Edward Robert
General BN: 26-27; LCAB:

115

BUMPUS, Jerry
  General ASF: 89
BUNCH, David R.
  "For Tomorrow, Daphalene"
    ASF: 89
BUNIN, Ivan Alexeyevich
  General LCAB: 25
  The Brothers [The Brethren]
    Fi: 421; SFC: 18; Wa:
    77
  "Conversation at Midnight"
    SFC: 18; Wa: 77
  "The Cup of Life" SFC: 19;
    Wa: 77
  Dark Alleys Fi: 421
  Derevnja Fi: 421
  Dry Valley Fi: 421; Ke:
    372-373
  The Gentleman from San Fran-
    cisco [Gospodin iz San
    Francisco] Fi: 422; Ke:
    373; Ma: 255; Po: 332-
    333; SFC: 19; Wa: 77
  "The Grammar of Love" SFC:
    19; Wa: 78
  The Life of Arsenyev Fi:
    422; Ke: 373
  Mitya's Love Fi: 422; Ke:
    373
  The Village Fi: 422; Ke:
    373; Ma: 255-256
BUNN, Alfred
  General EDT: 117
BUNNER, Henry Cuyler
  "The Love-Letters of Smith"
    ASF: 89
BUNUEL, Luis
  General Po: 333
BUNYAN, John
  General Be: 76-79; Bon:
    63-64; LCAB: 25
  Grace Abounding to the Chief
    of Sinners Be: 77-78;
    Bon: 64
  The Holy War EN: 11-12
  The Life and Death of Mr.
    Badman EN: 12; ENES1:
    27; ENES2: 34; Ma: 257
  The Pilgrim's Progress Be:
    76-79, 249; Bon: 63-64;
    EN: 12-14; ENE: 26-27;
    ENES1: 27; ENES2: 34;
    LCAB: 25; Ma: 257-259
BURGESS, Anthony [Joseph
    KELL]

General CFAE: 102; CN: 70-71;
    LCAB: 25; Po: 333-334; Sch:
    14-15
Abba Abba ENES2: 34
Beard's Roman Women ENES2:
    35
Beds in the East ENES1: 28
A Clockwork Orange CN: 71;
    ENE: 28; ENES1: 28;
    ENES2: 35; Ma: 260; Po:
    333; Sch: 15
The Clockwork Testament
    ENES2: 35
Devil of a State ENES1: 28;
    ENES2: 35
The Doctor Is Sick ENES1:
    28; ENES2: 35
Enderby ENE: 28; ENES1:
    28; ENES2: 35; Ma: 260-
    261; Sch: 15
Enderby Outside ENES1: 28;
    ENES2: 35
The Enemy in the Blanket
    ENES1: 29; ENES2: 36
The Eve of St. Venus ENES1:
    29; ENES2: 36
Honey for the Bears CN: 71;
    ENE: 28; ENES1: 29;
    ENES2: 36
Inside Mr. Enderby ENES1:
    29; ENES2: 36
The Long Day Wanes (Trilogy)
    CN: 71; ENES1: 29;
    ENES2: 36; Po: 333
M F ENES1: 29; ENES2: 36;
    Ma: 261; Sch: 16
"The Muse: A Sort of SF
    Story" Wa: 78
Napoleon Symphony ENES2:
    36
Nothing Like the Sun CN: 71;
    ENE: 28; ENES1: 29;
    ENES2: 36; LCAB: 25;
    Ma: 261; Po: 333; Sch:
    16
One Hand Clapping ENES1:
    29; ENES2: 36
The Right to an Answer CN:
    71; ENE: 28; ENES1: 29;
    ENES2: 36
Time for a Tiger ENE: 28;
    ENES1: 29; ENES2: 36
Tremor of Intent ENE: 28;
    ENES1: 29; ENES2: 36;
    Po: 333
A Vision of Battlements

ENES1: 30; ENES2: 36
The Wanting Seed CN: 71;
ENE: 28-29; ENES1: 30;
ENES2: 37; Po: 333;
Sch: 16
The Worm and the Ring
ENES1: 30; ENES2: 37
BURGESS, Thornton Waldo
General LCAB: 25
BURGOS, Carmen de
General Po: 334
BURGUET, Frantz-André
General Po: 334
Le protégé Po: 334
Le reliquaire Po: 334
Le roman de Blaise Po: 334
BURK, John Daly
General AD: 103
Bethlem Gabor AD: 103
Bunker-Hill; or The Death
of General Warren AD:
103
Female Patriotism AD: 103
BURKE, Edmund
General EC: 56-57
Reflections on the Revolution
in France EC: 56
BURKE, Kenneth
General APC: 168-169; ASF:
89; LCAB: 25; Po: 334-
335
"Three Seasons of Love"
PE: 68
Towards a Better Life Po:
335-336
BURKE, Thomas
"The Chink and the Child"
Wa: 78
BURN, David
General AL: 156-157
BURNETT, Frances Hodgson
The Secret Garden ENES1:
30
BURNETT, Whit
"Sherrel" SFC: 19; Wa: 78
BURNEY, Fanny
General Be: 84-85; Du:
25-26
Camilla ENES1: 30; ENES2:
37
Cecilia; or, Memoirs of an
Heiress Be: 84-85; ENE:
29; ENES1: 30; ENES2:
37; Ma: 262
Evelina Be: 84-85, 160;
Du: 25; EN: 14; ENE:

29; ENES1: 31; ENES2: 37-
38; LCAB: 6; Ma: 262-263
The Wanderer; or, Female Diffi-
culties ENE: 29; ENES1:
31; ENES2: 38
BURNS, John Horne
General CN: 71; LCAB: 25-
26
A Cry of Children CN: 72
The Gallery CN: 72; LCAB:
26; Po: 336
BURNS, Robert
General Ai: 82-84; EC: 57-
58; LCAB: 26
"Address to the Deil" PE: 68
"Death and Dr. Hornbook" PE:
68
"Epistle to John Lapraik" PE:
68
"Holy Willie's Prayer" PE: 68
"John Anderson My Jo, John"
PE: 68
"The Jolly Beggars" EC: 58;
PE: 68
"The Lea-Rig" PE: 68
"A Man's a Man for a' That"
LCAB: 26
"Mary Morison" PE: 68
"Tam O'Shanter" EC: 58;
ICBAP: 21; Ma: 264; PE:
69
"To a Mouse" Ma: 264-265;
PE: 69
"The Vision" LCAB: 26
"Ye Flowery Banks o' Bonie
Doon" PE: 69
BURR, Anne
Huui, Huui ADC: 63
Mert and Phil ADC: 63-64
BURRILL, Mary
Aftermath BAP: 42
They That Sit in Darkness
BAP: 42; MBA: 47-48
BURROUGHS, Charles
General MBA: 48
BURROUGHS, Edgar Rice
General ASF: 90; LCAB: 26
BURROUGHS, John
General Cla: 105; Po: 336
BURROUGHS, Margaret Taylor
Goss
General BAF: 51; BAW: 128
BURROUGHS, William S.
General ASF: 90; CFAE:
103-104; CN: 72; Ne: 23;
Po: 336-338

"The Beginning Is Also the
    End" WaS1: 26
Junkie Ne: 23
The Naked Lunch CFAE:
    104; CN: 72-73; LCAB:
    26; Ma: 266; Ne: 23;
    Po: 337-338
Nova Express CN: 73; Po:
    337
The Soft Machine CN: 74
The Ticket That Exploded
    CN: 74
"23 Skidoo Eristic Elite" Wa:
    78
BURROWS, Abe
Cactus Flower ADC: 64
Four Comedy Playlets (House
    on Dunkelmayer, Betty,
    Toreador, The Swingers)
    ADC: 64
_____, Robert GOLDMAN,
    Glenn PAXTON, and George
    WEISS
First Impressions ADC: 64
_____, Jo SWERLING, and
    Frank LOESSER
Guys and Dolls ADC: 64-65
_____, Jack WEINSTOCK,
    Willie GILBERT, and Frank
    LOESSER
How to Succeed in Business
    Without Really Trying
    ADC: 65
BURT, Maxwell Struthers
General Po: 338
BURTON, Robert
General Ba: 36-37
The Anatomy of Melancholy
    Ba: 36-37
BURUGA, Joseph
General BALE: 283
BURWELL, Adam Hood
General ECL: 119
BUSH, Josef
De Sade Illustrated ADC:
    66
BUSH, Roy
Two Daughters MBA: 48
BUSONI, Ferruccio
Doktor Faust DC2: 76
BUTCHER, James W., Jr.
General MBA: 48
The Seer MBA: 48
BUTLER, E.
The Smile and Wonder Cycle
    MBA: 48

BUTLER, Ellis Parker
"Pigs Is Pigs" WaS1: 26
BUTLER, Joseph
General EC: 59
BUTLER, Samuel (1612-1680)
General Bon: 25; LCAB: 26;
    Me: 135-138
Hudibras Bon: 25; ICBAP:
    21; Ma: 267; Me: 136-138
"The Ladies Answer" PE: 69
BUTLER, Samuel (1835-1902)
General BN: 28; TA: 110-111
Erewhon BN: 28; EN: 15;
    ENES1: 31; ENES2: 38;
    Ma: 268; TA: 110
Erewhon Revisited EN: 15-16;
    ENES1: 31
The Way of All Flesh BN: 28-
    29; EN: 16-17; ENE: 29-
    30; ENES1: 31; ENES2:
    38; Ma: 269; Po: 1899
BUTLER, Tommy
Selma MBA: 48-49
BUTOR, Michel
General Po: 338-342
A Change of Heart Fi: 31;
    Ke: 37
Degrees [Degrés] Fi: 31-32;
    Ke: 37; Po: 341, 1913-
    1914
Description de San Marco Fi:
    32
L'Emploi du temps Fi: 33-34;
    Ke: 37-38; Po: 341-342
Mobile Po: 341
La modification Po: 341
Passage de Milan Fi: 32-33;
    Ke: 38; Po: 341-342
Portrait de l'artiste en jeune
    singe Fi: 34
Réseau Aérien Po: 342
BUTTI, Enrico
Automaton Ke: 241
Enchantment Ke: 241
L'immorale Ke: 241
BUZZATI, Dino
General Br: 137; MD: 69;
    Po: 342
Un Caso Clinico Br: 137; MD:
    69; Po: 343
The Great Portrait Ke: 241
Una Lettera d'Amore Po: 343
A Love Affair Fi: 262
The Tartar Steppe Fi: 262;
    Ke: 241
BYNNER, Witter

General Po: 343
"Eden Tree" PE: 69
New Poems, 1960 Po: 343
BYRD, William II
General AP: 224-228; Da:
25
BYRNE, Seamus
General Br: 137
BYRON, Henry James
General EDT: 133
BYRON, Lord George Gordon
Noel
General Ai: 125-127; EDT:
120-129; Fog: 18-20;
ICBAP: 21; LCAB: 26-
27; Re: 136-142
"Age of Bronze" ICBAP: 21
Beppo Fog: 20
"By the Rivers of Babylon"
PE: 69
Cain EDT: 121-122, 124,
126-129; Fog: 20; Ma:
270; Re: 139
Childe Harold's Pilgrimage
Fog: 20; Ma: 270-271;
Re: 137, 140-141
Childe Harold's Pilgrimage--
Canto III ICBAP: 21
Child Harold's Pilgrimage--Canto
IV ICBAP: 21
"Darkness" PE: 69
The Deformed Transformed
DC1: 33; EDT: 128
"The Destruction of Senna-
cherib" PE: 69
Don Juan Ai: 126-127; Fog:
20-21; ICBAP: 21-22;
LCAB: 27; Ma: 271-273;
Re: 137-142
Don Juan--Canto III (Isles of
Greece) ICBAP: 22
"The Dream" PE: 69
English Bards and Scotch Re-
viewers Ma: 273-274
"Epistle to Augustus" PE:
69
"A Fragment" ("Could I Re-
mount the River of My
Years") PE: 69
"The Giaour" Fog: 21;
ICBAP: 22
"The Harp the Monarch Min-
strel Swept" PE: 69
Heaven and Earth EDT: 124
"If That High World" PE:
70

Manfred DC1: 34; EDT: 121-
122, 124-125, 128-129; Fog:
21; Ma: 274; Re: 141
Marino Faliero DC1: 34; EDT:
121-127, 129; Re: 138, 140
Mazeppa Fog: 21; ICBAP: 22
"My Soul Is Dark" PE: 70
"Ode to Napoleon Buonoparte"
ICBAP: 22
"On This Day I Complete My
Thirty-Sixth Year" PE: 70
"The Prisoner of Chillon" Ma:
275; PE: 70
"Prometheus" PE: 70
Sardanapalus DC1: 34; EDT:
121-122, 124-127
"Song of Saul Before His Last
Battle" PE: 70
"Soul" PE: 70
"Stanzas to the Po" PE: 70
The Two Foscari EDT: 121,
123, 127-128
"Vision of Judgment" Fog: 21;
ICBAP: 22; LCAB: 27;
PE: 70
"Waltz: An Apostrophic Hymn"
PE: 70; Re: 139
Werner EDT: 120, 122, 126-
127

C

C., W.
The First [Second] Part of the
Renowned Historie of Fragosa
King of Aragon ERP: 102
CABALLERO, Fernán
Clemencia Fi: 195; Ke: 184
"The Daughter of the Sun"
WaS1: 26
Elia o la españa trienta años ha
Ke: 184
The Family of Alvareda Fi:
195; Ke: 184
"The Flower of Ruins" WaS1:
26
Lagrimas Fi: 195
The Sea Gull Fi: 195; Ke:
185
"Silence in Life and Pardon in
Death" WaS1: 26
"Time Is Longer Than Fortune"
WaS1: 26
"The Two Friends" WaS1: 26
CABELL, James Branch

General ALL: 50-51; AN: 26-28; ASF: 91-92; LCAB: 27; Ne: 24-25; Po: 345-348; Wo: 49-50
"Balthazar's Daughter" ASF: 91
Beyond Life AN: 25
Chivalry AN: 25
"The Choices" ASF: 91; Wa: 78
Cords of Vanity AN: 25
The Cream of the Jest AN: 25; Ma: 276; Po: 348
Domnei AN: 25
Eagle's Shadow AN: 25
Figures of Earth AN: 25
Gallantry AN: 25
High Place AN: 26
"In Necessity's Mortar" ASF: 91; Wa: 78
"In the Second April" ASF: 91; Wa: 78
Jurgen AN: 26; Ma: 276-277; Po: 345
The King Was in His Counting House Po: 345
"Porcelain Cups" ASF: 91
"The Rat-Trap" Wa: 78
The Rivet in Grandfather's Neck Ma: 277
"The Sestina" ASF: 91; Wa: 78
"Simon's Hour" Wa: 78
Something About Eve AN: 26; Po: 345
"The Tenson" ASF: 91; Wa: 78
There Were Two Pirates AN: 26
CABLE, George Washington
General AF: 47-50; ALL: 51-52; AN: 29; ASF: 93-94; C1a: 106; Ho: 19-20, 143
"The Adventures of Françoise and Suzanne" ASF: 92
"The Angel of the Lord" ASF: 92
"Attalie Brouillard" ASF: 92; Wa: 79
"Au Large" Wa: 79
"Belles Demoiselles Plantation" AF: 48; ASF: 92; SFC: 19; Wa: 79; WaS1: 27
"Bras Coupé" ["The Story

of a Bras-Coupé"] ASF: 92; WaS1: 27
"Café des Exiles" SFC: 19; Wa: 79
"Caranco" ASF: 92
"Don Joaquin" SFC: 19; Wa: 79
"The Entomologist" ASF: 93; SFC: 19; Wa: 79
The Grandissimes AF: 47-49; AN: 28; Ho: 20, 143; LCAB: 27
"Gregory's Island" see "The Solitary"
"The 'Haunted House' in Royal Street" ASF: 93; SFC: 19; Wa: 79
"Jean-ah Poquelin" ASF: 93; SFC: 19; Wa: 79; WaS1: 27
John March, Southerner AN: 29; Ho: 20
"Madame Délicieuse" ASF: 93; SFC: 19; Wa: 79
"Madame Delphine" ASF: 93; SFC: 20; Wa: 79; WaS1: 27
"Père Raphaël" ASF: 93
"Posson Jone'" ASF: 93; SFC: 20; Wa: 79
"Salome Miller, the White Slave" ASF: 93
"'Sieur George" ASF: 93; SFC: 20; Wa: 79-80
"The Solitary" ASF: 93; Wa: 80; WaS1: 27
"The Story of a Bras-Coupé" see "Bras Coupé"
"The Taxidermist" ASF: 93; Wa: 80
"Tite Poulette" ASF: 93; SFC: 20; Wa: 80
Cade, Toni see BAMBARA, Toni Cade
CADOU, René-Guy
General Po: 348
CAEDMON
"Caedmon's Hymn" OMEP: 94-95
CAESAR, Adolph
The Square Root of Soul MBA: 49
Cafavy, Constantine P. see KABAPHES, Konstantinos Petrou
CAHAN, Abraham

General ASF: 94; JW: 184-186; Po: 348-349

"The Apostate of Chego-Chegg" ASF: 94; WaS1: 27

"Circumstances" WaS1: 27

"The Daughter of Avrom Leib" WaS1: 27

"Dumitru and Sigrid" WaS1: 27

"Fanny and Her Suitors" ["Fanny's Khasonim"] WaS1: 27

"A Ghetto Wedding" WaS1: 27

"The Imported Bridegroom" ASF: 94; WaS1: 27

"A Marriage by Proxy: A Story of the City" WaS1: 27

"A Providential Match" ["Mottke Arbel and His Romance"] WaS1: 27

"Rabbi Eliezer's Christmas" WaS1: 28

"Rafael Naarizokh Becomes a Socialist" WaS1: 28

The Rise of David Levinsky JW: 185-186; Po: 349

"A Sweatshop Romance" WaS1: 28

"Tzinchadzi of the Catskills" WaS1: 28

Yekl: A Tale of the New York Ghetto JW: 185; Po: 349

CAILLOIS, Roger
General Po: 349

CAIN, Brother
Epitaph to a Coagulated Trinity MBA: 49

CAIN, George
General BAF: 51
Blueschild Baby AAL: 147; BAF: 51-52; BAW: 134

CAIN, James M.
General AN: 29-30; ASF: 95; Po: 350
Mildred Pierce AN: 29

CAINE, Thomas Henry Hall [Hall CAINE]
General TA: 112

CAIRD, Mona
The Daughters of Danaus ENES2: 39

CAJANOV

Putesestvie Ke: 373

CALCANO, Eduardo
General Br: 137

CALDERON, George
Fountain Br: 137

CALDERON DE LA BARCA, Pedro
Absalom's Hair [Los Cabellos de Absalón] EDC: 76

El Alcalde de su Mismo see His Own Judge

El Alcalde de Zalamea see The Mayor of Zalamea

Las Armas de la Hermosura DC2: 76

El Astrologo Fingido see The False Astrologer

Basta Callar see It Is Enough to Keep Silent

La Bella Aurora DC2: 77

Beware of Smooth Water [Guardate del Agua Mansa] EDC: 76

The Blush of the Rose [La Purpura de la Rosa] DC2: 83; EDC: 76

Los Cabellos de Absalón see Absalom's Hair

Casa con Dos Puertas, Mala Es de Guardar see A House with Two Doors Is Difficult to Guard

La Cisma de Ingalaterra see The Schism of England

The Constant Prince [El Principe Constante] DC2: 77; EDC: 77; Ma: 278-279

Count Lucanor [El Conde Lucanor] EDC: 77

La Dama Duende see The Fairy Lady

Darlo Todo y No Dar Nada see Give Everything or Nothing

The Daughter of the Air [La Hija del Aire] DC2: 78; EDC: 77-78

Devotion to the Cross [La Devoción de la Cruz] DC2: 77-78; EDC: 78; Ma: 279

Echo and Narcissus [Eco y Narciso] DC2: 78; EDC: 78

En Esta Vida Todo Es Verdad y Todo Mentira see In This Life, Everything Is Both True and False

La Estatua de Prometeo see

Prometheus' Statue

The Fairy Lady [La Dama Duende] EDC: 78-79; Ma: 279-280

The False Astrologer [The Mock Astrologer; El Astrologo Fingido] DC2: 76-77; EDC: 79; Ma: 282-283

The Fortunes of Andromeda and Perseus [Las Fortunas de Andromeda y Perseo] EDC: 79

From Bad to Worse [Peor Está Que Estaba] EDC: 79

Give Everything or Nothing [Darlo Todo y No Dar Nada] EDC: 79

The Grand Duke of Grandia [El Gran Duque de Grandia] EDC: 79

The Great Theatre of the World [El Gran Teatro del Mundo] DC2: 78; EDC: 80

Guardate del Agua Mansa see Beware of Smooth Water

The Gulf of the Sirens [El Golfo de las Sirenas] EDC: 80

La Hija del Aire see The Daughter of the Air

His Own Judge [El Alcalde de su Mismo] EDC: 80

El Hombre Pobre Todo Es Trazas see Poverty Sharpens the Wits

A House with Two Doors Is Difficult to Guard [Casa con Dos Puertas, Mala Es de Guardar] DC2: 77; EDC: 80

La Iglesia Sitiada DC2: 78

In This Life, Everything Is Both True and False [En Esta Vida Todo Es Verdad y Todo Mentira] EDC: 80

It Is Enough to Keep Silent [Basta Callar] EDC: 80

El Jardin de Falerina DC2: 78

El Laurel de Apolo DC2: 78; EDC: 80

La Lepra de Constantino

DC2: 79

Life Is a Dream [La Vida es Sueño] DC2: 79-80; EDC: 80-82; LCAB: 27; Ma: 280-281

Love, the Greatest Enchantment [El Mayor Encanto Amor] DC2: 80

Luis Perez el Gallego DC2: 80

El Magico Prodigioso see The Wonder-Working Magician

Manañas de Abril y Mayo see Mornings in April and May

El Mayor Encanto Amor see Love, the Greatest Enchantment

El Mayor Monstruo los Celos see No Monster Like Jealousy

The Mayor of Zalamea [El Alcalde de Zalamea] DC2: 81; EDC: 82-83; Ma: 281-282

El Medico de su Honra see The Physician of His Own Honor

The Mock Astrologer see The False Astrologer

Mornings in April and May [Mañanas de Abril y Mayo] DC2: 81; EDC: 83

No Hay Más Fortuna Que Dios EDC: 83

No Monster Like Jealousy [El Mayor Monstruo los Celos] EDC: 83

No Siempre Lo Peor es Cierto DC2: 82

The Painter of His Own Dishonor [El Pintor de su Deshonra] DC2: 82; EDC: 84; Ma: 283

Peor Está Que Estaba see From Bad to Worse

Phantom Lady DC2: 82

The Physician of His Own Honor [El Medico de su Honra] DC2: 82; EDC: 84-85; Ma: 283-284

El Pintor de su Deshonra see The Painter of His Own Dishonor

Poverty Sharpens the Wits [El Hombre Pobre Todo Es Trazas] EDC: 84

El Principe Constante see The Constant Prince

Prometheus' Statue [La Estatua de Prometeo] EDC: 84

Purpura de la Rosa see The Blush of the Rose

The Schism of England [La Cisma de Ingalaterra] DC2: 77; EDC: 84

Secret Vengeance for Secret Insult [A Secreto Agravio, Secreta Venganza] DC2: 83; EDC: 84; Ma: 284-285

Le Selva Confusa DC2: 83

The Sibyl of the Orient [La Sibila del Oriente] DC2: 83; EDC: 84

El Tetraca de Jerusalen DC2: 83

There Are Dreams That Are True [Sueños Hay Que Verdad Son] DC2: 83; EDC: 85

The Three Greatest Marvels [Los Tres Mayores Prodigios] EDC: 85

The Tower of Babylon [La Torre de Babilonia] DC2: 83; EDC: 85

Las Tres Justicas en Una DC2: 83-84

La Vacante General DC2: 84

La Vida es Sueño see Life Is a Dream

Welcome, Trouble, If You Come Alone EDC: 85

The Wonder-Working Magician [El Magico Prodigioso] DC2: 80-81; EDC: 85-86; Ma: 285-286

CALDWELL, Ben

General BAP: 43-44; BAW: 135; MBA: 49-50

Black Quartet: Four New Black Plays MBA: 50

The Family Portrait; or My Son the Black Militant MBA: 50

The First Militant Preacher BAP: 44; MBA: 50

The Interview MBA: 50

The Job BAP: 44; MBA: 50

The King of Soul BAP: 44

Mission Accomplished MBA: 50

Prayer Meeting; or, The

First Militant Minister ADC: 66; BAP: 44; MBA: 50

Riot Sale BAP: 44; MBA: 50

Run Around MBA: 51

Top Secret MBA: 50

CALDWELL, Erskine

General ALL: 52; AN: 30; ASF: 95; CN: 74-75; X LCAB: 27-28; Ne: 26; Po: 350-351; Wo: 53-54

"August Afternoon" Wa: 80

The Bastard CN: 75

"Blue Boy" Wa: 80

"Country Full of Swedes" Wa: 80

"Daughter" Wa: 80; WaS1: 28

Episode in Palmetto CN: 75

Georgia Boy CN: 75

God's Little Acre AN: 30; CN: 75; Ma: 287; Ne: 26

Greta CN: 75

"The Growing Season" Wa: 80

"Indian Summer" Wa: 80

Journeyman Br: 137; CN: 75-76

"Kneel to the Rising Sun" ASF: 95; Wa: 80; WaS1: 28

"The Lonely Day" Wa: 80

"Masses of Men" Wa: 80

Miss Mamma Aimee CN: 76

"My Old Man's Baling Machine" Wa: 80

"The Negro in the Well" Wa: 80

"The People vs. Abe Lathan, Colored" Wa: 81

The Sacrilege of Alan Kent CN: 76; Wa: 81

"Saturday Afternoon" ASF: 95; Wa: 81

"Savannah River Payday" Wa: 81

"Slow Death" WaS1: 28

Summertime Island CN: 76

"The Sunfield" Wa: 81

"A Swell Looking Girl" Wa: 81

Tobacco Road Br: 138; CN: 76; Ma: 287-288

Tragic Ground AN: 30; CN: 76

Trouble in July CN: 76

"Where the Girls Were Different"

WaS1: 28
"Yellow Girl" Wa: 81
CALDWELL, Lewis A.H. [Abe
    NOEL]
    General BAF: 52
CALDWELL, Taylor
    General Po: 351
CALET, Henri
    General Po: 351-352
CALISHER, Hortense
    General CFAE: 105; CN:
        76-77; JW: 188; LCAB:
        28; Po: 352
    "Heartburn" ASF: 96; Wa:
        81
    In the Absence of Angels
        LCAB: 28
    "The Scream on Fifty-Seventh
        Street" WaS1: 28
    Textures of Life CN: 77
CALLAGHAN, Morley
    General CN: 77; Po: 352-
        353
    "Amuck in the Bush" Wa:
        81
    "Ancient Lineage" Wa: 81
    "An Autumn Penitent" Wa:
        81
    "The Blue Kimono" Wa: 81
    A Broken Journey CN: 77
    "A Cap for Steve" Wa: 81
    "The Cheat's Remorse" Wa:
        81
    "A Cocky Young Man" Wa:
        82
    "A Country Passion" Wa:
        82
    "An Escapade" Wa: 82
    "The Faithful Wife" Wa: 82
    "Father and Son" Wa: 82
    "Getting on in the World"
        Wa: 82
    "A Girl with Ambition" Wa:
        82
    "In His Own Country" Wa:
        82
    "It Had to Be Done" Wa: 82
    It's Never Over CN: 78
    "Last Spring They Came
        Over" Wa: 82
    "The Life of Sadie Hall" Wa:
        82
    "The Loved and the Lost"
        CN: 78; Wa: 82
    The Many Colored Coat CN:
        78

"Mr. and Mrs. Fairbanks" Wa:
    82
More Joy in Heaven CN: 78
No Man's Meat CN: 78
"Now That April's Here" Wa:
    82
A Passion in Rome CN: 78
"A Predicament" Wa: 82
"A Princely Affair" Wa: 83
"The Red Hat" Wa: 83
"A Sick Call" Wa: 83
"Soldier Harmon" Wa: 83
Strange Fugitive CN: 78-79
Such Is My Beloved CN: 79
That Summer in Paris Po: 352-
    353
They Shall Inherit the Earth
    CN: 79
"Two Fishermen" SFC: 20;
    Wa: 83
The Varsity Story CN: 79
"A Wedding Dress" Wa: 83
CALLANAN, Jeremiah J.
    "The Outlaw of Loch Lene"
        PE: 70
CALLIAS
    Alphabet Tragedy DC2: 84
CALLIMACHUS
    General LCAB: 28
LA CALPRENEDE, Gautier
    Cassandra Ke: 38
    Cleopatra Ke: 38
    Faramond Ke: 38
CALVERTON, Victor Francis
    General LCAB: 28
Calvin, Henry see HANLEY,
    Clifford
CALVINO, Italo
    General Po: 353
    "All at One Point" Wa: 83
    Il barone rampante Fi: 262
    The Castle of Crossed Destinies
        Fi: 262
    Il cavaliere inesistente Fi:
        262
    Le città invisibili Fi: 262
    Cosmicomics Fi: 262-263
    Marcovaldo Fi: 263
    I nostri antenati Fi: 263
    Il sentiero dei nidi di ragno
        Fi: 263
    Smog Fi: 263
    Il visconte dimezzato Fi: 263
CALVO SOTELO, Joaquin
    General Po: 353
    La Muralla Po: 354

CAMARGO, Manuel-Iván
  General Po: 354
CAMBA, Francisco
  El pecado de San Jesusito
    Ke: 185
  La revolución de Laino Ke:
    185
CAMBRIDGE, Ada
  General AL: 161-162
CAMDEN, William
  General SC: 42
  Britannia Hen: 51-52; SC:
    42
CAMERON, George Frederick
  General ECL: 121-122
CAMERON, Kenneth
  Papp ADC: 66
CAMINO GALICIA, León Felipe
  General Po: 354-356
CAMO, Pierre
  General Po: 356
CAMÕES, Luiz de
  El-Rei-Seleuco DC2: 84
  The Lusiad Ma: 289-290
CAMPANA, Dino
  General Po: 357
CAMPBELL, Bartley
  General AD: 105
  My Partner AD: 105
  The White Slave AD: 105
CAMPBELL, Dick
  General MBA: 51
CAMPBELL, Donald
  General Ai: 337
CAMPBELL, Festus Amtac
  In Portland's Valley of Beauty
    WIL: 21
CAMPBELL, George
  General WIL: 21-22
  First Poems WIL: 22-23
  A Play Without Scenery
    WIL: 22
CAMPBELL, Herbert
  General BAP: 44
  Middle Class Blacks MBA:
    51
CAMPBELL, James Edwin
  General AAPD: 57; BAW:
    136; LCAB: 28
CAMPBELL, John Wood
  General ASF: 96; LCAB:
    28
  "The Machine" WaS1: 28
  "Twilight" ASF: 96; WaS1:
    28
CAMPBELL, Joseph

General LCAB: 28
  "The Dancer" PE: 70
CAMPBELL, Owen
  General WIL: 23
CAMPBELL, Reginald
  The King's Enemies ENES2:
    39
CAMPBELL, Roy
  General Po: 357-358
  "The Zebras" ICBAP: 22
CAMPBELL, Thomas
  General Ai: 114; Re: 191-
    192
Campbell, William Edward March
  see MARCH, William
CAMPBELL, William Wilfred
  General ECL: 41-42
CAMPION, Edmund
  General SC: 42
CAMPION, Thomas
  "My Sweetest Lesbia" PE: 71
  "Now Winter Nights Enlarge"
    PE: 71
  Observations in the Art of Eng-
    lish Poesie Hen: 181
  "There Is a Garden in Her
    Face" PE: 71
  "Tune Thy Musicke to Thy
    Hart" (The First Book of
    Ayres, viii) PE: 71
  "When Thou Must Home to
    Shades of Under Ground"
    PE: 71
  "When to Her Cute Corinna
    Sings" PE: 71
CAMPISTRON, Jean de
  Tiridate DC2: 84
CAMPTON, David
  General MDAE: 143-144
  The Lunatic View Br: 138
CAMUS, Albert
  General Br: 138-139; LCAB:
    29; MD: 69-71; Po: 358-
    401
  "The Adulterous Woman" [La
    Femme Adultère"] Po: 394-
    395; SFC: 20; Wa: 83
  "The Artist at Work" ["Jonas,
    or The Artist at Work";
    "Jonas ou L'Artiste au
    Travail"] Po: 396; SFC:
    22; Wa: 87-88; WaS1: 29
  The Assassins [The Just As-
    sassins; The Just; Les
    Justes] Br: 139-140; DC2:
    86; EDC: 87-88; MD: 71;

Po: 396
Caligula Br: 140-142; DC2:
84-85; EDC: 86-87; LCAB:
29; MD: 71; Po: 367,
379-381
Carnets Po: 381
La Chute see The Fall
Cross Purposes see The
Misunderstanding
Devotion to the Cross [La
Devotion à la Croix] EDC:
87
L'Etat de Siège see State of
Siege
L'Etranger see The Stranger
"The Exile and the Kingdom"
[L'Exile et le Royaume]
Po: 394; Wa: 83-84;
WaS1: 28
The Fall [La Chute] Fi: 34-
36; Ke: 38-41; LCAB:
29; Ma: 291-292; Po:
360-361, 368-369, 371-373,
377-378, 381-386, 1305;
SFC: 21-22; Wa: 84-86;
WaS1: 29
"La Femme Adultère" see
"The Adulterous Woman"
"The Fire" Wa: 86
"The Growing Stone" Po:
370; SFC: 22; Wa: 87;
WaS1: 29
"The Guest" [L'Hôte] Br:
143; Po: 371, 395-396;
SFC: 22; Wa: 87; WaS1:
29
L'Homme Révolté see The
Rebel
Lyrical and Critical Essays
Po: 397
"Jonas, or The Artist at
Work" see "The Artist
at Work"
"Jonas, ou L'Artiste au
Travail" see "The Artist
at Work"
The Just Assassins see The
Assassins
Les Justes see The Assas-
sins
The Misunderstanding [Cross
Purposes; Le Malentendu]
Br: 142-143; DC2: 86;
EDC: 88; MD: 71-72;
MDAE: 102; Po: 370,
397-398

The Myth of Sisyphus LCAB:
29; Ma: 292; Po: 372, 398;
TMAP: 28
The Outsider see The Stranger
The Plague [La Peste] Po:
360, 363, 365, 368, 372-373,
376, 399-400
Possessed [Les Possédés] EDC:
88-89; MD: 72
The Rebel [L'Homme Révolté]
Po: 372, 377, 395
"The Renegade" [Le Renegat]
Po: 370, 401; SFC: 22;
Wa: 88; WaS1: 29
Requiem for a Nun [Requiem
pour une Nonne] EDC:
89; MD: 72; Po: 361, 401
"The Silent Men" SFC: 22;
Wa: 88
State of Siege [L'Etat de Siège]
Br: 143-144; DC2: 87;
EDC: 89; Fi: 36-38; Ke:
41-44; Ma: 292-294; MD:
71
The Stranger [The Outsider;
L'Etranger] Fi: 38-42; Ke:
44-48; Ma: 294-295; Po:
360-361, 363, 367-369, 372-
373, 376-378, 386-394; SFC:
22-24; Wa: 88-92; WaS1:
29-30
CANBY, Henry Seidel
General Po: 402
CANE, Melville
General Po: 402
"April Flurry" PE: 71
"Deep in Wagon-Ruts" PE: 71
"Hither and Thither" PE: 71
"Hopkinson" PE: 71
"January Garden" PE: 71
"Last Night It Snowed" PE:
71
"Presence of Snow" PE: 71
"Snow in April" PE: 72
"White Fog" PE: 72
CANETTI, Elias
General Po: 402-403
Auto da fe Fi: 263
Masse und Macht Po: 403
The Tower of Babel [Die
Blendung] Fi: 293-294;
Ke: 259; Po: 403
Canfield, Dorothy see FISHER,
Dorothy Canfield
CANIZARE, Jose
La Mas Ilustre Fregona DC2:

87
CANNAN, Denis [Dennis PUL-
    LEIN-THOMPSON]
    General Br: 144; MDAE:
        145-146
    Misery Me MDAE: 146
CANNAN, Gilbert
    General Mi: 224-225; TA:
        113
CANNON, Alice
    Great Day in the Morning
        ADC: 66
CANNON, David Wadsworth, Jr.
    General BAW: 137
CANNON, Noah Calwell W.
    General AAPD: 58
CANNON, Steve
    General BAF: 53
CANSINOS-ASSENS, Rafael
    General Po: 403
CANTWELL, Robert
    Land of Plenty LCAB: 29
CAPASSO, Aldo
    General Po: 403
CAPEK, Karel
    General Br: 144; MD: 72;
        Po: 404
    Adam the Creator [Adam
        Stvoritel] Br: 145: MD:
        72
    Bilǎ Nemoc see The White
        Plague
    Factory of the Absolute Ke:
        373-374; Po: 404
    Hordubal Ke: 374; Po:
        404-405
    Krakatit Ke: 374
    Loupeznik see The Outlaw
    The Makropulos Secret [The
        Makropulos Affair; Vec
        Makropulos] Br: 145;
        EDC: 89; MD: 73
    Meteor [Povetron] Po: 404-
        405
    Mother [Matka] Br: 145;
        EDC: 89
    An Ordinary Life [Obycejný
        Zivot] Ke: 374-375;
        Po: 404-405
    The Outlaw [Loupeznik] Br:
        146; DC2: 87
    Povĕtron see Meteor
    The Power and the Glory
        see The White Plague
    R.U.R or Rossum's Universal
        Robots Br: 146; DC2:

87-88; EDC: 89-90; LCAB:
    29; Ma: 296; MD: 73; Po:
    405
Vĕc Makropulos see The
    Makropulos Secret
War with the Newts Ke: 375
The White Plague [The Power
    and the Glory; Bilǎ Nemoc]
    Br: 146; MD: 73
_____ and Josef CAPEK
    The Fateful Game of Love
        [Lásky hra osudná] Br:
        145; MD: 72
    The Insect Comedy [From the
        Insect World; The Insect
        Play; The Insects; Life of
        the Insects; The World We
        Live In; Ze Zivota Hmyze]
        Br: 145; DC2: 87; EDC:
        90; MD: 72; Po: 403
CAPOTE, Truman
    General AN: 31; ASF: 97;
        CFAE: 107-109; CN: 79-
        80; LCAB: 29; MDAE: 148;
        Ne: 27; Po: 405-406
    "Among the Paths to Eden"
        ASF: 96; Wa: 92
    Breakfast at Tiffany's CN:
        80; LCAB: 29; Ma: 297;
        Po: 406
    "Children on Their Birthdays"
        ASF: 96; SFC: 25; Wa:
        92
    "A Christmas Memory" Wa: 93
    "A Diamond Guitar" ASF: 96;
        Wa: 93
    "The Duke in His Domain"
        ASF: 96
    The Grass Harp ADC: 66-67;
        Br: 146; CN: 80-81;
        LCAB: 30; MD: 73; MDAE:
        148
    "The Headless Hawk" ASF:
        96; SFC: 25; Wa: 93
    "House of Flowers" ASF: 97;
        Wa: 93
    "A House on the Heights"
        ASF: 97
    In Cold Blood CN: 81-82;
        Ma: 297-298; Po: 407
    "Jug of Silver" Wa: 93
    "Master Misery" ASF: 97;
        SFC: 25; Wa: 93; WaS1:
        30
    "Miriam" ASF: 97; SFC:
        25; Wa: 93

Other Voices, Other Rooms
    AN: 31; CFAE: 108-109;
    CN: 82-83; LCAB: 30;
    Ma: 298-299; Ne: 27;
    Po: 407-408
"Shut a Final Door" ASF:
    97; Wa: 93
"A Tree of Night" ASF: 97;
    SFC: 25; Wa: 93; WaS1:
    30
_____ and Harold ARLEN
House of Flowers ADC: 67
CAPUANA, Luigi
    Giacinta Fi: 263; Ke: 241
    Il Marchese di Roccaverdina
        Fi: 263; Ke: 241
    Profumo Fi: 263; Ke: 241
    Rassegnazione Fi: 263
CAPUS, Alfred
    La Veine DC2: 88
CARBALLIDO, Emilio
    General Po: 408
    Golden Thread DC2: 88
CARBERRY, H.D.
    General WIL: 23
CARBONELL, José Manuel
    General Po: 408
CARCANO, Francisco
    La hija de Marte Ke: 185
CARCO, Francis
    General Po: 408-409
    Les Innocents Ri2: 230
CAREW, Jan
    General WIL: 23-24
    Black Midas WIL: 24
    The Last Barbarian WIL:
        25-26
    Moscow Is Not My Mecca
        WIL: 26
    The Third Gift WIL: 26
    University of Hunger WIL:
        26
    The Wild Coast WIL: 25
CAREW, Thomas
    General Ba: 37-38; LCAB:
        30
    "Ask Me No More Where Jove
        Bestows" PE: 72
    "Celia Singing" PE: 72
    "The Complement" PE: 72
    "Disdain Returned" PE: 72
    "Mediocritie in Love Rejected"
        PE: 72
    "Perswasions to Enjoy" PE:
        72
    "Song" LCAB: 30

"The Spring" PE: 72
"A Rapture" PE: 72
"To A.L.: Persuasions to Love"
    PE: 72
"To My Inconstant Mistress"
    PE: 73
"Upon the King's Sicknesse"
    PE: 73
CAREY, George V.F.
    The Marriage Knight DC1: 34
CAREY, Henry
    General Li: 111
    Chronontonthologos DC1: 34
    The Contrivances DC1: 34
    The Honest Yorkshireman
        DC1: 34
CAREY, Peter
    "The Fat Man in History"
        WaS1: 30
CARIM, Enver
    General BALE: 283
CARLBERG, Gosta
    Bear Ye One Another's Burdens
        Ke: 348
CARLELL, Lodowick
    General LJCD: 229-230
    Osmond the Great Turk DC1:
        34
CARLETON, Will
    General LCAB: 30
CARLETON, William
    "A Pilgrimage to Patrick's Pur-
        gatory" WaS1: 30
    "The Three Tasks" Wa: 94
    "Wildgoose Lodge" ["Confessions
        of a Reformed Ribbonman"]
        WaS1: 30
CARLINO, Lewis John
    General MDAE: 150
    Cages ADC: 67
    Double Talk ADC: 67
    Epiphany Br: 146
    Exercise ADC: 67
    Telemachus Clay [Telemachus]
        ADC: 67-68; Br: 146
CARLYLE, Thomas
    General Ai: 133-135; LCAB:
        30; VP: 24-26
    The French Revolution Ma:
        300
    Heroes, Hero-Worship and the
        Heroic in History LCAB:
        30; Ma: 301-302
    History of Frederick II of
        Prussia Ma: 300-301
    Past and Present Ma: 302

Sartor Resartus Ma: 302-
303; VP: 24-26
CARMAN, Bliss
General ECL: 48-51; Po:
409
CARMICHAEL, Waverly Turner
General BAW: 138
CARMINES, Al
The Beast: A Meditation on
Beauty ADC: 68
Camp Meeting: 1840 ADC:
68
The Faggot ADC: 68
CAROSSA, Hans
General Po: 409
Ein Tag im Spätsommer 1947
Fi: 294
Stella Mystica Po: 409
CAROUTCH, Yvonne
General Po: 410
CARPENTER, John A.
The Birthday of the Infanta
DC1: 34
CARPENTIER, Alejo
General LCAB: 30; Po:
410
"El Acoso" Po: 410-411;
Wa: 94
"El año 59" WaS1: 30
El camino de Santiago Po:
411
"Los convidados de plata"
WaS1: 30
"Lord, Praised Be Thou"
WaS1: 31
"Manhunt" WaS1: 31
El siglo de las luces Po:
411
"Viaje a la Semilla" WaS1:
31
Carpio, Lope Felix de Vega
see LOPE [DE VEGA]
CARR, Clarence F.
General BAW: 138
CARR, Ernest J.
General WIL: 26
CARRANQUE DE RIOS, Andrés
Cinematografo Fi: 195
Uno Fi: 195
La vida difícil Fi: 195
CARRASQUILLA, Tomas
General LCAB: 30
Carre, John le see CORNWELL,
David John Moore
Carrera Andrade, Jorge see
ANDRADE, Jorge

CARRERE MORENO, Emilio
General Po: 412
CARRICK, James
With O'Leary in the Grave
ENES2: 39
CARRIO DE LA VANDERA, Alonso
El lazarillo de ciegos caminantes
LCAB: 30
CARROLL, Charles
General AP: 575-576
CARROLL, Lewis [Charles Lut-
widge DODGSON]
General BN: 30; VP: 27-28
Alice's Adventures in Wonderland
BN: 30-31; EN: 17; ENE:
30-31; ENES1: 31-32;
ENES2: 39; Ma: 304-305;
VP: 27-28
"The Hunting of the Snark"
LCAB: 50
"Jabberwocky" PE: 73, 127
Sylvie and Bruno ENES1: 32;
ENES2: 40
Sylvie and Bruno Concluded
ENES1: 32; ENES2: 40
Through the Looking-Glass
BN: 30-31; ENES1: 33;
ENES2: 40; Ma: 305-306;
VP: 27-28
CARROLL, Paul Vincent
General Br: 147; MBD: 39;
MD: 73; Mi: 225; Po:
412-413
The Bed of Procrustes [Things
That Are Caesar's] Br:
147; EDC: 91
Coggerers [The Conspirators]
Br: 147
The Devil Came from Dublin
[The Chuckeyhead Story]
Br: 147; EDC: 90
Green Cars Go East Br: 147
Kindred EDC: 90
The Old Foolishness Br: 147;
EDC: 90
Shadow and Substance Br:
147; EDC: 90-91; MBD:
39; MD: 73
Strings, My Lord, Are False
EDC: 91
Things That Are Caesar's see
The Bed of Procrustes
Wayward Saint EDC: 91
The White Steed Br: 147-148;
EDC: 91; MBD: 39; MD:
73

Wise Have Not Spoken EDC:
   91
CARROLL, Vinnette
   General BAP: 45; BAW:
      139; MBA: 51-52
   All the King's Men BAP: 45
   But Never Jam Today MBA:
      52
   Trumpets of the Lord BAP:
      45; MBA: 53
   Your Arms Too Short to Box
      with God MBA: 53-55
   _____ and Micki GRANT
   Croesus and the Witch BAP:
      45; MBA: 52
   Don't Bother Me, I Can't
      Cope BAP: 45, 90; MBA:
      52-53; 91-93
   I'm Laughin' But I Ain't
      Tickled MBA: 53
   The Ups and Downs of Theo-
      philus Maitland (Ward)
      BAP: 45; MBA: 53
CARROTHERS, James David
   General BAF: 68
CARSON, Robert [Mwina Imiri
      ABUBADIKA]
   The Education of Sonny Car-
      son MBA: 55
CARSWELL, Catherine
   General Ai: 219
CARTER, Martin
   General WIL: 27-28
   Poems of Resistance WIL:
      28
   Poems of Succession WIL:
      28
CARTER, Randolph
   Eugenia ADC: 68
CARTER, Steve
   General MBA: 56
   Eden ADC: 68; MBA: 56
   The Terraced Apartment
      BAP: 46
   Terraces ADC: 68; MBA:
      56
CARTEY, Wilfred
   House of Blue Lightning
      WIL: 28
CARTIGNY, Jean de
   The Voyage of the Wandering
      Knight see GOODYEAR,
      William [translator]
CARTON, Richard Claude
      [Richard Claude CRITCH-
      ETT]

General EDT: 134
CARTWRIGHT, Thomas
   General SC: 42
CARTWRIGHT, William
   General LJCD: 230-231
   The Lady Errant DC1: 35
CARUTHERS, William Alexander
   General AN: 31
   The Knights of the Horse-Shoe
      AN: 31
CARVALHO, Grimaldo
   General BAF: 53
CARY, Alice
   "Make Believe" PE: 73
CARY, Joyce
   General BN2: 21-23; CN:
      83-86; LCAB: 31; Po:
      413-417; Sch: 16-19
   The African Witch CN: 86;
      ENE: 31; ENES1: 33;
      ENES2: 40; Ma: 307; Po:
      413; Sch: 19-20
   Aissa Saved CN: 86; ENE:
      31-32; ENES1: 33; ENES2:
      40; Ma: 307-308; Sch: 19-
      20
   An American Visitor CN: 86-
      87; ENE: 32; ENES1: 33;
      ENES2: 40; Ma: 308-309;
      Po: 413, 417; Sch: 19-20
   Arabella CN: 87
   "The Breakout" Wa: 94
   "Bush River" Wa: 94
   The Captive and the Free CN:
      87; ENE: 32; Sch: 20
   Castle Corner CN: 87-88;
      ENE: 32; ENES1: 33;
      ENES2: 40; Ma: 309-310;
      Po: 417-418; Sch: 20
   Charley Is My Darling CN:
      88; ENES1: 33; ENES2: 40;
      Ma: 310; Po: 418; Sch: 20
   Cock Jarvis CN: 88
   Daventry CN: 88
   Except the Lord see also
      Second Trilogy CN: 88;
      ENE: 33; ENES1: 34;
      ENES2: 40; Ma: 310-311;
      Po: 418; Sch: 22
   A Fearful Joy CN: 88-89;
      ENE: 33; ENES1: 34;
      LCAB: 31; Ma: 311-312;
      Po: 417, 419; Sch: 20
   First Trilogy CN: 89; LCAB:
      31; Po: 419-421; Sch: 20
   Herself Surprised see also

First Trilogy CN: 90;
ENE: 33-34; ENES1: 34;
ENES2: 40; LCAB: 31;
Ma: 312-313; Sch: 20-22
The Horse's Mouth see also
First Trilogy BN2: 22;
CN: 90; ENE: 34-36;
ENES1: 34; ENES2: 40-
41; LCAB: 31; Ma: 313-
314; Po: 417, 421-422;
Sch: 20-22
A House of Children CN:
91; ENE: 36; ENES1: 34;
ENES2: 41
Mister Johnson BN2: 22;
CN: 91; EN: 17; ENE:
36-37; ENES1: 34; ENES2:
41; Ma: 314-315; Po:
413, 417, 422; Sch: 19-20
The Moonlight CN: 91; ENE:
37; ENES1: 34; Ma: 315-
316
Not Honour More see also
Second Trilogy CN: 92;
ENE: 37; ENES1: 34;
ENES2: 41; Ma: 316; Po:
422-423; Sch: 22
Prisoner of Grace see also
Second Trilogy CN: 92;
ENE: 37-38; ENES1: 35;
ENES2: 41; Ma: 317;
Po: 417, 423; Sch: 22
Second Trilogy (Political
Trilogy) BN2: 22; CN:
92; Po: 423; Sch: 22
To Be a Pilgrim see also
First Trilogy BN2: 22;
CN: 93; ENE: 38-39;
ENES1: 35; ENES2: 41;
LCAB: 31; Ma: 317-319;
Po: 423-424; Sch: 20-22
CARYLL, John
Sir Solomon Single DC1: 35
CASAL, Juan del
General LCAB: 31
CASANOVA DE SEINGALT,
Giacomo Girolamo
History of My Life LCAB:
31
CASARES, Adolfo Bioy
"The Child of His Friend"
Wa: 94
"The Feast of the Monster"
Wa: 94
CASELY-HAYFORD, Adelaide
General BALE: 283

CASELY-HAYFORD, Gladys May
General BALE: 283
CASELY-HAYFORD, Joseph
Ephraim
General BALE: 284
Ethiopia Unbound BALE: 284
CASEY, Bernie
Look at the People BAW: 141
CASEY, Bill
General ASF: 98
CASEY, Calvert
"En el Potosí" WaS1: 31
"In partenza" WaS1: 31
"Polacca brillante" WaS1: 31
"El regreso" WaS1: 31
CASEY, Gavin
General MAP: 139-140
CASEY, W.F.
The Suburban Groove Br:
148
CASONA, Alejandro
General Br: 148; Po: 3548-
3551
Los Arboles Muerin Pie DC2:
88
La dama del alba Po: 3551
Don Rodrigo Po: 3551-3552
Otra el Diablo DC2: 88
Probihido Suicidarse DC2: 88
La Sierna Varada DC2: 89
Siete Gritos en el Mar DC2:
89
Suicide Prohibited in Springtime
Br: 148
La Tercera Palabra DC2: 89
Las Tres Perfectas Casadas
DC2: 89
CASSILL, Ronald Verlin
General ASF: 98; Po: 424
"And in My Heart" ASF: 98;
Wa: 94
"The Biggest Band" ASF: 98;
LCAB: 31; WaS1: 31
"Fracture" Wa: 94
"Happy Marriage" ASF: 98;
Wa: 94
"Larchmoor Is Not the World"
SFC: 25; Wa: 95
"The Outer Island" ASF: 98
"The Puzzle Factory" SFC:
98
"This Hand, These Talons"
ASF: 98; Wa: 95
CASSOLA, Carlo
General Po: 424-425
Bebb's Girl [La ragazza di

Bube] Fi: 263; Ke: 241
Un cuore arido Ke: 241
CASTANEDA, Carlos
General LCAB: 31
CASTELLANOS, Rosario
"La tregua" WaS1: 31
CASTIGLIONE, Baldassare
The Book of the Courtier
LCAB: 31; Ma: 320-321
The Courtier see HOBY,
Sir Thomas [translator]
del CASTILLO, Michel
Tanguy Fi: 42
CASTILLO-PUCHE, José Luis
General Po: 425
Castro, Guillen de see GUIL-
LEN DE CASTRO
Castro, José María Ferreira de
see FERREIRA DE CAS-
TRO, José María
CASTRO ZAGAL, Oscar
General Po: 425
CATESBY, Mark
General Da: 50
CATHER, Willa
General ALL: 52-54; AN:
33-36; ASF: 101-103;
LCAB: 31-32; Ne: 28-30;
Po: 426-431; Wo: 57-60
"The Affair at Grover Station"
SFC: 25
Alexander's Bridge AN: 31-
32; Ne: 29
"Ardessa" Wa: 95
"Before Breakfast" ASF: 99;
SFC: 25; Wa: 95
"Behind the Singing Tower"
Wa: 95
"The Best Years" ASF: 99;
Po: 431; SFC: 26; Wa:
95
"The Bohemian Girl" ASF:
99; SFC: 26; Wa: 95
"The Clemency of the Court"
ASF: 99; SFC: 26; Wa:
95
"Coming, Aphrodite!" ["Com-
ing, Eden Bower!"] ASF:
99; SFC: 26; Wa: 95-96
"The Conversion of Sum Loo"
SFC: 26
"The Count of Crow's Nest"
ASF: 99; SFC: 26
"The Dance at Chevalier's"
SFC: 26
Death Comes for the Arch-

bishop AN: 32; LCAB: 32;
Ma: 322-323; Ne: 30; Po:
431-432; Wo: 59-60
"A Death in the Desert" ASF:
99; SFC: 26; Wa: 96
"The Diamond Mine" ASF: 99;
SFC: 26; Wa: 96
"Double Birthday" ASF: 99;
Wa: 96
"El Dorado: A Kansas Reces-
sional" Wa: 96
"Eleanor's House" SFC: 26;
Wa: 96
"The Elopement of Allen Poole"
ASF: 99; Wa: 96
"The Enchanted Bluff" SFC:
26; Wa: 96; WaS1: 31
"Eric Hermannson's Soul" ASF:
99; SFC: 26; Wa: 96
"The Fear That Walks by Noon-
day" SFC: 26
"Flavia and Her Artists" ASF:
99; SFC: 26; Wa: 96
"The Garden Lodge" ASF: 100;
Wa: 97
"A Gold Slipper" ASF: 100;
Wa: 97
"Her Boss" Wa: 97
"Jack-A-Boy" ASF: 100
"The Joy of Nelly Deane" ASF:
100; Wa: 97
A Lost Lady AN: 32; LCAB:
32; Ma: 323-324; Po: 430,
433
"Lou, the Prophet" ASF: 100;
SFC: 26; Wa: 97
Lucy Gayheart AN: 32
"The Marriage of Phaedra"
SFC: 26; Wa: 97
My Antonia AN: 32; LCAB:
32; Ma: 324-325; Ne: 29-30;
Po: 430, 433-434; Wo: 60
My Mortal Enemy Po: 434
"The Namesake" SFC: 27;
Wa: 97
"Nanette, An Aside" ASF:
100; SFC: 27; Wa: 97
"Neighbor Rosicky" ASF: 100;
SFC: 27; Wa: 97-98; WaS1:
31
"A Night at Greenway Court"
SFC: 27
O Pioneers! AN: 32-33; LCAB:
32; Ma: 325-326; Po:
430, 434-435
Obscure Destinies Po: 435

"The Old Beauty" ASF: 100;
SFC: 27; Wa: 98; WaS1:
31
"Old Mrs. Harris" ASF: 100;
SFC: 27; Wa: 98
"On the Divide" ASF: 100;
SFC: 27; Wa: 98
"On the Gull's Road" ASF:
100
One of Ours AN: 33; LCAB:
32; Po: 435-436
"Paul's Case" ASF: 100;
SFC: 27; Wa: 98; WaS1:
32
"Peter" ASF: 101; Wa: 99
"Peter Sadelack, Father of
Anton" SFC: 27
"The Prodigies" ASF: 101;
SFC: 27
"The Professor's Commence-
ment" Wa: 99
The Professor's House AN:
33; Ma: 326-328; Ne:
29-30; Po: 436-437; Wo:
60
"A Resurrection" SFC: 27
Sapphira and the Slave Girl
Po: 438
"Scandal" ASF: 101
"The Sculptor's Funeral"
ASF: 101; SFC: 27; Wa:
99
Shadows on the Rock AN:
33; Ma: 328; Po: 438
"A Singer's Romance" SFC:
27
"A Son of the Celestial"
SFC: 27; Wa: 99
The Song of the Lark AN:
33; Ma: 329
"A Tale of the White Pyramid"
SFC: 27
"Tom Outland's Story" Wa:
99
"Tommy, the Unsentimental"
ASF: 101; SFC: 27; Wa:
99
"The Treasure of Far Island"
ASF: 101; Wa: 99
"Two Friends" Wa: 99
"Uncle Valentine" ASF: 101;
Wa: 99
"A Wagner Matinée" ASF:
101; SFC: 27; Wa: 100
"The Willing Muse" Wa: 100
CATHERWOOD, Mary Hartwell

General AN: 36
CATTON, Bruce
General LCAB: 32
CATULLUS
Carmina Ma: 330
CAU, Jean
General Po: 438-439
CAUDWELL, Christopher
General Po: 439
CAULEY, Harry
The Paisley Convertible ADC:
69
CAUTE, David
General MDAE: 151
The Occupation ENES2: 41
Cavafy, Constantine Peter see
KABAPHES, Konstantinos
Petrou
CAVENDISH, George
The Life and Death of Cardinal
Wolsey Hen: 48; SC: 42-
43
CAVENDISH, Margaret, Duchess of
Newcastle
General ERP: 106
Nature's Pictures ERP: 106
CAVENDISH, William
General LJCD: 231
CAWTHORNE, W.A.
"The Kangaroo Islanders" Wa:
100
CAXTON, William
General Hen: 207-208
_____ [translator]
Blanchardyn and Eglantine
(Anon.) Hen: 207-208
The Golden Legend of Jacobus
de Voragine Hen: 206
The History of Reynard the
Fox (Anon.) Hen: 205
CAYROL, Jean
General Po: 440-441
Les corps étrangers Po: 440
Le déménagement Po: 440
L'Espace d'une nuit Po: 440
Le froid du soleil Po: 440
La Gaffe Po: 440
Je vivrai l'amour des autres
Ke: 48
La Noire Ke: 48
Les pleins et les Déliés Po:
440
CAZOTTE, Jacques
Le Diable amoureux Fi: 43
CEARD, Henry
Une Belle Journée Fi: 43;

Ke: 48
CELA, Camilo José
General Ma: 333; Po: 441-
443
La Catira Fi: 195; Ke: 185
"Don Anselmo" Wa: 100
The Family of Pasqual Duarte
[La familia de Pascual
Duarte] Fi: 196; Ke:
185-186; Po: 442, 444-446
The Hive [La colmena] Fi:
195-196; Ke: 185; Po:
442-444
"Marcelo Brito" Wa: 100
Mrs. Caldwell habla con su
hijo Fi: 197; Ke: 186
"The Mysterious Murder on
Blanchard Street" Wa:
100
Nuevas andanzas y desven-
turas de Lazarillo de
Tormes Fi: 197; Ke:
186; Po: 446
Pabellón de reposo Fi: 197;
Ke: 186
San Camilo Fi: 197
Toboggan of Hungry People
Fi: 197
CELAN, Paul
General Po: 447
"Dialogue in the Mountains"
Wa: 100
Ein Knirshen von eisernen
Schuhn ist im Kirsch-
baum Po: 447
Sprachgitter Po: 448
Todesfuge Po: 448
CELINE, Louis Ferdinand
General Po: 448-450
Casse-Pipe Fi: 43
Castle to Castle Fi: 43
Death on the Installment Plan
[Mort à Crédit] Fi: 43-
44; Ke: 48; Po: 449-451
Fairy Tale for Another Time
Fi: 44
Guignol's Band Fi: 44-45;
Ke: 48; Po: 451
Journey to the End of Night
[Voyage au bout de la
nuit] Fi: 45; Ke: 48-
49; Ma: 334-335; Po:
449-452
Mort à Crédit see Death on
the Installment Plan
North Fi: 46

Rigodon Fi: 46
Trifles for a Massacre Po: 449
Voyage au bout de la nuit see
Journey to the End of Night
CELTES, Conrad
Laus Diane DC2: 89
CENDRARS, Blaise
General Po: 452-453
Les Pâques à New York Po:
453
La Prose du Trans-Sibérien Po:
453
CENTLIVRE, Susanna
General EC: 59; Li: 112
CERDA, Mejia de la
Ines de Castro DC2: 89
CERF, Bennett Alfred
General LCAB: 32
CERNUDA, Luis
General Po: 453
CERTAD, Aquiles
General Br: 148
CERVANTES SAAVEDRA, Miguel
de
General LCAB: 33; Ma: 337-
338
El amante liberal Fi: 201; Ke:
190
Los Baños de Argel DC2: 89
La Casa Los Celos DC2: 89
El casamiento engañoso Fi:
201-202; Ke: 190
El celoso estremeño Fi: 202;
Ke: 190
El coloquio de los perros DC2:
89; Fi: 202; Ke: 190-191
El curioso impertinente Fi:
202
Don Quixote Fi: 202-211; Ke:
191-200; LCAB: 33; Ma:
336-337 see also SHELTON,
John [translator]
Las dos doncellas Fi: 211; Ke:
200
La Entrentenida DC2: 89
La española inglesa Fi: 211;
Ke: 200
Exemplary Novels [Novelas
ejemplares] Ke: 201 see
also MABBE, James [trans-
lator]
La fuerza de la sangue Fi:
211
La Galatea Fi: 211-212; Ke:
200
La gitanilla Fi: 212; Ke:

200-201
La ilustre fregona Fi: 212;
    Ke: 201
El licenciado Vidriera Fi:
    212; Ke: 201
Novelas ejemplares see
    Exemplary Novels
Numancia DC2: 90
Persiles and Sigismunda Fi:
    212-213; Ke: 201-202
El retablo de las marvillas
    DC2: 90; Po: 1695
Rinconete and Cortadillo Fi:
    213; Ke: 202
La señora Cornelia Fi: 213
El Trato de Argel DC2: 90
El viejo celoso DC2: 90; Fi:
    213

CESAIRE, Aimé
    General Po: 454
CESBRON, Gilbert
    General Po: 454
Chabaneix, Marie see NERVAT,
    Marie
CHABANEIX, Phillipe
    General Po: 454-455
CHAGAS, Manuel Pinheiro
    Novelas historicas Ke: 202
CHAISSAC, Gaston
    General Po: 455
CHAKOVSKI
    The Roads We Choose Ke:
        375
CHALLE, Robert
    Les Illustres Françoises Fi:
        46-47
CHAMBERS, Robert
    General Ai: 138
CHAMBERS, Robert W.
    General AN: 36
CHAMBERS, Whittaker
    General LCAB: 33
CHAMISSO, Adalbert von
    Peter Schlemihl Fi: 294;
        Wa: 100; WaS1: 32
CHAMSON, André
    General Po: 455
    Les Hommes de la route Fi:
        47
CHANDLER, Raymond
    General AN: 37; ASF: 103;
        Po: 455-456; Wo: 62
    "I'll Be Waiting" Wa: 101
    The Long Goodbye Wo: 62
    Playback Po: 456
CHANG, Eileen

"Blockade" WaS1: 32
"Jasmine Tea" WaS1: 32
CHANG T'IEN
    "After Her Departure" WaS1:
        32
    "The Bulwark" WaS1: 32
    "The Mid-Autumn Festival"
        WaS1: 32
    "On the Journey" WaS1: 32
    "Spring Breeze" WaS1: 32
CHANNING, William Ellery
    General AP: 229-231; Da:
        108-109
CHAO LIEN [formerly YÜ TA-FU]
    "Silver-grey Death" Wa: 101
    "Sinking" Wa: 101
CHAO, Shu-Li
    General Po: 456
    "The Marriage of Hsiao Erh-hei"
        WaS1: 32
CHAPMAN, George
    General ED: 216-219; NI:
        120-134, 147, 163-168; SC:
        43; TSD: 40-44
    All Fools DC1: 35; Ma: 339;
        NI: 143-144
    The Blind Beggar of Alexandria
        DC1: 35; EDC: 92; NI:
        145, 169; TSD: 42-43
    Bussy d'Ambois DC1: 35-36;
        EDC: 92-93; Ma: 339-340;
        NI: 134-137, 168-169; TSD:
        40-44
    Caesar and Pompey see The
        Tragedy of Caesar and
        Pompey
    Chabot, Admiral of France see
        The Tragedy of Chabot, Ad-
        miral of France
    The Conspiracy and Tragedy of
        Charles Duke of Byron [The
        Conspiracy of Byron; The
        Tragedy of Byron] DC1:
        37-39; EDC: 93-94; Ma:
        343-344; NI: 138-140, 169;
        TSD: 41-44
    Eastward Hoe DC1: 37; NI:
        114, 146, 170; TSD: 57
    The Fount of New Fashions
        DC1: 37
    The Gentleman Usher DC1:
        37; EDC: 94; Ma: 340-341;
        NI: 169; TSD: 43-44
    "Hero and Leander" ICBAP:
        22
    An Humorous Day's Mirth

NI: 170

"Hymnus in Noctem" (Shadow of Night, Part I) ICBAP: 22; PE: 73

Masque of the Middle Temple and Lincoln's Inn [The Memorable Mask of the Middle Temple and Lincoln's Inn] DC1: 37; NI: 145, 169

May-Day NI: 146

Monsieur D'Olive EDC: 94; NI: 146; TSD: 42

Northward Ho DC1: 38

"Ovid's Banquet of Sense" ICBAP: 22

Revenge for Honor see ANONYMOUS

The Revenge of Bussy D'Ambois DC1: 38; EDC: 94; Ma: 341-342; NI: 137-138, 169; TSD: 41, 44

The Second Maiden's Tragedy see MIDDLETON, Thomas

"The Shadow of Night" Ma: 342; PE: 73; SC: 43

Sir Giles Goosecap NI: 145-146, 169

"The Tears of Peace" PE: 73

The Tragedy of Byron see The Conspiracy and Tragedy of Charles Duke of Byron

The Tragedy of Caesar and Pompey [Caesar and Pompey] DC1: 36-37; EDC: 94; Ma: 342-343; NI: 140-141, 169; TSD: 41-44

The Tragedy of Chabot, Admiral of France [Chabot, Admiral of France] DC1: 39; EDC: 93; NI: 141-142, 169; TSD: 41, 43, 97

The Wars of Pompey and Caesar EDC: 94

The Widow's Tears DC1: 39; EDC: 95; Ma: 344; NI: 142-143; TSD: 43-44

CHAPMAN, John Jay
General LCAB: 33

CHAPMAN, Lonny
A Night at the Red Dog ADC: 69

CHAPURIN
Conscience DC2: 90

CHAR, René

General Br: 148; Po: 456-458

CHARBONNEAU, Robert
General Po: 458

Chardin, Pierre Teilhard de see TEILHARD DE CHARDIN, Pierre

CHARDONNE, Jacques
General Po: 458-459

CHARLES, Faustin
General WIL: 28
The Expatriate--Poems WIL: 28-29

CHARLES, Martha Evans [Marti CHARLES]
Jamimma BAP: 46; MBA: 56
Job Security BAP: 46; MBA: 56-57

CHARLES, the Rev. Norman
Infirmity Is Running MBA: 57

CHARLETON, Walter
The Ephesian Matron ERP: 107

CHARTIER, Emile-Auguste
General Po: 459-460

CHARYN, Jerome
General JW: 190

CHASE, Ilka
General LCAB: 33

CHASE, Mary Coyle
General MD: 73; MDAE: 152
Bernardine ADC: 69-70; Br: 148
Harvey ADC: 70; Br: 148; DC1: 39; MD: 73-74
Midgie Purvis ADC: 70
Mrs. McThing ADC: 70-71; Br: 149
The Next Half Hour ADC: 71; MD: 74

CHASE, Mary Ellen
General AN: 37; ASF: 103; Po: 460-461
"Marigolds" Wa: 101
"A Return to Constancy" Wa: 101
"Sure Dwelling" Wa: 101

CHATEAUBRIAND, François-René de
"Abencérage" Wa: 101; WaS1: 33
Atala Fi: 47; Ke: 49-50; Wa: 101; WaS1: 33
Les Aventures du dernier Abencérage Fi: 47
The Genius of Christianity Fi: 47; Ke: 50

The Martyrs Fi: 47; Ke:
50
The Natchez Fi: 47; Ke: 50
René Fi: 47-48; Ke: 50-51;
Wa: 101-102; WaS1: 33
CHATEAUBRIANT, Alphonse de
General Po: 461
CHATEAUBRUN
Ajax DC2: 90
CHATFIELD, E. Hale
General ICBAP: 22
CHATTERTON, Thomas
General EC: 59-60; Me:
142-145
Aella EC: 59; Me: 143
African Eclogues Me: 145
"Epistle to the Reverend Mr.
Catcott" Me: 144
CHAUCER, Geoffrey
General LCAB: 33; OMEP:
304-316
"An ABC" ICBAP: 22; PE:
73
The Book of the Duchess
ICBAP: 23; Ma: 345;
OMEP: 316-317
Book of Troilus LCAB: 33
The Canterbury Tales LCAB:
33-34; Ma: 346-347;
OMEP: 317-321
Canterbury Tales: "General
Prologue" OMEP: 321-322
Canterbury Tales: "Canon
Yeoman's Tale" OMEP:
330-331
Canterbury Tales: "Clerk's
Tale" OMEP: 327-328
Canterbury Tales: "Frank-
lin's Tale" OMEP: 325
Canterbury Tales: "Friar's
Tale" OMEP: 326
Canterbury Tales: "Knight's
Tale" LCAB: 33; OMEP:
322-323
Canterbury Tales: "Man of
Law's Tale" OMEP: 324
Canterbury Tales: "Mer-
chant's Tale" OMEP:
324-325
Canterbury Tales: "Miller's
Prologue and Tale"
OMEP: 323
Canterbury Tales: "Monk's
Tale" OMEP: 329
Canterbury Tales: "Nun's
Priest Tale" OMEP:

329-330
Canterbury Tales: "Pardoner's
Tale" OMEP: 328
Canterbury Tales: "Prioress'
Tale" OMEP: 328-329
Canterbury Tales: "Reeve's
Prologue and Tale" OMEP:
324
Canterbury Tales: "Squire's
Tale" OMEP: 325
Canterbury Tales: "Summoner's
Tale" OMEP: 326-327
Canterbury Tales: "Wife of
Bath's Prologue and Tale"
OMEP: 325-326
"The Complaint of Mars"
ICBAP: 23; PE: 73
"The Complaint of Venus" PE:
73
"Complaint to His Purse" PE:
73
"The Complaint Unto Pity"
ICBAP: 23; PE: 74
"Envoy to Scogan" PE: 74
"Fortune: Balades de Visage
Sanz Peinture" PE: 74
House of Fame ICBAP: 23;
OMEP: 331-332
Legend of Good Women
ICBAP: 23; OMEP: 333
The Parliament of Fowls
[Parlement of Foules]
ICBAP: 23; OMEP: 333-
334
"To Rosemounde" PE: 74
Troilus and Criseyde ICBAP:
23; LCAB: 33; Ma: 347-
348; OMEP: 335-337
Troilus and Criseyde--Book II
ICBAP: 23
"Truth, Balade de Bon Couseyl"
PE: 74
"Womanly Noblesse" PE: 74
CHAUDHURI, Pramatha
General Po: 461
CHAUFFIN, Yvonne
General Po: 461
Le Combat de Jacob Ke: 51
La Porte des Hebreux Ke:
51
Que votre volonte soit faite
Ke: 51
Les Rambourt Po: 461
CHAUNCEY, Anthony
Mini-Marvin MBA: 57
Chauncey, Harrell Cordell see

SALIM
CHAUNCY, Charles
General AP: 233-234; Da: 50

CHAYEFSKY, Paddy
General Br: 149; LCAB: 34; MD: 74; MDAE: 154; Po: 462
"A Few Kind Words from Newark" WaS1: 33
"The Giant Fan" WaS1: 33
Gideon ADC: 71; Br: 149; MD: 74; MDAE: 154; Po: 462
The Latent Heterosexual ADC: 71
The Middle of the Night ADC: 72
The Passion of Josef D. ADC: 72
The Tenth Man ADC: 72-73; Br: 149; LCAB: 34; MD: 74; MDAE: 154

CHEEVER, John
General ASF: 105; CFAE: 111-112; CN: 93; LCAB: 34; Po: 462-463
"The Angel of the Bridge" ASF: 104; WaS1: 33
"The Bella Lingua" WaS1: 33
"Clementina" WaS1: 33
"The Common Day" ASF: 104
"The Country Husband" ASF: 104; Wa: 102; WaS1: 33
"The Death of Justina" ASF: 104; WaS1: 33
"The Embarkment for Cythera" ASF: 104
"The Enormous Radio" ASF: 105; PE: 74; SFC: 28; Wa: 102; WaS1: 34
The Enormous Radio and Other Stories LCAB: 34
"Expelled" ASF: 104
"The Fourth Alarm" ASF: 104; WaS1: 34
"Goodbye, My Brother" ASF: 104; Wa: 102; WaS1: 34
"The Housebreaker of Shady Hill" ASF: 104; LCAB: 34; WaS1: 34
"The Music Teacher" ASF: 104; WaS1: 34
"O Youth and Beauty!" ASF: 105; WaS1: 34
"The Scarlet Moving Van" ASF: 105; WaS1: 34
"The Seaside Houses" ASF: 105; WaS1: 34
"The Swimmer" ASF: 105; Wa: 102; WaS1: 34
"A Vision of the World" ASF: 105; WaS1: 34
The Wapshot Chronicle CN: 93; LCAB: 34; Ma: 349; Po: 463
The Wapshot Scandal CFAE: 112; CN: 94; Ma: 349; Po: 463
"The World of Apples" ASF: 105; WaS1: 34
"The Wrysons" ASF: 105; WaS1: 34

CHEKHOV, Anton Pavlovich
General Br: 149-152; LCAB: 34; MD: 74-76; Po: 463-467
"About Love" Wa: 102
"An Acquaintance" see "A Gentleman Friend"
"After the Theatre" SFC: 28; Wa: 102
"Agafya" SFC: 28; Wa: 102; WaS1: 34
"Anna on the Neck" Wa: 102; WaS1: 34
"An Anonymous Story" SFC: 28; Wa: 102
"The Antagonists" Wa: 103
"Anyuta" Po: 467; SFC: 28; Wa: 103; WaS1: 35
"Ariadne" Wa: 103; WaS1: 35
"An Artist's Story" Wa: 103
"At a Country House" Wa: 103
"At Home" Wa: 103; WaS1: 35
"An Attack of Nerves" Wa: 103; WaS1: 35
The Bear [Medved] EDC: 95
"The Beauties" WaS1: 35
"Beautiful Women" Wa: 103
"The Bet" SFC: 28; Wa: 103
"The Betrothed" SFC: 28; Wa: 103
"Big Volodya and Little Volodya" WaS1: 35

The Bishop Fi: 422; Wa:
    103-104; WaS1: 35
The Black Monk [Cernyj
    Monax] Fi: 422; Ke:
    375; Po: 468-469; SFC:
    28; Wa: 104
A Boring Story see A
    Dreary Story
"The Boys" Wa: 104
"The Burbot" see "The
    Fish"
"The Butterfly" Wa: 104
Cajka see The Sea Gull
"Celovek v Futljare" see
    "The Man in a Case"
Cernyj Monax see The
    Black Monk
"The Chameleon" Wa: 104
Chayka see The Sea Gull
"The Chemist's Wife" Wa:
    104
The Cherry Orchard [Visnevyj
    Sad; Vishnyovy Sad] Br:
    152-154; DC2: 90-92;
    EDC: 95-97; LCAB: 34;
    Ma: 350-351; MD: 76-77;
    Po: 463-464, 471-473;
    TMAP: 175; TMBP: 259
"The Chorus Girl" SFC:
    28; Wa: 104
"La Cigalle" see "The
    Grasshopper"
"The Cook's Marriage" Wa:
    104
"The Crooked Mirror" Wa:
    104
"The Darling" ["Dusecka"]
    Po: 469; SFC: 28; Wa:
    104-105; WaS1: 35
"The Death of a Civil Ser-
    vant" Wa: 105
Djadja Vanya see Uncle
    Vanya
"A Doctor's Visit" SFC:
    28-29; Wa: 105
Drama Na Oxote see The
    Shooting Party
"Dreams" Wa: 105; WaS1:
    35
A Dreary Story [A Tedious
    Tale; A Boring Story]
    Fi: 422; Ke: 375; SFC:
    29; Wa: 105; WaS1: 35
The Duel Fi: 422-423;
    Ke: 375-376; SFC: 29;
    Wa: 105-106; WaS1: 35

"Dusecka" see "The Darling"
Dyadya Vanya see Uncle Vanya
"Easter Eve" Wa: 106; WaS1:
    35
"Enemies" SFC: 29; Wa: 106;
    WaS1: 35
"The Examining Magistrate"
    Wa: 106
"Fat and Thin" Wa: 106
"The Fish" ["The Burbot"]
    SFC: 29; Wa: 106
The Fit Ke: 376
"The Flutterer" see "The
    Grasshopper"
"A Gentleman Friend" SFC:
    29; Wa: 106; WaS1: 35
Good People Ke: 376
"Gooseberries" LCAB: 35;
    SFC: 29; Wa: 106-107;
    WaS1: 36
"The Grasshopper" ["The
    Flutterer"; The Philistines;
    "A Great Man"; "La Cigale"]
    SFC: 29; Wa: 107; WaS1:
    36
"Grisha" Wa: 107
"Gusev" Wa: 107; WaS1: 36
"Happiness" Wa: 107; WaS1:
    36
Harm of Tobacco DC2: 92;
    MD: 77
"Heartache" SFC: 29; Wa:
    107
"A Horse Name" WaS1: 36
The House with the Mezzanine
    Fi: 423; Ke: 376; Wa:
    107; WaS1: 36
"The Huntsman" SFC: 29;
    Wa: 107; WaS1: 36
"In Exile" SFC: 29; Wa: 107
"In Spring" Wa: 107
"In the Cart" see "The
    Schoolmistress"
In the Ravine Fi: 423; Ke:
    376; Po: 464; Wa: 107-
    108; WaS1: 36
"Ionych" Wa: 108; WaS1: 36
Ivanov Br: 154; DC2: 92;
    EDC: 97; MD: 77; Po:
    470
"The Kiss" SFC: 30; Wa:
    108; WaS1: 36
"The Lady of the Manor" Wa:
    108
"The Lady with the Dog" Fi:
    423; SFC: 30; Wa: 108;

WaS1: 36

"The Lament" see "Misery"

"Late-Blooming Flowers" Wa: 108

"The Letter" Wa: 108

"Lights" SFC: 30; Wa: 108; WaS1: 37

"Live Merchandise" Wa: 109

"The Lottery Ticket" SFC: 30; Wa: 109

"The Man in a Case" ["The Man in a Shell"; "Celovek v Futljare"] Po: 468; SFC: 30; Wa: 109

Medved see The Bear

"Misery" ["The Lament"] SFC: 30; Wa: 108-109; WaS1: 37

"A Misfortune" Wa: 109; WaS1: 37

Murder Fi: 423

"My Anniversary" Wa: 109

My Life Fi: 423; Ke: 376; SFC: 30; Wa: 109; WaS1: 37

Na Bolshoy Doroge see On the High Road

"Name Day" SFC: 30; Wa: 109

"Neighbors" Wa: 109

"A Nervous Breakdown" Wa: 109

"The New Villa" Wa: 109

"A Nightmare" Wa: 109

"Ninochka" Wa: 109

"Old Age" Wa: 109

"On Official Business" Wa: 110

"On the Cart" WaS1: 37

On the High Road [Na Bolshoy Doroge] EDC: 97

"On the Road" SFC: 30; Wa: 110

"One Man's Meat" Wa: 110

"One's Own Corner" Wa: 110

"Oysters" Wa: 110

Palata No. Shestoi see Ward No. 6

"The Party" SFC: 30; Wa: 110; WaS1: 37

"Peasant Wives" Wa: 110

Peasants Fi: 423; Ke: 376; Po: 464; SFC: 30; Wa: 110; WaS1: 37

"The Philistines" see "The Grasshopper"

Platonov, or a Country Scandal [Pyesa Bez Nazvaniya] Br: 154; DC2: 92; EDC: 97; MD: 77-78

"Polinka" SFC: 30; Wa: 110

"The Princess" Wa: 110

Pyesa Bez Nazvaniya see Platonov, or a Country Scandal

"Requiem" Wa: 110

"A Romance with a Double-Bass" Wa: 111

"Rothschild's Fiddle" SFC: 31; Wa: 111

"The Runaway" Wa: 111

"The Schoolmistress" ["In the Cart"] SFC: 31; Wa: 111

The Sea Gull [Chayka; Cajka] Br: 154-156; DC2: 92-93; EDC: 97-99; LCAB: 35; Ma: 351-352; MD: 78; Po: 468

"Sergeant Prishibeyev" see "Under-Officer Prishibeyev"

"The Service of the Dead" SFC: 31; Wa: 111

The Shooting Party [Drama Na Oxote] Ke: 376; Po: 469; Wa: 111

"Sleepy" ["Spat Khochetsia"] Po: 470-471; Wa: 111

"Sleepyhead" SFC: 31

"Small Fry" SF: 31; Wa: 111

Solomon DC2: 93

"Sorrow" Wa: 111; WaS1: 37

"Spat Khochetsia" see "Sleepy"

The Steppe Fi: 423-424; Ke: 376; SFC: 31; Wa: 111; WaS1: 37

Story of an Unknown Man Ke: 376; SFC: 31; Wa: 111

"The Student" SFC: 31; Wa: 111-112; WaS1: 37

"The Teacher of Literature" SFC: 31; Wa: 112; WaS1: 37

A Tedious Tale see A Dreary Story

"Thieves" Wa: 112

The Three Sisters [Tri Sestry] Br: 156-157; DC2: 93-94; EDC: 99-100; LCAB: 35; Lon: 32; Ma: 352-353; MD: 78; Po: 464, 471; TMBP: 186, 259; TMIP:

47

Three Years [Tri Goda] Fi:
424; Ke: 376; LCAB:
35; Po: 471; SFC: 31;
Wa: 112; WaS1: 37
"A Trifling Occurrence" Wa:
112
"The Trousseau" Wa: 112
"Two in One" Wa: 112
Uncle Vanya [Djadja Vanya;
Dyadya Vanya] see also
The Wood Demon Br:
157-158; DC2: 94-95;
EDC: 100-101; Ma: 353-
354; MD: 78-79; Po: 464,
469
"Under-Officer Prishibeyev"
["Sergeant Prishibeyev"]
SFC: 31; Wa: 112
"An Unpleasantness" Wa:
112
"An Upheaval" WaS1: 37
"Vanka" SFC: 31; Wa:
112; WaS1: 37
"Verochka" SFC: 31; Wa:
112-113
"Vint" Wa: 113
Vishnyovy Sad see The
Cherry Orchard
"A Visit to a Friend" Wa:
113; WaS1: 37
Visnevyj Sad see The
Cherry Orchard
"Volodya" Wa: 113
Ward No. 6 [Palata No.
Shestoi] Fi: 424; Ke:
376; LCAB: 35; Po: 470;
SFC: 32; Wa: 113; WaS1:
38
A Wedding EDC: 101; MD:
79
"The Wife" ["Zena"] Wa:
113
"The Witch" SFC: 32; Wa:
113
"A Woman's Kingdom" SFC:
32; Wa: 113; WaS1: 38
Wood Demon see also Uncle
Vanya EDC: 101-102
"Zena" see "The Wife"
CHERNYSHEVSKY, N.G.
What Is To Be Done? Fi:
424; Ke: 376-377
CHESNUTT, Charles Waddell
General AAF: 58-59; AAW:
44-45; AF: 52-53; ALL:

54-55; ASF: 107-109; BAF:
57-61; BAW: 145-148; Ho:
21-22; LCAB: 35
"Baxter's Procrustes" ASF:
106; BAF: 59; Wa: 114
"The Bouquet" Wa: 114
"A Busy Day in a Lawyer's Of-
fice" Wa: 114
"Cicely's Dream" WaS1: 38
The Colonel's Dream BAF: 61
The Conjure Woman AAF: 59;
AF: 52-53; BAF: 57-59,
61; BAW: 148; Ho: 21-22;
Ma: 355-356
"The Conjurer's Revenge"
ASF: 106; Wa: 114; WaS1:
38
"Dave's Neckliss" ASF: 106
"The Doll" Wa: 114
"The Goophered Grapevine"
ASF: 106; BAF: 59; Wa:
114; WaS1: 38
"The Gray Wolf's Ha'nt" ASF:
106; Wa: 114; WaS1: 38
"Her Virginia Mammy" Wa:
114; WaS1: 38
"Hot-Foot Hannibal" Wa: 114-
115; WaS1: 38
The House Behind the Cedars
AAF: 58; BAF: 60-61;
BAW: 148; Ho: 21, 143
"How Dasdy Came Through"
Wa: 115
"The March of Progress" ASF:
106
The Marrow of Tradition AAF:
59; AF: 53; BAF: 58, 60-
62; BAW: 148; Ho: 22; Ma:
356
"Mars Jeems's Nightmare"
ASF: 106; Wa: 115; WaS1:
38
"A Matter of Principle" ASF:
107; Wa: 115; WaS1: 38
"Mr. Taylor's Funeral" Wa:
115
"The Origin of the Hatchet
Story" ASF: 107; Wa: 115
"The Passing of Grandison"
Wa: 115; WaS1: 38
"Po' Sandy" ASF: 107; Wa:
115; WaS1: 38
"The Prophet Peter" Wa: 115
"Rena" ASF: 107
"The Sheriff's Children" ASF:
107; BAF: 59, 61; Wa: 115;

WaS1: 38
"Sis' Becky's Pickaninny"
    ASF: 107; Wa: 115; WaS1:
    38
"A Tight Boot" Wa: 115
"Tom's Warm Welcome" Wa:
    116
"Uncle Peter's House" ASF:
    107; Wa: 116
"Uncle Wellington's Wives"
    Wa: 116
"The Web of Circumstance"
    ASF: 107; Wa: 116;
    WaS1: 39
"The Wife of His Youth"
    AF: 53; ASF: 107; BAW:
    148; Wa: 116; WaS1: 39
The Wife of His Youth and
    Other Stories of the Color
    Line BAF: 61-62
CHESTER, Thomas
"Sir Launfal" OMEP: 296
CHESTERFIELD, Philip Dormer
    Stanhope, 4th Earl of
General EC: 60
Letters to His Son Ma: 357
CHESTERTON, Gilbert Keith
General LCAB: 35; Ma:
    358; Po: 473-475; Ri:
    170-185, 187-190; Sch:
    22-25; TA: 115
The Ball and the Cross
    ENES1: 35; ENES2: 41-
    42
"The Blue Cross" Wa: 116
"The Donkey" PE: 74
The Everlasting Man Ma:
    358-359
The "Father Brown" Stories
    Ri: 185-186
The Flying Inn ENES1: 35;
    ENES2: 42; Ri: 172
Four Faultless Felons ENES2:
    42
"The Green Man" Wa: 116
"The Hammer of God" Po:
    475; Wa: 116
Heretics Ma: 359; Ri: 188-
    189
Magic MD: 79; Ri: 189
The Man Who Knew Too Much
    ENES2: 42
The Man Who Was Thursday
    ENE: 39; ENES1: 35;
    ENES2: 42; Ma: 359-360;
    Ri: 172, 186-187

Manalive ENES2: 42
The Napoleon of Notting Hill
    · ENES1: 35; ENES2: 42;
    - Ma: 360-361; Ri: 172, 187;
    Ri2: 325
Orthodoxy Ma: 361; Ri: 185,
    189-190
The Paradoxes of Mr. Pond
    ENES2: 42
The Poet and the Lunatics
    ENES2: 42
"The Queer Feet" Wa: 116
The Return of Don Quixote
    ENES1: 35; ENES2: 43;
    Ri: 172
"The Rolling English Road"
    PE: 74
Tales of the Long Bow
    ENES2: 43
What's Wrong with the World
    Ma: 361
"The Yellow Bird" Wa: 116
CHETTLE, Henry
General ERP: 110; Hen:
    109; Log: 251-255
Hoffman DC1: 40
Kind-Heart's Dream ERP: 109-
    111
Piers Plainnes Seaven Yeres
    Prentiship [Piers Plainnes]
    ENES1: 35; ERP: 109-111
CHETWOOD, William Rufus
The Generous Free-Mason
    DC1: 40
CHEVALIER, P.E.
Rachel DC2: 95
CHEYNEY-COKER, Syl
General BALE: 284-285
CHIABRERA, Gabriello
Il Rapimento di Cefalo DC2:
    95
CHIANG KUEI [WANG I-CHIEN]
"Ah-yüan" Wa: 116
"The Shoe That Didn't Fit"
    Wa: 116
CHIARELLI, Luigi
General MD: 79
The Mask and the Face [Mask
    and Face; La Maschera e il
    Volto] Br: 158; MD: 79;
    Po: 475
CH'IEN Chung-shu
"Cat" WaS1: 39
"Inspiration" WaS1: 39
"Souvenir" WaS1: 39
CHILD, Lydia Maria

General AN: 37; ASF: 109
The Frugal Housewife AN: 37
"Jumbo and Zairee" ASF: 109
Philothea AN: 37

CHILD, Philip
General Po: 475-476

CHILDE, Wilfred Rowland
"Solemn and Gray, the Immense Clouds of Even" (from Ivory Palaces) PE: 74

CHILDERS, Erskine
General TA: 116
The Riddle of the Sands ENES2: 43

CHILDRESS, Alice
General AAPD: 355; AAW: 45; BAF: 62; BAP: 47; BAW: 150-151; Br: 158; MBA: 57-58
Florence BAP: 48; MBA: 58
Gold Through the Trees BAP: 48; MBA: 58
Just a Little Simple BAP: 48; MBA: 58
Like One of the Family BAF: 62
Mojo MBA: 58-59
The String ADC: 73; BAP: 48; MBA: 58-59
Trouble in Mind BAP: 48-49; Br: 158; MBA: 58-59
Wedding Band ADC: 73; BAP: 48-49; BAW: 151; MBA: 58-59
Wine in the Wilderness ADC: 73; BAP: 48; MBA: 58-59

CHILLINGWORTH, William
General Hen: 35

CHIN, Frank
The Chickencoop Chinaman ADC: 73
The Year of the Dragon ADC: 73

CHINWEIZU
General BALE: 285

CHIOINO, Jose
General Br: 158

CHISHOLM, Hugh
"Lament of the Lovers" PE: 74
"Notes on Progress" PE: 74

CHIVERS, Thomas Holley
General LCAB: 35

CHLUMBERG, Hans von
Miracle at Verdun [Wunder um Verdun] Br: 159; DC2: 95; MD: 79

CHOCANO, José Santos
General Po: 476

CHODOROV, Edward
Common Ground ADC: 73
Decision ADC: 73
Kind Lady ADC: 74
Oh, Men! Oh, Women ADC: 74
Those Endearing Young Charms ADC: 74
_____ and Arthur BARTON
Wonder Boy ADC: 74
_____ and H.S. KRAFT
Cue for Passion ADC: 74

CHODOROV, Jerome
Junior Miss ADC: 75
The Ponder Heart see also FIELDS, Joseph and Jerome CHODOROV Po: 476
Three Bags Full ADC: 74-75
_____ and Joseph FIELDS
Anniversary Waltz ADC: 75

CHODZKO, Ignacy
"The Guardian Angel" Wa: 117
"The Heir's Return" Wa: 117
"The Jubilee" Wa: 117
"The Last Court Session" Wa: 117
"My Grandfather's House" Wa: 117
"Samovar" Wa: 117

CHOMSKY, Noam
General LCAB: 35

CHOPIN, Kate
General AF: 56-57; ALL: 55; ASF: 111
At Fault AF: 56-57
"At the 'Cadian Ball" ASF: 109; Wa: 117
"Athénaïse" ASF: 109; Wa: 117
The Awakening AF: 56-57; ALL: 55; AN: 37
"Beyond the Bayou" ASF: 110
"Charlie" Wa: 117
"Désirée's Baby" ASF: 110; Wa: 117; WaS1: 39
"In and Out of Old Natchitoches" Wa: 117
"In Sabine" Wa: 117

"Lilacs" Wa: 117
"The Maid of Saint Philippe"
ASF: 110
"Miss McEnders" Wa: 117
"A No-Account Creole" ASF:
110; Wa: 118
"Ozéme's Holiday" ASF: 110;
Wa: 118
"A Point at Issue" ASF: 110;
Wa: 118
"Regret" ASF: 110; Wa:
118
"A Sentimental Soul" ASF:
110
"The Storm" ASF: 110; Wa:
118
"The Story of an Hour" ASF:
110; Wa: 118
"Vagabonds" ASF: 110; Wa:
118
"A Vocation and a Voice"
ASF: 110; Wa: 118
"Wiser Than a God" ASF:
111; Wa: 118
CHOROMANSKI, Michal
"The Banal Tale" Wa: 118
"The Cynical Tale" Wa: 118
"The Incredible Tale" Wa:
118
"The Insane Tale" Wa: 118
CHOU, Shu-Jen
General Po: 476
Ah Q and Others Po: 476
CHOYNOWSKI, Piotr
"A Deed" Wa: 118
"The Five Sulerzycki Gentle-
men" Wa: 118
"The Voyevod's Christmas
Eve" Wa: 119
CHRAIBI, Driss
General Po: 477
CHRISTIAN, Marcus
General BAW: 152
CHRISTIANSEN, Sigurd
Dream and Life Ke: 348
The Man with the Petrol
Station Ke: 348
Two Living and One Dead
Ke: 348
CHRISTIE, Agatha Miller
General MDAE: 156-157;
Po: 477
Endless Night Po: 477
Hidden Horizons EDC: 102
The Hollow EDC: 102
The Mousetrap EDC: 102;

MDAE: 156
The Murder at the Vicarage
ENES1: 35
Murder in Mesopotamia ENES1:
36
Spider's Web MDAE: 157
Ten Little Indians EDC: 102
Unexpected Guest EDC: 102
Witness for the Prosecution
EDC: 102
_____ and Gerald VERNER
Towards Zero EDC: 102
CHULKOV, Mikhail
The Comely Cook Fi: 424
The Mocker Fi: 424-425
CHUMANDRIN, Mikhail
Rable's Factory Ke: 377
CHURCH, Benjamin
The Choice Da: 50
CHURCH, Richard
General Po: 477
CHURCHILL, Charles
General EC: 61; ICBAP:
23; Me: 148-152
"The Apology" PE: 74
"The Candidate" ICBAP: 23
"The Dedication" ICBAP: 23
"The Duellist" Me: 148
"The Epistle to William Hogarth"
Me: 148
"Fragment of a Dedication to
P.W. Warburton" EC: 61;
Me: 149, 151-152; PE: 74
"The Ghost" ICBAP: 24
"Gotham" ICBAP: 24
"Night" PE: 75
The Rosciad Me: 148
CHURCHILL, Sir Winston [1874-
1965]
General LCAB: 35; Po: 478
CHURCHILL, Winston [1871-1947]
General AN: 38; ASF: 112;
Po: 478
"By Order of the Admiral"
ASF: 112
Coniston AN: 37; Ma: 362
The Crisis Ma: 363
The Crossing Ma: 363
The Dwelling-Place of Light
AN: 37
A Far Country AN: 37
The Inside of the Cup AN:
38
Mr. Crewe's Career AN: 38;
Ma: 364
A Modern Chronicle AN: 38

Richard Carvel Ma: 364-365
CIARDI, John Anthony
  General LCAB: 36; Po:
    478
  "Letter to Virginia Johnson"
    PE: 75
  "Metropolitan Ice Co." PE:
    75
  "Most Like an Arch This Mar-
    riage" ICBAP: 24
  "The Size of Song" PE: 75
  "Snowy Heron" ICBAP: 24
  "Tenzone" ICBAP: 24; PE:
    75; Po: 478-479
  "To Judith" PE: 75
  "To Judith Asleep" PE: 75
CIBBER, Colley
  General EC: 62; Li: 114-116
  An Apology for the Life of
    Colley Cibber, Comedian
    Ma: 366
  The Careless Husband DC1:
    40; EDC: 103; Ma: 366-
    367
  Damon and Phillida EDC:
    103
  The Double Gallant; or The
    Sick Lady's Cure EDC:
    103
  The Lady's Last Stake; or,
    The Wife's Resentment
    EDC: 103
  Love Makes a Man; or, The
    Fop's Fortune EDC: 103
  Love's Last Shift; or, The
    Fool in Fashion DC1: 40;
    EC: 62; EDC: 103; Li:
    115
  The Non-Juror DC1: 40;
    EDC: 103; Li: 115
  Perolla and Izadora EDC:
    104
  The Provok'd Husband; or,
    A Journey to London
    see also VANBRUGH, Sir
    John EDC: 104
  The Refusal; or The Lady's
    Philosophy DC1: 40;
    EC: 62; EDC: 104
  Richard III [The Tragical
    History of King Richard
    III] DC1: 40; EC: 62;
    EDC: 104; Li: 115-116
  The Rival Fools EDC: 104
  The Rival Queans, With the
    Humours of Alexander

the Great EDC: 104; Li:
  116
The School Boy; or, The Com-
  ical Rivals EDC: 104
She Wou'd and She Wou'd Not;
  or, The Kind Imposter EDC:
  104; Li: 116
The Tragical History of King
  Richard III see Richard III
Woman's Wit; or, The Lady in
  Fashion EDC: 104
Xerxes EDC: 104
Ximena; or The Heroick Daugh-
  ter EDC: 104
CICELLIS, Kay
  "The Way to Colonus" Wa: 119
CICERO, Marcus Tullius
  General LCAB: 36
CLANCIER, Georges-Emmanuel
  General Po: 479
CLANVOWE, Sir John
  "The Cuckoo and the Nightingale"
    ICBAP: 24; PE: 75
CLARE, John
  General Re: 195-196
  "Badger" PE: 75
  "Birds' Nests" PE: 75
  "The Hedgehog" PE: 75
  "I Am" PE: 75
  "I Hid My Love" PE: 75
  "An Invite to Eternity" PE:
    75
  "The Lark's Nest" PE: 76
  "Love and Beauty" ICBAP: 24;
    PE: 76
  "Mouse's Nest" PE: 76
  "The Nightingale's Nest" PE:
    76
  "Sand Martin" PE: 76
  "Schoolboys in Winter" PE: 76
  "The Skylark" PE: 76
  "The Sorrows of Love" PE: 76
  "A Vision" PE: 76
  "The Woodman" PE: 76
CLARENDON, Edward Hyde, Earl
  of
  General Bon: 73
Clarín see ALAS, Leopoldo
CLARK, Benjamin C.
  General LCAB: 36
CLARK, Benjamin P.
  General BAW: 152
CLARK, David R.
  "The Bee Space" PE: 76
  "Mountain Ash" PE: 76
  "Robin" PE: 76

"Tree" PE: 76

CLARK, Harold and Maxwell NURNBERG
Chalk Dust ADC: 75

CLARK, John Pepper
General BALE: 285-287; Br: 159; Po: 479
America, Their America BALE: 287
Casualties BALE: 286
"Ivbie" BALE: 286
The Masquerade BALE: 287; Br: 159
The Raft BALE: 286; Br: 159
A Reed in the Tide BALE: 287
Song of a Goat BALE: 285-287; Br: 159

CLARK, Ron and Sam BOBRICK
Norman, Is That You? ADC: 75

CLARK, Walter Van Tilburg
General AN: 38-39; ASF: 113; Po: 479-480; Wo: 64
"The Anonymous" Wa: 119; WaS1: 39
"The Buck in the Hills" ASF: 112; Wa: 119; WaS1: 39
The City of Trembling Leaves Ma: 368
"Hook" SFC: 32; Wa: 119; WaS1: 39
"The Indian Well" ASF: 112; Wa: 119; WaS1: 39
The Ox-Bow Incident AN: 38; Ma: 368-369; Po: 480-481; Wo: 64
"The Portable Phonograph" ASF: 112; Po: 481; SFC: 32; Wa: 119; WaS1: 39; Wo: 64
"The Rapids" SFC: 32; Wa: 119; WaS1: 39
The Track of the Cat AN: 38; LCAB: 36; Ma: 369-370
"The Watchful Gods" ASF: 112; Ma: 370-371; SFC: 32; Wa: 119-120; WaS1: 40
"Why Don't You Look Where You're Going?" Wa: 120
"The Wind and the Snow of Winter" ASF: 112; SFC: 32; Wa: 120; WaS1: 40

CLARK, William
Letters and Journals LCAB: 36

CLARKE, A.M.
General WIL: 29

CLARKE, Arthur C.
General LCAB: 36
Against the Fall of Night ENES2: 43
Childhood's End ENES2: 43-44
The City and the Stars ENES2: 44
The Deep Range ENES2: 44
Earthlight ENES2: 44
Imperial Earth ENES2: 44
Islands in the Sky ENES2: 44
"A Meeting with Medusa" WaS1: 40
"The Nine Billion Names of God" WaS1: 40
Prelude to Space ENES2: 44
Rendezvous with Rama ENES2: 44
The Sands of Mars ENES2: 44
"The Star" Wa: 120; WaS1: 40
"Summertime on Icarus" WaS1: 40
2001: A Space Odyssey ENES2: 44

CLARKE, Austin
General Br: 159; MBD: 39; Po: 481; WIL: 29-30
Amongst Thistles and Thorns WIL: 30
The Bigger Light WIL: 31
Black Fast DC1: 41
The Flame DC1: 41
"Four Stations in His Circle" Wa: 120
The Meeting Point WIL: 30-31
"The Motor Car" Wa: 120
The Plot Is Ready DC1: 41
Sister Eucharia DC1: 41
The Sons of Learning DC1: 41
Survivors of the Crossing WIL: 30
When He Was Free and Young and Used to Wear Silks WIL: 31

CLARKE, John Henrik
General BAF: 63; BAW: 155

"Santa Claus Is a White Man"
  ASF: 113
CLARKE, Marcus
  General AL: 168-171
  Chidiock Tichbourne AL:
    171
  His Natural Life AL: 168-
    171
CLAUDEL, Paul Louis Charles
  General Br: 159-163; LCAB:
    36; MD: 79-81; Po: 482-
    493
  Agamemnon DC2: 95
  And on the Seventh Day God
    Rested [The Seventh
    Day's Rest; Le Repos du
    Septième Jour] Br: 166;
    DC2: 96; EDC: 104-105;
    MD: 82; Po: 482-483,
    492-494
  L'Annonce Faite à Marie see
    The Tidings Brought to
    Mary
  The Book of Christopher
    Columbus [Le Livre de
    Christophe Columb] Br:
    163-164; DC2: 95; EDC:
    105; MD: 81
  Break of Noon [Partage de
    Midi] Br: 163; DC2: 96;
    EDC: 105; MD: 82; Po:
    487-488, 494
  The City [La Ville] Br:
    164; DC2: 98; EDC:
    105-106; MD: 82; Po:
    489, 493
  Crusts [Le Pain Dur] Br:
    164; EDC: 106; MD: 82;
    Po: 483, 486
  The East I Know [Connais-
    sance de l'Est] Po: 483,
    494
  L'Endormie [L'Endorme] Br:
    164; Po: 488
  The Exchange [L'Echange]
    Br: 164; EDC: 106; MD:
    82; Po: 483, 488-489
  La Femme et Son Ombre see
    The Woman and Her Shadow
  L'Histoire de Tobie et Sara
    see Tobias and Sara
  The Hostage [L'Otage] Br:
    165; DC2: 96; EDC:
    106-107; MD: 82; Po:
    482, 486
  The Humiliation of the Father
    [Le Père Humilé] Br: 165;
    EDC: 107; MD: 82; Po:
    486
  Le Jeune Fille Violaine see
    The Maid Violaine
  Joan of Arc at the Stake
    [Jeanne d'Arc au Bûcher]
    EDC: 107
  Le Livre de Christophe Columb
    see The Book of Christopher
    Columbus
  The Maid Violaine [La Jeune
    Fille Violaine] EDC: 107
  La muse qui est la grâce Po:
    494
  L'Otage see The Hostage
  L'Ours et la Lune EDC: 107
  Le Pain Dur see Crusts
  Partage de Midi see Break of
    Noon
  Le Père Humilé see The
    Humiliation of the Father
  Proteus [Protée] EDC: 107
  Le Repos du Septième Jour
    see And on the Seventh Day
    God Rested
  The Satin Slipper; or, The
    Worst Is Not Sure [Le Sou-
    lier de Satin; ou La Pire
    N'est Pas Toujours Sur] Br:
    165-166; DC2: 96-97; EDC:
    107-109; MD: 82; Po: 482,
    494
  The Seventh Day's Rest see
    And on the Seventh Day
    God Rested
  Le Testament d'Orphée Br:
    166
  Tête D'Or Br: 166-167; DC2:
    97; EDC: 109; MD: 82;
    Po: 482, 489, 495-496
  The Tidings Brought to Mary
    [L'Annonce Faite à Marie]
    Br: 167-168; DC2: 97-98;
    EDC: 109-110; MD: 81;
    Po: 482-483, 489, 493-494
  Tobias and Sara [L'Histoire de
    Tobie et Sara] EDC: 110
  La Ville see The City
  The Woman and Her Shadow
    [La Femme et Son Ombre]
    Br: 168
CLAUS, Hugo
  General Po: 496
CLAVEL, Bernard
  General Po: 496

CLAVELL, John
  General LJCD: 232
CLAY, Buriel, II
  Liberty Call ADC: 76;
    MBA: 60
CLAYTON, John
  General Da: 50
CLEAVER, Eldridge
  General AAL: 149-150;
    BAF: 63; BAW: 157-158
  Soul on Ice MDAE: 435
CLELAND, John
  General Be: 88-90
  Fanny Hill: Memoirs of a
    Woman of Pleasure Be:
    62, 88-90, 109; Du: 26;
    ENES1: 36; ENES2: 45
  Memoirs of a Coxcomb
    ENES1: 36; ENES2: 45
  The Woman of Honor
    ENES1: 36
CLEM, Charles Douglas
  General AAPD: 95; BAW:
    158-159
Clemens, Samuel Langhorne see
  TWAIN, Mark
CLEMO, Jack
  General Po: 502-503
CLERC, John [translator]
  Arnalt and Lucenda by Diego
    de SAN PEDRO ERP: 111
CLEVELAND, John
  General Ba: 38
  "Et Caetera" ICBAP: 24
  "The Hecatomb to His Mis-
    tress" PE: 76
  "The Senses Festival" PE: 76
Clezio, Jean Marie Gustave le
  see LE CLEZIO, Jean
  Marie Gustave
CLIFFORD, Carrie Williams
  General BAW: 159
  The Widening Light BAW:
    159
CLIFTON, Lucille
  Good News About the Earth
    BAW: 160
  Good Times BAW: 160
CLIMMONS, Artie
  My Troubled Soul MBA: 60
CLIVE, Catharine
  General Li: 118
  Every Woman in Her Humour
    Li: 118
  The Rehearsal Li: 118
CLOSSON, Herman

General Br: 168
CLOUGH, Arthur Hugh
  General ICBAP: 24; Ma:
    376-377; VP: 29-30
  "Ambarvalia" Ma: 372
  "Amours de Voyage" Ma: 372-
    373
  "Blank Misgivings of a Creature
    Moving About in Worlds Not
    Realised" ICBAP: 24; Ma:
    373; PE: 77; VP: 29
  "Blessed Are Those Who Have
    Not Seen" PE: 77
  The Bothie of Tober-na-Vuolich
    Ma: 373-374
  Dipsychus DC1: 41; ICBAP:
    24; Ma: 374-375
  "Easter Day. Naples, 1849"
    ICBAP: 25
  "Easter Day II" ICBAP: 25
  "Epi-strauss-ium" ICBAP: 25;
    Ma: 375; PE: 77
  "Is It True, Ye Gods, Who
    Treat Us" PE: 77
  "The Judgement of Brutus"
    ICBAP: 25
  "Love and Reason" PE: 77
  "Mari Magno" Ma: 375-376
  "Salsette and Elephanta"
    ICBAP: 25
  "Sa Majeste Très Chrétienne"
    ICBAP: 25
  "Say Not the Struggle Nought
    Availeth" LCAB: 37; Ma:
    377; PE: 77
  "To the Great Metropolis"
    ICBAP: 25
CLUCHEY, Rick
  The Cage ADC: 76
COBB, Chester
  General MAP: 142
COBB, Humphrey
  Paths of Glory see also
    HOWARD, Sidney Br:
    168; Po: 503
COBB, Irvin Shrewsbury
  General LCAB: 37-38
COBB, Joseph B.
  General ASF: 113
COBBET, Thomas
  A Practical Discourse of Prayer
    AP: 577
COBBETT, William
  General AP: 236-237
COBLE, Tom
  Time for the Gentle People

ADC: 76
COBO-BORDA, J.E.
General Po: 503
COBURN, D.L.
The Gin Game ADC: 76
COCCIOLI, Carlo
Manuel le Mexicain Fi: 48
The Strings of the Harp Fi:
263
COCTEAU, Jean
General Br: 168-169;
LCAB: 38; MD: 83; Po:
503-505
L'Aigle A Deux Têtes see
The Eagle with Two Heads
Antigone EDC: 110
Bacchus Br: 169-170; DC2:
98; EDC: 110; MD: 83
Beauty and the Beast [La
Belle et la Bête] Br:
170
The Blood of a Poet [Le
Sang d'un Poète] Br:
170; Po: 507
Le Boeuf sur le Toit see
The Ox on the Roof
Les Chevaliers de la Table
Ronde see Knights of
the Round Table
Le Coq et l'Arlequin Po:
505
The Eagle with Two Heads
[The Eagle Has Two
Heads; L'Aigle A Deux
Têtes] Br: 170-171;
EDC: 110-111; MD: 83
The Eiffel Tower Wedding
Party [Les Mariés de la
Tour Eiffel] Br: 171;
EDC: 113; MD: 84
Les Enfants Sacrés see
The Holy Terrors
Les Enfants Terribles see
The Holy Terrors
L'Eternel Retour Br: 171
The Grand Ecart Ke: 51
The Holy Terrors [Les En-
fants Sacrés; Les Mon-
stres Sacrés; Les Enfants
Terribles] Br: 171-
172; EDC: 111; Fi: 48;
Ke: 51; Ma: 378; MD:
84; Po: 505
The Human Voice [La Voix
Humaine] Br: 172;
DC2: 99; EDC: 111

The Infernal Machine [La Ma-
chine infernale] Br: 172-
173; DC2: 98-99; EDC:
111-112; LCAB: 38; Ma:
378-380; MD: 84; Po: 506
Intimate Relations [Problem
Parents; The Storm Within;
Les Parents Terribles] Br:
173-174; DC2: 99; EDC:
112; MD: 84
Knights of the Round Table
[Les Chevaliers de la Table
Ronde] Br: 174; DC2: 99;
EDC: 112; MD: 83
Léone Po: 506
La Machine à Ecrire see The
Typewriter
La Machine infernale see The
Infernal Machine
Les Mariès de la Tour Eiffel
see The Eiffel Tower Wed-
ding Party
Les Monstres Sacrés see The
Holy Terrors
Oedipus Rex [Oedipe-Roi] Br:
174; EDC: 112
Orpheus [Orphée] Br: 174-
175; DC2: 99; EDC: 112;
Ma: 380-381; MD: 84; Po:
506-507
The Ox on the Roof [Le Boeuf
sur le Toit] Br: 170; EDC:
112
Parade Br: 175; DC2: 99;
Po: 507
Les Parents Terribles see
Intimate Relations
Problem Parents see Intimate
Relations
Renaud et Armide Br: 175;
MD: 84
Romeo and Juliette [Roméo et
Juliette] Br: 176; MD:
84
Le Sang d'un Poète see The
Blood of a Poet
The Storm Within see Intimate
Relations
Thomas the Imposter Fi: 48;
Ke: 51
The Typewriter [La Machine à
Ecrire] Br: 176; EDC:
113; MD: 84
La Voix Humaine see The
Human Voice
CODJOE, Thomas A.

General BALE: 288; Po:
507
COFFEE, Lenore and William
Joyce COWEN
Family Portrait Br: 176
COFFEY, Charles
General Li: 120
The Beggar's Wedding DC1:
41
The Boarding-School DC1:
41
COFFEY, Tom
General Br: 176
COFFIN, Frank Barbour
General BAW: 162
COFFIN, Robert
General Po: 507-508
"Love, the Leaves Are Falling
Round Thee" PE: 77
COHAN, George M.
General Lon: 57
COHEN, Jean
General Po: 508
COHEN, Larry
Nature of the Crime ADC:
76
COHEN, Leonard Norman
General CFAE: 113; CN:
94; JW: 140, 325; Po:
508
Beautiful Losers CN: 94;
JW: 325
The Favourite Game CN: 94
"Go By Brooks, Love" PE:
77
COHEN, Matt
General JW: 328
The Colours of War JW: 328
"Columbus and the Fat Lady"
Wa: 120
The Disinherited JW: 328
COKAIN, Aston
The Obstinate Lady and the
Araucana LJCD: 232
COLE, Robert ["Bob"]
General BAP: 50-51; BAW:
162-163; MBA: 60
Black Patti's Troubadours
BAP: 51; MBA: 60
A Trip to Coontown BAP:
51; MBA: 60-61
_____ and J. Rosamond
JOHNSON
Red Moon BAP: 51; MBA:
60
Shoofly Regiment BAP: 51,

124; MBA: 60
COLE, Robert Wellesley
General BALE: 288
COLE, Tom
Medal of Honor Rag ADC: 76-
77; MBA: 61
COLE, William
General LCAB: 38
COLEMAN, Lonnie
A Place for Polly ADC: 77
COLEMAN, Val
The Jackhammer Br: 176
COLEMAN, Wanda
General BAF: 64
COLERIDGE, Mary Elizabeth
[Anodos]
General TA: 117
COLERIDGE, Samuel Taylor
General EDT: 138-140; Fog:
23-24, 28-31; ICBAP: 25;
LCAB: 38; Re: 110-119
"The Ballad of the Dark
Ladié" PE: 77
Biographia Literaria Ma: 382-
383; Re: 114-115
"Christabel" Fog: 26; ICBAP:
25; Ma: 383-384; Pe: 77-
78; Re: 112, 115-117
The Conversation Poems Fog:
26-27
"Dejection: An Ode" Fog:
27; ICBAP: 25; LCAB: 38;
Ma: 384-385; PE: 78-79;
Re: 114-115
"The Destiny of Nations" PE:
79
"The Eolian Harp" ICBAP:
25; PE: 79; Re: 117
"Fears in Solitude" PE: 79
"France: An Ode" PE: 79
"The Friend" ICBAP: 25
"Frost at Midnight" ICBAP:
25; PE: 79-80
"The Garden of Boccaccio" PE:
80
"The Hymn Before Sunrise, in
the Vale of Chamouni" Fog:
27; PE: 80; Re: 112
"Kubla Khan" Fog: 27-28;
ICBAP: 26; LCAB: 38;
Ma: 385-386; PE: 80-81;
Re: 113, 115-117
"Lewti" PE: 82
"Limbo" PE: 82
"Lines Composed in a Concert-
Room" ICBAP: 26

"Lines Written at Shurton
  Bars" PE: 82
"Monody on the Death of
  Chatterton" PE: 82
"The Nightingale" ICBAP:
  26; PE: 82
"No Plus Ultra" PE: 82
"Ode on the Departing Year"
  PE: 82
"On Donne's Poetry" PE:
  82
Osorio DC1: 42; EDT: 138-
  140
"The Pang More Sharp Than
  All" PE: 82
"The Picture" PE: 82
"Reflections on Having Left a
  Place of Retirement" PE:
  83
"Religious Musings" PE: 83
"Remorse" EDT: 138-140;
  Re: 115
"Rime of the Ancient Mariner"
  Fog: 24-26; ICBAP: 26;
  LCAB: 38; Ma: 386-388;
  PE: 83-85; Po: 4494, 4498;
  Re: 113-115, 117-118
"This Lime-Tree Bower My
  Prison" ICBAP: 26; PE:
  86
"The Three Graves" PE: 86
"Time, Real and Imaginary"
  ICBAP: 26; PE: 86
"To the River Otter" PE:
  86
"To William Wordsworth" PE:
  86
Zapolya EDT: 140
COLES, Erostine
Mimi La Crox MBA: 62
COLET, John
General Hen: 25
COLETTE, Sidonie-Gabrielle
General LCAB: 38-39; Po:
  508-511
Le Blé en herbe Fi: 48;
  Po: 510
"The Cat" Wa: 120
Chéri Fi: 48; Ke: 51; Ma:
  389-390; Po: 509-510;
  Wa: 120
Duo Fi: 48; Wa: 121
"L'Enfant malade" Wa: 121
Gigi Po: 510-511
The Last of Cheri [La Fin
  de Chéri] Fi: 49; Ke:

51-52; Po: 509-510; Wa:
  121
La Lune de pluie Fi: 49
Mitsou Fi: 49
The Pure and the Impure Ma:
  390
Le Toutounier Fi: 49; Wa:
  121
La Vagabonde Fi: 49
COLLE, Charles
Le Menteur DC2: 99
COLLETT, Camilla
The Governor's Daughters Ke:
  348
COLLIER, Eugenia
General BAF: 64
COLLIER, John
"De Mortuis" ASF: 113; Wa:
  121
"Thus I Refute Beelzy" Wa:
  121
"Wet Saturday" ASF: 113;
  WaS1: 40
COLLINS, Mortimer
Marquis and Merchant ENES1:
  36
Collins, Tom see FURPHY,
  Joseph
COLLINS, Wilkie
General BN: 32-33; Du: 27-
  28
Antonina ENES1: 36
Armadale EN: 17; ENES1: 37
Basil ENES1: 37
The Black Robe ENES1: 37
The Dead Secret ENES1: 37
The Haunted Hotel ENES1: 37
Heart and Science ENES1: 37
Hide and Seek ENES1: 37;
  ENES2: 45
Jezebel's Daughter ENES1: 37
The Law and the Lady ENES1:
  37
The Legacy of Cain ENES1:
  37
The Lighthouse DC1: 42
Man and Wife EN: 17; ENES1:
  37
The Moonstone BN: 32-33;
  Du: 27; EN: 17; ENE:
  39; ENES1: 37; ENES2:
  45; Ma: 391
The New Magdalen ENES1: 37
No Name BN: 33; EN: 17-18;
  ENES1: 37
Poor Miss Finch ENES1: 37

The Woman in White BN: 32-
33; Du: 27; EN: 18;
ENE: 40; ENES1: 38;
ENES2: 45; Ma: 392
COLLINS, William
General EC: 62-63; Me:
155-160
"Ode on the Death of Thom-
son" Me: 159
"Ode on the Poetical Charac-
ter" EC: 63; ICBAP:
26; Me: 155, 159-160;
PE: 86
"Ode on the Popular Super-
stitions of the Highlands
of Scotland Considered as
the Subject for Poetry"
EC: 63; ICBAP: 27; PE:
87
"Ode to Evening" EC: 63;
ICBAP: 27; LCAB: 39;
Me: 155-158; PE: 87
"Ode to Fear" ICBAP: 27;
PE: 87
"Ode to Liberty" ICBAP:
27; PE: 87
"Ode to Pity" ICBAP: 27;
PE: 87
"Ode to Simplicity" ICBAP:
27; PE: 87
"Ode Written in the Begin-
ning of the Year 1746"
("How Sleep the Brave")
ICBAP: 27
Persian Eclogues Me: 156
"Sonnet" ("When Phoebe
Form'd a Wanton Smile")
PE: 87
"Verses Humbly Address'd to
Sir Thomas Hanmer on
His Edition of Shakespeare's
Works" ICBAP: 27
COLLYER, Mary
Letters from Felicia to Char-
lotte ENES1: 38; ENES2:
45-46
COLLYMORE, Frank A.
General WIL: 31-32
Collected Poems WIL: 32
Flotsam WIL: 32
COLMAN, Benjamin
General AP: 239-240
COLMAN, George, The Elder
General EC: 63-64; Li:
121
The Jealous Wife DC1: 42

_____ and David GARRICK
The Clandestine Marriage DC1:
42; EC: 63; Li: 121
COLMAR, Andrew
Dancing for the Kaiser ADC:
77
COLOANE, Francisco A.
General Po: 511
COLTER, Cyrus
General ASF: 114; BAF: 65-
66; BAW: 168
"The Beach Umbrella" AAL:
151; BAW: 168; Wa: 121
The Beach Umbrella (Collection)
BAF: 66
"A Chance Meeting" Wa: 121
The Hippodrome BAF: 66
"A Man in the House" Wa:
121
"Moot" Wa: 121
The Rivers of Eros AAL:
151; BAF: 66; BAW: 168
COLUM, Padraic
General Br: 176; MBD: 40;
Mi: 226; Po: 511; TA:
118
"Eilis: A Woman's Story" Wa:
121
The Fiddler's House Br: 176
"The Flute Player's Story" Wa:
122
The Land Br: 176-177; DC1:
42
Thomas Muskerry Br: 177
COMBS, Frederick
Children's Mass ADC: 77
COMENIUS, Johann
Labyrinth of the World DC2:
100
COMFORT, Alexander
General EP: 78-79
The Almond Tree EP: 79
Cities of the Plain EP: 79
Elegies EP: 79
Haste to the Wedding EP: 79
Into Egypt EP: 79
"The Martyrdom of the House"
SFC: 32; Wa: 122
The Signal to Engage EP: 79
The Song of Lazarus EP: 78
A Wreath for the Living EP:
79
COMPTON, David Guy
The Steel Crocodile ENES2:
46
Synthajoy ENES2: 46

COMPTON-BURNETT, Ivy
  General BN2: 23-24; CN:
    94-95; LCAB: 39; Po:
    511-514; Ri: 195-201;
    Sch: 26-27
  Brothers and Sisters CN:
    95; ENE: 40; ENES1: 38;
    ENES2: 46; Ma: 393; Ri:
    202
  Bullivant and the Lambs
    [Mr. Bullivant and His
    Lambs] see also Man-
    servant and Maidservant
    CN: 96; Ma: 398
  Darkness and Day CN: 96;
    ENE: 40; ENES1: 38;
    ENES2: 46; Ma: 393
  Daughters and Sons CN:
    96; ENES1: 38; ENES2:
    46; Ma: 393-394
  Dolores CN: 96; ENES1:
    38; Ma: 394; Ri: 197,
    202
  Elders and Betters CN: 96;
    ENES1: 38; ENES2: 46;
    Ma: 394-395; Ri: 197,
    202
  A Family and a Fortune CN:
    96; EN: 18; ENE: 40;
    ENES1: 39; ENES2: 46;
    Ma: 395; Ri: 202
  A Father and His Fate CN:
    97; ENES1: 39; Ma: 395
  A God and His Gifts CN:
    97; ENE: 40; ENES1: 39;
    ENES2: 46; Ma: 395-396;
    Ri: 195-196
  A Heritage and Its History
    CN: 97; ENES1: 39;
    ENES2: 46; Ma: 396;
    Ri: 199, 202-203
  A House and Its Head CN:
    97; ENES1: 39; ENES2:
    46; Ma: 396-397
  The Last and the First
    ENES2: 46; Ma: 397;
    Ri: 197, 203
  Manservant and Maidservant
    see also Bullivant and
    the Lambs ENES1: 39;
    ENES2: 46; Ri: 198-199
  Men and Wives CN: 97;
    ENES1: 39; Ma: 397
  The Mighty and Their Fall
    CN: 97; ENE: 40;
    ENES1: 39; ENES2: 46;

    Ma: 397-398
  More Women Than Men CN:
    98; ENES1: 39; Ma: 398
  Mother and Son CN: 98;
    ENE: 40; ENES1: 40; Ma:
    398-399
  Parents and Children CN: 98;
    ENES1: 40; ENES2: 47;
    Ma: 399; Ri: 197-198
  Pastors and Masters CN: 98;
    ENE: 40-41; ENES1: 40;
    Ma: 399-400; Po: 514; Ri:
    203
  The Present and the Past CN:
    98; ENES1: 40; Ma: 400
  Two Worlds and Their Ways
    CN: 98; ENES1: 40; Ma:
    400; Ri: 199
CONDE, Carmen
  General Po: 514
  En manos del silencio Ke: 202;
    Po: 514
CONDON, Richard
  General Po: 514
CONFUCIUS
  General LCAB: 39
  The Analects LCAB: 39
CONGRAINS MARTIN, Enrique
  "Cuatro pisos, mil esperanzas"
    Wa: 122
  "Lima, hora cero" Wa: 122
CONGREVE, William
  General Bon: 38-39; Li: 125-
    129
  The Double Dealer Bon: 38;
    DC1: 42; EDC: 113; Li:
    126-127; Ma: 401-402
  Incognita ENES1: 40; ENES2:
    47
  Love for Love Bon: 38; DC1:
    43; EDC: 113-114; Li: 127;
    Ma: 402-403
  The Mourning Bride Bon: 38-
    39; DC1: 43; EDC: 114;
    Li: 126-127
  The Old Bachelor DC1: 43;
    EDC: 114-115; Li: 126;
    Ma: 403-404
  "Song: False Though She Be
    to Me and Love" PE: 87
  The Way of the World Bon:
    39; DC1: 43-44; EDC:
    115-116; LCAB: 39; Li:
    126-129; Ma: 404-405
CONKLE, E.P.
  Prologue to Glory ADC: 77-

78
Two Hundred Were Chosen
ADC: 78
CONLAN, James
The Priest in the Cellar
ADC: 78
CONN, Stewart
General Ai: 336; MDAE:
158
CONNELL, Evan Shelby, Jr.
General ASF: 114; CFAE:
115; CN: 99; Po: 515
"The Anatomy Lesson" Wa:
122
"Arcturus" Wa: 122
"The Condor and the Guests"
ASF: 114
The Diary of a Rapist CN:
99
"The Fisherman from Chihua-
hua" Wa: 122
"Guatemala" Wa: 122
Mrs. Bridge CN: 99; Ma:
406
Notes from a Bottle Found on
the Beach at Carmel Ma:
406-407
The Patriot CN: 99
"St. Augustine's Pigeon"
LCAB: 39; Wa: 122
"The Trellis" Wa: 122
"The Walls of Avila" Wa:
122
"The Yellow Raft" Wa: 122
CONNELL, Norreys [Conal
Holmes O'Connell
O'RIORDAN]
General Mi: 265-266
The Piper Br: 177, 523
CONNELL, Richard
"The Most Dangerous Game"
Wa: 122; WaS1: 40
CONNELLY, Marcus Cook
General Lon: 28; MD: 84;
Po: 515
The Flowers of Virtue ADC:
78
The Green Pastures ADC:
78-79; Br: 177; DC1:
44; Lon: 28; MD: 85;
Po: 515
A Story for Strangers ADC:
79; MD: 85
The Wisdom Tooth ADC:
79

_____ and Frank B. ELSER
The Farmer Takes a Wife ADC:
80
CONNER, Charles H.
General BAW: 168
Connor, Ralph [pseud.] see
GORDON, Charles William
CONOVER, Grandin
The Party on Greenwich Avenue
ADC: 80
CONRAD, Joseph [Jozef Konrad
KORZENIOWSKI]
General BN2: 26-32; LCAB:
39; Po: 516-539; Ri: 219-
253, 301-303; Sch: 28-41;
TA: 120-121
"After Thirty Years" Wa: 440
Almayer's Folly EN: 18; ENE:
41-42; ENES1: 40; ENES2:
47; Ma: 408-409; Po: 516,
525, 528, 535-536, 538-539,
1059; Ri: 230, 252-254;
Sch: 41-42
"Amy Foster" BN2: 29;
LCAB: 39; Po: 539-540;
Ri: 220, 227, 252, 254;
SFC: 33; Wa: 123; WaS1:
40
"An Anarchist" SFC: 33; Wa:
123
The Arrow of Gold BN2: 31;
EN: 18-19; ENE: 42;
ENES1: 40-41; ENES2: 47-
48; Po: 516, 540; Ri: 254-
255; Sch: 42
"Because of the Dollars" SFC:
33; Wa: 123
"The Black Mate" Po: 540;
SFC: 33; Wa: 124
"The Brute" Wa: 124
Chance BN2: 28-29; EN: 19-
20; ENE: 42-43; ENES1:
41; ENES2: 48; Po: 520-
521, 525, 527, 540-542; Ri:
221, 227-228, 238, 255-256;
Sch: 42-43
"Il Conde" Po: 542-543; Ri:
266; SFC: 36; Wa: 124
"The Duel" Ri: 256; SFC:
33; Wa: 124-125
"The End of the Tether" Po:
522, 532, 543; Ri: 236,
252, 257; SFC: 32; Wa:
125; WaS1: 40
"Falk" BN2: 29; Po: 523,

534, 543-544; Ri: 257;
SFC: 33-34; Wa: 125-126;
WaS1: 41

"Freya of the Seven Isles"
Ri: 258; SFC: 34; Wa:
126; WaS1: 41

"Gaspar Ruiz" Po: 544; Ri:
258; SFC: 34; Wa: 126

"Heart of Darkness" BN2:
28, 30; Ma: 409-411; Po:
519, 524, 526-527, 529-
533, 535, 544-555, 4561;
Ri: 219, 222, 224-225,
228, 230, 235-236, 238,
242, 244, 247, 250, 258-
266; Sch: 43-47; SFC:
34-36; TMAP: 62; Wa:
126-133; WaS1: 41

"The Idiots" Po: 555; Ri:
266; SFC: 36; Wa: 133-
134

"The Informer" Po: 556;
Ri: 267; SFC: 36; Wa:
134; WaS1: 41

"The Inn of the Two Witches"
Ri: 267; Wa: 134

"It's Good to Know Even
This in These Hard Times"
Wa: 440

"Karain" Ri: 220, 267; SFC:
36; Wa: 134; WaS1: 41-42

"The Lagoon" Po: 556-557;
Ri: 228, 267; SFC: 36-
37; Wa: 134-135; WaS1:
42

Lord Jim BN2: 28-29, 31;
EN: 20-22; ENE: 43-48;
ENES1: 41-42; ENES2:
48-50; LCAB: 40; Ma:
411-413; Po: 516, 520-
524, 527-529, 533-534,
538, 558-564, 1059, 1434,
4561; Ri: 219, 222-225,
227-228, 230, 238, 241-242,
245, 250, 267-273; Sch:
47-51

The Mirror of the Sea Po:
564-565; Ri: 302-303

The Nigger of the "Narcissus" BN2: 29-30; EN:
23-24; ENE: 48-50;
ENES1: 42-43; ENES2:
50; Ma: 413-415; Po:
520-521, 523, 525, 527,
529-530, 565-568; Ri:
222, 224, 244, 273-277,

302-303; Sch: 51-53

Nostromo BN2: 28-31; EN:
24-25; ENE: 50-53; ENES1:
43-44; ENES2: 51-52; LCAB:
40; Ma: 415-416; Po: 522,
526, 528, 530, 537, 568-572;
Ri: 219, 221-222, 224, 227-
230, 235, 237, 241-242, 244,
277-281; Sch: 53-56

One Day More Br: 178

An Outcast of the Islands EN:
25-26; ENE: 53-54; Po:
516, 525, 532-533, 535, 572-
573; Ri: 230, 252, 281;
Sch: 56

"An Outpost of Progress" Po:
573; SFC: 37; Wa: 135-
136; WaS1: 42

"The Partner" SFC: 37; Wa:
136

A Personal Record Po: 573;
Ri: 303

"The Planter of Malata" SFC:
37; Wa: 136

"Prince Roman" Ri: 220, 281;
SFC: 37; Wa: 136

The Rescue BN2: 29; EN:
26; ENE: 54-55; ENES1:
44; ENES2: 52; Po: 516,
525, 535, 538; Ri: 224, 227,
252, 282; Sch: 56

"The Return" SFC: 37; Wa:
136; WaS1: 42

The Rover ENE: 55-56;
ENES1: 44; ENES2: 52;
Po: 573-574; Ri: 220, 222,
227, 237, 282-283; Sch: 57

"The Second Wife" Wa: 440

The Secret Agent BN2: 28,
30-31; EDC: 116; EN: 26-
27; ENE: 56-59; ENES1:
45; ENES2: 52-53; Ma: 416-
418; Po: 523, 525, 528, 530,
574-581; Ri: 219, 221-222,
224, 229-230, 242, 246, 283-
289; Sch: 57-59

"The Secret Sharer" Ma:
418-420; Po: 529, 532, 534,
581-584; Ri: 222, 241, 252,
264, 289-292; SFC: 37-38;
TMAP: 62; Wa: 136-139;
WaS1: 42

A Set of Six Ri: 292

"The Shadow Line" BN2: 31;
Po: 529, 534, 537, 585;
Ri: 227, 230, 244, 252,

292-293; Sch: 59-60; Wa:
139-140; WaS1: 42
The Sisters Ri: 293
"A Smile of Fortune" Po:
585-586; Ri: 293; SFC:
38; Wa: 140
Suspense ENE: 59; Po:
586; Ri: 237, 293; Sch:
60
"The Tale" Po: 586; SFC:
38; Wa: 140-141
"Tomorrow" Po: 586; SFC:
38; Wa: 141
"Typhoon" BN2: 31; Po:
526, 537, 586-587; Ri:
222, 252, 294-295; SFC:
38-39; Wa: 141-142; WaS1:
42
Under Western Eyes EN:
27-28; ENE: 60-61;
ENES1: 46; ENES2: 53-
54; Ma: 420-421; Po:
522, 530, 587-589; Ri:
219, 221-222, 224, 228-
229, 239-241, 246, 250,
253, 295-297; Sch: 60-61
Victory BN2: 29, 31; EDC:
116; EN: 28-29; ENE:
61-63; ENES1: 46-47;
ENES2: 54; LCAB: 40;
Ma: 421-422; Po: 516,
523, 526, 528, 532, 534,
589-592; Ri: 219-221, 224,
227-228, 241-242, 245, 250,
297-300; Sch: 61-63
"The Warrior's Soul" SFC:
39; Wa: 142
"Youth" Po: 527, 529, 592-
593; Ri: 236, 238, 252,
300-301; SFC: 39; Wa:
142-143; WaS1: 43
_____ and Ford Madox FORD
The Inheritors ENE: 63;
ENES1: 47; Po: 521,
524, 556, 4561; Ri: 302,
360-361; Sch: 43
The Nature of a Crime
ENES1: 47; Po: 521;
Sch: 43
Romance ENES1: 47; Po:
521; Ri: 362; Sch: 43
CONRAD, Michael Georg
In Purpurner Finsterniss
Fi: 294
CONRADI, Hermann
Adam Man Ke: 259

CONROY, Jack
"The Siren" ASF: 114
CONSTABLE, Henry
General SC: 44
CONSTANT, Benjamin
Adolphe Fi: 49-50; Ke: 52;
LCAB: 40; Ma: 423; Wa:
143; WaS1: 43
Cécile Ke: 53
Wallenstein DC2: 100
Constant de Rebecque, Henri
Benjamin see CONSTANT,
Benjamin
CONTESSA, C.W.
"Meister Dietrich" Wa: 144
CONTON, William Farquhar
General BALE: 289
COOK, David
Happy Endings ENES2: 54
COOK, Fannie
Boot-Heel Doctor LCAB: 40
COOK, Will Marion
General BAW: 170-171; MBA: 62
Abyssinia BAP: 52
Bandanna Land BAP: 52
_____ and Paul Lawrence DUN-
BAR
Clorindy--The Origin of the
Cake-Walk BAP: 52, 70;
MBA: 62
Jes Lak White Folk BAP: 53;
MBA: 62
_____, Alex ROGERS, and J.A.
SHIPP
In Dahomey BAP: 53; MBA: 75
COOK[E], Ebenezer
General Da: 51
COOKE, John Esten
General AN: 39; Ma: 424
COOKE, Rose Terry
General AN: 39; ASF: 115;
LCAB: 40
"Cal Culver and the Devil"
Wa: 144
"Freedom Wheeler's Controversy
with Providence" Wa: 144
"How Celia Changed Her Mind"
ASF: 115
"Polly Mariner, Tailoress"
ASF: 115; Wa: 144
COOMBS, Orde
General BAF: 66-67
COOPER, Anna Julia
General BAW: 173-174
COOPER, Charles Edward [Varfelli
KARLEE, pseud.]

Love in Ebony BALE: 289
COOPER, Clarence L., Jr.
  General AAW: 45
  The Farm BAF: 67; BAW:
    174
  The Scene BAF: 67
COOPER, Edmund
  Seed of Light ENES2: 55
COOPER, Giles
  General Br: 178; MDAE:
    160
  Everything in the Garden
    MDAE: 160
COOPER, James Fenimore
  General AF: 74-79; ALL:
    62-64; AN: 43-47; Cla:
    19-21; Da: 95-96; Ho:
    32-37, 144-145; LCAB:
    40-41
  The Bravo AF: 74, 76
  The Chainbearer AN: 40;
    Ma: 425
  The Crater AN: 40
  The Deerslayer AF: 74;
    AN: 40; Ho: 34, 36;
    LCAB: 41; Ma: 425-426
  "Heart" ASF: 115
  The Heidenmauer AF: 74,
    76
  Home as Found AN: 40;
    Ho: 35, 144
  Homeward Bound AN: 40;
    Ho: 144
  "Imagination" ASF: 115
  The Last of the Mohicans
    AF: 76-77; AN: 40-41;
    Ho: 35-36; Ma: 426-428
  Lionel Lincoln Ho: 144
  Mercedes of Castile AN: 41
  The Pathfinder AN: 41;
    Ma: 428
  The Pilot Ma: 429
  The Pioneers AN: 41; Ho:
    34-36, 144; LCAB: 41;
    Ma: 429-430
  The Prairie AF: 74-75, 77;
    AN: 41-42; Ho: 34-36,
    144-145; Ma: 430-431
  Precaution AF: 76; AN:
    42
  The Red Rover AF: 74;
    AN: 42; Ma: 432
  The Redskins AN: 42;
    Ma: 432-433
  Satanstoe AF: 74; AN:
    42; Ho: 34, 36; Ma:

    433
  The Sea Lions AF: 74; AN:
    42
  The Spy AN: 42-43; Ma:
    433-434
  The Two Admirals AN: 43
  The Water-Witch AF: 74
  Wyandotté Ho: 36
COOPER, William [Harry Summer-
    field HOFF]
  General CFAE: 118; Sch: 63
  Scenes from a Married Life
    CN: 99
  Scenes from Provincial Life
    CN: 99-100
  Young People CN: 100
COOPER, William Arthur
  Thank God for a Song BAF:
    68; BAW: 174
COOVER, Robert
  General ASF: 116; CFAE:
    119; Po: 593
  "The Babysitter" ASF: 115;
    Wa: 144; WaS1: 43
  "The Brother" Wa: 144
  "The Elevator" WaS1: 43
  The Kid ADC: 80; TMAP:
    173
  "The Leper's Helix" ASF:
    115; Wa: 144
  "The Magic Poker" ASF: 116
  "The Pedestrian Accident"
    ASF: 116; Wa: 144
COPE, Jack
  "A Crack in the Sky" Wa:
    144
COPLAND, Robert
  General ERP: 116
COPPARD, A.E.
  "Adam and Eve and Pinch Me"
    SFC: 39; Wa: 144
  "Arabesque" Wa: 144
  "Emergency Exit" Wa: 144
  "Fifty Pounds" SFC: 39; Wa:
    145
  "The Higgler" SFC: 39; Wa:
    145
  "Olive and Camilla" Wa: 145
  "The Watercress Girl" Wa:
    145
  "A Wildgoose Chase" Wa: 145
  "Willie Waugh" SFC: 39; Wa:
    145
CORBET, Richard
  "The Fairies' Farewell" PE:
    88

CORELLI, Marie [Mary MACKAY]
General TA: 213-214
The Murder of Delicia
ENES2: 55
Vendetta ENES2: 55
COREY, Paul
General LCAB: 41
Acres of Antaeus LCAB: 41
CORKERY, Daniel
General Mi: 226-227
The Labour Leader Br: 178
The Threshold of Quiet
ENES2: 55
CORNEILLE, Pierre
Agésilas EDC: 116
Alidor DC2: 100
Andromeda EDC: 116
Attila DC2: 100; EDC: 116
Le Cid DC2: 100-101; EDC:
117-118; LCAB: 41;
Ma: 435-436
Cinna, or, the Clemency of
Augustus [Cinna, ou La
Clémence d'Auguste]
DC2: 101-102; EDC: 118;
Ma: 436-437
Clitandre DC2: 102; EDC:
118
The Comic Illusion [L'Illusion
Comique] DC2: 104; EDC:
118-119; Ma: 438-439
Death of Pompey [La Morte
de Pompée] EDC: 119
Don Sanche D'Aragon DC2:
102; EDC: 119
Le Galerie du Palais; ou
L'Amie Rivale see The
Palace Corridor; or The
Rival Friend
Hercalius DC2: 103; EDC:
119
Horatius [Horace] DC2:
103-104; EDC: 119-120;
Ma: 437-438
L'Illusion Comique see The
Comic Illusion
The Liar [Le Menteur] EDC:
120; Ma: 439
The Maidservant [La Suivante]
DC2: 107; EDC: 120
Médée DC2: 104; EDC:
120-121
Melite, or the False Letters
[Mélite, ou Les Fausses
Lettres] DC2: 105; EDC:
121

Le Menteur see The Liar
La Morte de Pompée see Death
of Pompey
La Morte de Solon DC2: 105
Nicomede DC2: 105; EDC:
121
Oedipe DC2: 105; EDC: 121
Othon DC2: 105; EDC: 121
The Palace Corridor; or The
Rival Friend [Le Galerie du
Palais; ou L'Amie Rivale]
DC2: 102-103; EDC: 121
Pertharites, King of the Lom-
bards [Petharite, Roi des
Lombards] DC2: 105; EDC:
121
Place Royale; or The Extrava-
gant Lover [La Place Royale;
ou l'Amoreux Extravagant]
DC2: 105; EDC: 121-122
Polyeucte DC2: 106; EDC:
122-123; Ma: 439-440
Pompée DC2: 106
Pulcherie EDC: 123
Rodogune, Princess of Parthia
DC2: 107; EDC: 123
Sequel to the Liar [La Suite de
Menteur] EDC: 123
Sertorius DC2: 107; EDC:
123
Sophonisbe EDC: 123
La Suite de Menteur see Se-
quel to the Liar
La Suivante see The Maidser-
vant
Surena DC2: 107; EDC: 123
Theodora, Virgin and Martyr
[Théodore] DC2: 107; EDC:
123
Tite et Berenice DC2: 107-
108; EDC: 123
The Widow; or The Betrayer
Betrayed [La Veuve; ou, La
Traître Trahi] DC2: 108;
EDC: 124
_____, MOLIERE, and Philippe
QUINAULT
Psyche DC2: 106-107; EDC:
124
_____ and MORATIN
La Estera DC2: 102
CORNEILLE, Thomas
Ariane DC2: 108
Comte D'Essex DC2: 108
Comtesse D'Orgueil DC2: 108
Stilicon DC2: 108

CORNWELL, David John More
  The Looking Glass War Po:
    594
  The Spy Who Came In From
    the Cold Po: 594
CORNY, Mikhail
  Sister Ke: 377
CORREGGIO, Giovanni
  Cefalo DC2: 108
CORROTHERS, James David
  General BAW: 176; LCAB:
    41
  In Spite of the Handicap
    BAW: 176-177
CORSO, Gregory Nanzia
  General ICBAP: 27; MDAE:
    161; Po: 594
CORTADA, J.
  Lorenzo Ke: 202
  El templario y la villana Ke:
    202-203
CORTAZAR, Julio
  General LCAB: 42; Po:
    594-595
  "All Fires the Fire" WaS1:
    43-44
  "Las armas secretas" Po:
    595-596; Wa: 145
  "At Your Service" WaS1:
    44
  "La Autopista del Sur" Wa:
    145
  "Axolotl" WaS1: 44
  "The Band" WaS1: 44
  "Bestiary" WaS1: 44
  "Blow-up" ["Las babas del
    diablo"] Wa: 145; WaS1:
    44
  "Los buenos servicios" Wa:
    145; WaS1: 44
  "La caracia" Wa: 145
  "Cartas de mamá" Wa: 145
  "Cefalea" WaS1: 44-45
  "Circe" WaS1: 45
  "The Condemned Door" Wa:
    145
  "Continuity of Parks" WaS1:
    45
  "Después del almuerzo" Wa:
    146
  "The Distances" WaS1: 45
  "End of the Game" ["Final
    del juego"] Wa: 146;
    WaS1: 45
  "The Gates of Heaven" ["Las
    puertas del cielo"] Wa:

  146; WaS1: 45
  "Homage to a Young Witch"
    WaS1: 45
  "House Taken Over" WaS1: 45
  "Instrucciones para John Howell"
    Wa: 146; WaS1: 45
  "The Isle at Noon" ["La isla a
    mediodia"] Wa: 146; WaS1:
    45
  "Lejana" Wa: 146
  "El móvil" Wa: 146
  "Neck of the Little Black Cat"
    WaS1: 45
  "The Night Face Up" WaS1: 45
  "Nurse Cora" WaS1: 46
  "Omnibus" WaS1: 46
  "The Other Heaven" ["El otro
    cielo"] Wa: 146; WaS1: 46
  "The Phases of Severo" WaS1:
    46
  "A Place Called Kindberg"
    WaS1: 46
  "Las puertas del cielo" see
    "The Gates of Heaven"
  "The Pursuer" WaS1: 46
  Rayuela Po: 596
  "The Reunion" WaS1: 46
  "The River" WaS1: 46
  "Secret Weapons" WaS1: 46
  "Siesta" Wa: 146
  "Silvia" Wa: 146
  "The Southern Throughway"
    WaS1: 46
  "Torito" WaS1: 46
  "A Yellow Flower" WaS1: 46
CORTES DE TOLOSA, Juan
  Lazarillo de Manzanares Fi:
    213
CORTEZ, Jayne
  Pissstained Stairs and the
    Monkey Man's Wares BAW:
    178
Corvo, Baron see ROLFE, Fred-
    erick
CORWIN, Norman
  The Rivalry ADC: 80
  Together Tonight ADC: 80
COSTAIN, Thomas B.
  General AN: 47
COSTELLO, Mark
  "Murphy's Xmas" ASF: 117
COSTIGAN, James
  Baby Want a Kiss ADC: 81
  Little Moon of Alban ADC:
    81
COTA, Rodrigo

Dialogo Entre el Amor y Un
　　Viejo DC2: 108
COTTER, Joseph Seamon, Jr.
　　General BAW: 178
COTTER, Joseph Seamon, Sr.
　　General AAPD: 96, 303;
　　　　AAW: 46; BAF: 69;
　　　　BAP: 53; BAW: 179-180;
　　　　LCAB: 42; MBA: 62
　　Caleb, The Degenerate
　　　　BAP: 53; MBA: 62-63
COTTON, Charles
　　"Bacon's Epitaph, Made by
　　　　His Man" PE: 88
　　"To Chloris. Stanzes Irre-
　　　　guliers" PE: 88
COTTON, John
　　General AP: 242-246; Da:
　　　　25-26
COUPERUS, Louis
　　General Po: 596
　　De boeken der kleine zielen,
　　　　die dingen die voorbijgaan
　　　　Po: 596
　　Eline Vere Po: 596
　　Herakles Po: 596
COURTELINE, Maurice
　　Bourbouroche DC2: 108
　　La Petit Malade DC2: 109
COURTHS-MAHLER, Hedwig
　　General Po: 596
COUSIN, Gabriel
　　General Br: 178; Po: 597
　　Le Drame du Fukuryu Maru
　　　　Br: 178
De COUVRAY, Louvet
　　Les Amours du Chevalier de
　　　　Faublas Fi: 50
COUVREUR, Jessie [Tasma]
　　General AL: 174-175
　　Uncle Piper of Piper's Hill
　　　　AL: 174
COVENTRY, Francis
　　The History of Pompey the
　　　　Little ENES2: 55
COVERDALE, Miles [ed.]
　　The Bible Hen: 221
COWAN, Peter
　　General MAP: 144-145
　　"The Empty Street" Wa:
　　　　146
　　Summer MAP: 144
　　The Tins MAP: 144-145
　　"The Tractor" Wa: 146
COWARD, Noel Pierce
　　General Br: 178; MBD:

40-41; MD: 85-86; MDAE:
　　164-165; Mi: 227-228
Ace of Clubs EDC: 124
Bittersweet EDC: 124
Blithe Spirit DC1: 45; EDC:
　　124-125; MBD: 40; MD: 86
Brief Encounter MD: 86
Cavalcade Br: 178; DC1: 45;
　　EDC: 125
A Conversation Piece Br: 179;
　　EDC: 125; MD: 86
Design for Living Br: 179;
　　DC1: 45; EDC: 125; Ma:
　　441; MD: 86
Easy Virtue Br: 179; EDC:
　　125
Fallen Angels EDC: 126
Hay Fever EDC: 126; MBD:
　　40; TMAP: 58
Home Chat EDC: 126
I'll Leave It to You EDC: 126
Island Fling EDC: 126
Look After Lulu EDC: 126;
　　MD: 86
Marquise EDC: 127
Nude with a Violin EDC: 127;
　　MD: 86
On with the Dance EDC: 127
Operette EDC: 127
Peace in Our Time Br: 179;
　　EDC: 127
Point Valaine Br: 179; EDC:
　　127
Pomp and Circumstance ENES1:
　　47
Post-Mortem DC1: 45; EDC:
　　127
Present Laughter Br: 179;
　　DC1: 45; EDC: 127-128;
　　MD: 86
Private Lives Br: 179; DC1:
　　45; EDC: 128; Ma: 441;
　　MBD: 40; MD: 86; Ri2:
　　267
Quadrille EDC: 128-129; MD:
　　86
Queen Was in the Parlor EDC:
　　129
Rat Trap EDC: 129
Relative Values EDC: 129
Sail Away MDAE: 164
Sigh No More EDC: 129
Sirocco EDC: 129
A Song at Twilight Br: 179;
　　EDC: 129
Suite in Three Keys MDAE:

164

This Happy Breed EDC: 129

This Year of Grace EDC: 129-130

Tonight at 8:30 EDC: 130; MD: 86

The Vortex Br: 179; EDC: 130; MD: 86

Waiting in the Wings EDC: 130

Words and Music EDC: 130

The Young Idea Br: 179; EDC: 130

COWDERY, Mae V.
General BAW: 181

COWEN, Ron
Inside Lulu ADC: 81
Summertree ADC: 81; Br: 180

COWLEY, Abraham
General Ba: 39-40; LCAB: 42
"Destinie" PE: 88
"Discourse Concerning Style" Ba: 40
Essays Ba: 40
"Hymn: To Light" PE: 88
"The Muse" PE: 88
"Of Wit" Ba: 39; PE: 88
"On Hope" ICBAP: 27
"On the Queen's Repairing Somerset House" PE: 88
"The Request" PE: 88
"The Resurrection" PE: 88
"To Mr. Hobs" ICBAP: 27
"To Sir William Davenant" ICBAP: 27
"To the Royal Society" ICBAP: 27

COWLEY, Malcolm
General Po: 597
Blue Juniata Ma: 442
Exile's Return Ma: 442
"The Long Voyage" PE: 88
"The Source" PE: 88

COWPER, William
General EC: 64-65; Ma: 443; Me: 165-168
"The Castaway" PE: 88
"The Flatting Mill" PE: 88
"Hark My Soul It Is the Lord" PE: 88
"John Gilpin" EC: 64-65
Memoir EC: 65

Olney Hymns Me: 167
Olney Hymns IX, "The Contrite Heart" PE: 89
Olney Hymns XI, "Jehovah Our Righteousness" PE: 89
The Task Me: 165-168
"To Mary Unwin" PE: 89

COX, Joseph Mason Andrew
General BAF: 69-70

COXE, George Hamilton
General ASF: 117

COXE, Louis Osborne
"Gunner's Mate" PE: 89
"The Middle Passage" ICBAP: 28
_____ and Robert CHAPMAN
Billy Budd ADC: 81

COYLE, J.J.
Ninety Day Mistress ADC: 82

COZZENS, James Gould
General ALL: 64-65; AN: 48; CN: 100-102; LCAB: 42; Ne: 30-31; Po: 597-602; Wo: 66-67
Ask Me Tomorrow CN: 102
By Love Possessed ALL: 65; AN: 47; CN: 102-104; LCAB: 42; Ma: 444; Po: 598, 600-604; Wo: 67
Castaway CN: 104; Po: 604
Cock Pit CN: 104
A Cure of Flesh see The Last Adam
"Eyes to See" ASF: 117
Guard of Honor CN: 104-105; LCAB: 42; Ma: 444-445; Ne: 31; Po: 600-601; Wo: 67
The Just and the Unjust AN: 47; CN: 105; Ne: 31; Po: 600, 604; Wo: 67
The Last Adam [A Cure of Flesh] CN: 105; LCAB: 42; Po: 604; Wo: 67
Men and Brethren AN: 47; CN: 106; Wo: 67
S.S. San Pedro CN: 106
The Son of Perdition CN: 106

CRABBE, George
General EC: 65-66; Me: 174-181
"Abel Keene" PE: 89
"The Borough" EC: 66; Me: 177
"The Library" ICBAP: 28

"Peter Grimes" PE: 89; Me:
175-176
"Procrastination" PE: 89
"Silford Hall" EC: 66; Me:
175-176
Tales in Verse, 1812 Me:
180-181
"The Village" EC: 66; Me:
177, 180; PE: 89
"Widow Goe" (The Parish
Register) ICBAP: 28
"The Workhouse" EC: 66
CRACKANTHORPE, Hubert
General TA: 123
"Anthony Garstin's Courtship"
WaS1: 47
"Battledore and Shuttlecock"
Wa: 147
"A Commonplace Chapter"
WaS1: 47
"A Dead Woman" WaS1: 47
"Etienne Mattou" WaS1: 47
"A Fellside Tragedy" Wa:
147
"Gaston Lalanne's Child"
WaS1: 47
"In Cumberland" WaS1: 47
"Lisa-la-Folle" WaS1: 47
"Modern Melodrama" WaS1:
47
"Profiles" WaS1: 47
"Saint-Pé" WaS1: 47
"The Struggle for Life"
WaS1: 47
"Study in Sentiment" see
"In Cumberland"
"Trevor Perkins" WaS1: 47
"The Turn of the Wheel"
Wa: 147; WaS1: 47
"The White Maize" WaS1: 47
"Yew Trees and Peacocks"
WaS1: 48
Craddock, Charles Egbert see
MURFREE, Mary Noailles
CRADDOCK, Thomas
General AP: 578
CRAFT, William
General LCAB: 42
CRAFTS, William
General Da: 109
The Sea-Serpent ADC: 82
Craigie, Pearl Mary Teresa
see HOBBES, John
Oliver
CRANE, Hart
General ALL: 65-67;

ICBAP: 28; LCAB: 42; Ma:
450-451; MP: 28-29; Po:
605-608
"The Air Plant" PE: 89
"And Yet This Great Wink of
Eternity" PE: 89
"At Melville's Tomb" ICBAP:
28; PE: 89-90
"Atlantis" ICBAP: 28; Ma:
446; PE: 89
"Ave Maria" Ma: 446-447; PE:
90
"Belle Isle" PE: 90
"Black Tambourine" ICBAP:
28; PE: 90; Po: 608
The Bridge ALL: 65; ICBAP:
28; Ma: 447-448; MP: 28-
29; PE: 90-91; Po: 608-
610
"The Bridge of Estador" PE:
91
"The Broken Tower" LCAB:
42-43; Ma: 448-449; PE:
91-92; Po: 611
"C 33" PE: 92
"Cape Hatteras" ICBAP: 28;
Ma: 449; PE: 92; Po: 611
"Chaplinesque" ICBAP: 28;
PE: 92; Po: 611
"Cutty Sark" PE: 92
"The Dance" Ma: 449-450; PE:
92
"Emblems of Conduct" ICBAP:
28; Po: 611-612
"Eternity" PE: 92
"The Fernery" PE: 92
"For the Marriage of Faustus
and Helen" ["For the Mar-
riage of Helen and Faustus"]
PE: 92-93; Po: 612
"The Harbor Dawn" Ma: 450;
PE: 93
"The Hurricane" PE: 93
"Indiana" PE: 93
"Key West" PE: 93; Po: 612
"Lachrymae Christi" ICBAP:
28; PE: 93
"Legend" ICBAP: 29; PE:
94; Po: 612
"The Mango Tree" PE: 94;
Po: 612
"The Mermen" PE: 94
"Moment Fugue" PE: 94
"National Winter Garden" PE:
94
"O Carib Isle!" PE: 94

"Paraphrase" PE: 94; Po: 612

"Passage" ICBAP: 29; PE: 94; Po: 613

"Pastorale" ICBAP: 29

"Possessions" PE: 94

"Poster" ("Voyage") PE: 94

Powhatan's Daughter Ma: 451-452

"Praise for an Urn" PE: 95

"Proem: To Brooklyn Bridge" PE: 95

"Quaker Hill" PE: 95

"Recitative" PE: 95

"Repose of Rivers" PE: 95

"The Return" PE: 95

"The River" Ma: 452; PE: 95; Po: 613

"The Sad Indian" PE: 95

"Southern Cross" PE: 95

"Three Songs" PE: 95-96

"To Zell, Now Bound for Spain" Po: 613

"The Tunnel" PE: 96

"Van Winkle" PE: 96

"Virginia" PE: 96

"Voyages" ICBAP: 29; Ma: 452-453; MP: 29; PE: 96-97; Po: 613-615

"Voyages II" ICBAP: 29

"The Wine Menagerie" ICBAP: 29; PE: 97

CRANE, Jonathan Townley
General ASF: 118

CRANE, Ronald Salmon
General LCAB: 43

CRANE, Stephen
General AF: 83-91; ALL: 67-68; AN: 51-53; ASF: 128-132; Cla: 22-23; Ho: 38-42, 145; ICBAP: 29; LCAB: 43

"An If He Wills, We Must Die" Wa: 147

"The Angel Child" ASF: 118; Wa: 147

"Apache Crossing" ASF: 118

"Art in Kansas City" ASF: 118-119

"Billie Atkins Went to Omaha" ["An Excursion Ticket"] ASF: 119; Wa: 147

"The Black Dog" ASF: 119

The Black Riders Cla: 22

"The Blue Battalions" [War Is Kind, 27] AF: 87; ICBAP: 29

"The Blue Hotel" AF: 86-87, 91; ASF: 119-120; Ma: 454; SFC: 39-40; Wa: 147-149; WaS1: 48

"The Bride Comes to Yellow Sky" ASF: 120-121; Ma: 454-455; SFC: 40; Wa: 149-150

"The Charge of William B. Perkins" SFC: 40; Wa: 150

"Charity, Thou Art a Lie" PE: 97

"The City Urchin and the Chaste Villagers" Wa: 150

"The Clan of No-Name" AF: 88; ASF: 121; SFC: 40; Wa: 150-151

"The Cry of a Huckleberry Pudding" SFC: 40; Wa: 151

"Dan Emmonds" ASF: 121; Wa: 151

"The Dark Brown Dog" ASF: 121

"Death and the Child" ASF: 121; SFC: 41; Wa: 151

"A Desertion" ASF: 121

"A Duel Between an Alarm Clock and a Suicidal Purpose" ASF: 121

"The Duel That Was Not Fought" ASF: 121

"An Episode of War" ASF: 122; SFC: 41; Wa: 151

"An Excursion Ticket" see "Billie Atkins Went to Omaha"

"An Experiment in Luxury" ASF: 122; Wa: 151

"An Experiment in Misery" ASF: 122; Wa: 151-152; WaS1: 48

"An Explosion of Seven Babes" ASF: 122

"The Fight" ASF: 122

"The Five White Mice" ASF: 122; SFC: 41; Wa: 152; WaS1: 48

"Flanagan and His Short Filibustering Adventure" ASF: 122

"Four Men in a Cave" ASF:

122; Wa: 152

George's Mother AF: 87, 91; Ho: 38, 40; Ma: 455; SFC: 41; Wa: 152

"A Ghoul's Accountant" ASF: 122

"God Rest Ye, Merry Gentlemen" ASF: 122; SFC: 41; Wa: 152

"Great Bugs at Onondaga" SFC: 122

"A Grey Sleeve" Wa: 153

"His New Mittens" ASF: 122; Wa: 153

"The Holler Tree" ASF: 123; Wa: 153

"Horses--One Dash" ASF: 123; SFC: 41; Wa: 153

"How the Ocean Was Formed" ASF: 123

"I Was in the Darkness" PE: 97

"In the Country of Rhymers and Writers" ASF: 123

"In the Tenderloin" ASF: 123; Wa: 153

"An Indiana Campaign" Wa: 153

"Just Plain Private Nolan" Wa: 153

"Killing His Bear" ASF: 123; Wa: 153

"The King's Favor" Wa: 153

"A Little Pilgrimage" ["A Little Pilgrim"] ASF: 123; Wa: 153; WaS1: 48

"The Little Regiment" ASF: 123; SFC: 41; Wa: 153

"The Lover and the Telltale" ASF: 123; Wa: 153

"Lynx-Hunting" ASF: 123; Wa: 153

Maggie: A Girl of the Streets AF: 84-85, 87, 89-91; AN: 49; Cla: 22; Ho: 38-40, 145; Ma: 456-457; SFC: 41; Wa: 153-155; WaS1: 48

"Making an Orator" Wa: 155

"A Man Adrift on a Slim Spar" ICBAP: 29; PE: 97

"A Man and-Some Others" ASF: 123; Wa: 155

"The Man in the Storm" ASF: 123-124; Wa: 156

"A Man Said to the Universe" Cla: 24; ICBAP: 29; PE: 97

"Manacles" Wa: 155

"Marines Signalling Under Fire at Guantanamo" SFC: 41; Wa: 155

"The Mesmeric Mountain" ASF: 124; Wa: 156

"The Monster" ASF: 124; Ho: 40; Ma: 457-458; SFC: 41-42; Wa: 156; WaS1: 48-49

"Moonlight on the Snow" ASF: 124; Wa: 157; WaS1: 49

"A Mystery of Heroism" ASF: 124-125; SFC: 42; Wa: 157

"Ol' Bennet and the Indians" ASF: 125

"An Ominous Baby" Wa: 157

"One Dash--Horses" WaS1: 49

"The Open Boat" AF: 83-86, 88; ASF: 125-127; Ma: 458-459; SFC: 42; Wa: 157-159; WaS1: 49

"The Pace of Youth" ASF: 127; Wa: 159

"A Poker Game" ASF: 127

"The Price of the Harness" ASF: 127; SFC: 42; Wa: 159

Private Fleming: His Various Battles Cla: 23; Ho: 40

The Red Badge of Courage AF: 84-91; AN: 49-51; Ho: 39-42, 145; LCAB: 43; Ma: 459-460; Po: 1526

"A Self-Made Man" ASF: 127; Wa: 159

"Shame" ASF: 127; Wa: 159

"Showing Off" Wa: 159

"The Silver Pageant" ASF: 127

"The Siren" Wa: 160

"The Squire's Madness" Wa: 160

"The Stove" ASF: 127

"A Tale of Mere Chance" ASF: 127

"A Tent in Agony" Wa: 160

"The Third Violet" Wa: 160; WaS1: 49

"Three Miraculous Soldiers" ASF: 127; Wa: 160; WaS1: 49

"The Trial, Execution and
Burial of Homer Phelps"
Wa: 160
"Twelve O'Clock" ASF: 127;
Wa: 160; WaS1: 49
"Uncle Jake and the Bell-
Handle" ASF: 128; Wa:
160
"The Upturned Face" ASF:
128; SFC: 42; Wa: 160;
WaS1: 49
"The Veteran" ASF: 128
"Virtue in War" SFC: 43;
Wa: 160
"War Is Kind" ICBAP: 29;
PE: 97
"War Memories" ASF: 128;
Wa: 160
"When Every One Is Panic-
Stricken" ASF: 128
"Why Did the Young Clerk
Swear? Or, The Unsatis-
factory French" ASF:
128; Wa: 160
"The Wise Men: A Detail of
American Life in Mexico"
ASF: 128
CRANMER, Thomas
General SC: 45
The Bible Hen: 221
CRAPSEY, Adelaide
"Niagara" PE: 97
"November Night" PE: 97
"Song: I Make My Shroud,
but No One Knows--"
PE: 98
"Suzanna and the Elders"
PE: 98
"Triad" PE: 98
CRASHAW, Richard
General Ba: 41-42; Ma:
461-463
"An Apology for the Prece-
dent Hymn" PE: 98
"Blessed Be the Paps Which
Thou Hast Sucked" Ma:
461
"Death more misticall and
high" Ba: 41
"Epiphany Hymn" Ba: 41;
PE: 98
"Epithalamium" PE: 98
"The Flaming Heart" PE:
98
"The Glorious Epiphanie of
Our Lord God" PE: 98

"The Holy Nativity" PE: 98
"Hymn in the Nativity" Ba:
42; PE: 98
"Hymn to Saint Teresa" Ma:
461
"A Hymn to the Name and Honor
of the Admirable Saint Ter-
esa" PE: 98
"In Memory of the Vertuous
and Learned Lady Madre de
Teresa..." PE: 98
"In the Glorious Epiphany of
Our Lord God" PE: 98
"The Mother of Sorrows" PE:
98
"Music's Duel" Ba: 41; PE:
99
"On a Prayer Book Sent to
Mrs. M.R." Ba: 41
"On Hope" ICBAP: 29
"On Our Crucified Lord, Naked
and Bloody" PE: 99
"On the Bleeding Wound of Our
Crucified Lord" ["On the
Wounds of Our Crucified
Lord"] ICBAP: 29; PE:
99
"Prayer" PE: 99
"Suppose He Had Been Tabled
at Thy Teates" PE: 99
"The Tear" LCAB: 43; PE:
99
"To the Name Above Every
Name, the Name of Jesus"
ICBAP: 29; PE: 99
"To the Noblest and Best of
Ladies, the Countess of
Denbigh" (1652 and 1653
versions) ICBAP: 30; PE:
99
"Upon the Bleeding Crucifix"
PE: 99
"The Weeper" Ba: 41-42;
ICBAP: 30; Ma: 463-464;
PE: 99-100
CRAVEN, Frank
The First Year ADC: 82
That's Gratitude ADC: 82
CRAWFORD, Charles
General Da: 79
CRAWFORD, Francis Marion
General AN: 53-54; LCAB:
43
"The Dead Smile" Wa: 161
CRAWFORD, Isabella Valancy
General ECL: 53-54

"The Canoe" ECL: 54; PE: 100

"The Dark Stag" ECL: 54; PE: 100

"The Lily Bed" ECL: 54; PE: 100

CRAWFORD, J.W.

The Dregs DC1: 45

CRAWFORD, Robert

The Brass Medallion MBA: 63

CREBILLON, Claude de

Athenian Letters Fi: 50

Les Egarements du coeur et de l'esprit Fi: 50-51; Ke: 53

Les Heureux orphelins Fi: 51

Lettres de la Duchesse de --- au Duc de --- Fi: 51

Lettres de la Marquise de M. au Comte de R. Fi: 51; Ke: 53

The Sofa Fi: 51; Ke: 53

CREBILLON, Prosper

Rhadamiste et Zenobie DC2: 109

CREELEY, Robert White

General ASF: 134; ICBAP: 30; LCAB: 43; MP: 30-31; Po: 615

"The Book" Wa: 161; WaS1: 49

"A Death" Wa: 161

"The Dishonest Mailmen" PE: 100

"The Dress" ASF: 134; Wa: 161

"The Flower" PE: 100

"For Love" Po: 616

"For W.C.W." PE: 100

"Le Fou" PE: 100

"The Grace" WaS1: 49

"I Know a Man" ICBAP: 30; PE: 100

"The Kind of Act Of" PE: 100

"The Language" PE: 100

"Mr. Blue" Wa: 161

"La Noche" PE: 100

"Love Comes Quietly" PE: 101

"Pieces" ICBAP: 30

"The Rhyme" PE: 101

"The Séance" Wa: 161

"They" PE: 101

"The Unsuccessful Husband" Wa: 161; WaS1: 49

"A Wicker Basket" LCAB: 43; MP: 31; PE: 101

"Zero" PE: 101

CREGAN, David

General MDAE: 167

Creighton, Anthony see OS-BORNE, John and Anthony CREIGHTON

CREVECOEUR, Hector St. Jean de

General AP: 247-252; Da: 64-65

Letters from an American farmer AP: 248-252; Da: 65

CREVEL, René

General Po: 616

CRICHTON, Robert

The Secret of Santa Vittoria LCAB: 43

CRIPPS, Arthur Shearly

"Amor Filius Misericordiae" Wa: 161

"Art Thou for Us, or for Our Adversaries?" Wa: 161

"The Black-Faced Lamb" Wa: 161

"A Bowed Head" Wa: 161

"The Burnt Offering" Wa: 161

"Charnwood Forest" Wa: 161

"Crimson and Snow White" Wa: 161

"Death in April" Wa: 162

"Fern Seed" Wa: 162

"In Blue and White" Wa: 162

"The Last Fence" Wa: 162

"The Leper Windows" Wa: 162

"A Lost Saint" Wa: 162

"The Miracle of the Nativity" Wa: 162

"New Light on an Old Champion" Wa: 162

"The Old Boy" Wa: 162

"On the Night of the Nativity" Wa: 162

"The Open Way" Wa: 162

"Our Lady of the Lake" Wa: 162

"The Place of Pilgrimage" Wa: 162

"The Riding of the Red Horse" Wa: 162

"The Scales of Passion" Wa: 162

"Times Go by Turns" Wa: 162

"A Trader's Story" Wa: 162

"Veld Fires" Wa: 162

CRISOLOGO, Mena Pecson
  Codigo Municipal DC2: 109
  Don Clixtofano de la Kota
    DC2: 109
  Maysa a Candidato DC2: 109
  Neneng DC2: 109
  Noble Rivalidad DC2: 109
  Pobre Don Celedonio DC2:
    109

CRISTOFER, Michael
  The Shadow Box ADC: 82

CRITCHELL, Laurence
  "Flesh and Blood" Wa: 163

CRITTENDEN, Jordan
  Unexpected Guests ADC: 82

CRNJANSKI, Miloš
  Migrations Fi: 425

CROCE, Benedetto
  General Po: 616-621
  La Poesia Po: 621

CROCKETT, Samuel Rutherford
  General Ai: 173; TA: 125

CROIX, N. Chrestien des
  Amnon et Thamar DC2: 109

CROMMELYNCK, Fernand
  General MD: 86-87; Po:
    621
  Les Amants Puérils Br: 180
  Chaud et Froid Br: 180
  Le Cocu Magnifique Br: 180
  Dardamelle ou Le Cocu Br:
    180
  Une Femme Qu'a le Coeur
    Trop Petit Br: 180
  La Folle Journée Br: 180
  Tripes d'Or Br: 180

CRONIN, Archibald Joseph
  General Ai: 251
  Grand Canary CN: 106
  The Keys of the Kingdom
    CN: 106

CROS, Charles
  General Po: 621

CROSBY, Harry Herbert
  General ICBAP: 30; Po:
    621-622

CROSBY, John
  General LCAB: 44

Cross, Mary Ann Evans see
  ELIOT, George

CROTHERS, Rachel
  General Lon: 28

As Husbands Go ADC: 83
Expressing Willie ADC: 83
Let Us Be Gay ADC: 83
A Little Journey ADC: 83
Susan and God ADC: 83-84
When Ladies Meet ADC: 84

CROUSE, Russel
  General Br: 180

CROWLEY, Mart
  The Boys in the Band ADC:
    84; Br: 181; TMAP: 55
  A Breeze from the Gulf ADC:
    85

CROWNE, John
  General Bon: 39; Li: 133
  The Married Beau Li: 133
  Sir Courtly Nice Li: 133

CROWNINSHIELD, Frank
  General LCAB: 44

CROXTON
  Play of the Sacrament see
    ANONYMOUS

CRUICKSHANK, Helen Burness
  General Ai: 228

Cruise O'Brien, Conor see
  O'BRIEN, Conor Cruise

CRUMP, Paul
  General BAF: 71
  Burn, Killer, Burn BAF: 71

CRUSE, Harold
  General BAW: 184

CRUTTWELL, Patrick
  General Po: 622

CSAK, Gyula
  Peace Be with the Guilty Br:
    181

CSOKOR, Franz Theodor
  General Po: 622
  Besetztes Gebiet DC2: 109-110
  Buchner's 'Woyzeck' DC2: 110
  Caesars Witwe DC2: 110
  Kalyso DC2: 110
  Pilatus DC2: 110
  3 November 1918 DC2: 110
  Der Verlorene DC2: 110

CUADRA, Jose de la
  General LCAB: 44

CUADRA, Pablo Antonio
  General Br: 181

CUCCI, Frank
  The Ofay Watcher ADC: 85

CUGOANO, Ottobah
  General BALE: 289

CULLEN, Countée Porter
  General AAPD: 98-99; AAW:
    46-47; BAF: 71-72; BAP:

54-55; BAW: 186-190; HR: 69-75; ICBAP: 30; Po: 622-623

"After a Visit" ICBAP: 30

Byword for Evil BAP: 55

"From the Dark Tower" ICBAP: 30; Po: 623

"Icarian Wings" ICBAP: 30

"Incident" PE: 101

One Way to Heaven BAF: 72-73; HR: 72; LCAB: 44

"The Shroud of Color" ICBAP: 30; PE: 101

"Yet Do I Marvel" HR: 70

CUMBERLAND, Richard

General EC: 66-67; Li: 135-136

Arundel ENES2: 55

The Brothers Li: 135

The Choleric Man DC1: 45

Henry ENES2: 55

John de Lancaster ENES2: 55

The Princess of Parma EC: 66

The West Indian DC1: 45; EC: 66; Li: 135-136

CUMMINGS, Edward Estlin

General ALL, 68-70; ICBAP: 31; LCAB: 44; Ma: 466-467; MP: 32-33; Po: 623-629

Actualities: I Po: 629

"All in Green Went My Love Riding" ICBAP: 31; PE: 101; Po: 629

"among these red pieces of" PE: 101

Anthropos, or the Future of Art ADC: 85; Br: 181; PE: 102

"anyone and noone" PE: 102

"Anyone Lived in a Pretty How Town" ICBAP: 31; PE: 102; Po: 629-30

"applaws)" PE: 102

"because you go away i give roses" PE: 102

"Bells" PE: 102

"The Bigness of Cannon" (La Guerre, I) ICBAP: 31; PE: 104; Po: 630

"! blac" PE: 102

"brIght" PE: 102

"Buffalo Bill's Defunct" (Por-traits, VIII) ICBAP: 31; PE: 102-103; Po: 630-631

"Chansons Innocentes I: in just-spring" PE: 103

"darling! because my blood can sing" PE: 103

"death is more than certain" PE: 103

The Enormous Room Ma: 465-466; Po: 631-632

"floatfloafloflf" PE: 103

"48" Po: 636

"goodbye Betty, don't remember me" PE: 103

"the greedy, the people" PE: 103

Him ADC: 85; Br: 181; DC1: 45-46; LCAB: 44; MD: 87; Po: 632

"I" ICBAP: 31; PE: 103; Po: 632

"i will be/ Moving in the Street of her" ICBAP: 31; PE: 104; Po: 632

"if everything happens that can't be done" LCAB: 44; PE: 103

"if up's the word; and a world grows greener" PE: 103

"(IM)C-A-T(MO)" ICBAP: 31; PE: 103; Po: 633

"Impression" PE: 103

"in heavenly realms of hellas" PE: 103

"In Just" ICBAP: 31; Po: 633

"it's/ so damn sweet when any-body--" PE: 104

"Jehovah Buried, Satan Dead" PE: 104

"A kike is the most danger-ous..." PE: 104

"Kind" ICBAP: 31; PE: 104; Po: 633

"Let's, From Some Loud Un-world's Most Rightful Wrong" ICBAP: 31; PE: 104; Po: 633

("Love's Function...") Po: 634

"Luck Means Finding" PE: 104

"a man who had fallen among thieves" PE: 104

"Memorabilia" ICBAP: 31; PE: 104; Po: 634

"The Mind's (i" Po: 634
"mortals)" PE: 104
"my father moved through
    dooms of love" PE: 104
"my sweet old etcetera" PE:
    104
"next to of course god
    america i" PE: 105
"no man, if men are gods"
    PE: 105
"no time ago" PE: 105
"Nobody Loses All the Time"
    PE: 105
"nonsun blob a" PE: 105
Nor Woman see "303"
"The Noster Was a Ship of
    Swank" ICBAP: 32; PE:
    105; Po: 634-635
"o pr" PE: 105
"(one!)" PE: 105; Po: 635
"1x1" PE: 105
"one's not half two" PE:
    105
"the people who" PE: 105
"Pity This Busy Monster,
    Manunkind" ICBAP: 32;
    PE: 105; Po: 635
"Poem" ("it's/ so damn sweet
    when anybody--") Po:
    635
"Poem" ("love's function is
    to fabricate unknownness")
    ICBAP: 32; PE: 106
"Portrait" PE: 106
"raise the shade" PE: 106
"Remarked Robinson Jefferson"
    Po: 636
"r-p-o-p-h-e-s-s-a-g-r" PE:
    106
Santa Claus ADC: 85; Br:
    182; DC1: 46
"Silence" (Poem 40 of 95
    Poems) PE: 106
"since feeling is first" PE:
    106
"the sky was" PE: 106
"so little he is" PE: 106
"Sonnet Entitled How to Run
    the World" ICBAP: 32;
    PE: 106; Po: 636
"Space being (don't forget to
    remember) Curved" PE:
    106
"Sunset" PE: 106
"ta" (Collected Poems, 52)
    PE: 106

"That Which We Who're Alive
    IN SPITE of Mirrors" PE:
    106
"these children singing in a
    stone a" PE: 106; Po: 636
"a thrown a" PE: 107
"305" ICBAP: 32; PE: 101
"303" (Nor Woman) ICBAP:
    32; PE: 101; Po: 634
"249" Po: 637
"275" ICBAP: 32; PE: 101;
    Po: 637
"262" ICBAP: 32; PE: 101;
    Po: 637
"up into the silence of the
    green" PE: 107
"the way to hump a cow is not"
    PE: 107
"what a proud dreamhorse pull-
    ing (smooth-loomingly)
    through" PE: 107
"What If a Much of a Which of
    a Wind" ICBAP: 32; LCAB:
    44; PE: 107; Po: 636
"When Faces Called Flowers
    Float Out of the Ground"
    PE: 107
"When God Lets My Body Be"
    PE: 107
")when what hugs stopping
    earth than silent is" PE:
    107
"when you are silent, shining
    host by guest" PE: 107
"who are these (wraith a cling-
    ing with a wraith)" PE:
    107
"Yes Is a Pleasant Country"
    PE: 107
CUNEY, Waring
    General BAW: 192-193
CUNEY-HARE, Maud
    General BAW: 193-194
    Antar of Araby BAP: 56
CUNNINGHAM, Allan
    General Ai: 121
Cunningham, E.V. [pseud.] see
    FAST, Howard
CUNNINGHAM, James Vincent
    General LCAB: 44; Po: 637
    "The Chase" PE: 107
    "Doctor Drink Epigram #1" PE:
    107
    "Meditation on Statistical Meth-
    od" PE: 107
    "Passion" PE: 107

"Reason and Nature" PE: 108

"Timor Dei" PE: 108

"To the Reader" PE: 108

"To What Strangers, What Welcome" PE: 108

Cunninghame-Graham, R.B. see GRAHAM, Robert Bontine Cunninghame

CUNQUEIRO, Alvaro
General Po: 637-638
Curial e Güelfa Fi: 214
Un hombre que se paracía a Orestes Fi: 214

CUOMO, George
General ASF: 135
"A Part of the Bargain" ASF: 135; Wa: 163
"Sing, Choir of Angels" ASF: 135; Wa: 163
"Sophisticated Lady" Wa: 163

CUPPY, William Jacob
General LCAB: 45

CUREL, François de
General Br: 182; MD: 87-88
L'Ame en Folie MD: 88
The Dance Before the Mirror [La Danse Devant Le Miroir] DC2: 110; MD: 88
La Fille Sauvage Br: 182
The Fossils [Les Fossiles] MD: 88
Lion's Meat [Le Repas du Lion] Br: 182; MD: 88

CURLEY, Daniel
"The Manhunt" ASF: 135

CURTIS, Jean-Louis
General Po: 638-639
Adélaide Po: 639
Chers Corbeaux Po: 639
Cygne Sauvage Po: 639
L'Echelle de soie Po: 639
Forêts de la Nuit Po: 639-640
Haute Ecole Po: 640
Les Juste Causes Po: 640
La Parade Po: 640
Un Saint au néon Po: 641

CURTY, Gene, Nitra SCHARF-MAN, and Chuck STRANG
The Lieutenant ADC: 85

CUSACK, Dymphna
General MAP: 148-149

Custance, Olive see DOUGLAS, Mrs. Alfred

CYNEWULF
"Christ" OMEP: 102-103
"Christ II" PE: 108
"Elene" OMEP: 105
"Fates of the Apostles" OMEP: 106; PE: 108
"Juliana" OMEP: 107

Cyrano de Bergerac, Savinien see de BERGERAC, Savinien Cyrano

CZAJKOWSKI, Michal
"The Battle of Moloczki" Wa: 163
"The Cavalry" Wa: 163
"The Proposal of a Zaporog Cossack" Wa: 163

D

D., H. see DOOLITTLE, Hilda

D., T.
The Bloody Banquet see ANONYMOUS

DABORNE, Robert
General NI: 329-330

DABROWSKA, Maria
General Po: 643
"A Change Came O'er the Scenes of My Dream" Wa: 163
"Consolation" Wa: 163
"Father Philip" Wa: 163
"Little John" Wa: 163
"Lucia from Pukucice" Wa: 163
"Miss Winczewska" Wa: 163
Nights and Days Fi: 425; Ke: 377
"A Piece of Glass" Wa: 164
"The Third Autumn" Wa: 164
"The Triumph of Dionysius" Wa: 164
"A Village Wedding" Wa: 164
"The Wild Plant" Wa: 164

DABROWSKI, Ignacy
"Twilight" Wa: 164

DACRE, Charlotte
Zofloya ENES1: 47

DADELSEN, Jean-Paul de
General Po: 643-644
"Poème pour la naissance de Jean-Louis Hoffet" Po: 643

DAGERMAN, Stig
General Po: 644

DAGHANI, Arnold

The Grave in the Cherry
Orchard Po: 644
DAHL, Roald
"Genesis and Catastrophe"
Wa: 164
DAHLBERG, Edward
General JW: 193-194; Po:
645; Wo: 70-71
Because I Was Flesh Po:
645
Bottom Dogs Wo: 70-71
Do These Bones Live Po:
645
DALE, Peter
"Wildflower" PE: 108
DALEY, Victor
General AL: 178-179
D'ALTON, Louis
General Br: 182
DALY, Augustin
General AD: 109-112; Lon:
57-58
Divorce AD: 110-111
The Last Word ADC: 85
Little Miss Million ADC: 86
Love in Tandem ADC: 86
Love on Crutches ADC: 86
Peg Woffington ADC: 86
Under the Gaslight ADC:
86
DALY, Carroll John
General ASF: 135
DALY, Victor
General BAF: 73; BAW:
195
Not Only War BAW: 195
DAMANI, Charu
General BALE: 289
DAMAS, Léon
"Sur un air de guitare" Wa:
164
DAMICO, James
The Trial of A. Lincoln
ADC: 86
DAMON, Samuel Foster
Genral Po: 646
DANA, Richard Henry, Jr.
General ALL: 70; LCAB:
45
Two Years Before the Mast
ALL: 70; AN: 54; Ma:
468
DANA, Richard Henry, Sr.
"The Little Beach Bird"
ICBAP: 32
"Paul Felton" ASF: 135

DANCOURT, Florent-Carton
Les Bourgeoises a la Mode
DC2: 110
Le Chevalier a la Mode DC2:
110
Colin-Maillard DC2: 110-111
L'Eclipse DC2: 111
DANDRIDGE, Raymond Garfield
General BAW: 196
DANE, Clemence [Winifred ASHTON]
General MD: 88; Mi: 228-
229
A Bill of Divorcement MD: 88
Come of Age MD: 88
Naboth's Vineyard Br: 58
Will Shakespeare MD: 88
DANIEL, Samuel
General ED: 221-222; NI:
283-291, 296, 298-301; SC:
45
"Are They Shadows That We
See?" PE: 108
Cleopatra see The Tragedie
of Cleopatra
A Defense of Rhyme SC: 45
"Delia" ICBAP: 32
"Epistles" SC: 45
Hymen's Triumph NI: 295-296
Musophilus SC: 45
Philotas DC1: 46; NI: 294-
295
The Queen's Arcadia NI: 295
Sonnet II (Delia) "Tears, vows,
and prayers win..." PE:
108
Sonnet 40 (Delia) "Delia!
These Eyes That So Ad-
mireth Thine" PE: 108
Sonnet 45 (Delia) "Care-
Charmer Sleep, Son of the
Sable Night" PE: 108
Tethy's Festival NI: 296
"To the Lady Margaret" PE:
108
The Tragedie of Cleopatra
[Cleopatra] DC1: 46; NI:
291-294
The Vision of the Twelve God-
desses NI: 296
DANIEL, Yuli
Atonement Fi: 425
The Man from Minap Fi: 425
This Is Moscow Speaking Fi:
425
DANIEL, Yuri
"Hands" Wa: 164

DANIELS, Ron
  Swing Low Sweet Steamboat
    MBA: 64
DANILOWSKI, Gustaw
  "Behind the Wall" Wa: 164
Dannenberger, Hermann see
  REGER, Erik
DANNER, Margaret
  General BAW: 197
D'ANNUNZIO, Gabriele
  General Br: 182; MD: 88-
    89; Po: 646-647
  The Child of Pleasure Fi:
    257; Ke: 237
  Crusade of the Innocent [La
    Crociata degli Innocenti]
    DC2: 111; MD: 89
  The Daughter of Jorio Br:
    182
  The Dead City [The City of
    Death; La Citta Morta]
    Br: 182; MD: 89
  Dream of a Morning in Spring
    [Sogno d'un Mattino di
    Primavera] Br: 183
  Dream of an Autumn Sunset
    [Sogno d'un Tramonto
    d'Autunno] Br: 183
  Episcopo and Company Ke:
    237
  Fedra DC2: 111
  The Flame of Life Ke: 237-
    238
  Forse che si forse che no
    Fi: 257
  Francesca da Rimini Br:
    183; MD: 89
  Il fuoco Fi: 257
  La Gioconda Br: 183; MD:
    89
  La Gloria Br: 183
  L'intrus Fi: 257; Ke: 238
  Sogno d'un Mattino di Prima-
    vera see Dream of a
    Morning in Spring
  Sogno d'un Tramonto
    d'Autunno see Dream
    of an Autumn Sunset
  The Triumph of Death Ke:
    238; Ma: 469
  Le vergini delle rocce Fi:
    257-258; Ke: 238
DANQUAH, Joseph Kwame
    Kyeretwie Boakye
  General BALE: 290
DANTE ALIGHIERI

  General LCAB: 45
  The Divine Comedy LCAB: 45;
    Ma: 470-471
  Paradiso LCAB: 45
  Vita Nuova Ma: 471-472
DAPONTE, Lorenzo
  Don Giovanni DC2: 111
DARIEN, George
  Biribi Fi: 51
DARIO, Rubén
  General Br: 183; LCAB: 45;
    Ma: 473-474; Po: 647-652
  Azul ... Ma: 473; Po: 652-
    653
  Emelina Po: 653
  Responso a Verlaine Po: 653
  Sinfonía en Gris Mayor Po:
    653
DARK, Eleanor
  General MAP: 151-152
  The Timeless Land MAP: 152
  "Urgent Call" WaS1: 49
  "Water in Moko Creek" WaS1:
    50
  "Wheels" WaS1: 50
  "Wind" WaS1: 50
DARLEY, George
  "Nepenthe" PE: 108
Darmesteter, Mary James see
  DUCLAUX, Mary
DARROW, Clarence
  General ASF: 135
DARTHES, Camilo
  General Br: 183
  _____ and Carlos S. DAMEL
  Los Chicos Crecen Br: 183
  La Hermana Josefina Br: 183
DARWIN, Charles
  General VP: 30-32
  The Voyage of the "Beagle"
    Ma: 475
DARYAN, Zarzant
  May Ke: 377
DAS, Manoj
  "The Crocodile's Lady" Wa:
    164
  "Farewell to the Ghost" Wa:
    165
  "The Last I Heard of Them"
    Wa: 165
  "A Letter from the Last Spring"
    Wa: 165
  "Mystery of the Missing Cap"
    Wa: 165
  "A Song for Sunday" Wa:
    165

"The Story of Baba Chakrad-
hari" Wa: 165
"Tragedy" Wa: 165
"A Trip into the Jungle"
Wa: 165
DATHORNE, Oscar Ronald
General WIL: 33
Dumplings in the Soup WIL:
33
The Scholar Man WIL: 33-34
DAUDET, Alphonse
L'Evangéliste Fi: 51; Ke:
53
"Father Gaucher's Elixir"
SFC: 43; Wa: 165
Fromont jeune et Risler aîné
Fi: 51; Ke: 53
"The Girl in Arles" SFC: 43;
Wa: 165
L'Immortel Fi: 51; Ke: 53
Jack Ke: 53
Kings in Exile Fi: 51-52;
Ke: 53; Ma: 476
The Little Good-for-Nothing
Ke: 54
La Lutte Pour La Vie DC2:
111
The Nabab Fi: 52; Ke: 54
Numa Roumestan Fi: 52;
Ke: 54
La Petite paroisse Fi: 52;
Ke: 54
"Poet Mistral" Wa: 165
Port Tarascon Fi: 52; Ke:
54
Rose et Ninette Ke: 54
Sapho [Sappho] Fi: 52; Ke:
54; Ma: 476
Tartarin of Tarascon Ke:
54-55; Ma: 476
Tartarin Over the Alps Fi:
52; Ke: 55
Le Tresor d'Arlatan Fi: 52
DAUDET, Léon
General Po: 653
DAUTHENDEY, Max
General Po: 653-654
"Das Abendrot zu Seta"
Wa: 165
"Auf dem Weg zu den
Eulenkäfigen" Wa: 165
"Die Segelboote von Yabase
im Abend heimkehren
sehen" Wa: 165
"Der unbeerdigte Vater"
Wa: 165

"Unter den Totentürmen" Wa:
165
"Zur Stunde der Maus" Wa:
166
DAVALOS, Marcelino
General Br: 183
DAVENANT, Sir William
General Ba: 43; ED: 223;
Li: 138-139; LJCD: 194-
197, 201, 208-209
The Cruel Brother DC1: 46
The First Day's Entertainment
at Rutland House DC1: 47;
LJCD: 200
Macbeth Bon: 40; LJCD:
199, 208
The Man's the Master DC1: 47;
Li: 139; LJCD: 201
The Platonic Lovers Bon: 40;
LJCD: 198-199
The Playhouse to Be Let DC1:
47; Li: 139
The Rivals EDC: 130; Li:
139
The Siege of Rhodes EDC:
131; Li: 139; LJCD: 197-
198
The Tempest; or, The En-
chanted Island LJCD: 200,
208-209
"To the Queen, Entertained at
Night by the Countess of
Anglesey" PE: 109
The Wits EDC: 131; LJCD:
198
DAVENPORT, Guy
General ASF: 136
"The Dawn in Erewhon" ASF:
136
"Tatlin!" ASF: 136
DAVENPORT, Robert
General LJCD: 232-234
The City-Night-Cap DC1: 47
King John and Matilda DC1:
47
A New Tricke to Cheat the
Devil DC1: 47
DAVIDSON, Donald
General Po: 654-655
"The Ninth Part of Speech"
PE: 109
Poems 1922-1961 Po: 655
"The Tall Men" PE: 109
"A Touch of Snow" ICBAP:
32; Po: 655
DAVIDSON, Frank Dalby

"Blood Will Tell" Wa: 166
"Fathers and Sons" Wa: 166
"Lady with the Scar" Wa: 166
"A Letter from Colleen" Wa: 166
"Nobody's Kelpie" Wa: 166
"Return to the Hunter" Wa: 166
"The Road to Yesterday" Wa: 166
"Tank-Sinkers" Wa: 166
"The Woman at the Mill" Wa: 166
"The Yarns Men Tell" Wa: 166

DAVIDSON, John
General Ai: 166; TA: 126-127
The Triumph of Mammon Br: 184

DAVIDSON, Norbert R., Jr.
General MBA: 67-68
Contraband MBA: 68
El Haji Malik ADC: 86; BAP: 56; MBA: 68

DAVIE, Donald Alfred
General ICBAP: 33; Po: 655-656
"Dorset" PE: 109
"The Fountain" ICBAP: 33
"Heigh-ho on a Winter Afternoon" PE: 109
"Hypochondriac Logic" PE: 109
"In the Stopping Train" PE: 109
"North Dublin" PE: 109
"To a Brother in the Mystery" PE: 109
"A Winter Talent" PE: 109

DAVIE, Elspeth
General Ai: 308

DAVIES, Hubert Henry
General Br: 184

DAVIES, John of Kidwelly
General ERP: 120

DAVIES, Kitchener
Stones of Emptiness DC1: 47

DAVIES, Robertson
General Po: 656
A Mixture of Frailties Po: 656

DAVIES, Samuel

General AP: 254-255; Da: 26-27

DAVIES, Sir John
General SC: 46
Nosce Teipsum ICBAP: 33; SC: 46
Orchestra ICBAP: 33; SC: 46

DAVIES, Stanley Jacob
General BALE: 290

DAVIES, William Henry
General Po: 656-657; TA: 128
"The Beauty Haunts Me Heart and Soul" PE: 109
"The Moon" PE: 109
"The Villain" PE: 109

Daviot, Gordon see MACKINTOSH, Elizabeth

DAVIS, Al
Black Sunlight MBA: 64

DAVIS, Arthur Hoey [Steele RUDD]
General AL: 183-185; Po: 657
"Starting the Selection" Wa: 656

DAVIS, Arthur P.
General BAF: 74

DAVIS, Buster
Doctor Jazz MBA: 64

DAVIS, Catherine
"Beware, Old Scrounger" PE: 109
"The Last Step" PE: 109
"The Leaves" PE: 110
"The Narrow House" PE: 110

DAVIS, Daniel Webster
General AAPD: 59; BAW: 201-202; LCAB: 45

DAVIS, Frank Marshall
General AAPD: 100; BAW: 203
Black Man's Verse BAW: 203
47th Street: Poems BAW: 203

DAVIS, George B.
General BAF: 74; BAW: 203
Coming Home BAF: 75; BAW: 203

DAVIS, Harold Lenoir
General AN: 55; ASF: 136; Po: 657
"Extra Gang" WaS1: 50
"Homestead Orchard" WaS1: 50

Honey in the Horn Po: 657-658

"The Kettle of Fire" WaS1: 50

"Old Man Isbell's Wife" WaS1: 50

"Open Winter" ASF: 136; WaS1: 50

"Shiloh's Waters" WaS1: 50

DAVIS, John
General AP: 257-258; Da: 109

DAVIS, Julia
The Anvil Br: 184

DAVIS, Nolan
General BAF: 75; BAW: 206
Six Black Horses BAF: 76

DAVIS, Ossie
General AAPD: 358; BAP: 58; BAW: 208-209; MBA: 65
Alice in Wonder [The Big Deal] BAP: 58-59; Br: 184; MBA: 65
Cotton Comes to Harlem MBA: 66-67
Countdown at Kusini MBA: 66-67
Curtain Call Mr. Aldridge, Sir MBA: 65
Last Dance for Sybil MBA: 65
Purlie Victorious AAPD: 358; ADC: 86-87; BAP: 59-60; BAW: 209; Br: 184; MBA: 65-66
School Teacher MBA: 66
_____, Peter UDELL, Philip ROSE, and Gary GELD
Purlie ADC: 87; BAP: 60; MBA: 66-67

DAVIS, Owen
General Br: 185; Lon: 58; MD: 89; Po: 658
The Donovan Affair ADC: 87
The Great Gatsby ADC: 87
Icebound Br: 185
The Insect Comedy ADC: 87
Jezebel ADC: 87
Just to Remind You ADC: 88
Mr. and Mrs. North ADC: 88

The Nervous Wreck ADC: 88
No Way Out ADC: 88; MD: 89
Sandalwood ADC: 88
Saturday Night ADC: 88
Sinners ADC: 88
The Snark Was a Boojum ADC: 88
_____ and Donald DAVIS
Ethan Frome ADC: 88-89; MD: 89
The Good Earth ADC: 89

DAVIS, Rebecca Harding
General AN: 55; ASF: 136-137
"John Lamar" ASF: 136
"Life in the Iron-Mills" ASF: 136
Margaret Howth AN: 55
"The Wife's Story" ASF: 136

DAVIS, Richard Harding
General AN: 55; APC: 101-102; ASF: 137; Po: 658
A Derelict Po: 658-659
"The Deserter" ASF: 137; WaS1: 50
"The Nature Faker" ASF: 137
Soldiers of Fortune Po: 659

DAVIS, Russell F.
Anything for a Friend BAF: 76

DAVIS, Thomas
General Po: 659

DAVISON, Frank Dalby
General MAP: 155-157
The White Thorntree MAP: 155-156

Davison, Lawrence H. [pseud.]
see LAWRENCE, David Herbert

DAVYS, Mary
The Lady's Tale ENES1: 47

DAWE, Bruce
General Po: 659

DAWES, Neville
General WIL: 34
The Last Enchantment WIL: 34-35

DAWKINS, Cecil
Displaced Person ADC: 89

DAY, Angel [translator]
Daphnis and Chloe by Longus ERP: 121

DAY, Clarence
General LCAB: 45-46

Life with Father LCAB: 45-
  46
DAY, Frank Parker
  Rockhound Po: 659-660
DAY, Holman
  General Po: 660
DAY, John
  General Log: 256-261
  The Blind Beggar of Bedinal
    Green DC1: 47
  The Isle of Gulls DC1: 47
  Law Tricks DC1: 48
  The Parliament of Bees DC1:
    48
  The Travails of Three Eng-
    lish Brothers see
    ANONYMOUS
DAY, Thomas
  General Be: 92-93
  Sanford and Merton Be: 92-
    93; EN: 29
DAY-LEWIS, Cecil
  General Po: 660
  "Children Look Down Upon
    the Morning-Gray" PE: 110
  "Come Live with Me and Be
    My Love" PE: 110
  "From Feathers to Iron" PE:
    110
  "The Image" PE: 110
  "An Italian Visit" PE: 110
  "The Magnetic Mountain" PE:
    110
  "Rest from Loving and Be
    Living" PE: 110
  "A Time to Dance" PE: 110
  "Transitional Poem" PE: 110
  "Word Over All" PE: 110
DAZAI OSAMU
  "Admonition" Wa: 166
  "Appeal to the Authorities"
    WaS1: 50
  "Bankruptcy" Wa: 166
  "Bottomless Abyss" Wa: 166
  "Cherries" Wa: 166
  "The Crackling Mountain" Wa:
    166
  "Family Happiness" Wa: 167
  "The Father" Wa: 167
  "Female Bandits" Wa: 167
  "Forsaking the Old Woman"
    Wa: 167
  "Das Gemeine" Wa: 167
  "The Great Red Drum" Wa:
    167
  "Great Strength" Wa: 167

"He Is Not What He Was" Wa:
  167
"The Indictment" Wa: 167
"Landlord for a Generation"
  Wa: 167
"Mermaid Sea" Wa: 167
"Metamorphosis" Wa: 167
"Monkey-Face Lad" Wa: 167
"Monkey Island" Wa: 167
"The Monkey's Grave" Wa:
  167
"Mount Yoshino" Wa: 167
"Obligation" Wa: 167
"Osan" Wa: 167
"The Refined Man" Wa: 168
"River of the Naked" Wa:
  168
"Romanesque" Wa: 168
"Run Melos" Wa: 168
"The Split-Tongue Sparrow"
  Wa: 168
"Stubborn in Poverty" Wa:
  168
"Those Two and Their Pathetic
  Mother" Wa: 168
"Villon's Wife" Wa: 168
D'AZEGLIO, Massimo
  Ettore Fieramosca Ke: 238
  Niccolò de' Lapi Ke: 238
D'COSTA, Jean
  Escape to Last Man Peak WIL:
    32
  Sprat Morrison WIL: 32
DEAKIN, Alfred
  General AL: 188-189
DEAN, Peyton
  Hamlet Jones MBA: 68-69
DEAN, Phillip Hayes
  General BAP: 61; MBA: 69
  American Night Cry: A Trilogy
    MBA: 69
  Every Night When the Sun Goes
    Down ADC: 89; MBA: 69-
    70
  Freeman ADC: 89; BAP: 61;
    MBA: 69-70
  The Owl Killer MBA: 69
  The Sty of the Blind Pig
    ADC: 89; BAP: 61-62;
    BAW: 210; MBA: 69-70
  This Bird of Dawning Singeth
    All Night Long BAP: 62
DeANDA, Peter
  Ladies in Waiting BAP: 60
De Andrade, Mario see
  ANDRADE, Mario de

De Beauvoir, Simone see
    BEAUVOIR, Simone de
De BOISSIERE, Ralph
    General WIL: 35
De BOOS, Charles
    Fifty Years Ago AL: 192
De BOSIS, Lauro
    General Po: 660
    Icaro LCAB: 21
DEBROSSES, Nelson
    General LCAB: 46
DeCAMP, Lyon Sprague
    General LCAB: 46
De Castro, Jose Maria Ferreira
    see CASTRO, Ferreira de
De Chardin, Pierre Teilhard
    see TEILHARD DE
    CHARDIN, Pierre
DECKER, Thomas
    General BALE: 290
DEE, John
    General SC: 46
DEE, Ruby
    General MBA: 70-71
DEEVY, Teresa
    General Br: 185
    In Search of Valour DC1:
        48
    Kati Roche DC1: 48
    The King of Spain's Daughter
        DC1: 48
    Strange Birth DC1: 48
    The Wild Goose DC1: 48
DEFILIPPIS-NOVOA, Francisco
    General Br: 185
De FILIPPO, Eduardo
    General Br: 185; MD: 89-
        90; Po: 661-662
    Big Magic [La Grande Magia]
        MD: 90
    The Boss Br: 185
    Christmas in the Cupiello
        Home [Natale in Case Cupi-
        ello] Br: 185
    Fear Number One [La Paura
        Numero Uno] MD: 90
    Filumena Maturano Br: 186
    La Grande Magia see Big
        Magic
    The Mayor of the Sanita
        [Il Sindaco del Rione
        Sanita] Br: 186
    Napoli Milionaria Br: 186
    Natale in Case Cupiello see
        Christmas in the Cupiello
        Home

La Paura Numero Uno see
    Fear Number One
Sabato, Domenica e Lumedi
    Br: 186
Il Sindaco del Rione Sanita see
    The Mayor of the Sanita
DEFOE, Daniel
    General Be: 102-110; Du: 31-
        33; LCAB: 46
    Captain Avery ENES2: 55
    Captain Singleton Be: 108;
        EN: 30; ENE: 63; ENES1:
        48; ENES2: 55-56; Ma:
        477
    The History of Colonel Jacque
        [The History of Colonel
        Jack; Colonel Jacque] Be:
        105; ENE: 64; ENES1: 48;
        ENES2: 56; Ma: 477-478
    A Journal of the Plague Year
        Be: 102, 105, 110; ENES1:
        48; ENES2: 56; Ma: 478
    The Memoirs of a Cavalier Be:
        108; ENES1: 49; ENES2:
        56
    Moll Flanders Be: 102-110;
        Du: 28-29; EN: 30; ENE:
        64-65; ENES1: 49; ENES2:
        56-57; LCAB: 46; Ma: 479-
        480
    Robinson Crusoe Be: 102-104,
        106-110; Du: 29-30; EN:
        30-32; ENE: 65-67; ENES1:
        50; ENES2: 57-58; LCAB:
        46-47; Ma: 480-481
    Roxana Be: 103-106; Du: 31;
        ENE: 67; ENES1: 51;
        ENES2: 58; Ma: 481-482
    A Tour Thro' the Whole Island
        of Great Britain Ma: 482-
        483
De FOREST, John William
    General AF: 94-96; AN: 55-
        56; ASF: 137-138; Cla:
        107; Ho: 42-43; LCAB: 47
    "A Gentleman of the Old School"
        ASF: 137
    Honest John Vane AF: 95;
        Cla: 107; Ho: 43
    Kate Beaumont AF: 95; AN:
        55; Cla: 107; Ho: 43
    Miss Ravenal's Conversion AF:
        94-96; AN: 55; Cla: 107;
        Ho: 42-43; LCAB: 47
    Playing the Mischief AF: 95;
        Cla: 107

A Union Officer in the Recon-
struction AF: 94; Cla:
107
A Volunteer's Adventures AF:
96; Cla: 107
Witching Times AF: 95; Ho:
43
"Yesebel" ASF: 137
DEGENHARDT, Franz Josef
General Po: 662
De Ghelderode, Michel see
GHELDERODE, Michel de
De Gourmant, Remy see
GOURMANT, Remy de
De GRAFT, Joseph Coleman
General BALE: 291
"Two Views from a Window"
BALE: 291
Visitor from the Past BALE:
291
De GRAFT-HANSON, J.O.
General BALE: 291
DeGRAZIA, Edward
Americans ADC: 90
DEGUY, Michel
General Po: 662-663
De HALES, Thomas
"Luve-Ron" OMEP: 384
DEHMEL, Richard
General Po: 663
DEI-ANANG, K.K.
General BALE: 291
DEI-ANANG, Michael Francis
General BALE: 292
DEKKER, Thomas
General ED: 226-227; ERP:
127-131; Hen: 113-114;
Log: 4-9, 18-19, 41-48;
TSD: 45-47
Britannia's Honour Log: 17-
18
Cupid and Psyche DC1: 48;
Log: 47
The Famous History of Sir
Thomas Wyatt see Sir
Thomas Wyatt
The Gull's Hornbook Ma:
484
The Honest Whore DC1: 48-
49; EDC: 131; Log: 11-
12, 48; Ma: 484-485;
TSD: 45-46
If It Be Not Good the Devil
Is in It DC1: 49; Log:
16, 47
If This Be Not a Good Play

TSD: 45
Keep the Widow Waking EDC:
131
London's Tempe, or the Field
of Happiness Log: 17-18
The Magnificent Entertainment
Given to King James Log:
17, 48
Match Me in London Log: 16
News from Hell ERP: 128
The Noble Soldier DC1: 49
Old Fortunatus DC1: 49;
EDC: 131-132; Log: 12-13,
47; Ma: 485; TSD: 45
Satiromastix; or The Untrussing
of the Humorous Poet DC1:
49; Log: 13-14, 47; Ma:
485-486
The Shoemaker's Holiday; or,
The Gentle Craft DC1:
49-50; EDC: 132; LCAB:
47; Log: 9-11, 46-48; Ma:
486-487; TSD: 45-46
Sir Thomas Wyatt [The Famous
History of Sir Thomas Wyatt]
DC1: 50; ED: 226-227;
Log: 47
The Sun's Darling Log: 17,
47; LJCD: 137
Troia Nova Triumphans Log:
17-18, 48
Twelfth Night TSD: 46
The Welsh Ambassador DC1:
50; Log: 48
The Whore of Babylon DC1:
50; EDC: 132; Log: 16, 47;
TSD: 46
The Wonderful Year ERP:
129, 131; Hen: 112
_____, Henry CHETTLE, and
William HAUGHTON
Patient Grissil DC1: 49; EDC:
133; Log: 14, 46
_____ and John FORD
The Witch of Edmonton see
also FORD, John, Thomas
DEKKER, and William ROW-
LEY EDC: 133; Log: 14-
15, 47; TSD: 45-46
_____ and Philip MASSINGER
The Virgin Martyr Log: 15;
TSD: 46
_____ and Thomas MIDDLETON
The Roaring Girl, or Moll Cut-
Purse see MIDDLETON,
Thomas and Thomas DEKKER

_____ and John WEBSTER
Northward Ho Log: 17, 47;
TSD: 46
Westward Ho Log: 17, 47-48;
TSD: 46
De la HOUSSAYE, Sidonie
"The Adventures of Fran-
çoise and Suzanne" WaS1:
50
"Alix de Morainville" WaS1:
50
"The Young Aunt with White
Hair" WaS1: 51
De la MARE, Walter
General EP: 83-87; LCAB:
47; Ma: 488-489; Po:
663-665
At First Sight ENES1: 51
"The Ghost" PE: 110
"The Guardian" Wa: 168
Henry Brocken ENES1: 51;
ENES2: 58
"The Horseman" PE: 110
"In the Forest" Wa: 168
"The Listeners" EP: 85-87;
ICBAP: 33; Ma: 488;
PE: 110-111; Po: 665-666
"The Looking Glass" Wa:
168
"Maerchen" PE: 111
"Maria-Fly" Wa: 168
Memoirs of a Midget ENES1:
51; ENES2: 59; Po: 666
"The Mocking Fairy" PE:
111
"Nostalgia" PE: 111
"Out of the Deep" SFC:
43; Wa: 168
"A Recluse" SFC: 43; Wa:
168
The Return ENES1: 51;
ENES2: 59
"The Riddle" Wa: 168
"Seaton's Aunt" Wa: 168
The Three Mulla-Mulgars
ENES1: 51
"The Traveller" EP: 87
DELANEY, Shelagh
General Br: 186; MBD:
41; MD: 90; MDAE:
171-172
The Lion in Love Br: 186;
EDC: 133; MD: 90;
MDAE: 172
A Taste of Honey Br: 186-
187; DC1: 50-51; EDC:

133-134; MBD: 41; MD: 90;
MDAE: 171-172; Po: 666;
TMBP: 104, 253
DELANY, Martin R.
General BAF: 76-77; BAW:
215-217
Blake BAF: 76-78
DELANY, Samuel R.
General BAF: 78-79; BAW:
218
Babel-17 BAF: 79
The Ballad of Beta-2 BAF:
79
Captives of the Flame BAF:
79
City of a Thousand Suns BAF:
79
Dhalgren BAF: 79-80
Driftglass BAF: 80
The Einstein Intersection BAF:
79-80
Empire Star BAF: 80
The Fall of the Towers BAF:
80
The Jewels of Aptor BAF: 80
Nova BAF: 80
The Tides of Lust BAF: 80;
BAW: 218
The Towers of Toron BAF:
80
Triton BAF: 80
De la ROCHE, Mazo [Mazo ROCHE]
"A Boy in the House" WaS1:
51
"Buried Treasure" WaS1: 51
"D'Ye Ken John Peel?" WaS1:
51
"The Son of a Miser: How Noel
Caron of St. Loo Proved
That He Was No Pinch-
Penny" WaS1: 51
"The Spirit of the Dance" WaS1:
51
"The Thief of St. Loo: An
Incident in the Life of An-
toine O'Neill, Honest Man"
WaS1: 51
De la Serna, Ramón see GOMEZ
DE LA SERNA, Ramón
De la Tailhede, Raymond see
LA TAILHEDE, Raymond de
De la Tour du Pin, Patrice see
LA TOUR DU PIN, Patrice
de
DELBLANC, Sven
Homunculus Fi: 294

DELEDDA, Grazia
  General Po: 667
  Anime oneste Ke: 241-242
  Ashes Ke: 242
  Elias Portolu Ke: 242
  The Mother [Le Madre] Ma:
    490; Po: 667
  Vecchio della montagna Ke:
    242
DELIBES, Miguel
  General Po: 667
  El camino Fi: 214; Ke:
    203; Po: 667-668
  Diary of a Hunter Fi: 214
  Five Hours with Mario Fi:
    214
  Las guerras de nuestros
    antepasados Fi: 214
  Long Is the Cypress' Shadow
    Fi: 214
  My Adored Son, Sisí Fi:
    214
  Parable of the Drowning Man
    Fi: 214
  El príncipe destronado Fi:
    214-215
  Las ratas Fi: 215; Po:
    668
  Still It Is Day Fi: 215
DELICADO, Francisco
  La lozana andaluza Fi:
    215, 264
De LISSER, Herbert G.
  General WIL: 35-36
  Arawak Girl WIL: 37
  The Cup and the Lip WIL:
    37
  Jane's Career: A Story of
    Jamaica [Jane: A Story
    of Jamaica] WIL: 36
  Morgan's Daughter WIL:
    37
  Psyche WIL: 37
  Under the Sun: A Jamaican
    Comedy WIL: 37
  The White Witch of Rosehall
    WIL: 37
DELL, Floyd
  General AN: 56; ASF:
    138; LCAB: 47; Po:
    668-669; Wo: 74-75
  "Jessica Screams" ASF:
    138; Po: 669
  Moon-Calf Po: 669
DELLA FAILLE, Pierre
  General Po: 670

DELLA PORTA, Giambattista
  Lo Astrologo DC2: 111
  Gli Duoi Fratelli Rivali DC2:
    111-112
  La Sorella DC2: 112
DELONEY, Thomas
  General ERP: 135-147; Hen:
    169; Ma: 491; SC: 47
  The Gentle Craft ENES2: 59;
    ERP: 135-147
  Jack of Newbury ENES1: 52;
    ENES2: 59; ERP: 135-147
  Thomas of Reading ENES1:
    52; ENES2: 59; ERP: 135-
    147
DEL RAY, Lester
  General LCAB: 47
De MATTEO, Donna
  Dear Mr. G ADC: 90
DEMBY, William
  General AAF: 71-72; AAW:
    48; BAF: 81-82; BAW:
    219
  Beetlecreek AAF: 71-72;
    BAF: 81-82; LCAB: 48;
    Po: 670
  The Catacombs AAF: 71-72;
    BAF: 81-82; Po: 670
De MILLE, James
  General ECL: 125-126
DEMING, Philander
  "John's Trial" Wa: 169
De Montherlant, Henry see
    MONTHERLANT, Henry de
De MORGAN, William Frend
  General TA: 129
  Alice-For-Short ENES1: 52
DEMPSTER, Roland Tombekai
  General BALE: 292
DENEVI, Marco
  General Po: 670
DENHAM, John
  General Ba: 43-44; LJCD:
    234-235
  Cooper's Hill Ba: 43-44;
    ICBAP: 33; PE: 111
DENIEHY, Daniel
  General AL: 194
DENKER, Henry
  A Case of Libel ADC: 90
  A Far Country ADC: 90
  The Headhunters ADC: 90
  Something Old, Something New
    ADC: 90
  Venus at Large ADC: 91
  What Did We Do Wrong? ADC:

91
_____ and Ralph BERKEY
    Time Limit ADC: 91
DENNEY, Reuel
    "The Rememberer" PE: 111
DENNIE, Joseph
    General AP: 259-261; Da:
        110
DENNIS, Doris L.
    Outcast MBA: 71
DENNIS, John
    General EC: 67; Li: 141
    Appius and Virginia DC1:
        51; Li: 141
    Iphigenia DC1: 51; Li:
        141
    Rinaldo and Armida Li: 141
DENNIS, Nigel Forbes
    General Br: 187; CFAE:
        121; MDAE: 174-175;
        Sch: 63
    Boys and Girls Come Out to
        Play CN: 107
    Cards of Identity Br: 187;
        CFAE: 121; CN: 107;
        DC1: 51; ENE: 67;
        LCAB: 48
    A House in Order CN: 107
    The Making of Moo Br: 187;
        DC1: 51
DENON, Vivant
    Point de Lendemain Fi: 52;
        Ke: 55
DENT, Arthur
    The Plaine Mans Path-Way
        to Heaven Hen: 29
DENT, Lester
    General ASF: 138
DENT, Peter
    "Movement (For F.C.)" PE:
        111
De PEDROLO, Manuel
    Cruma Br: 187
    Humans and No [Homes i
        No] Br: 187
DeQUINCEY, Thomas
    General Fog: 32-33
    Confessions of an English
        Opium Eater Ma: 492-
        493
DERLETH, August
    General Po: 671
De ROBERTO, Federico
    L'illusione Ke: 250
    I vicere Fi: 264; Ke:
        250

D'ERRICO, Ezio
    The Forest [La Foresta] Br:
        187
DERRIDA, Jacques
    Glas Fi: 52
DERWOOD, Gene
    General Po: 671
DERY, Tibor
    Mr. G.A. in X [Herr G.A. in
        X] Fi: 425; Ke: 377; Po:
        671
DESAINLIENS, Claude [Claudius
        HOLYBAND] [translator]
    Arnalt and Lucenda by Diego
        de SAN PEDRO ERP: 147
DESCHEVAUX-DUMESNIL, Suzanne
    "F---" WaS1: 51
Des Forêts, Louis-René see
        FORETS, Louis René des
DESHPANDE, Kusumavati
    "Wet and Shiny" Wa: 169
DESNICA, Vladan
    "Florjanović" WaS1: 51
    "Oko" WaS1: 51
    Summer Holidays in Winter
        [Summer Vacation During the
        Winter] Ke: 377; WaS1: 51
DESNOS, Robert
    General Po: 672
    Devil pour devil Fi: 52
    La Liberté ou l'amour Fi: 52
    Le Paysage Po: 672
DESROSIERS, Léo-Paul
    General Po: 672
Destouches, Louis Ferdinand see
        CELINE, Louis-Ferdinand
DETT, Robert Nathaniel
    General BAW: 221
De Unamuno, Miguel see UNA-
        MUNO, Miguel de
DEUTSCH, Babette
    "Visit to the Zoo" PE: 111
DEVAL, Jacques
    General Br: 188
    L'Age de Juliette EDC: 134
    Barricou EDC: 134
    Bathsheba EDC: 134
    La Beauté du Diable EDC:
        134
    Dans sa Candeur Naîve see
        Her Cardboard Lover
    Errand for Bernice EDC: 134
    Etienne EDC: 134
    Her Cardboard Lover [Dans sa
        Candeur Naîve] EDC: 135
    Il Etait Une Gare EDC: 135

Lorelei EDC: 135
Mademoiselle EDC: 135
Marriage Story EDC: 135
Oh, Brother! EDC: 135
Ombre Chère EDC: 135
Le Onzième Commandement
EDC: 135
Prayer for the Living [Prière
Pour les Vivantes] EDC:
135
La Rose de Septembre EDC:
136
Tovaritch EDC: 136
Ventôse EDC: 136
_____ and Lorenzo SEMPLE,
Jr.
Tonight in Samarkand [Ce
Soir à Samarcande] EDC:
136
DEVANEY, James
General MAP: 158; Po:
673
DEVAULX, Noël
General Po: 673
De VEAUX, Alex
General MBA: 71
de VERE, Edward, Earl of Ox-
ford
General SC: 47
DEVINE, Jerry
Children of the Wind ADC:
91
DEVLIN, Denis
General Po: 673-674
DeVOTO, Bernard
General APC: 73-74; LCAB:
48; Po: 674
DeVRIES, Peter
General ASF: 138; CFAE:
124; CN: 107; LCAB:
48; Po: 674-675
The Blood of the Lamb CN:
107; Ma: 494
Comfort Me with Apples CN:
108; Ma: 494
Let Me Count the Ways CN:
108; Ma: 494
The Mackerel Plaza CN:
108; LCAB: 48; Ma: 494-
495
Reuben, Reuben CN: 108;
Ma: 495
The Tents of Wickedness
CN: 108; Ma: 495
Through the Fields of Clover
CN: 108; Ma: 495

The Tunnel of Love CN: 108;
Ma: 495-496
The Vale of Laughter CN:
108; Ma: 496
DEWEY, John
General APC: 74; LCAB: 48
The Theory of Inquiry LCAB:
49
DEWHURST, Keith
General MDAE: 176
DEWS, William
Side Show ADC: 91
DHERY, Robert
La Grosse Valise Br: 188
La Plume de Ma Tante Br:
188
DHLOMO, Herbert Isaac Ernest
General BALE: 292-293
DHLOMO, Rolfus Reginald Ray-
mond
General BALE: 293
DHOTEL, André
General Po: 675
DIAZ-CANEJA, Guillermo
El sobre en blanco Ke: 203
DIAZ DUFOO, Carlos
General Br: 188
DIAZ GUTIERREZ, Jorge
General Br: 188
DIAZ MIRON, Salvador
General LCAB: 49
DIAZ RODRIGUEZ, Jesús
"El cojo" WaS1: 51
"No hay Dios que resista esto"
WaS1: 51
"No matarás" WaS1: 52
"El polvo a la mitad" WaS1:
52
DIAZ RODRIGUEZ, Manuel
General Po: 675
Sangre Patricia Po: 675-676
DIAZ SOSA, Rafael Angel
General Br: 188
DIAZ VILLAMIL, Antonio
General Br: 188
La Hoguera Br: 188
DIBDIN, Thomas John
General Li: 146
DICENTA Y BENEDICTO, Joaquin
General Br: 189; MD: 90
Juan Jose DC2: 112
DICK, Philip K.
General ASF: 139
"The Preserving Machine" Wa:
169
"The Stand-By Job" Wa: 169

"War Game" Wa: 169
DICKENS, Charles
  General BN: 35-40; Du:
    49-53; EDT: 152-156;
    LCAB: 49
  Barnaby Rudge BN: 40;
    Du: 33-34; EN: 32;
    ENE: 67-68; ENES1: 52;
    ENES2: 59-60; Ma: 497-
    498
  "The Black Veil" Wa: 169
  Bleak House BN: 41; Du:
    34-36; EN: 32-33; ENE:
    68-71; ENES1: 52-54;
    ENES2: 60-62; Ma: 498-
    499; Po: 581
  The Chimes ENES1: 54;
    ENES2: 62
  A Christmas Carol ENES1:
    54; ENES2: 62; Ma: 499-
    500
  "A Confession Found in a
    Prison in the Time of
    Charles the Second" Wa:
    169
  David Copperfield BN: 41-
    42; Du: 36-38; EN: 33-34;
    ENE: 71-72; ENES1: 54-
    55; ENES2: 62-64; LCAB:
    49; Ma: 500-501; Po:
    2086-2087
  Dombey and Son BN: 42;
    Du: 38-39; EN: 34-35;
    ENE: 72-73; ENES1: 55-
    56; ENES2: 64; Ma: 501-
    503
  "George Silverman's Explana-
    tion" Wa: 169
  Great Expectations BN: 43-
    44; Du: 39-41; EN: 35;
    ENE: 74-77; ENES1: 56-
    58; ENES2: 64-66; Ma:
    503-504
  Hard Times BN: 44; Du:
    41; EN: 35-36; ENE: 77-
    78; ENES1: 58-59; ENES2:
    66-67; Ma: 504-506; Po:
    2301
  The Haunted Man ENES1:
    60; ENES2: 67
  Is She His Wife? EDT: 153-
    154, 156
  The Lamplighter EDT: 154
  Little Dorrit BN: 45; Du:
    41-42; EN: 36; ENE:
    78-79; ENES1: 60-61;

  ENES2: 67-69; Ma: 506-507
  Martin Chuzzlewit BN: 45;
    Du: 42-43; EN: 36-37;
    ENE: 79; ENES1: 61;
    ENES2: 69-70; Ma: 507-508
  The Mystery of Edwin Drood
    BN: 43; Du: 43-44; EN:
    37; ENE: 73-74; ENES1:
    61-62; ENES2: 70-71; Ma:
    508-510
  Nicholas Nickleby BN: 45;
    Du: 44-45; EN: 38; ENE:
    80; ENES1: 62; ENES2:
    71; Ma: 510-511
  "No Thoroughfare" Wa: 169
  The Old Curiosity Shop Du:
    45; EN: 38; ENE: 80;
    ENES1: 62-63; ENES2:
    71-72; Ma: 511-512
  Oliver Twist BN: 45-46; Du:
    46; EN: 38-39; ENE: 80-
    81; ENES1: 63; ENES2: 72-
    73; LCAB: 49; Ma: 512-513
  Our Mutual Friend BN: 46;
    Du: 46-47; EN: 39-40;
    ENE: 81-83; ENES1: 64-
    65; ENES2: 73-74; Ma: 514-
    515
  The Pickwick Papers BN:
    46-47; Du: 48; EN: 40;
    ENE: 83-84; ENES1: 65;
    ENES2: 74; Ma: 515-516
  The Strange Gentleman EDT:
    153, 156
  A Tale of Two Cities Du: 48-
    49; EN: 40; ENE: 84;
    ENES1: 66; ENES2: 74-75;
    Ma: 516-517
  The Village Coquettes EDT:
    153, 156
  _____ and Wilkie COLLINS
  No Thoroughfare DC1: 51;
    EDT: 155
DICKENSON, John
  Arisbas ERP: 149
  Greene in Conceit ERP: 149
DICKERSON, Glenda
  General MBA: 71
  Jesus Christ, Lawd Today
    MBA: 71
  Owen's Song MBA: 71-72
DICKEY, James
  General ICBAP: 33; LCAB:
    49; Ma: 519-520; MP:
    34-35; Po: 676-678
  "Adultery" PE: 111

"Approaching Prayer" ICBAP:
  33; PE: 111
"Armor" ICBAP: 33
Buckdancer's Choice Ma:
  518; Po: 678
"Chenille" ICBAP: 33
"Cherrylog Road" ICBAP:
  33
Deliverance Ma: 518-519
"A Dog Sleeping on My Feet"
  ICBAP: 34; PE: 111
"Drinking from a Helmet"
  ICBAP: 34
"The Driver" ICBAP: 34;
  PE: 111-112
Drowning with Others Ma:
  519
"The Eye-Beaters, Blood,
  Victory, Madness, Buck-
  head and Mercy" Ma:
  519; PE: 112
"Falling" ICBAP: 34; PE:
  112
"The Fiend" ICBAP: 34
"The Firebombing" ICBAP:
  34; PE: 112
"The Heaven of Animals"
  LCAB: 49; MP: 34; PE:
  112
Helmets Ma: 519
"In Pursuit from Under" PE:
  112
"Inside the River" PE: 112
"The Lifeguard" PE: 112
"Mary Sheffield" PE: 112
"Orpheus Before Hades"
  ICBAP: 34; PE: 112
"The Owl King" PE: 112
"The Performance" ICBAP:
  34; PE: 112
"Slave Quarters" ICBAP:
  34
"Sled Burial, Dream Cere-
  mony" PE: 112
"Springer Mountain" ICBAP:
  34
"Turning Away" PE: 112
DICKEY, William
  General ICBAP: 34
DICKINSON, Emily
  General ALL: 71-76; Cla:
    25-28; ICBAP: 34; LCAB:
    50; Ma: 521-522
  "The Admirations--and--
    Contempts--of Time--"
    PE: 113

"After Great Pain, a Formal
  Feeling Comes" (No. 341)
  ICBAP: 35; PE: 113
"Apparently with No Surprise"
  PE: 113
"As by the Dead We Love to
  Sit" (No. 88) ICBAP: 35;
  PE: 113
"As Imperceptibly as Grief"
  PE: 113
"As Watchers Hang Upon the
  East" PE: 113
"At Half Past Three, a Single
  Bird" PE: 113
"Aurora Is the Effort" (No.
  1002) ICBAP: 35; PE: 113
"Because I Could Not Stop for
  Death" (No. 712) ICBAP:
  35; PE: 113-114
"Before I Got My Eye Put Out"
  PE: 114
"Before the Ice Is in the Pools"
  PE: 114
"A Bird Came Down the Walk"
  PE: 114
"Blazing in Gold" PE: 114
"Bustle in a House" (No. 1078)
  ICBAP: 35; PE: 114
"Butterfly Obtains" (No. 1685)
  ICBAP: 35; PE: 114
"Came a Wind Like a Bugle"
  PE: 115
"A Clock Stopped--Not the
  Mantel's" (No. 287) ICBAP:
  35; PE: 115
"Crickets Sang" (No. 1104)
  ICBAP: 35; PE: 115
"Crumbling Is Not an Instant's
  Act" PE: 115
"Dear Sue, Your--Riches--Taught
  Me--Poverty!" PE: 115
Death: A Sequence of Poems
  LCAB: 50
"Death Is a Dialogue Between"
  (No. 976) ICBAP: 35;
  PE: 115
"Elysium Is as Far as To" (No.
  1760) ICBAP: 35; PE:
  115
"Except the Smaller Size" PE:
  115
"'Faith' Is a Fine Invention"
  (No. 185) ICBAP: 35; PE:
  115
"Farther in Summer Than the
  Birds" PE: 115-116

"Feet of People Walking Home" (No. 7) ICBAP: 35; PE: 116

"For Every Bird a Nest" PE: 116

"Further in Summer Than the Birds" (No. 1068) ICBAP: 35

Further Poems LCAB: 50

"Go Make Thee Fair" (No. 318) ICBAP: 35

"Go Not Too Near a House of Rose" PE: 116

"The Harm of Years Is on Him" PE: 116

"He Put the Belt Around My Life" PE: 116

"The Heart Asks Pleasure First" PE: 116

"Hope Is a Strange Invention" PE: 116

"A House Upon the Height" PE: 116

"I Asked No Other Thing" PE: 116

"I Can Wade Grief" PE: 117

"I Cannot Dance Upon My Toes" PE: 116

"I Cannot Live with You" PE: 116

"I Died for Beauty" PE: 117

"I Dreaded That First Robin So" PE: 117

"I Felt a Funeral in My Brain" (No. 280) Cla: 27; ICBAP: 35; PE: 117

"I Had Not Minded Walls" (No. 398) ICBAP: 36; PE: 117

"I Have a King, Who Does Not Speak" PE: 117

"I Heard a Fly Buzz When I Died" (No. 465) ICBAP: 36; PE: 117-118

"I Know Some Lonely Houses off the Road" PE: 118

"I Like to See It Lap the Miles" (No. 585) ICBAP: 36; PE: 118

"I Meant to Have but Modest Needs" PE: 118

"I Never Hear the One Is Dead" PE: 118

"I Never Lost as Much but Twice" PE: 118-119

"I Never Saw a Moor" (No.

1052) ICBAP: 36; PE: 119

"I Should Have Been Too Glad, I See" PE: 119

"I Started Early, Took My Dog" (No. 520) ICBAP: 36; PE: 119

"I Taste a Liquor Never Brewed" (No. 214) ICBAP: 36; PE: 119

"I Years Had Been from Home" PE: 120

"If I Can Stop One Heart from Breaking" PE: 117

"If I Should Die" PE: 117

"If Pain for Peace Prepares" PE: 117

"If You Were Coming in the Fall" (No. 511) ICBAP: 36; PE: 117

"I'll Tell You How the Sun Rose" PE: 118

"Immured in Heaven!" PE: 118

"It Don't Sound So Terrible--Quite--as It Did" (No. 426) ICBAP: 36

"It Dropped So Low--in My Regard" PE: 119

"It Was Not Death, for I Stood Up" PE: 120

"It's Easy to Invent a Life" PE: 120

"I've Dropped My Brain--My Soul Is Numb" PE: 120

"The Lamp Burns Sure Within" (No. 233) ICBAP: 36; PE: 120

"The Last Night That She Lived" PE: 120

The Malay--Took the Pearl-- PE: 120

"A Mien to Move a Queen" PE: 120

"A Mine There Is No Man Would Own" PE: 120

"The Moon Upon Her Fluent Route" PE: 120

"More Life Went Out, When He Went" PE: 120

"Much Madness Is Divinest Sense" PE: 120

"My Life Had Stood--A Loaded Gun" (No. 754) ICBAP: 36; PE: 120-121

"My Wheel Is in the Dark!"

PE: 121

"The Nearest Dream Recedes--
Unrealized-- PE: 121

"No Brigadier Throughout the
Year" (No. 1561) ICBAP:
36; PE: 121

"No Rack Can Torture Me"
PE: 121

"Not with a Club the Heart
Is Broken" (No. 1304)
ICBAP: 36; PE: 121

"Of All the Souls That Stand
Create" PE: 121

"Of Bronze and Blaze" (No.
290) ICBAP: 37; PE:
121

"Of Death I Try to Think
Like This" PE: 121

"On This Wondrous Sea" PE:
122

"One Blessing Had I Than
the Rest" PE: 121

"One Day Is There of the
Series" (No. 814)
ICBAP: 37; PE: 121

"One Dignity Delays for All"
(No. 98) ICBAP: 37;
PE: 121

"One Life of So Much Conse-
quence" PE: 121

"One Need Not Be a Chamber
--to Be Haunted" PE:
122

"One Year Ago--Jots What?"
PE: 122

"The Only News I Know" PE:
122

"Our Journey Had Advanced"
PE: 122

"Pass to the Rendezvous of
Light" PE: 122

"Poets Light but Lamps" (No.
883) ICBAP: 37; PE:
122

"Poor Little Heart!" PE: 122

"Portraits Are to Daily Faces"
PE: 122

"Praise It--'Tis Dead" (No.
1384) ICBAP: 37; PE:
122

"Presentiment--Is That Long
Shadow--on the Lawn"
PE: 122

"Publication--Is the Auction"
PE: 122

"Renunciation Is a Piercing

Virtue" PE: 123

"Reverse Cannot Befall" (No.
395) ICBAP: 37; PE: 123

"The Robin Is the One" PE:
123

"A Route of Evanescence" PE:
123

"Safe in Their Alabaster
Chambers" PE: 123

"She Sweeps with Many-Colored
Brooms" PE: 123

"The Snow That Never Drifts"
PE: 123

"So Glad We Are" PE: 123

"Softened by Time's Consum-
mate Plush" PE: 123

"A Solemn Thing Within the
Soul" PE: 124

"Some Arrows Slay but Whom
They Strike" PE: 124

"The Soul Has Bandaged Mo-
ments--" PE: 124

"The Soul Selects Her Own Society" (No. 303) ICBAP:
37; PE: 124

"The Soul Should Always Stand
Ajar" PE: 124

"The Soul's Superior Instants"
(No. 306) ICBAP: 37; PE:
124

"Success Is Counted Sweetest"
PE: 124

"Summer Has Two Beginnings"
PE: 124

"Superfluous Were the Sun"
PE: 124

"There Are Two Ripenings"
PE: 124

"There Came a Day at Summer's
Full" (No. 322) ICBAP: 37;
PE: 124-125

"There Is No Frigate Like a
Book" PE: 125

"There's A Certain Slant of
Light" ALL: 76; PE: 125

"These Are the Days When
Birds Come Back" PE: 125

"This Consciousness That Is
Aware" PE: 125

"This Was a Poet" PE: 125

"Those Not Live Yet" PE:
125

"The Thought Beneath so Slight
a Film" PE: 125

"Tint I Cannot Take Is Best"
(No. 627) ICBAP: 37;

PE: 125
"Title Divine Is Mine" PE: 125
"To Hear an Oriole Sing" PE: 125
"To Lose One's Faith" PE: 125
"To Undertake Is to Achieve" PE: 126
"'Twas Like a Maelstrom, with a Notch" PE: 126
"'Twas Warm at First Like Us" PE: 126
"Two Butterflies Went Out at Noon" (No. 533) ICBAP: 37; PE: 126
"Water Makes Many Beds" (No. 1428) ICBAP: 37; PE: 126
"We Play at Paste--" PE: 126
"We Should Not Mind So Small a Flower" (No. 81) ICBAP: 37; PE: 126
"What Care the Dead, for Chanticleer" PE: 126
"What Soft Cherubic Creatures" (No. 401) ICBAP: 37; PE: 126
"When I Hoped I Feared" PE: 126
"When Roses Cease to Bloom, Sir" (No. 32) ICBAP: 38
"Where Ships of Purple Gently Toss" PE: 126
"A Wife--at Daybreak I Shall Be" PE: 127
"Wild Nights--Wild Nights" (No. 249) ICBAP: 38; PE: 127
"The Wind Drew Off" PE: 127
"The Wind--Tapped Like a Tired Man" PE: 127
"Wonder Is Not Precisely Knowing" PE: 127
"Your Riches--Taught Me-- Poverty" PE: 127
"You're Right--'The Way Is Narrow'" PE: 127
DICKINSON, John
General AP: 264-266; Da: 65-66
Letters from a Farmer in Pennsylvania AP: 264-

265
"Ode, On the French Revolution" AP: 265; Da: 66
DIDEROT, Denis
General LCAB: 50
Les Bijoux indiscret Fi: 52-53; Ke: 55
Les deux amis de Bourbonne Ke: 55
Est-il Bon? Est-il Mechant? DC2: 112
Le Fils Naturel DC2: 112
Jacques the Fatalist Fi: 53-54; Ke: 55-56
The Nun Ke: 56
Père de Famille DC2: 112
Rameau's Nephew Fi: 54-55; Ke: 56-57
La Religieuse Fi: 55-56
Supplément au Voyage de Bougainville Fi: 56
DIDION, Joan
Play It as It Lays Ma: 523
Di DONALDO, Pietro
"Christ in Concrete" Wa: 169
DIESBACH, Ghislain de
General Po: 678
DIEZ BARROSO, Victor Manuel
General Br: 189
DIEZ DE TEJADA, Vincente
General Po: 678
DIGBY, George
Elvira DC1: 52
DIGBY, Kenelm
General LJCD: 235
DIGGES, Leonard [translator]
Gerardo, the Unfortunate Spaniard by Gonzalo CESPEDES y MANESES ERP: 149-150
DIGGES, Thomas Atwood
Adventures of Alonso AN: 56
DIKOBE, Modikwe
General BALE: 293
DINESEN, Isak [Baroness Karen BLIXEN]
General LCAB: 20; Po: 678-680
"Alexander the Great" Wa: 170
"Alkmene" Wa: 170
Anecdotes of Destiny Ma: 524
The Angelic Avengers Ke: 346
"Babette's Feast" Wa: 170
"The Blank Page" Wa: 170
"The Cardinal's First Tale"

Wa: 170

"The Cardinal's Third Tale"
Wa: 170; WaS1: 52

"The Caryatides" Wa: 170

"The Cloak" Wa: 170

"A Consolatory Tale" Wa:
170; WaS1: 52

"Converse at Night in Copenhagen" Wa: 170

"Copenhagen Season" Wa:
170

"A Country Tale" Wa: 170

"The Deluge at Norderny"
Wa: 170-171

"The Diver" Wa: 171

"The Dreamers" Wa: 171

"The Dreaming Child" Wa:
171

"Echoes" Wa: 171

Ehrengard Ke: 346-347;
Po: 680; Wa: 171

"Familien de Cats" Wa: 171

"The Fish" Wa: 171

"The Heroine" Wa: 171

"The Immortal Story" Wa:
171

"The Invincible Slave Owners"
Wa: 171

Last Tales Ma: 524-525; Po:
680

"The Monkey" Po: 680-681;
Wa: 171-172

"Of Secret Thoughts and of
Heaven" Wa: 172

"The Old Chevalier" Wa:
172

Out of Africa Ma: 525

"The Pearl" Wa: 172

"Peter and Rosa" Wa: 172

The Poet Fi: 402; Wa: 172

"The Ring" Wa: 172; WaS1:
52

"The Roads Round Pisa" Wa:
172

"The Sailor-Boy's Tale" Wa:
172

Seven Gothic Tales Ma:
526

"Sorrow-Acre" Wa: 172;
WaS1: 52

"The Supper at Elsinore"
Wa: 172

"Tempests" Wa: 172

"The Wine of the Tetrarch"
Wa: 173

Winter's Tales Ma: 526-527

"The Young Man with the Carnation" Wa: 173

DING LING
"A Certain Night" WaS1: 52
"Diary of Miss Sophie" WaS1:
52

DIPOKO, Mbella Sonne
General BALE: 293-294

DISRAELI, Benjamin
General BN: 48-49; Du: 55-
56
Alroy ENES1: 66; ENES2: 75
Coningsby; or, The New Gen-
eration BN: 48; Du: 54;
ENE: 84; ENES1: 66;
ENES2: 75
Contarini Fleming BN: 49;
ENES1: 66; ENES2: 75
Endymion BN: 49; ENES1:
66
Henrietta Temple ENES1: 67;
ENES2: 75
Lothair BN: 48; ENES1: 67
Sybil; or, The Two Nations
BN: 49; Du: 54; ENE: 84-
85; ENES1: 67; ENES2: 75
Tancred; or, The New Crusade
Du: 54; ENE: 85; ENES1:
67
Venetia BN: 49; ENES1: 67
Vivian Grey BN: 48; Du:
55; ENES1: 67; ENES2:
76
The Young Duke ENES1: 67;
ENES2: 76

DIXON, Richard Watson
General TA: 130

DIXON, Thomas
General Po: 681
The Clansman DC1: 52; Po:
681-682
The Leopard's Spots Po: 682

DIZENZO, Charles
General MDAE: 177
An Evening for Merlin Finch
ADC: 91
A Great Career ADC: 92

DIZZY, Ras
General WIL: 37-38

DJOLETO, Amu
General BALE: 294

DOBIE, James Frank
General ASF: 139

DÖBLIN, Alfred
General Po: 682-683
The Amazon Fi: 294

Babylonische Wandrung Fi:
294
Berge Meere und Giganten
Fi: 294
Berlin Alexanderplatz Fi:
295; Ke: 260; Po: 683
"Die Ermordung einer Butter-
blume" Wa: 173
Hamlet or the Long Night
Comes to an End Fi: 295
November 1918 Fi: 295; Po:
683
Pardon Will Not Be Granted
Fi: 295-296
Wallenstein Fi: 296; Ke: 260
DOBSON, George
Dobson's Drie Bobs (Some-
times attributed to Dobson)
see ANONYMOUS
DOBSON, Henry Austin
General TA: 132
DODD, William
The Sisters ENES2: 76
DODERER, Heimito von
General Po: 683-687
The Demons [Die Dämonen]
Fi: 296; Ke: 260; Po:
686-687
Every Man a Murderer [Ein
Mord den Jeder Begeht]
Ke: 260; Po: 684, 687
Das letzte Abenteuer Po:
688
Die Posaunen von Jericho
Fi: 296; Po: 688
Die Strudelhofstiege Fi:
296; Ke: 260; Po: 686,
688
Ein Umweg Ke: 260; Po:
684
The Waterfalls of Slunj [Die
Wasserfälle von Slunj]
Po: 685, 688-689
Zwei Lugen Fi: 296
DODGE, Mary
"Our Contraband" ASF: 139
Dodgson, Charles Lutwidge
see CARROLL, Lewis
DODSLEY, Robert
Cleone Li: 148
The King and the Miller of
Mansfield Li: 148
DODSON, Owen
General AAPD: 306; AAW:
48; BAF: 83; BAP:
64-65; BAW: 226; LCAB:

50; MBA: 72
The Amistad BAP: 65; MBA:
72
The Ballad of Dorie Miller
BAP: 65
Bayou Legend BAP: 65; MBA:
72
Boy at the Window BAF: 83
A Christmas Miracle BAP: 65
"Come Home Early, Chile"
ASF: 140
Divine Comedy ADC: 92;
BAP: 65; MBA: 72
Everybody Join Hands BAP:
65
Freedom the Banner BAP: 65
Garden of Time ADC: 92;
BAP: 65; MBA: 72
New World A-Coming BAP: 65
Someday We're Gonna Tear Them
Pillars Down BAP: 65
Till Victory Is Won MBA: 72
With This Darkness BAP: 65
DOERING, Georg
Cervantes DC2: 113
DOLAN, Harry
General BAP: 66; BAW: 227
DOLBIER, Maurice
General LCAB: 50
DOMBROVSKIJ, Jurij
The Keeper of Antiquities Fi:
425
DOMINGUEZ, Franklin
Alberto y Ercilia Br: 189
Espigas Maduras Br: 189
Exodo Br: 189
El Vuelo de la Paloma Br: 189
DONAHOE, Edward
"Head by Scopas" SFC: 43;
Wa: 173
DONLEAVY, James Patrick
General CFAE: 125; CN:
108; LCAB: 50-51; MDAE:
179; Po: 689
The Beastly Beatitudes of
Balthazar B. Ma: 528
Fairy Tales of New York
MDAE: 179
The Ginger Man Br: 189;
CFAE: 125; CN: 109;
LCAB: 51; Ma: 528-529;
Po: 689
"The Saddest Summer of Samuel
S." ASF: 140; CN: 109;
Wa: 173
A Singular Man CN: 109;

Ma: 529; MDAE: 179;
Po: 689
DONNE, John
General Ba: 46-62; ICBAP:
38; LCAB: 51
"Aire and Angels" Ba: 53-
54; ICBAP: 38; PE: 127-
128
"An Anatomy of the World"
see "The First Anniver-
sary"
"The Anniversarie" PE: 128
The Anniversaries Ba: 56-
57; ICBAP: 38; PE: 128
"The Apparition" ICBAP:
38; PE: 128
"As Through a Looking-
Glass" Ba: 56
"Batter My Heart, Three
Person'd God" (Holy Son-
net 14) ICBAP: 38; Ma:
530
Biathanatos Ba: 60
"The Blossom" PE: 128
"Bracelet" (Elegy 11)
ICBAP: 38
"Broken Heart" ICBAP: 38;
PE: 129
"The Calme" Ba: 56; PE:
129
"Canonization" Ba: 52-54;
ICBAP: 38-39; LCAB:
51; Ma: 530-531; PE:
129-130
"Communitie" PE: 130
"The Computation" PE: 130
"Confined Love" PE: 130
"La Corona" Ba: 58; ICBAP:
39; PE: 141
"The Cross" PE: 130
"Crucyfying" PE: 130
"The Curse" ICBAP: 39;
PE: 130
"The Dampe" Ba: 52; PE:
130
"Death Be Not Proud" (Holy
Sonnet 10) ICBAP: 39
Devotions upon Emergent
Occasions Ba: 59-61;
Hen: 33
"The Dissolution" Ba: 53;
PE: 130
"The Dreame" (From Songs
and Sonnets) ICBAP:
39; PE: 131
"The Ecstasy" Ba: 52-55;

PE: 131-132
"Elegie Upon the Untimely Death
of the Incomparable Prince
Henry" PE: 134
Elegies Ba: 55; PE: 132-134
"Elegy 3" Ba: 55
"Elegy 7" Ba: 55; ICBAP:
39
"Elegy 10" Ba: 55
"Elegy 19: To His Mistress Go-
ing to Bed" Ba: 55
"Elegy on Mistress Boulstred"
PE: 134
"Elegy" on Prince Henry Ba:
59
"Elegy on the L.C." PE: 134
"Elegy on the Lady Marckham"
PE: 134
"Epithalamion Made at Lincolnes
Inne" Ba: 56; PE: 134
Essays in Divinity Hen: 34
"Expostulation" ICBAP: 39
"Extasie" ICBAP: 39; LCAB:
51; Ma: 531-532
"Farewell to Love" PE: 134
"A Fever" PE: 134
"The First Anniversary" ["An
Anatomy of the World"]
Ba: 56-57; ICBAP: 39;
LCAB: 51; PE: 135
"The Flea" Ba: 52; Ma: 533;
PE: 135
"Funerall Elegie" Ba: 54;
ICBAP: 39; PE: 136
"Go and Catch a Falling Star"
Ba: 53
"Going to Bed" (Elegy 19)
ICBAP: 39
"Good Friday, 1613. Riding
Westward" Ba: 58-59;
ICBAP: 39; Ma: 533-534;
PE: 136
"Good-Morrow" Ba: 52, 54;
ICBAP: 40; Ma: 534-535;
PE: 136-137
"Heroicall Epistle: Sapho to
Philaenis" ICBAP: 40
"His Picture" (Elegy 5) ICBAP:
40
"Holy Sonnet VIII" Ba: 58
"Holy Sonnet XII" Ba: 58
"Holy Sonnet XIII" Ba: 59
"Holy Sonnet XIV" Ba: 58-
59
"Holy Sonnet XVII" Ba: 58
"Holy Sonnets" Ba: 58-59;

LCAB: 51; PE: 137-139

"A Hymn to Christ, at the Author's Last Going into Germany" PE: 139-140

"Hymn to God My God, in My Sickness" Ba: 57-58; ICBAP: 40; LCAB: 51; PE: 140

"A Hymn to God the Father" PE: 140

"A Hymn to the Saints and to Marquis Hamilton" PE: 140

"If Poisonous Minerals" PE: 140

Ignatius His Conclave Ba: 59-61

"The Indifferent" PE: 140

"A Jet Ring Sent" PE: 140-141

"A Lecture Upon a Shadow" Ba: 53; ICBAP: 40; PE: 141

"Legacie" ICBAP: 40; PE: 141

"Letters to the Lady Carey and Mrs. Essex Riche, from Amyens" PE: 141

"The Litanie" PE: 141

"Lovers Infinitenesse" PE: 141

"Love's Alchemy" PE: 141-142

"Love's Deity" PE: 142

"Love's Diet" PE: 142

"Loves Growth" ICBAP: 40; PE: 142

"Love's Usury" PE: 142

"Man to Gods Image..." see "To the Countess of Huntingdon"

"The Message" PE: 142

Metaphysical Conceit ICBAP: 40

"Metempsychosis" see "The Progress of the Soul"

"Nativity" PE: 142

"Negative Love" PE: 143

"A Nocturnall Upon St. Lucies Day, Being the Shortest Day" Ba: 52-54; ICBAP: 40; PE: 143

"Obsequies to the Lord Harrington" PE: 143

"Of the Progress of the Soul" see "The Second Anniversary"

"Paradise and Calvarie" Ba: 57-58

Paradoxes and Problems Ba: 61

"Primrose" Ba: 52; ICBAP: 40; PE: 143

"The Progress of the Soul" ["Metempsychosis"] Ba: 56; PE: 144

"The Prohibition" PE: 144

"Relique" ICBAP: 40; PE: 144

"Resurrection Imperfect" PE: 144

"Sappho to Philaenis" PE: 144

"Satire 4" Ba: 55

Satires Ba: 55-56; ICBAP: 40-41; PE: 144-145

"Satyre III" (Kinde Pity Chokes My Spleene) Ba: 55-56; ICBAP: 40

"The Second Anniversary" ["Of the Progress of the Soul"] Ba: 56-57; ICBAP: 41; PE: 145-146

"Second Prebend Sermon" Ba: 61

Sermons Ba: 59-62; Hen: 32-33

"Song. Go and Catch a Falling Star" PE: 146

Songs and Sonnets Ba: 52-55

"Sonnet. The Token" PE: 146

"The Storme" Ba: 56; PE: 146-147

"The Sun Rising" ICBAP: 41; PE: 147

"To E. of D. with Six Holy Sonnets" PE: 147

"To Have Written Then" see "To the Countess of Bedford"

"To His Mistress Going to Bed" ICBAP: 41

"To Mr. Roland Woodward" PE: 147

"To Sir Henry Goodyer" PE: 147

"To Sir Henry Wotton, at His Going Ambassador to Venice" PE: 148

"To Sir Henry Wotton" ("Sir, More Than Kisses") PE: 147

"To Sir Rowland Woodward"
PE: 148
"To the Countess of Bedford"
["To Have Written Then"]
PE: 148
"To the Countess of Hunting-
don" ["Man to Gods
Image..."] ICBAP: 41;
PE: 148
"Twicknam Garden" PE:
148
"The Undertaking" ICBAP:
41; PE: 148
"Upon the Annunciation and
Passion Falling Upon One
Day, 1608" Ba: 59; PE:
148
"A Valediction: Forbidding
Mourning" Ba: 52;
ICBAP: 41; LCAB: 51;
Ma: 535-536; PE: 148-
149
"A Valediction: Of My
Name, in the Window"
ICBAP: 41; PE: 149-150
"A Valediction: Of the
Book" PE: 150
"A Valediction: Of Weeping"
Ba: 52; ICBAP: 41; PE:
150
"Virtuous Men" Ba: 54;
LCAB: 51
"What If This Present Were
the World's Last Night?"
(Holy Sonnet 13) ICBAP:
41
"Why Are We by All Crea-
tures Waited On?" (Holy
Sonnet 12) ICBAP: 41
"The Will" PE: 150
"Witchcraft by a Picture"
ICBAP: 41; PE: 150
"Woman's Constancy" PE:
151
DONNELLY, Ignatius
General LCAB: 51
DONOGHUE, Dennis
General BAW: 227
Legal Murder BAP: 66
DONOSO, José
"Santelices" WaS1: 52
"Summering" WaS1: 52
"Walk" WaS1: 52
DONOSO CORTES, Juan
General Po: 690
DOOLITTLE, Hilda [H.D.]

General ASF: 140; MP: 36;
Po: 690-692
"Helen in Egypt" MP: 36; Po:
690, 692
"Hermetic Definition" PE: 151
"Hipparchia" ASF: 140
"Murex" ASF: 140
"Oread" PE: 151
"The Pool" PE: 151
"Red Roses for Bronze" PE:
151
"Secret Name" ASF: 140
Tribute to Freud Po: 692
"The Walls Do Not Fall" PE:
151
"Winter Love (Espérance)" PE:
151
DORR, Donald
Jubilee MBA: 73
DORST, Tankred
Freedom for Clemens Br: 189
Great Diatribe at the Town
Wall [Grosse Schmahrede an
der Stadtmauer] Br: 189
Society in Autumn [Gesell-
schaft im Herbst] Br: 190
DOS PASSOS, John Roderigo
General ALL: 76-77; AN:
58-60; ASF: 141; Br: 190;
CN: 109-113; LCAB: 52;
MD: 90-91; Ne: 32-34;
Po: 693-697; Wo: 78-80
Adventures of a Young Man
see also District of Colum-
bia AN: 57; CN: 113
Airways, Inc. Br: 190; MD:
91
The Big Money see also
U.S.A. AN: 57; CN: 113;
LCAB: 52
Chosen Country CN: 113
District of Columbia CN: 113
First Encounter see also
One Man's Initiation--1917
CN: 113
Fortune Heights MD: 91
The 42nd Parallel see also
U.S.A. AN: 57; CN: 113-
114
The Grand Design see also
District of Columbia AN:
57; CN: 114
The Garbage Man [The Moon
Is a Gong] ADC: 92;
Br: 190; MD: 91; Po:
697

The Great Days CN: 114;
Po: 694
Manhattan Transfer AN:
57; CN: 114-115; LCAB:
53; Ma: 537; Ne: 32-33;
Po: 693, 697-698; Wo:
79
Midcentury CN: 115; Ma:
537-538
The Moon Is a Gong see
The Garbage Man
Most Likely to Succeed CN:
115
1919 see also U.S.A.
CN: 115
Number One see also District of Columbia AN:
57; CN: 116
One Man's Initiation--1917
CN: 116; Po: 698-699
Streets of the Night CN:
116; Po: 693
Three Soldiers AN: 57-58;
CN: 116-117; Ma: 538;
Po: 694, 699
U.S.A. CN: 117-118; LCAB:
53; Ma: 538-540; Ne: 33;
Po: 699-700
_____ and Paul SHYRE
U.S.A. ADC: 92
DOSTOEVSKY, Fyodor
General LCAB: 53
"Another Man's Wife and the
Husband Under the Bed"
SFC: 43; Wa: 173
"Bobok" WaS1: 52
The Brothers Karamazov
Fi: 425-431; Ke: 377-
382; LCAB: 53; Ma:
541-542
"A Christmas Tree and a
Wedding" SFC: 43; Wa:
173
"The Citizen" Wa: 173
"The Crawler" see "Polzunkov"
Crime and Punishment Fi:
431-435; Ke: 382-388;
LCAB: 53; Ma: 542-544
"The Crocodile" SFC: 43;
Wa: 174
The Devils see The Possessed
The Diary of Dostoevsky's
Wife LCAB: 53
The Double Fi: 438; Ke:

388-389; SFC: 44; Wa: 174;
WaS1: 53
The Dream of a Ridiculous Man
Fi: 438-439; SFC: 44; Wa:
174-175; WaS1: 53
The Eternal Husband Ke: 389;
LCAB: 53; SFC: 44; WaS1:
53
"A Faint Heart" SFC: 44; Wa:
175
The Friend of the Family see
The Village of Stepanchikova
The Gambler Fi: 439; Ke:
389; Ma: 544; SFC: 45;
Wa: 175; WaS1: 53
"A Gentle Creature" SFC: 45;
Wa: 175; WaS1: 53
"The Grand Inquisitor" SFC:
45; Wa: 175-176; WaS1: 53
"An Honest Thief" SFC: 45;
Wa: 176; WaS1: 53
The Idiot Br: 190; Fi: 439-
441; Ke: 390-392; LCAB:
53; Ma: 544-545
The Insulted and Injured Fi:
441-442; Ke: 392-393
The Landlady Fi: 442; Ke:
393; SFC: 46; Wa: 176-177;
WaS1: 53
Letters from the House of the
Dead Ke: 393-394
Letters from the Underworld
see Notes from Underground
A Little Hero Fi: 442; SFC:
46; Wa: 177; WaS1: 53
"A Meek One" Wa: 177
Mister Proxarcin [Mr. Prokharchin] Ke: 394; Wa:
177; WaS1: 53
Netochka Nezvanova Fi: 442;
Ke: 394
Notes from Underground [Letters from the Underworld]
Fi: 442-445; Ke: 394-396;
Ma: 545-546; SFC: 46-47;
Wa: 177-179; WaS1: 53-54
"A Novel in Nine Letters"
SFC: 47; Wa: 179; WaS1:
54
"The Peasant Marey" SFC:
47; Wa: 179; WaS1: 54
Polzunkov Ke: 396; SFC:
47; Wa: 179-180; WaS1:
54
Poor Folk [Poor People] Fi:

445-446; Ke: 396-397; Ma: 547; SFC: 47

The Possessed [The Devils; Les Possedes] Br: 190; Fi: 435-438; Ke: 397-400; LCAB: 53-54; Ma: 547-548

A Raw Youth Fi: 446; Ke: 400-401

"Stavrogin's Confession" Wa: 180

Uncle's Dream Ke: 401; SFC: 47; Wa: 180; WaS1: 54

"An Unpleasant Predicament" SFC: 48; Wa: 180

Vechnyi Muzh Fi: 446

"The Verdict" Wa: 180

The Village of Stepanchikova [The Friend of the Family] Fi: 446; Ke: 401-402; LCAB: 53; SFC: 44-45; Wa: 175; WaS1: 54

"A Weak Heart" WaS1: 54

"White Nights" SFC: 48; Wa: 180; WaS1: 54

DOUGALL, Lily A.
General ECL: 128

DOUGHTY, Charles Montagu
General Po: 700; TA: 133
Arabia Deserts Po: 700

DOUGLAS, Alfred Bruce
General TA: 134

DOUGLAS, Ellen
"Hold On" Wa: 180
"The House on the Bluff" Wa: 180

Douglas, Evelyn see BARLAS, John

DOUGLAS, Gavin
General Ai: 35-36; LCAB: 54
Aeneid Ai: 35

Douglas, George see BROWN, George Douglas

DOUGLAS, James
General Br: 191; TMIP: 40-41
Carrie TMIP: 41
The Ice Goddess Br: 191; TMIP: 40-42
North City Traffic Straight Ahead Br: 191; TMIP: 40-42
The Savages TMIP: 41

DOUGLAS, Keith

General LCAB: 54; Po: 701

"Deceased" ICBAP: 41

"Encounter with a God" ICBAP: 41

DOUGLAS, Lloyd C.
General AN: 60
The Robe AN: 60

DOUGLAS, Mrs. Alfred [Olive CUSTANCE; Olive Custance DOUGLAS]
General TA: 135

DOUGLAS, Norman
General Ai: 203; BN2: 33; Po: 701; Ri: 311-315; Sch: 64
Gymnasiast Po: 701
In the Beginning ENES1: 68; Ri: 311
Old Calabria Po: 702; Ri: 312, 315
South Wind ENES1: 68; Ri: 311-315; Sch: 65
They Went ENES1: 68; Ri: 311

DOUGLAS, O. [Anna BUCHAN]
General Ai: 214

Douglas, Olive Custance see DOUGLAS, Mrs. Alfred

DOUGLASS, Frederick [Frederick Augustus Washington BAILY]
General BAW: 229-232

DOVZHENKO, Oleksandr Petrovych
General Po: 702

DOWIE, Menie Muriel
Gallia ENES2: 76

DOWLAND, John
"Thou Mightie God, That Rightest Every Wrong" PE: 151

DOWNEY, Robert
What Else Is There? Br: 191

DOWNING, Henry Francis
General BAF: 84; BAW: 232; LCAB: 54
The American Cavalryman BAF: 84; BAW: 232

DOWNING, John Hyatt
General ASF: 141
"Rewards" Wa: 180

DOWSON, Ernest Christopher
General ICBAP: 42; LCAB: 54; TA: 136; VP: 32-33
"Apple Blossom in Brittany" Wa: 180
"The Diary of a Successful Man" Wa: 180

"The Dying of Francis Donne"
Wa: 181
"In Tempore Senectutis"
PE: 151
"Non Sum Qualis Eram Bonae
Sub Regno Cynarae" PE:
151
DOYLE, Arthur Conan
General Ai: 169; LCAB:
54; Po: 702; TA: 138
"The Disappearance of Lady
Frances Carfax" WaS1:
54
The Hound of the Baskervilles
ENE: 85
Musgrave Ritual Po: 702
"A Scandal in Bohemia" WaS1:
55
The Sign of the Four ENE:
85; ENES1: 68; ENES2:
76; Ma: 549
"The Speckled Band" Wa:
181; WaS1: 55
A Study in Scarlet ENES1:
68; ENES2: 76; Ma: 549-
550
DOYLE, Lynn [Leslie A. MONT-
GOMERY]
"Sham Fight" Wa: 181
DRABBLE, Margaret
General Sch: 65
"Crossing the Alps" Wa:
181
The Garrick Year ENES1:
68; ENES2: 76
Jerusalem the Golden ENES1:
68; ENES2: 76
The Millstone ENES1: 68-
69; ENES2: 76-77
The Needle's Eye ENES1:
69; ENES2: 77
A Summer Bird-Cage ENES1:
69; ENES2: 77
"A Voyage to Cythera" Wa:
181
The Waterfall ENES1: 69;
ENES2: 77
DRAHOS, Mary
Eternal Sabbath ADC: 92
Reunion of Sorts ADC: 92
DRAKE, Joseph Rodman
"The Culprit Fay" ICBAP:
42
DRAKE-BROCKMAN, Henrietta
General MAP: 160-161
DRAYTON, Geoffrey

General WIL: 38
Christopher WIL: 38
Three Meridians WIL: 38
Zohara WIL: 38-39
DRAYTON, Michael
General Log: 138-142, 145-
147; SC: 48
"Agincourt" PE: 151
"The Barons Warres" ICBAP:
42
"Clear Anchor" PE: 151
"Edward the Fourth to Mis-
tress Shore" PE: 151
"King John to Matilda" PE:
152
"Like an Adventurous Sea-Farer
Am I" PE: 152
"Love's Farewell" see also
"Since There's No Help,
Come Let Us Kiss and Part"
PE: 152
"Mary, the French Queene, to
Charles Brandon, Duke of
Suffolke" PE: 152
"Muses Elizium" ICBAP: 42
"Owen Tudor to Queene Kath-
erine" PE: 152
"Richard the Second to Queene
Isabel" PE: 152
"The Shepheard's Garland"
ICBAP: 42; PE: 152
"Since There's No Help, Come
Let Us Kiss and Part" see
also "Love's Farewell" PE:
152
Sir John Oldcastle Log: 141-
142
"To the Virginian Voyage" PE:
152
DREER, Herman
General BAF: 84-85; BAW:
233-234
DREISER, Theodore
General ALL: 77-80; AN:
62-66; ASF: 143; Br: 191;
Ho: 44-49; LCAB: 54-55;
Po: 702-709; Wo: 83-86
An American Tragedy [The
Case of Clyde Griffiths]
ALL: 79; AN: 60; Br:
191; Ho: 45-48; LCAB:
55; Ma: 551-552; Po: 704,
708, 710-712; Wo: 85
The Bulwark AN: 60-61; Ho:
47-48; Ma: 552-553; Po:
712-713

"Butcher Rogaum's Door"
  ASF: 141; WaS1: 55
"Chains" ASF: 141
"Convention" ASF: 142
"The Cruise of the Idlewild"
  ASF: 142; Wa: 181
The Financier Ma: 553-554;
  Po: 706
"Free" ASF: 142
"Fulfillment" ASF: 142
The "Genius" AN: 61; Ho:
  46; Ma: 554; Po: 713
"The Hand" ASF: 142
The Hand of the Potter ADC:
  92; Br: 191; MD: 91;
  Po: 714
"Her Boy" ASF: 142
Jennie Gerhardt AN: 61;
  Ma: 554-555; Po: 714;
  Wo: 85
Laughing Gas DC1: 52
"The Lost Phoebe" ASF:
  142; SFC: 48; Wa: 181;
  WaS1: 55
"Marriage--for One" ASF:
  142
"Married" ASF: 142
"The 'Mercy' of God" ASF:
  142
"Nigger Jeff" ASF: 142;
  Po: 714; WaS1: 55
"The Old Neighborhood" ASF:
  142
"Old Rogaum and His Theresa"
  ASF: 142
"Phantom Gold" ASF: 143
"The Prince Who Was a Thief"
  ASF: 143
"St. Columba and the River"
  ASF: 143
"The Shining Slave Makers"
  ASF: 143; WaS1: 55
Sister Carrie ALL: 79; AN:
  61-62; Ho: 45-46, 48-49;
  LCAB: 55; Ma: 555-557;
  Po: 714-717; Wo: 85
The Stoic Ho: 47; Ma: 557;
  Po: 706
The Titan AN: 62; Ma:
  557-558; Po: 706
"Typhoon" SFC: 48; Wa:
  181
"The Victor" Wa: 181
"When the Old Century Was
  New" ASF: 143; WaS1:
  55

DREXLER, Rosalyn
  General MDAE: 180
  An Evening of Bad Taste ADC:
    92
  Home Movies ADC: 93
  The Line of Least Existence
    ADC: 93
DRIEU LA ROCHELLE, Pierre
  General Po: 718-719
  L'Agent double Po: 718
  Les chiens de paille Po: 718
  La Duchesse de Friedland Po:
    718
  Le Feu follet Fi: 56
  L'Homme à cheval Po: 718
  L'Intermède Romain Po: 718
  Le Journal d'un délicat Po:
    718
  Mémoires de Dirk Raspe Po:
    718-719
  Le Souper de réveillon Po:
    718
Drinan, Adam see MACLEOD,
  Joseph
DRINKWATER, John
  General Mi: 229-230; TA:
    140
  Abraham Lincoln DC1: 52
  Robert E. Lee Br: 191
DRIVER, Donald
  Status Quo Vadis ADC: 93;
    Br: 192
DROSTE-HÜLSHOFF, Annette von
  "Bei uns zu Lande auf dem
    Lande" Wa: 181
  "Joseph: Eine Kriminalgesch-
    ichte" Wa: 182
  Die Judenbuche Fi: 296-297;
    Ke: 260; Wa: 182; WaS1:
    55
  "Ledwina" Wa: 182
DRUE, Thomas
  General LJCD: 236
  The Bloody Banquet see
    ANONYMOUS
DRUMMOND, William
  General Ai: 47; Ba: 62-63
DRUMMOND, William Henry
  General ECL: 130-131
  "Epilogue" to "For the King"
    PE: 152
DRYDEN, John
  General Bon: 8-11, 15-16,
    19-22; ICBAP: 42; LCAB:
    55-56; Li: 151-163; Ma:
    563-564; Me: 203-213

Absalom and Achitophel Bon:
11-12; ICBAP: 42; Ma:
559-560; Me: 187-193

Alexander's Feast, or The
Power of Music ICBAP:
42-43; Me: 198, 201-202;
PE: 152

All for Love; or, The World
Well Lost Bon: 17; DC1:
52-53; EDC: 136-137; Li:
155-157; Ma: 560-561

Amboyna; or, The Cruelties
of the Dutch to the Eng-
lish Merchants Bon: 17;
EDC: 137; Li: 157

Amphytryon; or, The Two
Socias [Amphitryon] DC1:
53; EDC: 138; Li: 157

"Anne Killigrew" ICBAP:
43

Annus Mirabilis Bon: 14-15;
ICBAP: 43; Me: 199-200

The Assignation; or, Love
in a Nunnery Bon: 17;
DC1: 53; EDC: 138; Li:
157

Astraea Redux Bon: 15;
ICBAP: 43; Me: 200,
202; PE: 153

Aureng-Zebe Bon: 18; DC1:
53; EDC: 138-139; Li:
157-158

"Baucis and Philemon" PE:
153

Cleomenes, the Spartan Hero
EDC: 139; Li: 158

The Conquest of Granada by
the Spaniards see also
"Zambra Dance" DC1:
53-54; EDC: 139-140;
Li: 159

Don Sebastian, King of
Portugal Bon: 18; DC1:
54; EDC: 140; Li: 158

"Eleonora" PE: 153

"Epilogue Spoken to the
King ... at Oxford ...
1681" PE: 153

"Epistle to Charleton" PE:
153

"Epistle to John Driden"
Bon: 14; Me: 199

"An Essay of Dramatic
Poesy" Bon: 20-22;
LCAB: 56; Ma: 561-562

An Evening's Love; or, The

Mock Astrologer Bon: 18;
EDC: 138, 140; Li: 159

Fables Bon: 15; Me: 200-201

"Heroique Stanzas ... to ...
Oliver late Lord Protector
of This Commonwealth
(1659)" PE: 153

The Hind and the Panther Bon:
12-13; ICBAP: 43; Me:
194-197

The Indian Emperor, or, The
Conquest of Mexico by the
Spaniards Bon: 18; DC1:
54; EDC: 140-141; Li:
159-160

The Kind Keeper; or, Mr.
Limberham EDC: 141; Li:
160

King Arthur; or, The British
Worthy EDC: 141; Li:
160

Love Triumphant; or, Nature
Will Prevail EDC: 141; Li:
160

Mac Flecknoe Bon: 13;
ICBAP: 43; Me: 187-194;
PE: 153-154

Marriage à-la-Mode Bon: 18;
DC1: 54; EDC: 141; Li:
160; Ma: 562-563

The Medal Bon: 14-15;
ICBAP: 43; Me: 190-194

The Mistaken Husband EDC:
141

"Ode: To the Pious Memory
of Mrs. Anne Killigrew"
Bon: 15; Me: 192, 199,
202; PE: 154

"On the Marriage of ... Mrs.
Anastasia Stafford" PE:
154

Religio Laici Bon: 14; ICBAP:
43; Me: 195-198; PE: 154

The Rival Ladies DC1: 54;
EDC: 141; Li: 160-161

Secret Love; or, The Maiden
Queen DC1: 54; EDC:
141-142; Li: 160-161

The Secular Masque Me: 201;
PE: 154

Sigismonda and Guiscardo Me:
201

Sir Martin Mar-All; or The
Feign'd Innocence Bon:
19; DC1: 55; EDC: 142;
Li: 160-161

"Song for St. Cecilia's Day,
1687" Bon: 14-15;
ICBAP: 43; LCAB: 56;
PE: 154-155
The Spanish Friar; or, The
Double Discovery Bon:
19; DC1: 55; EDC: 142;
Li: 157, 161; Ma: 564-
565
The State of Innocence and
Fall of Man Bon: 19;
EDC: 142; Li: 161-162
"To His Sacred Majesty"
PE: 155
"To Honor Dryden" PE: 155
"To My Dear Friend Mr
Congreve" PE: 155
"To My Honored Friend, Dr.
Charleton" ICBAP: 43;
PE: 155
"To My Honored Friend, Sir
Robert Howard" Me:
202; PE: 155
"To My Honoured Kinsman,
John Driden" Me: 198;
PE: 155
"To Sir Godfrey Kneller"
Me: 200; PE: 155
"To the Earl of Roscommon"
Me: 200
"To the Memory of Mr. Old-
ham" ICBAP: 44; Me:
198-201; PE: 155
"To the Pious Memory of the
Accomplisht Young Lady,
Mrs. Anne Killigrew"
ICBAP: 44
"To William Congreve" PE:
155
Troilus and Cressida; or,
Truth Found Too Late
EDC: 142; Li: 162-163
Tyrannick Love; or The Royal
Martyr [Tyrannic Love]
Bon: 19; DC1: 55; EDC:
142-143; Li: 163
"Upon the Death of the Lord
Hastings" PE: 155
Virgil, the Works of [trans-
lation] Bon: 22
The Wild Gallant Bon: 19;
DC1: 55; EDC: 143;
Li: 163
"Zambra Dance" see also
The Conquest of Granada
by the Spaniards PE:

156
_____ and William DAVENANT
The Tempest; or, The Enchanted
Island EDC: 143
_____ and Robert HOWARD
Indian Queen Bon: 18; EDC:
143; Li: 160
_____ and Nathaniel LEE
Duke of Guise DC1: 54; EDC:
143; Li: 158
DUBERMAN, Martin
General MDAE: 182
In White America ADC: 93;
TMAP: 175
The Memory Bank ADC: 93
Metaphors ADC: 93
Visions of Kerouac ADC: 93
DUBILLARD, Roland
General Br: 192
La maison d'or Br: 192; Po:
174
Naives Hirondelles Br: 192
Du BOIS, David Graham
...And Bid Him Sing BAF:
85
Du BOIS, Shirley Graham [Shirley
Lola GRAHAM]
General BAP: 67-68; MBA:
73
Tom-Tom BAP: 68; MBA: 73
Du BOIS, William Edward Burg-
hardt
General AAL: 156-158; AAPD:
102; AAW: 49; APC: 75;
ASF: 144; BAF: 86-87;
BAP: 68-69; BAW: 239-241;
HR: 76-77; LCAB: 56;
MBA: 73-74
The Black Flame Po: 719
"Children of the Moon" PE:
156
Dark Princess BAF: 87; BAW:
241
Haiti ADC: 93; BAP: 69;
MBA: 74
Mansart Builds a School BAF:
87
"Of the Coming of John" ASF:
144
The Ordeal of Mansart BAF:
88; BAW: 241
The Quest of the Silver Fleece
BAF: 88; BAW: 241
Star of Ethiopia BAP: 69;
MBA: 74
Worlds of Color BAF: 88;

BAW: 241

Du BOS, Charles
General Po: 719-720
Approximations Po: 719-721
Méditation sur la vie de
Baudelaire Po: 720
Qu'est-çe que la littérature?
Po: 720

Du BOS, René
General Po: 721

Du BOUCHET, André
General Po: 721

DUBUS, André
"The Doctor" Wa: 182

Ducasse, Isidore Lucien see
LAUTREAMONT, Comte
de

DUCIS, Jean
Hamlet DC2: 113

DUCK, Stephen
General Me: 215

DUCLAUX, Mary [Mary James
DARMESTETER; Agnes
Mary Frances ROBINSON]
General TA: 141

DUDEK, Louis
General Po: 721-722

Dudevant, Amantine see SAND,
George

DUDINTSEV, Vladimir
General Po: 722
Not by Bread Alone Ke:
402; Po: 722

DUDLEY, Sir Henry Bate
General Li: 164

DUEÑAS, Guadalupe
"La historia de Marquita"
WaS1: 55

DUES, Mike
General BALE: 294

DUFFETT, Thomas
General Li: 165
The Mock Tempest Li: 165

DUFFY, Maureen
General MDAE: 183

DUGAN, Alan
General ICBAP: 44; Po:
722

DuGard, Roger Martin see
MARTIN DU GARD,
Roger

DUGGAN, Maurice
"Along Rideout Road That
Summer" Wa: 182

DUHAMEL, Georges
General Po: 722

"Candide's Last Voyage" Wa:
182
"The Carter" Wa: 182
The Combat Br: 192
In the Shadow of the Statues
Br: 192
The Light Br: 192
"Meeting Salavin Again" Wa:
182
"The Origin and Prosperity of
Monkeys" Wa: 182
The Pasquier Chronicles Fi:
56; Ke: 57-58
Salavin's Journal Fi: 56; Ke:
58
"The Wreck" Wa: 182

DUJARDIN, Edouard
Les Lauriers sont coupés Fi:
56; Ke: 58; Po: 723, 1903,
1912

DUKES, Ashley
General Mi: 230

Dumarchais, Pierre see MACOR-
LAN, Pierre

DUMAS, (Fils), Alexandre
L'affaire Clemenceau Ke: 59
Camille [The Lady with the
Camelias; La Dame aux
Camelias] DC2: 113; EDC:
143-144; Ke: 59; Ma: 568
The Demi-Monde DC2: 113;
Ma: 568
L'Etrangère DC2: 113
Kean DC2: 113
The Lady with the Camelias
see Camille
Money Question [The Question
of Money] DC2: 113; Ma:
568

DUMAS, (Père), Alexandre
General LCAB: 56
Angèle EDC: 144
Antony DC2: 114; EDC: 144
Behind a Conspiracy; or, The
Son of Black Donald [L'En-
vers d'une Conspiration; ou,
Le Fils de Donald le Noir]
EDC: 144
The Black Tulip Ke: 58; Ma:
566
"Blanche de Beaulieu" Wa:
183
Le Bourgeois de Gand; ou, Le
Secrétaire du Duc d'Albe
see The Man from Ghent;
or, the Duke of Alba's Se-

cretary

Caligula EDC: 144

Charles VII and His Chief
Vassals [Charles VII Chez
Ses Grands Vassaux]
EDC: 144

The Chevalier of the Maison
Rouge Ma: 566

Christine à Fountainebleau
EDC: 144

The Corsican Brothers Ma:
566

The Count of Monte-Cristo
Fi: 56-57; Ke: 58; Ma:
566

The Countess de Charny Ma:
566

Le Dame de Monsoreau see
The Lady from Monsoreau

Les Demoiselles de Saint-Cyr
see The Ladies of Saint-
Cyr

L'Envers d'une Conspiration;
ou, Le Fils de Donald le
Noir see Behind a Con-
spiracy; or, The Son of
Black Donald

Une Fille du Régent see The
Regent's Daughter

Hamlet, Prince of Denmark
EDC: 144

Henry III and His Court
[Henri III et sa Cour]
DC2: 114; EDC: 145

L'Invitation à la Valse EDC:
145

La Jeunesse de Louis XIV
see The Youth of Louis
XIV

The Ladies of Saint-Cyr [Les
Demoiselles de Saint-Cyr]
EDC: 145

The Lady from Belle-Isle
[Mademoiselle de Belle-
Isle] EDC: 145

The Lady from Monsoreau [Le
Dame de Monsoreau] DC2:
114; EDC: 145

Lorenzino DC2: 114; EDC:
145

Mademoiselle de Belle-Isle
see The Lady from Belle-
Isle

The Man from Ghent; or, The
Duke of Alba's Secretary
[Le Bourgeois de Gand;

ou, Le Secrétaire du Duc
d'Albe] EDC: 145

Le Mari de la Veuve see The
Widow's Husband

A Marriage of Convenience:
Period Louix XV [Un Mariage
Sous Louis XV] EDC: 145

Memoirs of a Physician Ma:
566

L'Orferre du Roi Fi: 57

The Queen's Necklace Ma: 567

The Regent's Daughter [Une
Fille du Régent] EDC: 145

La Reine Margot Fi: 57

Romulus EDC: 145

"Souvenirs d'Antony" Wa: 183

La Testament de César EDC:
145

The Three Musketeers Fi: 57;
Ke: 58; LCAB: 56; Ma:
567

Twenty Years After Fi: 57;
Ma: 567

Le Vampire EDC: 145

The Vicomte de Bragelonne
Ma: 567

The Widow's Husband [Le Mari
de la Veuve] EDC: 146

The Youth of Louis XIV [La
Jeunesse de Louis XIV]
EDC: 146

DUMAS, Henry
General BAF: 88
Ark of Bones and Other Stories
BAF: 89
Jonoah and the Green Stone
BAF: 89

Du MAURIER, Daphne
General Po: 724
Frenchman's Creek ENE: 85
Rebecca Po: 724

Du MAURIER, George Louis
General BN: 49-50; TA: 142
The Martian ENES1: 69
Peter Ibbetson ENES1: 69
Trilby ENES1: 69; ENES2:
77

DUMITRIU, Petru
The Extreme Occident Ma: 569
Incognito Ma: 569

DUMMER, Jeremiah
The Diary of Jeremiah Dummer
AP: 579

DUNBAR, Paul Laurence
General AAPD: 62-64; AAW:
50-51; ASF: 145; BAF:

93-94; BAP: 70; BAW:
247-252; LCAB: 56; MBA:
75; Po: 724

"Anner 'Lizer's Stumblin'
Block" ASF: 144

Dream Lovers BAP: 70

Herrick BAP: 70

"The Independence of Silas
Bollender" Wa: 183

"Lincoln" LCAB: 57

"The Lynching of Jube Benson" ASF: 144

On the Island of Tanawana
BAP: 70

The Quibbler's Wife BAP:
70

"The Scapegoat" ASF: 145;
WaS1: 56

The Sport of the Gods BAF:
93; Po: 724

The Stolen Calf BAP: 70

Uncle Eph's Christmas BAP:
70

Winter Roses BAP: 70

DUNBAR, William
General Ai: 34; OMEP:
407-408; SC: 48

"The Golden Targe" OMEP:
408; PE: 156; SC: 48

"Hale, Sterne Superne!
Hale, in Eterne" PE:
156

"Lament for the Makaris"
PE: 156

"Meditation in Wintir" PE:
156

"My Heid Did Yak Yester-
nicht" PE: 156

"Petition of the Gray Horse"
PE: 156

"Strains of Sight" PE: 157

"The Thrissil and the Rois"
PE: 156

"To a Lady" PE: 156

"The Twa Maritt Wemen and
the Wedo" PE: 157

DUNBAR-NELSON, Alice Ruth
General ASF: 145; BAF:
95; BAW: 254; MBA: 74

The Dunbar Speaker and
Entertainer BAW: 254

Masterpieces of Negro Elo-
quence BAW: 254

Violets and Other Tales
BAF: 95

DUNCAN, Jane [Janet SANDI-
SON]
General Ai: 292

DUNCAN, Robert Edward
General ICBAP: 44; LCAB:
57; MP: 37; Po: 725

"Often I Am Permitted to Return
to a Meadow" ICBAP: 44

DUNCAN, Ronald
General MBD: 41; MDAE:
185

This Way to the Tomb Br:
192; DC1: 55; MBD: 41

DUNCAN, Sara Jeannette [Mrs.
COTES]
General ECL: 56-57

The Imperialist ECL: 56

DUNCAN, Thelma
The Death Dance BAP: 71;
MBA: 75

Sacrifice BAP: 71

DUNHAM, Katherine
General BAF: 96; BAW: 256-
257

Kasamance BAF: 96

A Touch of Innocence BAF:
96; BAW: 257

DUNLAP, William
General AD: 116-119; ALL:
80; Da: 110; Lon: 58-59

André AD: 116, 118; ADC:
93

Darby's Return AD: 118;
ADC: 94

The Father, or American
Shandyism AD: 119; ADC:
94

"It Might Have Been Better!
It Might Have Been Worse"
ASF: 145

The Stranger AD: 116

A Trip to Niagara; or, Travellers in America AD:
119; DC1: 55; Lon: 59

DUNN, Joseph H. and Ira KOL-
JONEN
Unnamable ADC: 94

DUNN, Max
General Po: 725

DUNNE, Finley Peter
General LCAB: 57

DUNNEHAUPT, Johann
Jacob DC2: 114

DUNNETT, Dorothy
General Ai: 323

DUNNING, Philip
Night Hostess ADC: 94

_____ and Philip HIGLEY
Remember the Day ADC: 94
_____ and Joseph SCHRANK
Page Miss Glory ADC: 94
DUNSANY, Lord Edward John
Moreton [Edward J.M.D.
PLUNKETT]
General Br: 193; MBD:
42; MD: 91; Mi: 230-
231; Po: 725; TA: 247
The Glittering Gate Br: 193
The Gods of the Mountain
DC1: 55; MD: 91
King Argimenes and the
Unknown Warrior Br:
193
A Night at the Inn Br: 193
The Tents of the Arabs Br:
193
"Two Bottles of Relish" Wa:
183; WaS1: 56
DUODU, Cameron
General BALE: 294
Dupin, Amantine see SAND,
George
DUPREY, Jean Pierre
General Po: 725-726
DURACK, Mary
General MAP: 162
Keep Him, My Country MAP:
162
DURANG, Christopher
Das Lusitania Songspiel
ADC: 94
A History of the American
Film ADC: 94-95; TMAP:
203
Titanic ADC: 95
The Vietnamization of New
Jersey ADC: 95
DURAS, Marguerite
General Br: 193; Po: 726-
727
L'Après-midi de Monsieur
Andesmas Fi: 57; Po:
728
Un Barrage contre la Pacifique
Fi: 57; Po: 726
"Le Boa" Wa: 183
"Les Chantiers" Wa: 183
Days in the Trees Br: 193
Destroy, She Said Fi: 57
Dix heures et demie du
soir en été Fi: 57-58
"Des Journées entières dans
les arbres" Po: 728

"Madame Dodin" Wa: 183
Le Marin de Gibralter Fi: 58;
Po: 726
Moderato Cantabile Fi: 58;
Ke: 59; Po: 728; Wa:
183; WaS1: 56
La Musica Br: 193-194
Ourika Fi: 58
Les Petits chevaux de Tarquina
Fi: 58
The Ravishing of Lol V. Stein
Fi: 58
The Square Br: 194; Fi: 58;
Ke: 59
The Viaduct Br: 194
Le Vice-Consul Fi: 59
La Vie tranquille Fi: 59
D'URFEY, Thomas
General Bon: 40-41; Li: 166-
167
DURHAM, Alice Marie
Golden Gloves MBA: 75
DURHAM, John S.
General BAF: 97
DURRELL, Lawrence
General BN2: 34-35; CFAE:
128-133; CN: 119; MDAE:
186-187; Po: 728-731; Sch:
66-68
Acte; or, The Prisoners of
Time DC1: 55; EDC: 146
The Alexandria Quartet BN2:
35; CFAE: 128-133; CN:
119-123; ENE: 85-88;
ENES1: 69-70; ENES2: 77-
78; LCAB: 57; Po: 730-
741; Sch: 68-71
"At Epidaurus" PE: 157
Balthazar ENE: 88-89;
ENES1: 70-71; Ma: 570-
571; Sch: 68-71
Bitter Lemons Ma: 571
The Black Book CN: 123-124;
ENES1: 71; Ma: 571-572;
Po: 730, 741
Clea see also The Alexandria
Quartet CN: 124; ENE:
89; ENES1: 71; Ma: 572-
573; Sch: 68-71
The Dark Labyrinth [Cefalû]
CN: 124; ENES1: 71; Ma:
573
An Irish Faustus Br: 194;
EDC: 146; Po: 741
Justine see also The Alex-
andria Quartet ENE: 89;

ENES1: 71; Ma: 573-574;
Sch: 68-71
A Key to Modern British Po-
etry Po: 741
Monsieur; or, The Prince of
Darkness ENES2: 78
Mountolive see also The
Alexandria Quartet CN:
124: ENE: 89-90; ENES1:
71; Ma: 574-575; Sch:
68-71
Nunquam ENES1: 71; ENES2:
78
Panic Spring CN: 124;
ENES1: 71
Pied Piper of Lovers CN:
124; Po: 741-742
Sappho EDC: 146
"Song for Zarathustra"
ICBAP: 44; PE: 157;
Po: 742
"To Argos" PE: 157
Tunc CN: 124; ENES1: 71;
ENES2: 78
White Eagles Over Serbia
CN: 124
DÜRRENMATT, Friedrich
General Br: 195-196; LCAB:
56; MD: 91-92; Po: 742-
748
The Anabaptists [Die Wieder-
täufer] EDC: 146; Po:
752
An Angel Comes to Babylon
[Ein Engel Kommt nach
Babylon] Br: 196; DC2:
114; EDC: 146; MD: 92;
Po: 742
Der Besuch der alten Dame
see The Visit
The Blind Man [Der Blinde]
Br: 197; DC2: 115;
EDC: 146-147
"Christmas" Wa: 183; WaS1:
56
A Dangerous Game Fi: 297;
Ke: 260
"The Director" Wa: 183
"The Dog" Wa: 184
Die Ehe des Herrn Missis-
sippi see The Marriage
of Mr. Mississippi
Ein Engel Kommt nach Baby-
lon see An Angel Comes
to Babylon
Es Steht Geschrieben see

It Is Written
Executioner see The Judge
and His Hangman
Frank the 5th, Opera of a Pri-
vate Bank [Frank der
Fünfte, Oper Einer Privat-
bank] Br: 197; DC2: 115;
EDC: 147; Po: 750
Greek Man Seeks Greek Maiden
[Grieche Sucht Griechen]
EDC: 147
Hercules and the Augean Stables
EDC: 147
Incident at Twilight Br: 197
It Is Written [Es Steht
Geschrieben] Br: 197;
DC2: 115; EDC: 147
The Judge and His Hangman
[Executioner; Der Richter
und sein Henker] Fi: 297;
Ke: 260; Po: 751; Wa:
184; WaS1: 56
The Marriage of Mr. Mississippi
[Die Ehe des Herrn Missis-
sippi] Br: 197-198; DC2:
115; EDC: 147-148; MD: 92;
Po: 742, 749-750
The Meteor [Der Meteor] Br:
198; DC2: 116; EDC: 148;
Po: 750
"The Nihilist" see "The Trap"
Once a Greek ... Fi: 297;
Wa: 184
Operation Wega [Das Unterneh-
men der Wega] Br: 198
"Die Panne" see "The Trap"
The Physicist [Die Physiker]
Br: 198; DC2: 116; EDC:
148-149; MD: 93; Po: 742,
751
"The Picture of Sisyphus" Wa:
184
"Pilate" Wa: 184
Play Strindberg EDC: 149
The Pledge [Das Versprechen]
Fi: 297; Ke: 260-261; Po:
752; Wa: 184
Portrait of a Planet EDC:
149
The Quarry Fi: 297-298
Der Richter und sein Henker
see The Judge and His
Hangman
Romulus the Great [Romulus
der Grosse] Br: 198-199;
DC2: 116; EDC: 149-150;

MD: 93; Po: 742, 751
"The Suspicion" Wa: 184
"The Torturer" Wa: 184;
    WaS1: 56
"The Town" Wa: 184
"The Trap" ["Die Panne"]
    Po: 750; Wa: 184
"The Tunnel" ["Der Tunnel"]
    Po: 752; Wa: 184; WaS1:
    56
Das Unternehmen der Wega
    see Operation Wega
Das Versprechen see The
    Pledge
The Visit [The Visit of the
    Old Lady; Der Besuch der
    alten Dame] Br: 199-200;
    DC2: 116-117; EDC: 150-
    151; LCAB: 56; MD: 92;
    Po: 742, 748-749, 1596
Die Wiedertäufer see The
    Anabaptists
"Weihnachten" Po: 752
Du RYER, Pierre
    Esther DC2: 117
    Saul DC2: 118
    Scevole DC2: 118
DUUN, Olav
    In Make-Believe Land Ke:
        348
    Menneske og Maktene Fi:
        402
    Our Own Age Ke: 348
DUVAL, John C.
    General ASF: 145
DUVIGNAUD, Jean
    General Po: 753
DWIGHT, Timothy
    General AP: 267-271; Da:
        66-67
    Travels in New-England and
        New-York AP: 268-271;
        Da: 67
    The Triumph of Infidelity
        Da: 66-67
DYER, Charles
    General MDAE: 189
    The Staircase EDC: 151;
        MDAE: 189
DYER, John
    General EC: 67-68; Me:
        218-219
    The Fleece Me: 218
    Grongar Hill EC: 67-68;
        ICBAP: 44; Me: 218
DYER, Sir Edward

General SC: 49
"A Modest Love" PE: 157
DYGASINSKI, Adolf
    "A Trip with Mademoiselle Jour-
        dan" Wa: 184
DYKES, James
    General BAW: 260
DYLAN, Bob
    General Po: 753
DYSON, Edward
    General AL: 197
    In the Roaring Fifties AL:
        197

E

Eagle, Solomon see SQUIRE,
    John Collings
EARLE, John
    General Ba: 63-64
EARLE, Victoria
    General LCAB: 57
EASMON, Raymond Sarif
    General BALE: 295
    The Burnt-Out Marriage BALE:
        295
Eastaway, Edward see THOMAS,
    Edward
EASTLAKE, William
    General ASF: 146; CFAE:
        135; CN: 125; Po: 755
    The Bronc People CN: 125
    Go In Beauty CN: 125
    Portrait of an Artist with
        Twenty-Six Horses CN:
        125
EASTMAN, Charles Alexander
    General ASF: 146
EASTMAN, Harold
    "The Mockingbird" ASF: 146
EASTON, Sidney
    General BAP: 71; BAW: 261
    Go Back Where You Stayed Last
        Night BAP: 72
    Lifeboat BAP: 72
    Miss Trudie Fair BAP: 72;
        Br: 200
EASTON, William Edgar
    General LCAB: 57; MBA: 76
    Christophe MBA: 76
    Dessalines ADC: 95; MBA:
        76
EATON, Geoffrey Dell
    Green Bush LCAB: 57
d'EAUBONNE, Françoise

General Po: 755
EBEN, Jacob Har
"Boaz of Dupra" Wa: 184
EBERHART, Richard
General LCAB: 57; Ma:
576; MDAE: 191; Po:
756-757
"Am I My Neighbor's Keeper"
ICBAP: 44; LCAB: 57
The Apparition MDAE: 191
"Experience Evoked" PE:
157
"From Letter I" PE: 157
"The Fury of Aerial Bombard-
ment" ICBAP: 44; PE:
157; Po: 757
"Grave Piece" PE: 157
"The Groundhog" LCAB:
57-58; PE: 157; Po: 757
"The Horse Chestnut Tree"
ICBAP: 44; PE: 158
"I Walked Out to the Grave-
yard to See the Dead" PE:
158
"Meditation" PE: 158
"On a Squirrel Crossing the
Road in Autumn, in New
England" PE: 158
"Orchard" PE: 158
"Seals, Terns, Time" PE:
158
"Throwing the Apple" ICBAP:
44; PE: 158; Po: 757
"Ur Burial" PE: 158; Po:
757-758
The Visionary Farms Br:
200; DC1: 55; MDAE:
92, 191
"The Young Hunter" PE:
158
EBNER-ESCHENBACH, Maria von
"Er lasst die Hand küssen"
Wa: 184; WaS1: 56
"Der Erstgeborene" Wa:
185
"Die Freiherrn von Gemper-
lein" Wa: 185
"Maslans Frau" Wa: 185
"Das Schädliche" Wa: 185
EBON [Tom DOOLEY]
General BAW: 261
ECHEGARAY, José
General Br: 201; Po: 758
The Cleansing Stain [Mancha
Que Limpia] Br: 201
The Great Galeoto Br: 201;

DC2: 118
ECHERUO, Michael Joseph Chukwu-
dalu
General BALE: 296
ECHEVERRIA, Esteban
General LCAB: 58
"El Matadero" Wa: 185
ECKELS, Jon B.
General BAW: 262
EDELMAN, Maurice
General LCAB: 58
EDELSTEIN, Hyman [Don SYNGE]
General JW: 144
EDGEWORTH, Maria
General Du: 57-58; LCAB:
58
The Absentee Du: 56; ENE:
90; ENES1: 72; Ma: 577
"Angelina; ou L'Amie Inconnue"
Wa: 185
Belinda ENES1: 72; ENES2:
78
Castle Rackrent Du: 56-57;
ENE: 90; ENES1: 72;
ENES2: 78; Ma: 577-578
The Double Disguise DC1: 55
Ennui ENES1: 72
Harrington ENES1: 72
Helen ENES1: 72
Lenora ENES1: 72; ENES2:
78
The Modern Griselda ENES1:
73
Ormond ENE: 90; ENES1:
73
Patronage ENES1: 73
Vivian ENES1: 73
EDIP-ADIVAR, Halide
"Everyday Men: The Pumpkin-
Seed Seller" WaS1: 56
EDMONDS, Irene
The Lost Gem MBA: 76
EDMONDS, Randolph S.
General AAPD: 311; BAP:
74; BAW: 263; MBA: 77
Bad Man BAP: 74
Bleeding Hearts BAP: 74
The Breeders BAP: 74; MBA:
77
Earth and Stars MBA: 77
Gangsters Over Harlem BAP:
74-75; MBA: 77
High Court of Historia BAP:
75
In the Land of Cotton MBA:
77

Meek Mose BAP: 75
Nat Turner BAP: 75; MBA: 77
The New Window BAP: 75
Old Man Pete BAP: 75
Prometheus and the Atom MBA: 77
Shades and Shadows MBA: 77
Six Plays for a Negro Theatre MBA: 77
Yellow Death BAP: 75; MBA: 77
EDMONDS, Walter D.
General Ma: 579
Chad Hanna Po: 758
"The Death of Red Peril" SFC: 48; Wa: 185
Rome Haul Po: 758
EDSCHMID, Kasimir
Sport Um Gagaly Fi: 298
EDSON, Russell
"One Wonders" PE: 158
EDWARDES, Richard
Clyomon and Clamydes see ANONYMOUS
Common Conditions see ANONYMOUS
Damon and Pithias DC1: 56
EDWARDS, Gus
The Offering ADC: 95
EDWARDS, Harry Stillwell
General Po: 759
"Elder Brown's Backslide" ASF: 146; Wa: 185
"His Defense" ASF: 146; Wa: 185
EDWARDS, Jonathan
General ALL: 80-82; AP: 276-294; Da: 28-29; ICBAP: 45; LCAB: 58
Sinners in the Hands of an Angry God AP: 282
EDWARDS, Junius
General BAF: 98
If We Must Die BAF: 98; BAW: 263
EDWARDS, Richard
General SC: 49
EGBUNA, Obi Benue
General BALE: 296
The Anthill BALE: 296
EGERTON, George
Keynotes ENES2: 78
EGGE, Peter
By the Deep Fjords Ke: 348-349
Guests Ke: 349
EGGLESTON, Edward
General AF: 98; AN: 67; ASF: 146; Ho: 136, 157; LCAB: 58
The Circuit Rider AF: 98
"The Gunpowder Plot" ASF: 146
The Hoosier School-Master AN: 67; Ho: 136
Roxy AF: 98; Ho: 136
"Uncle Sim's Boy" ASF: 146
EGUDU, Romanus
General BALE: 297
EGUILAZ, D. Luis de
Una Aventura de Tirso DC2: 118
La Cruz del Matrunonio DC2: 118
EGUREN, José María
General Po: 759
EHNI, René
General Po: 759
EHRENBERG, Il'ja
General LCAB: 58; Po: 759-760
The Extraordinary Adventures of Julio Jurenito and His Disciples [Xulio Xurenito] Fi: 446-447; Ke: 402
The Fall of Paris Ke: 402
In the Protochny Lane [In Protocnyj Lane] Ke: 402; Po: 760
The Ninth Wave Ke: 402
Ottepel see The Thaw
Out of Chaos Ke: 402-403
The Second Day Ke: 403
The Storm Ke: 403
The Summer of the Year 1925 Po: 760
The Thaw [Ottepel] Ke: 403; Po: 760
The Uncommon Life of Lasik Roitschwantz Ke: 403
Xulio Xurenito see The Extraordinary Adventures of Julio Jurenito and His Disciples
EICH, Günter
General Br: 201; Po: 760-761
Die Andere und Ich Br: 201
Geh Nicht Nach El Kuwehd Br: 201
Das Jahr Lazertis Br: 202
Die Mädchen aus Viterbo Br:

202
Träume, 1951 Br: 202
"Züge im Nebel" Wa: 185
EICHELBAUM, Samuel
General Br: 202
EICHENDORFF, Joseph von
General Po: 761
Ahnung und Gegenwart see
Presentiment and the
Present
Dichter und Ihre Gesellen
Fi: 298
"Dürande Castle" Wa: 186
"Die Entführung" Wa: 186
From the Life of a Good-for-
Nothing Fi: 298; Ke:
261; Wa: 186; WaS1: 57
The Marble Statue [Das
Marmorbild] Fi: 298;
Wa: 186; WaS1: 57
"Much Ado About Nothing"
Wa: 186
Presentiment and the Present
[Ahnung und Gegenwart]
Fi: 298; Ke: 261
EICHMAN, Mark
As to the Meaning of Words
ADC: 95
EIGNER, Laurence Noel
"Keep Me Still, I Do Not
Want to Dream" ICBAP:
45
EISLER, Hans
General Po: 761
EKELÖF, Gunnar
"Absentia Animi" Po: 762
EKWENSI, Cyprian Odiatu Duaka
General BALE: 298-300; Po:
761
An African Night's Entertain-
ment BALE: 300
Beautiful Feathers BALE:
299
Jagua Nana BALE: 299; Po:
761
People of the City BALE:
299
EKWERE, John
General BALE: 300
El Muhajir see MARVIN X
ELDER, Lonne, III
General AAPD: 363; BAP:
76; BAW: 264; MBA:
78
Ceremonies in Dark Old Men
ADC: 96; BAP: 76-77;

Ma: 580; MBA: 78-79
Charades MBA: 79
Part 2, Sounder MBA: 79
ELDERSHAW, M. Barnard
General MAP: 165
"The Plover" Wa: 187
"Shipwreck" Wa: 187
Tomorrow and Tomorrow MAP:
165
ELINSON, John
General LCAB: 58
ELIOT, George [Mary Ann Evans
CROSS]
General BN: 51-54; Du: 65-
68; ICBAP: 45; LCAB: 58
Adam Bede BN: 54; Du: 58-
59; EN: 40-41; ENE: 90-91;
ENES1: 73-74; ENES2: 78-
79; Ma: 581-582
"Amos Barton" Wa: 187
"A College Breakfast-Party"
ICBAP: 45
Daniel Deronda BN: 54-55;
Du: 59-60; EN: 41-42;
ENE: 92-93; ENES1: 74-75;
ENES2: 79-80; Ma: 582-583;
Po: 1786
Felix Holt, Radical BN: 55;
Du: 60; EN: 42; ENE:
93-94; ENES1: 75-76;
ENES2: 80; Ma: 583-585
"I Grant You Ample Leave"
ICBAP: 45; PE: 158
"In a London Drawing Room"
ICBAP: 45; PE: 158
"Janet's Repentance" Wa: 187
"The Lifted Veil" Wa: 187
Middlemarch BN: 55-56; Du:
60-63; EN: 42-44; ENE:
94-96; ENES1: 76-77;
ENES2: 79-82; LCAB: 58;
Ma: 585-587
The Mill on the Floss BN:
56; Du: 63-64; EN: 44;
ENE: 96-97; ENES1: 77-78;
ENES2: 83; LCAB: 59;
Ma: 587-588
"Mr. Gilfil's Love Story" Wa:
187
Romola BN: 56; Du: 64-65;
EN: 44-45; ENE: 97-98;
ENES1: 78-79; ENES2: 83-
84; Ma: 588-589
Scenes of Clerical Life BN:
56; ENES1: 79; ENES2:
84

Silas Marner BN: 57; Du:
    65; EN: 45; ENE: 98-99;
    ENES1: 79; ENES2: 84;
    Ma: 589-591; Po: 4033
The Spanish Gypsy EN: 45
ELIOT, John
  General AP: 296-297; Da:
    29
ELIOT, Marge
  General MBA: 80
ELIOT, Thomas Stearns
  General ALL: 82-87; APC:
    172-175; Br: 202-204;
    ICBAP: 45; LCAB: 59;
    Lon: 28-31; MBD: 42-
    47; MD: 93-95; MDAE:
    193-197; Mi: 231-233;
    MP: 38-41; Po: 762-807
  "The Ad-dressing of Cats"
    PE: 158
  "Animula" ICBAP: 45; PE:
    158; Po: 807
  "Ash-Wednesday" ALL: 87;
    ICBAP: 45; LCAB: 59;
    Ma: 592-593; MBD: 43;
    MP: 39, 41; PE: 158-
    160; Po: 786, 807-809
  "Aunt Helen" PE: 160
  "The Boston Evening Tran-
    script" PE: 160
  "Burbank with a Baedeker:
    Bleistein with a Cigar"
    PE: 160; Po: 790, 799,
    809
  "Burnt Norton" ICBAP: 46;
    PE: 160-161; Po: 809-810
  "Cape Ann" ICBAP: 46;
    PE: 161
  The Cocktail Party Br: 204-
    207; DC1: 56-60; EDC:
    151-154; LCAB: 59; Lon:
    26, 29-31; Ma: 593-595;
    MBD: 42-47; MD: 95-98;
    MDAE: 193-197; Po: 762,
    764-765, 776, 779, 782,
    805, 811-814; TMAP: 63,
    102
  The Confidential Clerk Br:
    207-208; DC1: 60-61;
    EDC: 154; Lon: 29; Ma:
    595-596; MBD: 43-44; MD:
    98; MDAE: 193-195, 197;
    Po: 776, 779, 782, 814-
    815
  "A Cooking Egg" PE: 161
  "Coriolan" DC1: 61; ICBAP:
    46; PE: 161; Po: 815
  "The Cultivation of Christmas
    Trees" PE: 161
  "Dans le Restaurant" PE: 161-
    162
  "A Dedication to My Wife" PE:
    162
  "Le Directeur" Po: 815
  "The Dry Salvages" ICBAP:
    46; LCAB: 59; MP: 39;
    PE: 162; Po: 815
  "East Coker" ICBAP: 46; PE:
    162-163; Po: 815-816
  The Elder Statesman Br:
    208-209; DC1: 61-62; EDC:
    154-155; Lon: 29-30; Ma:
    596-597; MBD: 43-44, 46;
    MD: 98-99; MDAE: 194,
    196-197; Po: 776, 816-817
  The Family Reunion Br: 209-
    211; DC1: 62-65; EDC:
    155-157; LCAB: 59-60; Lon:
    29-30; Ma: 598-599; MBD:
    43-46; MD: 99-101; MDAE:
    194; Po: 779, 782, 817-820
  "La Figlia Che Piange" PE:
    168
  "Five Finger Exercises" Po:
    820
  "Four Quartets" ALL: 83-84,
    87; ICBAP: 46; LCAB:
    60; Ma: 599-600; MP: 38-
    40; PE: 163-164; Po: 765,
    770, 773, 780, 809-810, 820-
    824; Ri2: 67, 70, 373
  "Gerontion" ICBAP: 46; Ma:
    601-602; MP: 39, 41; PE:
    165-166; Po: 825-827
  "Gus: The Theatre Cat" PE:
    166
  "The Hippopotamus" PE: 166;
    Po: 827
  "The Hollow Men" ICBAP: 46-
    47; Ma: 602-603; PE: 166-
    167; Po: 787, 799, 827-829
  "Hysteria" PE: 167; Po: 829
  "Jellicle Cats" PE: 167
  "Journey of the Magi" ICBAP:
    47; PE: 167-168; Po: 830-
    831
  "Landscapes" ICBAP: 47; Po:
    831
  "Lines to Ralph Hodgson Esgre"
    PE: 168
  "Little Gidding" ICBAP: 47;
    MP: 40; PE: 168; Po: 831

"Love Song of J. Alfred Pru-
frock" ICBAP: 47; Ma:
603-604; PE: 168-171; Po:
771, 780, 832-836

"Macavity: The Mystery Cat"
PE: 171

"Marina" ICBAP: 47; PE:
171; Po: 836-837

"Mr. Apollinax" PE: 171

"Mr. Eliot's Sunday Morning
Service" ICBAP: 47; PE:
171-172; Po: 837

Murder in the Cathedral Br:
211-214; DC1: 65-67; EDC:
157-160; Lon: 28-30; Ma:
605-606; MBD: 42-47; MD:
101-103; MDAE: 195; Po:
762, 777-778, 780, 782,
784, 792-794, 837-841

"The Naming of Cats" PE:
172

"New Hampshire" ICBAP:
47; PE: 172

Notes Towards the Definition
of Culture Po: 841

"Ode of Dejection" PE: 172;
Po: 841

"Old Deuteronomy" PE: 172

"Old Possum's Book of Practical Cats" PE: 172; Po:
792-793, 820, 841

On Poetry and Poets Po:
841-842

"Portrait of a Lady" PE:
172; Po: 779, 842

"Preludes" ICBAP: 48; PE:
172

"Rannoch, by Glencoe"
ICBAP: 48; PE: 172

"The Readers of the Boston
Evening Transcript"
ICBAP: 48

"Rhapsody on a Windy Night"
ICBAP: 48; PE: 173

The Rock Br: 214; DC1:
67; EDC: 160; MD: 103;
Po: 843

The Sacred Wood Po: 843

"A Song for Simeon" ICBAP:
48; PE: 173

"Sweeney Agonistes" Br:
214; EDC: 160-161; MBD:
44, 46; MD: 103; MDAE:
196-197; PE: 173; Po:
772, 843-844

"Sweeney Among the Night-

ingales" ICBAP: 48; PE:
173-174; Po: 844-845

"Sweeney Erect" ICBAP: 48;
PE: 174; Po: 771, 845

"To the Indians Who Died in
Africa" Po: 845

Tradition and the Individual
Talent Po: 845-846

"Triumphal March" (from the
unfinished Coriolan) PE:
174

"Usk" ICBAP: 48; PE: 174

"Virginia" ICBAP: 48; PE:
174

"The Waste Land" ALL: 82,
85, 87; ICBAP: 48; LCAB:
60; Ma: 606-608; MBD: 44;
MP: 39-40; PE: 174-179;
Po: 770, 772, 778, 785,
787, 789, 791, 794, 828-829,
846-859

"The Waste Land--I, Burial of
the Dead" ICBAP: 49

"The Waste Land--IV, Death by
Water" ICBAP: 49

"Whispers of Immortality" PE:
179; Po: 859

ELIZABETH I, Queen of England
General SC: 49-50

ELIZONDO, Jose F.
General Br: 215

ELKIN, Stanley Lawrence
General ASF: 147; CFAE:
137; JW: 196

"The Bailbondsman" ASF: 147

Boswell: A Modern Comedy
CN: 125

"I Look Out for Ed Wolfe" ASF:
147; LCAB: 60; WaS1: 57

ELLIOTT, George Paul
General ASF: 148; CFAE:
139; CN: 126

Among the Dangs LCAB: 60

"Children of Ruth" ASF: 147;
LCAB: 60

David Knudsen CN: 126

"Fever and Chills" ICBAP: 49

In the World CN: 126

"The NRACP" ASF: 147; WaS1:
57

"Sandra" Wa: 187

ELLIS, A.E.
The Rack ENE: 99

ELLIS, Havelock
General TA: 144

Kanga Creek MAP: 166

ELLISON, Harlan
  General ASF: 148
  "All the Sounds" WaS1: 57
  "Along the Scenic Route"
    WaS1: 57
  "Back to the Drawing Boards"
    WaS1: 57
  "Basilisk" WaS1: 57
  "Battlefield" WaS1: 57
  "The Beast That Shouted Love
    at the Heart of the World"
    WaS1: 57
  "A Boy and His Dog" ASF:
    148; WaS1: 58
  "Catman" WaS1: 58
  "The Crackpots" WaS1: 58
  "Croatoan" WaS1: 58
  "The Deathbird" WaS1: 58
  "Deeper Than the Darkness"
    WaS1: 58
  "Delusion of the Dragon
    Slayer" WaS1: 58
  "I Have No Mouth and I Must
    Scream" ASF: 148; WaS1:
    58
  "Knox" WaS1: 58
  "Night Vigil" WaS1: 58
  "One Life" WaS1: 58
  "Paingod" WaS1: 58
  "The Place with No Name"
    WaS1: 58
  "Pretty Maggie Moneyeyes"
    WaS1: 58
  "Punky and the Yale Men"
    WaS1: 58
  "Repent Harlequin! Said the
    Ticktockman" ASF: 148;
    Wa: 187; WaS1: 59
  "Run for the Stars" WaS1:
    59
  "Silent in Gehenna" WaS1:
    59
  "The Silver Corridor" WaS1:
    59
  "Status Quo at Troyden's"
    WaS1: 59
  "Wanted in Surgery" WaS1:
    59
  "Worlds to Kill" WaS1: 59
ELLISON, Ralph Waldo
  General AAF: 73-75; AAL:
    160-162, 168-171; AAW:
    52-53; AN: 68; ASF:
    149; BAF: 100-112; BAW:
    269-274; CFAE: 141-144;
    CN: 126-127; LCAB: 60;

  Ne: 34-35; Po: 860-861
  "Afternoon" AAL: 161-162;
    Wa: 187; WaS1: 59
  "Battle Royal" ASF: 148; Wa:
    188; WaS1: 59
  "The Birthmark" AAL: 161-
    162; Wa: 188; WaS1: 59
  "A Coupla Scalped Indians"
    WaS1: 59
  "Flying Home" AAL: 161-162;
    ASF: 148; BAF: 111; Wa:
    188; WaS1: 59
  "In a Strange Country" ASF:
    148; WaS1: 59
  Invisible Man AAF: 73-75;
    AAL: 160-161, 168-171;
    AAW: 52-53; AN: 67-68;
    BAF: 100-113; CFAE: 141-
    144; CN: 127-129; LCAB:
    60; Ma: 609-610; Ne: 34-
    35; Po: 861-866; TMAP: 127
  "King of the Bingo Game" AAL:
    161-162, 168; ASF: 148-149;
    BAF: 101, 110; Wa: 188;
    WaS1: 59-60
  "Mister Toussan" AAL: 161-
    162; Wa: 188; WaS1: 60
  Shadow and Act Ma: 610; Po:
    866-867
  "Slick Gonna Learn" AAL:
    161-162; Wa: 188
  "That I Had the Wings" AAL:
    161-162; ASF: 149; Wa:
    188; WaS1: 60
ELMSHE, Kenneth and Claibe
    RICHARDSON
  The Grass Harp ADC: 96
ELUARD, Paul
  General LCAB: 61; Po: 867-
    868
  "A Fernand Léger" Po: 869
  Capitale de la Douleur Po:
    869
  "Tout aiguisé de soif, tout af-
    famé de froid" Po: 869
ELYOT, Sir Thomas
  General Hen: 188-189; SC:
    50-51
  The Book Named the Governour
    ERP: 152-153; Hen: 189;
    SC: 50-51
EMANUEL, James A., Sr.
  General BAW: 276-277
  Panther Man BAW: 277
  The Treehouse and Other Poems
    BAW: 277

EMENYONU, Ernest
General BALE: 301
EMERSON, Ralph Waldo
General ALL: 87-92; C1a:
  29-36; ICBAP: 49; LCAB:
  61; Ma: 612-613
"The Adirondacs" PE: 179
The American Scholar Ma:
  611
"Bacchus" PE: 179; Po:
  4046
"The Bohemian Hymn" PE:
  179
"Brahma" ICBAP: 49; PE:
  179-180
"Compensation" PE: 180
"Concord Hymn" PE: 180
"Days" PE: 180
"Death" C1a: 32
"Each and All" PE: 180-181
English Traits ALL: 90
Essays: First and Second
  Series Ma: 611-612
"Ever the Rock of Ages Melts"
  ICBAP: 49; PE: 181
"Forbearance" PE: 181
"Give All to Love" ICBAP:
  49; PE: 181
"Guy" PE: 181
"Hamatreya" ICBAP: 49;
  PE: 181
Journals C1a: 31
"Monadnoc" PE: 181
Nature C1a: 31, 34; Ma:
  612
"Ode Inscribed to W.H. Chan-
  ning" ICBAP: 49; PE:
  181
"The Poet" PE: 181
"Power" PE: 181
"The Problem" PE: 181
"The Rhodora" PE: 181-182
"The Snow-Storm" ICBAP:
  49; PE: 182
"The Sphinx" C1a: 35; PE:
  182
"Terminus" PE: 182
"Threnody" PE: 182
"The Titmouse" PE: 182
"Uriel" ICBAP: 49
"Woodnotes" PE: 182
EMMANUEL, Pierre
General Po: 869
EMMONS, Richard
"The Fredoniad" ICBAP:
  49

EMPSON, William
General EP: 89-95; LCAB:
  61; Ma: 614; Po: 869-871
"The Ants" PE: 183
"Arachne" PE: 183; Po: 871
"Aubade" EP: 92
"The Beautiful Train" EP: 90;
  PE: 183
"Flighting for Duck" PE: 183
"Four Legs, Two Legs, Three
  Legs" EP: 92-93; PE: 183;
  Po: 871
The Gathering Storm EP: 90
"High Dive" PE: 183
"Ignorance of Death" PE: 183
"Invitation to Juno" ICBAP:
  49; PE: 183; Po: 871-872
"Legal Fiction" PE: 183
"Let It Go" PE: 183
"Missing Dates" ICBAP: 50;
  PE: 183; Po: 872
"Note on Local Flora" PE:
  183
Seven Types of Ambiguity EP:
  91; Po: 872
Some Versions of the Pastoral
  EP: 89-90, 93
The Structure of Complex Words
  EP: 93-95
"Success" PE: 183
"The Teasers" EP: 92; PE:
  184
"This Last Pain" EP: 92; PE:
  184
"To an Old Lady" EP: 90
"Ufa Nightmare" PE: 184
"Value Is in Activity" PE:
  184
"Your Teeth Are Ivory Towers"
  EP: 92
EMTAGE, James B.
General WIL: 39
Brown Sugar, a Vestigal Tale
  WIL: 39
ENAVATULLAH, Anwar
"The Unravelled Knot" Wa:
  188
ENCINA, Juan del
Auto del Repelon DC2: 118
Carnival Eclogues DC2: 118
ENDO, Shusaku
Ogon No Kuni Br: 215; DC2:
  118; Po: 872
The Silence Po: 872
ENGEL, Lehman and Joanna ROOS
Golden Ladder BAP: 78

ENGLAND, George A.
"The Empire of the Air"
WaS1: 60
"June 6, 2016" WaS1: 60
ENGLISH, Thomas Dunn
"Caesar Rowan" ICBAP: 50
"Momma Phoebe" ICBAP: 50
ENQUIST, Per Olov
Sekonden Fi: 402
"The Tracks in the Sea of
Tranquility" WaS1: 60
ENRIGHT, Dennis Joseph
"Busy Body Under a Cherry
Tree" Po: 873
ENRIGHT, Elizabeth
"I Forgot Where I Was" Wa:
188
"The Sardillion" SFC: 48;
Wa: 188
ENRIQUEZ GOMEZ, Antonio
El siglo pitagórico y Vida de
don Gregorio Guadaña
Ke: 203
ENZENSBERGER, Hans Magnus
General Po: 873
EOTVOS, Jozsef
The Carthusian Ke: 403
Hungary in 1514 Ke: 403
The Sisters Ke: 404
The Village Notary Ke: 404
EPHRON, Phoebe
Howie ADC: 96
_____ and Henry EPHRON
My Daughter, Your Son ADC:
96
Take Her, She's Mine ADC:
97
Three's a Family ADC: 97
EQUIANO, Olaudah [Gustavus
VASSA]
General BALE: 301-302;
BAW: 278
ERAPU, Laban
General BALE: 302
ERASMUS, Desiderius
The Praise of Folly Ma:
615-616
ERDMAN, Jean
The Coach with Six Insides
ADC: 97
Erenburg, Il'ja see EHREN-
BURG, Il'ja
Erickson, Walter [pseud.] see
FAST, Howard
ERNST, Max
Une Semaine de bonté Fi:
59
ERNST, Paul
General MD: 104
"The Blind Man" Wa: 188
"Das Eisenbahnwägelchen" Wa:
189
"Förster und Wilddieb" Wa:
189
"Das Opfer der Frau" Wa:
189
"Das Porzellangeschirr" Wa:
189
"Die Quittung" Wa: 189
"Second Vision" Wa: 189
"Das streitige Gut" Wa: 189
Wie die Flugel Brechen Ke:
261
"The Wife of the Signalman"
Wa: 189
ERROL, John
Moon on a Rainbow Shawl BAP:
78; MBA: 80
ERSKINE, Milton
A Time of the Key Br: 215
ERTZ, Susan
The Proselyte LCAB: 61
ERVINE, St. John Greer
General Br: 215; MD: 104;
Mi: 233-234; TA: 145
The Critics Br: 215
The First Mrs. Fraser MD:
104
The Foolish Lovers ENES2: 84
Jane Clegg Br: 215; MD:
104
John Ferguson Br: 215; MD:
104
The Magnanimous Lover Br:
215
Mary, Mary Quite Contrary
MD: 104
Mixed Marriage Br: 216; MD:
104
Private Enterprise Br: 216
The Ship MD: 104
The Wayward Man ENES2: 85
ESCOFFERY, Gloria
General WIL: 39
ESCUDERO, Pamplona
Los pueblos dormidos KE: 203
ESENIN, Sergei Alexandrovich
General Po: 873-874
ESPINA, Concha
General Po: 874
The Girl from Luzmela Fi:
215

High Altar Fi: 215
Mariflor Fi: 215; Ke: 203
The Metal of the Dead Fi: 215
A Novel of Love Fi: 215
The Prudent Virgin Fi: 215
The Red Beacon Fi: 215
The Red Chalice Fi: 215
Retaguardia Fi: 215
Rose of the Winds Fi: 215; Ke: 203
The Strongest One Fi: 216
To Wake Up and Die Fi: 216
A Valley in the Sea Fi: 216
Victoria in America Fi: 216
The Woman and the Sea Fi: 216
Yesterday's Flower Fi: 216
ESPINEL, Vicente
Marcos de Obregón Fi: 216
ESPRONCEDA, José de
Sancho Saldaña Ke: 203
ESTAUNIE, Edouard
General Po: 874
L'appel de la route Ke: 59
Les choses voient Ke: 59
L'empreinte Ke: 59
L'épave Ke: 59
Le ferment Ke: 59
Le labyrinthe Ke: 59
Solitudes Ke: 59
La vie secrète Ke: 59
ETHEREGE, Sir George
General Bon: 41-42; Li: 168-171
The Comical Revenge; or, Love in a Tub DC1: 67-68; EDC: 161; Li: 168-170
The Man of Mode; or, Sir Fopling Flutter Bon: 41-42; DC1: 68; EDC: 161; LCAB: 61; Li: 168-171, 328
She Would If She Could DC1: 68; EDC: 161-162; Li: 168-170
ETIEMBLE, René
General Po: 874-875
Blason d'un corps Fi: 59
L'Enfant de choeur Fi: 59
Peaux de couleuvre Fi: 59
EURIPIDES
General LCAB: 61
Aiegus DC2: 118

Alcestis DC2: 119-120; EDC: 162; LCAB: 61-62; Ma: 617
Alexandros DC2: 120
Andromache DC2: 120; EDC: 163; Ma: 617-618
Antiope DC2: 120
Bacchae DC2: 121-122; EDC: 163-164; LCAB: 62; Ma: 618-619
The Children of Heracles [Heracles; Heraclaidae] DC2: 126-127; EDC: 166; Ma: 619
Chrysippos DC2: 123
Cresphontes [Kresphontes] DC2: 123
Cyclops [Kyklóps] DC2: 123; EDC: 164; Ma: 619
Electra DC2: 123-124; EDC: 164-165; Ma: 619-620
Hecuba [Hekabē] DC2: 124-125; EDC: 165
Helen [Helena] DC2: 125; EDC: 165-166; Ma: 620-621
Heraclaidae see The Children of Heracles
Heracles see The Children of Heracles
Herakles Mad Ma: 621
Hippolytus DC2: 127-129; EDC: 166-168; Ma: 621-623
Hypsipyle DC2: 129
Ion DC2: 129-130; EDC: 168; Ma: 623
Iphigenia in Aulis [Iphigenèia è en Aulidi] DC2: 130; EDC: 168-169; Ma: 623-624
Iphigenia in Tauris [Iphigenèia è en Taurois] DC2: 130-131; EDC: 169; Ma: 624
Kresphontes see Cresphontes
Kyklóps see Cyclops
Medea DC2: 131-133; EDC: 169-170; LCAB: 62; Ma: 624-625; TMAP: 31, 33
Oedipus DC2: 133
Orestes DC2: 133-134; EDC: 170; Ma: 626
Palamedes DC2: 134
Peliades DC2: 134
Phoenician Women [Phoinissai] DC2: 134-135; EDC: 170-171; Ma: 626
Rhesus DC2: 135; EDC: 171
The Suppliants [Supplices; Suppliant Women] DC2: 135-

136; EDC: 171-172; Ma:
626-627
The Trojan Women [Tróiades]
DC2: 136-137; EDC: 172;
Ma: 627
EVANS, Abbie Huston
General Po: 875
EVANS, Augusta Jane
General AN: 68
EVANS, Caradoc
General Po: 875
"The Blast of God" Wa: 189
"The Earth Gives All and
Takes All" Wa: 189
EVANS, Don
General BAF: 114
Matters of Choice MBA: 80
Orrin ADC: 97; MBA: 80
Sugar-Mouth Sam Don't Dance
No More ADC: 97; MBA:
80
EVANS, Donald
General Po: 875-876
"En Monocle" ICBAP: 50
EVANS, George Essex
General AL: 200
"An Australian Symphony"
AL: 200
"Women of the West" AL:
200
EVANS, Mari
General BAW: 281
I Am a Black Woman BAW:
281
Evans, Mary Ann see ELIOT,
George
EVANS, Mike
Good Times MBA: 81
EVANS, Nathaniel
General Da: 79
"Aeolian Harp" ICBAP: 50
"Daphnis and Menalcas"
ICBAP: 50
"Occasioned by Hearing Him
Play on the Harmonica"
ICBAP: 50
EVANS, Zishaw
Zetta MBA: 81
EVANS-CHARLES, Martie
Jamimma ADC: 97
EVELING, Stanley
General MDAE: 198
EVELYN, John
General Bon: 74
EVERSON, William [Brother
Antoninus]

General Po: 76
"Jacob and the Angels" PE:
184
EVERWYN, Klaus Ewert
"Description of an Industrial Ac-
cident" Wa: 189
EVERYMAN
Everyman EDC: 172-173
EVREINOV, Nikolai Nikolaevich
General Br: 216; MD: 104-
105
The Beautiful Despot MD: 105
The Merry Death Br: 216;
MD: 105
The Theatre of the Soul [The
Back Stage of the Soul; Be-
hind the Curtain of the Soul]
Br: 216; MD: 105
EVTUSHENKO, Evgeniĭ Aleksandro-
vich
General Ma: 2375; Po: 876-
877
EWER, Ferdinand C.
"The Eventful Nights of August
20th and 21st, 1854" ASF:
150
EWING, Samuel
"American Miracle" PE: 184
EXTON, Clive
General MDAE: 199
No Fixed Abode MDAE: 199
EYEN, Tom
General MDAE: 200
Areatha in the Ice Palace ADC:
97
The Dirtiest Show in Town
ADC: 97
The White Whore and the Bit
Player MDAE: 200
Why Hanna's Skirt Won't Stay
Down ADC: 97-98
Women Behind Bars ADC: 98

F

FABBRI, Diego
General Br: 216
Jesus on Trial DC2: 137
FABRE, Ferdinand
L'Abbe Tigrane Ke: 60
Lucifer Ke: 60
Le Marquis de Pierrerue Ke:
60
Mon oncle Ke: 60
Norine Ke: 60

FABRICUS, Andreas
  Samson DC2: 137
FADEYEV, Alexander
  General Po: 879
  The Nineteen Po: 879
  The Rout Fi: 447; Ke: 404
  The Young Guard Ke: 404;
    Po: 879
FAIK, Sait
  "Love Letter" WaS1: 60
  "The Man Who Doesn't Know
    What a Tooth or a Tooth-
    ache Is" WaS1: 60
  "Sivriada Night" WaS1: 60
FAIKO Alexis
  Man with the Portfolio Br:
    216
Faille, Pierre Della see DELLA
  FAILLE, Pierre
FAIN, William
  "Harmony" Wa: 189
FAIR, Ronald L.
  General BAF: 114-115; BAW:
    283
  Hog Butcher BAF: 115
  Many Thousand Gone BAF:
    115; BAW: 283
  We Can't Breathe BAF:
    116
  World of Nothing BAF: 116
FAIRLEY, Ruth Ann
  General BAF: 116
FAIWOO, F. Kwasi
  General BALE: 303
FALCONER, William
  The Shipwreck Ai: 72
FALKBERGET, Johan
  The Bread of Night Ke: 349
  Christianus Sextus Ke: 349
  The Fourth Night Watch Ke:
    349
  Lisbeth of Jarnfield Ke:
    349
FALKNER, John Meade
  General TA: 146
FALLADA, Hans
  Bauern, Bonzen und Bomben
    Po: 880
  Little Man, What Now? Ke:
    261
  Once We Had a Child Ke:
    261
  Sparrow Farm Ke: 261
FALLON, Padraic
  General Br: 216
FALUDY, George

General JW: 145
FANGEN, Ronald
  An Angel of Light Ke: 349
  Duel Ke: 349
  Erik Ke: 349
  The Way of a Woman Ke: 349
FANN, Al
  King Heroin ADC: 98; MBA:
    81
FARAGOH, Francis Edwards
  General Br: 216
  Pinwheel Br: 216-217
FARGUE, Léon Paul
  General Po: 880-881
FARIAS, Armando Jiménez
  General Po: 881
FARMER, Philip José
  General ASF: 150; LCAB:
    62
  "The God Business" WaS1: 60
  "Son" WaS1: 60
FARQUHAR, George
  General Bon: 42-43; Li: 172-
    174
  The Beaux' Stratagem DC1:
    68; EDC: 173-174; Li: 173;
    Ma: 628
  The Constant Couple; or, A
    Trip to the Jubilee DC1:
    68-69; EDC: 174; Li: 174
  The Inconstant; or, The Way to
    Win Him DC1: 69; EDC:
    174
  Love and a Bottle Bon: 42;
    EDC: 174; Li: 174
  The Recruiting Officer DC1:
    69; EDC: 174; Li: 174;
    Ma: 628-629
  Sir Harry Wildair, Being the
    Sequel of a Trip to the
    Jubilee DC1: 69; EDC:
    174
  The Twin Rivals DC1: 69;
    EDC: 174; Li: 174
FARRELL, J.G.
  The Siege of Krishnapur
    ENES2: 85
  Troubles ENES2: 85
FARRELL, James Thomas
  General ALL: 92; AN: 69-70;
    ASF: 151; CN: 129-130;
    LCAB: 62; Ne: 35-37; Po:
    881-882; Wo: 88-90
  "The Benefits of an American
    Life" SFC: 48; Wa: 190
  Bernard Carr Trilogy CN:

130
Bernard Clare see also
    Bernard Carr Trilogy
    CN: 131
"Clyde" SFC: 48; Wa: 190
Danny O'Neill Pentalogy
    CN: 131
Eileen Rogers CN: 131
Father and Son AN: 68
Gas-House McGinty CN: 131
"Helen, I Love You" ASF:
    151; Wa: 190
Judgment Day see also
    Studs Lonigan Trilogy
    AN: 68; CN: 131-132;
    Po: 882-883
My Days of Anger see also
    Danny O'Neill Pentalogy
    AN: 68; CN: 132
No Star Is Lost AN: 68;
    Ne: 36
The Road Between see also
    Bernard Carr Trilogy
    CN: 132
"Studs" SFC: 48
Studs Lonigan Ne: 36; Po:
    883-884; Wa: 68; Wo: 90
Studs Lonigan Trilogy CN:
    132-133; Ma: 630; Po:
    881
This Man and This Woman
    AN: 69
"Two Sisters" SFC: 49; Wa:
    190
What Time Collects CN: 133
A World I Never Made see
    also Danny O'Neill Pental-
    ogy AN: 69; CN: 133;
    Ne: 36
Yet Other Waters AN: 69
Young Lonigan see also
    Studs Lonigan Trilogy
    AN: 69; CN: 133; Po:
    884; Wo: 89
Young Manhood of Studs
    Lonigan AN: 69
FARRELL, John
General AL: 202
FARRERE, Claude
General Po: 884
FARRINGTON, Conor
General Br: 217
FAST, Howard Melvin
General AN: 71; CFAE:
    147; CN: 134; JW: 201-
    202; LCAB: 62; Po:

884
The American CN: 134
Conceived in Liberty CN: 134
"The Day of Victory" Wa: 190
The Last Frontier CN: 134
The Proud and the Free CN:
    134
Spartacus CN: 134; Po: 884
The Unvanquished CN: 134
FATOBA, Femi
General BALE: 303
FATOUVILLE, Nolant de
La Precaution Inutile DC2:
    137
FAUCHOIS, René
General Br: 217
FAULKNER, William
General ALL: 93-99; AN: 81-
    89; ASF: 171-180; CN:
    134-152; LCAB: 62-63;
    MDAE: 201-202; Ne: 38-48;
    Po: 885-936; Wo: 94-97
Absalom, Absalom! ALL: 95-
    96, 98; AN: 71-72; CN:
    153-157; Ma: 631-632; Ne:
    40-41, 43-48; Po: 894-895,
    898, 912, 916, 921, 931, 937-
    944, 1010; Wo: 96-97
"An Absolution" ASF: 152
"Ad Astra" ASF: 152; Po:
    944; SFC: 49; Wa: 190
"All the Dead Pilots" ASF:
    152; SFC: 49; Wa: 190
"Ambuscade" ASF: 152
"Artist at Home" ASF: 152;
    Wa: 190
As I Lay Dying AN: 72-73;
    CN: 157-160; Ma: 632-633;
    Ne: 41-43, 46-48; Po:
    897, 934-935, 944-950
"Barn Burning" ASF: 152-153;
    Po: 951; SFC: 49; Wa:
    190-191; WaS1: 61
"The Bear" ALL: 95; ASF:
    153-157; LCAB: 63; Ma:
    634-635; Ne: 40, 42-46; Po:
    921, 951-958; SFC: 49-51;
    Wa: 191-196; WaS1: 61;
    Wo: 96-97
"A Bear Hunt" ASF: 157;
    SFC: 51; Wa: 196
"The Big Shot" ASF: 157
"Black Music" ASF: 157;
    SFC: 51; Wa: 196; WaS1:
    61
"The Brooch" ASF: 157;

Wa: 196
"By the People" ASF: 157
"Carcassonne" WaS1: 61
"Centaur in Brass" ASF:
    157; Wa: 196
"A Courtship" ASF: 157;
    Po: 958; SFC: 51; Wa:
    196-197
"Crevasse" Wa: 197
"Death Drag" ASF: 157; Wa:
    197
"Delta Autumn" ASF: 157;
    Po: 958; SFC: 51-52;
    Wa: 197-198; WaS1: 61
"Dr. Martino" SFC: 52; Wa:
    198; WaS1: 61
"Dry September" ASF: 158;
    Po: 958-959; SFC: 52;
    Wa: 198; WaS1: 61
"Elly" ASF: 158; Po: 959;
    SFC: 52; Wa: 198
"An Error in Chemistry"
    ASF: 158; Wa: 198
"Evangeline" ASF: 158
A Fable AN: 73; CN: 160-
    163; LCAB: 63; Ma:
    635-636; Ne: 43-46; Po:
    893, 910, 914, 919, 932,
    959-964
"Father Abraham" ASF: 158
"The Fire and the Hearth"
    ASF: 158-159; Po: 965;
    SFC: 52; Wa: 198-199;
    WaS1: 61
"Fool About a Horse" ASF:
    159
"Fox Hunt" SFC: 52; Wa:
    199
Go Down, Moses ASF: 159-
    162; Ma: 636-637; Ne:
    44-45, 47; Po: 893, 920,
    931, 965-968; SFC: 52-53;
    Wa: 199; WaS1: 61; Wo:
    96
"Gold Is Not Always" ASF:
    162; Po: 969; Wa: 199
"Golden Land" ASF: 162;
    Po: 969; Wa: 199; WaS1:
    62
"Hair" ASF: 162; Wa: 200
The Hamlet see also Snopes
    Trilogy ALL: 93; AN:
    74; CN: 163-165; Ma:
    637-638; Ne: 43-44, 48;
    Po: 907, 969-972, 1003;
    Wo: 96

"Hand Upon the Water" ASF:
    162; Wa: 200
"The Hill" ASF: 162
"Hog Pawn" ASF: 162
"Hong Li" ASF: 162
"Honor" ASF: 162
"The Horseswap" ASF: 162
"The Hound" ASF: 162; Po:
    973; SFC: 53; Wa: 200
Intruder in the Dust AN: 74-
    75; CN: 165-167; LCAB:
    63; Ma: 638; Po: 898, 906-
    907, 920, 973-974; Wo: 96
"A Justice" ASF: 162-163; Po:
    974; Wa: 200
"The Kingdom of God" ASF:
    163; Po: 974
"Knight's Gambit" ASF: 163;
    Po: 920, 975; SFC: 53;
    Wa: 200; WaS1: 62
Light in August AN: 75-76;
    CN: 167-172; LCAB: 63;
    Ma: 638-640; Ne: 40-47;
    Po: 894, 896, 914, 916, 919,
    922, 934, 975-983; Wo: 97
"Lion" ASF: 163; SFC: 53;
    Wa: 200
"Lizards in Jamshyd's Courtyard"
    ASF: 163
"Lo!" ASF: 163; Po: 984;
    Wa: 200
The Mansion see also Snopes
    Trilogy ALL: 93; AN: 76;
    CN: 172-173; Ma: 640; Ne:
    48; Po: 898, 984-985, 1003;
    Wo: 96
"Miss Zilphia Gant" ASF: 163;
    Wa: 200
"Mr. Arcarius" ASF: 163; Po:
    985; Wa: 200
"Mistral" ASF: 163; Po: 985;
    Wa: 200
"Monk" ASF: 164; SFC: 53;
    Wa: 200
Mosquitoes ALL: 99; AN:
    76; CN: 173-174; Po: 912,
    985-986
"Mountain Victory" Wa: 200
"Mule in the Yard" ASF: 164
"My Grandmother Millard" Wa:
    201
"Notes on a Horsethief" ASF:
    164
"Nympholepsy" ASF: 164
"An Odor of Verbena" ASF:
    164; SFC: 53; Wa: 201;

WaS1: 62

"Old Man" see also The
Wild Palms AN: 76; ASF:
164; CN: 175; Po: 933-
935, 987, 1024; Wa: 201;
WaS1: 62

"The Old People" ASF: 164;
Po: 988; SFC: 53; Wa:
201; WaS1: 62

"Once Aboard the Lugger"
WaS1: 62

"Out of Nazareth" ASF:
164

"Pantaloon in Black" ASF:
164-165; Wa: 202; WaS1:
62

"A Point of Law" ASF: 165

"Portrait of Elmer Hodge"
ASF: 165

"The Priest" ASF: 165

Pylon AN: 76-77; CN: 175-
176; Ne: 45, 47; Po:
988-989

"Race at Morning" ASF:
165; Po: 989; Wa: 202

"Raid" ASF: 165; Wa: 202

"Red Leaves" ASF: 165-166;
SFC: 53; Wa: 202; WaS1:
62

The Reivers CN: 176-177;
Ma: 640-641; Po: 928,
990-991; Wo: 96

Requiem for a Nun AN: 77;
CN: 177-178; Ma: 641;
Po: 904, 906-907, 910,
921, 932, 991-992

"Retreat" ASF: 166; Wa:
202

"Riposte in Tertio" ASF:
166; Wa: 202

"A Rose for Emily" ASF:
166-167; Po: 992-994;
SFC: 53-54; Wa: 203-
204; WaS1: 62

Sanctuary AN: 77-78; CN:
178-181; Ma: 642-643;
Ne: 42, 44-45; Po: 904,
906-907, 934, 994-998

Sartoris ALL: 98-99; AN:
78; CN: 181-183; Ma:
643-644; Ne: 48; Po:
907, 912, 920, 928, 934,
998-1000; Wo: 96

"Sepulture South" Wa: 204

"Shall Not Perish" ASF:
167; Po: 910; Wa: 205

"Shingles for the Lord" ASF:
167; Po: 1000; SFC: 54;
Wa: 205

"Skirmish at Sartoris" ASF:
167; Wa: 205

"Smoke" ASF: 168; SFC: 54;
Wa: 205

Snopes Trilogy CN: 183-184;
Ma: 644-645; Po: 1000-
1004

"Snow" ASF: 168

Soldier's Pay ALL: 99; AN:
78; CN: 184-185; LCAB:
63-64; Po: 896, 912, 920,
1004-1005

The Sound and the Fury ALL:
95-96; AN: 79-80; CN:
185-194; LCAB: 64; Ma:
645-647; Ne: 41-44, 46-48;
Po: 896-898, 912, 917, 919,
922, 934-935, 1005-1018; Wo:
96-97

"Spotted Horses" ASF: 168;
Po: 1018; SFC: 54-55; Wa:
205; WaS1: 62

"Sunset" ASF: 168

"The Tall Men" ASF: 168; Wa:
205-206; WaS1: 62

"That Evening Sun" ASF:
168-169; Po: 1019-1020;
SFC: 55; Wa: 206-207;
WaS1: 62-63

"That Will Be Fine" ASF: 169

"There Was a Queen" ASF:
169; Po: 1020; SFC: 55;
Wa: 207

These 13 Po: 1020

"Tomorrow" ASF: 169; Po:
1020-1021; Wa: 207

The Town see also Snopes
Trilogy ALL: 93; AN:
80; CN: 194-195; Ma: 647;
Ne: 45; Po: 898, 1003-
1004, 1021; Wo: 96

"Turnabout" ASF: 170; Wa:
207

"Twilight" ASF: 170

"Two Dollar Wife" Wa: 207

"Two Soldiers" ASF: 170;
Po: 910; Wa: 207

"Uncle Willy" ASF: 170; SFC:
55; Wa: 207; WaS1: 63

The Unvanquished AN: 81;
ASF: 170; Ma: 647; Po:
907, 921, 1021-1022

"Vendée" ASF: 170; Wa:

207

"Victory" ASF: 170; Po:
1023; Wa: 208

"Was" ASF: 170; Po: 1023;
SFC: 55-56; Wa: 208;
WaS1: 63

"Wash" ASF: 170-171; Po:
894-895, 1023-1024; SFC:
56; Wa: 208; WaS1: 63

"Weekend Revisited" ASF:
171

The Wild Palms AN: 81;
ASF: 171; CN: 195-196;
Ma: 648; Ne: 42-43, 45-
46; Po: 934, 1024-1025

The Wishing Tree Po: 896

_____ and Ruth FORD
A Requiem for a Nun (Requiem
pour une Nonne) ADC:
103; Br: 217; DC1: 69;
MDAE: 201-202

FAURE, Elie
General Po: 1025

FAURE-FREMIET, Philippe
General Br: 217

FAUSET, Arthur Huff
General BAF: 117; BAW:
285

"Symphonesque" ASF: 181

FAUSET, Jessie Redmon
General AAW: 54; BAF:
118-119; BAW: 287-288;
HR: 79-82

The Chinaberry Tree BAF:
118-119; BAW: 288; HR:
79-80

Comedy: American Style
BAF: 119-120

Plum Bun BAF: 120; BAW:
288

There Is Confusion BAF:
120; BAW: 288

FAUST, Irvin
"Jake Bluffstein and Adolph
Hitler" WaS1: 63

"Roar Lion Roar" ASF:
181; WaS1: 63

FAVENC, Ernest
General AL: 204

FAY, Theodore Sedgwick
General LCAB: 64

FEARING, Kenneth
General JW: 64; Po: 1025-
1026

"Ad" PE: 184

"The Face in the Bar Room

Mirror" PE: 184

"Green Light" PE: 184

"Obituary" PE: 184

"Portrait" PE: 184

"Radio Blues" PE: 184

"What If Mr. Jesse James Should
Someday Die?" PE: 184

"Yes, the Serial Will Be Con-
tinued" PE: 184

FEDIN, Konstantin
General Po: 1026

The Brothers Ke: 404

Cities and Years Fi: 447; Ke:
404-405

Early Joys Ke: 405

Koster Po: 1026

Neobyknovennoe leto Po: 1026

No Ordinary Summer Ke: 405

Pervye radosti Po: 1026

The Rape of Europe Ke: 405

Sanatorium Arktur Fi: 447;
Ke: 404

FEIERBERG, Mordekhai Ze'ev
"In the Evening" Wa: 208

"The Shadows" Wa: 209

FEIFFER, Jules
General LCAB: 64; MDAE:
203-204

God Bless ADC: 98; MDAE:
204

Jules Feiffer's Hold Me! ADC:
98

Knock Knock ADC: 98

Little Murders ADC: 98-99

The White House Murder Case
ADC: 99; MDAE: 204

_____, Dan GREENBURG,
Leonard MELFI, Sam
SHEPARD, and others
Oh! Calcutta! ADC: 99

Feikema, Feike see MANFRED,
Frederick

Feist, Gene see SLOAN,
Anthony

FELDMAN, Irving
General ICBAP: 50; JW:
65

Felipe, Carlos see FERNANDEZ,
Carlos

Felipe, León see CAMINO
GALICIA, León Felipe

FELLTHAM, Owen
General Ba: 64

Character of the Low Countries
Ba: 64

Resolves Divine, Morall, Poli-

ticall Ba: 64; Hen: 134
FELSEN, Henry Gregor
"First Skirmish" ASF: 181
FELTON, Haleemon Shaik
General BAP: 79
FENELON, François de
Les Aventures de Télémaque
Fi: 59
FENTON, Sir Geoffrey [translator]
Certaine Tragicall Discourses
by Matteo BANDELLO
ERP: 165-167; Hen: 153
FERAOUN, Mouloud
General Po: 1026
FERBER, Edna
General AN: 89; ASF: 181-182; JW: 205; Po: 1026-1027
"An Etude for Emma" ASF: 181
Cimarron LCAB: 64
Ferdinand, Val see SALAAM, Kalamu Ya
FERGUSON, Adam
General EC: 68
FERGUSON, Ira Lunan
General BAF: 121
FERGUSON, Merrill
The Village of Love WIL: 39-40
FERGUSSON, Erna
"Justice as Interpreted" ASF: 182
FERGUSSON, Francis
The King and the Duke DC1: 69
FERGUSSON, Robert
General Ai: 79; EC: 68-69
"Auld Reekie" PE: 184
"The Daft-Days" PE: 184
"The Farmer's Ingle" PE: 185
"The King's Birthday in Edinburgh" PE: 185
FERLINGHETTI, Lawrence
General LCAB: 64; Po: 1027
The Alligation see Three by Ferlinghetti
"A Coney Island of the Mind" LCAB: 64; PE: 185
Her Po: 1028
Pictures of the Gone World LCAB: 64

The Soldiers of No Country Br: 218
Three by Ferlinghetti [Three Thousand Red Ants; The Alligation; The Victims of Amnesia] ADC: 100
The Three Thousand Red Ants see also Three by Ferlinghetti Br: 218
The Victims of Amnesia see also Three by Ferlinghetti Br: 218
FERLITA, Ernst
Ballad of John Ogilvie ADC: 100
FERN, Fanny
General AN: 89
FERNANDEZ, Carlos [Carlos FELIPE]
General Br: 218
FERNANDEZ DE LA MORA, Gonzalo
General Po: 1028
FERNANDEZ MORENO, Baldomero
General Po: 1028
FERNANDEZ Y LIZARDI, Jose Joaquin
General LCAB: 64
FERREIRA, Antonio
Inez de Castro DC2: 137
FERREIRA DE CASTRO, José
General Po: 1028
A la e a neve Fi: 216
FERRETTI, Aurelio
General Br: 218
FERRIER, Susan Edmonstone
General Ai: 120; BN: 57
Marriage Ai: 120; BN: 57; ENES2: 85
FERRIL, Thomas Hornsby
General Po: 1029
FERRON, Jacques
"Cadieu" Wa: 209
FESSENDEN, Thomas Green
General AP: 299; Da: 111
FEUCHTWANGER, Lion
General Po: 1029-1030
Jefta und Seine Tochter Fi: 298-299
Josephus Fi: 299; Ke: 261
Jud Süss Fi: 299
Die Juden von Toledo Fi: 299
Narrenweisheit oder Tod und Verklärung des Jean-Jacques Rousseau Fi: 299
The Oppermanns Fi: 299;

Ke: 261
Paris Gazette Fi: 299; Ke: 261
Power Ke: 262; Ma: 649
Raquel Fi: 299
Success Fi: 299; Ke: 262
This Is the Hour Fi: 299
Tis Folly to Be Wise Fi: 299
FEYDEAU, Georges
General Br: 218; MD: 105
The Birdwatcher Br: 218
The Dupe [Le Dindon] Br: 219
Feu la Mère de Madame Br: 219
A Flea in Her Ear Br: 219
Going to Pot [On Purge Bébé] MD: 105
An Italian Straw Hat Br: 219
A Laxative for Baby see also Going to Pot Br: 219
Look After Lulu [Look Out for Lulu; Keep an Eye on Amélie!; Occupe-Toi d'Amélie] Br: 219-220; MD: 105
On Purge Bébé see Going to Pot
_____ and Maurice DESVALLIERES
Hotel Paradise [Hotel Paridiso; L'Hotel du Libre Echange] Br: 219; MD: 105
FICKE, Arthur Davison
General Po: 1030
FIDGE, George
The English Gusman ERP: 167
Hind's Ramble ERP: 167
FIEDLER, Leslie Aaron
General ASF: 182; JW: 209; LCAB: 64; Po: 1030-1031
"The Dancing of Reb Hershl with the Withered Hand" Wa: 209
"The First Spade in the West" ASF: 182; Wa: 209; WaS1: 63
"The Last Jew in America" ASF: 182; WaS1: 63
"The Last WASP in the World" ASF: 182; WaS1: 63
"Let Nothing You Dismay" SFC: 56; Wa: 209
Love and Death in the American Novel Po: 1031
No! In Thunder Po: 1031
"Nude Croquet" ASF: 182; Wa: 209
"Pull Down Vanity" Wa: 209
Pull Down Vanity and Other Stories Po: 1031
The Second Stone Po: 1031-1032
FIELD, Barron
General AL: 206-207
FIELD, Edward
General Po: 1032
FIELD, Eugene
"Little Boy Blue" PE: 185
FIELD, Michael [Kathleen Harris BRADLEY and Edith Emma COOPER]
General EDT: 163
FIELD, Nathan
General ED: 229; LJCD: 236-242
Woman Is a Weathercock DC1: 69
FIELDING, Gabriel [Alan Gabriel BARNSLEY]
General CFAE: 149; CN: 197; LCAB: 13; Po: 1032; Sch: 71-72
The Birthday King CFAE: 149; CN: 197; ENES1: 79; Po: 1033
Brotherly Love CN: 197; ENES1: 79
Eight Days CN: 197; ENES1: 79
Gentlemen in Their Season CN: 197-198; ENES1: 79
In the Time of Greenbloom CN: 198; ENES1: 79; Po: 1033
Through Streets Broad and Narrow CN: 198; ENES1: 80
FIELDING, Henry
General Be: 117-133; Du: 74-77; LCAB: 64-65; Li: 175-178
Amelia Be: 122-124, 127-132; Du: 68-69; EN: 45-46; ENE: 99-100; ENES1: 80; ENES2: 85; LCAB:

65; Ma: 650-651

Author's Farce Li: 176-177

The Coffee-House Politician
Li: 177

Deborah, or, A Wife for You
All DC1: 70; Li: 177

Don Quixote in England Be:
122; DC1: 70

Eurydice Hissed Li: 177

The Fathers DC1: 70

The Historical Register DC1:
70

The Intriguing Chambermaid
DC1: 70; Li: 177

Jonathan Wild Be: 121-125,
128, 132; EN: 46; ENE:
100-101; ENES1: 80-81;
ENES2: 86; Ma: 651-652

Joseph Andrews Be: 117-
122, 124-125, 130-131;
Du: 69-71; EN: 46-48;
ENE: 101-102; ENES1:
81; ENES2: 86; LCAB:
65; Ma: 652-654

The Letter Writers Li: 177

The Lottery DC1: 70; Li:
177

Love in Several Masques
DC1: 70

The Miser DC1: 70; Li:
177

The Mock Doctor Li: 176,
178

The Modern Husband DC1:
70; Li: 177

Pasquin DC1: 70; Li: 177-
178

Rape Upon Rape DC1: 70

Shamela Be: 124-125, 128-
129, 132; Du: 71; ENES1:
82; ENES2: 86

The Temple Beau DC1: 70-
71

Tom Jones Be: 117-121, 123-
132; Du: 71-74; EN: 48-
49; ENE: 102-105; ENES1:
82-84; ENES2: 86-88;
LCAB: 65; Ma: 654-656;
Ri2: 264

The Tragedy of Tragedies;
or The Life and Death of
Tom Thumb the Great [Tom
Thumb; A Tragedy] DC1:
71; Li: 178

Tumble-Down Dick Li: 176-
178

The Universal Gallant DC1: 71

The Wedding Day DC1: 71

FIELDING, Sarah
General Be: 137-138

The Countess of Dellwyn
ENES2: 88

David Simple Be: 137; ENES1:
84; ENES2: 88

The Governess ENES2: 88

FIELDS, Herbert, Dorothy FIELDS,
and Cole PORTER
Something for the Boys ADC:
100

FIELDS, James T.
"The Captain's Daughter" PE:
185

FIELDS, Joseph
The Doughgirls ADC: 100
_____ and Jerome CHODOROV
The French Touch ADC: 101
My Sister Eileen ADC: 101
The Ponder Heart see also
CHODOROV, Jerome ADC:
101; Po: 1032
_____, Jerome CHODOROV,
Leonard BERNSTEIN, Betty
COMDEN, and Adolph
GREEN
Wonderful Town ADC: 101-102
_____ and Peter DE VRIES
The Tunnel of Love ADC:
102

FIELDS, Julia
General BAW: 294

FIGUEROA, John J.
General WIL: 40
Love Leaps Here WIL: 40

FINAS, Lucette
Donne Fi: 59

Finch, Anne, Countess of
Winchilsea see WINCHILSEA,
Anne Finch, Countess of

FINDLAY, Roderick
"Jim and Miri" WaS1: 63

FINKEL, Donald
General ICBAP: 50; Po:
1033
"Hunting Song" ICBAP: 50
"In Gratitude" ICBAP: 50
"Simeon" ICBAP: 50

FINLAY, Ian
General Ai: 323

FINLAYSON, Roderick
"A Man of Good Religion"
Wa: 209

FIRBANK, Ronald [Arthur

ANNESLEY]
General BN2: 36-37; Po: 1033-1035; Ri: 322-326; Sch: 72-73
The Artificial Princess ENES1: 84; ENES2: 88; Ri: 327
Caprice ENES1: 84
Concerning the Eccentricities of Cardinal Pirelli ENES1: 84; Ri: 327
The Flower Beneath the Foot ENES1: 84; Ri: 327
Inclinations ENES1: 84; ENES2: 88
Odette d'Antrevernes ENES1: 84
Santal ENES1: 85
Sorrow in Sunlight ENES1: 85
A Study in Temperament ENES1: 85
Vainglory ENES1: 85; Ri: 327-328; Sch: 73
Valmouth ENES1: 85; Ri: 328

FISCHART, Johann
Geschichtklitterung Fi: 300

FISCHER, Ernst
General Po: 1035

FISCHER, Dorothy Canfield
General ASF: 183; AN: 89-90; LCAB: 65; Po: 1035
"The Apprentice" Wa: 209
"The Bedquilt" Wa: 209
"Flint and Fire" SFC: 25; Wa: 209

FISCHER, Robert and Arthur ALSBERG
Happiness Is Just a Little Thing Called a Rolls-Royce ADC: 102
_____ and Arthur MARX
The Impossible Years ADC: 102

FISCHER, Rudolph
General AAW: 54; BAF: 122-124; BAW: 297-298; HR: 85-86
"The City of Refuge" ASF: 183; Wa: 210
"Common Meter" ASF: 183; BAF: 123; HR: 85; Wa: 210; WaS1: 64
Conjure-Man Dies BAF: 124; BAP: 80; BAW: 298;
Br: 220; MBA: 82
"High Yaller" Wa: 210
"Miss Cynthie" ASF: 183; HR: 86; Wa: 210
"The Promised Land" Wa: 210
The Walls of Jericho BAF: 123-124; BAW: 298

FISHER, St. John
General Hen: 23; SC: 51-52

FISHER, Vardis
General AN: 90; ASF: 183; CN: 198; Po: 1036; Wo: 100-101
Adam and the Serpent see also The Testament of Man Series CN: 198
April: A Fable of Love CN: 199
Children of God: An American Epic AN: 90; CN: 199; Ma: 657
City of Illusion CN: 199
Dark Bridwell CN: 199
Darkness and the Deep see also The Testament of Man Series CN: 199
The Divine Passion see also The Testament of Man Series CN: 199
A Goat for Azazel see also The Testament of Man Series CN: 199
The Golden Rooms see also The Testament of Man Series CN: 199; Po: 1036
In Tragic Life see also The Vridar Hunter Tetralogy CN: 199-200
Intimations of Eve see also The Testament of Man Series CN: 200
The Island of the Innocent see also The Testament of Man Series CN: 200
Jesus Came Again see also The Testament of Man Series CN: 200
The Mothers: An American Saga of Courage CN: 200; Wo: 101
Mountain Man CN: 200
My Holy Satan see also The Testament of Man Series CN: 200
No Villain Need Be see also The Vridar Hunter Tetralogy

CN: 200

Orphans in Gethsemane see also The Testament of Man Series CN: 200

Passions Spin the Plot see also The Vridar Hunter Tetralogy CN: 200-201

Peace Like a River see also The Testament of Man Series CN: 201

Pemmican CN: 201

Tale of Valor CN: 201

The Testament of Man Series CN: 201

Toilers of the Hills CN: 201

The Valley of Vision see also The Testament of Man Series CN: 201

The Vridar Hunter Tetralogy CN: 201

We Are Betrayed see also The Vridar Hunter Tetralogy CN: 201-202

FISHER, William
The Waiters BAF: 124-125

FISKE, John
General C1a: 108
"Upon the Much-to-Be Lamented Desease of the Reverend Mr. John Cotton..." PE: 185

FITCH, Clyde
General AD: 121-124; Br: 220; Lon: 31
Barbara Frietchie AD: 122
Beau Brummel AD: 123; Br: 220
The City AD: 124; ADC: 102; Br: 220; DC1: 71
The Girl and the Judge ADC: 102
Her Own Way ADC: 103
The Last of the Dandies ADC: 103
The Masked Ball ADC: 103
Nathan Hale AD: 122; ADC: 103
Sapho ADC: 103
The Truth AD: 123; ADC: 103; Br: 220
_____ and Edith WHARTON
The House of Mirth ADC: 103

FitzGERALD, Edward
General LCAB: 65; VP: 33-34

The Rubáiyát of Omar Khayám LCAB: 65-66; Ma: 658
The Rubáiyát of Omar Khayyám [translation] VP: 33-34

FITZGERALD, Francis Scott
General ALL: 100-104; AN: 93-96; ASF: 190-193; LCAB: 66; Ne: 49-54; Po: 1037-1049; Wo: 105-108
"Absolution" ASF: 184; Po: 1049-1050; SFC: 56; Wa: 210; WaS1: 64
"The Adjuster" ASF: 184; Wa: 210
"Author's House" ASF: 184; Wa: 210
"Babes in the Woods" ASF: 184
"The Baby Party" SFC: 56; Wa: 211; WaS1: 64
"Babylon Revisited" ASF: 184-185; Ma: 659-660; Po: 1050-1051; SFC: 56; Wa: 210-211; WaS1: 64
"Basil and Cleopatra" ASF: 185; Wa: 211
The Beautiful and the Damned ALL: 103; AN: 90; Po: 1051
"Bernice Bobs Her Hair" ASF: 185
"The Boy Who Killed His Mother" ASF: 185
"The Bridal Party" Wa: 211
"The Camel's Back" ASF: 185
"The Captured Shadow" Wa: 211
"The Count of Darkness" ASF: 185
"Crazy Sunday" ASF: 185; Wa: 211-212
"The Cut-Glass Bowl" ASF: 185; Wa: 212; WaS1: 64
"Cyclone in Silent Land" ASF: 185
"Dearly Beloved" ASF: 185
"The Debutante" ASF: 186
"Design in Plaster" Wa: 212
"The Diamond as Big as the Ritz" ASF: 186; Ma: 660; SFC: 56; Wa: 212; WaS1: 64
"Diamond Dick and the First Law of Woman" ASF: 186
"Dice, Brass Knuckles and

Guitar" ASF: 186
"Emotional Bankruptcy" ASF: 186
"Family in the Wind" ASF: 186; Wa: 212; WaS1: 64
"The Fiend" ASF: 186
"First Blood" Wa: 212
"Flight and Pursuit" ASF: 186
"Forging Ahead" ASF: 186; Wa: 212
"The Freshest Boy" ASF: 186; Wa: 212
"A Full Life" ASF: 186
"Fun in the Artist's Studio" ASF: 186; Wa: 212
"Gods of Darkness" ASF: 186
The Great Gatsby ALL: 102-103; AN: 90-91; LCAB: 66; Ma: 660-662; Ne: 50-54; Po: 1042-1044, 1046, 1052-1067; Wo: 107-108
"Gretchen's Forty Winks" ASF: 186
"He Thinks He's Wonderful" ASF: 186; Wa: 212
"The I.O.U." ASF: 187
"The Ice Palace" ASF: 187; Wa: 212-213
"I'd Die for You" ASF: 187
"In the Darkest Hour" ASF: 187
"Jacob's Ladder" ASF: 187; Wa: 213
"The Jelly Bean" ASF: 187; Wa: 213
"Jemima, the Mountain Girl" ASF: 187
"John Jackson's Arcady" ASF: 187
"The Kingdom of the Dark" ASF: 187
"The Last of the Belles" ASF: 187; SFC: 56; Wa: 213
The Last Tycoon ALL: 100, 102-103; AN: 92; Ma: 663-664; Ne: 52-53; Po: 1044, 1067-1068; Wo: 108
"The Lees of Happiness" ASF: 187
"Lo, the Poor Peacock!" ASF: 187
"The Long Way Out" ASF: 187

"Love in the Night" ASF: 188
"Magnetism" ASF: 188
"Make Yourself at Home" ASF: 188
"A Man in the Way" Wa: 213
"May Day" ASF: 188; Po: 1068; SFC: 56-57; Wa: 213; WaS1: 64
"News of Paris--Fifteen Years Ago" ASF: 188
"A Night at the Fair" ASF: 188; Wa: 213
"No Harm Trying" ASF: 188; Wa: 213
"'O Russet Witch!'" ASF: 188
"The Offshore Pirate" ASF: 188; Wa: 213
"Offside Play" ASF: 188
"One Interne" Wa: 213
"One Trip Abroad" ASF: 188; Wa: 213-214
"The Ordeal" ASF: 189; Wa: 214
"Outside the Cabinet-Maker's" ASF: 189; Wa: 214
"Pat Hobby's Christmas Wish" ASF: 189; Wa: 214
"Pat Hobby's Secret" Wa: 214
"A Patriotic Short" ASF: 189; Wa: 214
"The Pearl and the Fur" ASF: 189
"The Perfect Life" Wa: 214
"The Pierian Springs and the Last Straw" ASF: 189; Wa: 214
"The Popular Girl" ASF: 189
"The Rich Boy" ASF: 189; Ma: 664; SFC: 57; Wa: 214; WaS1: 64
"The Rough Crossing" Wa: 214-215
"Salute to Lucie and Elsie" ASF: 189
"The Scandal Detectives" Wa: 215
"The Sensible Thing" ASF: 189; SFC: 57; Wa: 215
"Sentiment--And the Use of Rouge" ASF: 189
"A Short Trip Home" ASF: 189; Wa: 215
"Six of One--" ASF: 189; Wa: 215
"The Swimmers" ASF: 190;

Wa: 215
"Temperature" ASF: 190
Tender Is the Night ALL:
100, 102-103; AN: 92;
LCAB: 66; Ma: 665-666;
Ne: 51-52, 54; Po: 1038,
1044, 1046, 1068-1071; Wo:
106-108
"That Kind of Party" Wa:
215
"They Never Grow Older"
ASF: 190
This Side of Paradise ALL:
103; AN: 92-93; Ma:
666-667; Po: 1071-1072
"Three Acts of Music" ASF:
190
"Too Cute for Words" ASF:
190
"Two for a Cent" ASF: 190
"Two Old-Timers" ASF:
190; Wa: 215
"Two Wrongs" ASF: 190;
Wa: 215
"What to Do About It" ASF:
190
"Winter Dreams" ASF: 190;
Ma: 667-668; Po: 1072;
SFC: 57; Wa: 215;
WaS1: 64
"A Woman with a Past" Wa:
215
"Women in the House" ASF:
190
FITZGERALD, Robert David
General Po: 1072-1073
FITZGERALD, Zelda [Sayre]
General ASF: 195
"A Couple of Nuts" ASF:
195; WaS1: 64
"A Millionaire's Girl" ASF:
195
"Miss Ella" ASF: 195; WaS1:
65
"Our Own Movie Queen" ASF:
195
FITZMAURICE, George
General Br: 220-221; MBD:
47; Mi: 234; Po: 1073
The Country Dressmakers
Br: 221; DC1: 71
The Dandy Dolls Br: 221;
DC1: 71
The Enchanted Land Br:
221; MBD: 47
The Moonlighter Br: 221;

DC1: 71
The Ointment Blue, or, The
Ring of the Barna Men Br:
221
One Evening Gleam Br: 221
The Pie Dish Br: 221
The Toothache MBD: 47
FLAGG, Ann
General BAP: 80
FLANNER, Janet
General APC: 107; LCAB:
66
FLAUBERT, Gustave
General LCAB: 67
"Bibliomanie" Wa: 216
Bouvard and Pécuchet Fi: 59-
60; Ke: 60-61; Ma: 669;
Wa: 216; WaS1: 65
"Chevrin" Wa: 216
"Chronique Normande du dixième
siècle" Wa: 216
"La dernière heure" Wa: 216
"Deux mains sur une couronne"
Wa: 216
"La femme du monde" Wa: 216
"La fiancée et la tombe" Wa:
216
"La grande dame et le joueur de
vielle" Wa: 216
Hérodias Fi: 60-61; Ke: 61;
SFC: 57; Wa: 216-217;
WaS1: 65
"Une lecon d'histoire naturelle"
Wa: 217
La légende de Saint Julien
l'Hospitalier Fi: 61-62; Ke:
61
Madame Bovary Fi: 62-66; Ke:
61-65; LCAB: 67; Ma: 670-
671; Po: 1085, 1112; Ri2:
263
"Le main de fer" Wa: 217
"Matteo Falcone" Wa: 217
"Mémoires d'un fou" Wa: 217
"Le Moine des Chartreux" Wa:
217
"Le mort de Marguerite de
Bourgogne" Wa: 217
Novembre Fi: 66; Ke: 65
Une Nuit de Don Juan Ke: 66
"St. Julien" Ma: 671; SFC:
58; Wa: 217-218; WaS1: 65
Salammbô Fi: 66-67; Ke: 66-
67; Ma: 671-672
"San Pietro Ormano" Wa: 218
"Un secret de Philippe Prudent"

Wa: 218
A Sentimental Education Fi:
    67-70; Ke: 67-69; LCAB:
    67; Ma: 672-673
A Simple Heart Fi: 70-71;
    Ke: 69; Ma: 674; SFC:
    57; Wa: 218-219; WaS1: 65
"Smarh" Wa: 219
The Temptation of St. Anthony
    Fi: 71-72; Ke: 69-70; Ma:
    674-675
Trois Contes Fi: 72
FLECKER, James Elroy
    General Mi: 235-236; Po:
    1073; TA: 147
FLECKNOE, Richard
    The Damoiselles à la Mode
    DC1: 71
FLEG, Edmond
    General Po: 1074
FLEMING, Ian
    General LCAB: 67; Ma:
    676; Po: 1074-1075
    The Man with the Golden
    Gun Po: 1075
FLEMING, Peter
    Brazilian Adventure Ri2:
    460
FLEMING, Sarah Lee Brown
    General BAW: 299
FLERS, Robert de
    L'Habit vert Po: 1075
FLETCHER, Andrew
    General Ai: 59
FLETCHER, Giles
    General Ba: 65
    "Christ's Victory and Tri-
    umph" PE: 185
FLETCHER, John
    The Beggar's Bush see
    BEAUMONT, Francis and
    John FLETCHER
    The Bloody Brother see
    BEAUMONT, Francis and
    John FLETCHER
    Bonduca see BEAUMONT,
    Francis and John FLETCHER
    The Captain see BEAU-
    MONT, Francis and John
    FLETCHER
    The Faithful Shepherdess
    see BEAUMONT, Francis
    and John FLETCHER
    A King and No King see
    BEAUMONT, Francis and
    John FLETCHER

The Loyal Subject; or The
    Faithful General DC1: 72;
    ED: 208; LJCD: 43-44
The Maid's Tragedy see
    BEAUMONT, Francis and
    John FLETCHER
The Pilgrim DC1: 72; LJCD:
    46
Valentinian see BEAUMONT,
    Francis and John FLETCHER
The Wild-Goose Chase see
    BEAUMONT, Francis and
    John FLETCHER
_____ and Philip MASSINGER
Thierry and Theodoret see
    also BEAUMONT, Francis
    and John FLETCHER DC1:
    72
_____ and William SHAKESPEARE
The Two Noble Kinsmen see
    also BEAUMONT, Francis
    and John FLETCHER DC1:
    72; ED: 200-201; Ma: 681-
    682
FLETCHER, John Gould
    General ALL: 104; Po: 1075-
    1076
    Lincoln LCAB: 67
FLETCHER, Lucille
    Night Watch ADC: 103
FLETCHER, Phineas
    General Ba: 65; Hen: 35;
    NI: 330
FLEX, Walter
    Wanderer Between Two Worlds
    Ke: 262
FLEXNER, Hortense
    General Po: 1076
FLINT, F.S.
    "The Swan" PE: 185
FLINT, Timothy
    General AN: 97; ASF: 195
    The Lost Child AN: 96
FLIPPEN, Ruth Brooks
    General LCAB: 67
FLORES, Darío Fernández
    Lola, espejo escuro Po: 1076
FLORES, Jean de
    Aurelio and Isabell [Anonymous
    English translator] ERP:
    248-249
FLORES, Juan de
    Grimalte y Gradissa Fi: 216;
    Ke: 203
    Grisel y Mirabella Fi: 216;
    Ke: 204

FLORES, Mario
General Br: 221
FLOREZ, Fernandez
Volvoreta Ke: 204
FLOREZ, Wenceslao
El hombre que compro un
automovil Fi: 217
El sistema pelegrin Fi: 217
FLORIO, John
General SC: 52
FLOYD, Silas Xavier
General BAF: 125
FOERSTER, Norman
General LCAB: 67
FOGAZZARO, Antonio
General Po: 1076-1077
Daniele Cortis Fi: 264; Ke:
242; Ma: 683
"Eden Anto" WaS1: 65
"The Fiasco of Maestro Chieco"
WaS1: 65
Leila Fi: 264; Ke: 242;
Ma: 683
Little World of Nowadays Fi:
264
Little World of the Past Fi:
264; Ke: 242
Malombra Fi: 264
The Man of the World Ke:
242-243
Miranda Fi: 264; Po: 1077
The Mystery of the Poet Fi:
264; Ke: 243; Ma: 683
The Patriot Ma: 683-684
The Saint [Il Santo] Fi: 264;
Ke: 243; Ma: 684; Po:
1077
The Sinner Ma: 684
Valsolda Po: 1077
The Woman Ke: 243; Ma:
684
FOLEY, Martha
"One with Shakespeare" SFC:
58; Wa: 219
FOLLAIN, Jean
General Po: 1078
FONTAINE, Jean de la
Fables Ma: 1146
Le Papillon du Parnasse DC2:
137
FONTANE, Theodor
L'Adultera Fi: 300
Before the Storm Fi: 300;
Ke: 262
Cecile Fi: 300; Ke: 262
Effi Briest Fi: 300; Ke:

262-263; Ma: 685
Ellernklipp Ke: 263
Frau Jenny Treibel Fi: 300;
Ke: 263
Grete Minde Ke: 263
Irrungen, Wirrungen Fi: 301
Mathilde Möhring Fi: 301
Die Poggenpuhls Fi: 301
Quitt Ke: 263
Schach von Wuthenow Fi:
301; Ke: 263
Der Stechlin Fi: 301; Ke:
263-264
Stine Fi: 301; Ke: 264
Trials and Tribulations Ke:
264
Unterm Birnbaum Fi: 301
Unwiederbringlich Fi: 301;
Ke: 264
FOOTE, Horton
General MDAE: 207
The Trip to the Bountiful
MDAE: 207
FOOTE, Mary Hallock
General ASF: 195
"The Cup of Trembling" Wa:
219
"Friend Barton's Concern"
Wa: 219
"The Harshwood Bride" Wa:
219
"How the Pump Stopped at the
Morning Watch" Wa: 219
"In Exile" Wa: 219
"The Maid's Progress" ASF:
195; Wa: 219
"Maverick" Wa: 219
"On a Side Track" Wa: 219
"Pilgrims to Mecca" Wa: 219
"The Rapture of Hetty" Wa:
219
"The Story of Alcázar" Wa:
219
"A Touch of Sun" Wa: 219
"The Trumpeter" Wa: 220
"The Watchman" Wa: 220
FOOTE, Samuel
General EC: 69; Li: 179-180
The Englishman in Paris Li:
180
The Minor Li: 180
The Nabob EC: 69
FOOTE, Shelby
General ASF: 196; CFAE:
151; CN: 202; Po: 1078
"Child by Fever" ASF: 196

Follow Me Down CN: 202
"Rain Down Home" ASF:
    196
FORBES, Esther
General Po: 1078
la FORCE, Charlotte
Histoire secrete de Bourgogne
    Ke: 70
FORD, Ford Madox [HUEFFER,
    Joseph Leopold]
General BN2: 38-40; Po:
    1078-1083; Ri: 342-352,
    360-362; Sch: 74-77; TA:
    187
The Benefactor ENES1: 85
A Call ENES1: 85
An English Girl ENES1: 85;
    Po: 1081
The Fifth Queen; and How
    She Came to Court ENE:
    105; ENES1: 86; Ma:
    686; Sch: 77
The Fifth Queen Crowned
    ENES1: 86
The Fifth Queen Trilogy
    ENES1: 86; ENES2: 88;
    Po: 1079-1080, 1083; Ri:
    349
The Good Soldier BN2: 39-
    40; EN: 49-50; ENE:
    105-107; ENES1: 86;
    ENES2: 89; Ma: 686-687;
    Po: 1079, 1083-1089; Ri:
    342-346, 348, 350-357;
    Sch: 78-80
The "Half-Moon" ENES1: 86
Henry for Hugh ENES1: 86
Ladies Whose Bright Eyes
    ENE: 107; ENES1: 87;
    ENES2: 89; Po: 1089
Last Post ENE: 107; ENES1:
    87; Ri: 348; Sch: 80-81
A Little Less Than Gods
    ENES1: 87
A Man Could Stand Up--,
    ENES1: 87; ENES2: 89;
    Sch: 80-81
The Marsden Case ENES1:
    87; Ri: 343
Mr. Apollo ENES1: 87
Mr. Fleight ENE: 107;
    ENES1: 87
The New Humpty-Dumpty
    ENES1: 87
No Enemy ENES1: 87; Ri:
    343

No More Parades ENES1: 87;
    ENES2: 89; Sch: 80-81
The Panel ENES1: 87
Parade's End ENE: 107-108;
    ENES1: 88; ENES2: 89-90;
    Ma: 687-689; Po: 1079,
    1083, 1089-1091; Ri: 342-
    348, 350-351, 357-359; Ri2:
    464; Sch: 80-81
The Portrait ENES1: 88
Privy Seal ENES1: 88
Professor's Progress Po: 1081;
    Ri: 350
The Rash Act ENES1: 88
The Shifting of the Fire
    ENES1: 88
The Simple Life Limited
    ENES1: 88
Some Do Not ENES1: 89;
    ENES2: 90; Po: 1081; Ri:
    350; Sch: 80-81
Vive le Roy ENES1: 89
When the Wicked Man ENES1:
    89
The Young Lovell ENES1: 89
FORD, James Allan
General Ai: 316
FORD, John
General ED: 233-235; LJCD:
    120-126, 138, 147-150;
    TSD: 47-50
The Broken Heart DC1: 73-
    74; ED: 234; EDC: 175-
    176; LJCD: 129-133, 150-
    151; TSD: 47-49
The Chronicle Historie of Per-
    kin Warbeck see Perkin
    Warbeck
The Fancies, Chaste and Noble
    EDC: 176; LJCD: 137
The Great Favourite; or The
    Duke of Lerma DC1: 74
An Ill Beginning Has a Good
    End EDC: 176
The Lady's Trial EDC: 176;
    LJCD: 137, 151
The Late Murder of the Son
    Upon the Mother LJCD:
    151
The Lover's Melancholy ED:
    233; EDC: 176; LJCD:
    136, 151; TSD: 49
Love's Sacrifice DC1: 74;
    EDC: 176; LJCD: 135-136,
    151; TSD: 50
Perkin Warbeck [The Chronicle

Historie of Perkin Warbeck]
DC1: 74-75; ED: 233;
EDC: 176-177; LJCD:
133-135, 151; TSD: 47-50
The Queen; or, The Excel-
lency of Her Sex EDC:
177
The Spanish Gypsy LJCD:
151; TSD: 50
'Tis Pity She's a Whore
DC1: 75; EDC: 177-178;
LJCD: 127-129, 150; Ma:
690; TSD: 47-49
The Welsh Ambassador see
DEKKER, Thomas
_____ and Thomas DEKKER
The Sun's Darling see
DEKKER, Thomas
_____, Thomas DEKKER, and
William ROWLEY
The Witch of Edmonton see
also DEKKER, Thomas
and John FORD DC1:
75-76; LJCD: 136-137,
151; EDC: 178
FORD, Nick Aaron
General BAF: 126
FORD, Robert Edgar
General BAW: 303
FORDE, A.N.
General WIL: 40
FORDE, Emanuel
General ERP: 168
Ornatus and Artesia ENES1:
89; ERP: 168
FOREMAN, Richard
Evidence ADC: 103
Pandering to the Masses: A
Misrepresentation ADC:
104
Rhoda in Potatoland ADC:
104
_____, Richard and Stanley
SILVERMAN
Hotel for Criminals ADC:
104
FORETS, Louis-René des
General Po: 1091
Le Bavard Fi: 72
FORNERET, Xavier
"A neuf heures à Paris" Wa:
220
"Un Oeil entre deux yeux"
Wa: 220
"Un Rêve c'est" Wa: 220
FORNES, María Irene

General MDAE: 209
Cap-a-Pie ADC: 104
Fefu and Her Friends ADC:
104
FORRELLAT, Luisa
Siempre en capilla Ke: 204
FORRELLDAD, Luisa
General Po: 1092
FORREST, David
General MAP: 167-168
"The Keeper of the Night" Wa:
220
FORREST, Leon
The Bloodworth Orphans BAF:
126
There Is a Tree More Ancient
Than Eden BAF: 126; BAW:
304
FORSBERG, Rolf
A Tenth of an Inch Makes the
Difference Br: 221
FORSTER, Edward Morgan
General BN2: 41-44; LCAB:
67-68; Po: 1092-1099; Ri:
370-388, 403-404; Sch: 82-
89; TA: 148-149
Abinger Harvest Ri: 377, 403
"Albergo Empedocle" Ri: 389;
SFC: 58; Wa: 220; WaS1:
65
"Ansell" WaS1: 65
"Arthur Snatchfold" WaS1: 66
"The Celestial Omnibus" Po:
1099; Ri: 389; SFC: 58-59;
Wa: 220; WaS1: 66
"The Classical Annex" WaS1:
65
"Co-ordination" Wa: 223
"The Curate's Friend" SFC:
59; Wa: 223
"Dr. Woolacott" WaS1: 66
"The Eternal Moment" Ri: 389;
SFC: 59; Wa: 221; WaS1:
66
The Hill of Devi Po: 1099-
1100
Howard's End BN2: 42-43;
EN: 50; ENE: 108-110;
ENES1: 89-90; ENES2: 90-
91; Ma: 691-692; Po: 1092,
1094, 1097, 1100-1103, 4560-
4561; Ri: 370, 372, 377-379,
382-384, 389-392; Ri2: 464;
Sch: 89-91; TMBP: 158
The Longest Journey BN2:
42-43; EN: 50-51; ENE:

110-111; ENES1: 90-91; ENES2: 91; Ma: 692-693; Po: 1092, 1103-1104; Ri: 370, 372, 377-378, 384, 392; Sch: 91

"The Machine Stops" Ri: 392-393; SFC: 59; Wa: 221; WaS1: 66

Marianne Thornton Po: 1104

Maurice Ri: 372, 393; Sch: 91-92; ENES1: 91; ENES2: 91

"Mr. Andrews" SFC: 59; Wa: 221-222

"The Obelisk" WaS1: 66

"The Other Boat" WaS1: 66

"Other Kingdom" SFC: 59; Wa: 222

"The Other Side of the Hedge" SFC: 59; Wa: 222; WaS1: 66

A Passage to India BN2: 41-44; EN: 51; ENE: 111-115; ENES1: 91-93; ENES2: 91-93; LCAB: 68; Ma: 693-694; Po: 1092-1095, 1097, 1099, 1104-1112; Ri: 370, 372, 374, 377-379, 381-384, 393-401; Sch: 92-96

"The Point of It" SFC: 59; Wa: 222; WaS1: 66

"The Purple Envelope" WaS1: 66

"The Road from Colonus" Ri: 401; SFC: 59-60; Wa: 222-223; WaS1: 66

A Room with a View BN2: 43; EN: 52; ENE: 115-116; ENES1: 93; ENES2: 93-94; Ma: 694-696; Po: 1092, 1112; Ri: 370, 372, 377, 402; Sch: 97

"The Story of a Panic" SFC: 60; Wa: 223; WaS1: 66

"The Story of the Siren" Po: 1112; Ri: 402; SFC: 60; Wa: 223-224

"The Torque" WaS1: 66

"What Does It Matter?" WaS1: 66

Where Angels Fear to Tread EN: 52; ENE: 116; ENES1: 93-94; ENES2: 94; Ma: 696-697; Po: 1095, 1112-1113; Ri: 370, 372, 377, 383, 402; Sch: 97

FORSTER, William
    General AL: 210

FORSYTH, James
    General MDAE: 210

Fort, Gertrud von Le see LE FORT, Gertrud von

FORT, Keith
    "The Coal Shoveller" ASF: 197; Wa: 224

FORTE, Christine
    General BAF: 126

FORTEN, Charlotte L. [Mrs. Frances GRIMKE]
    General BAW: 305

FORTESCUE, Sir John
    The Gouvernance of England Hen: 95

FORTESCUE, Thomas [translator]
    The Forest by Pedro MEXIA ERP: 169

FORTUNE, Timothy Thomas
    General AAPD: 64; BAW: 306
    Dreams of Life BAW: 306

FORZANO, Giovacchino
    Sly Br: 221

FOSCOLO, Ugo
    Last Letters of Jacopo Ortis Fi: 264-265; Ke: 243

FOSTER, Alex
    Community Kitchen MBA: 82

FOSTER, Greg
    Freeze MBA: 82-83
    Mainline Blues MBA: 83

FOSTER, Hannah Webster
    General AN: 97

FOSTER, Michael
    General WIL: 40
    Things WIL: 41

FOSTER, Paul
    Balls ADC: 104
    Elizabeth I ADC: 104
    Hurrah for the Bridge Br: 222
    Marcus Brutus ADC: 104
    The Recluse ADC: 104
    Tom Paine ADC: 104; Br: 222

FOUGERET DE MONBRON, Jean-Louis
    Margot la Ravaudeuse Fi: 72

Foulis, Hugh see MUNRO, Neil

FOUQUE, Baron de la Motte
    Undine Fi: 72

Fournier, Henri Alban see
  ALAIN-FOURNIER
FOWLER, Frank
  General AL: 212
FOWLER, William
  General Ai: 44
FOWLES, John
  General CFAE: 153; LCAB:
    68; Sch: 97-98
  The Collector CN: 202;
    ENES1: 94; ENES2: 94;
    Ma: 698; Po: 1116
  Daniel Martin ENES2: 94
  The French Lieutenant's
    Woman CN: 202; ENES1:
    94-95; ENES2: 94-95;
    LCAB: 68; Ma: 698-699;
    Po: 1116; Sch: 98
  The Magus CN: 202; ENES1:
    95; ENES2: 95; Ma: 699-
    700; Po: 1116; Sch: 98-
    99
FOWOWE, Oyeleke
  General BALE: 304
FOX, George
  General Bon: 64
FOX, John, Jr.
  General ASF: 197
  "The Army of the Callahan"
    Wa: 224
  "The Battle-Prayer of Parson
    Small" Wa: 224
  "Christmas for Big Ames"
    Wa: 224
  "Christmas Night with Satan"
    Wa: 224
  "A Crisis for the Guard"
    Wa: 224
  "A Cumberland Vendetta"
    Wa: 224
  "The Goddess of Happy Val-
    ley" Wa: 224
  "Grayson's Baby" ASF: 197;
    Wa: 224
  "A Mountain Europa" Wa:
    224
  "On Hell-fer-Sartain Creek"
    Wa: 224
  "On the Road to Hell-fer-
    Sartain" Wa: 224
  "The Pardon of Becky Day"
    Wa: 224
  "The Pope of Big Sandy"
    Wa: 225
  "A Purple Rhododendron"
    Wa: 225

FOXE, John
  General SC: 53
  Book of Martyrs Hen: 27-28;
    SC: 53
FRAIBERG, Louis Benjamin
  General LCAB: 68
FRAME, Janet
  General CN: 202
  "A Boy's Will" Wa: 225
  "Keel and Kool" WaS1: 67
  "The Lagoon" WaS1: 67
  "Miss Gibson and the Lumber
    Room" Wa: 225
  Owls Do Cry CN: 202
  "The Reservoir" WaS1: 67
  Scented Gardens for the Blind
    CN: 203
  "Swans" WaS1: 67
  "Two Sheep" Wa: 225
FRANCE, Anatole
  General Po: 1116-1117
  The Amethyst Ring Fi: 72;
    Ke: 70
  At the Sign of the Reine
    Pédauque [La Rôtisserie de
    la Reine Pédauque] Ke:
    70-71; Ma: 701; Po: 1116
  Balthasar Ke: 71
  Books of My Friend Fi: 72;
    Ke: 71
  Crainquebille Ke: 71
  The Crime of Sylvester Bonnard
    [Le Crime de Sylvestre Bon-
    nard] Fi: 72-73; Ke: 71;
    Ma: 701; Po: 1117
  The Desires of Jean Servien
    Fi: 73; Ke: 71
  The Dressmaker's Form Ke:
    71
  The Elm on the Mall Fi: 73;
    Ke: 71
  The Gods Are Athirst Fi: 73;
    Ke: 72; Ma: 701-702
  L'Ille des Pinguons see Pen-
    guin Island
  Jocaste Po: 1117-1118
  M. Bergeret in Paris Fi: 73;
    Ke: 72
  Le Mannequin d'Osier Po:
    1118
  A Mummer's Tale Ke: 72
  On the White Stone Ke: 72
  The Opinions of Jerome Coig-
    nard Ke: 72
  Penguin Island [L'Ille des
    Pinguons] Fi: 73; Ke:

72-73; Ma: 702; Po: 1116

Procurator of Judea [Le Pro-
curateur de Judée] Ke:
73; Po: 1118

Le Puits de Sainte Claire
Ke: 73

The Revolt of the Angels [La
Révolte des Anges] Fi:
73; Ke: 73-74; Ma: 703;
Po: 1116

La Rôtisserie de la Reine
Pédauque see At the
Sign of the Reine
Pédauque

Les Sept femmes de la Barbe-
Bleue Fi: 73

Thaïs Fi: 73; Ke: 74;
LCAB: 68; Ma: 703;
Po: 1118

FRANCES, José
Judith Po: 1119

FRANCIS, Lord Jeffrey
General Ai: 112

FRANCIS, Robert
"The Big Tent" PE: 185

FRANCK, Hans
"Die Südsee-Insel" Wa: 225
"Taliter?" Wa: 225

FRANCONI, Gabriel-Tristan
Untel de l'Armée Française
Fi: 73

FRANK, Bruno
Der Reisepass Fi: 301
Storm in a Teacup [Storm
over Patsy; Sturm im
Wasserglas] Br: 222

FRANK, Gerold
General LCAB: 68

FRANK, Leonhard
Im Letzten Wagen Fi: 302
Karl und Anna Br: 222

FRANK, Waldo
General AN: 98; ASF: 197;
JW: 213; LCAB: 68;
Po: 1119-1120
The Bridegroom Cometh
AN: 97
Chalk Face AN: 97
City Block AN: 97
The Dark Mother AN: 97
The Death and Birth of
David Markand AN: 97
Holiday AN: 97
The Invaders AN: 97
Island in the Atlantic AN:
97

Not Heaven AN: 97
Rahab AN: 97
Summer Never Ends AN: 97
The Unwelcome Man AN: 98

FRANKAU, Pamela
General LCAB: 68

FRANKEN, Rose
Another Language ADC: 105;
Br: 222
Claudia ADC: 105
Doctors Disagree ADC: 105
The Hallams ADC: 105; Br:
222
Outrageous Fortune ADC:
105; Br: 222
Soldier's Wife ADC: 105-106

FRANKENBERG, Lloyd
"I Lazarus" PE: 185

FRANKLIN, Benjamin
General AP: 307-342; Da:
31-34; LCAB: 68
"An Arabian Tale" Da: 33
Autobiography AP: 317, 320,
322-325, 327-331, 336-337;
Da: 32-33; LCAB: 68;
Ma: 704-705
"Dissertation on Liberty and
Necessity" AP: 317

FRANKLIN, J.E.
General AAPD: 366; BAF:
127; BAP: 81; BAW: 308
Black Girl ADC: 106; BAP:
81; BAW: 308; MBA: 83-
84
_____ and Micki GRANT
The Prodigal Sister ADC:
106; BAP: 81; MBA: 83-84

FRANKLIN, Miles
General MAP: 171-172
All That Swagger MAP: 172
Old Blastus of Bandicoot
MAP: 172
Ten Creeks Run MAP: 172
Up the Country MAP: 172

FRANKO, Ivan
General Po: 1120
Zakhar Ke: 405

FRASER, Fitzroy
General WIL: 41
The Coming of the Harvest
WIL: 41
Wounds in the Flesh WIL: 41

FRASER, George M.
Flash for Freedom ENES1:
95; ENES2: 95
Flashman ENES1: 95; ENES2:

96
Flashman at the Charge
    ENES2: 96
Flashman in the Great Game
    ENES2: 96
Royal Flash ENES1: 95;
    ENES2: 96
FRASER, George Sutherland
    General Ai: 307
FRATTI, Mario
    General Br: 222
FRAUNCE, Abraham
    General SC: 53
    The Arcadian Rhetorike Hen:
        193
FRAYN, Michael
    General MDAE: 213
FRAZER, Sir James George
    General Ai: 162; TA: 150
    "The Golden Bough" Ai:
        162; TA: 150
FREDERIC, Harold
    General AF: 100-103; ALL:
        104-105; AN: 98; ASF:
        198; Ho: 49-50, 145-146
    "The Copperhead" AF: 101-
        102
    "Cordelia and the Moon"
        ASF: 197
    The Damnation of Theron
        Ware AF: 100-103; ALL:
        105; AN: 98; Ho: 50,
        145-146; Ma: 706-707
    "A Day in the Wilderness"
        AF: 101
    "The Deserter" AF: 101
    "The Eve of the Fourth"
        AF: 101
    Gloria Mundi Ho: 49
    "In the Shadow of Gabriel"
        ASF: 197
    The Market-Place AF: 100-
        101; Ho: 49
    "Marsena" AF: 101
    "The Martyrdom of Maev"
        ASF: 197
    "My Aunt Susan" AF: 101
    "The Path of Murtogh" ASF:
        198
    Seth's Brother's Wife AF:
        102; Ho: 50
    "The Truce of the Bishop"
        ASF: 198
    "The Two Rochards" ASF:
        198
    "The War Widow" AF: 101;

ASF: 198
    "The Wooing of Teige" ASF:
        198
FREDERICK, John Towner
    Druida LCAB: 69
FREDRO, Alexander
    Mr. Joviality DC2: 138
FREED, Donald
    Inquest ADC: 106
FREEDMAN, Ralph
    General Po: 1120
FREEMAN, David E.
    Creeps ADC: 106
    Jesse and the Bandit Queen
        ADC: 106
FREEMAN, H. Lawrence
    General BAP: 82
FREEMAN, H.W.
    Joseph and His Brethren
        ENES2: 96
FREEMAN, John
    General TA: 151
FREEMAN, Mary Eleanor Wilkins
    General AF: 106-107; ALL:
        105; AN: 99; ASF: 201;
        LCAB: 69
    "Amanda and Love" ASF: 199;
        WaS1: 67
    "The Apple Tree" ASF: 199;
        Wa: 225
    "Arethusa" ASF: 199; Wa:
        225
    "The Balking of Christopher"
        Wa: 225
    "The Bar Lighthouse" ASF:
        199
    "A Church Mouse" Wa: 225
    "A Conflict Ended" ASF: 199;
        SFC: 60; Wa: 225
    "A Conquest of Humility" ASF:
        199
    "Coronation" ASF: 199
    "Evelina's Garden" Wa: 225
    "A Gala Dress" SFC: 60; Wa:
        226
    "Gentian" ASF: 199; SFC:
        60; Wa: 226
    "The Great Pine" Wa: 226
    "An Honest Soul" Wa: 226
    "A Humble Romance" ASF:
        200
    "An Independent Thinker"
        ASF: 200; Wa: 226
    Jane Field AN: 98
    "Life Everlastin'" ASF: 200
    "A New England Nun" AF:

106; ASF: 200; Wa: 226
"A New England Prophet"
ASF: 200
"An Object of Love" ASF:
200
"Old Lady Pingree" Wa:
226
"Old Woman Magoun" ASF:
200
"On the Walpole Road" Wa:
226
Pembroke AN: 99
"A Poetess" ASF: 200
"The Revolt of 'Mother'"
AF: 106; ASF: 200; Wa:
226
"Sister Liddy" ASF: 200;
Wa: 226
"A Solitary" ASF: 200
"Symphony in Lavender"
Wa: 226
"A Taste of Honey" Wa:
226
"The Three Old Sisters and
the Old Beau" AF: 107;
ASF: 200; Wa: 226
"Two Old Lovers" ASF: 200;
SFC: 60; Wa: 226
"A Village Lear" ASF: 200;
SFC: 60; Wa: 227
"A Village Singer" ASF:
201
"A Wayfaring Couple" ASF:
201; Wa: 227
"The White Birch" Wa: 227
FRENAUD, André
General Po: 1120-1121
FRENCH, Alice see also
THANET, Octave
"Trusty, No. 49" Wa: 227
FRENEAU, Philip
General ALL: 106; AP:
344-347; Da: 67-68
"The American Village" PE:
185
"The Beauties of Santa Cruz"
PE: 185
"The Indian Burying Ground"
Da: 67-68; ICBAP: 51;
PE: 185
"The Wild Honey Suckle" PE:
186
FRENSSEN, Gustav
Otto Babendiek Ke: 264
FREUD, Sigmund
General LCAB: 69

FREUDENBERGER, Daniel
A Sorrow Beyond Dreams
ADC: 107
Freyre, Ricardo Jaimes see
JAIMES FREYRE, Ricardo
FREYTAG, Gustave
The Ancestors Ke: 264
Debit and Credit Fi: 302; Ke:
264
The Lost Manuscript Ke: 264
FRIEDEL, Johann
Eleonore Fi: 302
FRIEDMAN, Bruce Jay
General ASF: 201; JW: 216;
Po: 1121
Black Angels LCAB: 69
"Brazzaville Teen-ager" Wa:
227
"The Canning of Mother Dean"
Wa: 227
"Far from the City of Class"
Wa: 227
"A Foot in the Door" Wa: 227
"The Humiliation" Wa: 227
"The Imposing Proportions of
Jean Shrimpton" Wa: 227
"The Investor" Wa: 227
"The Man They Threw Out of
Jets" Wa: 227
A Mother's Kisses CN: 203
Scuba Duba ADC: 107; Br:
223; MDAE: 214
"Show Biz Connections" Wa:
227
Steambath ADC: 107
Stern CN: 203
"The Subversive" Wa: 227
"When You're Excused, You're
Excused" WaS1: 67
"Yes, We Have No Richard"
Wa: 228
FRIEDRICH, Otto
"Freedom of the Press" ASF:
201
FRIEL, Brian
General Br: 223; MBD: 47;
TMIP: 46-50
"Among the Ruins" WaS1: 67
Crystal and Fox TMIP: 49
The Enemy Within TMIP: 46,
50
"Foundry House" Wa: 228;
WaS1: 67
Freedom of the City TMIP:
37, 49
The Gentle Island TMIP: 50

Lovers TMIP: 48, 50-51
The Loves of Cass McGuire
    TMIP: 48, 51
The Mundy Scheme TMIP:
    49, 52
Philadelphia, Here I Come!
    Br: 223; TMIP: 47-53
A Saucer of Larks TMIP:
    50
"The Widowhood System"
    Wa: 228
FRIEL, George
    General Ai: 290
FRINGS, Ketti
    The Long Dream ADC: 107
    Look Homeward, Angel ADC:
        107-108
    Mr. Sycamore ADC: 108
FRISBY, Terence
    General MDAE: 215
    The Bandwagon MDAE:
        215
    The Subtopians MDAE: 215
FRISCH, Max
    General Br: 223-224; LCAB:
        69; MD: 105-106; Po:
        1122-1125
    Als der Krieg zu Ende War
        see When the War Came
        to an End
    Andorra Br: 224-225; DC2:
        138; EDC: 179; MD: 106;
        Po: 1122
    Answer from the Silence Fi:
        302
    Biedermann and the Firebugs
        see The Firebugs
    Biedermann und die Brand-
        stifter see The Firebugs
    Bin oder die Reise nach
        Peking Fi: 302; Po:
        1125
    Biography [Biografie] EDC:
        180
    The Chinese Wall [Die
        Chinesische Mauer] Br:
        225; DC2: 138-139; EDC:
        180-181
    Count Öderland [Graf Öder-
        land] Br: 225; DC2:
        139; EDC: 181; MD: 106
    Don Juan; or, The Love of
        Geometry [Don Juan, oder
        Die Liebe zur Geometrie]
        Br: 225; DC2: 139; EDC:
        181; MD: 106

The Firebugs [Mr. Biedermann
    and the Arsonists; Bieder-
    mann and the Firebugs; The
    Fire Raisers; Biedermann und
    die Brandstifter] Br: 225-
    226; DC2: 138; EDC: 179-
    180; LCAB: 69; MBD: 71;
    MD: 106; Po: 1126; TMBP:
    156
Graf Öderland see Count
    Öderland
The Great Wrath of Philipp
    Hotz [The Great Fury of
    Philipp Hotz; Die Grosse Wut
    des Philipp Hotz] Br: 226
Homo Faber Fi: 302-303; Ke:
    265; Po: 1126
A House in Berlin Br: 226
I'm Not Stiller see Stiller
Jürg Reinhart Fi: 303
Mein Name Sei Gantenbein see
    A Wilderness of Mirrors
Mr. Biedermann and the Arson-
    ists see The Firebugs
Montauk Fi: 303
Now They Sing Once More [Nun
    Singen Sie Wieder] Br:
    224; EDC: 182; Po: 1122
Santa Cruz Br: 226; DC2:
    139; EDC: 182; Po: 1127
Die Schwierigen Fi: 303
Stiller [I'm Not Stiller] Fi:
    303-304; Ke: 265; Po:
    1127-1128
When the War Came to an End
    [Als der Krieg zu Ende
    War] EDC: 182; Po: 1122
A Wilderness of Mirrors [Mein
    Name Sei Gautenbein] Fi:
    303, 304; Po: 1127
FROISSART, Jean
    Chronicles Ma: 708
    The Chronicles of England,
        translator Sir John Bouchier,
        Lord Berners Hen: 46
FROMENTIN, Eugene
    Dominique Fi: 73-74; Ke:
        74-75
FROST, Frances
    "Cradle Song" PE: 186
FROST, Robert
    General ALL: 107-109; ASF:
        202; ICBAP: 51; LCAB:
        69; Ma: 711-712; MD: 106;
        MP: 42-44; Po: 1128-1150
    "A-Wishing Well" ICBAP: 51

"Accidentally on Purpose"
PE: 186
"Acquainted with the Night"
ICBAP: 51; PE: 186;
Po: 1150-1151
"After Apple-Picking" ICBAP:
51; Ma: 709; PE: 186;
Po: 1151
"And All We Call American"
PE: 186
"The Armful" ICBAP: 51
"Away!" PE: 186
"The Axe-Helve" PE: 186;
Po: 1151
"The Bear" PE: 186
"Beech" PE: 187
"Bereft" PE: 187
"Birches" ICBAP: 51; PE:
187
"The Birthplace" PE: 187
"The Black Cottage" PE:
187
"Blueberries" Po: 1151
"Bond and Free" PE: 187
"A Boy's Will" MP: 43; PE:
187; Po: 1151
"Brown's Descent" PE: 187
"Build Soil" ICBAP: 51
"The Census-Taker" ICBAP:
51; Po: 1152
"The Cockerel Buying Habit"
Wa: 228
"The Cocoon" PE: 187
"Come In" ICBAP: 51; PE:
187; Po: 1152
"A Concept Self-Conceived"
PE: 187
"The Death of the Hired Man"
ICBAP: 51; Ma: 709-710;
PE: 187-188; Po: 1137,
1152
"The Demiurge's Laugh" PE:
188; Po: 1152
"Desert Places" ICBAP: 52;
PE: 188; Po: 1152-1153
"Design" ICBAP: 52; PE:
188; Po: 1153
"Devotion" PE: 188
"Directive" ICBAP: 52;
LCAB: 69; PE: 188-189;
Po: 1153-1154
"The Discovery of the
Madeiras" PE: 189
"Doom to Bloom" PE: 189
"The Draft Horse" ICBAP:
52; PE: 189; Po: 1154-

1155
"Dust of Snow" ICBAP: 52;
PE: 189; Po: 1155
"The Egg and the Machine"
PE: 190
"An Empty Threat" PE: 190
"Etherealizing" PE: 190
"Far-away Meadow" in "The
Last Mowing" PE: 190
"The Fear" ICBAP: 52; PE:
190; Po: 1137
"The Figure in the Doorway"
PE: 190
"Forgive, O Lord" PE: 190
"For Once, Then, Something"
ICBAP: 52; PE: 190
"From Sight to Insight" ICBAP:
52
"Gathering Leaves" PE: 190
"Ghost House" PE: 190
"The Gift Outright" PE: 190
"Going for Water" PE: 190
"Good-Bye and Keep Cold"
ICBAP: 52
"The Grindstone" PE: 191
"Happiness Makes Up in Height"
PE: 191
"The Hill Wife" ICBAP: 52;
PE: 191
"Home Burial" ICBAP: 53;
LCAB: 69; PE: 191; Po:
1137
"The Housekeeper" Po: 1137
"Hyla Brook" Po: 1146
"I Will Sing You One-O"
ICBAP: 53; PE: 191
In the Clearing (Collection of
Poems) ICBAP: 53; Po:
1155
"In the Home Stretch" PE:
191
"In Time of Cloudburst" PE:
191
"In White" ICBAP: 53
"In White and Design" PE:
191
"Iota Subscript" Po: 1156
"Iris by Night" ICBAP: 53
"A Just Judge" Wa: 228
"Kitty Hawk" ICBAP: 53;
PE: 191
"The Last Mowing" PE: 191
"A Leaf Trader" PE: 191
"Leaves Compared with Flowers"
PE: 192
"Lesson for Today" ICBAP:

53; PE: 192

"A Line-Storm Song" PE: 192

"The Literate Farmer and the Planet Venus" PE: 192

"Locked Out: As Told to a Child" PE: 192

"A Lone Striker" PE: 192

"Love and a Question" PE: 192; Po: 1156

"The Lovely Shall Be Choosers" PE: 192; Po: 1156

"Maple" PE: 192

"Masque of Mercy" ICBAP: 53; MD: 106; PE: 192; Po: 1140, 1156-1157

"Masque of Reason" DC1: 76; ICBAP: 53; MD: 107; PE: 193; Po: 1140, 1157

"Meeting and Passing" PE: 193

"Mending Wall" ICBAP: 53; Ma: 710-711; MP: 43; PE: 193-194; Po: 1157-1158

"Moon Compasses" PE: 194

"The Most of It" PE: 194

"The Mountain" PE: 194

"Mowing" PE: 194; Po: 1158

"Nature's First Green Is Gold" PE: 194

"The Need of Being Versed in Country Things" PE: 194; Po: 1146

"Neither Out Far Nor in Deep" ICBAP: 53; PE: 195

"Never Again Would Birds' Song Be the Same" PE: 195

"New Hampshire" PE: 195

"Not All There" PE: 195

"Nothing Gold Can Stay" ICBAP: 53; PE: 195; Po: 1158-1159

"October" PE: 195

"The Oft-Repeated Dream" PE: 195

"An Old Man's Winter Night" ICBAP: 53; PE: 195; Po: 1159

"Old Welch Goes to Show" Wa: 228

"On a Tree Fallen Across the Road" PE: 195

"On the Heart's Beginning to Cloud the Mind" PE: 196

"Once by the Pacific" ICBAP: 54; PE: 195-196; Po: 1159

"Once Looking Up by Chance at the Constellations" PE: 196

"Once More Brevity" PE: 196

"The Onset" ICBAP: 54

"The Original and Only" Wa: 228

"Our Hold on the Planet" Po: 1159-1160

"Out, Out--" ICBAP: 54; PE: 196; Po: 1160

"The Oven Bird" ICBAP: 54; PE: 196; Po: 1146, 1160

"The Pasture" PE: 196

"Paul's Wife" Po: 1161

"The Pauper Witch of Grafton" PE: 196

"A Prayer in Spring" PE: 196

"Provide, Provide" PE: 196

"Putting in the Seed" PE: 197

"Quandary" PE: 197

"Range-Finding" ICBAP: 54; PE: 197; Po: 1161

"Reluctance" PE: 197

"The Road Not Taken" ICBAP: 54; PE: 197; Po: 1161-1162

"The Rose Family" ICBAP: 54; PE: 197; Po: 1162

"The Runaway" PE: 197

"The Same Thing Over and Over" Wa: 228

"Sand Dunes" PE: 197; Po: 1162

"The Self-Seeker" PE: 197; Po: 1137

"A Semi-Revolution" PE: 198

"A Servant to Servants" ICBAP: 54; PE: 198; Po: 1137, 1162

"The Silken Tent" ICBAP: 54; PE: 198

"Sitting by a Bush in Broad Sunlight" PE: 198

"Snow" ICBAP: 54; PE: 198

"A Soldier" PE: 198

"Span of Life" ICBAP: 54; PE: 198

"Spring Pools" ICBAP: 54; PE: 198; Po: 1163

"Stopping by Woods on a Snowy Evening" ICBAP: 54-55; LCAB: 70; Ma: 712-713;

PE: 198-199; Po: 1163-
  1164
"Storm Fear" PE: 199
"The Subverted Flower" PE:
  199; Po: 1165
"The Thatch" PE: 199
"To Earthward" PE: 200;
  Po: 1165
"To the Thawing Wind" PE:
  200
"Trap Nests" Wa: 228
"Tree at My Window" PE:
  200
"Trespass" PE: 200
"The Tuft of Flowers" PE:
  200
"Two Look at Two" PE: 200
"Two Tramps in Mud Time"
  ICBAP: 55; LCAB: 70;
  PE: 200; Po: 1165
"Unharvested" PE: 200
"The Vanishing Red" PE:
  201
"West-Running Brook" ICBAP:
  55; PE: 201; Po: 1165
"Wild Grapes" PE: 201
"A Wishing Well" PE: 201;
  Po: 1166
"Witch of Coös" ICBAP: 55;
  PE: 201; Po: 1166
"A Witness Tree" PE: 201
"The Wood-Pile" ICBAP:
  55; PE: 201-202; Po:
  1166
"A Young Birch" PE: 202
FROUDE, James Anthony
  The Lieutenant's Daughter
    ENES2: 96
  The Nemesis of Faith ENES1:
    95
  The Spirit's Trials ENES2:
    96
FRY, Christopher
  General Br: 227-228; MBD:
    48-49; MD: 107-109;
    MDAE: 218-220; Mi: 236-
    237; Po: 1166-1170
  The Boy with a Cart Br:
    228; DC1: 76; EDC:
    182; MBD: 48; MD: 109;
    MDAE: 218; Po: 1170-
    1171
  Curtmantle Br: 228; DC1:
    76; EDC: 182-183; MBD:
    49; MDAE: 219; Po: 1171-
    1172

The Dark Is Light Enough Br:
    229; DC1: 76-77; EDC:
    183; MBD: 48-49; MD: 109-
    110; Po: 1167
The Firstborn Br: 229; DC1:
    77; EDC: 183-184; MD:
    110; MDAE: 220; Po: 1172
The Lady's Not for Burning
    Br: 229; DC1: 77-78; EDC:
    184-185; Ma: 714-715; MBD:
    49; MD: 110; MDAE: 220;
    Po: 1172
The Lark MDAE: 218-219
A Phoenix Too Frequent Br:
    229-230; DC1: 78; EDC:
    185-186; MBD: 49; MD:
    110; Po: 1173
Ring Around the Moon MD:
    110-111
A Sleep of Prisoners Br: 230;
    DC1: 78; EDC: 186; MBD:
    48-49; MD: 111; MDAE:
    219-220; Po: 1173
Thor, with Angels Br: 230;
    DC1: 78; EDC: 186; MD:
    111
Tiger at the Gates MDAE: 218
"Venus Observed" Br: 230-
    231; DC1: 78-79; EDC:
    187; Ma: 715-716; MD: 111;
    PE: 202; Po: 1173
FRYE, Northrop
  General LCAB: 70; Po: 1173-
    1175
  Anatomy of Criticism Po: 1175
  The Critical Zodiac LCAB: 70
  The Well-Tempered Critic Po:
    1175
FUCHS, Daniel
  General JW: 218
FUENTES, Carlos
  General LCAB: 70; Po: 1176
  "By the Mouth of the Gods"
    see "The Gods Speak"
  "Chac Mool" Wa: 228; WaS1:
    67
  A Change of Skin Ma: 717
  "The Cost of Life" Wa: 228
  The Death of Artemio Cruz [La
    muerte de Artemio Cruz]
    Ma: 717-718; Po: 1176
  "The Doll Queen" Wa: 228
  "The Gods Speak" ["By the
    Mouth of the Gods"] Wa:
    228-229; WaS1: 67
  "In Defense of Trigolibia"

Wa: 229
"Litany of the Orchids" Wa: 229
"The Man Who Invented Gunpowder" Wa: 229
"El muñeco" Wa: 229
"The Old Morality" Wa: 229
"Pantera en jazz" Wa: 229
"Pastel rancio" Wa: 229
"A Pure Soul" Wa: 229
La región más transparente Po: 1176-1177
"Tlactocatzine, the One from the Flemish Garden" Wa: 229
"To the Sea Serpent" Wa: 229
"Trigo errante" Wa: 229
"The Two Helens" Wa: 229; WaS1: 67-68
"What Fortune Brought" Wa: 229
Where the Air Is Clear Ma: 718

FÜHMANN, Franz
Bohmen am Meer Fi: 304
Das Judenauto Fi: 304

FULLER, Charles H., Jr.
General BAF: 127
The Brownsville Raid ADC: 108; MBA: 84-85
Candidate! BAP: 83
In My Many Names and Days BAP: 83; MBA: 84
In the Deepest Part of Sleep ADC: 108; BAP: 83; MBA: 84-85
The Layout MBA: 84
The Perfect Party BAP: 83
The Rise BAP: 83
The Village: A Party BAP: 83

FULLER, Henry Blake
General AF: 110; AN: 99; ASF: 202; Ho: 136-137, 157
"Dr. Gowdy and the Squash" ASF: 202; Wa: 229-230
"The Downfall of Abner Joyce" ASF: 202; Wa: 230
"The Greatest of These" ASF: 202; Wa: 230
"Little O'Grady vs. the Grindstone" ASF: 202; Wa: 230

"Pasquale's Picture" ASF: 202
"Waldo Trench Regains His Youth" Wa: 230

FULLER, Hoyt W.
General BAF: 127; BAW: 313

FULLER, James
Rebel Without a Cause Br: 231

FULLER, Margaret
General ALL: 110-112

FULLER, Roy
General Po: 1177
The Carnal Island ENES2: 96
Fantasy and Fugue ENES2: 96
The Father's Comedy ENES2: 96
Image of a Society ENES2: 96
My Child, My Sister ENES2: 96
The Perfect Fool ENES2: 96
The Ruined Boys ENES2: 96
The Second Curtain ENES2: 96

FULLER, Stephany
Moving Deep BAW: 313

FULLER, Thomas
General Ba: 65-66; Hen: 54; LJCD: 242
The Holy State and The Profane State Ba: 66; Hen: 136

FULWELL, Ulpian
Like Will to Like DC1: 79

FURETIERE, Antoine
Roman bourgeois Fi: 74; Ke: 75

FURMAN, Roger
General BAP: 84; BAW: 315; MBA: 85
Fat Tuesday MBA: 85
The Long Black Block BAP: 84; MBA: 85

FURMANOV, Dmitri
Capaev Ke: 405

FURNBERG, Louis
General Po: 1177

FÜRPHY, Joseph [Tom COLLINS]
General AL: 217-221
Such Is Life AL: 217-221; Po: 1177

FURTH, George
Twigs [four plays: Emily, Celia, Dorothy, and Ma] ADC: 108
_____ and Stephen SONDHEIM
Company ADC: 108-109

FUTRELLE, Jaques
"The Flying Eye" WaS1: 68
"The Problem of Cell 13"
ASF: 203
FYLES, Franklin and David
BELASCO
The Girl I Left Behind Me
Br: 231

G

GAARD, David
And Puppy Dog Tails ADC:
109
GABRE-MEDHIN, Tsegaye
General BALE: 304
GADDA, Carlo Emilio
Acquainted with Grief Fi:
265
That Awful Mess on Via
Merulana Fi: 265; Ke:
243
GADDIS, William
General Po: 1179
GADENNE, Paul
General Po: 1179
L'Avenue Ke: 75
L'Invitation chez Les Stirl
Ke: 75
La plage de Scheveningen
Ke: 75
Siloe Ke: 75
GAGER, William
Oedipus DC1: 79
GAGLIANO, Frank
Conerico Was Here to Stay
ADC: 109
Night of the Dunce ADC:
109
Prince of Peasantmania ADC:
109
GAINES, Ernest J.
General AAF: 82-84; AAW:
55; ASF: 203; BAF: 129-
130; BAW: 316-317
The Autobiography of Miss
Jane Pittman AAF: 83;
AAL: 176; BAF: 130-
131; Ma: 719
Bloodline AAF: 83; AAL:
176; BAF: 130-131; Ma:
719
"Bloodline" ASF: 203; Wa:
230
Catherine Carmier AAF:

83; AAL: 176; BAF: 131
"Just Like a Tree" ASF: 203;
Wa: 230
"A Long Day in November"
ASF: 203; Wa: 230; WaS1:
68
Of Love and Dust AAF: 83;
AAL: 176; BAF: 131
"The Sky Is Gray" ASF: 203;
Wa: 230
"Three Men" ASF: 203
GAINES, Frederick
Ghost Dancer ADC: 109
Jerusalem ADC: 109
Wilde! ADC: 109
_____ and Dale F. MENTEN
The House of Leather: An
Ante-Bellum Rock Musical
ADC: 109
GAINES, J.E. [Sonny Jim]
Don't Let It Go to Your Head
ADC: 109; BAP: 84; MBA:
86
Heaven and Hell's Agreement
ADC: 109; BAP: 84; MBA:
86
Sometimes a Hard Head Makes a
Soft Behind BAP: 84; MBA:
86
What If It Had Turned Up
Heads? ADC: 109; BAP:
84
GAINES-SHELTON, Ruth
The Church Fight BAP: 85
GAINSFORD, Thomas
The Historie of Trebizond ERP:
170-171
GAISER, Gerd
General Po: 1179
Galdós, Benito Pérez see PEREZ
GALDOS, Benito
GALE, Zona
General AN: 99; ASF: 204;
Po: 1180
Birth Po: 1180
"Bridal Pond" ASF: 204; Wa:
230
Miss Lulu Bett ADC: 110;
Br: 231
Mister Pitt ADC: 110
The Neighbors ADC: 110; Br:
231
"The Story of Jeffro" ASF:
204
GALICH, Manuel
General Br: 231

GALLANT, Mavis
"Acceptance of Their Ways"
WaS1: 68
"The Legacy" Wa: 230
"Orphan's Progress" Wa:
230
GALLEGOS, Rómulo
General Po: 1180-1181
La Alborada Po: 1182
Cantaclaro Po: 1182
Doña Bárbara Po: 1182-1183
El último Solar Po: 1183
GALLICO, Paul
General APC: 107; ASF:
204
"The Enchanted Doll" Wa:
231
GALLIE, Menna
General Po: 1183-1184
You're Welcome to Ulster
ENES2: 97
GALLIVAN, G.P.
General Br: 231
Decision at Easter Br: 232
Mourn the Ivy Leaf Br:
232
GALSWORTHY, John
General BN2: 44-46; Br:
232; LCAB: 70; MBD:
50-51; MD: 111-112; Mi:
237-239; Po: 1184-1185;
Ri: 417-427, 433-434;
Sch: 99-103; TA: 153-
154
"The Apple Tree" Po: 1185-
1186; Ri: 420; Wa: 231
Bit of Love EDC: 187; MD:
112-113
The Burning Spear ENES1:
96
Caravan Ri: 426
The Country House ENES1:
96; ENES2: 97
The Dark Flower ENES2: 97
The Eldest Son Br: 232;
MD: 113
End of the Chapter ENES2:
97
Escape EDC: 187-188; MD:
113
Exiled EDC: 188
A Family Man EDC: 188;
MD: 113
The First and the Last MD:
113
The Forest EDC: 188; MD:

113
Forsyte Saga BN2: 46; EN:
52; ENE: 116-117; ENES1:
96; ENES2: 97; LCAB: 70;
Ma: 720-721; Po: 1186-
1187; Ri: 418, 424, 428-431;
Sch: 103-104
The Foundations MD: 113
Fraternity BN2: 46; EN: 53;
ENES1: 96; ENES2: 97;
Po: 1187; Ri: 418, 420,
432
The Fugitive Br: 232; EDC:
188; MD: 113
In Chancery see also Forsyte
Saga ENES2: 97; Ri: 430
Indian Summer of a Forsyte
see Forsyte Saga
The Island Pharisees ENES2:
97
"The Japanese Quince" Ri:
432; Wa: 231; WaS1: 68
Jocelyn ENES1: 96; ENES2:
97; Ri: 420, 432
Joy MD: 113
"The Juryman" Wa: 231
"Justice" Br: 233; DC1: 79;
EDC: 188; MBD: 50; MD:
113; Po: 1187; Wa: 231
The Little Dream MD: 113
The Little Man Br: 233
Loyalties Br: 233; DC1: 79;
EDC: 188; MBD: 51; MD:
113; Po: 1188; Ri: 433
The Man of Property see also
The Forsyte Saga EN: 53;
ENE: 117; ENES1: 96;
ENES2: 97-98; Po: 1185;
Ri: 418, 420, 428-431
"Manna" SFC: 60; Wa: 231
The Mob Br: 233; EDC:
189; MD: 113
A Modern Comedy ENES2: 98;
Ri: 418
Old English EDC: 189
Over the River Ri: 419
The Patrician ENES2: 98
The Pigeon Br: 233; DC1:
80; MD: 113
"Quality" Wa: 231
The Roof EDC: 189; MD:
113
Saint's Progress Ri: 432
"The Salvation of Swithin For-
syte" Wa: 231
The Show EDC: 189; MD:

113
The Silver Box Br: 233-
234; DC1: 80; EDC: 189;
LCAB: 70; MD: 114
The Silver Spoon see For-
syte Saga
The Skin Game Br: 234;
EDC: 189; MD: 114; Ri:
434
Strife Br: 234; DC1: 80;
MD: 114
Swan Song see also Forsyte
Saga ENES2: 98
"Ultima Thule" Po: 1188;
Wa: 231
The White Monkey Ri: 431
Windows EDC: 189; MD:
114
GALT, John
General Ai: 117-118; BN:
58; Du: 78-79
Annals of the Parrish Du:
78; ENES1: 96; ENES2:
98
The Ayrshire Legatees
ENES2: 98
Bogle Corbet ENES2: 98
The Earthquake ENES2: 98
Eben Erskine ENES2: 98
The Entail Du: 78; ENES1:
96; ENES2: 98
The Gathering of the West
BN: 58; ENES2: 98
Glenfell ENES2: 98
The Last of the Lairds
ENES2: 98
Lawrie Todd ENES2: 98
The Majolo ENES2: 98
The Member ENES2: 99
The Provost Ai: 117; Du:
78; ENES2: 99
The Radical ENES2: 99
Ringan Gilhaize ENES2: 99
Rothelan ENES2: 99
Sir Andrew Wylie ENES2:
99
Southennan ENES2: 99
The Spacewife ENES2: 99
Stanley Buxton ENES2: 99
The Steam-Boat ENES2: 99
The Stolen Child ENES2: 99
GALVEZ, Manuel
General Po: 1188-1189
Escenas de la guerra del
Paraguay Po: 1189
La maestra normal Po:

1189
Perdido en su noche Po: 1190
GAMBOA, Don Federico
General Br: 234
GAMBOA, Jose Joaquin
General Br: 234
The Gentleman, Death, and the
Devil [El Caballero, la
Muerte, y el Diablo] Br:
234
Gana, Alberto Blest see BLEST
GANA, Alberto
Gandía, Manuel Zeno see ZENO
GANDIA, Manuel
GANGANHARA
Gangadasapratapvilasa DC2:
140
GANIVET, Angel
La conquista del reino de Maya
Ke: 204
Los trabajos de Pío Cid Ke:
204
GANT, Lisbeth A.
General BAF: 132
GANTIER, Joaquin
General Br: 235
GANTILLON, Simon
General Br: 235
Cyclone Br: 235
Maya Br: 235
GARBORG, Arne
A Free Thinker Ke: 349
The Lost Father Ke: 349
Menfolk Ke: 349
Peace Ke: 350
Peasant Students Ke: 350
She Who Stayed with Mother
Ke: 350
The Son Came Home Ke: 350
Weary Men Ke: 350
GARCES, Enrique
General Br: 235
GARCIA, Carlos
La desordenada codicia de los
bienes ajenos Fi: 217
GARCIA CALDERON, Ventura
"Juventud" Wa: 231
GARCIA LOPEZ, Angel
General Po: 1190
GARCIA LORCA, Federico
General Br: 235-236; LCAB:
70; Ma: 725-726; MD:
114-115; Po: 1190-1195
The Abandoned Church [Iglesia
abandonada] Po: 1202
Amor de Don Perlimplin con

Belisa en su jardin see
The Love of Don Perlimp-
lin for Belisa in His Garden
Asi que pasen cinco años
see When Five Years
Pass
The Audience [The Public;
El público] Br: 239;
EDC: 189-190; Po: 1204
Balada Triste Po: 1196
Blood Wedding [Bitter Olean-
der; Bodas de sangre]
Br: 236-237; DC2: 239-
240; EDC: 190-191; LCAB:
70-71; Ma: 722-723; MD:
115; Po: 1197-1198
Burla de don Pedro a caballo
Po: 1198
The Butterfly's Evil Spell
[The Spell of the Butter-
fly; The Witchery of the
Butterfly; El malefico de
la mariposa] Br: 237;
EDC: 193; MD: 116; Po:
1203
Canción de Jinete Po: 1199
Canciones Po: 1199
La Casa de Bernarda Alba
see The House of Ber-
narda Alba
La casada infiel Po: 1201
Córdoba, lejana y sola Po:
1201
El Diván del Tamarit Po:
1202
Doña Rosita the Spinster; or,
The Language of the
Flowers [Doña Rosita la
soltera, o El lenguaje de
las flores] Br: 237-238;
EDC: 191; MD: 116; Po:
1202
Gypsy Ballads [Romancero
gitano] Po: 1206
The House of Bernarda Alba
[La Casa de Bernarda Al-
ba] Br: 238; DC2:
240-241; EDC: 191-192;
LCAB: 70; Ma: 723-724;
MD: 115-116; Po: 1199-
1201
Iglesia abandonada see
The Abandoned Church
In the Frame of Don Cristó-
bal see The Puppet
Farce of Don Cristóbal

Lament for the Death of a Bull-
fighter [Llanto por Ignacio
Sánchez Mejias] Po: 1202-
1203
The Love of Don Perlimplin for
Belisa in His Garden [The
Lass, the Sailor, and the
Student; Amor de Don Per-
limplin con Belisa en su
jardín] Br: 238-239; DC2:
240; EDC: 192; Ma: 724-
725; MD: 115; Po: 1196
El malefico de la mariposa see
The Butterfly's Evil Spell
Mariana Pineda Br: 239; DC2:
241; EDC: 192-193; MD:
116; Po: 1203
Muerte de Antoñito el Camborio
Po: 1203
Pantomime of Don Christopher
see The Puppet Farce of
Don Cristóbal
Poema del cante jondo Po:
1203-1204
Poet in New York [Poeta en
Nueva York] Po: 1204
"Preciosa y el aire" Po: 1204
The Public see The Audience
El público see The Audience
The Puppet Farce of Don Cris-
tóbal [In the Frame of Don
Cristóbal; Pantomime of Don
Christopher; Retabillo de Don
Cristóbal] Br: 239; DC2:
240; EDC: 193; MD: 116;
Po: 1205
Puppet Show of the Cachiporra
[Los Titeres de Cachiporra]
Br: 239
Romance de la luna, luna Po:
1205
"Romance sonámbulo" Po: 1205
Romancero gitano see Gypsy
Ballads
San Rafael. Córdoba Po: 1206
Shoemaker's Prodigious Wife
[La zapatera prodigioso]
Br: 240; DC2: 241; EDC:
193; MD: 117; Po: 1208
The Spell of the Butterfly see
The Butterfly's Evil Spell
Thus Five Years Pass see
When Five Years Pass
Los Titeres de Cachiporra see
Puppet Show of the Cachi-
porra

Trip to the Moon Po: 1207
When Five Years Pass [Thus
Five Years Pass; Asi que
pasen cinco años] Br:
240; DC2: 239; EDC:
193; MD: 115; Po: 1196
The Witchery of the Butterfly
see The Butterfly's Evil
Spell
Yerma Br: 240-241; DC2:
241-242; EDC: 193-194;
LCAB: 70; Ma: 726-727;
MD: 116; Po: 1207-1208
La zapatera prodigioso see
The Shoemaker's Prodigious
Wife
GARCIA MARQUEZ, Gabriel
General LCAB: 71; Po:
1208-1209
"Artificial Roses" WaS1: 68
"Baltazar's Marvelous After-
noon" WaS1: 68
"Big Mama's Funeral" WaS1:
68
"Bitter Sorrow for Three
Sleepwalkers" WaS1: 68
"Blancaman the Good, Vendor
of Miracles" WaS1: 69
"Blue-dog Eyes" WaS1: 69
Cien años de soledad Po:
1209
"The Day After Saturday"
["One Day After Saturday"]
Wa: 231; WaS1: 69
"Death Constant Beyond
Love" WaS1: 69
"Eve Inside Her Cat" WaS1:
69
"Los funerales de la Mamá
Grande" Wa: 515
"The Handsomest Drowned
Man in the World" WaS1:
69
"The Incredible and Sad Tale
of Innocent Erendira and
Her Heartless Grandmother"
WaS1: 69
"The Last Voyage of the Ghost
Ship" WaS1: 69
"Montiel's Widow" WaS1: 69
"Nabo" WaS1: 69
"The Night of the Curlews"
WaS1: 69
"One Day After Saturday"
see "The Day After Sat-
urday"

"One of These Days" WaS1:
69
"The Other Rib of Death" WaS1:
69
"The Sea of Lost Time" WaS1:
69
"Someone Has Disturbed the
Roses" WaS1: 69
"There Are No Thieves in This
Town" WaS1: 70
"The Third Resignation" WaS1:
70
"Tubal-Cain Forges a Star"
WaS1: 70
"Tuesday Nap" ["Tuesday Si-
esta"] Wa: 232; WaS1: 70
"A Very Old Man with Enormous
Wings" WaS1: 70
GARCIA MORENTE, Manuel
General Po: 1209-1210
GARCIA PAVON, Francisco
General Po: 1210-1211
GARCIA VELLOSO, Enrique
General Br: 241
GARÇON, Maurice
General Po: 1211
GARDINER, Dorothy
The Golden Lady LCAB: 71
GARDNER, Erle Stanley
General ASF: 204
GARDNER, Herb
The Goodbye People ADC: 110
Thieves ADC: 110
A Thousand Clowns ADC: 110;
TMAP: 171
GARDNER, Isabella
"Mea Culpa" ICBAP: 55
"Summer Remembered" PE:
202
"The Widow's Yard" ICBAP:
55; LCAB: 71; PE: 202
GARDNER, John
Grendel Ma: 728
The Sunlight Dialogues Ma:
728-729
GARDONYI, Geza
The Invisible Man Ke: 405
GARIBALDI, Giuseppe
Cantoni, il volontario Fi: 265
I mille Fi: 265
The Rule of the Monk Fi: 265
Garioch, Robert see SUTHER-
LAND, Robert Garioch
GARLAND, Hamlin
General AF: 113-117; ALL:
112-113; AN: 100-101;

ASF: 206-207; C1a: 36-37; Ho: 51-53; LCAB: 71; Po: 1211-1216

"Among the Corn Rows" ASF: 205; Wa: 232

Back-Trailers from the Middle Border Po: 1212

Boy Life on the Prairie AF: 114; Po: 1216

"A Branch Road" ASF: 205; Wa: 232

"Chicago Studies" AF: 116; C1a: 37; Ho: 53; Po: 1216

"A Common Case" ASF: 205; Wa: 232

"The Creamery Man" Wa: 232

Crumbling Idols AF: 116

"Daddy Deering" Wa: 232

A Daughter of the Middle Border Po: 1212

"A Day's Pleasure" Wa: 232

"Delmar of Pima" ASF: 205

"A Girl from Washington" see "A Meeting in the Foothills"

"A Girl of Modern Tyre" ASF: 205

"John Boyle's Conclusion" ASF: 205; Po: 1216; Wa: 232

"The Land of the Straddle-Bug" ASF: 205; Wa: 232

A Little Norsk see "Ol' Pap's Flaxen"

Main-Travelled Roads AF: 113, 115-116; C1a: 36-37; Ho: 52; Ma: 730-731

"A Meeting in the Foothills" Wa: 232

Miller of Boscobel Po: 1216-1217

"The Moccasin Ranch" ASF: 205

"Mrs. Ripley's Trip" Wa: 232

"Ol' Pap's Flaxen" Wa: 232

"The Return of a Private" ASF: 206; Ho: 52; Wa: 232

"Rising Wolf--Ghost Dancer" ASF: 206; Wa: 233

Roadside Meetings LCAB: 71

Rose of Dutcher's Coolly

AF: 113, 115; Ho: 52; Ma: 731-732

"The Silent Eaters" ASF: 206; Wa: 233; WaS1: 70

A Son of the Middle Border AF: 113, 115, 117; AN: 100; C1a: 37; Ho: 52-53; Ma: 732; Po: 1212, 1217

A Spoil of Office AN: 100; Ho: 52; Po: 1217

"The Story of Howling Wolf" ASF: 206; Wa: 233

"Ten Years Dead" ASF: 206; Wa: 233

Trail-Makers of the Middle Border Po: 1212

"Under the Lion's Paw" ASF: 206; Wa: 233

"Up the Coulé" ASF: 206; Wa: 233

GARNEAU, Saint-Denys
General Po: 1217

GARNET, Henry Highland
General LCAB: 71

GARNETT, David
General BN2: 47; Sch: 104
Lady into Fox Po: 1217
A Man in the Zoo Po: 1217

GARNETT, Edward William
General Mi: 239

GARNIER, Robert
Bradamante DC2: 140
Hippolyte DC2: 140
Marc-Antoine DC2: 140
La Troade DC2: 140

GARRARD, Lewis Hector
Wah-to-yah and the Taos Trail LCAB: 71

GARRETT, Jimmy
General BAW: 319; MBA: 86
And We Own the Night: A Play of Blackness ADC: 110; BAP: 85; MBA: 86-87

GARRICK, David
General EC: 69-70; Li: 183-187
The Jubilee EC: 70

GARRIGUE, Jean
"Dialog for Belvedere" PE: 202
"A Dream" ICBAP: 55
"The Little Pony" ICBAP: 55
"Proem" ICBAP: 55
"A Water Walk by Villa D'Este" ICBAP: 55

GARRO, Elena

A Solid Home [Un Hogar
Solido] Br: 241
GARRY, Flora
General Ai: 266
GARSHIN, Vsevolod
"Four Days" Wa: 233
"From the Reminiscences of
Private Ivanov" Wa: 233
"The Incident" Wa: 233
"The Meeting" Wa: 233
"Nadezhda Nikolaevna" Wa:
233
"Night" Wa: 233
"The Red Flower" Wa: 233
GARSON, Barbara
General MDAE: 223
Mac Bird! ADC: 110-111;
LCAB: 71; MDAE: 223;
Po: 1218; TMBP: 223
GARTH, Sir Samuel
General Me: 221-222
The Dispensary ICBAP: 55;
Me: 221-222; PE: 202
GARVEY, Mrs. Amy Ashwood
Hey! Hey! BAP: 86
GARY, Romain
General Po: 1218
Les Racines du ciel Po:
1218-1219
GASCAR, Pierre
General Po: 1219
The Animals see also Les
Bêtes Ke: 75; Wa: 234
Les Bêtes see also The
Animals Po: 1219
"The Dogs" Wa: 234
"The Horses" Wa: 234
"The House of Blood" Wa:
234
Le Meilleur de la Vie Po:
1220
Les moutons de feu Ke: 75
The Season of the Dead Ke:
75-76; Wa: 234
GASCOIGNE, George
General ED: 238-239; ERP:
175; Ma: 734-735; SC:
53-54; TSD: 50
The Adventures of Master
F.J. EN: 53; ENES1:
97; ENES2: 99-100; ERP:
173-183; Hen: 154; Ma:
733; SC: 53
The Complaint of Philomene
SC: 54
"The Constancy of a Lover

Hath Thus Sometimes Been
Briefly Declared" PE: 202
"Gascoigne's Woodmanship" PE:
202
"Good Morrow" PE: 202
Jocasta Ma: 733-734
"The Lullaby of a Lover" PE:
202
The Steel Glass SC: 53-54
GASCOYNE, David
General ICBAP: 56; Po:
1220-1221
"The Diabolical Principle" PE:
203
"Phantasmagoria" ICBAP: 56
"Winter Garden" PE: 203
GASHE, Marina
General BALE: 304
GASKELL, Elizabeth
General BN: 59-60; Du: 80-
81
Cousin Phillis ENES1: 97;
ENES2: 100
Cranford BN: 60; Du: 79;
EN: 53; ENE: 117-118;
ENES1: 97; ENES2: 100
A Dark Night's Work ENES1:
97; ENES2: 100
"The Heart of John Middleton"
WaS1: 70
Mary Barton BN: 60; Du:
79-80; EN: 53-54; ENE:
118; ENES1: 97; ENES2:
100-101
My Lady Ludlow ENES1: 98
North and South BN: 60;
Du: 80; EN: 54; ENE:
118; ENES1: 98; ENES2:
101
Ruth EN: 54; ENE: 118;
ENES1: 98; ENES2: 101
"The Sexton's Heart" WaS1:
70
Sylvia's Lovers EN: 54; ENE:
118; ENES1: 98; ENES2:
102
Wives and Daughters EN: 54-
55; ENE: 119; ENES1: 98-
99; ENES2: 102
GASS, William Howard
General ASF: 208
"Icicles" ASF: 208; Wa: 234;
WaS1: 70
"In the Heart of the Heart of
the Country" ASF: 208;
Ma: 736; Wa: 234; WaS1:

70

"Mrs. Mean" ASF: 208

Omensetter's Luck CN: 203;
LCAB: 72; Ma: 736

"Order of Insects" WaS1:
70

"The Pederson Kid" ASF:
208; Wa: 234; WaS1: 70

"Willie Masters' Lonesome
Wife" ASF: 208

Gasset, José Ortega y see
ORTEGA Y GASSET, José

GATES, Lewis E.
General Po: 1221

GATHERU, Reuel John Mugo
General BALE: 305

GATTI, Armand
General Br: 241; Po:
1221

Chant Publique Devant Deux
Chaises Electriques Br:
241

Le Crapaud-Buffle Br: 241

Imaginary Life of Auguste G.
DC2: 140

V Comme Vietnam Br: 241

GAUCLERE, Yassu
General Po: 1221

GAUTIER, Théophile
"L'Ame de la maison ou la
Vie et la Mort d'un Gril-
lon" Wa: 234

The Amorous Corpse Fi:
75; Ke: 76

Arria Marcella Fi: 74;
Wa: 234; WaS1: 71

"Avatar" WaS1: 71

Le Capitaine Fracasse Fi:
74; Ke: 76

"The Dead Lemon" ["Clari-
monde"; "The Beautiful
Vampire"] Wa: 234-235;
WaS1: 71

"Elias Wildmanstadius" Wa:
235

"Fortunio" Wa: 235; WaS1:
71

"Jettatura" Wa: 235

"King Candaules" ["Le Roi
Candaule"] Wa: 235;
WaS1: 71

Mademoiselle de Maupin Fi:
74-75; Ke: 76

"The Mummy's Foot" WaS1:
71

"The Mummy's Tale" WaS1:

71

"Omphale" Wa: 235; WaS1: 71

"One of Cléopâtra's Nights"
["Une Nuit de Cléopatre"]
Wa: 235; WaS1: 71

"Onuphrius" Wa: 235

"Le Roi Candaule" see "King
Candaules"

The Romance of the Mummy
Ke: 76

Spirite Fi: 75; WaS1: 71

"La Toison d'or" Wa: 235

"The Twin Knight" WaS1: 71

GAVIDIA, Francisco
General Br: 241

GAY, Cedric
Survival MBA: 87

GAY, John
General EC: 71-72; Li: 188-
191; Me: 224-228

Achilles DC1: 80; Li: 189

Acis and Galatea EC: 71; Li:
189

The Beggar's Opera DC1: 80;
EC: 71-72; EDC: 194-196;
Li: 189-191; Ma: 737-738;
TMIP: 17

The Captives DC1: 80

Dione DC1: 80

"Mr. Pope's Welcome from
Greece" PE: 203; Me: 227

The Mohocks DC1: 80-81; EC:
71-72; EDC: 196; Li: 189

Polly DC1: 81; EC: 71-72;
EDC: 196-197; Li: 189-191

Rural Sports Me: 225

"Saturday" (The Shepherd's
Week) PE: 203; Me: 226-
227

The Shepherd's Week EC: 71-
72; Me: 225-228

Three Hours After Marriage
DC1: 81; EC: 72; Li:
189-190

Trivia EC: 71; Me: 224, 227

The What D'Ye Call It DC1:
81; EC: 71; EDC: 197;
Li: 190

GAYLE, Addison, Jr.
General BAF: 132

GAZZO, Michael V.
A Hatful of Rain ADC: 111;
Br: 242

The Night Circus ADC: 112

GEDDES, Virgil
The Earth Between Br: 242

GEIJERSTAM, Gustaf
  Boken om Lille Bror Ke:
    350
  Kvinnomakt Ke: 350
GEISMAR, Maxwell David
  General LCAB: 72
GELBART, Larry
  The Sly Fox ADC: 112
GELBER, Jack
  General Br: 242; LCAB:
    72; MD: 117; MDAE:
    224-225; Po: 1222; TMAP:
    158-163
  The Apple ADC: 112; Br:
    242; DC1: 81; MD: 117;
    MDAE: 224-225; Po: 1222;
    TMAP: 158-163
  Barbary Shore ADC: 112;
    TMAP: 163
  The Connection ADC: 112-
    113; Br: 242-243; DC1:
    81-82; LCAB: 72; MD:
    117; MDAE: 224-225;
    Po: 1222-1223; TMAP:
    158-164
  The Cuban Thing ADC:
    113; TMAP: 164
  Rehearsal ADC: 113; MBA:
    87; TMAP: 164
  Sleep ADC: 113; TMAP:
    161, 164
  Square in the Eye ADC:
    113-114; Br: 243; TMAP:
    159-160, 164-165
GELLERT, Christian
  Das Leben der Schwedischen
    Gräfin von G ** Fi: 304
GENET, Jean
  General Br: 243-245; LCAB:
    72; MD: 117-118; Po:
    1223-1230
  Adame Miroir Br: 245; DC2:
    141
  Albert Giacometti's Studio
    Br: 245
  The Balcony [Le Balcon]
    Br: 245-247; DC2: 141-
    142; EDC: 197-199;
    LCAB: 72; MD: 119;
    MDAE: 225; Po: 1227,
    1229, 1230-1231; TMAP:
    160; TMBP: 185
  The Blacks [Les Negres]
    Br: 247-249; DC2: 142-
    143; EDC: 199-200;
    LCAB: 72; MD: 119-
    120; Po: 1227, 1229, 1232;
    TMAP: 171
  Deathwatch [Haute Surveillance]
    Br: 249; DC2: 143; EDC:
    200-201; MD: 119; Po: 1229
  The Maids [Les Bonnes] Br:
    250-251; DC2: 144; EDC:
    201-202; MD: 119; MDAE:
    298; Po: 1229, 1231; TMAP:
    174
  Nôtre-Dame-des-Fleurs Po:
    1232-1233
  Paolo Paoli Br: 251
  The Screens [Les Paravents]
    Br: 251-252; DC2: 144-145;
    EDC: 202-203; MD: 120;
    Po: 1233-1234
  The Tight Rope Walker Br:
    252
GENEVOIX, Maurice
  Raboliot Fi: 75
GENNARI, Genevieve
  La Fugue Irlandaise Fi: 75
GENTILE, Giovanni
  General Po: 1234
GEORGE, Crispin
  General BALE: 305
GEORGE, Henry
  General C1a: 108-109
GEORGE, Stefan
  General Po: 1235-1238
  Algabal Po: 1239
  Das Jahr der Seele Po: 1239
  Lukretia Po: 1239
  Das neue Reich Po: 1239
  Der Siebente Ring Po: 1239-
    1240
GEORGE, Walter Lionel
  General TA: 155
GEORGHIU, Constantin Virgil
  La meurtre de Kyrallesa Po:
    1244
GERALDY, Paul
  General Br: 252
  Robert et Marianne Br: 252
GERARD DE NERVAL [Gerard
    LABRUNIE]
  General LCAB: 72
GERHARD, Adele
  General Po: 1240
GERHARDIE, William Alexander
  General LCAB: 73
  Resurrection LCAB: 73
GERIMA, Haile
  Bush Mama MBA: 87-88
GERNSBACK, Hugo

General LCAB: 73
GEROULD, Katherine F.
"The Great Tradition" ASF:
209; Wa: 235
"Wesendonck" ASF: 209;
Wa: 235
GERRY, Bill
"Understand What I Mean?"
SFC: 61; Wa: 235
GERSHE, Leonard
Butterflies Are Free ADC:
114
GERSHON, Karen
"Swiss Morning" (Vierwald-
stättersee) PE: 203
GERSTACKER, Friedrich
Germelshausen Ke: 265
GERSTENBERG, Heinrich von
Ugolino DC2: 145
GESPEDES Y MANESES, Gonzalo
Gerardo, the Unfortunate
Spaniard see DIGGES,
Leonard [translator]
GETA, Hosidus
Medea DC2: 145
GHELDERODE, Michel de
General Br: 252-255; MD:
120-121; Po: 1240-1242
La Balade du Grand Macabre
see The Grand Macabre's
Stroll
Barabbas Br: 255; EDC:
203
The Blind Men [Les Aveugles]
Br: 255
La Cavalier Bizarre see
The Strange Rider
Christopher Columbus [Chris-
tophe Columb] Br: 255;
Po: 1243
Chronicles of Hell [The
Pomps of Hell; Fastes
d'Enfer] Br: 255; DC2:
145; Po: 1243
The Death of Doctor Faust
[Le Mort du Docteur
Faust] Br: 255; EDC:
203; Po: 1243-1244
Don Juan Br: 256
D'Un Diable Qui Precha Mer-
veilles see Of a Devil
Who Preached Wonders
Ecole des Bouffons see
School for Buffoons
Escurial Br: 256; EDC:
203

Fastes d'Enfer see Chronicles
of Hell
Les Femmes au Tombeau see
The Women at the Tomb
The Grand Macabre's Stroll [La
Balade du Grand Macabre]
Br: 256
Hop, Signor! Br: 256; EDC:
203
Mademoiselle Jaïre Br: 256;
EDC: 203
Magie Rouge see Red Magic
The Magpie on the Gallows [La
Pié sur la Gibet] Br: 256
Marie la Miserable Br: 257
Le Mort du Docteur Faust see
The Death of Doctor Faust
Of a Devil Who Preached Won-
ders [D'Un Diable Qui
Precha Merveilles] Br: 257
Pantagleize Br: 257; DC2:
145-146; EDC: 203; MD:
121
La Pié sur la Gibet see The
Magpie on the Gallows
The Pomps of Hell see Chroni-
cles of Hell
Red Magic [Magic Rouge] Br:
257; DC2: 146; EDC: 204;
Po: 1243
Saint Francois d'Assise Br:
257
School for Buffoons [Ecole des
Bouffons] Br: 257
Sortie de l'Acteur Br: 257;
MD: 121
Splendors of Hell EDC: 204
The Strange Rider [La Cavalier
Bizarre] Br: 258
Three Actors and Their Drama
[Trois Acteurs, un Drame]
Br: 258; MD: 121
The Women at the Tomb [Les
Femmes au Tombeau] Br:
258
GHEON, Henri
General Br: 258; MD: 121;
Po: 1244
La Mystere de L'Invention de
la Croix Br: 258; DC2:
146
Oedipe Br: 258
Les Trois Miracles de Sainte
Cécile Br: 258; DC2:
146
GHISELIN, Brewster

"Bath of Aphrodite" PE:
203
"Gull in the Great Basin"
PE: 203
GIACOSA, Guiseppe
General Br: 258
Like Falling Leaves Br: 258
GIBBON, Edward
General EC: 73; LCAB: 73
Autobiography EC: 73
The History of the Decline
and Fall of the Roman
Empire EC: 73; LCAB:
73; Ma: 739-740
Gibbon, Lewis Grassic see
MITCHELL, James Leslie
GIBBONS, Stella
Cold Comfort Farm ENES2:
102
GIBBS, Barbara
"Dry Canyon, September"
PE: 203
"In a Garden, I and II" PE:
203
GIBBS, Wolcott
Season in the Sun ADC: 115
GIBSON, Walker
"Billiards" PE: 203
"Thaw" PE: 203
GIBSON, Wilfrid Wilson
General Mi: 239-240
GIBSON, William
General MD: 121
The Body and the Wheel ADC:
115
A Cry of Players ADC: 115
Dinny and the Witches
ADC: 115
Golda ADC: 115
The Miracle Worker ADC:
115-116; Br: 258; DC1:
82; LCAB: 73; MD: 121
The Seesaw Log MDAE: 227
Two for the Seesaw ADC:
116; Br: 258; DC1: 82;
MD: 121
GICARU, Muga
General BALE: 305
GIDE, André
General Br: 259; LCAB:
73; MD: 122; Po: 1245-
1257
Ajax MD: 122
Bathsheba [Bethsabé] EDC:
204; MD: 122
Cahiers d'André Walter see

The Notebooks of André
Walter
The Caves of the Vatican [Laf-
cadio's Adventures; The
Vatican Cellars; The Vatican
Swindle; Les Caves du Vati-
can] EDC: 205; Fi: 75-76;
Ke: 77-79; Ma: 741-742;
Po: 183, 1257-1259
Corydon Fi: 76; Ke: 79; Po:
1256, 1259
The Counterfeiters [Les Faux
Monnayeurs] Fi: 76-78;
Ke: 79-82; LCAB: 73; Ma:
742-743; Po: 1256, 1260
"El Hadj" SFC: 61; Wa: 236
The Fruits of the Earth [Les
Nourritures terrestres]
Fi: 78; Ke: 82-83; Ma:
743; Po: 1262-1263
Geneviève Fi: 78-79; Ke:
83; SFC: 61; Wa: 235
The Immoralist [L'Immoraliste]
Br: 259; Fi: 79-80; Ke:
83-85; Ma: 744-745; Po:
1254, 1261-1262; SFC: 61-
62; Wa: 236-237; WaS1:
71-72
Isabelle Fi: 80; Ke: 85;
SFC: 62; Wa: 237
Journal Po: 1262
King Candaules [Le Roi Can-
daule] Br: 259; DC2: 146;
EDC: 204; MD: 122; Po:
1247
Lafcadio's Adventures see
The Caves of the Vatican
Marshlands [Paludes] Fi: 80-
81; Ke: 85-86; Po: 1257,
1263, 4343; SFC: 62; Wa:
237
The Notebooks of André Walter
[Cahiers d'André Walter]
Fi: 81; Ke: 76-77; Po:
1258
Les Nourritures terrestres see
The Fruits of the Earth
Oedipus [Oedipe] Br: 259-
260; DC2: 146; EDC: 204;
MD: 122; Po: 1263
Paludes see Marshlands
The Pastoral Symphony [La
Symphonie Pastorale] Fi:
81-82; Ke: 86-87; Ma:
745-746; Po: 1248, 1266;
SFC: 62-63; Wa: 237-238;

WaS1: 72
Perséphone Br: 260; EDC: 204; MD: 122
Philoctetes [Philoctète] Br: 260; DC2: 146; EDC: 204; MD: 122
La Porte étroite see Strait Is the Gate
Le Procès see The Trial
Prometheus Misbound [Le Prométhée mal enchaîné] Fi: 82; Ke: 87-88; Ma: 746; Po: 1257, 1265
The Return [Le Retour] MD: 122
The Return of the Prodigal [Le retour de l'enfant prodique] Br: 260; Fi: 82; Ke: 88; MD: 122; Po: 1265; SFC: 64; Wa: 238; WaS1: 72
Robert, ou l'Intérêt Général EDC: 204; Fi: 82; Ke: 88; SFC: 64; Wa: 239
Le Roi Candaule see King Candaules
Saül Br: 261; DC2: 147; EDC: 205; MD: 122; Po: 1247, 1265
The School for Wives Fi: 82-83; Ke: 88; Wa: 239
Strait Is the Gate [La Porte étroite] Fi: 83-84; Ke: 88-90; Ma: 746-747; Po: 1248, 1264; SFC: 64-65; Wa: 239-240; WaS1: 72
La Symphonie Pastorale see The Pastoral Symphony
La tentative amoureuse Fi: 84; Ke: 90
Theseus [Thesée] Fi: 84; Ke: 90; Po: 1266; SFC: 65; Wa: 240
Travels in the Congo [Voyage au Congo] Po: 1267
The Treatise of the Narcissus [Le Traité du Narcisse] Fi: 84; SFC: 65-66
Le Treizième Arbre EDC: 205; MD: 122
The Trial [Le Procès] Po: 1264-1265
Urien's Voyage [Le Voyage d'Urien] Fi: 84-85; Ke: 90-91; Po: 1267
The Vatican Cellars see The

Caves of the Vatican
The Vatican Swindle see The Caves of the Vatican
Voyage au Congo see Travels in the Congo
Le Voyage d'Urien see Urien's Voyage
_____ and BARRAULT, J.J.
Le Procès DC2: 147
GIJSEN, Marnix
General Po: 1267-1268
GILBERT, Herman Cromwell
That Uncertain Sound BAF: 132
GILBERT, Mercedes
General BAF: 133; BAW: 325
Aunt Sara's Wooden God BAF: 133
GILBERT, Sir William Schwenck
General Br: 261; EDT: 174-185; MBD: 51-52; VP: 34-35
Broken Hearts EDT: 183
Engaged EDT: 182
The Gondoliers EDT: 181; Ma: 748
The Grand Duke EDT: 180, 182; Ma: 748-749
Gretchen DC1: 82; EDT: 183; MBD: 51
The Happy Land EDT: 184
H.M.S. Pinafore Ma: 749
Iolanthe EDT: 184; Ma: 749
The Mikado Ma: 750
The Ne'er-Do-Well EDT: 183
Our Island Home EDT: 183
The Pirates of Penzance Ma: 751
Princess Ida EDT: 181; Ma: 751
Ruddigore Ma: 751-752
The Sorcerer Ma: 752
Thespis Ma: 752-753
Trial by Jury DC1: 82; EDT: 181; Ma: 753
Utopia, Limited Ma: 753-754
_____ and Arthur Seymour SULLIVAN
Patience DC1: 82; EDT: 182; Ma: 750; MBD: 51-52
The Yeoman of the Guard DC1: 82; EDT: 180; Ma: 754; MBD: 51; VP: 35
GILBERT, Stephen
Monkeyface ENES2: 102
Ratman's Notebooks ENES2:

102
GILBERT, Zack
    General BAW: 326
GILDON, Charles
    General EC: 74
    The Battle of the Authors
        EC: 74
    Love's Victim; or The Queen
        of Wales DC1: 83
    The Patriot DC1: 83
GILL, Peter
    General MDAE: 228
GILLETTE, William
    General AD: 126-129; Lon:
        59
    Clarice ADC: 117
    Electricity AD: 126
    Held by the Enemy AD: 127-
        128
    Secret Service AD: 126-129;
        ADC: 117
    Too Much Johnson ADC:
        117
    _____ and Arthur Conan
        DOYLE
    Sherlock Holmes AD: 128-
        129; ADC: 117-118; Lon:
        59
GILMAN, Charlotte Perkins
    "The Yellow Wallpaper"
        ASF: 209
Gil Polo, Gaspar see POLO,
    Gaspar Gil
GILROY, Frank Daniel
    General LCAB: 73; MDAE:
        230
    The Only Game in Town
        ADC: 118
    Present Tense (four plays:
        Present Tense, Come Next
        Tuesday, Twas Brillig,
        and So Please Be Kind)
        ADC: 118
    The Subject Was Roses
        ADC: 118; Br: 261
    That Summer--That Fall
        ADC: 118
    Who'll Save the Plowboy?
        ADC: 118-119; MDAE:
        230
GINER, Gloria
    General Po: 1268
GINSBERG, Allen
    General ALL: 113-114;
        ICBAP: 56; JW: 69-
        70; LCAB: 74; MP: 45;

Po: 1268-1270
"Ankor Wat" ICBAP: 56
Empty Mirror ALL: 113
"Howl" JW: 69; MP: 45; Po:
    1270-1271
Howl and Other Poems ALL:
    113
"Kaddish" ADC: 119; ALL:
    113; ICBAP: 56; JW: 69;
    MP: 45
Reality Sandwiches and Later
    Poems ALL: 113
A Supermarket in California Po:
    1271
"A White Paper" ICBAP: 56
Wichita Vortex Sutra LCAB:
    74
GIOFFRE, Marissa
    Bread and Roses MBA: 88
GIONO, Jean
    General Br: 261; Po: 1271-
        1274
    Les Ames fortes Ke: 91
    Angelo Fi: 85; Ke: 91
    Battles in the Mountain Fi:
        85; Ke: 91
    Blue Boy Fi: 85; Ke: 91
    Le Bout de la route Br: 261;
        DC2: 147; Po: 1273-1274
    Le chant du monde see Song
        of the World
    Colline Fi: 85
    "The Corn Dies" SFC: 66;
        Wa: 240
    Deux cavaliers de l'orage see
        Two Riders of the Storm
    Domitien Br: 261
    La Femme du boulanger Br:
        262; DC2: 147; Po: 1273-
        1274
    Le Grand Théâtre Po: 1275
    Le Grand Troupeau Fi: 85-86;
        Ke: 91
    Les grands chemins Fi: 86;
        Ke: 91
    Harvest Ke: 91
    Hill of Destiny Ke: 91
    The Horseman on the Roof [Le
        Hussard sur le toit] Fi:
        86; Ke: 91-92; Ma: 755;
        Po: 1275
    Joy of Man's Desiring Ke: 92
    Lanceurs de graines Br:
        262; DC2: 147; Po: 1273-
        1274
    Lovers Are Never Losers Ke:

92
The Malediction [Le Moulin de Pologne] Ke: 92; Po: 1275-1276
Mort d'un personnage Fi: 86; Ke: 92
La Naissance de l'Odyssee Fi: 86; Ke: 92
Noe Ke: 92
Pauline Ke: 92
Pour saluer Melville Fi: 86; Po: 1276
Que ma joie demeure Fi: 87
Regain Fi: 87
Un roi sans divertissement Fi: 87; Ke: 92; Po: 1273
"Solitude de la pitié" Po: 1276; Wa: 240
Song of the World [Le chant du monde] Ke: 92; Ma: 755; Po: 1274
The Straw Man Ke: 92-93
The Trilogy of Pan Ke: 93
Two Riders of the Storm [Deux cavaliers de l'orage] Fi: 85; Ke: 91; Po: 1274-1275
Un de Baumugnes Fi: 87
Le Voyage en Caleche Br: 262
Les vraies richesses Ke: 93
GIOVANINETTI, Silvio
General Br: 262
GIOVANNI, Nikki
General AAL: 178-179; AAPD: 177; BAF: 133; BAW: 328
GIPSON, Frederick
General ASF: 210
Hound Dog Man LCAB: 74
GIRAUDOUX, Jean
General Br: 262-264; LCAB: 74; MD: 123-124; Po: 1276-1280
The Adventures of Jerome Bardini Fi: 87; Ke: 93
Amphitryon 38 Br: 264; DC2: 147-148; EDC: 205-206; Ma: 756; MD: 124
The Apollo of Bellac [L'Apollon de Bellac] Br: 264; EDC: 206
L'Apollon de Marsac EDC: 206
Band of Angels see Duel of Angels

Bella Fi: 87
Cantiques des Cantiques see Song of Songs
The Chosen Ones Fi: 87; Ke: 93
Combat avec l'ange Fi: 87
Le Dernier rêve Ke: 93
Duel of Angels [Band of Angels; For Lucretia; Pour Lucrece] Br: 265; DC2: 150; EDC: 206, 208; Ma: 757; MD: 125; Po: 1278, 1285
Eglantine DC2: 148; Fi: 87; Ke: 93; Po: 1280-1281
Electra [Electre] Br: 265-266; DC2: 148; EDC: 206-207; LCAB: 74; Ma: 757-758; MD: 124; Po: 1278, 1281
The Enchanted [Intermezzo] Br: 266; DC2: 148; EDC: 207-208; Po: 1283-1284
La Folle de Chaillot see The Madwoman of Chaillot
For Lucretia see Duel of Angels
La Guerre de Troie n'aura pas lieu see The Tiger at the Gates
l'Impromptu de Paris see Paris Impromptu
Intermezzo see The Enchanted
Judith Br: 266-267; DC2: 149; EDC: 208; Ma: 758-759; MD: 125; Po: 1278, 1284-1285
Juliette in the Land of Men Fi: 87; Ke: 93
Last Dream of Edmond About Fi: 87
The Liar Fi: 88
The Madwoman of Chaillot [La Folle de Chaillot] Br: 267-268; DC2: 149; EDC: 208-209; Ma: 759-760; MD: 124-125; Po: 1281-1282
My Friend from Limousin Fi: 88; Ke: 93
Ondine Br: 268-269; DC2: 149-150; EDC: 209; Ma: 760-761; MD: 125; Po: 1285
Paris Impromptu [l'Impromptu de Paris] EDC: 210; MD: 125
Pour Lucrece see Duel of Angels

Prière de la Tour Eiffel Po: 1285

The School for the Indifferent Fi: 88; Ke: 93

Siegfried Br: 269-270; DC2: 150; EDC: 210; Ma: 761-762; MD: 126; Po: 1286

Simon the Pathetic [Simon le pathetique] Fi: 88; Ke: 93; Po: 1286

Sodom and Gomorrah [Sodome et Gomorrhe] Br: 270; DC2: 150; EDC: 210; MD: 126; Po: 1278

Song of Songs [Cantiques des Cantiques] Br: 270; DC2: 150; EDC: 210

Le Supplement au Voyage de Cook see Virtuous Island

Suzanne et le Pacifique Fi: 88

The Tiger at the Gates [The Trojan War Will Not Take Place; La Guerre de Troie n'aura pas lieu] Br: 270-271; DC2: 151; EDC: 210-212; LCAB: 74; Ma: 762-763; MD: 125; Po: 1282-1283

Virtuous Island [Le Supplement au Voyage de Cook] DC2: 151; EDC: 212; MD: 126

GIRONELLA, José Maria
General Po: 1287

The Cypresses Believe in God [Los cipreses creen en Dios] Fi: 217; Ke: 204; Ma: 764; Po: 1287

"Death of the Sea" Wa: 241

"Goya and the Mountain" Wa: 241

Un Hombre see Where the Soil Was Shallow

La marea Ke: 204

Un millon de muertes Fi: 217

"Miracle in the Town" Wa: 241

The Peace Has Broken Out Fi: 217

"The Red Egg" Wa: 241

"Ryki, Bird-King" Wa: 241

"The Suicidal Twin and His Brother" Wa: 241

"Three Plates on the Table" ["Wishing Becomes Reality"] Wa: 241

Where the Soil Was Shallow [Un Hombre] Ke: 204; Po: 1288

GISSING, George Robert
General BN2: 48-50; Du: 83-84; TA: 157

Born in Exile Du: 82; EN: 55; ENE: 119; ENES1: 99; ENES2: 102-103; Ma: 765-766

The Crown of Life ENE: 119; ENES1: 99; ENES2: 103

Demos Du: 82; EN: 55; ENE: 119; ENES1: 99; ENES2: 103; Ma: 766-767

Denzil Quarrier ENES1: 99; ENES2: 103

The Emancipated ENES1: 99; ENES2: 103

Eve's Ransom ENES1: 99

"House of Cobwebs" Wa: 241

"Humplebee" Wa: 241

In the Year of Jubilee Du: 82; ENE: 119; ENES1: 99; ENES2: 103; Ma: 767

Isabel Clarendon EN: 55; ENES1: 99; ENES2: 103; Ma: 767-768

A Life's Morning ENES1: 99-100; ENES2: 104

The Nether World Du: 82; EN: 55; ENE: 119; ENES1: 100; ENES2: 104; Ma: 768-769

New Grub Street Du: 82; EN: 55; ENE: 120; ENES1: 100; ENES2: 104; Ma: 769-770

The Odd Women ENE: 120; ENES1: 100; ENES2: 104

Our Friend the Charlatan ENES1: 100

"A Poor Gentleman" Wa: 241

The Private Papers of Henry Ryecroft BN2: 49; Du: 82; ENE: 120; ENES1: 100; ENES2: 104; Ma: 770-771

Thyrza EN: 55; ENE: 120; ENES1: 100; ENES2: 105; Ma: 772

The Unclassed BN2: 50; EN: 56; ENES1: 100;

ENES2: 105; Ma: 772-773
Veranilda ENE: 120; ENES1:
  101
The Whirlpool EN: 56;
  ENES1: 101; ENES2: 105;
  Ma: 773
Workers in the Dawn EN:
  56; ENE: 120; ENES1:
  101; ENES2: 105; Ma:
  773-774
GIUSSO, Lorenzo
  General Po: 1288
GLADKOV, F.V.
  Cement Fi: 447; Ke: 405-
  406
  Energy Ke: 406
GLAPTHORNE, Henry
  General LJCD: 242-243
GLASGOW, Ellen
  General ALL: 114-116; AN:
  102-104; ASF: 211; Ho:
  54-56, 146; LCAB: 74;
  Po: 1288-1291; Wo: 111-
  112
  "The Artless Age" Wa: 241;
  WaS1: 72
  Barren Ground AN: 101;
  Ho: 56, 146; Ma: 775;
  Po: 1291; Wo: 112
  The Battle-Ground AN: 101;
  Ho: 146
  "Between Two Shores" ASF:
  210; Wa: 241
  "Dare's Gift" ASF: 210;
  Wa: 242; WaS1: 72
  The Deliverance AN: 101;
  Ho: 55; Ma: 775-776;
  Po: 1291-1292
  "The Difference" ASF: 210;
  WaS1: 72
  In This Our Life AN: 101
  "Jordan's End" ASF: 210;
  Wa: 242; WaS1: 72
  Life and Gabriella AN: 101
  The Miller of Old Church
  AN: 101; Ma: 776
  "The Past" ASF: 210; WaS1:
  72
  "A Point in Morals" ASF:
  210; Wa: 242
  "The Professional Instinct"
  ASF: 210; Po: 1292; Wa:
  242; WaS1: 72
  "Romance and Sally Byrd"
  ASF: 210; WaS1: 72
  Romance of a Plain Man AN:

101; Po: 1292
The Romantic Comedians AN:
  102; Ma: 777
"The Shadowy Third" ASF:
  210; WaS1: 72
The Sheltered Life AN: 102;
  AN: 102; Ho: 146; Ma:
  777-778; Po: 1292-1293
They Stooped to Folly AN:
  102; Ma: 778; Po: 1293
"Thinking Makes It So" ASF:
  210; WaS1: 72
Vein of Iron AN: 102; Ho:
  146; Ma: 778-779
Virginia AN: 102; Ho: 146;
  Ma: 779-780
The Voice of the People AN:
  102; Po: 1293
"Whispering Leaves" ASF: 210;
  Wa: 242; WaS1: 72
The Woman Within Ma: 780
GLASPELL, Susan
  General Br: 271; Lon: 59;
  Po: 1293
  Alison's House ADC: 119; Br:
  272
  Bernice Br: 272
  "The Busy Duck" Wa: 242
  Chains of Dew Br: 272
  Close the Book Br: 272
  The Comic Artist ADC: 119;
  Br: 272
  "The Escape" Wa: 242
  "The Hearing Ear" Wa: 242
  The Inheritors ADC: 119; Br:
  272
  "A Jury of Her Peers" ASF:
  211; Wa: 242; WaS1: 73
  The Outside Br: 272
  The People Br: 272
  "The Preposterous Motive" Wa:
  242
  Suppressed Desires Br: 272
  Tickless Time Br: 272
  Trifles ADC: 119; Br: 272
  The Verge ADC: 119-120; Br:
  273
  Woman's Honor Br: 273
GLASSER, Barry
  Screen Play ADC: 120
GLASSER, Ronald J.
  365 Days ADC: 120
GLASSER, William
  Beehive ADC: 120
GLASSMAN, Stephen, Gene ALLAN,
  and Ron DANTE

Billy ADC: 120

GLATSTEIN, Jacob
"Citizen God" SFC: 66; Wa: 242

GLEBOV, Anatol
Inga Br: 273

GLEN, Duncan [Ronald Eadie MUNRO]
General Ai: 332

GLISSANT, Edouard
La Lézarde Fi: 88

GLOVER, Denis
General Po: 1293-1294

GLUCHOWSKI, Bruno
"The Water Cannon" Wa: 242

GLYN, Elinor Sutherland
Three Weeks ENES1: 101

GNAPHEUS, Guliemus
Acolastvs DC2: 151

GOBINEAU, Joseph-Arthur de
Les Pléiades Ke: 93

GODARD, Jean-Luc
General Po: 1294

GODDARD, William
General AP: 580

GODDEN, Margaret Rumer
General CFAE: 158; CN: 203-204; Sch: 104
The Battle of the Villa Fiorita ENES1: 101
Black Narcissus CN: 204; ENES1: 101
Breakfast with the Nikolides CN: 204; ENES1: 101
A Breath of Air ENES1: 101
China Court ENES1: 101
Chinese Puzzle ENES1: 101
"Down Under the Thames" Wa: 243
An Episode of Sparrows ENES1: 101
A Fugue in Time ENES1: 102
The Greengage Summer ENES1: 102
Gypsy, Gypsy ENES1: 102
In This House of Brede ENES1: 102
"The Little Black Ram" Wa: 243
Kingfishers Catch Fire CN: 204; ENES1: 102
The Lady and the Unicorn ENES1: 102
"The Oyster" Wa: 243

"The Red Doe" Wa: 243
The River CN: 204; ENES1: 102
Take Three Tenses: A Fugue in Time CN: 204
"Time Is a Stream" Wa: 243
"Why Not Live Sweetly" Wa: 243

GODFREY, David
"The Hard-Headed Collector" Wa: 243

GODFREY, Thomas
General AD: 131-132; Da: 52; Lon: 59-60
The Prince of Parthia AD: 131-132; ADC: 120; Lon: 59

GODSEY, Edwin
General Po: 1294

GODWIN, Francis
The Man in the Moon ENES1: 102; ENES2: 105; ERP: 186-190; Hen: 173

GODWIN, Gail
"A Sorrowful Woman" ASF: 212; Wa: 243

GODWIN, William
General Be: 143-146; Du: 85-87; EC: 74-75
Caleb Williams Be: 143-146; Du: 84-85; EN: 56; ENE: 120-121; ENES1: 102-103; ENES2: 105-106
Cloudesley ENE: 121; ENES1: 103
Deloraine ENE: 121; ENES1: 103
Fleetwood; or, The New Man of Feeling EN: 56; ENE: 121; ENES1: 103; ENES2: 106
Imogen; A Pastoral Romance ENE: 121
Mandeville, a Tale of the Seventeenth Century Du: 85; ENE: 122; ENES1: 103
St. Leon: A Tale of the Sixteenth Century Be: 145; Du: 85; EN: 57; ENE: 122; ENES1: 103-104; ENES2: 106-107

GODWIN, William, Jr. [pseud. SYPHAX]
"The Executioner" Wa: 243

GOEBBELS, Joseph
Michael Po: 1294-1295

GOERING, Reinhard
General Po: 1295
Jung Schuk Fi: 304
Naval Battle [Seeschlacht]
Br: 273
GOES, Albrecht
General Po: 1295
The Burnt Offering [Das
Brandopfer] Ke: 265;
Po: 1295
Restless Night [Unruhige
Nacht] Ke: 265; Po:
1295; Wa: 243
GOETEL, Ferdynand
"The Child Who Was Mur-
dered" Wa: 244
"My Husband Is Dying" Wa:
244
"The Pilgrim of Karapet"
Wa: 244
GOETHE, Johann Wolfgang von
General LCAB: 74-75
Clavigo DC2: 151-152
Egmont DC2: 152; EDC:
212; Ma: 781
Elective Affinities [Die
Wahlverwandtschaften]
Fi: 304-306; Ke: 265-266;
Ma: 781-782; Po: 1086
"Fairy Tale" Wa: 244;
WaS1: 73
Faust DC2: 152-161; EDC:
212-222; LCAB: 75; Lon:
28; Ma: 783-784
Faust, Part II DC2: 161-
162
Gotter DC2: 162
Goetz von Berlichingen with
the Iron Hand see also
Gotz von Berlichingen's
Right Hand EDC: 222-
223
Gotz von Berlichingen's Right
Hand see also Goetz von
Berlichingen with the Iron
Hand DC2: 163
Der Gross-Cophta DC2: 163
Hermann and Dorothea Fi:
306; Ke: 266-267
Iphigenie auf Taurus DC2:
163-164; EDC: 223-224
Jahrmarktsfest zu Plunders-
weilern DC2: 164
Die Leiden des jungen
Werthers see The Sor-
rows of Young Werther

Magic Flute DC2: 164
Das Märchen Fi: 306; Ke:
267
The Natural Daughter [Die
Naturliche Tochter] DC2:
164-165; EDC: 225
Novelle Fi: 306-307
Pandora DC2: 165
Satyros DC2: 165
The Sorrows of Young Werther
[Werther; Die Leiden des
jungen Werthers] Fi: 307-
309; Ke: 267-269; Ma:
784-786; Po: 2098
Stella DC2: 165; EDC: 225
Torquato Tasso DC2: 165-166;
EDC: 225-226
Werther see The Sorrows of
Young Werther
Wilhelm Meister Fi: 309-311;
Ke: 269-271
Wilhelm Meister's Apprenticeship
Ma: 786-787
Wilhelm Meister's Travels Ma:
787-789
GOETZ, Augustus and Ruth
GOETZ
The Heiress ADC: 120-121
The Immoralist ADC: 121
GOFFE, Thomas
General LJCD: 243-244
Orestes DC1: 83
GOGARTY, Oliver St. John
General Po: 1295-1296
"The Crab Tree" PE: 203
"Golden Stockings" PE: 203
"Non Dolet" PE: 203
"Per Iter Tenebricosum" PE:
203
GOGOL, Nikolay Vasilyevich
General Br: 273; LCAB: 75
Alfred Br: 273
"The Carriage" Wa: 244;
WaS1: 73
"Christmas Eve" Wa: 244;
WaS1: 73
Dead Souls Fi: 447-449; Ke:
406-408; LCAB: 75; Ma:
790-791
Diary of a Madman Fi: 449;
Ke: 408; Ma: 791-792;
Wa: 244; WaS1: 73
"A Dread Wild Boar" Wa: 244
"The Enchanted Spot" ["The
Enchanted Place"] Wa:
245; WaS1: 73

Evenings on a Farm Near
  Dikanka Fi: 449
The Fair at Sorochinsk Ke:
  408
The Gamblers [Igrokhi] Br:
  273; EDC: 226
The Inspector-General [The
  Revizor] Br: 273-274;
  DC2: 166; EDC: 226;
  LCAB: 75; Ma: 792-793
"Ivan Fyodorovich Shponka
  and His Aunt" Wa: 245;
  WaS1: 73
"Kolyaska" Wa: 245
"Leaving the Theater" Wa:
  245
"The Lost Letter" Wa: 245;
  WaS1: 73
The Marriage, an Utterly In-
  credible Occurrence Br:
  274; EDC: 226-227
"The May Night, or The
  Drowned Woman [Maiden]"
  Wa: 245; WaS1: 73
Mirgorod Fi: 449
"The Nevsky Prospect" SFC:
  66; Wa: 245; WaS1: 73
"The Nose" SFC: 67; Wa:
  245-246; WaS1: 73
The Old World Landowners
  Fi: 449; Ke: 408; SFC:
  67; Wa: 246; WaS1: 74
"The Overcoat" LCAB: 75;
  Ma: 793-794; SFC: 67;
  Wa: 246-247; WaS1: 74
"The Portrait" SFC: 67;
  Wa: 247; WaS1: 74
"The Quarrel Between Ivan
  Ivanovitch and Ivan Niki-
  forovitch" ["The Two
  Ivans"] SFC: 67; Wa:
  247; WaS1: 74
The Revizor see The In-
  spector General
"Rome" Wa: 247-248; WaS1:
  74
"St. John's Eve" Wa: 248;
  WaS1: 74
St. Petersburg Cycle Fi:
  449
"The Sorochinsty Fair" Wa:
  248; WaS1: 74
Taras Bulba Fi: 449-450;
  Ke: 408; Ma: 794-795;
  Wa: 248; WaS1: 74
"The Teacher" Wa: 248

"A [The] Terrible Vengeance"
  Wa: 248; WaS1: 74
"The Two Ivans" see "The
  Quarrel Between Ivan Ivano-
  vitch and Ivan Nikiforovitch"
Vij [Viy and Vii] Fi: 450;
  Ke: 409; SFC: 67; Wa:
  248; WaS1: 75
Zapiski Sumasshedshego Fi:
  450
GOLBERG, Mécislas
  General Po: 1296
GOLD, Herbert
  General ASF: 212; CFAE:
    159-160; CN: 204; JW:
    221; LCAB: 75; Po: 1296
  The Age of Happy Problems
    Ma: 796
  A Death on the East Side
    LCAB: 76
  Fathers Ma: 796
  "The Heart of the Artichoke"
    ASF: 212; Wa: 249
  The Man Who Was Not with It
    CN: 204-205
  The Optimist AN: 104; CN:
    205; LCAB: 76; Ma: 796
  Salt CN: 205
  "Susanna at the Beach" Wa:
    249
  Therefore Be Bold CN: 205;
    Ma: 796
  "Where a Man Dwells" Wa: 249
  "The Witch" ASF: 212; Wa:
    249
GOLD, Lloyd
  A Grave Undertaking ADC:
    121
GOLD, Michael [Irwin GRANICH]
  General ASF: 212; JW: 224
  Jews Without Money JW: 224
  "Love on a Garbage Dump"
    ASF: 212
GOLD, Mike
  General Br: 274
  Fiesta Br: 274
  Hoboken Blues Br: 274
GOLDING, Arthur
  General Hen: 212
GOLDING, William Gerald
  General BN2: 51-52; CFAE:
    161-169; CN: 205-207;
    LCAB: 76; MDAE: 231;
    Po: 1296-1300; Sch: 105-
    108
  The Brass Butterfly Br:

274-275; MDAE: 231
"Envoy Extraordinary"
MDAE: 231; Wa: 249
Free Fall CFAE: 162, 165,
169; CN: 207-208; ENE:
122-123; ENES1: 104;
ENES2: 107; Ma: 797-798;
Po: 1300; Sch: 108-109
The Inheritors BN2: 51;
CFAE: 162, 164, 168;
CN: 208-209; ENE: 123;
ENES1: 104; ENES2:
107-108; Ma: 798-799;
Po: 1297, 1299-1302;
Sch: 109
Lord of the Flies BN2: 51-
52; CFAE: 162-163, 165-
169; CN: 209-214; ENE:
123-126; ENES1: 104-105;
ENES2: 108; Ma: 800-801;
MDAE: 434; Po: 1297,
1299-1300, 1302-1308; Sch:
109-111
Pincher Martin [The Two
Deaths of Christopher
Martin] BN2: 52; CFAE:
162-163, 166-168; CN:
214-216; ENE: 126-127;
ENES1: 105; ENES2:
108-109; LCAB: 76;
Ma: 801-802; Po: 1299-
1300, 1308-1310; Sch:
111-112
The Pyramid BN2: 52;
CFAE: 165, 167, 169;
CN: 216; ENE: 127;
ENES2: 109; Po: 1310;
Sch: 112
The Scorpion God ENES2:
109
The Spire BN2: 52; CFAE:
163-164, 167-169; CN:
216-217; ENE: 127-128;
ENES1: 105-106; ENES2:
109; LCAB: 76; Ma: 802-
803; Po: 1310-1312; Sch:
112-113
The Two Deaths of Chris-
topher Martin see Pincher
Martin
GOLDMAN, James
The Lion in Winter ADC:
121-122; Br: 275
GOLDONI, Carlo
Baruffe Chiozzotte see The
Chioggian Brawls
The Boars [Rusteghi] EDC:
227
La Bottega del Caffe see The
Coffee House
Il Bugiardo see The Liar
Il Campiello see The Public
Square
La Casa Nova see The New
House
The Chioggian Brawls [Baruffe
Chiozzotte] EDC: 227
The Clever Lady's Maid [La
Cameriera Brillante] EDC:
227
The Coffee House [La Bottega
del Caffe] EDC: 227
The Fan [Il Ventaglio] EDC:
227
The Father of a Family [Il
Padre di Famiglia] EDC:
227
La Guerra see The War
The Liar [Il Bugiardo] EDC:
228
The Mistress of the Inn [Mine
Hostess; La Locandiera]
EDC: 228; Ma: 804
The New House [La Casa Nova]
EDC: 228
Il Padre di Famiglia see The
Father of the Family
The Public Square [Il Campiello]
EDC: 228
Rusteghi see The Boars
Servant of Two Masters [Il
Servitore de Due Padroni]
EDC: 228
The True Friend [Il Vero Am-
ico] EDC: 228
Il Ventaglio see The Fan
The War [La Guerra] EDC:
228
GOLDSCHMIDT, Meir
"Aron and Esther" WaS1: 74
"Avrohmehe Nattergal" WaS1:
75
"The Battle of Marengo" WaS1:
75
"Bewitched No. 1" WaS1: 75
"A Christmas in the Country"
WaS1: 75
"The Fickle Girl on Graahede"
WaS1: 75
"God's Angel from Rørvig"
WaS1: 75
"The Last Lucifer Match"

WaS1: 75
"Maser" WaS1: 75
"Paolo and Giovanna" WaS1: 75
"The Photographers and Mephistopheles" WaS1: 75
"Poison" WaS1: 75
GOLDSMITH, Clifford
What a Life Br: 275
GOLDSMITH, Martin
Night Shift ADC: 122
GOLDSMITH, Oliver (1730?-1774)
General Be: 150-152; Du: 88; EC: 75-77; LCAB: 76; Li: 195-196; Me: 233-237
"Ballad of Edwin and Angeline" (The Vicar of Wakefield) PE: 203
The Deserted Village Be: 151; EC: 77; LCAB: 76; Ma: 805; Me: 233-237; PE: 203-204
"An Elegy on the Death of a Mad Dog" PE: 204
The Good Natur'd Man DC1: 83; EC: 76-77; EDC: 229; Li: 195-196
Life of Nashe EC: 75
Retaliation EC: 77; Me: 236; PE: 204
She Stoops to Conquer; or, The Mistakes of a Night DC1: 83; EC: 76-77; EDC: 229; Li: 196; Ma: 805-806
The Traveller, or a Prospect of Society EC: 77; Me: 234-237; PE: 204
The Vicar of Wakefield Be: 150-152; Du: 87-88; EC: 77; EN: 57; ENE: 128-129; ENES1: 106; ENES2: 109-110; LCAB: 76; Ma: 806-807
GOLDSMITH, Oliver (1794-1861)
General ECL: 138
Goldsmith, Peter [pseud.] see PRIESTLEY, John Boynton
GOLL, Yvan
Genral Po: 1312
Methusalem Br: 275
GOLOVANOV, Yaroslav
Forge of Thunder Ke: 409

GOLUBIEW, Antoni
Boleslaw the Brave Fi: 450
GOMBROWICZ, Witold
General Po: 1313-1314
"Adventures on the Banbury" Wa: 249
Cosmos Fi: 450
Ferdydurke Fi: 450; Po: 1313-1314
"Five Minutes Before Sleep" Wa: 249
Le mariage Po: 1313
Pornografia [La Pornographie] Fi: 450-451; Po: 1313
"A Supper at the Countess Kotlubaj's" Wa: 249
Trans-Atlantic Fi: 451
GOMEZ DE LA SERNA, Gaspar
General Po: 1314
GOMEZ DE LA SERNA, Ramón
General Po: 1314-1316
"The After-Dinner Guest" Wa: 249
"Aunt Martha" Wa: 249
"Beltran's Daughter" Wa: 249
"The Blind Man and the Courtesan" Wa: 249
"Blue Cholera" Wa: 249
"The Bottle and the Candlestick" Wa: 250
"The Cheerful Barbershop" Wa: 250
"The Christmas Crib-Maker" Wa: 250
"Christmas Eve, 2500 A.D." Wa: 250
"A Christmas Story About a Stained Glass Window" Wa: 250
"The Defender of the Cemetery" Wa: 250
"The Diseased One" Wa: 250
"Doña Juana the Mad" Wa: 250
"Doña Urraca of Castile" Wa: 250
"The Explorers" Wa: 250
"The Fatal Lady" Wa: 250
"Fear of the Sea" Wa: 250
"The Fragrance of the Mimosas" Wa: 250
"The Gentleman from Olmedo" Wa: 250
"A Gift for the Doctor" Wa: 250
"The Great Grippe Victim"

Wa: 250
"The Greenhouse" Wa: 250
Greguería Po: 1314-1316
"His Liver Presented Itself"
    Wa: 250
"The Hypersensitive Woman"
    Wa: 251
"Ildefonso Cuadrado" Wa:
    251
"Leopold and Teresa" Wa:
    251
"The Malice of the Acacia
    Flowers" Wa: 251
"The Man in the Gallery"
    Wa: 251
"The Man with Big Feet"
    Wa: 251
"María Yarsilovna" Wa: 251
"The Master of the Atom"
    Wa: 251
"The Millionaire's Son" Wa:
    251
"Of Another Race" Wa: 251
"Olvido" Wa: 251
"One Cup Short" Wa: 251
"The Opera Glasses and the
    Glove" Wa: 251
"Pandora's Box" Wa: 251
"Postponement of Destiny"
    Wa: 251
The Recluse of Burgos" Wa:
    251
"The Red-Head" Wa: 251
"The Roughnecks" Wa: 251
"The Russian" Wa: 252
"The Sated One" Wa: 252
"The Seven Princes of Lara"
    Wa: 252
"She + She - He + He" Wa:
    252
"The Snow Coat" Wa: 252
"The Storm" Wa: 252
"The Surrealist Son" Wa:
    252
"That Novel" Wa: 252
"Tonight in Russia" Wa:
    252
"The Town of the Brunette"
    Wa: 252
"The Trials and Adventures
    of a Non-Hatter" Wa:
    252
"The Triangular House" Wa:
    252
"The Turk with the Spikenard"
    Wa: 252

"The Turkey Hen" Wa: 252
"The Two Sailors" Wa: 252
"The Vegetarian" Wa: 252
"The Virgin Painted Red" Wa:
    252
"The White-Bearded Old Man"
    Wa: 252
"The Widow, and the Widower's
    Toast" Wa: 253
"The Woman Abandoned in the
    Flea Market" Wa: 253
"The Woman Who Dressed Like
    a Man" Wa: 253
"The Woman with the Twangy
    Voice" Wa: 253
"Women of Assignation" Wa:
    253
"The Young Alcira" Wa: 253
GOMULICKI, Wiktor
    "A Quintet" Wa: 253
    "Under the Umbrella" Wa:
        253
GONCHAROV, Ivan
    "A Cruel Illness" Wa: 253
    "A Happy Error" Wa: 253
    The Journey of the Frigate
        Pallas Fi: 451
    Oblomov Fi: 451-452; Ke:
        409-410; LCAB: 76
    An Ordinary Story Fi: 452;
        Ke: 410
    The Precipice Fi: 452; Ke:
        410-411
    The Ravine Fi: 452; Ke: 411
GONCOURT, Edmond de
    Cherie Fi: 88; Ke: 93-94
    La Faustin Fi: 88; Ke: 94
    La Fille Elisa Fi: 88-89; Ke:
        94
    The Zemganno Brothers Fi:
        89; Ke: 94
    _____ and Jules de GONCOURT
    Charles Demailly Fi: 89; Ke:
        94
    En 18 Fi: 89; Ke: 94
    Germinie Lacerteux Fi: 89;
        Ke: 94; Ma: 808
    The Goncourt Journals Ma:
        808
    Madame Gervaisais Fi: 89;
        Ke: 94
    Manette Salomon Fi: 89; Ke:
        94; Ma: 808
    Renée Mauperin Fi: 89; Ke:
        94
    Soeur Philomène Fi: 89; Ke:

94
GONZAGA, Curzio
Gli Inganni DC2: 166
GONZALES, Esteban
La vida y hechos de Esteban-
illo González Fi: 256;
Ke: 203
GONZALEZ, Anson
General WIL: 41-42
The Love Song of Boysie B
and Other Poems WIL: 42
_____ and Victor QUESTEL
Score WIL: 42
GONZALEZ, Joaquin Victor
Mis Montanas LCAB: 76
GONZALEZ, N.M.V.
"Where's My Baby Now?" Wa:
253
GONZALEZ PRADA, Manuel
General Po: 1316
GONZALEZ-RUANO, César
General Po: 1316-1317
GOODHART, William
Generation ADC: 122
GOODMAN, Paul
General ASF: 213; ICBAP:
56; JW: 74-75; LCAB:
77; MDAE: 234; Po:
1317
"The Architect from New
York" ASF: 213; Wa:
253
The Empire City JW: 74;
Po: 1317
"A Prayer for Dew" SFC:
68; Wa: 254
GOODRICH, Frances and Albert
HACKETT
Bridal Wise ADC: 122
The Diary of Anne Frank
ADC: 122-123
The Great Big Doorstep
ADC: 123
Up Pops the Devil ADC: 123
GOODWIN, Ruby Berkley
General BAF: 134
GOODYEAR, William [translator]
The Voyage of the Wandering
Knight by Jean de
CARTIGNY ERP: 193
GOODYERE, Sir Henry
"Elegie on the Untimely Death
of the Incomparable
Prince, Henry" PE: 204
GOOGE, Barnabe
General SC: 55

"Cupido Conquered" PE: 204
GOOLDEN, Barbara
The Sleeping Sword ENES2:
110
GORAKHPURI, Firaq
General Po: 1317
GORDIMER, Nadine
General CN: 217-218; Po:
1318
"The Amateur" Wa: 254
"Another Part of the Sky" Wa:
254
"A Bit of Young Life" Wa:
254
"The Catch" Wa: 254
"Charmed Lives" Wa: 254
"Check Yes or No" Wa: 254
"The Defeated" Wa: 254
"Enemies" Wa: 254
"Face from Atlantis" Wa: 254
"Friday's Footprint" Wa: 254
"The Gentle Art" Wa: 254
"Happy Event" Wa: 254
"Horn of Plenty" Wa: 254
"The Hour and the Years" Wa:
254
"An Image of Success" Wa:
255
"Is There Nowhere Else Where
We Can Meet?" Wa: 255
"The Kindest Thing to Do" Wa:
255
The Late Bourgeois World CN:
218
"Livingstone's Companions"
Wa: 255; WaS1: 75
"Message in a Bottle" Wa: 255
"Monday Is Better Than Sunday"
Wa: 255
"No Place Like--" Wa: 255
"Oh, Woe Is Me" Wa: 255
"Our Bovary" Wa: 255
"Out of Season" Wa: 255
"The Prisoner" Wa: 255
"A Satisfactory Settlement" Wa:
255
"Six Feet of the Country" Wa:
255
"The Soft Voice of the Serpent"
Wa: 255
"A Style of Her Own" Wa:
255
"Tenants of the Last Tree
House" Wa: 255
"The Train from Rhodesia" Wa:
255; WaS1: 75

"The Umbilical Cord" Wa:
  256
"La Vie Boheme" Wa: 256
"A Watcher of the Dead" Wa:
  256
"Which New Era Would That
  Be?" Wa: 256
"The White Goddess and the
  Mealie Question" Wa: 256
"Why Haven't You Written?"
  Wa: 256
A World of Strangers CN:
  218
GORDIN, Jacob
General MD: 126
GORDON, Adam Lindsay
General AL: 227-228
GORDON, Caroline
General AN: 104; ASF:
  215-216; CN: 218-219;
  LCAB: 77; Po: 1318-
  1320; Wo: 114-115
Aleck Maury, Sportsman
  AN: 104; CN: 219; Ma:
  809
"All Lovers Love the Spring"
  ASF: 213; Wa: 256
"The Brilliant Leaves" ASF:
  213; SFC: 68; Wa: 256
"The Burning Eyes" ASF:
  213; Wa: 256
"The Captive" ASF: 214;
  Po: 1320; SFC: 68; Wa:
  256-257; Wo: 115
"Emmanuele! Emmanuele!"
  ASF: 214; Wa: 257
"The Enemies" ASF: 214;
  Wa: 257
"The Forest of the South"
  ASF: 214; SFC: 68; Wa:
  257
The Garden of Adonis CN:
  219
Green Centuries CN: 219
"Hear the Nightingale Sing"
  ASF: 214; SFC: 68;
  Wa: 257
"Her Quaint Honor" ASF:
  214; Wa: 257
"The Ice House" ASF: 214;
  SFC: 68; Wa: 257
"The Last Day in the Field"
  ASF: 214; Wa: 257
"The Long Day" ASF: 214;
  SFC: 68; Wa: 257
The Malefactors AN: 104;

CN: 219-220; Ma: 809; Po:
  1318; Wo: 115
"Mr. Powers" ASF: 214; Wa:
  257
"A Narrow Heart: The Portrait
  of a Woman" Wa: 258
None Shall Look Back CN:
  220; Ma: 809-810
"Old Red" ASF: 215; Po:
  1320; SFC: 68; Wa: 258
"The Olive Garden" ASF: 215;
  Wa: 258
"One Against Thebes" ASF:
  215; SFC: 69; Wa: 258-259
"One More Time" ASF: 215;
  Wa: 258
Penhally CN: 220
"The Petrified Woman" ASF:
  215; Wa: 258
"The Presence" ASF: 215;
  Wa: 258
The Strange Children CN:
  220-221; Ma: 810; Po:
  1320; Wa: 258; Wo: 114
"Summer Dust" see "One
  Against Thebes"
"To Thy Chamber Window,
  Sweet" Wa: 259
"Tom Rivers" ASF: 215; Wa:
  259
The Women on the Porch CN:
  221; Po: 1318
GORDON, Charles William [Ralph
  CONNOR]
General ECL: 62; Po: 515-
  516
GORDON, Eugene F.
General BAF: 135
GORDON, Mildred
General LCAB: 77
GORDON, Rex
Utopia Minus X ENES2: 110
GORDON, Ruth
Leading Lady ADC: 123
Over Twenty-One ADC: 123-
  124
A Very Rich Woman ADC:
  124
Years Ago ADC: 124
GORDON, Steve
Tough to Get Help ADC: 124
GORDON, Stuart and Bury St.
  EDMUND
Warp ADC: 124
GORDON, Taylor
General BAW: 331

Born to Be BAW: 331
GORDON, William
    History of the American Revolution AP: 580
GORDONE, Charles
    General AAPD: 371; BAP: 87; BAW: 331-333; MBA: 88
    Gordone Is a Muthah BAP: 88; MBA: 88
    The Last Chord MBA: 89
    No Place to Be Somebody ADC: 124-125; BAP: 88-89; MBA: 89-90
GORE, Catherine
    Cecil ENES1: 106
    Mrs. Armytage ENES1: 107
    The Two Aristocracies ENES1: 107
GORE, Christopher
    Brothers ADC: 125
GORKY, Maxim [Alexei PESHKOV]
    General Br: 275; LCAB: 77; MD: 126-127; Po: 1321-1322
    The Artamonov Business Ke: 411
    "At the Salt Marsh" Wa: 259
    "Boles" Wa: 259
    "Chelkash" Wa: 259
    Children of the Sun [Deti Solntsa] EDC: 229
    "The Coachman" Wa: 259
    The Confession Ke: 411
    Counterfeit Coin DC2: 166
    Country People EDC: 229
    "Creatures That Once Were Men" Wa: 259
    Dachniki see Summerfolk
    Delti Solntsa see Children of the Sun
    Dostigaeff and the Others EDC: 230
    Egor Bulychev and Others see Yegor Bulichov and the Others
    Enemies DC2: 166
    Foma Gordeyev Ke: 411; Ma: 811
    Forty Years see The Life of Klim Samgin
    "He Ran Off" Wa: 259
    "The Hermit" WaS1: 75
    "Kain and Artyom" Wa: 259
    "Karamora" Wa: 259
    "Konovalov" Wa: 259
    The Life of Klim Samgin [Forty Years; Zhizn' Klima Samgina] Fi: 452; Ke: 411; Po: 1323
    The Lower Depths [Na Dne] Br: 275-276; DC2: 166-167; EDC: 230; Ma: 811-812; MD: 127-128; Po: 1323; TMAP: 164
    "Makar Chudra" Wa: 259
    "The Mistake" Wa: 259
    Mother [Mat'] Fi: 452; Ke: 411; Ma: 812; Po: 1323
    "My Fellow Traveller" Wa: 259
    Na Dne see The Lower Depths
    Night Lodging [Nachtasyl] Br: 276; EDC: 230
    "Old Izergil" Wa: 260
    "On a Raft" Wa: 260
    "One Autumn Evening" Wa: 260
    "The Orlovs" Wa: 260
    Orphan Paul Ke: 411
    "Out of Boredom" Wa: 260
    Queer People DC2: 167
    "A Rolling Stone" Wa: 260
    Somov and Others [Somov i Drugie] EDC: 230
    The Spy Ke: 412
    "The Story of a Hero" Wa: 260
    Summerfolk [Dachniki] EDC: 231
    The Survivors EDC: 231; MD: 128
    "A Tale of Unrequited Love" Wa: 260
    The Three Ke: 412
    "Twenty-Six Men and a Girl" Wa: 260
    "Vanka Mazin" Wa: 260
    Varenka Olessova Ke: 412
    Vassa Zheleznova Br: 276
    Wives Friend DC2: 167
    Yegor Bulichov and the Others [Egor Bulychev and Others] Br: 276; DC2: 167; EDC: 231; MD: 127
    Zhizn 'Klima Samgina see The Life of Klim Samgin
    The Zikovs [Zykovs; Zykovy] DC2: 167; EDC: 231;

MD: 128
GOROSTIZA, Celestino
  The Color of Our Skin [El
    Color de Nuestra Piel]
    Br: 276
GOROSTIZA, Manuel de
  Contingo, Pan y Celolla DC2:
    167
  Indulgencia Para Todos DC2:
    167
GOSS, Clay
  General BAW: 333; MBA:
    90
  Andrew ADC: 125; BAP:
    89; MBA: 90
  Home Cookin' MBA: 90
  Mars MBA: 90
  (on) Of Being Hit BAP: 89;
    MBA: 90
  Spaces in Time MBA: 90
GOSS, John
  "Bird Song" SFC: 69; Wa:
    260
GOSSE, Edmund
  General Po: 1324; TA: 159
  Father and Son Po: 1324
GOSSON, Stephen
  General Hen: 102; SC: 55
  The Ephemerides of Phialo
    ERP: 194
  The Schoole of Abuse Hen:
    102; SC: 55
GOTLIEB, Phyllis
  Ordinary Moving JW: 147
  Sunburst JW: 147
GOTTER, Wilhelm
  Jahrmarkt DC2: 167
GOTTHELF, Jeremias
  The Black Spider Ke: 271;
    Wa: 260; WaS1: 75
GOUDGE, Elizabeth
  The Bird in the Tree
    ENES1: 107
  The Heart of the Family
    ENES1: 107
  Pilgrim's Inn ENES1: 107
GOULD, Nat
  General AL: 232
GOURMONT, Remy de
  General Po: 1324-1325
  The Horses of Diomede Ke:
    95
  Lilith DC2: 167
  Sixtine Ke: 95
GOVER, Robert
  General CN: 221

GOW, James E. and Arnaud
    d'USSEAU
  Deep Are the Roots ADC: 125;
    Br: 276; DC1: 83
  Legend of Sarah ADC: 126
  Tomorrow the World ADC: 126
GOW, Ronald
  General MDAE: 235
GOWER, John
  General OMEP: 341-342
  Confessio Amantis OMEP: 342
GOYEN, William
  General ASF: 216; CN: 221;
    Po: 1326
  "The Children of Old Somebody"
    WaS1: 76
  "The Enchanted Nurse" ASF:
    216; WaS1: 76
  "Ghost and Flesh, Water and
    Dirt" Wa: 260
  "The Grasshopper's Burden"
    Wa: 260; WaS1: 76
  The House of Breath CN:
    222
  In a Farther Country CN:
    222
  "The Letter in the Cedarchest"
    Wa: 261
  "The Moss Rose" WaS1: 76
  "Nests in a Stone Image"
    WaS1: 76
  "Old Wildfoot" WaS1: 76
  "Pore Perrie" WaS1: 76
  "The Rescue" ASF: 216;
    WaS1: 76
  "The White Rooster" ASF:
    216; Wa: 261
GOYTISOLO, Juan
  General Po: 1325
  "Autumn in the Port When It
    Drizzles" Wa: 261
  The Circus [El circo] Fi:
    217; Ke: 205
  Count Julian Fi: 217-218
  Duelo en el Paraíso Ke: 205;
    Po: 1326
  "Face and Cross" Wa: 261
  Fiestas Fi: 218; Ke: 205;
    Po: 1326
  Fin de fiesta Fi: 218
  "The Friends" Wa: 261
  "The Guard" Wa: 261
  "Here Below" Wa: 261
  The Island [La isla] Fi: 218;
    Ke: 205
  Juan the Landless Fi: 218

Juegos de manos Ke: 205

Marks of Identity Fi: 218-
219

"The Night Patrol" Wa: 261

La resaca see The Undertow

Sleight of Hand Fi: 219

Sorrow at Paradise House
Fi: 219

"Suburbs" Wa: 261

The Undertow [La resaca]
Fi: 219; Ke: 205

"The Voyage" Wa: 261

GOZZANO, Guido
General Po: 1326

GOZZI, Carlo
Love of the Three Oranges
DC2: 168

GRABBE, Christian
Aschenbrodel DC2: 168

Don Juan und Faust DC2:
168

Hermannsschlacht DC2: 168

Herzog DC2: 168

Jest, Satire, Irony and Deeper Significance DC2: 168

Napoleon DC2: 168-169

GRACIAN, Baltasar
El criticón Fi: 219; Ke:
205

GRACQ, Julien
General Po: 1326-1327

Un Balcon en Forêt Fi: 89-
90

Un Beau ténébreux Fi: 90;
Po: 1327

The Castle of Argol [Au
Chateau d'Argol] Fi: 90;
Po: 1327

Le Rivage des Syrtes Fi:
90

GRAF, Oskar Maria
General Po: 1327-1328

Das Leben meiner Mutter
Po: 1327

Wir sind Gefangene Po: 1327

GRAHAM
"The White Threshold" PE:
204

GRAHAM, Donald L.
General BAW: 334

GRAHAM, James Marquis
General Ai: 50

GRAHAM, Lorenz
General BAW: 336

GRAHAM, Robert Bontine Cunninghame [R.B. CUN-

NINGHAME-GRAHAM]
General Ai: 195-196; Po:
1328; TA: 161

"The Grave of the Horseman"
Wa: 261

GRAHAM, William Sydney
General Ai: 309-310

GRAHAME, Kenneth
General Ai: 170; Po: 1328;
TA: 161

"The Secret Drawer" Wa: 261

GRAINVILLE, Cousin de
Le dernier homme Ke: 95

GRAMKO, Ida
General Br: 276

GRANBERRY, Edwin
"A Trip to Czardis" SFC: 69;
Wa: 261-262

GRANDVAL, Charles de
Le Valet Astrologue DC2: 169

GRANGE, John
General SC: 56

The Golden Aphroditis ERP:
195-196; SC: 56

Granich, Irwin [pseud.] see
GOLD, Michael

GRANIN, Daniel
Dem Gewitter entgegen Po:
1328

Idu Na Grozu Ke: 412

Those Who Seek Ke: 412

GRANT, James
General Ai: 141

GRANT, John Wesley
General BAW: 338

GRANT, Micki
General BAP: 90

GRANT, Robert
The Chippendales Po: 1329

GRANVILLE-BARKER, Harley
General Br: 276-277; MBD:
52-53; Mi: 240-241; Po:
1329; TA: 162

Ann Leete [The Marrying of
Ann Leete] Br: 277; MD:
129

The Family of the Oldroyds
DC1: 84

Farewell to the Theatre MD:
128

His Majesty MBD: 53; MD:
128; Po: 1329

The Madras House Br: 277;
MBD: 52-53; MD: 128-129

The Marrying of Ann Leete
see Ann Leete

Our Visitor DC1: 84
The Secret Life MD: 129
The Voysey Inheritance Br:
277; MD: 129
Waste Br: 277; DC1: 84;
MBD: 53; MD: 129; Po:
1330
The Weather Hen DC1: 84
GRASS, Günter
General Br: 278; Po: 1330-
1331
"The Advantages of Wind
Hens" Wa: 262
Askese Po: 1331
Die Blechtrommel see The
Tin Drum
Die bösen Köche see The
Wicked Cooks
Cat and Mouse [Katz und
Maus] Fi: 311-312; Ke:
271-272; Ma: 813; Po:
1332-1333, 1335-1336
Dog Years [Hundejahre] Fi:
312-313; Ke: 272; Po:
1334-1335
"Five Birds" Wa: 262
The Flood [Hochwasser]
EDC: 231
The Flounder Fi: 313-314
From the Diary of a Snail
Fi: 314
Hochwasser see The Flood
Hundejahre see Dog Years
Katz und Maus see Cat and
Mouse
"The Left-Handers" Wa:
262
Local Anesthetic Fi: 314
Mister, Mister EDC: 231
Onkel, Onkel see Uncle,
Uncle
The Plebians Rehearse for the
Uprising [Die Plebejer
Proben den Aufstand]
Br: 278; EDC: 231-232;
MDAE: 471; Po: 1336;
TMBP: 222
Thirty-Two Teeth [Zweiund-
dreissig Zähne] EDC:
232
The Tin Drum [Die Blech-
trommel] Fi: 314-317;
Ke: 272; Ma: 813-815;
Po: 1331-1334
Das Treffen in Telgte Fi:
317

Uncle, Uncle [Onkel, Onkel]
EDC: 232
The Wicked Cooks [Die bösen
Köche] EDC: 232; Po:
1334
Zweiunddreissig Zähne see
Thirty-Two Teeth
GRAU, Jacinto
General Br: 278; MD: 129;
Po: 1337
Bibi Carabe DC2: 169
El Burlador que no se Burla
MD: 129
El Conde Alarcos Br: 278;
DC2: 169
Las Grafas de Don Telesforo
DC2: 169
En Ildaria Br: 278
El Senor Pigmalion DC2:
169
Tabarin DC2: 169
GRAU, Shirley Ann
General ASF: 217; CFAE: 171;
CN: 222; Po: 1337
"The Beach Party" Wa: 262
"The Black Prince" ASF: 217
"Eight O'Clock One Morning"
ASF: 217
The Hard Blue Sky CN: 222;
Ma: 816
The House on Coliseum Street
CN: 222
The Keepers of the House
CFAE: 171; CN: 222; Ma:
816
"The Land and the Water" Wa:
262
"The Longest Day" Wa: 262
"Sea Change" Wa: 262
"Stanley" Wa: 262
"The Way Back" Wa: 262
GRAVES, Richard
General Be: 154-155
Columella Be: 154-155;
ENES2: 110
The Spiritual Quixote Be:
154-155; ENES1: 107;
ENES2: 110
GRAVES, Robert
General CFAE: 174-175; EP:
99-107; LCAB: 77; Ma:
818-819; MP: 46-47; Po:
1337-1346; Sch: 114-115
"Apple Island" PE: 204
"The Bard" PE: 204
"The Castle" PE: 204

"Certain Mercies" ICBAP:
56
Claudius the God ENES2:
111; Ma: 817
"The Cool Web" PE: 204
Count Belisarius ENES2:
111
"Ecstasy of Chaos" PE: 205
"Goliath and David" ICBAP:
56
"Hercules at Nemea" Po:
1346
Hercules, My Shipmate
ENES2: 111
I, Claudius ENES2: 111;
Ma: 817-818
"It's a Queer Time" ICBAP:
56
"Language of the Seasons"
Po: 1346
"The Legs" MP: 47; Po:
1346
My Head! My Head! ENES2:
111
"Pure Death" PE: 205
"The Return of the Goddess
Artemis" PE: 205
"Rocky Acres" PE: 205
"Saint" ICBAP: 56; PE:
205
"The Second Fated" PE:
205
"Sick Love" PE: 205
"To Juan at the Winter Sol-
stice" ICBAP: 56; PE:
205; Po: 1346-1347
"Vanity" Po: 1347
Watch the North Wind Rise
ENES2: 111
"What Did You Say?" PE:
205
"The White Goddess" MP:
47; PE: 205; Po: 1338,
1342, 1345
Work in Hand Po: 1342
GRAY, Cecil
General WIL: 42
Gray, Pearl Zane see GREY,
Zane
GRAY, Simon
General MDAE: 237; TMBP:
57
Butley TMBP: 57
Otherwise Engaged TMBP:
57-58
Plaintiffs and Defendants

TMBP: 58
Two Sundays TMBP: 58
GRAY, Sir Alexander
General Ai: 220
GRAY, Thomas
General EC: 78-79; LCAB:
77; Me: 241-251
"The Bard" EC: 78; Me: 242,
245; PE: 205
Elegy Written in a Country
Churchyard EC: 79-80;
ICBAP: 57; LCAB: 77;
Ma: 820-821; Me: 241-251;
PE: 205-206
"Ode on a Distant Prospect of
Eton College" EC: 78;
ICBAP: 57; Me: 242-244,
247; PE: 206-207
"Ode on the Death of a Favorite
Cat Drowned in a Tub of
Gold Fishes" EC: 79; Me:
245, 248-249; PE: 207
"Ode I: On the Spring" EC:
79; ICBAP: 57; Me: 249;
PE: 207
"The Progress of Poesy" Me:
249; PE: 207
"Sonnet on the Death of Richard
West" ICBAP: 57; Me:
243-244, 247-248; PE: 207
GREBAN, Arnoul
Acts of the Apostles DC2: 169
GREEN, A. [Alexander GRINEVSKI]
Crimson Sails Ke: 412
GREEN, Carolyn
Janus ADC: 126-127
GREEN, Henry [Henry Vincent
YORKE]
General BN2: 52-54; CN:
222-224; LCAB: 77; Po:
1347-1349; Ri: 438-442;
Sch: 115-116
Back BN2: 53; CN: 224;
ENE: 129; ENES1: 107;
ENES2: 111; Po: 1350; Ri:
442
Blindness CN: 224; ENES1:
107; ENES2: 111
Caught CN: 224; ENES1:
108; ENES2: 111; Ri: 442
Concluding CN: 224; ENE:
129; ENES1: 108; ENES2:
111; LCAB: 77; Po: 1347,
1349; Ri: 441
Doting BN2: 53; CN: 225;
ENE: 129-130; ENES1: 108;

ENES2: 111; Po: 1349;
Ri: 441-442
Living CN: 225; ENES1:
108; ENES2: 112; Ri:
439, 441
Loving BN2: 53; CN: 225;
EN: 57; ENE: 130;
ENES1: 108; ENES2:
112; LCAB: 77; Po:
1349-1350; Ri: 438-439,
441-443; Sch: 116-117
Mood Ri: 438
Nothing CN: 225-226; ENE:
130; ENES1: 108; ENES2:
112; Po: 1349; Ri: 441,
443
Party Going BN2: 53; CN:
226; EN: 57; ENE: 130;
ENES1: 108-109; ENES2:
112; Ri: 439, 441, 443
GREEN, Julien
General Br: 278-279; MD:
129; Po: 1350-1353
Adrienne Mesurat Fi: 90
"The Apprentice Psychiatrist"
Wa: 262
L'Autre sommeil Fi: 90
Avarice House Fi: 90; Ke:
95
"Christine" Wa: 262
The Closed Garden Fi:
90; Ke: 95; Ma: 822
The Dark Journey Fi: 90;
Ke: 95
The Dreamer Fi: 90; Ke:
95-96
Each in His Darkness Fi:
90
Epaves Fi: 90-91
Journal Po: 1351, 1353
The Keys of Death Fi: 91;
Wa: 262
Léviathan Fi: 91; Wa: 263
Le Malfaiteur see The
Transgressor
Midnight Fi: 91; Ke: 96;
Ma: 822
Mille chemins ouverts Po:
1351
Moira Fi: 91; Ke: 96
Mont-Cinère Fi: 91
L'Ombre Br: 279
Partir avant le jour Po:
1351
The Pilgrim on the Earth
Fi: 91; Ke: 97; Wa:

263
South [Sud] Br: 279; DC1:
84; MD: 129-130; Po: 1353
Terre lointaine Po: 1351
Then Shall the Dust Return Fi:
91; Ke: 97
The Transgressor [Le Malfaiteur]
Fi: 91; Po: 1353
Le Visionnaire Fi: 91
Le Voyager sur la terre Ke:
97
GREEN, Paul
General Br: 279; Lon: 31-
32; MBA: 95; MD: 130;
MDAE: 240; Po: 1354
The Common Glory ADC: 127;
MD: 130
The Field God ADC: 127;
Br: 279
The House of Connelly ADC:
127; Br: 279; DC1: 84;
MD: 130
Hymn to the Rising Sun Br:
280
In Abraham's Bosom ADC:
127; Br: 280; DC1: 84;
MD: 130
The Lost Colony ADC: 127;
DC1: 84; MD: 130
Peer Gynt ADC: 127-128;
MD: 131
Roll, Sweet Chariot ADC: 128;
LCAB: 77; MD: 131
Shroud My Body Down Br: 280;
MD: 131
Tread the Green Grass Br:
280; DC1: 84; MD: 131
Wilderness Road ADC: 128;
MDAE: 240
_____ and Kurt WEILL
Johnny Johnson ADC: 128;
Br: 280; MD: 130
_____ and Richard WRIGHT
Native Son see also WRIGHT,
Richard ADC: 128-129;
BAP: 214-215; Br: 280,
761; MBA: 95; MD: 131;
TMAP: 127
GREENBERG, A.
"Don Nahum" Wa: 263
GREENBERG, Samuel B.
General JW: 77
GREENBERG, Stanley R.
Pueblo ADC: 129
GREENBURG, Dan
Arf ADC: 129

The Great Airplane Snatch
ADC: 129
GREENE, Bert
The Summer of Daisy Miller
ADC: 129
GREENE, Charles
The Legend of Toby Kingdom
MBA: 95
GREENE, Graham
General BN2: 54-57; Br:
280; CFAE: 179-188; CN:
226-231; LCAB: 78; MBD:
53; MD: 131; MDAE:
242-244; Po: 1354-1362;
Sch: 117-124
"Across the Bridge" SFC:
69; Wa: 263
"The Basement Room" LCAB:
78; Po: 1362-1363; SFC:
69; Wa: 263; WaS1: 76
"The Blue Film" WaS1: 76
Brighton Rock BN2: 56;
CFAE: 181, 185-186;
CN: 231-233; EN: 57-58;
ENE: 130-131; ENES1:
109; ENES2: 112; Po:
1358, 1360, 1362-1364; Sch:
124
"Brother" Wa: 263
A Burnt-Out Case BN2: 55-
56; CFAE: 182, 186-187;
CN: 233-234; ENE: 131-
132; ENES1: 109; ENES2:
112; Ma: 823-824; Po:
1364-1365; Sch: 124-125
Carving a Statue Br: 280-
281; EDC: 232
The Comedians CFAE: 182;
CN: 234; ENE: 132;
ENES1: 109; ENES2: 112-
113; Ma: 824; Po: 1365-
1366; Sch: 125
The Complaisant Lover Br:
281; DC1: 85; EDC:
232-233; LCAB: 78; MD:
131; MDAE: 243; TMBP:
40
The Confidential Agent CN:
234-235; EN: 58; ENE:
132; ENES1: 110; ENES2:
113
"The Destructors" Wa: 263;
WaS1: 76
The End of the Affair BN2:
56; CFAE: 181, 185; CN:
235-236; EN: 58-59; ENE:

132-133; ENES1: 110; ENES2:
113; Ma: 824-825; Po: 1360,
1366; Sch: 125
"The End of the Party" Wa:
264
England Made Me [The Ship-
wrecked] CN: 236-237;
ENES1: 110; ENES2: 113
A Gun for Sale [This Gun for
Hire] CN: 237; ENE: 133;
ENES1: 110; ENES2: 113;
Po: 1358
The Heart of the Matter BN2:
55-57; CFAE: 184, 186; CN:
237-239; EN: 59-60; ENE:
133-134; ENES1: 110-111;
ENES2: 113; LCAB: 78;
Ma: 825-827; Po: 1360,
1362, 1366-1367; Sch: 126
"The Hint of an Explanation"
Po: 1367; Wa: 264
The Honorary Consul ENES1:
111; ENES2: 113
The Human Factor ENES2: 114
"The Innocent" Wa: 264
It's a Battlefield CN: 239; EN:
60; ENES1: 111; ENES2:
114; Po: 1367
The Labyrinthe Ways see The
Power and the Glory
The Living Room Br: 281;
DC1: 85; EDC: 233; MBD:
53; MD: 131; MDAE: 242-
243; Po: 1367-1368
Loser Takes All CN: 239;
ENES1: 111; ENES2: 114;
Po: 1368
The Man Within CN: 240; EN:
60; ENES1: 111; ENES2:
114
The Ministry of Fear CN: 240;
EN: 60; ENES1: 111;
ENES2: 114; Ma: 827-828
The Name of Action CN: 240;
ENES1: 111
Orient Express see Stamboul
Train
Our Man in Havana CFAE:
187; CN: 240-241; ENE:
134; ENES1: 112; ENES2:
114; Ma: 828
The Potting Shed Br: 281;
DC1: 85-86; EDC: 233-234;
LCAB: 78; MBD: 53; MD:
132; MDAE: 242-244; Po:
1368-1369

The Power and the Glory [The Labyrinthe Ways] BN2: 56-57; Br: 281; CFAE: 183-184, 186-187; CN: 241-243; EN: 60-61; ENE: 134-136; ENES1: 112; ENES2: 114-115; Ma: 828-830; MBD: 53; Po: 1360, 1362, 1369-1370; Sch: 126-127

The Quiet American CFAE: 183-185, 188; CN: 243-244; EN: 62; ENE: 136; ENES1: 112; ENES2: 115; Ma: 830-831; Po: 1358, 1370-1371; Sch: 127

The Return of A.J. Raffles EDC: 234

Rumour at Nightfall CN: 244; EN: 62; ENES1: 112; ENES2: 115

"The Second Death" Po: 1371; SFC: 69; Wa: 264

The Shipwrecked see England Made Me

Stamboul Train [Orient Express] CN: 244; EN: 62; ENES1: 112; ENES2: 115

The Third Man CFAE: 180; CN: 245; EN: 62; ENES1: 112-113; ENES2: 115; Sch: 127

This Gun for Hire see A Gun for Sale

Travels with My Aunt ENES1: 113; ENES2: 115; Sch: 128

"Under the Garden" Po: 1371; Wa: 264

"A Visit to Morin" Po: 1371; Wa: 264

GREENE, Robert
General ED: 242-244; ERP: 207-242; Hen: 161; PS: 57-68, 88-91; SC: 56-57; TSD: 51-53

Alphonsus King of Aragon [The Comical History of Alphonsus King of Aragon] DC1: 86; EDC: 234; PS: 74-75, 91; TSD: 52

Black Book's Messenger ERP: 211, 223

Card of Fancy ERP: 219, 221-222

Ciceronis Amor: Tullies Love ENES1: 113; ENES2: 115; ERP: 211

The Comical History of Alphonsus King of Aragon see Alphonsus King of Aragon

Francesco's Fortunes ERP: 232

Friar Bacon and Friar Bungay [Honorable Historie of Friar Bacon and Friar Bungay] DC1: 86; ED: 242; EDC: 234-235; PS: 69-72, 91; TSD: 51-53

George a Green, the Pinner of Wakefield PS: 78, 92; TSD: 52

Groatsworth of Wit ERP: 210-213, 216-217, 228, 230, 232, 234, 236, 241; SC: 57

Gwydonius ERP: 216, 221-222; Hen: 159; SC: 57

Historie of Orlando Furioso, One of the Twelve Peeres of France see Orlando Furioso

Honorable Historie of Friar Bacon and Friar Bungay see Friar Bacon and Friar Bungay

James IV [Scottish Historie of James IV] DC1: 86-87; EDC: 235; PS: 72-74, 91; TSD: 51-52

John of Bordeux see also ANONYMOUS PS: 78-79; TSD: 52

Locrine see ANONYMOUS

Mamillia ERP: 219, 221, 232-233, 239, 241

Menaphon ENES1: 113; ERP: 211, 217-218, 220, 226, 233

Morando ERP: 220

Never Too Late ERP: 232

Orlando Furioso [Historie of Orlando Furioso, One of the Twelve Peeres of France] DC1: 87; EDC: 235; PS: 76-78, 92; TSD: 51

Pandosto ENES1: 113; ENES2: 115; ERP: 212, 217, 219, 221-222, 225-226, 229, 238; Hen: 160

Philomena ERP: 238

Planetomachia ERP: 214

Repentance of Robert Greene ERP: 216; SC: 57

Scottish Historie of James IV

see James IV

Selimus DC1: 87; PS: 301-310; TSD: 52

"The Shepherd Wife's Song" PE: 207

The Spanish Masquerado ERP: 217

"Sweet Are the Thoughts" PE: 208

_____ and Thomas LODGE
A Looking Glass for London and England see also LODGE, Thomas and Robert GREENE PS: 75-76, 91; TSD: 52

GREENFELD, Josh
I Have a Dream ADC: 129; MBA: 95-96

GREENLEE, Sam
General BAF: 136; BAW: 342

Blues for an African Princess BAW: 342

The Spook Who Sat by the Door BAF: 136; MBA: 96

GREENOUGH, Henry
General LCAB: 78

GREENOUGH, Sarah Dana
General LCAB: 78

GREENRIDGE, Gertrude
Ma Low's Daughters MBA: 96

GREENWALD, Robert
I Have a Dream MBA: 97

GREENWOOD, Frank J.
General BAW: 342

Burn, Baby, Burn! BAP: 92

The Cotton Curtain MBA: 97

GREENWOOD, Walter
Love on the Dole ENES2: 115

GREGORY I, Pope
Pastoral Care see ALFRED THE GREAT [translator]

GREGORY, André
Alice in Wonderland ADC: 129-130

The Seagull ADC: 130

GREGORY, Horace
"Bridgewater Jones: Impromptu in a Speakeasy" PE: 208

"Chorus for Survival" PE: 208

"O Metaphysical Head" PE: 208

"O Mors Aeterna" PE: 208

"Under the Stone I Saw Them Flow" (from Chorus for Survival) PE: 208

GREGORY, Lady Isabella Augusta
General Br: 281-282; MBD: 54; MD: 132; Mi: 241-243; Po: 1372-1373; TA: 164

Aristotle's Bellows Br: 282

The Caravans Br: 282

Dave MD: 132

Dervorgilla Br: 282

The Dragon Br: 282

The Full Moon Br: 282

The Gaol Gate MD: 132

The Golden Apple Br: 282

Grania Br: 283; DC1: 87; MD: 132

Hyacinth Halvey MD: 132

The Image Br: 283

The Jester Br: 283

Kincora Br: 283

MacDonough's Wife MD: 132

The Spreading of the News Br: 283; DC1: 87; MD: 133

Story Brought by Brigit MD: 133

Twenty-Five MD: 133

White Cockade MD: 133

The Wrens Br: 283; MD: 133

GREKOVA, I.
Behind the Control Room Ke: 412

GRENFELL, Julian
"Into Battle" ICBAP: 57

"Prayer for Those on the Staff" ICBAP: 57

GRESSIEKER, Hermann
The Emperor Br: 283

Royal Gambit [Heinrich VIII und Seine Frauen] Br: 283

GREVILLE, Fulke
General Hen: 56; NI: 330-334; SC: 57-58

Alaham DC1: 88

"All My Senses, Like Beacons Flame" PE: 208

Caelica SC: 57-58

Caelica, "Sonnet 2" PE: 208

Caelica, "Sonnet 7" PE: 208

Caelica, "Sonnet 16" PE: 208

Caelica, "Sonnet 22" PE: 208

Caelica, "Sonnet 38" PE: 208

Caelica, "Sonnet 69" PE: 208
Caelica, "Sonnet 87" PE: 208
Caelica, "Sonnet 99" PE: 208
Caelica, "Sonnet 100" PE:
　208
"Down in the Depth of Mine
　Iniquity" PE: 209
Mustapha DC1: 88
"The Treatie of Humane
　Learning" ICBAP: 57
GREY, Zane [GRAY, Pearl Zane]
　General ASF: 217; Po:
　1347
"Avalanche" Wa: 264
"Canyon Walls" Wa: 264
"Monty Price's Nightingale"
　Wa: 264
"The Secret of Quaking Asp
　Cabin" Wa: 264
The Vanishing American
　LCAB: 78
GRIEG, John Y.T.
　Lothian Cameron ENES2:
　115
GRIEG, Nordahl
　The Ship Sails On Fi: 402
Grieve, Christopher Murray
　see MacDIARMID, Hugh
GRIFFIN, Benjamin
　Whig and Tory Li: 198
GRIFFIN, Gerald
　General BN: 61
"The Barber of Bantry"
　WaS1: 76
"The Black Birds and the
　Yellow Hammers" WaS1:
　76
"Card Drawing" WaS1: 76
"The Great House" WaS1:
　77
"The Half-Sir" WaS1: 77
"A Night at Sea" WaS1: 77
"Sir Dowling O'Hartigan"
　WaS1: 77
"Touch My Honour, Touch
　My Life" WaS1: 77
"The Village Ruin" WaS1:
　77
GRIFFIN, John Howard
　General LCAB: 78-79
　The Devil Rides Outside
　　AN: 105; LCAB: 78-79
　Nuni LCAB: 78-79
GRIFFIN, Oscar
　Miss Ann Is Still Alive MBA:
　97

GRIFFITH, Elizabeth
　The History of Lady Barton
　　ENES2: 116
GRIFFITH, George
　"The Lord of Labour" WaS1:
　　77
GRIGGS, Sutton Elbert
　General AAW: 55; BAF: 137-
　　138; BAW: 344-345; LCAB:
　　79
　The Hindered Hand BAF: 138;
　　BAW: 345
　Imperium in Imperio BAF: 138
　Overshadowed BAF: 138
　Pointing the Way BAF: 138
　Unfettered BAF: 138
GRIGOROVICH, Dmitri
　"Karelin's Dream" Wa: 265
　The Village Fi: 452; Wa: 265
GRILLO, John
　General MDAE: 246
　Hello, Goodbye, Sebastian
　　MDAE: 246
GRILLPARZER, Franz Serafin
　The Ancestress [Die Ahnfrau]
　　DC2: 169-170; EDC: 236;
　　Ke: 272
　Der Arme Spielmann see The
　　Poor Minstrel
　Blanca from Castile [Blanka von
　　Kastilien] EDC: 236
　Ein Bruderzwist in Habsburg
　　see Family Strife in Habs-
　　burg
　A Dream Is Life [Der Traum
　　ein Leben] DC2: 171; EDC:
　　236-237
　Esther EDC: 237
　A Faithful Servant of His Master
　　[Ein Treuer Diener Seines
　　Herrn] DC2: 172; EDC:
　　237
　Family Strife in Hapsburg [Ein
　　Bruderzwist in Habsburg]
　　DC2: 170; EDC: 237-238
　The Golden Fleece [Das Goldene
　　Vliess] DC2: 170; EDC:
　　238
　Hero and Leander [Des Meeres
　　und der Liebe Wellen] DC2:
　　171; EDC: 238-239
　The Jewess of Toledo [Die
　　Judin von Toledo] DC2:
　　170; EDC: 239
　King Ottakar, His Rise and Fall
　　[König Ottakars Glück und

Ende] DC2: 170; EDC:
239

Das Kloster bei Sendomir Fi:
317

Libussa DC2: 171; EDC:
239-240

Medea DC2: 171

Des Meeres und der Liebe
Wellen see Hero and
Leander

Melusina DC2: 171

The Poor Minstrel [The Poor
Player; Der Arme Spiel-
mann] Fi: 317; Ke: 272-
273; Wa: 265-266; WaS1:
77

Sappho DC2: 171; EDC:
240

Thou Shalt Not Lie [Weh
Dem, Der Lugt] EDC:
240-241

Der Traum ein Leben see
A Dream Is Life

Ein Treuer Diener Seines
Herrn see A Faithful
Servant of His Master

Weh Dem, Der Lugt see
Thou Shalt Not Lie

GRIMES, Nikki
Poems by Nikki BAW: 345

GRIMKE, Angeline Weld
General BAP: 92; BAW:
346-347; HR: 87
Mara HR: 87
Rachel BAP: 92; BAW:
347; HR: 87; MBA: 98

GRIMKE, Charlotte L. Forten
General AAPD: 65

GRIMM, Friedrich Melchior
Correspondance litteraire
LCAB: 79

GRIMM, Hans
"Dina" Wa: 266

GRIMMELSHAUSEN, Franz
The Female Vagrant Ke:
273
Simplicissimus Fi: 318-319;
Ke: 273
Vogelnest Ke: 274

GRIMMELSHAUSEN, Johann Jakob
Christoffel von
Courasche Fi: 318

GRIN, Alexander
The Golden Chain Fi: 452
Jessy and Morgiana Fi:
452-453

The Road to Nowhere Fi: 453
Scarlet Sails Fi: 453; WaS1:
77
She Who Runs on the Waves
Fi: 453
The Shining World Fi: 453

GRONNIOSAW, James Albert Ukaw-
saw
General BALE: 306

GROSJEAN, Jean
General Po: 1373-1374

GROSSE, Karl
Der Genius Fi: 319

GROSSI, Tommaso
Marco Visconti Ke: 243

GROSVENOR, Verta Mae [VERTA
MAE]
General BAW: 347

GROTIUS [Hugo de GROOT]
Adamus Exul DC2: 172

GROTOWSKI, Jerzy
General Po: 1374

GROULX, Lionel
General Po: 1374

GROVE, Frederick Philip [Felix
Paul GREVE]
General Po: 1375
"The Boat" Wa: 266
"The Desert" Wa: 266
Our Daily Bread LCAB: 79
"Snow" Wa: 266

GRUNDY, Sydney
General EDT: 187

GRYPHIUS, Andreas
Cardenio et Celinde DC2: 172
Carolus Stuardus DC2: 172
Catherina von Georgien DC2:
172
Gelibte Dornrose DC2: 172
Horribilicribrifax DC2: 173
Papinianus DC2: 173

GUARE, John
General MDAE: 248
Cop-Out ADC: 130
The House of Blue Leaves ADC:
130
Landscape of the Body ADC:
130
Marco Polo Sings a Solo ADC:
130
Muzeeka ADC: 130
Rich and Famous ADC: 130

GUARINI, Giovanni
Il Pastor Fido DC2: 173-174

GUAZZO, Stefano
General Hen: 192

GUEHENNO, Jean
General Po: 1375
GUENON, René
General Po: 1375
GUERARD, Albert
General Po: 1376
GUERIN, Raymond
General Po: 1376
GUERRAZZI, F.D.
Pasquale Paoli Fi: 265
Il secolo che muore Fi: 265-266
The Seige of Florence Ke: 243
GUEVARA, Velez de
La Nina de Gomez Arias DC2: 174
GUICCIARDINI, Francesco
The Historie ... Conteining the Warres of Italie, tr. Geoffrey FENTON Hen: 49
GUILLEMIN, Henri
General Po: 1376
GUILLEN, Jorge
General Po: 1376-1379
Advenimiento Po: 1379
Cántico Po: 1379-1380
Clamor Po: 1379, 1381
Gran silencio Po: 1381
Homenaje Po: 1381
Luzar de Lázaro Po: 1381-1382
GUILLEN, Nicolás
General Po: 1382
GUILLEN DE CASTRO
El Cerco de Tremecen DC2: 174
El Conde Alarcos DC2: 174
Donde no esta su Dueno DC2: 174
La Mocedades del Cid DC2: 174
La Tragedia por los Celos DC2: 174
GUILLEVIC, Eugène
General Po: 1382-1383
Terraqué Po: 1382
GUILLOUX, Louis
General Po: 1383
Angelina Fi: 92
Les Batailles perdues Fi: 92
Compagnons Fi: 92
La Confrontation Fi: 92
Dossier Confidential Fi: 92

Hymenee Fi: 92
Le Jeu de patience Fi: 92
La Maison du peuple Fi: 92
Le Pain des rêves Fi: 92-93
Parpagnacco ou la conjuration Fi: 93
Le Sang noir Fi: 93; Po: 1383
GUILPIN, Everard
General SC: 58
GUIMARÃES ROSA, Joao
General Po: 1383
"Buriti" Wa: 654
"A Love Story" Wa: 654
"Message from the Mountain" Wa: 654
"My People" Wa: 654
"The Return of the Prodigal Husband" Wa: 654
"The Third Bank of the River" Wa: 654
"The Time and Turn of Augusto Matraga" Wa: 654
GUIMERA, Angel
Marta of the Lowlands Br: 283
GUIN, Wyman
"Beyond Bedlam" Wa: 266
GUIRALDES, Ricardo
General Po: 1384
Don Segundo Sombra LCAB: 79; Po: 1384-1387
GUITRY, Sacha
General Br: 283; Po: 1387
Quand Jouons-Nous la Comedie Br: 283
GUMILEV, Nikolay
General Po: 1387-1388
Poisoned Tunic DC2: 175
Gunn, Bill see GUNN, William Harrison
GUNN, Neil M.
General Ai: 239-240; Po: 1388
"Blaeberries" Wa: 266
"Dance of the Stones" Wa: 266
"Down to the Sea" Wa: 266
"Henry Drake Goes Home" Wa: 266
"Love's Dialectic" Wa: 266
"The Moor" Wa: 266
"Paper Boats" Wa: 266
"Such Stuff as Dreams" Wa: 267
"Symbolical" Wa: 267

"Whistle for Bridge" Wa:
267
GUNN, Thom
General LCAB: 79; Po:
1388
"The Corridor" PE: 209
"Elegy on the Dust" PE:
209
"Helen's Rape" ICBAP: 57
"In Santa Maria Del Popolo"
ICBAP: 57
"On the Move" ICBAP: 57;
PE: 209
"Waking in a Newly-Built
House" ICBAP: 57
"The Wound" PE: 209
GUNN, William Harrison [Bill
GUNN]
General BAF: 138; BAP:
92-93; BAW: 348; MBA:
98
Black Picture Show ADC:
131; BAP: 93; MBA:
98-99
GUNNARSSON, Gunnar
Blessed Are the Poor in
Spirit Ke: 350
GURAZADA APPARAO
"Kanyaka" WaS1: 77
"Reform" WaS1: 78
GURIK, Robert
General JW: 426
GURNEY, A.R. Jr.
Children ADC: 131
The David Show ADC: 131
Scenes from American Life
ADC: 131
The Wayside Motor Inn ADC:
131
GURNEY, Ivor
General Po: 1389
GUSTAFSON, Ralph
General Po: 1389
GUTHRIE, Alfred Bertram, Jr.
General AN: 105; ASF:
106; CN: 245; LCAB:
79; Po: 1389
The Big Sky CN: 245; Ma:
832
"Mountain Medicine" ASF:
217
These Thousand Hills CN:
245
The Way West AN: 105;
CN: 245-246
GUTHRIE, Thomas Anstey

General Po: 1389
GUTHRIE, Tyrone
General LCAB: 79
GUTIERREZ, Garcia
El Trovador DC2: 175
GUTIERREZ NAJERA, Manuel
General LCAB: 79
GUTIERREZ-SOLANA, José
General Po: 1389-1390
GUTZKOW, Karl
Blasedow und Seine Sohne Ke:
274
Doubting Girl Ke: 274
Wally die Zweiflerin Fi: 319
GUY, Rosa
General BAF: 139; BAW:
348
Bird at My Window BAF: 139
GUZMAN, Martin Luis
The Eagle and the Serpent
Ma: 833
GUZMAN, Nicomedes
"A Coin in the River" WaS1:
78
GWALA, Mafika Pascal
General BALE: 306
GYLLENSTEN, Lars
The Blue Ship Fi: 402
Cain's Memoirs Fi: 402
The Cave in the Desert Fi:
402
The Death of Socrates Fi: 402
Diarium Spirituale Fi: 402
In the Shadow of Don Juan Fi:
402
Infantilia Fi: 402
Juvenilia Fi: 402
Lotus in Hades Fi: 402
Palace in the Park Fi: 403
The Senator Fi: 403
Senilia Fi: 403

H

HABIB, Rowley
"The Visitors" Wa: 267
HABINGTON, William
General LJCD: 244
HACK, Peter
Die Schone Helena DC2: 175;
Po: 1578
HACKET, Harley
On Toby Time MBA: 99
HACKETT, Francis
General Po: 1391

HAECKER, Hans-Joachim
  Don't Turn Around [Drecht
    Euch Nicht Um] Br: 284
HAGER, L.N.
  Comedy of the Crocodile DC2:
    175
HAGGARD, Henry Rider
  General TA: 166
  Allan Quartermain ENE:
    136; ENES2: 116
  Ayesha ENES2: 116
  Cetywayo and His White
    Neighbors ENE: 136
  Dawn ENE: 136
  King Solomon's Mines ENE:
    137; ENES2: 116
  She ENE: 137; ENES1: 113;
    ENES2: 116
  The Witch's Head ENE: 137
HAHN, Emily
  General LCAB: 79
HAIK, Farjallah
  General Po: 1391
HAILEY, Oliver
  And Where She Stops Nobody
    Knows ADC: 131
  Father's Day ADC: 131
  Hey You, Light Man! ADC:
    131; Br: 284
  Who's Happy Now? ADC:
    132
HAINES, William Wister
  Command Decision ADC:
    132; Br: 284; DC1: 88
HAIRSTON, William
  General BAP: 93; BAW:
    349
  Walk in Darkness BAP: 93;
    MBA: 99
AL-HAKIM, Tawfiq
  General Po: 1391
HAKLUYT, Richard
  General Hen: 67-68; SC:
    59
HALBE, Max
  Youth [Jugend] Br: 284
HALCON, Manuel
  General Po: 1391-1392
HALDANE, John Burdon Sand-
    erson
  General LCAB: 79-80
HALDEMAN-JULIUS, Emanuel
  Dust LCAB: 80
HALE, Edward Everett
  General ASF: 218; LCAB:
    80

"A Man Without a Country"
    ASF: 218; Ma: 834
HALE, John
  General MDAE: 250
HALE, Nancy
  "Rich People" Wa: 267
  "A Summer's Long Dream" ASF:
    218
HALE, Sarah Josepha
  General ASF: 218
  "The Silver Mine" ASF: 218
HALEY, Alex
  General MBA: 100
  Roots MBA: 100
HALIBURTON, Thomas Chandler
  General ECL: 65-68
HALIFAX, Sir George Savile, Mar-
    quis of
  General Bon: 74-75
HALL, Adrian
  Billy Budd ADC: 132
HALL, Bob and David RICHMOND
  The Passion of Dracula ADC:
    132
HALL, Donald
  General Ma: 835; Po: 1392
  "The Body of Politics" PE:
    209
  "Cold Water" PE: 209
  "Exile" PE: 209
  "The Grass" PE: 209
  "The Snow" PE: 209
  "The Stump" PE: 209
  "Swan" PE: 209
  "Wedding Party" PE: 209
  "Wells" PE: 209
HALL, Edward
  Chronicle Hen: 47; SC: 60
HALL, Hazel
  General Po: 1392
HALL, J. Parsons
  "All Her Own Fault" Wa: 267
  "Poor Mary Ann" Wa: 267
  "The Reserved Husband" Wa:
    267
  "The Slave of the Needle" Wa:
    267
HALL, James Norman
  General ASF: 218; Da: 111
  "The Backwoodsman" ASF:
    218; Wa: 267
  "The War Belt" WaS1: 78
HALL, Joseph
  General Ba: 66-67; Hen:
    31; SC: 59
  Characters of Vertues and

Vices Ba: 66-67
HALL, Marguerite Radclyffe
  The Well of Loneliness
    ENES2: 116
HALL, Oakley
  "The Crown" ASF: 219
  "The Retaining Wall" ASF:
    219
  Warlock LCAB: 80
HALL, Prince
  General LCAB: 80
HALL, Willis
  General Br: 284
  The Long and the Short and
    the Tall Br: 284
HALLAM, Arthur Henry
  "Long Hast Thou Wandered
    on the Happy Mountain"
    ICBAP: 58
  "The Palace of Art" ICBAP:
    58
HALLE, Adam de la
  Le Jeu de la Feuillee DC2:
    175
HALLECK, Fitz-Greene
  General Da: 111-112
HALLEY, Anne
  "Dear God, the Day Is Grey"
    PE: 209
HALLIWELL, David
  General MDAE: 253
HALM, Friedrich
  "Die Freundinnen" Wa: 267
  Griseldis DC2: 175
  "Das Haus an der Verona-
    brücke" Wa: 268
  "Die Marzipan-Lise' Wa: 268
HALPER, Albert
  General JW: 228; Po: 1392
HALSEY, Margaret
  General LCAB: 80
HAMILTON, Alexander
  General AP: 350-354; Da:
    69
  The Federalist AP: 352-354
HAMILTON, Dr. Alexander
    (1712-1756)
  The Itinerarium... AP:
    580-581
HAMILTON, Edmond
  General LCAB: 80
  "The Man Who Evolved"
    WaS1: 78
HAMILTON, Elizabeth
  General Ai: 98
HAMILTON, Patrick

Angel Street ADC: 133; EDC:
    241
  Duke in Darkness EDC: 241
  Rope's End EDC: 241
HAMILTON, William
  General Ai: 63
HAMMEL, Claus
  General Po: 1392
HAMMERSTEIN, Oscar II and
    Georges BIZET
  Carmen Jones ADC: 133
  _____, Benjamin F. GLAZER,
    and Richard RODGERS
  Carousel ADC: 133-134
  _____ and Jerome KERN
  Music in the Air ADC: 134
  Show Boat ADC: 134-135
  _____, Joshua LOGAN, and
    Richard RODGERS
  South Pacific see also
    RODGERS, Richard and
    Oscar HAMMERSTEIN II
    ADC: 135
  _____, Frank MANDEL, Laurence
    SCHWAB, and Sigmund ROM-
    BERG
  The New Moon ADC: 135
  _____ and Richard RODGERS
  Allegro see also RODGERS,
    Richard and Oscar HAMMER-
    STEIN II ADC: 136
  The King and I ADC: 136
  Oklahoma see also RODGERS,
    Richard and Oscar HAMMER-
    STEIN II ADC: 136-137
  _____ and Sigmund ROMBERG
  Sunny River ADC: 137
HAMMETT, Samuel Dashiell
  General ASF: 219
  "The Big Knockover" ASF:
    219
  The Maltese Falcon Ma: 836
HAMMON, Briton
  General BAW: 352; LCAB:
    80
HAMMON, Jupiter
  General AAPD: 66-67; AAW:
    55-56; BAW: 353-354; LCAB:
    80
HAMP, Pierre
  General Br: 284
HAMPTON, Christopher
  General MDAE: 255; TMBP:
    61-63
  The Philanthropist MDAE:
    255; TMBP: 61-63, 235

Savages TMBP: 61-62
Total Eclipse TMBP: 61-63
When Did You Last See My
  Mother? TMBP: 62
HAMSUN, Helmut
Ved Rigets Pont DC2: 175
HAMSUN, Knut
General Po: 1393
August Fi: 403
Chapter the Last Ke: 350
Children of the Times Ke:
  350
Editor Lynge Ke: 350-351
Growth of the Soil Fi: 403;
  Ke: 351; Ma: 837
Hunger Fi: 403; Ke: 351;
  Ma: 837
Mysteries Fi: 403; Ke: 351;
  Ma: 837-838
New Soil Ke: 351
Pan Fi: 403; Ke: 351; Ma:
  838
The Ring Is Closed Fi: 403;
  Ke: 351
The Road Leads On Ke: 352
Segelfoss Town Ke: 352;
  Ma: 838
Siste Kapitel Fi: 403
"Under the Autumn Star"
  Wa: 268; WaS1: 78
Victoria Fi: 403; Ke: 352;
  Ma: 838
The Women at the Pump Ke:
  352
HANDKE, Peter
General Po: 1393
The Goalie's Anxiety at the
  Penalty Kick Fi: 319
Wunschloses Ungluck Fi:
  319
HANKIN, St. John [Emile
  CLAVERING]
General Br: 284; MBD:
  55; Mi: 243; TA: 167
HANLEY, Clifford [Henry CAL-
  VIN]
General Ai: 322
HANLEY, James
General BN2: 58; CN: 246;
  MDAE: 257
Boy CN: 246
Captain Bottell CN: 246
The Closed Harbour CN:
  246
Drift CN: 246
Ebb and Flood CN: 246

Emily CN: 246
An End and a Beginning CN:
  246
The Furys CN: 247; ENES2:
  116
Hollow Sea CN: 247
The House in the Valley CN:
  247
Levine CN: 247
No Directions CN: 247
The Ocean CN: 247
Our Time Is Gone CN: 247
Resurrexit Dominus CN: 247
Sailor's Song CN: 247
Say Nothing CN: 247
The Secret Journey CN: 247;
  ENES2: 116
Stoker Bush CN: 247
The Welsh Sonata CN: 248
What Farrar Saw CN: 248
Winter Song CN: 248
HANLEY, William
General LCAB: 80; MBA:
  101
Mrs. Dally Has a Lover [Mrs.
  Dally] ADC: 137-138; Br:
  285
Slow Dance on the Killing
  Ground ADC: 138; Br:
  285; MBA: 101
Whisper into My Good Ear
  ADC: 138
HANNAH, Barry
General ASF: 220
"Behold the Husband in His
  Perfect Agony" ASF: 220
HANNAY, James
General BN: 61
HANSBERRY, Lorraine
General AAPD: 375-376; AAW:
  56; BAP: 95-96; BAW:
  356-358; Br: 285; LCAB:
  80; MBA: 102-103; MD:
  133; Po: 1394
Les Blancs AAPD: 376; ADC:
  138; BAP: 96, 98-99; MBA:
  103-104, 107
The Drinking Gourd MBA: 103
A Raisin in the Sun AAL: 182;
  AAPD: 375-376; AAW: 56;
  ADC: 138-139; BAP: 96-99;
  Br: 285-286; DC1: 88; Ma:
  839; MBA: 104-109; MD:
  133; Po: 1394
_____ and Robert NEMIROFF
The Sign in Sidney Brustein's

Window AAPD: 376; ADC:
139-140; BAP: 98, 100;
BAW: 358; Br: 286; Ma:
839-840; MBA: 106, 108
To Be Young, Gifted and
Black ADC: 140; BAP:
100; MBA: 106, 108
HANSEN, Martin A.
General Po: 1394
"The Birds" WaS1: 78
"The Bridegroom's Oak" WaS1:
78
"Early Morning" WaS1: 78
"The Easter Bell" WaS1: 78
"The Gardener, the Beast,
and the Child" WaS1: 78
"Haavn" WaS1: 78
"The Homecoming" WaS1: 78
Jonathan's Journey Fi: 403;
Ke: 352
The Liar Fi: 403-404; Ke:
352
Lucky Kristoffer Fi: 404
"The Man from the Earth"
WaS1: 79
"The Messenger" WaS1: 79
"The Midsummer Festival"
WaS1: 79
"Night in March" WaS1: 79
"The Owl" WaS1: 79
"The Righteous One" WaS1:
79
"Sacrifice" WaS1: 79
"September Fog" WaS1: 79
"The Soldier and the Girl"
WaS1: 79
"The Thornbush" WaS1: 79
"Tirad" WaS1: 79
"The Waiting Room" WaS1:
79
HARBEN, William N.
General ASF: 220
"The Heresy of Abner Cali-
han" Wa: 268
"Jim Trundle's Crisis" Wa:
268
"The Whipping of Uncle Henry"
Wa: 268
HARBURG, Edgar Y. and Fred
SAIDY
Finian's Rainbow DC1: 88
HARBY, Isaac
General JW: 377
Alberti ADC: 140
The Gordian Knot ADC:
140

HARDIE, John Jackson
General MAP: 176
HARDING, Samuel
Sicily and Naples DC1: 88
HARDY, Alexandre
La Belle Egyptienne DC2: 175
Didon se Sacrifiant DC2: 176
Mariamne DC2: 176
Morte D'Achilles DC2: 176
La Morte de Daire DC2: 176
HARDY, Frank
General MAP: 179-180
Power Without Glory MAP:
179-180
The Unlucky Australians MAP:
179
HARDY, Thomas
General BN: 63-65; Du: 96-
100; EP: 115-128; ICBAP:
58; LCAB: 80-81; Po: 1394-
1413; TA: 169-170; VP: 36-
39
"Absent-Mindedness in a Parish
Choir" Wa: 268
"According to the Mighty Work-
ing" PE: 209
"After a Journey" PE: 210
"After the Last Breath" PE:
210
"Afterwards" ICBAP: 58; PE:
210; Po: 1413
"Ah, Are You Digging on My
Grave?" Po: 1414
"An Ancient to Ancients" PE:
210
"And There Was a Great Calm"
EP: 126
"At Castle Boterel" ICBAP:
58; PE: 210
"Barbara of the House of
Grebe" Wa: 268
"Beeny Cliff" ICBAP: 58; PE:
210
"Beyond the Last Lamp" EP:
122
"The Blinded Bird" ICBAP: 58
"A Broken Appointment" Po:
1414
"The Burghers" ICBAP: 58
"Channel Firing" EP: 126;
ICBAP: 58; PE: 210; Po:
1414
"The Chapel-Organist" ICBAP:
58
"The Chéval-Glass" ICBAP:
58

"The Commiteeman of 'The Terror'" Wa: 268

"A Commonplace Day" PE: 210

"Contretemps" ICBAP: 58; PE: 210

"The Convergence of the Twain" EP: 117, 123; ICBAP: 58; PE: 210-211

"Conversation at Dawn" EP: 118

"The Dance of the Phoenix" ICBAP: 58

"The Darkling Thrush" ICBAP: 59; LCAB: 81; PE: 211

"Death Divided" EP: 117

Desperate Remedies Du: 88; EN: 62-63; ENE: 137-138; ENES1: 113-114; ENES2: 116-117; Po: 1410, 1414-1415

"The Distracted Preacher" Wa: 268

"The Doctor's Legend" Wa: 268

"Doom and She" ICBAP: 59; PE: 211

"A Dream or No" ICBAP: 59

"Drinking Song" ICBAP: 59

"A Drizzling Easter Morning" PE: 211

"Drummer Hodge" PE: 211

The Duchess of Hamptonshire Po: 1415

"During Wind and Rain" EP: 119; ICBAP: 59; PE: 211; Po: 1415

The Dynasts EP: 118-123, 125, 127; ICBAP: 59; Ma: 841-842; Po: 1396, 1415-1419; TA: 170; VP: 37-39

"The Face at the Casement" ICBAP: 59

"The Fallow Deer at the Lonely House" PE: 211

Far from the Madding Crowd BN: 65; Du: 88-89; EN: 63; ENE: 138-139; ENES1: 114; ENES2: 117; LCAB: 81; Ma: 842-843; Po: 1409-1411, 1419-1420

"A Few Crusted Characters" Wa: 268

"The Fiddler of the Reels"

Wa: 268-269

"Former Beauties" ICBAP: 59; PE: 211; Po: 1420

"Friends Beyond" EP: 125; PE: 211

"The Garden Seat" PE: 212

"George Meredith" PE: 212

"The Glory" EP: 117

"God-Forgotten" ICBAP: 59; PE: 211

"The Going" PE: 212

The Hand of Ethelberta Du: 89; EN: 63; ENE: 139; ENES1: 114; ENES2: 118; Po: 1420

"He Abjures Love" PE: 212

"The Head Above the Fog" ICBAP: 59

"Her Death and After" ICBAP: 59

"Her Father" PE: 212; Po: 1420

"The House of Hospitalities" ICBAP: 59

"I Found Her Out There" ICBAP: 59; PE: 212

"I Leant Upon a Coppice Gate" PE: 212

"If You Had Known" ICBAP: 59; PE: 212

"An Imaginative Woman" Wa: 269

"The Impercipient at a Cathedral Service" PE: 212; Po: 1421

"In Tenebris, I" PE: 212

"In the Days of Crinoline" PE: 212

"In Time of 'The Breaking of Nations'" PE: 212

Jude the Obscure BN: 65-66; Du: 89-91; EN: 63-64; ENE: 140-143; ENES1: 114-115; ENES2: 118-119; Ma: 843-845; Po: 1398, 1401, 1409, 1421-1426; Ri2: 457

"The Lacking Sense" PE: 212

A Laodicean Du: 91; ENE: 143; ENES1: 115; ENES2: 119; Po: 1426

"Last Week in October" ICBAP: 59

"The Last Words to a Dumb Friend" PE: 213

"A Man" ICBAP: 59

"The Man He Killed" LCAB: 81; PE: 213

"The Marchioness of Stonehenge" Wa: 269

"The Masked Face" PE: 213

The Mayor of Casterbridge BN: 66; Du: 91-92; EN: 64-65; ENE: 143-145; ENES1: 115-116; ENES2: 119-120; Ma: 845-846; Po: 1396, 1427-1432

"A Mere Interlude" WaS1: 79

"The Milkmaid" PE: 213

"The Missed Train" PE: 213

"The Moth-Signal" ICBAP: 60; PE: 213

"My Cicely" ICBAP: 60

"Nature's Questioning" ICBAP: 60; PE: 213

"Near Lanivet, 1872" PE: 213

"Neutral Tones" EP: 125; ICBAP: 60; PE: 213-214

"A Night in November" PE: 214

"The Noble Lady's Tale" ICBAP: 60

"Nobody Comes" PE: 214

"Old Mrs. Chundle" WaS1: 79

"On a Heath" PE: 214

"On an Invitation to the United States" PE: 214

"On the Departure Platform" PE: 214

"On the Western Circuit" Wa: 269; WaS1: 79

"The Oxen" PE: 214

A Pair of Blue Eyes Du: 92; EN: 65-66; ENE: 146; ENES1: 116; ENES2: 120-121; Po: 1410-1411, 1432

"Poems of 1912-13" VP: 38

"Poems of Pilgrimmage" Po: 1432

"Postponement" PE: 214

The Return of the Native BN: 66-67; Du: 92-93; EN: 66-67; ENE: 146-149; ENES1: 116-117; ENES2: 121; EP: 127; LCAB: 81; Ma: 846-847; Po: 1409, 1432-1436

"The Revisitation" PE: 214

"The Rift" ICBAP: 60

"The Roman Road" PE: 214

"The Romantic Adventures of a Milkmaid" SFC: 69; Wa: 269; WaS1: 80

"The Sacrilege" ICBAP: 60; PE: 214

"Seen by the Waits" PE: 214

"The Shadow on the Stone" PE: 214

"She Did Not Turn" ICBAP: 60

"She to Him" PE: 215

"The Sign-Seeker" ICBAP: 60; PE: 215

"Souls of the Slain" Po: 1436

"Squire Petrick's Lady" SFC: 70; Wa: 269

"The Subalterns" EP: 126; ICBAP: 60; PE: 215

"The Sun on the Letter" ICBAP: 60

"A Sunday Morning Tragedy" ICBAP: 60

"The Telegram" PE: 215

Tess of the d'Urbervilles BN: 67; Du: 93-95; EN: 67-68; ENE: 149-152; ENES1: 117-118; ENES2: 121-123; Ma: 848-849; Po: 1398, 1436-1442

"The Three Strangers" Po: 1442-1443; SFC: 70; Wa: 269

"To a Motherless Child" PE: 215

"To an Unborn Pauper Child" PE: 215

"To My Father's Violin" PE: 215

"To Please His Wife" Wa: 269

"The Torn Letter" EP: 123

"A Tradition of 1804" SFC: 70; Wa: 269

"A Tragedy of Two Ambitions" Po: 1443; SFC: 70; Wa: 269-270

"A Trampwoman's Tragedy" EP: 118; ICBAP: 60

"Transformations" PE: 215

The Trumpet-Major Du: 95; ENE: 152; ENES1: 118; ENES2: 123; Po: 1443-1444

Two on a Tower EN: 68;

ENE: 152; ENES1: 118;
ENES2: 123-124; Po: 1444
"The Two Wives" ICBAP:
60; PE: 215
Under the Greenwood Tree
BN: 67; Du: 95-96;
ENE: 152-153; ENES1:
118; ENES2: 124; Ma:
849-850; Po: 1444
"Under the Waterfall" ICBAP:
60
"The Voice" PE: 215
"The Waiting Supper" Wa:
270
"A Wasted Illness" ICBAP:
61
The Well-Beloved ENE: 153;
ENES1: 118; ENES2: 124;
Po: 1444-1445
"Wessex Heights" EP: 117,
123-124; ICBAP: 61; PE:
215
"Who's in the Next Room?"
PE: 215
"The Withered Arm" SFC:
70; Wa: 270
"The Woman I Met" PE: 215
The Woodlanders BN: 67;
Du: 96; EN: 68; ENE:
154-155; ENES1: 118-119;
ENES2: 124-125; Ma:
851-852; Po: 1445-1446
"Your Last Drive" PE: 215
HARE, Bill
God Says There Is No Peter
Ott ADC: 140
HARE, David
General MDAE: 260
HARECKI, Maksim
Two Souls Ke: 412
HARIHARA
Ram Lila DC2: 176
Samkhaparabhava Vyayoga
DC2: 176
HARINGTON, Sir John
General SC: 60
HARKNESS, Margaret
Captain Lobe ENES2: 125
A City Girl ENES2: 125
George Eastmond--Wanderer
ENES2: 125
A Manchester Shirtmaker
ENES2: 125
Out of Work ENES2: 125
Harland, Henry see LUSKA,
Sidney [pseud.]

HARPER, Frances Ellen Watkins
General AAPD: 68; AAW: 56;
BAF: 140-141; BAW: 362-
363; LCAB: 81
HARPER, Ken
General MBA: 109
Wiz MBA: 109-110
HARPER, Michael S.
General BAW: 365
Song: I Want a Witness BAW:
365
HARPUR, Charles
General AL: 235-236
HARRIGAN, Edward
General AD: 134-136; Lon:
60
Notoriety ADC: 140
Reilly and the Four Hundred
AD: 134
HARRINGTON, James
General Bon: 75
Oceanea Hen: 122
HARRIS, Alexander
General AL: 238-239
The Emigrant Family AL: 238-
239
Settlers and Convicts AL:
238-239
HARRIS, Bill
Warn the Wicked MBA: 110
HARRIS, Corra
General ASF: 220
HARRIS, Elmer
Johnny Belinda ADC: 140
HARRIS, Frank
General TA: 172
"The Best Man in Garotte"
Wa: 270
"Elder Conklin" Wa: 270
"First Love" Wa: 270
"A Fool's Paradise" Wa: 270
"A French Artist" Wa: 270
"Gulmore the Boss" Wa: 270
"In the Vale of Tears" Wa:
270
"The Interpreter" Wa: 270
"The Irony of Chance" Wa:
270
"Love Is My Sin" Wa: 270
"A Modern Idyll" Wa: 270
"Profit and Loss" Wa: 270
"The Sheriff and His Partner"
Wa: 271
"The Yellow Ticket" Wa: 271
HARRIS, George Washington
General ASF: 223-224

"Bill Ainsworth's Quarter Race" ASF: 220

"Dad's Dog School" ASF: 220

"Frustrating a Funeral" ASF: 220; WaS1: 80

"How Sut Lovengood Dosed His Dog" ASF: 220

"The Knob Dance" ASF: 220

"Mrs. Yardley's Quilting" ASF: 220

"Old Skissim's Middle Boy" ASF: 221; WaS1: 80

"Playing Old Sledge for the Presidency" ASF: 221

"Rare Ripe Garden Seed" ASF: 221

"A Snake-Bit Irishman" ASF: 221

"Sut Lovengood at Bull's Gap" ASF: 221

"Sut Lovengood Blown Up" ASF: 221

"Sut Lovengood Escapes Assassination" ASF: 221

"Sut Lovengood, on the Puritan Yankee" ASF: 221

"Sut Lovengood Reports What Bob Dawson Said, After Marrying a Substitute" ASF: 221

"Sut Lovengood Travels with Old Abe" ASF: 221

"Sut Lovengood's Adventures in New York" ASF: 221

"Sut Lovengood's Big Dinner Story" ASF: 221

"Sut Lovengood's Big Music Box Story" ASF: 222

"Sut Lovengood's Chest Story" ASF: 222

"Sut Lovengood's Daddy 'Acting Horse'" ASF: 222

"Sut Lovengood's Hark from the Tombs Story" ASF: 222

"Sut Lovengood's Shirt" ASF: 222

"Sut Lovingood Allegory" ASF: 222

"Sut Lovingood Come to Life" ASF: 222

"Sut Lovingood's Dream: Tartarus and What He Saw There" ASF: 222

"Sut Lovingood's Hog Ride" ASF: 222

"Sut Lovingood's Love-Feast of Varmints Held at Nashville, March 28th and 29th" ASF: 222

"Well! Dad's Dead" ASF: 223

HARRIS, Joel Chandler

General AF: 120-121; ALL: 116-117; ASF: 225; LCAB: 81

"Ananias" Wa: 271

"At Teague Poteet's" ASF: 224

"Azalia" ASF: 224

Brer Rabbit Ma: 853

"The Cause of the Difficulty" Wa: 271

"The Comedy of War" ASF: 224

"Free Joe and the Rest of the World" ASF: 224; Wa: 271

"A Ghost Story" ASF: 224

"Little Compton" ASF: 224; Wa: 271

"Mingo" ASF: 224; Wa: 271

"Mr. Rabbit Grossly Deceives Mr. Fox" ASF: 224

"Mombi: Her Friends and Her Enemies" ASF: 224; Wa: 271

Nights with Uncle Remus AF: 121

"A Story About the Little Rabbits" ASF: 224

Tales of Uncle Remus Ma: 853-854

"Tar-Baby" ASF: 225

"Where's Duncan?" Wa: 271

Harris, John Beynon see WYNDHAM, John

HARRIS, Mark

General CN: 248; JW: 231; LCAB: 82; Ma: 855; Po: 1446

Something About a Soldier CN: 248

Trumpet to the World CN: 248; LCAB: 82

Wake Up, Stupid CN: 248

HARRIS, Mrs. Helen Webb

Frederick Douglas BAP: 101

Ganifrede BAP: 101

HARRIS, Neil

General MBA: 110

Cop and Blow ADC: 141;

MBA: 110
Players Inn ADC: 141;
    MBA: 110-111
So Nice, They Named It Twice
    ADC: 141; MBA: 111
Straight from the Ghetto
    MBA: 111
HARRIS, Ted
    Silhouettes ADC: 141
HARRIS, William Chandler
    General LCAB: 82
HARRIS, Wilson
    General WIL: 42-46
    The Age of the Rainmakers
        WIL: 50
    Ascent to Omai WIL: 49-50
    Black Marsden WIL: 51
    Companions of the Day and
        Night WIL: 51
    "Couvade" Wa: 271
    Eternity to Season WIL: 46
    The Eye of the Scarecrow
        ENES2: 126; WIL: 48
    The Far Journey of Oudin
        WIL: 47
    Fetish WIL: 46
    Heartland WIL: 48
    "Kanaima" Wa: 271
    Palace of the Peacock WIL:
        46-47
    The Secret Ladder WIL:
        47-48
    The Sleepers of Roraima
        WIL: 50
    Tumatumari WIL: 49
    The Waiting Room WIL: 48-
        49
    The Whole Armour WIL: 47
HARRISON, Eric
    General Po: 1446
HARRISON, Harry
    General LCAB: 82
HARRISON, Henry Sydnor
    General Po: 1446
HARRISON, James
    An Exhortation to the Scots
        LCAB: 82
HARRISON, Paul Carter
    General AAPD: 379; MBA:
        111
    Doctor Jazz MBA: 111
    _____ and Coleridge-Taylor
        PERKINSON
    The Great Mac Daddy ADC:
        141; BAP: 102-103;
        BAW: 370; MBA: 111-112

HARRISON, Susie Frances ["SERA-
        NUS"]
    General ECL: 142
HARRISON, William
    General SC: 60
HARROWER, Elizabeth
    General MAP: 182
    The Long Prospect MAP: 182
    The Watch Tower MAP: 182
HARRY, Myriam
    L'Ile de volupté Ke: 97
HARRY THE MINSTREL
    General Ai: 33
HARSA
    Nagananda DC2: 176
HARSDOERFFER, George
    Frauenzimmer-Gespraechspiele
        DC2: 176
HART (BECKWITH), Julia C.
    General ECL: 143-144
HART, Moss
    General Br: 286; JW: 380;
        Lon: 60; MD: 133; MDAE:
        261
    Christopher Blake ADC: 141-
        142; Br: 286; MD: 133
    The Climate of Eden ADC:
        142; Br: 286; DC1: 88;
        MD: 133
    Light Up the Sky ADC: 142;
        MD: 133
    _____ and Irving BERLIN
    As Thousands Cheer ADC:
        142
    Face the Music ADC: 142
    _____ and George S. KAUFMAN
    The American Way ADC: 142-
        143
    The Fabulous Invalid see also
        KAUFMAN, George S. and
        Moss HART ADC: 143
    George Washington Slept Here
        ADC: 143
    I'd Rather Be Right see also
        KAUFMAN, George S. and
        Moss HART ADC: 143
    The Man Who Came to Dinner
        see also KAUFMAN, George
        S. and Moss HART ADC:
        143
    Merrily We Roll Along see also
        KAUFMAN, George S. and
        Moss HART ADC: 144
    Once in a Lifetime see also
        KAUFMAN, George S. and
        Moss HART ADC: 144

You Can't Take It with You
see also KAUFMAN,
George S. and Moss HART
ADC: 144; Lon: 60; Po:
1447
_____ and Cole PORTER
Jubilee ADC: 144
_____ and David ROSE
Winged Victory ADC: 145;
MD: 133
_____, Kurt WEILL, and Ira
GERSHWIN
Lady in the Dark ADC:
145; Br: 286; DC1: 89;
MD: 133
HART, Richard
"Letter from Madrid" PE:
216
HART, Stanley
Some of My Best Friends
ADC: 145
HARTE, Bret
General AF: 124-125; ALL:
117-118; AN: 105; ASF:
227; C1a: 109; LCAB:
82
Gabriel Conroy AN: 105
"High-Water Mark" ASF:
226
"The Idyl of Red Gulch"
Wa: 271
"In the Carquinez Woods"
ASF: 226
"An Ingénue of the Sierras"
ASF: 226
"The Judgment of Bolinas
Plain" ASF: 226
"The Luck of Roaring Camp"
AF: 124; ASF: 226;
Ma: 856; Wa: 271-272
"The Mystery of the Hacienda"
ASF: 226
"The Outcasts of Poker Flat"
ASF: 226; Wa: 272
"The Passing of Enriquez"
ASF: 226; Wa: 272
"The Right Eye of the Com-
mander" ASF: 226
"The Story of a Mine" ASF:
226
"Tennessee's Partner" ASF:
226-227; Wa: 272; WaS1:
80
"Thankful Blossom" ASF:
227
"What Happened at the Fonda"

ASF: 227
HARTLEY, Leslie Poles
General BN2: 59; CFAE: 190;
CN: 248-249; LCAB: 82;
Po: 1447-1448; Ri: 450-452;
Sch: 128
The Betrayal ENES2: 126
The Boat CN: 249; ENES2:
126; Ri: 450
The Brickfield ENES2: 126
"Conrad and the Dragon"
WaS1: 80
"The Crossways" WaS1: 80
Eustace and Hilda see also
Eustace and Hilda Trilogy
CN: 249; ENES2: 126
Eustace and Hilda Trilogy
CN: 249; ENES2: 126; Ri:
450, 452
"The Face" Ri: 450
Facial Justice CN: 249;
ENES1: 119; ENES2: 126;
Ri: 453
"Fall in at the Double" WaS1:
80
The Go-Between CFAE: 190;
CN: 249; ENES2: 126;
Po: 1449; Ri: 450, 452-453
The Harness Room ENES2:
126
The Hireling CN: 250; ENES2:
126
"The Killing Bottles" WaS1:
80
The Love-Adept ENES2: 126
My Fellow Devils CN: 250;
ENES2: 127
My Sisters' Keeper ENES2:
127; Ri: 450
"Pains and Pleasures" WaS1:
80
A Perfect Woman CN: 250;
ENES2: 127; Ri: 453
"Please Do Not Touch" WaS1:
80
Poor Clare ENES2: 127
"The Prayer" WaS1: 80
"The Pylon" WaS1: 80
The Shrimp and the Anemone
see also Eustace and Hilda
Trilogy CN: 250; ENES2:
127; Ri: 452-453
Simonetta Perkins CN: 250;
ENES2: 127
The Sixth Heaven see also
Eustace and Hilda Trilogy

CN: 250
"Someone in the Lift" WaS1: 80
"A Summons" WaS1: 80
"Travelling Grave" Wa: 272
"A Very Present Help" Ri: 450
The Will and the Way ENES2: 127
HARTLEY, Marsden
General Po: 1449
Androscoggin Po: 1449
HARTOG, Jan de
The Inspector ENE: 155
HARTUNG, Hugo
General Po: 1449
HARVEY, Gabriel
General Hen: 106; SC: 61
"Gloss" PE: 216
"Sonnet: Gorgon, or the Wonderful Year" PE: 216
"A Stanza Declarative: To the Lovers of Admirable Works" PE: 216
"The Writer's Postscript: Or a Friendly Caveat to the Second Shakerley of Powles" PE: 216
HASEK, Jaroslav
The Good Soldier Schweik Fi: 453; Ke: 412; Po: 1450
HASENCLEVER, Walter
General Br: 286; Po: 1450
Antigone Br: 286; DC2: 177; Po: 1450
Beyond [Jenseits] Br: 286
"Christoph Kolumbus oder die Entdeckung Amerikas" Po: 1450
Ehen werden im Himmel geschlossen DC2: 177; Po: 1450
Her Man on Wax [Napoleon Greift Ein] Br: 286; Po: 1450
Jenseits see Beyond
"Konflikt in Assyrien" Po: 1450
Men [Die Menschen] Br: 286
Napoleon Greift Ein see Her Man on Wax
The Saviour [Der Retter] Br: 287
The Son [Der Sohn] Br:

287; Po: 1450
HASSALL, Christopher
Christ's Comet Br: 287
HASTINGS, Michael
Lee Harvey Oswald ADC: 145
HATCH, James and C. Bernard JACKSON
Fly Black Bird [The Blackbird] BAP: 103, 120; MBA: 112
HAUFF, Wilhelm
"Die Betterin vom Pont des Arts" Wa: 272
Lichtenstein Ke: 274
"Othello" Wa: 272
"The Picture of the Kaiser" Wa: 272
HAUGHTON, William
General Log: 261
HAUN, Mildred
"Barshia's Horse He Made, It Flew" Wa: 272
HAUPTMANN, William
Comanche Café ADC: 146
Domino Courts ADC: 146
Heat ADC: 146
HAUPTMANN, Carl
Marianne DC2: 177; Po: 1458
HAUPTMANN, Gerhart
General Br: 287-288; MD: 134-136; Po: 1450-1457
Agamemnon [Agamemnon's Death; Agamemnons Tod] Br: 289; DC2: 177; Po: 1862
And Pippa Dances [Und Pippa Tanzt] Br: 293; MD: 139
Der Arme Heinrich see Poor Heinrich
The Assumption of Hannele [Hanneles Himmelfahrt] Br: 289; DC2: 179; MD: 138
Atlantis Ke: 274
Atrides Tetralogy [Die Atriden] MD: 136; Po: 1457
Bahnwärter Thiel see Flagman Thiel
The Beaver Coat [The Thieves' Comedy; Der Biberpelz] Br: 289, 293; DC2: 177; EDC: 242; Ma: 857; MD: 136; Po: 1455, 1458
Before Sunrise [Before Dawn; Vor Sonnenaufgang] Br: 289; DC2: 181; EDC: 242; MD: 139
Before Sunset [Vor Sonnenun-

tergang] EDC: 242; MD: 139; Po: 1463-1464

Biberpelz see The Beaver Coat

Bow of Ulysses Br: 289; DC2: 177

"Carnival" Wa: 272; WaS1: 81

Charlemagne's Hostage [Kaiser Karls Geisel] MD: 138

Colleague Crampton [Kollege Crampton] Br: 289; MD: 138

The Coming of Peace see The Reconciliation

The Commemoration Masque [Festspiel in Deutschen Reimen] Br: 290; DC2: 178; MD: 137

The Conflagration [The Red Cock; Der Rote Hahn] Br: 292; DC2: 181; EDC: 242; MD: 139; Po: 1455

The Darkness [Die Finsternisse] Br: 290; DC2: 178; EDC: 242; MD: 137

The Daughter of the Cathedral [Die Tochter der Kathedrale] DC2: 181; EDC: 242

Dorothea Angermann DC2: 177; EDC: 242

Drayman Henschel see Henschel the Teamster

Einsame Menschen see Lonely Men

Elektra Br: 290; DC2: 178; EDC: 242-243; MD: 137; Po: 1862

Erbe des Tiberius MD: 137

Fasching Fi: 319-320

The Feast of Peace see The Reconciliation

Festspiel in Deutschen Reimen see The Commemoration Masque

Der Finsternisse see The Darkness

Flagman Thiel [Signalman Thiel; Bahnwärter Thiel] Fi: 319; Ke: 274; Wa: 273; WaS1: 81

The Flight of Gabriel Schilling [Gabriel Schillings Flucht] Br: 290; MD: 137

Florian Geyer Br: 290; DC2: 178; EDC: 243; MD: 137

The Fool in Christ [Der Narr in Christo Emanuel Quint] Fi: 320; Ke: 274-275; Po: 1461-1462

Das Friedensfest see The Reconciliation

Fuhrmann Henschel see Henschel the Teamster

Gabriel Schillings Flucht see The Flight of Gabriel Schilling

Germanen und Romer Br: 290; DC2: 179; EDC: 243; MD: 137; Po: 1459

The Golden Harp [Die Goldene Harfe] EDC: 243; MD: 137

The Great Dream [Der Grosse Traum] Po: 1452, 1459

Griselda Br: 291; DC2: 179

Hamlet EDC: 243

Hamlet in Wittenberg EDC: 243; MD: 137-138

Hanneles Himmelfahrt see The Assumption of Hannele

Henry of Avë see Poor Heinrich

Henschel the Teamster [Drayman Henschel; Fuhrmann Henschel] Br: 291; EDC: 242; MD: 137

Herbert Englemann see also ZUCKMAYER, Carl DC2: 179; MD: 138; Po: 1460

"The Heretic of Soana" ["Der Ketzer von Soana"] DC2: 180; Po: 1460; Wa: 273

Im Wirbel der Berufung Ke: 275

Indipohdi Br: 291; MD: 138

Die Insel der Grossen Mutter Ke: 275

Iphigenia in Aulis [Iphigenie in Delphi] see also Elektra Br: 291; DC2: 179-180; EDC: 243; MD: 138; Po: 1460, 1862

Kaiser Karls Geisel see Charlemagne's Hostage

"Der Ketzer von Soana" see "The Heretic of Soana"

Kollege Crampton see Colleague Crampton

Lonely Men [Lonely Lives;

Einsame Menschen] Br:
291-292; DC2: 177-178;
EDC: 243-244; MD: 136-
137; Po: 1458

Magnus Garbe DC2: 180;
MD: 138; Po: 1461

Marianne MD: 138

Michael Kramer Br: 292;
DC2: 180; EDC: 244;
MD: 138; Po: 1461

The Miracle of the Sea [Das
Meerwunder] Ke: 275;
Wa: 273

Der Narr in Christo see
The Fool in Christ

Peter Brauer MD: 138

"Phantom" Wa: 273

"Pima grüsst zum Geburstag"
Po: 1462

Poor Henrich [Henry of Ave;
Der Arme Heinrich] Br:
292; DC2: 180; MD: 136

Promethidenlos DC2: 180

The Rats [Die Ratten] Br:
292; DC2: 180; EDC:
244; MD: 138

The Reconciliation [The Feast
of Peace; The Coming of
Peace; Das Friedensfest]
Br: 290; DC2: 178-179;
EDC: 244; MD: 137; Po:
1459

The Red Cock see The
Conflagration

Rose Bernd Br: 292; EDC:
244; MD: 138

Der Rote Hahn see The
Conflagration

Schluck und Jau Br: 292;
MD: 139; Po: 1462

"Der Schuss im Park" Wa:
273

Die Schwarze Maske MD:
139

Signalman Thiel see Flagman
Thiel

The Sunken Bell [Die Ver-
sunkene Glocke] Br:
292-293; DC2: 181; EDC:
244; Ma: 857; MD: 139;
Po: 1463

The Thieves' Comedy see
The Beaver Coat

Die Tochter der Kathedrale
see The Daughter of the
Cathedral

Und Pippa Tanzt see And Pippa
Dances

Veland EDC: 244; MD: 139

Die Versunkene Glocke see
The Sunken Bell

Vor Sonnenaufgang see Before
Sunrise

Vor Sonnenuntergang see Before Sunset

The Weavers [Die Weber] Br:
293; DC2: 181-182; EDC:
245; Ma: 857-858; MD: 139-
140; Po: 1464

The White Savior [The White Redeemer; Der Weisse Heiland]
Br: 293; MD: 140

HAUSTED, Peter
General LJCD: 244-245
The Rival Friends DC1: 89
Senile Odium DC1: 89

HAUTEROCHE, Noel
Les Bourgeoises de Qualite
DC2: 182

HAVEL, Vaclav
General Br: 293
The Garden Party [Zahradni
Slavnost] Br: 294
The Memorandum [Notification;
Vyrozumeni] Br: 294; DC2:
182

HAVIGHURST, Walter
General Po: 1464

HAVOC, June
Marathon '33 ADC: 146

HAWES, Stephen
General SC: 62
The Pastime of Pleasure SC:
62

HAWES, William P.
"A Bear Story and No Mistake!"
ASF: 228
"A Shark Story" ASF: 228

HAWKES, John
General ASF: 228-229; CFAE:
192; CN: 250-251; LCAB:
82; MDAE: 263-264; Ne:
55; Po: 1465-1466
The Beetle Leg CN: 251
The Cannibal CFAE: 192; CN:
251; Ne: 55; Po: 1467
"Charivari" ASF: 228; Wa:
273
"Death of an Airman" ASF:
228
"The Goose on the Grave" ASF:
228; CN: 251; Wa: 273

"The Grandmother" Wa: 273
The Innocent Party MDAE: 264
The Lime Twig CFAE: 192; CN: 252; Ne: 55; Po: 1465
"The Nearest Cemetery" Wa: 273
"The Owl" ASF: 228; CN: 252; Wa: 273
Second Skin CFAE: 192; CN: 252
"The Traveler" ASF: 228
Hawkins, Anthony Hope see HOPE, Anthony
HAWKINS, Odie
General BAF: 142
HAWKINS, Sir John
General Hen: 65
HAWTHORNE, Julian
General ASF: 230
"The Minister's Oath" ASF: 230
HAWTHORNE, Nathaniel
General AF: 130-139; ALL: 118-126; AN: 111-118; ASF: 253-265; Cla: 39-42; Ho: 57-69, 146-148; LCAB: 82-83
"Alice Doane's Appeal" ASF: 230-231; Ma: 859-860; SFC: 70-71; Wa: 274; WaS1: 81
"The Ambitious Guest" ASF: 231; Ma: 860; SFC: 71; Wa: 274; WaS1: 81
The American Notebooks Ma: 860-861
"The Antique Ring" ASF: 231; Wa: 275
"The Artist of the Beautiful" ASF: 231-232; Ma: 861-862; SFC: 71; Wa: 275-276; WaS1: 81
"The Battle-Omen" ASF: 232
"The Birthmark" ASF: 233; Ma: 862-863; SFC: 71-72; Wa: 276-277; WaS1: 81
The Blithedale Romance AF: 131-132, 135-136, 138; AN: 105-106; Cla: 39; Ho: 60-69, 146-148; LCAB: 83; Ma: 863-865; Po: 534, 4145
"A Book of Autographs" ASF: 233
"The Canterbury Pilgrims" ASF: 234; Ma: 865; SFC: 72; Wa: 277
"The Celestial Railroad" ASF: 234; Ma: 865-866; SFC: 72; Wa: 278
"The Chimaera" ASF: 234
"Chippings with a Chisel" ASF: 234; Wa: 278
"The Christmas Banquet" ASF: 234; Ma: 866-867; SFC: 72-73; Wa: 278
"Circe's Palace" ASF: 234
"The Custom House" AF: 133; Ho: 68-69; Ma: 867-868
"David Swann: A Fantasy" ASF: 234; Wa: 278
"The Devil in Manuscript" ASF: 234; Wa: 278; WaS1: 81
Doctor Grimshawe's Secret AN: 106-107; Ma: 868
"Dr. Heidegger's Experiment" ASF: 234; Ma: 868-869; SFC: 73; Wa: 278-279
A Dolliver Romance AN: 107
"Drowne's Wooden Image" ASF: 234-235; Ma: 869; SFC: 73; Wa: 279; WaS1: 81-82
"Earth's Holocaust" ASF: 235; Ma: 869-870; SFC: 73; Wa: 279; WaS1: 82
"Edward Randolph's Portrait" ASF: 235; SFC: 73; Wa: 279; WaS1: 82
"Egotism; or, The Bosom Serpent" ASF: 235-236; Ma: 870-871; SFC: 73; Wa: 279
"Endicott and the Red Cross" ASF: 236; Ma: 871; SFC: 73; Wa: 279-280; WaS1: 82
The English Notebooks Ma: 871-872
"Ethan Brand" ASF: 236-237; Ma: 872-873; SFC: 73-74; Wa: 280-282; WaS1: 82
"Fancy's Show Box" ASF: 237; SFC: 74-75; Wa: 282; WaS1: 82
Fanshawe AN: 107; Ho: 61, 147-148; Ma: 873-874
"Feathertop" ASF: 237; Ma: 874; SFC: 75; Wa: 282; WaS1: 82
"Fire Worship" SFC: 75; Wa: 282-283

"Fragments from a Journal of
a Solitary Man" ASF:
237; SFC: 75
"The Gentle Boy" ALL: 125;
ASF: 237-238; Ma: 875-
876; SFC: 75; Wa: 283
"The Golden Fleece" ASF:
238
"The Golden Touch" ASF:
239
"The Gorgon's Head" ASF:
238
"Graves and Goblins" ASF:
238
"The Gray Champion" ASF:
238; Ma: 876; SFC: 75-
76; Wa: 283-284; WaS1:
82
"The Great Carbuncle" ASF:
238; Ma: 876-877; SFC:
76; Wa: 284
"The Great Stone Face" ASF:
238-239; Ma: 877; SFC:
76; Wa: 284
"The Hall of Fantasy" ASF:
239; Cla: 41; SFC: 76;
Wa: 284
"The Haunted Mind" ASF:
239; SFC: 76; Wa: 284-
285; WaS1: 82
"The Hollow of the Three
Hills" ASF: 239; Ma:
877-878; SFC: 76; Wa:
285; WaS1: 82
The House of the Seven
Gables AF: 130-135; AN:
107-108; Ho: 60-63, 65-
69, 147-148; LCAB: 83-
84; Ma: 878-879
"Howe's Masquerade" ASF:
239; Wa: 285; WaS1: 82
"The Intelligence Office"
ASF: 239; SFC: 76; Wa:
285
"The Interrupted Nuptials"
ASF: 239
"John Inglefield's Thanksgiv-
ing" ASF: 240; SFC:
76
"Lady Eleanor's Mantle" ASF:
240; Ma: 879-880; SFC:
76; Wa: 285; WaS1: 82-
83
"Legends of the Province
House" Ma: 880
"The Lily's Quest" ASF: 240;

SFC: 76; Wa: 285
"Little Annie's Ramble" ASF:
240
"Main-Street" ASF: 240
"The Man of Adamant" ASF:
240; Ma: 880-881; SFC: 76;
Wa: 286
The Marble Faun AF: 130-131,
133, 136-137, 139; ALL:
126; Cla: 39, 42; Ho: 59-
69, 147; Ma: 881-882; Po:
1802, 1819, 1821-1822
"The Maypole of Merry Mount"
ALL: 125; ASF: 241;
LCAB: 84; Ma: 882-883;
SFC: 77; Wa: 286-287;
WaS1: 83
"The Minister's Black Veil"
ASF: 241-242; Ma: 883-885;
SFC: 77; Wa: 287-288; WaS1:
83
"The Minotaur" ASF: 242
"The Miraculous Pitcher" ASF:
242
"Mr. Higginbotham's Catastrophe"
ASF: 242; Ma: 885; Wa:
288; WaS1: 83
"Monsieur du Miroir" ASF:
243; SFC: 77; Wa: 288-289
Mosses from an Old Manse Ma:
885-886
"Mrs. Bullfrog" ASF: 243;
SFC: 77; Wa: 288
"My Kinsman, Major Molineux"
AF: 134; ASF: 243-245;
Cla: 40; LCAB: 84; Ma:
886-887; SFC: 77-78; Wa:
289-291; WaS1: 83
"The New Adam and Eve" ASF:
245; SFC: 78; Wa: 291
"Night Sketches" ASF: 245
"The Old Apple Dealer" ASF:
245; Wa: 291
"Old Esther Dudley" ASF:
245; Wa: 291-292; WaS1: 83
"The Old Manse" ASF: 246
"Old News" ["The Old Tory"]
ASF: 246
"An Old Woman's Tale" Wa:
292
"P.'s Correspondence" ASF:
246
"The Paradise of Children"
ASF: 246
"Peter Goldthwaite's Treasure"
ASF: 246; SFC: 78; Wa:

292; WaS1: 83
"The Pomegranate Seeds"
ASF: 246
"The Procession of Life"
ASF: 246; SFC: 78; Wa:
292
"The Prophetic Pictures"
ASF: 246; Ma: 887-888;
SFC: 78; Wa: 292; WaS1:
84
"The Pygmies" ASF: 246
"Rappaccini's Daughter" ASF:
246-248; Ma: 888-889; SFC:
78-79; Wa: 292-294; WaS1:
84
"Roger Malvin's Burial" ASF:
248-249; Ma: 889-890;
SFC: 79-80; Wa: 294-295;
WaS1: 84
The Scarlet Letter AF: 131-
136, 138-139; AN: 109-
111; Cla: 39-42; Ho: 58-
69, 146-148; LCAB: 83-84;
Ma: 891-892; Po: 1732,
4131
"A Select Party" ASF: 250;
SFC: 80; Wa: 295
Septimius Felton AN: 111;
Ma: 892
"The Seven Vagabonds" ASF:
250; Wa: 295
"The Shaker Bridal" ASF:
250; SFC: 80; Wa: 295-
296
"Sights from a Steeple" ASF:
250
"Sketches from Memory" ASF:
250
"The Snow Image" ASF:
250; SFC: 80; Wa: 296
"Sunday at Home" ASF:
250; SFC: 80; Wa: 296
"Sylph Etherege" Wa: 296
"The Three Golden Apples"
ASF: 250
"The Threefold Destiny"
ASF: 250; SFC: 80; Wa:
296
"The Toll-Gatherer's Day"
ASF: 250
Twice-Told Tales Ma: 892-
893
"The Village Uncle" ASF:
250-251; Wa: 296
"A Virtuoso's Collection"
ASF: 251; SFC: 80; Wa:

296
"Wakefield" ASF: 251; Ma:
893-894; SFC: 80; Wa: 296-
297; WaS1: 84
"The Wedding Knell" ASF:
251; Wa: 297; WaS1: 84
"The White Old Maid" ASF:
251; Wa: 297
"The Wives of the Dead" ASF:
251; SFC: 80; Wa: 297
"Young Goodman Brown" AF:
134, 137; ASF: 251-253;
Cla: 40; LCAB: 84; Ma:
894-895; SFC: 80-81; Wa:
297-301; WaS1: 85
HAY, George Campbell
General Ai: 307
HAY, Ian
Hattie Stowe Br: 294
HAY, John
General ASF: 267
"The Blood Seedling" Wa:
301; WaS1: 85
"The Foster-Brother" Wa:
301; WaS1: 85
"Jim Bludso" PE: 216
"Kane and Abel" Wa: 301;
WaS1: 85
"The Minstrel" ASF: 267
"Shelby Cabell" Wa: 301;
WaS1: 85
HAY, John MacDougall
General Ai: 219
Gillespie Ai: 219
HAY, Julius
General Br: 294
HAY, William Gosse
General MAP: 185-189
The Escape of the Notorious Sir
William Heans MAP: 185-
189; Po: 1467
HAYCOX, Ernest
General AN: 118; ASF: 267
HAYDEN, John
Lost Horizons ADC: 146
HAYDEN, Robert Earl
General AAPD: 184; AAW:
57; BAW: 371-372; ICBAP:
61
"The Diver" AAPD: 184; PE:
216
"Frederick Douglass" AAPD:
184; PE: 216
"Full Moon" PE: 216
"The Peacock Room" PE: 216
"The Rabbi" PE: 216

HAYDEN, Sterling
  General LCAB: 84
HAYES, Alfred
  General CN: 252
  All Thy Conquests CN: 252
  The Girl on the Via Flaminia
    CN: 252
  "The Shrunken Head" PE:
    216
HAYES, Joseph
  Calculated Risk ADC: 146
  The Desperate Hours ADC:
    146-147; Br: 294
  Is Anyone Listening? ADC:
    147
HAYLEY, William
  General Li: 202
HAYNES, Lemuel
  General LCAB: 84
HAYWOOD, Eliza
  General Be: 160
  Betsy Thoughtless Be: 160;
    ENES1: 119; ENES2: 127
  Idalia ENES1: 119
  Love in Excess ENES1: 119
  Memoirs of Utopia ENES1:
    119
HAZAZ, Haiyim
  "A Flowing River" Wa: 301
  "The Sermon" Wa: 301
HAZELTON, George C.
  Mistress Nell ADC: 147
  ———— and Harry BENRIMO
    The Yellow Jacket ADC:
    147
HAZLITT, William
  General Fog: 34; LCAB:
    84; Ma: 896-897
  Liber Amoris Ma: 897-898
HEAD, Bessie
  General BALE: 306-307
HEAD, Richard
  The English Rogue ENES1:
    119
HEANEY, Seamus
  General Po: 1467
HEARD, Josephine Henderson
  General BAW: 372
HEARD, Nathan C.
  General BAF: 142
  A Cold Fire Burning BAF:
    143
  Howard Street BAF: 143;
    BAW: 373
  To Reach a Dream BAF:
    143; BAW: 373

HEARN, Lafcadio
  General ALL: 126-128; AN:
    118-119; ASF: 268; LCAB:
    85; Po: 1467-1469
  Chita: A Memory of Last Island
    Ma: 899; Po: 1469
  Glimpses of Unfamiliar Japan
    Ma: 899
  "Karma" ASF: 267
  "Of a Promise Kept" ASF:
    267
  "A Passional Karma" ASF: 267
  "The Story of Itō Norisuké"
    ASF: 267
  "The Story of Kōgi the Priest"
    ASF: 267
HEARNE, John
  General WIL: 51-53
  The Autumn Equinox WIL: 55
  The Faces of Love WIL: 54-55
  The Land of the Living WIL:
    55-56
  Stranger at the Gate WIL: 54
  Voices Under the Window WIL:
    53-54
HEATH, Roy A.K.
  A Man Come Home WIL: 56
HEATH-STUBBS, John
  "Pharos" Po: 1469
HEAVYSEGE, Charles
  General ECL: 146
  Saul: A Drama in Three Parts
    ECL: 146
HEBBEL, Friedrich
  Agnes Bernauer DC2: 182
  "Anna" Wa: 301
  "Barbier Zitterlein" Wa: 301
  "The Cow" Wa: 302; WaS1:
    85
  Gyges und Sein Ring DC2:
    182
  Herodes und Mariamne DC2:
    182-183
  Maria Magdalena DC2: 183;
    LCAB: 85
  Moloch DC2: 183
  "Der Rubin" Wa: 302
  "Schnock" Wa: 302
HEBERT, Anne
  General Po: 1469
  "Les Chambres de bois" Wa:
    302
  "Un grand mariage" Wa: 302
  "La Mort de Stella" Wa: 302
  "Le Printemps de Catherine"
    Wa: 302

"Le Torrent" Wa: 302
HECHT, Anthony
General ICBAP: 61; Po:
1470
"Ostia Antica" PE: 216; Po:
1470
HECHT, Ben
General AN: 119; JW: 237;
LCAB: 85; Po: 1470
A Flag Is Born ADC: 147;
MD: 140
Lily of the Valley ADC: 147
To Quito and Back ADC:
147-148; Br: 295; DC1:
89; MD: 140
Winkelberg ADC: 148
_____ and Gene FOWLER
The Great Magoo ADC: 148;
MD: 140
_____ and Charles MacARTHUR
The Front Page ADC: 148;
DC1: 89; MD: 140
Ladies and Gentlemen ADC:
148-149
Swan Song ADC: 149; MD:
140
Twentieth Century ADC:
149
HEDDEN, Worth Tuttle
Love Is a Wound Po: 1470-
1471
HEGARTY, Walter
The Price of Chips ENES2:
127
HEGGEN, Thomas
General ASF: 268; LCAB:
85
"Night Watch" SFC: 81;
Wa: 302
_____ and Joshua LOGAN
Mister Roberts ADC: 149;
Br: 295; DC1: 89
HEIDENSTAM, Verner von
Saint Bridget's Pilgrimage
Ke: 352
The Tree of the Folkungs
Ke: 352
HEIFNER, Jack
Vanities ADC: 150
HEIJERMANS, Hermann
General Br: 295; MD: 140
Ghetto Br: 295
The Good Hope [Op Hoop van
Zegen] Br: 295; MD:
141
Ora et Labora Br: 295

HEINE, Heinrich
General LCAB: 85
"Aus den Memoiren des Herrn
von Schnabelewopski" see
"From the Memoirs of Herr
von Schnabelewopski"
"The Baths of Lucca" WaS1:
85
Das Buch Le Grand Fi: 320
"Florentine Night" WaS1: 85
"From the Memoirs of Herr von
Schnabelewopski" Fi: 320;
WaS1: 85
"Die Harzreise" WaS1: 85
"The Journey from Munich to
Genoa" WaS1: 86
"The Rabbi of Bacherach"
WaS1: 86
HEINESEN, William
"Arcadian Afternoon" Wa: 302
"Ascension" Wa: 302
"Atalanta" Wa: 302
"The Ballad of Double-Simon and
Kildse-Kalsa" Wa: 303
The Black Pot Fi: 404; Ke:
352
"Doda" Wa: 303
"Don Juan of the Blubber
Works" Wa: 303
"Gamaliel's Bewitchment" Wa:
303
The Good Hope Fi: 404
"The Gryla" Wa: 303
"The Heavens Smile" Wa: 303
"The Hour of the Wolf" Wa:
303
"Knives" Wa: 303
"Leonard and Lenora" Wa: 303
The Lost Musicians Fi: 404
"The Madman's Garden" Wa:
303
"The Modern Age" Wa: 303
"The Moon over Mount Horeb"
Wa: 303
Mother Pleiades Fi: 404
"The Night of the Storm" Wa:
303
Noatun Fi: 404
"The Rush of the River" Wa:
303
"Smoking Mirror" Wa: 303
"The Soul" Wa: 303
Stormy Daybreak Fi: 404
"The Story of the Poet Lin Pe
and His Tame Crane" Wa:
303

Tarnet ved Verdens Ende
   Fi: 404
"Tartaros" Wa: 304
"The Virgin Birth" Wa: 304
"The Winged Darkness" Wa:
   304; WaS1: 86
HEINLEIN, Robert Anson
   General ASF: 268; LCAB:
      85
   "All You Zombies" ASF:
      268; Wa: 304
   "And He Built a Crooked
      House" WaS1: 86
   "Blowups Happen" Wa: 304
   "By His Bootstraps" ASF:
      268; Wa: 304; WaS1: 86
   "Common Sense" ASF: 268;
      Wa: 304; WaS1: 86
   "Coventry" ASF: 268; Wa:
      304; WaS1: 86
   "Destination Moon" Wa: 304
   "The Devil Makes the Law"
      see "Magic Inc."
   "The Future Revisited" Wa:
      304
   "Gentlemen, Be Seated"
      WaS1: 86
   "The Green Hills of Earth"
      WaS1: 86
   "Gulf" ASF: 269; Wa: 304
   "If This Goes On" ASF:
      269; Wa: 304; WaS1: 86
   "Jerry Is a Man" Wa: 304
   "Let There Be Light" Wa:
      304
   "Life-Line" ASF: 269; Wa:
      304; WaS1: 86
   "Magic, Inc." ASF: 269;
      WaS1: 86
   "The Man Who Sold the Moon"
      Wa: 304
   "The Man Who Travelled in
      Elephants" WaS1: 86
   "The Menace from Earth"
      Wa: 305
   "Misfit" Wa: 305; WaS1: 86
   "My Object All Sublime" Wa:
      305
   "Requiem" ASF: 269; WaS1:
      86
   "Searchlight" WaS1: 87
   "Sky Lift" WaS1: 87
   "Solution Unsatisfactory"
      ASF: 239; Wa: 305
   "Space Jockey" WaS1: 87
   "They" ASF: 269; Wa: 305;

   WaS1: 87
   "Universe" ASF: 269; Wa:
      305; WaS1: 87
   "The Unpleasant Profession of
      Jonathan Hoag" ASF: 269;
      Wa: 305
   "Waldo" ASF: 269; Wa: 305;
      WaS1: 87
   "We Also Walk Dogs" WaS1: 87
   "The Year of the Jackpot"
      WaS1: 87
HEINSE, Wilhelm
   Ardinghello und die Glückseeli-
      gen Inseln Fi: 320; Ke:
      275
   Laidion Ke: 275
HEIREMANS, Luis Alberto
   General Br: 295
HEISELER, Bernt von
   General Po: 1471
   Philoktet DC2: 183
HEISELER, Henry von
   General Po: 1471
HEISSENBÜTTEL, Helmut
   General Po: 1471
HELIODORUS
   An Aethiopian History see
      UNDERDOWNE, Thomas
      [translator]
HELLER, Joseph
   General CFAE: 193-194; CN:
      253; JW: 240; MDAE: 265
   Catch-22 ADC: 150; CFAE:
      193-194; CN: 253-254; JW:
      240; LCAB: 85; Ma: 900-
      901; MDAE: 265; Po: 1471-
      1475, 2189
   Something Happened JW: 240;
      Ma: 901-902
   We Bombed in New Haven
      ADC: 150; Br: 295; Ma:
      902
HELLMAN, Geoffrey Theodore
   General LCAB: 85
HELLMAN, Lillian
   General Br: 296; JW: 383;
      LCAB: 85-86; Lon: 32; MD:
      141; MDAE: 267-268; Po:
      1475
   Another Part of the Forest
      ADC: 150-151; Br: 296;
      DC1: 89; Ma: 903; MD:
      141; Po: 1475-1476
   The Autumn Garden ADC:
      151; Br: 296; DC1: 89;
      Lon: 32; MD: 141; Po:

1476

The Children's Hour ADC: 151-152; Br: 297; DC1: 89; Ma: 903; MD: 141-142

Days to Come ADC: 152; Br: 297; MD: 142

The Lark ADC: 152; MDAE: 268

The Little Foxes ADC: 152-153; Br: 297; DC1: 90; Ma: 904; MD: 142

Montserrat ADC: 153; DC1: 90; MD: 142

My Mother, My Father and Me ADC: 153

Pentimento Ma: 904

The Searching Wind ADC: 153-154; Br: 297; DC1: 90; MD: 142

Toys in the Attic ADC: 154; Br: 297-298; DC1: 90; LCAB: 86; Lon: 32; Ma: 904-905; MD: 142; Po: 1476

An Unfinished Woman Ma: 905

Watch on the Rhine ADC: 154; Br: 298; Ma: 905; MD: 142

_____, Leonard BERNSTEIN, and Richard WILBUR

Candide ADC: 155

HELWIG, David

"The Best Name of Silence" PE: 217

HEMINGE, William

The Fatal Contract DC1: 90

The Jewes Tragedy DC1: 90

HEMINGWAY, Ernest

General ALL: 128-134; AN: 122-127; ASF: 288-298; CN: 254-264; ICBAP: 61; LCAB: 86-87; Ne: 56-63; Po: 1476-1511; Wo: 120-123

Across the River and Into the Trees AN: 119; CN: 265-266; LCAB: 87; Ne: 61-62; Po: 1512

"After the Storm" ASF: 270; Po: 1512-1513; SFC: 82; Wa: 305; WaS1: 87

"An Alpine Idyll" ASF: 270; Po: 1513; SFC: 82; Wa: 305-306; WaS1: 87

"Banal Story" ASF: 270; Wa: 306

"The Battler" ASF: 270; Ma: 906; Po: 1513; SFC: 82; Wa: 306; WaS1: 87

"Big Two-Hearted River" ASF: 270-271; Ma: 906-908; Po: 1513-1514; SFC: 82; Wa: 306-307; WaS1: 87

"The Butterfly and the Tank" ASF: 271; Wa: 307

"A Canary for One" ASF: 271; Po: 1514; SFC: 82; Wa: 307-308

"The Capital of the World" ASF: 271-272; Po: 1514-1515; SFC: 82; Wa: 308; WaS1: 87

"Cat in the Rain" ASF: 272; Po: 1515; SFC: 82-83; Wa: 308; WaS1: 87

"Che Ti Dice La Patria?" ASF: 272; SFC: 83; Wa: 308

"A Clean Well-Lighted Place" ASF: 272-274; LCAB: 87; Ma: 908-909; Po: 1515-1517; SFC: 83; Wa: 308-310; WaS1: 88

"Cross-Country Snow" ASF: 274; SFC: 83; Wa: 310

"The Dangerous Summer" Po: 1499; Wa: 310

"A Day's Wait" ASF: 274; Po: 1517; Wa: 310-311

Death in the Afternoon Po: 1481, 1483

"The Denunciation" ASF: 274; Wa: 311

"The Doctor and the Doctor's Wife" ASF: 274; Po: 1517; SFC: 83; Wa: 311; WaS1: 88

"The End of Something" ASF: 2741; Po: 1517; SFC: 83-84; Wa: 311-312

"The Faithful Bull" ASF: 274; WaS1: 88

A Farewell to Arms ALL: 128; AN: 120; CN: 266-269; LCAB: 87; Ma: 909-911; Ne: 58-62; Po: 1477, 1491, 1518-1524; Wo: 121

"Father and Sons" ASF: 274-275; SFC: 84; Wa: 312;

WaS1: 88

The Fifth Column Po: 1487

"Fifty Grand" ASF: 275; Po: 1524; SFC: 84; Wa: 312

For Whom the Bell Tolls ALL: 128; AN: 120-121; CN: 269-272; Ma: 911-912; Ne: 57-59; Po: 1481, 1487, 1491, 1525-1526; Wo: 121

"The Gambler, the Nun, and the Radio" ASF: 275; Po: 1526-1527; SFC: 84; Wa: 312-313; WaS1: 88

"Get a Seeing-Eye Dog" ASF: 275; Wa: 313

"God Rest You Merry, Gentlemen" ASF: 275; Po: 1527; Wa: 313; WaS1: 88

"The Good Lion" ASF: 275; WaS1: 88

The Green Hills of Africa Po: 1481-1482, 1527-1528

"Hills Like White Elephants" ASF: 276; Po: 1528; SFC: 84; Wa: 313; WaS1: 88

"Homage to Switzerland" ASF: 276; SFC: 84; Wa: 313

"In Another Country" ASF: 276; Ma: 913; Po: 1528; SFC: 84; Wa: 314

In Our Time Po: 1528-1529

In Our Time "Chapter III" ASF: 272

In Our Time "Chapter V" ASF: 272

In Our Time "Chapter VI" ASF: 272

In Our Time "Chapter IX" ASF: 272

In Our Time "Chapter XV" ASF: 272

"Indian Camp" ASF: 276; Ma: 913-914; Po: 1529-1530; SFC: 85; Wa: 314-315; WaS1: 88

Islands in the Stream Ma: 914-915

"Judgment of Manitou" ASF: 277

"The Killers" ASF: 277; Ma: 915-916; Po: 1530-1531; SFC: 85; Wa: 315-316; WaS1: 88-89

"The Last Good Country" ASF: 277

"The Light of the World" ASF: 277-278; Ma: 917; Po: 1532; SFC: 85; Wa: 316; WaS1: 89

"A Man of the World" ASF: 278; Wa: 317

"Mr. and Mrs. Elliot" ASF: 278; Po: 1480; Wa: 317

"The Mother of a Queen" ASF: 278; Wa: 317

A Moveable Feast LCAB: 87; Ma: 917-918; Po: 1498, 1511, 1532-1533

"My Old Man" ASF: 278; Po: 1533; SFC: 86; Wa: 317

"A Natural History of the Dead" ASF: 278-279; Po: 1533; SFC: 86; Wa: 317

"Night Before Battle" ASF: 279; Wa: 317

"Night Before Landing" ASF: 279

"Nobody Ever Dies" ASF: 279; Wa: 317; WaS1: 89

"Now I Lay Me" ASF: 279; Po: 1533; SFC: 86; Wa: 317-318

The Old Man and the Sea ALL: 128; AN: 121; ASF: 279-282; CN: 272-276; LCAB: 87; Ma: 918-920; Ne: 58, 60; Po: 1483, 1534-1538; SFC: 86-87; Wa: 318-321; WaS1: 89; Wo: 121

"Old Man at the Bridge" ASF: 282; Wa: 321-322

"On the Quai at Smyrna" ASF: 282; Po: 1539; Wa: 322; WaS1: 89

"On Writing" ASF: 282

"One Reader Writes" ASF: 283; Wa: 322

"Out of Season" ASF: 283; SFC: 88; Wa: 322

"A Pursuit Race" ASF: 283; SFC: 88; Wa: 322

"The Revolutionist" ASF: 283; Wa: 322; WaS1: 89

"The Sea Change" ASF: 283; Po: 1539; Wa: 322

"Sepi Jingan" ASF: 283

"The Short Happy Life of

Francis Macomber" ASF: 283-285; Ma: 920-921; Po: 1539-1541; SFC: 88-89; Wa: 322-325; WaS1: 89-90

"A Simple Enquiry" SFC: 89; Wa: 325

"The Snows of Kilimanjaro" ASF: 285-287; Ma: 921-923; Po: 1541-1544; SFC: 89; Wa: 325-327; WaS1: 90

"Soldier's Home" ASF: 287; Ma: 923-924; Po: 1544; SFC: 90; Wa: 327; WaS1: 90

The Spanish Earth Po: 1491

"Summer People" ASF: 287

The Sun Also Rises ALL: 128; AN: 121-122; CN: 276-280; LCAB: 87; Ma: 924-926; Ne: 57, 61-62; Po: 1477, 1498-1499, 1544-1551; Wo: 121-122

"Ten Indians" ASF: 287; Po: 1551; SFC: 90; Wa: 327

"The Three-Day Blow" ASF: 287; SFC: 90; Wa: 327; WaS1: 90

"Three Shots" ASF: 287; WaS1: 90

To Have and Have Not AN: 122; CN: 280-281; Po: 1487, 1551

"Today Is Friday" ASF: 287; Wa: 328

The Torrents of Spring AN: 122; CN: 281; Ne: 60; Po: 1480, 1551-1552

"The Undefeated" ASF: 288; Ma: 926; Po: 1552; SFC: 90; Wa: 328

"Under the Ridge" ASF: 288; Wa: 328; WaS1: 90

"Up in Michigan" ASF: 288; Po: 1552; SFC: 90; Wa: 328

"A Very Short Story" ASF: 288; SFC: 90; Wa: 329

"A Way You'll Never Be" ASF: 288; Po: 1552-1553; SFC: 90; Wa: 328-329

"Wine of Wyoming" ASF: 288; Wa: 329

_____ and Benjamin F.

GLAZER
The Fifth Column ADC: 155; Br: 298

HENDERSON, David
General BAW: 373

HENDERSON, Elliott Blaine
General LCAB: 87

HENDERSON, George Wylie
General AAW: 57; BAF: 143; BAW: 373; LCAB: 87-88
Jule BAF: 143-144; LCAB: 87-88
Ollie Miss BAF: 143-144; LCAB: 87-88

HENDERSON, Hamish
General Ai: 316

HENDRICKS, Jon
Evolution of the Blues MBA: 112

HENDRIKS, Arthur Lemiere
General WIL: 56-57
Madonna of the Unknown Nation WIL: 58
Muet WIL: 57
On This Mountain and Other Poems WIL: 57
Seven Jamaican Poets WIL: 57-58
These Green Islands WIL: 57

HENDRY, James Findlay
General Ai: 296

HENLEY, William Ernest
General TA: 174; VP: 39-40
"Invictus" PE: 217
"Space and Dread and the Dark" ICBAP: 61; PE: 217
"The Ways of Death" PE: 217

HENRIQUEZ URENA, Max
General Po: 1553

HENRY VIII, King of England
General SC: 62

HENRY, Lord Cockburn
General Ai: 119

Henry, O. [William Sydney PORTER] see O. HENRY

HENRY, Robert
General LCAB: 88

HENRYSON, Robert
General Ai: 31-32; LCAB: 88; OMEP: 409; SC: 62
"The Annunciation" PE: 217
Moral Fables OMEP: 410-411
Orpheus and Eurydice Ai: 32; OMEP: 410

"The Preaching of the Swallow" PE: 217
"Robene and Makyne" PE: 217
"Sum Practysis of Medecyne" PE: 217
"The Tale of the Cock and the Fox" OMEP: 410
"The Tale of the Wolf and the Wether" Ai: 32; OMEP: 410
Testament of Cresseid Ai: 32; ICBAP: 61; OMEP: 410-411; PE: 217; SC: 62

HENSCHKE, Alfred
The Circle of Chalk [The Chalk Circle; Der Kreidekreis] Br: 298
HENSEN, Herwig
General Br: 298
HENSHAW, James Ene
General BALE: 307
HENSON, Josiah
General LCAB: 88
HENTZ, Caroline Lee Whiting
General AN: 128
Ernest Linwood AN: 128
HEPPENSTALL, Rayner
General Po: 1553
HERBERT, C.L.
General WIL: 58
HERBERT, Edward, First Baron Herbert of Cherbury
General Ba: 68
"Tears, Flow No More" PE: 226
"To Her Hair" PE: 226
HERBERT, F. Hugh
The Best House in Naples ADC: 155
For Keeps ADC: 155
For Love of Money ADC: 156
A Girl Can Tell ADC: 156
Kiss and Tell ADC: 156
The Moon Is Blue ADC: 156
_____ and Hans KRALY
Quiet, Please! ADC: 156
HERBERT, George
General Ba: 69-74; ICBAP: 61; Ma: 928-929
"Aaron" PE: 217
"Affliction, I" PE: 217-218
"Affliction, II" PE: 218

"Affliction, III" PE: 218
"Affliction, IV" PE: 218
"Affliction, V" PE: 218
"The Agony" ["The Agonie"] ICBAP: 61; PE: 218
"The Altar" PE: 218-219
"Anagram of the Virgin Mary" ICBAP: 61; PE: 219
"Artillerie" PE: 219
"Assurance" ICBAP: 62
"The Bag" ICBAP: 62; PE: 219
"The Banquet" PE: 219
"The Bunch of Grapes" ICBAP: 62; PE: 219
"Business" PE: 219
"Christmas" ICBAP: 62; PE: 219
"The Church" Ba: 69; ICBAP: 62; PE: 219
"The Church Militant" Ba: 71; ICBAP: 62; PE: 219
"Church-monuments" PE: 219-220
"The Church Porch" Ba: 69; PE: 220
"The Collar" Ba: 70-71; ICBAP: 62; LCAB: 88; PE: 220
"Confession" PE: 220
"The Coronet" Ba: 70
"The Cross" PE: 220
"Dialogue" PE: 220
"Discipline" PE: 220
"Dooms Day" PE: 221
"Easter" ICBAP: 62; PE: 221
"Easter-Wings" Ba: 70; PE: 221
"The Elixir" Ba: 72
"Employment (II)" ICBAP: 62
"The Flower" ICBAP: 62; PE: 221
"The Foil" Ba: 73; PE: 221
"Frailtie" ICBAP: 62; PE: 221
"The Glimpse" PE: 221
"Grief" PE: 221
"The Holdfast" PE: 221
"The Holy Communion" PE: 221
"Home" PE: 221
"I Gave to Hope a Watch of Mine" PE: 222
"The Invitation" PE: 222
"Jordan" Ba: 70, 74; ICBAP:

62; PE: 222
"Jordan I" Ba: 71, 74; PE: 222
"Life" PE: 222
"Love" ICBAP: 62; PE: 222
"Love I" PE: 222
"Love II" PE: 222
"Love (III)" Ba: 73; ICBAP: 62; PE: 222
"Love-Joy" ICBAP: 62; PE: 222
"Love Unknown" ICBAP: 63; PE: 222
"Man" PE: 223
"The Odour" PE: 223
"Paradise" ICBAP: 63; PE: 223
"A Parodie" Ba: 73; PE: 223
"Peace" Ba: 74; ICBAP: 63; PE: 223
"The Pearl" PE: 223
"The Pilgrimage" ICBAP: 63; PE: 223
"Prayer" Ba: 71, 73; ICBAP: 63; PE: 223
"Prayer II" PE: 223
"Providence" Ba: 72; ICBAP: 63; PE: 223
"The Pulley" PE: 224
"The Quidditie" PE: 224
"The Quip" ICBAP: 63; PE: 224
"Redemption" Ba: 72; ICBAP: 63; PE: 224
"The Reprisall" PE: 224
"The Rose" Ba: 69; ICBAP: 63; PE: 224
"The Sacrifice" Ba: 72-73; PE: 224
"Sepulchre" PE: 224
"The Sinner" PE: 225
"Sinnes Round" PE: 225
"The Sonne" Ba: 70; PE: 225
"The Temper" Ba: 70; ICBAP: 63; PE: 225
"The Temper I" PE: 225
The Temple Ba: 69-74
"The Thanksgiving" PE: 225
"They Did Accuse Me of Great Villainy" PE: 225
"To All Angels and Saints" PE: 225

"Trinity Sunday" PE: 225
"A True Hymne" PE: 225
"Ungratefulnesse" PE: 225
"Vanitie" Ba: 71; PE: 225
"Virtue" Ba: 69, 73; ICBAP: 63; PE: 225-226
"The Windows" ICBAP: 63; PE: 226
"The World" PE: 226
"A Wreathe" Ba: 70; PE: 226
HERBERT, John
Fortune and Men's Eyes ADC: 156-157
HERBERT, Sir Alan Patrick
General Mi: 243-244
HERBERT, William
"What Ys He, Thys Lordling, That Cometh Vrom the Vyth" PE: 226
HERBERT, Xavier
General MAP: 192-196
Capricornia MAP: 192-196
Poor Fellow My Country MAP: 192-196
Seven Emus MAP: 194
Soldiers' Women MAP: 194
HERCULES, Frank
General BAF: 144; WIL: 58
I Want a Black Doll BAF: 144-145; WIL: 58
Where the Hummingbird Flies BAF: 145; BAW: 374; WIL: 58
HERCZEG, Ferenc
General Br: 298
HERFORD, Oliver
General LCAB: 88
HERGESHEIMER, Joseph
General ALL: 135; AN: 128-129; ASF: 300; LCAB: 88; Ne: 63-64; Po: 1553; Wo: 126-127
"Asphodel" Wa: 329
"Bread" Wa: 329
The Bright Shawl and Linda Condon Po: 1553-1554
"The Crystal Chandelier" Wa: 329
Cytherea AN: 128
"The Great Wall" Wa: 329
"Juju" Wa: 329
"A Little Number in Piqué" Wa: 329
The Limestone Tree AN: 128
"Oak" Wa: 329
"Rosemary Roselle" Wa: 329

Three Black Pennys AN:
128
Wild Oranges Po: 1554
HERLIHY, James Leo
General Ma: 930; MDAE:
271
Stop, You're Killing Me
(three plays: Laughs,
Etc., Terrible Jim Fitch,
and Bad Bad Jo-Jo) ADC:
157
_____ and William NOBLE
Blue Denim ADC: 157
HERMAN, Yury
Our Acquaintances Ke:
412-413
Hermite see TRISTAN
L'HERMITE
HERMLIN, Stephan
General Po: 1554
"The Commandant" WaS1:
90
"Journey of a Painter in
Paris" WaS1: 90
"The Way of the Bolsheviks"
WaS1: 90
HERNANDEZ, Jose
Martin Fierro LCAB: 88
HERNANDEZ, Luisa Josefina
General Br: 298
The Real Guests [Los
Huespedes Reales] Br:
299
HERNANDEZ, Miguel
General Po: 1554
HERNE, James A.
General AD: 139-144; ALL:
134-135; Lon: 32-33
Drifting Apart AD: 140-
141; ADC: 157; DC1:
90
Margaret Fleming AD: 139-
144; ADC: 157; DC1:
90; Lon: 33
The Reverend Griffith Daven-
port AD: 139, 142, 144;
ADC: 158; DC1: 91;
Lon: 33
Sag Harbor AD: 144
Shore Acres AD: 139-140,
142-143; DC1: 91; Lon:
32
HERNTON, Calvin
General BAF: 145
Scarecrow BAF: 145
HERODOTUS

General LCAB: 88
The History of the Persian
Wars Ma: 931-932
HERON, Haly
General SC: 63
HERRERA, Ernesto
General Br: 299
HERRERA Y REISSIG, Julio
General Po: 1554-1555
HERRERO, Juan Luis
"Isla de Pinos" WaS1: 90
HERRICK, Robert (1591-1674)
General Ba: 75-76; LCAB:
88-89; Ma: 934-935
"Ah Ben" see "An Ode for
Him"
"All Things Decay and Die"
PE: 226
"Another Grace for a Child"
PE: 226
"The Apparition of His Mistress
Calling Him to Elysium"
PE: 226
"The Argument of His Book"
PE: 226
"The Bracelet: To Julia" PE:
226
"Care a Good Keeper" PE:
227
"The Carkanet" ICBAP: 63;
PE: 227
"Cherry-Ripe" PE: 227
"The Coming of Good Luck"
PE: 227
"Corinna's Going A-Maying"
Ba: 75-76; ICBAP: 64;
Ma: 933; PE: 227
"Counsell" PE: 227
"Delight in Disorder" Ba:
76; ICBAP: 64; Ma: 933;
PE: 227
"A Dirge Upon the Death of the
Right Valiant Lord, Bernard
Stuart" ICBAP: 64
"Divination by a Daffodill" PE:
227
"Empires of Kings" PE: 227
"The Faerie Temple: Or,
Oberons Chappell" ICBAP:
64; PE: 228
"Farewell Frost, or Welcome the
Spring" PE: 228
"The Funeral Rites of the
Rose" ICBAP: 64; PE:
228
"Good Friday: Rex Tragicus,

or Christ Going to His
Crosse" ICBAP: 64; PE:
228
Hesperides Ba: 75-76; Ma:
934
"His Age, Dedicated to His
Peculiar Friend, Master
John Wickes, under the
Name of Posthumus" PE:
228
"His Farewell to Sack" PE:
228
"His Grange, or Private
Wealth" PE: 228
"His Poetrie His Pillar" PE:
228
"His Winding-Sheet" PE:
228
"The Hock-Cart, or Harvest
Home" Ba: 75; ICBAP:
64; PE: 228
"How Roses Came Red"
ICBAP: 64; PE: 228
"Julia's Petticoat" PE: 228-
229
"The Kisse. A Dialogue"
PE: 229
"Love" PE: 229
"The Mad Maid's Song" PE:
229
"A Meditation for His Mis-
tresse" PE: 229
"The Night Piece, to Julia"
PE: 229
"No Spouse but a Sister"
PE: 229
"A Nuptiall Song" PE: 229
"Oberon's Feast" ICBAP:
64; PE: 229
"Oberons Palace" ICBAP:
64
"An Ode for Him" ["Ah Ben"]
PE: 229
"The Pillar of Fame" PE:
229
"The School or Perl of Putney
... Mistresse Portman"
PE: 229
"The Sick Rose" PE: 229
"A Ternary of Littles Upon a
Pipkin of Jelly Sent to a
Lady" PE: 229-230
"A Thanksgiving to God, for
His House" PE: 230
"This Crosse-Tree Here"
PE: 227

"This Great Realme of Poetry"
PE: 230
"To Anthea Lying in Bed" PE:
230
"To Blossoms" PE: 230
"To Daffodils" PE: 230
"To Electra" PE: 230
"To His Mistresse Objecting to
Him Neither Toying nor Talk-
ing" PE: 230
"To Live Merrily and to Trust
to Good Verses" PE: 230
"To M. Denham, on His Pro-
spective Poem" ICBAP: 64;
PE: 230
"To Meadows" PE: 230
"To Perilla" ICBAP: 64; PE:
230
"To Sylvia" PE: 230
"To the Reverend Shade of His
Religious Father" ICBAP:
64; PE: 231
"To the Virgins to Make Much
of Time" LCAB: 89; PE:
231
"The Transfiguration" PE:
231
"Upon Julia Weeping" PE: 232
"Upon Julia's Clothes" Ba:
75; ICBAP: 65; Ma: 935-
936; PE: 231-232
"Upon Julia's Voice" PE: 232
"Upon Prig" PE: 232
"Upon Sylvia" PE: 230
"The Vine" PE: 232
"The Vision" PE: 232
"The Watch" PE: 232
HERRICK, Robert (1868-1938)
General ALL: 135; AN: 129-
130; ASF: 300; Po: 1555-
1556; Wo: 130
"The Master of the Inn" ASF:
300
Together AN: 129
Herrmann, Gerhart see MOSTAR,
Gerhart Herrmann
HERRON, Shaun
Through the Dark and Hairy
Wood ENES2: 127
The Whore Mother ENES2: 127
HERSEY, John
General AN: 130; CFAE:
195-196; CN: 281-282;
LCAB: 89; Po: 1556
A Bell for Adano CN: 282;
Ma: 937

The Child Buyer CN: 282;
Ma: 937-938; Po: 1556
"A Fable South of Cancer"
ASF: 301
The Marmot Drive CN: 282
A Single Pebble CN: 282;
Ma: 938
The Wall AN: 130; CFAE:
196; CN: 282-283; Ma:
938
The War Lover AN: 130;
CN: 283; Ma: 939; Po:
1556-1557
White Lotus CN: 283
HERZEN, Alexander
"The Thieving Magpie" Wa:
329
Who Is to Blame? Fi: 453
HERZMANOVSKY-ORLANDO,
Fritz von
General Po: 1557
HESIOD
General LCAB: 89
Theogony Ma: 940
Works and Days Ma: 940-941
HESSE, Hermann
General LCAB: 89; Po:
1557-1566
Beneath the Wheel [Under the
Wheel; The Prodigy; Un-
term Rad] Fi: 320; Ke:
279; Ma: 942; Po: 1557,
1564, 1574
Berthold Fi: 320
"A Child's Soul" SFC: 90;
Wa: 329-330; WaS1: 90
Death and the Lover Ke:
275-276
Demian Fi: 320-321; Ke:
276; Ma: 942-943; Po:
1557, 1562, 1564-1565
"Diary from a Health Resort"
["Guest at a Spa"] SFC:
91; Wa: 330
The Glass Bead Game [Das
Glasperlenspiel; Magister
Ludi] Fi: 321-323; Ke:
276-278; Ma: 944-945; Po:
1562-1563, 1566-1569
Das Haus der Träume Po:
1569
Hermann Lauscher Po: 1562
"Heumond" Po: 1570; Wa:
330
"Iris" Wa: 330
"Journey to the East"
["Morgenlandfahrt"] Fi:
323-324; Ke: 276; Ma: 945-
946; Po: 1563, 1565, 1571-
1572; SFC: 91; Wa: 330;
WaS1: 91
"King Yu" SFC: 91; Wa: 330
"Klein and Wagner" Fi: 324;
Ke: 276; Po: 1570; Wa:
330
"Klingsor's Last Summer" Wa:
330-331; WaS1: 91
König Yu. Eine Geschichte aus
dem alten China Po: 1570
Kurgast Fi: 324; Po: 1571;
Wa: 331
"Morgenlandfahrt" see "Jour-
ney to the East"
Narcissus and Goldmund
[Narziss und Goldmund] Fi:
324-325; Ma: 946-947; Po:
1564
Peter Camenzind Fi: 325; Po:
1564
Piktors Verwandlungen Po:
1559
"The Poet" Wa: 331
The Prodigy see Beneath the
Wheel
Rosshalde Ke: 278; Po: 1564
Siddhartha Fi: 325-326; Ke:
278; Ma: 947-949; Po:
1560, 1564, 1572-1573; SFC:
91; Wa: 331; WaS1: 91
"The Steep Road" Wa: 331
Steppenwolf Fi: 326-328; Ke:
278-279; Ma: 949-950; Po:
1557, 1560, 1562, 1564-1565,
1573-1574
"The Trip to Nuremberg" Wa:
331
Under the Wheel see Beneath
the Wheel
Unterm Rad see Beneath the
Wheel
"Youth, Beautiful Youth" Wa:
331-332
"zu einer Tokkata von Bach"
Po: 1574-1575
HEWETT, Dorothy
General MAP: 387
The Chapel Perilous MAP:
386
HEWLETT, Maurice Henry
General TA: 175-176
HEY, Richard
The Fish with the Gold Dagger

[Der Fisch mit dem Goldenen Dolch] Br: 299

Thymian und Drachentod Br: 299

Woe to Him Who Doesn't Lie [Weh dem der Nicht Lügt] Br: 299

HEYEN, William
General Po: 1575

HEYERT, Murray
"The New Kid" ASF: 301

HEYM, Georg
General Po: 1575-1576
Bariolomeo Ruggieri [Atalanta Oder Die Angst] DC2: 183; Po: 1575-1576
Der Irre Fi: 328
"Jonathan" Wa: 332
"The Lunatic Asylum" WaS1: 91

HEYM, Stefan
The Crusaders LCAB: 89

HEYSE, Paul
Andrea Delfin Fi: 328
"L'Arrabiata" Wa: 332
"David and Jonathan" Wa: 332
"Furia" Wa: 332
"Geteiltes Herz" Wa: 332
"Grenzen der Menschheit" Wa: 332
"Die Hexe vom Korso" Wa: 332
"Himmlische und irdische Liebe" Wa: 332
"The Last Centaur" Wa: 332
"Mädchen von Treffi" Wa: 332
Mary of Magdala [Maria von Magdala] Br: 299
"Nino and Maso" Wa: 332
"Die Stickerin von Treviso" Wa: 332
"Unvergessbare Worte" Wa: 332
"Der verlorene Sohn" Wa: 332
"Der Weihnachtsfund" Wa: 332

HEYWARD, Dorothy
Set My People Free ADC: 158
_____ and DuBose HEYWARD
Mamba's Daughters see also HEYWARD, DuBose ADC: 158; Br: 299

Porgy see also HEYWARD, DuBose ADC: 158
_____, DuBose HEYWARD, and George GERSHWIN
Porgy and Bess see also HEYWARD, DuBose ADC: 159-160
_____ and Howard RIGSBY
South Pacific ADC: 160

HEYWARD, DuBose
General AN: 131; ASF: 301; Po: 1576
Brass Ankle ADC: 160; DC1: 91
"The Brute" ASF: 301; Wa: 333
"Dorothy Grumpet, Graduate Lady" Wa: 333
"The Half Pint Flask" ASF: 301
Mamba's Daughters see also HEYWARD, Dorothy and DuBose HEYWARD AN: 130
Porgy see also HEYWARD, Dorothy and DuBose HEYWARD AN: 131; Po: 1577
Porgy and Bess see also HEYWARD, Dorothy, DuBose HEYWARD, and George GERSHWIN Po: 1577
"The Winning Loser" ASF: 301; Wa: 333
"A Yoke of Steers" PE: 232

HEYWOOD, Donald
How Come, Lawd? BAP: 104
Ol' Man Satan BAP: 104

HEYWOOD, John
General ED: 246-248; SC: 63; TSD: 53-54
The Four Prentices of London DC1: 91
Johan, Johan DC1: 92; TSD: 53-54
Play of the Wether DC1: 93; ED: 247; TSD: 53

HEYWOOD, Thomas
General ED: 250-251; Hen: 115; Log: 105-107, 110, 118-120; TSD: 54-56
The "Age" Plays [The Ages] DC1: 91; Log: 109, 120
Appius and Virginia see WEBSTER, John
The Captives, or The Lost Recovered DC1: 91; EDC: 245

A Challenge for Beauty
DC1: 91; EDC: 245
The English Traveller DC1:
92; EDC: 245; Log: 109;
TSD: 56
The Fair Maid of the West
Log: 120; TSD: 56
Henry IV DC1: 92
If You Know Not Me, You
Know Nobody. Part I
TSD: 56
King Edward the Fourth
EDC: 245
London's Jus Honorarium
Log: 120
Love's Mistress; or The
Queen's Masque DC1: 92;
Log: 109, 120
A Maidenhead Well Lost EDC:
246
Play of Love DC1: 92-93
The Rape of Lucrece DC1:
93; EDC: 246; Log:
110; TSD: 55
The Royal King and the
Loyal Subject EDC: 246
Sir Thomas More Log: 120,
136
Troia Britannica Log: 120;
TSD: 55
The Wise Woman of Hogsdom
DC1: 93
Wit and Witless DC1: 93
A Woman Killed with Kindness
DC1: 93-94; EDC: 246-
247; Log: 107-109, 120;
TSD: 54-56
_____ and Richard BROME
The Late Lancashire Witches
see also BROME, Richard
and Thomas HEYWOOD
DC1: 92; Log: 121
_____ and William ROWLEY
Fortune by Land and Sea
EDC: 247
HIBBERD, Jack
General MAP: 389
HIDALGO, José Luis
General Po: 1577
HIDEO, Nagata
Demon of Pleasure DC2:
183-184
HIERRO, José
"Para un esteta" Po: 1577
HIGGINS, Aidan
Langrishe, Go Down ENES2:

128
HIGGINSON, Thomas Wentworth
"The Monarch of Dreams" ASF:
301; Wa: 333
HIKMET, Nazim
C'est un dur métier que l'exil
Po: 1577-1578
HILBERRY, Conrad
"Hamster Cage" PE: 232
HILDESHEIMER, Wolfgang
General Br: 300; Po: 1578
The Delay [Die Verspätung]
Br: 300
Nightpiece Br: 300
"Das Opfer Helena" Po: 1578
Plays in Which Darkness Falls
[Plays in Which It Grows
Dark; Spiele in Denen Es
Dunkel Wird] Br: 300
Tynset Fi: 328
Die Verspätung see The Delay
"A World Ends" Wa: 333
HILDRETH, Richard
General AN: 131
The Slave AN: 131
HILL, Aaron
General EC: 80; Li: 205
King Henry the Fifth; or The
Conquest of France DC1:
94
The Prompter EC: 80
Zara DC1: 94
HILL, Abram
General AAPD: 314; BAP:
105; BAW: 376; MBA: 113
Anna Lucasta BAP: 105
Hell's Half Acre BAP: 105
Power of Darkness BAP: 105-
106
Walk Hard, Talk Loud BAP:
105-106
Walk Hard, Walk Tall MBA:
113
_____ and John SILVERA
On Striver's Row see also
SILVERA, John and Abram
HILL BAP: 105-106; MBA:
113
HILL, Errol
Man, Better Man BAP: 107
HILL, Frederick S.
The Six Degrees of Crime
ADC: 161
HILL, Geoffrey
"Funeral Music" PE: 232
"Lachrimae Verae" PE: 232

"The Martyrdom of Saint
Sebastian" PE: 232
"Pavana Dolorosa"
["Lachrimae Sonnet II"] PE:
232
"Picture of a Nativity" PE:
232
"September Song" PE: 233
HILL, Leslie Pinkney
General BAW: 379
Jethro BAP: 107
HILL, Leubrie and Alex ROGERS
Dark Town Follies BAP:
107
HILL, Mars
Man in the Family MBA:
114
HILL, Roy L.
Corrie J. Carroll and Other
Poems BAW: 380
HILLYER, Robert
General Po: 1578-1579
Riverhead AN: 131
HILTON, James
Goodbye, Mr. Chips Ma:
951
Lost Horizon Ma: 951
HILTON, Walter
The Scale of Perfection Hen:
19-20
HIMES, Chester B.
General AAF: 68-70; AAL:
191; AAW: 58; ASF:
302; BAF: 148-150; BAP:
108; BAW: 382-383; LCAB:
89; Po: 1579
Black on Black BAF: 150-
151
Blind Man with a Pistol
BAF: 151
Cast the First Stone BAF:
151
Cotton Comes to Harlem
BAF: 149, 151; BAP:
108
"Crazy in the Stir" WaS1:
91
"Da-Da-Dee" WaS1: 91
"He Knew" WaS1: 91
"Headwaiter" WaS1: 91
The Heat's On BAF: 151
"Heaven Has Changed" WaS1:
91
"His Last Day" WaS1: 91
If He Hollers Let Him Go
AAL: 189; BAF: 151-

152; BAP: 108
Lonely Crusade BAF: 152
"Lunching at the Ritzmore"
WaS1: 91
"Mama's Missionary Money"
WaS1: 91
"A Nigger" ASF: 301-302;
WaS1: 92
Pinktoes BAF: 152
"Pork Chop Paradise" WaS1:
92
"Prediction" ASF: 302; WaS1:
92
The Primitive AAF: 69
"Prison Mass" WaS1: 92
Run Man Run BAF: 152
"So Softly Smiling" WaS1: 92
"Tang" WaS1: 92
Third Generation BAF: 152-
153
"To What Red Hell?" WaS1: 92
"Two Soldiers" WaS1: 92
HINDE, Thomas [Thomas CHITTY]
The Day the Call Came CN:
283
Happy as Larry CN: 283
High CN: 283
Mr. Nicholas CN: 284
HINE, Daryl
General ICBAP: 65
HINES, Barry
A Kestrel for a Knave ENES1:
119
HINGA, Edward
General BALE: 307
HINOJOSA, José Maria
General Po: 1579
HINOJOSA, Rolando R.
General ASF: 302-303
"Fira the Blond" ASF: 302
"Por Esas Cosas Que Pasan"
ASF: 302
HINTON, James
"Mediators to the Goatherd"
Wa: 333
Hinton, Richard W. [pseud.] see
ANGOFF, Charles
HIPPIUS-MEREZHKOVSKAJA,
Zinaida
General Po: 1579-1580
HIVNOR, Robert
General MDAE: 272
The Ticklish Acrobat DC1:
94; MDAE: 272
HOAGLAND, Everett
General BAF: 153; BAW:

384
HOBBES, John Oliver [Pearl
 Mary Teresa CRAIGIE]
 General TA: 124
 Robert Orange ENES1: 119
 The School for Saints ENES1:
 120
HOBBES, Thomas
 General Ba: 77-79; Bon:
 55-56
 Leviathan Ba: 77-79; Bon:
 55-56; Hen: 121-122
HOBSON, Richard
 Memphis Is Gone ADC: 161
HOBY, Sir Thomas [translator]
 The Courtier by Baldassare
 CASTIGLIONE Hen: 211
HOCCLEVE, Thomas
 General OMEP: 390-391
 "Complaint" OMEP: 391
 "Letter of Cupid" OMEP:
 390-391
HOCHHUTH, Rolf
 General Br: 300; LCAB:
 89
 The Deputy [The Representa-
 tive; Der Stellvertreter]
 Br: 300-301; DC2: 184-
 185; EDC: 247-249; Po:
 1581-1583
 Guerillas EDC: 249
 Soldiers; An Obituary for
 Geneva [Soldaten. Nekro-
 log auf Genf. Tragödie]
 Br: 301; DC2: 185;
 EDC: 249-250; Po: 1580-
 1581
HOCHWÄLDER, Fritz
 General Br: 301-302; Po:
 1583
 Crown Colony see The
 Strong Are Lonely
 Donadieu Br: 302
 Donnerstag see Thursday
 Esther Br: 302
 Faith Is Not Enough see
 The Strong Are Lonely
 The Fugitive [Der Flüchtling]
 Br: 302; DC2: 186
 Das Heilige Experiment see
 The Strong Are Lonely
 Die Herberge Br: 302
 Der Himbeerpflucker see
 The Raspberry Picker
 Hotel du Commerce Br:
 302

Liebe in Florenz Br: 302
Meier Helmbrecht Br: 303
Der Offentliche Anklager Br:
 303
1003 Br: 303
The Raspberry Picker [Der Him-
 beerpflucker] Br: 303
The Strong Are Lonely [Faith
 Is Not Enough; Crown Colony;
 Das Heilige Experiment] Br:
 303; DC2: 186
Thursday [Donnerstag] Br:
 302
HODGE, Merle
 Crick Crack Monkey WIL: 58-
 59
HODGES, Frenchy Jolene
 General BAW: 384
HODGSON, Ralph
 General Po: 1583
 "February" PE: 233
 "The Muse and the Mastiff" PE:
 233
 "The Skylark" PE: 233
 "Time" PE: 233
 "To Deck a Woman" PE: 233
HODGSON, William Hope
 The Boats of the Glen Carig
 ENES2: 128
HODGSON, William Noel
 "By All the Glories of the Day"
 PE: 233
HOEL, Sigurd
 A Day in October Ke: 352
 A Fortnight Before Frost
 Comes Ke: 352
 I Have Fallen in Love with
 Another Ke: 353
 The Road to the End of the
 World Ke: 353
 Sinners in Summertime Ke:
 353
HOFF, H.S.
 Scenes from Provincial Life
 ENES1: 120
HOFFMAN, Charles Fenno
 "Queen Meg" WaS1: 92
HOFFMAN, Daniel
 General ICBAP: 65
 "A Little Geste" ICBAP: 65
HOFFMAN, William
 Gilles de Rais ADC: 161
HOFFMANN, Ernst Theodor Ama-
 deus
 "The Adventure of New Year's
 Night" ["A New Year's Eve

Adventure"; "Die Aben-
teuer der Silvester-Nacht"]
Fi: 328; Wa: 333, 336;
WaS1: 92
"Account of the Life of a
Noted Man" Wa: 333
"Der Artushof" Wa: 333
"The Automaton" ["Automata"]
Wa: 33; WaS1: 92
"The Baron of B." WaS1:
92
Die Bergwerke Zu Falun DC2:
186
"The Choice of a Bride"
Wa: 333
"The Contest of the Minstrels"
Wa: 333-334
The Cooper of Nuremberg
Ke: 279
"Counselor Krespel" see
"Rat Krespel"
"The Cousin's Corner Window"
Wa: 334
"The Deserted House" Wa:
334; WaS1: 93
The Devil's Elixirs Fi: 328-
329; Ke: 279-80
Don Juan Fi: 329
"The Enemy" Wa: 334
"The Entail" Ke: 280; Wa:
334
"Das Fräulein von Scudéri"
["Mademoiselle de Scudéry"]
Fi: 329; Ke: 281; Wa:
335; WaS1: 93
"Gambler's Luck" Wa: 334
"Das Gelübde" see "The
Vow"
"The Golden Pot" Fi: 329-
330; Ke: 280; Wa: 334;
WaS1: 93
"Die Heimatochare" Wa: 334
"The Hold" Wa: 334
"Ignaz Denner" Wa: 335
"The Jesuit Church in G."
Wa: 335
Der Kampf der Sanger Ke:
280
"The King's Bride" ["The
King's Betrothed"] Ke:
280; Wa: 335
"Knight Gluck" ["Ritter
Gluck"] Fi: 331; Wa:
335
Kreisleriana Fi: 330
"Little Zack" ["Little Zaches

Called Cinnabar"; "Klein
Zaches Genannt Zinnobar"]
Fi: 330; Ke: 280-281; Wa:
335
"The Lost Reflection" Wa: 335
"The Loved One" Wa: 335
"Luck" Wa: 335
"The Magnetizer" ["Der Magnet-
iseur"] Ke: 281; Wa: 335
Die Marquise de la Pivadière
Fi: 330; Wa: 335
"Master Flea" ["Meister Floh"]
Ke: 281; Wa: 335-36
"Master Johannes Wacht" Wa:
336
"Master Martin the Cooper and
His Assistants" Wa: 336
"The Mines of Falun" Fi: 330;
Ke: 281; Wa: 336
"The Mysterious Child" see
"The Strange Child"
Nucracker and Mouse King Fi:
330; Ke: 281; Wa: 336
"The Pause" WaS1: 93
"The Poet and the Composer"
Wa: 336
"The Primogeniture" Wa: 336
"Princess Brambilla" [Prinzessin
Brambilla"] Fi: 330; Ke:
281; Wa: 336; WaS1: 93
"Rat Krespel" ["Counselor
Krespel"; "The Story of
Krespel"] Fi: 330-331; Wa:
334; WaS1: 92-93
"The Recovery" Wa: 336
"Ritter Gluck" see "Knight
Gluck"
"The Sandman" Fi: 331; Ke:
281; Wa: 336-337; WaS1:
93
"Serapion" Ke: 281; Wa:
337
"Signor Formica" Wa: 337
"The Sinister Guest" Wa: 337
"The Story of Krespel" see
"Rat Krespel"
"The Strange Child" ["The
Mysterious Child"] Ke: 282;
Wa: 336
"The Strange Sufferings of a
Theatre Director" Wa: 337
Tomcat Murr Fi: 331; Ke:
282
"The Vow" ["Das Gelübde"]
Fi: 329; Ke: 282; Wa:
337

HOFMANNSTHAL, Hugo von
General Br: 303-304; MD: 142-143; Po: 1584-1591
The Adventurer and the Singer [Der Abenteurer und die Sängerin] EDC: 250
Die Aegyptische Helen see The Egyptian Helen
Alcestis [Alkestis] DC2: 186; EDC: 250; MBD: 44; Po: 1591
Andreas Fi: 331-332
Arabella Br: 304; DC2: 186; EDC: 250; MD: 144; Po: 1592
Ariadne in Naxos [Ariadne Auf Naxos] DC2: 186; EDC: 250-251; MD: 144; Po: 1592
Aufzeichnungen zu Reden in Skandinavien Po: 1592
Die beiden Götter EDC: 251; Po: 1585
Das Bergwerk zu Falun see The Mine at Falun
Der Brief des Lord Chandos an Francis Bacon see The Letter of Lord Chandos
The Cavalier of the Rose [The Rose Bearer; Der Rosenkavalier] Br: 306; DC2: 187; EDC: 251; MD: 144; Po: 1597-1598
Cristina's Journey Home [Christinas Heimreise] EDC: 251-252; Po: 1593-1594
Dame Kobold see The Phantom Lady
Death and the Fool [The Fool and Death; Der Tor und der Tod] Br: 304; DC2: 188; EDC: 252; MD: 145
The Death of Titian [Der Tod des Tizian] EDC: 252
The Difficult Man [Der Schwierige] Br: 304-305; DC2: 186-188; EDC: 252-253; MBD: 53; MD: 144; Po: 1598-1601; TMBP: 259
The Egyptian Helen [Die Aegyptische Helen] EDC: 253; Po: 1591

Electra [Elektra] Br: 305; DC2: 186-187; EDC: 253; MD: 144; Po: 1594-1595
The Emperor and the Witch [Der Kaiser und die Hexe] EDC: 253; Po: 1596
Das Erlebnis des Marschalls von Bassompierre Ke: 282; Po: 1585-1586
Everyman [Via Crusis; Jedermann] Br: 305; DC2: 187; EDC: 253-254; MD: 144; Po: 1590, 1595-1596
The Fool and Death see Death and the Fool
Die Frau Ohne Schatten see The Woman Without a Shadow
Das Gerettete Venedig see Venice Preserv'd
Die Grafin Pompila DC2: 187
The Great World Theatre of Salzburg see The Salzburg Great Theatre of the World
Horseman's Story [Reitergeschichte] Fi: 332; Ke: 282; Po: 1585-1586, 1597; Wa: 337; WaS1: 93-94
The Incorruptible Man [Der Unbestechliche] Br: 306; EDC: 254
Jedermann see Everyman
Der Kaiser und die Hexe see The Emperor and the Witch
"Der Kaiser von China spricht" Po: 1590-1591
Das Kleine Welttheatre see The Little Theatre of the World
Das Leben ein Traum EDC: 254
The Letter of Lord Chandos [Der Brief des Lord Chandos an Francis Bacon] Po: 1593
The Little Theatre of the World [Das Kleine Welttheatre] EDC: 254-255; Po: 1596
Das Märchen der 672. Nacht Fi: 332; Po: 1596
The Mine at Falun [Das Bergwerk zu Falun] MD: 144
Oedipus and the Sphinx [Oedipus und die Sphinx]

EDC: 255; Po: 1597

The Phantom Lady [Dame Kobold] Br: 306

Raoul Richter, 1896 Fi: 332

Reitergeschichte see Horseman's Story

The Rose Bearer see The Cavalier of the Rose

Der Rosenkavalier see The Cavalier of the Rose

The Salzburg Great Theatre of the World [The Great World Theatre of Salzburg; Salzburger Grosse Welttheatre] Br: 306; DC2: 187; EDC: 254; MD: 144; Po: 1590

Der Schüler DC2: 188; Po: 1598

Der Schwierige see The Difficult Man

Semiramis Po: 1585

Silvia Po: 1601

Sommerreise Fi: 332; Po: 1601

"Tale of the Merchant's Son and His Servant" WaS1: 94

Der Tod des Tizian see The Death of Titian

Der Tor und der Tod see Death and the Fool

The Tower [Der Turm] Br: 306; DC2: 188; EDC: 255; MD: 145; Po: 1601-1602

Der Unbestechliche see The Incorruptible Man

"Under the Copper-Beech Tree" WaS1: 94

Venice Preserv'd [Das Gerettete Venedig] Br: 305; DC2: 187; EDC: 255-256; Po: 1595

Via Crusis see Everyman

"Die Wege und die Begegnungen" WaS1: 94

"Weltgeheimnis" Po: 1602

The White Fan [Der weisse Fächer] Br: 306; EDC: 256; Po: 1602

The Woman Without a Shadow [Die Frau Ohne Schatten] EDC: 256; MD: 144

HOGAN, David
"The Leaping Trout" Wa:
337

HOGARTH, William
General EC: 81

HOGG, James
General Ai: 101-102; BN: 68; Du: 101; Re: 198

"The Barber of Duncow" WaS1: 94

"The Cameronian Preacher's Tale" WaS1: 94

"Mary Burnet" WaS1: 94

"Mr. Adamson of Laverhope" WaS1: 94

The Private Memoirs and Confessions of a Justified Sinner Ai: 102; BN: 68; Du: 100-101; ENES1: 120; ENES2: 128

"Tibby Hyslop's Dream" WaS1: 94

HOLAN, Vladimir
General Po: 1603

HOLBERG, Ludvig
Jacob von Tyboe DC2: 188

Jeppe of the Hill [Jeppe paa Bjerget] EDC: 256

HOLCROFT, Thomas
General Be: 162-164; Li: 208

The Adventures of Hugh Trevor [Hugh Trevor] Be: 163; EN: 69; ENES1: 120; ENES2: 128

Alwyn Be: 163; EN: 68; ENES1: 120

Anna St. Ives Be: 163; EN: 68-69; ENES1: 120; ENES2: 128

Manthorn, the Enthusiast ENES1: 120; ENES2: 128

Memoirs of Bryan Perdue ENES1: 120; ENES2: 128

HOLDEN, Inez
Born Old; Died Young ENES1: 120

HÖLDERLIN, Friedrich
Hyperion Fi: 332-333; Ke: 282

Tod des Empedokles DC2: 188-189

HOLIDAY, Barton
General LJCD: 245

HOLIFIELD, Harold
General BAP: 109; BAW: 386

Cow in the Apartment MBA:

114

HOLINSHED, Raphael
The Chronicles of England,
Scotlande, and Irelande
Hen: 49; SC: 64

HOLLAND, Edwin C.
Corsair ADC: 161

HOLLAND, Mignon
General BAW: 386

HOLLANDER, John
General ICBAP: 65; Po:
1603
"Icarus Before Knossos"
ICBAP: 65

HOLLAR, Constance
General WIL: 59

HOLLEY, Mrs. Mary
General LCAB: 89

HOLLOWAY, John Wesley
General BAW: 387

HOLLOWAY, Lucy Ariel Williams
General BAW: 387

HOLMAN, M. Carl
General LCAB: 89

HOLME, Constance
Beautiful End ENES2: 129
Crump Folk Going Home
ENES2: 129
He-Who-Came? ENES2: 129
The Lonely Plough ENES2:
129
The Old Road from Spain
ENES2: 129
The Splendid Fairing ENES2:
129
The Things Which Belong--
ENES2: 129
The Trumpet in the Dust
ENES2: 129

HOLMES, John
General Po: 1603
"Herself" ICBAP: 65; PE:
233; Po: 1603

HOLMES, John Clellon
Go CN: 284

HOLMES, John Haynes and
Reginald LAWRENCE
If This Be Treason Br: 307

HOLMES, Oliver Wendell, Sr.
General ALL: 135-136;
AN: 131-132; Cla: 43-
44; Ho: 137, 157; LCAB:
90
"The Chambered Nautilus"
Cla: 43; PE: 233
"The Deacon's Masterpiece"

Cla: 44; ICBAP: 65; PE:
233
Elsie Venner ALL: 136; AN:
131; Cla: 44; Ho: 157
The Guardian Angel ALL:
136; AN: 131
"In Memory of Abraham Lincoln"
LCAB: 90
"The Living Temple" PE: 233
A Mortal Antipathy ALL: 136;
AN: 131
"The Peau de Chagrin of State
Street" PE: 233
"Two Sonnets: Harvard" PE:
233
"The Two Streams" PE: 233-
234

HOLMES, R. Ernest
General BAF: 153

HOLOFCENER, Lawrence
Before You Go ADC: 161

HOLT, Will and Linda HOPKINS
Me and Bessie MBA: 114-115

HOLTBY, Winifred
South Riding ENES2: 129

HO LUNG, Richard
General WIL: 59

HOLZ, Arno
General Po: 1603-1604
Die Sozialaristokraten DC2:
189
_____ and Johannes SCHLAF
Die Familie Selicke EDC: 256

HOME, John
General Ai: 70; Li: 211-212
Alfred DC1: 94
Alonzo DC1: 94
Douglas Ai: 70; DC1: 94;
Li: 211-212
The Fatal Discovery DC1: 95;
Li: 212
The Siege of Aquilea Ai: 70;
Li: 212

HOME, William Douglas
General MDAE: 274
Aunt Edwina EDC: 256
Bad Soldier Smith EDC: 256
The Chiltern Hunters Br: 307
Iron Duchess EDC: 256;
MDAE: 274
Now Barabbas Br: 307
The Reluctant Debutant EDC:
257; MDAE: 274
Yes, M'Lord EDC: 257

HOMER
General LCAB: 90

The Iliad LCAB: 90; Ma: 952-953

The Odyssey LCAB: 90; Ma: 953-954

HONIG, Edwin
General Po: 1604

Hood, George see BROWN, George Douglas

HOOD, Thomas
General Re: 200
"Autumn" PE: 234
"The Death Bed" PE: 234
Lamia DC1: 95
"Ruth" PE: 234

HOOK, Theodore Edward
General BN: 68

HOOKER, Richard
General SC: 64
Of the Lawes of Ecclesiasticall Polity Hen: 110-111; SC: 64

HOOKER, Thomas
General AP: 357-360; Da: 52
The Poor Doubting Christian AP: 357-358

HOOLE, John
General Li: 213

HOOPER, Johnson Jones
General ASF: 303
"The Captain Attends a Camp Meeting" ASF: 303
"The 'Tallapoonsy Vollantares' Meet the Enemy" ASF: 303; WaS1: 94

HOPE, Alec Derwent
General Po: 1604
"Agony Column" PE: 234
The Wandering Islands Po: 1604

HOPE, Anthony [Anthony Hope HAWKINS]
General TA: 173
A Man of Mark ENE: 155
Prisoner of Zenda ENE: 155

HOPE, Thomas
Anastasius ENES2: 129

HOPKINS, Bill
The Divine and the Decay CN: 284

HOPKINS, Charles
Boadicea, Queen of Britain Li: 214

HOPKINS, Gerard Manley
General EP: 133-141;
ICBAP: 65; LCAB: 90;
Ma: 956-957; TA: 178;
VP: 41-43
"The Alchemist in the City" PE: 234
"As Kingfishers Catch Fire" (No. 57) ICBAP: 65; PE: 234
"Binsey Poplars Felled 1879" PE: 234
"The Blessed Virgin Compared to the Air We Breathe" PE: 234
"The Caged Skylark" (No. 39) ICBAP: 66; PE: 234
"The Candle Indoors" (No. 46) ICBAP: 66; PE: 234
"Carrion Comfort" (No. 64) ICBAP: 66; PE: 235
"Duns Scotus's Oxford" PE: 235
"The Escorial" PE: 235
"Felix Randal" (No. 53) ICBAP: 66; PE: 235
"God's Grandeur" (No. 31) ICBAP: 66; Ma: 955; PE: 235-236; VP: 41
"The Habit of Perfection" (No. 22) ICBAP: 66; PE: 236
"Harry Ploughman" (No. 71) ICBAP: 66; PE: 236
"Heaven-Haven" (No. 9) ICBAP: 66; PE: 236
"Henry Purcell" (No. 45) ICBAP: 66; PE: 236
"Hurrahing the Harvest" (No. 38) ICBAP: 66; PE: 237
"I Must Hunt Down the Prize" (No. 88) ICBAP: 66
"I Wake and Feel the Fell of Dark, Not Day" (No. 67) ICBAP: 67; PE: 237
"Inversnaid" (No. 56) ICBAP: 67; PE: 237
"The Leaden Echo and the Golden Echo" LCAB: 91; PE: 237
"The Loss of the Eurydice" (No. 41) EP: 141; ICBAP: 67; PE: 237
"Margaret Clitheroe" PE: 237
"The May Magnificent" PE: 237
"My Own Heart Let Me More Have Pity On" (No. 69) ICBAP: 67; PE: 237
"No Worst, There Is None"

(No. 65) ICBAP: 67; PE:
237-238

"Nothing Is So Beautiful as
Spring" PE: 237

"On a Piece of Music" PE:
238

"Patience, Hard Thing! The
Hard Thing but to Pray"
(No. 68) ICBAP: 67;
PE: 238

"Pied Beauty" (No. 37)
ICBAP: 67; PE: 238

"Ribblesdale" (No. 58)
ICBAP: 67

"St. Thecla" (No. 136)
ICBAP: 67

"The Shepherd's Brow" (No.
75) ICBAP: 67; PE:
238-239

"Soliloquy of One of the Spies
Left in the Wilderness"
PE: 239

"Sonnet to St. Alphonsus Rodriguez" PE: 239

"Soul, Self; Come, Poor Jack-
self, I Do Advise" PE:
239

"Spelt from Sibyl's Leaves"
(No. 61) ICBAP: 67;
PE: 239

"Spring" (No. 33) ICBAP:
67; PE: 239-240

"Spring and Fall: To a Young
Child" (No. 55) ICBAP:
67; Ma: 957; PE: 240;
VP: 42

"The Starlight Night" PE:
240

"Terrible Sonnets" VP: 42-
43

"That Nature Is a Heraclitean
Fire and of the Comfort of
the Resurrection" (No. 72)
ICBAP: 67-68; PE: 240

"Thee, God, I Come From, to
Thee Go" PE: 241

"Thou Art Indeed Just, Lord,
If I Contend" (No. 74)
ICBAP: 68; PE: 241

"To Oxford II" PE: 241

"To R.B. [Robert Bridges]"
(No. 76) ICBAP: 68;
PE: 241

"To Seem the Stranger Lies
My Lot, My Life" (No. 66)
ICBAP: 68; PE: 241

"Tom's Garland" PE: 241; VP:
43

"A Vision of the Mermaids" (No.
2) ICBAP: 68

"The Windhover, to Christ Our
Lord" (No. 36) EP: 136,
139, 141; ICBAP: 68; Ma:
957-959; PE: 241-243; VP:
42-43

"The Woodlark" (No. 138)
ICBAP: 68

"The Wreck of the Deutschland"
(No. 28) EP: 138, 141;
ICBAP: 68-69; LCAB: 91;
Ma: 959-960; PE: 243-245;
TA: 178; VP: 42

HOPKINS, John
General MDAE: 275

HOPKINS, Linda
General MBA: 116
Inner City BAP: 109

HOPKINS, Pauline Elizabeth
General BAF: 153-154; BAW:
390; MBA: 117
Contending Forces BAF: 154;
BAW: 390

HOPKINSON, Abdur-Rahman [Slade]
General WIL: 59
The Friend WIL: 60

HOPKINSON, Francis
General AP: 361-363; Da: 79
"Ode Sacred to the Memory of
His Late Gracious Majesty
George II" ICBAP: 69
"Prologue in Praise of Music:
Ode on Music" ICBAP: 69

Hopley-Woolrich, Cornell George
see WOOLRICH, Cornell

HORACE
General LCAB: 91
Ars Poetica Ma: 961
Odes Ma: 961-963

Horatius Flaccus, Quintus see
HORACE

HORGAN, Paul
General ASF: 303

HORIA, Vintila
God Was Born in Exile Fi: 453

HORNE, Frank M.
General BAF: 154; BAW: 391

HORNE, Richard Henry
General AL: 242-243
"Australian Explorers" AL:
242
Cosmo De Medici DC1: 95
The Death of Marlowe DC1: 95

Hildebrand DC1: 95
Judas Iscariot DC1: 95
Spirit of Peers and People:
A National Tragi-Comedy
DC1: 95
HOROVITZ, Israel
General MDAE: 277
Acrobats ADC: 162
Alfred Dies see The Wake-
field Plays
Alfred the Great see The
Wakefield Plays
Dr. Hero ADC: 162
The Honest-to-God Schnozzola
ADC: 162
The Indian Wants the Bronx
ADC: 162; Br: 307
It's Called the Sugar Plum
ADC: 162
Line ADC: 162
Morning ADC: 162; MDAE:
277
Our Father's Failing see
The Wakefield Plays
The Primary English Class
ADC: 162-163
Rats ADC: 163
The Wakefield Plays [a Mass
trilogy: Alfred the Great;
Our Father's Failing; and
Alfred Dies] ADC: 163
HORTON, George Moses
General AAPD: 69-70; AAW:
58; BAW: 393-394; LCAB:
91
HORVATH, Oedon von
General Br: 307; Po: 1604-
1605
HOSEIN, Clyde
General WIL: 60
HOSIDIUS
Medea DC2: 189
HOSKINS, John
"Absence" PE: 245
"Of the Loss of Time" PE:
245
HOUGH, Emerson
Heart's Desire Po: 1605
HOUGHTON, William Stanley
General Br: 307; Mi:
244; TA: 180
Hindle Wakes Br: 307
HOUGRON, Jean
General Po: 1605
HOUSMAN, Alfred Edward
General EP: 145-153; ICBAP:

69; LCAB: 91; Po: 1605-
1613; TA: 181-182; VP:
44-45
"Be Still, My Soul, Be Still"
(Shropshire Lad, 48) EP:
150; ICBAP: 69; PE: 245;
Po: 1613
"Bredon Hill" (Shropshire Lad,
21) PE: 245
"Bring in this timeless grave to
throw" (Shropshire Lad, 46)
EP: 151; Po: 1613
"The Carpenter's Son" (Shrop-
shire Lad, 47) EP: 145;
ICBAP: 69; PE: 245; Po:
1613
"The Chestnut Casts His Flam-
beaux" (Last Poems, 9) PE:
245
"Crossing Alone the Nighted
Ferry" (More Poems, 23)
PE: 245
"The Deserter" EP: 148; Po:
1613-1614
"Eight O'Clock" (Last Poems,
15) PE: 245
"1887" (Shropshire Lad, 1) PE:
245-246
"Epitaph on an Army of Mer-
cenaries" (Last Poems, 37)
ICBAP: 69; PE: 246
"Fancy's Knell" (Last Poems,
41) PE: 246
"Farewell to Barn and Stack and
Tree" (Shropshire Lad, 8)
PE: 246
"The Farms of Home I've Lost in
Even" (More Poems, 14) PE:
246
"For My Funeral" Po: 1614
"He Standing Hushed" (More
Poems, 28) ICBAP: 69; PE:
246; Po: 1614
"Hell Gate" (Last Poems, 31)
PE: 246; Po: 1615
"Her Strong Enchantments Fail-
ing" (Last Poems, 3) PE:
246; Po: 1615
"Here in the Beechen Forest"
PE: 246
"Hypermnestra" Po: 1615
"I Hoed and Trenched and
Weeded" (Shropshire Lad,
63) PE: 247
"I to My Perils" (More Poems,
6) PE: 247

"If It Chance Your Eye
Offend You" (Shropshire
Lad, 45) PE: 246
"The Immortal Part" (Shrop-
shire Lad, 43) PE: 247;
Po: 1615
"Into My Heart an Air That
Kills" (Shropshire Lad, 40)
PE: 247
"Is My Team Plowing?" (Shrop-
shire Lad, 27) ICBAP:
69; PE: 247; Po: 1615-
1616
"It Nods and Curtseys and
Recovers" (Shropshire
Lad, 16) PE: 247
"The Land of Biscay" ICBAP:
69; Po: 1616
"The Lent Lily" (Shropshire
Lad, 29) PE: 247
"Loveliest of Trees" (Shrop-
shire Lad, 2) PE: 247-
248
"March" (Shropshire Lad, 10)
PE: 248
"The Merry Guide" (Shrop-
shire Lad, 42) PE: 248
"The Night Is Freezing Fast"
(Last Poems, 20) PE:
248
"Now Dreary Dawns the East-
ern Light" (Last Poems,
28) PE: 248
"Now Hollow Fires Burn Out
to Black" (Shropshire
Lad, 60) PE: 248
"The Olive" PE: 248
"On Moonlit Heath and Lone-
some Bank" (Shropshire
Lad, 9) PE: 248
"On Wenlock Edge the Wood's
in Trouble" ICBAP: 69;
PE: 248; Po: 1616
"The Oracles" (Last Poems,
25) EP: 152; ICBAP:
69; PE: 248; Po: 1616
"Others, I Am Not the First"
(Shropshire Lad, 30) PE:
249
"The Recruit" (Shropshire
Lad, 3) ICBAP: 69; PE:
249; Po: 1617
"Reveille" (Shropshire Lad, 8)
PE: 249
"Revolution" (Last Poems,
36) PE: 249

A Shropshire Lad EP: 145-148,
150-151; ICBAP: 70; LCAB:
91; Ma: 964-965; Po: 1617-
1618; TA: 181; VP: 44
"The Stars Have Not Dealt Me
the Worst They Could Do"
Po: 1619
"Tell Me Not Here; It Needs Not
Saying" (Last Poems, 40)
PE: 249
"Terence, This Is Stupid Stuff"
(Shropshire Lad, 62) PE:
249; Po: 1619
"This Time of Year a Twelve-
month Past" (Shropshire Lad,
25) PE: 250
"To an Athlete Dying Young"
(Shropshire Lad, 19) PE:
249; Po: 1620
"The True Lover" (Shropshire
Lad, 53) PE: 250
"Wake Not for the World-Heard
Thunder" Po: 1620
"We'll to the Woods No More"
(Last Poems, Preface) PE:
250
"When I Came Last to Ludlow"
(Shropshire Lad, 58) PE:
250
"When Israel Out of Egypt
Came" (More Poems, 2) PE:
250
"When Smoke Stood Up from
Ludlow" (Shropshire Lad, 7)
PE: 250
"White in the Moon the Long
Road Lies" (Shropshire Lad,
36) PE: 250
"With Rue My Heart Is Laden"
(Shropshire Lad, 54) PE:
250
"With Seed the Sowers Scatter"
(More Poems, 32) PE: 250
HOUSMAN, Laurence
General Mi: 244-245
Bethlehem Br: 307
Jacob's Ladder Br: 307
Little Plays of St. Francis (1st
series) Br: 308
Old Testament Plays Br: 308
St. Martin's Pageant Br: 308
Victoria Regina Br: 308; EDC:
257
_____ and Harley GRANVILLE-
BARKER
Prunella, or Love in a Garden

EDC: 257
HOWARD, Bronson
General AD: 147-150; Lon:
60
The Amateur Benefit AD:
148-149; DC1: 95; Lon:
60
Aristocracy AD: 147
The Banker's Daughter AD:
148-150; ADC: 163
The Henrietta AD: 147, 150;
ADC: 163
One of Our Girls AD: 148
Saratoga AD: 147
Shenandoah AD: 147-148;
ADC: 163
Young Mrs. Winthrop AD:
148
HOWARD, Edward
The Six Days Adventure
DC1: 95
The Woman's Conquest DC1:
95
HOWARD, Garland
Change Your Luck ADC:
163
HOWARD, Henry, Earl of Surrey
General SC: 65
"Dyvers Thy Death" PE:
440
"Give Place Ye Lovers" PE:
440
"Good Ladies" PE: 440
"How Each Thing Save the
Lover in Spring Reviveth
to Pleasure" ("When
Windesor Walles Sustained
My Wearied Arme") PE:
440
"In the Rude Age" PE: 440
"London Hast Thou Accused
Me" PE: 440
"Love That Doth Reign and
Live Within My Thought"
ICBAP: 124; PE: 440
"The Means to Attain Happy
Life" PE: 440
"Norfolk Sprang Thee"
(Thomas Clere Sonnet)
PE: 441
"O Happy Dames" PE: 441
"Prisoned in Windsor, He
Recounteth His Pleasure
There Passed" ICBAP:
124; PE: 441
"The Soote Season" PE: 441

"Wyatt Resteth Here" PE: 441
HOWARD, James H.W.
General BAF: 155
HOWARD, John Hayden
"Beyond Words" ASF: 304
HOWARD, Richard
"Waiting for Ada" PE: 250
HOWARD, Sallie
The Jackal BAP: 109
HOWARD, Sidney Coe
General Br: 308; Lon: 33-34;
MD: 145; Po: 1620
Alien Corn ADC: 163; Br:
308; Lon: 34
Dodsworth ADC: 163-164; Br:
308; Lon: 34
The Ghost of Yankee Doodle
ADC: 164; Br: 308-309
Half Gods ADC: 164; Br:
309
The Late Christopher Bean
ADC: 164; Lon: 34
Lucky Sam McCarver Br: 309
Madam, Will You Walk? ADC:
164; Br: 309; DC1: 96
Ned McCobb's Daughter ADC:
164; Br: 309; Lon: 34
Ode to Liberty ADC: 164
Paths of Glory see also COBB,
Humphrey ADC: 165
Quest ADC: 165
The Silver Cord ADC: 165;
Br: 309-310; DC1: 96; MD:
146
Swords ADC: 165
They Knew What They Wanted
ACC: 165-166; Br: 310;
Lon: 33; MD: 146
_____, Will IRWIN, Raymond
SCOTT, and Bernard
HANIGHEN
Lute Song ADC: 167; MD:
146
_____ and Paul de KRUIF
Yellow Jack ADC: 166; Br:
310; DC1: 96; Lon: 33;
MD: 146
_____ and Charles MacARTHUR
Salvation ADC: 167
HOWARD, Sir Robert
General Bon: 43; Li: 216
The Great Favourite; or The
Duke of Lerma see FORD,
John
HOWARD, Vilma
The Tam MBA: 117

HOWARTH, Donald
General MDAE: 279
HOWE, Edgar Watson
General AF: 142-143; ALL:
136-137; AN: 132; ASF:
304; LCAB: 91; Po: 1621
"Doctor Gilkerson" Wa: 337
The Story of a Country Town
AF: 142-143; ALL: 136-
137; AN: 132; LCAB:
91-92
HOWE, Joseph
General ECL 147-148
HOWELL, Constance
A More Excellent Way
ENES2: 129
HOWELL, James
General Ba: 80; ERP: 252-
253; Hen: 138
Dodona's Grove ERP: 252-
253
HOWELLS, William Dean
General AD: 155-157; AF:
148-153; ALL: 137-140;
AN: 134-139; ASF: 306-
307; Cla: 46-50; Ho:
70-77, 148-149; LCAB:
92; Po: 1621-1638
"The Angel of the Lord"
ASF: 304
Annie Kilburn Ho: 73; Po:
1638
April Hopes Ho: 77; Po:
1638-1639
A Boy's Town Ho: 77; Po:
1639
"A Case of Metaphantasmia"
ASF: 304
Certain Delightful English
Towns Po: 1621
A Chance Acquaintance Po:
1637, 1740
"A Circle in the Water" ASF:
304
Colonel Sellers as a Scientist
see also TWAIN, Mark
and William Dean HOWELLS
Po: 1639
"The Critical Bookstore"
ASF: 304-305
Criticism and Fiction Cla:
50; Ho: 76; Po: 1640
A Dangerous Ruffian see
The Garroters
The Day of Their Wedding
Po: 1622

"A Day's Pleasure" ASF: 305
"A Difficult Case" ASF: 305;
WaS1: 94
"A Dream" ASF: 305
"Editha" ASF: 305; Po: 1640;
Wa: 338
Fennel and Rue ASF: 305; Ho:
73
"Flitting" ASF: 305
A Foregone Conclusion Ho: 74;
Po: 1640
The Garroters [A Dangerous
Ruffian] AD: 157
A Hazard of New Fortunes AF:
153; ALL: 140; An: 133;
Ho: 72, 74-75; Ma: 966-967;
Po: 1630-1632, 1641
"His Apparition" ASF: 305
An Imperative Duty AN: 133;
Po: 1637, 1641-1642
"The Independent Candidate"
ASF: 305
Indian Summer AN: 133; Ho:
74; Ma: 967-968; Po: 1642
The Kentons Po: 1642
Lady of the Aroostook AN:
133
The Landlord at Lion's Head
AF: 151; Ho: 75-76, 149;
Po: 1642-1643
The Leatherwood God Ho: 71,
76; Po: 1637
A Letter of Introduction AD:
156
"Letters of an Alturian Travel-
ler" ASF: 305
London Films Po: 1621
"The Magic of a Voice" ASF:
305
The Minister's Charge Ho: 74;
Po: 1643
A Modern Instance AF: 150,
153; ALL: 140; AN: 133;
Ho: 74, 76-77, 149; Ma:
968-969; Po: 1643-1644
"A Pair of Patient Lovers"
ASF: 306
A Parting and a Meeting Po:
1622
"A Pedestrian Tour" ASF:
306
A Previous Engagement AD:
156
Questionable Shapes Ho: 148
"A Romance of Real Life"
ASF: 306; Po: 1648; Wa:

338
"Scene" ASF: 306; Po:
1648-1649
A Sea Change; Or Love's
Stowaway DC1: 96
Seven English Cities Po:
1621
Shadow of a Dream Ho: 73,
76, 148; Po: 1637, 1649
"A Shaker Village" Po: 1622
"A Sleep and a Forgetting"
WaS1: 94
The Son of Royal Langbrith
Po: 1740
Their Wedding Journey AF:
152; AN: 134; Ho: 73,
76; Po: 1630, 1649-1650
"Though One Rose from the
Dead" ASF: 306
Through the Eye of the
Needle Po: 1632
Traveler from Altruvia AN:
134; Po: 1632, 1649
The Undiscovered Country
AF: 152-153; ALL: 140;
Po: 1622, 1637, 1650
The Vacation of the Kelwyns
AN: 135
A Woman's Reason AN: 134
Years of My Youth LCAB:
92
_____ and Paul KESTER
The Rise of Silas Lapham
AD: 155; ADC: 167;
AF: 152-153; ALL: 140;
AN: 133-134; Ho: 72-77,
149; LCAB: 92; Ma: 969-
970; Po: 1631-1632, 1637,
1645-1648
HOWES, Barbara
"The Heart of Europe" PE:
250
"In the Cold Country" PE:
251
"Portrait of an Artist" PE:
251
HOYT, Charles H.
General AD: 159-160; Lon:
60-61
A Runaway Colt AD: 159
A Texas Steer AD: 160
A Trip to Chinatown AD:
159
HRONSKY, Jozef
The World on a Quagmire Fi:
453

HROTSVITHA OF GANDERSHEIM
Abraham DC2: 189
Calimachus DC2: 189
Dulcitius DC2: 189-190
Gallicanus DC2: 190
Gesta Ottonis DC2: 190
Paphnutius DC2: 190
Sapientia DC2: 190
HSIAO HUNG
"At the Foot of the Mountain"
WaS1: 95
"The Bridge" WaS1: 95
"A Cry in the Wilderness"
WaS1: 95
"Flight from Danger" WaS1:
95
"Hands" WaS1: 95
"On the Oxcart" WaS1: 95
"Vague Expectations" WaS1:
95
HUBBARD, Elbert
General ASF: 308
"How I Found My Brother"
ASF: 308
HUBBARD, Frank McKinney
General LCAB: 92
HUBBARD, Lafayette Ronald
"Fear" ASF: 308
HUBBARD, William
General AP: 366
HUCH, Ricarda
Aus Bimbos Seelenwanderungen
Po: 1650
Der Grosse Krieg Ke: 283
"Der letzte Sommer" Wa: 338
Von den Königen und der Krone
Po: 1650
HUCHEL, Peter
General Po: 1650-1651
HUDSON, Hoyt Hopewell
General LCAB: 93
HUDSON, Lois Phillips
The Bones of Plenty LCAB:
93
HUDSON, William Henry
General Po: 1651; TA: 185
A Crystal Age ENES1: 120;
ENES2: 129
Fan ENES1: 121; ENES2: 130
Far Away and Long Ago Ma:
971
Green Mansions ENES1: 121;
ENES2: 130; Ma: 971-972;
Po: 1651
Hampshire Days Ma: 972-973
The Purple Land ENE: 155;

ENES1: 121; ENES2: 130;
Ma: 973-974
Hueffer, Joseph Leopold Ford
Hermann Madox see
FORD, Ford Madox
HUERTA, Garcia de la
La Raquel DC2: 190
HUGHES, Allison
General MBA: 118
HUGHES, Babette
Murder! Murder! Murder!
BAP: 110
HUGHES, Hatcher
Hell-Bent fer Heaven ADC:
167
_____ and Elmer RICE
Wake Up, Jonathan see also
RICE, Elmer ADC: 167
_____ and Alan WILLIAMS
It's a Grand Life ADC:
168
HUGHES, John
Calypso and Telemachus Li:
217
The Siege of Damascus Li:
217
HUGHES, Langston
General AAL: 192, 195-196;
AAPD: 113-115, 319;
AAW: 59-61; ALL: 140-
141; ASF: 310; BAF:
158-162; BAP: 112-113;
BAW: 400-401; Br: 310-
311; HR: 91-100; ICBAP:
70; LCAB: 93; Ma: 975-
976; MBA: 118; Po: 1651-
1654; Wo: 132-133
Angelo Herndon Jones MBA:
119
Ballad of the Brown King
BAP: 115; Br: 311
"Berry" Wa: 338
"Big Meeting" ASF: 308;
Wa: 338
The Big Sea HR: 98
Black Nativity BAP: 115,
117; Br: 311; MBA:
119-120
"Blessed Assurance" ASF:
308; Wa: 338
"The Blues I'm Playing"
ASF: 308; Wa: 338;
WaS1: 95
"Christmas Song" ASF: 308;
Wa: 338
"Cora Unashamed" ASF:

308; Wa: 338
"Daybreak in Alabama" PE: 251
Don't You Want to Be Free?
BAP: 113; Br: 311-312;
MBA: 119
Drums of Haiti [Emperor of Haiti;
Troubled Island] BAP: 113;
Br: 312; MBA: 119
"Du, Meine Zuversicht" see
"Blessed Assurance"
Esther BAP: 115; Br: 312
"Father and Son" ASF: 308;
Wa: 338; WaS1: 95
Fine Clothes to the Jew AAL:
192; HR: 97
"The Folks at Home" see
"Home"
Front Porch BAP: 113-114;
Br: 312
The Gold Piece MBA: 119
"A Good Job Gone" ASF: 308;
Wa: 338
Gospel Glow [Gospel Glory]
BAP: 115; Br: 312
"Home" ASF: 308; Wa: 338
Jerico-Jim Crow BAP: 115-116;
Br: 312; MBA: 119
Joy to My Soul BAP: 114
Just a Little Simple Br: 312
Langston Hughes Said MBA:
120
Laughing to Keep from Crying
AAL: 192; BAF: 162
"Little Dog" ASF: 309; Wa:
339
Little Ham BAP: 114, 116; Br:
312; MBA: 119
"Mary Winowsky" AAW: 60;
ASF: 309; BAF: 159; Po:
1654; Wa: 339
"Minstrel Man" Po: 1654
"Mother and Child" ASF: 309;
Wa: 339
Mulatto ADC: 168; BAP: 114,
116-117; Br: 312; Ma: 975;
MBA: 119-121
Not Without Laughter BAF:
162; HR: 94; Po: 1654
"On the Road" ASF: 309; Wa:
339
"On the Way Home" ASF: 309;
Wa: 339
"One Christmas Eve" ASF:
309; Wa: 339
The Panther and the Lash
Po: 1654-1655

"Passing" Wa: 339
"Poor Little Black Fellow"
ASF: 309; Wa: 339
Port Town BAP: 116; Br:
313
"Powder-White Face" ASF:
309; Wa: 339
The Prodigal Son ADC: 168;
BAP: 116-117; Br: 313
"Professor" ASF: 309; Wa:
339
"Red-Headed Baby" ASF:
309; Wa: 339
"Rejuvenation Through Joy"
ASF: 309; Wa: 339
"Sailor Ashore" ASF: 309;
Wa: 339
Scottsboro Blues BAP: 114
Scottsboro Limited MBA:
120
Simple Speaks His Mind BAF:
162
Simple Stakes a Claim BAF:
162-163
Simple Takes a Wife BAF:
163
Simple's Uncle Sam BAF:
159, 163
Simply Heavenly ADC: 168;
BAP: 114-115, 117; Br:
313; MBA: 120-121
"Slave on the Block" ASF:
309; SFC: 91; Wa: 339
"Slice Him Down" Wa: 340
"Something in Common" Wa:
340
Soul Gone Home AAPD:
319; BAP: 115; Br: 313;
MBA: 120
"Spanish Blood" ASF: 309
Street Scene BAP: 115,
117; MBA: 120
The Sun Do Move BAP: 116;
Br: 313; MBA: 120
"'Tain't So" Wa: 340
"Theme for English B" PE:
251
Troubled Island see Drums
of Haiti
Way Down South BAP: 117-
118
"Ways and Means" Wa: 340
Ways of White Folks AAL:
192; BAF: 163-164
The Weary Blues AAL: 192;
HR: 92, 94

"Who's Passing for Who?" Wa:
340
_____ and Arna BONTEMPS
When the Jack Hollers BAP:
26, 115; Br: 313
_____ and Jobe HUNTLEY
. Tambourines to Glory AAPD:
319; ADC: 168; BAF: 163;
BAP: 116-117; Br: 313;
MBA: 120-121
_____ and Zora Neale HURSTON
Mule Bone BAP: 116; MBA:
120
_____ and Jan MEYEROWITZ
The Barrier AAL: 192; ADC:
168; BAP: 115, 117; Br:
311; MBA: 119
HUGHES, Richard [Arthur WAR-
REN]
General BN2 59-60; CFAE:
197; Mi: 245-246; Po: 1655;
Sch: 129
"The Cart" Wa: 340
A Comedy of Good and Evil
Br: 313
The Fox in the Attic
CN: 284; ENE: 156; ENES1:
121; ENES2: 130; Ma: 977
A High Wind in Jamaica [The
Innocent Voyage] BN2: 60;
CFAE: 197; CN: 284; ENE:
156; ENES1: 121; ENES2:
130; Ma: 978; Po: 1655-
1656; Sch: 129
The Human Predicament ENES1:
121; ENES2: 130
In Hazard CN: 284; ENES1:
121; ENES2: 130; Ma: 977
The Innocent Voyage see A
High Wind in Jamaica
"Llwyd" Wa: 340
"Poor Man's Inn" Wa: 340
The Wooden Shepherdess
ENES1: 121; ENES2: 130;
Ma: 978
HUGHES, Ted
General ICBAP: 70; LCAB:
93; MDAE: 280; MP: 48;
Po: 1656-1657
"Childbirth" ICBAP: 70
"A Childish Prank" PE: 251
"Crow" MP: 48
"Full Moon and Little Frieda"
PE: 251
"Gog" PE: 251
"The Hawk in the Rain" ICBAP:

70; PE: 251; Po: 1657
"Lupercalia" ICBAP: 70
"Pike" PE: 251
"Wodwo" PE: 251
_____ and Peter BROOK
Orghast at Persepolis MDAE:
280
HUGHES, Thomas
General BN: 68
The Misfortunes of Arthur
DC1: 96
Tom Brown's School Days
ENE: 156; ENES2: 130
HUGO, Richard Franklin
General ICBAP: 70
HUGO, Victor Marie
Bug-Jargal Fi: 93
Les Burgraves EDC: 258
Cromwell EDC: 258
Le Dernier Jour d'un con-
damné Fi: 93
Han D'Islande Fi: 93; Ke:
97
Hernani DC2: 190-191;
EDC: 258-259
The Hunchback of Notre Dame
Fi: 93-94; Ke: 97-98; Ma:
979
Lucretia Borgia DC2: 191
The Man Who Laughs Fi:
94; Ke: 98
Marion de Lorme EDC: 259
Mary Tudor [Marie-Tudor]
DC2: 191; EDC: 259
Les Misérables Fi: 94-95;
Ke: 98-99; LCAB: 93;
Ma: 979-980
Ninety-Three Fi: 95; Ke:
99
Ruy Blas EDC: 259
The Toilers of the Sea Fi:
95; Ke: 99-100; Ma:
980-981
HUGUENIN, Jean-René
General Po: 1657-1658
HUIDOBRO, Vicente
General Po: 1658
HULME, Thomas Ernest
General Po: 1658-1659
HUME, Alexander
General Ai: 43-44
HUME, David
General Ai: 65; EC: 82-
83; LCAB: 93
Dialogues Concerning Natural
Religion EC: 83; Ma:

982
An Enquiry Concerning Human
Understanding EC: 82
History of England Ma: 982-
983
"Of Criticism" EC: 83
"Of Tragedy" EC: 83
A Treatise of Human Nature
EC: 82-83; Ma: 983
HUME, Fergus
General AL: 248
HUMPHREY, William
General ASF: 311; CN: 285
Home from the Hill CN: 285
The Ordways CN: 285
HUMPHREYS, David
General Da: 79
HUMPHRIES, Rolfe
"Little Fugue" PE: 251; Po:
1659
"Polo Grounds" PE: 251
HUNEKER, James Gibbons
General AN: 140; ASF: 311;
Po: 1659-1660
"Pan" Wa: 340
HUNT, Hamlen
"Tonight We Eat Leaning" SFC:
91; Wa: 340
HUNT, Leigh
General Fog: 36; Re: 203-204
"Abou Ben Adhem" PE: 251
"Jenny Kissed Me" PE: 251
HUNT, Violet
The Desirable Alien at Home in
Germany Po: 1660
HUNTER, Eddie
General BAP: 118; BAW: 403
How Come? BAP: 118
HUNTER, Evan
General ASF: 311
HUNTER, Frederic
The Hemingway Play ADC:
168
HUNTER, Kristin [Mrs. John I.
LATTANY]
General BAF: 165; BAW: 405
God Bless the Child BAF: 165
The Landlord BAF: 165
The Survivors BAF: 165
HUNTER, Norman Charles
A Day by the Sea Br: 314;
MDAE: 281
HUNTER, Robert
Androboros DC1: 97
HUNTER-DUVAR, John
General ECL: 150

HURD, Richard
　General EC: 84
　Letters on Chivalry and
　　Romance EC: 84
HURLBURT, William
　Bride of the Lamb Br: 314
　Recessional Br: 314
HURST, Fannie
　General AN: 140; LCAB:
　　93-94
　Lummox AN: 140
　A President Is Born AN:
　　140
HURSTON, Zora Neale
　General AAF: 62-63; AAW:
　　61; ASF: 311-312; BAF:
　　166-169; BAW: 407-408;
　　HR: 102-107; LCAB: 94;
　　MBA: 122
　"Black Death" ASF: 311;
　　WaS1: 95
　"Drenched in Light" ASF:
　　311; Wa: 341
　"The Gilded Six-Bits" ASF:
　　311; Wa: 341
　"John Redding Goes to Sea"
　　ASF: 311; Wa: 341
　Jonah's Gourd Vine BAF:
　　169
　Moses, Man of the Mountain
　　BAF: 169
　Seraph on the Suwanee BAF:
　　167, 169
　"Spunk" ASF: 311; Wa:
　　341
　"Sweat" ASF: 311; Wa:
　　341; WaS1: 95
　Their Eyes Were Watching
　　God BAF: 167-169; HR:
　　105-107
HUTCHESON, Francis
　General EC: 84-85
HUTCHINSON, Alfred
　General BALE: 308
HUTCHINSON, Lionel
　Man from the People WIL:
　　60
　One Touch of Nature WIL:
　　60-61
HUTCHINSON, Thomas
　General AP: 581-582
HUXLEY, Aldous
　General BN2: 61-63; CN:
　　285-288; ICBAP: 70;
　　LCAB: 94; Po: 1660-
　　1669; Ri: 465-482, 492-

　　495; Sch: 130-135
Adonis and the Alphabet Ri:
　492
After Many a Summer Dies the
　Swan CN: 289; EN: 69;
　ENE: 156; ENES1: 121;
　ENES2: 130; LCAB: 94;
　Ma: 984; Po: 1664, 1667,
　1669; Ri: 466, 468, 473, 479,
　483
"After the Fireworks" Wa:
　341
Antic Hay CN: 289-290; EN:
　69; ENE: 156; ENES1: 121-
　122; ENES2: 130-131; LCAB:
　94; Po: 1664, 1669; Ri:
　475-476, 483-484; Sch: 136
Ape and Essence CN: 290;
　ENES1: 122; ENES2: 131;
　Po: 1669-1670; Ri: 467, 474,
　484; Ri2: 327
"Beauty" ICBAP: 71
Beyond the Mexique Bay Ri:
　488, 493, 495
"The Birth of God" PE: 252
Brave New World BN2: 62;
　CN: 290-291; EN: 69; ENE:
　157; ENES1: 122; ENES2:
　131; LCAB: 94; Ma: 984-
　985; Po: 1664, 1666, 1670-
　1672; Ri: 467, 470, 473-476,
　482, 484-487; Ri2: 322,
　326-328, 331, 466, 507; Sch:
　136-137
Brave New World Revisited Ri:
　485-486, 494
Brief Candles Ri: 477
"Chawdron" Wa: 341
"The Cicadas" PE: 252
"The Claxtons" Wa: 341
"A Country Walk" Wa: 341
Crome Yellow CN: 292; EN:
　69; ENE: 158; ENES1: 122;
　ENES2: 131; Ma: 985-986;
　Po: 1665, 1672; Ri: 468,
　473, 475-476, 482, 487-488
"Cynthia" Wa: 341
"The Death of Lully" Wa: 341
Do What You Will Ri: 492
The Doors of Perception Ri:
　495
Ends and Means Ri: 492-494
"Eupompus Gave Splendour to
　Art by Numbers" Wa: 341
Eyeless in Gaza CN: 292; EN:
　70; ENE: 158; ENES1: 122-

123; ENES2: 131-132;
LCAB: 94; Ma: 986-987;
Ri: 468, 470, 476, 479,
482, 488; Sch: 137
"The Farcical History of
Richard Greenow" Wa:
341
"Frad" Wa: 341
The Genius and the Goddess
CN: 292-293; ENE: 158;
ENES1: 123; ENES2: 132;
Po: 1667; Ri: 479
"The Gioconda Smile" Po:
1672; Ri: 488; SFC: 91;
Wa: 341-342
"Green Tunnels" Wa: 342
"Happily Ever After" Wa:
342; WaS1: 95
"Happy Families" Wa: 342
"In the Chaos of the Moon's"
PE: 252
Island BN2: 62; CN: 293;
ENE: 158; ENES1: 123;
ENES2: 132; Ma: 987;
Po: 1665-1666, 1673; Ri:
468-470, 475, 489; Ri2:
526; Sch: 137
"Leda" ICBAP: 71; PE:
252; Po: 1673; Ri: 495
"Little Mexican" Wa: 342
Mortal Coils Ri: 482
Music at Night Ri: 495
"Nuns at Luncheon" SFC:
91; Wa: 342
The Olive Tree, and Other
Essays Ri: 492
The Perennial Philosophy
Ri: 493
Point Counter Point BN2:
62; CN: 293-294; EN:
70; ENE: 158-159; ENES1:
123-124; ENES2: 132-133;
LCAB: 94; Ma: 988-989;
Po: 1674-1675; Ri: 467,
475-476, 480, 482, 490-
491; Sch: 137-138
"The Reef" PE: 252
"The Rest Cure" Wa: 342
"Sir Hercules" Wa: 342
"Soles Occidere et Redire
Possunt" ICBAP: 71
Those Barren Leaves CN:
294; EN: 70; ENE: 159;
ENES1: 124; ENES2:
133; Ri: 491
"Tide" PE: 252

"The Tillotson Banquet" Wa:
342
Time Must Have a Stop CN:
295; EN: 71; ENE: 159;
ENES1: 124; ENES2: 133;
Po: 1667; Ri: 479, 491-492
"Two or Three Graces" Wa:
342
"Uncle Spencer" Wa: 342
The World of Light Br: 314;
DC1: 97; Ri: 494
"The Yellow Mustard" PE: 252
"Young Archimedes" SFC: 92;
Wa: 342
HUXLEY, Thomas Henry
General VP: 45-46
HUYSMANS, Joris-Karl
Against the Grain Fi: 95-96;
Ke: 100; Ma: 990
The Cathedral Ke: 100
Un Dilemme Fi: 96
Downstream Fi: 96; Ke: 101
En ménage Fi: 96; Ke: 101
En rade Fi: 96; Ke: 101
En route Fi: 96; Ke: 101;
Ma: 990
Là-bas Fi: 96; Ke: 100-101
Marthe Fi: 97; Ke: 101
The Oblate Fi: 97; Ke: 102
A rebours LCAB: 94
St. Lydwine Ke: 102
Les Soeurs Vatard Fi: 97; Ke:
102
HYDE, Douglas
General Mi: 246
The Twisting of the Rope Br:
314

I

Ibáñez, Vicente Blasco see
BLASCO IBAÑEZ, Vicente
IBARBOUROU, Juana de
General Po: 1677
IBSEN, Henrik
General Br: 314-319; LCAB:
94; MD: 146-153
Brand Br: 319-320; DC2:
191-192; EDC: 260-261; Ma:
991-992; MD: 153-154
Bygmester Solness see The
Master Builder
Catiline [Catalina; Catilina;
Katilina] Br: 320; DC2:
192; EDC: 261; MD: 154

The Doll's House [Et Dukke-
hjem] Br: 320-321; DC2:
192-193; EDC: 261-262;
Ma: 992-993; MBD: 67;
MD: 154-155; MDAE:
400; TMBP: 112

The Emperor and Galilean
[Kejser og Galilaeer] Br:
321; DC2: 194; EDC:
262-263; MD: 155

An Enemy of the People [En
Folkenfiend] Br: 321-
322; DC2: 194; EDC:
263; LCAB: 94; Ma: 993;
MD: 155-156

The Feast at Solhaug [Gildet
Paa Solhaug] Br: 322;
DC2: 194; EDC: 263;
MD: 156

Fru Inger til Ostraat see
Lady Inger of Østeraad

Fruen fra Havet see Lady
from the Sea

Ghosts [Gengangere] Br:
322-324; DC2: 195-197;
EDC: 264-265; LCAB:
95; Ma: 994-995; MD:
156-157

Gildet Paa Solhaug see The
Feast at Solhaug

Haermaendene Paa Helgeland
see Vikings at Helgeland

Hedda Gabler Br: 324-325;
DC2: 197-198; EDC:
265-268; LCAB: 95; Ma:
995-996; MD: 157-158;
Po: 37; TMAP: 37

The Hero's Grave MD: 158

John Gabriel Borkman Br:
325; DC2: 198; EDC:
268; MD: 158

Katilina see Catiline

Kejser og Galilaeer see The
Emperor and Galilean

Kjaemphøien see The War-
rior's Barrow

Kjaerlighedens Komodie see
Love's Comedy

Kongs-Emnerne see The
Pretenders

Lady from the Sea [The Sea
Woman; Fruen fra Havet]
Br: 326; DC2: 198-199;
EDC: 269; Ma: 996-997;
MD: 158-159

Lady Inger of Østeraad [Fru

Inger til Ostraat] DC2:
195; EDC: 269; MD: 159

League of Youth [De Unges For-
bund] Br: 326; DC2: 199;
EDC: 269; MD: 159

Little Eyolf [Lille Eyolf] Br:
326-327; DC2: 199; EDC:
269-270; MD: 159; MDAE:
60; Po: 38; TMAP: 58

Love's Comedy [Kjaerlighedens
Komodie] Br: 327; DC2:
199; EDC: 270; MD: 159-
160

The Master Builder [Bygmester
Solness] Br: 327-328; DC2:
199-201; EDC: 270-271; Ma:
997-998; MD: 160

Nar Vi Döde Vagner see When
We Dead Awaken

Olaf Liljekrans Br: 328; EDC:
271

Peer Gynt Br: 328-329; DC2:
201-202; EDC: 271-273;
LCAB: 95; Ma: 998-999;
MD: 160-162; TMAP: 63

The Pillars of Society [Sanfun-
dets Støtter] Br: 329; DC2:
202; EDC: 273-274; Ma:
999-1000; MD: 162

The Pretenders [Kongs-Emnerne]
Br: 330; DC2: 202-203;
EDC: 274; MD: 162

Rosmersholm Br: 330-331;
DC2: 203-204; EDC: 274-
275; LCAB: 95; Ma: 1000-
1001; MD: 162-163

St. John's Eve [Sancthansnat-
ten] Br: 331; EDC: 275;
MD: 163

Samfundets Støtter see The
Pillars of Society

The Sea Woman see Lady from
the Sea

De Unges Forbund see League
of Youth

Vikings at Helgeland [Haer-
maendene Paa Helgeland] Br:
331; DC2: 204; EDC: 275

Vildanden see The Wild Duck

The Warrior's Barrow [Kjaem-
phøien] Br: 331; EDC:
275

When We Dead Awaken [Nar
Vi Döde Vagner] Br: 332;
DC2: 204-205; EDC: 275-
276; Ma: 1001-1002; MD:

163-164
The Wild Duck [Vildanden]
  Br: 332-334; DC2: 205-
  206; EDC: 276-278; LCAB:
  95; Ma: 1002-1003; MD:
  164-165
ICAZA, Jorge
  General Br: 334
  El chulla Romero y Flórez
    Po: 1677
  En las calles Po: 1677
  Huasipungo Po: 1677-1678
Iceberg Slim see BECK, Robert
IGNATOW, David
  General ICBAP: 71; JW:
  84; Po: 1678
IGUH, Thomas Orlando
  General BALE: 309
IJIMERE, Obotunde [Ulli BEIER]
  General BALE: 309
IKE, Vincent Chukwuemeka
  General BALE: 309
IKIDDEH, Ime
  General BALE: 310
IKOR, Roger
  General Po: 1678
ILF AND PETROV
  Diamonds to Sit On Ke:
    413
  The Little Golden Calf Ke:
    413
ILHAN, Attilâ
  General Po: 1678-1679
IMBRIE, McCrea and Neil
    SELDEN
  Someone's Comin' Hungry
    ADC: 169
IMBUGA, Francis D.
  General BALE: 310
IMLAY, Gilbert
  The Immigrants Ma: 1004
IMMERMANN, Karl
  The Epigones Ke: 283
  Munchhausen Ke: 283
INCHBALD, Elizabeth
  General Li: 220
  Nature and Art ENES2: 133
  A Simple Story ENES2: 133
INGE, William
  General Br: 334-335; LCAB:
  95; Lon: 34; MD: 165;
  MDAE: 283-285; Po:
  1679
  All Fall Down MDAE: 284
  The Boy in the Basement
    Br: 335; MD: 165

Bus Riley's Back in Town Br:
  335; MD: 165
Bus Stop ADC: 169; Br: 335;
  DC1: 97; Ma: 1005; MD:
  166; Po: 1679
Come Back, Little Sheba ADC:
  169; Br: 335-336; DC1: 97;
  Ma: 1005-1006; MD: 166;
  Po: 1679
The Dark at the Top of the
  Stairs ADC: 170; Br: 336;
  DC1: 97; Ma: 1006; MD:
  166; Po: 1679
Dialogue for Two Men see The
  Love Death Plays
Farther Off from Heaven ADC:
  170
Glory in the Flower Br: 336;
  MD: 166
An Incident at the Standish
  Arms Br: 336
The Last Pad ADC: 170
A Loss of Roses ADC: 170;
  Br: 336-337; DC1: 97;
  LCAB: 95; Ma: 1006-1007;
  MD: 166; MDAE: 284
The Love Death Plays [six
  plays: The Wake; Venus
  and Adonis; Dialogue for Two
  Men; Midwestern Manic; The
  Love Death; and The Star]
  ADC: 170
The Mall Br: 337
Memory of Summer Br: 337
Midwestern Manic see The
  Love Death Plays
Natural Affection ADC: 170-
  171; Br: 337; MD: 166;
  MDAE: 284
Overnight ADC: 171
People in the Wind Br: 337;
  MD: 166
Picnic ADC: 171; Br: 337;
  DC1: 97; Ma: 1007; MD:
  166-167; MDAE: 283-284;
  Po: 1679
The Rainy Afternoon Br:
  338
A Social Event Br: 338; MD:
  167
Splendor in the Grass Br:
  338; MD: 167; MDAE: 284
The Star see The Love Death
  Plays
The Strains of Triumph Br:
  338

Summer Brave ADC: 171;
Br: 338; MD: 167
The Tiny Closet ADC: 171;
Br: 338
To Bobolink, for Her Spirit
Br: 338
Venus and Adonis see The
Love Death Plays
The Wake see The Love
Death Plays
Where's Daddy? ADC: 171-
172
INGRAHAM, Joseph Holt
General AN: 140
Pierce Fleming AN: 140
INGRAM, Kenneth E.
General WIL: 61
INGRASSIA, Anthony
Fame ADC: 172
INNAURATO, Albert
Earth Worms ADC: 172
Gemini ADC: 172
The Transfiguration of Benno
Blimpie ADC: 172
Ulysses in Traction ADC:
172
Innes, Michael see STEWART,
John Innes Mackintosh
INOUE, Yasushi
Tempyō Po: 1679-1680
INVERNIZIO, Carolina
Storia d'una sartina Fi: 266
IONESCO, Eugène
General Br: 338-342; LCAB:
95-96; MD: 167-169; Po:
1680-1692
The Aerial Pedestrian [The
Airborne Pedestrian; The
Pedestrian of the Air; The
Stroller in the Air; Le
Piéton de l'air] Br: 342-
343; DC2: 210; EDC:
285-286; Ma: 1014; Po:
1681, 1687
Amédée, or How to Get Rid
of It [Amédée, ou Comments
s'en Debarrasser] Br:
343; DC2: 207; EDC:
278; Ma: 1008; MD: 169
L'Avenir est dans les Oeufs,
ou Il Faut de Tout pour
Faire un Monde see The
Future Is in the Eggs, or
It Takes Everything to
Make a World
The Bald Soprano [The Bald

Prima-Donna; La Cantatrice
chauve] Br: 343-344; DC2:
207-208; EDC: 278-279; Ma:
1008-1009; MD: 169; Po:
1683, 1687, 1689, 1692-1693
The Berenger Plays LCAB:
96
The Chairs [Les Chaises] Br:
344-345; DC2: 208-209;
EDC: 279-281; Ma: 1009-
1010; MD: 169; Po: 1693-
1694; TMBP: 224
Exit the King [The King Dies;
Le Roi se Meurt] Br: 345-
346; EDC: 281; Ma: 1010-
1011; MD: 170; Po: 174,
1681
Frenzy for Two Br: 346
The Future Is in the Eggs, or
It Takes Everything to Make
a World [L'Avenir est dans
les Oeufs, ou Il Faut de Tout
pour Faire un Monde] Br:
346; EDC: 281
Hunger and Thirst [La Soif et
la Faim] Br: 346-347; DC2:
209; EDC: 281-282; Po:
1695
Improvisation, or The Shepherd's
Chameleon [L'Impromptu de
l'Alma, or Le Cameleon du
Berger] Br: 347; DC2:
209; EDC: 282; MD: 170
Jack, or The Submission
[Jacques, ou La Soumission]
Br: 347; DC2: 209; EDC:
282; Ma: 1011; MD: 169-170
Jeux de Massacre see Wipe
Out Games
The Killer [Tueur sans Gages]
Br: 347-348; DC2: 209-210;
EDC: 282-283; Ma: 1011-
1012; MD: 170; Po: 1681,
1685, 1687, 1695
The King Dies see Exit the
King
The Lesson [La Leçon] Br:
348-349; DC2: 210; EDC:
283-284; Ma: 1012-1013; MD:
170; Po: 1683, 1689
Maid to Marry Br: 349
The New Tenant [Le Nouveau
Locataire] Br: 349; DC2:
210; EDC: 284; MD: 170
The Pedestrian of the Air see
The Aerial Pedestrian

The Picture [Le Tableau]
Br: 349; EDC: 284; MD:
170
Le Piéton de l'air see The
Aerial Pedestrian
"Rhinoceros" ["Le Rhinocéros"]
Br: 349-350; DC2: 210-
211; EDC: 284-285; LCAB:
96; Ma: 1013-1014; MD:
170; Po: 1681, 1685, 1687,
1695; WaS1: 95-96
Le Roi se Meurt see Exit
the King
La Soif et la Faim see
Hunger and Thirst
The Stroller in the Air see
The Aerial Pedestrian
Le Tableau see The Picture
Tueur sans Gages see The
Killer
Victims of Duty [Victimes du
Devoir] Br: 351; DC2:
211-212; EDC: 286; Ma:
1014-1015; MD: 170; Po:
1687, 1689, 1696
Wipe Out Games [Jeux de
Massacre] EDC: 286
IOOR, William
The Battle of Eutaw Springs
ADC: 172
Independence ADC: 173
IREDELL, James
General AP: 582
IRELAND, David
General MAP: 198
The Chantic Bird MAP: 198
The Flesheaters MAP: 198
The Unknown Industrial
Prisoner MAP: 199
IRELE, Abiola
General BALE: 310
Iron, Ralph see SCHREINER,
Olive
IRVINE, Weldon
Young, Gifted and Broke
MBA: 122
IRVING, Washington
General AF: 157-159; ALL:
142-145; AP: 369-378;
ASF: 314-317; Da: 98-99;
LCAB: 96
"The Adventure of My Aunt"
Wa: 343
"The Adventure of My Uncle"
ASF: 312; SFC: 92; Wa:
343

"The Adventure of the German
Student" ASF: 312; SFC:
92; Wa: 343; WaS1: 96
"The Adventure of the Mysteri-
ous Picture" SFC: 92; Wa:
343
"The Adventure of the Mysteri-
ous Stranger" Wa: 343
The Adventures of Captain
Bonneville ALL: 142
"The Angler" Wa: 343
"Annette Delarbre" Wa: 343
Astoria ALL: 142
"The Bold Dragoon" Wa: 343
"Buckthorne and His Friends"
SFC: 92
"Buckthorne, or The Young
Man of Great Expectations"
ASF: 312; Wa: 343
A Chronicle of the Conquest of
Granada AF: 158; Ma:
1016
"The Devil and Tom Walker"
ASF: 312; Wa: 343
"Dolph Heyliger" ASF: 312;
Wa: 343
"The Grand Prior of Minorca"
ASF: 312
A History of New York [Knick-
erbocker's History] AF:
157-159; ALL: 144; AP:
372-378; Da: 99; Ma: 1016-
1017
In the Rocky Mountains and the
Far West ALL: 142
"John Bull" ASF: 312
"The Legend of Prince Ahmed
al Kamel" Wa: 343
"The Legend of Sleepy Hollow"
AF: 158-159; ALL: 144;
ASF: 312-313; Da: 98-99;
LCAB: 96; Ma: 1017-1018;
SFC: 92; Wa: 344; WaS1:
96
"The Legend of the Rose of the
Alhambra" Wa: 344
"Life of Capt. James Lawrence"
Da: 98
"May-Day" ASF: 313
"On Passaic Falls" Da: 99
"The Pride of the Village" Wa:
344
"Rip Van Winkle" AF: 158-
159; ALL: 144; ASF: 313;
Da: 98-99; Ma: 1018-1019;
SFC: 92-93; Wa: 344-345;

WaS1: 96
"The Rookery" ASF: 313
Salmagundij... AP: 372-374
"The Seven Sons of Lara"
    ASF: 314
Sketch Book LCAB: 96
The Sketch Book of Geoffrey
    Crayon, Gent. AF: 158-
    159; AP: 373-375
"The Spectre Bridegroom"
    AF: 159; ASF: 314; SFC:
    93; Wa: 345; WaS1: 96
"The Story of the Young
    Italian" ASF: 314; SFC:
    93; Wa: 345
"The Story of the Young
    Robber" ASF: 314; Wa:
    345; WaS1: 96
"The Stout Gentleman" ASF:
    314
"The Student of Salamanca"
    Wa: 345
A Tour on the Prairies ALL:
    142
U.S.A. ALL: 142
"The Wife" Wa: 345-346
"Wolfert Webber" ASF: 314;
    Wa: 346
IRWIN, James [Edward J.
    MOORE]
The Sea Horse ADC: 173
IRZYKOWSKI, Karol
Paluba Fi: 453; Ke: 413
ISAAKIAN, Avetik
General Po: 1696
ISHAM, John W.
The Octoroons MBA: 122
Oriental America MBA: 122
ISHERWOOD, Christopher
General BN2: 63-64; Br:
    351; CFAE: 200; CN:
    295-296; MBD: 26-27; Mi:
    246-247; Po: 1696-1697;
    Sch: 138-139
All the Conspirators CN:
    296; ENES1: 124; ENES2:
    133
"Ambrose" WaS1: 96
The Ascent of F6 see also
    AUDEN, Wystan Hugh and
    Christopher ISHERWOOD
    Po: 1697-1698
The Berlin Stories Ma: 1020
The Dog Beneath the Skin
    see also AUDEN, Wystan
    Hugh and Christopher

ISHERWOOD Po: 1698
Down There on a Visit BN2:
    63-64; CN: 296; ENES1:
    124; ENES2: 133; Ma: 1020
Goodbye to Berlin CN: 296;
    ENES2: 134; Sch: 139
"The Hero" WaS1: 96
I Am a Camera Br: 351
A Meeting by the River ENES1:
    124; ENES2: 134
The Memorial CN: 296;
    ENES1: 124; ENES2: 134
Mr. Norris Changes Trains
    ENES1: 124; ENES2: 134
"On Ruegen Island" WaS1: 96
Prater Violet CN: 296; ENES1:
    124; ENES2: 134; Ma: 1021;
    SFC: 93; Wa: 346
Ramakrishna and His Disciples
    LCAB: 96
A Single Man CN: 297;
    ENES1: 124-125; ENES2:
    134; Ma: 1021-1022
The World in the Evening CN:
    297; ENES1: 125; ENES2:
    134
ISKANDER, Fazil
The Goatibex Constellation Fi:
    453
Sandro from Chegem Fi: 453
ISLA Y ROJO, José Francisco
Fray Gerundio Ke: 205-206
ISLAM, Kazi Nazrul
General Po: 1698
ISVARAN, Manjeri S.
"At His Nativity" WaS1: 97
"Consummation" WaS1: 97
"Sivaratri" WaS1: 97
Itallie, Jean-Claude van see
    VAN ITALLIE, Jean-Claude
IVANOV, Viacheslav
General Po: 1698
IVANOV, Vsevolod
Armored Train No. 14-69
    Br: 351; MD: 170
"The Kid" SFC: 93; Wa: 346
"Runaway Island" Wa: 346
IWASZKIEWICZ, Jaroslaw
The Fame and the Glory
    Po: 1698-1699
Lovers of Marona Po: 1698-
    1699
Mother Joanna of the Angels
    Po: 1698-1699
IZEVBAYE, Daniel S.
General BALE: 311

J

JABAVU, Noni [Helen NON-
TANDO]
General BALE: 311
JABES, Edmond
Je bâtis ma demeure Po:
1701
La question du livre Po:
1701
JACCOTTET, Philippe
General Po: 1701
JACK, Sam
Creole Show MBA: 123
JACKER, Corinne L.
Harry Outside ADC: 173
My Life ADC: 173
Jackman, Marvin see MARVIN
X
JACKMAN, Oliver
Saw the House in Half WIL:
61
JACKSON, Blyden
General BALE: 170
Operation Burning Candle
BAF: 170
JACKSON, C. Bernard
Departure MBA: 123
The Second Earthquake
MBA: 123
Sweet Nutcracker MBA: 123
JACKSON, Charles
"The Boy Who Ran Away"
Wa: 346
JACKSON, Elaine
General BAP: 120
Cockfight ADC: 173; MBA:
123
Toe Jam MBA: 123
JACKSON, Helen Hunt
General ASF: 317
Ramona AN: 140-141
JACKSON, James Thomas
General MBA: 124
JACKSON, Mae
General BAF: 171
JACKSON, Shirley
General ASF: 318
"After You, My Dear Al-
phonse" Wa: 346; WaS1:
97
"The Beautiful Stranger"
WaS1: 97
"The Bus" WaS1: 97
"Charles" WaS1: 97
"The Daemon Lover" WaS1:

97
"Elizabeth" ASF: 318
"Flower Garden" ASF: 318;
WaS1: 97
Hangsaman CN: 297
"The Island" WaS1: 97
"The Little House" WaS1: 97
"The Lottery" ASF: 318; SFC:
93-94; Wa: 346; WaS1: 97
"On the House" WaS1: 97
"The Phantom Lover" see "The
Daemon Lover"
"The Possibility of Evil" WaS1:
98
"The Rock" WaS1: 98
"Seven Types of Ambiguity"
ASF: 318
"The Summer People" Wa: 347;
WaS1: 98
"The Villager" WaS1: 98
"The Visit" WaS1: 98
We Have Always Lived in the
Castle CN: 297; Po: 1701
"The Witch" ASF: 318; Wa:
347
JACOB, Marcel
General Po: 1702
JACOB, Max
Le Cornet à dés Po: 1702
Saint Matorel Po: 1702
Jacob, Porfirio Barba see BARBA
JACOB, Porfirio
JACOB, Violet
General Ai: 199
JACOBI, Friedrich Heinrich
Edward Allwills Papiere Ke:
283
JACOBS, William Wymark
General Mi: 247; Po: 1702;
TA: 189
JACOBSEN, Hans Jacob
Fair Play Fi: 404
Father-and-Son Journey Fi:
405
A Firm Grip on Life Fi: 405
Mirage Fi: 405
JACOBSEN, Jens Peter
Marie Grubbe Fi: 405; Ke:
353
Mogens Ke: 353
Niels Lyhne Fi: 405; Ke:
353
JACOBSEN, Jørgen-Frantz
Barbara Fi: 405
JACOBSON, Dan
General CN: 297-298

"Beggar My Neighbor" Wa: 347

The Beginners CN: 298

A Dance in the Sun CN: 298

Evidence of Love CN: 298

The Price of Diamonds CN: 298

The Trap CN: 298

"The Zulu and the Zeide" Wa: 347

JAEGER, Frank
Den Unge Jaegers Lidelser Fi: 405

JAEGER, Hans
From the Christiania Boheme Ke: 353

JAFFE, Dan
Dan Freeman Po: 1703

JAGO, Richard
"Edge-Hill" PE: 252

JAHNN, Hans Henny
General Po: 1703
Fluss Ohne Ufer Fi: 333; Po: 1703-1704
The Memoirs of Gustav Anias Horn Fi: 333
Die Nacht aus Blei Po: 1704
Perrudja Fi: 333

JAIMES FREYRE, Ricardo
General LCAB: 96
Los Conquistadores Br: 352

JAKOBSDOTTIR, Svava
"Accident" WaS1: 98

JAKOBSON, A.
Fight Without a Frontline DC2: 212
Life in a Citadel DC2: 212
Two Camps DC2: 212

JAKOBSON, Roman
General LCAB: 97

JALOUX, Edmond
General Po: 1704

JAMES I, King of Scotland
General Ai: 30
The Kingis Quair Ai: 30; ICBAP: 71; OMEP: 411-412

JAMES VI, King of Scotland
General Ai: 45

JAMES, Adeola
General BALE: 311

JAMES, Alice
Diary LCAB: 97

JAMES, Brian
General MAP: 200

"Bungally" Wa: 347

"Coming Down from Tip-Top" Wa: 347

"Dolf" Wa: 347

"Jacob's Escape" Wa: 347

"Joe Waite's Lantern" Wa: 347

"Prayers for Rain" Wa: 347

"The Reign of Eugene Ham" Wa: 347

"Untimely Aid" Wa: 347

JAMES, C.L.R.
General WIL: 61-62
Beyond a Boundary WIL: 62
Minty Alley WIL: 62

JAMES, George Payne Rainsford
General BN: 69

JAMES, Henry
General AD: 162-165; AF: 164-173; ALL: 145-154; AN: 152-164; ASF: 339-348; Br: 352; Cla: 53-56; Ho: 79-96, 149-152; LCAB: 97-98; MD: 170-171; Po: 1705-1751

"The Abasement of the North-mores" ASF: 318; Po: 1751; SFC: 94; Wa: 347-348

"Adina" ASF: 319; SFC: 94; Wa: 348; WaS1: 98

The Album MD: 171

"The Altar of the Dead" ASF: 319; SFC: 94; Wa: 348; WaS1: 98

The Ambassadors AF: 164, 166, 169-170, 172-173; ALL: 145, 148-150, 152-153; AN: 141-142; Ho: 82-83, 85-87, 89-95, 150-151; LCAB: 98; Ma: 1023-1024; Po: 1706, 1720, 1723, 1725, 1728, 1730-1731, 1740, 1752-1761

The American AD: 164; ADC: 173; AF: 171; ALL: 145, 148, 151; AN: 142-143; Br: 352; Ho: 82-83, 85-87, 89, 92-94, 151; Ma: 1024-1026; MD: 171; Po: 1730-1731, 1761-1766

The American Scene Ho: 89; Po: 1766-1767

The Art of Fiction Po: 1767

The Art of the Novel Po: 1767

The Aspern Papers AF: 165; ALL: 148-149; An: 143;

ASF: 319-320; Ho: 91,
93; Ma: 1026-1027; Po:
1768-1769; SFC: 94-95;
Wa: 348-349; WaS1: 98
"At Isella" ASF: 320; SFC:
95; Wa: 349
"The Author of Beltraffio"
ASF: 320; Ma: 1027-
1028; Po: 1770; SFC: 95;
Wa: 349-350
Autobiography Po: 1770-1771
The Awkward Age ALL: 148-
149, 151; AN: 143-144;
Ho: 82-83, 86-89, 91; Ma:
1028-1030; Po: 1725,
1742, 1771-1773
"The Beast in the Jungle"
AF: 172; ALL: 148; ASF:
321-322; Ho: 150; Ma:
1030-1031; Po: 1773-1775;
SFC: 95-96; Wa: 350-
352; WaS1: 98-99
"The Beldonald Holbein" ASF:
322; Po: 1775-1776; SFC:
96; Wa: 352; WaS1: 99
"The Bench of Desolation"
ALL: 148; ASF: 322; Po:
1776; SFC: 96; Wa: 352-
353; WaS1: 99
"Benvolio" ASF: 322; SFC:
97; Wa: 353; WaS1: 99
"The Birthplace" ASF: 322;
Po: 1742-1743, 1776-1777;
SFC: 97; Wa: 353; WaS1:
99
The Bostonians AF: 170;
ALL: 148; AN: 144; Ho:
82-84, 88-91, 93, 149, 151;
LCAB: 98; Ma: 1032-
1033; Po: 1725-1726, 1733,
1736, 1746, 1777-1779
"Broken Wings" ASF: 322;
SFC: 97; Wa: 353; WaS1:
99
"Brooksmith" ASF: 322;
Po: 1780; SFC: 97; Wa:
353-354; WaS1: 99
"A Bundle of Letters" ASF:
323; SFC: 97; Wa: 354;
WaS1: 99
"The Chaperon" ASF: 323;
SFC: 97; Wa: 354; WaS1:
99
"Collaboration" ASF: 323;
Wa: 354; WaS1: 100
Confidence AN: 144; Po:

1780
"Covering End" ASF: 323;
SFC: 97; Wa: 354; WaS1:
100
"The Coxon Fund" ASF: 323;
SFC: 97; Wa: 354; WaS1:
100
"Crapy Cornelia" ASF: 323;
Po: 1780-1781; SFC: 97;
Wa: 354; WaS1: 100
"Crawford's Consistency" SFC:
97; Wa: 354-355
Daisy Miller AD: 164; ADC:
174; ALL: 148; AN: 144-
145; ASF: 323-324; Br:
352; Ho: 83, 89; Ma: 1033-
1035; MD: 171; Po: 1740,
1781-1783; SFC: 98; Wa:
355-356; WaS1: 100
"A Day of Days" ASF: 324;
SFC: 98; Wa: 356-357;
WaS1: 100
"De Grey" ASF: 325; SFC:
99; Wa: 357
"The Death of the Lion" ASF:
324-325; SFC: 98-99; Wa:
357; WaS1: 100
"The Diary of a Man of Fifty"
ASF: 325; SFC: 99; Wa:
357; WaS1: 100
Disengaged ADC: 174; MD:
171
English Hours LCAB: 98
"The Escape" Wa: 357
"Eugene Pickering" ASF: 325;
SFC: 99; Wa: 357-358;
WaS1: 100
"Europe" ASF: 325; Po: 1783;
SFC: 99; Wa: 358
The Europeans ALL: 151-153;
AN: 145; Ho: 83, 85, 90,
95; Ma: 1035-1036; Po:
1783-1784
"The Figure in the Carpet"
AF: 172; ASF: 325-326;
Ma: 1036-1037; Po: 1784-
1786; SFC: 99-100; Wa:
358-359; WaS1: 100
"Flickerbridge" ASF: 326;
SFC: 100; Wa: 359; WaS1:
100
"Fordham Castle" ASF: 326;
SFC: 100; Wa: 359; WaS1:
100
"Four Meetings" ASF: 326;
Po: 1786-1787; SFC: 100;

Wa: 359-360; WaS1: 100

French Poets and Novelists
Po: 1787

"The Friends of the Friends"
ASF: 326; SFC: 100;
Wa: 360; WaS1: 101

"Gabrielle de Bergerac" ASF:
326; SFC: 100; Wa: 360

"Georgina's Reasons" ASF:
326; SFC: 100; Wa: 360;
WaS1: 101

"The Ghostly Rental" ASF:
327; Po: 1787-1788; SFC:
101; Wa: 360-361

"The Given Case" SFC:
101; Wa: 361

"Glasses" ASF: 327; SFC:
101; Wa: 361; WaS1: 101

The Golden Bowl AF: 164,
169, 173; ALL: 145, 148-
150, 152-154; AN: 145-
146; Ho: 82, 85, 87-91,
93-96, 150; Ma: 1037-
1038; Po: 1720, 1728,
1742, 1788-1792

"The Great Condition" SFC:
101; Wa: 361

"The Great Good Place"
ASF: 327; Po: 1792-
1793; SFC: 101; Wa:
361; WaS1: 101

"Greville Fane" ASF: 327;
SFC: 101; Wa: 361-362;
WaS1: 101

"Guest's Confession" ASF:
327; Wa: 362; WaS1: 101

Guy Domville AD: 163;
ADC: 174; Br: 352;
DC1: 98; MD: 171

The High Bid ADC: 174;
Br: 352; DC1: 98; MD:
171

"The Impressions of a Cousin"
ASF: 327; SFC: 101;
Wa: 362; WaS1: 101

"In the Cage" ASF: 327-
328; Ho: 84; Po: 1793-
1794; SFC: 102; Wa:
362; WaS1: 101

The Innocents Br: 352-353

"An International Episode"
ASF: 328; Po: 1794;
SFC: 101-102; Wa: 362-
363; WaS1: 101

The Ivory Tower AF: 169;
ALL: 150; AN: 146;

Po: 1794-1795

"John Delavoy" SFC: 102; Wa:
363; WaS1: 101

"The Jolly Corner" AF: 172;
ASF: 328-329; Po: 1795-
1796; SFC: 102-103; Wa:
363-364; WaS1: 101

"Julia Bride" ASF: 329; Po:
1711; SFC: 103; Wa: 364;
WaS1: 102

"Lady Barberina" ASF: 329;
SFC: 103; Wa: 364-365

"A Landscape Painter" ASF:
329; Po: 1796; SFC: 103;
Wa: 365

"The Last of the Valerii" ASF:
329; SFC: 103; Wa: 365;
WaS1: 102

"The Lesson of the Master"
ASF: 329; Po: 1796; SFC:
103-104; Wa: 365-366; WaS1:
102

"The Liar" AF: 165; ASF:
329; Po: 1797; SFC: 104;
Wa: 366; WaS1: 102

"A Light Man" ASF: 329; Po:
1797; SFC: 104; Wa: 366

"A London Life" ASF: 329;
Wa: 366

"Longstaff's Marriage" SFC:
104; Wa: 366

"Lord Beaupré" ASF: 330;
SFC: 104; Wa: 367

"Louisa Pallant" ASF: 330;
Po: 1797; Wa: 367; WaS1:
102

"Madame de Mauves" ALL:
148; ASF: 330; Cla: 55;
Po: 1731, 1735-1736, 1798-
1799; SFC: 104-105; Wa:
367-368; WaS1: 102

"The Madonna of the Future"
AF: 172; ASF: 330; Po:
1799; SFC: 105; Wa: 368;
WaS1: 102

"The Marriages" ASF: 331;
Po: 1799; SFC: 105; Wa:
368; WaS1: 102

"Master Eustace" ASF: 331;
SFC: 105; Wa: 368; WaS1:
102

"Maud-Evelyn" ASF: 331;
Po: 1799-1800; SFC: 105-
106; Wa: 368-369; WaS1:
102

"The Middle Years" ASF:

331; Po: 1800; SFC:
106; Wa: 369; WaS1: 102

"Miss Gunton of Poughkeepsie"
ASF: 331; SFC: 106;
Wa: 369

"The Modern Warning" ASF:
331; SFC: 106; Wa: 369;
WaS1: 103

"Mora Montravers" ASF:
331; SFC: 106; Wa: 369;
WaS1: 103

"A Most Extraordinary Case"
ASF: 331; SFC: 106;
Wa: 369-370

"Mrs. Medwin" Po: 1800;
SFC: 106; Wa: 369;
WaS1: 102

"My Friend Bingham" SFC:
106; Wa: 370

"A New England Winter" ASF:
331; SFC: 106; Wa: 370;
WaS1: 103

"The Next Time" ASF: 331;
Po: 1800; SFC: 106-107;
Wa: 370

"Nona Vincent" ASF: 331;
SFC: 107; Wa: 370

Notebooks Ho: 94

"Osborne's Revenge" ASF:
332; SFC: 107; Wa: 370

The Other House AD: 163-
164; ADC: 174; AF: 168;
AN: 146; Br: 352; DC1:
98; MD: 171

The Outcry AD: 163; ADC:
174; AN: 146-147; Br:
352; DC1: 98

"Owen Wingrave" ASF: 332;
SFC: 107; Wa: 370-371;
WaS1: 103

"Pandora" ASF: 332; Po:
1706, 1800; SFC: 107;
Wa: 371; WaS1: 103

"The Papers" ASF: 332;
SFC: 107; Wa: 371; WaS1:
103

Parisian Sketches Po: 1801

"A Passionate Pilgrim" ASF:
332; Po: 1801; SFC:
107-108; Wa: 371; WaS1:
103

"Paste" ASF: 332; Po:
1801; SFC: 108; Wa: 371-
372; WaS1: 103

"The Patagonia" ASF: 332;
SFC: 108; Wa: 372; WaS1:
103

"The Path of Duty" SFC: 108;
Wa: 372; WaS1: 103

"The Pension Beaurepas" ASF:
332; SFC: 108; Wa: 372;
WaS1: 103

"The Point of View" ASF:
332; SFC: 108; Wa: 372;
WaS1: 103

"Poor Richard" ASF: 333;
SFC: 108; Wa: 372; WaS1:
103

The Portrait of a Lady AF:
165, 170-172; ALL: 149-151,
153; AN: 147-148; Cla: 56;
Ho: 80, 82-85, 88-94, 150-
151; LCAB: 98; Ma: 1038-
1040; Po: 1735-1736, 1738-
1741, 1750, 1801-1811, 2302

The Princess Casamassima AF:
170; ALL: 145, 151, 153;
AN: 148; Ho: 82, 87-95,
150; LCAB: 98; Ma: 1040-
1042; Po: 1721, 1725-1726,
1736, 1746, 1811-1815

"The Private Life" ASF: 333;
SFC: 108; Wa: 372-373

"A Problem" SFC: 109; Wa:
373

"Professor Fargo" ASF: 333;
SFC: 109; Wa: 373; WaS1:
103

"The Pupil" AF: 172; ASF:
333; Po: 1742, 1815-1816;
SFC: 109; Wa: 373-374;
WaS1: 103-104

"Pyramus and Thisbe" Wa:
374

"The Real Thing" AF: 172;
ASF: 333-334; Po: 1816-
1818; SFC: 109-110; Wa:
374-375; WaS1: 104

The Reprobate DC1: 98; MD:
172

The Reverberator AN: 149;
Po: 1706, 1818

Roderick Hudson AF: 170;
ALL: 145, 151, 153; AN:
149; Ho: 86, 88-89, 91-93;
Ma: 1042-1043; Po: 1714,
1721, 1723, 1726, 1741-1742,
1818-1820

"The Romance of Certain Old
Clothes" ASF: 334; Po:
1820; SFC: 110; Wa: 375;
WaS1: 104

"Rose-Agathe" ASF: 334; WaS1: 104

"A Round of Visits" ASF: 334-335; Po: 1820; SFC: 110; Wa: 375-376

The Sacred Fount AF: 166; ALL: 148-149; AN: 149-150; Ho: 79, 82, 84-85, 89, 92, 94, 150-151; Ma: 1043-1045; Po: 1725, 1820-1824

The Saloon Br: 352

The Sense of the Past AN: 150; Po: 1707, 1824-1825

"The Siege of London" ASF: 335; Po: 1825; SFC: 110; Wa: 376

"Sir Dominick Ferrand" ASF: 335; SFC: 110; Wa: 376

"Sir Edmund Orme" ASF: 335; SFC: 111; Wa: 376; WaS1: 104

"The Solution" ASF: 335; SFC: 111; Wa: 376; WaS1: 104

"The Special Type" ASF: 335; SFC: 111; Wa: 376

The Spoils of Poynton ALL: 148-149, 151; AN: 150; Ho: 82, 84-85, 87-88, 93-94; Ma: 1045-1046; Po: 1738, 1742, 1750, 1825-1830

"Still Waters" Wa: 376

"The Story in It" ASF: 335; SFC: 111; Wa: 376; WaS1: 104

"The Story of a Masterpiece" ASF: 335; Po: 1830; SFC: 111; Wa: 376-377

"The Story of a Year" ASF: 335; SFC: 111; Wa: 377; WaS1: 104

Summersoft MD: 172

"The Sweetheart of M. Briseux" SFC: 111; Wa: 377

Tenants ADC: 174; MD: 172

"The Third Person" ASF: 335; SFC: 111; Wa: 377

"The Tone of Time" ASF: 335; SFC: 112; Wa: 377; WaS1: 104

"A Tragedy of Error" ASF: 335; Po: 1831; SFC: 112; Wa: 377

The Tragic Muse ALL: 148; AN: 150; Ho: 82-85, 88-89, 92, 151; Ma: 1046-1047; Po: 1736, 1741-1742, 1831-1833

"Travelling Companions" ASF: 336; SFC: 112; Wa: 377-378; WaS1: 104

"The Tree of Knowledge" ASF: 336; Po: 1833; SFC: 112; Wa: 378; WaS1: 104

"The Turn of the Screw" AF: 166, 168-169, 172-173; ALL: 148; ASF: 336-339; Cla: 54, 56; Ho: 82-83; LCAB: 98-99; Ma: 1047-1049; Po: 1733, 1833-1843; SFC: 112-114; Wa: 378-383; WaS1: 104-105, 150

"The Two Faces" Po: 1843; SFC: 115; Wa: 383; WaS1: 105

"The Velvet Glove" ASF: 339; Po: 1723; Wa: 383; WaS1: 105

"Very Modern Rome" Po: 1843

Washington Square ALL: 148; AN: 150-151; Ho: 83, 90, 149-150; Ma: 1049-1051; Po: 1843; Wa: 383-384; WaS1: 105

Watch and Ward AN: 151; Ho: 89; Po: 1844

"The Way It Came" ASF: 339

What Mazie Knew AF: 167, 172; ALL: 148-149, 151-153; AN: 151; Ho: 82, 84-85, 87-88, 95-96; Ma: 1051-1053; Po: 1742, 1844-1847

"The Wheel of Time" ASF: 339; SFC: 115; Wa: 384

William Wetmore Story and His Friends Po: 1847

The Wings of the Dove AF: 164, 169, 171; ALL: 145, 148-153; AN: 151-152; Cla: 53; Ho: 82, 84, 86, 88-95, 150; LCAB: 99; Ma: 1053-1054; Po: 1720, 1728, 1733, 1739-1741, 1847-1852

JAMES, Montagu Rhodes

General TA: 190

"The Ashtree" SFC: 115; Wa: 384

"The Diary of Mr. Poynter"

SFC: 115; Wa: 384
JAMES, William
  General APC: 57-59
  The Varieties of Religious
    Experience APC: 57
JAMES DE TERZA, Maria Elena
    [Malena SANDOR]
  Una Mujer Libre Br: 353
JAMESON, Storm
  A Cup of Tea for Mr. Thur-
    gill ENES2: 134
  A Moment of Truth ENES2:
    134
  There Will Be a Short Inter-
    val ENES2: 134
JAMISON, Roscoe Conkling
  General BAW: 417
JAMMES, Francis
  General Po: 1852-1853
JANIN, Jules
  L'Âne mort et la femme
    guillotinée Fi: 97
JANVIER, Ludovic
  La Baigneuse Fi: 97
JARDIEL PONCELA, Enrique
  General Br: 551; Po: 1853
JARNES, Benjamin
  Locura y muerte de nadie
    Po: 1853
  The Madness and Death of
    Nobody Fi: 220; Ke:
    206
  The Paper Guest Fi: 220
  Paula and Paulita Fi: 220
  The Red and the Blue Fi:
    220
  Scenes on the Brink of Death
    Fi: 220
  Summer Salon Fi: 220
  Theory of the Top-String
    Fi: 220; Ke: 206
  The Useless Professor Fi:
    220
  The Wind's Sweetheart Fi:
    220
JARRELL, Randall
  General ALL: 154; LCAB:
    99; Ma: 1056-1058; MP:
    49-50; Po: 1854-1855
  "The Black Swan" PE: 252
  "Burning the Letters" PE:
    252
  "A Camp in a Prussian
    Forest" PE: 252
  "Cinderella" ICBAP: 71
  "The Death of the Ball Turret

Gunner" Ma: 1055; PE:
    252-253; Po: 1856
  "Eighth Air Force" Ma: 1055;
    PE: 253
  "Eland" MP: 50
  "The Emancipators" PE: 253;
    Po: 1856
  "A Front" ICBAP: 71; Po:
    1856
  "The Girl Dreams That She Is
    Giselle" PE: 253
  "Hohensalzburg" PE: 253
  "Hope" PE: 253
  "The House in the Wood" PE:
    253
  "A Hunt" PE: 253
  "Jerome" PE: 253
  "King's Hunt" PE: 253
  "Losses" ICBAP: 71; PE:
    253; Po: 1856
  "The Lost World" ICBAP: 71;
    Ma: 1055-1056; PE: 253
  "Love in Its Separate Being"
    PE: 253
  "The Metamorphosis" PE: 253
  "The Night Before the Night
    Before Christmas" PE: 253
  "On the Railway Platform" PE:
    254
  Pictures from an Institution
    Ma: 1056; Po: 1856
  "A Quilt-Pattern" PE: 254
  "A Rhapsody on Irish Themes"
    PE: 254
  "Seele im Raum" PE: 254
  "The Sleeping Beauty: Varia-
    tion of the Prince" PE:
    254
  "Soul" PE: 254
  "Thinking of the Lost World"
    ICBAP: 71; PE: 254
  "The Venetian Blind" PE: 254
  "A Well-to-Do Invalid" PE:
    254
  "Where the Rainbow Ends" Po:
    1857
  The Woman at the Washington
    Zoo Ma: 1058
JARRETTE, Alfred Q.
  General BAF: 172; BAW: 417
JARRY, Alfred
  General Br: 353; MD: 172;
    Po: 1857
  César-Antéchrist Br: 353
  Cuckold Ubu [Ubu Cocu] Br:
    354

Gestes et opinions du Docteur
Faustroll Fi: 97
King Ubu [King Turd; Ubu
Roi; Pere Ubu] Br: 354-
355; DC2: 212-213; MD:
172; Po: 1857-1858
Ubu Enchained [Ubu En-
chaine] Br: 355
JARRY, Hawke
General BAF: 172
Black Schoolmaster BAF:
172
JAVELLANA, Stevan
Without Seeing the Dawn Po:
1858
JEANETTE, Gertrude
General BAP: 121
A Bolt from the Blue BAP:
121; MBA: 124
Light in the Cellar BAP:
121
This Way Forward BAP:
121; MBA: 124
JEFFERIES, Richard
General BN: 69; TA: 191
After London ENES1: 125
Hodge and His Masters
ENES1: 125
JEFFERS, Robinson
General ALL: 154-157; Br:
355; ICBAP: 71; LCAB:
99; Ma: 1059; MD: 172;
MDAE: 286-287; MP: 51-
52; Po: 1858-1860
"Apology for Bad Dreams"
ALL: 155
At the Birth of an Age ALL:
155
Cawdor ALL: 155
"Christmas Card" PE: 254
The Cretan Woman ADC:
174-175; Br: 355-356;
MDAE: 286-287
"The Cruel Falcon" ICBAP:
71
Dear Judas MD: 172
"Fire on the Hills" PE: 254
"Give Your Heart to the
Hawks" PE: 254
"Greater Grandeur" PE: 254
"Hurt Hawks" PE: 254; Po:
1861
"Margrave" PE: 254
Medea ADC: 175; Br: 356;
DC1: 98; MD: 172-173
"Meditation on Saviours" PE:

254
"Nova" PE: 254
"Ocean" PE: 254
"The Purse-Seine" PE: 255
"Rearmament" ICBAP: 71
"Return" ICBAP: 72
"Roan Stallion" ALL: 155;
ICBAP: 72; Ma: 1059-1060;
PE: 255; Po: 1861
"Science" PE: 255
"Shine, Perishing Republic"
PE: 255
Tamar ALL: 155; Ma: 1060;
Po: 1861
The Tower Beyond Tragedy
ADC: 175; ALL: 155; Br:
356; DC1: 98; MD: 173;
Po: 1862
JEFFERSON, Joseph, III
Rip Van Winkle ADC: 175-176
JEFFERSON, Roland S.
The School on 103rd Street
BAF: 172
JEFFERSON, Thomas
General AP: 381-396; Da:
70-72
The Declaration of Independence
AP: 381, 389, 393, 395; Da:
70, 72
JEFFREY, William
General Ai: 250
JELLICOE, Ann
General Br: 356; MBD: 55;
MDAE: 289; TMBP: 67-68
The Giveaway TMBP: 67-68
The Knack Br: 356-357; DC1:
98; EDC: 286-287; TMBP:
18, 67-68, 171
The Rising Generation Br:
357; TMBP: 68
Shelley; or, The Idealist
MDAE: 289; TMBP: 68
The Sport of My Mad Mother
Br: 357; DC1: 98; EDC:
287; MBD: 55; TMBP: 67-
68
JENKINS, Deaderick Franklin
General BAF: 173
It Was Not My World BAW:
418
JENKINS, John E.
"Ginx's Baby" WaS1: 105
JENKINS, Robin
General Ai: 297-298
JENKINS, William Fitzgerald
General LCAB: 99

JENSEN, Johannes V.
    The Long Journey Ke: 353;
        Ma: 1061
    "Potowatomi's Daughter" Po:
        1862
    The Trek of the Cimbri Ke:
        353
JENSEN, Thit
    Stygge Krumpen Ke: 353
JEPHSON, Robert
    General Li: 222
    Braganza Li: 222
    The Law of Lombardy DC1:
        98-99; Li: 222
JEROME, Jerome Klapka
    General EDT: 192; TA:
        192
    All Roads Lead to Calvary
        ENES1: 125
    Anthony John ENES1: 125
    "Blasé Billy" Wa: 384
    "The Choice of Cyril Har-
        john" Wa: 384
    "In Remembrance of John
        Ingerfield and of Anne,
        His Wife" Wa: 385
    "Johnson and Emily, or the
        Faithful Ghost" Wa: 385
    "Malvina Brittany" Wa: 385
    "The Man Who Went Wrong"
        Wa: 385
    "The Materialization of
        Charles Mivanway" Wa:
        385
    "The Passing of the Third
        Floor Back" EDC: 287;
        Wa: 385
    Paul Kelver ENES1: 125
    "The Philosopher's Joke"
        Wa: 385
    "The Soul of Nicholas Sny-
        ders" Wa: 385
    They and I ENES1: 125
    Tommy and Co. ENES1:
        125
    "The Woman of the Saeter"
        Wa: 385
JEROME, Judson
    "Aubade" PE: 255
    "From Beowulf to Thomas
        Hardy" PE: 255
JERROLD, Douglas William
    General EDT: 194-195
    Black Ey'ed Susan; or All
        in the Downs DC1: 99
    "Ephraim, Rue: The Vic-

    tim of Society" Wa: 385
    "A Lay of St. Gengulphus"
        Wa: 385
    "The Lesson of Life" Wa: 385
    A Man Made of Money ENES1:
        125
    "The Mayor of Hole-Cum-
        Corner" Wa: 385
    "Mr. Peppercorn at Home" Wa:
        385
    Mutiny at the Nore DC1: 99
    "The Papers of a Gentleman-at-
        Arms" Wa: 385
    "The Preacher Parrot" Wa:
        385
    St. Giles and St. James
        ENES1: 125
    "The Sick Giant and the Doctor
        Dwarf" Wa: 386
    The Story of a Feather ENES1:
        125
    "A Wine Cellar" Wa: 386
JERRY, Bongo
    General WIL: 62-63
JESSE, Fryniwyd Marsh Tennyson
    [Mrs. H. M. HARWOOD]
    General Mi: 248
JESSYE, Eva Alberta
    General BAW: 420
    My Spirituals BAW: 420
JETHA, Nazara
    General BALE: 312
JEWETT, Sarah Orne
    General AF: 176-179; ALL:
        157-158; AN: 164; ASF:
        351-352; Cla: 110; Ho:
        96-97; LCAB: 99
    "Andrew's Fortune" Wa: 386
    "Aunt Cynthy Dallett" Wa:
        386
    "Autumn Holiday" ASF: 349;
        Wa: 386
    "A Bit of Shore Life" Wa:
        386
    "A Born Farmer" Wa: 386
    "Confession of a House-Breaker"
        Wa: 386
    A Country Doctor Ma: 1062-
        1063
    The Country of the Pointed
        Firs AF: 176-179; ALL:
        158; ASF: 349-350; Ho:
        96-97; Ma: 1063-1065
    "The Courting of Sister Wisby"
        ASF: 350; Wa: 386
    "Dan's Wife" ASF: 350

"A Dark Night" ASF: 350;
Wa: 386
Deephaven ASF: 350; Ho:
97; Ma: 1065-1067
"The Dulham Ladies" ASF:
350; Wa: 386
"A Dunnet Shepherdess"
ASF: 350; Wa: 386
"An Every-Day Girl" Wa:
387
"Fame's Little Day" Wa: 387
"Farmer Finch" Wa: 387
"The First Sunday in June"
Wa: 387
"The Flight of Betsey Lane"
Wa: 387
"The Foreigner" ASF: 350;
Wa: 387
"A Garden Story" Wa: 387
"The Girl with the Cannon
Dresses" Wa: 387
"The Gray Man" Wa: 387
"The Gray Mills of Farley"
Wa: 387
"The Green Bowl" Wa: 387
"The Growtown 'Bugle'" Wa:
387
"A Guest at Home" Wa: 387
"The Guests of Mrs. Timms"
ASF: 350; Wa: 388
"The Hilton's Holiday" Wa:
388
"The Honey Tree" Wa: 388
"In a Country Practice" Wa:
388
"Jenny Garrow's Lovers" Wa:
388
"The King of Folly Island"
ASF: 350; Wa: 388
"Lady Ferry" ASF: 351;
Wa: 388
"A Landlocked Sailor" Wa:
388
"The Landscape Chamber"
ASF: 351; Wa: 388
"Law Lane" Wa: 388
"A Lost Lover" Wa: 388
"Marsh Rosemary" Wa: 388
"Martha's Lady" Wa: 388
"Miss Manning's Minister"
Wa: 388
"Miss Peck's Promotion" Wa:
388
"Miss Tempy's Watchers"
ASF: 351; Wa: 389
"The Mistress of Sydenham
Plantation" Wa: 389
"A Native of Winby" Wa: 389
"A Neighbor's Landmark" Wa:
389
"The New Methuselah" Wa:
389
"A New Parishioner" Wa: 389
"The Only Rose" ASF: 351;
Wa: 389
"Paper Roses" Wa: 389
"The Parshley Celebration" Wa:
389
"The Passing of Sister Barsett"
Wa: 389
"Peach-Tree Joe" Wa: 389
"Peg's Little Child" Wa: 389
"A Pinch of Salt" Wa: 389
"The Queen's Twin" Wa: 389
"River Driftwood" ASF: 351
"Sister Peacham's Turn" Wa:
389
"A Sorrowful Guest" Wa: 390
"A Spring Sunday" Wa: 390
"The Spur of the Moment" Wa:
390
"A Stage Tavern" Wa: 390
"Stolen Pleasures" Wa: 390
"Tom's Husband" Wa: 390
The Tory Lover AF: 176; AN:
164; Ho: 97
"A White Heron" ASF: 351;
SFC: 115; Wa: 390; WaS1:
105-106
"William's Wedding" ASF: 351;
Wa: 390
JEWSBURY, Geraldine
General BN: 69
Constance Herbert ENES2:
134
The Half-Sisters ENES1: 126;
ENES2: 135
Marian Withers ENES1: 126;
ENES2: 135
Zoe ENES2: 135
JHABVALA, R. Prawer
General Ma: 1068; Po: 1862
Jimenez, A. see FARIAS, Ar-
mando Jimenez
JIMENEZ, Juan Ramón
General LCAB: 99; Ma:
1069-1070; Po: 1863-1867
"Los Caminos de la Tarde"
Po: 1868
"¿Como era, Dios mio, cómo
era?" Po: 1868
Crepúsculo Po: 1868

"Mademoiselle" Po: 1868
Platero and I [Platero y yo]
Ma: 1069; Po: 1868-1869
Tercera antología poética Po:
1869
Viene una música lánguida
Po: 1869
La Viudita Po: 1870
JIMENEZ MARTOS, Luis
General Po: 1870
JIMINEZ RUEDA, Julio
General Br: 357
JOANS, Ted
General AAPD: 191; BAF:
173
JOB, Thomas
Land's End ADC: 176
Thérèse ADC: 176
JODELLE, Etienne
Cleopatra Captive DC2: 213
Didon se Sacrifiant DC2:
213
JOFRE, Hermogenes
Los Martires Br: 357
JOHN, Frank
Black Songs WIL: 63
JOHNSON, Adolphus
General BAW: 422
JOHNSON, Alvin Saunders
Spring Storm LCAB: 99
JOHNSON, B.S.
Albert Angelo ENES1: 126;
ENES2: 135
Christie Malry's Own Double-
Entry ENES2: 135
House Mother Normal ENES2:
135
See the Old Lady Decently
ENES2: 135
Travelling People ENES2:
135
Trawl ENES2: 135
The Unfortunates ENES2:
135
JOHNSON, Charles
General Li: 224
The Country Lasses Li: 224
Faith and the Good Thing
BAF: 173-174
The Force of Friendship
Li: 224
The Generous Husband DC1:
99; Li: 224
Love in a Chest Li: 224
The Village Opera DC1: 99
JOHNSON, Charles Bertram

General BAW: 423
JOHNSON, Edward
General AP: 397-399
Wonder-Working Providence...
AP: 397-398
JOHNSON, Edward Austin
General LCAB: 99
JOHNSON, Emily Pauline
General ECL: 152-153
JOHNSON, Eyvind
Bobinack Fi: 405
The Clouds over Metapontion
Fi: 405; Ke: 354
Commentary on a Falling Star
Fi: 405
The Days of His Grace Fi:
406
Dreams of Roses and Fire
Fi: 406; Ke: 354
His Grace's Days Ke: 354
Krilon Fi: 406; Ke: 354
Life's Long Day Fi: 406; Ke:
354
Nagra Steg Mot Tystnaden Fi:
406
Night Maneuvers Fi: 406
The Novel about Olof Fi: 406;
Ke: 354
Put Away the Sun Fi: 406
Rain at Dawn Fi: 406
Strandernas Svall Ke: 354
The Swell on the Beaches Fi:
406
Town in Darkness Fi: 406
JOHNSON, Fenton
General AAPD: 116; AAW:
62; BAF: 174-175; BAW:
425; LCAB: 100
A Little Dreaming BAW: 425
Visions of the Dusk BAW:
425
JOHNSON, Geoffrey
General Po: 1870
JOHNSON, Georgia Douglas
General AAPD: 117, 321;
AAW: 62; BAP: 122; BAW:
427
Attucks BAP: 122
An Autumn Love Cycle BAW:
427
Bronze: A Book of Verse
BAW: 427
Frederick Douglass BAP: 122
A Sunday Morning in the South
BAP: 122
William and Ellen Craft BAP:

122
JOHNSON, Hall
General BAP: 122; BAW:
428
Run, Little Chillun! BAP:
122-123; BAW: 428; Br:
357; MBA: 125
JOHNSON, Herman
Nowhere to Run, Nowhere to
Hide ADC: 176; BAP:
123; MBA: 125-126
JOHNSON, J. Rosamond
General BAP: 123
JOHNSON, James Weldon
General AAPD: 118-119;
AAW: 62-63; BAF: 175-
177; BAW: 431-434; HR:
110-116; ICBAP: 72;
LCAB: 100; Po: 1870-
1871
The Autobiography of an Ex-
Coloured Man BAF: 175-
177; HR: 111-116
God's Trombones HR: 112,
115
JOHNSON, Joe
General BAF: 177
JOHNSON, Josephine Winslow
"John, Chapter VI" Wa: 390
Now in November LCAB:
100
"Safe" Wa: 390
JOHNSON, Linton Kwesi
Dread Beat Blood WIL: 63
JOHNSON, Lionel Pigot
General TA: 193
"By the Statue of King
Charles at Charing Cross"
PE: 255
"Comely and Calm He Rides"
PE: 255
"The Dark Angel" ICBAP:
72; PE: 255
"Oxford" PE: 255
JOHNSON, Pamela Hansford
General CFAE: 202; CN:
298-299; LCAB: 100;
Sch: 140
An Avenue of Stone see also
Trilogy CN: 299
Catherine Carter CN: 299
Cork Street, Next to the
Hatters CN: 299
An Error of Judgement CN:
299
The Humbler Creation CN:

299
An Impossible Marriage CN:
299
The Last Resort CN: 299
Night and Silence Who Is Here?
CN: 299
The Philistines CN: 299
This Bed Thy Centre CN: 299
Trilogy CN: 300
The Trojan Brothers CN: 300
The Unspeakable Skipton CN:
300; ENE: 159
Winter Quarters CN: 300
JOHNSON, Reginald Vel
The Trap Play ADC: 176
JOHNSON, Richard
The Seven Champions of
Christendom ERP: 260-261
JOHNSON, Richard T., Daniel
HOLLYWOOD, and Jersey
MEADOWS
All the Girls Came Out to Play
ADC: 176
JOHNSON, Samuel (1696-1722)
General AP: 401-402; Da: 53
JOHNSON, Samuel (1709-1784)
General Be: 169-175; Du:
103-104; EC: 85-96; LCAB:
100; Me: 255-269
"The Battle of the Pygmies and
Cranes" EC: 94; Me: 266
The Dictionary EC: 90-91
The Idler EC: 93; Ma: 1071
Irene EC: 95
A Journey to the Western Is-
lands of Scotland EC: 93;
Ma: 1071-1072
Life of Addison EC: 89
Life of Richard Savage EC:
123; Ma: 1073
Life of Swift EC: 90
Lives of the Poets EC: 89
London EC: 94; Me: 258,
260-261, 263-264, 267-269;
PE: 255
"On the Death of Dr. Robert
Levet" ICBAP: 72; Me:
262, 265, 269; PE: 255
The Rambler EC: 92-93;
LCAB: 100; Ma: 1073-1074
Rasselas Be: 169-175, 248;
Du: 101-103; EC: 91-92;
EN: 71; ENE: 159-161;
ENES1: 126-127; ENES2:
135-136; Ma: 1075-1076;
Me: 257

The Vanity of Human Wishes
    EC: 94; ICBAP: 72;
    LCAB: 100; Ma: 1076-
    1077; Me: 257-269; PE:
    255-256
The Vision of Theodore PE:
    256; Me: 265
JOHNSON, Samuel, of Cheshire
    Hurlothrumbo Li: 225
JOHNSON, Uwe
    General Po: 1871-1872
    "An Absence" ["Eine Reise
        wegwohin, 1960"] Wa:
        390
    "Eine Kneipe geht verloren"
        Po: 1872
    Jahrestage Fi: 333
    Speculations About Jacob
        [Mutmassungen über Jakob]
        Fi: 333-334; Ke: 283; Po:
        1872-1873
    "A Tavern Vanishes" Wa:
        390
    The Third Book About
        Achim Fi: 334
JOHNSON, Vel
    Section D MBA: 126
JOHNSON, William Matthews
    General BAF: 178
JOHNSTON, Denis
    General Br: 357; MBD:
        55; Mi: 248
    Blind Man's Buff Br: 357
    A Bride for the Unicorn
        Br: 357
    The Dreaming Dust Br: 357
    The Golden Cuckoo Br:
        358
    The Moon in the Yellow River
        Br: 358
    The Old Lady Says "No!"
        Br: 358
    The Scythe and the Sunset
        Br: 358
    Storm Song Br: 358
    Strange Occurrence on Ire-
        land's Eye Br: 358
JOHNSTON, George
    General MAP: 202-203
    A Cartload of Clay MAP:
        202
    My Brother Jack MAP: 202-
        203
JOHNSTON, Jennifer
    The Captains and the Kings
        ENES2: 136

The Gates ENES2: 136
How Many Miles to Babylon?
    ENES2: 136
JOHNSTON, Mary
    General AN: 165; LCAB: 100
JOHNSTON, Richard Malcolm
    General ASF: 352
    "The Expensive Treat of Colonel
        Moses Grice" WaS1: 106
    "The Goosepond School" WaS1:
        106
    "How Mr. Bill Williams Took the
        Responsibility" WaS1: 106
    "Mr. Fortner's Marital Claims"
        Wa: 391; WaS1: 106
    "Mr. Neelus Peeler's Conditions"
        WaS1: 106
    "Mr. Williamson Slippey and His
        Salt" WaS1: 106
    "Old Friends and New" ASF:
        352; Wa: 391
JOHNSTOUN, James
    [Supplement to] The Countess
        of Pembroke's Arcadia by
        Philip SIDNEY ERP: 261
JOLAOSO, Mabel
    General BALE: 312
JONAS, George
    General JW: 149
JONES, A.H.
    The Masqueraders DC1: 99
JONES, Arnold
    Cinderella Everafter MBA:
        126
JONES, David
    General LCAB: 100; MP:
        52-53; Po: 1873-1876
    The Anathemata LCAB: 100;
        MP: 53; Po: 1873-1877
    Epoch and Artist Po: 1874-
        1875, 1877
    In Parentheses ENES1: 127;
        LCAB: 100; MP: 53; Po:
        1873-1875, 1877-1878
    "Rite and Fore-Time" PE:
        256
    "The Tribune's Visitation" PE:
        256
JONES, Edward Smyth
    General BAW: 439
JONES, Eldred Durosimi
    General BALE: 312
JONES, Elinor
    Colette ADC: 176
JONES, Gayl
    General BAF: 178

Corregidora BAF: 179
Eva's Man BAF: 179
"White Rat" WaS1: 106
JONES, Glyn
The Island of Apples ENES2:
137
The Learning Lark ENES2:
137
The Valley, the City, the
Village ENES2: 137
JONES, Henry Arthur
General Br: 358; EDT:
200-201; MBD: 56; MD:
173; Mi: 249-250; TA:
194-195
The Case of Rebellious Susan
MD: 173
Chance, the Idol MD: 173
The Crusaders MD: 173
The Dancing Girl MD: 173
The Hypocrites MD: 174
Judah MD: 174
The Lackey's Carnival Br:
358; MD: 174
The Liars Br: 358; MD:
174
Michael and His Lost Angel
Br: 359; DC1: 99; MD:
174
The Middleman MD: 174
Mrs. Dane's Defence EDT:
200; MD: 174
The Physician Br: 359;
DC1: 99; MD: 174
The Silver King MD: 174
The Tempter MD: 174
JONES, Howard Mumford
O Strange New World LCAB:
101
JONES, J. McHenry
General BAF: 179; BAW:
441
JONES, Jack
Rhonda Roundabout Br:
359
JONES, James
General AN: 165; CFAE:
203-204; CN: 300; LCAB:
101; Po: 1878
From Here to Eternity AN:
165; CFAE: 203-204; CN:
300-301; LCAB: 101; Ma:
1078; Po: 1878-1879
Go to the Widow-Maker CN:
301; Po: 1879
"The Ice-Cream Headache"

ASF: 353; LCAB: 101
The Pistol AN: 165
Some Came Running AN: 165;
CN: 301; Po: 1879
The Thin Red Line CFAE:
204; CN: 301-302; Ma:
1079; Po: 1879-1880
JONES, John Beauchamp
General LCAB: 101
JONES, Joseph S.
Solon Shingle [The People's
Lawyer] DC1: 99
JONES, Joshua Henry, Jr.
General BAW: 442
By Sanction of Law BAW: 442
JONES, Le Roi [Imamu Amiri
BARAKA]
General AAL: 200-202, 214-
217; AAPD: 194-196, 385-
388; AAW: 63-64; ASF:
65; BAF: 22-24; BAP: 13-
15; BAW: 54-56; Br: 359;
ICBAP: 72; LCAB: 101;
MBA: 10-13; MP: 21-22;
Po: 1880-1881; TMAP: 117-
132
"The Alternative" ASF: 65;
WaS1: 10
Arm Yourself or Harm Yourself
MBA: 14
The Baptism AAL: 215; AAPD:
387; ADC: 177; BAP: 15;
MBA: 14; Po: 1880-1881;
TMAP: 125, 129
"Black Art" PE: 33
"Black Dada Nihilismus" PE:
33
A Black Mass [Black Masses]
AAL: 215; ADC: 177; BAP:
15, 19; MBA: 14; TMAP:
125, 132-133
Blues People TMAP: 127
"A Chase (Alighieri's Dream)"
ASF: 65; BAF: 24; Wa:
37; WaS1: 10
Dante see The System of
Dante's Hell
"Death of Horatio Alger" ASF:
65; WaS1: 10
The Death of Malcolm X MBA:
14-15
Dutchman AAL: 200-201, 214-
217; AAPD: 385-388; ADC:
177-178; BAP: 15-17, 19;
Br: 359-360; Ma: 1080;
MBA: 15-17, 21-22; Po:

1882; TMAP: 117-118, 121, 123-129, 131, 133

The Eighth Ditch MBA: 17

Experimental Death Unit # 1 AAL: 215; ADC: 178; BAP: 19; MBA: 17-18; TMAP: 118, 123

Four Black Revolutionary Plays MBA: 17

"Going Down Slowly" WaS1: 10

Great Goodness of Life: A Coon Show AAL: 215; ADC: 178; MBA: 17; TMAP: 119, 133

"Heroes Are Gang Leaders" Wa: 37; WaS1: 10

Home on the Range BAP: 17; MBA: 18, 22; TMAP: 133

"Hymn for Lanie Poo" PE: 33

"In Memory of Radio" PE: 33

J-E-L-L-O ADC: 178; MBA: 18

Madheart AAL: 215-216; AAPD: 388; ADC: 178; BAP: 17, 19; MBA: 18; Po: 1882-1883; TMAP: 125-126, 132-133

The Motion of History MBA: 22

Murderous Angels MBA: 22

Police BAP: 17; MBA: 18-19

A Recent Killing ADC: 178; BAP: 19; MBA: 19, 22; TMAP: 129, 134

Roi MBA: 22

"Round Trip" WaS1: 10

S-1: A Play MBA: 22; TMAP: 134

"Salute" WaS1: 10

"The Screamer" MBA: 19; WaS1: 10

Sidney Poet Heroical ADC: 178; MBA: 19, 22; TMAP: 134

The Slave AAL: 200-202, 214-216; AAPD: 385-388; ADC: 178-179; BAP: 17-19; Br: 360; MBA: 19-20, 22; Po: 1880, 1882; TMAP: 119, 121, 123-125, 129, 134-135

Slave Ship AAL: 215, 217; AAPD: 385, 387; ADC: 179; BAP: 18-19; MBA: 20, 22-23; Po: 1883; TMAP: 118-119, 125, 128, 135

"Suppose Sorrow Was a Time Machine" WaS1: 10

The System of Dante's Hell [Dante] BAF: 22, 24-25; MBA: 14; Po: 1883; TMAP: 120-121, 125

Tales AAL: 216; BAF: 22, 25

The Toilet AAL: 200-202, 215-216; AAPD: 386-388; ADC: 179-180; BAP: 18-20; Br: 360; MBA: 20-21, 23; Po: 1880; TMAP: 121, 123, 125, 129, 135

Two Plays for L.A. MBA: 23

"Uncle Tom's Cabin: Alternate Ending" WaS1: 10

"Words" ASF: 65; WaS1: 10

JONES, Madison
A Buried Land LCAB: 101

JONES, Marion Patrick
Pan Beat WIL: 63

JONES, Preston
Bradleyville Trilogy see A Texas Trilogy

The Last Meeting of the Knights of the White Magnolia see also A Texas Trilogy ADC: 180

The Oldest Living Graduate see also A Texas Trilogy ADC: 180

A Place on the Magdalena Flats ADC: 180

Sante Fe Sunshine ADC: 180

A Texas Trilogy [three plays: Lu Ann Hampton Laverty Oberlander; The Last Meeting of the Knights of the White Magnolia; and The Oldest Living Graduate] ADC: 180

JONES, Ralph H.
General BAF: 180

JONES, Silas
General BAF: 180
Waiting for Mongo ADC: 181; MBA: 127

JONES, Sir William
General EC: 96

JONES, Tom and Harvey SCHMIDT

The Fantasticks ADC: 181
I Do! I Do! ADC: 181
JONES, Walter
    Dudder Love ADC: 181
    Jazznite ADC: 181; BAP:
      125; MBA: 127
    Nigger Nightmare MBA: 127
JONES-QUARTEY, K.A.B.
    General BALE: 313
JONG, Erica
    Fear of Flying Ma: 1081
JONSON, Ben
    General Ba: 81-86; ED:
      256-269; ICBAP: 72;
      LCAB: 101; Ma: 1087-
      1089; NI: 7-42, 81-82,
      96-111, 113-114; TSD:
      57-68
    The Alchemist DC1: 100-
      101; ED: 258, 266, 269;
      EDC: 287-289; Ma: 1082-
      1083; NI: 50-54, 111;
      TSD: 58, 60, 62-67
    "Apologetical Dialogue" Ba:
      84
    Bartholomew Fair DC1: 101;
      ED: 258, 262, 267-269;
      EDC: 289-290; Ma: 1083-
      1084; NI: 54-57, 111;
      TSD: 59, 61-68
    The Case Is Altered DC1:
      101-102; EDC: 290-291;
      NI: 77, 114; TSD: 61
    Catiline, His Conspiracy
      DC1: 102; ED: 259; EDC:
      290-291; Ma: 1084-1085;
      NI: 63-65, 114; TSD:
      59-61, 68
    "A Celebration of Charis"
      Ba: 84; PE: 256-257
    "A Celebration of Charis I"
    "His Excuse for Loving"
      PE: 257
    "A Celebration of Charis 4"
    "Her Triumph" PE: 257
    Chlorida: Rites to Chloris
      and Her Nymphs DC1:
      102; NI: 81
    Christmas His Masque
      [Christmas His Show]
      NI: 114
    "Come, My Celia, Let Us
      Prove" Ba: 84; PE: 257
    Cynthia's Revels, or The
      Fountain of Self-Love
      DC1: 102-103; EDC: 291;

      NI: 73-74, 113-114; TSD:
      58, 61, 63, 67
    The Devil Is an Ass DC1:
      103; ED: 258, 267; EDC:
      291; NI: 74-75, 114
    Discoveries Ba: 85
    "Drink to Me, Celia" Ba: 84
    Eastward Hoe see CHAPMAN,
      George
    "An Elegy" ICBAP: 72
    "Elegy on the Death of Lady
      Jane Pawlet" PE: 257
    Epicene [Epicoene] see also
      The Silent Woman ED:
      258, 267; EDC: 291-292;
      LCAB: 101; Ma: 1085-1086;
      NI: 57-59, 111; TSD: 58-
      60, 65-66
    Epigrammes Ba: 85
    "An Epistle Mendicant" PE:
      257
    "An Epistle to a Friend, to Per-
      suade Him to the Warres"
      PE: 257
    "Epistle to Elizabeth Countesse
      of Rutland" PE: 257
    "An Epistle to Katherine, Lady
      Aubigny" PE: 257
    "Epistle to Mr. Arthur Squib"
      PE: 257
    "Epitaph on Elizabeth, L.H."
      Ba: 84; ICBAP: 73; PE:
      257-258
    "Epitaph on Solomon Pavy"
      Ba: 84; ICBAP: 73; PE:
      258
    "Eupheme: Or, The Faire
      Fame Left to Posteritie of
      That Truly Noble Lady, the
      Lady Venetia Digby" PE:
      258
    Every Man in and Every Man
      Out NI: 111-112
    Every Man in His Humour DC1:
      103-104; EDC: 292-293;
      Ma: 1086-1087; NI: 65-66;
      TSD: 59, 63
    Every Man Out of His Humour
      DC1: 104-105; EDC: 293-
      294; Ma: 1087; NI: 72-73
    "Famous Voyage" Ba: 84
    "A Fit of Rime Against Rime"
      Ba: 84; ICBAP: 73; PE:
      258
    "The Ghyrlond" ICBAP: 73
    The Gypsies Metamorphosed

DC1: 105; EDC: 294;
NI: 80, 113-114

Haddington Masque [The Mask
at Lord Haddington's Mar-
riage; or, The Hue and
Cry After Cupid] DC1:
105; NI: 78; TSD: 61

Hymenaei DC1: 105; NI:
78, 114

"Hymn to Diana" PE: 258

"A Hymne on the Nativitie
of My Saviour" ICBAP:
73; PE: 258

"A Hymne to God the Father"
PE: 258

"Inviting a Friend to Supper"
PE: 258

"It Was a Beauty That I Saw"
PE: 258

"Let Me Be What I Am" Ba:
84

Love's Welcome at Bolsover
NI: 81

The Magnetic Lady; or,
Humours Reconciled ED:
258; EDC: 294; NI: 75-
76; TSD: 64

The Mask at Lord Hadding-
ton's Marriage; or, The
Hue and Cry After Cupid
see Haddington Masque

The Mask of Owls NI: 81

The Masque of Augurs DC1:
105; EDC: 294; NI: 80;
TSD: 67

The Masque of Beauty DC1:
105; NI: 78

The Masque of Blacknesse
DC1: 105; NI: 77, 114

Masque of Gipsies TSD: 62

Masque of Queenes DC1:
105; NI: 79; TSD: 61

Mercury Vindicated DC1:
106; NI: 113; TSD: 60

Mortimer, His Fall DC1:
106; EDC: 294; NI: 76-
77

"My Answer. The Poet to
the Painter" PE: 258

"My Picture Left in Scotland"
PE: 258

The New Inn; or The Light
Heart DC1: 106; ED:
258, 267; EDC: 294; NI:
71-72, 112; TSD: 60,
62-63

Oberon the Fairy Prince NI:
79, 113

"An Ode: High Spirited
Friend" PE: 258

"On a Lover's Dust Made Sand
for an Hour Glass" PE:
258

"On Lucy Countesse of Bedford"
PE: 259

"On My First Daughter" PE:
259

"On My First Son" Ba: 84;
PE: 259

"On Something That Walkes
Some-where" PE: 259

Pan's Anniversary; or, The
Shepherds' Holiday Ni:
114; PE: 259

"The Pattern of Piety" PE:
259

"The Picture of the Body" PE:
259

Pleasure Reconciled to Virtue
EDC: 294

Poetaster; or, The Arraignment DC1: 106-107; EDC:
295; NI: 67-69, 112; TSD:
61, 64, 67

Prince Henry's Barriers NI:
81

"Queene and Huntresse"
("Hymn," Cynthia's Revels)
ICBAP: 73; PE: 259

"The Reverse" ICBAP: 73

The Sad Shepherd DC1: 107;
NI: 114

Sejanus, His Fall DC1: 107-
108; EDC: 295-296; Ma:
1089-1090; NI: 60-63, 112;
TSD: 59-64, 66-67

The Silent Woman see also
Epicene DC1: 108; TSD:
58, 61, 66

"The Sinners Sacrifice"
ICBAP: 73

"A Song" ICBAP: 73; PE:
259

The Staple of News DC1:
108; ED: 258, 267; EDC:
296; NI: 69-71, 112; TSD:
64

A Tale of a Tub DC1: 108;
ED: 258; NI: 76; TSD:
59

"Though Beautie Be the Marke
of Praise" PE: 257

Timber Ba: 85; Hen: 181;
LCAB: 102
"To Celia: Drink to Me Only
with Thine Eyes" Ba: 84;
LCAB: 102; PE: 259-260
"To Heaven" Ba: 84; ICBAP:
73; PE: 260
"To His Lady, Then Mrs.
Cary" PE: 260
"To John Donne" Ba: 84;
ICBAP: 73; PE: 260
"To Mary Lady Wroth" PE:
260
"To Penshurst" Ba: 85;
ICBAP: 73; PE: 260
"To Sir Lucklesse Woo-all"
PE: 260
"To Sir William Sidney, on
His Birthday" Ba: 84
"To the Immortall Memorie,
and Friendship of That
Noble Paire, Sir Lucius
Cary, and Sir H. Morison"
Ba: 84; PE: 260-261
"To the Memory of My Be-
loved, the AUTHOR Mr.
William Shakespeare" PE:
261
The Vision of Delight Ba:
84; EDC: 296; NI: 79
Volpone; or, The Fox DC1:
108-110; ED: 256-258,
266, 269; EDC: 296-299;
LCAB: 102; Ma: 1090-
1091; NI: 42-50, 113;
TSD: 57-66, 68, 81
"Why I Write Not of Love"
PE: 261
JOPLIN, Scott
General BAW: 445-446
Treemonisha BAP: 125-126;
MBA: 127-129
JORDAN, Norman
General AAPD: 197
JORDAN, Thomas
General LJCD: 245
JORGENSEN, Johannes
General Po: 1884
Foraarssagn Ke: 354
En Fremmed see A Stranger
Hjemvee Ke: 354
Livets Trae see The Tree
of Life
Our Lady of Denmark Fi:
406
Spring Legend Fi: 406

A Stranger [En Fremmed] Fi:
406; Ke: 354
Summer [Sommer] Fi: 406; Ke:
354
The Tree of Life [Livets Trae]
Fi: 406; Ke: 354
JOSELOVITZ, Ernest
Hagar's Children ADC: 181
JOSEPH, Robert L.
Face of a Hero ADC: 181-182
Isle of Children ADC: 182
JOSIKA, Miklos
The Czechs in Hungary Ke:
413
The Reckless Ke: 413
JOSSET, Andre
Elizabeth la Femme sans Homme
Br: 360
JOUHANDEAU, Marcel
General Po: 1885
JOUVE, Pierre-Jean
General Po: 1885-1886
Paulina, 1880 Po: 1886
JOUVET, Louis
General Po: 1886
JOVANOVICH, William
General LCAB: 102
JOVELLANOS, Gaspar de
El Delincuente Honrado DC2:
213
JOVINE, Francesco
Signora Ava Fi: 266
Le terre del Sacramento Fi:
266
JOYCE, James
General BN2: 66-71; Br:
361; LCAB: 102; MBD:
56-57; MD: 174-175; Po:
1886-1929; Ri2: 12-23, 46-
47; Sch: 141-153
"After the Race" Po: 1929;
SFC: 115; Wa: 391; WaS1:
106
"Alone" PE: 261
"Araby" Po: 1926, 1929-1932;
SFC: 115; Wa: 391-393;
WaS1: 106-107
"Bahnofstrasse" Po: 1932
"The Boarding House" Po:
1932-1933; SFC: 115-116;
Wa: 393; WaS1: 107
Chamber Music Po: 1933-1934
"Chamber Music 36" PE: 261
"Clay" Po: 1934-1936; SFC:
116; Wa: 393-395; WaS1:
107

"Counterparts" Po: 1936;
   SFC: 116; Wa: 395; WaS1:
   107
"The Dead" Ma: 1092-1093;
   Po: 1937-1941; SFC: 116-
   117; Wa: 395-398; WaS1:
   107
Dubliners BN2: 68-69; Po:
   1901-1902, 1941-1948; Ri2:
   13-15, 19, 24-29; TMIP:
   103
"Ecce Puer" PE: 261; Po:
   1948
"An Encounter" Po: 1949;
   SFC: 117-118; Wa: 398-
   399; WaS1: 107
"Eveline" Po: 1949-1950;
   SFC: 118; Wa: 399-400;
   WaS1: 107
Exiles Br: 361; DC1: 110;
   EDC: 299-301; Ma: 1093-
   1094; MBD: 57; MD: 175-
   176; MDAE: 419; Po:
   1894-1895, 1950-1953; Ri2:
   13, 15, 17, 46
Finnegans Wake BN2: 67-69,
   71; EN: 71-76; ENE: 162-
   170; ENES1: 127-131;
   ENES2: 137-139; LCAB:
   102; Lon: 50; Ma: 1094-
   1096; Po: 1890, 1893,
   1899-1900, 1902-1907,
   1909-1911, 1916, 1922-1925,
   1928, 1953-1982; Ri2: 14-
   17, 19, 21-22, 29-34, 553;
   Sch: 153-160
Giacomo Joyce Po: 1982
"Grace" Po: 1982-1984; SFC:
   118; Wa: 400-401; WaS1:
   107
"I Hear an Army" PE: 261
"Ivy Day in the Committee
   Room" Po: 1984-1985;
   SFC: 118; Wa: 401-402;
   WaS1: 107
Letters LCAB: 102
"A Little Cloud" Po: 1985;
   SFC: 118-119; Wa: 402;
   WaS1: 107
"A Mother" Po: 1985-1986;
   SFC: 119; Wa: 402-403;
   WaS1: 108
"A Painful Case" Po: 1986-
   1987; SFC: 119; Wa:
   403-404; WaS1: 108
A Portrait of the Artist as

a Young Man BN2: 68-71;
   EN: 76-79; ENE: 170-174;
   ENES1: 131-132; ENES2:
   139-141; LCAB: 103; Ma:
   1096-1097; Po: 1890, 1895-
   1896, 1899-1903, 1907, 1916,
   1926-1928, 1987-2002, 2029;
   Ri2: 13-17, 19, 21, 34-38,
   47, 409; Sch: 160-165
"The Sisters" Po: 2002-2005;
   SFC: 119-120; Wa: 404-405;
   WaS1: 108
Stephen Hero ENE: 174-175;
   ENES1: 132; ENES2: 141;
   Po: 1895, 1899, 1903, 1909,
   1914, 2005-2007, 2029; Ri2:
   15-18, 22, 46-47; Sch: 160-
   165
"Tilly" Po: 2007
"Two Gallants" Po: 2007; SFC:
   120; Wa: 405-406; WaS1:
   108
Ulysses BN2: 67-71; EN: 79-
   86; ENE: 175-185; ENES1:
   132-139; ENES2: 141-146;
   LCAB: 103; Ma: 1097-1099;
   MDAE: 387; Po: 1890, 1893-
   1896, 1899-1900, 1903, 1905-
   1907, 1910-1911, 1913-1914,
   1916, 1924-1925, 1927-1928,
   2008-2054; Ri2: 13-17, 19,
   21, 38-46, 368; Sch: 165-177
JOZSEF, Atilla
   General Po: 2054
JUA, Chakula Cha
   Langston & Company BAP:
   126
JUDD, Sylvester
   General AN: 166
JUDRIN, Roger
   General Po: 2054
JUHASZ, Ferenc
   "The Boy Changed into a Stag"
   PE: 261
JULIAN OF NORWICH
   General Hen: 128
JULIEN, Max
   Cleopatra Jones MBA: 129
   The Mack MBA: 129
   Naked as a Jailbird MBA: 129
   Thomasine and Bushrod BAP:
   126; MBA: 129
JULIUS, Duke Heinrich
   Susanna DC2: 213
   Von Einem Wirthe Oder Gast-
   geber DC2: 213

JÜNGER, Ernst
  General Po: 2055-2057
  Arbeiter see The Working-
    man
  Auf den Marmorklippen see
    On the Marble Cliffs
  Der Friede see The Peace
  The Glass Bees Fi: 334
  Heliopolis Fi: 334; Ke: 283
  On the Marble Cliffs [Auf
    den Marmorklippen] Fi:
    335; Ke: 283; Po: 2057-
    2058
  The Peace [Der Friede] Po:
    2058
  The Slingshot Fi: 335
  The Storm of Steel [In Stahl-
    gewittern] Fi: 335; Ke:
    284; Po: 2058
  Sturm Po: 2059
  Visit to Godenholm Ke: 284
  The Workingman [Arbeiter]
    Ke: 284; Po: 2057
"JUNIUS"
  General EC: 96-97
JUSTICE, Donald Rodney
  General ICBAP: 73; Po: 2059
  "The Metamorphosis" ICBAP:
    73
JUVENAL
  General Ma: 1100

                    K

KABAPHES, Konstantinos Petrou
  General LCAB: 103; Ma:
    331-332; Po: 439-440
KACHINGWE, Aubrey
  General BALE: 313
KAFFKA, Margit
  Colors and Years Ke: 413
KAFKA, Franz
  General LCAB: 103; Po:
    2061-2085
  "Eine alltägliche Verwirrung"
    see "A Common Confusion"
  "Ein altes Blatt" see "An
    Old Page"
  America [Amerika] Fi: 335-
    336; Ke: 284-85; Ma:
    1101; Po: 1590-1591, 2072-
    2073, 2080-2081, 2083,
    2086-2087
  "Auf der Galerie" see "In
    the Gallery"

"Before the Law" ["Vor dem
  Gesetz"] Po: 2083, 2114-
  2115; SFC: 120; Wa: 406
"Beim Bau der Chinesischen
  Mauer" Po: 1590-1591
"Ein Bericht für eine Akademie"
  see "A Report to an Academy"
"Ein Besuch im Bergwerk" Ke:
  289; Po: 2089; Wa: 406
"Blumfeld, an Elderly Bachelor"
  SFC: 120; Wa: 406; WaS1:
  108
"The Bucket Rider" Wa: 406
"The Burrow" Fi: 336; Ke:
  285; Ma: 1101-1102; SFC:
  120-121; Wa: 407; WaS1: 108
"The Cares of a Family Man"
  SFC: 121; Wa: 407-408;
  WaS1: 108
The Castle [Das Schloss] Fi:
  336-339; Ke: 285-288; Ma:
  1102-1103; Po: 2064, 2071-
  2073, 2077-2078, 2080, 2084,
  2105-2108
"Children on a Country Road"
  SFC: 121; Wa: 408
"A Common Confusion" ["Eine
  alltägliche Verwirrung"] Po:
  2083, 2085; SFC: 121; Wa:
  408
"The Conscription of Troops"
  Wa: 408
"Conversation with a Praying
  Man" Wa: 408
"A Country Doctor" ["Ein
  Landarzt"] Fi: 339-340; Ke:
  288-289; Ma: 1103-1104;
  Po: 2095-2097; SFC: 121;
  Wa: 408-409; WaS1: 108
"Description of a Struggle" Fi:
  340; SFC: 121; Wa: 409
"A Dream" SFC: 121; Wa: 410
"Das Ehepaar" see "The Mar-
  ried Couple"
"Eleven Sons" SFC: 121; Wa:
  410
"First Sorrow" SFC: 121; Wa:
  410
"Forschungen eines Hundes"
  see "Investigations of a Dog"
"A Fratricide" SFC: 121; Wa:
  410; WaS1: 108
"The Giant Mole" SFC: 121;
  Wa: 410
"Give It Up!" SFC: 121; Wa:
  410

"The Great Wall of China"
   Fi: 340; Ke: 289; Po:
   2064, 2081; SFC: 122;
   Wa: 410-411; WaS1: 108-
   109
"Der Heizer" see "The
   Stoker"
"A Hungry Artist" ["A Hunger
   Artist"; "Ein Hunger-
   künstler"] Fi: 341; Ke:
   289; Ma: 1105; Po: 2090-
   2092; SFC: 122; Wa: 411-
   412; WaS1: 109
"The Hunter Gracchus" ["Der
   Jäger Gracchus"] Ke:
   289; Po: 2094; SFC:
   122-123; Wa: 412; WaS1:
   109
"A Hybrid" Wa: 412
"An Imperial Message" SFC:
   123; Wa: 412
"In Our Synagogue" SFC:
   123; Wa: 412
"In the Gallery" ["Auf der
   Galerie"] Po: 2087-2088;
   SFC: 123; Wa: 412-413;
   WaS1: 109
"In the Penal Colony" ["In
   der Strafkolonie"] Fi:
   341-343; Ke: 289-290;
   Ma: 1106; Po: 2092-2094;
   SFC: 123; Wa: 413-414;
   WaS1: 109
"Investigations of a Dog"
   ["Forschungen eines
   Hundes"] Fi: 343; Ke:
   290; Po: 2083, 2090;
   SFC: 123-124; Wa: 414;
   WaS1: 109
"Jackals and Arabs"
   ["Schakale und Araber"]
   Po: 2105; SFC: 124;
   Wa: 414
"Der Jäger Gracchus" see
   "The Hunter Gracchus"
"Josephine the Singer"
   ["Josephine the Songstress";
   "Josefine, die Sängerin";
   "The Mouse Folk"] Fi: 343;
   Ke: 292; Po: 2083, 2094;
   SFC: 124; Wa: 414-415;
   WaS1: 109
"The Judgment" ["Das Ur-
   teil"] Ke: 290-291; Ma:
   1107; Po: 2068, 2109;
   SFC: 124; Wa: 415-416;

WaS1: 109-110
"The Knock at the Manor Gate"
   Wa: 416
"Der Kreisel" Wa: 416
"Ein Landarzt" see "A Country
   Doctor"
The Letter to His Father Po:
   2068
"The Levy of Troops" SFC:
   124; Wa: 416
"A Little Woman" SFC: 124;
   Wa: 416
"The Married Couple" ["Das
   Ehepaar"] Po: 2089-2090;
   SFC: 125; Wa: 416
"Memoirs of the Kalda Railroad"
   SFC: 125; Wa: 416
"The Merchant Messner" SFC:
   125; Wa: 417
"Metamorphosis" ["Die Verwand-
   lung"] Fi: 343-345; Ke:
   291-292; Ma: 1108-1109; Po:
   2068, 2077, 2083, 2109-2114;
   SFC: 125-126; Wa: 417-419;
   WaS1: 110
"My Neighbor" SFC: 126; Wa:
   419
"Das nächste Dorf" see "The
   Next Village"
"The New Advocate" Wa: 419;
   WaS1: 110
"The Next Village" ["Das
   nächste Dorf"] Po: 2083;
   SFC: 126; Wa: 419
"An Old Page" ["An Old Manu-
   script"; "Ein altes Blatt"]
   Po: 2085; SFC: 126; Wa:
   419
"On a Little Railway in Russia"
   SFC: 126; Wa: 419
"On Parables" ["Von den
   Gleichnissen"] Po: 2114
"On the Train" Wa: 420
Le Procès see The Trial
"Prometheus" SFC: 126; Wa:
   420
Der Prozess see The Trial
"A Report to an Academy" ["Ein
   Bericht für eine Akademie"]
   Ke: 293; Po: 2088-2089;
   SFC: 126-127; Wa: 420;
   WaS1: 110
"Schakale und Araber" see
   "Jackals and Arabs"
Das Schloss see The Castle
"The Silence of the Sirens"

["Das Schweigen der
Sirenen"] Po: 2108; Ke:
293; Wa: 420; WaS1: 111
Die Sorge des Hausvaters
Po: 2108
"Das Stadtwappen" Wa: 420
"The Stoker" ["Der Heizer"]
Po: 2090; SFC: 127; Wa:
420-421; WaS1: 111
The Trial [Le Procès; Der
Prozess] Br: 361; Fi:
345-350; Ke: 293-296;
LCAB: 103; Ma: 1109-
1110; Po: 2064, 2069,
2071-2073, 2077-2078, 2080-
2081, 2084, 2098-2104;
TMBP: 164
"Das Urteil" see "The Judg-
ment"
"Die Verwandlung" see
"Metamorphosis"
"The Village Schoolteacher"
WaS1: 111
"Von den Gleichnissen" see
"On Parables"
"Vor dem Gesetz" see "Be-
fore the Law"
"Wedding Preparations in the
Country" Wa: 421
"The White Horse" SFC:
127; Wa: 421
KAHIGA, Hannah
General BALE: 313
KAHIGA, Samuel
General BALE: 313
KAHN, Arthur Lee
Baby of the Family DC1:
110-111
Burglary a la Mode DC1:
111
The Fox DC1: 111
The Last of the Hargroves
DC1: 111
Putting It Over DC1: 111
We-Uns of Tennessee DC1:
111
KAHN, Hannah
"Ride a Wild Horse" PE:
261
KAIN, Gylan
General BAW: 448
KAISER, Georg
General Br: 361-362; MD:
176-177; Po: 2115-2117
Adrienne Ambrossat MD:
177

Alain und Elise MD: 177
Alkibiades Saved [Der Gerettete
Alkibiades] Br: 362; DC2:
214; MD: 177
Bellerophon Br: 362; DC2:
213; MD: 177; Po: 2118
Der brand im Opernhaus see
Fire in the Opera House
The Burghers of Calais [Die
Bürger von Calais] Br:
362; DC2: 213; MD: 177;
Po: 2117
The Coral see Gas Trilogy
David und Goliath MD: 177
Der Englische Sender MD: 177
Europa MD: 177
Fire in the Opera House [Der
brand im Opernhaus] MD:
177
Flight to Venice [Flucht nach
Venedig] Br: 362; MD:
177
Das Floss der Medusa see The
Raft of the Medusa
Das Frauenopfer MD: 177
From Morn till Midnight [Von
morgens bis mitternacht] Br:
363; DC2: 214; MD: 179;
Po: 2119
Der Gärtner von Toulouse MD:
177
Gas Trilogy [The Coral; Gas I;
Gas II; Die Koralle] Br:
363; DC2: 214; MD: 177-
178; Po: 2116-2117
Gats MD: 177
Der Geist der Antike MD:
177
Der Gerettete Alkibiades see
Alkibiades Saved
Gillies and Jeanne [Gillies und
Jeanne] DC2: 214; MD:
178
Griechische Dramen Po: 2118
Hellseherei MD: 178
Hölle Weg Erde Br: 363; MD:
178
The Jewish Widow [Die Jüdische
Witwe] Br: 363; MD: 178;
Po: 2118
Kanzlist Krehler MD: 178
King Cuckold [König Hahnrei]
MD: 178
Klawitter MD: 178
Kolportage MD: 178
König Hahnrei see King

Cuckold
Die Koralle see Gas Trilogy
Die Lederköpfe MD: 178
Das Los des Ossian Balvesen
MD: 178
Mississippi MD: 178
Der Mutige Seefahrer MD:
178
Napoleon in New Orleans
MD: 178
Nebeneinander MD: 178
Noli Me Tangere MD: 178
Oktobertag see The
Phantom Lover
Papiermühle MD: 178
Pferdewechsel MD: 178
The Phantom Lover [Oktober-
tag] Br: 363; MD: 178
Der Präsident MD: 178
The Protagonist [Der Pro-
tagonist] Br: 363; MD:
178
Pygmalion Br: 363; DC2:
214; MD: 178; Po: 2118
The Raft of the Medusa
[Das Floss der Medusa]
Br: 364; MD: 177
Rektor Kleist Br: 364;
DC2: 214; MD: 178
Rosamunde Floris MD: 179
Schellenkönig Br: 364; DC2:
214; Po: 2118
Der Silbersee MD: 179
Der Soldat Tanaka DC2:
214; MD: 179; Po: 2118
Die Spieldose MD: 179
Twice Oliver [Zweimal
Oliver] Br: 364; DC2:
215; MD: 179; Po: 2116
Villa durea Po: 2116
Von morgens bis mitternacht
see From Morn Till Mid-
night
Der Zentaur MD: 179
Zwei Krawtten MD: 179
Zweimal Amphitryon Br:
364; DC2: 214; MD: 179;
Po: 2116, 2118
Zweimal Oliver see Twice
Oliver
KALCHEIM, Lee H.
General MDAE: 290
The Morning After Br: 364
KALIDASA
Malavikagnimitram DC2: 215
The Recovered Ring [Shak-

untala] DC2: 215-217;
LCAB: 103; Po: 1524
Vikram and the Nymph DC2:
217-218
KALVE, Aivars
Tumbleweed Fi: 454
KAMBAN, Gudmundur
Ragnar Finnsson Ke: 354
Thirtieth Generation Ke: 354
KAMES, Henry Home, Lord
General EC: 97
KANDINSKY, Wassily
General Po: 2119-2120
KANE, Hamidou
L'Aventure ambiguë Po: 2120
KANE, Harnett Thomas
General Po: 2120
KANIN, Fay
Goodbye, My Fancy ADC:
182
_____ and Michael KANIN
His and Hers ADC: 182
Rashomon ADC: 182-183
KANIN, Garson
Born Yesterday ADC: 183
Come on Strong ADC: 183
Dreyfus in Rehearsal ADC:
183
A Gift of Time ADC: 183;
TMAP: 171
The Live Wire ADC: 183-184
The Rat Race ADC: 184
The Smile of the World ADC:
184
Kanin, Michael see KANIN, Fay
and Michael KANIN
KANT, Hermann
Die Aula Fi: 350; Po: 2120
KANTOR, MacKinley
Andersonville AN: 166; Ma:
1111; Po: 2120-2121
KAPLAN, Justin
Mr. Clemens and Mark Twain
LCAB: 103
KARAGHO, Patrick
General BALE: 314
KARAMZIN, Nikolay
"Anecdote" Wa: 421
"A Knight of Our Time" Wa:
421
"Martha the Mayoress"
["Marfa..."] Wa: 421
"My Confession" Wa: 421
"The Sensitive and the Cold"
Wa: 421
KARCHMER, Sylvan

"A Fistful of Alamo Heroes"
  ASF: 353
KARIARA, Jonathan
  General BALE: 314
KARIUKI, Joseph Elijah
  General BALE: 314
KARIUKI, Josiah Mwangi
  General BALE: 315
KASACK, Hermann
  General Po: 2121
  "The Dream of Death" Wa:
    421
  Fälschungen Fi: 350; Wa:
    421
  Das Grosse Netz Fi: 350
  Die Stadt Hinter dem Strom
    Fi: 350-351
KASOMA, Kabwe
  General BALE: 315
KASPROWICZ, Jan
  Napierski's Revolt DC2: 218
KASS, Jerome
  Monopoly ADC: 184
  Saturday Night ADC: 184
KASSAM, Amin
  General BALE: 315
KASSAM, Sadru
  General BALE: 315
KASSAM, Yusef
  General BALE: 316
KÄSTNER, Erich
  General Po: 2121
  Drei Männer im Schnee see
    Three Men in the Snow
  Emil and the Detective [Emil
    und die Detektive] Ke:
    296; Po: 2121-2122
  Emil and the Triplets [Emil
    und die drei Zwillinge]
    Ke: 296; Po: 2121-2122
  Fabian Ke: 296
  Das Fliegende Klassenzimmer
    Ke: 296; Po: 2121-2122
  Punktchen und Anton Ke:
    296; Po: 2121-2122
  Die Schule der Diktatoren
    Br: 364
  Three Men in the Snow [Drei
    Männer im Schnee] Ke:
    296; Po: 2121-2122
KATAYEV, Valentin Petrovich
  General MD: 179; Po:
    2122-2123
  The Blue Scarf Br: 364
  The Embezzlers Ke: 413
  For the Power of the Soviets

    Ke: 413
  Forward, oh Time Ke: 413
  The Grass of Oblivion Fi:
    454; Po: 2122
  The Holy Well Po: 2122
  The Little House MD: 179
  Lonely White Sail Ke: 413
  A Million Torments MD: 179
  "Our Father Who Art in Heaven"
    Wa: 421
  The Path of Flowers Br: 365
  The Sacred Well Fi: 454
  Squaring the Circle Br: 365;
    MD: 179
KATTAN, Naim
  General JW: 334
  La memorie et la promesse JW:
    334
KATZ, Leon
  Dracula: Sabbat ADC: 184
KAUFMAN, Bob
  General BAW: 451
KAUFMAN, George S.
  General Br: 365; JW: 392;
    Lon: 35; MD: 179-180;
    MDAE: 293-294; Po: 2123
  The Butter and Egg Man ADC:
    184
  Hollywood Pinafore ADC: 185;
    MD: 180
  _____ and Marc CONNELLY
  The Beggar on Horseback ADC:
    185; Br: 365; MD: 180
  Dulcy ADC: 185
  Merton of the Movies ADC:
    185; TMAP: 203
  _____ and Katharine DAYTON
  First Lady ADC: 185
  _____ and Edna FERBER
  Bravo! ADC: 186
  Dinner at Eight ADC: 186; Br:
    365-366; DC1: 111; MD:
    180
  The Land Is Bright ADC: 186
  The Royal Family ADC: 186-
    187; MD: 180
  Stage Door ADC: 187
  Theatre Royal Br: 366
  _____ and Moss HART
  The American Way see also
    HART, Moss and George S.
    KAUFMAN Br: 365
  The Fabulous Invalid see also
    HART, Moss and George S.
    KAUFMAN MD: 180
  I'd Rather Be Right see also

HART, Moss and George S.
KAUFMAN MD: 180
The Man Who Came to Dinner
see also HART, Moss and
George S. KAUFMAN Br:
366; MD: 180
Merrily We Roll Along see
also HART, Moss and
George S. KAUFMAN DC1:
111
Once in a Lifetime see also
HART, Moss and George S.
KAUFMAN Br: 366
You Can't Take It with You
see also HART, Moss and
George S. KAUFMAN Br:
366; DC1: 111; MD: 181;
Po: 2123
_____ and Nunnally JOHNSON
Park Avenue MD: 180
_____ and Leueen MacGRATH
Fancy Meeting You Again
ADC: 187; MD: 180
The Small Hours ADC: 187;
Br: 366
_____, Morrie RYSKIND,
George GERSHWIN, and
Ira GERSHWIN
Let 'Em Eat Cake ADC: 187
Of Thee I Sing ADC: 187;
DC1: 111; Lon: 35; MD:
180
_____ and Howard TEICHMAN
The Solid Gold Cadillac ADC:
188
_____ and Alexander WOOLL-
COTT
The Dark Tower ADC: 188;
Br: 365
KAUFMAN, Wallace
"Smethport, Pennsylvania"
PE: 261
KAUFMANN, Richard
Heaven Pays No Dividends
Ke: 296
KAVANAGH, Patrick
General LCAB: 103; Po:
2123-2125
"Advent" PE: 261
Come Dance with Kitty Stob-
ling Po: 2124
The Green Fool ENES2: 146
"Primrose" PE: 261
Tarry Flynn ENES2: 146
KAVERIN, Veniamin
Artist Unknown see The

Unknown Artist
Before the Mirror Fi: 454
Fulfillment of Desires Fi: 454;
Po: 2126
The Open Book Fi: 454; Po:
2126
A Piece of Glass Ke: 414
Searches and Hopes Ke: 414
Skandalist Fi: 454
Two Captains Fi: 454; Po:
2126
The Unknown Artist [Artist Un-
known] Fi: 454; Ke: 413-
414
Xudoznik neizvesten Po: 2125
KAWABATA, Yasunari
General Po: 2126
"The Izu Dancer" Wa: 422
"A Man Who Does Not Smile"
WaS1: 111
Snow Country Ma: 1112; Po:
2126-2127
KAY-SHUTTLEWORTH, James
Phillips
Ribblesdale ENES1: 139
Scarsdale ENES1: 139
KAYANJA, Lydia
General BALE: 316
KAYE-SMITH, Sheila
General TA: 196
The End of the House of Alard
ENES2: 146
Joanna Godden ENES2: 146
The Lardners and the Laurel-
woods ENES2: 146
Little England ENES2: 146
Mrs. Gailey ENES2: 146
Susan Spray ENES2: 146
Sussex Gorse ENES2: 147
Tamarisk Town ENES2: 147
The View from the Parsonage
ENES2: 147
KAYIRA, Legson
General BALE: 316
KAYPER-MENSAH, Albert William
General BALE: 317
KAZAKOV, Jurij
General Po: 2127
"Adam and Eve" Wa: 422
"Antlers" Wa: 422
"Autumn in the Woods" Wa:
422
"Here Comes a Dog" Wa: 422
"Morning Calm" Wa: 422
"The Outsider" Wa: 422
KAZAN, Molly

The Alligators ADC: 188
Rosemary ADC: 188
KAZANTZANKIS, Nikos
General LCAB: 104; Po:
2127-2128
Bios Kai Politeia tou Alexi
Zormpa see Zorba the
Greek
The Fratricides [Aderphop-
hades] Po: 2128-2129
God's Pauper [St. Francis,
a Novel; Ophtōhaulos tou
Theou] Ma: 1115; Po:
2131
The Greek Passion [Ho
Christo Xanastauronetai]
Ma: 1113; Po: 2130
Kuros Po: 2130
The Last Temptation of Christ
Ma: 1113
The Odyssey: A Modern
Sequel [Odysseias] Ma:
1113-1114; Po: 2130-2131
Ophtōhaulos tou Theou see
God's Pauper
Report to Greco Ma: 1114-
1115
St. Francis, a Novel see
God's Pauper
Zorba the Greek [Bios Kai
Politeia tou Alexi Zormpa]
Ma: 1115-1116; Po: 2129
KEANE, E. McG.
L'Oubli WIL: 63-64
KEANE, John B.
General Br: 366; TMIP:
58-61
Big Maggie TMIP: 59, 61-
62
The Field Br: 366
The Highest House on the
Mountain Br: 367; TMIP:
62
Mame Fadden TMIP: 60
Many Young Men of Twenty
Br: 367; TMIP: 50, 60-
61
No More in Dust Br: 367;
TMIP: 59, 62
The Rain at the End of the
Summer TMIP: 62
Sharon's Grave Br: 367;
TMIP: 63
Sive Br: 367; TMIP: 59-
61, 63
The Year of the Hiker Br:

367
KEATS, John
General EDT: 202-203; Fog:
38-41; ICBAP: 74; LCAB:
104; Ma: 1117-1119; Re:
174-183
"La Belle Dame Sans Merci"
Fog: 42-43; ICBAP: 74;
LCAB: 104; PE: 262; Re:
177-178
"Bright Star" PE: 262
"Endymion" Fog: 43; ICBAP:
74; LCAB: 104; Re: 178,
180, 183
"Epistle to Charles Cowden
Clarke" PE: 263
Epistle to John Hamilton Rey-
nolds Fog: 43
"The Eve of St. Agnes" Fog:
43-44; ICBAP: 74; LCAB:
104; PE: 263-264; Re: 177-
178, 180, 183
"The Eve of St. Mark" PE:
264
"Fairy's Song" PE: 264
"The Fall of Hyperion" Fog:
44; ICBAP: 74; PE: 264-
265; Re: 178-179
"The Great Odes" Fog: 41;
Re: 179, 182-183
"Hyperion" Fog: 44-45; PE:
265; Re: 178-179, 182
"I Stood Tip-toe" Fog: 45;
PE: 266
"If by Dull Rhymes Our Eng-
lish Must Be Chained" PE:
265
"Isabella; or the Pot of Basil"
Fog: 45; ICBAP: 74; PE:
265; Re: 180, 183
"Lamia" Fog: 45; PE: 266;
Re: 177-178, 181
"Nebuchadnezzar's Dream" PE:
266
"Ode on a Grecian Urn" Fog:
41-42; ICBAP: 74; LCAB:
104; PE: 266-269; Re:
177, 180
"Ode on Indolence" PE: 269-
270
"Ode on Melancholy" Fog: 42;
ICBAP: 74; PE: 270
"Ode to a Nightingale" Fog:
42; ICBAP: 74-75; LCAB:
104; PE: 271-273; Re:
177, 182

"Ode to Psyche" Fog: 42;
ICBAP: 75; PE: 273

"On First Looking into Chapman's Homer" ICBAP:
75; PE: 273-274

"On Seeing the Elgin Marbles for the First Time" PE:
274

"On Sitting Down to Read King Lear Once Again"
ICBAP: 75; PE: 274

"On Visiting the Tomb of Burns" PE: 274

"Sleep and Poetry" Fog:
45; ICBAP: 75; PE:
274

"To Autumn" Fog: 41;
ICBAP: 75; PE: 274-275;
Re: 181-182

"To Sleep" ICBAP: 75; PE:
275

"To ___; What Can I Do to Drive Away Remembrance from My Eyes" PE: 275-276

"What the Thrush Said" PE:
276

"When I Have Fears That I May Cease to Be" PE:
276

"Why Did I Laugh Tonight? No Voice Will Tell" PE:
276

"Written in the Cottage Where Burns Was Born"
PE: 276

KEBLE, John
"Easter Eve" PE: 276

KEELER, Harry S.
General ASF: 353

KEES, Weldon
General Po: 2132
"The Locusts, the Plaza, the Room" PE: 276

KELEMAN, Stanley
General LCAB: 104

Kell, Joseph see BURGESS, Anthony

KELLER, David
"The Menace" WaS1: 111
"The Revolt of the Pedestrians" WaS1: 111

KELLER, Gottfried
The Abused [Misused] Love Letters Ke: 296; Wa:
423

"The Banner of the Upright Seven" ["Das Fähnlein der sieben Aufrechten"] Ke: 296; Wa:
423

"Die Berlocken" Wa: 422

Clothes Make the Man [Kleider Machen Leuter] Fi: 351;
Ke: 296; Wa: 422; WaS1:
111

"The Dance Legend" Wa: 422

"Dietegen" Wa: 423

"Don Correa" Wa: 423

"Dorothea's Flower-Basket" Wa:
423

"Die Drei Gerechten Kammacher" see "Three Righteous (or Decent) Comb Makers"

"Eugenia" Wa: 423

"Das Fähnlein der sieben Aufrechten" see "The Banner of the Upright Seven"

"Die Geisterseher" Wa: 423

Green Henry [Der Grüne Heinrich] Fi: 351; Ke: 297

Kleider Machen Leuter see Clothes Make the Man

"Der Landvogt von Greifensee"
Fi: 351; Wa: 423

Die Leute von Seldwyla Fi:
351

Martin Salander Fi: 351; Ke:
297-298

"Der Narr auf Manegg" Wa:
423

"Pankraz, Der Schmoller" Fi:
351; Wa: 423

"The Poor Baroness" Wa: 423

"Regine" Wa: 423

"Regula Amrain and Her Youngest Son" Wa: 423

"Romeo und Julia auf dem Dorfe" see "A Village Romeo and Juliet"

"Der Schlimm-heilige" Wa:
423

"Der Schmied seines Glückes"
Wa: 423

Seven Legends Ke: 298

Short Novels of Zurich Ke:
298

Das Sinngedicht Fi: 352; Ke:
298; Wa: 422-423

"Three Righteous (or Decent) Comb Makers" ["Die Drei Gerechten Kammacher"]
Fi: 351; Ke: 298; Wa:

424; WaS1: 111

"Ursula" Ke: 298; Wa: 424

"Das verlorene Lachen" Ke: 299; Wa: 424

"A Village Romeo and Juliet" ["Romeo und Julia auf dem Dorfe"] Fi: 351-352; Ke: 298-299; Wa: 424; WaS1: 111

"The Virgin and the Devil" Wa: 424

"The Virgin and the Nun" Wa: 425

"The Virgin as Knight" Wa: 425

KELLEY, William Melvin
General AAF: 80-82; AAW: 64; ASF: 354; BAF: 182-183; BAW: 454

"Cry for Me" BAF: 183

Dancers on the Shore BAF: 183-184

dem AAF: 81-82; BAF: 182-184

A Different Drummer AAF: 81-82; BAF: 182-184

A Drop of Patience BAF: 184-185

Dunford Travels Everywhere AAF: 81; BAF: 182, 185

"The Life You Save" ASF: 353

"The Poker Party" ASF: 354; WaS1: 111

"Saint Paul and the Monkeys" ASF: 354

KELLY, George Edward
General Br: 367-368; LCAB: 104; Lon: 61; MD: 181; Po: 2132

Behold the Bridegroom ADC: 189; Br: 368

Craig's Wife ADC: 189; Br: 369; DC1: 112; MD: 181

Daisy Mayme ADC: 189; Br: 369

The Deep Mrs. Sykes ADC: 189; Br: 370; MD: 181

The Fatal Weakness ADC: 189; Br: 370; MD: 181

Maggie the Magnificent ADC: 190; Br: 370

Philip Goes Forth ADC: 190; Br: 370-371

Reflected Glory ADC: 190; Br: 371

The Show Off ADC: 190-191; Br: 371-372; MD: 181

The Torch-Bearers ADC: 191; Br: 372; DC1: 112; MD: 181-182

KELLY, Hugh
General Li: 226

False Delicacy DC1: 112; Li: 226

A Word for the Wise DC1: 112

KELLY, Tim
A Darker Flower Br: 372

KEMAL, Yashar
General Po: 2132

KEMBLE, John Philip
General Li: 228

KEMENY, Sigismund
The Enthusiasts Ke: 414

Gyulai Pal Ke: 414

Stormy Times Ke: 414

KEMP, Arnold
Eat of Me: I Am the Saviour BAF: 185

KEMP, Robert
General Ai: 285

KEMP, William
Kemp's Nine Days Wonder ERP: 262

Kempadoo, Peter see LAUCH-MONEN

KEMPE, Margery
General Hen: 129

KENDALL, Henry
General AL: 255-257

KENEALLY, Thomas
General MAP: 206-210

An Awful Rose MAP: 385

Bring Larks and Heroes MAP: 206-209

The Chant of Jimmie Blacksmith MAP: 207-210

The Fear Show Po: 2133

The Place at Whitton Po: 2133

Three Cheers for the Paraclete MAP: 207, 210; Po: 2133

KENNAWAY, James
General Ai: 326

KENNEDY, Adrienne
General BAP: 128; BAW: 456; MBA: 130-131

Cities in Bezique [two plays: The Owl Answers and A Beast's Story] ADC: 191; BAP: 128; BAW: 456;

MBA: 131-132

The Funnyhouse of a Negro
ADC: 191; BAP: 128-129;
BAW: 456; Br: 372;
MBA: 131-132

In His Own Write BAP: 129;
BAW: 456

A Rat's Mass ADC: 191;
BAP: 128-129

Sun MBA: 132

KENNEDY, Charles Rann
The Admiral ADC: 191

The Servant in the House
ADC: 191-192

The Seventh Trumpet ADC:
192

The Terrible Week ADC:
192

KENNEDY, John Pendleton
General AF: 182-184; ALL:
158; AN: 166; Ho: 98-
99

Horse-Shoe Robinson AF:
182-184; AN: 166; Ho:
98-99

Quodlibet AF: 182

The Red Book AF: 182;
Ho: 98

Rob of the Bowl AF: 182-
184; AN: 166; Ho: 98

Swallow Barn AF: 182-184;
Ho: 98-99

KENNEDY, Joseph Charles
"Poets" ICBAP: 75

KENNEDY, Ludovic
Murder Story Br: 372

KENNEDY, Mark
General BAF: 185; BAW:
456

The Pecking Order BAF:
186

KENNEDY, Rev. G.A. Studdert
"There Was Rapture of
Spring in the Morning"
["Woodbine Willie"] PE:
276

Kennedy, X.J. see KENNEDY,
Joseph Charles

KENNER, Hugh
General Po: 2133

KENT, George E.
General BAF: 186

KENT, Lena [Lettice Ada KING]
General WIL: 64

KENTE, Gibson
General BALE: 317

KENYATTA, Jomo
General BALE: 317

KERMAN, Sheppard
Mr. Simian Br: 372

KEROUAC, Jack
General AN: 167; ASF: 354;
CFAE: 206-207; CN: 302;
LCAB: 104-105; Ne: 64-65;
Po: 2133-2135

Desolation Angels CN: 302

The Dharma Bums CN: 303;
Ma: 1120; Po: 2135

Dr. Sax AN: 166

Maggie Cassidy AN: 166

On the Road AN: 167; CN:
303; Ma: 1120-1121; Ne:
65; Po: 2136

The Subterraneans AN: 167;
CFAE: 207; CN: 304; Ma:
1122; Ne: 65; Po: 2136

KERR, Alfred
General Po: 2136

KERR, Berrilla
The Elephant in the House
ADC: 192

KERR, Jean
Finishing Touches ADC: 192

Jenny Kissed Me ADC: 192

King of Hearts ADC: 192-193

Mary, Mary ADC: 193

Poor Richard ADC: 193

KERR, Walter
Sing Out, Sweet Land! ADC:
193

_____ and Leo BRADY
Count Me In ADC: 194

_____ and Jean KERR
Song of Bernadette ADC: 194

_____, Jean KERR, and Jay
GORNEY
Heaven on Earth ADC: 194

Touch and Go ADC: 194

KESEY, Ken
General CFAE: 209

One Flew Over the Cuckoo's
Nest CFAE: 209; CN:
304; Ma: 1123-1124; Po:
2137

Sometimes a Great Notion Ma:
1124; Po: 2137

KESSELRING, Joseph
Arsenic and Old Lace ADC:
194; Br: 372; MD: 182

Four Twelves Are 48 ADC:
194; MD: 182

There's Wisdom in Women ADC:

194-195

KESSLER, Lyle
  Watering Place ADC: 195
KETRON, Larry
  Augusta ADC: 195
KEYES, Daniel
  "Flowers for Algernon" WaS1:
    111
KEYES, Frances Parkinson
  General Po: 2137
KEYSERLING, Eduard von
  General Po: 2137-2138
  "Der Beruf" Wa: 425
  Ein Frühlingsopfer DC2:
    218; Po: 2137-2138
  "Zur Psychologie des Kom-
    forts" Po: 2138
  Sultry Days Ke: 299
KGOSITSILE, Keorapetse William
  General BALE: 318; BAW:
    459
KHAFULA, John J.B.
  General BALE: 318
KHAN, Ismith
  General WIL: 64
  The Jumbie Bird WIL: 64-
    65
  The Obeah Man WIL: 65
KHAN, Shafa'ath Ahmed
  General BALE: 319
KHANYILE, Edmund
  General BALE: 319
KHARMS, Daniil
  The Old Woman Fi: 454-455
KHLEBNIKOV, Velimir
  General Po: 2138
KHVYL'OVY [Mykola FITIL'OV]
  Woodcocks Ke: 414
KIBERA, Leonard
  General BALE: 319
  "It's a Dog's Share in Our
    Kinshasa" WaS1: 112
  "Silent Song" WaS1: 112
  "The Stranger" WaS1: 112
  "The Tailor" WaS1: 112
  Voices in the Dark BALE:
    319
KICHIZO, Nakamura
  A Vicarage DC2: 218
KIELLAND, Alexander
  Garman and Worse Ke:
    354-355
  Skipper Worse Ke: 355
KIELY, Benedict
  "A Ball of Malt and Madame
    Butterfly" Wa: 425

"A Bottle of Brown Sherry" Wa:
  425
Call for a Miracle ENES1: 139;
  ENES2: 147
The Captain with the Whiskers
  ENES1: 139; ENES2: 147
The Cards of the Gambler
  ENES1: 139; ENES2: 147
"A Cow in the House" Wa:
  425
Dogs Enjoy the Morning
  ENES1: 139; ENES2: 147
"A Great God's Angel Standing"
  Wa: 425
"Heroes in the Dark House"
  Wa: 425
"Homes on the Mountain" Wa:
  425
Honey Seems Bitter ENES1:
  139; ENES2: 147
"The House in Jail Square" Wa:
  425
In a Harbour Green ENES1:
  139; ENES2: 147
"A Journey to the Seven
  Streams" Wa: 425
Land Without Stars ENES1:
  139; ENES2: 147
"The Little Bishop" Wa: 425
"The Little Wrens and Robins"
  Wa: 425
"The Pilgrims" Wa: 426
"The Shortest Way Home" Wa:
  426
"Soldier, Red Soldier" Wa:
  426
"Ten Pretty Girls" Wa: 426
There Was an Ancient House
  ENES1: 140; ENES2: 147
"A View from the Treetops"
  Wa: 426
"The White Wild Bronco" Wa:
  426
KIERKEGAARD, S.
  Journal of a Seducer Ke:
    355
KIERLAND, Joseph Scott
  Drum-Taps ADC: 195
KIGGE, James
  General BALE: 320
KIIK, Heino
  Tondiöömaja Fi: 455
KILGORE, James
  General BAF: 186
KILLENS, John Oliver
  General AAW: 64; BAF:

187; BAP: 129-130; BAW: 463

And Then We Heard the Thunder BAF: 187-188; BAW: 463

Ballad of the Winter Soldiers BAP: 130

The Cotillion BAF: 188; BAW: 463

Odds Against Tomorrow BAP: 130

'Sippi BAF: 188; BAW: 463

Slaves BAP: 130

Youngblood BAF: 188; BAW: 463

KILLIGREW, Henry
Pallantas and Eudora [The Conspiracy] DC1: 112

KILLIGREW, Thomas
General LJCD: 246-247
The Parson's Wedding DC1: 112

KILMER, Joyce
General Po: 2139
"Trees" ICBAP: 75; PE: 276; Po: 2139

KILPATRICK, Lincoln
Deep Are the Roots MBA: 132

KILROY, Thomas
General TMIP: 67-68
The Big Chapel ENES2: 147; TMIP: 49, 67
The Death and Resurrection of Mr. Roche TMIP: 68-69
Talbot's Box TMIP: 69
Tea, Sex, and Shakespeare TMIP: 69

KILTY, Jerome
Dear Liar ADC: 195
The Little Black Book ADC: 195

KIM, Richard
The Martyred Po: 2139-2140

KIMBALL, F.M.
The Great Fugue ADC: 195

KIMENYE, Barbara
General BALE: 320

KING, Delphine
General BALE: 320
Dreams of Twilight BALE: 320

KING, Francis

A Domestic Animal ENES1: 141
The Needle ENES2: 148

KING, Grace Elizabeth
General AF: 186-187; ASF: 355; Po: 2140
"The Crippled Hope" Wa: 426
"In the French Quarter, 1870" ASF: 354
Monsieur Motte ASF: 354

KING, Henry
General Ba: 86; Hen: 34
"The Exequy" Ba: 86; PE: 276-277

King, Kennedy see BROWN, George Douglas

KING, Martin Luther, Jr.
General BAW: 466

KING, Norman
The Shadow of Doubt Br: 373

KING, Woodie, Jr.
General BAF: 189; BAP: 131; MBA: 132-133
A Black Quartet MBA: 133
The Long Night MBA: 133
Right On! BAP: 131

KINGSLEY, Charles
General BN: 70-71; Du: 104-105
Alton Locke Du: 104; EN: 86-87; ENES1: 140; ENES2: 148; Ma: 1125
Hereward the Wake EN: 87; ENES2: 148; Ma: 1126
Hypatia EN: 87; ENES1: 140; ENES2: 148; Ma: 1126
Two Years Ago EN: 87; ENE: 185; ENES1: 140; ENES2: 148
The Water Babies LCAB: 105
Westward Ho! EN: 87; ENE: 185; ENES1: 140; ENES2: 148; Ma: 1126-1127
Yeast Du: 104; EN: 87; ENES1: 140; ENES2: 148; Ma: 1127-1128

KINGSLEY, Henry
General AL: 261-263; BN: 71-72
Geoffrey Hamlyn AL: 261-263; ENES1: 140
The Hillyars and the Burtons AL: 261-262; ENES1: 140
Mademoiselle Mathilde ENES1: 140
"Magdalen at Michael's Gate" ICBAP: 75

Oakshott Castle ENES1: 140
Ravenshoe AL: 261, 263;
ENES1: 140
Silcote of Silcotes ENES1:
141
KINGSLEY, Sidney
General LCAB: 105; Lon:
35; MD: 182
Darkness at Noon ADC:
196; Br: 373
Dead End ADC: 196; Br:
373; Lon: 35
Detective Story ADC: 196-
197; Br: 373; DC1:
112; MD: 182
Lunatics and Lovers ADC:
197
Men in White ADC: 197;
Br: 373; DC1: 112; MD:
182
Night Life ADC: 197
The Patriots ADC: 197-198;
DC1: 112; Lon: 35
The World We Make ADC:
198; Br: 373; DC1: 113;
MD: 182
KINKEL, Johanna
Hans Ibeles in London Fi:
352
KINNELL, Galway
General ICBAP: 75-76; Po:
2140
"The Bear" PE: 277
"The Descent" PE: 277
"Easter" ICBAP: 76; PE:
277
"First Communion" PE: 277
"First Song" ICBAP: 76;
PE: 277; Po: 2141
"Flower Herding on Mount
Monadnock" Po: 2140
"How Many Nights" PE: 277
"The Porcupine" PE: 277
"Seven Streams of Nevis"
PE: 277
"Spindrift" PE: 277
"The Supper After the Last"
PE: 277
"The Thief" PE: 277
"To Christ Our Lord" PE:
278
"Vapor Trail Reflected in the
Frog Pond" PE: 278
"What a Kingdom It Was"
Po: 2140
"Where the Track Vanishes"

PE: 278
KINOY, Ernest
Leadbelly MBA: 133
KINSELLA, Thomas
General Po: 2141
"Downstream" PE: 278
"First Light" PE: 278
"Navigators" PE: 278
"Wormwood" LCAB: 105
KIPLING, Rudyard
General Du: 105-107; LCAB:
105; Ma: 1131; Po: 2141-
2156; TA: 198-199; VP:
47-48
"The Arrest of Lieutenant Go-
lightly" Po: 2157; Wa:
426
"As Easy as A.B.C." SFC:
127; Wa: 426
"At the End of the Passage"
Wa: 426
"At the Pit's Mouth" Wa: 426
"Aunt Ellen" Wa: 426
"Baa, Baa, Black Sheep" Wa:
426
"Beauty Spots" Wa: 427
"Below the Mill Dam" WaS1:
112
"Beyond the Pale" Wa: 427
"Black Jack" Wa: 427
"Bread Upon the Waters" Wa:
427
"The Bridge-Builders" Wa:
427
"The Bronckhorst Divorce Case"
Wa: 427
"Brother Square-Toes" SFC:
127; Wa: 427
"Brugglesmith" Wa: 427
"The Brushwood Boy" Ma:
1129; SFC: 127; Wa: 427
"The Bull That Thought" Wa:
427-428
Captains Courageous ENES1:
141; ENES2: 149; Ma: 1129;
Po: 2155
"The Children of the Zodiac"
SFC: 127; Wa: 428
"The Church That Was at
Antioch" Wa: 428; WaS1:
112
"Cold Iron" Wa: 428
"The Comprehension of Private
Copper" Po: 2157; Wa:
428; WaS1: 112
"A Conference of the Powers"

Wa: 428

"The Conversion of Aurelian
McGoggin" SFC: 127;
Wa: 428

"The Courting of Dinah Shadd"
Wa: 428

"Danny Deever" PE: 278

"Dayspring Mishandled" SFC:
127; Wa: 428; WaS1: 112

"The Devil and the Deep Sea"
Po: 2157; Wa: 429

"The Disturber of Traffic"
Wa: 429

"The Dog Hervey" Wa: 429;
WaS1: 112

"The Drums of the Fore and
Aft" Wa: 429

"East and West" Wa: 429

"The Edge of the Evening"
Wa: 429

"The Enemies to Each Other"
SFC: 127-128; Wa: 429

"The Enlightenments of
Pagett, M.P." Wa: 429

"An Error in the Fourth
Dimension" Po: 2157;
Wa: 429

"The Eye of Allah" SFC:
128; Wa: 429

"Fairy-Kist" Wa: 429

"False Dawn" SFC: 128;
Wa: 429

"The Finest Story in the
World" Wa: 430

"A Friend of the Family"
Wa: 430

"Friendly Brook" SFC: 128;
Wa: 430; WaS1: 112

"A Friend's Friend" Wa:
430

"The Gardener" Po: 2158;
Wa: 430; WaS1: 112

"An Habitation Enforced"
SFC: 128; Wa: 430;
WaS1: 112

"The Head of the District"
SFC: 128; Wa: 430

"His Private Honour" Wa:
430

"The House Surgeon" Po:
2158; Wa: 430; WaS1:
112

"How Fear Came" Wa: 430

"If" Po: 2158

"In the House of Suddhoo"
Wa: 430-431

"In the Interest of the Brethren"
Wa: 431

"In the Presence" Wa: 431

"In the Rukh" Wa: 431

"In the Same Boat" Wa: 431;
WaS1: 112

"The Janeites" Wa: 431

The Jungle Books Ma: 1129;
Po: 2158-2159

"Kaa's Hunting" SFC: 128;
Wa: 431

Kim Du: 105; ENE: 186;
ENES1: 141; ENES2: 149;
Ma: 1130; Po: 2155, 2159-
2161

"The King's Ankus" Wa: 431

"The Knife and the Naked
Chalk" Wa: 431

"The Legs of Sister Ursula"
Wa: 431

The Light That Failed ENE:
186; ENES1: 141; ENES2:
149; Ma: 1130-1131; Po:
2155, 2161

"Little Foxes" Wa: 431

"Love-o'-Women" SFC: 128;
Wa: 431

"M'Andrew's Hymn" PE: 278

"The Madness of Private Orth-
eris" Wa: 431

"A Madonna of the Trenches"
SFC: 128; Wa: 431; WaS1:
112

"The Maltese Cat" Wa: 431

"The Man Who Was" Wa: 432

"The Man Who Would Be King"
Po: 2161-2162; SFC: 128;
Wa: 432; WaS1: 113

"The Mark of the Beast" SFC:
128; Wa: 432

"Mary Postgate" Po: 2162;
SFC: 128; Wa: 432; WaS1:
113

"The Miracle of Purun Bhagat"
Wa: 432

"The Moral Reformers" Wa:
433

"Mrs. Bathurst" Po: 2162-
2163; Wa: 432-433; WaS1:
113

"My Son's Wife" SFC: 128;
Wa: 433; WaS1: 113

"My Sunday at Home" Wa:
433

"Naboth" Wa: 433

"Namgay Doola" Wa: 433

The Naulahka ENE: 186;
ENES1: 141; ENES2:
149; Po: 2163
"On Greenhow Hill" SFC:
128; Wa: 433
"On the City Wall" Wa: 433
"On the Gate" Wa: 433
".007" Wa: 433
"The Other Man" Wa: 433
"The Phantom Rickshaw"
SFC: 129; Wa: 433
"Pig" Wa: 433-434
"A Priest in Spite of Him-
self" SFC: 129; Wa:
434
"The Prophet and the Coun-
try" Wa: 434
"Puck of Pook's Hill" Po:
2163
"The Puzzler" WaS1: 113
"The Record of Badalia
Herodsfoot" Wa: 434
"Red Dog" Wa: 434
"The Rescue of Pluffles"
SFC: 129; Wa: 434
"The Return of Imray" Wa:
434
"Rimini" Po: 2163
"A Sahib's War" Wa: 434
"The Satisfaction of a Gentle-
man" Wa: 434
"Sea Constables: A Tale of
'15" Wa: 434; WaS1:
113
"The Ship That Found Her-
self" Wa: 434
Something of Myself Po:
2163-2164
"The Song of the Exiles" Po:
2164
Stalky & Company Po:
2155, 2164
"The Story of Muhammed Din"
Wa: 434
"The Strange Ride of Morrow-
bie Jukes" Wa: 434;
WaS1: 113
"Swept and Garnished" Wa:
434; WaS1: 113
"Teem: A Treasure Hunter"
Po: 2164; Wa: 434
"The Tender Achilles" SFC:
129; Wa: 435
"They" Po: 2164; SFC:
129; Wa: 435; WaS1: 113
"The Tie" Wa: 435

"To Be Filed for Reference" Wa:
435
"To the True Romance" Po:
2165
"Tods' Amendment" SFC: 129;
Wa: 435
"The Tomb of His Ancestors"
Wa: 435
"The Tree of Justice" Wa: 435
"Uncovenanted Mercies" Wa:
435
"Unprofessional" SFC: 129;
Wa: 435; WaS1: 113
"The Village That Voted the
Earth Was Flat" Po: 2165;
Wa: 435
"The Vortex" WaS1: 113
"A Wayside Comedy" Po: 2165;
Wa: 435; WaS1: 113
"The White Seal" Wa: 436
"William the Conqueror" Wa:
436
"Wireless" Po: 2165-2166; Wa:
436
"The Wish House" SFC: 129;
Wa: 436; WaS1: 113
"With the Night Mail" Wa: 436
"Without Benefit of Clergy" Po:
2165; SFC: 129; Wa: 436
"The Woman in His Life" WaS1:
113
"Wressley of the Foreign Of-
fice" Wa: 436
KIPPHARDT, Heinar
General Br: 373
The Adventures of Joel Brand
[Joel Brand: Geschichte
Eines Geschäfts] Br: 373
The Case of J. Robert Oppen-
heimer [In the Matter of J.
Robert Oppenheimer; In der
Sache J. Robert Oppenheim-
er] Br: 374; DC2: 218;
LCAB: 105
Der Hand des Generals Br:
374
KIRBY, William
General ECL: 156
The Golden Dog ECL: 156
KIRK, Hans
The Slave Ke: 355
KIRKE, John
General LJCD: 247
KIRKLAND, Caroline M.
General ASF: 355
A New Home--Who'll Follow?

LCAB: 105
KIRKLAND, Jack
 The Man with the Golden
  Arm ADC: 198
 Mr. Adam ADC: 198
 Suds in Your Eye ADC:
  198
 Tobacco Road ADC: 198-
  199
 Tortilla Flat ADC: 199
KIRKLAND, Joseph
 General AF: 189-190; AN:
  167
 The Captain of Company K
  AF: 190; AN: 167
 The McVeys AF: 190
 Zury: The Meanest Man in
  Spring County AF: 190;
  AN: 167; LCAB: 106
KIRKMAN, Francis
 General ERP: 263
KIRKWOOD, James
 P.S., Your Cat Is Dead!
  ADC: 199
KIRONDE, Erisa
 General BALE: 321
KIRSHON, Vladimir Mikailovich
 The Miraculous Alloy MD:
  182
 _____ and Andrei V.
  USPENSKII
 Red Rust Br: 374; MD:
  182
KIRSTEIN, Lincoln
 White House Happening ADC:
  199
KISTEMAECKERS, Henri
 General Br: 374
KITTOWE, Robert
 Loves Load-Starre ERP:
  263
KIVI, Aleksis
 Seven Brothers Ke: 355
KIZER, Carolyn
 General ICBAP: 76; Po:
  2166
KIZINGA, Nallumba
 General BALE: 321
KLEIN, Abraham Moses
 General JW: 152-153, 335;
  Po: 2166-2167
 Herschel of Ostropol Po:
  2167
 The Second Scroll JW:
  335; Po: 2167-2168
KLEIST, Heinrich von

Amphitryon DC2: 218-219;
  EDC: 301-302
The Battle of Arminius [Die Her-
  mannsschlact] DC2: 219;
  EDC: 302
"The Beggar Woman of Locarno"
  Wa: 436; WaS1: 113-114
The Broken Jug [Der Zer-
  brochene Krug] DC2: 222;
  EDC: 302-303
Cathy from Heilbronn; or, The
  Trial by Fire [Das Kätchen
  von Heilbronn; oder, Die
  Feuerprobe] DC2: 219-220;
  EDC: 303
The Duel [Der Zweikampf] Fi:
  355-356; Wa: 437; WaS1:
  114
The Earthquake in Chile Fi:
  352-353; Ke: 299; Wa: 437;
  WaS1: 114
The Engagement in Santo Domin-
  go [Die Verlobung in St.
  Domingo] Fi: 355; Wa:
  437; WaS1: 114
The Feud of the Schroffensteins
  [Die Familie Schroffenstein]
  DC2: 219; EDC: 303
The Foundling Fi: 353; Wa:
  437-438; WaS1: 114-115
Die Heilige Cäcilie oder die Ge-
  walt der Musik see St.
  Cecilia or the Power of Music
Die Hermannsschlact see The
  Battle of Arminius
Das Kätchen von Heilbronn;
  oder, Die Feuerprobe see
  Cathy from Heilbronn; or
  The Trial by Fire
The Marquise von O... Fi:
  353-354; Wa: 438; WaS1:
  115
Michael Kohlhaas Fi: 354-355;
  Ke: 300; Wa: 438-439; WaS1:
  115
Penthesilea DC2: 220; EDC:
  303-304
Prince Frederick of Homburg
  [Prinz Friedrich von Hom-
  burg] DC2: 220-222; EDC:
  304-306; LCAB: 106
Robert Guiskard DC2: 222;
  EDC: 306
St. Cecilia or the Power of Mu-
  sic [Die Heilige Cäcilie oder
  die Gewalt der Musik] Fi:

353; Wa: 439; WaS1: 115

Die Verlobung in St. Domingo
see The Engagement in
Santo Domingo

Der Zerbrochene Krug see
The Broken Jug

Der Zweikampf see The
Duel

KLIEWER, Warren
The Violators Po: 2168

KLINE, Otis Adelbert
General ASF: 355

KLINGER, Friedrich von
Fausts Leben, Thaten und
Hollenfahrt Ke: 300
Geschichte Giafars des
Barmeciden Ke: 300
Sturm und Drang DC2: 222
Die Zwillinge DC2: 222-223

KLOPSTOCK, Friedrich
Die Fruhlingfeier DC2: 223
Hermann DC2: 223

KLOSSOWSKI, Pierre
Le Baphomet Po: 2168
Roberte Po: 2168

KNEE, Allan
Santa Anita '42 ADC: 199

KNIGHT, Damon Francis
General LCAB: 106

KNIGHT, Eric
"Flurry at the Sheep Dog
Trial" Wa: 439

KNIGHT, Etheridge
General AAL: 221; BAF:
189; BAW: 468

KNIGHT, G. Wilson
General Po: 2168

KNIGHT, Sarah Kemble
The Journal of Madam Knight
AP: 403-404; Da: 54

KNISTER, Raymond
General Po: 2168

KNOTT, Frederick
Dial "M" for Murder EDC:
306
Mr. Fox of Venice EDC:
306
Wait Until Dark EDC: 306-
307
Write Me a Murder EDC:
307

KNOWLES, James Sheridan
General EDT: 207
The Hunchback EDT: 207

KNOWLES, John
General CFAE: 211-212;

CN: 304; Po: 2169

Indian Summer CN: 304; Ma:
1132

Morning in Antibes CN: 305

A Separate Peace CFAE: 211-
212; CN: 305; Ma: 1132-
1133; Po: 2169-2171

KNOX, Alexander
The Closing Door Br: 374

KNOX, John
General Ai: 40-41; SC: 67

KNUDSEN, Jakob
Fremskridt Ke: 355

KOCH, Christopher
General MAP: 211-212
The Boys in the Island MAP:
211-212
Across the Sea Wall MAP: 212

KOCH, Kenneth
General ICBAP: 76; JW: 86;
MDAE: 296; Po: 2171-2172
Washington Crossing the Dela-
ware Br: 374
"When the Sun Tries to Go On"
ICBAP: 76

KOCHANOWSKI, Jan
Dismissal of Grecian Envoys
DC2: 223

KOCHETOV, V.
The Brothers Yershov Ke:
414
The Zhurbins Ke: 414

KODA, Rohan
"The Bearded Man" WaS1:
115
"Destiny" WaS1: 116
"Encounter with a Skull" WaS1:
116
"Love Bodhisattva" WaS1: 116
"Snowflakes Dancing" WaS1:
116
"A Sword" WaS1: 116
"Viewing of a Painting" WaS1:
116

KODOLANYI, Janos
Watershed Ke: 415

KOEPPEN, Wolfgang
Der Tod in Rom Fi: 356

KOESTLER, Arthur
General CN: 305-306; LCAB:
106; Po: 2172
The Act of Creation Ma: 1134;
Po: 2172
The Age of Longing CN: 306;
ENES2: 149; Fi: 356; Ke:
300

Arrival and Departure CN:
306-307; ENES2: 149; Fi:
356; Ke: 300; Ma: 1135-
1136

The Call-Girls ENES2: 150;
Fi: 356

Darkness at Noon Br: 375;
CN: 307; ENES2: 150;
Fi: 356; Ke: 300-301;
Ma: 1136-1137; Po: 2172-
2174; Ri2: 324

The Ghost in the Machine
Ma: 1137; Po: 2172

The Gladiators CN: 308;
ENES2: 150; Fi: 356;
Ke: 301; Ma: 1138

Scum of the Earth Ke: 301

The Sleepwalkers Ma: 1138-
1139; Po: 2172

Thieves in the Night CN:
308; ENES2: 150; Fi:
356; Ke: 301-302; Ma:
1139-1140

KOJEVE, Alexandre
General Po: 2174

KOKOSCHKA, Oskar
General Br: 375; Po: 2174
The Burning Bush [Schaus-
piel der Brennende Dorn-
busch] Br: 375
Hiob Br: 375
Mörder, Hoffnung der Frauen
Br: 375; Po: 2174
Orpheus und Euridike Br:
375
Sphinx and Strawman [Sphinx
und Strohmann] Br: 376

KOLLONTAY, A.
"The Love of Three Generations" Wa: 439

KOLMAR, Gertrud
General Po: 2174-2175

KOLOKOLOV, Nikolay
Honey and Blood Fi: 455

KOLROSS, Johannes
Beel DC2: 223

KOMAROV, Matvej
Van'ka Kain Fi: 455

KOMEY, Ellis Ayitey
General BALE: 321

KOMROFF, Manuel
"Hamlet's Dagger" SFC:
129; Wa: 439

KONADU, Samuel Asare
General BALE: 322

KONOPNICKA, Maria
"My Children's Dolls" Wa: 439
"Smoke" Wa: 439
"The Wine Fortress" Wa: 439
"Wojciech Zapala" Wa: 440

KONOVALOV, Grigory
The University Ke: 415

KONSTANTINOV, Konstantin
"Day by Day" Wa: 440

KONSTANTINOVIC, Radomir
Give Us Today Ke: 415
The Pure and the Defiled Ke:
415

KONWICKI, Tadeusz
A Contemporary Dreambook Ke:
415

KOPISCH, August
"Ein Carnevalsfest" Wa: 440

KOPIT, Arthur
General Br: 376; LCAB:
106; MD: 182-183; MDAE:
298; Po: 2175; TMAP: 170-
176
Chamber Music MDAE: 298;
TMAP: 173-174
The Day the Whores Came Out
to Play Tennis ADC: 199-
200; Br: 376; TMAP: 173,
175-176
Indians ADC: 200; MDAE:
298; TMAP: 171-177
Oh Dad, Poor Dad, Mama's
Hung You in the Closet and
I'm Feeling So Sad ADC:
200-201; Br: 376; DC1:
113; TMAP: 171-173, 175,
177-178
Sing to Me Through Open Windows ADC: 201; TMAP:
178
Wings TMAP: 174, 178, 206-
207

KOPS, Bernard
General Br: 376; MDAE: 300
Change for an Angel Br: 376
The Dream of Peter Mann Br:
376
Enter Solly Gold Br: 376;
MDAE: 300
Goodbye, World Br: 377
The Hamlet of Stepney Green
Br: 377; DC1: 113
Home Sweet Honeycomb MDAE:
300
Stray Cats and Empty Bottles
Br: 377

KOPTA, Josef

The Third Company Ke:
415
KORNEICHUK, Alexander
Partisans in the Steppes of
the Ukraine Br: 377
A Virburnum Grove MD:
183
KORNFELD, Paul
General Br: 377
Heaven and Hell [Himmel
und Hölle] Br: 377
The Seduction [Die Verfüh-
rung] Br: 377
KOROLENKO, Vladimir
"Makar's Dream" Wa: 440
Korzeniowski, Jozef Konrad
see CONRAD, Joseph
KOSINSKI, Jerzy [Joseph
NOVAK]
General JW: 243; LCAB:
106
Being There Ma: 1141
Cockpit Ma: 1141-1142
The Painted Bird JW: 243;
Ma: 1142-1143
Steps JW: 243; Ma: 1143
KOSTYLEV, Valentin
Ivan the Terrible Ke: 415
KOSZTOLANYI, Dezso
Anna Edes Ke: 415
The Bloody Poet Ke: 415
KOTZEBUE, August von
Pizarro DC2: 223
Stranger DC2: 224
Die Verlaumder [Slanderer]
DC2: 224
Die Verwandtschaften DC2:
224
KOTZWINKLE, William
"Follow the Eagle" WaS1:
116
KOUTOUKAS, H.M.
General MDAE: 301
Kouyoumdjian, Dikran see
ARLEN, Michael
KOZAKOV, Mikhail
"The Man Who Kissed the
Ground" Wa: 440
KRAMER, Horace
Marginal Land LCAB: 106
KRAMER, Theodor
General Po: 2175-2176
KRAMM, Joseph
The Shrike ADC: 201; Br:
377
KRAMP, Willy

Die Jünglinge Ke: 302
KRASINSKI, Zygmunt
Undivine Comedy [Undivine
Faust] DC2: 224
KRASNA, Norman
Dear Ruth ADC: 202
John Loves Mary ADC: 202
Kind Sir ADC: 202
Small Miracle ADC: 202
Sunday in New York ADC:
202-203
Who Was That Lady I Saw You
With? ADC: 203
_____ and Groucho MARX
Time for Elizabeth ADC: 203
KRASZEWSKI, Josef Ignacy
"Abracadabra" Wa: 440
"Adam" Wa: 440
"The Biography of an Organist
of Sokal" Wa: 440
"The Butterfly" Wa: 440
"A Cemetery Story" Wa: 441
"A Concert in Krynica" Wa:
441
"A Country Fair in Yanovka"
Wa: 441
"Old-Fashioned Letter Writing"
Wa: 441
"Psiarek" Wa: 441
"The Treasure" Wa: 441
"The Woman at the Church
Door" Wa: 441
KRATT, Ivan
Baranov's Island Ke: 415
Ross Colony Ke: 415
KRAUS, Karl
General Br: 377-378; Po:
2176
"Die Dritte Walpurgisnacht"
Po: 2176
Die Fackel Br: 378
Last Days of Mankind [Die
letzten Tage der Mensch-
heit] Br: 378; DC2: 224;
Po: 2177
KRAUSE, Herbert
Wind Without Rain LCAB:
106
KRAUSS, Ruth
General MDAE: 303
KREISEL, Henry
General JW: 338
KRESTOVSKII, V.V.
Panurge's Herd Fi: 455; Ke:
415
Peterburskie Trushchoby Fi:

455

KREUDER, Ernst
"Phantom der Angst" Wa:
441

KREVE, Vincas
General Po: 2177

KRIGE, Uys
"The Charcoal Burners" Wa:
441
"The Coffin" Wa: 441
"Death of a Zulu" Wa: 441
"The Dream" Wa: 441

KRISHNAMURTI, Jiddu
General Po: 2177

KRISTENSEN, Tom
Haervaerk Fi: 406-407
Livets Arabesk Fi: 407

KRLEZA, Miroslav
General Po: 2177
The Return of Philip Latino-
vicz Fi: 455

KRONENGOLD, A.J.
Tubstrip ADC: 203

KRUCZKOWSKI, Leon
Ethel and Julius DC2: 224

de KRÜDENER, M.
Valerie Fi: 97

KRUDY, Gyula
Autumn Races Ke: 416
The Red Mailcoach Ke: 416

KRUSE, Hinrich
General Po: 2177-2178

KRUSENSTJERNA, Agnes von
Froknama von Pahlen Ke:
355

KRUTCH, Joseph Wood
General Po: 2178
The Modern Temper LCAB:
106

KTOROVA, Alla
The Face of Firebird Fi:
455

KUBIN, Alfred
The Other Side Fi: 356

KUFFNER, Christop
Cervantes in Algiers DC2:
225

KULIEV, Kaisyn
General Po: 2178

KULISH, Mykola
The People's Malakhiy DC2:
225

KUNCEWICZ, Maria
The Stranger Fi: 455

KUNCZ, Aladar
Black Monastery Ke: 416

Clouds Over a City Ke: 416

KUNDERA, Milan
The Joke Fi: 455

KUNENE, Raymond Mazisi
General BALE: 322

KUNERT, Günter
General Po: 2178

KUNITZ, Stanley
General JW: 89; LCAB: 106;
Po: 2179
"Among the Gods" PE: 278
"Careless Love" PE: 278
"Father and Son" ICBAP: 76;
LCAB: 107
"Geometry of Moods" PE: 278
"Hermetic Poem" PE: 278
"Journal for My Daughter" PE:
278
"Night Letter" PE: 278
"Prophecy on Lethe" PE: 278
"The Science of the Night" PE:
279
"The Scourge" PE: 279
Selected Poems 1928-1958 Po:
2179
"The Surgeons" PE: 279
"The Testing-Tree" PE: 279

KUNTAMBILA, Jonathan
General BALE: 322

KUPRIN, Alexander I.
"At the Circus" WaS1: 116
"The Bracelet of Garnets" see
"The Garnet Bracelet"
"Delirium" WaS1: 116
The Duel Fi: 455-456
"Emerald" WaS1: 116
"The Enquiry" WaS1: 116
"The Garnet Bracelet" ["The
Bracelet of Garnets"] Wa:
441; WaS1: 116
In Honour's Name Ke: 416
"In the Dark" WaS1: 116
"The Jewess" WaS1: 116
"The Last Debut" WaS1: 116
Liquid Sun Ke: 416
"Off the Street" WaS1: 116
The Pit Fi: 456
"A Quiet Life" WaS1: 117
"River of Life" Wa: 441;
WaS1: 117
"Staff-Captain Rybnikov"
WaS1: 117
Sulamif' Fi: 456
"The Swamp" WaS1: 117

KURNITZ, Harry
Once More, with Feeling ADC:

203
Reclining Figure ADC: 203
A Shot in the Dark ADC:
204
KURZ, Hermann
"Die blasse Apollonia" Wa:
442
"Horoscope" Wa: 442
KURZ, Isolde
"Anno Pestis" Wa: 442
"Die Dame von Forli" Wa:
442
"Der heilige Sebastian" Wa:
442
"Die Humanisten" Wa: 442
"Die Mär von der schönen
Galiana" Wa: 442
"Schuster und Schneider"
Wa: 442
"Unsere Carlotta" Wa: 442
"Die Verdammten" Wa: 442
KUTTNER, Henry
General ASF: 356; LCAB:
107
"The Fairy Chessmen" ASF:
356
"Piggy Bank" ASF: 356
KUVAYEV, Oleg
The Territory Fi: 456
KUZMIN, Mikhail
General Po: 2180
The Quiet Guard Ke: 416
Travellers on Land and Sea
Ke: 416
Wings Fi: 456; Ke: 416
KVARES, Donald
Leona Is a Funny Name
ADC: 204
Springtime for Mahler ADC:
204
KYD, Thomas
General ED: 272-273; PS:
93, 104; TSD: 68-70
Cornelia EDC: 307; PS:
99, 105
The Spanish Tragedy DC1:
113-114; ED: 272-273;
EDC: 307-309; Ma: 1144-
1145; PS: 94-99, 104-
105; TSD: 68-70
The Ur-Hamlet DC1: 114
KYNASTON, Francis
General Ba: 87
KYNE, Peter B.
General AN: 168

L

LA BAR, Tom
Whitsuntide ADC: 204
LACAN, Jacques
General Po: 2181
LA CAPRIA, Raffaele
Ferito a morte Ke: 243
LACLOS, Pierre de
Les liaisons dangereuses Fi:
97-99; Ke: 102-103
LACRETELLE, Jacques de
General Po: 2181
LACY, Ernest
Rinaldo, the Doctor of Florence
DC1: 114
LACY, John
The Dumb Lady DC1: 114
LADD, Joseph Brown
General Da: 80
LADOO, Harold Sonny
General WIL: 65
No Pain Like This Body WIL:
65
Yesterdays WIL: 65
Lady Gregory see GREGORY,
Lady Isabella Augusta
LA FARGE, Oliver
General AN: 168; ASF: 356
"All the Young Men" ASF:
356
"Captain Tom and Mother
Carey's Chickens" Wa: 442
"Haunted Ground" Wa: 442
"North Is Black" ASF: 356;
Wa: 442
"Old Century River" Wa: 442
"La Spécialté de M. Duclos"
ASF: 356; Wa: 442
LAFAYETTE, Madame de
La Comtesse de Tende Fi:
99-100; Ke: 103
La Princesse de Clèves Fi:
100-102; Ke: 103-104
Zaïde Ke: 104
LA FERRERE, Gregorio de
General Br: 378
The Crackpots [Locos de
Overano] Br: 378
The Women of Barranco [Las
de Barranco] Br: 378
LAFFAN, Kevin
General MDAE: 304
La Fontaine see FONTAINE,
Jean de la
LAFORET, Carmen

General Po: 2181-2182
La isla y los demonios Fi:
    220; Ke: 206
La llamada Po: 2182
La mujer nueva Ke: 206
Nada Fi: 220; Ke: 206;
    Po: 2181-2182
Un noviazgo Fi: 220
LAFOURCADE, Enrique
    King Ahab's Feast [La fiesta
    del Rey Acab] Po: 2182
LAGERKVIST, Pär Fabian
    General Br: 378-379; MD:
        183; Po: 2182-2185
    Barabbas EDC: 309; Fi:
        407; Ke: 355-356; Ma:
        1147; Po: 2183, 2185
    Bödeln see The Hangman
    "The Children's Campaign"
        Wa: 443
    The Death of Ahasuerus
        Fi: 407; Ke: 356; Ma:
        1147; Po: 2183, 2185
    The Difficult Hour see The
        Trying Hour
    The Dwarf [Dvärgen] Br:
        379; Fi: 407; Ke: 356;
        Ma: 1148; Po: 2186
    The Eternal Smile [Det Eviga
        Leendet] Fi: 407; Ke:
        356; Ma: 1148; Po: 2184,
        2186-2187
    L'être invisible see The
        Invisible One
    "Father and I" SFC: 129;
        Wa: 443; WaS1: 117
    "The Fragment" Wa: 443
    Han Som Fick Leva Oun Sitt
        Liv see The Man Who
        Was Given Life to Live
        Again
    The Hangman [Bödeln] Br:
        379; EDC: 310; Fi: 407;
        Ke: 356; Ma: 1148;
        WaS1: 117
    Himlens Hemlighet see The
        Secret of Heaven
    The Holy Land [Det Heliga
        Landet] Fi: 407; Ke:
        356; Ma: 1149; Po: 2185
    The Invisible One [L'être in-
        visible; Den Osynlige]
        EDC: 310
    The King [Konungen] Br:
        379; EDC: 310; Ma: 1149
    The Last Man [Sista Manskan]

DC2: 225; EDC: 310; Ma:
    1149
Let Man Live [Låt Manniskan
    Leva] EDC: 310; MD: 183
"The Lift That Went Down into
    Hell" Wa: 443
Livet EDC: 310
The Man Who Was Given Life to
    Live Again [Han Som Fick
    Leva Oun Sitt Liv] EDC:
    310
The Man Without a Soul [Man-
    nen Utan Själ] EDC: 311;
    MD: 183
Mariamne Fi: 407
"Maurice Fleury" Wa: 443
Midsummer Night's Dream in the
    Workhouse [Midsommardröm i
    Fattighuset] EDC: 311
Modern Theatre Po: 2183, 2187
Den Osynlige see The Invisible
    One
The Philosopher's Stone [De
    Vises Sten] Br: 379; EDC:
    311
The Pilgrim Fi: 408
Pilgrim at Sea Ma: 1149; Po:
    2183, 2185
The Secret of Heaven [Himlens
    Hemlighet] Br: 379; EDC:
    311; Ma: 1149
The Sibyl [Sibyllan] Fi: 408;
    Ke: 356; Ma: 1150; Po:
    2183-2184, 2187
Sista Manskan see The Last
    Man
"The Strange Country" Wa:
    443
The Trying Hour [The Difficult
    Hour; Den Svara Stunden]
    Br: 379; EDC: 311
De Vises Sten see The Philos-
    opher's Stone
LAGERLÖF, Selma
    General Po: 2187-2188
    Anna Svard Ke: 356
    Charlotte Lowenskold Ke: 356
    The Emperor of Portugallia Ke:
        357
    The Girl from Marsh Croft Ke:
        357
    Gösta Berlings Saga see The
        Story of Gosta Berling
    Jerusalem Ke: 357-358; Ma:
        1151-1152
    Kristuslegender Po: 2188-

2189
Lilliecrona's Home Ke: 358
The Miracles of Antichrist
    Ke: 358
The Outcast Ke: 358
Outlawed Ke: 358
The Ring of the Lowenskolds
    Ke: 358
The Story of Gosta Berling
    [Gösta Berlings Saga]
    Fi: 408; Ke: 357; Ma:
    1151
The Tale of a Manor Ke:
    358
Thy Soul Shall Bear Witness
    Ke: 359
The Treasure Ke: 359
The Wonderful Adventures of
    Nils Ke: 359
LAGROLET, Jean
General Po: 2189
LA GUMA, Alex
General BALE: 323-324
"Coffee for the Road" WaS1:
    117
"The Gladiators" WaS1: 117
"A Matter of Taste" WaS1:
    117
LAINE, Henry Allen
General BAW: 470
LAMB, Arthur Clifton
God's Great Acres BAP:
    132
Millsboro Memorial MBA:
    134
Roughshod Up the Mountain
    BAP: 132
Shades of Cotton Lips MBA:
    134
LAMB, Charles
General Fog: 47; LCAB:
    107; Ma: 1153
"The Old Familiar Faces"
    PE: 279
LAMB, Myrna
Apple Pie ADC: 204
Crab Quadrille MBA: 134
LAMMING, George
General Po: 2189; WIL:
    65-71
Cannot Shot and Glass Beads
    WIL: 75
The Emigrants WIL: 71-72
In the Castle of My Skin
    LCAB: 107; WIL: 71
Natives of My Person WIL:

75
Of Age and Innocence WIL:
    72-73
The Pleasures of Exile WIL:
    73
Season of Adventure WIL: 73-
    74
Water with Berries WIL: 74-
    75
"A Wedding in Spring" Wa:
    443
LA MOTTE, Ellen N.
The Backwash of War Po:
    2189
LAMPE, Friedo
General Po: 2190
LAMPEDUSA, Giuseppe Tomasi di
The Leopard [Il Gattopardo]
    Fi: 266-267; Ke: 253; Ma:
    1154; Po: 4270-4273
"Lighea" Po: 4270-4271
LAMPELL, Millard
The Wall ADC: 204
LAMPMAN, Archibald
General ECL: 70-73
"Heat" ECL: 72
LANDOLFI, Tommaso
"Wedding Night" Wa: 443
LANDOR, Walter Savage
General Fog: 49; Ma: 1155-
    1156; Re: 207-208
"Dirce" PE: 279
Imaginary Conversations Ma:
    1155
"Mild Is the Parting Year and
    Sweet" PE: 279
"Mother I Cannot Mind My
    Wheel" PE: 279
"On Lucretia Borgia's Hair"
    PE: 279
"Proud Word You Never Spoke"
    PE: 279
"Rose Aylmer" PE: 279
"Yes; I Write Verses Now and
    Then" ICBAP: 76; PE:
    279
LANE, Rose Wilder
General LCAB: 107
LANG, Andrew
General Ai: 155; TA: 201-
    202
LANG, John
General AL: 266
Botany Bay AL: 266
LANGA, Mandlenkosi
General BALE: 324

LANGEVIN, André
General Po: 2190
LANGGÄSSER, Elizabeth
General Po: 2190-2191
"Beginning of the Season"
Wa: 443
The Indelible Seal [Das
Unauslöschliche Siegel]
Fi: 356-357; Ke: 302; Po:
2190-2191
Proserpine Po: 2190
The Quest Fi: 357; Ke:
302; Po: 2190
"Untergetaucht" Ke: 302;
Po: 2191
LANGLAND, William
Piers Plowman ICBAP: 76;
OMEP: 362-368
The Vision of William, Con-
cerning Piers the Plowman
Ma: 1157-1158
LANGLEY, Adria Locke
A Lion in the Streets AN:
168
LANGNER, Lawrence
Moses Br: 379
LANIER, Sidney
General ALL: 159; AN:
168; Cla: 57-58; LCAB:
107; Ma: 1159-1160
"Betrayal" ICBAP: 77
"Corn" ICBAP: 77; PE:
279
"In Absence" ICBAP: 77
"June Dreams, in January"
ICBAP: 77
"Life and Song" ICBAP: 77
"The Marshes of Glynn" Cla:
58; ICBAP: 77; Ma: 1159;
PE: 279-280
"My Springs" PE: 280
"Night and Day" PE: 280
"Song of the Chattahoochee"
ICBAP: 77
"Sunrise" ICBAP: 77; PE:
280
"The Symphony" ICBAP:
77; PE: 280
Tiger-Lilies AN: 168
LANKAUSKAS, Romualdas
"One More Day" Wa: 443
"So Short Is the Month of
August" Wa: 444
"Sprites Live in the Woods"
Wa: 444
"Wandering Sand" Wa: 444

LANNEL, Jean de
Romant Satyrique Fi: 102
LANUSSE, Armand
General BAW: 475; LCAB:
107
LARBAUD, Valéry
General Po: 2191-2194
A. O. Barnabooth Ke: 104
Fermina Márquez Fi: 102; Ke:
104; Po: 2194
LARDNER, Ring
General ALL: 160-161; ASF:
358; LCAB: 107; Po: 2194-
2195; Wo: 137-138
"Alibi Ike" ASF: 356; SFC:
130; Wa: 444; WaS1: 117
"Anniversary" Wa: 444
"The Battle of the Century"
Wa: 444
"A Busher's Letters Home" ASF:
356; Wa: 444
"A Caddy's Diary" ASF: 356;
SFC: 130; Wa: 444; WaS1:
117
"Champion" ASF: 356; Wa:
444; WaS1: 117
"A Chip of the Old Block" ASF:
357; Wa: 444
"Contract" Wa: 444
"Cured!" ASF: 357
"A Day with Conrad Green"
Wa: 444
"Dinner" Wa: 445
"Ex Parte" ASF: 357; SFC:
130; Wa: 445
"The First Game" ASF: 357
"The Golden Honeymoon" ASF:
357; SFC: 130; Wa: 445;
WaS1: 117
"Gullible's Travels" ASF: 357
"Haircut" ASF: 357; Po: 2195;
SFC: 130; Wa: 445; WaS1:
117
"Harmony" Wa: 445
"Horseshoes" SFC: 130; Wa:
445
"Hurry Kane" Wa: 446
"I Can't Breathe" ASF: 357;
Wa: 446; WaS1: 118
"Insomnia" ASF: 357; Wa:
446; WaS1: 118
"The Love Nest" ASF: 357;
SFC: 130; Wa: 446
"The Maysville Minstrel" Wa:
446
"My Roomy" ASF: 357; SFC:

130; Wa: 446; WaS1: 118
"Nora" Wa: 446
"Now and Then" Wa: 446
"The Pennant Pursuit" ASF:
    357
"Rhythm" Wa: 446
"Some Like Them Cold" ASF:
    357; SFC: 130; Wa: 446;
    WaS1: 118
"Sun Cured" Wa: 446
"There Are Smiles" Wa:
    446
"A Visit to the Garrison"
    Wa: 447
"Who Dealt?" Wa: 447
"The Young Immigrants"
    ASF: 357
"Zone of Quiet" ASF: 358;
    Wa: 447
LARKIN, Philip Arthur
    General CN: 308; ICBAP:
        77; LCAB: 107; Ma:
        1161-1162; MP: 54; Po:
        2196-2197
    "Absences" PE: 280
    "Arrival" PE: 280
    "An Arundel Tomb" PE:
        280
    "At Grass" PE: 280
    "Deceptions" PE: 280
    "The Dedicated" PE: 280
    "Dry-Point" PE: 281
    A Girl in Winter CN: 309;
        Ma: 1161
    "Going" PE: 281
    "Here" PE: 281
    High Windows Ma: 1161
    "How Distant" PE: 281
    Jill CN: 309
    "Maiden Name" ICBAP: 77
    "Modesties" PE: 281
    "Naturally the Foundation
        Will Bear Your Expenses"
        ICBAP: 77; Po: 2197
    "Next, Please" PE: 281
    "Poem VII" [from XX Poems]
        PE: 281
    "Reasons for Attendance"
        PE: 281
    "Solar" PE: 281
    "Toads" PE: 281
    "Waiting for breakfast while
        she brushed her hair"--
        "Coda" to The North Ship
        PE: 281
    "Wants" PE: 281

"The Whitsun Weddings" Ma:
    1162-1163; PE: 281
LA ROCHE, Sophie von
    Erscheinungen am See Oneida
        Ke: 302
LA ROCHEFOUCAULD LIANCOURT,
    François Alexandre Frederic,
    duc de
    General LCAB: 108
La Rochelle, Pierre Drieu see
    DRIEU LA ROCHELLE,
    Pierre
LA ROSE, Anthony John
    Foundations: A Book of Poems
        WIL: 75-76
LARRA, Mariano José de
    El doncel de Don Enrique el
        Doliente Ke: 206
    No más mostrador [Quitting
        Business] DC2: 225
LARRETA, Enrique
    La gloria de Don Ramiro Po:
        2197
LARSEN, J. Anker
    The Philosopher's Stone Ke:
        359
LARSEN, Karl
    Spring Ke: 359
LARSEN, Lance
    The Hashish Club ADC: 205
LARSEN, Nella
    General AAW: 64; BAF: 190-
        191; BAW: 476; HR: 117-
        118
    Passing BAF: 191-192; HR:
        118
    Quicksand BAF: 191-192; BAW:
        476; HR: 118
LARSON, Clinton F.
    The Mantle of the Prophet
        DC1: 114
LARTEGUY, Jean
    Les Centurions Fi: 102
    Les Mercenaires Fi: 102
    Les Pretoriens Fi: 102
LA RUSSO, Louis, II
    Lamppost Reunion ADC: 205
    Wheelbarrow Closers ADC:
        205
LA SALE, Antoine de
    Le Petit Jehan de Saintre Fi:
        156
    Réconfort de Mme du Fresne
        Fi: 156; Ke: 104
LA SALLE, Ferdinand
    Franz von Sickingen DC2:

225
LASHIN, Orrie, and Milo
   HASTINGS
   Class of '29 ADC: 205
LASHLEY, Cliff
   General WIL: 76
LASKER-SCHÜLER, Else
   General Po: 2197-2199
LASKI, Marghanita
   The Offshore Island Br:
   379
LASKY, Victor
   General LCAB: 108
LASSWITZ, Kurd
   On Two Planets Fi: 357
LA TAILHEDE, Raymond de
   General Po: 2199
LATHAM, Philip
   "The Xi Effect" ASF: 359
LATIMER, Hugh
   General Hen: 27; SC: 68
LATORRE, Mariano
   General Po: 2199-2200
LA TOUR du PIN, Patrice de
   General Po: 2200
LATTIMORE, Richmond
   "Witness to Death" ICBAP:
   77; PE: 282
LAUCHMONEN [Peter KEMPADOO]
   General WIL: 76
   Guiana Boy WIL: 76
   Old Thom's Harvest WIL:
   76-77
LAUD, William
   General Hen: 38
LAUGHLIN, James
   "Go West Young Man" ICBAP:
   78; PE: 282; Po: 2200
LAURENCE, Margaret
   General Po: 2200-2201
   "The Drummer of All the
   World" Wa: 447
   "Goodman's Master" Wa: 447
   "The Merchant of Heaven"
   Wa: 447
   "Nanuk" Wa: 447
   "The Perfume Sea" Wa: 447
   "To Set Our House in Order"
   Wa: 447
   "The Tomorrow-Tamer" Wa:
   447
   "The Voice of Adamo" Wa:
   447
LAURENTS, Arthur
   General Br: 380; MD: 183;
   MDAE: 306

The Bird Cage ADC: 205; Br:
   380; MD: 183-184
A Clearing in the Woods ADC:
   205; Br: 380; DC1: 114;
   MD: 184; MDAE: 306; Po:
   2201
The Enclave ADC: 206
The Home of the Brave ADC:
   206; Br: 380; DC1: 114;
   MD: 184
Invitation to a March ADC:
   206; Br: 380; MDAE: 306
The Time of the Cuckoo ADC:
   206; Br: 380; DC1: 115;
   MD: 184
_____, Leonard BERNSTEIN,
   and Stephen SONDHEIM
West Side Story ADC: 207
_____, Richard RODGERS, and
   Stephen SONDHEIM
Do I Hear a Waltz? ADC: 207
_____, Jule STYNE, and Stephen
   SONDHEIM
Gypsy ADC: 207-208
LAUTREAMONT, Comte de [Isidore
   Lucien DUCASSE]
   General LCAB: 56
   Les Chants de Maldoror Fi:
   102-103
LAVANT, Christine
   General Po: 2201
LAVIN, Mary
   General Po: 2201-2202
   "An Akoulina of the Irish Mid-
   lands" WaS1: 118
   "At Sallygap" Wa: 448; WaS1:
   118
   "The Becker Wives" Wa: 448;
   WaS1: 118
   "Bridal Sheets" WaS1: 118
   "Brother Boniface" Wa: 448
   "The Bunch of Grapes" Wa:
   448
   "The Cemetery" Wa: 448
   "The Cuckoo-Spit" Wa: 448;
   WaS1: 118
   "A Cup of Tea" Wa: 448; WaS1:
   118
   "A Fable" Wa: 448
   "Frail Vessel" Wa: 448
   "A Gentle Soul" WaS1: 118
   "The Great Wave" Wa: 448;
   WaS1: 118
   "The Green Grave and the Black
   Grave" Wa: 448; WaS1:
   118

"Grief" Wa: 448
"Happiness" Wa: 448; WaS1: 118
"A Happy Death" Wa: 448; WaS1: 118
"The Haymaking" Wa: 449
"Heart of Gold" WaS1: 119
"In a Café" WaS1: 119
"In the Middle of the Fields" Wa: 449; WaS1: 119
"The Joy Ride" Wa: 449
"Lilacs" Wa: 449
"The Little Prince" Wa: 449; WaS1: 119
"The Long Ago" Wa: 449
"Love Is for Lovers" WaS1: 119
"Loving Memory" Wa: 449; WaS1: 119
"A Memory" WaS1: 119
The Middle of the Fields Po: 2202
"Miss Holland" WaS1: 119
"A Mock Auction" WaS1: 119
"My Vocation" WaS1: 119
"The New Gardener" WaS1: 119
"An Old Boot" WaS1: 119
"One Evening" WaS1: 119
"One Summer" Wa: 449; WaS1: 119
"The Pastor of Six Mile Bush" WaS1: 119
"The Patriot Son" Wa: 449; WaS1: 119
"Posy" Wa: 449
"A Pure Accident" WaS1: 120
"The Sand Castle" Wa: 449; WaS1: 120
"Sarah" Wa: 449; WaS1: 120
"Say Could That Lady Be I?" Wa: 449
"Scylla and Charybdis" Wa: 449
"A Single Lady" Wa: 449
"The Small Bequest" WaS1: 120
"A Story with a Pattern" Wa: 449; WaS1: 120
"Sunday Brings Sunday" Wa: 449; WaS1: 120
"Tom" WaS1: 120
"Tomb of an Ancestor" WaS1: 120

"A Tragedy" Wa: 450; WaS1: 120
"Trastevere" WaS1: 120
"A Visit to the Cemetery" Wa: 450
"What's Wrong with Aubretia?" WaS1: 120
"The Widow's Son" Wa: 450; WaS1: 120
"The Will" Wa: 450; WaS1: 120
"A Woman Friend" WaS1: 120
"The Yellow Beret" WaS1: 120

LAW, William
General EC: 97-98
A Serious Call EC: 97

LAWLER, Ray
The Summer of the Seventeenth Doll Br: 380; DC1: 115; Po: 2202

LAWRENCE, David Herbert
General BN2: 73-77; Br: 380; EP: 160-170; ICBAP: 78; LCAB: 108; MAP: 213-215; MBD: 58; MD: 184; Mi: 250-252; MP: 56; Po: 2203-2240; Ri2: 60-74, 85-87; Sch: 178-192; TA: 204-205
Aaron's Rod EN: 87-88; ENE: 187; ENES1: 141-142; ENES2: 150-151; Ma: 1164-1165; Po: 2219, 2240; Ri2: 71, 74; Sch: 193
"Almond Blossom" Po: 2227-2228
Apocalypse Po: 2240
"Baby Tortoise" PE: 282
"Bavarian Gentians" PE: 282; Po: 2210, 2228, 2240
"The Blind Man" Po: 2241; Ri2: 75; SFC: 130; Wa: 450; WaS1: 120
"The Blue Moccasins" SFC: 131; Wa: 450
"The Border Line" Po: 2241; SFC: 131; Wa: 451; WaS1: 121
The Boy in the Bush MAP: 214-215; Ri2: 75
"The Captain's Doll" EP: 160; Po: 2241; Ri2: 69, 75; Sch: 193; SFC: 131; Wa: 451; WaS1: 121

"The Christening" Wa: 451;
    WaS1: 121
A Collier's Friday Night EDC:
    311; MBD: 58
"Corot" PE: 282
"The Crown" Po: 2208
The Daughter-in-Law EDC:
    311; MBD: 58
"The Daughters of the Vicar"
    Po: 2234, 2241; SFC:
    131; Wa: 451; WaS1: 121
David Br: 380; DC1: 115;
    EDC: 311; MD: 184; Po:
    2242
"A Doe at Evening" ICBAP:
    78
"End of Another Home Holi-
    day" PE: 282
"England, My England" Po:
    2242; SFC: 131; Wa: 452
"The Enkindled Spring" PE:
    282
"The Escaped Cock" see
    "The Man Who Died"
Etruscan Places Po: 2242
"Fanny and Annie" Po:
    2242; SFC: 131; Wa:
    452
"Fantasia of the Unconscious"
    Po: 2213, 2216-2217
"Fish" PE: 282
"A Fly in the Ointment" Wa:
    452
"The Flying Fish" Wa: 452
"The Fox" Ma: 1165-1166;
    Po: 2213, 2242-2244; Ri2:
    69, 75; SFC: 132; Wa:
    452-453; WaS1: 121
"A Fragment of Stained Glass"
    Wa: 453
"Giorno Dei Morti" EP: 169
"Gipsy" PE: 282
"Glad Ghosts" SFC: 132;
    Wa: 453
"Gloire de Dijon" PE: 282
"Goose Fair" Wa: 453
"The Hands of the Betrothed"
    PE: 282
"Her Turn" Wa: 453
"Honour and Arms" see
    "The Prussian Officer"
"The Horse Dealer's Daughter"
    LCAB: 108; Po: 2244;
    Ri2: 76; SFC: 32; Wa:
    453-454; WaS1: 121
"In Love" Wa: 454

"Jimmy and the Desperate Wom-
    an" SFC: 132; Wa: 454;
    WaS1: 121
John Thomas and Lady Jane
    ENES2: 151
Kangarooo BN2: 74; EN: 88;
    ENE: 187-188; ENES1: 142;
    ENES2: 151; Ma: 1166-1167;
    MAP: 213-215; Po: 2219,
    2244-2246; Ri2: 76; Sch: 193
Lady Chatterley's Lover BN2:
    75-76, 112; EN: 88-89; ENE:
    188-191; ENES1: 142-143;
    ENES2: 151-152; LCAB:
    108; Ma: 1167-1168; Po:
    2210, 2219, 2221, 2246-2256;
    Ri2: 60, 69, 71, 77; Sch:
    194-197
"The Ladybird" Ri2: 69, 76;
    SFC: 132; Wa: 454; WaS1:
    121
"The Last Laugh" Po: 2257;
    SFC: 132; Wa: 454; WaS1:
    121
Last Poems Po: 2257
Look! We Have Come Through
    Po: 2258
The Lost Girl EN: 89; ENE:
    191-192; ENES1: 143;
    ENES2: 152; Ri2: 77-78;
    Sch: 197
"Lotus and Frost" PE: 282
"Love Among the Haystacks"
    Wa: 454; WaS1: 121
"Love on the Farm" ICBAP:
    78; PE: 282
"The Lovely Lady" SFC: 132;
    Wa: 454-455; WaS1: 121
"The Man Who Died" Ma:
    1168-1169; Po: 2210, 2223,
    2234, 2259; Ri2: 78; Sch:
    197; SFC: 132-133; Wa:
    455-456; WaS1: 121
"The Man Who Loved Islands"
    Po: 2222-2223, 2236-2237,
    2259; SFC: 133; Wa: 456;
    WaS1: 122
"The Man Who Was Through with
    the World" Po: 2222-2223;
    Wa: 456
"Masses and Classes" Po:
    2259
"Medlars and Sorb Apples" PE:
    282
Merry-Go-Round EDC: 312
"The Miracle" see "The Horse

Dealer's Daughter"
"A Modern Lover" Po: 2229-
2230; Wa: 456
"Monkey Nuts" Wa: 456
Mornings in Mexico Po:
2260
"Mother and Daughter" SFC:
133; Wa: 456
"New Eve and Old Adam"
Wa: 457; WaS1: 122
"New Heaven and Earth" PE:
282
"None of That" SFC: 133;
Wa: 457
"Odour of Chrysanthemums"
Po: 2260; SFC: 133; Wa:
457; WaS1: 122
"The Old Adam" Wa: 457
"Once" Wa: 457
"The Overtone" SFC: 133;
Wa: 457-458; WaS1: 122
Pansies Po: 2260
"Piano" EP: 169; ICBAP:
78; PE: 283; Po: 2261
The Plumed Serpent BN2:
73, 77; EN: 89; ENE:
192-193; ENES1: 143;
ENES2: 152; Ma: 1169-
1170; Po: 2261-2262; Ri2:
71, 78-79; Sch: 197-198
"A Prelude" Wa: 458
"The Primrose Path" SFC:
133; Wa: 458
"The Princess" Po: 2234,
2262; SFC: 133-134; Wa:
458; WaS1: 122
"The Prussian Officer" Po:
2212, 2236, 2262-2263;
Ri2: 61; SFC: 134; Wa:
458-459; WaS1: 122
"Psychoanalysis and the Un-
conscious" Po: 2217
The Rainbow EN: 89-90;
ENE: 193-194; ENES1:
144-145; ENES2: 152-154;
Ma: 1170-1172; Po:
2206-2207, 2219, 2221,
2224, 2229, 2263-2266;
Ri2: 60, 62, 66, 79-81;
Sch: 198-200
"The Reality of Peace" Po:
2208
"The Rocking-Horse Winner"
Ma: 1172-1173; Po:
2266-2269; Ri2: 81; SFC:
134; Wa: 459-460; WaS1:

122
"St. Mawr" EN: 90-91; Ma:
1173-1174; Po: 2269; Ri2:
72, 81; Sch: 202-203; SFC:
135; Wa: 460-461; WaS1:
122
"Samson and Delilah" SFC:
134; Wa: 461
Sea and Sardinia Po: 2269-
2270
"Second Best" SFC: 134; Wa:
461; WaS1: 122
"The Shades of Spring" Po:
2229-2230, 2270; SFC: 134;
Wa: 461; WaS1: 122
"The Shadow in the Rose Gar-
den" SFC: 134-135; Wa:
461-462; WaS1: 123
"The Ship of Death" LCAB:
109
"A Sick Collier" Wa: 462
"Smile" SFC: 135; Wa: 462
"Snake" EP: 161, 168-169;
ICBAP: 78; PE: 283; Po:
2227-2228, 2270
"The Soiled Rose" see "The
Shades of Spring"
"Song of a Man Who Has Come
Through" ICBAP: 78; PE:
283; Po: 2258, 2271
"Song of a Man Who Is Loved"
Po: 2258
"Song of a Man Who Is Not
Loved" Po: 2258
Sons and Lovers BN2: 74;
EN: 91; ENE: 194-197;
ENES1: 145-146; ENES2:
154; LCAB: 109; Ma: 1174-
1176; Po: 2213, 2219, 2221,
2232, 2271-2275; Ri2: 60, 69,
71, 81-83; Sch: 200-202
"Strike-Pay" Wa: 462
Studies in Classic American Lit-
erature Po: 2275-2276; Ri2:
66
"Sun" SFC: 135; Wa: 462;
WaS1: 123
"Surgery for the Novel" Po:
2213
"The Thimble" Wa: 462; WaS1:
123
"Things" SFC: 136; Wa: 462;
WaS1: 123
"The Thorn in the Flesh" Po:
2212; SFC: 136; Wa: 462
"Tickets, Please" Po: 2277;

Wa: 462-463; WaS1: 123
"Tortoise Shout" PE: 283
"Tortoises" Po: 2277
Touch and Go EDC: 312;
  MD: 184
The Trespasser BN2: 77;
  ENE: 197; ENES1: 146;
  ENES2: 155; Po: 2277-
  2278; Ri2: 83; Sch: 203
Twilight in Italy Po: 2278
"Two Blue Birds" SFC: 136;
  Wa: 463
"Two Marriages" Wa: 463
"The Undying Man" Wa:
  463
"The Virgin and the Gipsy"
  Po: 2279; Sch: 203; Wa:
  463; WaS1: 123
"Wedding Morn" Po: 2279
"Whether or Not" PE: 283
The White Peacock EN: 92;
  ENE: 197; ENES1: 146-
  147; ENES2: 155; Ma:
  1176-1177; Po: 2204,
  2279-2281; Ri2: 71, 83;
  Sch: 204
"The White Stocking" SFC:
  136; Wa: 463
The Widowing of Mrs. Holroyd
  EDC: 312; MBD: 58
"The Wild Common" PE: 283
"Wintry Peacock" SFC: 136;
  Wa: 463; WaS1: 123
"The Witch à la Mode" Wa:
  463; WaS1: 123
"The Woman Who Rode Away"
  Po: 2213, 2234; SFC:
  136; Wa: 463-464; WaS1:
  123
Women in Love BN2: 75-77;
  EN: 92-93; ENE: 197-200;
  ENES1: 147-148; ENES2:
  155-157; LCAB: 109; Ma:
  1177-1178; Po: 2206-2208,
  2219, 2221, 2224, 2229,
  2232, 2281-2286; Ri2: 60,
  62-63, 66, 69, 71-72, 83-
  85; Sch: 204-207
"You Touched Me" SFC: 136;
  Wa: 464
_____ and Walter GREENWOOD
  My Son's My Son EDC: 312;
  MBD: 58
LAWRENCE, George Alfred
  General BN: 72
LAWRENCE, Jerome

General MDAE: 308
_____ and Robert E. LEE
  Auntie Mame ADC: 208
  A Call on Kuprin ADC: 208
  First Monday in October ADC:
  208
  The Gang's All Here ADC:
  208-209
  The Incomparable Max ADC:
  209
  Inherit the Wind ADC: 209
  The Night Thoreau Spent in
  Jail ADC: 209
  Only in America ADC: 209
_____ , Robert E. LEE, and
  Jerry HERMAN
  Mame ADC: 209-210
LAWRENCE, Thomas Edward
  General Po: 2286-2288
  Seven Pillars of Wisdom Ma:
  1179; Po: 2289
LAWRENCE, Walter MacArthur
  General WIL: 77
LAWSON, Henry
  General AL: 278-282; Po:
  2290-2293
  "The Babies in the Bush" Wa:
  464; WaS1: 123
  "Brighten's Sister-in-Law" Wa:
  464
  "The Bush Undertaker" Po:
  2291; Wa: 464
  "A Double-Buggy at Lahey's
  Creek" Wa: 464
  "The Drover's Wife" Po: 2291;
  Wa: 464; WaS1: 123
  "The Green Lady" WaS1: 123
  "A Hero in Dingo Scrubs" Wa:
  465
  Joe Wilson Po: 2293
  "Joe Wilson's Courtship" Wa:
  465
  "No Place for a Woman" Po:
  2291; Wa: 465
  "A Sketch of Mateship" Wa:
  465
  "Telling Mrs. Baker" Wa: 465
  "The Union Buries Its Dead"
  Wa: 465
  "Water Them Geraniums" Po:
  2291; Wa: 465
  While the Billy Boils AL: 281
LAWSON, John Howard
  General Br: 381; LCAB: 109;
  MD: 184
  Gentlewoman ADC: 210; Br:

381; MD: 184

The International ADC: 210;
Br: 381; MD: 184

Loud Speaker ADC: 210;
Br: 381; MD: 184

Marching Song ADC: 210;
Br: 381; DC1: 115; MD:
184

Nirvana ADC: 210; Br:
381

Parlor Magic Br: 382

The Processional ADC: 210;
Br: 382; DC1: 115; MD:
184-185; Po: 2293-2294

The Pure in Heart ADC:
210; Br: 382; MD: 185

Roger Bloomer ADC: 211;
Br: 382; DC1: 115; MD:
185

Success Story ADC: 211;
Br: 382; DC1: 115; MD:
185

LAXNESS, Halldór Kiljan

General Po: 2294

The Atom Station Fi: 408;
Ke: 359

The Beauty of the Skies Fi:
408

The Bell of Iceland Fi: 408;
Ke: 359

The Happy Warriors Fi: 408

The House of the Poet Fi:
408

Independent People Fi: 408;
Ke: 359; Ma: 1180

Kristnihald under Jökli Po:
2294

The Light of the World Fi:
408

A Local Chronicle Fi: 408

Olaf the Poet Ke: 359-360

The Palace of the Summerland
Fi: 408-409

Salka Valka Fi: 409; Ke:
360

LAYAMON

"Brut" Ma: 1181; OMEP:
257-258

LAYE, Camara

Le Regard du Roi LCAB:
109

"Les Yeux de la Statue"
WaS1: 123

LAYTON, Irving

General JW: 158; Po: 2295

LAZARUS, Emma

General JW: 92-93

LAZECNIKOV, I.I.

Ice Palace Ke: 416

The Infidel Ke: 416

The Last Page Ke: 416

LAZIO, Carl

Lets Eat Hair! The Chinese
Icebox (Two Playlets) Br:
382

LEA, Tom

The Brave Bulls AN: 168

"Quite a Beach" ASF: 359

The Wonderful Country LCAB:
109

LEACH, Wilford, and John BRAS-
WELL

Demon ADC: 211

Gertrude ADC: 211

LEACOCK, John

The Fall of British Tyranny:
Or American Liberty Tri-
umphant DC1: 115

LEACOCK, Stephen

General Po: 2296-2297

Arcadian Adventures Po: 2296

Sunshine Sketches of a Little
Town Po: 2297

LEAKEY, Caroline

General AL: 283-284

The Broad Arrow AL: 284

LEAKS, Sylvester

General BAF: 193; BAW: 478

LEAR, Edward

General VP: 48-49

"The Dong with a Luminous
Nose" PE: 283

"Jumblies" PE: 283

"The Owl and the Pussycat"
PE: 283

"The Pobble Who Has No Toes"
PE: 283

LEAR, Norman

General LCAB: 109

LEAUTAUD, Paul

General Po: 2297-2298

Le Petit Ami Ke: 104; Po:
2298

LEAVIS, Frank Raymond

General LCAB: 109; Po:
2299-2304

"Criticism and Philosophy" Po:
2304

The Great Tradition Po: 2304

"How to Teach Reading" Po:
2305

LE CARDONNEL, Louis

General Po: 2305
Le Carré, John see CORN-
    WELL, David John Moore
LE CLEZIO, Jean-Marie-Gustave
    General Po: 2305-2306
    The Book of Flights Fi: 103
    "A Day in Old Age" WaS1:
        124
    "Fever" WaS1: 124
    Fever [Collection] Po: 2306
    The Flood [Le Déluge] Fi:
        48, 103
    The Giants Fi: 103
    The Interrogation Fi: 103
    Journeys to the Other Side
        Fi: 103
    "Martin" WaS1: 124
    Le Procès verbal Po: 2306
    Terra Amata Fi: 103; Po:
        2306
    War Fi: 104
LEDUC, Violette
    General Po: 2306
    L'Affamée Fi: 104
    La Bâtarde Po: 2306-2307
    Thérèse et Isabelle Po: 2307
LEDWIDGE, Francis
    General TA: 206
LEDYARD, John
    General AP: 582
LEE, Arthur
    General AP: 582-583
LEE, Audrey
    The Clarion People BAF:
        193
LEE, C.Y.
    "The Casanova of Kearny
        Street" Wa: 466
LEE, Don L.
    General AAL: 222; AAPD:
        201; BAW: 482
    "But He Was Cool or: He
        Even Stopped for Green
        Lights" PE: 284
    Think Black! AAL: 223;
        AAPD: 201
LEE, George Washington
    General AAW: 65; BAF:
        194; BAW: 482
    Beale Street Sundown BAF:
        194
    River George BAF: 194
LEE, Harper
    General LCAB: 109; Po:
        2307
    To Kill a Mockingbird Po:

2307-2308
LEE, Jim
    The Shoeshine Parlor MBA:
        134
LEE, John M.
    Counter Clockwise BAF: 194
LEE, Leslie
    General MBA: 135
    Between Then and Now MBA:
        135
    The First Breeze of Summer
        ADC: 211; BAP: 133; MBA:
        135-136
    The War Party MBA: 136
LEE, Nathaniel
    General Li: 232-233
    Constantine the Great DC1:
        116; Li: 233
    Gloriana DC1: 116
    Lucius Junius Brutus EDC:
        312; Li: 233
    Mithradates DC1: 116
    Nero DC1: 116; Li: 233
    The Rival Queens; or The Death
        of Alexander the Great DC1:
        116; EDC: 312; Li: 233
    Sophonisba; or Hannibal's Over-
        throw DC1: 116; EDC:
        312; Li: 233
    Tragedy of Nero, Emperor of
        Rome EDC: 312
LEE, Robert
    Foundation WIL: 77
LEE, Sophia
    The Recess ENES1: 148
Lee, Vernon see PAGET, Violet
LEE-HAMILTON, Eugene
    General TA: 207
    "The New Medusa" ICBAP:
        78
LeFANU, Joseph Sheridan
    General BN: 72
    Carmilla ENES2: 157; Wa:
        466
    The Cock and Anchor ENES1:
        148
    "The Drunkard's Dream" Wa:
        466
    "The Evil Guest" Wa: 466
    The Fortunes of Colonel Torlogh
        O'Brien ENES1: 148
    "Green Tea" SFC: 136; Wa:
        466
    Guy Deverell ENES1: 148
    Haunted Lives ENES1: 149
    The House by the Church-Yard

ENES1: 149
"Mr. Justice Harbottle" Wa:
466
"The Room in the Dragon
Volant" Wa: 467
"A Strange Adventure in the
Life of Miss Laura Mild-
may" Wa: 467
"A Strange Event in the Life
of Schalken the Painter"
Wa: 467
Uncle Silas BN: 72; ENES1:
149
Willing to Die ENES1: 149
Wylder's Hand ENES1: 149
LE FORT, Gertrud von
General Po: 2310
"Die Abberufung der Jung-
frau von Barby" Wa:
465
Am Tor des Himmels [At the
Gate of Heaven] Ke:
302; Wa: 465
"Die Consolata" Wa: 465
"Das Gericht des Meeres"
Wa: 465
Die Letzte am Schafott [The
Last at the Scaffold] Fi:
357; Ke: 302; Po: 2311;
Wa: 465
"Pilate's Wife" Wa: 466
The Pope from the Ghetto
Ke: 302
"Die Tochter Farinatas" Wa:
466
"Der Turm der Beständigkeit"
Wa: 466
"Die Unschuldigen" Wa: 466
The Veil of Veronica Ke:
302-303
The Wedding of Magdeburg
Ke: 303
The Wreath of Angels Ke:
303
LE GALLIENNE, Richard
General Po: 2311; TA:
209
LEGARE, Hugh Swinton
General Da: 112
Léger, Alexis St. Léger see
see PERSE, Saint-John
LEGER, Jean
Tragédie de Rhodes DC2:
225
LEGGE, Thomas
Richardus Tertius DC1:

116
LEGGETT, William
"The Rifle" ASF: 359
LE GOFFIC, Charles
General Po: 2311-2312
LE GRAND, Alexandre
L'innocent criminel DC2: 225
LE GUIN, Ursula
General ASF: 359-360
"The New Atlantis" ASF: 359;
WaS1: 124
"Nine Lives" ASF: 359; WaS1:
124
"Vaster than Empires and More
Slow" ASF: 359; WaS1:
124
"The Word for World Is Forest"
ASF: 359; WaS1: 124
LEHAI, Joy
General BALE: 324
LEHMANN, Rosamond
General CN: 309; Po: 2312;
Ri2: 93-96; Sch: 207-208
The Ballad and the Source
CN: 309; ENES1: 149;
ENES2: 157; Ri2: 94-95
Dusty Answer CN: 309;
ENES1: 149; ENES2: 157;
Ri2: 95
The Echoing Grove CN: 309;
ENES1: 149; ENES2: 157;
Ri2: 94
"The Gypsy's Baby" Ri2: 93
Invitation to the Waltz CN:
309; ENES1: 149; ENES2:
157; Ri2: 95
No More Music Ri2: 93
A Note in Music CN: 310;
ENES1: 149; ENES2: 157;
Ri2: 94-95
A Sea-Grape Tree ENES2:
157; Ri2: 94
The Weather in the Streets
CN: 310; ENES1: 149-150;
ENES2: 158; Ri2: 94
LEHMANN, Wilhelm
General Po: 2312-2313
Michael Lippstock Fi: 357
LEHR, Wilson, Ira BILOWIT, and
Alfred BROOKS
Of Mice and Men ADC: 211
LEIBER, Franz
General LCAB: 109
LEIBER, Fritz
"The Man Who Made Friends
with Electricity" WaS1: 124

LEIMERT, John
  "John Thomas's Cube" Wa:
    467
  "The Swiss Watch" Wa: 467
Leinster, Murray see JENKINS,
    William Fitzgerald
LEITCH, Maurice
  General Po: 2313
  The Liberty Lad ENES2: 158
  Poor Lazarus ENES2: 158
LEIVICK, Halper
  In the Days of Job DC2:
    226; MD: 185
LELAND, Henry Perry
  General LCAB: 110
LEM, Stanislaw
  "In Hot Pursuit" WaS1: 124
  The Investigation Fi: 456
  Solaris Fi: 456
LE MAY, Leon Pamphile
  General Po: 2313
LE MIERRE
  Barnvelt DC2: 226
LEMON, Mark
  General EDT: 208
LEÑERO, Vicente
  General Po: 2314
LENGYEL, Joszef
  An Angry Old Man Ke:
    416-417
LENNOX, Charlotte Ramsay
  General Be: 179-180
  The Female Quixote Be:
    179-180; ENES2: 158;
    LCAB: 110
  Henrietta ENES2: 158
LE NOIRE, Rosetta
  General MBA: 136
  Bubbling Brown Sugar MBA:
    136-140
  Come Laugh and Cry with
    Langston Hughes MBA:
    137
LENORMAND, Henri-René
  General Br: 383; MD:
    185; Po: 2314-2315
  L'amour magicien see Love
    the Magician
  Asie Br: 384; DC2: 226;
    LCAB: 110; Po: 2315
  The Coward [Le lâche] Br:
    384; DC2: 226; MD:
    186
  Crépuscle du téâtre see
    In Theatre Street
  La dent rouge Br: 384;

MD: 185-186
The Dream Doctor [Eater of
  Dreams; Le mangeur des rêves]
  Br: 384; DC2: 226; MD:
  186
Equator [Shadow of Evil; L'ombre
  du mal] Br: 384; DC2: 227;
  MD: 185
The Failures [Les rates] Br:
  384-385; DC2: 226; MD: 186
La folle du ciel Br: 385
L'homme et ses fantômes see
  Man and His Phantoms
The House on the Ramparts [La
  maison des ramparts] Br:
  385
In Theatre Street [Crépuscle
  du théâtre] Br: 385; MD:
  185
Le lâche see The Coward
Love the Magician [L'amour
  magicien] Br: 383; DC2:
  226
Man and His Phantoms [L'homme
  et ses fantômes] Br: 385;
  DC2: 226-227; MD: 186;
  Po: 2316
Le mangeur des reves see
  The Dream Doctor
Mixture Br: 385; DC2: 227;
  MD: 186
L'ombre du mal see Equator
The Possessed [Les possédés]
  Br: 385
Les rates see The Failures
A Secret Life [Une vie secrète]
  Br: 385-386; MD: 186
Shadow of Evil see Equator
Simoon [Le Simoun] Br: 386;
  DC2: 227
Three Rooms DC2: 227
Time Is a Dream [Le Temps
  est un songe] Br: 386;
  MD: 186
Terre de Satan Br: 386
Une vie secrète see A Secret
  Life
LENZ, J.M.R.
  Der Landprediger Fi: 357
  Zerbin oder die Neuere Philos-
    ophie Fi: 357
LENZ, Siegfried
  General Po: 2316
  Brot und Spiele Fi: 357
  Duel with the Shadow Fi:
    357

An Exemplary Life Fi: 357
"Die Festung" Wa: 467
The German Lesson Fi: 358
"Ein Hans aus lauter Liebe"
    Wa: 467
Heimatmuseum Fi: 358
"Der langere Arm" Wa: 467
"Der sechste Geburtstag"
    Wa: 467
"Der seelische Ratgeber"
    Wa: 467
Time of the Guiltless [Zeit
    der Schuld-Losen] Br:
    386
Topic of Conversation Fi:
    358
Der Waldbruder Fi: 358;
    Ke: 303
LEON, Ricardo
El amor de los amores Ke:
    208
La casta de hidalgos Ke:
    208
Los centauros Ke: 208
El hombre nuevo Ke: 208
Rojo y gualdo Ke: 208
Los trabajadores de la muerte
    Ke: 209
LEONARD, Hugh
General Br: 386; TMIP:
    76-78
All the Nice People see
    Mick and Mick
The Au Pair Man TMIP: 79
The Big Birthday Br: 386;
    TMIP: 79-80
Da TMIP: 76, 78
Irishmen: A Suburb of
    Babylon TMIP: 80
A Leap in the Dark TMIP:
    80
Madigan's Lock TMIP: 77,
    80
Mick and Mick [All the Nice
    People] Br: 386
The Passion of Peter McGinty
    TMIP: 80-81
The Patrick Pearse Motel
    TMIP: 81, 90
The Poker Session Br: 386;
    TMIP: 81
The Quick and the Dead
    TMIP: 48
Stephen D Br: 387; TMIP:
    77-78, 81-82
Summer TMIP: 82

A Walk on the Water TMIP:
    78
LEONOV, Leonid Maksimovich
General Po: 2317
The Badgers Fi: 456; Ke:
    417
"The End of a Petty Man" Wa:
    467
Invasion Br: 387
Locusts Ke: 417
Road to the Ocean Fi: 456;
    Ke: 417
The Russian Forest [Russkii
    Les'] Fi: 456; Ke: 417-
    418; Po: 2317
Skutarevsky Fi: 456; Ke:
    418
Soviet River Fi: 456; Ke:
    418
The Taking of Velikoshumsk
    Ke: 418
The Thief Fi: 456-457; Ke:
    418
LEONT'EV, Konstantin
In My Own Land Ke: 418
LEOPARDI, Giacomo
La Virtu Indiana DC2: 227
LE PAN, Douglas
General Po: 2317-2318
LEPROHON [MULLINS], Rosanna
    Eleanor
General ECL: 158
LERA, Angel María de
General Po: 2318
LERMONTOV, Mikhail
Bela Ke: 419
The Demon: An Eastern Tale
    Ma: 1182
"Fragment of a Story Once Be-
    gun" see "Shtoss"
Geroy Nashego Vremeni Fi:
    457
A Hero of Our Time Fi: 457;
    Ke: 419; LCAB: 110; Ma:
    1182-1183
Masquerade DC2: 227-228
"Shtoss" Ke: 419; Wa: 467
Spaniards DC2: 228
Strange Man DC2: 228
"Taman" WaS1: 125
Two Brothers DC2: 228; Ma:
    1183
LERNER, Alan Jay, and Frederick
    LOEWE
My Fair Lady ADC: 212
LE ROY, Jean

General Po: 2318
LE SAGE, Alain-René
Gil Blas of Santillane Fi:
104; Ke: 104-105; Ma:
1184
LESKOV, Nikolai
"Administrative Grace" WaS1:
125
"The Alexandrite" Wa: 468;
WaS1: 125
"The Amazon" WaS1: 125
"Ancient Psychopaths" WaS1:
125
"Antukà" WaS1: 125
"An Apparition in the Engi-
neers' Castle" WaS1:
125
At Knives Point Fi: 457-
458; Ke: 419
"The Battle-axe" WaS1:
125
"The Beauteous Aza" WaS1:
125
"Boyarin Nikita Yurievich"
WaS1: 125
"Boyarinya Marfa Andreyevna"
WaS1: 125
"Brahmadatta and Radovan"
WaS1: 125
"The Bugbear" WaS1: 125
The Bullsheep Ke: 420
"A Case That Was Dropped"
WaS1: 125
Cathedral Folk [The Cathe-
dral Clergy] Fi: 458; Ke:
420; LCAB: 110
"The Cattle-Pen" WaS1:
125
"Children of Cain" see
"Sheramur"
"Christ Visits a Muzhik"
WaS1: 126
"Christmas Night in a Railway
Carriage" see "A Journey
with a Nihilist"
"The Co-Functionaries: A
Bucolic Tale on a Histori-
cal Canvas" WaS1: 126
"The Darner" WaS1: 126
"The Dead Estate" WaS1:
126
"Deception" WaS1: 126
The Devil's Puppets Fi:
458
"The Enchanted Pilgrim"
WaS1: 126

"The Enchanted Wanderer" SFC:
136; Wa: 468
"An Enigmatic Incident in an In-
sane Asylum" WaS1: 126
An Enigmatic Man Ke: 420
"Episcopal Justice" WaS1: 126
"The Featherbrains" see "De-
ception"
"The Felon of Ashkelon" WaS1:
126
"Figura" WaS1: 126
"Fish Soup Without Fish"
WaS1: 126
"The Hour of God's Will" WaS1:
126
"Idle Dancers" see "The
Pustoplyasians"
"The Improvisers" WaS1: 126
"In a Coach" WaS1: 126
"Interesting Men" WaS1: 126
"Iron Will" WaS1: 126
"A Journey with a Nihilist"
WaS1: 127
"Kolyvan Husband" WaS1: 127
"The Lady and the Wench"
WaS1: 127
"Lady Macbeth of Mtsensk" Fi:
458; Ke: 420; Wa: 468;
WaS1: 127
"The Lefthander" WaS1: 127
"Leon the Butler's Son" WaS1:
127
Levsha Fi: 458
"The Life of a Peasant Marty-
ress" WaS1: 127
"The Little Fool" WaS1: 127
"A Little Mistake" WaS1: 127
"Man of Darkness" WaS1: 127
"The Man on Watch" Wa: 468
"The Melamed of Österreich"
WaS1: 127
"The Mind Takes Its Own and
the Devil His Own" WaS1:
127
"The Mocker" WaS1: 127
"The Moscow Ace" see "The
Darner"
"The Mountain" WaS1: 127
"The Musk-ox" WaS1: 127
"Mysterious Omens" WaS1:
128
Night Owls Fi: 458; Ke: 420
WaS1: 128
No Way Out Fi: 458; Ke: 420
Nowhere Ke: 420
"Offended Before Christmas"

WaS1: 128

"Pamphalon the Mountebank"
WaS1: 128

"Pavlin" WaS1: 128

"Pearl Necklace" WaS1: 128

"The Pustoplyasians" WaS1:
128

"The Pygmy" WaS1: 128

"Rabbit Warren" WaS1: 128

"The Robber" WaS1: 128

"A Robbery" WaS1: 128

"Russian Cryptomatrimony"
WaS1: 128

The Sealed Angel Ke: 420;
WaS1: 128

"The Sentry" WaS1: 128

"Sheramur" WaS1: 128

"A Short History of a Case
of Private Derangement"
WaS1: 128

"The Spirit of Mme. de Gen-
lis" WaS1: 128

"The Tale of the Crosseyed
Lefthander from Tula and
the Steel Flea" see "The
Lefthander"

"The Tale of Theodore the
Christian and His Friend
Abraham the Hebrew"
WaS1: 129

"Three Good Deeds" see
"The Pygmy"

"The Toupee Artist" WaS1:
129

"The Unbaptized Priest"
WaS1: 129

"The Unmercenary Engineers"
WaS1: 129

"Vexation of Spirit" WaS1:
129

"The Voice of Nature" Wa:
468

White Eagle Fi: 458; WaS1:
129

"The Wild Beast" WaS1: 129

"A Winter's Day" WaS1: 129

"Yid Somersault" WaS1: 129

Zakhudalyi Rod Ke: 420

LESLIE, Peter
The Extremist ENES2: 158

LESORT, Paul-Andre
General Po: 2318

LESPERANCE, Jean-Talon
"Rosalba; or, Faithful to
Two Lovers" Wa: 468

LESSING, Bruno

"The End of Our Task" Wa:
468

"The Unconverted" Wa: 468

"Urim and Turim" Wa: 468

LESSING, Doris
General CFAE: 216; CN:
310; LCAB: 110; MDAE:
309-310; Po: 2318-2319;
Sch: 208-210

African Stories Ma: 1185

The Antheap CN: 310; WaS1:
129

"The Black Madonna" WaS1:
129

Briefing for a Descent into Hell
ENES1: 150; ENES2: 158-
159; Ma: 1185-1186; Sch:
210

Children of Violence CN: 310;
ENE: 200; ENES1: 150;
ENES2: 159; Ma: 1186-1187;
Sch: 211

"The Day Stalin Died" Wa:
468

"The De Wets Come to Kloof
Grange" Wa: 468

"Dialogue" Wa: 468; WaS1:
129

Each His Own Wilderness Br:
387

Eldorado CN: 311

"England versus England" Wa:
469

"The Eye of God in Paradise"
Wa: 469

"Flavors of Exile" Wa: 469

The Four-Gated City ENES1:
150; ENES2: 159; Ma:
1187-1189; Sch: 211

"Getting Off the Altitude" Wa:
469

The Golden Notebook CN:
311; ENE: 200; ENES1:
150-151; ENES2: 159-160;
LCAB: 110; Ma: 1189-1190;
Sch: 211-212

The Grass Is Singing CN:
311; ENE: 200; ENES1:
151; ENES2: 160; Ma: 1190-
1191

"The Habit of Loving" Wa:
469

A Home for the Highland Cattle
CN: 311

Hunger CN: 311

In Pursuit of the English

ENE: 200

Landlocked see also Children of Violence CN: 312; ENES2: 160; Sch: 211

"'Leopard' George" Wa: 469; WaS1: 129

"A Letter from Home" Wa: 469

"A Man and Two Women" Ma: 1191; Wa: 469

Martha Quest see also Children of Violence CN: 312; ENES2: 161; Sch: 211

The Memoirs of a Survivor ENES2: 161

"No Witchcraft for Sale" Wa: 469

"Notes for a Case History" Wa: 469

"The Nuisance" Wa: 469

"The Old Chief Mshlanga" Wa: 469; WaS1: 129

"Old John's Place" Wa: 469

The Other Woman CN: 312

"Outside the Ministry" Wa: 469

"Plants and Girls" Wa: 469

A Proper Marriage see also Children of Violence CN: 312; ENES2: 161; Sch: 211

Retreat to Innocence CN: 312; ENE: 201; ENES2: 161

A Ripple in the Storm see also Children of Violence CN: 312; ENES2: 161; Sch: 211

"A Room" Wa: 469

"The Second Hut" Wa: 469; WaS1: 129

Shikasta ENES2: 161

"Story of Two Dogs" Wa: 470

The Summer Before the Dark ENES1: 151; ENES2: 161; Ma: 1191-1192

"A Sunrise on the Veld" Wa: 470; WaS1: 129

"The Temptation of Jack Orkney" WaS1: 130

"To Room Nineteen" Wa: 470; WaS1: 130

"Two Potters" Wa: 470; WaS1: 130

"Winter in July" Wa: 470

"A Woman on a Roof" Wa: 470

LESSING, Gotthold Ephraim

Der Dorfjunker DC2: 228

Emilia Galotti DC2: 228-229; EDC: 312-314; Ma: 1193-1194

Faust DC2: 229

The Freethinker [Der Freigeist] DC2: 229; EDC: 314

Das Horoskop DC2: 229

The Jews [Die Juden] DC2: 229-230; EDC: 314

Der Junge Gelehrte see The Young Scholar

Die Kleinen DC2: 230

Die Matrone von Ephesus EDC: 314

Minna von Barnhelm; or, The Soldier's Fortune [Minna von Barnhelm; or Das Soldaten-glück] DC2: 230; EDC: 315-316; Ma: 1194

Miss Sara Sampson DC2: 231; EDC: 316

Nathan the Wise [Nathan der Weise] DC2: 230-231; EDC: 316-318; Ma: 1194-1195

Philotas DC2: 231; EDC: 318-319

Samuel Henzi DC2: 231

The Treasure [Der Schatz] EDC: 319

The Young Scholar [Der Junge Gelehrte] DC2: 230; EDC: 319

LESTER, Julius

General BAF: 195; BAW: 484

L'ESTRANGE, Sir Roger

General Bon: 75

LE SUEUR, Meridel

"Annunciation" SFC: 137; Wa: 466

"Breathe Upon These Slain" SFC: 137; Wa: 466

LETTS, Winifred M. [Mrs. W.H. VERSCHOYLE]

General Mi: 252

LEVER, Charles

General BN: 73

The Knight of Gwynne ENES2: 161

Lord Kilgobbin ENES2: 161

LEVERSON, Ada

General Po: 2319

Bird of Paradise ENES1: 151

"The Blow" Wa: 470
"Claude's Aunt" Wa: 470
"In the Change of Years"
Wa: 470
The Limit ENES1: 151
Love at Second Sight ENES1:
151
Love's Shadow ENES1: 151
"Mimosa" Wa: 470
"The Quest of Sorrow" Wa:
470
"Suggestion" Wa: 470
Tenterhooks ENES1: 151
The Twelfth Hour ENES1:
151
LEVERTOV, Denise
General ICBAP: 78; JW:
97; MP: 57-58; Po: 2320-
2321
"At the Edge" ICBAP: 78
"The Coming Fall" ICBAP:
78
"The Dead" PE: 284
"The Disclosure" ICBAP:
78
"The Five Day Rain" PE:
284
"The Fountain" Po: 2321
"The Garden Wall" ICBAP:
78; PE: 284
"The Goddess" ICBAP: 79
"Illustrious Ancestors" PE:
284
"Losing Track" PE: 284
"Love Song" Po: 2321
"The Malice of Innocence"
PE: 284
"The Necessity" Po: 2321
"The 90th Year" PE: 284
"Olga Poems" ICBAP: 79
"Say the Word" Wa: 470
"Six Variations" PE: 284
The Sorrow Dance Po: 2321-
2322
"A Stir in the Air" PE: 284
"The Stonecarver's Poem"
PE: 284
"The Third Dimension"
ICBAP: 79
"With Eyes at the Back of
Our Heads" PE: 284
LEVI, Carlo
Christ Stopped at Eboli Ke:
243-244
The Watch Fi: 267; Ke:
244

LEVI, Peter
General Po: 2322
LEVI, Stephen
Daphne in Cottage D ADC:
212
LEVIN, Ira
Critic's Choice ADC: 213
Dr. Cook's Garden ADC: 213
General Seeger ADC: 213
Interlock ADC: 213
No Time for Sergeants ADC:
213
Veronica's Room ADC: 213
LEVINE, Norman
General JW: 341; Po: 2322-
2323
LEVINE, Richard N., and C.
Robert HOLLOWAY
The American Nightmare ADC:
213
LEVI-STRAUSS, Claude
Tristes tropiques Ke: 105
LEVITT, Saul
The Andersonville Trial ADC:
214
LEVY, Benn Wolfe
General MDAE: 312; Mi: 252
Madame Bovary ADC: 214
The Rape of the Belt Br: 387;
MDAE: 312
Return to Tyassi DC1: 116;
MDAE: 312
Springtime for Henry ADC:
214
LEVY, Jacques
Berchtesgaden ADC: 214
LEVY, Melvin
Gold Eagle Guy Br: 387
LEWES, George Henry
General EDT: 209
Captain Bland DC1: 117
Ranthorpe ENES1: 151
Rose, Blanche and Violet
ENES1: 151
LEWIN, John
The House of Atreus ADC:
215
_____ and Michael VALENTI
Blood Red Roses ADC: 215
LEWIS, Alfred Henry
General ASF: 360
"The Mills of Savage Gods"
Wa: 471
LEWIS, Alun
General Po: 2323
"Ha, Ha! Among the Trumpets"

PE: 284
"The Orange Grove" Wa:
471
"The Raid" SFC: 137; Wa:
471
"Raider's Dawn" PE: 284
"The Reunion" Wa: 471
"Tudor Witch" Wa: 471
"The Wanderers" Wa: 471
"Ward 0.3b" Wa: 471
LEWIS, Arthur H.
General LCAB: 110
LEWIS, Cecil Day
General Ma: 1196
Starting Point ENES2: 164
LEWIS, Clive Staples
General Po: 2324-2328; Ri2:
112-122, 133-138; Sch:
212-215
The Allegory of Love Ri2:
137-138
Christian Reflections Ri2:
135
The Chronicles of Narnia
ENES2: 161-162; Ma:
1197; Ri2: 122-126; Sch:
215-216
"Dark Tower" Ri2: 118-119,
135
An Experiment in Criticism
Ri2: 135
The Four Loves Ma: 1197-
1198
The Great Divorce Ri2: 126
The Horse and His Boy
ENES2: 162; Sch: 215-
216
The Last Battle ENES2:
162; Sch: 215-216
The Lion, the Witch, and the
Wardrobe ENES2: 162;
Sch: 215-216
The Magician's Nephew
ENES2: 162; Sch: 215-
216
Of Other Worlds Ri2: 118
Out of the Silent Planet
ENE: 201; ENES1: 152;
ENES2: 162; Ma: 1198;
Ri2: 127-130, 522; Sch:
216-217
Perelandra ENE: 201;
ENES1: 152; ENES2:
162-163; Ma: 1199; Ri2:
127-129; Sch: 216-217
The Pilgrim's Regress Ri2:
126
Prince Caspian ENES2: 163;
Sch: 215-216
"The Ransom Trilogy" ["The
Space Trilogy"] Po: 2324-
2327; Ri2: 126-132
The Screwtape Letters Ri2:
132
The Silver Chair ENES2: 163;
Sch: 215-216
That Hideous Strength ENE:
201; ENES1: 152; ENES2:
163; Ma: 1199-1200; Ri2:
127-131; Sch: 216-217
Till We Have Faces ENES1:
153; ENES2: 163; Ma:
1200-1201; Po: 2328-2329;
Ri2: 116-118, 132-133; Sch:
218
The Voyage of the "Dawn Tread-
er" ENES2: 163; Sch: 215-
216
LEWIS, Henry Clay
General ASF: 361
"The Curious Widow" ASF:
361; WaS1: 130
"My Early Life" ASF: 361
"Stealing a Baby" ASF: 361;
WaS1: 130
"A Struggle for Life" ASF:
361; WaS1: 130
"Valerian and the Panther"
ASF: 361
LEWIS, Ira
The Sponsor ADC: 215
LEWIS, James Franklin
General Po: 2329
"Dawn in the Study" PE: 285;
Po: 2329
"In Memoriam" ICBAP: 79;
PE: 285; Po: 2329
LEWIS, Janet
General AN: 168; Po: 2329-
2330
The Ghost of Monsieur Scarron
Po: 2329
The Invasion Po: 2330
The Trial of Soren Qvist Po:
2329
The Wife of Martin Guerre Po:
2329
LEWIS, Matthew Gregory
General Be: 183-184; Du:
108; EDT: 212-213; Li:
234
Adelgitha EDT: 212

Feudal Tyrants ENES1: 153
The Monk Be: 183-184; Du:
107-108; EN: 93; ENE:
201-202; ENES1: 153;
ENES2: 164
The Twins DC1: 117; EDT:
212; Li: 234
LEWIS, Meriwether
General LCAB: 110
LEWIS, Milton, and Julian FUNT
The Dancer ADC: 215
LEWIS, O.F.
"Alma Mater" WaS1: 130
LEWIS, Oscar
The Children of Sánchez Ma:
1202
LEWIS, Richard
General Da: 54
"The Fate Changer" WaS1:
130
LEWIS, Saunders
General Po: 2330-2331
LEWIS, Sinclair
General ALL: 161-163; AN:
170-173; ASF: 360-361;
CN: 312-316; LCAB:
110-111; Ne: 65-67; Po:
2331-2337; Wo: 141-143
Ann Vickers AN: 169; CN:
316
Arrowsmith ALL: 162; AN:
169; CN: 317-319; Ma:
1203-1205; Ne: 67; Po:
2338-2339; Wo: 142
Babbitt ALL: 162; AN:
169; CN: 319-320; LCAB:
111; Ma: 1205-1206; Ne:
66; Po: 2339-2340; Wo:
142
Bethel Merriday CN: 320
Cass Timberlane AN: 169;
CN: 320; Ma: 1206-1207
Dodsworth ALL: 162; AN:
169; Br: 387; CN: 320-
321; LCAB: 111; Ma:
1207-1208; Po: 2331, 2341
Elmer Gantry ALL: 162;
AN: 169; CN: 321-322;
LCAB: 111; Ma: 1208-
1209; Ne: 67; Po: 2341
Free Air CN: 322
Gideon Planish AN: 169;
CN: 322
The God-Seeker AN: 169;
CN: 322
"The Hidden People" WaS1:
130
The Innocents CN: 322
It Can't Happen Here AN:
169
The Job CN: 323
Kingsblood Royal AN: 170;
CN: 323; Po: 2341-2342
Main Street ALL: 162; AN:
170; CN: 323-324; LCAB:
111; Ma: 1209-1210; Ne:
65; Po: 1289-1290, 2342;
Wo: 142
The Man Who Knew Coolidge
AN: 170; CN: 324; Ne:
67
Mantrap ALL: 162; CN: 324
"Nature, Incorporated" ASF:
360
Our Mr. Wrenn AN: 170; CN:
324-325
The Prodigal Parents CN: 325
"The Scarlet Sign" ASF: 360;
Po: 2342
The Trail of the Hawk CN:
325
"A Woman by Candlelight" ASF:
360
Work of Art AN: 170; CN:
325
World So Wide CN: 325
"Young Man Axelbrod" WaS1:
130
_____ and John MOFFIT
It Can't Happen Here ADC:
215; Br: 287; CN: 322
LEWIS, Wyndham
General BN2: 78-80; LCAB:
112; Po: 2343-2348; Ri2:
158-172, 176-183; Sch: 218-
222
The Apes of God EN: 93;
ENES1: 153; ENES2: 164;
Ri2: 158-159, 161; Sch:
222
Art of Being Ruled Ri2: 182
"Beau Séjour" Wa: 471; WaS1:
130
"Bestre" WaS1: 131
"Brotcotnaz" Wa: 471; WaS1:
131
"Cantleman's Spring Mate"
SFC: 137; Wa: 471; WaS1:
131
The Childermass EN: 93;
ENES1: 153; Ri2: 161, 164
"The Cornac and His Wife"

Wa: 471
"The Death of the Ankou"
   Wa: 471; WaS1: 131
The Demon of Progress in
   the Arts Ri2: 162
"Doppelgänger" Wa: 472
"The French Poodle" WaS1:
   131
The Human Age see also
   The Childermass; Monstre
   Gai; Malign Fiesta EN:
   93; ENES1: 153; ENES2:
   164; Po: 2348-2349; Ri2:
   161, 172-174; Sch: 222
Malign Fiesta ENES1: 153
Men Without Art Ri2: 181-
   182
Monstre Gai ENES1: 153;
   Po: 2349
"My Disciple" Wa: 472
Paleface Ri2: 167
The Red Priest Ri2: 174
The Revenge for Love EN:
   93; ENES1: 154; ENES2:
   164; Ri2: 159-160, 162,
   168-169, 171, 174
The Roaring Queen ENES1:
   154; Ri2: 176
"The Rot" Wa: 472
Self-Condemned EN: 94;
   ENES1: 154; ENES2:
   164; Po: 2349-2350; Ri2:
   159-162, 174-175
"Sigismund" Wa: 472
Snooty Baronet EN: 94;
   ENES1: 154; ENES2:
   165; Ri2: 160, 171, 175
Tarr EN: 94; ENES1: 154;
   ENES2: 165; Ri: 160-
   161, 168-169, 175-176;
   Sch: 222
Time and Western Man Ri2:
   167, 178-182
"Time the Tiger" Wa: 472
The Trial of Man Po: 2350
"Unlucky for Pringle" Wa:
   472
The Vulgar Streak ENES1:
   154; ENES2: 165; Ri2:
   159, 171, 176
"The War Baby" Wa: 472
The Wild Body Po: 2350;
   Ri2: 161
"The Writer and the Absolute"
   Ri2: 181
LEWISOHN, Ludwig

General AN: 174; JW: 252;
   LCAB: 112; Po: 2350-2351
"The Bolshevik" Wa: 472
The Case of Mr. Crump AN:
   173
"The Saint" Wa: 472
"Writ of Divorcement" Wa:
   472
LEYDEN, John
   General Ai: 113
LEZAMA LIMA, Jose
   Paradiso Po: 2351
LHOTE, André
   General Po: 2351
LIANG, Lee Kok
   "When the Saints Go Marching"
      Wa: 472
LIASHKO, N.
   "The Song of the Chains" SFC:
      137
LIBEDINSKII, Yuri
   The Birth of a Hero Ke: 420
   The Week Ke: 421
LIBEN, Meyer
   General ASF: 362
   "Justice Hunger" Wa: 472
LIBERATORE, Umberto
   General Po: 2351
LIBRI, Bartolomeo de
   St. John Beheaded DC2: 231
LIDIN, Vladimir
   Ships Are Sailing Ke: 421
LIDMAN, Sara
   General Po: 2351
   Bara Mistel Fi: 409
   Hjortronlandet Fi: 409
   Jag Och Min Son Fi: 409
   Med Fem Diamanter Fi: 409
   Regnspiran Fi: 409
   Tjardalen Fi: 409
LIDMAN, Sven
   As Through Fire Ke: 360
LIE, Jonas
   Adam Schrader Fi: 409; Ke:
      360
   The Barque "Future" Fi: 409
   The Commodore's Daughter Fi:
      409
   The Daughters of the Port Com-
      mander Ke: 360
   Dyre Rein Fi: 409; Ke: 360
   East of the Sun, West of the
      Moon, and Behind the Tower
      of Babel Fi: 409; Ke: 360
   "The Eight-Oared Boat" see
      "The Søndmøre Boat"

Et Samlio Ke: 360

Evil Powers [Forces of Evil]
  Fi: 409-410; Ke: 360

The Family at Gilje Fi: 410;
  Ke: 360

Faste Forland Fi: 410; Ke:
  360

Finneblod Ke: 360

Forces of Evil see Evil
  Powers

Go Onward Fi: 410; Ke:
  360

Livsslaven see The Slave
  of Life

Maelstrom Fi: 410

Maisa Jons Fi: 410; Ke:
  360

The Man of Second Sight Ke:
  360-361

A Marriage Fi: 410

Niobe Fi: 410; Ke: 361

"The Nordfjord House" WaS1:
  131

Old Rutland Ke: 361

The Pilot and His Wife Fi:
  410; Ke: 361

Rutland Fi: 410

The Slave of Life [Livsslaven]
  Fi: 410; Ke: 360

"The Søndmøre Boat" WaS1:
  131

Thomas Ross Fi: 410; Ke:
  361

The Ulfvungs Fi: 410; Ke:
  361

The Visonary Fi: 410; Ke:
  361

A Vortex Ke: 361

When the Iron Curtain Falls
  Fi: 410

When the Sun Sets Fi: 410;
  Ke: 361

LIEBLING, Abbott Joseph
  General LCAB: 112

LIGHTHALL, William Douw
  General ECL: 160

LIGHTS, Frederick
  All Over Nuthin' MBA: 140

LILAR, Suzanne
  Le Burlador Br: 387

LILJENQUIST, Don C.
  Woman Is My Idea ADC:
  215

LILLO, Baldomero
  General LCAB: 112

LILLO, George

General EC: 98; Li: 235-236

Arden of Feversham see
  ANONYMOUS

The Christian Hero DC1: 117

The Elmerick DC1: 117

The Fatal Curiosity DC1: 117;
  Li: 235-236

The London Merchant DC1:
  117-118; EC: 98; LCAB:
  112; Li: 235-236

LILLY, John
  General LCAB: 112

LIMBOUR, Georges
  General Po: 2352

LIMON, José
  "Frost in the Rio Grande Valley"
  PE: 285

LINARES RIVAS, Manuel
  General Br: 388
  Aire de Fuera Br: 388
  La Fuerza del Mal Br: 388
  La Garra Br: 388

LINCOLN, Victoria
  "Down in the Reeds by the
  River" Wa: 472

LIND, Jakov
  "Hurrah for Freedom" Wa:
  473
  "Journey Through the Night"
  Wa: 473
  "Resurrection" Wa: 473
  Soul of Wood Fi: 410; Wa:
  473

LINDEGREN, Erik
  General Po: 2352
  "Portrait-Elegy" Po: 2352

Lindesay, Ethel Florence see
  RICHARDSON, Henry Handel

LINDNER, Robert
  "The Jet-Propelled Couch"
  WaS1: 131

LINDO, Archie
  General WIL: 77

LINDSAY, David
  General Ai: 217-218; ED:
  276; Po: 2352; SC: 68
  The Adventures of Monsieur de
  Mailly Ai: 217; ENES2:
  165
  A Voyage to Arcturus Ai:
  218; ENES2: 165

LINDSAY, Howard
  General Br: 388
  She Loves Me Not ADC: 215
  _____ and Russel CROUSE
  The Great Sebastians ADC:

216

Life with Father ADC: 216;
MD: 186

Life with Mother ADC: 216-
217

The Prescott Proposals ADC:
217

Remains to Be Seen ADC:
217

State of the Union ADC:
217-218; MD: 186

Strip for Action ADC: 218;
MD: 186

Tall Story ADC: 218

_____, Russel CROUSE, and
Irving BERLIN

Call Me Madam ADC: 218

_____, Russel CROUSE, Oscar
HAMMERSTEIN II, and
Richard RODGERS

The Sound of Music ADC:
218-219

_____ and Bertrand ROBIN-
SON

O Promise Me ADC: 219

Your Uncle Dudley ADC:
219

_____ and Damon RUNYON

A Slight Case of Murder
ADC: 219

LINDSAY, Jack

Clue of Darkness Po: 2353

Life Rarely Tells Po: 2353

The Roaring Twenties Po:
2353

LINDSAY, Maurice

General Ai: 312

LINDSAY, Norman

General MAP: 219-222; Po:
2353-2354

Dust or Polish? MAP: 222

Halfway to Anywhere MAP:
219-220

Miracles by Arrangement
MAP: 222

Pan in the Parlour MAP:
222

Redheap MAP: 220-222

LINDSAY, Powell

General BAP: 134; BAW:
490

LINDSAY, Sir David

General Ai: 37

The Satire of the Three
Estates [Ane Satire of
the Thrie Estatis] Ai:

37; DC1: 118

LINDSAY, Vachel

General ALL: 163-164; LCAB:
112; Ma: 1211-1212; Po:
2354-2356

"Abraham Lincoln Walks at Midnight" PE: 285

"The Congo" PE: 285

"General William Booth Enters
into Heaven" PE: 285; Po:
2356

"The Santa Fe Trail" PE: 285

Linebarger, Paul see SMITH,
Cordwainer

LING SHU-HUA

"Embroidered Pillows" WaS1:
131

"The Eve of the Mid-Autumn
Festival" WaS1: 131

"Little Liu" WaS1: 131

LINGARD, Joan

General Ai: 334

LINKLATER, Eric

General Ai: 265

LINN, John Blair

General AP: 405; Da: 112-
113

LINNA, Väinö

General Po: 2356-2357

Taalla Pohjantahden Alla Ke:
361

The Unknown Soldier [Tunte-
maton Sotilas] Ke: 361; Po:
2357

LINNEY, Romulus

Holy Ghosts ADC: 219

Love Suicide at Schofield Barracks ADC: 219

The Sorrows of Frederick ADC:
219

LINS, Osman

"The Betrothal" Wa: 473

"A Dot in the Circle" Wa: 473

LINS DO REGO, Jose

General Ma: 1213

LINTON, Eliza

General BN: 73

The World Well Lost ENES2:
165

LIPATOV, Vil

Lida Varaksina Po: 2357

Skazanie o direktore Proncha-
tove Po: 2357

LIPPARD, George

General AN: 174

LIPPMANN, Walter

General APC: 62-63
A Preface to Politics APC:
63
LIPTON, Lawrence
General Po: 2358
LISTER, Richard Percival
"Target" ICBAP: 79; PE:
285
LIVESAY, Dorothy
General Po: 2358
"The Glass House" SFC:
137; Wa: 473
LIVINGS, Henry
General Br: 388; MDAE:
314
The Arson Squad Br: 388
Big Soft Nellie Br: 388
Eh? Br: 388; MDAE: 314;
Po: 2358
Jack's Horrible Luck Br:
388
Kelly's Eye Br: 389; MDAE:
314; Po: 2358
Stop It, Whoever You Are
Br: 389
LIVINGSTON, Myrtle
For Unborn Children BAP:
135
LIVINGSTON, William
General AP: 407-408
LIVY
History [Annals] Ma: 1214-
1215
LIYONG, Taban lo
General BALE: 325-326
Another Nigger Dead BALE:
326
Eating Chiefs BALE: 325
Fixions BALE: 325-326
The Last Word BALE: 325-
326
LLEWELLYN, Martin
General LJCD: 247-248
LLORENS, David
General BAW: 491
LLOYD, Charles
Edmund Oliver ENES1: 154
LO HUA-SHENG [HSÜ Ti-shan]
"The Vain Labors of a Spider"
WaS1: 131
"Yü-kuan" WaS1: 131
LOBANOV, M.E.
Boris Godunov DC2: 231-
232
LOBATO, Monteiro
General Po: 2358

LOBEIRA, Vasco de
Amadís de Gaul Ma: 1216
LOCKE, Alain LeRoy
General BAW: 494-495
Locke, David Ross see NASBY,
Petroleum V.
LOCKE, John
General Bon: 57-59
LOCKHART, John Gibson
General Ai: 129-130
Some Passages in the Life of Mr.
Adam Blair Ai: 130; ENES1:
154; Po: 1732
LOCKRIDGE, Ross, Jr.
General AN: 174
Raintree County AN: 174; Po:
2358-2359
LODEIZEN, Hans
General Po: 2359
LODGE, George Cabot
Cain DC1: 118
Herakles DC1: 118
LODGE, Thomas
General ED: 278-279; ERP:
272-286; Hen: 162; PS:
154-155, 158-160; SC: 69
Euphues's Shadow ERP: 281
A Fig for Momus SC: 69
Forbonius and Prisceria ERP:
272, 277, 279, 281; Hen:
161
A Margarite of America ERP:
273, 281
Robert Second Duke of Nor-
mandy [Robin the Devil]
ERP: 276, 281, 285
Rosalynde ENES1: 154; ENES2:
165; ERP: 271-286; Hen:
161
"Satire 5" [from A Fig for
Momus] PE: 285
Wit's Misery ERP: 285
The Wounds of Civil War DC1:
118; PS: 155-156, 160
LODGE, Thomas [translator]
The Workes of SENECA Hen:
214
_____ and Robert GREENE
A Looking Glass for London and
England see also GREENE,
Robert and Thomas LODGE
ED: 278; PS: 156, 160
LOESSER, Frank
The Most Happy Fella ADC:
219-220
LOGAN, James

General AP: 409-410; Da: 54

LOGAN, John
Jack Ruby, All-American Boy
ADC: 220

LOGAN, John Burton
General ICBAP: 79; MP: 59; Po: 2359-2360
"Big Sur: Partington" PE: 285
"A Century Piece for Poor Heine" LCAB: 112; MP: 59; PE: 285; Po: 2360
"Lines for Michael in the Picture" MP: 59; PE: 285
"The Picnic" PE: 285
"The Rescue" PE: 286
"Shore Scene" PE: 286
"A Trip to Four or Five Towns" PE: 286

LOGAN, Joshua
The Wisteria Trees ADC: 220-221

LOGINOV, Victor
Otherwise It Wouldn't Be Love Ke: 421

LOMAX, Pearl Cleage
General BAP: 135; BAW: 498

LONDON, Jack [John GRIFFETH]
General ALL: 164-166; AN: 175-176; ASF: 366-368; Cla: 111-112; Ho: 100-102; LCAB: 112-113; Po: 2360-2364; Wo: 147-148
"All Gold Canyon" ASF: 362; WaS1: 132
"The Apostate" ASF: 362; Wa: 473
"Bâtard" ["Diable--A Dog"] ASF: 362; Wa: 473
"The Bones of Kahelili" ASF: 362; Wa: 473
Burning Daylight Po: 2363
The Call of the Wild AN: 174; Ho: 100-102; Ma: 1217; Po: 2361, 2364; Wa: 474; WaS1: 132
"The Chinago" ASF: 362 Wa: 474
"A Curious Fragment" ASF: 362; Wa: 474
"A Day's Lodging" ASF: 362
"The Death of Ligoun" Wa: 474

"Diable--A Dog" see "Bâtard"
The Divine Fire Ho: 100
"The Dream of Debs" Wa: 474
"The Enemy of All the World" Wa: 474
"A Goboto Night" ASF: 362
"The God of His Fathers" ASF: 362-363; Wa 474
"Goliah" ASF: 363
"The Great Interrogation" ASF: 363; Wa: 474
"The Grit of Woman" Wa: 474
"In a Far Country" ASF: 363; SFC: 137; Wa: 474
"The Inevitable White Man" Wa: 474
The Iron Heel AN: 174-175; Ho: 100; Po: 2363-2364
John Barleycorn AN: 175
"The Kanaka Surf" ASF: 363; Wa: 474-475
"Keesh, the Son of Keesh" ASF: 363; Wa: 475
"Koolan the Leper" ASF: 363; Wa: 475
"The Law of Life" ASF: 363; Wa: 475
"The League of Old Men" ASF: 363; Wa: 475
"Like Argus of the Ancient Times" ASF: 363; Wa: 475
The Little Lady of the Big House Po: 2363
"Local Color" Wa: 475
"Love of Life" ASF: 363; Wa: 475
Martin Eden AN: 175; Ho: 100-101; LCAB: 113; Po: 2361
"The Master of Mystery" ASF: 363
"Mauki" ASF: 364; Wa: 475
"The Men of Forty-Mile" ASF: 364; Wa: 475
"The Mexican" ASF: 364; Wa: 475
"The Minions of Midas" Wa: 475
"The Mistake of Creation" ASF: 364
"A Night's Swim in Yeddo Bay" ASF: 364
"An Odyssey of the North" ASF: 364; Wa: 475
"On the Makaloa Mat" Po: 2365; Wa: 475

"The One Thousand Dozen"
ASF: 364
"A Piece of Steak" ASF:
364; Wa: 475; WaS1: 132
"Planchette" Wa: 476
"The Priestly Prerogative"
ASF: 364; Wa: 476
"The Red One" ASF: 364;
WaS1: 132
The Road AN: 175
"The Scarlet Plague" ASF:
364
The Sea Wolf AN: 175; Ho:
101; Ma: 1217-1218; Po:
2361, 2365
"The Seed of McCoy" ASF:
364; Wa: 476
"The Shadow and the Flash"
Wa: 476
"Shin Bones" ASF: 365;
Wa: 476
"The Sickness of Lone Chief"
ASF: 365; Wa: 476
"The Son of the Wolf" ASF:
365; Ho: 101; Po: 2366;
Wa: 476
"The Story of Jees Uck" Wa:
476
"The Strength of the Strong"
Wa: 476
"The Sun-Dog Trail" ASF:
365; Wa: 476
"The Tears of Ah Kim" ASF:
365; Wa: 476
"The Terrible Solomons" ASF:
365
"A Thousand Deaths" ASF:
365
"To Build a Fire" ASF:
365; Po: 2366; Wa: 476-
477; WaS1: 132
"To the Man on Trail" ASF:
365; Wa: 477
"Told in the Drooling Ward"
WaS1: 132
"The Unexpected" ASF:
365; Wa: 477
The Valley of the Moon Po:
2363
"War" ASF: 365-366
"The Water Baby" ASF:
366; Wa: 477
"The Whale Tooth" ASF:
366; Wa: 477
"When Alice Told Her Soul"
Wa: 477

"When God Laughs" ASF: 366;
Wa: 477
"Which Make Men Remember"
Wa: 477
White Fang Po: 2361
"The White Silence" ASF: 366;
Wa: 477
"The Wife of a King" ASF:
366; Wa: 477; WaS1: 132
"The Wisdom of the Trail" ASF:
366; Wa: 477
"The Wit of Porportuk" ASF:
366; Wa: 477
"Yah! Yah! Yah!" Wa: 478
LONDON, Roy
Mrs. Murray's Farm ADC:
221
LONG, Sumner Arthur
Never Too Late ADC: 221
LONGFELLOW, Henry Wadsworth
General ALL: 166-169; AN:
177; Cla: 59-60; ICBAP:
79; LCAB: 113
"Aftermath" PE: 286
"Chaucer" ICBAP: 79; PE:
286
The Courtship of Miles Standish
Ma: 1219
"The Cross of Snow" ICBAP:
79; PE: 286
"Divina Commedia," Sonnet I
PE: 286
"Evangeline" Ma: 1219
"The Falcon of Ser Federigo"
PE: 286
"The Fire of Drift-Wood" PE:
286
"Helen of Tyre" PE: 286
"Hymn to the Night" PE: 286
Hyperion Cla: 59-60
"In the Churchyard at Cam-
bridge" PE: 286
"Jugurtha" PE: 286
"Killed at the Ford" PE: 286
"My Lost Youth" PE: 286
"The Occultation of Orion"
ICBAP: 79; PE: 287
"Paul Revere's Ride" PE: 287
"Seaweed" PE: 287
"Serenade" ICBAP: 79; PE:
287
"Snow-Flakes" PE: 287
The Song of Hiawatha Cla:
59-60; LCAB: 113; Ma:
1219-1220
"The Tide Rises, the Tide

Falls" PE: 287

LONGFORD, Lady Christine
General Br: 389

LONGHI, Vincent J.
Climb the Greased Pole ADC: 221
Lincoln Mask ADC: 221

LONGINUS, Cassius
General LCAB: 113
On the Sublime Ma: 1221-1222

LONGSTREET, Augustus Baldwin
General ASF: 370
"A Dance" ASF: 369
"The Fight" ASF: 369
"The Gander Pulling" ASF: 369
"Georgia Theatrics" ASF: 369
"The Horse-Swap" Wa: 478
"The Mother and Her Child" ASF: 369; WaS1: 132

LONGUS
Daphnis and Chloë see also DAY, Angel [translator] Ma: 1223

LÖNS, Hermann
General Po: 2366

LONSDALE, Frederick [Lionel Frederick LEONARD]
General MDAE: 315; Mi: 252-253
Aren't We All? Br: 389
But for the Grace of God Br: 389
The Day After Tomorrow ADC: 222
The High Road ADC: 222
The Last of Mrs. Cheyney Br: 389
On Approval Br: 389

LOOMIS, Edward
General AN: 177; Po: 2367
The Mothers Po: 2366-2367
"Wounds" ASF: 370; Wa: 478

LOOS, Anita
Chéri ADC: 222
Darling, Darling ADC: 222
Gigi ADC: 222
Happy Birthday ADC: 222-223
The King's Mare ADC: 223
_____ and John EMERSON
Gentlemen Prefer Blondes ADC: 223

_____, Joseph FIELDS, Jule STYNE, and Leo ROBIN
Gentlemen Prefer Blondes ADC: 223

LOPE [de Vega]
El acero de Madrid see The Waters of Madrid
Las almenas de Toro DC2: 232
Los amantes sin amor DC2: 232
Amar, servir y esperar DC2: 232
El arenal de Sevilla DC2: 232; EDC: 540
Los Benavides DC2: 232
The Birth of Ursón and Valentín [El nacimiento de Ursón y Valentín] EDC: 540
Las bizarrías de Belisa see The Gallantries of Belisa
La buena guarda see The Good Custodian
El caballero de Olmedo see The Knight from Olmedo
El caballero del milagro see Sir Miracle Comes a Cropper
El capellán de la Virgen DC2: 233
El casamiento en la muerte DC2: 233
Castelvines y Monteses DC2: 233
El castigo sin venganza see Justice Without Revenge
Los cautivos de Argel EDC: 540
El cerco de Santa Fé see The Siege of Santa Fé
El cerco de Tremecen DC2: 233
Comedia famosa de Don Manuel DC2: 233
The Commanders of Cordoba [Los comendadores de Córdoba] EDC: 540
La corona de Hungría see The Hungarian Crown
La creation del mundo DC2: 233
El cuerdo en su casa DC2: 234
La dama boba see The Idiot Lady
The Deserved Crown [La corona merecida] EDC: 540
La discreta enamorada DC2:

234

The Dog in the Manger [El perro del hortelano] DC2: 238; EDC: 540

Don Lope de Cardona DC2: 234; EDC: 540

Los donaires de Matico see The Witty Sayings of Matico

Donde no esta su dueno DC2: 234

La Dorotea DC2: 234-235; Ma: 2208

The Duke of Viseo [El duque de Viseo] EDC: 541

Los embustes de Celauro DC2: 235

El esclavo de Roma see The Slave of Rome

Estrella de Sevilla see Star of Seville

The Example for Married Women and the Test of Patience [El ejemplo de casadas y prueba de la paciencia] EDC: 541

The Fairs of Madrid [Las ferias de Madrid] EDC: 541

La fianza satisfecha see The Outrageous Saint

Lo fingido verdadero see Make-Believe Becomes Truth

Las fortunas de Diana DC2: 235

The Fortunate Son [El hijo venturoso] EDC: 541

Fuenteovejuna see The Sheep Well

The Gallant of La Membrilla [El galán de la Membrilla] EDC: 542

The Gallantries of Belisa [Las bizarrías de Belisa] EDC: 542

The Good Custodian [La buena guarda] EDC: 542

El gran Castrucho DC2: 236

El gran duque de Moscovia [Le gran duc de Moscou] DC2: 236; EDC: 542

The Greatest Virtue of a King [La mayor virtud de un rey] EDC: 542

La hermosa Ester DC2: 236; EDC: 542

El hijo de Reduán see Reduan's Son

El hijo venturoso see The Fortunate Son

Humility and Pride [La humildad y la soberbia] EDC: 542

The Hungarian Crown [La corona de Hungría] EDC: 542

The Idiot Lady [La dama boba] DC2: 234; EDC: 542

La ilustre Fregona DC2: 236

The Inn of the Court [El meson de la corte] EDC: 543

Justice Without Revenge [El castigo sin venganza] DC2: 233; EDC: 543

The King and the Farmer [El villano en su rincón] DC2: 239; EDC: 543

The King, the Greatest Alcalde [El mejor alcalde el rey] DC2: 236-237; EDC: 543; Ma: 2208

The King Without a Kingdom [El rey sin reino] EDC: 543

The Knight from Olmedo [El caballero de Olmedo] DC2: 232-233; EDC: 543-544

El lacayo fingido DC2: 237

The Life of St. Peter Nolasco [La vida de San Pedro Nolasco] EDC: 544

Lo que ha de ser see What Must Be, Must Be

The Madmen of Valencia [Los locos de Valencia] EDC: 544

Make-Believe Becomes Truth [Lo fingido verdadero] EDC: 544

El mayor imposible DC2: 237; EDC: 544

La mayor victoria DC2: 237

La mayor virtud de un rey see The Greatest Virtue of a King

El mejor alcalde el rey see The King, the Greatest Alcalde

El mesón de la corte see The Inn of the Court

La moza de cántaro DC2: 237; EDC: 544

El nacimiento de Ursón y Valentín see The Birth of Urson and Valentin

El niño inocente de la guardia DC2: 237

La ocasión perdida DC2: 237

The Outrageous Saint [La fianza satisfecha] DC2: 237; EDC: 544-545

The Peace of Kings and the Jewess of Toledo [Las paces de los reyes y judia de Toledo] DC2: 238; EDC: 545

Peribáñez and the Commander of Ocaña DC2: 238; EDC: 545

El perro del hortelano see The Dog in the Manger

El Perseo EDC: 545

Persistence Until Death [Porfiar hasta morir] EDC: 545

Los pleitos de Ingalaterra EDC: 545

El pradoso aragones DC2: 238

El príncipe despeñado DC2: 238

El príncipe inocente DC2: 238

El príncipe melancólico DC2: 238

Reduán's Son [El hijo de Reduán] EDC: 545

El rey sin reino see The King Without a Kingdom

El robo de Dina DC2: 238

Rome Burned [Roma abrasada] EDC: 546

Santiago el verde DC2: 239

The Sheep Well [Fuenteovejuna] DC2: 235-236; EDC: 541-542; LCAB: 183; Ma: 2208-2209

The Siege of Santa Fé [El cerco de Santa Fé] EDC: 546

Sir Miracle Comes a Cropper [El caballero del milagro] EDC: 546

The Slave of Rome [El esclavo de Roma] EDC: 546

Star of Seville [Estrella de Sevilla] DC2: 239; LCAB: 183

Triunfo de la humildad DC2: 239

The True Lover [El verdadero amante] DC2: 239; EDC: 546

The Valencian Widow [La viuda valenciana] EDC: 546

La vida de San Pedro Nolasco see The Life of St. Peter Nolasco

El villano en su rincón see The King and the Farmer

The Waters of Madrid [El acero de Madrid] EDC: 546

What Must Be, Must Be [Lo que ha de ser] EDC: 546

The Witty Sayings of Matico [Los donaires de Matico] EDC: 546

LOPEZ, Sabatino
General MD: 186; Po: 2367

LOPEZ ALBUJAR, Enrique
"El campeon de la muerte" Wa: 478
"El licenciado Aponte" Wa: 478

LOPEZ ANGLADA, Luis
General Po: 2367

LOPEZ DE HARO, Rafael
General Po: 2367

LOPEZ DE SAA, Leopoldo
General Po: 2368

LOPEZ DE UBEDA, Francisco
La picara Justina [The Rogue Justina] Fi: 224; Ke: 209

LOPEZ PANCHECO, Jesus
Central electrica Fi: 224

LOPEZ RUBIO, José
General Br: 389
Alberto Br: 389; Po: 2368
Los manos son inocentes Po: 2368

LOPEZ VELARDE, Ramón
General LCAB: 113
"Novedad de la Patria" Po: 2368
"Suave Patria" Po: 2368

LOPEZ Y FUENTES, Gregorio
General Po: 2368-2369

Lorca, Federico García see GARCIA LORCA, Federico

LORD, James, and Marguerite DURAS
The Beast in the Jungle ADC:

223
LORD, Tracy
The Philadelphia Story Br:
390
LORDE, André
General BAW: 500
LOREDANO, Giovanni Francesco
La Dianea Fi: 267
LORENZINI, Carlo
Pinocchio Ke: 244
LORENZO, Pedro de
General Po: 2369
LORTZ, Richard
Voices ADC: 223
LOTI, Pierre
Au Maroc Fi: 104
Aziyadé Fi: 104
A Common Soldier Ke: 105
The Disenchanted Fi: 104;
Ke: 105
Fantôme d'Orient Fi: 104
Fleurs d'ennui Fi: 104
Madame Chrysanthemum Fi:
104; Ke: 105
Le mariage de Loti Fi:
104-105
Matelot Fi: 105
My Brother Yves Fi: 105;
Ke: 105
Pêcheur d'islande Fi: 105;
Ke: 105
Ramuntcho Fi: 105; Ke:
105
Le roman d'un Spahi Fi:
105; Ke: 105
LOUŸS, Pierre
The Girl and the Puppet Br:
390
LOVECRAFT, Howard Phillips
General ASF: 371-372;
LCAB: 114; Po: 2369
"At the Mountains of Mad-
ness" ASF: 370; WaS1:
132
"The Call of Cthulhu" ASF:
370; Wa: 478; WaS1: 132
"The Colour of Outer Space"
WaS1: 133
"Dagon" WaS1: 133
"Dreams in the Witch House"
ASF: 370; WaS1: 133
"The Dunwich Horror" ASF:
370; WaS1: 133
"The Festival" ASF: 370
"The Haunter of the Dark"
ASF: 370; WaS1: 133

"He" WaS1: 133
"The Horror at Red Hook" ASF:
370; WaS1: 133
"The Hound" ASF: 370
"The Lair of the Star-Spawn"
ASF: 370
"The Music of Erich Zann"
SFC: 137; Wa: 478
"The Nameless City" ASF:
370; WaS1: 133
"The Other Gods" WaS1: 133
"The Outsider" ASF: 371;
WaS1: 133
"Pickman's Model" WaS1: 133
"The Picture in the House"
WaS1: 133
"Polaris" ASF: 371; WaS1:
133
"The Rats in the Walls" ASF:
371; WaS1: 133
"The Shadow Out of Time"
ASF: 371; WaS1: 133
"The Shadow Over Innsmouth"
ASF: 371; WaS1: 133
"The Shunned House" ASF:
371; WaS1: 133
"The Statement of Randolph
Carter" ASF: 371
"The Temple" WaS1: 134
"The Terrible Old Man" ASF:
371
"The Thing on the Doorstep"
ASF: 371; WaS1: 134
"Through the Gates of the Sil-
ver Key" ASF: 371; WaS1:
134
"The Tomb" WaS1: 134
"The Whisperer in Darkness"
ASF: 371; WaS1: 134
LOVELACE, Earl
General WIL: 77-78
The Schoolmaster WIL: 78-79
While Gods Are Falling WIL:
78
LOVELACE, Richard
General Ba: 87-88; ICBAP:
79; Ma: 1224-1225
"Advice to my best Brother.
Coll: Francis Lovelace"
ICBAP: 80; PE: 287
"Ant" PE: 287
"La Bella Bona-Roba" LCAB:
114; PE: 288
"A Black Patch on Lucasta's
Face" PE: 287
"Cupid Far Gone" PE: 287

"Elinda's Grove" PE: 287
"The Falcon" Ba: 87; PE: 287
"The Grasshopper" Ba: 87-88; ICBAP: 80; PE: 287-288
"Gratiana Dancing and Singing" PE: 288
"Loose Saraband" Ba: 87
"Mock-Song" Ba: 88
"The Scrutinie" Ba: 87; PE: 288
"The Snayle" Ba: 88; ICBAP: 80; PE: 288
"Song: No, No, Fair Heretic. It Needs Must Be" PE: 288
"Song: To Amarantha, that she would dishevell her haire" PE: 288
"To Althea, from Prison" PE: 288
"To Lucasta" Ba: 88; PE: 288
"To My Dear Friend Mr. E.R." PE: 288
The Vintage to the Dungeon Ba: 88

LOVELICH, Henry
"Merlin" OMEP: 273

LOVELL, George William
General EDT: 213
The Wife's Secret DC1: 118

LOVER, Samuel
General BN: 73

LOWBURY, Edward
General ICBAP: 80; Po: 2369-2370

LOWELL, Amy
General ALL: 169; Po: 2370
"A Fairy Tale" ICBAP: 80
"The Hammers" ICBAP: 80
"Meeting-House Hill" PE: 288
"Night Clouds" PE: 289
"The Overgrown Pasture" ICBAP: 80
"Patterns" ICBAP: 80; PE: 289
"Sunshine" PE: 289

LOWELL, James Russell
General ALL: 170-171; Cla: 62-65; LCAB: 114
"Agassiz" PE: 289
"Auspex" PE: 289

The Biglow Papers Cla: 63-64; Ma: 1226
"The Cathedral" PE: 289
"The Courtin'" PE: 289
"A Fable for Critics" ICBAP: 80; Ma: 1226-1227
"Fitz Adam's Story" PE: 289
"Ode Recited at the Harvard Commemoration" Cla: 62; LCAB: 114; PE: 289
"To the Dandelion" PE: 289
"Washers of the Shroud" Cla: 62

LOWELL, Robert
General ALL: 171-174; ICBAP: 80; LCAB: 114; MDAE: 317-319; MP: 60-62; Po: 2370-2378
"Adam and Eve" PE: 289
"After Surprising Conversions" PE: 289
"As a Plane Tree by the Water" PE: 289
"At the Indian Killer's Grave" PE: 290
Benito Cereno see also The Old Glory ADC: 224; MDAE: 317-319; Po: 2379
"Between the Porch and the Altar" PE: 290
"Beyond the Alps" PE: 290; Po: 2379
"Caligula" PE: 290
"Central Park" Po: 2379
"Children of Light" PE: 290
"Christmas Eve Under Hooker's Statue" ICBAP: 80
"Colloquy in Black Rock" PE: 290
"Commander Lowell 1887-1950" PE: 290
"Dea Roma" Po: 2379
"The Dead in Europe" ICBAP: 81
"The Death of the Sheriff" ICBAP: 81; PE: 290
"The Dolphin" PE: 290
"The Drinker" PE: 290
"Dunbarton" PE: 290
"During Fever" PE: 291
Endicott and the Red Cross see also The Old Glory ADC: 224; Br: 390; MDAE: 318
"The Exile's Return" ICBAP: 81; PE: 291

"Ezra Pound" PE: 291
"Fall Weekend at Milgate"
    PE: 291
"Father's Bedroom" PE: 291
"The First Sunday in Lent"
    ICBAP: 81; PE: 291
"Fishnet" PE: 291
"For Sale" PE: 291
"For the Union Dead" ICBAP:
    81; Ma: 1228-1229; MP:
    62; PE: 291; Po: 2379-
    2380
"Grandparents" PE: 291
"Hawthorne" PE: 291; Po:
    2380-2381
"High Blood" PE: 291
"Home After Three Months
    Away" PE: 292
Imitations Ma: 1229-1230;
    MDAE: 318; Po: 2381
"In Memory of Arthur Win-
    slow" PE: 292
"July in Washington" PE:
    292
Land of Unlikeness Po:
    2372
Life Studies Ma: 1230-1231;
    Po: 2371, 2373
Lord Weary's Castle Ma:
    1231-1232; Po: 2371-2372,
    2381-2382
"Man and Wife" PE: 292; Po:
    2382
"Mary Winslow" ICBAP: 81;
    PE: 292; Po: 2382
"Memories of West Street and
    Lepke" PE: 292
"The Mills of the Kavanaughs"
    ICBAP: 81; Po: 2383
"Mr. Edwards and the Spider"
    PE: 292
"Mother Marie Therese" PE:
    292
My Kinsman, Major Molineux
    see also The Old Glory
    Br: 390; MDAE: 317
"My Last Afternoon with Uncle
    Devereux Winslow" ICBAP:
    81; PE: 293; Po: 2383
"Napoleon Crosses the Bere-
    zina" PE: 292
"Near the Ocean" Ma: 1232-
    1233; PE: 292; Po:
    2383-2384
"The Neo-Classical Urn" PE:
    293

"Nostaligie de la Boue" PE:
    293
Notebook 1967-1968 Ma: 1233;
    Po: 2384
The Old Glory [three plays:
    Endicott and the Red Cross,
    My Kinsman, Major Molineux,
    and Benito Cereno] ADC:
    224-225; Br: 390; Ma: 1234;
    MDAE: 317-319; Po: 2384
Phaedra MDAE: 317-319; Po:
    2384
"A Prayer for My Grandfather
    to Our Lady" PE: 293
Prometheus Bound ADC: 225;
    MDAE: 317-318; Po: 2385
"The Public Garden" PE: 293;
    Po: 2385
"The Quaker Graveyard in Nan-
    tucket" ICBAP: 81; PE:
    293; Po: 2385
"Sailing Home from Rapallo" PE:
    293
"1790" Po: 2385-2386
"Skunk Hour" ICBAP: 81;
    LCAB: 114; MP: 61; PE:
    293
"The Slough of Despond" PE:
    293
"Soft Wood" PE: 293
"'Sunthin' in the Pastoral Line"
    PE: 293
"Terminal Days at Beverly
    Farms" PE: 294
"To Speak of Woe That Is in
    Marriage" PE: 294
"Ulysses and Circe" PE: 294
"Vanity of Human Wishes" Po:
    2386
"Waking Early Sunday Morning"
    ICBAP: 81
"Waking in the Blue" PE: 294
"Washers of the Shroud"
    ICBAP: 81; PE: 294
"Where the Rainbow Ends" PE:
    294
You Knocked Yourself Out
    [adaptation of UNGARETTI's
    Tu ti spezzasti] Po: 2373
LOWENFELS, Walter
    General ICBAP: 81; Po: 2386
LOWENSTEIN, Daniel Casper von
    Agrippina DC2: 242
    Cleopatra DC2: 242
    Epicharis DC2: 242
    Ibrahim Bassa DC2: 242

Sophonisbe DC2: 242-243
LOWRY, Malcolm
General CN: 326; Po: 2386-
2390
"The Bravest Boat" Wa:
478; WaS1: 134
"The Bulls of the Resurrec-
tion" Wa: 478
Dark as the Grave Wherein
My Friend Is Laid ENES1:
155; ENES2: 165-166;
Ma: 1235; Po: 2390-2391
"Economic Conference, 1934"
Wa: 478
"Elephant and Colosseum"
Wa: 478-479; WaS1: 134
"Enter One in Sumptuous
Armor" Wa: 479
"The Forest Path to the
Spring" Po: 2388; Wa:
479; WaS1: 134
"Ghostkeeper" Wa: 479
"Gin and Goldenrod" Wa:
479; WaS1: 134
Hear Us O Lord from Heaven
Thy Dwelling Place Ma:
1235-1236
"Hotel Room in Chartres"
Wa: 479
"In Le Havre" Wa: 479
"The Last Address" Wa:
479
Lunar Caustic ENES1: 155;
ENES2: 166; Po: 2391;
Wa: 479
October Ferry to Gabriola
ENES1: 155; ENES2:
166
"On Board the West Hard-
away" Wa: 479
"Present Estate of Pompeii"
Wa: 479-480; WaS1: 134
"Strange Comfort Afforded by
the Profession" Wa: 480;
WaS1: 134
"Through the Panama" Po:
2388, 2391; Wa: 480;
WaS1: 134
Ultramarine CN: 326;
ENES1: 155; ENES2:
166; Ma: 1236
Under the Volcano CN: 326-
328; ENE: 202-203;
ENES1: 155-156; ENES2:
166-167; Ma: 1236-1238;
Po: 2391-2396

LOY, Mina
General Po: 2396
"Apology of Genius" ICBAP:
82
"Der Blinde Junge" ICBAP:
82
LOZANO, Rafael
General Po: 2396
LOZANO GARCIA, Lazaro, and
LOZANO GARCIA, Carlos
General Br: 390
LU HSÜN [LU Xun, also CHOU
Shu-jên]
"Benediction" WaS1: 134
"Brothers" WaS1: 134
"Diary of a Madman" WaS1:
134-135
"Divorce" WaS1: 135
"Dragon Boat Festival" WaS1:
135
"A Happy Family" WaS1: 135
"In a Restaurant" WaS1: 135
"K'ung I-chi" WaS1: 135
"Medicine" WaS1: 135
"The New Year's Sacrifice"
WaS1: 135
"Remorse" WaS1: 135
"Soap" WaS1: 135
"Storm in a Teacup" Wa: 480;
WaS1: 135
"The True Story of Ah Q"
WaS1: 135
"Upstairs in the Wineshop"
WaS1: 135
"A Warning to the People"
WaS1: 135
"The White Light" Wa: 480;
WaS1: 135
LUBBOCK, Percy
General Po: 2396
LUBIN, Armen
General Po: 2397
LUCA DE TENA, Juan Ignacio
General Po: 2398
Do lo pintado a lo vivo DC2:
352
Quien soy yo? DC2: 352
LUCAS, Curtis
General BAF: 196; BAW:
501
Flour Is Dusty BAF: 196
LUCAS, Edward Verrall
General TA: 210
LUCAS, Frank Lawrence
Land's End Br: 390
LUCAS, Hippolyte

Rachel DC2: 243
Luce, Clare Boothe see
    BOOTHE, Clare
LUCE, G.H.
    "Climb Cloud, and Pencil
        All the Blue" PE: 294
LUCE, William
    The Belle of Amherst ADC:
        226
LUCIAN
    General Ma: 1239
LUCIE-SMITH, Edward
    General WIL: 79
    Confessions and Histories
        WIL: 79-80
    "Rock-Shooting at Sunset"
        PE: 408
    Towards Silence WIL: 80
    A Tropical Childhood WIL:
        79
LUCO CRUCHAGO, German
    General Br: 391
    La Viuda de Apablaza Br:
        391
LUCRETIUS
    De rerum natura Ma: 1240-
        1241
LUDLAM, Charles
    General MDAE: 320
    Camille: A Tearjearker
        ADC: 226
    Caprice ADC: 226
    Conquest of the Universe
        ADC: 227
    Eunuchs of the Forbidden City
        ADC: 227
    Der Ring Gott Farblonjet
        ADC: 227
LUDWIG, Jack
    General JW: 344; Po: 2398
    Confusions Po: 2398
    "Requiem for Bibul" Po:
        2398
    "A Woman of Her Age" Po:
        2398
LUDWIG, Otto
    Aus dem Regen in die Traufe
        Fi: 358; Ke: 303
    Between Heaven and Earth
        [Zwischen Himmel und
        Erde] Fi: 359; Ke: 303;
        Wa: 480
    Die Buschnovelle Ke: 303
    Die Emanzipation der Domes-
        tiken Ke: 303
    Der Erbförster DC2: 243;

Wa: 480
    Das Hausgesinde Ke: 303
    Die Heiteretei Fi: 358; Ke:
        303-304
    Maria Fi: 358-359; Ke: 304
    Die Wahrhaftige Geschichte von
        den Drei Wünschen Ke: 304
    Zwischen Himmel und Erde see
        Between Heaven and Earth
LUGONES, Leopoldo
    General Po: 2398-2399
LUKACS, Georg
    General Po: 2399-2401
    L'ame et les formes Po: 2399
    The Meaning of Contemporary
        Realism Po: 2401
    Studies in European Realism
        Po: 2401
LUKE, Peter
    General MDAE: 321
    Hadrian the Seventh MDAE:
        321
LUKIN, Nikolai
    The Fate of the Discovery Ke:
        421
LUKIN, V.I.
    Scepetil'nik DC2: 243
LUMMENAEUS, Jacobus
    Amnon DC2: 243
LUMPKIN, Grace
    "White Man" Wa: 480
LUNACHARSKI, Anatol
    Faust and the City DC2: 243
LUNDKVIST, Artur
    General Po: 2402
LUPSET, Thomas
    A Compendious and a Very
        Fruteful Treatyse,
        Teachynge the Waye of
        Dyenge Well Hen: 25-26
LUPTON, Thomas
    All for Money DC1: 118
LUS, Peter
    "My Heart Is as Black as the
        Soil of This Country" Wa:
        480
Lusin see LU Hsün [CHOU, Shu-
    jên]
LUSKA, Sidney
    General JW: 254
LUTHULI, Albert John Mvumbi
    General BALE: 327
LUTYENS, David Bulwer
    Mary Stuart Po: 2402
LUZI, Mario
    General Po: 2402

LVOV, S.
  Save Our Souls Ke: 421
LYASHKO, N.
  The Blast Furnace Ke: 421
  The Breath of a Dove Ke:
    421
  "The Rainbow" Wa: 481
  "The Song of the Chains"
    Wa: 481
LYDGATE, John
  General OMEP: 392
  The Dance of Death OMEP:
    393
  Siege of Thebes OMEP:
    394-395
LYLY, John
  General ED: 282-284; ERP:
    289-320; PS: 126-131,
    136, 140-142; SC: 70;
    TSD: 71-72
  Alexander, Campaspe and
    Diogenes DC1: 118-119;
    EDC: 319
  Campaspe Ma: 1242; PS:
    133-134, 142
  "Cupid and Campaspe" PE:
    294
  Endymion, the Man in the
    Moon DC1: 119; ED:
    282-283; EDC: 319-320;
    Ma: 1242-1243; PS: 132;
    TSD: 71-72
  Euphues ERP: 289-320;
    Hen: 156; SC: 70
  Euphues and His England
    see also Euphues EN:
    95; Ma: 1243-1244
  Euphues: The Anatomy of
    Wit see also Euphues
    ED: 284; EN: 94-95;
    ENES1: 156; ENES2: 167;
    Ma: 1243-1244
  Galathea EDC: 320; PS:
    134-135
  Love's Metamorphosis DC1:
    119; EDC: 320; PS:
    132-133; TSD: 71
  Midas EDC: 320; PS: 135;
    TSD: 71
  Mother Bombie EDC: 320;
    PS: 135
  Pappe with an Hatchet Hen:
    104
  Sapho and Phao EDC: 320-
    321; PS: 134; TSD: 71
  Woman in the Moon EDC:

321; PS: 135
LYNCH, Benito
  El inglés de los güesos Po:
    2403
LYON, Harris Merton
  General ASF: 372; Po: 2403-
    2404
  "In the Black-and-Tan" Wa:
    481
  "The Man with the Broken
    Fingers" ASF: 372; Wa:
    481
  "The Riding Beggar" ASF:
    372; Wa: 481
  "Scarlet and White" ASF: 372
  "The 2000th Christmas" WaS1:
    136
  "The Weaver Who Clad the
    Summer" Wa: 481
LYON, Kate
  "Lorraine's Last Voyage" ASF:
    372
LYTLE, Andrew Nelson
  General ASF: 373; CN: 328;
    Po: 2404
  "Alchemy" ASF: 373; Po:
    2404; Wa: 481
  At the Moon's End CN: 328
  The Hero with the Private Parts
    Po: 2404
  "The Hind Tit" ASF: 373
  "Jerico, Jerico, Jerico" ASF:
    373; Po: 2405; Wa: 481
  The Long Night CN: 328; Po:
    2405
  "The Mahagony Frame" ASF:
    373; Po: 2405; Wa: 481
  "Mister McGregor" ASF: 373;
    Po: 2405-2406; Wa: 481
  A Name for Evil CN: 328; Po:
    2406
  The Velvet Horn AN: 177;
    CN: 328-329; Po: 2406-
    2407
LYTTELTON, George, Lord
  General EC: 98
Lytton, Edward George Bulwer
    Lytton see BULWER-
    LYTTON, Edward George
Lytton, Edward Robert Bulwer-
    Lytton see BULWER-
    LYTTON, Edward Robert

M

MABBE, James
   General ERP: 322-323;
      LJCD: 248
MABBE, James [translator]
   The Rogue, or the Life of
      Guzman de Alfarache by
      Mateo ALEMAN ERP:
      322-323
   Exemplary Novels by Miguel
      de CERVANTES SAAVEDRA
      ERP: 322-323
MABLEY, Edward
   Glad Tidings ADC: 227
   _____ and Leonard MIMS
      Temper the Wind DC1: 119
McALMON, Robert
   General ASF: 374; Po:
      2409
   "Distinguished Air" ASF:
      373
   "The Lodging House" ASF:
      373
   "Miss Knight" ASF: 373
MacARDLE, Dorothy
   The Old Man Br: 391
MACAULAY, Rose
   General BN2: 81; Ri2:
      193-197; Po: 2409-2410;
      Sch: 223; TA: 211
   Abbots Verney ENES1: 156
   And No Man's Wit ENES1:
      156
   Crewe Train ENES1: 156;
      Ri2: 193
   Dangerous Ages ENES1:
      156; Ri2: 194-195
   The Furnace ENES1: 156
   Going Abroad ENES1: 156;
      Po: 2410; Ri2: 193
   The Lee Shore ENES1: 156;
      Ri2: 195
   The Making of a Bigot
      ENES1: 157
   "The Mind Is Its Own Place"
      Wa: 482
   Orphan Island ENES1: 157;
      Ri2: 196
   Potterism ENES1: 157; Ri2:
      195-196
   They Were Defeated ENES1:
      157; Ri2: 197
   Told by an Idiot ENES1:
      157; Po: 2410; Ri2: 194-
      196; TA: 211

   The Towers of Trebizond
      ENES1: 157; Po: 2410; Ri2:
      193, 195-196
   Two Blind Countries Ri2: 196
   Views and Vagabonds ENES1:
      157; Po: 2411; Ri2: 193,
      195
   What Not Ri2: 195
   The World My Wilderness
      ENES1: 157; Ri2: 195
MACAULAY, Thomas Babington
   General VP: 49-50
   The History of England from the
      Accession of James the
      Second Ma: 1245-1246
MACAULEY, Robie
   The Disguises of Love AN:
      177
   "The Invaders" SFC: 138; Wa:
      482
MacBETH, George
   General Ai: 330-331; ICBAP:
      82
MacBETH, Robert
   General AAPD: 391; BAP:
      136; BAW: 504; MBA: 141
   A Black Ritual MBA: 141
MacCAIG, Norman
   General Ai: 294
   "Celtic Cross" PE: 294
   "Go-Between" PE: 294
   "Lark in the Air" PE: 294
McCALL, James Edward
   General BAW: 505
MacCARTHY, John Bernard
   General Br: 391
   Kinship Br: 391
McCARTHY, Mary
   General ASF: 375; CFAE:
      219-220; CN: 329; LCAB:
      115; Ne: 71; Po: 2411-2412
   "Artists in Uniform" ASF:
      374; Wa: 482
   Birds of America Ma: 1247
   A Charmed Life AN: 180;
      CN: 329-330; Ma: 1247-
      1248; Po: 2412-2413
   "The Cicerone" ASF: 374; Wa:
      482
   "The Company Is Not Respon-
      sible" ASF: 374; Wa: 482
   The Company She Keeps AN:
      180; CN: 330; Ma: 1248
   "Cruel and Barbarous Treat-
      ment" ASF: 374; Wa: 482
   "The Friend of the Family"

Wa: 482

"Genial Host" Wa: 482

"Ghostly Father, I Confess"
ASF: 374; Wa: 482

The Group CFAE: 220;
CN: 330-331; Ma: 1248-
1249; Ne: 71; Po: 2413

The Groves of Academe CN:
330; Ma: 1249-1250

"The Hounds of Summer"
ASF: 374; Wa: 482

"The Man in the Brooks Brothers Shirt" ASF: 374;
Wa: 483

Memories of a Catholic Childhood Ma: 1250

The Oasis CN: 331; Ma:
1250-1251; Po: 2413-2414

"The Old Men" ASF: 374;
Wa: 483

"Portrait of the Intellectual
as a Yale Man" ASF:
374; Wa: 483

"Rogue's Gallery" Wa: 483

"The Unspoiled Reaction"
ASF: 374; SFC: 154;
Wa: 483

"The Weeds" ASF: 375; Wa:
483

McCLEARY, Dorothy
"Something Jolly" SFC:
154; Wa: 483

McCLELLAN, George Marion
General AAPD: 71; BAF:
197; BAW: 506; LCAB:
115

McCLURE, Michael
General MDAE: 323
The Beard ADC: 227;
MDAE: 323
General Gorgeous ADC:
227
Gorf ADC: 227
The Meatball ADC: 228

McCLUSKEY, John
Look What They Done to My
Song BAF: 197-198

MacCOLLA, Fionn [Thomas
Douglas MacDONALD]
General Ai: 275

McCOMAS, Annette
Are You Still in Your Cabin
Uncle Tom? MBA: 141

McCOMBIE, Thomas
General AL: 286

McCOURT, Edward

General Po: 2414

McCRAE, George Gordon
General AL: 288

McCRAE, Hugh
General Po: 2414

McCRONE, Guy
General Ai: 259

McCULLERS, Carson
General ALL: 174-175; AN:
181; ASF: 377; Br: 391;
CFAE: 221-223; CN: 331-
333; LCAB: 115; MDAE:
324-325; Ne: 72; Po: 2414-
2419

The Ballad of the Sad Café
ALL: 175; AN: 181; ASF:
375-76; Br: 391-393; CN:
333-334; Ma: 1252-1253;
Po: 2418-2420; SFC: 154;
Wa: 483-484; WaS1: 136

Clock Without Hands ALL:
175; CFAE: 222; CN: 334;
Ma: 1253-1254; Ne: 72;
Po: 2419, 2421

"Correspondence" ASF: 376;
Wa: 484

"A Domestic Dilemma" ASF:
376; Wa: 484

The Heart Is a Lonely Hunter
ALL: 175; AN: 181;
CFAE: 222-223; CN: 335-
336; LCAB: 115; Ma: 1254-
1256; Ne: 72; Po: 2421-
2422

"The Jockey" Wa: 484; WaS1:
136

The Member of the Wedding
ADC: 228; ALL: 175; AN:
181; Br: 393-394; CFAE:
223; CN: 336; LCAB: 115;
Ma: 1256-1257; MD: 186;
Ne: 72; Po: 2422-2423

The Mortgaged Heart Ma:
1257-1258

Reflections in a Golden Eye
ALL: 175; AN: 181; CN:
337; LCAB: 115; Ma:
1258-1259

"The Sojourner" ASF: 376;
Wa: 484-485; WaS1: 136

The Square Root of Wonderful
ADC: 228; Br: 394

"Sucker" Wa: 485

"A Tree. A Rock. A Cloud."
ASF: 377; Wa: 485; WaS1:
136

"Wunderkind" ASF: 377
_____, G. WOOD, and Theo-
dore MANN
F. Jasmine Addams ADC:
229
McCULLOCH, Thomas
General ECL: 162
McDermot, T.H. see REDCAM,
Tom
MacDIARMID, Hugh [Christopher
Murray GRIEVE]
General Ai: 244-246; MP:
63-64; Po: 2423-2425
Collected Poems LCAB: 78
A Drunk Man Looks at the
Thistle Ai: 245
"The Eemis Stane" PE: 294
"Ex Vermibus" PE: 295
"Farmer's Death" PE: 295
"Gairmscoile" PE: 295
"In Memoriam James Joyce"
Po: 2425-2426
"Lament for the Great Music"
Po: 2426
"Lourd on My Hert as Winter
Lies" PE: 295
"The Man in the Moon" PE:
295
"Moonstruck" PE: 295
"O Wha's Been Here Afore
Me, Lass" PE: 295
Sangschaw Ai: 245
"The Skeleton of the Future"
PE: 295
"Somersault" PE: 295
"The Spur of Love" PE:
295
"The Watergaw" PE: 295
"Yet Ha'e I Silence Left, the
Croon o' A'" PE: 295
MacDONAGH, Donagh
General Br: 394
Happy as Larry Br: 394
MacDONALD, Cynthia
"Departure" PE: 295
"Inventory" PE: 295
"Objects d'Art" PE: 295
MacDONALD, Dwight
General LCAB: 116
MacDONALD, George
General Ai: 143; BN: 74;
LCAB: 116
Alec Forbes of Howglen
ENES1: 157
"The Broken Swords" Wa:
485

"The Castle" Wa: 485
"Cross Purposes" Wa: 485
"The Cruel Painting" Wa: 485
"The Fairy Fleet" ["The Cara-
soyn"] Wa: 485
"The Giant's Heart" Wa: 485
"The Golden Key" Wa: 485
"A Hidden Life" Wa: 485
Home Again ENES2: 167
"The Light Princess" Wa: 485
Lilith BN: 74; ENES1: 157
Mary Marston ENES2: 167
Phantastes BN: 74; ENES1:
157; ENES2: 167
"The Shadows" Wa: 485
McDONALD, Ian
The Humming-Bird Tree WIL:
80-81
MacDONALD, Ross [Kenneth
MILLAR]
The Galton Case LCAB: 125
McDOUGALL, Colin
Execution Po: 2426
MacDOUGALL, Ursula
"Titty's Dead and Tatty Weeps"
Wa: 486
MacDowell, Katherine Sherwood
see BONNER, Sherwood
McEVOY, Charles Alfred
General Mi: 253
McEVOY, Joseph Patrick
General Po: 2426-2427
God Loves Us Br: 394
MacEWEN, Gwendolyn
General Po: 2427
Julian the Magician Po: 2427
McFARLANE, Basil
General WIL: 81
Jacob and the Angel WIL: 81
Seven Jamaican Poets WIL:
81
McFARLANE, John Ebenezer Clare
General WIL: 81-82
The Challenge of Our Time
WIL: 82
The Magdalen WIL: 82
McFARLANE, R.L.C.
General WIL: 82-83
McFEE, William
General Po: 2427
McGAHERN, John
General Po: 2427
The Barracks ENES2: 167
The Dark ENES2: 167; Po:
2427-2428
The Leavetaking ENES2: 168

McGEE, Thomas D'Arcy
    General ECL: 164-165
MacGILL, Patrick
    The Rat Pit ENES2: 168
MACGILLIVRAY, James Pitten-
        drigh
    General Ai: 197
McGINLEY, Phyllis
    General Po: 2428-2429
McGIRT, James E.
    General AAPD: 72; AAW:
        66; BAF: 198; BAW:
        508-509
McGONAGALL, William
    General Ai: 148-149
McGRATH, John
    General MDAE: 326
    Events While Guarding the
        Bofors Gun ADC: 229
McGRATH, Russell
    Invitation to a Beheading
        ADC: 229
McGRAW, Patricia Washington
    Profile of Four Black Women
        MBA: 142
McGUIRE, Ken
    Grin and Bare It ADC: 229
McGUIRE, Michael
    The Children ADC: 229
MACHA, Karel H.
    "The Evening at Bezdez"
        Wa: 486
    Gypsies Ke: 421
    The Hangman Ke: 421
    "The Krkonoshe Pilgrimage"
        Wa: 486
    "Marinka" Wa: 486
    Pictures from My Life Ke:
        421
MACHADO DE ASSIS, Joaquim
        M.
    "Admiral's Night" Wa: 486
    "Um Almôço" Wa: 486
    "The Animal Game" Wa: 486
    Dom Casmurro Ma: 1260;
        Po: 98
    "Education of a Stuffed Shirt"
        Wa: 486
    Epitaph of a Small Winner
        Ma: 1260
    "Ernesto de Tal" Wa: 486
    "Un Esqueleto" Wa: 486
    "Father Versus Mother" Wa:
        486
    "Final Request" Wa: 486
    "Um Homen Superior" Wa:

    486
    "The Looking Glass" Wa: 486
    "Midnight Mass" Wa: 487
    "El Mulher Préto" Wa: 487
    "Onze Anos Depuis" Wa: 487
    "Pílades e Orestes" Wa: 487
    "The Psychiatrist" Wa: 487
    "The Rod of Justice" Wa: 487
    "The Secret Heart" Wa: 487
    "Sem Olhos" Wa: 487
    "Valério" Wa: 487
    "A Woman's Arms" Wa: 487
MACHADO Y RUIZ, Antonio
    General Po: 2429-2434
    Las adelfas Po: 2432
    "Anoche, cuando dormía" Po:
        2434-2435
    "The Crime Was in Granada"
        see "El crimen fue en
        Granada"
    "El crimen fue en Granada"
        Po: 2434
    De un cancionero apócrifo Po:
        2435
    "Es una tarde cenicienta y mus-
        tia" Po: 2435-2436
    "Fue una clara tarde" Po:
        2436
    "Galerías" Po: 2436
    "Hacia un ocaso radiante" Po:
        2437
    "Hastío" Po: 2437
    El hombre que marió en la guerra
        Po: 2432
    Juan de Mañara Po: 2437-2438
    "Muerte de Abel Martín" Po:
        2438
    Out of an Apocrypha Songbook
        see De un cancionero apó-
        crifo
    "Poema de un día" Po: 2438
    "Por un ventanal, entró la
        lechuza" Po: 2438
    "Siesta" Po: 2439
    Soledades Po: 2439
    "La tierra de Alvargonzáles"
        Po: 2439
MACHADO Y RUIZ, Manuel
    General Po: 2439
    Las adelfas Po: 2439
    El hombre que marió en la guerra
        Po: 2439
    Juan de Mañara DC2: 243;
        Po: 2440
MACHAR, Agnes Maule ["FIDELIS"]
    General ECL: 168

MACHEN, Arthur
  General Po: 2440-2441; TA:
    212-213
  "The Angels of Mons" ["The
    Bowmen"] Po: 2441; Wa:
    487
  The Great God Pan ENES2:
    168
  The Hill of Dreams ENES1:
    157; ENES2: 168
  "The Novel of the White Pow-
    der" Wa: 487
  "The Shining Pyramid" Wa:
    487
  "The White People" Wa: 487
MACHIAVELLI, Nicolo
  Clizia DC2: 244
  Mandragola DC2: 244
  The Prince LCAB: 116; Ma:
    1261-1262
MACIAS PICAVEA, Ricardo
  La tierra de campos Ke:
    209
MacINNES, Colin
  Absolute Beginners ENES2:
    168
  City of Spades ENES2: 168
  Mr. Love and Justice ENES2:
    168
MacIntyre, John see BRAN-
    DANE, John
McIVER, Ray
  General BAP: 136
  God Is a (Guess What?) ADC:
    229; BAP: 137; MBA:
    142
MACK, Lorenz
  "A Ferryman Died" Wa: 488
McKAY, Claude
  General AAPD: 124-125;
    AAW: 66; ASF: 378;
    BAF: 199-201; BAW:
    513-515; HR: 121-130;
    ICBAP: 82; LCAB: 116;
    Po: 2441; WIL: 83-86
  "The Agricultural Show"
    ASF: 378; Wa: 488
  Banana Bottom BAF: 200-
    202; BAW: 515; WIL:
    86
  Banjo BAF: 200, 202; BAW:
    514; HR: 124-125, 127;
    LCAB: 116; WIL: 86
  "Brownskin Blues" Wa: 488;
    WaS1: 136
  Gingertown BAF: 202; HR:
    125
  "The Harlem Dancer" ICBAP:
    82; Po: 2441
  "Highball" ASF: 378; WaS1:
    136
  Home to Harlem BAF: 199,
    202; HR: 122, 127; LCAB:
    116; Po: 2441-2442
  "If We Must Die" HR: 127;
    PE: 296
  "The Little Sheik" WaS1: 136
  A Long Way from Home WIL:
    86
  "Mattie and Her Sweetman"
    WaS1: 136
  "Near-White" Wa: 488; WaS1:
    136
  "The Prince of Porto Rico"
    WaS1: 136
  Selected Poems of Claude McKay
    WIL: 86
  "The Strange Burial of Sue"
    ASF: 378; Wa: 488; WaS1:
    136
  "Truant" ASF: 378; Po:
    2442; Wa: 488
  "When I Pounded the Pavement"
    WaS1: 136
MACKAY, John Henry
  The Anarchists Ke: 304
  Der Freiheitsucher Ke: 304
  Der Schwimmer Fi: 359
Mackay, Mary see CORELLI,
    Marie
MacKAYE, James Morrison Steele
  General AD: 167-169; Lon:
    62
  Hazel Kirke AD: 168
  Paul Kauvar AD: 169
MacKAYE, Percy Wallace
  General Br: 394; Lon: 61;
    MD: 186-187; Po: 2442
  Caliban ADC: 230
  George Washington ADC: 230
  The Scarecrow ADC: 230; Br:
    394; MD: 187
  Wakefield DC1: 119
  Washington, the Man Who Made
    Us DC1: 119
McKEE, John
  Livin Is a Hard Way to Die
    MBA: 142
MACKEN, Walter
  General Br: 395
  The Silent People ENES2: 168
McKENNA, James

General TMIP: 84-85
At Bantry TMIP: 85
The Scatterin' TMIP: 84-86
MACKENZIE, Henry
General Ai: 78; Be: 187-
188; Du: 108-109
The Force of Fashion DC1:
119-120
Julia de Roubigné EN: 95;
ENES2 170
The Man of Feeling Be: 187-
188; Du: 108; EN: 96;
ENES1: 158; ENES2:
170
The Man of the World EN:
96; ENES2: 170
MACKENZIE, Kenneth Ivo
General MAP: 225-226; Po:
2443-2444
Chosen People MAP: 225
Dead Men Rising MAP: 225-
226
The Refuge MAP: 225-226
The Young Desire It MAP:
225
Mackenzie, Seaforth see MAC-
KENZIE, Kenneth Ivo
MACKENZIE, Sir Compton
General Ai: 225-226; Po:
2443; Sch: 224; TA:
215
Carnival ENES2: 168
Extraordinary Women ENES2:
168
Extremes Meet ENES2: 169
The Four Winds of Love Ai:
226; EN: 95; ENES2:
169
Guy and Pauline EN: 95;
ENES2: 169
Keep the Home Guard Turning
ENES2: 169
The Lunatic Republic ENES2:
169
The Monarch of the Glen
ENES2: 169
The Passionate Elopement
ENES2: 169
Poor Relations ENES2: 169
The Red Tapeworm ENES2:
169
Rich Relatives ENES2: 169
Rockets Galore ENES2:
169
Scotch on the Rocks ENES2:
169

Sinister Street EN: 95; ENES2:
169
Sylvia Scarlett EN: 95; ENES2:
169
The Three Couriers ENES2:
169
The Vanity Girl ENES2: 169
Vestal Fire ENES2: 169
Water on the Brain ENES2:
169
MACKENZIE, Sir George
General Ai: 58
McKEON, Richard Peter
General LCAB: 116
MACKEY, William Wellington
General MBA: 142
Behold! Cometh the Vanderkel-
lans ADC: 230; BAP: 138;
MBA: 143
Billy No Name ADC: 230;
BAP: 138
Family Meeting BAP: 138;
MBA: 143
Saga MBA: 143
MACKIE, Alastair
General Ai: 324
MACKIE, Albert David
General Ai: 272
MACKINTOSH, Elizabeth [Gordon
DAVIOT; Josephine TEY]
General Ai: 253
Autumn Fire Po: 2444
Brat Farrar ENES2: 170
The Daughter of Time ENES2:
170
Expensive Halo ENES2: 170
The Franchise Affair ENES2:
170
Kif ENES2: 170
Leith Sands Br: 184
The Man in the Queue ENES2:
170
Miss Pym Disposes ENES2: 170
The Privateer ENES2: 171
Queen of Scots Br: 184
Richard of Bordeaux Br: 184
A Shilling for Candles ENES2:
171
The Singing Sands ENES2:
171
To Love and Be Wise ENES2:
171
MACKLIN, Charles
General EC: 99; Li: 237-238
Convent Garden Theatre DC1:
120

Love a la Mode Li: 238
The Man of the World Li: 238
McLACHLAN, Alexander
  General ECL; 169-170
Maclaren, Ian see WATSON, John
McLAVERTY, Michael
  General Po: 2445
  Call My Brother Back
    ENES2: 171
  "The Game Cock" Wa: 488
  In This Thy Day ENES2: 171
  "Pigeons" Wa: 488
MacLEAN, Alistair
  HMS Ulysses ENES1: 158
MacLEAN, Katherine
  "Pictures Don't Lie" ASF: 378
  "Unhuman Sacrifice" ASF: 378
MACLEAN, Sorley
  General Ai: 295
MacLEISH, Archibald
  General ALL: 175; Br: 395; LCAB: 116; Lon: 36; Ma: 1264-1265; MD: 187; MDAE: 328-330; Po: 2445-2446
  Air Raid MD: 187
  "L'An Trentiesme de Mon Eage" PE: 296
  "... & Forty-Second Street" PE: 296
  "Ars Poetica" ICBAP: 82; PE: 296; Po: 2446
  Conquistador LCAB: 116; Ma: 1263
  "'Dover Beach'--A Note to That Poem" PE: 296; Po: 2446
  "Dr. Sigmund Freud Discovers the Sea Shell" PE: 296
  "Einstein" PE: 296
  "Eleven" PE: 296
  "The End of the World" PE: 296; Po: 2446
  "Epistle to Be Left in the Earth" PE: 296
  The Fall of the City ADC: 230; DC1: 120-121; MD: 187
  "The Hamlet of A. Mac-Leish" ICBAP: 82; PE:

296; Po: 2447
  Herakles ADC: 230; Po: 2447
  "Hypocrite Auteur" PE: 296; Po: 2447
  J.B. ADC: 230-232; Br: 395-396; Lon: 36; Ma: 1263-1264; MD: 187-188; MDAE: 91-92, 191, 329-330; Po: 2448-2454
  "Lines for an Interment" PE: 296
  "Memorial Rain" PE: 297
  "Men" PE: 297
  Nobodaddy Br: 396; DC1: 121-122; MD: 188
  "'Not Marble nor the Gilded Monuments'" PE: 297
  Panic ADC: 232; Br: 396; MD: 188
  "Pony Rock" PE: 297
  Scratch ADC: 232
  "Songs for Eve" ICBAP: 82
  This Music Crept by Me on the Water Br: 396; DC1: 121; MD: 188; MDAE: 329
  "You, Andrew Marvell" PE: 297
McLELLAN, Robert
  General Ai: 283-284
MacLENNAN, Hugh
  General CN: 337-338; Po: 2454-2455
  Barometer Rising CN: 338; Po: 2455
  Each Man's Son CN: 338-339; Po: 2455-2456
  The Precipice CN: 339
  Return of the Sphinx CN: 339
  Two Solitudes CN: 339-340
  The Watch That Ends the Night CN: 340; Po: 2456-2457
Macleod, Fiona see SHARP, William
MACLEOD, Joseph [Adam DRINAN]
  General Ai: 272
MacLEOD, Leroy
  General LCAB: 117
MacLIAMMOIR, Michael
  General Br: 397
  Ill Met by Moonlight Br: 397; EDC: 321
  Where Stars Walk EDC: 321
MCLLVANNEY, William
  General Ai: 337

MAC LOW, Jackson
    General MDAE: 331; Po:
        2457
McLUHAN, Herbert Marshall
    General LCAB: 117
MacMAHON, Bryan
    General Br: 397
    The Honey Spike Br: 397
    Song of the Anvil Br: 397
McMAHON, Frank
    Borstal Boy ADC: 232-233;
        TMIP: 48
MacMANUS, Francis
    General Po: 2457-2458
    Watergate ENES1: 158
MacMECHAN, Archibald
    General Po: 2458
    "The Sarah Stands By" Po:
        2458
McMURTY, Larry
    General Po: 2458
    All My Friends Are Going to
        Be Strangers Ma: 1266
    Horseman, Pass By Ma:
        1266-1267
    The Last Picture Show Ma:
        1267-1268; Po: 2459
    Leaving Cheyenne Ma: 1268
    Moving On Ma: 1268-1269
McNALLY, Terrence
    And Things That Go Bump in
        the Night ADC: 233;
        MDAE: 333
    Bad Habits ADC: 233
    Botticelli ADC: 233
    Next ADC: 233; MDAE:
        333
    Noon ADC: 233
    The Ritz ADC: 233
    Sweet Eros ADC: 234
    Tour ADC: 234
    Where Has Tommy Flowers
        Gone? ADC: 234
    Whiskey ADC: 234
    Witness ADC: 234
        and Giles COOPER
    The Lady of the Camellias
        ADC: 234
MacNAMARA, Brinsley [John
    WELDON]
    General Br: 397; Mi: 254
    The Glorious Uncertainty Br:
        397
    The Land for the People Br:
        397
    Look at the Heffermans! Br:

397
The Master Br: 397
McNEAL, Claude
    Felix ADC: 234
MacNEICE, Louis
    General Br: 398; EP: 172-
        186; Ma: 1271; MP: 64-65;
        Po: 2459-2462
    "Areopagus" Ma: 1270
    Autumn Journal Ma: 1270; PE:
        297; Po: 2460, 2462
    Autumn Sequel Po: 2460, 2462
    Blind Fireworks Po: 2463
    Christopher Columbus DC1:
        122
    The Dark Tower DC1: 122;
        MDAE: 486
    "Eclogue from Iceland" PE:
        297
    "Entirely" PE: 297
    "Explorations" EP: 183
    "Leaving Barra" PE: 297
    "Meeting Point" PE: 297
    "The Pale Panther" MP: 65;
        PE: 297
    "Perseus" ICBAP: 82; Ma:
        1270-1271; PE: 297; Po:
        2463
    "Prayer Before Birth" Ma:
        1271; PE: 297
    "The Riddle" ICBAP: 82; PE:
        298; Po: 2463
    "Round the Corner" Po: 2463
    "Snow" EP: 174, 176; Ma:
        1272; PE: 298; Po: 2464
    "The Streets of Laredo" PE:
        298
    "The Stygian Banks" Ma:
        1272
    "The Sunlight on the Garden"
        PE: 298
    "Les Sylphides" PE: 297
    Ten Burnt Offerings EP: 175
    "These Days Are Misty" PE:
        298
    Visitations Ma: 1272
    "Western Landscape" PE: 298
    "You Who Will Soon Be Unrecap-
        turable" PE: 298
McNEILE, Herman Cyril
    Bulldog Drummond ENES2: 171
McNEILL, Anthony
    General WIL: 87
    Hello Ungod WIL: 88
    Reel from "The Life Movie" WIL:
        88

Seven Jamaican Poets WIL:
87
McNEILL, Janet
A Child in the House ENES1:
158
The Maiden Dinosaur ENES1:
158; ENES2: 171
The Small Widow ENES2:
171
Talk to Me ENES1: 158;
ENES2: 171
McNEILLY, Wilfred Glassford
The Green Grassy Slopes
ENES2: 171
McNULTY, Matthew Edward
General Po: 2465
The Lord Mayor Br: 398
MacORLAN, Pierre
General Po: 2465
MACPHERSON, Ian
General Ai: 274
MACPHERSON, James
General Ai: 74; EC: 99;
Me: 272-275
Fragments of Ancient Poetry,
Collected in the High-
lands of Scotland Me:
272-273
The Poems of Ossian EC:
99; Me: 272-275
McPHERSON, James Alan
General BAF: 203
"Gold Coast" ASF: 378;
Wa: 488; WaS1: 136
"Hue and Cry" ASF: 379;
Wa: 488
Hue and Cry [Collection]
BAF: 203-204
"A Solo Song: For Doc"
ASF: 379; WaS1: 137
MacPHERSON, Jay
The Boatman Po: 2466
MACRI, Oreste
General Po: 2466
MacSWINEY, Terence
The Revolutionist Br: 398
McTAIR, Roger
General WIL: 88
MACU, Ridgeway E.
General BALE: 327
MADACH, Imre
The Tragedy of Man DC2:
244-245; Po: 17-18
MADARIAGA, Salvador de
Guía del lector Po: 2466
El enemigo de Dios Ke:

209; Po: 2466
MADDOX, Gloria D.
Rare Cut Glass MBA: 143
MADDY, Pat [ABISODU; AMADOU]
General BALE: 327
MADISON, Bishop James
General AP: 583
MADISON, James
General AP: 411-417; Da:
73-74
The Federalist AP: 412-417;
Da: 73
MADSEN, Svend Age
"Here" WaS1: 137
Maestro Solnes see PLANCHART,
Julio
MAETERLINCK, Maurice
General Br: 398-399; MD:
188-190; Po: 2467-2468
L'Abbe-Setubal see Father
Setubal
Aglavaine and Selysette Br:
399-400; DC2: 245; EDC:
321; MD: 190
Alladine and Palomides Br:
400; EDC: 321; MD: 190
Ariadne and Bluebeard; or The
Useless Deliverance [Blue-
beard and Aryan; Ariane et
Barbebleu] Br: 401; EDC:
321; MD: 190
The Betrothal [Les fiançailles]
Br: 400; EDC: 321; MD:
190
The Blind [Les aveugles] Br:
400; EDC: 322; MD: 190
The Blue Bird [L'oiseau bleu]
Br: 400-401; DC2: 245;
EDC: 322; MD: 190-191
The Burgomaster of Stilemonde
[Le Bourgmestre de Stil-
monde] Br: 401; EDC:
322
The Death of Tintagiles [La
mort de Tintagiles] Br:
401; EDC: 322; MD: 190
Father Setubal [L'Abbe-Setubal]
EDC: 322
Les fiançailles see The Be-
trothal
The Home [Interior; L'interieur]
Br: 401; DC2: 245; EDC:
322; MD: 190
The Intruder [L'intruse] Br:
401; DC2: 245; EDC: 323;
MD: 190

Joyzelle Br: 401-402; EDC:
323; MD: 190

The Last Judgment [Le juge-
ment dernier] EDC:
323

Mary Magdaleine [Marie Mag-
deleine] Br: 402; EDC:
323; MD: 190

Monna Vanna Br: 402;
EDC: 323; MD: 190

La mort de Tintagiles see
The Death of Tintagiles

L'oiseau bleu see The Blue
Bird

Pelléas and Mélisande
[Pelléas et Mélisande]
Br: 402-403; DC2: 245-
246; EDC: 323-324; MD:
191; Po: 2468-2469

The Power of the Dead [La
puissance des morts] EDC:
324

Princess Maleine Br: 403;
DC2: 246; EDC: 324;
MD: 191

The Seven Princesses [Les
sept princesses] Br:
403; EDC: 324; MD: 191

Sister Béatrice [Soeur
Beatrice] Br: 403; EDC:
324; MD: 191

Treasure of the Humble DC2:
246

MAEZTU, Ramiro de
General Po: 2469

MAGDALANY, Philip
Criss-Crossing ADC: 234
Section Nine ADC: 235
Watercolor ADC: 235

MAGEE, J.G.
"High Flight" PE: 298

MAGGIORE, Giuseppe
"Seven and a Half" ["Sette
e mezzo"] Po: 2469

MAHABIR, Dennis
The Cutlass Is Not for Killing WIL: 88-89

MAHONY, Francis Sylvester
"The Bells of Shandon" PE:
298

MAHONEY, William
General BAF: 204
Black Jacob BAF: 204-205

Maiakovskii, Vladimir Vladimirovich see MAYAKOVSKY,
Vladimir Vladimirovich

MAIDSTONE, Richard
"The Fifty-First Psalm" PE:
298

MAILER, Norman
General ALL: 175-177; AN:
178; ASF: 379-380; CFAE:
227-231; CN: 340-342; JW:
258; LCAB: 117; MDAE:
334-335; Ne: 68; Po: 2473-
2480
Advertisements for Myself Ma:
1273-1274; Po: 2480-2481
An American Dream CFAE:
231; CN: 342-343; Ma:
1274-1275; Ne: 68; Po:
2481-2483
Armies of the Night Ma: 1275-
1276; Po: 2483
Barbary Shore AN: 177; CN:
344; Ma: 1276-1277
"A Calculus at Heaven" WaS1:
137
Cannibals and Christians Ma:
1277-1278; Ne: 68
The Deer Park ADC: 235;
AN: 177; CN: 344-345;
LCAB: 117; Ma: 1278-1279;
MDAE: 334-335; TMBP: 144
"The Man Who Studied Yoga"
ASF: 379; Wa: 488; WaS1:
137
The Naked and the Dead AN:
177; CFAE: 229; CN: 345-
346; LCAB: 117; Ma: 1279-
1280; Po: 2483-2484
Of a Fire on the Moon Ma:
1280-1281
"The Paper House" ASF: 379
The Presidential Papers Po:
2484-2485
"The Time of Her Time" LCAB:
117; WaS1: 137
"Way Out" ASF: 379
Why Are We in Vietnam? CN:
346-347; Po: 2485

MAILLU, David
General BALE: 328

MAIMAME, J. Arthur
General BALE: 328

MAINE, Charles Eric
Fire Past the Future ENES1:
158

MAINWARING, Daniel
"Fruit Tramp" ASF: 381
One Against the Earth Po:
2485

MAIR, Charles
General ECL: 172-173
MAIRET, Jean
Sophonisbe DC2: 246
MAIS, Roger
General WIL: 89-93
And Most of All Man WIL:
93
Atalanta at Calydon WIL:
93
Black Lightning WIL: 94
Brother Man WIL: 94
The Hills Were Joyful To-
gether WIL: 93-94
The Three Novels of Roger
Mais WIL: 94
MAISTRE, Joseph Marie, comte
de
General LCAB: 117
MAISTRE, Xavier de
"La Jeune Sibérienne" Wa:
489
MAITLAND, Sir Richard
General LCAB: 118
MAJOR, Clarence
General BAF: 205; BAW:
524
All-Night Visitors BAF:
205
No BAF: 205-206
Reflex and Bone Structure
BAF: 206
MAKAL, Mahmut
General Po: 2485
MALAMUD, Bernard
General ALL: 178-179; ASF:
383-385; CFAE: 233-237;
CN: 347-348; JW: 260-
261; LCAB: 118; Ne:
68-69; Po: 2486-2491
"Angel Levine" ASF: 381;
SFC: 138; Wa: 489; WaS1:
137
The Assistant ALL: 178-
179; CFAE: 235-237; CN:
349-350; JW: 261; LCAB:
118; Ma: 1282-1283; Ne:
69; Po: 2486, 2488, 2491-
2493
"Behold the Key" ASF: 381;
Wa: 489; WaS1: 137
"Benefit Performance" ASF:
381; Wa: 489
"The Bill" ASF: 381; Wa:
489
"Black Is My Favorite Color"

ASF: 381; Wa: 489; WaS1:
137
"A Choice of Profession" ASF:
381; Wa: 489-490; WaS1:
137
Dubin's Lives ALL: 178
"The First Seven Years" ASF:
381; Wa: 490; WaS1: 137
The Fixer ALL: 179; CFAE:
235-236; CN: 350-351;
LCAB: 118; Ma: 1283-1284;
Po: 2493-2495
"The German Refugee" ASF:
381; Wa: 490
"The Girl of My Dreams" ASF:
382; Wa: 490; WaS1: 137
"The Glass Blower of Venice"
ASF: 382; Wa: 490; WaS1:
137
"Idiots First" ASF: 382; Ma:
1284; Po: 2495; Wa: 490;
WaS1: 138
"The Jewbird" ASF: 382; Wa:
490; WaS1: 138
"The Lady of the Lake" ASF:
382; Po: 2496; Wa: 490;
WaS1: 138
"The Last Mohican" ASF: 382;
Wa: 490-491; WaS1: 138
"Life Is Better Than Death"
ASF: 382; Wa: 491; WaS1:
138
"The Loan" ASF: 382; Po:
2496; Wa: 491; WaS1: 138
"The Magic Barrel" ASF: 382-
383; Ma: 1284-1285; Wa:
491-492; WaS1: 138
"The Maid's Shoes" ASF: 383;
Wa: 492; WaS1: 138
"The Mourners" ASF: 383;
Wa: 492
"Naked Nude" ASF: 383; Wa:
492; WaS1: 138
The Natural ALL: 178-179;
CFAE: 235, 237; CN: 351-
352; Ma: 1285-1286; Ne:
69; Po: 2496-2497
A New Life ALL: 178-179;
CFAE: 234, 236-237; CN:
352-353; Ma: 1286-1287; Ne:
69; Po: 2488, 2497-2498;
TMAP: 59
Pictures of Fidelman CFAE:
236; Ma: 1287; Po: 2498
"Pictures of the Artist" ASF:
383

"A Pimp's Revenge" ASF:
  383; Wa: 492; WaS1: 138
"The Place Is Different Now"
  Wa: 492
"The Prison" ASF: 383;
  SFC: 138; Wa: 492
"The Silver Crown" ASF:
  383; Wa: 492; WaS1: 138
"Still Life" ASF: 383; Wa:
  492; WaS1: 138
"A Summer's Reading" ASF:
  383; Wa: 492
"Take Pity" ASF: 383; Po:
  2498-2499; Wa: 492-493;
  WaS1: 139
The Tenants Ma: 1288
MALAPARTE, Curzio
  General Po: 2499
  The Skin Ke: 244
MALCOLM X [Malcolm LITTLE]
  General BAW: 525-526
  The Autobiography of Mal-
    colm X BAW: 526
MALECHA, Herbert
  "The Trial" Wa: 493
MALEGUE, Joseph
  Augustin ou le maitre est
    là Ke: 105
MALERBA, Luigi
  Il pataffio Fi: 267
  The Serpent Fi: 267
MALEWSKA, Hanna
  General Po: 2499
MALGONKAR, Manohar
  "Bachcha Lieutenant" Wa:
    493
  "Hush" Wa: 493
  "A Little Sugar--A Little
    Tea" Wa: 493
  "Maggie" Wa: 493
  "A Pinch of Snuff" Wa: 493
  "A Question of Tactics" Wa:
    493
  "The Rise of Kistu" Wa: 493
  "Suleman's Courier" Wa: 493
  "This Is to Recommend" Wa:
    493
  "Top Cat" Wa: 493
  "Two Red Roosters" Wa:
    493
MALIK, Abdul [Delano de
  COTEAU]
  General WIL: 94-95
  Black Up WIL: 95
MALLALIEU, H.B.
  "Lines from Europe" PE:

298
MALLARME, Stéphane
  General LCAB: 118; Ma:
    1290-1291
  The Afternoon of a Faun [L'ap-
    res-midi d'un faune] Ma:
    1289
  Herodiade DC2: 246; Ma:
    1289
  "Igitur" Ma: 1289-1290
  "A Throw of the Dice" [Un coup
    de des"] Ma: 1291-1292
MALLEA, Eduardo
  General LCAB: 118; Po: 2500
  All Green Shall Perish [Todo
    verdor perecerá] Ma: 1293;
    Po: 2502
  La bahía del silencio see The
    Bay of Silence
  The Bay of Silence [La bahía
    del silencio] Ma: 1293; Po:
    2500
  Fiesta in November Ma: 1293-
    1294
  Historia de una pasión argentina
    Po: 2501
  Posesíon Po: 2501
  La sala de espera Po: 2502
  Todo verdor perecerá see All
    Green Shall Perish
MALLESON, Miles
  The Fanatics Br: 403
MALLET, David
  Mustapha Li: 240
MALLET-JORIS, Françoise
  General Po: 2502-2503
  The House of Lies Ke: 106;
    Po: 2502
  Le Jeu du Souterrain Fi: 105
  The Red Room Ke: 106
MALLOCH, George Reston
  General Ai: 213
MALLOCK, William Hurrell
  General BN: 74; TA: 216
  "Chorus from a Tragedy"
    ICBAP: 82
  "Melancholy" ICBAP: 82
  The New Republic BN: 74
  The Old Order Changes ENES1:
    158
MALMBERG, Bertil
  Die Excellenz DC2: 246
MALORY, Sir Thomas
  Le Morte d'Arthur ENE: 203-
    204; ENES1: 159; ENES2:
    171-172; Hen: 149-150;

Ma: 1295-1296

MALRAUX, André
General LCAB: 118; Po:
2503-2514
Antimémoires Po: 2514-2516
La Condition humaine see
Man's Fate
The Conquerors Fi: 105-
106; Ke: 106; Ma: 1297
Days of Wrath [Days of Con-
tempt; Le temps du mépris]
Fi: 106-107; Ke: 106-
107; Ma: 1297-1298; Po:
2519
L'Espoir see Man's Hope
Man's Fate [La Condition
humaine] Fi: 107-108;
Ke: 107-109; Ma: 1298-
1299; Po: 2516-2518
Man's Hope [L'Espoir] Fi:
108-110; Ke: 109-110;
Ma: 1299-1300
The Metamorphosis of the
Gods [La Metamorphose
des Dieux] Po: 2518
Les Noyers de l'Altenburg
see The Walnut Trees of
Altenburg
Paper Moons Fi: 110; Ke:
107
The Royal Way [La Voie
royale] Fi: 110-111; Ke:
110-111; Ma: 1300-1301;
Po: 2520-2521
Le temps du mepris see
Days of Wrath
The Temptation of the West
Fi: 111
The Voices of Silence [Las
Voix du silence] Po:
2521-2522
La Voie royale see The
Royal Way
The Walnut Trees of Alten-
burg [Les Noyers de
l'Altenburg] Fi: 111-112;
Ke: 111-112; Ma: 1301-
1302; Po: 2519

MALTZ, Albert
General ASF: 386
The Black Pit ADC: 235;
Br: 404; DC1: 122
"Good-by" WaS1: 139
"The Happiest Man on Earth"
WaS1: 139
"Man on the Road" Wa: 493;

WaS1: 139
"Incident on a Street Corner"
WaS1: 139
Private Hicks Br: 404
"Season of Celebration" WaS1:
139
"The Way Things Are" WaS1:
139
_____ and George SKLAR
Peace on Earth see also
SKLAR, George and Albert
MALTZ ADC: 235

MALYSKIN, A.
People from the Backwoods
Ke: 421

MAMET, David
General TMAP: 181-182
American Buffalo ADC: 235-
236; TMAP: 183
Dark Pony TMAP: 183
Duck Variations ADC: 236;
TMAP: 183-184
A Life in the Theatre ADC:
236; TMAP: 182, 184, 207
Reunion TMAP: 184
Sexual Perversity in Chicago
ADC: 236; TMAP: 184-185
Water Engine TMAP: 185
The Woods TMAP: 185-186

MAMIN-SIBIRYAK, D.N.
Three Ends Ke: 422

MANDEL, Eli
General JW: 160; Po: 2523
Out of Place JW: 160
Another Time JW: 160

MANDEL, Loring
Advise and Consent ADC:
236-237
Project Immortality ADC: 237

MANDEL'SHTAM, Osip Emel'evich
General Po: 2523-2525
Acmeist Manifesto Po: 2526
"Insomnia" ["Bessonnica"]
Po: 2525
Notes Towards a Supreme Fic-
tion [Vos'mistišija] Po:
2526
Tristia Po: 2526

MANDEVILLE, Bernard
General EC: 100
The Fable of the Bees EC:
100

MANDEVILLE, Sir John
Travels Hen: 64

Mandiargues, Pieyre de see
PIEYRE DE MANDIARGUES,

André
MANFRED, Frederick [Feike FEIKEMA]
General AN: 178; CN: 353-354; Po: 2526-2528
Boy Almighty CN: 354
The Brother see also World's Wanderer CN: 354
The Buckskin Man's Tales Po: 2528
The Chokecherry Tree CN: 354
Conquering Horse Po: 2528
The Giant see also World's Wanderer CN: 354
The Golden Bowl CN: 354; Po: 2528
Lord Grizzly CN: 354; Po: 2528-2529
Morning Red CN: 354
The Primitive see also World's Wanderer CN: 354-355
Riders of Judgment CN: 355; Po: 2529
This Is the Year CN: 355
World's Wanderer CN: 355
MANFREDI CANO, Domingo
General Po: 2529
MANGAN, James Clarence
"The Man in the Cloak" Wa: 494
"The Thirty Flasks" Wa: 494
"The Three Rings" Wa: 494
MANGLIS, Yannis
"Benghazi" Wa: 494
"The Boy with the Red Rose" Wa: 494
"Coffin" Wa: 494
"The Diving Suit" Wa: 494
"The Feast of Saint Paraskevi" Wa: 494
"The Fellow Travelers" Wa: 494
"The Forest" Wa: 494
"The Gambler" Wa: 494
"Ghosts" Wa: 494
"Gypsy Wedding" Wa: 494
"Half Moon" Wa: 494
"Maaleche" Wa: 494
"Madalena" Wa: 494
"The Miracle" Wa: 495
"My Friend from Munich" Wa: 495
"The Old Man" Wa: 495

"The Partners" Wa: 495
"The Photographs" Wa: 495
"Revenge" Wa: 495
"The Secret of Captain Antonis the Bear" Wa: 495
"The Sluggard" Wa: 495
"A Strange Fellow" Wa: 495
"The Twins" Wa: 495
"The Wanderer" Wa: 495
"The Wedding" Wa: 495
"When You Fight for Freedom" Wa: 495
MANGUA, Charles
General BALE: 328-329
Son of Woman BALE: 329
A Tail in the Mouth BALE: 328
MANHEIM, Ralph
"The Girl Who Loved Seders" SFC: 138; Wa: 495
MANHOFF, William
The Owl and the Pussycat ADC: 237; Br: 404
MANIFOLD, John
"Fife Tune" PE: 298
MANIFOLD, John Streeter
"Smoko with the Balkans" WaS1: 139
MANKOWITZ, Wolf
General MDAE: 336-337; Po: 2529
The Bespoke Overcoat MDAE: 337
MANLEY, Mary de la Rivière
General Be: 191; Li: 241
The Secret History of Queen Zarah and the Zarazians ENES1: 159
Secret Memoirs and Manners of Several Persons of Quality of Both Sexes from the New Atlantis Be: 191; ENES1: 159
MANN, Heinrich
General MD: 191; Po: 2530-2531
"Abdanken" Wa: 495
Die Arme Tonietta MD: 191; Po: 2531
Die Armen Fi: 359; Ke: 304
Der Atem Fi: 359
Auferstehung Ke: 304; Po: 2530; Wa: 496
Die Branzilla Fi: 359; Ke: 304; Po: 2531-2532; Wa: 496

Die Göttinnen Fi: 359; Ke: 304; Po: 2530

The Head Fi: 359; Ke: 304

Henri Quatre Fi: 359-360; Ke: 304; Po: 2532-2533

Im Schlaraffenland Fi: 360; Ke: 304; Po: 2532

Kaiserreich Trilogy Po: 2533

Die Kleine Stadt Fi: 360; Po: 2533-2534

Kobes Fi: 360; Ke: 305; Wa: 496

The Little Superman Ke: 305

Madame Legros DC2: 246; EDC: 325; Po: 2534

Pippo Spano Ke: 305; Wa: 496

Professor Unrat Fi: 360

Royal Women Fi: 360

The Small Town Ke: 305

Der Tyrann Ke: 305; Po: 2530; Wa: 496

Der Untertan Fi: 360

"Zola" Po: 2534

MANN, Klaus

General Po: 2535

Anja and Esther Br: 404

"Le Dernier Cri" WaS1: 139

"The Monk" WaS1: 139

"Three Star Hennessy" WaS1: 139

Treffpunkt im Unendlichen Po: 2535

MANN, Leonard

General MAP: 229

A Murder in Sydney MAP: 229; Po: 2535

MANN, Thomas

General LCAB: 119; Po: 2535-2569

"At the Prophet's" SFC: 138; Wa: 496

Der Bajazzo see The Dilettante

"Bashan and I" see "A Man and His Dog"

The Beloved Returns Fi: 361; Ke: 305-306

Betrachtungen eines Unpolitishchen Po: 2573

The Black Swan [Die Betrogene] Ma: 1303; SFC: 138-139; Po: 2573-2574; Wa: 496

The Blood of the Walsungs [Wälsungenblut] Fi: 376; Ke: 306-307; Ma: 1303-1304; 497; WaS1: 140

Buddenbrooks Fi: 361-362; Ke: 306-7; Ma: 1303-1304; Po: 2574-2576

Confessions of Felix Krull, Confidence Man Fi: 367-368; Ke: 307-308; Ma: 1304-1305; Po: 2569-2572

"Death" SFC: 139; Wa: 497

Death in Venice [Der Tod in Venedig] Fi: 362-364; Ke: 308-311; Ma: 1306-1307; Po: 2597-2605; SFC: 139-141; Wa: 497-500; WaS1: 140

The Dilettante [Der Bajazzo] Ke: 311; Po: 2569; SFC: 141; Wa: 500

"The Disillusionment" SFC: 141; Wa: 500

"Disorder and Early Sorrow" SFC: 141; Wa: 500-501; WaS1: 140

Doctor Faustus Fi: 365-367; Ke: 311-314; LCAB: 119; Ma: 1307-1308; Po: 2576-2585

"Das Eisenbahnunglück" see "Railway Accident"

Der Erwählte see The Holy Sinner

"Fallen" ["Gefallen"] Fi: 368; Ke: 314; SFC: 141; Wa: 501; WaS1: 140

"The Fight Between Jappe and Do Escobar" SFC: 142; Wa: 501

Fiorenza Ke: 314

"Friedrich und die grosse Koalition" Po: 2589

"Geist und Kunst" Po: 2589

Die Geschichten Jaakobs Fi: 368; Po: 2589

"Gladius Dei" Fi: 368; Po: 2590; SFC: 142; Wa: 501; WaS1: 140

"A Gleam" SFC: 142; Wa: 501

"Herr und Hund" see "A Man and His Dog"

The Holy Sinner [Der Erwählte] Fi: 368-369; Ke: 314-315; Ma: 1308-1309; Po: 2586-2588

"The Infant Prodigy" Wa:
501-502; WaS1: 140
Joseph and His Brothers
[Joseph und seine Brüder]
Ma: 1309-1310; Po: 2592-
2594
Joseph Novels Fi: 369-370;
Ke: 315-317
Joseph the Provider [Joseph
der Ernährer] Po: 2591-
2592
Königliche Hoheit Fi: 370;
Po: 2594; Wa: 502
"Little Herr Friedemann"
Fi: 370; Ke: 317; SFC:
142; Wa: 502
"Little Lizzy" SFC: 142;
Wa: 502
Lotte in Weimar Po: 2594-
2595
The Magic Mountain [Der
Zauberberg] Fi: 371-374;
Ke: 318-321; LCAB: 119;
Ma: 1310-1311; Po: 2609-
2616
"A Man and His Dog" ["Herr
und Hund"] Ke: 321;
Po: 2590-2591; SFC:
142-143; Wa: 502-503
Mario and the Magician
[Mario und der Zauberer]
Fi: 374; Ke: 321; Ma:
1312; Po: 2595-2596; SFC:
143; Wa: 503-504; WaS1:
140-141
"Meerfahrt mit Don Quijote"
Po: 2596
"Railway Accident" ["Das
Eisenbahnunglück"]
LCAB: 119; SFC: 144;
Po: 2586; Wa: 504
Royal Highness Fi: 374;
Ke: 321-322
"Schwere Stunde" see "A
Weary Hour"
"The Tables of the Law"
SFC: 144; Wa: 504
Theodor Storm Po: 2597
"Tobias Mindernickel" SFC:
144; Wa: 504
Der Tod in Venedig see
Death in Venice
Tonio Kröger Fi: 375;
Ke: 322-323; Ma: 1312-
1314; Po: 2605-2607;
SFC: 144-145; Wa: 504-

505; WaS1: 141
The Transposed Heads [Die Ver-
tauschten Köpfe] Ke: 323;
Po: 2608; SFC: 145-146;
Wa: 505-506
Tristan Fi: 375-376; Ke:
323-324; Po: 2607-2608;
SFC: 146; Wa: 506
Die Vertauschten Köpfe see
The Transposed Heads
Wälsungenblut see The Blood
of the Walsungs
"The Wardrobe" Ke: 324;
SFC: 146; Wa: 506
"The Way to the Churchyard"
SFC: 146; Wa: 506
"A Weary Hour" ["Schwere
Stunde"] Fi: 375; Po:
2597; SFC: 146; Wa: 506-
507
"The Will to Happiness" SFC:
146; Wa: 507; WaS1: 141
Der Zauberberg see The
Magic Mountain
Mannan, Laila see SANCHEZ,
Sonia
MANNERS, J. Hartley
Peg o' My Heart ADC: 237
MANNING, Frederic
General MAP: 230-231
Her Privates We ENES2: 172-
173; MAP: 231; Po: 2616
Manning, Lawrence see PRATT,
Fletcher and Lawrence
MANNING
MANNING, Mary
General Br: 404
Youth's the Season Br: 404
MANNING, Olivia
General CN: 355
The Balkan Trilogy ENES1:
160
Friends and Heroes CN: 355
The Great Fortune CN: 356
The Spoilt City CN: 356
MANNYNG, Robert, of Brunne
"Handlyng Synne" OMEP:
242
MANSFIELD, Katherine [Kathleen
Beauchamp MURRY]
General LCAB: 119; Po:
2616-2619; Ri2: 215-227,
231-232; TA: 233-234
"All Serene" Wa: 507
"The Aloe" see "Prelude"
"The Apple Tree" Wa: 507

"At Lehmann's" Wa: 507;
WaS1: 141
"At the Bay" Ma: 1315; Po:
2619; Ri2: 227; SFC:
147; Wa: 507; WaS1: 141
"Bains Turcs" Wa: 507;
WaS1: 141
"Bank Holiday" WaS1: 141
"The Baron" Wa: 507;
WaS1: 141
"A Birthday" Wa: 507;
WaS1: 141
"Bliss" Ma: 1315-1316;
SFC: 147; Wa: 508
Bliss, and Other Stories Ri2:
217, 223, 225, 228
"The Canary" Wa: 508
"Carnation" WaS1: 141
"The-Child-Who-Was-Tired"
Ri2: 228; SFC: 147; Wa:
508
"The Common Round" SFC:
147; Wa: 508
"A Cup of Tea" SFC: 147;
Wa: 508
"The Daughters of the Late
Colonel" Ri2: 228; SFC:
147-148; Wa: 508-509;
WaS1: 142
"A Dill Pickle" SFC: 148;
Wa: 509
"The Doll's House" Ma:
1316; Ri2: 228; SFC:
148; Wa: 509; WaS1: 142
The Dove's Nest Ri2: 224
"The Education of Audrey"
WaS1: 142
"Die Einsame" WaS1: 142
"The Escape" SFC: 148;
Wa: 509; WaS1: 142
"Feuille d'Album" Wa: 509
"The Fly" Ma: 1316-1317;
Po: 2619-2622; Ri2:
229; SFC: 148; Wa: 509-
510; WaS1: 142
"Frau Brechenmacher Attends
a Wedding" Wa: 510;
WaS1: 142
"Frau Fischer" Wa: 510
"The Garden Party" Ma:
1317-1318; Po: 2623-2624;
Ri2: 217, 230; SFC:
148-149; Wa: 510-511;
WaS1: 142
"Germans at Meat" Wa: 511;
WaS1: 142

"Her First Ball" Po: 2624;
SFC: 149; Wa: 511
"Honeymoon" SFC: 149; Wa:
511
"How Pearl Button Was Kid-
napped" Wa: 511; WaS1:
142
"An Ideal Family" Wa: 511
In a German Pension Ri2: 215,
223
"An Indiscreet Journey" SFC:
149; Wa: 511; WaS1: 142
"Je ne Parle pas Français" Ri2:
230; SFC: 149; Wa: 512;
WaS1: 142
Journal of Katherine Mansfield
Ri2: 217, 231-232
"A Journey to Bruges" Wa:
512
"The Lady's Maid" Wa: 512
"The Life of Ma Parker" Wa:
512
"The Little Governess" Wa:
512
"The Man Without a Tempera-
ment" Po: 2624; Ri2: 231;
SFC: 149; Wa: 512
"Marriage à la Mode" Po:
2624; Ri2: 231; SFC: 149;
Wa: 512; WaS1: 142
"The Mating of Gwendolen" Po:
2624
"Millie" Wa: 512
"Miss Brill" Po: 2625; Ri2:
231; SFC: 149; Wa: 512-
513; WaS1: 142-143
"Mr. and Mrs. Dove" Wa: 513
"Mr. Reginald Peacock's Day"
SFC: 149; Wa: 513
"The Modern Soul" WaS1: 143
The Mystery of Maata Ri2:
232
"New Dresses" Wa: 513; WaS1:
143
"Ole Underwood" Wa: 513
"Pension Séguin" Wa: 513;
WaS1: 143
"Pictures" SFC: 149; Wa:
513; WaS1: 143
"Poison" SFC: 149; Wa: 513
"Prelude" ["The Aloe"] Ma:
1318; Po: 2625; SFC: 149;
Wa: 513; WaS1: 143
"Psychology" SFC: 150; Wa:
513
"Revelations" SFC: 150; Wa:

514

The Scrapbook of Katherine Mansfield LCAB: 119; Ri2: 218, 231

"The Singing Lesson" SFC: 150; Wa: 514; WaS1: 143

"The Sister of the Baroness" WaS1: 143

"Six Years After" WaS1: 143

"Something Childish but Very Natural" SFC: 150; Wa: 514

"Spring Picture" WaS1: 143

"The Stranger" SFC: 150; Wa: 514; WaS1: 143

"A Suburban Fairy Tale" WaS1: 143

"Sun and Moon" Wa: 514; WaS1: 143

"The Swing of the Pendulum" Wa: 514; WaS1: 143

"Taking the Veil" WaS1: 143

"This Flower" WaS1: 143

"The Tiredness of Rosabel" SFC: 150; Wa: 514; WaS1: 144

"A Truthful Adventure" WaS1: 144

"Violet" WaS1: 144

"The Voyage" Wa: 514

"A Wedding" SFC: 150; Wa: 514

"The Wind Blows" SFC: 150; Wa: 514; WaS1: 144

"The Woman at the Store" Wa: 514; WaS1: 144

"The Wrong House" WaS1: 144

"The Young Girl" WaS1: 144

MANSON, Harley
The Green Knight DC1: 122
The Noose-Knot Ballad DC1: 122

MANSOUR, Joyce
General Po: 2626

MANTERO, Manuel
General Po: 2626

MANUEL, Don Juan
"La mujer brava" Wa: 515

MANZONI, Alessandro
The Betrothed Fi: 267-268; Ke: 244-245; Ma: 1319-1320

MAO DUN [MAO TUN or TUNG; also SHEN YEN-PING]
"Autumn Harvest" WaS1: 144
"Autumn in Kuling" WaS1: 144
"Creation" WaS1: 144
"Spring Silkworms" WaS1: 144
"Suicide" WaS1: 144

MAO TSE-TUNG
General Po: 2626-2627

MAPANJE, Jack
General BALE: 329

MARAGALL, Juan
General Po: 2627

MARAI, S.
Divorce in Buda Ke: 422

MARAJ, Jagdip
The Flaming Circle WIL: 95

MARAÑON, Gregorio
General Po: 2628

MARASCO, Robert
Child's Play ADC: 237-238

MARCADE, Eustache de
Passion D'Arras DC2: 246

MARCEAU, Félicien
General Po: 2628
The Egg Br: 404

MARCEL, Gabriel
General Br: 404-405; MD: 191-192; Po: 2628-2633
Ariadne [Le chemin de Crête] Br: 405
La chapelle ardente Br: 405
La coeur de autres Br: 405
Les coeurs avides [La Soif] Br: 405; MD: 192
Le dard Br: 406
L'emissaire Br: 406
Le fanal Br: 406
La grace Br: 406
L'horizon Br: 406
L'iconoclaste Br: 406
A Man of God [Un homme de Dieu] Br: 406; DC2: 247; MD: 192
Mon temps n'est pas le vôtre Br: 407
Le monde cassé Br: 407
Le mort de demain Br: 407
Le quator en la dièse Br: 407
Le regard neuf Br: 407
Rome n'est plus dans Rome Br: 407
Le signe de la croix Br: 407
La soif Br: 408; DC2: 247

MARCH, William [W.E.M. CAMP-
BELL]
General ASF: 387; AN:
178; CN: 356; LCAB:
29; Po: 2633
"Aesop's Last Fable" ASF:
386; WaS1: 144
The Bad Seed AN: 178;
CN: 356; Po: 2633-2634
Come In at the Door CN:
356
Company K CN: 356;
LCAB: 29
"The Dappled Fawn" ASF:
387
"A Haircut in Toulouse"
SFC: 150; Wa: 515
"The Little Wife" ASF: 387;
Po: 2634; SFC: 150;
Wa: 515
The Looking Glass CN: 356
"A Memorial to the Slain"
ASF: 387
"Nine Prisoners" ASF: 387
"Personal Letter" ASF: 387;
SFC: 150; Wa: 515
"A Sum in Addition" SFC:
150; Wa: 515
The Tallons CN: 357
"The Unploughed Patch"
ASF: 387
Marcus Aurelius see AURELIUS
ANTONIUS, Marcus
MARCUS, Frank
General MDAE: 339
Bamboula BAP: 138
Green Room EDC: 325
The Killing of Sister George
EDC: 325
Mrs. Mouse Are You Within?
EDC: 325
MARCUS, Pesach
"Higher and Higher" WaS1:
144
MARGETSON, George Reginald
General BAW: 526-527
MARGUERITE DE NAVARRE
Heptameron Fi: 112
MARIA DE JESUS, Carolina
General Po: 2634
MARIAS, Julián
General Po: 2634
MARIE DE FRANCE
Lais Ma: 1321-1322
MARIN, Juan
"Black Port" WaS1: 145

"A Flight into Mystery" WaS1:
145
"Julian Aranda's Death" WaS1:
145
"Lazarus" WaS1: 145
"The Man at the Funeral" WaS1:
145
"The Man Hunt" WaS1: 145
"Nuptial" WaS1: 145
"Percival Lawrence's Crime"
WaS1: 145
MARINETTI, Francesco T.
General Br: 408
MARISSEL, André
General Po: 2634-2635
MARIVAUX, Pierre
General LCAB: 119
Actors in Good Faith [Les
Acteurs de bonne foi] DC2:
247; EDC: 325
L'Amour et la vérité see
Love and Truth
Annibal see Hannibal
The Argument [La dispute]
EDC: 325
Arlequin, poli par l'amour see
Harlequin Polished by Love
A Case of Mistaken Identity
[La méprise] EDC: 326
A Case of Sincerity EDC:
326
Le chemin de la fortune DC2:
247
The Colony [La colonie] EDC:
326
La commère see The Gossip
La dénouement imprevu see
The Unforeseen Solution
La dispute see The Argument
Double Inconstancy [La double
inconstance] DC2: 247;
EDC: 326
L'école des mères see A
School for Mothers
L'epreuve see The Test
The Faithful Wife [La femme
fidèle] EDC: 326
False Confessions [Les fausses
confidences] DC2: 247-
248; EDC: 326-327
The False Servant [La fausse
suivante] DC2: 248; EDC:
327
A Father, Prudent and Just;
or Crispin the Jolly Rogue
[La père prudent et equit-

able] EDC: 327

Félicie EDC: 327

La femme fidèle see The
The Faithful Wife

The Fop Reformed [Le petit-
maître corrige] EDC:
327

The Game of Love and Chance
[Le jeu de l'amour et du
hasard] EDC: 327

The Gossip [La commère]
EDC: 327

Hannibal [Annibal] EDC:
327

Harlequin Polished by Love
[Arlequin, poli par l'amour]
EDC: 327

L'héritier du village see
The Village Heir

L'heureux strategeme see
The Lucky Strategem

The Inheritance [Le legs]
EDC: 328

The Island of Reason [L'ile
de la raison] EDC: 328

The Island of Slaves [L'ile
des esclaves] EDC: 328

Le jeu de l'amour et du hasard see The Game of
Love and Chance

Joy Unforseen [La joie im-
prévue] EDC: 328

Le legs see The Inheritance

Love and Truth [L'amour et
la verite] EDC: 328

The Lucky Strategem [L'heureux stratagème] EDC:
328

La meprise see A Case of
Mistaken Identity

The Mother as a Confidante
[La mere confidente]
EDC: 328

Oaths All Too Rashly Taken
[Les serments indiscrets]
DC2: 248; EDC: 328

Le paysan parvenu Fi:
112-113; Ke: 112

La père prudent et equitable
see A Father, Prudent
and Just...

Le petit-maître corrige see
The Fop Reformed

Pharsamon Fi: 113

Plutus Triumphant see The
Triumph of Plutus

Le préjugé vaincu see Victory
Over Prejudice

The Prince in Disguise; or, The
Illustrious Imposter [Le
prince travesti; ou L'illustre
aventurier] EDC: 328-329

The Provincial Lady [La provin-
ciale] EDC: 329

La réunion des amours see
Two Kinds of Love Recon-
ciled

A School for Mothers [L'école
des meres] DC2: 247; EDC:
329

Les serments indiscrets see
Oaths All Too Rashly Taken

The Sincere Ones [Les sinceres]
EDC: 329

Surprise of Love [Second Surprise of Love] DC2: 248;
EDC: 329

Télémaque travesti Fi: 113

The Test [L'epreuve] DC2:
247; EDC: 329

The Triumph of Love [Le triomphe de l'amour] EDC:
329

The Triumph of Plutus [Le
triomphe de Plutus; Plutus
Triumphant] EDC: 328-329

Two Kinds of Love Reconciled
[La réunion des amours]
EDC: 329

The Unforeseen Solution [La
dénouement imprévu] EDC:
329

Victory Over Prejudice [Le
préjugé vaincu] EDC: 329

La vie de Marianne Fi: 113-
114; Ke: 112

The Village Heir [L'héritier du
village] EDC: 330

MARKANDAYA, Kamala
General Ma: 1323; Po: 2635

MARKFIELD, Wallace
General JW: 263

MARKHAM, Edwin
General ICBAP: 83; LCAB:
120; Po: 2635
"The Man with the Hoe" PE:
298

MARKHAM, Gervase
General ERP: 324; NI: 334-
335
The English Arcadia ERP:
324

MARKS, Leo
  The Girl Who Couldn't Quite
    Br: 408
MARKWEI, Matei
  General BALE: 329
MARLOWE, Christopher
  General ED: 288-299; LCAB:
    120; PS: 7-13, 25, 38-
    43; SC: 71-72; TSD: 73-
    84
  Dido, Queen of Carthage
    [Tragedy of Dido, Queen
    of Carthage] DC1: 122-
    123; ED: 295; EDC: 341-
    342; PS: 24-25, 51-52;
    TSD: 73, 75, 77, 82
  Doctor Faustus [The Tragical
    History of Dr. Faustus]
    DC1: 123-127; ED: 201,
    288-289, 292, 294-297;
    EDC: 336-341; LCAB:
    120; Ma: 1324-1325; PS:
    14-18, 43-47; TSD: 73-
    84, 88
  Edward II DC1: 127-128;
    ED: 290, 295-296; EDC:
    330-331; LCAB: 120; Ma:
    1325-1326; PS: 23-24,
    51; TSD: 74, 77-79, 81-
    82, 84
  Hero and Leander ED: 295;
    ICBAP: 83; Ma: 1326-
    1327; SC: 71-72
  The Jew of Malta DC1:
    128-129; ED: 295-297;
    EDC: 331-333; Ma: 1327-
    1329; PS: 21-23, 49-50;
    TSD: 73-74, 76-79, 81-83
  The Massacre at Paris DC1:
    129; EDC: 333; PS: 24,
    51; TSD: 77, 79
  "The Passionate Shepherd to
    His Love" ICBAP: 83;
    PE: 298; SC: 71
  Tamburlaine the Great ED:
    288, 295, 297; EDC:
    333-336; Ma: 1329-1330;
    TSD: 73-83
  Tamburlaine, Part I DC1:
    129-130; ED: 291; PS:
    18-20, 47-49; TSD: 74-
    76, 80, 83-84
  Tamburlaine, Part II DC1:
    130; PS: 20-21, 49;
    TSD: 77, 82
  Tamburlaine, Parts I & II

  DC1: 130-132; TSD: 76-77
MARMION, Shakerly
  General LJCD: 248-249
MARMONTEL, Jean-François
  Les Incas Ke: 112-113
MARQUAND, John Phillips
  General ALL: 179; AN: 179-
    180; ASF: 388; CN: 357-
    358; LCAB: 120; Ne: 70-
    71; Po: 2635-2638; Wo: 151
  B.F.'s Daughter AN: 178; CN:
    358
  "Deep Water" SFC: 150; Wa:
    515
  Don't Ask Questions see
    H.M. Pulham, Esq.
  "The End Game" ASF: 388;
    Wa: 515
  "Good Morning, Major" ASF:
    388; SFC: 150; Wa: 515
  H.M. Pulham, Esq. [Don't Ask
    Questions, English title]
    AN: 178; CN: 358; Ma:
    1331; Po: 2638
  The Late George Apley CN:
    359; Ma: 1331-1332; Po:
    2638-2639
  Life at Happy Knoll CN: 359
  Melville Goodwin, U.S.A. AN:
    179; CN: 359; Ma: 1332
  Point of No Return Br: 408;
    CN: 360; Ma: 1332; Po:
    2639-2640
  Repent in Haste CN: 360
  Sincerely, Willis Wayde AN:
    179; CN: 360
  So Little Time AN: 179; CN:
    360
  Timothy Dexter Revisited Po:
    2640
  Wickford Point CN: 360-361;
    Ma: 1332-1333
  Women and Thomas Harrow CN:
    361; Ma: 1333; Po: 2640
  _____ and George S. KAUFMAN
  The Late George Apley ADC:
    238
MARQUES, René
  General Br: 408; Po: 2640
  The Little Cart [La carreta]
    Br: 408; DC2: 248
  Un niño azul para esa sombra
    Br: 409
  Palm Sunday Br: 409; DC2:
    248
  The Sun and the MacDonalds

[El sol y los MacDonald]
Br: 409
Márquez, Gabriel García see
GARCIA MARQUEZ, Gabriel
MARQUIS, Don
General APC: 40-41; ASF:
388; LCAB: 120; Po:
2641
Sons of the Puritans Po:
2641
MARQUIS, Thomas Guthrie
General ECL: 176
MARRANT, John
General BAW: 527
MARRYAT, Frederick
General BN: 75-76
Frank Mildmay ENES2: 173
Jacob Faithful ENES1: 160;
ENES2: 173
Japhet in Search of a Father
ENES2: 173
Joseph Rushbrook ENES2:
173
The King's Own ENES1: 160;
ENES2: 173
Mr. Midshipman Easy ENE:
204; ENES2: 173
Newton Forster ENES2: 173
Percival Keene ENES2: 173
Peter Simple ENES2: 173
The Phantom Ship ENES2:
173
The Pirate ENES2: 173
Poor Jack ENES2: 173
The Privateersman ENES2:
173
Snarleyyow ENES2: 173
MARSCHALL, Josef
General Po: 2641
MARSE, Juan
Si te dicen que caí Fi: 224
Ultimas tardes con Teresa
Fi: 224
MARSH-CALDWELL, Anne
Emilia Wyndham ENES1:
160
MARSHALL, Alan
General MAP: 233-234; Po:
2642
How Beautiful Are Thy Feet
MAP: 233
MARSHALL, Joyce
"The Old Woman" Wa:
515
MARSHALL, Paule

General AAF: 77-79; ASF:
388; BAF: 207; BAW: 528
"Barbados" WaS1: 145
"Brooklyn" WaS1: 145
Brown Girl, Brownstones AAF:
77; BAF: 207-208; BAW:
528
The Chosen Place, the Timeless
People AAF: 78-79; BAF:
208; BAW: 528
"Reena" ASF: 388; Wa: 516
Soul Clap Hands and Sing
AAF: 78; BAF: 208
"To Da-duh, In Memoriam"
WaS1: 145
MARSON, Una
General WIL: 95
MARSTON, John
General ED: 302-303; NI:
177-197, 218-219, 232-239;
SC: 72; TSD: 85-88
Antonio and Mellida DC1: 132-
133; EDC: 342; NI: 205-
210, 241-243; TSD: 85-86,
88
Antonio's Revenge DC1: 133;
EDC: 342-343; NI: 241-243;
TSD: 85-88
City Pageant NI: 245
"Cras" [Satire 4] PE: 299
The Dutch Courtesan DC1:
133-134; EDC: 343; NI:
202-205, 241; TSD: 86-87
Histriomastix; or, The Player
Whipt DC1: 134; EDC:
343; NI: 212-214, 244; TSD:
86-87
The Insatiate Countess NI:
216, 245
Jack Drum's Entertainment
EDC: 343; NI: 215-216,
244-245; TSD: 85
Lust's Dominion see ANONY-
MOUS
The Malcontent DC1: 134;
EDC: 343-344; NI: 198-202,
239-240; TSD: 86-88
"The Metamorphosis of Pygmal-
ion's Image" PE: 299; SC:
72
Parasitaster, or The Fawn
DC1: 134; EDC: 344; NI:
211-212, 244; TSD: 87
What You Will DC1: 134;
EDC: 344; NI: 214-215,
244

The Wonder of Women; or,
The Tragedy of Sophonisba
DC1: 134; EDC: 344;
NI: 210-211, 243-244;
TSD: 85, 87-88
_____, George CHAPMAN, and
Ben JONSON
Eastward Ho! see also
CHAPMAN, George EDC:
344-345; NI: 216-218,
245; TSD: 86
MARSTON, John Westland
General EDT: 218
The Patrician's Daughter
EDT: 218
MARTI, José
General LCAB: 120
MARTIAL
Epigrams of Martial Ma:
1334
MARTIN, David
General MAP: 236-237; Po:
2642
The Hero of Too MAP: 237
Where a Man Belongs MAP:
236
MARTIN DESCALZO, José Luis
La frontera de Dios Ke:
209
MARTIN DU GARD, Maurice
Les Mémorables Po: 2642
MARTIN DU GARD, Roger
General Po: 2642-2646
La belle saison Fi: 114;
Po: 2646
Le consultation Fi: 114-115
Devenir! Fi: 115; Ke: 113
L'été 1914 Fi: 115; Ke: 113
Jean Barois Fi: 115; Ke:
113; Ma: 1335; Po: 2647
La mort du pere Fi: 115
Le penitencier Fi: 115
The Postman Ma: 1335-1336
La sorellina Fi: 115
Un taciturne Br: 409
Les Thibault [The World of
the Thibaults] Fi: 115-
116; Ke: 113-114; Ma:
1336-1337; Po: 2647
L'une de nous Fi: 116; Ke:
114; Po: 2647-2648
MARTIN GAITE, Carmen
El balneario Fi: 224
Retahilas Fi: 224
Ritmo lento Fi: 224
MARTIN SANTOS, Luis

General Po: 2648
Tiempo de silencio Fi: 225;
Po: 2648
MARTINEAU, Harriet
General BN: 76
Deerbrook ENES1: 160
MARTINEZ ESTRADA, Ezequiel
General Po: 2648
MARTINEZ FERRANDO, Jesus
Ernesto
General Po: 2649
MARTINEZ OLMEDILLA, Augusto
General Po: 2649
Martínez Ruiz, José see AZORIN
MARTINEZ SIERRA, Gregorio
General Br: 409-410; MD:
192; Po: 2656
Amanecer see Dawn
Cada uno y su vida EDC:
345
El corazón ciego EDC: 345
Dawn [Amanecer] EDC: 345
Don Juan de España DC2:
320
La humilde verdad Ke: 209
The Kingdom of God [El reino
de Dios] Br: 410; DC2:
320; EDC: 345; MD: 192
Madame Pepita EDC: 345
Mama EDC: 345
Nuestra esperanza Br: 410
The Palace of Sadness [El
palacio triste] EDC: 345
Poor John [Pobrecito Juan]
EDC: 345
Primavera en otoño Br: 410;
DC2: 320; Po: 2656
El reino de Dios see The
Kingdom of God
The Romantic Young Lady
[Sueno de una noche de
agosto] EDC: 346
Sol de la tarde Ke: 209
Sueño de una noche de agosto
see The Romantic Young
Lady
Tú eres la paz Ke: 209
_____ and Eduardo MARQUINO
Road to Happiness EDC: 346
_____ and Maria MARTINEZ
SIERRA
Cradle Song Br: 410; EDC:
346
MARTINI, Fausto Maria
Ridi, Pagliaccio Br: 410
MARTINSON, Harry

Aniara Po: 2656
The Nettles Bloom Ke: 361
MARTORELL, Joannot
Tirant lo blanc Fi: 225
MARTYN, Edward
General Br: 410; MBD:
58-59; MD: 192; Mi:
254; Po: 2656-2657; TA:
218
The Bending of the Bough
Br: 410-411
The Dream Physician Br:
411; MD: 192
The Enchanted Sea Br:
411; MD: 192
Grangecolman Br: 411;
MD: 192
The Heather Field Br: 411;
DC1: 135; MBD: 58;
MD: 192-193; Po: 2657
Maeve Br: 411; MD: 193
The Place Hunters Br: 412
Regina Eyre DC1: 135; Po:
2657
Romulus and Remus MD:
193
The Tale of a Town Br:
412; MD: 193
MARTYR, Peter
General Hen: 65
MARVELL, Andrew
General Ba: 89-93; ICBAP:
83; LCAB: 120-121; Ma:
1341
"Antipodes in Shoes" ICBAP:
83
"Bermudas" Ba: 93; ICBAP:
83; Ma: 1338; PE: 299
"Clorinda and Damon" PE:
299
"The Coronet" Ba: 92-93;
ICBAP: 83; PE: 299
"Damon the Mower" ICBAP:
83; PE: 299-300
"Daphnis and Chloe" ICBAP:
83; PE: 300
"The Definition of Love"
Ba: 92-93; ICBAP: 83;
PE: 300
"A Dialogue Between the
Resolved Soul and Created
Pleasure" ICBAP: 83;
PE: 301
"A Dialogue Between the
Soul and Body" Ba: 92;
ICBAP: 84; PE: 301

"A Dialogue Between the Two
Horses" ICBAP: 84
"An Epitaph Upon _____" PE:
301
"Eyes and Tears" PE: 301
"The First Anniversary" Ba:
97; PE: 301
"Fleckno, an English Priest at
Rome" PE: 301
"The Gallery" ICBAP: 84; PE:
301
"The Garden" Ba: 94; ICBAP:
84; LCAB: 121; Ma: 1338-
1340; PE: 302-303
"An Horatian Ode Upon Crom-
well's Return from Ireland"
Ba: 96-97; ICBAP: 84; Ma:
1340; PE: 303-304
"Hortus" ICBAP: 84
"The Last Instructions to a
Painter" Ba: 93; ICBAP:
84
"The Loyall Scott" PE: 304
"Mourning" PE: 304
"The Mower Against Gardens"
Ba: 93; ICBAP: 84; PE:
304
"Mower Poems" PE: 304
"The Mower to the Glo-Worms"
ICBAP: 84; PE: 305
"The Mower's Song" Ba: 92;
ICBAP: 84; PE: 304
"Musicks Empire" Ba: 93;
PE: 305
"The Nymph Complaining for the
Death of Her Fawn" Ba:
94-95; ICBAP: 85; PE:
305-306
"On a Drop of Dew" Ba: 93;
PE: 306
"The Picture of Little T.C. in
a Prospect of Flowers"
ICBAP: 85; PE: 306
"To His Coy Mistress" Ba:
95-96; ICBAP: 85; LCAB:
121; Ma: 1341-1342; PE:
306-308
"Tom May's Death" PE: 308
"The Unfortunate Lover" Ba:
92-93; ICBAP: 85; PE:
308
"Upon Appleton House" Ba:
96; ICBAP: 85
"Upon the Death of the Lord
Hastings" PE: 308
"Upon the Hill and Grove at

Bill-Borow" Ba: 93; PE:
308
MARVIN X [M.E. JACKMAN;
El MUHAJIR]
General MBA: 144
The Black Bird MBA: 144
Flowers for the Trashman
MBA: 144
Take Care of Business MBA:
144
MARX, Henry
L'homme en marche Br:
412
MARY, André
General Po: 2658
MASEFIELD, John
General Br: 412; EP: 190-
198; Ma: 1343-1344; MBD:
59; Mi: 254-256; Po:
2658-2659
"Alfred Noir" PE: 308
"August 1914" EP: 197
"C.L.M." PE: 308; Po:
2659
"Cargoes" EP: 196-197;
ICBAP: 85; PE: 308;
Po: 2659
The Coming of Christ Br:
412; DC1: 135
"Dauber" EP: 192-193, 197;
ICBAP: 85; Po: 2659
"The Everlasting Mercy"
EP: 192-193, 197; ICBAP:
85
A King's Daughter Br: 412
"The Lost Orchard" PE:
309
"The Racer" PE: 308
Reynard the Fox EP: 191-
192, 196-197
"Sea Fever" EP: 195, 197;
PE: 308
"Tomorrow" LCAB: 121
"The Wanderer" EP: 197
MASIYE, Andreya Sylvester
General BALE: 329-330
The Lands of Kazembe
BALE: 330
MASON, Charles Welsh
Merlin--A Piratical Love
Story ENES2: 173
MASON, Clifford
Gabriel BAP: 139
Midnight Special MBA: 145
Sister Sadie MBA: 145
MASON, George

General AP: 583-584
MASON, John
General NI: 335
The Turke DC1: 135
MASON, Judi Ann
Livin' Fat ADC: 239; MBA:
145
MASON, William
General EC: 100
MASSINGER, Philip
General ED: 306-307; LJCD:
91-95, 104-105, 115-117;
TSD: 88-90
The Beggar's Bush see BEAU-
MONT, Francis and John
FLETCHER
Believe as You List DC1: 135;
EDC: 346; LJCD: 100, 118
The Bondman DC1: 135; EDC:
347; LJCD: 101; Ma: 1345;
TSD: 89
The City Madam DC1: 135;
EDC: 347; LJCD: 100;
TSD: 89
The Custom of the Country see
BEAUMONT, Francis and
John FLETCHER
The Double Marriage see BEAU-
MONT, Francis and John
FLETCHER
The Duke of Milan DC1: 135-
136; LJCD: 101, 118
The Emperor of the East DC1:
136; EDC: 347; LJCD: 101-
102; TSD: 90
The Guardian LJCD: 103
The Knight of Malta see
BEAUMONT, Francis and
John FLETCHER
Love's Cure LJCD: 104
The Maid of Honour EDC:
347; LJCD: 102, 117-118;
Ma: 1345; TSD: 89-90
A New Way to Pay Old Debts
DC1: 136; ED: 306; EDC:
347-348; LJCD: 95-97, 117-
118; Ma: 1345-1346; TSD:
88-89
The Picture EDC: 348; LJCD:
104, 117-118
Renegado; or, The Gentleman
of Venice EDC: 348; LJCD:
103, 117; TSD: 90
The Roman Actor DC1: 136;
EDC: 348; LJCD: 97-98;
Ma: 1346; TSD: 89

The Spanish Curate LJCD: 118

Thierry and Theodoret see FLETCHER, John and Philip MASSINGER

The Unnatural Combat DC1: 136; LJCD: 102

A Very Woman; or, The Prince of Tarent EDC: 348; LJCD: 103, 118; TSD: 89

_____ and Nathan FIELD
The Fatal Dowry DC1: 136; EDC: 348; LJCD: 98-99, 117

The Virgin Martyr EDC: 348; LJCD: 99, 118; TSD: 88, 90

MASSON, André
General Po: 2660

MASTEROFF, Joe, John KANDER, and Fred EBB
Cabaret ADC: 239

MASTERS, Edgar Lee
General ALL: 179-180; AN: 180; Br: 412; LCAB: 121; Po: 2660-2661

Across Spoon River Po: 2661

Althea Br: 412

The Bread of Idleness Br: 413

Children of the Market Place AN: 180

Eileen Br: 413

The Leaves of the Tree Br: 413

Lichee Nuts Po: 2661

The Locket Br: 413

Maximilian Br: 413

The New Spoon River Po: 2662

"A One-Eyed View" Po: 2662

"The Pasture Rose" Po: 2662

Spoon River Anthology Ma: 1347-1348; Po: 2662-2663

The Trifler Br: 413

MASTRONARDI, Lucio
Il maestro di Vigevano Ke: 245

MASUCCIO, Salernitano
Novella 33 Ke: 245

MATA, Gonzalo Humberto

General Po: 2664

MATA DOMINGUEZ, Pedro
General Po: 2664
Un grito en la noche Ke: 209

MATERNUS, Curiatus
Domitius DC2: 248

MATHER, Cotton
General AP: 422-432; Da: 35
Magnalia Christi Americana AP: 425-426, 428-432; Da: 35
Manductio Ad Ministerium AP: 432

MATHER, Increase
General AP: 435-437; Da: 36

MATHER, Richard
General AP: 439-440

MATHERS, Peter
General MAP: 239-240
Trap MAP: 239

MATHESON, Richard
"Return" Wa: 516

MATHEUS, John Frederick
General BAF: 209; BAW: 535
'Cruiter BAP: 139; MBA: 145
"Fog" ASF: 389
Ouanga BAP: 139; MBA: 145
Ti Yvette BAP: 139

MATHEWS, Cornelius
General AN: 180; ASF: 389
Behemoth: A Legend of the Mound-Builders AN: 180

MATHEWSON, Christopher
A Shriek to Melt the Texas Moon ADC: 239

MATHIS, Sharon Bell
General BAF: 209

MATSHIKIZA, Todd
General BALE: 330

MATSHIWULWANE, Mboza
General BALE: 300

MATTERA, Don
General BALE: 331

MATTHEWS, James
General BALE: 331

Matthews, Mrs. W.E. see EARLE, Victoria

MATTHIESSEN, Francis Otto
General Po: 2664
American Renaissance LCAB: 121

MATURIN, Charles Robert
General Du: 109
The Albigenses ENES1: 160;

ENES2: 174
Fatal Revenge ENES1: 160;
ENES2: 174
Melmoth the Wanderer Du:
109; EN: 94; ENE: 204-
205; ENES1: 160-161;
ENES2: 174
The Milesian Chief ENES1:
161; ENES2: 174
The Wild Irish Boy ENES1:
161; ENES2: 174
Women ENES1: 161; ENES2:
174
MATUTE, Ana María
General Po: 2664-2665
Los Abel Ke: 209
"The Apprentice" Wa: 516
"The Beautiful Dawn" Wa:
516
"Bernardino" Wa: 516
"The Birds" Wa: 516
"The Black Sheep" Wa: 516
"The Boy Next Door" Wa:
516
"The Boy Who Found a Violin
in a Granary" Wa: 516
"The Boy Who Was the
Devil's Friend" Wa: 516
"The Boy Whose Friend Died"
Wa: 516
"The Boys" Wa: 516
"The Celebration" Wa: 516
"Christmas for Carnavalito"
Wa: 516
"Coal Dust" Wa: 516
"Conscience" Wa: 517
"The Cotton Field" Wa: 517
"Doing Nothing" Wa: 517
"The Dry Branch" Wa: 517
En esta tierra Fi: 225; Ke:
209
"Fausto" Wa: 517
"A Few Kids" Wa: 517
Fiesta al noroeste Fi: 226;
Ke: 209-210
"The Fire" Wa: 517
"The Friend" Wa: 517
"The Good Children" Wa:
517
Los hijos muertos Fi: 226;
Ke: 210
"The Island" Wa: 517
"King of the Zennos" Wa:
517
"The Laundress' Son" Wa:
517

"The Little Blue-Eyed Negro"
Wa: 517
Little Theater [Pequeño teatro]
Fi: 226; Po: 2665
"The Lost Dog" Wa: 517
"The Merry-Go-Round" Wa:
517
The Merchants Fi: 226
"The Metalworker" Wa: 517
"Miss Vivian" Wa: 517
"Mr. Clown" Wa: 518
"The Moon" Wa: 518
"News of Young K." Wa: 518
"No tocar" Wa: 518
"The Ones from the Store" Wa:
518
"The Pastry Shop Window" Wa:
518
Pequeño teatro see Little
Theater
Primera memoria Fi: 226; Ke:
210
"The Rabble" Wa: 518
"Rather a Sword" Wa: 518
"Reason" Wa: 518
"The Repentent One" Wa: 518
"The Rescue" Wa: 518
"Roads" Wa: 518
"The Round" Wa: 518
"The Schoolmaster" Wa: 518
"Shadows" Wa: 518
"Sin of Omission" Wa: 518
Los soldados lloran de noche
Ke: 210
"The Son" Wa: 518
"A Star on Her Skin" Wa:
519
"Thirst and the Child" Wa:
519
La trampa Fi: 226
"The Treasure" Wa: 519
"The Trees" Wa: 519
"The Ugly Girl" Wa: 519
MAUGHAM, William Somerset
General BN2: 82-83; Br:
413-414; LCAB: 121; MBD:
59-60; MD: 193-194; Mi:
256-257; Po: 2666-2670;
Ri2: 250-261, 266-268; Sch:
225-227; TA: 220-221
"The Artistic Temperament of
Stephen Carey" Wa: 519
Ashenden ENES2: 174; Ri2:
255
"The Back of Beyond" Wa:
519

"A Bad Example" Wa: 519
"Before the Party" Wa: 519
The Breadwinner Br: 414;
   DC1: 137; EDC: 348;
   Ri2: 267
Caesar's Wife Br: 414; EDC:
   348-349
Cakes and Ale EN: 96;
   ENE: 205; ENES1: 161;
   ENES2: 174; Ma: 1349-
   1350; Ri2: 251, 253, 260-
   261; Po: 2670; Sch: 228
Camel's Back EDC: 349
Caroline EDC: 349
Catalina Ri2: 252
Christmas Holiday ENES1:
   161; Ri2: 255, 262
The Circle [Le Cercle] Br:
   414; DC1: 137; EDC:
   349; MBD: 60; MD: 194;
   Po: 2671; Ri2: 258, 266-
   268
"The Colonel's Lady" Wa:
   519
The Constant Wife Br: 414-
   415; EDC: 349-350; MD:
   194; Ri2: 266
"The Creative Impulse" Wa:
   519
"Daisy" Wa: 519
Don Fernando Ri2: 256
"The Door of Opportunity"
   SFC: 151; Wa: 519
East of Suez Br: 415; EDC:
   350; MD: 194; Ri2: 258
The Explorer EDC: 350;
   ENES1: 161
"The Facts of Life" SFC:
   151; Wa: 519
"The Fall of Edward Bernard"
   SFC: 151; Wa: 519-520
"Fear" Wa: 520
For Services Rendered Br:
   415; EDC: 350; MD: 194;
   Ri2: 254, 266
"The Force of Circumstance"
   Wa: 520
The Hero ENES1: 161;
   ENES2: 174
Home and Beauty Br: 415
"The Human Element" Wa:
   520
Jack Straw Br: 415
"Jane" Wa: 520
Lady Frederick Br: 415;
   EDC: 350

The Land of Promise Br: 416;
   EDC: 350
Landed Gentry EDC: 350
Letter EDC: 351
"The Lion's Skin" SFC: 151;
   Wa: 520
Liza of Lambeth ENES1: 161;
   ENES2: 174; Ma: 1350-1351;
   Po: 2671; Ri2: 252, 262
"Mackintosh" Wa: 520
The Magician ENES1: 161; Ri2:
   262
The Making of a Saint ENES2:
   174
A Man of Honour Br: 416;
   EDC: 351
Marriages Are Made in Heaven
   EDC: 351
The Merry-Go-Round ENES1:
   162
"Mr. Know-All" SFC: 151;
   Wa: 520
The Mob Br: 416
The Moon and Sixpence BN2:
   83; EN: 96; ENES1: 162;
   Ma: 1351-1352; Ri2: 251,
   258, 261-262; Sch: 228
Mrs. Craddock ENES1: 162;
   ENES2: 174; Po: 2671; Ri2:
   252, 255, 263
The Narrow Corner ENES1:
   162; Ri2: 252
The Noble Spaniard Br: 416;
   DC1: 137
Of Human Bondage BN2: 83;
   EN: 96; ENE: 205; ENES1:
   162; Ma: 1352-1354; Po:
   2671; Ri2: 251-253, 255-259,
   261, 263-265; Sch: 228
On a Chinese Screen Po: 2672
Our Betters Br: 416; DC1:
   137; EDC: 351; MD: 194;
   Ri2: 267
"The Outstation" Ri2: 265;
   Wa: 520; WaS1: 145
The Painted Veil ENES1: 162;
   Ri2: 252, 265
Penelope Br: 416
"The Pool" Wa: 520
"Princess September and the
   Nightingale" Wa: 520
"Rain" Ri2: 265; SFC: 151;
   Wa: 520-521
The Razor's Edge BN2: 83;
   EN: 96; ENES1: 162; Ri2:
   252, 258-259, 265; Sch: 228

"Red" Wa: 521
Sacred Flame EDC: 351
"Sanatorium" Wa: 521; WaS1:
145
Sheppey Br: 416-417;
EDC: 351; MD: 194; Ri2:
254
Smith Br: 417
The Summing Up Ma: 1354-
1355; Ri2: 255-256, 268
The Tenth Man EDC: 352
Theatre ENES1: 162; Ri2:
265
Then and Now Ri2: 260
"The Traitor" Wa: 521
"The Treasure" Wa: 521
Trembling of a Leaf Ri2: 260
The Unattainable Br: 417
"The Unconquered" Wa:
521
The Unknown Br: 417; EDC:
352; Ri2: 266
Up at the Villa Ri2: 265-
266
"The Vessel of Wrath" Wa:
521
"Virtue" Wa: 521
"The Yellow Streak" Wa:
521
MAULNIER, Thierry
General Po: 2672
La maison de la nuit Br:
417; Po: 2672
MAUPASSANT, Guy de
General LCAB: 122
"All Over" Wa: 521
L'Ame étrangère Fi: 116
"Amour" Wa: 521
L'Angelus Fi: 116
"The Apparition" SFC: 151;
Wa: 521
"At Sea" Wa: 522
"The Avenger" Wa: 522
"Ball-of-Fat" see "Tallow
Ball"
"Bed No. 29" Wa: 522
Bel-Ami Fi: 116; Ke: 114-
115; Ma: 1356
Boule de Suif Fi: 116
"The Bringer of Sleep" Wa:
522
"By Horseback" Wa: 522
"A Corsican Bandit" Wa:
522
"A Coward" Wa: 522
"The Cripple" Wa: 522

"Darkness" Wa: 522
"Decorated" Wa: 522
Le demande DC2: 248
"The Devil" SFC: 151; Wa:
522
"Le diable" see "The Devil"
"A Divorce Case" Wa: 522
"Dreams" Wa: 522
"The Drowned Man" ["Lost at
Sea"] Wa: 522
"Duchoux" Wa: 522
"A Duel" Wa: 522
"En famille" see "A Family Af-
fair"
"The False Gems" SFC: 151
"A Family Affair" SFC: 152;
Wa: 523
"Father and Son" see "The
Hautots, Father and Son"
"Fear" SFC: 152; Wa: 523
"Fly: Recollections of a Boat-
man" Wa: 523
Fort comme la mort Fi: 116
"Happiness" SFC: 152; Wa:
523
"The Hautots, Father and Son"
SFC: 152; Wa: 523
"He?" Wa: 523
"Him" SFC: 152
"The Horla" Fi: 116-117; SFC:
152; Wa: 523
"In the Wood" Wa: 523
"The Inheritance" Wa: 523
"The Inn" SFC: 152; Wa:
523
"The Jewels" Wa: 523
"Little Rogue" Wa: 523
"The Lock of Hair" Wa: 524
"Lost at Sea" see "The
Drowned Man"
"A Mad Man" Wa: 524
"The Mad Woman" Wa: 524
"Madame Tellier's House" see
also "La maison Tellier"
Wa: 524
"Mademoiselle Cocotte" Wa:
524
"Mademoiselle Fifi" Wa: 524
"Mademoiselle Perle" Wa: 524
"La maison Tellier" see also
"Madame Tellier's House"
SFC: 152
"The Mask" Wa: 524
The Master Passion Ke: 115
"La mère sauvage" see also
"The Savage Mother" SFC:

152
"Miss Harriet" SFC: 152
"Monsieur Parent" Wa: 524
Mont-Oriol Fi: 117; Ke:
115; Ma: 1356-1357
"Moonlight" SFC: 152; Wa:
524
"Mount of Olives" Wa: 524
"My Uncle Jules" Wa: 524
"The Necklace" SFC: 152-
153; Wa: 524-525; WaS1:
145
"A Night's Entertainment"
Wa: 525
"Old Amiable" Wa: 525
"On the Journey" Wa: 525
"On the Water" SFC: 153
One Life Fi: 117; Ke: 115
Our Heart Fi: 117; Ke:
116
"Paul's Woman" Wa: 525
"A Piece of String" SFC:
153; Wa: 525
Pierre et Jean Fi: 117-118;
Ke: 116; Ma: 1357
Pierrot Ke: 116
"The Protector" Wa: 525
"Queen Hortense" Wa: 525
"The Rondoli Sisters" Wa:
525
"The Savage Mother" see
also "La mère sauvage"
Wa: 525
"Simon's Papa" Ke: 116;
SFC: 153; Wa: 526
"The Skinned Hand" SFC:
153; Wa: 526
"Une soirée" SFC: 153
"The Spasm" Wa: 526
"Story of a Farm Girl" SFC:
153; Wa: 526
"Suicides" Wa: 526
"Tallow Ball" SFC: 153; Wa:
526
"The Tellier House" see
"La maison Tellier"
"The Test" Wa: 526
"Two Friends" ["A Fishing
Excursion"] Wa: 526
"Two Little Soldiers" SFC:
153; Wa: 526
"Useless Beauty" Wa: 526
Une vendetta Ke: 116
"The Victim" Wa: 526
"Waiter, a Bock" Wa: 526
"Who Knows?" SFC: 153;

Wa: 527
"The Will" Wa: 527
A Woman's Life Ma: 1357-1358
"Yvette" Fi: 118; SFC: 153;
Wa: 527
MAURETTE, Mme. Marcelle
La servante DC2: 247
MAURIAC, Claude
General Po: 2672-2673
L'agrandissement Fi: 118
All Women Are Fatal Fi: 118;
Ke: 116-117
Le dialogue intérieur Po:
2673
The Dinner Party Fi: 118;
Ke: 117; Ma: 1359
The Marquise Went Out at Five
Fi: 118; Ke: 117; Ma:
1359
MAURIAC, François
General Br: 417-418; MD:
194; Po: 2673-2678
Un Adolescent d'autrefois Fi:
118
Les Anges noirs see The
Dark Angels
Asmodee Br: 418; DC2: 249
Le Baiser au lépreux see A
Kiss for the Leper
"Conte de Noél" Wa: 527
"Coups de Couteau" Wa: 527
The Dark Angels [Les Anges
noirs] Fi: 118; Ke: 117;
Po: 2679
"Le Démon de la connaissance"
Wa: 527
The Désert of Love [Le Desert
de l'amour] Fi: 118; Ke:
117; Ma: 1360; Po: 2679
The End of Night [La Fin de
la nuit] Fi: 118-119; Ke:
117; Po: 2680
The Enemy Fi: 119; Ke: 117
L'Enfant chargé de chaînes see
Young Man in Chains
Feu sur la terre, ou Le Pays
sans chemin Br: 418
Flesh and Blood Fi: 119; Ke:
118
The Frontenac Mystery Fi:
119; Ke: 118
The Frontenacs Ma: 1360-1361
Galigai Fi: 119
Génitrix Fi: 119; Ke: 118;
Ma: 1361-1362; Po: 2680
"Insomnie" Wa: 527

A Kiss for the Leper [Le
Baiser au lépreux] Fi:
119-120; Ke: 118-119;
Ma: 1362-1363; Po: 2679
The Lamb Fi: 120; Ke:
119; Ma: 1363
The Lines of Life Fi: 120;
Ke: 119
The Little Misery Ke: 119
The Loved and the Unloved
Ke: 119
Les Mal aimés Br: 418;
DC2: 249
Nest of Vipers see The
Vipers' Tangle
Le Noeud de vipères see
The Vipers' Tangle
Passage du Malm Br: 418
La Pharisienne see Woman
of the Pharisees
Question of Precedence Ke:
119-120; Ma: 1363
"Rank" Wa: 527
The River of Fire Ke: 120
The Stuff of Youth Ke:
120
That Which Was Lost Ke:
120
"Thérèse à l'hôtel" Wa:
527
"Thérèse chez le docteur"
Wa: 527
Therese Desqueyroux Fi:
120-121; Ke: 120; Ma:
1363-1364; Po: 2681-2682;
Wa: 527; WaS1: 146
The Unknown Sea Fi: 121;
Ke: 120-121
The Vipers' Tangle [Le
Noeud de vipères; Nest
of Vipers] Fi: 120; Ke:
121; Ma: 1365-1366; Po:
2681
The Weakling Fi: 121
Woman of the Pharisees [La
Pharisienne] Fi: 121;
Ke: 121; Po: 2681
Young Man in Chains
[L'Enfant chargé de
chaînes] Fi: 121; Ke:
121-122; Wa: 528; Po:
2679-2680
MAURICE, Frederick Denison
Eustace Conway ENES1:
162
MAUROIS, Andre

General Po: 2683-2684
Atmosphere of Love Ke: 122
"Le Départ" Wa: 528
The Family Circle Ke: 122
Prométhée Po: 2685
Terre promise Ke: 122
The Weigher of Souls Ke: 122
MAURRAS, Charles
General Po: 2685-2686
Mavor, Osborne Henry see
BRIDIE, James
MAXWELL, Gavin
General Ai: 302
MAXWELL, Marina
General MBA: 145
Play Mas MBA: 146
MAXWELL, William
"The Absent-Minded Heart"
SFC: 154; Wa: 528
MAY, Elaine
Adaptation ADC: 239
MAY, James Boyer
General Po: 2686
MAY, Thomas
General LJCD: 249
MAYAKOVSKY, Vladimir Vladi-
mirovich
General Br: 418; MD: 194-
195; Po: 2469-2472
The Bathhouse [Banya] EDC:
324; MD: 195
The Bedbug [La punaise;
Klop] Br: 418; DC2: 249;
EDC: 324; MD: 195; Po:
2473
Buffle DC2: 249
Mystery-Bouffe [Misteriya-Buff]
EDC: 325; MD: 195
The Tragedy of Vladimir Maya-
kovsky MD: 195
MAYER, Edwin Justus
Children of Darkness ADC:
239-240; Br: 419
The Last Love of Don Juan
ADC: 240
_____, Kurt WEILL, and Ira
GERSHWIN
The Firebrand of Florence
ADC: 240
MAYER, Tom
General ASF: 389; Po: 2686
MAYFIELD, Julian
General AAPD: 393; AAW:
67; BAF: 210; BAP:
140; BAW: 537; MBA: 146
The Grand Parade BAF:

210-211
  The Hit BAF: 211
  The Long Night BAF: 211;
    MBA: 146
  The Other Foot BAP: 140;
    Br: 419; MBA: 146
  Uptight BAP: 140-141
MAYHEW, Henry
  The Wandering Minstrel DC1:
    137
MAYHEW, Jonathan
  General AP: 441
MAYNE, Fanny
  Jane Rutherford ENES2:
    175
MAYNE, Jasper
  General LJCD: 249
MAYNE, Rutherford [Samuel J.
    WADDELL]
  General Br: 419; Mi: 257-
    258
  The Drone Br: 419
  The Troth Br: 419
  The Turn of the Road Br:
    419
MAZRUI, Ali A.
  General BALE: 331-332
  The Trial of Christopher
    Okigbo BALE: 331-332
MAZZANTI, Carlos
  El sustituto Po: 2687
MBITI, John Samuel
  General BALE: 332
MEADES, Anne
  The History of Sir William
    Harrington ENES2: 175
MEANS, E.K.
  "The Late Figger Bush" Wa:
    528
MEANS, Sterling M.
  General BAW: 539
MEDBOURNE, Matthew
  Tartuffe; or The French
    Puritan DC1: 137
MEDEK, Rudolf
  Anabasis Ke: 422
  The Fiery Dragon Ke:
    422
  Great Days Ke: 422
  The Island in the Storm Ke:
    422
  The Mighty Dream Ke: 422
MEDIO, Dolores
  General Po: 2687
  "Andrés" Wa: 528
  "The Bellboy" Wa: 528

Bibiana Fi: 226
"A Cape for Braulio" Wa: 528
"The Courtyard" Wa: 528
Diary of a Schoolteacher Fi:
  226
The Fish Stays Afloat Fi: 227
"Five Letters from Germany"
  Wa: 528
"Giddy-up, Nicolas" Wa: 528
"The Hand Organ" Wa: 528
"The Handful of Dry Grass"
  Wa: 528
"Hi, Boss!" Wa: 528
"Injustice" Wa: 529
"The Last Toy Drum" Wa:
  529
"Little Miguel's Baby Carriage"
  Wa: 529
"The Marten" Wa: 529
"Miracle in Santaolaya" Wa:
  529
"Mr. Garcia" Wa: 529
"Nina" Wa: 529
"Pause" Wa: 529
"The Picture" Wa: 529
Public Servant Fi: 227
"The Second Time" Wa: 529
"Shall We Go, Timotheo?" Wa:
  529
"The Strongest One" Wa: 529
"Teresa, a Solo Composed of
  Memories for a Man" Wa:
  529
"Tomorrow" Wa: 529
"Unpunished Crime" Wa: 529
"Uphill" Wa: 529
We Riveros Fi: 227
MEDNICK, Murray
  General MDAE: 341
  The Hunter ADC: 240; MDAE:
    341
MEDOFF, Mark
  The Halloween Bandit ADC:
    240
  The Wager ADC: 240
  When You Comin' Back, Red
    Ryder? ADC: 240-241
Meinhard, Carl see BERNAUER,
  Rudolph and Carl MEINHARD
MEIRELES, Cecilia
  General Po: 2688
MEJIA VALLEJO, Manuel
  El día señalado Po: 2688
MELBANCKE, Brian
  Philotimus ERP: 325-326;
    Hen: 158

MELDON, Maurice
  Aisling Br: 419
MELEZH, Ivan
  General Po: 2688
MELFI, Leonard
  Birdbath ADC: 241
  Cinque ADC: 241
  Halloween ADC: 241
  Night ADC: 241
  Stars and Stripes ADC:
    241
  Times Square ADC: 241
MELFORD, Larry
  General BAF: 212
MELL, Max
  Der Nibelunge Not DC2:
    249; Po: 2688
Melmoth, Sebastian see WILDE,
    Oscar
MEL'NIKOV-PECHERSKY, Pavel
  Grandma's Yarns Fi: 458
  In the Forests Fi: 458
  The Krasil'nikovs Fi: 458
  Olden Times Fi: 458
  On the Hills Fi: 458-459
MELVILLE, Herman
  General AF: 193-200; ALL:
    180-190; AN: 195-202;
    ASF: 408-413; Cla: 67-
    73; Ho: 103-117, 152-154;
    LCAB: 122; Ma: 1388-
    1389
  "America, I" PE: 309
  "The Apparition: A Retro-
    spect" PE: 309
  "The Apple-Tree Table"
    ASF: 389; Cla: 68; Ma:
    1367; SFC: 154; Wa:
    529-530; WaS1: 146
  "Art" PE: 309
  "Bartleby the Scrivener"
    AF: 198, 200; ASF: 389-
    394; Cla: 68, 70-73; Ma:
    1367-1368; SFC: 154-155;
    Wa: 530-533; WaS1: 146-
    147
  Battle-Pieces Cla: 69
  "The Bell-Tower" ASF:
    394; Cla: 68, 73; Ma:
    1368-1369; SFC: 155;
    Wa: 533-534; WaS1: 147
  "Benito Cereno" AF: 200;
    ALL: 183; ASF: 394-
    398; Cla: 67-69, 71-73;
    Ho: 110, 114-115, 153;
    Ma: 1369-1370; SFC: 155-

  156; Wa: 534-538; WaS1:
    147-148
  "The Berg" PE: 309
  "Billy Budd" AF: 193, 195-
    196, 198-200; ALL: 181, 184,
    188-189; ASF: 398-403; Cla:
    72; Ho: 107-110, 112-116,
    152-154; Ma: 1370-1371; SFC:
    156-159; Wa: 538-544; WaS1:
    148
  "Billy in the Darbies" ICBAP:
    85; PE: 309
  Clarel ALL: 186, 188; Cla:
    73; ICBAP: 86; Ma: 1371-
    1372
  "Cock-A-Doodle-Doo" ASF:
    403-404; Cla: 70; Ma: 1372-
    1373; SFC: 159; Wa: 544-
    545; WaS1: 148-149
  "Commemorative of a Naval Vic-
    tory" PE: 309
  The Confidence Man AF: 194,
    196, 198; ALL: 181-182;
    AN: 181-182; Cla: 69-70;
    Ho: 108-116, 152-154;
    LCAB: 122-123; Ma: 1373-
    1374
  "The Conflict of Convictions"
    PE: 309
  "Daniel Orme" ASF: 404; Ma:
    1374; SFC: 160; Wa: 545
  "The Encantadas" ASF: 404-
    405; Cla: 70; Ma: 1374-
    1375; SFC: 160; Wa: 545-
    546; WaS1: 149
  "The Fiddler" ASF: 405; Ma:
    1375-1376; SFC: 160; Wa:
    546; WaS1: 149
  "Fragments from a Writing
    Desk" ASF: 405
  "The 'Gees" ASF: 405; Ma:
    1376; Wa: 546
  "The Haglets" PE: 309
  "The Happy Failure" ASF:
    405; Ma: 1376; SFC: 160;
    Wa: 546; WaS1: 149
  "I and My Chimney" ASF:
    406; Cla: 68, 71-72; Ma:
    1376-1377; SFC: 160-161;
    Wa: 546-547; WaS1: 149
  "In a Bye-Canal" PE: 309
  Israel Potter ALL: 181-182;
    AN: 182-183; Cla: 69;
    Ho: 105, 109-110, 113, 154;
    Ma: 1377-1378
  "Jimmy Rose" ASF: 406; Ma:

1378; SFC: 161; Wa:
547; WaS1: 149
"The Lightning-Rod Man"
ASF: 406; Cla: 71; Ma:
1379; SFC: 161; Wa:
547-548; WaS1: 149
"The Little Good Fellows"
ICBAP: 86; PE: 309
"The Loiterer" ICBAP: 86
"The Maldive Shark" PE:
309
"The March into Virginia"
ICBAP: 86
Mardi AF: 194-195; ALL:
182-183, 184, 188; AN:
183-184; Cla: 68; Ho:
107, 109-110, 112, 116-
117, 152, 154; Ma: 1379-
1380
"The Martyr" LCAB: 123
Moby Dick AF: 193-200;
ALL: 181-184, 186, 188-
190; AN: 184-190; Cla:
67, 69-73; Ho: 104-117,
152-154; LCAB: 123;
Ma: 1381-1384
"Monody" PE: 309
"Naples in the Time of Bomba"
ICBAP: 86
"The Night March" PE: 310
Omoo ALL: 182-183; AN:
190-191; Ho: 109; Ma:
1384-1385
"The Paradise of Bachelors
and the Tartarus of
Maids" ASF: 407; Cla:
71, 73; Ma: 1385-1386;
SFC: 161; Wa: 548;
WaS1: 149
"Pebbles" PE: 310
"The Piazza" ASF: 407;
Cla: 67, 71; Ma: 1386;
SFC: 161; Wa: 548-549;
WaS1: 149-150
Pierre AF: 194; ALL: 181-
182, 188-189; AN: 191-
192; Cla: 70; Ho: 108,
111-113, 116-117, 152-153;
Ma: 1386-1388
"Poor Man's Pudding and
Rich Man's Crumbs" ASF:
407-408; Ma: 1389; SFC:
162; Wa: 549; WaS1:
150
"A Rail Road Cutting Near
Alexandria in 1855" PE:

310
Redburn AF: 194-195, 197;
ALL: 181-183, 188; AN:
192-193; Ho: 107-108, 110,
112-113, 115-116; Ma: 1389-
1390
"Rip Van Winkle's Lilac" ASF:
408
"The Rose Farmer" ICBAP: 86
"Rose Window" ICBAP: 86
"Stockings in the Farm-House
Chimney" ICBAP: 86
"Time's Betrayal" ICBAP: 86
"The Town-Ho's Story" Cla:
71; Ho: 110, 114-115, 152
"Trophies of Peace" ICBAP:
86
"The Two Temples" ASF: 408;
Ma: 1391; Wa: 549; WaS1:
150
Typee ALL: 181-183, 188; AN:
193-194; Cla: 71-72; Ho:
107, 115, 117, 152-153; Ma:
1391-1392
"Under the Rose" ASF: 408
"When Forth the Shepherd
Leads the Flock" ICBAP:
86
White Jacket AF: 198, 200;
ALL: 181-183, 188; AN:
194-195; Cla: 73; Ho: 106-
107, 112-114, 116-117; Ma:
1392-1393
MENANDER
Arbitration [Epitrepontes] DC2:
251; EDC: 352
Dyskolos Ma: 1394-1395
The Girl from Samos [Samia]
EDC: 352
The Grouch [Dyskolos; Curmud-
geon] DC2: 249-251; EDC:
352-353
Hypobolimaios DC2: 251
The Shearing of Glycera [Peri-
keiromene; Rape of Locks]
DC2: 251-252; EDC: 353
Sikyonios DC2: 252
MENARD, John Willis
General AAPD: 72
MENCKEN, Henry Louis
General ALL: 190-192; APC:
68-70; ICBAP: 86; LCAB:
123-124; Po: 2689-2702
The American Language Po:
2703
Notes on Democracy Po: 2704

The Philosophy of Friedrich
Nietzsche Po: 2704
MENCKEN, Sara Haardt
General ASF: 414
MENDES, Alfred H.
General WIL: 95-96
Black Fauns WIL: 96
Pitch Lake WIL: 96
MENDOZA, Hector
General Br: 419
MENESES, Porfirio
"Contrabando" Wa: 549
MENKEN, Adah Isaacs
General JW: 101
MENOTTI, Gian-Carlo
General MD: 195
Amahl and the Night Visitors
ADC: 241
Amelia Goes to the Ball
ADC: 242
The Consul ADC: 242; MD:
195
The Labyrinth ADC: 242
The Last Savage ADC:
242-243
Maria Golovin ADC: 243
Martin's Lie ADC: 243
The Medium ADC: 243;
MD: 195
The Old Maid and the Thief
ADC: 243
The Saint of Bleecker Street
ADC: 244
The Telephone ADC: 244;
MD: 195
The Unicorn, the Gorgon,
and the Manticore ADC:
244
MERA, Juan León
Cumandá LCAB: 124
MERAS, Icchokas
Striptease, or Paris-Rome-
Paris Fi: 459
MERCER, David
General MDAE: 344
Belcher's Luck MDAE: 344
MEREDITH, George
General BN: 77-80; Du:
115-118; LCAB: 124; Ma:
1409-1410; VP: 51-52
The Adventures of Harry
Richmond BN: 78-79;
Du: 112; EN: 96-97;
ENE: 205; ENES1: 164;
Ma: 1396-1397
The Amazing Marriage BN:

77; Du: 109-110; EN: 97;
ENE: 205; ENES1: 163;
ENES2: 175; Ma: 1397-1398
Beauchamp's Career BN: 78;
Du: 110; EN: 97; ENE:
205-206; ENES1: 163;
ENES2: 175; Ma: 1398-1399
"The Case of General Opler and
Lady Camper" SFC: 162;
Wa: 550
Celt and Saxon EN: 98
"Daphne" ICBAP: 86
Diana of the Crossways Du:
110; EN: 98; ENE: 206;
ENES1: 163; ENES2: 175;
Ma: 1399-1401
"Dirge in the Woods" PE: 310
"Earth and a Wedded Woman"
ICBAP: 86
The Egoist BN: 78; Du:
110-111; EN: 98-99; ENE:
206-207; ENES1: 163-164;
ENES2: 175-176; LCBAP:
124; Ma: 1401-1402
Evan Harrington BN: 78; Du:
111-112; EN: 99; ENE:
207; ENES1: 164; ENES2:
176; Ma: 1402-1403
"The House on the Beach"
SFC: 162; Wa: 550
"In the Woods" PE: 310
"The Lark Ascending" PE:
310
Lord Ormont and His Aminta
BN: 78; Du: 112; EN:
99; ENE: 207; ENES1: 164;
ENES2: 176; Ma: 1403-1404
"Love in the Valley" PE: 310
"Lucifer in Starlight" ICBAP:
87; PE: 310
"Margaret's Bridal Eve"
ICBAP: 87
"Meditation Under Stars" PE:
310
Modern Love ICBAP: 87; Ma:
1404-1406; VP: 51-52
"Modern Love," [Sonnet 1]
PE: 310
"Modern Love," [Sonnet 3]
PE: 310
"Modern Love," [Sonnet 4]
PE: 310
"Modern Love," [Sonnet 9]
PE: 310
"Modern Love," [Sonnet 13]
PE: 310

"Modern Love," [Sonnet 14]
PE: 311
"Modern Love," [Sonnet 19]
PE: 311
"Modern Love," [Sonnet 23]
ICBAP: 87; PE: 311
"Modern Love," [Sonnet 26]
PE: 311
"Modern Love," [Sonnet 30]
PE: 311
"Modern Love," [Sonnet 31]
PE: 311
"Modern Love," [Sonnet 50]
PE: 311
"The Nuptials of Atilla"
ICBAP: 87
"Ode to the Spirit of Earth
in Autumn" ICBAP: 87
"Odes in Contribution to the
Song of French History"
ICBAP: 87
"The Old Chartist" ICBAP:
87; PE: 311
One of Our Conquerors BN:
78-79; Du: 112-113; EN:
99-100; ENE: 207;
ENES1: 164; ENES2:
176; Ma: 1406-1407
The Ordeal of Richard Fev-
erel BN: 77-79; Du:
113-114; EN: 100-101;
ENE: 207-208; ENES1:
164-165; ENES2: 176-177;
Ma: 1407-1408
"Pass We to Another Land"
ICBAP: 87
"Periander" ICBAP: 87;
PE: 311
"Phantasy" ICBAP: 87
"The Rape of Aurora"
ICBAP: 87
Rhoda Fleming BN: 79; Du:
114-115; EN: 101; ENE:
207; ENES1: 165; ENES2:
177; Ma: 1410-1411
Richard Feverel see The
Ordeal of Richard Feverel
Richmond Roy EN: 101
Sandra Belloni; or, Emilia in
England BN: 79; Du:
115; EN: 101-102; ENE:
208-209; ENES1: 165;
ENES2: 177; Ma: 1411-
1412
The Satirist DC1: 137
The Shaving of Shagpat BN:

79; Du: 115; EN: 102;
ENES1: 165; ENES2: 177
"The Tale of Chloe" SFC: 162;
Wa: 550
"The Teaching of the Nude"
ICBAP: 87
"The Test of Manhood" ICBAP:
87
The Tragic Comedians BN: 78;
Du: 115; EN: 102; ENE:
209; ENES1: 165; Ma: 1412
Vittoria EN: 103; ENE: 209;
ENES1: 165-166; ENES2:
177
"The Woods of Westermain"
ICBAP: 87; PE: 311
"Youth in Memory" PE: 311
MEREDITH, William
General ICBAP: 88
"Battlewagon" PE: 311
"Wedding Song" PE: 311
MERES, Francis
Poetrie SC: 72
MEREZHKOVSKY, Dmitriy Serge-
yevich
General Po: 2704
MEREZHKOVSKY, K.D.
Julian the Apostate Ke: 422
The Romance of Leonardo da
Vinci Ke: 422
MERI, Veijo
General Po: 2704
MERIMEE, Prosper
Les Ames du Purgatoire Fi:
121
"The Blue Room" SFC: 162;
Wa: 550; WaS1: 150
The Capture of the Redoubt
[L'Enlèvement de la redoute]
Fi: 122; Ke: 122; Wa: 550;
WaS1: 150
Carmen Fi: 121; Ke: 122;
Wa: 550; WaS1: 150
1572. Chronique du règne de
Charles IX Fi: 122
Colomba Fi: 122; Ke: 122;
Wa: 550; WaS1: 150
The Double Mistake [La Double
Méprise] Fi: 122; Ke: 122;
Wa: 550; WaS1: 150
L'Enlèvement de la redoute see
The Capture of the Redoubt
The Etruscan Vase [Le Vase
étrusque] Fi: 122; Ke:
122; WaS1: 150
"Federigo" WaS1: 150

"The Game of Backgammon"
Wa: 550; WaS1: 150
"Lokis" WaS1: 150
"Mateo Falcone" Fi: 122;
Ke: 122; SFC: 162; Wa:
550; WaS1: 150
Le Vase étrusque see The
Etruscan Vase
La Vénus d'Ille Fi: 122; Ke:
122; Wa: 550; WaS1:
150-151
"La Vision de Charles XI"
Wa: 551; WaS1: 151
MERIWETHER, Louise M.
General BAF: 212; BAW:
542
Daddy Was a Number Runner
BAF: 212-213; BAW: 542
MERLIN, Frank
I Got Shoes Br: 420
MERRILL, James
General ICBAP: 88; Po:
2705
"The Book of Ephraim" PE:
312
"Dreams About Clothes" PE:
312
"18 West 11th Street" PE:
312
"From the Cupola" ICBAP:
88
The Immortal Husband DC1:
137
Nights and Days Po: 2705
"In Nine Sleep Valley" PE:
312
"Syrinx" PE: 312
"The Thousand and Second
Night" ICBAP: 88
MERRIMAN, Henry Seton
Barlasch of the Guard ENES1:
166
Dross ENES1: 166
Flotsam ENES1: 166
From One Generation to Another
ENES1: 166
The Grey Lady ENES1: 166
In Kedar's Tents ENES1:
166
The Isle of Unrest ENES1:
166
The Last Hope ENES1: 166
The Phantom Future ENES1:
166
Prisoners and Captives
ENES1: 166

Roden's Corner ENES1: 166
The Slave of the Lamp ENES1:
166
The Sowers ENES1: 166
Suspense ENES1: 166
The Velvet Glove ENES1: 167
The Vultures ENES1: 167
With Edged Tools ENES1: 167
Young Mistley ENES1: 167
MERRITT, Abraham
General LCAB: 124
MERSON, Susan
Reflections of a China Doll
ADC: 245
MERTON, Thomas
General APC: 85; Po: 2705-
2708
No Man Is an Island Po: 2708
"St. Malachy" PE: 312
MERVILLE, M.M. and T. SAUVAGE
Farvas DC2: 252
MERWIN, William Stanley
General ICBAP: 88; LCAB:
124; MDAE: 345; MP: 66-
67; Po: 2709
"The Annunciation" PE: 312
"Beginning" PE: 312
"December Among the Vanished"
PE: 312
"Dictum: For a Masque of
Deluge" ICBAP: 88
"The Drunk in the Furnace"
ICBAP: 88
"Evening with Loe Shore and
Cliffs" PE: 312
"Folk Art" PE: 312
"For Now" PE: 312
"For the Anniversary of My
Death" PE: 312
"In a Clearing" PE: 312
"In the Time of the Blossoms"
PE: 312
"Learning a Dead Language"
PE: 313
"Lemuel's Blessing" LCAB:
125; MP: 66; PE: 313
"Leviathan" ICBAP: 88; Po:
2709
The Lice MP: 66
"The Locker Room" Wa: 551
"Memory of Spring" PE: 313
"Odysseus" PE: 313
"The Port" PE: 313
"The Prodigal Son" PE: 313
"Psalm: Out Fathers" PE:
313

"Signs" PE: 313

"Under Black Leaves" PE: 313

"Whenever I Go There" PE: 313

"When You Go Away" PE: 313

"You, Genoese Mariner" ICBAP: 88

MESNIL, Armand du
  Valdieu Ke: 122

METCALFE, James
  "Pray in May" PE: 313

MEUNIER, Lucien
  Les Modes DC2: 252

MEURICE, Paul
  La Famille Aubry Ke: 122-123

MEXIA, Pedro
  The Forest see FORTESCUE, Thomas [translator]

MEYER, Annie
  Black Souls MBA: 146

MEYER, Conrad Ferdinand
  The Amulet [Das Amulett] Fi: 376; Ke: 324; Wa: 551; WaS1: 151
  Angela Borgia Ke: 324; Wa: 551; WaS1: 151
  Gustav Adolfs Page see The Page of Gustavus Adolphus
  Der Heilige see The Saint
  Jurg Jenatsch Fi: 377; Ke: 324
  Das Leiden eines Knaben see The Suffering of a Boy
  The Monk's Wedding [Die Hochzeit des Mönchs] Fi: 376-377; Ke: 324; Wa: 551-552; WaS1: 151
  The Page of Gustavus Adolphus [Gustav Adolfs Page] Ke: 324; Wa: 551; WaS1: 151
  Plautus in the Convent Ke: 324; Wa: 552
  Die Richterin see The Woman Judge
  The Saint [Der Heilige] Fi: 376; Ke: 324-325; Wa: 551; WaS1: 151
  The Shot from the Pulpit [Der Schuss von der Kanzel] Fi: 377; Ke: 325; Wa: 552; WaS1: 151
  The Suffering of a Boy [Das Leiden eines Knaben] Fi: 377; Ke: 325; Wa: 551; WaS1: 151
  The Temptation of Pescara [Die Versuchung des Pescara] Fi: 377; Ke: 325; Wa: 552; WaS1: 151
  The Woman Judge [Die Richterin] Fi: 377; Ke: 325; Wa: 552; WaS1: 151

MEYER, Cord
  "Waves of Darkness" SFC: 162; Wa: 552

MEYER-ECKHARDT, Victor
  "Die Gemme" Wa: 552

MEYERS, Patrick
  Feedlot ADC: 245

MEYERS, William
  Spiro Who? ADC: 245

MEYNELL, Alice Christiana Gertrude Thompson
  General TA: 222

MEYNELL, Viola
  General Po: 2710

MEZU, Sebastian Okechukwu
  General BALE: 333

MHANGWANE, Sam
  General BALE, 333

MICHAEL, James Lionel
  General AL: 294

MICHAELS, Sidney
  Dylan ADC: 245
  Tchin-Tchin ADC: 245

MICHAUT, M.G.
  La Jalousie du Barbouille DC2: 252

MICHAUX, Henri
  General Po: 2710-2711
  "Chant de mort" Po: 2712
  "Clown" Po: 2712

MICHEAUX, Oscar
  General AAW: 67; BAF: 213; BAW: 543-544
  Hallelujah MBA: 146
  The Wind from Nowhere BAF: 213

MICHELET, Jules
  General LCAB: 125

MICHELSEN, Hans Gunter
  General Br: 420

MICHENER, James A.
  General AN: 202; ASF: 414
  "Mutiny" Po: 2712
  Tales of the South Pacific Ma:

1413
"Until They Sail" ASF: 414
MICKEL, Karl
    General Po: 2712
MICKSON, E.K.
    General BALE: 334
MIDDLETON, Christopher
    General ICBAP: 88
    Chinon of England ERP:
        327
    "Male Torso" PE: 313
MIDDLETON, O.E.
    "Not for a Seagull" Wa:
        552
MIDDLETON, Richard
    "The Bird in the Garden"
        Wa: 552
    "Fate and the Artist" Wa:
        552
    "The Ghost Ship" Wa: 552
    "A Tragedy in Little" Wa:
        553
MIDDLETON, Thomas
    General ED: 310-311; Log:
        52-59, 66, 77-79; TSD:
        91-95
    The Ant and the Nightingale:
        Or Father Hubburd's Tales
        ERP: 329
    Blurt, Master Constable; or
        The Spaniard's Night Walk
        EDC: 353; Log: 79
    A Chaste Maid in Cheapside
        DC1: 138-139; EDC: 353-
        354; Log: 61-62, 82; Ma:
        1414-1415; TSD: 92-95
    The Family of Love DC1:
        139; EDC: 354; Log: 65,
        80; Ma: 1415; TSD: 92,
        94
    A Game at Chess DC1: 139;
        EDC: 354-355; Log: 63-
        64, 84; Ma: 1415-1416;
        TSD: 91, 93-95
    Honest Whore see DEKKER,
        Thomas
    The Inner-Temple Masque
        Log: 66
    A Mad World, My Masters
        EDC: 355; Log: 63, 80-
        81; Ma: 1416-1417; TSD:
        94-95
    The Mayor of Queenborough;
        or, Hengist, King of Kent
        DC1: 139-140; EDC: 355;
        Log: 64, 82; TSD: 94

    Michaelmas Term DC1: 140;
        EDC: 355-356; Log: 62, 81;
        Ma: 1417; TSD: 92, 94-95
    More Dissemblers Besides Women
        DC1: 140; EDC: 356
    No Wit, No Help Like a Woman's
        DC1: 140; EDC: 356; Log:
        66; TSD: 92
    The Phoenix DC1: 140; EDC:
        356; Log: 65, 80; Ma:
        1417-1418; TSD: 92, 94
    The Puritan Log: 81; TSD:
        92
    The Revenger's Tragedy see
        TOURNEUR, Cyril
    The Second Maiden's Tragedy
        DC1: 16; EDC: 357; Log:
        239-244; TSD: 41, 91
    A Trick to Catch the Old One
        DC1: 141; EDC: 357; Log:
        62-63, 80; Ma: 1418-1419;
        TSD: 93
    The Viper and Her Brood
        EDC: 357
    The Widow EDC: 357
    The Witch DC1: 141; EDC:
        357; Log: 66, 82
    Women Beware Women DC1:
        141-142; EDC: 358; Log:
        60-61, 83; Ma: 1419-1420;
        TSD: 91-94
    Your Five Gallants DC1: 142;
        EDC: 358-359; Log: 80;
        Ma: 1420; TSD: 94
    _____ and Thomas DEKKER
    The Roaring Girl; or, Moll
        Cut-Purse DC1: 140-141;
        EDC: 359; Log: 15, 47,
        63, 81-82
    _____, Philip MASSINGER, and
        William ROWLEY
    The Old Law; or, A New Way
        to Please DC1: 16; EDC:
        361; TSD: 94
    _____ and William ROWLEY
    The Changeling DC1: 138;
        EDC: 359-361; Log: 59-60,
        83; Ma: 1421-1422; TSD:
        91-95
    A Fair Quarrel DC1: 139;
        EDC: 361; Log: 65-66, 82;
        Ma: 1422-1423; TSD: 91,
        93
    The Spanish Gypsy EDC:
        361; Log: 83-84; Ma: 1423;
        TSD: 92-93

———— and John WEBSTER
Anything for a Quiet Life
EDC: 359; Log: 82

MIDWOOD, Bart
The Dance of Mata Hari ADC:
245

MIGUEIS, José Rodrigues
Uma aventura inquietante Fi:
227
A escola do paraiso Fi: 227
Lodo Fi: 227
Pascoa feliz Fi: 227
Saudades para a dona gen-
ciana Fi: 227

MIHURA, Miguel
General Br: 420; Po: 2713
La bella Dorotea DC2: 252
Maribel y la extrana familia
DC2: 252
A media luz los tres DC2:
253
Mi adorado Juan DC2: 253
Ninette un Senor de Murcia
DC2: 253
Sublime Decision DC2: 253
Three Top Hats [Tres som-
breros de copa] Br: 420;
DC2: 253

MIKHALKOV, Sergei Vladimirovich
The Crayfish MD: 195

MIKSZATH, Kálmán
"The Big Spender" WaS1:
151
"The First Narrative" WaS1:
151
"The Golden Maid" WaS1:
152
"Lapaj, the Famous Bagpiper"
WaS1: 152
"The Late Lamb" WaS1: 152
"The Lottery" WaS1: 152
"The Novel of Two Manors"
WaS1: 314
"Pali Szücs's Luck" WaS1:
152
"Poor Janos Gelyi's Horses"
WaS1: 152
"The Queen's Skirt" WaS1:
152
St. Peter's Umbrella Ke:
422
"The Second Narrative" WaS1:
152
The Siege of Beszterce Ke:
422
"That Black Stain" WaS1:

152
"That Which Poisons the Soul"
WaS1: 152
"The Virgin Mary of Gozon"
WaS1: 152
"Where Has Magda Gal Gone?"
WaS1: 152

MILBURN, George
"The Apostate" Wa: 553
"A Pretty Cute Little Stunt"
Wa: 553
"The Wish Book" SFC: 162;
Wa: 553

MILES, Josephine
General Po: 2713

MILES, Judy
General WIL: 96-97

MILGATE, Rodney
A Refined Look at Existence
MAP: 385

MILL, John Stuart
General LCAB: 125; VP: 53-
54

MILLAR, Ronald
The Affair MDAE: 347

MILLAY, Edna St. Vincent
General ALL: 192-193; ASF:
414; Br: 420; LCAB: 125;
Ma: 1427-1429; MD: 195;
Po: 2713-2715
Aria da Capo ADC: 246; Br:
421; Ma: 1424; MD: 196;
Po: 2716
The Buck in the Snow Ma:
1424-1425
Conversations at Midnight Br:
421
"Euclid Alone Has Looked on
Beauty Bare" Ma: 1425;
PE: 313-314
A Few Figs from Thistles Ma:
1425-1426
"God's World" PE: 314
The Harp-Weaver and Other
Poems Ma: 1426-1427
Huntsman, What Quarry? LCAB:
125; Ma: 1427
The King's Henchman Br:
421; DC1: 142; MD: 196
"Justice Denied in Massachu-
setts" ICBAP: 88
The Lamp and the Bell Br:
421
"Memorial to D.C.: Elegy" PE:
314
"Oh, Oh, You Will Be Sorry

for That Word" PE: 314
"Oh, Sleep Forever in the
Latmian Cave" PE: 314
"On Hearing a Symphony of
Beethoven" PE: 314
The Princess Marries the
Page Br: 421
"Renascence" Po: 2716
Renascence and Other Poems
Ma: 1429-1430
"The Return" PE: 314
Second April Ma: 1430
"Sonnets" LCAB: 125
Two Slatterns and a King
Br: 421
The Wall of Dominoes Br:
421
"What's This of Death, from
You Who Never Will Die?"
PE: 314
"The White Peacock" ASF:
414
Wine from These Grapes
Ma: 1430-1431
MILLEN, Gilmore
Sweet Man BAW: 710-711;
Po: 2716
MILLER, Arthur
General ALL: 193-194; ASF:
415; Br: 421-425; JW:
396; LCAB: 125-126; Lon:
36-39; MD: 196-198;
MDAE: 351-358; Po: 2717-
2725
After the Fall ADC: 246-
247; ALL: 193-194; Br:
425-426; DC1: 142; Lon:
38; Ma: 1432; MD: 198;
MDAE: 351-352, 354-357;
Po: 2725-2728
All My Sons ADC: 247-248;
ALL: 193-194; Br: 426-
428; DC1: 143; Lon: 37;
Ma: 1432-1433; MD:
198; Po: 2728-2729; TMAP:
190; TMBP: 255
The Creation of the World
and Other Business ADC:
248-249; ALL: 194
The Crucible ADC: 249-251;
ALL: 193-194; Br: 428-
430; DC1: 143-144; Lon:
36-39; Ma: 1433-1434;
MD: 198-199; MDAE: 351-
354, 356-357; Po: 2729-
2730

Death of a Salesman ADC:
251-254; ALL: 193-194; Br:
430-436; DC1: 144-147;
Lon: 29, 37-39; Ma: 1434-
1435; MD: 199-201; Po:
2730-2734
An Enemy of the People ADC:
254; DC1: 147; MD: 201;
MDAE: 352, 357; Po: 2735
"Fame" ASF: 414; Wa: 553
"Fitter's Night" ASF: 415;
Wa: 553
Honors at Dawn Br: 436
"I Don't Need You Any More"
ASF: 415; Wa: 553
Incident at Vichy ADC: 254-
255; ALL: 193-194; Br:
436-437; Ma: 1435-1436;
MD: 201; MDAE: 352-355;
Po: 2735
The Man Who Had All the Luck
ADC: 255; ALL: 194; Br:
437; DC1: 147; MD: 201
A Memory of Two Mondays
ADC: 255; ALL: 193-194;
Br: 437; MD: 201
The Misfits ASF: 415; Br:
437-438; DC1: 147; MD:
201; MDAE: 354; Po: 2735-
2736
"Monte Sant' Angelo" ASF:
415; Wa: 553; WaS1: 152
"Please Don't Kill Anything"
ASF: 415; Wa: 553
The Price ADC: 255-256;
ALL: 194; Br: 438; MDAE:
352, 357; Po: 2736; TMBP:
185
"The Prophecy" Wa: 553
The Pussycat and the Expert
Plumber Who Was a Man Br:
438
"A Search for a Future" Wa:
553
They Too Arise Br: 438
A View from the Bridge ADC:
256-257; ALL: 193-194; Br:
438-439; DC1: 147-148;
Lon: 37; Ma: 1436; MD:
201-202; MDAE: 352-355,
389; Po: 2736; TMAP: 28
_____ and Stanley SILVERMAN
Up from Paradise ADC: 257
Miller, Cincinnatus Hiner see
MILLER, Joaquin
MILLER, Flournoy

Runnin' Wild BAP: 141
MILLER, Henry
General ALL: 195-196; AN:
202-204; ASF: 416; CN:
361-365; LCAB: 126; Ne:
73-74; Po: 2737-2743; Wo:
155-156
Black Spring CN: 365
Just Wild About Harry Po:
2743
Nexus see also The Rosy
Crucifixion CN: 365
Plexus see also The Rosy
Crucifixion CN: 365
The Rosy Crucifixion CN:
365
Sexus see also The Rosy
Crucifixion CN: 365;
Po: 2743
The Smile at the Foot of the
Ladder ASF: 415; CN:
365
Tropic of Cancer AN: 202;
CN: 365-367; LCAB:
126; Ma: 1437; Ne: 73;
Po: 2743-2745
Tropic of Capricorn CN:
367; LCAB: 127
MILLER, Hugh
General Ai: 137
MILLER, James
The Universal Passion Li:
243
MILLER, Jason
Nobody Hears a Broken Drum
ADC: 257
That Championship Season
ADC: 257-258
MILLER, Joaquin
General Cla: 112-113;
LCAB: 126
MILLER, Kelly
General BAF: 214; BAW:
546
MILLER, May
General BAF: 214; BAW:
547
Christophe's Daughters
BAP: 142
Graven Images BAP: 142-
143; MBA: 147
Harriet Tubman BAP: 143
Riding the Goat BAP: 143;
MBA: 147
Scratches BAP: 143
MILLER, Merle

The Sure Thing CN: 368
That Winter CN: 368
MILLER, Peter
General Po: 2745-2746
MILLER, Samuel
General AP: 443-444
Brief Retrospect of the Eight-
eenth Century AP: 443-444
MILLER, Schuyler
"The Cave" WaS1: 152
MILLER, Susan
Cross Country ADC: 258
MILLER, Vassar
General Po: 2746
MILLER, Walter M., Jr.
General ASF: 417
"Anybody Else Like Me?" Wa
553
"The Big Hunger" WaS1: 153
"Blood Bank" WaS1: 153
A Canticle for Leibowitz Po:
2746
"Check and Checkmate" WaS1:
153
"Cold Awakening" WaS1: 153
"Command Performance" WaS1:
153
"Conditionally Human" WaS1:
153
"Crucifixus Etiam" ASF: 416;
WaS1: 153
"The Darfsteller" ASF: 417
"Dark Benediction" WaS1: 153
"Death of a Spaceman" ["Me-
mento Homo"] WaS1: 153
"The Hoofer" WaS1: 153
"I Made You" WaS1: 153
"Memento Homo" see "Death
of a Spaceman"
"No Moon for Me" WaS1: 153
"Please Me Plus" WaS1: 153
"Six and Ten Are Johnny"
WaS1: 153
"The Soul-Empty Ones" WaS1:
153
"The Ties That Bind" WaS1:
153
"The Yokel" WaS1: 153
MILLS, Alison
Francisco BAF: 215
MILNE, Alan Alexander
General MD: 202; Mi: 258
Ariadne EDC: 362
Chloe Marr ENES1: 167
Dover Road EDC: 362
Four Days' Wonder ENES1:

167
The Fourth Wall EDC: 362
Give Me Yesterday EDC: 362
The Great Broxopp EDC: 362
The House at Pooh Corner ENES1: 167
Ivory Door EDC: 362
The Lucky One EDC: 362; MD: 202
Meet the Prince EDC: 362
Michael and Mary EDC: 362
Mr. Pim Passes By EDC: 363; ENES1: 167; MD: 202
Once on a Time ENES1: 167
Other People's Lives EDC: 363
Perfect Alibi EDC: 363
The Red House Mystery ENES1: 167
Sarah Simple EDC: 363
Success EDC: 363
They Don't Mean Any Harm EDC: 363
To Have the Honor EDC: 363
The Truth About Blayds EDC: 363
Two People ENES1: 167
Winnie-the-Pooh ENES1: 167; ENES2: 177
MILNER, Ronald
General AAPD: 395; BAP: 143-144; BAW: 548; MBA: 148
Black Quartet MBA: 150
How's the World Treating You? Br: 439
The Monster BAP: 144
The Warning--A Theme for Linda ADC: 258; BAP: 144; MBA: 148-149
What the Winesellers Buy ADC: 258; BAP: 144; MBA: 149-151
Who's Got His Own AAPD: 395; BAP: 144-145; MBA: 149-150
_____ and Charles MASON
Season's Reasons MBA: 150-151
MILOSZ, Czeslaw
General Po: 2747

MILOSZ, Oscar
General Po: 2747
MILTON, David Scott
Duet ADC: 258
MILTON, John
General Hen: 119-120; ICBAP: 88-89; LCAB: 126; Ma: 1444-14446
"Ad Patrem" ICBAP: 89
"L'Allegro" ICBAP: 89; Ma: 1440; PE: 314-315
"L'Allegro" and "Il Penseroso" LCAB: 127; PE: 315
"Areopagitica" Hen: 118; Ma: 1438-1439
"At a Solemn Music" PE: 315
"At a Vacation Exercise in the College" PE: 315-316
Comus DC1: 148-149; Ma: 1439-1440
"Cyriack, this three years day these eyes" [Sonnet 22] PE: 316
"The Doctrine of Divorce" Hen: 118
"Elegy Five: 'In Adventum Veris'" ["On the Coming of Spring"] ICBAP: 89
"An Epitaph on the Marchioness of Winchester" PE: 316
"Epitaphium Damonis" ["On the Death of Damon"] ICBAP: 89
"How Soon Hath Time" [Sonnet 7] "On His Having Arrived at the Age of Twenty-Three" ICBAP: 89; PE: 316
"I Did but Prompt the Age to Quit Their Clogs" [Sonnet 12] ICBAP: 89; PE: 316
"Lady that in the prime of earliest youth" [Sonnet 9] PE: 316
"Lawrence of Virtuous Father Virtuous Son" [Sonnet 20] PE: 316
"Lycidas" ICBAP: 89; LCAB: 127; Ma: 1440-1441; PE: 316-319
"Methought I Saw My Late Espoused Saint" [Sonnet 23] PE: 319
"Of Reformation" Hen: 117
"On His Blindness" see "Sonnet XIX"
"On His Deceased Wife" see

"Sonnet XXIII"

"On Shakespeare 1630" PE: 320

"On the Death of a Fair Infant Dying of a Cough" ICBAP: 90; PE: 320

"On the Late Massacre in Piemont" see "Sonnet XVIII"

"On the Lord General Fairfax, at the Siege of Colchester" [Sonnet 15] PE: 321

"On the Morning of Christ's Nativity Composed 1629" ICBAP: 90; LCAB: 127; Ma: 1442; PE: 321-322

"On the University Carrier" and "Another on the Same" PE: 322

"On Time" ICBAP: 90; PE: 322

Paradise Lost Be: 209; ICBAP: 90-91; LCAB: 126-127; Ma: 1442-1443; Ri2: 137-138

Paradise Lost--Book I ICBAP: 91

Paradise Lost--Book II ICBAP: 91

Paradise Lost--Book III ICBAP: 91

Paradise Lost--Book IV ICBAP: 91

Paradise Lost--Book V ICBAP: 91

Paradise Lost--Book VI ICBAP: 91

Paradise Lost--Book VIII ICBAP: 91

Paradise Lost--Book IX ICBAP: 91

Paradise Lost--Box X ICBAP: 92

Paradise Lost--Book XI ICBAP: 92

Paradise Lost--Book XII ICBAP: 92

Paradise Regained Be: 209; ICBAP: 92; LCAB: 126; Ma: 1443-1444

Paradise Regained--Books I and II ICBAP: 92

"Paraphrase of Psalm 114" PE: 322

"The Passion" ICBAP: 92; PE: 322

"Il Penseroso" ICBAP: 92; Ma: 1440; PE: 315, 322

Samson Agonistes DC1: 149-152; LCAB: 127; Ma: 1446-1447

"Sonnet VII" ["On His Having Arrived at the Age of Twenty-Three"] ICBAP: 92

"Sonnet XII" ["I Did but Prompt"] ICBAP: 92

"Sonnet XVI" ["To the Lord General Cromwell, May, 1652"] ICBAP: 92; PE: 322

"Sonnet XVIII" ["On the Late Massacre in Piemont"] ICBAP: 93; LCAB: 127; PE: 320-321

"Sonnet XIX" ["On His Blindness"] ICBAP: 93; Ma: 1441; PE: 319-320

"Sonnet XXIII" ["On His Deceased Wife"] ICBAP: 93

"The Tenure of Kings and Magistrates" Hen: 119

"To Mr. Lawrence" PE: 322

"To Mr. H. Lawes, on His Aires" [Sonnet 13] PE: 322

"To the Lord General Cromwell, May, 1652" see "Sonnet XVI"

"Upon the Circumcision" PE: 322

"When I Consider How My Light Is Spent" see "Sonnet XIX"

"When the Assault Was Intended to the City" [Sonnet 8] PE: 323

MIMS, Harley
General BAW: 548

MINOT, Stephen
"Journey to Ocean Grove" Wa: 554
"Sausage and Beer" ASF: 417

MIRBEAU, Octave
General MD: 202; Po: 2747-2748
Epidemic DC2: 253
Le Journal d'une femme de chambre Fi: 122
The Torture Garden [Le Jardin des supplices] Ke: 123; Po: 2748

MIRK, John
The Festival Hen: 20-21

MIRO, Gabriel

General Po: 2748-2749
Dentro del cercado Fi: 227
Nuestro padre San Daniel
Fi: 227
El obispo leproso Fi: 228
MISHIMA, Yukio
General Po: 2749-2750
Confessions of a Mask Ma:
1448; Po: 2749-2750
The Decay of the Angels
Ma: 1448
"Patriotism" Wa: 554; WaS1:
154
Runaway Horses Ma: 1448-
1449
Sailor Who Fell from Grace
with the Sea Ma: 1449;
Po: 2749-2750
The Sound of Waves Ma:
1449
The Temple of Dawn Ma:
1449-1450
The Temple of the Golden
Pavilion Ma: 1450; Po:
2749-2750
MISTRAL, Gabriela
General Po: 2751-2752
"Meciendo" Po: 2752
"¿Para Qué Viniste?" Po:
2752
MITCHELL, Irene Musillo
"Scenes from the Thistledown
Theatre" WaS1: 154
MITCHELL, James Leslie [Lewis
Grassic GIBBON]
General Ai: 267-268
Cloud Howe ENES2: 177
Gay Hunter ENES1: 167;
ENES2: 177
Grey Granite ENES2: 177
Image and Superscription
ENES2: 177
The Lost Trumpet ENES2:
177-178
A Scots Quair Ai: 267-268;
Po: 1244-1245
Spartacus ENES2: 178
Stained Radiance ENES2:
178
Sunset Song ENES1: 168;
ENES2: 178
The Thirteenth Disciple
ENES2: 178
Three Go Back ENES1: 168;
ENES2: 178
MITCHELL, Julian

The Undiscovered Country
ENES1: 168
MITCHELL, Langdon
Becky Sharp ADC: 259
Major Pendennis ADC: 259
The New York Idea ADC: 259;
Br: 439-440
MITCHELL, Leroy E., Jr.
General BAW: 549
MITCHELL, Loften
General AAPD: 396; BAF:
215; BAP: 147; BAW: 551;
MBA: 152
The Bancroft Dynasty MBA:
152
Blood in the Night BAP: 148
The Cellar BAP: 148; MBA:
152
Cocktails MBA: 152
Crossroads MBA: 152
The Depression Years BAP:
148
Harlem Homecoming MBA: 152
A Land Beyond the River ADC:
259; BAP: 148-149; Br:
440; MBA: 152
Star of Morning BAP: 148;
MBA: 152
Tell Pharoah MBA: 152
_____ and Irving BURGIE
Ballad for Bimshire BAP: 148;
MBA: 152-153
MITCHELL, Margaret
Gone with the Wind AN: 204;
Po: 2753-2754
MITCHELL, Silas Weir
General AF: 202-203; AN:
204; ASF: 417; Po: 2754
"The Autobiography of a
Quack" ASF: 417; Wa:
554
"The Case of George Dedlow"
Wa: 554
"The Fourteenth Guest" Wa:
554
"Hephzibah Guinness" Wa:
554
"A Madeira Party" Wa: 554
"A Man and a Woman" Wa:
554
"Miss Helen" Wa: 554
Roland Blake AF: 203; AN:
204
"The Sins of the Fathers" Wa:
554
"Thee and You" Wa: 554

"Was He Dead?" ASF: 417;
    Wa: 554
MITCHELL, William Ormond
    General Po: 2754
    The Kite Po: 2754
    Who Has Seen the Wind Po:
        2754-2755
MITCHISON, Naomi
    General Ai: 258
MITFORD, Jessica
    General LCAB: 127
MITFORD, Mary Russell
    General BN: 80
    Our Village ENES1: 168;
        ENES2: 178
MITFORD, Nancy
    General CN: 368
    Don't Tell Alfred CN: 368;
        ENES1: 168
MITRA, Premendra
    "The Great Big City" Wa:
        555
MITTELHOLZER, Edgar Austin
    General WIL: 97-100
    The Aloneness of Mrs. Chat-
        ham WIL: 107
    Children of Kaywana WIL:
        101-102
    Eltonsbrody WIL: 106
    The Harrowing of Hubertus
        WIL: 103
    The Jilkington Drama WIL:
        108
    Kaywana Blood WIL: 104-
        105
    Latticed Echoes WIL: 105-
        106
    The Life and Death of Sylvia
        WIL: 102-103
    The Mad MacMullochs WIL:
        105
    A Morning at the Office [A
        Morning in Trinidad]
        LCAB: 127; WIL: 100-
        101
    My Bones and My Flute WIL:
        103
    Of Trees and the Sea WIL:
        103-104
    The Piling of Clouds WIL:
        106-107
    Shadows Move Among Them
        WIL: 101
    A Swarthy Boy WIL: 107
    A Tale of Three Places WIL:
        104

Thunder Returning WIL: 106
A Tinkling in the Twilight WIL:
    105
Uncle Paul WIL: 107
The Weather Family WIL: 105
The Weather in Middenshot
    WIL: 102
With a Carib Eye WIL: 104
The Wounded and the Worried
    WIL: 107
MOBERG, Vilhelm
    General Po: 2755
    Bad Conduct Mark Ke: 361
    The Emigrants Ke: 361-362;
        Po: 2756
    The Last Letter Home Ke:
        362; Po: 2755-2756
    Soldat med Brutet Gevar Fi:
        411
    Unto a Good Land Ke: 362;
        Po: 2756
    Utvandrarna Po: 2755-2756
MODISANE, Bloke William
    General BALE: 334
MODUPE, Prince
    General BALE: 335
MOERS, Hermann
    When the Thistle Blooms [Zur
        Zeit der Distelblute] Br:
        440
MOFFETT, Cleveland
    General ASF: 417
MOFFITT, John
    "Along the Curb" ICBAP: 93
    "Nightmare's Nest" ICBAP:
        93
    "The Signals" ICBAP: 93
    "The Well" ICBAP: 93
MOFOKENG, Zakes
    General BALE: 335
Mogin, Georges see NORGE,
    Géo
MOGIN, Jean
    A Chacun Selon Sa Faim Br:
        440
    La Fille à la Fontaine Br:
        440
MOHRT, Michel
    General Po: 2756
MOIR, David Macbeth
    General Ai: 136
MOISE, Penina
    General JW: 103
MOLETTE, Barbara and Carlton
    MOLETTE
    Rosalee Pritchett ADC: 259;

BAP: 149-150; MBA:
156
_____, Carlton MOLETTE, and
Charles MANN
Doctor B.S. Black MBA:
156
MOLETTE, Carleton W.
General BAW: 552
MOLIERE [Jean Baptiste POQUE-
LIN]
General LCAB: 127
Les amants magnifiques see
The Magnificent Lovers
L'amour médecin DC2: 253
The Amorous Quarrel [Le
dépit amoureux] DC2:
255; EDC: 368
Amphitryon DC2: 253-254;
EDC: 369; Ma: 1451
L'avare see The Miser
The Blunderer; or, The
Mishaps [L'etourdi; ou
Les contre-temps] EDC:
369
The Bourgeois Gentleman
[Le bourgeois gentil-
homme] DC2: 254-255;
EDC: 369-370; Ma: 1451-
1452
Le dépit amoureux see The
Amorous Quarrel
The Doctor in Spite of Him-
self [L'médecin malgré
lui] DC2: 255; EDC:
370
Don Garcia of Navarre, or
The Jealous Prince [Dom
Garcie de Navarre, ou
Le prince jaloux] DC2:
255; EDC: 370
Don Juan, or The Feast with
the Statue [Don Juan, ou
Le festin de pierre] DC2:
255-256; EDC: 371-372;
LCAB: 128; Ma: 1452-
1453
L'école des femmes see The
School for Wives
L'école des maris see The
School for Husbands
L'étourdi; ou Les contre-
temps see The
Blunderer...
Les femmes savantes see
The Learned Ladies
Les fourberies de Scapin

see The Rogueries of Scapin
George Dandin; or The Abashed
Husband [Georges Dandin;
ou Le mari confondu] DC2:
257; EDC: 372-373
The Imaginary Invalid [The
Hypochondriac; Le malade
imaginaire] DC2: 256-257;
EDC: 373; Ma: 1453
L'impromptu de Versailles DC2:
256
The Learned Ladies [Les
femmes savantes] EDC:
373
The Magnificent Lovers [Les
amants magnifiques] EDC:
373-374
Le malade imaginaire see The
Imaginary Invalid
Le médecin malgré lui see The
Doctor in Spite of Himself
The Misanthrope [Le mis-
anthrope] DC2: 257-258;
EDC: 374-376; LCAB: 128;
Ma: 1453-1454; Po: 1601
The Miser [L'avare] DC2:
254, 258; EDC: 376; LCAB:
128; Ma: 1454-1455
Monsieur de Pourceaugnac
EDC: 376
La princesse d'Elide EDC:
376
Le registre d'Hubert DC2:
259
The Ridiculous Snobs [Les
précieuses riducules] DC2:
258-259; EDC: 376
The Rogueries of Scapin [Les
fourberies de Scapin] DC2:
256; EDC: 377
The School for Husbands
[L'école des maris] DC2:
259; EDC: 377
The School for Wives [L'école
des femmes] DC2: 259-
260; EDC: 377-378; Ma:
1455
Sganarelle DC2: 260
Tartuffe, or The Imposter
[Tartuffe, ou L'imposteur]
DC2: 260-261; EDC: 378-
380; Ma: 1455-1456
_____, Pierre CORNEILLE, and
Philippe QUINAULT
Psyché DC2: 259; EDC:
380

MOLINA CAMPOS, Enrique
General Po: 2757
MOLL, Ernest George
General Po: 2757
MOLLOY, Edward A.
The Comforter ADC: 260
Consider the Lilies ADC: 260
Five Star Saint ADC: 260
Guimpes and Saddles ADC: 260
MOLLOY, Michael
General Br: 440
MOLNAR, Ferenc
General Br: 440; MD: 202
Carnival [Farsang] Br: 441;
EDC: 380
Csoda a hegyek közt see
Miracle in the Mountains
Delicate Story EDC: 380
The Devil [Az ördög] Br:
441; EDC: 380
Egi es földi szerelem see
Launzi
Egy, ketto, három see
One, Two, Three
A farkas see The Wolf
Farsang see Carnival
The Glass Slipper Br: 441
The Good Fairy [A jó tünder]
Br: 441; EDC: 380-381
The Guardsman [Where Ignor-
ance Is Bliss; A testör]
Br: 441; DC2: 261;
EDC: 381
A hattyú see The Swan
Játék a kastélyban see
The Play's the Thing
Launzi [Egi és földi szere-
lem] Br: 441; EDC:
381
Liliom Br: 441; DC2: 261;
EDC: 381; MD: 202-203
Miracle in the Mountains
[Csoda a hegyek kozt]
EDC: 381; MD: 203
Olympia Br: 441
One, Two, Three [Egy, ketto,
három] EDC: 381
Az ördög see The Devil
The Phantom Rival [The Tale
of the Wolf] Br: 441
The Play's the Thing [Játék
a kastélyban] EDC:
382; MD: 203
The Red Mill Br: 441

The Swan [A hattyu] Br: 441;
EDC: 382
The Tale of the Wolf see The
Phantom Rival
A testor see The Guardsman
Unknown Girl EDC: 382
Where Ignorance Is Bliss see
The Guardsman
The Wolf [A farkas] EDC:
382
MOMADAY, N. Scott
"Angle of Geese" PE: 323
"The Bear" PE: 323
"Before an Old Painting of The
Crucifixion" PE: 323
"Buteo Regalis" PE: 323
House Made of Dawn Ma: 1457
MOMBERT, Alfred
General Po: 2757
MONKHOUSE, Allan Noble
General Mi: 259; TA: 224
MONRO
"The Garden" PE: 323
MONROE, Harold
"Trees" PE: 323
MONROE, Harriet
General LCAB: 128; Po:
2758
MONSARRAT, Nicholas
General Po: 2758
MONSEY, Derek
Less Than Kind DC1: 152
MONTAGU, Elizabeth
General EC: 101
MONTAGU, Lady Mary Wortley
General EC: 101
MONTAGUE, Charles Edward
General TA: 225
"Action" Wa: 555
A Hind Let Loose Po: 2759
MONTAGUE, John
General LCAB: 128
"The Cry" Wa: 555
"Death of a Chieftain" Wa:
555
"The Trout" LCAB: 128
MONTAIGNE, Michel Eyquem de
General LCAB: 128
MONTALBAN, Juan Perez de
Secundo Tomo de las Comedias
DC2: 261
El Valor Perseguido DC2:
262
MONTALE, Eugenio
General LCAB: 128; Po:
2759-2762

La Bufera e altro Po: 2762
"Elegia di pico Farnese" Po:
2762
Farfalla di Dinard Fi: 268
Occasioni Po: 2763
"L'Orto" Po: 2763
Ossi di seppia Po: 2763
MONTALVO, Garci
Amadis de Gaula Fi: 228;
Ke: 210
MONTALVO, Juan
General LCAB: 128
MONTAURIER, Jean
Comme a travers le feu Ke:
123
MONTCHRETIEN, Antoine de
David ou l'Adultere DC2:
262
Ecossoise DC2: 262
Hector DC2: 262
Sophonisbe DC2: 262
MONTE, Eric
General MBA: 157
Cooley High BAP: 150;
MBA: 157
This Is Our World MBA:
157
MONTEFORTE TOLEDO, Mario
General Po: 2763
MONTEMAYOR, Jorge de
Diana Fi: 228; Ke: 210
MONTESQUIEU, Charles de
Secondat, Baron de
Lettres persanes Fi: 122-
123
MONTESQUIOU, Robert de
General Po: 2764
MONTGOMERIE, Alexander
General Ai: 43; ICBAP:
93; NI: 336-337
The Cherry and the Slae
LCAB: 129
MONTGOMERIE, William
General Ai: 273
MONTGOMERY, Marion
General Po: 2764
"Ye Olde Bluebird" ASF:
417
MONTGOMERY, Robert
Lotta ADC: 260
Subject to Fits: A Response
to Dostoyevsky's "The
Idiot" ADC: 260
_____ and Joseph CHAIKIN
Electra ADC: 260
MONTHERLANT, Henry Millon

de
General Br: 442-443; LCAB:
129; MD: 203; Po: 2764-
2770
The Bachelors Fi: 123; Ke:
123
Les Bestiaires Br: 443
Brocéliande Br: 443; EDC:
382; Po: 2770
The Bullfighters Ke: 123
The Cardinal of Spain [Cardinal
d'Espagne] Br: 443; DC2:
262; EDC: 382-383; Po:
2770-2771
Celles qu'on prend dans ses
bras see Women One Takes
in One's Arms
Chaos and Night Fi: 123; Ke:
123
The City Whose Prince Is a
Child [La Ville dont le
prince est un enfant] Br:
446; DC2: 264; EDC: 383;
MD: 204; Po: 2767
The Civil War [La Guerre
Civile] Br: 444; EDC:
383
Demain il fera jour see To-
morrow the Dawn
Demon of Good Fi: 123
Desert Love Ke: 123
Don Juan Br: 444; DC2:
263; EDC: 383; Po: 2770
The Exile [L'Exil] Br: 444;
EDC: 383; Po: 2772
Fils de personne see No
Man's Son
Les Garçons Po: 2766
La Guerre civile see The
Civil War
Un Incompris see Misunder-
stood
The Lepers Ke: 123
Malatesta Br: 444; DC2: 263;
EDC: 384; MD: 204; Po:
2772
The Master of Santiago [Le
Maître de Santiago] Br:
444-445; DC2: 263; EDC:
384; Ke: 123; MD: 204;
Po: 2767, 2770, 2772
Misunderstood [Un incompris]
Br: 444; EDC: 384
No Man's Son [Fils de Per-
sonne] Br: 445; DC2: 263;
EDC: 384

Les Olympiques Ke: 123
Pasiphaë EDC: 384; LCAB:
129
Pity for Women Fi: 123
Port-Royal Br: 445; DC2:
263; EDC: 384-385; MD:
204; Po: 2770, 2772-2773
Queen After Death; or, How
to Kill Women [La Reine
Morte; ou Comment on tue
les Femmes] Br: 445-
446; DC2: 263-264; EDC:
385; MD: 204; Po: 2767,
2773-2774
Le Songe Fi: 123; Ke: 123
Tomorrow the Dawn [Demain
il Fera Jour] Br: 446;
EDC: 385
La Ville dont le prince est
un enfant see The City
Whose Prince Is a Child
Un Voyageur solitaire est un
diable Po: 2774
Women One Takes in One's
Arms [Celles Qu'on Prend
dans ses Bras] Br: 443-
444; DC2: 262; EDC:
386; MD: 203; Po: 2767
Young Girls Fi: 123
MONTIEL BALLESTEROS, Adolfo
Gaucho Tierra Po: 2774
MONVEL, Jacques de
Les Victimes Cloitrees DC2:
264
MOOCK, Armando
General Br: 446; Po: 2774
MOODIE, Susanna
General ECL: 77-78
Roughing It in the Bush
ECL: 77-78
Life in the Clearing ECL:
78
MOODY, Anne
Mr. Death: Four Stories
BAF: 216
MOODY, Michael Dorn
The Shortchanged Review
ADC: 260
MOODY, Ralph
General LCAB: 129
MOODY, William Vaughn
General Br: 447; Cla:
113-114; Lon: 39; MD:
204; Po: 2775
The Death of Eve Br: 447;
MD: 204

The Faith Healer ADC: 260;
Br: 447; MD: 204
The Fire-Bringer ADC: 261;
Br: 447; DC1: 152; MD:
204
The Great Divide ADC: 261;
Br: 447; MD: 204
The Masque of Judgment ADC:
261; DC1: 152; MD: 204
"An Ode in Time of Hesitation"
PE: 323; Po: 2775
MOORCOCK, Michael
Behold the Man ENES2: 178
MOORE, Bai Tamia Johnson
Ebony Dust BALE: 335
MOORE, Brian
General CFAE: 243-244; CN:
368; Po: 2775-2777; Sch:
228-229
An Answer from Limbo CN:
369; ENE: 209; Ma: 1458
Catholics Ma: 1458-1459
The Emperor of Ice-Cream
CFAE: 244; CN: 369; ENE:
209; Ma: 1459; Po: 2777
The Feast of Lupercal CN:
369; ENE: 209-210; Ma:
1459-1460; Po: 2775-2776
I Am Mary Dunne CFAE: 243;
Ma: 1460-1461
The Lonely Passion of Judith
Hearne CN: 370; ENE:
210; Ma: 1461; Po: 2775-
2776
The Luck of Ginger Coffey
CN: 369-370; ENE: 210;
Ma: 1461-1462; Po: 2776-
2777
"Uncle T" Wa: 555
MOORE, C.L.
see also her pseudonyms Law-
rence O'DONNELL and Lewis
PADGETT
General ASF: 418; LCAB:
129
"The Bright Illusion" WaS1:
154
"The Fairy Chessmen" ASF:
418
"No Woman Born" WaS1: 154
"There Shall Be Darkness"
ASF: 418
"Vintage Season" ASF: 418
MOORE, Edward
General EC: 102; Li: 244
The Foundling EC: 102; Li:

244

The Gamester DC1: 152;
    Li: 244

Moore, Edward J. see IRWIN,
    James

MOORE, George

General BN2: 84-86; Br:
    447-448; LCAB: 129;
    MBD: 61; Mi: 259-260;
    Po: 2777-2782; Sch:
    230-234; TA: 227

"Agnes Lahens" Wa: 555

"Albert Nobbs" Wa: 555;
    WaS1: 154

"Alms-Giving" Wa: 555

Aphrodite in Aulis ENES1:
    168; ENES2: 178

"An Art Student" see
    "Mildred Lawson"

The Bending of the Bough
    DC1: 152; MBD: 58

The Brook Kerith ENES1:
    168; ENES2: 178; Ma:
    1463-1464; Po: 2781-2782;
    Sch: 234-235

"A Clerk's Quest" Wa: 555

Confessions of a Young Man
    ENES2: 178; Po: 2782-
    2783

Diarmuid and Grania Po:
    2783

A Drama in Muslin EN:
    103; ENES1: 168; ENES2:
    178; Ma: 1464-1465; Po:
    2783; Sch: 235

Esther Waters BN2: 85-86;
    EN: 103; ENE: 210;
    ENES1: 169; ENES2: 178-
    179; LCAB: 129; Ma:
    1465-1466; Po: 2783-2784;
    Sch: 235-236

Evelyn Innes ENES2: 179;
    Po: 2784; Sch: 236

"The Exile" Wa: 556; WaS1:
    154

"Fugitives" Wa: 556

"Hail and Farewell" ENES1:
    169; ENES2: 179; Po:
    2784-2785

Héloïse and Abélard ENES1:
    169; ENES2: 179; Po:
    2781

"Henrietta Marr" Wa: 556;
    WaS1: 154

"Home Sickness" Wa: 556

"In the Clay" Wa: 556;

WaS1: 154

"Julia Cahill's Curse" Wa:
    556; WaS1: 154

The Lake BN2: 85; ENES1:
    169; ENES2: 179; Sch: 236

"A Letter to Rome" WaS1:
    154

"Liodin and Curithir" Po:
    2781; WaS1: 154

"Marban and Luachet" Po:
    2781

A Mere Accident ENES2: 179;
    Po: 2785

Mike Fletcher ENES1: 169;
    ENES2: 179

"Mildred Lawson" Wa: 556;
    WaS1: 154

A Modern Lover EN: 103;
    ENES1: 169; ENES2: 179;
    Ma: 1466-1467; Po: 2786

A Mummer's Wife EN: 103;
    ENE: 210-211; ENES1: 169;
    ENES2: 179; Ma: 1467-
    1468; Po: 2786-2787; Sch:
    236

"Peronnik the Fool" WaS1:
    155

"A Play-House in the Waste"
    Wa: 556

"Priscilla and Emily Lofft" Wa:
    556; WaS1: 155

"A Remembrance" Po: 2787

"Sarah Gwynn" Wa: 556;
    WaS1: 155

Sister Teresa ENE: 211;
    ENES2: 180; Po: 2787;
    Sch: 236

"So on He Fares" Wa: 556;
    WaS1: 155

"Some Parishioners" Wa: 556;
    WaS1: 155

Spring Days ENES2: 180

A Story-Teller's Holiday
    ENES2: 180

"The Sweetness of the Past"
    Po: 2788

Ulick and Soracha Po: 2781

The Untilled Field Po: 2788

Vain Fortune ENES2: 180

"The Way Back" Wa: 556;
    WaS1: 155

"The Wedding Gown" Wa:
    556; WaS1: 155

The Wild Goose BN2: 85; Wa:
    556; WaS1: 155

"Wilfred Holmes" Wa: 557;

WaS1: 155
"The Window" WaS1: 155
MOORE, Honor
Mourning Pictures ADC:
261
MOORE, John
General Ai: 72
MOORE, Marianne
General ALL: 196-197;
LCAB: 129; Ma: 1471-
1472; MP: 68-69; Po:
2789-2794
"Apparition of Splendor"
ICBAP: 93; PE: 323;
Po: 2794-2795
"Bird-Witted" ICBAP: 93;
Ma: 1469; PE: 323
"Black Earth" PE: 323
"Camilla Sabina" PE: 323
"A Carriage from Sweden"
PE: 323
"Critics and Connoisseurs"
PE: 323; Po: 2795
"Dream" ICBAP: 94; Po:
2795
"Elephants" PE: 324
"A Face" PE: 324
"The Fish" ICBAP: 94; Ma:
1469; PE: 324; Po: 2795
"The Frigate Pelican" PE:
324
"He 'Digesteth Harde Yron'"
Ma: 1469-1470; PE: 324
"The Hero" PE: 324
"The Icosaphere" PE: 324;
Po: 2796
"In Distrust of Merits" Ma:
1470; PE: 324; Po: 2796
"The Jerboa" Ma: 1470;
PE: 324-325
"Marriage" PE: 325
"Mathematics" Po: 2796
"The Mind Is an Enchanting
Thing" PE: 325
"The Monkeys" PE: 325;
Po: 2796
"Nevertheless" PE: 325
"No Swan So Fine" ICBAP:
94; PE: 325
"Novices" PE: 325
"O to Be a Dragon" ICBAP:
94; PE: 325
"An Octopus" ICBAP: 94;
PE: 325
"The Pangolin" ICBAP: 94;
PE: 325

"The Past Is the Present" PE:
325
"Poetry" PE: 325
"Roses Only" PE: 325
"St. Nicholas" ICBAP: 94
"See in the Midst of Fair
Leaves" PE: 326
"Silence" PE: 326
"Snakes, Mongooses, Snake-
charmer and the Like" PE:
326
"Spenser's Ireland" LCAB:
129; PE: 326
"The Steeple-Jack" Ma: 1472;
PE: 326
"Tell Me, Tell Me" ICBAP:
94; PE: 326
"Then the Ermine" ICBAP:
94; PE: 326
"To a Snail" ICBAP: 94; PE:
326; Po: 2796
"Tom Fool at Jamaica" PE:
326; Po: 2797
"What Are Years?" ICBAP:
94; PE: 326
"The Wood-Weasel" PE: 326
MOORE, Merrill
General Po: 2797
"Granny Weeks" PE: 327
"The Gun Barrel Looked at Him
with Love in Its Single Eye-
hole" PE: 327
"The Sound of Time Hangs
Heavy in My Ears" PE:
327
MOORE, Nicholas
"Alteration" PE: 327
"Unity Quitbread at Eltham"
PE: 327
MOORE, Pamela
General Po: 2797-2798
MOORE, Rosalie
"The Grasshopper Man" PE:
327
MOORE, Thomas
General Fog: 50; Re: 211-
212
"Irish Melodies" Re: 212
"Lalla Rookh" Re: 211-212
"The Songs of Fionnuala" PE:
327
MOORE, Thomas Sturge
General Mi: 261; Po: 2798;
TA: 229
Daimonassa Br: 448
"From Titian's 'Bacchanal' in

the Prado at Madrid"
ICBAP: 94
Judith Br: 448
"Love's Faintness Accepted"
PE: 327
Mariamne Br: 448
"Silence (I)" ICBAP: 94
"To Silence" ICBAP: 94;
PE: 327
MOORHOUSE, Frank
"The American, Paul Jonson"
WaS1: 155
Conference-Ville MAP: 242-243
Tales of Mystery and Romance
MAP: 242-243
MOPELI-PAULIS, Attwell Sidwell
General BALE: 336
MORA, Ferenc
Golden Coffin Ke: 423
Song of the Wheatfields Ke:
423
MORAES, Dom
General Po: 2798
MORAES, Vinicius de
General Po: 2798
MORALES, Rafael
General Po: 2799
MORAN, Michael
Jinx Bridge ADC: 261
MORAND, Paul
General Po: 2799
"Mr. U" Po: 2799
MORANTE, Elsa
Arturo's Island [L'Isola di
Arturo] Ke: 245-246;
Po: 2799-2800
The House of Liars Ke:
246
MORATIN, Leandro Fernandez
de
La Estera DC2: 264
El Si De Las Niñas DC2:
264
El Viejo y la Niña DC2:
264
MORAVIA, Alberto
General Br: 448; Po: 2800-2802
Agostino [Two Adolescents]
Fi: 270; Ke: 247; Po:
2803; SFC: 163; Wa: 557
The Automaton [L'Automa]
Po: 2803; Wa: 557
Beatrice Cenci Br: 448;
DC2: 264; EDC: 405;

Po: 2803
"The Chimpanzee" Wa: 557
"The Chinese Vase" Wa: 557
"The Comics" Wa: 557
The Conformist Fi: 268; Ke:
246
Conjugal Love Fi: 268; Ke:
246
"Crime at the Tennis Club"
Wa: 557
"Disobedience" ["Luca"] Wa:
557
Il Disprezzo see A Ghost at
Noon
The Empty Canvas Fi: 268-269; Ke: 246
The Fancy Dress Party Fi:
269; Ke: 246
A Ghost at Noon [Il Disprezzo]
Fi: 269; Ke: 246; Po:
2803
"Going to the People" Wa: 557
"In a Strange Land" Wa: 557
The Indifferent Ones [Gli In-differenti] Fi: 269; Ke:
246-247; Po: 2804
The Lie Fi: 269
"Luca" see "Disobedience"
"Measurements" Wa: 557
Mistaken Ambitions Fi: 269-270
"Mother's Boy" Wa: 557
"The Negro and the Old Man
with the Bill-Hook" Wa:
557
"Rain in May" Wa: 557
"Scatter-Brains" Wa: 557
"A Sick Boy's Winter" Wa:
558
"Tired Courtesan" Wa: 558
Two: A Phallic Novel Fi:
270
Two Adolescents see Agostino
Two Women Fi: 270; Ke:
247; Ma: 1473
The Woman of Rome Fi: 270;
Ke: 247; Wa: 1473
MORDAUNT, Thomas Osbert
"Sound, Sound the Clarion"
PE: 327
MORE, Hannah
Coelebs in Search of a Wife
ENES2: 180
MORE, Henry
General Ba: 98-99; Bon: 59;
Hen: 39

MORE, Paul Elmer
General APC: 178-179;
LCAB: 129-130; Po:
2804-2805
The Shelbourne Essays Po:
2806
MORE, Sir Thomas
General Hen: 130; SC: 74-
76
The Confutacyon of Tyndales
Answere Hen: 96
The Dialogue of Comfort
Hen: 129; SC: 75
The History of King Richard
III Hen: 47
Utopia Hen: 96-98; Ma:
1474-1475; Ri2: 518; SC:
74-76
MOREAU, Louis
"The Face" SFC: 163; Wa:
558
Moreno, Baldomero Fernández
see FERNANDEZ MORENA,
Baldomero
MORETO, Augustin
El Desden Con el Desden
DC2: 265
Escarraman DC2: 265
El Lindo don Diego DC2:
265
MORGAN, Charles Langbridge
General BN2: 87; Br:
448; CN: 370; MD: 204;
MDAE: 360-361; Mi: 261-
262; Po: 2806-2807
A Breeze in Morning CN:
370
The Burning Glass Br:
448; MD: 204; Po: 2806-
2807
The Flashing Stream Br:
448; MD: 204; Po: 2807
The Fountain see Sparken-
broke Trilogy
The Gunroom CN: 370
The Judge's Story CN: 370;
Po: 2806
Portrait in a Mirror see also
Sparkenbroke Trilogy
ENES2: 180
The River Line MD: 205;
Po: 2806-2807
Sparkenbroke Trilogy CN:
370; Po: 2807
The Voyage CN: 371
MORGAN, David

Second Wind ADC: 261
MORGAN, Edwin
General Ai: 317-318
MORGAN, Lady [Sydney OWENSON]
General BN: 80
The Novice of St. Dominick
ENES2: 180
St. Clair ENES2: 180
The Wild Irish Girl ENES2:
180
MORGENSTERN, Christian
General Po: 2807-2808
Galgenlieder Po: 2808
MORI OGAI
"The Abe Family" Wa: 558
"As If" Wa: 558
"The Boat on the River Takase"
Wa: 558
"The Courier" Wa: 558
"The Dancing Girl" Wa: 558
"Exorcising Demons" Wa: 558
"Half a Day" Wa: 558
"Hanako" Wa: 558
"Kuriyama Daizan" Wa: 558
"The Last Phrase" Wa: 558
"Last Will and Testament of
Okitsu Yagoemon" Wa: 558
"Living Alone" Wa: 558
"Play" Wa: 559
"A Record of Froth on the
Water" Wa: 559
"Sahashi Jingorō" Wa: 559
"Sanshō the Bailiff" ["Sanshō
the Steward"] Wa: 559;
WaS1: 155
"Sleeping Late" Wa: 559
"The Snake" Wa: 559
"Tsuge Shirōzaemon" Wa: 559
"Under Reconstruction" Wa:
559
"Yasui's Wife" Wa: 559
MORICZ, Zsigmond
Be Good Til You Die Ke: 423
Golden Mud Ke: 423
Transylvania Ke: 423
MORIER, James Justinian
General BN: 81
The Adventures of Hajji Baba
of Ispahan BN: 81;
ENES2: 181
MÖRIKE, Eduard
"The Farmer and His Son"
Wa: 559
"The Hand of Jezerte" Wa:
559
"Lucie Gelmeroth" Wa: 559

Mozart auf der Reise nach Prag Fi: 377-378; Wa: 599; WaS1: 155
Painter Nolten Fi: 378; Ke: 325
"The Stuttgart Hutzelmännlein" Wa: 560
"The Treasure" Wa: 560
MORITZ, Karl Philipp
Anton Reiser Fi: 378; Ke: 325; LCAB: 130
MORLEY, Christopher
General AN: 204; APC: 41; Po: 2808-2810
MORRIS, A.G.
"Panahard and Mr. Snaith" SFC: 163; Wa: 560
MORRIS, Garrett
The Secret Place ADC: 261
MORRIS, John [John HEARNE and Morris CARGHILL]
Candywine Fever WIL: 108
Fever Grass WIL: 108
MORRIS, Mervyn
General WIL: 108-109
The Pond WIL: 109
Seven Jamaican Poets WIL: 109
MORRIS, Ralph
The Life and Astonishing Adventures of John Daniel ENES2: 181
MORRIS, William
General Ma: 1476-1477; VP: 55-57
"The Chapel in Lyoness" ICBAP: 95; PE: 327
"The Defence of Guenevere" ICBAP: 95; PE: 327; VP: 55-57
The Defence of Guenevere and Other Poems VP: 55-57
"A Dream" WaS1: 156
A Dream of John Ball ENES1: 169; ENES2: 181
"The Earthly Paradise" ICBAP: 95; VP: 56
"Gertha's Lovers" WaS1: 156
"Golden Wings" PE: 328; WaS1: 156
"The Haystack in the Floods" ICBAP: 95; PE: 328
"The Hollow Land" PE: 328; WaS1: 156

The House of the Wolfings ENES1: 169; ENES2: 181
"The Judgment of God" PE: 328
"King Arthur's Tomb" ICBAP: 95; PE: 328
"Lindenborg Pool" WaS1: 156
"Lonely Love and Loveless Death" PE: 328
News from Nowhere ENES1: 170; ENES2: 181-182
"The Nymph's Song of Hylas" [The Life and Death of Jason, Book 4] PE: 328
"Rapunzel" PE: 328; VP: 57
The Roots of the Mountains ENES2: 182
Sigurd the Volsung VP: 55
"Sir Galahad" ICBAP: 95
The Story of the Glittering Plain ENES2: 182; WaS1: 156
"The Story of the Unknown Church" PE: 328; WaS1: 156
The Sundering Flood ENES2: 182
"Svend and His Brethren" WaS1: 156
The Water of the Wondrous Isles ENES1: 170; ENES2: 182
The Well at the World's End ENES2: 182
The Wood Beyond the World ENES2: 182
MORRIS, Wright
General AN: 205; CFAE: 246-247; CN: 371-372; Ne: 74-75; Po: 2810-2813
Cause for Wonder CN: 372
Ceremony in Lone Tree CFAE: 246; CN: 372; LCAB: 130; Ma: 1478; Ne: 75; Po: 2814
The Deep Sleep CN: 372
The Field of Vision CFAE: 247; CN: 372-373; Ma: 1478-1479; Ne: 75; Po: 2814
The Home Place CN: 373
The Huge Season AN: 205; CN: 373; Ma: 1479
In Orbit CFAE: 246; CN: 373; Ne: 75; Po: 2814-2815

The Inhabitants CN: 373
Love Among the Cannibals
    CN: 373-374; Ma: 1479;
    Wa: 560
Man and Boy CN: 374
The Man Who Was There CN:
    374
My Uncle Dudley CN: 374;
    Ma: 1479-1480
One Day CFAE: 247; CN:
    374; LCAB: 130; Po:
    2815
What a Way to Go CN: 374-
    375
The Works of Love CN: 375
The World in the Attic CN:
    375
MORRISON, Arthur
    General TA: 230
    A Child of the Jago ENES1:
        170; ENES2: 182
    To London Town ENES1:
        170
MORRISON, John
    General MAP: 245
    "The Battle of Flowers" Wa:
        560
    "The Lonely One" Wa: 560
    "The Sleeping Doll" Wa:
        560
    "To Margaret" Wa: 560
MORRISON, Nancy Brysson
    General Ai: 277
MORRISON, Toni
    General AAF: 85-86; BAF:
        217
    The Bluest Eye AAF: 85-
        86; BAF: 217-218; Ma:
        1481
    Song of Solomon AAF: 86
    Sula AAF: 85-86; BAF:
        218; Ma: 1481
MORSE, Jedidiah
    General AP: 584
MORSELLI, Enrico Luigi
    General Br: 449
MORSTIN, Ludwik Hieronim
    General Po: 2815
LA MORTIERE
    Motifs de retraite Fi: 123
MORTIMER, John
    General Br: 449; MDAE:
        364
    Call Me a Liar Br: 449
    David and Broccoli Br:
        449

The Dock Brief Br: 449
I Spy Br: 449
Two Stars for Comfort Br:
    449
What Shall We Tell Caroline?
    Br: 449
The Wrong Side of the Park
    Br: 449
MORTIMER, Penelope
    The Pumpkin Eater CN: 375;
        ENES1: 170
MORTON, Thomas
    General AP: 445-446; Da:
        55
    "Rise Oedipus" PE: 328
    Speed the Plough DC1: 153
    Zorinski Li: 245
MOSCHEROSCH, Johann Michael
    Soldaten-Leben Ke: 325-326
MOSCOSO VEGA, Luis A.
    General Br: 450
MOSEL, Tad
    General MDAE: 366
    All the Way Home ADC: 262
MOSENSOHN, Yigal
    "Corporal Sonnenberg" Wa:
        560
    "Sergeant Green" Wa: 560
    "Sheep" Wa: 560
MOSES, Gilbert
    General AAPD: 397; BAP:
        151; BAW: 556
    Roots MBA: 158
MOSS, Carlton
    Prelude to Swing MBA: 158
MOSS, Grant
    Death Come Creeping in the
        Room MBA: 158
MOSS, Howard
    General ICBAP: 95
    "The City Lion" PE: 328
    "Persistence of Song" ICBAP:
        95
MOSTAR, Gerhart Herrmann
    General Br: 450
    The Birthday [Die Geburt] Br:
        450
    Bis Der Schnee Schultz Br:
        450
    Meier Helmbrecht Br: 450
    Putsch Imx Paris Br: 450
    Der Zimmerherr Br: 450
MOTJUWADI, Stanley
    General BALE: 336
MOTLEY, John Lothrop
    General LCAB: 130

MOTLEY, Willard
General AAL: 234; AAW:
68; ASF: 418; BAF: 218-
219; BAW: 558; CN: 375;
Po: 2815
"The Almost White Boy"
WaS1: 156
"The Beautiful Boy" Wa:
560
"Bedroom Scene" Wa: 561
"The Beer Drinkers" Wa:
561
"The Boy" WaS1: 156
"The Boy Grows Up" Wa:
561; WaS1: 156
"Boy Meets Boy" Wa: 561
"The Concert" Wa: 561
"Father Burnett's Vestry"
Wa: 561
"How the Road Was Built"
Wa: 561
Knock on Any Door AAL:
234; BAF: 219-220; CN:
375-376; Ma: 1482; Po:
2815
Let No Man Write My Epitaph
BAF: 220; CN: 376; Ma:
1482; Po: 2815
Let Noon Be Fair BAF: 220
"Needles" Wa: 561
"Niño de Noche" Wa: 561
"Street Walker" Wa: 561
"V-Female" Wa: 561
We Fished All Night BAF:
221; CN: 376; Po: 2815
"Weasel Takes a Woman" Wa:
561
MOTOJICHO
Daybreak Dreams MBA: 159
MOTSISI, Moses Casey
General BALE: 336
MOTTEUX, Peter Anthony
General Bon: 43-44; Li:
246
Farewell Folly Li: 246
MOTTRAM, R.H.
The Spanish Farm Trilogy
ENES2: 183
MOUNTFORT, William
Greenwich Park Li: 248
MOURLET, Michel
General Po: 2816
MOWAT, David
General MDAE: 367
MOWATT, Anna Cora
General AD: 183-185; ALL:

233; Lon: 62
Fashion, or Life in New York
AD: 184-185; ADC: 262
MPHAHLELE, Ezekiel
General BALE: 337-339; Po:
2816
"Across Down Stream" WaS1:
156
The African Image BALE: 338
"A Ballad of Oyo" WaS1: 156
"The Barber of Bariga" WaS1:
156
Down Second Avenue BALE:
337-338
"Down the Quiet Street" WaS1:
156
"Grieg on a Stolen Piano" WaS1:
157
"He and the Cat" WaS1: 157
"In Corner B" WaS1: 157
"The Leaves Were Falling" WaS1:
157
"The Living and the Dead"
Wa: 561; WaS1: 157
The Living and the Dead and
Other Stories BALE: 338
"The Master of Doornvlei" WaS1:
157
"Mrs. Plum" WaS1: 157
"Out Brief Candle" WaS1: 157
"A Point of Identity" WaS1:
157
"Reef Train" WaS1: 157
"The Suitcase" WaS1: 157
"Tomorrow You Shall Reap"
WaS1: 157
Voices in the Whirlwind BALE:
338
"We'll Have Dinner at Eight"
WaS1: 157
"The Woman" WaS1: 157
"The Woman Walks Out" WaS1:
157
MPHANDE, John
General BALE: 339
MQAYISA, Khayalethu
Confused Mhlaba BALE: 339
MROZEK, Slawomir
General Br: 450
"Art" Wa: 561
Tango Br: 450
MTSHALI, Oswald Mbuyseni
[Joseph]
General BALE: 340
MUCHA, Jiri
The Problems of Lieutenant

Knap Ke: 423

MUELAS, Federico
General Po: 2816

MUGOT, Hazel
General BALE: 340

MUHAJIR, El [Marvin X; Marvin
JACKMAN]
The Black Bird BAP: 152
Take Care of Business BAP:
152

MUIR, Edwin
General Ai: 231; EP: 200-
205; ICBAP: 95; LCAB:
130; Po: 2817-2824
"The Animals" PE: 329; Po:
2824
"The Annunciation" ICBAP:
95
"Ballad of Hector in Hades"
ICBAP: 95; PE: 329
"Ballad of the Flood" PE:
329
"Ballad of the Soul" PE:
329
"The Combat" PE: 329
"The Covenant" PE: 329
"The Days" PE: 329
"Dialogue" PE: 329
"The Enchanted Knight"
ICBAP: 95; PE: 329
"The Gate" PE: 329
"The Groove" PE: 329
"The Horses" PE: 329
"The Human Fold" PE: 329
"The Island" ICBAP: 95
"The Journey Back" EP:
201; PE: 329; Po: 2824
"The Labyrinth" PE: 329-
330
"The Little General" PE:
330
The Marionette ENES2: 183
"Milton" ICBAP: 96
"The Mythical Journey" PE:
330
"The Narrow Place" PE:
330
"One Foot in Eden" PE: 330
"Orpheus' Dream" PE: 330
"Outside Eden" PE: 330
Poor Tom ENES2: 183
"The Recurrence" PE: 330
"The Return" ICBAP: 96
"Telemachos Remembers"
ICBAP: 96
The Three Brothers ENES2:

183
"The Three Mirrors" PE: 330
"To J.F.H." PE: 330
"The Toy Horse" ICBAP: 96;
PE: 330; Po: 2825
"The Transfiguration" LCAB:
130
"Troy" ICBAP: 96
"Twice-Done, Once-Done" PE:
330
"Variations on a Time Theme"
ICBAP: 96; PE: 330
"The Voyage" PE: 330
"The Wheel" PE: 330
"The Window" PE: 330

MUIR, John
General APC: 102; Cla: 114

MUJIA, Ricardo
Bolívar en Junín Br: 451

MUJZHEL, V.
A Year Ke: 423

MUKASA-SSALI, Paul
General BALE: 341

MUKHERJI, Shankar [Sankar]
General Po: 2825

MULAISHO, Dominic
General BALE: 341

MULIKITA, Fwanyanga Matale
General BALE: 341

MULOCK, Dinah Maria
General BN: 81
Avillion ENES2: 183
John Halifax, Gentleman BN:
81; ENES1: 170; ENES2:
183

MUMFORD, Lewis
General APC: 75-76

MUNCH-PETERSEN, Gustaf
General Po: 2825

MUNDAY, Anthony
General ERP: 331-335; Log:
125-129, 135; SC: 76-77
The Downfall of Robert, Earl
of Huntington [The Death of
Robert, Earl of Huntington]
Log: 127-128
"I Serve a Mistress Whiter Than
the Snow" PE: 331
John a Kent and John a Cumber
Log: 127
Zelauto ERP: 331-335; Hen:
157

MUNDAY, Anthony [translator]
Palmerin D'Oliva [ANONYMOUS]
Hen: 213

MUNFORD, Robert

General AD: 171; Da: 81
The Candidates DC1: 153
MUNGER, Mrs. Dell H.
The Wind Before the Dawn
LCAB: 130
MUÑIZ, Carlos
General Po: 2825
MUNK, Kaj
General Br: 451; MD: 205
Death of Ewald DC2: 265
He Sits at the Melting Pot
Br: 451; DC2: 265
An Idealist Br: 451; DC2:
265
The Word [Ordet] Br: 451;
DC2: 265; MD: 205; Po:
2826
MUNONYE, John
General BALE: 342
MUNRO, Alice
"Boys and Girls" Wa: 562
"The Dance of the Happy
Shades" WaS1: 157
"Day of the Butterfly" WaS1:
158
"The Office" Wa: 562
"The Shining House" Wa:
562
"The Time of Death" WaS1:
158
"Walker Brothers Cowboy"
Wa: 562
"Winter Wind" WaS1: 158
MUNRO, Charles Kirkpatrick
[Charles Walden Kirkpatrick
MacMULLAN]
General Mi: 262-263
Munro, Hector Hugh see SAKI
MUNRO, Neil [Hugh FOULIS]
General Ai: 200; TA: 232
Munro, Ronald Eadie see
GLEN, Duncan
MUNTHE, Axel
General Po: 2828
MURDOCH, Iris
General BN2: 88-90; CFAE:
252-256; CN: 376-378;
LCAB: 131; MDAE: 368;
Po: 2828-2837; Sch:
237-240
An Accidental Man ENES1:
171; ENES2: 183
The Bell BN2: 89-90; CFAE:
254-255; CN: 378-379;
ENE: 211-212; ENES1:
171; ENES2: 183; Ma:

1483-1484; Po: 2830-2832,
2834, 2837-2838; Sch: 240
The Black Prince ENES1: 171;
ENES2: 183-184; Ma: 1484
Bruno's Dream CFAE: 255;
ENE: 212; ENES1: 171;
ENES2: 184; Ma: 1484-1485;
Po: 2839; Sch: 240
A Fairly Honourable Defeat
ENES1: 171-172; ENES2:
184; Sch: 240
The Flight from the Enchanter
CFAE: 254-255; CN: 379-
380; ENE: 212-213; ENES1:
172; ENES2: 184; Ma: 1485-
1486; Po: 2831, 2839; Sch:
240
The Italian Girl CN: 380;
ENE: 213-214; ENES1:
172; ENES2: 184; Ma: 1486-
1487; Po: 2832; Sch: 240-
241
The Nice and the Good CN:
380; ENE: 214; ENES1: 172;
ENES2: 184-185; Ma: 1487-
1488; Po: 2839; Sch: 241
The Red and the Green CN:
380-381; ENE: 214; ENES1:
172; Ma: 1488; Po: 2840;
Sch: 241
The Sacred and Profane Love
Machine ENES2: 185
The Sandcastle CN: 381-382;
ENE: 214-215; ENES1: 172;
ENES2: 185; Ma: 1489-
1490; Po: 2831-2832, 2834
The Sea, the Sea ENES2: 185
A Severed Head CFAE: 254;
CN: 382; ENE: 215-216;
ENES1: 172; ENES2: 185;
Ma: 1490-1491; Sch: 241
The Time of the Angels CN:
382-383; ENE: 216; ENES1:
173; ENES2: 185; Ma:
1491-1492; Po: 2830
Under the Net BN2: 88-90;
CFAE: 252-253, 255-256;
CN: 383-384; ENE: 216-
218; ENES1: 173; ENES2:
185; LCAB: 131; Ma: 1492-
1493; Po: 2830-2831, 2834,
2840-2841; Sch: 241-242
The Unicorn BN2: 89; CFAE:
255; CN: 384; ENE: 218;
ENES1: 173; ENES2: 186;
Ma: 1493-1495; Sch: 242

An Unofficial Rose CN: 385;
ENE: 218-219; ENES1:
173; ENES2: 186; Ma:
1495-1496; Po: 2830, 2841
A Word Child ENES2: 186
MURDOCH, Walter
General Po: 2841-2842
MURDOCK, Frank
Davy Crockett DC1: 153
MURDOCK, John
The Triumph of Love DC1:
153
MURE, Sir William
General Ai: 48
MURFREE, Mary Noailles [pseud.
Charles Egbert CRAD-
DOCK]
General AF: 205-206; AN:
205; ASF: 118
"A-Playin' of Old Sledge at
the Settlemint" ASF:
117; Wa: 562
"The Bushwackers" ASF:
118; Wa: 562
"The Casting Vote" Wa: 562
"The Dancin' Party at Har-
rison's Cove" Wa: 562
"Drifting Down Lost Creek"
ASF: 118; Wa: 562
"The 'Harnt' That Walks Chil-
howee" ASF: 118; Wa:
562
In the Tennessee Mountains
AF: 206
"The Mystery of Witch-Face
Mountain" Wa: 562
"Over on T' Other Mounting"
ASF: 118
"The Panther of Jolton's
Ridge" Wa: 562
"The Phantom of Bogue
Holauba" Wa: 562
"The Phantoms of the Foot-
Bridge" Wa: 563
The Prophet of the Great
Smokey Mountains AN:
205
"The Raid of the Guerilla"
Wa: 563
"The Riddle of the Rocks"
Wa: 563
"The Romance of Sunrise
Rock" Wa: 563
"Star in the Valley" Wa:
563
"Taking the Blue Ribbon at

the County Fair" Wa: 563
MURO, Amado Jesus
General ASF: 419
MURPHY, Arthur
General EC: 102; Li: 249-
250
All in the Wrong DC1: 153
The Way to Keep Him DC1:
153
MURPHY, John
General Br: 451
MURPHY, Richard
General LCAB: 131
MURPHY, Thomas
General TMIP: 89-91
Famine TMIP: 91
The Morning After Optimism
TMIP: 91-92
On the Inside TMIP: 91-92
On the Outside TMIP: 91-92
The Sanctuary Lamp TMIP:
93
Snakes and Reptiles TMIP:
93
A Whistle in the Dark Br:
451; TMIP: 89-90, 93-94
The White House TMIP: 94
MURRAY, Albert
General BAF: 221-222; BAW:
562
Trainwhistle Guitar BAF: 222
MURRAY, Charles
General Ai: 201
MURRAY, Gilbert
General Po: 2842-2843
MURRAY, John
The Prince of Mandalore BAP:
152-153
_____ and Allen BORETZ
Room Service ADC: 263
MURRAY, Judith Sargent Stevens
General AP: 584
MURRAY, Thomas Cornelius
General Br: 451-452; MD:
205; Mi: 263; Po: 2843;
TA: 232
Aftermath Br: 452
Autumn Fire Br: 452; DC1:
153; MD: 205
Birthright Br: 452
The Blind Wolf Br: 452
Maurice Harte Br: 452
The Pipe in the Fields Br:
452
Sovereign Love Br: 452
Spring Br: 452

MURRY, John Middleton
General Po: 2844-2846
The Necessity of Communism
Po: 2847
The Problem of Style Po:
2847
Shakespeare Po: 2847
Murry, Kathleen Beauchamp see
MANSFIELD, Katherine
MUSAUS, Johann Karl August
von
Grandison der Zweite Ke:
326
MUSIL, Robert
General Po: 2847-2850
The Blackbird [Die Amsel]
Po: 2850; WaS1: 158
"The Completion of Love"
see "The Perfecting of a
Love"
Drei Frauen Po: 2850-2851
"Grigia" Fi: 378; Ke: 326;
Po: 2851; Wa: 563; WaS1:
158
"The Lady from Portugal"
["The Portuguese Lady,"
"Die Portugiesin"] Fi:
378-379; Ke: 326-327;
Wa: 563; WaS1: 158
The Man Without Qualities
[Der Mann ohne Eigenschaf-
ten] DC2: 266; Fi: 378-
379; Ke: 326; Po: 2847,
2849-2850, 2852-2856
"The Perfecting of a Love"
["The Completion of Love"]
Fi: 380; Wa: 563; WaS1:
158
"Die Portugiesin" see "The
Lady from Portugal"
Die Schwärmer Br: 452;
DC2: 265; Ke: 327; Po:
2856-2857
The Temptation of Silent
Veronika [Die Versuchung
der Veronika] Fi: 380;
Po: 2858; Wa: 564; WaS1:
158
"Tonka" Fi: 380-381; Ke:
327; Po: 2857; Wa: 564;
WaS1: 158
Vinzenz und die Freundin
bedeutender Männer Po:
2859
Young Törless [Die Ver-
wirrungen des Zöglings

Törless] Fi: 381; Ke: 327;
Po: 2849, 2858-2859
MUSINGA, V.E.
General BALE: 342
MUSSET, Alfred Louis Charles de
Barberine EDC: 386
Bettine EDC: 386
The Candle-Stick [Le Chande-
lier] EDC: 386
A Caprice [Un Caprice] DC2:
266; EDC: 386
Les Caprices de Mariamne see
The Follies of Marianne
Carmosine EDC: 386
La Confession d'un enfant du
siècle Fi: 123
The Cup and the Lip [La Coupe
et les Lèvres] EDC: 386
"Les Deux Maîtresses" Wa:
564
"Emmeline" Wa: 564
Fantasio DC2: 266; EDC:
386
The Follies of Marianne [Les
Caprices de Mariamne] DC2:
266; EDC: 387
Il ne faut jurer de rien see
You Can't Be Sure of Any-
thing
Lorenzaccio DC2: 266; EDC:
387-388
"Mimi Pinson" Wa: 564
No Trifling with Love [On Ne
Badine Pas Avec l'Amour]
DC2: 266; EDC: 388
La Nuit Vénitienne... see
A Venetian Night...
"Le Secret de Javotte" Wa:
564
A Venetian Night; or, Laur-
ette's Wedding [La Nuit
Vénitienne; ou, Les Noces
de Laurette] EDC: 388
You Can't Be Sure of Anything
[Il ne faut jurer de rien]
EDC: 388
MUSTAPHA, Matura
Black Slaves, White Chains
MBA: 159
Rum an' Coca-Cola MBA: 159
MUSYOKI, Thomas
General BALE: 342
MUTIGA, Joe
General BALE: 342
MUTWA, Vusamazulu Credo
General BALE: 343

MWANGI, Meja
  General BALE: 343
  Kill Me Quick BALE: 343
MWAURA, Joshua
  General BALE: 343
MWAURA, Mike
  General BALE: 343
MYERBERG, Michael
  Dear Judas ADC: 263
MYERS, Leopold Hamilton
  General BN2: 90; Ri2:
    285-289; Sch: 242
  The "Clio" Ri2: 285-286
  The Near and the Far
    ENES1: 174; ENES2:
    186; Ri2: 285-289
  The Orissers ENES2: 186;
    Ri2: 285-286
  The Pool of Vishnu ENES2:
    186; Ri2: 288
  The Root and the Flower
    ENES2: 186; Ri2: 288-
    289
  Strange Glory Ri2: 285-286
MYERS, Walter D.
  General BAF: 223

N

NABBES, Thomas
  General LJCD: 250-251
NABOKOV, Vladimir [see also
    V. SIRIN]
  General ASF: 420-421; Br:
    452-453; CFAE: 258-263;
    CN: 385-387; LCAB:
    131; MDAE: 369-370; Ne:
    75-78; Po: 2861-2868
  Ada or Ardor: A Family
    Chronicle Ma: 1497; Po:
    2868-2869
  "The Admiralty Needle" Wa:
    564
  "An Affair of Honor" Wa:
    564; WaS1: 158
  "The Assistant Producer"
    ASF: 419; Wa: 565
  "The Aurelian" Wa: 565
  "Bachmann" Wa: 565; WaS1:
    158
  Bend Sinister CN: 387;
    Ke: 423; Ma: 1497-1498;
    Ne: 77; Po: 2869-2870
  "Benevolence" WaS1: 158
  Camera Obscura [Laughter

    in the Dark] CN: 387
  "Christmas" WaS1: 159
  "A Christmas Story" ASF: 419;
    Wa: 565; WaS1: 159
  "The Circle" Wa: 565
  "Cloud, Castle, Lake" ["Cloud,
    Lake, Tower"] ASF: 419;
    Wa: 565
  "Conversation Piece, 1945" see
    "Double Talk"
  Dar see The Gift
  "A Dashing Fellow" Wa: 565;
    WaS1: 159
  Death [Smert'] Br: 453
  Dedushka see The Grandfather
  The Defense CN: 387-388;
    Ma: 1498; Ne: 78; Wa:
    565
  Despair [Otchayanie] CN:
    388; Ma: 1498-1499; Ne:
    76-77; Po: 2880
  "Details of Sunset" WaS1:
    159
  "The Doorbell" Wa: 565;
    WaS1: 159
  "Double Talk" ASF: 419; Wa:
    565; WaS1: 159
  Eugene Onegin [translation of
    Pushkin] Po: 2870-2871
  The Event [Sobytie] Br: 453;
    MDAE: 369
  The Exploit CN: 388
  "The Eye" ["Sogtyadatai"]
    CN: 388; Wa: 565
  "The Fight" Wa: 565; WaS1:
    159
  "First Love" ASF: 419; Wa:
    565
  "A Forgotten Poet" ASF: 419;
    Wa: 565
  The Gift [Dar] CN: 388-389;
    Ke: 423; Ma: 1499; Ne:
    76; Po: 2870
  The Grandfather [Dedushka]
    Br: 453
  "Guidebook to Berlin" ["A Guide
    to Berlin"] Wa: 565; WaS1:
    159
  Invitation to a Beheading
    [Priglashenie Na Kazn']
    CFAE: 262; CN: 389; Ne:
    78; Po: 2883-2884
  Izobretenie Val'sa see The
    Waltz Invention
  "Khvat" see "A Dashing
    Fellow"

King, Queen, Knave CN: 389
"Lance" ASF: 419
Laughter in the Dark see Camera Obscura
"A Letter That Never Reached Russia" WaS1: 159
"Letter to Russia" Wa: 566
"Lips to Lips" ASF: 419; Wa: 566
Lolita CFAE: 259-263; CN: 389-392; Ke: 423-424; Ma: 1499-1501; Ne: 76-78; Po: 2871-2880
"The Magician" Wa: 566
"A Matter of Chance" WaS1: 159
"Music" Wa: 566
"Notification" Wa: 566
"A Nursery Tale" WaS1: 159
"The Offense" Wa: 566
Otchayanie see Despair
Pale Fire CFAE: 259, 263; CN: 392-393; Ke: 424; LCAB: 131; Ma: 1501-1502; Ne: 76-78; Po: 2880-2882
"The Passenger" WaS1: 159
"Perfection" Wa: 566
Pnin CFAE: 263; CN: 393; Ke: 424; Ma: 1502-1503; Ne: 77; Po: 2882
The Pole [Polius] Br: 453
"Port" Wa: 566; WaS1: 159
"The Potato Elf" ASF: 419; Wa: 566; WaS1: 159
Priglashenie Na Kazn' see Invitation to a Beheading
"The Razor" Wa: 566; WaS1: 159
The Real Life of Sebastian Knight CFAE: 259-261, 263; CN: 393-394; Ke: 424-425; Ma: 1503; Ne: 77; Po: 2884-2885
"Recruitment" Wa: 566
"The Return of Chorb" Wa: 566; WaS1: 159
"Scenes from the Life of a Double Monster" ASF: 420; Wa: 566
"The Scoundrel" see "An Affair of Honor"
"Signs and Symbols" ASF:

420; Wa: 566; WaS1: 159
Skital'tsy see The Wanderers
Smert' see Death
Sobytie see The Event
"Soglyadatai" see "The Eye"
Solus Rex CN: 394
"Spring in Fialta" ASF: 420; Wa: 566; WaS1: 160
"The Storm" WaS1: 160
"Terror" Wa: 567; WaS1: 160
"That in Aleppo Once..." ASF: 420; Wa: 567
"Time and Ebb" ASF: 420; Wa: 567
The Tragedy of Mister Morn [Tragediya Gospodina Morna] Br: 453
"Triangle in a Circle" ASF: 420; Wa: 567
Ultima Thule CN: 394
"The Vane Sisters" Wa: 567; WaS1: 160
"A Visit to a Museum" Wa: 567
The Waltz Invention [Izobretenie Val'sa] ADC: 263; Br: 453-454; MDAE: 369
The Wanderers [Skital'tsy] Br: 454

NAGAI KAFU
"The River Sumida" WaS1: 160
NAGENDA, John
General BALE: 344
NAHAM, Rabbi Bratylav
"A Story About a Clever Man and a Simple Man" Wa: 567
NAHARRO, Torres
Comedia Jacinta DC2: 267
Comedia Serafina DC2: 267
NAIPAUL, Shiva
General WIL: 109
The Chip-Chip Gatherers WIL: 110-111
Fireflies WIL: 110
NAIPAUL, Vidiadhar Surajprasad
General LCAB: 131; Po: 2885-2886; WIL: 111-116
An Area of Darkness WIL: 122-123
"A Christmas Story" WaS1: 160
"The Enemy" WaS1: 160
A Flag on the Island Wa:

567; WIL: 124-125

"Gopi" WaS1: 160

"Greenie and Yellow" Wa: 567

Guerillas ENES2: 186; WIL: 127

"Gurudeva" WaS1: 160

"Heart" Wa: 567

A House for Mr. Biswas ENES1: 174; ENES2: 186-187; Po: 2885-2886; WIL: 118-120

In a Free State Wa: 567; WIL: 126-127

The Loss of Eldorado WIL: 125-126

"Man-man" Wa: 567

The Middle Passage WIL: 120-121

Miguel Street ENES2: 187; WIL: 117-118

The Mimic Men ENES2: 187; WIL: 123-124

Mr. Stone and the Knight's Companion ENES1: 174; ENES2: 187-188; WIL: 121-122

"The Mourners" WaS1: 160

"My Aunt Gold Teeth" WaS1: 160

The Mystic Masseur ENES2: 188; Po: 2885; WIL: 116-117

"One Out of Many" Wa: 567; WaS1: 160

The Overcrowded Barracoon WIL: 127

The Suffrage of Elvira ENES2: 188; WIL: 117

"Tell Me Who to Kill" Wa: 568; WaS1: 160

Najera, Manuel Gutierrez see GUTIERREZ NAJERA, Manuel

NAKASA, Nathaniel Ndzivane General BALE: 344-345

NALE ROXLO, Conrado General Br: 454; Po: 2886-2888

Cristina's Pact [El pacto de Cristina] Br: 454

Judith y las rosas Br: 455; DC2: 294; Po: 2888

The Mermaid Tail [La cola de la sirena] Br: 455

Una viuda difícil Br: 455; DC2: 294; Po: 2886

NALKOWSKA, Zofia "Happiness" Wa: 568

NAPIER, Lonne L. Play Me No Carols MBA: 159

NARAYAN, Rasipuram Krishnaswami General Po: 2888-2890

"A Breach of Promise" Wa: 568

The Guide Po: 2890

"A Horse and Two Goats" Wa: 568

NASBY, Petroleum V. [David Ross LOCKE] General ASF: 421-422; AN: 174

"A Fictitious Fact" ASF: 421

NASH, N. Richard The Girls of Summer ADC: 263-264

Keep It in the Family ADC: 264

The Rainmaker ADC: 264; DC1: 153

See the Jaguar ADC: 264

NASH, Ogden "Literary Reflection" PE: 331

"The Turtle" PE: 331

NASHE, Thomas General ED: 313-314; ERP: 339-358; Hen: 107; PS: 108-112, 118-123; SC: 77-78

"Adieu, Farewell Earth's Bliss" ICBAP: 96

The Anatomie of Absurditie Hen: 105

"If I Must Die" [from The Unfortunate Traveller] PE: 331

"Litany in Time of Plague" PE: 331

Pierce Penniless Hen: 106; SC: 77

"Spring the Sweete Spring, Is the Yere's Pleasant King" PE: 331

Summer's Last Will and Testament PS: 112-114; TSD: 71

The Terrors of the Night SC: 77

The Unfortunate Traveller ENES1: 174; ENES2: 188; ERP: 339-358; Hen: 166-

167; Ma: 1504; PS: 108-
110; SC: 77-78
NATANSON, Jacques
General Br: 455
L'Eté Br: 455
Le Greluchon Délicat Br:
455
NATHAN, George Jean
General Po: 2890-2891
NATHAN, Robert
General AN: 205-206; CN:
394; Po: 2891
Autumn CN: 394
The Bishop's Wife CN: 394
The Color of Evening CN:
395
The Devil with Love CN:
395
The Fiddler in Barly CN:
395
Jonah CN: 395
Long After Summer CN:
395
The Mallot Diaries CN: 395
Mr. Whittle and the Morning
Star CN: 395
One More Spring CN: 395
The Orchid CN: 395
Peter Kindred CN: 395
Portrait of Jennie CN: 395
The Puppet Master CN: 396
Road of Ages CN: 396
Sir Henry CN: 396
So Love Returns CN: 396
A Star in the Wind CN:
396
Stonecliffe CN: 396
There Is Another Heaven
CN: 396
The Wilderness Stone CN:
396
Winter in April AN: 205;
CN: 396
The Woodcutter's House
CN: 396
NAUGHTON, Bill
General MDAE: 372
Alfie ENES1: 174
NAVEL, Georges
General Po: 2891
NAVROZOV, Lev
Welcome to Soviet America
ADC: 264
NAZARETH, Peter
General BALE: 345
NDEBELE, Njabulo

General BALE: 345
NDU, Pol Nnamuzikam
General BALE: 346
NEAL, John
General ASF: 422; Da: 113
"Courtship" WaS1: 161
"David Whicher" ASF: 422;
WaS1: 161
"The Haunted Man" WaS1:
161
"The Ins and Outs" WaS1:
161
"Otter-Bag" WaS1: 161
"Robert Steele" WaS1: 161
"The Utilitarian" WaS1: 161
"The Young Phrenologist"
WaS1: 161
NEAL, Larry
General BAF: 223; BAP:
153-154; BAW: 566; MBA:
160
NEAL, Robert
General AN: 206
NEALE, Thomas
General LJCD: 251
NEERA, Anna
Senio Ke: 247
NEIDIG, William J.
General ASF: 422
NEIHARDT, John G.
General Po: 2891-2892
A Cycle of the West Po: 2892
NEILSON, John Shaw
General Po: 2892-2894
NEKRASOV, N.A.
Zizn' i Poxozdenija Tixona
Trostnikova Fi: 459
NEKRASOV, Viktor Platonovich
General Po: 2894
Home Town Ke: 425
Kira Georgievna Ke: 425
NEMCOVA, Bozhena
Babicka Ke: 425
"Babs" Wa: 568
"The Castle and the Village"
Wa: 568
Karla Ke: 425; Wa: 568
"Poor People" Wa: 568
"Wild Bára" Wa: 568
NEMECEK, Zdenek
General Po: 2895
NEMEROV, Howard
General CFAE: 267; CN:
396; JW: 107; LCAB: 131;
Ma: 1505-1506; Po: 2895-
2896

Federigo, or, The Power of
Love CN: 397
The Homecoming Game CFAE:
267; CN: 397; Ma: 1505
The Melodramatists CN: 397
"Painting a Mountain Stream"
PE: 331
"Runes" PE: 331
"The Sanctuary" PE: 331
"Santa Claus" PE: 331
"The View" PE: 331
NEMES, Gyorgy
One Brief Moment Ke: 425
NEMIROFF, Robert
General MBA: 160
_____, Charlotte ZALTZBERG,
Judd WOLDIN, and Robert
BRITTAN
Raisin ADC: 264
NEMTSOV, Vladimir
The Golden Bottom Ke: 425
NEOGY, Rajat
General BALE: 346
NERUDA, Pablo
General LCAB: 131; Ma:
1507; Po: 2896-2898
The Grapes and the Wind
[Las uvas y el viento]
Po: 2899
Residence on Earth [Residen-
cia en la tierra] Po:
2899
NERVAL, Gérard de
Aurélia Fi: 123-124; Ke:
123-124
"L'Histoire de la reine du
matin et de Soliman,
prince des Génies" Wa:
568
L'Imagier de Harlem DC2:
267
"Jemmy" Wa: 568
Le Marquis de Fayolle Fi:
124; Ke: 124; Wa: 568
Octavie Fi: 124; Ke: 124
Roman tragique Fi: 124
Sylvie Fi: 124; WaS1:
161
Voyage en Orient Fi: 124;
Ke: 124
NERVAT, Marie
General Po: 2900
NERVO, Amado
General Po: 2900
NESBIT, Edith [E. NESBIT;
Mrs. Hubert BLAND]

General LCAB: 19; TA: 235
NEULS, Jan
The Struggle for Coal Ke:
425
NEUTSCH, Erik
Spur der Steine Fi: 381
NEVEUX, Georges
General Br: 455; MD: 205;
Po: 2900-2901
NEVEUX, Pol
General Po: 2901
NEVILLE, Edgar
General Po: 2901
NEVILLE, Mary
Arthur; or, A Knight of Our
Own Day ENES2: 188
NEVILLE, Michael
Ballymurphy ADC: 265
NEWBOLT, Henry John
General TA: 236
NEWBY, Percy Howard
General CFAE: 270; CN:
397; LCAB: 132; Po:
2901-2902; Sch: 242-243
Agents and Witnesses ENES2:
189
The Barbary Light CN: 397;
ENES2: 189
A Guest and His Going CN:
397; ENES2: 189; Ma:
1508; Po: 2902
A Journey to the Interior CN:
398; ENES2: 189; Ma: 1508
Kith ENES2: 189
Mariner Dances ENES2: 189
One of the Founders ENES2:
189
The Picnic at Sakkara CN:
398; ENES2: 189; Ma:
1508; Po: 2902
The Retreat CN: 398; ENES2:
189; Ma: 1508-1509; Po:
2902
Revolution and Roses CN:
398; ENES2: 189; Po:
2902
A Season in England ENES2:
189
The Snow Pasture CN: 398;
ENES2: 189
Something to Answer For
ENES2: 189
A Step to Silence CN: 398;
ENES2: 189; Po: 2902
The Young May Moon CN:
398; ENES2: 189

NEWCASTLE, Margaret Caven-
dish, Duchess of
General Bon: 76
NEWLOVE, John
Black Night Window Po:
2902
NEWMAN, Frances
General Po: 2903
NEWMAN, John Henry
General VP: 58-59
Apologia pro Vita Sua VP:
58-59
Callista ENES1: 174;
ENES2: 190
"Dream of Gerontius" PE:
331; VP: 59
The Idea of a University
LCAB: 132
"Lead, Kindly Light" PE:
331
Loss and Gain ENES1: 174;
ENES2: 190
"The Pillar of the Cloud"
PE: 331
NEWSOME, Mary Effie Lee
General BAF: 224
NEWTON, John
"How Sweet the Name of
Jesus Sounds" PE: 332
NEXO, Martin Andersen
General Po: 2903
Pelle, the Conqueror Ke:
362
NEZVAL, V.
Atlantis DC2: 267
NG'OMBE, James
General BALE: 347
NGUBIAH, Stephen N.
A Curse from God BALE:
347
NGUGI WA THIONG'O [James]
General BALE: 348-351;
LCAB: 132
The Black Hermit BALE:
349
A Grain of Wheat BALE:
349-350
Homecoming BALE: 348-349
"A Meeting in the Dark" Wa:
569
The River Between BALE:
348-350
Weep Not, Child BALE:
348-350
NGULUBE, Bayahi L.
General BALE: 351

NICHOLAS, Arthur
General WIL: 127-128
NICHOLAS, Robert
"Sunrise Poem" PE: 332
NICHOLS, Anne
Abie's Irish Rose ADC: 265
_____ and Alfred VAN RONKEL
Pre-Honeymoon ADC: 265
NICHOLS, Peter
General MDAE: 373; TMBP:
72-73
The Brick Umbrella TMBP:
73
Chez Nous EDC: 388
The Continuity of Man TMBP:
73
Daddy Kiss It Better TMBP:
74
A Day in the Death of Joe Egg
[Joe Egg] EDC: 388-389;
TMBP: 72, 74
Forget Me Not Lane EDC:
389; TMBP: 72, 74
Freeway EDC: 389; TMBP:
73
The Gorge TMBP: 74
Hearts and Flowers TMBP:
74
The Hooded Terror TMBP:
74
Joe Egg see A Day in the
Death of Joe Egg
The National Health; or Nurse
Norton's Affair EDC:
389; MDAE: 373; TMBP:
72-75
When the Wind Blows TMBP:
75
NICHOLS, Robert
The Decapitated Taxi Br:
456
The Wax Engine Br: 456
_____ and Maurice BROWN
Wings Over Europe Br: 456
Nicholson, David see ROC, John
NICHOLSON, Norman
General MDAE: 374; Po:
2903-2904
The Fire of the Lord ENES1:
174
The Green Shore ENES1: 175
A Match for the Devil Br:
456
The Old Man of the Mountains
Br: 456
NICOL, Abioseh [Davidson S.W.H.

NICOL]
General BALE: 351
NICOLE, Christopher
General WIL: 128
The Amyot Crime WIL: 129
Blood Amyot WIL: 128
Dark Noon WIL: 128
The Deviator WIL: 129
The Eliminator WIL: 129
King Creole WIL: 129
The Self-Lovers WIL: 129
Shadows in the Jungle WIL: 128
White Boy WIL: 129
NICOLSON, Harold
General Po: 2904
Diaries and Letters Po: 2904
NIEDECKER, Lorine
General Po: 2904
NIEDZWIECKI, Zygmunt
"The Eyes" Wa: 569
"A Fable" Wa: 569
"Marinated Fish" Wa: 569
"The Quarrelsome Woman" Wa: 569
"The Winning Number" Wa: 569
NIEMOJEWSKI, Andrzej
"Ptak" Wa: 569
NIETZSCHE, Friedrich Wilhelm
Beyond Good and Evil Ma: 1510
The Birth of Tragedy Ma: 1510-1512
Thus Spake Zarathustra LCAB: 132; Ma: 1512-1513; Po: 2129
NIEVO, Ippolito
The Castle of Fratta Ma: 1514
Confessions of an Italian Fi: 270; Ke: 247-248
NIHOLIC-MICKI, D.
Judas Did Not Betray God Ke: 425
NIKOLAEVA, Galina
A Battle on the Way Ke: 425-426
NIMIER, Richard
The Blue Hussar Ke: 124
Les Epées Ke: 124
NIMIER, Roger
General Po: 2905
NIMS, John Frederick
General Po: 2905
"Love Poem" PE: 332
"The Magical View of Nature" PE: 332
"Penny Arcade" PE: 332
"Winter in the Park" PE: 332
NIN, Anaïs
General ASF: 424; Po: 2905-2906
"The All-Seeing" ASF: 423; Wa: 569
"Birth" ASF: 423; WaS1: 161
"The Child Born Out of the Fog" ASF: 423
Children of the Albatross Ma: 1515
Collages Ma: 1515
The Diary of Anaïs Nin Ma: 1515-1516
"Djuna" ASF: 423
The Four-Chambered Heart Ma: 1516-1517
"Hedja" ASF: 423; WaS1: 161
The House of Incest Ma: 1517
"Houseboat" ASF: 423
"Je suis le plus malade des surréalistes" ASF: 423
Ladders to Fire Ma: 1517
"The Mouse" ASF: 423; WaS1: 161
"Ragtime" ASF: 423; WaS1: 161
Seduction of the Minotaur Ma: 1517-1518; Po: 2906
A Spy in the House of Love Ma: 1518-1519
"Stella" ASF: 423; WaS1: 162
"Under a Glass Bell" ASF: 423; Wa: 569
"The Voice" ASF: 423; WaS1: 162
"Winter of Artiface" ASF: 423; Ma: 1519; WaS1: 162
Nirala see TRIPATHI, Suryakant
NISSENSON, Hugh
General JW: 265
"The Well" ASF: 425
NIVEN, Frederick
General Ai: 216-217
NIVEN, Larry
"Flash Crowd" ASF: 425
NIZAN, Paul
Antoine Bloye Fi: 124
Le Cheval de Troie Fi: 125
La Conspiration Fi: 125
NJAU, Rebecca

General BALE: 351
NKOSI, Lewis
General BALE: 352-353
The Rhythm of Violence
BALE: 352-353; Po: 2906
NNOLIM, Charles
General BALE: 353
NOAH, Mordecai Manuel
General AD: 173-174; JW:
398-399
She Would Be a Soldier AD:
173-174
NOAILLES, Anna de
General Po: 2907
NOBIKOV, Gregory
Newsboy Br: 456
NOBLE, Gil
The Life and Times of Fred-
erick Douglass MBA:
160
NODIER, Charles
La Fée aux miettes Fi:
125; Ke: 124; Wa: 569
"The Four Talismans" Wa:
569
"Franciscus Columna" Wa:
569
"Une Heuere ou la vision"
Wa: 570
"L'Histoire d'Helene Gillet"
Wa: 570
"L'Histoire du Calife Hakem"
Wa: 570
"L'Homme et la fourmi" Wa:
570
Jean Sbogar Fi: 125; Wa:
570
"Jean-Francois Les Bau-
Bleus" Wa: 570
"Legende de Soeur Beatrix"
Wa: 570
"Lydie or the Resurrection"
Wa: 570
"Mademoiselle de Marsas"
Wa: 570
"Paul or the Resemblance"
Wa: 570
"Le Peintre de Saltzbourg"
Wa: 570
"La plus petite des pantouf-
fles" Wa: 570
Smarra Fi: 125
"Le Songe d'or" Wa: 570
Trilby Fi: 125; Ke: 124;
Wa: 570
NOËL, Marie

General Po: 2907
Petit-jour Po: 2907
Nolan, Brian see O'BRIEN, Flann
NOLL, Bink
"My Estate" PE: 332
NOMBELA Y TABARES, Julio
The Lust for Riches Ke: 211
NOONAN, John Ford
General MDAE: 375
Goodby and Keep Cold ADC:
266
Older People ADC: 266
Where Do We Go from Here?
ADC: 266
The Year Boston Won the Pen-
nant ADC: 266; MDAE:
375; TMAP: 173
NOONE, John
The Night of Accomplishment
ENES2: 190
NORFORD, George
General BAW: 568
Head of the Family BAP: 154
Joy Exceeding Glory BAP:
154; MBA: 160
NORGE, Géo
General Po: 2907-2908
NORIEGA HOPE, Carlos
General Br: 456
NORMAN, Frank
Fings Ain't Wot They Used T'Be
MDAE: 376
NORRIS, Frank
General AF: 208-212; ALL:
197-199; AN: 207-209; ASF:
425-426; Cla: 74-76; Ho:
118-120, 154; LCAB: 132;
Po: 2908-2913
Blix AN: 206; Ho: 120; Ma:
1520; Po: 2913-2914
"A Case for Lombroso" Po:
2910; Wa: 570
"A Deal in Wheat" ASF: 425;
Wa: 570-571
"Dying Fires" ASF: 425; Wa:
571
"The Great Corner in Hannibal
and St. Jo." ASF: 425
"Grettir at Drangey" Wa:
571
"Grettir at Thorhall-stead"
Wa: 571
"His Single Blessedness" Po:
2910; Wa: 571
"Lauth" ASF: 425; Wa: 571
McTeague AF: 209, 211; ALL:

197-198; AN: 206; Cla: 75-76; Ho: 119-120, 154; LCAB: 132; Ma: 1520-1521; Po: 2908, 2912, 2914-2915

A Man's Woman AN: 206; Po: 2913, 2915

Moran of the Lady Letty Po: 2913

The Octopus AF: 209-212; ALL: 197-198; AN: 206-207; Cla: 75-76; Ho: 118-120, 154; Ma: 1522-1523; Po: 2909, 2912, 2916-2917

The Pit AF: 211-212; ALL: 197-198; AN: 207; Ho: 119; Ma: 1523-1524; Po: 2912

The Responsibilities of the Novelist Ma: 1524

"A Reversion to Type" Po: 2910

"The Salvation Boom in Matabeleland" Wa: 571

"Son of a Sheik" Po: 2910

"Toppan" ["Unequally Yoked"] Wa: 571

Vandover and the Brute AF: 209; ALL: 197-198; AN: 207; Cla: 76; Ho: 120; Ma: 1524-1525; Po: 2908, 2912, 2918

NORRIS, Hoke
General LCAB: 132-133

NORRIS, John
General Bon: 59-60
"My Estate" PE: 332

NORRIS, Kathleen
General AN: 209

NORTH, Christopher [John WILSON, 1785-1854]
General Ai: 122

NORTH, Roger
General EC: 102-103

NORTH, Thomas [translator]
The Morall Philosophie of Doni by BIDPAI ERP: 359-360

NORTJE, Kenneth Arthur
General BALE: 353-354

NORTON, Charles Eliot
General Po: 2918

NORTON, Thomas and Thomas SACKVILLE
Gorboduc, or Ferrex and

Porrex DC1: 154; ED: 272-273, 316; EDC: 389; Ma: 1526-1527

NORWID, Cyprian
"Ad leones" Wa: 571
"The Bracelet" Wa: 571
"Civilization" Wa: 571
"Dominic" Wa: 571
"The Kind Guardian, or Bartlomiej Becomes Alphonse" Wa: 571
"Lord Singleworth's Secret" Wa: 571
"Menego" Wa: 571
"Stigma" Wa: 571

NOSSACK, Hans Erich
General Br: 457; Po: 2918-2919
Die Rotte Kain Br: 457
Ein Sonderfall Br: 457

NOTT, Kathleen
The Emperor's Clothes LCAB: 133

NOURISSIER, François
General Po: 2919

NOURSE, Joan and Philip NOURSE
The Happy Faculty ADC: 266

Novak, Joseph [pseud.] see KOSINSKI, Jerzy

NOVAK, Slobodan
General Po: 2919

NOVALIS [Friedrich von HARDENBERG]
Atlantis Fi: 382
Eros und Fabel Fi: 382
Heinrich von Ofterdingen Fi: 382; Ke: 327
Hyazinth und Rosenblute Fi: 382
Die Lehrlinge zu Sais Fi: 382

NOVAS CALVO, Lino
General Po: 2920
"La abuela reina y el sobrina Delfín" WaS1: 162
"Cayo Canas" WaS1: 162
"Un dedo encima" WaS1: 162
"Nadie a quien matar" WaS1: 162
"The Night of Ramón Yendía" WaS1: 162
"El otro cayo" WaS1: 162
"La vaca en la azotea" WaS1: 162

NOWLAN, Alden

General Po: 2920
NOYES, Alfred
General Po: 2920-2921; TA:
    237
"For the Eightieth Birthday
    of George Meredith" PE:
    332
NTIRU, Richard
General BALE: 354
NUGENT, Elliott
General Br: 457
A Place of Our Own ADC:
    266
_____ and J.C. NUGENT
The Poor Nut ADC: 266
_____ and James THURBER
The Male Animal see also
    THURBER, James and
    Elliott NUGENT ADC:
    266-267
NWACHUKWU, Shakespeare
    C.N.
General BALE: 354
NWANKWO, Nkem
General BALE: 355
Danda BALE: 355
NWAPA, Flora
General BALE: 355-356
Efuru BALE: 356
NWOGA, Donatus Ibe
General BALE: 356
NYE, Bill
General ASF: 426
NZEKWU, Onuora
General BALE: 357
NZERIBE, Grace Nnenna
General BALE: 357

O

OAKES, Urian
General AP: 447
"An Elegy Upon the Death
    of the Reverend Mr.
    Thomas Shepard" Da: 55
OAKLEY, Barry
General MAP: 247
OATES, Joyce Carol
General ALL: 199-200;
    ASF: 430-431; Po: 2923
"Accomplished Desires" ASF:
    430
The Assassins Ma: 1528
"At the Seminary" WaS1:
    162

"Bodies" Wa: 572
"The Children" WaS1: 162
"The Dead" ASF: 430; Wa:
    572; WaS1: 162
"Did You Ever Slip on Red
    Blood?" WaS1: 162
Do with Me What You Will Ma:
    1528
"Dreams" ASF: 430
Expensive People Ma: 1528
A Garden of Earthly Delights
    Ma: 1529
"The Girl" WaS1: 163
"The Heavy Sorrow of the Body"
    ASF: 430
"How I Contemplated the World
    from the Detroit House of
    Correction and Began My
    Life Over Again" ASF:
    430; WaS1: 163
"The Loves of Franklin Am-
    brose" ASF: 430; Wa:
    572
Marriages and Infidelities Ma:
    1529
"The Metamorphosis" ASF:
    430; WaS1: 163
"Narcotic" WaS1: 163
"Normal Love" ASF: 430;
    WaS1: 163
Ontological Proof of My Exist-
    ence ADC: 267
"Pastoral Blood" WaS1: 163
"Plot" ASF: 430; Wa: 572
"Puzzle" WaS1: 163
Sunday Dinner ADC: 267
Sweet Enemy ADC: 267
Them Ma: 1529-1530
"Waiting" WaS1: 163
"Where Are You Going, Where
    Have You Been?" ASF:
    430; Wa: 572; WaS1: 163
"Wild Saturday" Wa: 572
Wonderland Ma: 1530
"You" Wa: 572
OBALDIA, René de
L'Air du Large Br: 457
Du Vent dans les Branches de
    Sassafras Br: 457
OBELER, Arch
Night of the Auk Br: 457
OBENG, R.E.
General BALE: 357
OBEY, André
General Br: 458; MD: 205-
    206

Bataille de la Marne Br:
458

Une Fille Pour du Vent Br:
458

Lazare Br: 458

Loire Br: 458

Lucrece see Le Viol de
Lucrece

Noah [Noe] Br: 458; DC2:
267; MD: 206

Venus and Adonis Br: 458;
DC2: 267

Le Viol de Lucrece [Lucrece]
Br: 458

OBIECHINA, Emmanuel
General BALE: 358

O'BRIEN, Conor Cruise
General LCAB: 44
Murderous Angels MDAE:
377

O'BRIEN, Edna
General Po: 2923; TMIP:
101-103

August Is a Wicked Month
ENES2: 190

Casualties of Peace ENES2:
190

A Cheap Bunch of Nice
Flowers TMIP: 104

The Country Girls ENES2:
190; Po: 2923-2924;
TMIP: 103

The Gathering ADC: 267;
TMIP: 104-105

Girl with Green Eyes ENES2:
190; TMIP: 103

Girls in Their Married Bliss
ENES2: 190; Po: 2923;
TMIP: 103

"Irish Revel" Wa: 572

The Lonely Girl Po: 2923

Night ENES2: 190

"An Outing" Wa: 572

A Pagan Place ENES2: 190;
Po: 2924; TMIP: 101,
105

"The Rug" Wa: 572

O'BRIEN, Fitz-James
General LCAB: 133
"The Diamond Lens" ASF:
431; Wa: 572
"How I Overcame My Gravity"
ASF: 431
"The Pot of Tulips" ASF:
431; Wa: 572
"What Was It? A Mystery"

ASF: 431; Wa: 572
"The Wondersmith" Wa: 572

O'BRIEN, Flann [Brian NOLAN,
Brian O'NOLAN]
General Po: 3022
At Swim--Two Birds ENES1:
175; ENES2: 190-191; Po:
3022
The Dalkey Archive ENES1:
175; ENES2: 191
"Donagate" Wa: 573
The Hard Life ENES1: 175;
ENES2: 191
"John Duffy's Brother" Wa:
573
"The Marble Crown" Wa: 573
The Third Policeman ENES1:
175; ENES2: 191; Po: 3023
"Two in One" Wa: 573

O'BYRNE, Dermot
General Po: 2924

O'CASEY, Sean
General Br: 459-461; MBD:
62-65; MD: 206-208; MDAE:
379; Mi: 264-265; Po: 2924-
2933
"The Bald Primaqueera" Po:
2933
Bedtime Story Br: 462; EDC:
389; Po: 2934
Behind the Green Curtain Br:
462; EDC: 390
The Bishop's Bonfire Br:
462; EDC: 390; MD: 208
Cock-a-Doodle-Dandy Br:
462-463; DC1: 154; EDC:
390; Ma: 1531; MBD: 63,
65; MD: 208; Po: 2934-
2935
The Crimson in the Tri-Colour
Br: 463
The Drums of Father Ned Br:
463; DC1: 154; EDC: 391;
MBD: 64; MD: 208; Po:
2935
Drums Under the Window EDC:
391
The End of the Beginning
EDC: 391
Feathers from the Green Crow
Po: 2935
The Frost in the Flower Br:
463
The Hall of Healing EDC:
391; Po: 2935
The Harvest Festival Br: 463

I Knock at the Door EDC:
391

Juno and the Paycock Br:
464; DC1: 154-155; EDC:
391-392; Ma: 1532-1533;
MBD: 62-65; MD: 208;
Po: 2936

Kathleen [Cathleen] Listens
In Br: 464; DC1: 155;
EDC: 390; MBD: 63;
MD: 208-209; Po: 2936

The Moon Shines on Kylena-
moe Br: 464

Nannie's Night Out Br:
465; DC1: 155; EDC:
392; MBD: 62; MD: 209;
Po: 2936

Oak Leaves and Lavender;
or, A World on Wallpaper
Br: 465; DC1: 155;
EDC: 392; MD: 209

Pictures in the Hallway
EDC: 392

The Plough and the Stars
Br: 465-466; DC1: 155;
EDC: 392-393; Ma:
1533-1534; MBD: 62-65;
MD: 209; Po: 2937-2938

A Pound on Demand EDC:
393; MD: 209

Purple Dust Br: 466; DC1:
155; EDC: 393; Ma:
1534-1535; MBD: 63-64;
MD: 209; Po: 2938

Red Roses for Me Br: 467;
DC1: 155; EDC: 394;
LCAB: 133; Ma: 1535-
1536; MBD: 64-65; MD:
209; Po: 2938

The Robe of Rosheen Br:
467

The Shadow of a Gunman
Br: 467-468; DC1: 155;
EDC: 394-395; Ma: 1536-
1537; MBD: 62; MD: 209;
Po: 2939

The Shifting Heart DC1:
156

The Silver Tassie Br: 468-
469; DC1: 156; EDC:
395; Ma: 1537-1538; MBD:
65; MD: 209-210; Po:
2940

The Star Turns Red Br:
469; DC1: 156; EDC:
395; MD: 210; Po: 2940

Time to Go Br: 469; EDC:
395

Within the Gates Br: 469-470;
DC1: 156; EDC: 395-396;
Ma: 1538-1539; MD: 210;
Po: 2940-2941

OCHARAN MAZAS, Don Luis de
Marichu Ke: 211

O'CONNOR, Edwin
General ASF: 432; Po: 2941-
2942

All in the Family CN: 398;
Ma: 1540

The Edge of Sadness CN:
399; Ma: 1540; Po: 2942

The Last Hurrah CN: 399;
Ma: 1540-1541; Po: 2943

"Parish Reunion" Wa: 573

O'CONNOR, Flannery
General ALL: 200-203; AN:
209; ASF: 438-444; CFAE:
273-281; CN: 399-402;
LCAB: 133; Ne: 78-79;
Po: 2943-2956

"The Artificial Nigger" ASF:
432; Ma: 1542-1543; Po:
2956; SFC: 163; Wa: 573-
574; WaS1: 163

"The Barber" ASF: 432; Wa:
574; WaS1: 164

"The Capture" ASF: 432, 438;
Wa: 574; WaS1: 166

"A Circle in the Fire" ASF:
432; Wa: 574; WaS1: 164

"The Comforts of Home" ASF:
432; Wa: 574-575; WaS1:
164

"The Crop" ASF: 432; Wa:
575; WaS1: 164

"The Displaced Person" ASF:
433; Ma: 1543; Po: 2957;
SFC: 163; Wa: 575-576;
WaS1: 164

"The Enduring Chill" ASF:
433; Wa: 576; WaS1: 164

"Enoch and the Gorilla" ASF:
433; WaS1: 164

"Everything That Rises Must
Converge" ALL: 202; ASF:
433-434; CFAE: 280; Ma:
1543-1544; Po: 2957-2958;
Wa: 576-577; WaS1: 164

"The Geranium" ASF: 434;
WaS1: 164

"Good Country People" ASF:
434; Ma: 1544-1545; Po:

2958; SFC: 163-164; Wa:
577; WaS1: 164
"A Good Man Is Hard to Find"
ALL: 202; ASF: 434-435;
CFAE: 275; Ma: 1545-
1546; Po: 2959-2960; SFC:
164; Wa: 577-579; WaS1:
165
"Greenleaf" ASF: 435; Po:
2960; Wa: 579; WaS1:
165
"The Heart of the Park"
ASF: 435; WaS1: 165
"Judgement Day" ASF:
435; Wa: 579; WaS1:
165
"The Lame Shall Enter First"
ASF: 435-436; Po: 2960-
2961; Wa: 579-580; WaS1:
165
"A Late Encounter with the
Enemy" ASF: 436; SFC:
164; Wa: 580
"The Life You Save May Be
Your Own" ASF: 436; Po:
2961; Wa: 580-581; WaS1:
165
"Mary Ann: The Story of a
Little Girl" ASF: 436
Mystery and Manners Ma:
1546-1547
"Parker's Back" ASF: 436;
Po: 2961; Wa: 581;
WaS1: 165
"The Partridge Festival"
ASF: 437; Wa: 581
"The Peeler" ASF: 437;
WaS1: 165
"Revelation" ASF: 437; Wa:
581-582; WaS1: 165
"The River" ASF: 437;
SFC: 164; Wa: 582; WaS1:
165
"A Stroke of Good Fortune"
ASF: 437; Po: 2962;
Wa: 582; WaS1: 165
"A Temple of the Holy Ghost"
ASF: 437; SFC: 164;
Wa: 582-583; WaS1: 166
"The Train" ASF: 437;
Wa: 583; WaS1: 165
"The Turkey" see "The
Capture"
"A View of the Woods" ASF:
438; Wa: 583; WaS1:
166

The Violent Bear It Away ALL:
202-203; CFAE: 274, 277-
280; CN: 402-404; Ma:
1547-1548; Ne: 79; Po:
2962-2964
"Why Do the Heathen Rage?"
ASF: 438; WaS1: 166
"Wildcat" ASF: 438; WaS1:
166
Wise Blood ALL: 202-203; AN:
209; CFAE: 274-275, 277-
280; CN: 405-406; LCAB:
133; Ma: 1548-1550; Ne:
79; Po: 2965-2966
"A Woman on the Stairs" see
"A Stroke of Good Fortune"
"You Can't Be Any Poorer Than
Dead" ASF: 438; WaS1:
166
O'CONNOR, Frank [Michael
O'DONOVAN]
General Br: 470; Po: 2966-
2967
"Achilles Heel" WaS1: 166
"An Act of Charity" WaS1:
166
"After Fourteen Years" WaS1:
166
"The American Wife" Wa: 583
"Bones of Contention" WaS1:
166
"The Bridal Night" WaS1: 166
"The Cheapjack" Wa: 583
"The Cheat" WaS1: 166
"The Corkerys" WaS1: 166
"Counsel of Oedipus" WaS1:
166
"Daydreams" WaS1: 167
"Don Juan (Retired)" WaS1:
167
"The Drunkard" Wa: 583;
WaS1: 167
Dutch Interior ENES2: 191
"The Eternal Triangle" WaS1:
167
"Expectations of Life" WaS1:
167
"Father and Son" WaS1: 167
"First Confession" WaS1: 167
"First Confession and Repent-
ence" SFC: 164; Wa: 583
"The Genius" WaS1: 167
"The Grand Vizier's Daughter"
WaS1: 167
"Guests of the Nation" SFC:

164; Wa: 584; WaS1: 167

"The Holy Door" WaS1: 167

"The House That Johnny Built" WaS1: 167

"The Impossible Marriage" WaS1: 167

"In the Train" Br: 470; SFC: 164; Wa: 584; WaS1: 167

"Judas" Po: 2967-2968; SFC: 164; Wa: 584; WaS1: 167

"A Life of Your Own" WaS1: 168

"The Long Road to Ummera" WaS1: 168

"The Luceys" WaS1: 168

"Mac's Masterpiece" Wa: 584

"The Mad Lomasneys" Wa: 584; WaS1: 168

"The Majesty of the Law" SFC: 164; Wa: 584; WaS1: 168

"The Man of the House" Wa: 584

"The Man of the World" WaS1: 168

"The Mass Island" WaS1: 168

"Michael's Wife" WaS1: 168

"Music When Soft Voices Die" WaS1: 168

"My Oedipus Complex" SFC: 164; Wa: 584; WaS1: 168

"Out-and-Out Free Gift" WaS1: 168

"The Paragon" WaS1: 168

"The Party" WaS1: 168

"Patriarch" Wa: 584

"Peasants" WaS1: 168

"The Pretender" Wa: 585; WaS1: 168

"Requiem" WaS1: 169

The Saint and Mary Kate ENES2: 191

"The School for Wives" WaS1: 169

"The Sentry" WaS1: 169

"September Dawn" WaS1: 169

A Set of Variations Po: 2968; WaS1: 169

"Song Without Words" WaS1: 169

"The Star That Bids the Shepherd Fold" WaS1: 169

"The Stepmother" WaS1: 169

"The Study of History" Wa: 585

"The Teacher's Mass" WaS1: 169

"The Thief" WaS1: 169

"Unapproved Route" WaS1: 169

"Uprooted" Po: 2968; SFC: 164; Wa: 585; WaS1: 169

"Vanity" WaS1: 169

O'CONNOR, John
Come Day--Go Day ENES2: 191

O'CONNOR, William Van
General Po: 2968

OCRUTNI, Joseph
"Rumkowsky" Wa: 585

OCTAVIAN
Damnation of Antony DC2: 267

OCULI, Okello
General BALE: 358

ODETS, Clifford
General ALL: 203-204; Br: 470-471; JW: 402-403; LCAB: 133; Lon: 39-40; MD: 210-211; MDAE: 380-381; Po: 2969-2970

Awake and Sing ADC: 267-268; Br: 471-472; DC1: 156-157; Lon: 60; Ma: 1551-1552; MD: 211; Po: 2970-2971

The Big Knife ADC: 268-269; Br: 473; DC1: 157; MD: 212

Clash by Night ADC: 269; Br: 473; DC1: 157; MD: 212

The Country Girl [In England, A Winter Journey] ADC: 269-270, 273; Br: 473; MD: 212; MDAE: 381

The Flowering Peach ADC: 270; Br: 473; DC1: 157; MD: 212; MDAE: 380-381

Golden Boy ADC: 270-271; Br: 473-474; DC1: 157; Ma: 1552-1553; MD: 212

I Can't Sleep ADC: 271

Night Music ADC: 271; Br: 474; DC1: 157; Lon: 40; MD: 212

Paradise Lost ADC: 271-272;

Br: 474-475; DC1: 157;
MD: 212-213
Rocket to the Moon ADC:
272; Br: 475; DC1: 157;
MD: 213
The Russian People ADC:
272
Till the Day I Die ADC:
272-273; Br: 475; MD:
213
Waiting for Lefty ADC:
273; Br: 475-476; DC1:
158; Lon: 40; Ma: 1553-
1554; MD: 213; Po: 2971
A Winter Journey see The
Country Girl
_____, William GIBSON,
Charles STROUSE, and
Lee ADAMS
Golden Boy ADC: 273-274
ODOEVSKY, Vladimir Fëdrovich
"Beethoven's Last Quartet"
Wa: 585
"A City Without Name" Wa:
585
"The Dead Body That Be-
longed to No One Knew
Whom" Wa: 565
"Elsa" Wa: 585
"How Collegiate Councillor
Ivan Bogdanovich Otno-
shenie Was Unable to
Offer Holiday Greetings to
His Superior on Easter
Sunday" Wa: 585
"How Dangerous It Is for
Girls to Walk in Groups
on the Nevskij Prospekt"
Wa: 585
"The Improvisor" Wa: 585
"Kosmorama" Wa: 585
"Opere del Cavaliere Giam-
batista Piranesi" Wa: 586
Russian Nights Fi: 459
"The Salamander" Wa: 586
"Sebastian Bach" Wa: 586
"Sylphida" Wa: 586
O'DONNELL, Frank J. Hugh
Anti-Christ Br: 476
The Shaws of Synge Street
Br: 476
O'DONNELL, George Marion
"Return" PE: 332
O'DONNELL, Lawrence [Cath-
erine L. MOORE]
"The Children's Hour" WaS1:

169
"Vintage Season" WaS1: 169
O'DONNELL, Peadar
Adrigoole ENES2: 192
Islanders ENES2: 192
The Knife ENES2: 192
O'DONOVAN, John
General Br: 476
The Less We Are Together
Br: 476
O'Donovan, Michael see
O'CONNOR, Frank
O'DOWD, Bernard Patrick
General Po: 2971
O'DUFFY, Eimar
Asses in Clover ENES1: 175
King Goshawk and the Birds
ENES1: 175
The Lion and the Fox ENES1:
175
Miss Rudd and Some Lovers
ENES1: 175
Printer's Errors ENES1: 175
The Spacious Adventures of the
Man in the Street ENES1:
175
The Wasted Island ENES1:
175; ENES2: 192
OE KENZABURO
"The Catch" WaS1: 170
"Sheep" Wa: 586
OEHLENSCHLAGER, Adam
Amleth DC2: 268
O'FAOLAIN, Julia
Women in the Wall ENES2: 192
O'FAOLAIN, Sean
General Ma: 1555-1556; Po:
2971-2973
"Admiring the Scenery" Wa:
586; WaS1: 170
Bird Alone ENES1: 176;
ENES2: 192
"The Bombshop" Wa: 586
"A Born Genius" Wa: 586
"A Broken World" Wa: 586;
WaS1: 170
"Childybawn" Wa: 586
Come Back to Erin ENES1:
176; ENES2: 192; Po:
2973-2974
"Discord" Wa: 586
"Fugue" Wa: 586
"The Fur Coat" Wa: 586
I Remember! I Remember! Ma:
1555; Wa: 586
"Lady Lucifer" Wa: 587

"Lilliput" Wa: 587
"Lovers of the Lake" Wa:
587; WaS1: 170
"The Man Who Invented Sin"
Ma: 1555; SFC: 165;
Wa: 587
"Midsummer Night Madness"
Wa: 587; WaS1: 170
A Nest of Simple Folk
ENES1: 176; ENES2: 192
"No Country for Old Men"
Wa: 587
"The Old Master" Wa: 587
"One True Friend" Wa: 587
"The Patriot" Wa: 587
"A Shadow, Silent as a Cloud"
Wa: 587
"The Silence of the Valley"
Po: 2974; Wa: 587;
WaS1: 170
"Sinners" Wa: 587
"The Small Lady" SFC: 165;
Wa: 587; WaS1: 170
"The Sugawn Chair" Wa:
588
"Teresa" Wa: 588
"A Touch of Autumn in the
Air" Wa: 588
"Unholy Living and Half Dy-
ing" Wa: 588
"Up the Bare Stairs" Wa:
588
Vive Moi! Ma: 1556
OFFENBACH, Jacques
Tales of Hoffman DC2: 268
OFFORD, Carl
General BAF: 225; BAW:
570
The White Face BAF: 225
O'FLAHERTY, Liam
General BN2: 91-92; Ma:
1558; Po: 2974-2975
The Assassin ENES1: 176;
ENES2: 192
"The Bath" WaS1: 170
"The Black Rabbit" Wa:
588
The Black Soul ENES1:
176; ENES2: 192
"The Blackbird's Mate"
WaS1: 170
"The Caress" Wa: 588;
WaS1: 170
"The Conger Eel" Wa: 588
"The Cow's Death" Wa:
588

"The Ditch" WaS1: 170
"The Fairy Goose" Wa: 588;
WaS1: 170
Famine Ma: 1557; ENES1:
176; ENES2: 192
"Galway Bay" Wa: 588; WaS1:
170
"Going into Exile" WaS1: 171
"The Hawk" Wa: 588; WaS1:
171
"His First Flight" Wa: 588
The House of Gold ENES1:
176; ENES2: 193
The Informer ENES1: 176;
ENES2: 193; Ma: 1557-
1558; Po: 2975
"The Inquisition" WaS1: 171
Insurrection ENES1: 176;
ENES2: 193
Land ENES1: 176; ENES2:
193
"The Letter" WaS1: 171
The Martyr ENES1: 176;
ENES2: 193
"Milking Time" WaS1: 171
"The Mirror" Wa: 588; WaS1:
171
Mr. Gilhooley ENES1: 176;
ENES2: 193
"The Mountain Tavern" WaS1:
171
"The Outcast" WaS1: 171
"The Parting" WaS1: 171
"The Pedlar's Revenge" WaS1:
171
"The Post Office" Wa: 589;
WaS1: 171
"Proclamation" WaS1: 171
The Puritan ENES1: 177;
ENES2: 193; Ma: 1558
"The Reaping Race" Wa: 589
"Red Barbara" Wa: 589;
WaS1: 171
The Return of the Brute
ENES2: 193
"The Rockfish" Wa: 589;
WaS1: 171
Skerrett ENES2: 193
"Sport: The Kill" WaS1:
171
"Spring Sowing" Wa: 589;
WaS1: 171
"A Strange Disease" WaS1:
171
"The Stream" Wa: 589
"The Tent" WaS1: 172

"The Terrorist" WaS1: 172
"Three Lambs" Wa: 589
Thy Neighbour's Wife ENES1:
    177; ENES2: 193
"The Tramp" WaS1: 172
"Trapped" Wa: 589
"Two Lovely Beasts" Wa:
    589
"The Tyrant" WaS1: 172
"Unclean" WaS1: 172
"The Wave" Wa: 589
"The Wedding" Wa: 589
The Wilderness ENES2: 193
"The Wounded Cormorant"
    Wa: 589; WaS1: 172
OGALI, Ogali A.
    General BALE: 359
OGILVIE, William G.
    Cactus Village WIL: 130
    The Ghost Bank WIL: 130
OGOT, Grace Akinye
    General BALE: 360
O'GRADY, Rohan
    O'Houlihan's Jest Po: 2975
OGUNYEMI, Wale
    General BALE: 360
    Kiriji BALE: 360
O'HAGAN, Thomas
    General ECL: 178
O'HARA, Frank
    General ICBAP: 96; LCAB:
        133; MDAE: 383; MP:
        69-70; Po: 2975-2976
    "The Day Lady Died" LCAB:
        133; MP: 69; PE: 332
    "Early on Sunday" PE: 332
    "Essay on Style" PE: 332
    The General Returns from
        One Place to Another Br:
        476; MDAE: 383
    "Music" PE: 332
    "A Step Away from Them"
        PE: 332
O'HARA, John
    General ALL: 204-205; AN:
        210; ASF: 446; CFAE:
        284-285; CN: 406-407;
        LCAB: 133-134; MDAE:
        384; Ne: 79; Po: 2976-
        2977
    "All the Girls He Wanted"
        Wa: 589
    Appointment in Samarra
        CFAE: 285; CN: 407-
        408; Ma: 1559; Ne: 79;
        Po: 2977

"Are We Leaving Tomorrow?"
    SFC: 165; Wa: 589
The Big Laugh CN: 408
Butterfield 8 CN: 408
"The Chink in the Armor"
    ASF: 445; Wa: 589
"Conversation in the Atomic Age"
    Wa: 590
"Decision" ASF: 445; Wa: 590
"Do You Like It Here?" Wa:
    590
"The Doctor's Son" ASF:
    445; Wa: 590
Elizabeth Appleton CN: 408
A Family Party CN: 408
The Farmer's Hotel CN: 408
"A Few Trips and Some Poetry"
    Wa: 590
From the Terrace CN: 408-
    409; Ma: 1559-1560
"The Gangster" ASF: 446;
    Wa: 590
"The Girl on the Baggage
    Truck" Wa: 590
Hope of Heaven CN: 409
"Horizon" ASF: 446; Wa:
    590
"Imagine Kissing Peter" Wa:
    590
"Leonard" ASF: 446
The Lockwood Concern CN:
    409
"Miss W." Wa: 590
Ourselves to Know CN: 409;
    Ma: 1560
"Over the River and Through
    the Woods" ASF: 446; Wa:
    590
Pal Joey ASF: 446; DC1:
    158
"Price's Always Open" Wa:
    590
"Radio" ASF: 446; Wa: 590
A Rage to Live CN: 409; Ma:
    1560-1561
"Someone to Trust" Wa: 590
"Summer's Day" ASF: 446;
    Wa: 590
Ten North Frederick AN:
    209; CN: 410; Ma: 1561
"Transaction" ASF: 446; Wa:
    590
"We're Friends Again" Wa:
    590
"Zero" ASF: 446
O'HARA, Kane

General Li: 254
The Golden Pippin Li: 254
Midas Li: 254
O. HENRY [William Sydney
    PORTER]
  General ALL: 223-224; ASF:
    429; LCAB: 141; Ma:
    927; Po: 3250-3251; Wo:
    163
  "According to Their Lights"
    Wa: 591
  "An Afternoon Miracle" see
    "The Miracle of Lava
    Canyon"
  "The Atavism of John Tom
    Little Bear" ASF: 426;
    Wa: 591
  "The Badge of Policeman
    O'Roon" ASF: 427
  "Blind Man's Holiday" Wa:
    591
  "The Caballero's Way" ASF:
    427; Wa: 591
  Cabbages and Kings Po:
    3251
  "A Call Loan" ASF: 427
  "The Call of the Tame" Wa:
    591
  "The Chair of Philanthro-
    mathematics" ASF: 427;
    Wa: 591
  "A Chaparral Christmas
    Gift" ASF: 427; Wa:
    591
  "The Complete Life of John
    Hopkins" SFC: 165; Wa:
    591
  "The Duel" Wa: 591
  "The Duplicity of Hargraves"
    Wa: 591
  "Elsie in New York" ASF:
    427
  "The Ethics of Pig" ASF:
    427
  "The Fool-Killer" SFC: 165;
    Wa: 591
  "The Furnished Room" ASF:
    427; SFC: 165; Wa: 591
  "The Gift of the Magi" ASF:
    427; SFC: 165; Wa: 591
  "The Green Door" Wa: 591
  "The Handbook of Hymen"
    ASF: 427; Wa: 591
  "The Hiding of Black Bill"
    ASF: 427; Wa: 592
  "Hostages to Momus" ASF:
    427
  "Hygeia at the Solito" ASF:
    427
  "The Last Leaf" ASF: 427;
    Wa: 592
  "The Last of the Troubadours"
    ASF: 428
  "Let Me Feel Your Pulse" Wa:
    592
  "The Lonesome Road" ASF:
    428; Wa: 592
  "Lost on Dress Parade" Wa:
    592
  "The Marquis and Miss Sally"
    ASF: 428
  "The Memento" Wa: 592
  "The Miracle of Lava Canyon"
    ["An Afternoon Miracle"]
    ASF: 426; Wa: 592
  "The Moment of Victory" ASF:
    428
  "A Municipal Report" ASF:
    428; SFC: 165; Wa: 592;
    WaS1: 172
  "A Night in New Arabia" ASF:
    428
  "The Passing of Black Eagle"
    ASF: 428; Wa: 592
  "The Pendulum" Wa: 592
  "The Plutonian Fire" ASF:
    428
  "The Poet and the Peasant"
    Wa: 592
  "Princess and the Puma" ASF:
    428
  "The Proof of the Pudding"
    ASF: 428; SFC: 165; Wa:
    592
  "The Ransom of Mack" ASF:
    428; Wa: 592
  "The Ransom of Red Chief"
    ASF: 428
  "Roads to Destiny" ASF: 428
  "The Roads We Take" Wa:
    592
  "The Rose of Dixie" Wa: 592
  "The Snow Man" Wa: 593
  "Telemachus, Friend" ASF:
    428
  "Thimble, Thimble" Wa: 593
  "Tommy's Burglar" ASF: 428
  "Two Renegades" ASF: 428-
    429
  "The Venturers" ASF: 429;
    Wa: 593
  "Vereton Villa" ASF: 429;

Wa: 593
"While the Auto Waits" Wa:
593
"The Whirligig of Life" SFC:
165; Wa: 593
OJAIDE, Tanure
General BALE: 361
OJENKI [Alvin SAXON, Jr.]
General BAW: 572
OJIKE, Mazi Mbonu
General BALE: 361
OKAFOR-OMALI, Dilim
General BALE: 361
OKAI, John Atukwei
General BALE: 361-362
The Oath of the Fontomfrom
and Other Poems BALE:
362
OKARA, Gabriel Imomotimi
Gbaingbain
General BALE: 362-363
The Voice BALE: 362-363
OKECHUKWU, Ikechukwu
General BALE: 363
O'KEEFE, John
General Li: 256
Omai Li: 256
She's Eloped Li: 256
OKEKE, Uche
General BALE: 364
O'KELLY, Seumas
General Br: 476; Mi: 265;
Po: 2978
"At the Burning of the Sod"
Wa: 593
"Both Sides of the Pond"
Wa: 593
The Bribe Br: 476
"The Building" Wa: 593
"The Gray Lake" Wa: 593
The Parnellite Br: 477
"The Prodigal Daughter" Wa:
593
The Shuiler's Child Br:
477
The Weaver's Grave Po:
2978; Wa: 593
"The White Goat" Wa: 593
OKIGBO, Christopher
General BALE: 365-367;
Po: 2978-2979
"Distances" BALE: 365
Heavensgate BALE: 365-
366
Labyrinths BALE: 367
Laments BALE: 365

Limits BALE: 365-366
Path of Thunder BALE: 366-
367
OKOLA, Lennard
General BALE: 368
OKONKWO, Rufus
General BALE: 368
OKPAKU, Joseph Ohiomogben
General BAF: 225; BALE:
368
Born Astride the Grave BALE:
368; BAP: 155
OKPEWHO, Isidore
General BALE: 369
OKUDZAVA, Bulat
General Po: 2979
Putesestvie Diletantov Fi:
459
OKWU, Edward C.
General BALE: 369
OLADELE, Francis
General BALE: 369
OLDENBOURG, Zoë
Destiny of Fire Po: 2979
OLDHAM, John
General Bon: 27; Me: 277-
278
"Sardanapalus" Me: 278
"Satyr Addressed to a Friend"
PE: 333
"A Satyr Upon a Woman" PE:
333
"Satyrs Upon the Jesuits"
Bon: 27; ICBAP: 96; Me:
277-278
OLESHA, Iurii
General Po: 2979
"The Chain" Wa: 593
The Conspiracy of Feelings
[Zagovor Chuvsty] Po:
2980-2981
Envy [Zavist'] Fi: 459-460;
Ke: 426; LCAB: 134; Po:
2981; Wa: 594
"In Summer" Wa: 594
Liompa Fi: 460
"Love" Wa: 594
Three Fat Men Ke: 426
OLIPHANT, Carolina
General Ai: 99
OLIPHANT, Margaret
General Ai: 147; BN: 81-82
A Beleaguered City BN: 81;
ENES1: 177
Miss Marjoribanks BN: 82;
ENES1: 177

The Perpetual Curate ENES1:
177
Phoebe, Junior ENES1: 177
Salem Chapel ENES1: 177;
ENES2: 193
A Son of the Soil ENES2:
193
OLISAH, Sunday Okenwa
General BALE: 370
OLIVER, Diane
"Neighbors" ASF: 447; Wa:
594
Oliver, George see ONIONS,
George Oliver
Oller, Narcís
La febre d'or Fi: 228-229
OLLIER, Claude
Le Maintien de l'ordre Fi:
125
La Mise en scène Fi: 125
OLLIVER, Albert
L'Etoile de Seville DC2: 268
OLMO, Lauro
General Po: 2981
OLSEN, Tillie
General ASF: 447; Po:
2981
"Hey Sailor, What Ship?"
Wa: 594
"I Stand Here Ironing" ASF:
447; Wa: 594
"The Iron Throat" ASF:
447
"O Yes" ASF: 447; Wa:
594
"Tell Me a Riddle" ASF:
447; Wa: 594; WaS1: 172
OLSON, Charles
General ICBAP: 96; MP:
71-72; Po: 2982
"Anecdotes of the Late War"
LCAB: 134
"The Death of Europe (a
Funeral Poem for Rainer
M. Gerhardt)" PE: 333
"The Kingfishers" ICBAP:
96; LCAB: 134; MP: 71;
PE: 333; Po: 2982
Maximus LCAB: 134; MP:
72
"The Moon Is the Number 18"
PE: 333
"On First Looking Out
Through Juan de la Cosa's
Eyes" PE: 333
"The Praises" PE: 333

"Variations Done for Gerald
Van de Wiele" PE: 333
OLSON, Elder
General Po: 2982
OLSON, Lawrence
"Great Abaco" PE: 333
OLSSON, Hagar
General Po: 2982-2983
Chitambo Fi: 411
O'MORRISON, Kevin
Ladyhouse Blues ADC: 274
OMOTOSO, Kole
General BALE: 371
ONADIPE, Kola
General BALE: 371
ONDAATJE, Michael
The Collected Works of Billy
the Kid ADC: 274
O'NEAL, John
General MBA: 161
When the Opportunity Scratches,
Itch It MBA: 161
O'NEAL, Ron
General MBA: 161
O'NEILL, Eugene Gladstone
General ALL: 205-210; Br:
477-491; LCAB: 134-135;
Lon: 40-47; MD: 213-223;
MDAE: 386-390; Po: 2983-
3003
Abortion ADC: 274; ALL:
208; Br: 491
Ah, Wilderness! ADC: 274-
275; Br: 492-493; DC1:
158; Ma: 1562; MD: 223;
MDAE: 389; Po: 3003-3004
All God's Chillun Got Wings
ADC: 275; Br: 493-494;
DC1: 158; MD: 223
Anna Christie ADC: 275-276;
Br: 494-495; DC1: 159;
Ma: 1562-1563; MD: 223;
Po: 3004
Before Breakfast ADC: 276;
Br: 495; MD: 223-224
Beyond the Horizon ADC:
277; Br: 495-496; DC1:
159; Lon: 41; MD: 224;
Po: 3005
Bound East for Cardiff see
also S.S. Glencairn ADC:
277; Br: 496; MD: 224
Bread and Butter ADC: 277;
Br: 496
Chris [Chris Christopherson]
ADC: 277; Br: 496; MD:

224

Days Without End ADC: 277-278; ALL: 210; Br: 496-497; DC1: 159; Lon: 40, 43, 46; MD: 224-225; Po: 3005

Desire Under the Elms ADC: 278-280; ALL: 207-208; Br: 497-499; DC1: 160; LCAB: 135; Lon: 42-45; Ma: 1563-1564; MD: 225; Po: 3005-3008

Diff'rent ADC: 280; Br: 499-500; DC1: 160; MD: 225-226

The Dreamy Kid ADC: 280; Br: 500; MD: 226

Dynamo ADC: 280-281; Br: 500-501; DC1: 160; MD: 226

The Emperor Jones ADC: 281-282; Br: 501-502; DC1: 160-161; Ma: 1564; MD: 226

Exorcism ADC: 282; Br: 502; MD: 227

The First Man ADC: 282; Br: 502-503; MD: 227

Fog ADC: 282; Br: 503; Lon: 46

The Fountain ADC: 282-283; Br: 503; DC1: 161; MD: 227

Gold ADC: 283; Br: 503-504; MD: 227

The Great God Brown ADC: 283-284; Br: 504-505; DC1: 161-162; Lon: 40-41; MBD: 57; MD: 227-228; Po: 3008-3009; TMAP: 54, 74

The Hairy Ape ADC: 284-285; ALL: 208; Br: 505-507; DC1: 162; LCAB: 135; Lon: 40; Ma: 1564-1565; MD: 228; Po: 3009-3010; TMAP: 35

Hughie ADC: 285-286; Br: 507; Lon: 45; MD: 228; MDAE: 387, 389; Po: 3010

The Iceman Cometh ADC: 286-288; ALL: 207-209; Br: 507-510; DC1: 163-164; Lon: 40-42, 44-45; Ma: 1565-1567; MD: 228-

230; MDAE: 56, 388; Po: 3011-3012

Ile ADC: 288; Br: 510; DC1: 164

In the Zone see also S.S. Glencairn ADC: 288; Br: 510; DC1: 164; MD: 230; Po: 3013

Lazarus Laughed ADC: 289; Br: 510-511; DC1: 164-165; Lon: 40, 45; MD: 230-231; Po: 3013

Long Day's Journey Into Night ADC: 289-292; ALL: 208-209; Br: 511-513; DC1: 165-166; Lon: 42-43, 45-47; Ma: 1567-1568; MD: 231-232; MDAE: 386-390; Po: 3014-3015; TMAP: 41

The Long Voyage Home see also S.S. Glencairn ADC: 292; MD: 232

Marco Millions ADC: 292; Br: 513-514; DC1: 166; Lon: 40; MD: 232; Po: 3015-3016

A Moon for the Misbegotten ADC: 293-294; ALL: 209; Br: 514-515; DC1: 166; MD: 232; MDAE: 386-387; Po: 3016

The Moon of the Caribbees see also S.S. Glencairn ADC: 294; ALL: 208; Br: 515; DC1: 166; MD: 232

More Stately Mansions ADC: 294-295; Br: 515; Lon: 47; MDAE: 387-389; Po: 3017

Mourning Becomes Electra ADC: 295-297; ALL: 208; Br: 515-519; DC1: 166-168; LCAB: 135; Lon: 41, 43-47; Ma: 1568-1569; MD: 232-234; Po: 3017-3019

Now I Ask You ADC: 297; Br: 519

The Personal Education ADC: 297

Recklessness ADC: 297

The Reckoning ADC: 297

The Revelation of John the Divine ADC: 297

The Rime of the Ancient Mariner ADC: 297; Br: 519

The Rope ADC: 297; Br:

519

Servitude ADC: 297; Br: 519; Lon: 40; MD: 234

Shell-Shock ADC: 297; Br: 519

The Sniper ADC: 297

S.S. Glencairn [four plays: Moon of the Caribbees; In the Zone; Bound East for Cardiff; and The Long Voyage Home] ADC: 298; Br: 519; Lon: 46; MD: 234

Strange Interlude ADC: 298-299; Br: 519-521; DC1: 168-169; Lon: 41-42; Ma: 1569-1570; MD: 234-235; Po: 3020

The Straw ADC: 299; Br: 521; MD: 235

A Tale of Possessors Self-Dispossessed ADC: 299-300

Thirst ADC: 300; ALL: 208; Br: 521

"Tomorrow" Po: 3020

A Touch of the Poet ADC: 300-301; ALL: 209; Br: 521-522; DC1: 169; Lon: 40, 45; Ma: 1570-1571; MD: 235; MDAE: 388; Po: 3020-3021

Warnings ADC: 301

The Web ADC: 301; Br: 522; Po: 3021

Welded ADC: 301; Br: 522-523; DC1: 169; MD: 235-236

Where the Cross Is Made ADC: 301; Br: 523; MD: 236

A Wife for a Life ADC: 301

ONETTI, Juan Carlos

General LCAB: 135

"Avenida de mayo--Diagonal--Avenida de mayo" WaS1: 172

"Dreaded Hell" Wa: 594

"A Dream Come True" Wa: 594

"Esbjerg, on the Coast" Wa: 594

"The Face of Misfortune" Wa: 594; WaS1: 172

"The House in the Sand" Wa: 594

"Masquerade" Wa: 595

"The Nameless Tomb" Wa: 595

"El posible Baldi" WaS1: 172

"Welcome, Bob" Wa: 595

ONIONS, George Oliver [Oliver ONIONS; George OLIVER]

General TA: 238

"The Beckoning Fair One" Wa: 595

O'Nolan, Brian see O'BRIEN, Flann

ONWUKA, Wilfred

General BALE: 372

OPOKU, Samuel K.

General BALE: 372

OPPEN, George

General JW: 110; Po: 3023

OPPENHEIM, E. Phillips

General Po: 3023

OPPENHEIM, James

"Memories of Whitman and Lincoln" LCAB: 135

"Slag" WaS1: 172

ORDWAY, Joe

Entertaining Mrs. Sloane Br: 523

O'REILLY, Dowell

General AL: 298

O'REILLY, John Boyle

General AL: 300-301

Moondyne AL: 300-301

"A White Rose" PE: 333

ORIANI, Alfredo

Vortice Fi: 270

O'Riordan, Conal Holmes O'Connell see CONNELL, Norreys

ORLOVITZ, Gil

General Po: 3023-3024

"The Rooster" ICBAP: 96

ORLOVSKY, Peter

General Po: 3024

ORM

"The Ormulum" OMEP: 242-243

ORNITZ, Samuel Badisch

General JW: 268

ORR, Christine

Hogmanay ENES2: 193

ORRERY, Roger Boyle, Earl of [Roger BOYLE]

General Bon: 44; Li: 257

The History of Henry the Fifth DC1: 32

Parthenissa ERP: 94-95

The Tragedy of Zoroastres

Bon: 44
ORTEGA, Philip D.
  "The Coming of Zamora"
    ASF: 447
ORTEGA Y GASSET, José
  General Po: 3024-3028
  The Dehumanization of Art
    Po: 3028-3029
  Goethe from Within Po:
    3029
  The Modern Theme Ma:
    1572
  Notes on the Novel Po:
    3029
  The Revolt of the Masses
    Ma: 1572-1573; Po: 3030
ORTON, Joe
  General MBD: 65-66; MDAE:
    392; Po: 3030; TMBP:
    79-82
  Crimes of Passion; Erping-
    ham Camp; The Ruffian
    on the Stair TMBP: 82
  Entertaining Mr. Sloane
    TMBP: 79-82
  Funeral Games TMBP: 82
  Loot MDAE: 392; TMBP:
    79-83
  What the Butler Saw MBD:
    66; MDAE: 392; TMBP:
    73, 80, 83
ORTUÑEZ DE CALAHORRA,
    Diego
  The Mirror of Knighthood
    see A., L. [trans-
    lator], PARRY, Robert
    [translator], TYLER,
    Margaret [translator]
ORWELL, George
  General BN2: 93-94; CN:
    410-414; LCAB: 135; Po:
    3030-3042; Ri2: 300-317,
    331-337; Sch: 243-248
  Animal Farm CN: 414-415;
    EN: 103-104; ENE: 219;
    Ma: 1574-1575; Po: 3042-
    3043; Ri2: 301-306, 313,
    318-319, 335; Sch: 248-
    249; SFC: 165-166; Wa:
    595-596; WaS1: 173
  Burmese Days CN: 415-
    416; EN: 104; ENE:
    219-220; ENES1: 177;
    ENES2: 194; Po: 3043;
    Ri2: 301, 306, 316, 319-
    320; Sch: 249

A Clergyman's Daughter CN:
    416; EN: 104; ENE: 220;
    ENES1: 178; ENES2: 194;
    Ri2: 305-306
Collected Essays, Journalism and
    Letters LCAB: 135-136
Coming Up for Air CN: 416-
    417; EN: 104; ENE: 220;
    ENES1: 178; ENES2: 194;
    Ri2: 302, 304, 306, 311-312,
    320-321, 523; Sch: 249
Down and Out in Paris and Lon-
    don ENES1: 179; ENES2:
    194; Po: 3043-3044; Ri2:
    332, 335; Sch: 249
"England, Your England" Po:
    3044
"The English People" Ri2:
    304
Homage to Catalonia ENE:
    220; ENES2: 194; Po: 3044;
    Ri2: 303-304, 313, 331-334,
    336-337; Sch: 250
Keep the Aspidistra Flying
    CN: 417; EN: 104; ENE:
    220; ENES1: 178-179;
    ENES2: 195; MDAE: 397;
    Po: 3044-3045; Ri2: 321;
    Sch: 250
Nineteen Eighty Four CN:
    417-421; EN: 104-105; ENE:
    220-222; ENES1: 179;
    ENES2: 195; LCAB: 135;
    Ma: 1575-1576; Po: 3045-
    3051; Ri2: 301-302, 316,
    321-331, 466; Sch: 250-252
The Road to Wigan Pier BN2:
    93; ENE: 222; ENES1: 179-
    180; ENES2: 195; Po:
    3051-3052; Ri2: 302, 311-
    312, 331, 333-334, 336-337;
    Sch: 252
"Shooting an Elephant" Po:
    3052; Ri2: 332-333
"Why I Write" Po: 3052
ORY, Carlos Edmundo de
  General Po: 3052
ORZESZKOWA, Eliza
  Bene Nati Ke: 426
  The Boor Ke: 426
  "The Chain Links" Wa: 596
  "The Generous Lady" Wa:
    596
  Meir Ezofowicz Ke: 426
  "On a Winter Evening" Wa:
    596

On the Banks of the Nieman
  Ke: 426
"The Strong Samson" Wa:
  596
"Whose Fault Is It?" Wa:
  596
OSADEBAY, Dennis Chukude
  General BALE: 373
OSAHON, Naiwu
  General BALE: 373
OSBORN, Paul
  A Bell for Adano ADC: 302
  The Innocent Voyage ADC:
    302
  Morning's at Seven ADC:
    302
  On Borrowed Time ADC:
    302
  Point of No Return ADC:
    303; Br: 523
  The World of Suzie Wong
    ADC: 303
OSBORNE, John
  General Br: 523-524; LCAB:
    136; MBD: 66-68; MD:
    236; MDAE: 396-401; Po:
    3053-3056; TMBP: 91-121
  The Blood of the Bambergs
    Br: 524; EDC: 396;
    TMBP: 262
  A Bond Honoured Br: 524;
    EDC: 396; MDAE: 396;
    TMBP: 105, 118-119, 121,
    265
  The Devil Inside Him TMBP:
    118
  The Entertainer Br: 524-
    525; DC1: 169-170; EDC:
    396-397; Ma: 1577; MD:
    236-237; MBD: 66-67;
    MDAE: 397, 399; TMBP:
    93, 108, 113, 115, 119-
    121, 253
  The Hotel in Amsterdam Br:
    525; EDC: 397; MDAE:
    399; TMBP: 95, 103, 105,
    119, 122
  Inadmissible Evidence Br:
    525; DC1: 170; EDC:
    397-398; Ma: 1577-1578;
    MBD: 66; MDAE: 398;
    TMBP: 94, 102, 110-111,
    114, 118-120, 122
  Look Back in Anger Br:
    526-527; DC1: 170; EDC:
    398-400; LCAB: 136;

  Ma: 1578-1579; MBD: 66-67;
    MD: 237-238; MDAE: 396-
    401; Po: 3056-3058; TMBP:
    91-93, 96, 98, 100-110, 112-
    123, 223, 253; TMIP: 20, 27
  Luther Br: 527; DC1: 170;
    EDC: 400-401; Ma: 1579-
    1580; MBD: 66-68; MD:
    238; MDAE: 397, 399-400;
    Po: 3058-3059; TMBP: 93-
    94, 96-99, 102, 104-108, 111-
    112, 117, 119-120, 123
  A Patriot for Me Br: 527;
    EDC: 401-402; MDAE: 399-
    400; TMBP: 111, 119-120,
    121, 123
  A Place Calling Itself Rome
    TMBP: 119
  Plays for England see also
    Under Plain Cover Br:
    527-528; TMBP: 119
  A Sense of Detachment TMBP:
    124
  A Subject of Scandal and Con-
    cern Br: 528; DC1: 170;
    EDC: 402
  Time Present Br: 528; EDC:
    402; MDAE: 399; TMBP:
    102-103, 118-119, 124
  Tom Jones Po: 3059
  Under Plain Cover see also
    Plays for England EDC:
    402; TMBP: 113, 262
  West of Suez EDC: 402;
    TMBP: 72, 101, 120, 124
  The World of Paul Slickey Br:
    528; DC1: 171; EDC: 402;
    MBD: 66; MD: 238; MDAE:
    398; Po: 3059; TMBP: 124
  _____ and Anthony CREIGHTON
  Epitaph for George Dillon Br:
    525; DC1: 170; EDC: 402-
    403; MDAE: 396; TMBP:
    94, 105, 108, 111-112, 115,
    118-119, 121-122
  Personal Enemy TMBP: 118
OSGOOD, Lawrence
  Pigeons ADC: 303
OSKISON, John Milton
  General ASF: 448
OSOFISAN, Femi
  General BALE: 373
OSORIO, Luis Enrique
  General Br: 528
OSORIO, Miguel Angel
  General Po: 3060

OSTENSO, Martha
  Wild Geese Po: 3060
OSTER, Pierre
  General Po: 3060
OSTROVSKIJ, Nikolay Alexeye-
    vich
  That's How Steel Was Tem-
      pered Ke: 427
OSTROVSKY, Alexander Niko-
    laevich
  General Br: 528
  Easy Money DC2: 268
  The Forest [Les] EDC:
      403
  The Girl with No Dowry
      [Bespridannitsa] EDC:
      403
  Marriage DC2: 268
  Poor Bride DC2: 268
  A Profitable Job [Dokhodnoye
      Mesto] EDC: 403
  Storm DC2: 268; Ke: 426
  Talents and Admirers DC2:
      268
O'SULLIVAN, Seumas
  "Birds" PE: 333
  "Nelson Street" PE: 333
  "The Sheep" PE: 333
OTIS, James
  General AP: 449-450
OTIS, Mary
  Seize the Day ADC: 303
OTTLIK, Geza
  School at the Border Ke:
      427
OTWAY, Thomas
  General Bon: 44-45; Li:
      258-261
  The Atheist EDC: 403; Li:
      259
  Caius Marius DC1: 171; Li:
      259
  Don Carlos, Prince of Spain
      EDC: 403; Li: 260
  The Orphan; or, The Un-
      happy Marriage EDC:
      403-404; Li: 260
  The Soldier's Fortune EDC:
      404
  Venice Preserved; or A Plot
      Discovered Bon: 44-45;
      DC1: 171; EDC: 404-
      405; Li: 259-261
OUIDA [Marie Louise de la
    RAMEE]
  General BN: 82

  Under Two Flags BN: 82
OUSMANE, Sembene
  "Ses Trois Jours" Wa: 596
  "Vehi-Ciosane" Wa: 596
OVECHKIN, Valentin
  Greetings from the Front Ke:
      427
  "One of the Many" Wa: 596
  "Praskovya Maksimovna" Wa:
      596
OVERBURY, Sir Thomas
  General Ba: 100; Hen: 133
OVID
  Amores Ma: 1581
  Ars Amatoria Ma: 1581-1582
  Heroides Ma: 1582
  The Metamorphoses Ma: 1582-
      1583
OVIEDO Y VALDES, Gonzalo Fer-
    nandez de
  Claribalte Ke: 211
OWEN, Alun
  General Br: 528; MDAE: 403
  Progress to the Park DC1:
      171
  The Rough and Ready Lot
      DC1: 171
  The Ways of Love DC1: 171
OWEN, Walter
  General Po: 3060
OWEN, Wilfred
  General EP: 208-214; ICBAP:
      97; MP: 73; Po: 3061-
      3064; TA: 239
  "All Sounds Have Been as
      Music" Po: 3064
  "Anthem for Doomed Youth"
      EP: 211, 213; PE: 333
  "At a Cloory Near the Ancre"
      EP: 211
  "Dulce et Decorum Est" EP:
      211; PE: 334
  "Exposure" EP: 213
  "Futility" EP: 209, 213;
      ICBAP: 97
  "Greater Love" EP: 210-211,
      213; LCAB: 136; PE: 334;
      Po: 3064
  "Hospital Barge at Cerisy"
      ICBAP: 97
  "Miners" EP: 209; PE: 334
  "The Parable of the Old Man
      and the Young" PE: 334
  "Purple" Po: 3065
  "The Seed" EP: 213
  "The Show" EP: 209; PE:

334; Po: 3065
"Strange Meeting" EP: 210,
213; ICBAP: 97; PE:
334; Po: 3065
OWENS, Daniel
Arife and Pendabus MBA:
162
Emily T MBA: 162
OWENS, Rochelle
General MDAE: 405
Beclch ADC: 303
Futz ADC: 304; Br: 529;
MDAE: 405
The Karl Marx Play ADC:
304
OWENS, William A.
General ASF: 448
"Hangerman John" ASF:
448
Walking on Borrowed Land
Po: 3065
OWOMOYELA, Oyekan
General BALE: 374
OXLEY, James Macdonald
General ECL: 181
OYAMO [Charles F. GORDON]
General MBA: 162
The Breakout ADC: 304;
MBA: 162
Chimpanzee MBA: 162
His First Step BAP: 156;
MBA: 162
His First Step [Part I] ADC:
304
Lovers MBA: 162
The Thieves MBA: 163
Willie Bignigga MBA: 163
OYEJIDE, Lekan
General BALE: 374
OYEWOLE, Abiodun
Comments MBA: 163
OYONO-MBIA, Guillaume
General BALE: 374
OZ, Amos
"The Nomad and the Viper"
Wa: 596
OZICK, Cynthia
General ASF: 448; JW:
270
"Envy; or, Yiddish in Amer-
ica" WaS1: 173
"Usurpation (Other People's
Stories)" WaS1: 173
"Virility" WaS1: 173

P

PADGETT, Lewis [Catherine L.
MOORE and Henry KUTTNER]
"Piggy Bank" WaS1: 173
"The Twonky" WaS1: 173
"When the Bough Breaks"
WaS1: 173
PAGANO, Jo
"The Disinherited" SFC: 166;
Wa: 597
PAGE, Thomas Nelson
General AF: 214; ALL: 210-
211; AN: 210; ASF: 449-
450; Cla: 115
"The Burial of the Guns" ASF:
448
"Elsket" ASF: 448
"The Gray Jacket of No. 4"
ASF: 448
In Ole Virginia ALL: 210
"Little Darby" ASF: 448
"Marse Chan" AF: 214; ASF:
448; Wa: 597; WaS1: 173
"Meh Lady" ASF: 449; Wa:
597; WaS1: 173
"No Haid Pawn" ASF: 449;
Wa: 597; WaS1: 173
"The Old Gentleman of the
Black Stock" ASF: 449
"Old Jabe's Marital Experiment"
ASF: 449
"Ole 'Stracted" ASF: 449; Wa:
597; WaS1: 173
"Polly: A Christmas Recollec-
tion" ASF: 449
Red Rock ALL: 210
"A Soldier of the Empire" ASF:
449
"Unc' Edinburg's Drowndin'"
ASF: 449; Wa: 597
PAGET, Violet [Vernon LEE]
General Po: 2308-2309; TA:
241
Miss Brown Po: 2309
PAGNOL, Marcel
General Br: 529; MD: 238;
Po: 3067-3068
Souvenirs d'enfance Po: 3068
Topaze [Monsieur Topaze] MD:
238; Po: 3067
PAIN, Barry Eric Odell
General TA: 242
PAINE, Albert B.
"The Black Hands" WaS1: 173
PAINE, Thomas

General AP: 452-461; Da: 75-76

The Age of Reason AP: 458-460; Ma: 1584

Common Sense AP: 456, 458-459; Ma: 1585-1586

The Crisis AP: 458; Ma: 1586

The Rights of Man AP: 455-456, 458-459; Ma: 1586-1587

PAINTER, William

General SC: 78

The Palace of Pleasure ERP: 362-370; Hen: 152-153; SC: 78

PALACIO VALDES, Armando

La aldea perdida Ke: 211

La alegría del capitán Ribot Ke: 211

"Las burbujas" Po: 3068

El cuarto poder Ke: 211

La espuma Ke: 211

La fe Ke: 211

La hermana San Sulpicio Ke: 211-212

El idilio de un enfermo Ke: 212

José Ke: 212

Marta y María Ke: 212

Los mayos de Cadiz Ke: 212

Maxima Ke: 212

La novela de un novelista Fi: 229

Riverita Ke: 212

El señorito Octavio Fi: 229; Ke: 212

Tristán o el pesimismo Ke: 212

PALANGYO, Peter K.

General BALE: 375

Dying in the Sun BALE: 375

PALAPRAT, Jean

Le Bourru DC2: 268

PALAZZESCHI, Aldo

The Sisters Materassi Fi: 270-271

PALEY, Grace

"Goodbye and Good Luck" Wa: 597

"The Used-Boy Raisers" WaS1: 174

PALMA, Clemente

"Los canastros" Wa: 597

"Una historia vulgar" Wa: 597

"El hombre del cigarillo" Wa: 597

"La leyenda de hachisch" Wa: 597

"Un paseo extraño" Wa: 597

PALMA, Ricardo

General Po: 3069

PALMER, C. Everard

General WIL: 130

Baba and Mr. Big WIL: 131

Big Doc Bitterfoot WIL: 130

A Broken Vessel WIL: 130

The Cloud with the Silver Lining WIL: 130

A Cow Called Boy WIL: 131

The Hummingbird People WIL: 130-131

My Father, Sun-Sun Johnson WIL: 131

The Sun Salutes You WIL: 130

The Wooing of Beppo Tate WIL: 131

Palmer, Edward Vance see PALMER, Vance

PALMER, Eustace

General BALE: 375

PALMER, Herbert

General Po: 3069-3070

PALMER, Jon Phillips

The Starting Five MBA: 163

PALMER, Nettie [Janet Gertrude PALMER]

General Po: 3070

PALMER, Vance

General MAP: 252-254; Po: 3070-3072

"The Foal" Wa: 598

Golconda MAP: 253; Po: 3072

The Passage MAP: 253-254

"The Rainbow Bird" Wa: 598

PALTOCK, Robert

The Life and Adventures of Peter Wilkins ENES2: 196

PALUDAN, Jacob

Jorgen Stein Ke: 362

PANAS, Alexander

Mr. Tambo, Mr. Bones ADC: 304

PANETTA, George

Kiss Mama ADC: 304

Mike Downstairs ADC: 304

PANFEROV, F.I.

Bruski Ke: 427

In the Name of the Young Ke:

427
PANNELL, Lynn K.
It's a Shame MBA: 163
PANNWITZ, Rudolf
General Po: 3072-3073
PANOVA, Vera
General Po: 3073
The Bright Shore Ke: 427
Kruzhilikha Ke: 427
Seasons of the Year Ke:
427-428
PANTIN, Raoul
Journey WIL: 131
PANZINI, Alfredo
La Madonna di Mama Fi:
271
PAPINI, Giovanni
General Po: 3073-3074
Le Buffonate Po: 3074
The Devil Po: 3074
PARANDOWSKI, Jan
"Aegean Civilization" Wa:
598
"Cherry" Wa: 598
"A Conversation with a
Shadow" Wa: 598
"Encyclopedists" Wa: 598
"Lascaux" Wa: 598
"Max von Trott" Wa: 598
"The Mediterranean Hour"
Wa: 598
"Miedzy lampa a switem" Wa:
598
"The Milestone" Wa: 598
"The Olympic Wreath" Wa:
598
"The Phonograph" Wa: 598
"Poczajow" Wa: 598
"The Prayer of Aristides"
Wa: 598
"Rodecki" Wa: 598
"Roscher" Wa: 599
"Tableau" Wa: 599
"The Telescope of Galileo"
Wa: 599
PARDO BAZAN, Emilia
General Po: 3075-3076
"Accidente" WaS1: 14
Adam and Eve Fi: 229
A Christian Woman Fi: 229;
Ke: 213
La cuestión palpitante Po:
3077
Dulce dueño Fi: 229
Insolacion Fi: 229; Ke:
213

"Jesusa" WaS1: 14
La madre naturaleza Fi: 229;
Ke: 213; Po: 3077
Memorias de un solteron Fi:
229
Morrina Ke: 213
"La nina martir" WaS1: 14
Pascual Lopez Fi: 229; Ke:
213
Los Pazos de Ulloa Fi: 229-
230; Ke: 213-214; Po:
3077-3078
La piedra angular Ke: 214
La quimera Fi: 230; Ke: 214
El saludo de las brujas Ke:
214
La sirena negra Fi: 230; Po:
3078
El tesoro de Gaston Ke: 214
La tribuna Ke: 214
Un viaje de novios Ke: 214
PAREJA Y DIEZ CANSECO, Al-
fredo
General Po: 3078
PARKER, Dorothy
General APC: 42; ASF: 450;
JW: 113; LCAB: 136; Po:
3079
"The Actress" PE: 334
"The Banquet of Crow" WaS1:
174
"Big Blonde" ASF: 450; SFC:
166; Wa: 599; WaS1: 174
"Clothe the Naked" WaS1:
174
Ladies of the Corridor Br:
529
"Mr. Durant" SFC: 167; Wa:
599
"The Sexes" ASF: 450; Wa:
599
"Soldiers of the Republic"
ASF: 450; WaS1: 174
"Standard of Living" Wa: 599
"Such a Pretty Little Picture"
ASF: 450; WaS1: 174
"A Telephone Call" SFC:
167; Wa: 599
"Too Bad" WaS1: 174
"The Waltz" ASF: 450
"You Were Perfectly Fine"
ASF: 450; Wa: 599
PARKER, Gilbert
General ECL: 186-187
PARKER, Matthew
General SC: 78

PARKER, Rod
And Whose Little Boy Are
You? ADC: 304
PARKER, Theodore
General AAL: 211-212
PARKES, Frank Kobina [Francis
Ernest KOBINA]
General BALE: 375
PARKMAN, Francis
General AAL: 212; Cla:
116-117
The Conspiracy of Pontiac
Cla: 116
The Oregon Trail Cla: 116
Vassall Morton AN: 210
PARKS, Gordon
General BAF: 226-227; BAP:
156-157; BAW: 577-578;
MBA: 163
The Learning Tree BAF:
227; BAP: 157
PARNELL, Thomas
General Me: 280-281
"Hymn to Contentment" Me:
280; PE: 334
PARRA, Nicanor
General Po: 3080
PARRA, Teresa de la
General Po: 3080
PARRINGTON, Vernon Louis
General LCAB: 136
PARRY, Robert
Moderatus ERP: 371-372
PARRY, Robert [translator]
Mirror of Knighthood by
Diego ORTUNEZ DE CALA-
HORRA ERP: 371-372
PARSONS, Elizabeth
"The Nightingale Sing" WaS1:
174
PARTRIDGE, Eric
General LCAB: 136
PASCAL, Blaise
General LCAB: 136
PASCOLI, Giovanni
General Br: 529; Po: 3080
PASINETTI, Pier-Maria
General Po: 3081
La confusione Ke: 248; Po:
3081
Rosso veneziano Ke: 248
PASO, Alfonso
General MD: 238; Po: 3081
PASOLINI, Pier Paolo
General Po: 3081-3082
Biciclettone Po: 3083

PASSEUR, Steve
Je vivrai un grand amour Br:
529
N'importe quoi pour elle Br:
529
No Fury [L'Acheteuse] Br:
529
Une Vilaine femme Br: 530
PASTERNAK, Boris
General Ma: 1589; Po: 3083-
3092
"Aerial Ways" Wa: 599
"The Cave" Wa: 599
"The Childhood of Luvers"
["Detstvo Lyuvers"] Po:
3092; Wa: 599-600
Doctor Zhivago Fi: 460-462;
Ke: 428-431; LCAB: 136;
Ma: 1588-1589; Po: 3092-
3108
"The History of a Contraoctave"
Wa: 600
"The Last Summer" Wa: 600
"Letters from Tula" Wa: 600
"The Narrative" Wa: 600
"The Sign of Apelles" Wa:
600
"Tale" WaS1: 174
PATCHEN, Kenneth
General ICBAP: 97; Po:
3108
"Bury Them in God" WaS1:
174
PATEL, Ravji
General Po: 3108
PATER, Walter Horatio
General BN: 82-83; Du: 119-
120; LCAB: 136; TA: 243-
244; VP: 60-61
"Apollo in Picardy" Wa: 600
"The Child in the House" Wa:
600
"Denys L'Auxerrois" Wa: 600
"Duke Carl of Rosenmold" Wa:
600
"Emerald Uthwart" Wa: 601
"An English Poet" Wa: 601
Gaston de Latour ENES1: 180
"Gaudioso, the Second" Wa:
601
Marius the Epicurean BN: 83;
Du: 118-119; ENES1: 180;
ENES2: 196; VP: 61
"Sebastian Van Storck" SFC:
167; Wa: 601; WaS1: 174
PATERSON, Andrew Barton [The

Banjo]
General AL: 306-308; Po:
3108-3109
"Waltzing Matilda" AL: 306-
308
PATMORE, Coventry
General VP: 61-62
"Amelia" PE: 335
"Angel in the House" ICBAP:
97; PE: 335; VP: 62
"The Azalea" PE: 335
"The Day After Tomorrow"
PE: 335
"Departure" PE: 335
"Eros and Psyche" ICBAP:
97
"King Cophetua the First"
ICBAP: 97
"Love at Large" ICBAP:
97; PE: 335
"Pain" ICBAP: 97
"Psyche's Discontent" ICBAP:
97
"The Rod, the Root and the
Flower" ICBAP: 97
"Sponsa Dei" ICBAP: 97
"Tired Memory" PE: 335
"To the Body" ICBAP: 98
"To the Unknown Eros"
ICBAP: 98
"The Toys" PE: 335
"Tristitia" PE: 335
"The Victories of Love" PE:
335
PATON, Alan
General CFAE: 287-288;
CN: 422; Po: 3109
Cry, the Beloved Country
CFAE: 287-288; CN:
422-423; Ma: 1590-1591;
Po: 3110
"Death of a Tsotsi" Wa:
601
"Debbie Go Home" Wa: 601
"A Drink in the Passage"
Wa: 601
"Ha'penny" Wa: 601
"Life for a Life" Wa: 601
"Sponono" Wa: 601
Too Late the Phalarope Br:
530; CN: 423; Po: 3110
"The Waste Land" Wa: 601
PATRICK, John [John Patrick
GOGGAN]
General MDAE: 407
The Curious Savage ADC:

305; Br: 530
Everybody Loves Opal ADC:
305
Good as Gold ADC: 305
The Hasty Heart ADC: 305;
Br: 530
Lo and Behold! ADC: 305
The Story of Mary Surratt
ADC: 305-306
The Teahouse of the August
Moon ADC: 306; Br: 530
PATRICK, Robert
General MDAE: 408
Fred and Harold ADC: 306
The Haunted Host ADC: 306
Kennedy's Children ADC:
306-307
One Person ADC: 307
Play by Play ADC: 307
PATTERSON, Charles
Black Ice MBA: 164
Legacy MBA: 164
PATTERSON, Lindsay
General BAF: 227-228
PATTERSON, Orlando
General BAF: 228; WIL:
131-132
An Absence of Ruins BAF:
228; WIL: 133
The Children of Sisyphus
BAF: 228; WIL: 132-133
Die the Long Day BAF: 228;
WIL: 133
PATTON, Frances Gray
"A Piece of Bread" SFC:
167; Wa: 601
PATTULO, George
"The More Abundant Life" Wa:
602
PAUL, Jean [RICHTER]
Hesperus Fi: 382-383; Ke:
327
The Invisible Lodge Fi: 383;
Ke: 328
Katzenberger Fi: 383
Siebenkas Fi: 383
Titan Fi: 383; Ke: 328
The Twins Fi: 383
Wutz Fi: 383
PAULDING, James Kirke
General AF: 216-217; AN:
211; AP: 464-465; ASF:
451; Da: 100; Ho: 138-139,
157
The Bucktails ADC: 307
"The Creole's Daughter" AF:

217

The Diverting History of John
Bull and Brother Jonathan
AP: 464

"The Dumb Girl" ASF: 450-
451; Wa: 602

The Dutchman's Fireside AF:
216; AN: 210-211; Ho:
138

The Lion of the West ADC:
307

The Puritan and His Daughter
AF: 216; AN: 211; AP:
465

Salmagundi;... AP: 464-
465

Salmagundi: Second Series
AP: 464-465

Sheppard Lee AN: 211

Westward Ho! AF: 217

PAULHAN, Jean
General Po: 3111-3119
Le Clair et l'obscur Po:
3119

Les Fleurs de Tarbes Po:
3119

Progrès en amour assez lents
Po: 3120

PAUSEWANG, Gudrun
Der Weg nach Tongay Fi:
383; Po: 3120; Wa: 602

PAUSTOVSKII, Konstantin
General Po: 3120

PAVESE, Cesare
General Po: 3121-3124
Among Women Only Fi: 271
The Beach Fi: 271
The Beautiful Summer Fi:
271

The Comrade Fi: 271-272
The Devil in the Hills Fi:
272

Fuoco grande Ke: 248
The Harvesters Fi: 272
The House on the Hill Fi:
272-273

Lavorare stanca Po: 3124
The Moon and the Bonfires
[La Luna e i falò] Fi:
273; Ke: 248; Po: 3124

The Political Prisoner Fi:
273

PAVLENKO, Pyotr Andreyevich
Happiness Ke: 431-432
In the Fast Ke: 432

PAVLOVA, Karolina

A Double Life Fi: 462

PAWLEY, Thomas
General BAP: 158; MBA:
164

Crispus Attucks BAP: 158
FFV (First Family of Virginia)
BAP: 158

Judgment Day BAP: 158;
MBA: 164

Messiah BAP: 158
Smokey BAP: 158
The Tumult and the Shouting
BAP: 158

PAYNE, Daniel Alexander
General AAPD: 73; BAW:
583-584

PAYNE, Henry Nevil
General Li: 263
The Siege of Constantinople
Li: 263

PAYNE, John Howard
General AD: 177-181; Da:
113; EDT: 232; Lon: 62-
63

Brutus AD: 179-180
"Home Sweet Home" PE: 335
_____ and Washington IRVING
Charles II, or The Merry Monarch ADC: 307

PAYRO, Roberto Jorge
General LCAB: 137

PAZ, Octavio
General LCAB: 137; Ma:
1592; Po: 3125-3126

El laberinto de la soledad Po:
3126

Libertad bajo palabra Po:
3127

Piedra de sol Po: 3127
"Puerta condenada" Po: 3128
"La rama" Po: 3128

p'BITEK, J.P. Okot
General BALE: 376-378
Song of Lawino BALE: 376-
378

Song of Ocol BALE: 377
Song of Prisoner BALE: 376-
377

PEA, Enrico
Moscardino Fi: 274; Ke: 248
Il servitore del diavolo Ke:
248

Il volto santo Ke: 248

PEACE, Ernest E.
General BAW: 585

PEACOCK, Reginald

General Hen: 22

PEACOCK, Thomas Love
General BN: 84; Du: 120-
121; LCAB: 137; Re:
215-216
Crotchet Castle Du: 120;
ENE: 222; ENES1: 180;
ENES2: 196
Gryll Grange ENE: 222;
ENES1: 180; ENES2: 196
Headlong Hall EN: 105;
ENE: 222; ENES1: 181;
ENES2: 196
Maid Marian ENE: 222;
ENES1: 181; ENES2: 196
Melincourt EN: 105; ENE:
222; ENES1: 181; ENES2:
197
The Misfortunes of Elphin
EN: 105; ENE: 223;
ENES1: 181; ENES2: 197
Nightmare Abbey Du: 120;
ENE: 223; ENES1: 181;
ENES2: 197
"War Song" PE: 335

PEAKE, Mervyn
General Po: 3128
Gormenghast ENES2: 197
Titus Alone ENES2: 197
Titus Groan ENES2: 197

"The Pearl-Poet" see individual
titles under ANONYMOUS

PEARSE, Patrick H.
"Barbara" Wa: 602
"Brigid of the Wind" see
"The Keening Woman"
"The Dearg-Daol" Wa: 602
"Eoineen of the Birds" Wa:
602
"Iosagan" Wa: 602
"The Keening Woman" Wa:
602
"The Mother" Wa: 602
"The Priest" Wa: 602
"The Singer" Wa: 602
"The Thief" Wa: 602
"The Wood" Wa: 602

PEARSON, Kesketh
General LCAB: 137

PEELE, George
General ED: 320; PS:
143-144, 150; TSD: 95-
97
The Arraignment of Paris
DC1: 172; ED: 320;
PS: 145, 151; TSD: 95-
97
"Bathsheba's Song" [from The
Love of King David and Fair
Bathsheba] PE: 335
The Battle of Alcazar DC1:
172; ED: 320; PS: 145-146,
151
David and Bethsabe [The Love
of King David and Fair Beth-
sabe] DC1: 172; ED: 320;
PS: 146, 151-152; TSD:
95-96
Edward I DC1: 172; ED:
320; PS: 146, 151
The Hunting of Cupid DC1:
172
The Life and Death of Jack
Strawe see ANONYMOUS
Merry Conceited Jests ERP:
376
Old Wives Tale DC1: 173;
ED: 320; PS: 144-145, 151;
TSD: 95-96

PEGUY, Charles
General Po: 3128-3134
Jeanne d'Arc Po: 3134
Notre Jeunesse Po: 3134

PELLEGRIN, S.J.
Polydore DC2: 269

PELLERIN, Jean-Victor
Terrain vague Br: 530
Têtes de rechange Br: 530

PELLEW, J.D.C.
"The Temple" PE: 335

PELLICO, Silvio
Francesca da Rimini DC2: 269
Tommaso Moro DC2: 269

PENN, William
General AP: 469-474; Da:
38

PENRY, John
General SC: 79

PENZOLDT, Ernst
General Po: 3135

PEPYS, Samuel
General Bon: 76-77
Diary Bon: 76-77; LCAB:
137; Ma: 1593-1594

PERAZA, Luis
El hombre que se fue Br:
530

PERCIVAL, James Gates
General Da: 114

PERCY, Thomas
General EC: 103-104
"On the Ancient Metrical

Romances" EC: 103
PERCY, Walker
    General CFAE: 289-290;
        CN: 423; Po: 3135-3137
    The Last Gentleman CN:
        423; Ma: 1595; Po: 3135-
        3136
    The Moviegoer CN: 424;
        Ma: 1595-1596; Po: 3135-
        3138
PERCY, William
    General NI: 337-338
    A Forest Tragaedye in Vacun-
        ium DC1: 173
PERCY, William Alexander
    General Po: 3138
    Lanterns on the Levee Po:
        3138
PEREDA, Jose Maria de
    El buey suelto Fi: 230
    "Coats of Arms and Bags of
        Money" Wa: 603
    De tal palo, tal astilla Fi:
        230; Ke: 215
    Don Gonzalo Gonzalez de la
        Gonzalera Fi: 230; Ke:
        215
    "The End of a Race" Wa:
        603
    "The Levy" Wa: 603
    Pedro Sanchez Fi: 230;
        Ke: 215
    Peñas Arriba Fi: 230-231;
        Ke: 215
    La puchera Fi: 230; Ke:
        215
    El sabor de la tierruca Fi:
        231
    Sotileza Fi: 231; Ke: 215
PEREIRA, Francesca Yetunde
    General BALE: 379
PERELMAN, Sidney Joseph
    General JW: 273; LCAB:
        137
    The Beauty Part ADC: 308;
        Br: 530; MDAE: 409
    "Call Me Monty and Grovel
        Freely" WaS1: 175
    "Dial 'H' for Heartburn"
        WaS1: 175
PERET, Benjamin
    General Po: 3139-3140
PERETZ, Isaac Loeb
    General MD: 238
    Three Gifts MD: 239
PERETZ, Itzhak L.

"The Adventures of a Melody"
    Wa: 603
"Bontsha the Silent" Wa: 603
"Devotion Without End" WaS1:
    175
"Hear, O Israel" Wa: 603
"If Not Higher" Wa: 603
"The Kabbalists" Wa: 603
PERETZ, Y.L.
    Bay Nakht Oyfn Altn Mark
        DC2: 269
PEREZ DE ARCE, Camilo
    General Br: 531
PEREZ DE AYALA, Ramón
    General Po: 3140-3142
    A.M.D.G. Fi: 231; Ke: 215;
        Po: 3141
    Bajo el signo de Artemisa Fi:
        231
    Belarmino y Apolonio Fi:
        231; Ke: 215-216; Po:
        3140, 3142
    La caída de los limones Fi:
        231; Ke: 216; Po: 3143
    El curandero de su honra Fi:
        231
    Luna de miel, luna de hiel
        Fi: 231; Ke: 216
    Luz de domingo Ke: 216
    Novelas poematicas Ke: 216
    La pata de la raposa Fi: 231-
        232; Ke: 216; Po: 3141
    Prometeo Ke: 216; Po: 3143
    La revolución sentimental Po:
        3143
    Tigre Juan Fi: 232; Ke:
        216-217
    Tinieblas en las cumbres Fi:
        232; Ke: 217; Po: 3141
    Los trabajos de Urbano y
        Simona Fi: 232
    Troteras y danzaderas Ke:
        217; Po: 3141
PEREZ DE HITA, Ginés
    Historia de los bandos de los
        Zegríes y Abencerrajes Ke:
        226
PEREZ GALDOS, Benito
    General Br: 231, 531; MD:
        239; Po: 3144-3151
    El abuelo Fi: 232; Ke: 217
    Aita Tettauen Fi: 232; Ke:
        217; Po: 3152
    El amigo Manso Fi: 232-233;
        Ke: 217-218; Ma: 1597;
        Po: 3152-3153

Angel Guerra Fi: 233; Ke: 218; Ma: 1597-1598
Antón Caballero MD: 239
Aquel Po: 3153
El audaz Ke: 218
El caballero encantado Fi: 233
Cádiz Ke: 218; Po: 3153
Carlos VI en La Rapita Fi: 233; Ke: 218
Casandra Ke: 218
Los cien mil hijos de San Luis Fi: 233
La corte de Carlos IV Ke: 218; Po: 3153
La de Bringas Fi: 233-234; Ke: 219; Po: 3154
La de los tristes destinos DC2: 140; Ke: 219; Po: 3154
La desheredada Fi: 234-235; Ke: 219; Ma: 1598-1599; Po: 3154-3155
El doctor Centeno Fi: 235; Ke: 219
Doña Perfecta DC2: 139; Fi: 235-236; Ke: 219-220; Ma: 1599; Po: 3155-3156
Electra MD: 239
Episodios nacionales Fi: 236; Ke: 220; Po: 3156-3157
España tragica Fi: 236
La familia de León Roch Fi: 236; Ke: 220-221; Po: 3157-3158
La fontana de oro Fi: 236-237; Ke: 221; Po: 3158
Fortunata y Jacinta Fi: 237-238; Ke: 221-222; Ma: 1599-1600; Po: 3159-3160
Gloria Fi: 238-239; Ke: 222-223; Po: 3160
The Grandfather Br: 231
Halma Fi: 239; Ke: 223
La incógnita Fi: 239; Ke: 223
Juan Martín, el Empecinado Fi: 239; Po: 3161
La Loca de la Casa DC2: 140; Po: 3161
Marianela Fi: 239-240; Ke: 223-224; Ma: 1601; Po: 3161-3162
"Mi calle" Po: 3162

Miau Fi: 240; Ke: 224
Misericordia Fi: 240-241; Ke: 224; Ma: 1601; Po: 3162-3163
Nazarín Fi: 241; Ke: 224
El 19 de marzo y el 2 de mayo Ke: 219
Los Pepes Po: 3163
"El pórtico de la gloria" WaS1: 175
Lo prohibido Fi: 241-242; Ke: 224-225; Po: 3163
Realidad DC2: 140; Fi: 242; Ke: 225; Ma: 1602
La sombra Fi: 242; Ke: 225
Tormento Fi: 242-243; Ke: 225; Po: 3163-3164
Torquemada Fi: 243
Torquemada en el purgatorio Ke: 226; Po: 3164
Torquemada en la cruz Ke: 225
Torquemada en la hoguera Fi: 243; Ke: 225-226; Po: 3164-3165
Torquemada y San Pedro Fi: 243; Ke: 226; Po: 3165
Tristana Fi: 243-244; Ke: 226
Zaragoza Ke: 226; Po: 3165
PEREZ LUGIN, Alejandro
La casa de la Troya Ke: 226-227
PERINET, Joachim
Kasper der Fagottist DC2: 269
PERKINS, Eugene
General BAP: 159; BAW: 587
Fred MBA: 164
Our Street BAP: 159
PERLOW, Isaac
"In Thy Blood Live" Wa: 603
PEROL, Jean
General Po: 3165-3166
PERR, Harvey
Rosebloom ADC: 308
PERROS, Georges
General Po: 3166
PERRY, Felton
General MBA: 165
Buy the Bi and By MBA: 165
Or MBA: 165
PERRY George Sessions
General ASF: 451; Po: 3166

PERRY, Richard
  Changes BAF: 229
PERRY, Shaunielle
  General MBA: 165
  Music Magic MBA: 165
PERSE, St.-John [Alexis Saint-
    Leger LEGER]
  General Po: 3166-3173
  Amers Po: 3173
  Anabasis [Anabase] Ma:
    1603; Po: 3167, 3173-
    3174
  Chronique Ma: 1603; Po:
    3174-3175
  Eloges and Other Poems Ma:
    1603-1604
  Exil Ma: 1604; Po: 3175
  Neiges Po: 3175
  Oiseaux Po: 316
  "Pictures for Crusoe" Ma:
    1604
  Seamarks Ma: 1604-1605
  Vents Ma: 1605
PERSOV, S.
  "The Outcome" Wa: 603
PERYALIS, Notis
  Masks of Angels Br: 531
PERZYNSKI, Wlodzimierz
  "The Laundry of Conscience"
    Wa: 603
  "The Perishing World" Wa:
    603
PESSOA, Fernando
  General LCAB: 137; Po:
    3176-3177
PETERKIN, Julia
  General ASF: 451; AN:
    211; Po: 3177
  "Ashes" Wa: 604; WaS1:
    175
  "Green Thursday" WaS1:
    175
  "Meeting" WaS1: 175
  "The Red Rooster" WaS1:
    175
  "A Sunday" WaS1: 175
PETERS, Lenrie [Leopold]
  General BALE: 379
  The Second Round LCAB:
    137-138
PETERS, Paul and George
    SKLAR
  Stevedore ADC: 308; Br:
    531
PETERS, Samuel
  General AP: 584-585

PETERSEN, Don
  Does a Tiger Wear a Necktie?
    ADC: 309
PETERSEN, Nis
  Spilled Milk Ke: 362
PETERSON, Louis
  General AAPD: 399; BAP:
    160; BAW: 589; Br: 531
  Entertain a Ghost BAP: 160-
    161
  Mrs. Patterson MBA: 165
  Take a Giant Step AAPD: 399;
    BAP: 160-162; Br: 531;
    MBA: 166
PETRAKIS, Harry Mark
  General ASF: 451
PETRARCH, Francesco
  Le Rime of Petrarch [Can-
    zoniere] Ma: 1606
PETRONIUS, Gaius
  The Satyricon Ma: 1607-1608
PETRY, Ann
  General AAF: 70-71; AAW:
    69; BAF: 230-231; BAW:
    590-591; LCAB: 138
  Country Place BAF: 232
  "In Darkness and Confusion"
    AAF: 70; ASF: 452; BAW:
    590; Wa: 604
  "Miss Muriel" Wa: 604
  Miss Muriel and Other Stories
    BAF: 232
  The Narrows AAF: 71; BAF:
    232
  The Street AAF: 70; AN:
    211; BAF: 232-233
  "The Witness" ASF: 452;
    BAF: 231; WaS1: 175
PETTIE, George
  General SC: 79
  A Petite Pallace of Pettie His
    Pleasure ERP: 377-380;
    Hen: 155
PETTITT, Henry
  General EDT: 234
PETTY, Sir William
  General Bon: 77
PEYREFITTE, Roger
  General Po: 3177
  The Exile of Capri Po: 3178
PHARIS, Gwen
  The Courting of Marie Jenvrin
    DC1: 173
  One Man's House DC1: 173
  Pasque Flowers DC1: 173
  Still Stands the House DC1:

173
PHARR, Robert Deane
General BAF: 233; BAW:
592
The Book of Numbers BAF:
233-234
S.R.O. BAF: 234
The Soul Murder Case BAF:
234
PHELPS, Elizabeth Stuart
General ASF: 452
"The Angel Over the Right
Shoulder" ASF: 452
PHILIPPE, Charles-Louis
General Po: 3178
PHILIPS, Ambrose
General EC: 104; Li: 265
The Distressed Mother DC1:
173-174; EC: 104; Li:
265
Humphry, Duke of Gloucester
DC1: 174; Li: 265
PHILIPS, Watts
The Dead Heart DC1: 174
PHILLIPS, David Graham
General AN: 211-212; ASF:
452; LCAB: 138; Po:
3179
The Plum Tree AN: 211
PHILLIPS, Edward
The Stage Mutineers Li:
267
PHILLIPS, Jane
General BAF: 234
Mojo Hand BAF: 234
PHILLIPS, Jonas B.
General JW: 405
PHILLIPS, Stephen
General Mi: 266; TA: 244-
245
PHILLIPS, Thomas Hal
"The Shadow of an Arm"
SFC: 167; Wa: 604
PHILLPOTS, Eden
General Mi: 267
PICASSO, Pablo
Desire Caught by the Tail
DC2: 269
PICCOLOMINI, Alessandro
Ortensio DC2: 269
PICCOLOMINI, Enea Silvio
The Goodly History of the
Lady Lucrece [Anon.
English trans. of 1567]
ERP: 190-191
The Historie of Eurialus

and Lucretia see ALLEN,
Charles [translator]
PICHAMURTHI, N.
General Po: 3180
PICHETTE, Henri
General Po: 3180
The Epiphanies [Les Epiphanies]
Br: 531
PICKENS, William
General BAW: 594
"The Vengeance of the Gods"
WaS1: 175
PICKERZNG
Horestes DC1: 174
PICO, Pedro E.
General Br: 532
PICON, Jacinto Octavio
Juanita Tenorio Ke: 227
PICON-SALAS, Mariano
General Po: 3180
PIERCE, Ovid Williams
General Po: 3180
PIERPONT, John
General Da: 114
PIERSON, Helen W.
"Chip" ASF: 453
PIETERSE, Cosmo George Leipoldt
General BALE: 380
PIEYRE DE MANDIARGUES, André
General Po: 3181
La Motocyclette Fi: 125
"The Tide" WaS1: 139
PIKE, Albert
General ASF: 453
PILLAI, Thakazhi Sivasankara
"The Flood" Wa: 604
PIL'NYAK, Boris
General Po: 3182
Krasnoye Derevo Fi: 462
Machines and Wolves Fi: 462;
Ke: 432
Mahagony Fi: 462; Ke: 432
Mother Earth Fi: 462
The Naked Year Fi: 462-463;
Ke: 432
The Ripening of the Fruit Ke:
432
Soljanoj Ambar Fi: 463
The Volga Falls to the Caspian
Sea Fi: 463; Ke: 432
PINDAR
The Odes Ma: 1609-1610
Pindar, Peter see WOLCOT, John
Pineda, Rafael see DIAZ SOSA,
Rafael Angel
PINERA, Virgili

General Br: 532; Po: 3182
PIÑERO, Miguel
  Eulogy for a Small-Time Thief
    ADC: 309
  Midnight Moon at the Greasy
    Spoon ADC: 309
  Short Eyes ADC: 309
  The Sun Always Shines for
    the Cool ADC: 309
PINERO, Sir Arthur Wing
  General Br: 532; EDT:
    241-247; MBD: 68-69;
    MD: 239-240; Mi: 267-
    269; Po: 3183; TA: 245
  The Amazons EDC: 405
  The Benefit of the Doubt
    Br: 532; EDC: 405
  The Big Drum EDC: 405
  The Cabinet Minister EDT:
    241
  Child Man EDC: 405
  A Cold June EDC: 405
  Dandy Dick EDC: 405
  Dr. Harmer's Holidays EDC:
    405
  The Enchanted Cottage EDC:
    405-406
  The Freaks EDC: 406
  The Gay Lord Quex EDC:
    406
  His House in Order EDC:
    406; EDT: 242-243; MD:
    240
  The Hobby Horse EDC: 406
  Imprudence EDC: 406
  In Chancery EDC: 406
  Iris DC1: 174; EDC: 406;
    MD: 240
  The Ironmaster EDC: 406
  Lady Bountiful EDC: 406
  Late of Mockford's EDT:
    246
  Letty EDC: 407; MD: 240
  The Magistrate DC1: 174;
    EDC: 407
  Mayfair EDC: 407
  Mid-Channel DC1: 174; EDC:
    407; MD: 240
  The Notorious Mrs. Ebbsmith
    Br: 532; DC1: 174;
    EDC: 407; MD: 240
  Playgoers EDC: 407; EDT:
    246-247
  Preserving Mr. Panmure
    EDC: 407
  The Princess and the Butter-

fly, or, The Fantastics Br:
  532; DC1: 175; EDC: 407;
  EDT: 242; MD: 240
The Profligate DC1: 175;
  EDC: 407
The Rector; The Story of Four
  Friends EDC: 408
The School Mistress DC1:
  175; EDC: 408; MD: 240
A Seat in the Park EDC:
  408; EDT: 246-247
The Second Mrs. Tanqueray
  Br: 533; DC1: 175; EDC:
  408; EDT: 241-244; MD:
  240; Po: 3183
The Squire EDT: 241, 244
Sweet Lavender EDC: 408
The Thunderbolt EDC: 408
The Times EDC: 408; EDT:
  241
Trelawny of the "Wells" DC1:
  175; EDC: 408-409; EDT:
  243; MD: 240-241
The Weaker Sex EDC: 409
PING HSIN [Hsieh WAN-YING]
  "Since Her Departure" WaS1:
    176
  "The West Wind" WaS1: 176
PINGET, Robert
  General Po: 3183-3185
  Baga Fi: 126
  Between Fantoine and Agapa
    Fi: 126
  Clope to the Dossier Fi: 126
  Dead Letter [Lettre morte]
    Br: 533
  Le Fiston Fi: 126
  The Fox and the Compass Fi:
    126
  Graal Flibuste Fi: 126; Ke:
    124
  The Inquisitory [L'Inquisitoire]
    Br: 533; Fi: 126; Ke:
    124; Po: 3185
  Lettre morte see Dead Letter
  Mahu ou le materiau Fi: 126-
    127
  The Old Tune [La Manivelle]
    Br: 533
  Passacaille Fi: 127
  Quelqu'un Fi: 127; Po: 3185
PINNER, David
  General MDAE: 410
PINO, Bernardino [Pino da CAGLI]
  Gli Ingiusti sdegni DC2: 270
PINSKI, David

"Beruria" Wa: 604
"The Wall" Wa: 604
"Zerubabel" Wa: 604
PINTER, Harold
  General Br: 533-535; LCAB:
    138; MBD: 69-73; MD:
    241; MDAE: 414-419; Po:
    3186-3193; TMBP: 135-189
  The Basement [Originally The
    Compartment] Br: 535;
    EDC: 409; Ma: 1611;
    MBD: 73; TMBP: 147,
    169, 172, 188-189
  The Birthday Party Br:
    535-536; DC1: 175-176;
    EDC: 409-411; Ma: 1611-
    1612; MBD: 69-73; MD:
    241; MDAE: 414, 416-
    418, 512-513; Po: 3193;
    TMBP: 16, 135-136, 138-
    141, 143-144, 147-149,
    155-156, 158-159, 160,
    162-165, 167, 173-176,
    178, 180-182, 184-189,
    257
  The Caretaker Br: 536-
    537; DC1: 176; EDC:
    411-413; LCAB: 138; Ma:
    1613-1614; MBD: 69-72;
    MD: 241-242; MDAE: 414-
    418; Po: 3194-3195; TMAP:
    171; TMBP: 18, 135-139,
    143, 145-149, 151-154,
    156-157, 160-161, 165-169,
    171-174, 176, 178-179,
    182, 184-190, 257
  The Collection Br: 537-538;
    DC1: 176; EDC: 413;
    Ma: 1614-1615; MBD:
    70; MD: 242; MDAE:
    418; Po: 3195; TMBP:
    136, 144, 147, 158, 164,
    188, 190, 262
  The Dumb Waiter Br: 538;
    DC1: 176; EDC: 414;
    Ma: 1615-1616; MBD:
    70; MD: 242; MDAE:
    103, 415; Po: 3195;
    TMBP: 138, 141-145, 149,
    156, 159, 161, 169, 178,
    184, 186, 188, 190
  The Dwarfs Br: 538; DC1:
    176-177; EDC: 414-415;
    Ma: 1616; MBD: 72-73;
    MDAE: 415, 419; Po:
    3195; TMBP: 136, 148,

161, 167, 171, 175, 177, 187,
    190, 257
  The Homecoming Br: 538-539;
    EDC: 415-417; Ma: 1616-
    1618; MBD: 70-73; MDAE:
    414-418; Po: 3196-3197;
    TMBP: 135-136, 138-139,
    141, 144-148, 150-153, 158-
    159, 162-163, 165-169, 171-
    172, 176, 178, 181-182, 184-
    188, 190-191
  Landscape Br: 539; EDC:
    417; Ma: 1618-1619; MBD:
    69-72; MDAE: 414, 416;
    TMBP: 136, 138, 148, 153,
    156-158, 162, 165, 176-177,
    186-187, 191
  The Lover Br: 539; EDC:
    417-418; Ma: 1619; MD:
    242; TMAP: 36; TMBP:
    144, 158, 161, 178, 188, 191
  Night EDC: 418; TMBP: 135,
    138, 156, 167, 186
  A Night Out Br: 539; DC1:
    177; EDC: 418; MD: 242;
    TMBP: 158, 176, 187, 191,
    257
  Night School Br: 539; EDC:
    418; MD: 242
  No Man's Land EDC: 418;
    MBD: 71; TMBP: 79
  Old Times EDC: 418; Ma:
    1620; MBD: 71-73; TMAP:
    223; TMBP: 79, 135, 137-
    138, 151, 153-154, 165, 169,
    174, 179, 185, 188
  The Room Br: 539-540; DC1:
    177; EDC: 418-419; Ma:
    1620-1621; MBD: 72-73;
    MD: 242; TMBP: 136, 138,
    144, 149, 156-157, 161, 168,
    178, 186-188, 191, 257
  Silence EDC: 419; Ma: 1621-
    1622; MBD: 71; TMBP:
    138, 153, 156, 158-159, 165,
    177, 186, 188
  A Slight Ache Br: 540; DC1:
    177; EDC: 420; Ma: 1622-
    1623; MBD: 69, 72-73; MD:
    242; MDAE: 414-415, 418;
    Po: 3198; TMBP: 136, 139,
    142, 144, 149, 158, 166-167,
    170-171, 176, 178, 184, 187-
    188, 191-192, 257
  Tea Party Br: 540; EDC:
    420-421; Ma: 1623; MBD:

70; Po: 3198; TMBP:
141, 147, 158, 187, 192;
Wa: 604
PIOZZI, Hester Lynch Thrale
General EC: 105
PIPPIN, Don and Steve BROWN
The Contrast ADC: 309
PIRANDELLO, Luigi
General Br: 540-543; LCAB:
138; MD: 242-244; Po:
3199-3212
All for the Best [Tutto per
bene] Br: 543-544;
EDC: 421; MD: 248
L'altro figlio see The Other
Son
L'amica delle mogli see The
Wives' Friend
"An Annuity for Life" WaS1:
176
As Before, Better Than Be-
fore [As at First but
Better Than at First;
Come prima, meglio di
prima] Br: 544; EDC:
421; MD: 245
As You Desire Me [Come tu
mi vuoi] DC2: 270; EDC:
421; MD: 245
At the Gate [At the Exit;
All'uscita] EDC: 421;
MD: 245
Il berretto a sonagli see
Cap and Bells
"A Breath" WaS1: 176
But It's Not a Serious Affair
[It Is Only in Jest; but
It's Not in Earnest; Ma
non è una cosa seria]
Br: 546; EDC: 422; MD:
246
"By Himself" WaS1: 176
"La camera in attesa" Wa:
604
"Candelora" WaS1: 176
Cap and Bells [Il berretto
a sonagli] Br: 544;
DC2: 270; EDC: 422;
MD: 245
"Captivity" WaS1: 176
Chee Chee [Cecè] Br: 544;
MD: 245
"The Choice" WaS1: 176
Ciascuno a suo modo see
Each in His Own Way
"Ciaula scopre la luna"

WaS1: 176
Clothing the Naked [To Clothe
the Naked; Naked; Vestire
gli ignudi] Br: 544; EDC:
425; LCAB: 138; MD: 248
Come prima, meglio di prima
see As Before, Better Than
Before
Come tu mi vuoi see As You
Desire Me
Così è (se vi pare) see Right
You Are (If You Care to
Think So)
"A Day" WaS1: 176
"The Destruction of Man" WaS1:
176
Diana and Tuda [Diana e la
Tuda] Br: 544; DC2:
270; EDC: 422; MD: 245;
Po: 3213
The Diary of Serafino Gubbio,
Cinema Operator Ke: 248
The Doctor's Duty [The Duty
of a Physician; Il dovere del
medico] EDC: 422; MD:
245
"Double Tombs for Two" WaS1:
176
A Dream (But Perhaps It
Isn't) [Sogno (ma forse no)]
EDC: 422
Each in His Own Way [Ciascuno
a suo modo] Br: 544-545;
DC2: 270; EDC: 422; MD:
245; Po: 3212
Each in His Role see The
Rules of the Game
Either or One or of No One
[O di uno o di nessuno]
MD: 246
Enrico IV see Henry IV
The Festival of Our Lord of the
Ship [Sanctuary of Our Lord
of the Ship; In a Sanctuary;
Sagra del Signore della
nave] EDC: 422; MD: 247
"Flight" WaS1: 176
"The Fly" WaS1: 176
Il fu Mattia Pascal see The
Late Mattia Pascal
The Game as He Played It
see The Rules of the Game
"The Gentle Touch of Death"
WaS1: 176
The Giants of the Mountain
[I giganti della montagna]

see The Mountain Giants
La giara see The Jar
Il giuoco delle parti see
The Rules of the Game
Grafting [L'innesto] Br:
545; EDC: 422; MD: 246
"Happiness" WaS1: 176
Henry IV [Enrico IV] Br:
545-546; DC2: 270-271;
EDC: 422-423; LCAB:
138; Ma: 1624; MD: 245-
246; Po: 3213
"The Haunted House" ["Gran-
ella's House"] Wa: 605
If Not So, or Other People's
Reasons [Se non così, o
La ragione degli altri]
Br: 547; EDC: 423
"The Illustrious Corpse"
WaS1: 177
The Imbecile [L'imbecille]
EDC: 423; MD: 246
In a Sanctuary see The
Festival of Our Lord of
the Ship
"In Silence" WaS1: 177
L'innesto see Grafting
It Is Only in Jest see But
It's Not a Serious Affair
It Is So (If You Think So)
see Right You Are (If
You Care to Think So)
The Jar [La giara] MD:
246; Po: 3214; SFC: 167;
Wa: 605
"The Journey" WaS1: 177
"Juggler's Balls" WaS1:
177
The Late Mattia Pascal [Il fu
Mattia Pascal] Fi: 274;
Ke: 249; Po: 3213
Lazarus [Lazzaro] EDC:
424; MD: 246
The Life I Gave You [La vita
che ti diedi] Br: 546;
EDC: 424; MD: 248
Limes of Sicily see Sicilian
Limes
Liolà Br: 546; EDC: 424;
MD: 246
"The Little Fan" Wa: 605;
WaS1: 177
"The Little Garden" WaS1:
177
"The Long Dress" WaS1:
177

"Il lume dell' alta casa" Wa:
605
Lumíe di Sicilia see Sicilian
Limes
Ma non è una cosa seria see
But It's Not a Serious Affair
Man, Beast, and Virtue
[L'uomo, la bestia e la virtù]
Br: 546; EDC: 424; MD:
248
The Man with the Flower in His
Mouth [L'uomo dal fiore in
bocca] EDC: 424; MD:
248; Po: 3217
"A Mere Formality" WaS1: 177
La morsa see The Vise
"Mortal Remains" WaS1: 177
The Mountain Giants [The Giants
of the Mountain; I giganti
della montagna] Br: 546;
DC2: 271; EDC: 424; Po:
3214
Mrs. Morli, One and Two [La
signora Morli, una e due]
Br: 548; EDC: 424; MD:
248
Naked see Clothing the Naked
Naked Masks Br: 547
The New Colony [La nuova
colonia] Br: 547; EDC:
425; MD: 246
No One Knows How [One Does
Not Know How; Non si sa
come] EDC: 425; MD: 246
"Nothing" WaS1: 177
O di uno o di nessuno see
Either of One or of No One
"Old Music" WaS1: 177
One, None and a Hundred
Thousand Fi: 274; Ke:
249
The Other Son [L'altro figlio]
EDC: 425; MD: 245
The Outcast Fi: 274
The Patent [La patente] MD:
246
Pensaci Giacomino see Think
It Over, Giacomino
The Pleasure of Honesty [The
Pleasure of Respectability;
Il piacere dell' onestà] Br:
547; EDC: 425; MD: 246-
247
"Prima notte" Wa: 605
Quando si è qualcuno see
When Someone Is Somebody

Questa sera si recita a sog-
getto see Tonight We
Improvise

"Remedy: Geography" WaS1:
177

Right You Are (If You Care
to Think So) [It Is So
(If You Think So); Così
è (se vi pare)] Br: 547-
548; DC2: 272; EDC:
425-426; LCAB: 138; Ma:
1625; MD: 245; Po: 3212

The Rights of Others [La
ragione degli altri] MD:
247

"The Rose" WaS1: 177

The Rules of the Game [Each
in His Role; The Game as
He Played It; Il giuoco
delle parti] Br: 545;
EDC: 426; MD: 246

Sagra del Signore della
nave see The Festival
of Our Lord of the Ship

Sanctuary of Our Lord of
the Ship see The Festi-
val of Our Lord of the
Ship

"Schoolmistress Boccarmè"
WaS1: 177

"Scialle nero" WaS1: 177

Se non così, o La ragione
degli altri see If Not
So; or, Other People's
Reasons

"The Shrine" WaS1: 177

Si gira Fi: 274-275

Sicilian Limes [Limes of
Sicily; Lumíe di Sicilia]
EDC: 426; MD: 246

La signora Morli, una e due
see Mrs. Morli, One and
Two

Six Characters in Search of
an Author [Sei personaggi
in cerca d'autore] Br:
548-550; DC2: 272-274;
EDC: 426-428; LCAB:
138; Ma: 1625-1627; MD:
247; Po: 2315-2317

Sogno (ma forse no) see
A Dream (But Perhaps
It Isn't)

"Stefano Giogli, uno e due"
WaS1: 177

"The Straw Bird" WaS1: 177

Suo marito Fi: 275; Ke: 249

"There's Someone Who Is Laughing" WaS1: 178

Think It Over, Giacomino [Think,
Giacomino; Think of It, Giacomino; Pensaci Giacomino]
Br: 550; EDC: 428; MD:
246

To Clothe the Naked see
Clothing the Naked

To Find Oneself [Trovarsi]
Br: 550; EDC: 428; MD:
248

Tonight We Improvise [Questa
sera si recita a soggetto]
Br: 550; DC2: 274; EDC:
428-429; MD: 247

"The Tragedy of a Character"
WaS1: 178

"The Trap" WaS1: 178

The Turn Fi: 275

Tutto per bene see All for
the Best

"The Umbrella" WaS1: 178

L'uomo dal fiore in bocca see
The Man with the Flower
in His Mouth

L'uomo, la bestia e la virtù
see Man, Beast, and Virtue

I vecchi e i giovani Fi: 274

Vestire gli ignudi see Clothing
the Naked

The Vise [La morsa] EDC:
429; MD: 246

"Visit" WaS1: 178

"Visiting the Sick" WaS1: 178

La vita che ti diedi see The
Life I Gave You

"War" SFC: 167; Wa: 605

"The Wave" WaS1: 178

"The Wet Nurse" WaS1: 178

"The Wheelbarrow" WaS1: 178

"When I Was Mad" WaS1: 178

When Someone Is Somebody
[Quando si è qualcuno] Br:
550; MD: 247

The Wives' Friend [L'amica delle
mogli] MD: 245

"World News" WaS1: 178

"The Wreath" WaS1: 178

PISCATOR, Irwin
General Br: 551

PITCAIRNE, Archibald
General Ai: 59

PITCHER, Oliver
General BAW: 595

PITHAN, Pudumai
  "Redemption" Wa: 605
PITTMAN, Arthur
  Possibilities ADC: 310
PIX, Mary Griffith
  The French Beau Li: 269
  The Spanish Wives Li: 269
PLA, Josefina
  General Br: 551
PLAATJE, Solomon Tshekiso
  General BALE: 380
  Mhudi BALE: 380
PLANCHART, Julio
  La Republica de Cain Br:
    551
PLANCHE, James Robinson
  General EDT: 249-250
  Angelo DC2: 274
  Charles XII, or The Siege of
    Stralsund DC2: 274
PLANCHON, Roger
  Edward II DC2: 274
  La Remise DC2: 275
PLATER, Alan
  General MDAE: 421
  Close the Coalhouse Door
    MDAE: 421
PLATH, Sylvia
  General ICBAP: 98; LCAB:
    138-139; Ma: 1633-1635;
    MP: 75-76; Po: 3217-3222
  "The Applicant" PE: 335
  "Ariel" Ma: 1628-1629; MP:
    75; PE: 335-336; Po:
    3220
  "Arrival of the Bee Box"
    PE: 336
  "The Bee Meeting" PE: 336
  "The Beekeeper's Daughter"
    PE: 336
  The Bell Jar Ma: 1629-1630
  "Black Rook in Rainy Weather"
    PE: 336
  "Brasilia" PE: 336
  The Colossus and Other
    Poems Ma: 1630-1632;
    Po: 3220
  "The Couriers" PE: 336
  "Cut" PE: 336
✓ "Daddy" ICBAP: 98; Ma:
    1632-1633; PE: 336
  "The Daughters of Blossom
    Street" Wa: 605
  "The Disquieting Muses" PE:
    336
  "Edge" PE: 337

"Event" PE: 337
"Fever 103°" PE: 337
"The Fifteen-Dollar Eagle" Wa:
  605
"The Fifty-Ninth Bear" Wa:
  605
"In Plaster" ICBAP: 98
"Johnny Panic and the Bible of
  Dreams" Wa: 605
"Lady Lazarus" PE: 337
"Leaving Early" PE: 337
"Lesbos" PE: 337
"Little Fugue" PE: 337
"Love Letter" PE: 337
"Magi" PE: 337
"The Manor Garden" PE: 337
"Morning Song" PE: 337
"Parliament Hill Fields" PE:
  337
"Poppies in July" PE: 337
"Private Ground" PE: 338
"Sheep in Fog" PE: 338
"Snakecharmer" PE: 338
"Strings" PE: 338
"The Surgeon at 2 A.M." PE:
  338
"The Swarm" PE: 338
"The Tour" PE: 338
"Tulips" PE: 338
Winter Trees Ma: 1635
"Wintering" PE: 338
"The Wishing Box" Wa: 605
"You're" PE: 338
"Zoo Keeper's Wife" PE: 338
PLATO
  General LCAB: 139
  The Apology LCAB: 139
  The Republic LCAB: 139;
    Ma: 1636-1637
  Symposium Ma: 1637
PLATO, Ann
  General AAPD: 73; BAW:
    596
PLAUTUS, Titus Maccius
  Amphitruo [Amphitryon] DC2:
    275; EDC: 429-430; Ma:
    1638-1639
  Asinaria EDC: 430
  Aulularia DC2: 275; EDC:
    430
  Bacchides EDC: 430
  Captivi DC2: 276; EDC: 430
  The Carthaginian [Poenulus]
    DC2: 278; EDC: 430
  Casina EDC: 430
  Curculio DC2: 276; EDC:

430

Epidicus DC2: 276; EDC: 430-431

Faeneratrix DC2: 276

Menaechmi [The Twin Menaechmi] DC2: 276-277; EDC: 431; LCAB: 139; Ma: 1639-1640

Mercator DC2: 277

Miles Gloriosus DC2: 277; EDC: 431

Mostellaria DC2: 277-278; EDC: 431

Persa DC2: 278; EDC: 431

Poenulus see The Carthaginian

The Pot of Gold LCAB: 139

Pseudolus DC2: 278; EDC: 431-432

Rudens DC2: 278; EDC: 432

Stichus DC2: 279; EDC: 432

Trinummus EDC: 432

Truculentus DC2: 279; EDC: 432

The Twin Menaechmi see Menaechmi

PLENZDORF, Ulrich
Die Neuen Leiden des Jungen W. Fi: 383-384

PLIEVIER, Theodor
Stalingrad Fi: 384

PLINIUS SECUNDUS, Gaius
Natural History Ma: 1641

PLIVIER, Theodor
General Po: 3222

PLOMER, William
General Po: 3222
"Bed Number Seventeen" Wa: 605
"Black Peril" Wa: 606
"A Brutal Sentimentalist" Wa: 606
"The Child of Queen Victoria" Wa: 606
"Down on the Farm" Wa: 606
"Ever Such a Nice Boy" Wa: 606
"Folk Tale" Wa: 606
"The Island" Wa: 606
"Local Colour" Wa: 606
"Mother Kamchatka: Or Mr. Mainchance in Search of the Truth" Wa: 606

"A Museum Piece" Wa: 606
Museum Pieces Po: 3222
"Nakamura" Wa: 606
"Nausica" Wa: 606
"The Night Before the War" Wa: 606
"No Ghost" Wa: 606
"The Owl and the Pussy Cat" Wa: 606
"A Piece of Good Luck" Wa: 606
"The Portrait of an Emperor" Wa: 606
"Portraits in the Nude" Wa: 606
"The Sleeping Husband" Wa: 607
"Stephen Jordan's Wife" Wa: 607
"Thy Neighbor's Creed" SFC: 168; Wa: 607
"Ula Masondo" Wa: 607
"A Wedding Guest" Wa: 607
"When the Sardines Came" Wa: 607

PLOTINUS
General LCAB: 139

Plunkett, Edward J.M.D. see DUNSANY, Lord Edward John Moreton

PLUNKETT, James
Strumpet City ENES1: 181; ENES2: 197-198
The Trusting and the Maimed Po: 3222

PLUNKETT, Joseph
General Po: 3223

PLUTARCH
Parallel Lives [Lives] LCAB: 139; Ma: 1642

PLUTZIK, Hyam
Horatio Po: 3223

PODHORETZ, Norman
General Po: 3223-3224
Making It Po: 3224

POE, Edgar Allan
General AF: 221-226; ALL: 213-221; ASF: 470-480; Cla: 77-82; Ho: 121-122; LCAB: 139-140
"Al Aaraaf" ICBAP: 98; PE: 338-339
"The Angel of the Odd" ASF: 453; SFC: 168; Wa: 607; WaS1: 178
"Annabel Lee" PE: 339

"The Assignation" ASF: 453; SFC: 168; Wa: 607

"The Balloon Hoax" SFC: 168; Wa: 607

"The Bells" ICBAP: 98; PE: 339

"Berenice" ASF: 453; SFC: 168; Wa: 608; WaS1: 178

"The Black Cat" ASF: 454; SFC: 168; Wa: 608; WaS1: 178-179

"Bon-Bon" ASF: 454; Wa: 608

"The Cask of Amontillado" ASF: 454-455; Ma: 1643-1644; SFC: 168-169; Wa: 609-610; WaS1: 179

"The City in the Sea" ICBAP: 98; PE: 339

"The Colloquy of Monos and Una" ASF: 455; SFC: 169; Wa: 610; WaS1: 179

"The Conqueror Worm" ICBAP: 98; PE: 339

"The Conversation of Eiros and Charmion" ASF: 455; SFC: 169; Wa: 610

"A Descent into the Maelstrom" ASF: 456; SFC: 169; Wa: 610-611; WaS1: 179

"The Devil in the Belfry" ASF: 456; SFC: 169; Wa: 611; WaS1: 179

"Diddling Considered as One of the Exact Sciences" ASF: 456; Wa: 611

"The Domain of Arnheim" ASF: 456; Wa: 611; WaS1: 179

"Dream-Land" PE: 339

"Duc de L'Omelette" ASF: 456-457; Wa: 611; WaS1: 179

"Eldorado" ICBAP: 98; PE: 339

"Eleonora" ASF: 457; SFC: 169; Wa: 611-612; WaS1: 179

"An Enigma" ICBAP: 98; PE: 339

Eureka ALL: 214

"Evening Star" ICBAP: 99; PE: 340

"The Facts in the Case of M. Valdemar" ASF: 457; SFC: 169; Wa: 612

"The Fall of the House of Usher" AF: 225-226; ASF: 457-459; Cla: 77-78, 81-82; LCAB: 140; Ma: 1644-1645; SFC: 170-171; Wa: 612-615; WaS1: 179-180

"For Annie" PE: 340

"Four Beasts in One" ASF: 459; SFC: 171; Wa: 615; WaS1: 180

"The Gold Bug" ASF: 459; Ma: 1645-1646; SFC: 171; Wa: 615-616; WaS1: 180

"Hans Pfaal" ["The Unparalleled Adventure of One Hans Pfaal"] ASF: 460; SFC: 171; Wa: 627

"The Haunted Palace" PE: 340

"Hop-Frog" ASF: 460; SFC: 171; Wa: 616; WaS1: 180

"How to Write a Blackwood Article" ASF: 460; SFC: 171; Wa: 616

"Hymn" ICBAP: 99

"The Imp of the Perverse" ASF: 460; Wa: 616; WaS1: 180

"Introduction" ICBAP: 99; PE: 340

"The Island of the Fay" ASF: 460; SFC: 171; Wa: 616; WaS1: 180

"Israfel" ICBAP: 99; PE: 340

"The Journal of Julius Rodman" ASF: 461

"King Pest" ASF: 461; SFC: 171-172; Wa: 616

"The Lake: To_____" PE: 340

"Landor's Cottage" ASF: 461; Wa: 616

"Lenore" ICBAP: 99; PE: 340

"Ligeia" AF: 221; ASF: 461-462; Cla: 77, 79, 81; Ma: 1646-1647; SFC: 172; Wa: 616-618; WaS1: 180

"The Lighthouse" ASF: 462; Wa: 618

"Lionizing" ASF: 462-463; SFC: 172; Wa: 618

"The Literary Life of Thingum Bob, Esq." ASF: 463; Wa:

618

"Loss of Breath" ASF: 463;
SFC: 172; Wa: 618;
WaS1: 180

"The Man of the Crowd"
ASF: 463; SFC: 173;
Wa: 619

"The Man That Was Used Up"
ASF: 463; SFC: 173;
Wa: 619; WaS1: 180

"MS. Found in a Bottle"
ASF: 463; Ma: 1647-1648;
SFC: 174; Wa: 619;
WaS1: 180

"The Masque of the Red
Death" ASF: 463-464;
Cla: 81; Ma: 1648-1649;
SFC: 173; Wa: 619-620;
WaS1: 180

"Mellonta Tauta" ASF: 464;
Wa: 620

"Mesmeric Revelation" ASF:
464; SFC: 173; Wa: 620

"Metzengerstein" ASF: 464;
SFC: 173; Wa: 620-621

"Morella" ASF: 464-465;
SFC: 173-174; Wa: 621;
WaS1: 180

"The Murders in the Rue
Morgue" ASF: 465; Ma:
1649; SFC: 174; Wa:
621; WaS1: 181

"The Mystery of Marie Roget"
ASF: 466; Ma: 1649-
1650; SFC: 174; Wa:
621-622

"Mystification" ASF: 466

The Narrative of Arthur
Gordon Pym AF: 221-222,
224; AN: 212; Ho: 121-
122, 155; LCAB: 140;
Ma: 1650-1651; Wa: 622-
623; WaS1: 181

"Never Bet the Devil Your
Head" ASF: 466; SFC:
174; Wa: 623

"The Oblong Box" ASF:
466; SFC: 174; Wa:
623

"The Oval Portrait" ASF:
466; SFC: 174; Wa: 624;
WaS1: 181

"The Philosophy of Furni-
ture" ASF: 466

"The Pit and the Pendulum"
ASF: 466; Ma: 1651-

1652; SFC: 174-175; Wa:
624; WaS1: 181

"The Power of Words" ASF:
467; SFC: 175; Wa: 624

"A Predicament" ASF: 467;
Wa: 624; WaS1: 181

"The Premature Burial" ASF:
467; SFC: 175; Wa: 624

"Psyche Zenobia" see "How to
Write a Blackwood Article"

"The Purloined Letter" ASF:
467; Wa: 625; WaS1: 182

"The Raven" Cla: 80; ICBAP:
99; LCAB: 140; PE: 340

"The Scythe of Time" Wa:
625

"Shadow--A Parable" ASF:
467; Wa: 625

"The Signora Zenobia" see
"How to Write a Blackwood
Article"

"Silence--A Fable" ASF: 467;
SFC: 175; Wa: 625; WaS1:
182

"Siope--A Fable" see "Silence
--A Fable"

"The Sleeper" PE: 340

"Some Passages in the Life of
a Lion" see "Lionizing"

"Some Words with a Mummy"
ASF: 467; Wa: 625

"The Spectacles" ASF: 468;
SFC: 175; Wa: 625; WaS1:
182

"The Sphinx" Wa: 625; WaS1:
182

"Stanzas" PE: 340

"A Succession of Sundays" see
"Three Sundays in a Week"

"The System of Doctor Tarr
and Professor Fether" ASF:
468; SFC: 175; Wa: 625-
626; WaS1: 182

"A Tale of Jerusalem" SFC:
175; Wa: 626

"A Tale of the Ragged Mountains" ASF: 468; SFC:
176; Wa: 626

"The Tell-Tale Heart" ASF:
468-469; Cla: 81; Ma:
1652-1653; SFC: 176; Wa:
626-627; WaS1: 182

"Thou Art the Man" ASF:
469; Wa: 627

"The Thousand-and-Second Tale
of Scheherazade" ASF:

469; SFC: 176; Wa: 627

"Three Sundays in a Week"
ASF: 469; SFC: 176;
Wa: 627

"To Helen" ICBAP: 99; PE:
340-341

"To One in Paradise" PE:
341

"Ulalume" Cla: 78, 80;
ICBAP: 99; PE: 341

"The Unparalleled Adventures
of One Hans Pfaal" see
"Hans Pfaal"

"The Valley of Unrest" PE:
342

"The Visionary" see "The
Assignation"

"Von Kempeln and His Dis-
covery" ASF: 469; Wa:
627

"William Wilson" AF: 221;
ASF: 469-470; Cla: 81;
Ma: 1653-1654; SFC:
176; Wa: 627-628; WaS1:
182

POGODIN, Nikolai Federovich
After the Ball MD: 248
The Aristocrats Br: 551;
MD: 248
The Creation of the World
MD: 248

POGOREL'SKIJ [Aleksej Alek-
seevich PEROVSKIJ]
"The Baleful Consequences
of an Unbridled Imagina-
tion" Wa: 628
"The Black Chicken, or
The Subterranean Dwellers"
Wa: 628
The Double Ke: 432
"The Fifth Evening" Wa:
628
"The First Evening" Wa:
628
"The Fourth Evening" Wa:
628
"The Hypnotist" Wa: 629
"Izidor and Anjuta" Wa:
629
"The Journey by Stagecoach"
Wa: 629
"The Poppy-Seed-Cake
Woman of the Lafërtov"
Wa: 629; Ke: 432

POHL, Frederick
"The Tunnel Under the

World" ASF: 481

Poirier, Louis see GRACG, Julien

POLEVOJ, Nikolaj Fëdrovich
"The Felicity of Madness" Wa:
629
"The Painter" Wa: 629

POLGAR, Alfred
General Po: 3224

POLIDORI, John
"The Vampyre" Wa: 629

POLITE, Charlene Hatcher
General BAP: 235
The Flagellants BAF: 235-236
Sister and the Victims of Foul
Play BAF: 236

POLLOCK, Channing
Mr. Moneypenny Po: 3224

POLO, Gaspar Gil
Diana enamorada Fi: 217; Ke:
227

POLOTAN, Kerima
"Cost Price" Wa: 629
"The Virgin" Wa: 629

POMBO, Rafael
General Po: 3225

PONCELA, Serrano
General Po: 3225

PONGE, Francis
General Po: 3225-3227
"The Goat" ["La Chèvre"] Po:
3228
Le Grand recueil Po: 3228

PONTEN, Josef
General Po: 3228-3229
Die Bockreiter Ke: 328; Wa:
629
Die Insel Ke: 328
Die Meister Ke: 328
"Die Uhr von Gold" Wa: 629
Volk auf dem Wege Po: 3229

PONTOPPIDAN, Henrik
General Ma: 1655; Po: 3229
The Kingdom of the Dead Fi:
411; Ke: 362-363
Lucky Peter Fi: 411; Ke:
363
Man's Heaven Fi: 411; Ke:
363
The Promised Land Fi: 411;
Ke: 363
Sandinge Parish Fi: 411

POOLE, Ernest
"An Author's Predicament"
ASF: 481
The Harbor Po: 3229

POPE, Alexander

General EC: 106-109;
ICBAP: 99; LCAB: 141;
Ma: 1659-1660; Me: 318-
334
"Artimesia" EC: 117
"Autumn" PE: 342
"Brutus" ICBAP: 99
The Dunciad EC: 112-113;
ICBAP: 99; Ma: 1656-
1657; Me: 311-316; PE:
343-344
Dunciad--Book I ICBAP: 99
Dunciad--Book IV ICBAP:
100
"Elegy to the Memory of an
Unfortunate Lady" EC:
112; ICBAP: 100; Me:
298-300; PE: 343
Eloisa to Abelard EC: 112;
ICBAP: 100; Me: 298-
300; PE: 343-344
"Epilogue to the Satires"
EC: 114-115; ICBAP:
100; PE: 344
"Epistle to Augustus" ICBAP:
100
"Epistle to Dr. Arbuthnot"
EC: 114-115; ICBAP:
100; Me: 307-310; PE:
344-345
"Epistle to Harley" EC: 117;
Me: 317
"Epistle to Miss Blount"
PE: 345
Epistles to Several Persons
EC: 115-116; Me: 303-
306
An Essay on Criticism EC:
109-110; ICBAP: 100;
Ma: 1657-1658; Me: 291-
293; PE: 345
An Essay on Man EC: 113-
114; ICBAP: 100; Ma:
1658-1659; Me: 300-303;
PE: 345-346
Essay on Man--Epistle II
ICBAP: 100
The Iliad [translation of
HOMER] EC: 116-117
Imitations of Horace EC:
114-115; Me: 306-311
"Moral Essays--Epistle I"
["To Sir Richard Temple,
Lord Cobham"] Me: 305;
PE: 350
"Moral Essays--Epistle II"

["To a Lady"; "Of the Char-
acters of Women"] ICBAP:
101; Me: 304-306; PE: 349
"Moral Essays--Epistle III"
["To Allen, Lord Bathurst";
"Of Avarice and Allied
Vices"] ICBAP: 101; Me:
304; PE: 349
"Moral Essays--Epistle IV" ["To
Richard Boyle, Earl of Bur-
lington"; "Of the Use of
Riches"] ICBAP: 101; Me:
305-306, 309; PE: 350
"Moral Essays--Epistle V" ["To
Mr. Addison"] EC: 117;
Me: 316-317; PE: 349
"Ode for Musick on St. Cecilia's
Day" EC: 117; Me: 317;
PE: 346
"Ode on Solitude" Me: 317;
PE: 346
Pastorals EC: 110; Me: 289-
291; PE: 346
"Phryne" EC: 117
The Rape of the Lock EC:
110-111; ICBAP: 101; LCAB:
141; Ma: 1660-1661; Me:
293-298; PE: 347-348
"Satire II" PE: 348
"Solitude" PE: 348
"Spring" PE: 348
"Summer" PE: 349
"Timon's Villa" [From "To the
Right Honourable Richard
Earl of Burlington"] PE:
349
"To Allen, Lord Bathurst" see
"Moral Essays--Epistle III"
"To a Lady" see "Moral Es-
says--Epistle II"
"To Augustus" ["The First
Epistle of the Second Book
of Horace Imitated"] Me:
309-310; PE: 349
"To Lord Bolingbroke" ["The
First Epistle of the First
Book of Horace Imitated"]
Me: 309-310; PE: 349
"To Mr. Addison" see "Moral
Essays--Epistle V"
"To Mr. Bethel" ["The Second
Satire of the Second Book of
Horace"] PE: 349
"To Mr. Fortescue" ["The First
Satire of the Second Book
of Horace Imitated"] PE:

350

"To Richard Boyle, Earl of
Burlington" see "Moral
Essays--Epistle IV"

"To Sir Richard Temple,
Lord Cobham" see "Moral
Essays--Epistle I"

"To Venus" ["The First Ode
of the Fourth Book of
Horace Imitated"] PE:
350

Windsor Forest EC: 110;
ICBAP: 101; Me: 289-
291; PE: 350

"Winter" PE: 350

POPOVIC, Aleksandar
General Po: 3230
Deadly Motorism [Smrtonosna
Motoristika] EDC: 432
The Goldwinged Duck [Utva
Ptica Zlatorkrila] EDC:
432
Hats Off! [Kape Dole] EDC:
432
Second Door Left [Druga
Vrata Levo] EDC: 433

Poquelin, Jean Baptiste see
MOLIERE

PORCHE, François
General Br: 551; MD: 248
Les Butors et la Finette
MD: 248

PORTER, Bernard H.
General Po: 3230-3231

PORTER, Eleanor
Pollyana Po: 3231-3232

PORTER, Hal
General MAP: 257-259; Po:
3232
A Bachelor's Children MAP:
257
"Francis Silver" Wa: 629
A Handful of Pennies MAP:
257
Mr. Butterfly MAP: 257
"Otto Ruff" Wa: 630
The Right Thing MAP: 257
"Say to Me Ronald" Wa:
630
The Tilted Cross MAP: 257-
259
The Watcher on the Cast-Iron
Balcony Po: 3233

PORTER, Henry
The Two Angry Women of
Abington DC1: 177

PORTER, Jane
The Scottish Chiefs ENES2:
198
Thaddeus of Warsaw ENES2:
198

PORTER, Katherine Anne
General ALL: 221-223; ASF:
485-488; CN: 424-425;
LCAB: 141; Ne: 80-81;
Po: 3233-3239; Wo: 159-160
"The Circus" ASF: 482; SFC:
176-177; Wa: 630; WaS1:
182
"The Cracked Looking-Glass"
ASF: 482; Po: 3239; SFC:
177; Wa: 630
"A Day's Work" ASF: 482;
SFC: 177; Wa: 630
"The Days Before" Wa: 630
"The Downward Path to Wisdom"
ASF: 482; Po: 3239; SFC:
177; Wa: 631
"The Fig Tree" ASF: 482;
Wa: 631; WaS1: 182
"Flowering Judas" ASF: 482;
Ma: 1662-1663; Po: 3240-
3241; SFC: 177; Wa: 631-
632; WaS1: 183
"The Grave" ASF: 482-483;
Po: 3241-3242; SFC: 178;
Wa: 632-633; WaS1: 183
"Hacienda" ASF: 483; Po:
3243; SFC: 178; Wa: 633;
WaS1: 183
"He" ASF: 483; SFC: 178;
Wa: 633; WaS1: 183
"Holiday" ASF: 483; Wa:
633-634; WaS1: 183
"The Jilting of Granny Weather-
all" ASF: 483; Po: 3243-
3244; SFC: 178; Wa: 634;
WaS1: 183
"The Journey" see "The Old
Order"
"The Last Leaf" ASF: 483;
Wa: 634
"The Leaning Tower" ASF:
483-484; SFC: 178; Wa:
634-635
"Magic" ASF: 484; Wa: 635;
WaS1: 183
"María Concepción" ASF:
484; Po: 3244; SFC: 178-
179; Wa: 635
"The Martyr" ASF: 484; Wa:
635

"Noon Wine" ASF: 484;
LCAB: 141; Ne: 81; Po:
3244-3245; SFC: 179; Wa:
635-636; WaS1: 183; Wo:
160
"Old Mortality" ASF: 484;
Ma: 1663-1664; SFC:
179-180; Wa: 636-637;
WaS1: 183
"The Old Order" ["The
Journey"] ASF: 483;
SFC: 180; Wa: 637;
WaS1: 183
The Old Order [Collection]
Po: 3245
"Pale Horse, Pale Rider"
ASF: 484-485; Ma: 1664;
Po: 3246; SFC: 180;
Wa: 637-638; WaS1: 184
"Rope" ASF: 485; SFC:
180; Wa: 638; WaS1: 184
Ship of Fools CN: 425-427;
Ma: 1665-1666; Ne: 80-
81; Po: 3246-3249; Wo:
159-160
"The Source" ASF: 485;
Wa: 638; WaS1: 184
"That Tree" ASF: 485; SFC:
180; Wa: 638
"Theft" ASF: 485; Po:
3250; SFC: 180; Wa:
638; WaS1: 184
"Virgin Violeta" ASF: 485;
Wa: 638
"The Witness" ASF: 485;
Wa: 639
PORTER, Peter
"A Christmas Recalled" PE:
351
Porter, William Sydney see
O. HENRY
PORTILLO DE TRAMBLEY,
Esther
"The Apple Trees" ASF:
489
PORTMAN, Julie A.
Riot ADC: 310
PORTO-RICHE, Georges de
General MD: 248-249
A Loving Wife [L'Amoureuse]
MD: 249
POST, Melville Davisson
General ASF: 489
"An Act of God" Wa: 639
"The Adopted Daughter"
Wa: 639

"The Age of Miracles" Wa: 639
"The Angel of the Lord" ["The
Broken Stirrup"] Wa: 639
"The Bradmoor Murder" Wa:
639
"The Corpus Delicti" ASF:
489; Wa: 639
"The Edge of the Shadow" Wa:
639
"The Riddle" Wa: 639
"The Spread Rails" Wa: 639
Postl, Karl Anton see SEALS-
FIELD, Charles
POSTON, Ted
General BAF: 236
"The Revolt of the Evil Fairies"
ASF: 489
POTOCKI, Jan
"Princess Brambilla" Wa: 639
POTOK, Chaim
The Chosen JW: 275
POTTER, Dennis
General MDAE: 422
POULET, Georges
General Po: 3252
POUND, Ezra
General ALL: 224-230; ICBAP:
101; LCAB: 142; Ma: 1670;
MDAE: 423-424; MP: 77-
79; Po: 3252-3285
"The Alchemist" PE: 351
"Ballad of the Goodly Fere"
PE: 351
"Ballatetta" PE: 351
Cantos ALL: 225-226, 228-
230; ICBAP: 101; LCAB:
142; Ma: 1667-1668; MP:
77-79; Po: 3285-3296
"Canto 2" PE: 351; Po: 3287
"Canto 4" Po: 3287
"Canto 15" Po: 3290
"Canto 20" PE: 351
"Canto 75" PE: 351; Po: 3292
"Canto 86" PE: 351
"Canto 88" PE: 351; Po: 3291
"Canto 89" Po: 3291
"Canto 91" ICBAP: 101; PE:
351; Po: 3285
"Canto 93" PE: 351
"Canto 97" PE: 351
"Canto 101" PE: 351
"Canto 110" PE: 351
"Canto 112" PE: 352
Cathay Po: 3296
"The Chinese Cantos" [Numbers
52-61] Po: 3290

"Effects of Music upon a
Company of People" PE:
352
"Fan Piece, for Her Imperial
Lord" ICBAP: 101; PE:
352
"The Garden" PE: 352
"Homage to Sextus Propertius"
ICBAP: 101; MP: 79;
PE: 352; Po: 3297
Hugh Selwyn Mauberley ALL:
226; ICBAP: 101; LCAB:
142; Ma: 1668-1669; MP:
78; PE: 352-353; Po:
3298-3300
"In a Station of the Metro"
ICBAP: 101-102; PE:
353; Po: 3300
"Liu Ch'e" PE: 353
Mauberley see Hugh Selwyn
Mauberley
"Near Perigord" PE: 353;
Po: 3301
"A Pact" ICBAP: 102; PE:
353; Po: 3301
"Papyrus" PE: 353; Po:
3301-3302
Pavannes and Divisions
LCAB: 142
Personae MP: 79
The Pisan Cantos Ma: 1669-
1670; Po: 3288, 3290,
3294-3295
"Portrait d'une Femme" PE:
354; Po: 3302
"The Return" PE: 354; Po:
3302
Rock-Drill Po: 3286, 3295
"The Seafarer" Po: 3302
"Separation on the River
Kiang" Po: 3303
Thrones Po: 3285-3286
Usura LCAB: 142
The Women of Trachis Br:
551; DC1: 177; MDAE:
423; Po: 3303-3304
POURRAT, Henri
Gaspard des montagnes
Fi: 127
Trésor des contes Po: 3304
POWELL, Adam Clayton, Sr.
General BAF: 237; BAW:
600
POWELL, Anthony
General BN2: 95-96; CFAE:
292-293; CN: 427-428;

Po: 3304-3306; Sch: 253-
255
The Acceptance World see also
A Dance to the Music of Time
CN: 428; ENE: 223; ENES1:
181; Ma: 1671
Afternoon Men CN: 428; ENE:
223; ENES1: 181; ENES2:
198; Ma: 1671; Po: 3305-
3306
Agents and Patients CN: 428;
ENE: 223; ENES1: 181;
ENES2: 198; Ma: 1671-1672;
Po: 3306
At Lady Molly's see also A
Dance to the Music of Time
CN: 428; ENE: 223; ENES1:
182; Ma: 1672
Books Do Furnish a Room
ENES1: 182; Ma: 1672-
1673
A Buyer's Market see also A
Dance to the Music of Time
CN: 428; ENE: 223-224;
ENES1: 182; Ma: 1673
Casanova's Chinese Restaurant
see also A Dance to the
Music of Time CN: 428-429;
ENE: 224; ENES1: 182; Ma:
1673
A Dance to the Music of Time
BN2: 95-96; CFAE: 293;
CN: 429-430; ENE: 224-225;
ENES1: 182; ENES2: 198;
LCAB: 142; Ma: 1674-1675;
Po: 3306-3308
From a View to a Death CN:
430; ENE: 224; ENES1:
182; ENES2: 198; Ma:
1675; Po: 3305-3306
The Kindly Ones see also A
Dance to the Music of Time
CN: 430; ENE: 224; ENES1:
182; Ma: 1675-1676
The Military Philosophers see
also A Dance to the Music
of Time CN: 430-431; ENE:
224; ENES1: 182; Ma: 1676
The Music of Time see A
Dance to the Music of Time
A Question of Upbringing see
also A Dance to the Music
of Time CN: 431; ENE:
225; ENES1: 182; Ma: 1676-
1677
The Soldier's Art see also A

Dance to the Music of Time
CN: 431; ENE: 225;
ENES1: 182; Ma: 1677
Temporary Kings ENES1:
182; Ma: 1677-1678
The Valley of Bones see also
A Dance to the Music of
Time CN: 431; ENE:
225; ENES1: 183; Ma:
1678
Venusberg CN: 431; ENE:
225; ENES1: 183; ENES2:
198; Ma: 1678; Po: 3305-
3306
What's Become of Waring CN:
431-432; ENE: 226;
ENES1: 183; ENES2: 198;
Ma: 1679; Po: 3305
POWELL, Dawn
General LCAB: 142
POWER, Richard
The Hungry Grass ENES2:
199
The Land of Youth ENES2:
199
POWERS, James Farl
General ASF: 491-492;
CFAE: 295-297; CN:
432; LCAB: 143; Po:
3309-3311
"The Blessing" ASF: 490;
Wa: 639
"Blue Island" ASF: 490;
Wa: 639
"A Couple of Nights Before
Christmas" SFC: 180;
Wa: 640
"Dawn" ASF: 490; Wa:
640
"Death of a Favorite" ASF:
490; SFC: 180; Wa: 640
"Defection of a Favorite"
ASF: 490; Wa: 640
"The Devil Was a Joker"
ASF: 490; Wa: 640
"The Forks" ASF: 490; Po:
3311; SFC: 180; Wa:
640
"God Writes a Bad Hand"
Wa: 640
"He Don't Plant Cotton" ASF:
490; Wa: 640-641
"Interlude in a Bookshop"
Wa: 640
"Jamesie" ASF: 490; SFC:
181; Wa: 641

"The Keystone" ASF: 490; Po:
3311; Wa: 641
"Lions, Harts, and Leaping
Does" ASF: 490; SFC:
181; Wa: 641
"Look How the Fish Live" ASF:
490; SFC: 181; Wa: 641
"The Lord's Day" ASF: 490;
Wa: 641
"A Losing Game" ASF: 491;
Wa: 641
Morte D'Urban CFAE: 296-
297; CN: 432-433; LCAB:
143; Po: 3312-3313
"The Old Bird, a Love Story"
ASF: 491; Wa: 641
"The Poor Thing" ASF: 491;
Wa: 641
"Presence of Grace" ASF:
491; Wa: 641
"Priestley Fellowship" Wa:
642
"Prince of Darkness" ASF:
491; SFC: 181; Wa: 642;
WaS1: 184
"Renner" ASF: 491; Wa:
642
"The Trouble" ASF: 491; Wa:
642
"The Valiant Woman" ASF:
491; Po: 3313; SFC: 181;
Wa: 642; WaS1: 184
"Zeal" ASF: 491; SFC: 181;
Wa: 642
POWYS, John Cowper
General BN2: 97-98; Po:
3314-3317; Ri2: 357-367,
371-375; Sch: 256-258
All or Nothing ENES1: 183;
ENES2: 199
Atlantis ENES1: 183; ENES2:
199; Ri2: 357, 358, 367
Autobiography Ri2: 358-362,
364, 366, 372-374
The Brazen Head ENES1:
183; ENES2: 199
The Complex Vision Ri2:
360, 373
Ducdame ENES1: 183;
ENES2: 199; Ri2: 357-359,
361, 365, 367
A Glastonbury Romance EN:
105; ENES1: 183-184;
ENES2: 199; Po: 3317;
Ri2: 357-358, 360, 362,
364-368; Sch: 258

Homer and the Aether Ri2: 364

In Defence of Sensuality Ri2: 374

The Inmates ENES1: 184; ENES2: 199

Lucifer Po: 3317; Ri2: 371, 374

Maiden Castle ENES1: 184; ENES2: 199; Ri2: 357- 358, 365, 368- 369

The Maiden of Culture Ri2: 372

Morwyn ENES1: 184; ENES2: 199; Ri2: 357, 369

Odes and Other Poems Ri2: 374

Owen Glendower ENE: 226; ENES1: 184; ENES2: 199; Po: 3318; Ri2: 357, 365, 367, 369; Sch: 258

A Philosophy of Solitude Ri2: 360, 372, 374

Porius ENE: 226; ENES1: 184; ENES2: 200; Po: 3317; Ri2: 357, 359, 360, 367, 369- 370

Rodmoor ENES1: 184-185; ENES2: 200; Ri2: 357, 365, 370

Samphire Ri2: 374

Visions and Revisions Ri2: 374

Weymouth Sands ENES1: 185; ENES2: 200; Ri2: 357- 358, 370

Wolf Solent ENE: 226; ENES1: 185; ENES2: 200; Po: 3316- 3317; Ri2: 357- 358, 360, 364- 365, 367, 370- 371; Sch: 258

Wood and Stone ENES1: 185; ENES2: 200; Ri2: 357, 365, 371, 394

POWYS, Llewelyn
General Po: 3318
Apples Be Ripe ENES2: 200

POWYS, Theodore Francis
General BN2: 98- 99; Po: 3319- 3320; Ri2: 387- 394; Sch: 259
"Bottle's Path" SFC: 181; Wa: 642
Fables Ri2: 387- 388

Innocent Birds ENES2: 200

Kindness in a Corner ENES2: 200; Ri2: 393

"The Left Leg" Ri2: 387

Mark Only Ri2: 387

Mr. Tasker's Gods ENES1: 185; ENES2: 200; Ri2: 393

Mr. Weston's Good Wine BN2: 99; ENE: 226; ENES2: 200; Po: 3320; Ri2: 387, 390, 393- 394

Mockery Gap ENES2: 200; Ri2: 387, 394

The Soliloquy of a Hermit Ri2: 394

Unclay ENES2: 200; Ri2: 387

Prada, Manuel González see GONZALEZ PRADA, Manuel

PRADO, Pedro
"The Laugh in the Desert" WaS1: 184
"Moonlight" WaS1: 184
"Summer Picture: The Cripple" WaS1: 184
"When You Are Poor" WaS1: 184
"The Wise Woman" WaS1: 184

PRADO NOGUEIRA, José Luis
General Po: 3321

PRAED, Rosa
General AL: 311
Affinities Po: 3321

PRAMOEDYA ANANTA TOER
"Things Vanished" WaS1: 184

PRATOLINI, Vasco
General Po: 3321
Cronache di poveri amanti Fi: 275
A Hero of Our Times Ke: 249
Metello Ke: 248; Po: 3321
Il quartiere Fi: 275
Una storia italiana Ke: 249; Po: 3322
A Tale of Poor Lovers Ke: 249

PRATT, Edwin John
General Po: 3322- 3324
The Cachalot Po: 3324
"The Shark" PE: 354

PRATT, Fletcher and Lawrence MANNING
"City of the Living Dead" WaS1: 185

PRAZ, Mario
General LCAB: 143
The Romantic Agony LCAB:
143
PREM CHAND, Munshi [Munshi
Dhanpat RAI]
"The Chess Player" WaS1:
185
"The Old Aunt" WaS1: 185
PRESCOTT, Harriet E.
"Down the River" ASF: 492
PRESCOTT, William Hickling
General Cla: 117-118
The Conquest of Mexico
Cla: 118
Ferdinand and Isabella LCAB:
143
Preshkov, Alexei see GORKI,
Maxim
PRESTON, Thomas
Cambises, King of Persia
DC1: 177-178
PREVERT, Jacques
General Po: 3325-3326
PREVOST, Antoine François
Cleveland Fi: 127; Ke: 124
Le Doyen de Killerine Fi:
127; Ke: 124
Histoire d'une Grecque mod-
erne Fi: 127-128; Ke:
125
Histoire de Marguerite d'Anjou
Fi: 128
Manon Lescaut Fi: 128-129;
Ke: 125
Mémoires d'un honnête homme
Ke: 125
Mémoires d'un homme de
qualité Fi: 129; Ke:
125-126
PRICE, Donald
"Character of a Broad" Wa:
642
PRICE, Reynolds
General ASF: 493; CN:
433; Po: 3326-3327
"A Chain of Love" ASF:
492
A Generous Man CN: 434;
LCAB: 143; Po: 3327
A Long and Happy Life CN:
434
"The Names and Faces of
Heroes" ASF: 492; Wa:
643
"A Sign of Blood" ASF:

492; Wa: 643
"Uncle Grant" ASF: 492; Wa:
643
"Waiting at Dachau" LCAB:
143
"Walking Lessons" ASF: 493;
Wa: 643
"The Warrior Princess Ozimba"
ASF: 492-493; Wa: 643
PRICE, Richard
General EC: 118
PRICHARD, Katharine Susannah
General MAP: 263-266; Po:
3327-3328
Black Opal MAP: 265
Coonardoo MAP: 266
Intimate Strangers MAP: 266
The Roaring Nineties MAP:
265
Working Bullocks MAP: 265-
266
PRIDEAUX, James
The Last of Mrs. Lincoln ADC:
310
The Orphans ADC: 310
Postcards ADC: 310
PRIESTLEY, Eric John
General BAF: 237
PRIESTLEY, John Boynton [Peter
GOLDSMITH]
General Br: 551-552; CN:
434; LCAB: 143; MBD:
73-74; MD: 249; MDAE:
426-427; Mi: 269-270; Po:
3328-3330; Sch: 260
Adam in Moonshine CN: 434
Angel Pavement CN: 434;
ENES1: 185; ENES2: 201;
Ma: 1680
Bees on the Boat Deck Br:
552, EDC: 433
Benighted CN: 434; ENES1:
186; ENES2: 201
Bright Day CN: 435; ENES1:
186; ENES2: 201
Cornelius Br: 552; EDC:
433
The Dangerous Corner Br:
552; DC1: 178; EDC: 433;
MD: 249
Daylight on Saturday CN:
435; ENES2: 201
Desert Highway DC1: 178;
EDC: 433
Eden End Br: 552; EDC:
433; MD: 249

Ever Since Paradise Br: 552; DC1: 178; EDC: 433; MD: 249
Faraway CN: 435
Festival at Farbridge CN: 435; ENES2: 201
The Glass Cage EDC: 433-434
The Golden Fleece Br: 552
The Good Companions ENES1: 186; ENES2: 201; Ma: 1680
Goodnight, Children EDC: 434
Home Is Tomorrow Br: 552; EDC: 434
I Have Been Here Before Br: 552; DC1: 178; EDC: 434; MD: 249
The Image Men ENES2: 201
An Inspector Calls Br: 552-553; DC1: 178; EDC: 434; Ma: 1680; MBD: 74; MD: 249
Johnson Over Jordan Br: 553; EDC: 434; MD: 249
Laburnum Grove Br: 553; EDC: 434
The Linden Tree Br: 553; DC1: 178; EDC: 434-435; Ma: 1680-1681; MD: 249
Literature and Western Man Po: 3330
The Long Mirror DC1: 178; EDC: 435
Lost Empires ENES2: 201
Music at Night Br: 553; DC1: 178; EDC: 435; MD: 249-250
People at Sea Br: 553; EDC: 435
Roundabout EDC: 435
Saturn Over the Water CN: 435
The Scandalous Affair of Mr. Kettle and Mrs. Moon EDC: 435
Summer Day's Dream Br: 553; EDC: 435; MD: 250
They Came to the City Br: 553; EDC: 435
They Walk the City CN: 435
Time and the Conways Br: 553; DC1: 179; EDC: 435; MD: 250
When We Are Married Br: 553; EDC: 436
_____ and Jacquetta HAWKES
Dragon's Mouth EDC: 436; MD: 249
The White Countess DC1: 179; EDC: 436; MBD: 48
_____ and Edward KNOBLOCK
Good Companions EDC: 436
PRINCE, Frank Templeton
General Po: 3330
"The Old Age of Michelangelo" PE: 354
PRINCE, Thomas
General AP: 475-476
A Chronological History of New England... AP: 476
PRIOR, Matthew
General EC: 118-119; Me: 337-339
Alma EC: 118-119; Me: 338
"The Lady Who Offers Her Looking Glass to Venus" PE: 354
"The Mice, a Tale" Me: 339
"An Ode" PE: 354
Predestination Me: 338
Solomon Me: 337-338
"To a Child of Quality of Five Years Old, the Author Supposed Forty" PE: 354
"To the Honourable Charles Montague, Esq." ICBAP: 102; PE: 354
"Written in the Beginning of Mezeray's History of France" PE: 354
PRISCO, Michele
General Po: 3330
PRITCHARD, Norman Henry II
General BAF: 238
PRITCHETT, V.S.
General Po: 3331; Sch: 261
"The Ape" SFC: 182; Wa: 643
"The Sailor" Wa: 643
"The Scapegoat" Wa: 643
PROCTOR, Adelaide Anne
"The Pilgrims" PE: 354
PROKOSCH, Frederic
General AN: 213; CFAE: 302; CN: 435; Po: 3331
Age of Thunder CN: 435
The Asiatics CN: 435
A Ballad of Love CN: 436
The Conspirators CN: 436

The Idols of the Cave CN: 436

The Night of the Poor CN: 436

Nine Days to Mukalla CN: 436

The Seven Sisters CN: 436

The Seven Who Fled CN: 436

The Skies of Europe CN: 436

Storm and Echo CN: 436

A Tale for Midnight CN: 436

PROPERTIUS

General Ma: 1682-1683

PROUD, Robert

General AP: 585

PROUST, Marcel

General LCAB: 143; Po: 3332-3354

A la recherche du temps perdu see Remembrance of Things Past

A l'ombre des jeunes filles en fleurs see Within a Budding Grove

Un Amour de Swann Fi: 129; Ke: 137; Po: 3356, 3358

The Captive Fi: 129; Ke: 126; Ma: 1684

Cities of the Plain Fi: 130; Ke: 126-127; Ma: 1684-1685

"Combray" Fi: 130; Po: 3359-3360

Contre Sainte-Beuve Po: 3380-3381

The Fugitive [The Sweet Cheat Gone; La fugitive] Fi: 130; Ke: 139; Ma: 1690-1691

The Guermantes Way Ke: 127; Ma: 1685

Jean Santeuil Fi: 130-131; Ke: 127-128; Ma: 1685-1687; Po: 3381-3384

La Mort de Baldassare Silvande Fi: 131

The Past Recaptured see Time Recaptured

Pleasures and Days Fi: 131; Ke: 129

Portraits de peintres Po: 3384

Remembrance of Things Past [A la recherche du temps perdu] Fi: 131-139; Ke: 129-137; LCAB: 143; Ma: 1688-1689; Po: 3354-3380

Swann's Way [Du côté de chez Swann] Fi: 139-140; Ke: 137-139; Ma: 1689-1690; Po: 3358, 3363

The Sweet Cheat Gone see The Fugitive

Time Recaptured [The Past Recaptured] Fi: 140; Ke: 139-140; Ma: 1687-1688

Within a Budding Grove [A l'ombre des jeunes filles en fleurs] Fi: 129; Ke: 140-141; Ma: 1691-1692; Po: 3370

PRUS, Boleslaw

"Antek" Wa: 643

"The Barrel-Organ" Wa: 643

"The Converted One" Wa: 643

The Doll [Lalka] Ke: 432-433

The Emancipationists Ke: 433

"Graveyard Stories" Wa: 643

"The Harvest Contest" Wa: 643

Lalka see The Doll

"A Legend of Ancient Egypt" Wa: 644

"Mr. Wesolowski and His Walking Stick" Wa: 644

The Outpost Fi: 463; Ke: 433

Pharaoh Ke: 433

"The Saxonian Garden" Wa: 644

"Under the Fence" Wa: 644

PSICHARI, Ernest

General Po: 3385

PURDY, Alfred Wellington

General Po: 3385

PURDY, James

General ASF: 494-495; CFAE: 304-305; CN: 437; LCAB: 144; Po: 3385-3387

"About Jessie Mae" Wa: 644

Cabot Wright Begins CN: 437; Po: 3387-3388

"The Color of Darkness" ASF: 493; Wa: 644; WaS1: 185

"Cutting Edge" ASF: 493; Wa: 644; WaS1: 185

"Daddy Wolf" ASF: 493; Po: 3388; Wa: 644; WaS1: 185

"Don't Call Me by My Right
Name" ASF: 493; Wa:
644; WaS1: 185
"Encore" ASF: 493; Wa:
644
Eustace Chisholm and the
Works CN: 437
"Eventide" ASF: 493; Wa:
644; WaS1: 185
"Everything Under the Sun"
ASF: 493; Wa: 645
"A Good Woman" LCAB:
144; Wa: 645
"Goodnight, Sweetheart"
ASF: 494; Wa: 645
"Home by Dark" ASF: 494;
Wa: 645; WaS1: 185
"The Lesson" ASF: 494;
Wa: 645
Malcolm CFAE: 304-305;
CN: 437-438; Po: 3388-
3389
"Man and Wife" Wa: 645
"Mr. Evening" ASF: 494;
Wa: 645
"Mrs. Benson" Wa: 645
The Nephew CN: 438; Po:
3390
"Night and Day" ASF: 494;
Wa: 645
"Plan Now to Attend" Wa:
645
"Sermon" ASF: 494; Wa:
645
"63: Dream Palace" ASF:
494; Wa: 645; WaS1:
185
"Sound of Talking" Wa:
645
"Why Can't They Tell You
Why?" ASF: 494; Wa:
646; WaS1: 185
"You May Safely Gaze" Wa:
646
"You Reach for Your Hat"
Wa: 646
PUSHKIN, Alexander
General LCAB: 144
"An Amateur Peasant Girl"
see "The Peasant-Miss"
Angelo DC2: 279
The Blackamoor of Peter the
Great Fi: 463
Boris Godunov DC2: 279;
Ma: 1693-1694
The Bronze Horseman: A

Petersburg Tale Ma: 1694
The Captain's Daughter Fi:
463; Ke: 433; Ma: 1694-
1695; SFC: 182; Wa: 646
Dubrovskii Fi: 463
"The Egyptian Nights" SFC:
182; Wa: 646
Eugene Onegin LCAB: 144;
Ma: 1695-1696
Feast in Time of Plague DC2:
279
"History of the Village Goryuk-
hino" SFC: 182; Wa: 646
Kamennyy Gost DC2: 279
"The Lady-Rustic" see "The
Peasant-Miss"
"The Lonely Cottage on Vasil-
evskij Island" Wa: 646
"The Peasant-Miss" ["Mistress
into Maid"] SFC: 182; Wa:
646
The Queen of Spades Fi:
463-464; Ke: 433; Ma:
1696-1697; SFC: 182; Wa:
646; WaS1: 185-186
Ruslan and Lyudmila Ma:
1697-1698
"The Shot" SFC: 182; Wa:
647
"The Snowstorm" SFC: 182;
Wa: 647
"The Station Master" SFC:
182; Wa: 647; WaS1: 186
"The Undertaker" SFC: 182;
Wa: 647
PUTINAS, Vincas Mykolaitis
In the Shadow of Altars Ke:
433-434
The Rebels Ke: 434
PUTNAM, Phelps
"Ballad of a Strange Thing"
PE: 354
"The Five Seasons" PE: 354
"Hasbrouck and the Rose" PE:
354
PUTRAMENT, Jerzy
General Po: 3390
PYNCHON, Thomas
General ASF: 496; CFAE:
307; LCAB: 144; Po:
3390-3391
The Crying of Lot 49 AF:
168; CN: 439; LCAB: 144;
Ma: 1699
"Entropy" ASF: 495; Wa:
647; WaS1: 186

Gravity's Rainbow Ma: 1700
"A Journey into the Mind of
  Watts" WaS1: 186
"Low-lands" ASF: 495; WaS1:
  186
"Mortality and Mercy in Vi-
  enna" ASF: 495; WaS1:
  186
"The Secret Integration"
  ASF: 495; WaS1: 186
"Under the Rose" ASF: 496
V. CN: 439; LCAB: 144;
  Ma: 1701; Po: 3391-3392

Q

Q see QUILLER-COUCH,
  Arthur Thomas [Q]
QUARLES, Francis
  General Ba: 101
QUASIMODO, Salvatore
  General Po: 3393-3397
QUAYLE, Ada
  The Mistress WIL: 134
QUEIROS, Eça de
  A ilustre casa de Ramires
    Fi: 245
  Alves e cia Fi: 244
  The City and the Mountains
    Fi: 244; Ke: 227
  Cousin Bazilio Fi: 244
  O crime do padre Amaro
    Fi: 244-245; Ke: 227
  O primo Basilio Fi: 245;
    Ke: 227
  Os Maias Ke: 227
  The Mandarin Fi: 245; Ke:
    227
  The Relic Fi: 245; Ke: 227
QUEIROZ, Rachel de
  General Po: 3397
  As Três Marias Po: 3397
QUENEAU, Raymond
  General Po: 3398-3400
  Chene et chien Fi: 140
  Les Enfants du Limon Fi:
    140
  Les Fleurs bleues Fi: 140
  Fly in the Ointment Ke: 141
  Saint Glinglin Ke: 141
  The Sunday of Life Ke:
    141
QUENNELL, Peter
  General Po: 3400
QUESTEL, Victor D.

General WIL: 134
QUESTY, Joanni
  General BAW: 604
QUEVEDO, Francesco
  Como Ha De Ser El Privado
    DC2: 279
QUEVEDO, Francisco de
  El buscón Fi: 245-246; Ke:
    227-228
  La hora de todos Fi: 246
QUILLER-COUCH, Arthur Thomas
  [Q]
  General Po: 3400; Ta: 249
QUINAULT, Philippe
  Agrippa DC2: 280
  Astrate DC2: 280
QUINCY, Eliza Susan
  General AP: 585
QUINN, Roderic
  General AL: 314
QUINTERO, Serafin
  General Br: 553
  La Prisa Br: 553
QUIROGA, Elena
  General Po: 3400-3401
  Algo pasa en la calle see
    Something's Happening in
    the Street
  Blood [La sangre] Fi: 246;
    Ke: 228
  Bus One Fi: 246
  La enferma see The Sick Wom-
    an
  I Write Your Name Fi: 246
  The Mask [La careta] Fi:
    246; Ke: 228
  Northwind [Viento del norte]
    Fi: 246; Ke: 228
  The Other City Fi: 246
  Profound Present Fi: 246
  Sadness Fi: 246
  La sangre see Blood
  The Sick Woman [La enferma]
    Fi: 246-247; Ke: 228
  Something's Happening in the
    Street [Algo pasa en la
    calle] Fi: 247; Ke: 228
  Sonorous Solitude Fi: 247
  Viento del norte see North-
    wind
  The Young Placida Fi: 247
QUIROGA, Horacio
  General LCAB: 144; Po:
    3401
  "A la deriva" WaS1: 186
  "En la noche" Wa: 647

"Gloria tropical" Wa: 647
"El hombre muerte" WaS1: 186
"Las moscas" WaS1: 186
"Los pescadores de vigas" Wa: 647
"La voluntad" Wa: 647

R

RAABE, Wilhelm
Abu Telfan Ke: 328
Die Akten des Vogelsangs Fi: 384
Alte Nester Fi: 384
Altershausen Fi: 384
"The Black Galley" Wa: 647
The Burial Cart Ke: 328
The Cake Eater Ke: 328-329
Die Chronik der Sperlingsgasse Fi: 384; Ke: 329
Else von der Tanne Fi: 384; Wa: 647
"Die Gänse von Bützow" Wa: 647
"Gedelöcke" Wa: 648
"Die Hämelschen" Wa: 648
Hastenbeck Ke: 329
"Holunderblüte" Wa: 648
Horacker Ke: 329
"Höxter und Corvey" Wa: 648
The Hunger-Pastor Ke: 329
Im Alten Eisen Fi: 384; Ke: 329
"Die Innerste" Wa: 648
"Das letzte Recht" Wa: 648
"Der Marsch nach Hause" Wa: 648
Das Odferd Ke: 329
Pfisters Mühle Fi: 384; Ke: 329
Prinzessin Fisch Ke: 329
"Der Reiches Krone" Wa: 648
Stopfkuchen Fi: 384
"The Student from Wittenberg" Wa: 648
Unruhige Gaste Ke: 329
"Zum wilden Mann" Wa: 648; WaS1: 187
RABE, David

General TMAP: 189-192
The Basic Training of Pavlo Hummel ADC: 310-311; TMAP: 190-193
In the Boom Boom Room [Boom Boom Room] ADC: 311; TMAP: 190, 193-194
The Orphan ADC: 311; TMAP: 191, 194
Sticks and Bones ADC: 311-312; TMAP: 189-192, 194-195
Streamers ADC: 312; TMAP: 190, 192, 195-196
RABELAIS, François
General LCAB: 144-145
Gargantua and Pantagruel Fi: 140-146; Ke: 141-146; Ma: 1702-1703; Po: 1910
The Works of Rabelais see also URQUHART, Sir Thomas [translator]
RABY, Peter
The Three Musketeers ADC: 312
RACINE, Jean Baptiste
General LCAB: 145
Alcestii DC2: 280
Alexander the Great [Alexandre Le Grand] DC2: 280; EDC: 436; Ma: 1704
Andromache [Andromaque] DC2: 280-281; EDC: 437-438; LCAB: 145; Ma: 1704-1705
Athalie DC2: 281-282; EDC: 438-439; Ma: 1705
Bajazet; or, The Tragedy of Roxane DC2: 282; EDC: 439; Ma: 1706
Bérénice DC2: 282-283; EDC: 439-440; Ma: 1706-1707
Britannicus DC2: 283; EDC: 440-441; Ma: 1707
Esther DC2: 283; EDC: 441; Ma: 1707
Iphigénie DC2: 283-284; EDC: 441-442; Ma: 1707-1708
The Litigants [Les Plaideurs] DC2: 286; EDC: 442
Mithridate DC2: 284; EDC: 442; Ma: 1708
Phaedra [Phèdre] DC2: 284-286; EDC: 443-446; LCAB: 145; Ma: 1708-1710
The Thebans; or The Enemy

Brothers [La Thébaïde;
ou, Les Frères Ennemis]
DC2: 286-287; EDC: 446;
Ma: 1710
RADCLIFFE, Ann
General Be: 196-198; Du:
122
The Castles of Athlin and
Dunbayne ENES1: 186;
ENES2: 201
Gaston de Blondeville
ENES1: 186; ENES2: 201
The Italian ENES1: 186;
ENES2: 201
The Mysteries of Udolpho
Be: 196-197; Du: 121;
EN: 106; ENE: 226;
ENES1: 186; ENES2: 201;
LCAB: 144; Ma: 1711
The Romance of the Forest
Du: 121-122; ENES1:
186-187; ENES2: 202;
Ma: 1711-1712
A Sicilian Romance ENES1:
187
RADDALL, Thomas Head
General Po: 3403
RADIGUET, Raymond
General Po: 3403-3404
Le Bal du comte d'Orgel Fi:
147; Po: 3404
Le Diable au corps Fi: 147;
Ke: 146
Radvanyi, Netty see SEGHERS,
Anna
RAFF, William Jourdan
Harlem MBA: 166
RAFFALT, Reinhard
The Successor [Der Nach-
folger] Br: 554
RAGNI, Gerome, James RADO,
and Galt MacDERMOT
Hair ADC: 312-313; Br:
554
RAHMAN, Aishah
Lady Day BAP: 163
Transcendental Blues MBA:
167
Unfinished Women Cry in No
Man's Land While a Bird
Dies in a Gilded Cage
MBA: 167
RAIMONDI, Giuseppe
General Po: 3405
RAIMUND, Ferdinand
Der Alpenkonig und der

Menschenfeind DC2: 287
Der Bauer Als Mullionar DC2:
287
Die Gelesselte Phantasie DC2:
287
Der Verschwender DC2: 287
RAINE, Kathleen
General EP: 216-217; ICBAP:
102; Po: 3405-3406
"The Crystal Skull" ICBAP:
102
"The Invisible Spectrum" PE:
354
"The Pythoness" ICBAP: 102;
PE: 355
"Winter Fire" PE: 355
RAINOLDE, Richard
The Foundacion of Rhetorike
Hen: 191
RAKESH, Mohan
"Savorless Sin" WaS1: 187
RAKOSI, Carl
General Po: 3406
"A Journey Far Away" PE:
355
RALEIGH [or RALEGH], Sir Walter
General Hen: 69-70; SC:
80-81
"As You Came from the Holy
Land" PE: 355
The History of the World Hen:
52
"The Last Booke of the Ocean
to Scinthia" ICBAP: 102
"The Lie" LCAB: 145; PE:
355
"The Ocean's Love to Cynthia"
PE: 355
"The Pilgrimage" PE: 355
"Walsingham" PE: 355
RALPH, James
General EC: 119; Li: 272
The Fall of the Earl of Essex
Li: 272
RAMIREZ ANGEL, Emiliano
General Po: 3406
RAMKEESOON, Peter
Sunday Morning Coming Down
WIL: 134
Ramón, Juan see JIMENEZ, Juan
Ramón
RAMOS, Graciliano
General Po: 3406-3407
Angústia Po: 3407
Vidas Sêcas Po: 3407
RAMOS, José Antonio

General Br: 554
RAMSAY, Allan
General Ai: 60; EC: 120
RAMUZ, Charles-Ferdinand
General Po: 3407-3410
Farinet ou la fausse monnaie
Po: 3411
La Grande peur dans la montagne Po: 3411
Le Règne de l'esprit malin
Po: 3411
RAND, Ayn
General Po: 3411-3412
Atlas Shrugged Ma: 1713
The Fountainhead AN: 213;
Ma: 1713; Po: 3411-3412
RANDALL, Bob
6 rms riv vu ADC: 313
RANDALL, Dudley
General BAF: 238; BAW:
609
Randolph, Georgiana Ann see
RICE, Craig
RANDOLPH, Thomas
General LJCD: 251-253
Praeludium DC1: 179
RANGANAYAKAMMA, Muppala
General Po: 3412
RANIELLO, John
A Comedy Tonight [three
plays: Misses; Image and
Likeness; and Comedy Tonight] ADC: 313
RANIERI, Antonio
Ginevra Ke: 250
RANKINS, William
General Log: 261-262
RANSOM, John Crowe
General ALL: 231-232;
APC: 182-184; ICBAP:
102; LCAB: 145-146; Ma:
1720-1721; MP: 80-82;
Po: 3412-3418
"Amphibious Crocodile" PE:
355
"Antique Harvesters" Ma:
1714; PE: 355
"Bells for John Whiteside's
Daughter" Ma: 1714-
1715; PE: 355-356; Po:
3418-3419
"Blackberry Winter" PE:
356
"Blue Girls" ICBAP: 102;
Ma: 1715; PE: 356;
Po: 3419

"Captain Carpenter" ICBAP:
102; LCAB: 146; Ma: 1715-
1716; PE: 356; Po: 3419-
3420
"Conrad in Twilight" PE: 356;
Po: 3420
"Dead Boy" Ma: 1716; PE:
357; Po: 3420
"The Equilibrists" ICBAP:
102; Ma: 1717; PE: 357;
Po: 3420-3421
"The First Travels of Max"
PE: 357
"Fresco: From the Last Judgment" Po: 3421
"God Without Thunder" Po:
3421
"Grace" PE: 357
"Here Lies a Lady" Ma: 1717-
1718; PE: 357
"Janet Waking" ICBAP: 103;
Ma: 1718; PE: 357-358
"Lady Lost" PE: 358
"Little Boy Blue" ICBAP:
103; PE: 358; Po: 3421
"Master's in the Garden Again"
ICBAP: 103; LCAB: 146;
Po: 3421-3422
"Miller's Daughter" PE: 358
"Miriam Tazewell" Ma: 1718-
1719; PE: 358; Po: 3422
The New Criticism Ma: 1719
"Night Voices" PE: 358
"Noonday Grace" PE: 358
"Old Mansion" PE: 358
"Painted Head" Ma: 1719-
1720; PE: 358-359; Po:
3422
"Parting Without a Sequel" PE:
359
"Philomela" ICBAP: 103; PE:
359; Po: 3422
"Piazza Piece" PE: 359
"A Poem Nearly Anonymous"
Po: 3423
"Prelude to an Evening"
ICBAP: 103; Ma: 1721;
PE: 359; Po: 3423
"The School" PE: 359
"Spectral Lovers" Ma: 1721-
1722; PE: 359
"Spiel of Three Mountebanks"
PE: 359
"The Swimmer" PE: 360
"The Tall Girl" PE: 360
"Two in August" ICBAP:

103; PE: 360; Po: 3423
"Vaunting Oak" PE: 360
"Vision by Sweetwater" PE: 360
"Winter Remembered" PE: 360
RAO, Raja
General Po: 3423-3424
The Cat and Shakespeare Po: 3423-3424
"Companions" Wa: 648
"The Cow of the Barricades" Wa: 648; WaS1: 187
The Cow of the Barricades and Other Stories Po: 3425
"In Khandesh" Wa: 648; WaS1: 187
Kanthapura Po: 3425-3426
"Narsiga" Wa: 648; WaS1: 187
"The True Story of Kanakapala, Protector of God" Wa: 648
RAPHAEL, Frederic
General CFAE: 309; CN: 439; Po: 3426
The Earlsdon Way CN: 439-440
The Graduate Wife CN: 440
The Limits of Love CN: 440
Lindmann CN: 440
Obbligato CN: 440
The Trouble with England CN: 440
A Wild Surmise CN: 440
RAPHAEL, Lennox
General BAP: 164
Che! ADC: 313; BAP: 164; MBA: 167
RAPHAELSON, Samson
Accent on Youth Br: 554
Hilda Crane Br: 554
Jason Br: 554
The Perfect Marriage Br: 554
Young Love Br: 554
Rappoport, Solomon see ANSKY, S.
RASCOE, Burton
The Bookman's Daybook LCAB: 146
RASMUSSEN, Emil Michael
General BAF: 239; BAW: 612
RASPUTIN, Valentin

Upstream, Downstream Fi: 464
RASSER, Johann
Spil von Kinderzucht DC2: 287
RASTELL, John
The Nature of the Four Elements see ANONYMOUS
Of Gentleness and Nobility DC1: 179
RAT, Maurice
General Po: 3426
RATTIGAN, Terence Mervyn
General Br: 555; MD: 250; MDAE: 429-430; Mi: 270-271; Po: 3426
Adventure Story DC1: 179; EDC: 447
After the Dance EDC: 447
The Browning Version Br: 555; EDC: 447; MD: 250
The Deep Blue Sea Br: 555; EDC: 447-448; MD: 250
Flare Path Br: 555; EDC: 448; MD: 250
French Without Tears Br: 555; EDC: 448
Harlequinade EDC: 448; MD: 250
Heart to Heart Br: 555; EDC: 448
In Praise of Love EDC: 448
Man and Boy Br: 555; EDC: 449
Man to Man EDC: 449
Nelson: A Portrait in Miniature Br: 555
O Mistress Mine [Love in Idleness, in England] Br: 555; EDC: 448-449; MD: 250
Ross Br: 555-556; EDC: 449; MDAE: 430
Separate Tables Br: 556; DC1: 179; EDC: 449-450; MD: 250
Sleeping Prince EDC: 450
Variations on a Theme Br: 556; EDC: 450; MD: 250
While the Sun Shines EDC: 450; MD: 250
Who Is Sylvia? Br: 556; EDC: 450
The Winslow Boy Br: 556; DC1: 179; EDC: 450-451; MD: 250
_____ and Anthony MAURICE
Follow My Leader EDC: 451

RAVENSCROFT, Edward
General Li: 273-274
The Anatomist Bon: 45; Li: 273
The Citizen Turned Gentleman Li: 273
The Italian Husband Li: 273
King Edgar and Alfreda Li: 273
The Wrangling Lovers Li: 273
RAWLINGS, Marjorie Kinnan
General ASF: 497; Po: 3427
"Alligators" ASF: 496
"Black Secret" Wa: 648
"Cocks Must Crow" ASF: 496; Wa: 649
"Cracker Chidlings" ASF: 496
"A Crop of Beans" Wa: 649
"The Enemy" Wa: 649
"Gal Young Un" ASF: 496; Wa: 649
"Jacob's Ladder" ASF: 497; Wa: 649
"Lord Bill of the Suwannee River" Po: 3427
"A Mother in Mannville" ASF: 497; Wa: 649
The Sojourner AN: 213
The Yearling AN: 213
RAWLINS, Thomas
The Rebellion DC1: 179
RAWLINSON, A.R.
Birthmark Br: 556
RAWSON, Clayton
General ASF: 497
RAY, Henrietta Cordelia
General AAPD: 74
RAY, R.J.
The Gombeen Man Br: 556
RAYFIEL, David
Nathan Weinstein, Mystic, Connecticut Br: 556
RAYNAL, Paul
General Br: 556; MD: 250
Le Maître de Son Coeur Br: 557
Le Matériel Humain Br: 557
The Unknown Warrior [Le Tombeau sous l'Arc de Triomphe] Br: 557; MD: 250-251
RAZAF, Andy [Andreamanen-

tania Paul RAZAFINKERIEFO]
General BAP: 164-165; BAW: 614; MBA: 167
Hot Chocolate MBA: 167
READ, Sir Herbert
General LCAB: 146; Po: 3427-3432; Sch: 261
"The Analysis of Love" PE: 360
"Beata l'Alma" PE: 360
"The End of War" ICBAP: 103; PE: 360
"Equation a+b+c=X" PE: 360
"Execution of Cornelius Vane" ICBAP: 103
"Fear" ICBAP: 103
The Green Child ENES1: 187; ENES2: 202; Po: 3433
"John Donne Declines a Benefice" PE: 360
"The Lament of St. Denis" PE: 360
"Love and Death" PE: 360
"Mutations of the Phoenix" PE: 361
"The Narrow Labyrinth Has Light" PE: 361
"Nuncio" PE: 361
"The Retreat" PE: 361
"A World Within a War" PE: 361
READ, Opie
General ASF: 497
READ, Piers Paul
Upstart ENES1: 187
READE, Charles
General BN: 85-86; Du: 123-124; EDT: 257-258
Art: A Dramatic Tale ENES2: 202; WaS1: 187
The Bloomer ENES2: 202
Christie Johnstone EN: 106; ENE: 226-227; ENES2: 202
The Cloister and the Hearth BN: 86; Du: 123; EN: 106; ENE: 227; ENES1: 187; ENES2: 202; Ma: 1723
Clouds and Sunshine ENES2: 202; WaS1: 187
Foul Play ENES2: 202
Gold EDT: 258
Griffith Gaunt ENES1: 187; ENES2: 202
Hard Cash BN: 85; Du: 123; EN: 106; ENE: 227; ENES2: 202; Ma: 1723-1724

It Is Never Too Late DC1: 180

It Is Never Too Late to Mend BN: 85; EDT: 258; EN: 106; ENE: 227; ENES1: 187; ENES2: 202; Ma: 1724-1725

The Jilt ENES2: 202

Love Me Little, Love Me Long ENES2: 202

Nance Oldfield EDT: 257

Peg Woffington ENES2: 202; Ma: 1725

A Perilous Secret ENES2: 202

Put Yourself in His Place EN: 106; ENES2: 203

A Simpleton ENES2: 203

Singlehart and Doubleface ENES2: 203

A Terrible Temptation ENES2: 203

The Wandering Heir ENES2: 203

White Lies ENES2: 203

A Woman-Hater ENES2: 203

———— and Tom TAYLOR

Masks and Faces EDT: 257

REAGE, Pauline

The Story of O Fi: 147; Po: 3433

REANEY, James

General Po: 3433-3434

"The Bicycle" Po: 3434

Colours in the Dark Po: 3434

The Easter Egg DC1: 180

The Killdeer DC1: 180

REARDON, Dennis J.

The Happiness Cage ADC: 314

The Leaf People ADC: 314

Siamese Connections ADC: 314

REASON, Charles D.

General BAW: 615

REASON, Charles Lewis

General AAPD: 74-75

REBHUN, Paul

Susanna DC2: 287

REBREANU, Liviu

Ion Fi: 464

RECHY, John Francisco

General CFAE: 311

City of Night CFAE: 311, 394; CN: 440-441;

LCAB: 146

REDCAM, Tom [Thomas Henry McDERMOT]

General WIL: 134-136

REDDING, Saunders

General AAW: 70; BAF: 239; BAW: 617

Stranger and Alone BAF: 239-240

REDFORD, John

Wit and Science DC1: 180

REDGROVE, Peter

General ICBAP: 103

"Mr. Waterman" WaS1: 187

REDMOND, Eugene

General BAP: 165; BAW: 622; MBA: 167

The Face of the Deep BAP: 165; BAW: 622

REED, Henry

"Naming of Parts" PE: 361; Po: 3435

REED, Ishmael

General AAF: 84-85; BAF: 240-241; BAW: 624-625

Flight to Canada BAF: 241-242

The Free-Lance Pallbearers AAL: 240; BAF: 242

"I Am a Cowboy in the Boat of Ra" BAF: 240; PE: 361

The Last Days of Louisiana Red AAF: 84; BAF: 242-243

Mumbo Jumbo AAF: 84-85; BAF: 243

Yellow Back Radio Broke Down AAF: 84; AAL: 240; BAF: 243; MBA: 168

REED, Joseph

Dido Li: 275

REED, Mark

Petticoat Fever ADC: 314

Yes, My Darling Daughter ADC: 314; Br: 557

REEDS, F. Anton

"Forever Is Not So Long" WaS1: 187

REEL, Arthur

Cain and Artyom ADC: 314

REESE, Lizette Woodworth

General Po: 3435

"Tears" Po: 3435

REEVE, Clara

General Be: 200-201

The Old English Baron ENES1: 187

REEVES, Donald
  General BAW: 626
REGE, P.S.
  General Po: 3436
REGER, Erik
  Union der festen Hand Po:
    3436
REGIS, Leon and François de
    VEGNES
  Bastos le Hardi Br: 557
  Le Grande Pénitence Br:
    557
REGNIER, Henri de
  General Po: 3436-3437
  Médailles d'argile Po: 3437
  "Le Sang de Marsyas" Po:
    3437
REGNIER, Paule
  General Po: 3437
REGOYOS, Darío de
  España negra Po: 3438
REID, Alastair
  General Ai: 325
REID, Forrest
  General Po: 3438
  At the Door of the Gate
    ENES2: 203
  The Bracknels ENES2: 203
  Brian Westby ENES2: 203
  Demophon ENES2: 203
  The Garden God ENES2:
    203
  The Gentle Lover ENES2:
    203
  The Kingdom of Twilight
    ENES2: 203
  Pender Among the Residents
    ENES2: 203
  Peter Waring ENES2: 203
  Pirates of the Spring ENES2:
    204
  The Retreat ENES2: 204
  The Spring Song ENES2:
    204
  Uncle Stephen ENES2: 204
  Young Tom ENES2: 204
REID, Thomas
  General EC: 120
REID, Thomas Mayne
  General BN: 86
REID, Victor Stafford
  General WIL: 136-138
  The Leopard WIL: 139-140
  New Day LCAB: 146;
    WIL: 138-139
  Sixty-Five WIL: 140

  The Young Warriors WIL: 140
REIMANN, Brigitte
  Franziska Linkerhand Fi: 385
REINACHER, Edward
  General Po: 3438
REINER, Carl
  Something Different ADC: 314
Reissig, Julio Herrera y see
    HERRERA y REISSIG, Julio
RELLA, Ettore
  Sign of Death DC1: 180
REMARQUE, Erich Maria
  All Quiet on the Western Front
    [Im Westen nichts Neues]
    Fi: 385; Ke: 329-330; Ma:
    1726; Po: 3438
  Die Traumbude Fi: 385
REMINGTON, Frederic
  General ASF: 497
REMIRO DE NAVARRA, Baptista
  Los peligros de Madrid Ke:
    228
REMIZOV, Aleksej
  Pjataja Jazva Fi: 464
  Prud Fi: 464
  "Sisters of the Cross" Wa:
    649
REMY-NERIS, André
  General Po: 3439
RENARD, Jean-Claude
  General Po: 3439
RENAULT, Mary
  General Po: 3439; Sch: 261-
    262
  The Bull from the Sea ENE:
    227; ENES1: 187
  The Charioteer ENE: 227;
    ENES1: 187
  Fire from Heaven ENES1: 188
  The Friendly Young Ladies
    ENES1: 188
  Kind Are Her Answers ENES1:
    188
  The King Must Die ENE: 227;
    ENES1: 188; LCAB: 146;
    Po: 3439
  The Last of the Wine ENE:
    227-228; ENES1: 188
  The Mask of Apollo ENES1:
    188
  North Face ENES1: 188
  Purposes of Love ENES1:
    188
  Return to Night ENES1: 188
Renéville, André Rolland de see
    ROLLAND DE RENEVILLE,

André
RENGIFO, Cesar
General Br: 557
RENN, Ludwig
General Po: 3440
REPIDE, Pedro de
General Po: 3440
REPPLIER, Agnes
General Po: 3440
REQUENA, Maria Asuncion
General Br: 557-558
RESNIK, Muriel
Any Wednesday ADC: 315
REUTER, Gabriele
Aus Guter Familie Fi: 385
REVERDY, Pierre
General Po: 3440-3442
"Voyages sans fin" Po: 3442
REVUELTAS, José
"La frontera increíble" WaS1: 187
"Los hombres en el pantano" WaS1: 188
"Lo que solo uno escucha" WaS1: 188
REXROTH, Kenneth
General Po: 3442-3443
"The Homestead Called Damascus" PE: 361
Rey, Lester del see DEL REY, Lester
REYBAUD, Louis
Jérôme Paturot à la d'une position sociale Ke: 146
REYES, Albert
The War of the Worlds ADC: 315
REYES, Alfonso
General Po: 3443-3445
"Ancorajes" Po: 3445-3446
"Era un jardín..." Po: 3446
REYES, José Trinidad
General Br: 558
REYLES, Carlos
General Po: 3446
El embrujo de Sevilla Po: 3446
REYMONT, Wladyslaw [Ladislas]
The Comedienne Fi: 465
"The Confession" Wa: 649
"Death" Wa: 649
The Dreamer Ke: 434; Wa: 649
"A Dusk" Wa: 649
The Ferments Fi: 465

"Franek" Wa: 649
"The Graveyard" Wa: 649
"I Have Killed" Wa: 649
The Insurrection Fi: 465
The Last Diet Fi: 465
"Lili" Wa: 649
Nil Desperandum Fi: 465
"On a Certain Day" Wa: 650
"On the Edge" Wa: 650
"Pages of a Diary" Wa: 650
The Peasants Fi: 465; Ke: 434; Ma: 1727
"The Pilgrimage to Jasna Gora" Wa: 650
"The Princess" Wa: 650
The Promised Land Fi: 465; Ke: 434
"The Return" Wa: 650
"Righteously" Wa: 650
"The Riot" Wa: 650
"A Sacrifice" see "Lili"
"The Shadow" Wa: 650
"Tomek Baran" Wa: 650
"Work!" Wa: 650
REYNOLD, Gonzague de
General Po: 3446
REYNOLDS, Evelyn [Eve LYNN]
General BAW: 627
REYNOLDS, Henry
General Ba: 102
Mythomystes Ba: 102; Hen: 181
REYNOLDS, John
The Triumphs of God's Revenge ERP: 384
REYNOLDS, Jonathan
Rubbers ADC: 315
Yanks 3 Detroit 0 Top of the Seventh ADC: 315
REYNOLDS, Sir Joshua
General EC: 121
REYNOSA, Rodrigo de
Coplas de las Comrades DC2: 287
REZNIKOFF, Charles
General JW: 117; Po: 3447
REZVANI, Medjid Khan
General Po: 3447
RHODES, Eugene Manlove
General ASF: 498; Po: 3447-3448
"Beyond the Desert" ASF: 497; Wa: 650
"No Mean City" ASF: 497
RHODES, Hari
General BAF: 244

RHONE, Trevor
  Comic Strip MBA: 168
  Smile Orange MBA: 168
RHYS, Jean
  General Po: 3448-3449; Sch:
    262; WIL: 140-141
  After Leaving Mr. Mackenzie
    ENES1: 188; ENES2:
    204; WIL: 141
  Good Morning, Midnight
    ENES1: 188; ENES2:
    204; WIL: 141
  Quartet ENES1: 189; ENES2:
    204; WIL: 141
  Sleep It Off Lady WIL: 142
  Tigers Are Better Looking
    WIL: 142
  Voyage in the Dark ENES1:
    189; ENES2: 204; WIL:
    141
  Wide Sargasso Sea ENES1:
    189; ENES2: 205; Po:
    3448; WIL: 141-142
RIBEMONT-DESSAIGNES, Georges
  Le Bourreau du Pérou Br:
    558
RIBEYRO, Julio
  "Una aventura nocturna"
    Wa: 650
  "De color modesto" Wa: 650
  "Los gallinazos sin plumas"
    Wa: 650
  "La piel de un indio no cuesta
    cara" Wa: 650
RIBMAN, Ronald
  General MDAE: 431
  The Ceremony of Innocence
    ADC: 315; Br: 558
  Cold Storage ADC: 315;
    MBA: 168
  Fingernails Blue as Flowers
    ADC: 316
  Harry, Noon and Night ADC:
    316; Br: 558
  The Journey of the Fifth
    Horse ADC: 316; Br:
    558
  Passing Through from Exotic
    Places [three plays: Sun-
    stroke; The Burial of
    Esposito; and The Son
    Who Hunted Tigers in
    Jakarta] ADC: 316
  The Poison Tree ADC: 316;
    MBA: 168-169
RICARDOU, Jean

  La Prise de Constantinople Fi:
    147
RICE, Elmer
  General Br: 558-559; JW:
    410-411; LCAB: 146-147;
    Lon: 47-48; MD: 251; Po:
    3449-3450
  The Adding Machine ADC:
    316-317; Br: 559-560; DC1:
    180; JW: 411; MD: 251;
    Po: 3449
  American Landscape ADC:
    317; Br: 560; MD: 251
  Between Two Worlds ADC:
    317; Br: 560; MD: 251
  Black Sheep ADC: 317; Br:
    560
  Close Harmony Br: 560
  Cock Robin Br: 560
  Counsellor-at-Law ADC: 317-
    318; Br: 560; MD: 251
  Cue for Passion ADC: 318;
    Br: 560
  Dream Girl ADC: 318; Br:
    561; MD: 251
  Flight to the West ADC: 318;
    Br: 561; MD: 251-252
  The Grand Tour ADC: 318-
    319; Br: 561; MD: 252
  The Home of the Free Br:
    561
  The House in Blind Alley Br:
    561
  Judgment Day ADC: 319; Br:
    561; MD: 252
  The Left Bank ADC: 319; Br:
    561; DC1: 180
  Love Among the Ruins ADC:
    319; Br: 561
  A New Life ADC: 319; Br:
    562; MD: 252
  Not for Children ADC: 319;
    Br: 562; DC1: 180; MD:
    252
  On Trial ADC: 319-320; Br:
    562; Po: 3450
  The Passing of Chow-Chow
    Br: 562
  See Naples and Die ADC:
    320; Br: 562
  The Sidewalks of New York
    ADC: 320; Br: 562
  Street Scene ADC: 320-321;
    Br: 562-563; DC1: 180-181;
    MD: 252
  The Subway ADC: 321; Br:

563; DC1: 181; MD: 252;
Po: 3449-3450
Two on an Island ADC: 321;
Br: 563
Wake Up, Jonathan see also
HUGHES, Hatcher and
Elmer RICE Br: 563
We, the People ADC: 321;
Br: 563; MD: 252
The Winner ADC: 321-322;
Br: 563
_____, Kurt WEILL, and
Langston HUGHES
Street Scene ADC: 322
RICH, Adrienne
General ICBAP: 103; LCAB:
147; MP: 83; Po: 3450
"The Celebration in the
Plaza" PE: 361
"The Mirror in Which Two
Are Seen as One" PE:
361
RICH, Barnaby
General ERP: 387-393;
Hen: 158; SC: 81-82
Brusanus ERP: 390, 393
Dialogue Between Mercury
and an English Soldier
ERP: 392
Don Simonides ERP: 388,
391
Farewell ERP: 388-393
"Sappho" SC: 81
RICHARD, Jean-Pierre
General Po: 3450-3451
RICHARDS, Beah
General BAW: 628; MBA:
169
A Black Woman Speaks
MBA: 169
RICHARDS, Ivor Armstrong
General LCAB: 147; Po:
3451-3453
Goodbye Earth and Other
Poems Po: 3453
"Not No" PE: 361
RICHARDSON, Dorothy Miller
General BN2: 100-101;
LCAB: 147; Po: 3454-
3456; Ri2: 402-412; Sch:
262-265; TA: 250
Backwater ENES2: 205
Clear Horizon ENES2: 205
Dawn's Left Hand ENES2:
205; Ri2: 405
Deadlock ENES2: 205; Ri2:

405
"Excursion" WaS1: 188
Honeycomb ENES2: 205
Interim ENES2: 205; Po:
3455; Ri2: 408
"Nook on Parnassus" WaS1:
188
Oberland ENES2: 205; Ri2:
403
"Ordeal" WaS1: 188
Pilgrimage EN: 107; ENES1:
189; ENES2: 205; Po:
3457-3458; Ri2: 402-411
Pointed Roofs EN: 107;
ENES2: 205; Ri2: 404, 409
Revolving Lights ENES2: 205;
Ri2: 412
The Trap ENES2: 206
"Tryst" WaS1: 188
The Tunnel ENES2: 206; Po:
3455; Ri2: 408, 412
"Visit" WaS1: 188
"Visitor" WaS1: 188
RICHARDSON, Henry Handel
[Ethel Florence LINDESAY;
Henrietta RICHARDSON;
Ethel Florence Lindesay
ROBERTSON]
General MAP: 270-281; Po:
3458; TA: 252
"The Bath" Wa: 651
"The Coat" Wa: 651
"The End of a Childhood"
MAP: 274, 278; Wa: 651
The Fortunes of Richard
Mahony ENE: 228; MAP:
270-280; Po: 3458-3462
The Getting of Wisdom MAP:
271-272, 275-276
"The Life and Death of Peterle
Lüthy" Wa: 651
"Mary Christina" Wa: 651
Maurice Guest ENE: 228;
MAP: 274-277, 279; Po:
3462-3463
"The Professor's Experiment"
Wa: 651
"Sister Ann" Wa: 651
"Succedaneum" Wa: 651;
WaS1: 188
Ultima Thule MAP: 271
The Young Cosima MAP: 274,
276, 280; Po: 3464
RICHARDSON, Howard and William
BERNEY
Dark of the Moon see also

BERNEY, William and
Howard RICHARDSON
DC1: 181
RICHARDSON, Jack
General Br: 564; LCAB:
147; MD: 252; Po: 3464
Gallows Humor ADC: 322;
Br: 564; DC1: 181; MD:
252; Po: 3465
Lorenzo ADC: 323; Br:
564; DC1: 181
The Prodigal ADC: 323;
Br: 564; DC1: 181;
LCAB: 147; MD: 252;
MDAE: 432; Po: 3465
Xmas in Las Vegas ADC:
323; Br: 564
RICHARDSON, John
General ECL: 81-82
"A Canadian Campaign" ECL:
81
"Kensington Gardens in 1830"
ECL: 81
Wacousta; or, The Prophecy.
A Tale of the Canadas
ECL: 81
RICHARDSON, Mel
The Breach BAP: 167
RICHARDSON, Nola
General BAF: 244
Richardson, Robert Shirley see
LATHAM, Philip
RICHARDSON, Samuel
General Be: 207-217; Du:
128-130; LCAB: 147
Clarissa [Clarissa Harlowe]
Be: 89, 118, 208-217;
Du: 124-126; EN: 107-
108; ENE: 228-229;
ENES1: 189-191; ENES2:
206-207; LCAB: 147-148;
Ma: 1728-1729; Po: 1436-
1437
Pamela Be: 89, 121, 125,
209-216; Du: 126-128;
EN: 109; ENE: 229-230;
ENES1: 191-192; ENES2:
207-208; LCAB: 147; Ma:
1729-1730
Pamela II Du: 128
Sir Charles Grandison Be:
210, 213-214; Du: 128;
EN: 109-110; ENE: 231;
ENES1: 192; ENES2: 208;
LCAB: 148; Ma: 1731
RICHARDSON, Willis

General AAPD: 330; BAF:
244; BAP: 169; BAW: 630;
HR: 131-132; MBA: 170
Alimony Rastus BAP: 169
Antonio Maceo BAP: 169
Attucks, the Martyr BAP:
169
The Black Horseman BAP:
169
The Broken Banjo BAP: 169;
MBA: 170
The Chip Woman's Fortune
ADC: 323; BAP: 169-171;
MBA: 170
Compromise BAP: 170
The Deacon's Awakening BAP:
170
The Elder Dumas BAP: 170
The Flight of the Natives MBA:
170
A Ghost of the Past BAP: 170
The House of Sham BAP: 170
The Idle Head BAP: 170
In Menelik's Court BAP: 170
The King's Dilemma BAP: 170
Meek Mose BAP: 170
Miss or Mrs. BAP: 171
Mortgaged BAP: 171
Near Calvary BAP: 171
RICHLER, Mordecai
General CFAE: 313-314; CN:
441; JW: 347-348; Po: 3465-
3466
The Acrobats CN: 441; JW:
347; Po: 3466
The Apprenticeship of Duddy
Kravitz CN: 441; JW: 348;
Po: 3466-3467
A Choice of Enemies CN: 441
Stick Out Your Neck CN: 441
"The Summer My Grandmother
Was Supposed to Die" Wa:
651
RICHTER, Conrad
General AN: 213; ASF: 498;
CN: 442; Po: 3467-3468
Always Young and Fair CN:
442
The Awakening Land see Ohio
Trilogy
"Brothers of No Kin" Wa:
651
The Fields see also Ohio
Trilogy CN: 442; Ma:
1732
The Free Man CN: 442

The Grandfathers CN: 442
The Lady CN: 443; Ma:
  1732
"The Laughter of Leen" Wa:
  651
The Light in the Forest CN:
  443; Ma: 1732-1733; Po:
  3468
Ohio Trilogy CN: 443; Ma:
  1733; Po: 3467
The Sea of Grass CN: 443;
  LCAB: 148; Ma: 1733-
  1734
A Simple Honorable Man CN:
  443; LCAB: 148; Ma:
  1734; Po: 3468
Tacey Cromwell CN: 443;
  Ma: 1734
The Town see also Ohio
  Trilogy CN: 444; Ma:
  1734-1735
The Trees see also Ohio
  Trilogy CN: 444; Ma:
  1735
The Waters of Kronos CN:
  444; Po: 3468
RICKWOOD, Edgell
General Po: 3468
RICTUS, Jehan
General Po: 3468-3469
RIDEOUT, Ransom
Goin' Home Br: 564
RIDING, Laura
General Po: 3469
RIDLER, Anne
General Br: 564; MDAE:
  433; Po: 3469
The Shadow Factory Br:
  565; Po: 3469
Trial of Thomas Cranmer
  Po: 3469-3470
RIDRUEJO, Dionisio
Poesía en armas Po: 3470
Primer libro de amor Po:
  3470
RIEHL, Wilhelm Heinrich
"Der Stadtpfeifer" Wa: 651
"Der stumme Ratsherr" Wa:
  651
RIGGS, Lynn
General Lon: 63
The Cream in the Well Br:
  565
Green Grow the Lilacs
  ADC: 323-324; Br: 565
Russet Mantle Br: 565

RILEY, Clayton
Gilbeau ADC: 324; MBA: 170-
  171
RILEY, James Whitcomb
General ALL: 232-233; LCAB:
  148
"Lincoln--The Boy" LCAB:
  148
RILKE, Rainer Maria
General LCAB: 148; Po:
  3470-3482
"The Angel of the Meridian"
  Po: 3482
"Archaic Torso of Apollo" Po:
  3483
"Aus der Kinderzeit" Po:
  3486
"Der aussätzige König" Po:
  3486
"The Beggar and the Proud
  Maiden" Wa: 652
"Birth of Venus" ["Geburt der
  Venus"] Po: 3490
Das Buch der Bilder Po:
  3486-3487
Duineser Elegien Po: 3487-
  3489
Les Fenêtres Po: 3489
"Die Fensterrose" Po: 3489-
  3490
"Geburt der Venus" see
  "Birth of Venus"
"Der Geist Ariel" Po: 3490
"Gesang der Frauen an den
  Dichter" Po: 3490
Geschichten vom Lieben Gott
  Po: 3491
"Herbst" Po: 3491
Die Hochzeitsmenuett DC2:
  288
"Die Kathedrale" Po: 3491-
  3492
"Leichen-Wäsche" Po: 3492
"Das Marienleben" Po: 3492
Mir zur Feier Po: 3493
Murillo DC2: 288
Neue Gedichte Po: 3493-3494
The Notebooks of Malte Laurids
  Brigge Fi: 385-386; Ke:
  330; Po: 3483-3485
Ode an Bellman Po: 3495
Ohre Gegenwart DC2: 288
Puppen Po: 3495
"Requiem auf den Tod eines
  Knaben" Po: 3495
"Römische Fontane, Borghese"

Po: 3496
"Sankt Sebastian" Po: 3496
"Der Schaunde" Po: 3496
Sonette an Orpheus Po: 3496-3498
"Spanische Tänzerin" Po: 3498
"Spätherbst in Venedig" Po: 3498
Das Stundenbuch Po: 3498-3499
Das Tagliche Leben DC2: 288
Der Turm Po: 3499
"Die Turnstunde" WaS1: 188
"Das Wappen" Po: 3500
"Zu der Zeichnung, John Keats im Tode darstellend" Po: 3500

RIMANELLI, Giose
General Po: 3500
The Day of the Lion Ke: 250
Original Sin Ke: 250
Una posizione sociale Ke: 250

RIMBAUD, Arthur
General LCAB: 148; Ma: 1737-1738
The Drunken Boat Ma: 1736
The Illuminations Ma: 1736-1737
A Season in Hell Ma: 1738-1739

RINEHART, Mary Roberts
General AN: 213
_____ and Avery HOPWOOD
The Bat ADC: 324

RINSER, Luise
General Po: 3500

RINTELS, David W.
Clarence Darrow ADC: 324

RIORDAN, J.W.
James Joyce's Dubliners ADC: 325

RIOS, Juan
General Br: 565

RISSE, Heinz
General Po: 3501

RISTIC, Marko
Sans Mesure Po: 3501

Ritchie, Anna Cora Mowatt see MOWATT, Anna Cora

RITTENHOUSE, David
General AP: 586

RITTNER, Tadeusz
"The Clock" Wa: 652
"Gold" Wa: 652

RIVAS [Angel el Perez de SAAVED-RA]
El Desengano en un Sueno DC2: 288
Don Alvaro DC2: 288

RIVE, Richard
General BALE: 381

RIVERA, José Eustacio
La vorágine Po: 3501-3502

RIVERA, Tomás
"...and the earth did not part" ASF: 498-499
"His Hand in His Pocket" ASF: 499
"Trapped" ASF: 499

RIVERS, Conrad Kent
General AAPD: 225; BAF: 245; BAW: 632-633

RIVES, Amélie [Princess TROUBET-ZKOY]
"A Brother to Dragons" Wa: 652
"Virginia of Virginia" Wa: 652

RIVERS, Joan, Edgar ROSENBERG, and Lester COLODNY
Fun City ADC: 325

RIVET, Renée
General Po: 3502

RIVIERE, Jacques
General Po: 3502-3503
Aimée Po: 3503

ROA BASTOS, Augusto Antonio
General LCAB: 148
"Borrador de un informe" Wa: 40
"The Carpincho Hunters" WaS1: 188
"The Excavation" WaS1: 188
Hijo de hombre Po: 3503-3504
"Lying in State" WaS1: 188
"Nocturnal Games" WaS1: 189
"Private Audience" WaS1: 189
"Slaughter" WaS1: 189
"To Tell a Story" WaS1: 189

ROACH, Eric
General WIL: 143-144
Belle Fanto WIL: 144

ROBB, John S.
General ASF: 499

ROBBE-GRILLET, Alain
General LCAB: 149; Po: 3504-3515

L'Année dernière à Marienbad
  see Last Year at Marienbad
"Behind the Automatic Door"
  Wa: 652; WaS1: 189
La Belle captive Fi: 147
"A Corridor" Wa: 652; WaS1:
  189
Dans le labyrinthe see In
  the Labyrinth
"The Dressmaker's Dummy"
  Wa: 652; WaS1: 189
"The Escalator" Wa: 652;
  WaS1: 189
The Gum Erasers [Les
  Gommes] Fi: 147-148; Ke:
  146; Po: 3516
L'Immortelle Fi: 148
In the Labyrinth [Dans le
  labyrinthe] Fi: 148;
  Ke: 146-147; Po: 3515-
  3516
Jealousy [La Jalousie] Fi:
  148-149; Ke: 147; LCAB:
  149; Po: 3517-3518
Last Year at Marienbad
  [L'Année dernière à Mari-
  enbad] Fi: 149; Ke:
  147; Po: 3515
La Maison de rendez-vous Fi:
  149
Project for a Revolution in
  New York Fi: 149-150
Un Regicide Fi: 150
"The Replacement" Wa:
  652; WaS1: 189
"Scene" Wa: 652; WaS1:
  189
"The Secret Room" Wa:
  652-653; WaS1: 189
"The Shore" Wa: 653;
  WaS1: 189
Topologie d'une cité fantome
  Fi: 150
The Voyeur [Le Voyeur] Fi:
  150-151; Ke: 147-148;
  Po: 3518-3519
"The Way Back" Wa: 653;
  WaS1: 189
"The Wrong Direction" Wa:
  653; WaS1: 189
ROBERTS, Charles George
  Douglas
  General ECL: 89-92
"The Last Barrier" Wa: 653
"The Moonlight Trail" Wa:
  653

"When Twilight Falls on the
  Stump Lots" WaS1: 189
ROBERTS, Elizabeth Madox
  General AN: 214; ASF: 499;
    LCAB: 149; Ne: 81-82; Po:
    3520-3521; Wo: 166-167
"The Betrothed" Wa: 653
A Buried Treasure AN: 214;
  Ne: 82
Black Is My Truelove's Hair
  AN: 214
"Death at Bearwallow" Wa: 653
The Great Meadow AN: 214;
  Ne: 82; Po: 3521; Wo: 167
"The Haunted Palace" Wa: 653
He Sent Forth a Raven AN:
  214; Ne: 82; Po: 3522
Jingling in the Wind AN: 214
My Heart and My Flesh AN:
  214
"On the Mountainside" Wa:
  653
The Time of Man AN: 214;
  Ne: 82
ROBERTS, Henry
  General ERP: 393
ROBERTS, Kenneth
  General AN: 215; Po: 3522-
    3523
  Lydia Bailey AN: 215
ROBERTS, Walter Adolphe
  General WIL: 144-145
  The Pomegranate WIL: 145
  The Single Star WIL: 145
Robertson, Ethel Florence Lindesay
  see RICHARDSON, Henry
  Handel
Robertson, Henrietta Richardson
  see RICHARDSON, Henry
  Handel
ROBERTSON, Lanie
  Back County Crimes ADC:
    325
ROBERTSON, Thomas William
  General Br: 565; EDT: 264-
    265; MBD: 74
  Caste Br: 565; EDC: 451;
    EDT: 265
  Ours Br: 565
ROBIN, Armand
  General Po: 3523-3524
Robinson, Agnes Mary Frances
  see DUCLAUX, Mary
ROBINSON, David V.
  Promenade, All! ADC: 325
ROBINSON, Edwin Arlington

General ALL: 233-237; Cla: 83-84; ICBAP: 103; LCAB: 149; Ma: 1744-1745; Po: 3525-3536

Amaranth Po: 3537

"Amaryllis" PE: 361; Po: 3537

Avon's Harvest Po: 3537

"Battle After War" ICBAP: 103; PE: 361; Po: 3537

"Ben Jonson Entertains a Man from Stratford" ICBAP: 104

"The Book of Annandale" Ma: 1740

"Captain Craig" ICBAP: 104; Ma: 1740-1741; Po: 3538

"Cassandra" PE: 361

"The Clerks" PE: 361

"Cliff Klingenhagen" PE: 361

"Conrad in Twilight" ICBAP: 104

"Credo" PE: 362; Po: 3538

"The Dark Hills" PE: 362

"Demos" PE: 362

"Dionysus in Doubt" PE: 362

"En Passant" PE: 362; Po: 3538

"Eros Turannos" PE: 362

"The Field of Glory" PE: 362

"Firelight" ICBAP: 104; PE: 362; Po: 3538

"Flammonde" PE: 362; Po: 3538-3539

"For a Dead Lady" Ma: 1741; PE: 362-363; Po: 3539

"The Garden" ICBAP: 104

"The Gift of God" PE: 363

"The Glory of the Nightingales" ICBAP: 104

"The Growth of 'Lorraine'" PE: 363

"Hillcrest" Po: 3539

"The House on the Hill" PE: 363

"How Annandale Went Out" PE: 363

"Isaac and Archibald" PE: 363

"Karma" PE: 363

"King Jasper" ICBAP: 104

"Lost Anchors" ICBAP: 104; PE: 363; Po: 3540

"Luke Havergal" Ma: 1741-1742; PE: 363-364; Po: 3540

"The Man Against the Sky" Ma: 1742-1743; PE: 364; Po: 3540-3541

"The Man Who Died Twice" PE: 364

"The Master" LCAB: 149

Merlin Ma: 1743-1744; Po: 3541

"Miniver Cheevy" PE: 364; Po: 3541

"Mr. Flood's Party" ICBAP: 104; Ma: 1744; PE: 365; Po: 3542

"New England" PE: 365; Po: 3542

"The Night Before" Po: 3542-3543

"An Old Story" PE: 365

"On the Way" PE: 365

"Richard Cory" ICBAP: 104; LCAB: 149; Ma: 1745-1746; PE: 365-366; Po: 3543

"Scattered Lives" ASF: 499

"The Sheaves" PE: 366; Po: 3543

"Sonnet: Oh for a Poet" PE: 366

Talifer LCAB: 149; Po: 3544

"The Tree in Pamela's Garden" ICBAP: 104; PE: 366; Po: 3544-3545

Tristram ALL: 237; ICBAP: 104; Ma: 1746

"Veteran Sirens" ICBAP: 104; PE: 366; Po: 3545

"The Whip" PE: 366

ROBINSON, Frank M.
"The Wreck of the Ship John B" WaS1: 190

ROBINSON, Garrett
Land of Lem MBA: 171

ROBINSON, Lennox
General Br: 565-566; MBD: 74-75; Mi: 271-272; TA: 254

The Big House Br: 566

The Clancy Name Br: 566

Crabbed Youth and Age Br: 566

The Dreamers Br: 566

Harvest Br: 566

The Lost Leader Br: 566
Patriots Br: 566
Portrait Br: 566
The Round Table Br: 566
The Whiteheaded Boy Br:
566
ROBINSON, Michael Massey
General AL: 315-316
ROBINSON, Rose
Eagle in the Air BAF: 246
ROBINSON, Rowland E.
General ASF: 500
ROBLES, Emmanuel
General Po: 3545
Montserrat Br: 566
ROBLETO, Hernan
General Br: 567
ROC, John [David NICHOLSON]
Fire ADC: 326; Br: 567
ROCHE, Guillaume
General Br: 567
Le Voyageur Br: 567
_____ and André OBEY
La Souriante Madame Beudet
Br: 567
ROCHE, Louis [Louis AUPPER-
GARD]
Le Retour de la Sainte DC2:
288
ROCHE, Maurice
Compact Fi: 151
ROCHEFORT, Christiane
Warrior's Rest Ke: 148;
Po: 3545-3546
Rochefoucauld, La see La
ROCHEFOUCAULD LIAN-
COURT, François Alex-
andre Frederic, duc de
ROCHE-GUILHEN
Rare en Tout DC2: 288
Rochester, John Wilmot, 2nd
Earl of see WILMOT,
John, Earl of Rochester
ROD, Edouard
La Course à la mort Ke:
148
La-Haut Ke: 148
La Sacrifiée Ke: 148
Le Silence Ke: 149
La Vie Po: 3546
La Vie privée de Michel
Teissier Ke: 149
RODGERS, Carolyn M.
General AAPD: 226; BAW:
637
RODGERS, Richard and Oscar

HAMMERSTEIN II
Allegro see also HAMMER-
STEIN, Oscar II, and Richard
RODGERS DC1: 182
Oklahoma see also HAMMER-
STEIN, Oscar II, and Richard
RODGERS DC1: 182
South Pacific see also HAM-
MERSTEIN, Oscar II, Joshua
LOGAN and Richard RODGERS
DC1: 182
RODGERS, William Robert
Awake! and Other Wartime
Poems LCAB: 150
RODMAN, Howard
The Explorer DC1: 181
RODO, José Enrique
General Po: 3547-3548
"Ariel" LCAB: 150; Po: 3548
RODRIGUEZ, Claudio
General Po: 3548
Rodríguez Alvarez, Alejandro see
CASONA, Alejandro
RODRIGUEZ DEL PADRON, Juan
Siervo libre de amor Fi: 247
RODRIGUEZ MOÑINO, Antonio
General Po: 3552
ROEPKE, Gabriela
General Br: 567
The White Butterfly [Mariposa
blanca] Br: 567
ROETHKE, Theodore
General ALL: 237-239; ICBAP:
105; LCAB: 150; Ma:
1751-1752, 1754-1755; MP:
84-85; Po: 3552-3558
"The Abyss" ICBAP: 105;
PE: 366; Po: 3559
"The Auction" PE: 366
"The Big Wind" PE: 366
"The Boy and the Bush" PE:
366
"Bring the Day" PE: 366
"Child on Top of a Greenhouse"
PE: 366
"Cuttings (later)" PE: 367
"The Dance" PE: 367
"Death Piece" Po: 3559
"The Decision" PE: 367
"The Donkey" PE: 367
"The Dying Man" PE: 367
"Elegy" PE: 367
"Elegy for Jane" PE: 367
"The Far Field" ICBAP: 105;
Ma: 1747-1748; PE: 367
The Far Field [Collection] Po:

3559
"A Field of Light" PE: 367
"Four for Sir John Davies"
    PE: 367
"Frau Bauman, Frau Schmidt,
    and Frau Schwartze" PE:
    367
"The Gentle" ICBAP: 105;
    PE: 367; Po: 3560
"Give Way, Ye Gates" PE:
    368
"I Knew a Woman" ICBAP:
    105; PE: 368; Po: 3560
"I Need, I Need" PE: 368
"I Waited" PE: 368
"In a Dark Time" ICBAP:
    105; LCAB: 150; PE:
    368; Po: 3560
"In Evening Air" PE: 368
"Infirmity" PE: 368
"Journey to the Interior"
    PE: 368
"The Kitty-Cat Bird" PE:
    368
"The Lamb" PE: 369
"A Light Breather" PE:
    369
"The Long Alley" PE: 369
"The Long Waters" ICBAP:
    105; PE: 369
"The Longing" ICBAP:
    105; PE: 369
"The Lost Son" Ma: 1748-
    1749; PE: 369
"Luke Havergal" ICBAP:
    105
"The Marrow" PE: 369
"Meditation at Oyster River"
    ICBAP: 105; PE: 369;
    Po: 4710
"Meditations of an Old Woman"
    PE: 369
"The Motion" PE: 369
"My Papa's Waltz" ICBAP:
    105; PE: 370
"North American Sequence"
    MP: 85; PE: 370; Po:
    3561
"O Lull Me, Lull Me" PE:
    370
"Once More, the Round"
    PE: 370
"Open House" ICBAP: 106;
    Ma: 1750-1751; PE: 370;
    Po: 3561
"Orchids" PE: 370

"The Partner" PE: 370
"Praise to the End" ICBAP:
    106; Ma: 1752-1754
"The Restored" PE: 370
"The Right Thing" PE: 370
"Root Cellar" PE: 370
"The Rose" ICBAP: 106; PE:
    370
"The Sequel" PE: 370
"The Serpent" PE: 370
"The Shape of Fire" PE: 370-
    371
"Song" PE: 371; Po: 3561
"The Tree, the Bird" PE:
    371
"Unfold! Unfold!" ICBAP:
    106; PE: 371
"The Vigil" PE: 371
"The Visitant" PE: 371
"The Waking" Ma: 1755-1756;
    PE: 371
"A Walk in Late Summer" PE:
    371
"Where Knock Is Open Wide"
    ICBAP: 106; PE: 371; Po:
    3561
"Words for the Wind" Ma:
    1756-1757
"The Wraith" PE: 371
ROGERS, Alex
    General BAP: 172-173; BAW:
    637
_____ and J.A. SHIPP
    Abyssinia BAP: 173
    Bandanna Land BAP: 173
_____, J.A. SHIPP, and Bert
    WILLIAMS
    Mr. Lode of Koal BAP: 173
ROGERS, Elymas Payson
    General AAPD: 75; BAW:
    638
ROGERS, Ira
    General MBA: 171
ROGERS, Joel Augustus
    General BAW: 639
    She Walks in Beauty BAF:
    246
ROGERS, Robert
    Ponteach, or The Savages of
    America ADC: 326
ROGERS, William Allen
    General LCAB: 150
Rohmer, Sax see WARD, Arthur
    Sarsfield
ROJAS, Carlos
    General Po: 3562

ROJAS, Fernando de
La Celestina [Tragicomedia
de Calisto y Melibea]
DC2: 289-293; Fi: 197-
201; Ke: 186-190
ROJAS, Manuel
General LCAB: 150; Po:
3562
Hijo de ladrón Po: 3562-3563
Lanchas en la bahía Po:
3563
ROJAS, Ricardo
Ollantay Po: 3563
ROJAS GONZALEZ, Francisco
General Po: 3563
Rojas y Zorilla see ZORILLA,
Francisco Rojas y
ROKEAH, David
General Po: 3563-3564
ROLDAN, Belisario
El Bronce Br: 567
La Niña a la Moda Br: 567
ROLFE, Frederick [Baron
CORVO]
General Ri2: 423-428; Po:
3564; TA: 255
The Armed Hands Ri2: 427
The Desire and Pursuit of
the Whole ENES2: 208;
LCAB: 150; Po: 3564-
3565; Ri2: 423-424, 426-
427
Don Renato Ri2: 427-428
Don Tarquinio ENES2: 208
Hadrian the Seventh ENES1:
193; ENES2: 208; Po:
3565; Ri2: 423-427
A History of the Borgias
Ri2: 425
In His Own Image Ri2: 427
Nicholas Crabbe ENES2:
208; Ri2: 424, 427
_____ and C.H.C. PIRIE-
GORDON
Hubert's Arthur Ri2: 424,
426
ROLLAND, Romain
General MD: 252-253; Po:
3565-3570
L'Ame enchantée Fi: 151;
Po: 3570
Clérambault Ke: 149
Colas Breugnon Ke: 149
Jean-Christophe Fi: 151-
152; Ke: 149; Ma: 1758-
1759; Po: 3570-3571

Mélusine Po: 3571
ROLLAND DE RENEVILLE, André
General Po: 3571
ROLLE, Richard
The Form of Living Hen: 17-
18
"Jhesu, God Sonn" PE: 371
ROLLERI, William
Night Shift MBA: 171
ROLLINS, Bryant
Danger Song BAF: 247
RØLVAAG, Ole
General AN: 215; Po: 3572
Giants in the Earth AN: 215;
LCAB: 150; Po: 3572-3573
ROMAINS, Jules [Louis FARI-
GOULE]
General Br: 568; MD: 253;
Po: 3573-3574
Amedée et les Messieurs en
Rang Br: 568; MD: 253
L'Armée dans la Ville Br: 568;
MD: 253
The Body's Rapture Ke: 149
Boen Br: 568
Cromedeyre-le-Vieil Br: 568;
MD: 253
The Death of a Nobody [La
Mort de quelqu'un] Ke:
149-150; Po: 3574
The Dictator [Le Dictateur]
Br: 568; MD: 253
Doctor Knock [Knock; ou, Le
Triomphe de la médicine]
Br: 569; MD: 253
Donogoo [Donogoo Tonka; ou,
Les Miracles de la science]
Br: 568; MD: 253
Grâce encore pour la terre!
Br: 568; MD: 253
Les Hommes de bonne volonté
see Men of Good Will
Jean le Maufranc Br: 568;
MD: 253
Jean Musse; ou L'Ecole de
l'hypocrisie Br: 569; MD:
253
Knock... see Doctor Knock
Le Mariage de M. Le Trouhadec
Br: 569; MD: 253
Men of Good Will [Les Hommes
de bonne volonté] Fi: 152;
Ke: 150; Po: 3574
La Mort de quelqu'un see The
Death of a Nobody
The Proud and the Meek Ke:

150
Psyche Ke: 150
Verdun Ke: 150
When the Ship Ke: 150
ROMAN, Lawrence
Under the Yum-Yum Tree
ADC: 326-327
ROMANO, Octavio
"A Rosary for Doña Marina"
ASF: 500
ROMANOV, Panteleymon Serge-
yevich
Three Pairs of Silk Stockings
[Comrade Kislyakov] Ke:
434
ROMERIL, John
Chicago, Chicago MAP: 385
ROMERO, Emilio
"Balseros del Titicaca" Wa:
653
ROMERO, Fernando
"De regreso" Wa: 653
"El nido extraño" Wa: 654
"Santos Tarqui" Wa: 654
ROMERO, José Rubén
General Po: 3575
La vida, inútil de Pito Pérez
LCAB: 150; Po: 3575
ROMERO, Luis
The Current Fi: 247
Letter from the Past [Carta
de ayer] Fi: 247; Po:
3575-3576
La noria Ke: 229; Po: 3575-
3576
The Old Voices Fi: 247
The Others Fi: 247
The Treadmill Fi: 247
ROMERO MURUBE, Joaquín
General Po: 3576
ROOS, Audrey and William
ROOS
Speaking of Murder ADC:
327
ROPER, Moses
General BAW: 641
ROPER, William
The Life of Sir Thomas More
Hen: 54
ROPSHIN, V. [Boris Viktorovich
SAVINSKY]
What Never Happened Ke:
434
Rosa, Joao Guimarães see
GUIMARÃES ROSA, Joao
ROSALES, Luis

General Po: 3576
ROSCOE, Theodore
"Corday and the Seven League
Boots" ASF: 500
"The Wonderful Lamp of Thibaut
Corday" ASF: 500
ROSE, Reginald
This Agony, This Triumph
ADC: 327
The Porcelain Year Br: 569
ROSEGGER, Peter
Erdsegen Fi: 386
ROSEN, Arnold
General LCAB: 151
ROSENBERG, Isaac
General LCAB: 151; Po:
3576-3577; TA: 256
"August 1914" ICBAP: 106
"Break of Day in the Trenches"
ICBAP: 106
"Dead Man's Dump" ICBAP:
106
"Marching" ICBAP: 106
Moses Br: 569
ROSENFELD, Isaac
General ASF: 500; JW: 277;
Po: 3577
An Age of Enormity Po:
3577-3578
"Bazaar of the Senses" SFC:
182; Wa: 654
"The Brigadier" ASF: 500;
Wa: 654
"Coney Island Revisited" ASF:
500
"The Hand That Fed Me" Wa:
654
"King Solomon" Wa: 654
ROSENFELD, Paul
General Po: 3578
ROSENKRANTZ, Palle
The Hermit Ke: 363
ROSINI, Giovanni
Luisa Strozzi Ke: 250
ROSS, Alan
"Radar" PE: 372
ROSS, John M.
General MBA: 172
The Purple Lily BAP: 174
Wanga Doll BAP: 174; MBA:
172
ROSS, Judith
An Almost Perfect Person
ADC: 328
ROSS, Lillian
General LCAB: 151

Ross, Martin see SOMERVILLE,
    Edith Oenone
ROSS, Sinclair
    General Po: 3578
    As for Me and My House
        Po: 3578-3579
    "Circus in Town" Wa: 654
    "Cornet at Night" Wa: 655
    "The Lamp at Noon" Wa:
        655
    "Not by Rain Alone" Wa:
        655
    "The Painted Door" Wa:
        655
ROSS, William Wrightson Eustace
    General Po: 3579
ROSSETTI, Christina Georgina
    General LCAB: 151; Ma:
        1760-1762; VP: 63-64
    "Acme" PE: 372
    "Amor Mundi" PE: 372
    "A Birthday" ICBAP: 106;
        PE: 372; VP: 63
    "The Convent Threshold"
        LCAB: 151
    "Eve" PE: 372
    "Goblin Market" ICBAP:
        106; Ma: 1760; PE: 372
    "Good Friday" PE: 372
    "Heartsease in My Garden
        Bed" PE: 372
    "Rest" PE: 372
    "Restive" PE: 372
    "Sleeping at Last" PE: 372
    "Spring" PE: 372
    "Spring Quiet" PE: 373
    "To My Fior-di-Lisa" PE:
        373
    "A Triad" ICBAP: 106
    "Two Thoughts of Death,
        II" PE: 373
    "Up-Hill" PE: 373
ROSSETTI, Dante Gabriel
    General LCAB: 151; Ma:
        1764-1765; VP: 65-67
    "Ave" PE: 373
    "The Blessed Damozel"
        ICBAP: 106; LCAB:
        151; Ma: 1763; PE: 373;
        VP: 66
    "Body's Beauty" [House of
        Life, Sonnet 78] PE:
        373
    "Bridal Birth" [House of Life,
        Sonnet 2] ICBAP: 107;
        PE: 373

"The Bride's Prelude" ICBAP:
    107
"The Card Dealer" ICBAP:
    107; PE: 373
"Chimes" ICBAP: 107
"The Cloud Confines" PE:
    374
"The Dark Glass" [House of
    Life, Sonnet 34] ICBAP:
    107; PE: 374
"Death's Songsters" [House of
    Life, Sonnet 87] ICBAP:
    107; PE: 374
"For a Venetian Pastoral" PE:
    374
"Heart's Hope" [House of Life,
    Sonnet 5] ICBAP: 107; PE:
    374
The House of Life ICBAP:
    107; Ma: 1763-1764; VP:
    65-67
"Jenny" ICBAP: 107; PE:
    374
"A Last Confession" ICBAP:
    107; PE: 374; VP: 66
"Love Enthroned" [House of
    Life, Sonnet 1] PE: 374
"The Lovers' Walk" [House of
    Life, Sonnet 12] PE: 374
"Mary Magdalene" PE: 374
"Memorial Thresholds" [House
    of Life, Sonnet 81] ICBAP:
    107; PE: 374
"The Monochord" [House of
    Life, Sonnet 79] PE: 375
"My Sister's Sleep" ICBAP:
    107; PE: 375
"Nuptial Sleep" PE: 375
"On Mary's Portrait Which I
    Painted Six Years Ago"
    ICBAP: 107; PE: 375
"The Paris Railway-Station"
    ICBAP: 107
"The Portrait" PE: 375
"Rose Mary" ICBAP: 108
"St. Luke the Painter" ["House
    of Life, Sonnet 74"] ICBAP:
    108; PE: 375-376
"The Sea-Limits" PE: 375
"Silent Noon" [House of Life,
    Sonnet 19] PE: 375
"The Song-Throe" [House of
    Life, Sonnet 61] PE: 375
"A Sonnet Is a Moment's Monu-
    ment" [House of Life Intro-
    ductory Sonnet] PE: 375

"The Stream's Secret" PE:
376
"Transfigured Life" [House
of Life, Sonnet 60] PE:
376
"The Vase of Life" [House of
Life, Sonnet 95] ICBAP:
108; PE: 376
"Willowwood" [House of Life,
Sonnets 49-52] PE: 376;
VP: 66
"Woodspurge" ICBAP: 108;
PE: 376
ROSTAND, Edmond
General Br: 569; MD: 253-
254; Po: 3579
Chantecler Br: 569; EDC:
451-452; Ma: 1766; MD:
254
Cyrano de Bergerac Br:
570; DC2: 293; EDC:
452-453; LCAB: 151;
Ma: 1766-1767; MD: 254;
Po: 3580-3581
The Eaglet [L'Aiglon] Br:
569; EDC: 451; Ma:
1768; MD: 254; Po:
3580
The Faraway Princess [La
Princesse Lointaine] Br:
570; EDC: 453
The Last Night of Don Juan
[La Derniere nuit de Don
Juan] DC2: 293; EDC:
454
The Romantics [Les Roman-
esques] Br: 570; EDC:
454
The Woman of Samaria [La
Samaritaine] EDC: 454
ROSTAND, Maurice
General Po: 3581
ROSTEN, Leo
General LCAB: 151
The Education of H*Y*M*A*N
K*A*P*L*A*N Br: 570
ROSTEN, Norman
Mister Johnson Br: 570
ROTH, Eugen
General Po: 3581
ROTH, Henry
General ASF: 501; JW:
280-281; Po: 3581
"At Times in Flight" ASF:
500-501; Wa: 655
"Broker" ASF: 501; Wa:

655
Call It Sleep CN: 444-445;
JW: 280-281; Ma: 1769;
Po: 3582-3583
"The Dun Dakotas" ASF: 501;
Wa: 655
"Final Dwarf" ASF: 501
"If We Had Bacon" ASF: 501
"Petey and Yotsee and Mario"
ASF: 501
"Somebody Always Grabs the
Purple" ASF: 501
"The Surveyor" ASF: 501
ROTH, Joseph
General Po: 3583-3584
Beichte eines Mörders Po:
3585
Hiob Po: 3585
Die Hundert Tage Fi: 386;
Ke: 330
Der Leviathan Fi: 386
The Radetsky March Ke: 330;
Po: 3585
Der Stumme Prophet Po: 3585-
3586
ROTH, Philip
General ASF: 503-504; CFAE:
315-316; CN: 445; JW:
284-286; Ne: 82; Po:
3586-3588
"The Contest for Aaron Gold"
AFS: 502
"The Conversion of the Jews"
ASF: 502; Wa: 655; WaS1:
190
"Courting Disaster, or Serious
in the Fifties" ASF: 502;
WaS1: 190
"Defender of the Faith" ASF:
502; Wa: 655-656; WaS1:
190
"Eli, the Fanatic" ASF: 502;
Wa: 656; WaS1: 190
"Epstein" ASF: 502; Wa:
656; WaS1: 190
Goodbye, Columbus ASF:
502-503; CFAE: 316; CN:
445-446; JW: 284; Ma:
1770-1771; Po: 3588; Wa:
656; WaS1: 190
The Great American Novel Ma:
1771
"'I Always Want You to Admire
My Fasting'; or Looking at
Kafka" ASF: 503; WaS1:
190

"In Trouble" WaS1: 190
Letting Go CFAE: 315; CN:
446; JW: 285; Ma: 1771-
1772; Po: 3588-3589
"Marriage à la Mode" ASF:
503
My Life as a Man JW: 286
"Novotny's Pain" ASF: 503
"On the Air" ASF: 503
Our Gang Ma: 1772-1773
Portnoy's Complaint JW:
285; Ma: 1773-1774; Po:
3589
"Salad Days" WaS1: 190
"Whacking Off" Po: 3590;
Wa: 656
When She Was Good CN:
446-447; Ma: 1774
"You Can't Tell a Man by the
Song He Sings" ASF:
503
ROTH, Samuel
General Po: 3590
ROTIMI, Olawale
General BALE: 382
The Gods Are Not to Blame
BALE: 382
Ovonramwen Nogbaisi BALE:
382
ROTROU, Jean
Cosroes DC2: 293
Les Deux Sosies DC2: 294
Martyrdom of Adriere DC2:
294
Venceslas DC2: 294
Le Veritable Saint Genest
DC2: 294
ROUD, Gustave
General Po: 3590-3591
ROUSSEAU, Jean Jacques
General LCAB: 152
Confessions LCAB: 152;
Ma: 1775
Emile Fi: 152-153; Ke: 151;
Ma: 1775-1776
The New Héloïse [La Nouvelle
Héloïse] Fi: 153-155;
Ke: 151-153; Ma: 1776-
1777
ROUSSEL, Raymond
General Br: 570; Po: 3591-
3592
ROUSSET, Jean
General Po: 3593
ROUSSIN, André
General MD: 254-255; Po:

3593
ROWCRAFT, Charles
General AL: 318
ROWE, Elizabeth Singer
General EC: 121
ROWE, George Clinton
General AAPD: 76
ROWE, Nicholas
General EC: 122; Li: 278-
279
The Ambitious Stepmother DC1:
182; EDC: 454
The Fair Penitent DC1: 182;
EC: 122; EDC: 454; Li:
279
Jane Shore [The Tragedy of
Jane Shore] DC1: 182;
EC: 122; Li: 279
Lady Jane Gray [The Tragedy
of Lady Jane Grey] DC1:
182; Li: 279
The Royal Convert DC1: 182
Tamerlane DC1: 183; EC:
122; Li: 279; Lon: 59
Ulysses DC1: 183; Li: 279
ROWE, Richard [Peter POSSUM]
General AL: 319-320
ROWLEY, Samuel
General Log: 262-263
When You See Me You Know Me
DC1: 183
ROWLEY, William
General Log: 263-269
All's Lost by Lust DC1: 183
The Birth of Merlin DC1: 183
ROWLEY, William
The Witch of Edmonton see
FORD, John, Thomas DEK-
KER, and William ROWLEY
ROWSE, Alfred Leslie
General Po: 3593
ROWSON, Susanna
Charlotte Temple Ma: 1778
Roxlo, Conrado Nalé see NALE
ROXLO, Conrado
ROY, Gabrielle
General Po: 3593-3594
Alexandre Chenevert, Caissier
Po: 3595
Bonheur d'occasion Po: 3594
Rue Deschambault Po: 3595
"Wilhelm" Wa: 656
ROY, Jesse H. and Geneva C.
TURNER
Bridging a Gap BAP: 174
ROY, Jules

General Po: 3595

ROY, Namba
General WIL: 146
Black Albino WIL: 146

ROYAL, A. Bertrand
General BAF: 248

ROZANOV, Vasilij
General Po: 3595-3596

ROZANOV, Victor
General Br: 571

ROZEWICZ, Tadeusz
General Po: 3596

RUBADIRI, James David
General BALE: 383

RUBIN, Ramón
General Po: 3596

RUBIO, José
Alberto DC2: 294

RUBIO, Rodrigo
General Po: 3596

Rudd, Steele see DAVIS,
Arthur Hoey

RUDKIN, David
General Br: 571; MDAE:
434
Afore Night Came Br: 571;
DC1: 183; MDAE: 434

RUEDA, Lope de
Comedia enfemia DC2: 294-
295
Olives [Las aceitunas] DC2:
295

RUFFNER, Henry
"Judith Bensaddi" ASF: 504

RUGANDA, John
General BALE: 383

RUHENI, Mwangi
The Minister's Daughter
BALE: 383

RUIZ IRIARTE, Víctor
General Po: 3597

Ruiz, José Martínez see
AZORIN

RUKEYSER, Muriel
General JW: 121
"Boy with His Hair Cut
Short" PE: 376
"The Childless Years Alone
Without a House" PE:
376
"Effort at Speech Between
Two People" PE: 376
"They Came to Me and Said,
'There Is a Child'" PE:
376

RULFO, Juan

General LCAB: 152; Po: 3597
"La cuesta de las comadres"
WaS1: 190
En la madrugada Po: 3597
"El llano an llamas" Po: 3598;
WaS1: 191
"Luvina" Wa: 657; WaS1:
191
"The Man" WaS1: 191
"No oyes ladrar los perros"
Wa: 657; WaS1: 191
Pedro Páramo Po: 3598
"Talpa" WaS1: 191

RUNG, Otto
The Bird of Paradise Ke: 363
A Girl in Two Mirrors Ke:
363

RUNYON, Damon
General ASF: 504; Po: 3599

RUSH, Benjamin
General AP: 478-479

RUSH, James
Now a Way of Life ADC: 328

RUSKIN, John
General LCAB: 152; VP: 68-
70
Fors Clavigera Ma: 1779
Modern Painters Ma: 1779-
1780
Praeterita Ma: 1780-1781
The Queen of the Air Ma:
1781
The Seven Lamps of Architec-
ture Ma: 1781-1782
The Stones of Venice Ma:
1782
Time and Tide Ma: 1782
Unto This Last Ma: 1783
"A Walk in Chamouni" ICBAP:
108

RUSS, George B.
General BAF: 248

RUSSELL, Bertrand
General Po: 3599-3600
Portraits from Memory Po:
3600

RUSSELL, Charles M.
General ASF: 505; Po: 3600

RUSSELL, Charlie L.
General BAP: 175; BAW:
644
Five on the Black Hand Side
ADC: 328; BAP: 175;
MBA: 172
Revival BAP: 175

RUSSELL, Eric Frank

General LCAB: 152
RUSSELL, George William [AE]
General Mi: 272-273; Po:
3601-3603; TA: 257-258
The Avatars ENES2: 208
Deidre DC1: 19
The Interpreters ENES2:
208
"Self-Discipline" PE: 376
RUSSELL, John
"The Price of the Head"
SFC: 183; Wa: 657
RUSSO, Luigi
General Po: 3604
RUTEBEUF
Miracle de Théophile DC2:
295
RUTENBORN, Guenther
The Sign of Jonah [Das
Zeichen des Jona] Br:
571
RUTHERFORD, Mark [William
Hale WHITE]
General AN: 260; BN:
87; Du: 167-168; Po: .
4641; TA: 302
The Autobiography of Mark
Rutherford AN: 260;
EN: 128; ENE: 267;
ENES1: 239; ENES2: 258
Catherine Furze AN: 260;
EN: 128; ENES1: 239;
ENES2: 258
Clara Hopgood AN: 260;
EN: 128; ENE: 267;
ENES1: 240; ENES2: 258
"The Love of Woman" Wa:
657
Mark Rutherford's Deliverance
EN: 128-129; ENES1:
240; ENES2: 259
"Michael Trevanion" Wa:
657
Miriam's Schooling ENES1:
240; ENES2: 259; Wa:
657
"Mr. Whitaker's Retirement"
Wa: 657
"A Mysterious Portrait" Wa:
657
The Revolution in Tanner's
Lane EN: 129; ENE:
267; ENES1: 240; ENES2:
259
RUTTER, Joseph
General LJCD: 253-254

RWAKYAKA, Proscovia
General BALE: 384
RYERSON, Florence and Colin
CLEMENTS
Harriet ADC: 328-329
Strange Bedfellows ADC: 329
RYGA, George
General Po: 3604
Ecstasy of Rita Joe Po: 3604
RYMER, Thomas
General Bon: 77
RZEWUSKI, Henryk
"Prince Karol Radziwill" Wa:
657
"A Sermon at the Bar Confeder-
acy" Wa: 657
"Tadeusz Reyten" Wa: 657
"The Zaporog Sich" Wa: 657
RZHREVSKAYA, Elena
Many Years Later Ke: 434

S

S., J.
Andromana DC1: 183
S., W.
Locrine see ANONYMOUS
SAAR, Ferdinand von
"Marianne" Wa: 658
Schloss Kostenitz Fi: 387
"Die Troglodytin" Wa: 658
SAAVEDRA PEREZ, Alberto
General Br: 571
SABA, Umberto
General Po: 3605
Il Canzoniere Po: 3605
SABATIER, Robert
General Po: 3606
SABATO, Ernesto
General Po: 3606
Sobre héroes y tumbas Po:
3606
El túnel Po: 3606-3608
La vieja bandera Po: 3608
SABERHAGEN, Fred
General ASF: 505
"The Face of the Deep" ASF:
505
"Goodlife" WaS1: 191
"In the Temple of Mars" WaS1:
191
"Patron of the Arts" WaS1:
191
"The Peacemaker" WaS1: 191
"Starsong" ASF: 505

SA-CARNEIRO, Mário de
General Po: 3608-3609
SACHAROW, Lawrence
Concept ADC: 329
SACHS, Hans
Alcestis DC2: 295
Der David mit Batseba DC2:
295
Das Hoffgesindt Veneris
DC2: 295
Master Bechnesser Walther
DC2: 295
Tragedia der Richter Simson
DC2: 295
SACHS, Maurice
General Po: 3609
SACHS, Nelly
General Po: 3609-3610
SACKLER, Howard
General MDAE: 435
The Great White Hope ADC:
329; Br: 571; MDAE:
435; Po: 3610-3611
SACKVILLE, Thomas, Earl of
Dorset
General ED: 315-316; SC:
82
"The Complaint of Henry,
Duke of Buckingham"
ICBAP: 108; PE: 376
Gorboduc see NORTON,
Thomas and Thomas
SACKVILLE
SACKVILLE-WEST, Victoria
General Sch: 265
All Passion Spent ENES1:
193
The Challenge ENES1: 193
The Dark Island ENES1:
193
Devil at Westease ENES1:
193
The Dragon in Shallow Waters
ENES1: 193
The Easter Party ENES1:
193
The Edwardians ENES1:
193; Po: 3611
Family History ENES1: 193
Grand Canyon ENES1: 193
Grey Wethers ENES1: 193
Heritage ENES1: 193
No Signposts in the Sea
ENES1: 193
Seducers in Ecuador ENES1:
194

SADE, Marquis de
General LCAB: 152
Juliette Ke: 153
Justine Ke: 153
SADEEK, Sheik M.
General WIL: 146
SADEH, Pinhas
General Po: 3611
SADOVEANU, Mihail
The Hatchet Fi: 465
SAFFIN, John
General AP: 586
SAGAN, Françoise
General Po: 3611-3613
Aimez-vous Brahms? Ke: 153;
Po: 3613
A Certain Smile Ke: 153; Po:
3613-3614
Those Without Shadows Ke:
153
SAHKOOR, Salahudin
Armageddon MBA: 172
SAID, Junus
"Fidgety" Wa: 658
SAINER, Arthur
General MDAE: 436
Saint Augustine see AUGUSTINE,
Saint
Saint-Denys Garneau, Hector de
see GARNEAU, Saint-Denys
Hector de
SAINT-EVREMOND, Charles de
Marquetel de Saint Denis de
General Bon: 78
SAINT-EXUPERY, Antoine de
General LCAB: 153; Po:
3614-3617
La Citadelle Ke: 154; Po:
3616
Flight to Arras [Pilote de
guerre] Fi: 155; Ma:
1784-1785
The Little Prince [Le Petit
Prince] Fi: 155; Ke:
154; Ma: 1785; Po: 3616-
3617
Night Flight [Vol de nuit]
Fi: 155; Ke: 154; Ma:
1785-1786
Southern Mail [Courrier sud]
Fi: 155; Ke: 154; Ma:
1786-1787
Terre des hommes Fi: 155
Wind, Sand and Stars Ke:
154; Ma: 1787-1788
The Wisdom of the Sands Ma:

1788-1789
ST. JOHN, Bruce
General WIL: 147
ST. OMER, Garth
General WIL: 147
J--Black Bam and the Masqueraders WIL: 149
Nor Any Country WIL: 149
A Room on the Hill WIL: 148
Shades of Grey WIL: 148
Syrop WIL: 148
SAINT-PIERRE, Bernardin de
La Chaumière Indienne Fi: 155
Paul and Virginia Fi: 155-156; Ke: 154-155
SAINTE-BEUVE, Charles
General LCAB: 153
Volupté Fi: 155; Ke: 153-154
SAINTSBURY, George Edward Bateman
General Po: 3618; TA: 259
SAINT-SORLIN, Desmarets de
Europe DC2: 295
SAKI [Hector Hugh MUNRO]
General Ma: 1790; Po: 2826-2827; Ri2: 274-281; TA: 230-231
"The Achievement of the Cat" Wa: 658
Beasts and Super-Beasts Po: 2827; Ri2: 280
Chronicles of Clovis Ri2: 276, 278
"Esme" Wa: 658
"Filboid Studge" Wa: 658
"The Forbidden Buzzards" Wa: 658
"The Hounds of Fate" Wa: 658
"The Lumber Room" Wa: 658
"The Mappined Life" Wa: 658
"The Music on the Hill" Wa: 658
"The Occasional Garden" Wa: 658
"The Open Window" Po: 2827-2828
Reginald Ri2: 280
Reginald in Russia Ri2: 280

"The Reticence of Lady Anne" Wa: 658
The Rise of the Russian Empire Ri2: 275
"The Sheep" Wa: 659
"The She-Wolf" Wa: 659
"The Soul of Laploshka" Wa: 659
The Square Egg Ri2: 279
"Sredni Vashtar" Ma: 1790; Wa: 659
"The Stampeding of Lady Bastable" Wa: 659
"The Story of St. Vespaluus" Wa: 659
"Tea" Wa: 659
"Tobermory" Wa: 659
Toys of Peace Ri2: 275
"The Treasure Ship" Wa: 659
The Unbearable Bassington ENES1: 171; Ri2: 274, 279-281
When William Came ENES1: 171; Ri2: 274-275
SALA, George Augustus Henry
General BN: 88
SALAAM, Kalamu ya [Val FERDINAND]
General BAF: 248
Black Liberation Army MBA: 172
Blk Love Song #1 BAP: 176
SALACROU, Armand
General Br: 572; LCAB: 153; MD: 255; Po: 3618-3619
L'Archipel Lenoir... see The Lenoir Archipelago...
Atlas-Hôtel Br: 573; EDC: 454; MD: 255
Boulevard Durand Br: 573; MD: 255
The Bridge of Europe [Pont de l'Europe] Br: 574; EDC: 455; MD: 255
Dieu le Savait Br: 573; MD: 255
Les Fiancés du Havre EDC: 455
A Free Woman [Une Femme libre] Br: 573; EDC: 455; MD: 255
The Frenzied Ones [Les Frénétiques] Br: 573; EDC: 455
Histoire de rire see When the

Music Stops

L'Inconnue d'Arras see The Unknown Women of Arras

The Lenoir Archipelago; or One Must Not Touch Immobile Things [L'Archipel Lenoir; ou Il ne faut pas toucher aux choses immobiles] Br: 572-573; EDC: 455; Po: 3619

A Man Like the Others [Un Homme comme les autres] Br: 573; EDC: 455

La Marguerite Br: 573

Nights of Wrath [Les Nuits de la colère] Br: 574; EDC: 455; MD: 255

Patchouli, ou Les Desordres de l'amour Br: 574; EDC: 455; MD: 255

Pont de l'Europe see The Bridge of Europe

Poof Br: 574

Shore Leave [Tour à terre] EDC: 456

The Unknown Women of Arras [L'Inconnue d'Arras] Br: 574-575; EDC: 456; MD: 255

When the Music Stops [Histoire de rire] Br: 575; EDC: 456; MD: 255

The World Is Round [La Terre est ronde] Br: 575; EDC: 456

SALAS BARBADILLO, Alonso de

The Correction of Vices Fi: 247

The Curious and Wise Alexander Fi: 247

The Daughter of Celestina [La ingeniosa Elena] Fi: 247; Ke: 229

The Discourteous Courtier Fi: 247

Don Diego, Nocturnal Adventurer Fi: 247-248; Ke: 229

Flora, Clever and Too Clever Fi: 248

The Fortunate Fool Fi: 248

The House of Virtuous Pleasure Fi: 248

La ingeniosa Elena see The Daughter of Celestina

The Post Office of the God

Momus Fi: 248

The Proper Gentleman Fi: 248

El sagaz Estancio Ke: 229

SALAZAR BONDY, Sebastian

General Br: 575

"Volver al pasado" Wa: 659

SALES, Sir William

Theophania ERP: 397-398

SALIM [Harrell Cordell CHAUNCEY]

General MBA: 173

We Heard from Martin MBA: 173

SALIMU [Netti McGRAY]

General MBA: 173

Growin' Into Blackness MBA: 173

SALINAS, Pedro

General LCAB: 153; Po: 3619-3620

"The Breakfast" Wa: 659

El chantajista Po: 3620

El contemplado Po: 3621

"The Neophyte Author" Wa: 659

"No te veo" Po: 3621

Presagios Po: 3621

Todo mas claro Po: 3621

La voz a ti debida Po: 3621-3622

SALINGER, Jerome David

General AN: 216; ASF: 509-512; CFAE: 317-327; CN: 447-448; JW: 288; LCAB: 153; Ne: 83-85; Po: 3622-3639

"Blue Melody" ASF: 505; Wa: 659

"Both Parties Concerned" Wa: 660

"A Boy in France" Wa: 660

The Catcher in the Rye AN: 215-216; CFAE: 318-326; CN: 448-458; JW: 287-288; LCAB: 153; Ma: 1791-1792; Ne: 83-85; Po: 3622, 3626, 3629-3630, 3634, 3639-3652

"De Daumier-Smith's Blue Period" ASF: 505; Ma: 1792-1793; Wa: 660; WaS1: 191

"Down at the Dinghy" ASF: 505; Wa: 660; WaS1: 191

"Elaine" ASF: 505; Wa: 660

"For Esmé--with Love and

Squalor" ASF: 505-506;
Ma: 1793-1794; Po: 3622,
3652-3653; Wa: 660-661;
WaS1: 192

"Franny" ASF: 506; Ma:
1794-1796; Ne: 85; Wa:
661-663; WaS1: 192

Franny and Zooey CFAE:
324-326; LCAB: 154; Po:
3653-3655

"A Girl I Knew" ASF: 506;
Wa: 663

"Go See Eddie" ASF: 506;
Po: 3655; Wa: 663

"The Hang of It" Wa: 663

"Hapworth 16, 1924" ASF:
506; Po: 3623-3624; Wa:
663

"The Heart of a Broken
Story" Wa: 663

"I'm Crazy" ASF: 506; Wa:
663

"The Inverted Forest" ASF:
506; Wa: 663

"Just Before the War with
the Eskimos" ASF: 506;
Po: 3625; Wa: 663;
WaS1: 192

"The Last Day of the Last
Furlough" ASF: 506;
Wa: 663

"The Laughing Man" ASF:
506; Wa: 663-664; WaS1:
192

"The Long Debut of Lois Tag-
gett" ASF: 507; Wa:
664

Nine Stories CFAE: 321;
Po: 3655

"Once a Week Won't Kill You"
Wa: 664

"A Perfect Day for Banana-
fish" ASF: 507; Ma:
1796-1797; Po: 3655; Wa:
664-665; WaS1: 192

"Personal Notes of an Infantry-
man" Wa: 665

"Pretty Mouth and Green My
Eyes" ASF: 507; Po:
3655-3656; Wa: 665; WaS1:
192

"Raise High the Roofbeam,
Carpenters" ASF: 507;
CFAE: 325; LCAB: 153;
Ma: 1797; Po: 3656;
Wa: 665

"Seymour: An Introduciton"
ASF: 507-508; CFAE: 325;
LCAB: 153; Ma: 1798; Po:
3627-3628, 3656-3657; Wa:
665-666

"Slight Rebellion Off Madison"
ASF: 508; Wa: 666

"The Stranger" Wa: 666

"Teddy" ASF: 508; Po:
3657; Wa: 666; WaS1: 192

"This Sandwich Has No Mayon-
naise" ASF: 508; Wa: 666

"Uncle Wiggily in Connecticut"
ASF: 508; Po: 3658; Wa:
666-667; WaS1: 192

"The Varioni Brothers" ASF:
508; Wa: 667

"The Young Folks" ASF: 508;
Wa: 667

"A Young Girl in 1941 with No
Waist at All" ASF: 508; Wa:
667

"Zooey" ASF: 509; Ma:
1798-1800; Ne: 85; Wa:
667-668; WaS1: 192

SALIŅS, Gunars
General Po: 3658

SALKEY, Andrew
General WIL: 149-151
The Adventures of Catullus
Kelly WIL: 153
"Anancy" Wa: 668
"Anancy's Score" WIL: 154
Drought WIL: 152
Earthquake WIL: 152
Escape to an Autumn Pavement
WIL: 151
Georgetown Journal WIL: 154
Havana Journal WIL: 153-154
Hurricane WIL: 152
Jamaica WIL: 154
Joey Tyson WIL: 154
Jonah Simpson WIL: 153
The Late Emancipation of Jerry
Stover WIL: 152-153
A Quality of Violence WIL: 151
Riot WIL: 152

SALMON, André
General Po: 3658-3659

SALTYKOV-SHCHEDRIN, Mikhail
The Golovlyovs Fi: 465; Ke:
434-435
The History of a Town Fi:
465
Monrepos the Refuge Ke: 435

SALTUS, Edgar

General ASF: 513; AN:
216
SALUTIN, Rick
General JW: 431
SALVADOR, Tomás
General Po: 3659
Los atracadores Ke: 229
Cabo de vara Ke: 229
Cuerda de presos Ke: 229
Diálogos en la oscuridad Ke:
229
Division 250 Ke: 229
El haragan Ke: 229
Historias de Valcanillo Ke:
229
SAMAIN, Albert
Polypheme DC2: 296
SAMKANGE, Stanlake J.T.
General BALE: 384
SAMONA, Carmelo
Brothers Fi: 275
SAMPSON, William
General LJCD: 254
The Vow Breaker; or The
Fair Maiden of Clifton
DC1: 184
SAMUELS, Lesser and Frank
LOESSER
Greenwillow ADC: 330
SANCHEZ, Florencio
General Br: 575-576; Po:
3659- 3660
Barranca abajo see Down
Hill
Canillita Br: 576
Los Curdas Br: 576
Los derechos de la salud Br:
576
El desalojo Br: 576
Down Hill [Barranca abajo]
Br: 576
En familia Br: 576
The Immigrant's Daughter
[La gringa] Br: 576-577;
DC2: 296; Po: 3659
Mano Santa Br: 577
Marta Gruni Br: 577
Moneda Falsa Br: 577
Los muertos Br: 577
My Son the Doctor [M' hijo
el dotor] Br: 577; DC2:
296
Nuestros hijos Br: 577
El pasado de una vida Br:
577
La pobre gente Br: 577

La tigra Br: 577
SANCHEZ, Luis Alberto
El Perú... Po: 3660
SANCHEZ, Sonia [Laila MANNAN]
General AAL: 244; AAPD:
228, 403; BAP: 176-177;
BAW: 647; MBA: 173
The Bronx Is Next BAP: 177;
MBA: 173
Sister Son/ji ADC: 330; BAP:
177; MBA: 173-174
Uh Huh, but How Do It Free
Us BAP: 177
SANCHEZ DIAZ, Ramón
General Po: 3660
SANCHEZ FERLOSIO, Rafael
Alfanhuí Fi: 248; Po: 3660
SANCHO, Ignatius ["AFRICANUS"]
General BALE: 385
SAND, George [Armandine Aurore
Lucile DUPIN]
The Actress and the Nun Ke:
155
Les Beaux Messieurs de Bois-
Doré Ke: 155
Consuelo Fi: 156; Ke: 155;
LCAB: 154; Ma: 1801
La Danielle Fi: 156
Elle et lui Ke: 155
Indiana Fi: 156; Ke: 155; Ma:
1801
Jacques Fi: 156; Ke: 155
Lélia Fi: 156-157; Ke: 155-
156
Lucrezia Floriani Ke: 156
"Mattea" Wa: 668
Mauprat Fi: 157
"Melchior" Wa: 668
"Métella" Wa: 668
La Petite Fadette Ke: 156
Story of My Life Fi: 157
Valentine Ke: 156
SANDBURG, Carl
General ALL: 239-241; LCAB:
154; Po: 3660-3663
Abraham Lincoln Ma: 1802
"Broken-Face Gargoyles" PE:
376
"Caboose Thoughts" PE: 377
"Chicago" PE: 377
Chicago Poems Ma: 1802; Po:
3663-3664
"Cool Tombs" PE: 377
"Early Lynching" PE: 377
"A Fence" ICBAP: 108; PE:
377; Po: 3664

"Fog" PE: 377
"Lost" PE: 377
"Nocturne in a Deserted
   Brickyard" PE: 377
"Number Man" PE: 377
"On a Flimmering Flume You
   Shall Ride" PE: 377
The People, Yes Ma: 1803;
   Po: 3664
"Plaster" Po: 3664
Remembrance Rock Ma: 1803
Smoke and Steel LCAB: 154
"To the Ghost of John Milton"
   PE: 377
"Wind Song" PE: 377
SANDERS, Thomas E.
   "Legacy" PE: 377
SANDERSON, Robert
   General Hen: 34
Sandison, Janet see DUNCAN,
   Jane
Sandor, Malena see JAMES DE
   TERZA, Maria Elena
SANDOZ, Mari
   General Po: 3665-3666
   Cheyenne Autumn Po: 3666
SANDYS, George
   General Da: 56; LJCD:
   254
SANGSTER, Charles
   General ECL: 190
SANJUAN, José María
   General Po: 3666
Sankar see MUKHERJI, Shankar
SANKEY, Tom
   The Golden Screw ADC:
   330
SAN PEDRO, Diego de
   Arnalte and Lucenda see
   also CLERC, John [trans-
   lator]; DESAINLIENS,
   Claude [translator] Fi:
   248
   Carcel de amor Fi: 248; Ke:
   229-230
   Tractado de amores Ke: 230
SANSBURYE, John
   General NI: 338
SAN SECONDO, Rosso di
   The Desired Guest [L'Ospite
   desiderato] Br: 578
SANSOM, William
   General CFAE: 330; CN:
   458; Po: 3667; Sch:
   265-266
   "Among the Dahlias" Wa:

668
A Bed of Roses ENES2: 209
The Body CN: 458; ENES2:
   209
"Building Alive" Wa: 668
"Caffs, Pools, and Bikes" Wa:
   669
The Cautious Heart ENES2:
   209
"A Change of Office" Wa: 669
"The Cliff" SFC: 183; Wa:
   669
"A Country Walk" Wa: 669
"Difficulty with a Bouquet" Wa:
   669
"Episode at Gastein" Wa: 669
The Face of Innocence ENES2:
   209
"Fireman Flower" Wa: 669
"The Forbidden Lighthouse"
   Wa: 669
"Friends" Wa: 669
"From the Water Junction" Wa:
   669
"The Girl on the Bus" Wa:
   669
Goodbye ENES2: 209
Hans Feet in Love ENES2: 209
"Hot and Cold" Wa: 669
"How Claeys Died" SFC: 183;
   Wa: 669
"Journey into Smoke" Wa: 669
The Last Hours of Sandra Lee
   ENES2: 209
"A Last Word" Wa: 669
"Life, Death" Wa: 669
"The Long Sheet" Wa: 669
The Loving Eye ENES2: 209
"A Mixed Bag" Wa: 669
"Murder" Wa: 670
"Old Man Alone" Wa: 670
"On Stony Ground" Wa: 670
"Outburst" Wa: 670
"The Peach-House Potting-Shed"
   Wa: 670
"A Smell of Fear" Wa: 670
"Something Terrible, Something
   Lovely" Wa: 670
"Three Dogs in Sienna" Wa:
   670
"Time and Place" Wa: 670
"Time Gents, Please" Wa: 670
"Tutti Frutti" Wa: 670
"Various Temptations" Wa:
   670
"The Vertical Ladder" Wa: 670

"A Visit to the Dentist" Wa:
670
"The Wall" Wa: 670
"The Witnesses" Wa: 670
"A Woman Seldom Found" Wa:
670
"The World of Glass" Wa:
671
A Young Wife's Tale ENES2:
209
SANTAYANA, George
General AN: 217; APC:
76-77; Cla: 118-119;
LCAB: 154; Po: 3667-
3680
"I Sought on Earth a Garden
of Delight" PE: 377
The Last Puritan AN: 216-
217; Po: 3680-3681
The Life of Reason Po: 3681
Lucifer; or The Heavenly
Truce DC1: 184; Po:
3681
Metanoia Po: 3681
My Host the World Po: 3682
"O World" PE: 377
SANTEE, Ross
General ASF: 513
SANTOS CHOCANO, José
General Po: 3682
SANTOVENIA Y ECHAIDE, Eme-
terio Santiago
General Po: 3682
SAPORTA, Marc
Composition No I Fi: 157
SAPPHO
General Ma: 1804-1805
SARAH, Roberto [Andres
TERBAY]
General Br: 578
Some Day Br: 578
SARDOU, Victorien
Delia Harding Br: 578
Divorçons Br: 578
Fédora Br: 578
Gismonda Br: 578
Theodora DC2: 296; Po:
3682-3683
SARDUY, Severo
General Po: 3683
SARGESON, Frank
General Po: 3683
The Hangover Po: 3683-
3684
"In the Department" Wa:
671

Joy of the Worm Po: 3683-3684
"A Man and His Wife" Wa: 671
A Time for Showing DC1: 184
SARMENT, Jean
General Br: 578; MD: 255
As-Tu Du Coer MD: 256
La Couronne de Carton Br:
579; MD: 256
Facilité Br: 579
Je suis trop grand pour moi
Br: 579; MD: 256
Leopold le bien-aimé MD: 256
Madelon Br: 579
Le Mariage d'Hamlet Br: 579;
MD: 256
Les Plus beaux yeux du monde
MD: 256
Rude Awakening [Le Pêcheur
d'ombres] Br: 579; MD:
256
SARMIENTO, Domingo
General LCAB: 154
SAROYAN, William
General ALL: 241; AN: 217;
ASF: 513; Br: 579-580;
CN: 458-459; LCAB: 154;
Lon: 48-49; MD: 256;
MDAE: 438; Po: 3684-3686;
Wo: 170-171
Across the Board on Tomorrow
Morning ADC: 330-331; Br:
580; MD: 256
The Adventures of Wesley Jack-
son AN: 217; CN: 459
"Antranik of Armenia" Wa:
671
"The Ants" Wa: 671
"Aspirin Is a Member of the
N.R.A." Wa: 671
"At Sundown" Wa: 671
The Beautiful People ADC:
331; Br: 580; DC1: 184
The Cave Dwellers ADC: 331;
Br: 580; MD: 256;
MDAE: 438
"Citizens of the Third Grade"
Wa: 671
"Corduroy Pants" Wa: 671
"The Crusader" Wa: 671
"The Daring Young Man on the
Flying Trapeze" ASF: 513
Don't Go Away Mad Br: 580
"The Fifty-Yard Dash" Wa:
671
Get Away, Old Man ADC:
331; Br: 580; DC1: 184;

MD: 256

Hello, Out There ADC: 331;
Br: 580; DC1: 184; MD:
256

The Human Comedy AN:
217; CN: 459; Ma: 1806;
Wo: 170-171

Jim Dandy ADC: 331; Br:
580; DC1: 184

"The Journey to Hanford"
Wa: 671

The Laughing Matter CN:
459

"Laughing Sam" Wa: 671

"The Living and the Dead"
ASF: 513; SFC: 183;
Wa: 671

The London Comedy, or Sam
the Highest Jumper of
Them All ADC: 331

"Love, Here Is My Hat"
WaS1: 192

Love's Old Sweet Song ADC:
332; Br: 580-581; DC1:
184; MD: 256-257

"My Cousin Dikran, the
Orator" Wa: 672

My Heart's in the Highlands
ADC: 332; Br: 581;
DC1: 185; MD: 257

My Name Is Aram Wo: 170

"O.K., Baby, This Is the
World" Wa: 672

"1, 2, 3, 4, 5, 6, 7, 8"
SFC: 183; Wa: 672

Rock Wagram CN: 459; Wo:
171

Sam Ego's House Br: 581

"Seventy Thousand Assyrians"
ASF: 513; Wa: 672

"Some Day I'll Be a Millionaire Myself" Wa: 672

Subway Circus Br: 581

"The Summer of the Beautiful
White Horse" Wa: 672

Sunset Sonata see The
Time of Your Life

Talking to You ADC: 332;
Br: 581; MD: 257

"The Three Swimmers and
the Grocer from Yale"
Wa: 672

The Time of Your Life ADC:
332-333; Br: 581; DC1:
185; MD: 257; Po: 3686

Tracy's Tiger CN: 459

"Two Days Wasted in Kansas
City" Wa: 672

"With a Hey Nonny, Nonny"
ASF: 513

_____ and Henry CECIL

Settled Out of Court ADC:
333

SARRAUTE, Nathalie

General LCAB: 154-155; Po:
3686-3692

Between Life and Death Fi:
157

Fools Say Fi: 157

The Golden Fruits [Les Fruits
d'or] Fi: 157-158; Ke: 156;
Po: 3692

Martereau Fi: 158; Ke: 156;
Po: 3693

The Planetarium Fi: 158; Ke:
157; Po: 3693

Portrait of a Man Unknown
[Portrait d'un inconnu] Fi:
158; Ke: 157; Po: 3694

Le Silence suivi de le mensonge
Fi: 158

Tropismes Fi: 158-159; Ke:
157

Vous les entendez? Fi: 159

SARRAZIN, Albertine

L'Astragale Fi: 159

La Cavale Fi: 159

Journal de prison Fi: 159

SARTRE, Jean-Paul

General Br: 581-584; LCAB:
155; MD: 257-259; Po:
3694-3734

The Age of Reason Fi: 159;
Ke: 157-158; Po: 3737

Altona see The Condemned of
Altona

Anti-Semite and Jew [Réflex-
ions sur la question juive]
Po: 3755

Bariona Br: 584; Po: 3735

"Baudelaire" Po: 3735-3736

Being and Nothingness [L'Etre
et le néant] Po: 3740-3741

"Black Orpheus" LCAB: 155

"La Chambre" see "The
Room"

Les Chemins de la liberté see
Roads to Freedom

"Childhood of a Leader" Wa:
672

The Chips Are Down [Les
Jeux sont faits] MD: 260;

Po: 3743

The Condemned of Altona
[Altona; The Loser Wins;
Les Séquestrés d'Altona]
Br: 584-586; DC2: 296-
297; EDC: 456-457; Ma:
1807; MD: 261; Po: 3757-
3759

Critique de la Raison Dia-
lectique Po: 3738-3739

Death Without Burial, or Men
Without Shadows see
The Victors

The Devil and the Good Lord
[Le Diable et le Bon Dieu]
see Lucifer and the Lord

Dirty Hands [Red Gloves;
Les Mains sales; Crime
Passionnel] Br: 586-587;
DC2: 297-298; EDC: 458-
459; Ma: 1808-1809; MD:
260

"Erostratus" Wa: 672

L'Etre et le néant see Being
and Nothingness

The Flies [Les Mouches] Br:
587-589; DC2: 298-300;
EDC: 459-460; Ma: 1809-
1810; MD: 260-261; Po:
3747-3748

Huis-clos [In camera] see
No Exit

"Intimacy" SFC: 183; Wa:
672

Les Jeux son faits see The
Chips Are Down

Kean; or Disorder and Genius
[Kean; ou Desordre et
Genie] Br: 589; DC2:
300; EDC: 460; MD: 260

The Loser Wins see The
Condemned of Altona

Lucifer and the Lord [The
Devil and the Good Lord;
Le Diable et le Bon Dieu]
Br: 590-591; DC2: 297;
EDC: 458; Ma: 1808;
MD: 259; Po: 3739

Les Mains sales see Dirty
Hands

"The Making of a Leader"
SFC: 183; Wa: 672

Morts sans sépultures see
The Victors

Les Mouches see The
Flies

Le Mur see The Wall

Nausea [La Nausée] Fi: 159-
161; Ke: 158-160; LCAB:
155; Ma: 1810-1811; Po:
3749-3754

Nekrassov Br: 592; DC2:
301; EDC: 460-461; MD:
261; Po: 3754

No Exit [In camera; Huis-clos]
Br: 592-594; DC2: 301-302;
EDC: 461-462; LCAB: 155;
Ma: 1811-1812; MD: 259-
260; MDAE: 58, 106; Po:
3742-3743; TMAP: 33

Paths of Liberty see Roads
to Freedom

Qu'est-ce que la littérature?
Po: 3755

Red Gloves see Dirty Hands

The Reprieve Fi: 161; Ke:
160

The Respectful Prostitute [La
Putain respectueuse] Br:
594-595; DC2: 302; EDC:
462; Ma: 1812; MD: 261;
Po: 3755

Roads to Freedom [Les Chemins
de la liberté] Fi: 161; Ke:
160; Ma: 1812-1813; Po:
3737

"The Room" ["La Chambre"]
Po: 3736-3737; Wa: 672-673

Saint-Genet Po: 3756

Les Séquestrés d'Altona see
The Condemned of Altona

Situations Po: 3759

"The Transcendance of the Ego"
Po: 3760

Trojan Women [Adaptation of
Euripides' play] DC2: 302;
Po: 3760

Troubled Sleep Br: 595; Ke:
160

The Victors [Death Without
Burial, or Men Without
Shadows; Morts sans sépul-
tures] Br: 591-592; DC2:
300-301, 303; EDC: 462;
MD: 260

The Wall [Le Mur] Po: 3749;
SFC: 183; Wa: 673

SASSOON, Siegfried Loraine
General Po: 3761-3762; TA:
260

"Acceptance" PE: 377

"Counter-Attack" ICBAP: 108

"Died of Wounds" ICBAP: 108

"Everyone Sang" PE: 378

"The Imperfect Lover" PE: 378

"The Kiss" ICBAP: 108

Memoirs of a Fox-Hunting Man ENES1: 194; ENES2: 209

Memoirs of an Infantry Officer ENE: 231; ENES1: 194; ENES2: 209

"The Messenger" PE: 378

Sherston's Progress ENES1: 194; ENES2: 209

SASTRE, Alfonso
General Br: 595; MD: 261; Po: 3762-3764

Anna Kleiber Br: 595

The Condemned Squad [Escuadra hacia la muerte] Br: 595; DC2: 303; MD: 261; Po: 3763, 3765

Death in the Neighborhood Br: 595

Every Man's Bread Br: 595

Pathetic Prologue Br: 596

SASTRI, Sripanda Subrahmanya
"Attar of Roses" Wa: 673

SATCHELL, William
"After His Kind" Wa: 673

"The Babes in the Bush" Wa: 673

"The Black Mirror" Wa: 673

"The Divided Note" Wa: 673

"From a Northern Gumfield" Wa: 673

"The Great Unemployed Scheme" Wa: 674

"The Man Who Went North" Wa: 674

"A Martyr to Circumstantial Evidence" Wa: 674

"The Stiff 'Un" Wa: 674

"Te Kotiro Ma" ["The White Girl"] Wa: 674

"The Yellow Dwarf: A Tale of a Mine" Wa: 674

SATIE, Erik
General Po: 3765

SAUL, Oscar
Medicine Show Br: 596

_____ and Louis LANTZ
The Revolt of the Beavers ADC: 334; Br: 596

SAUMAGNE, Henri
L'Autre Messie Br: 596

Bas-Noyard Br: 596

Madame Marie Br: 596

Terminus Br: 596

SAUNDERS, Frank G.
Balloons in Her Hair MBA: 174

SAUNDERS, James A.
General MDAE: 440

The Italian Girl MDAE: 440

A Scent of Flowers DC1: 185

SAUNDERS, Margaret Marshall
General ECL: 193

SAUVAGEOT, Marcelle
General Po: 3765

SAVAGE, Richard
General EC: 123

Love in a Veil EC: 123

SAVEL'EV, A.
Syn Krest'janskij Ke: 435

SAVERY, Henry [Simon STUKELEY]
General AL: 322

Quintus Servinton AL: 322

SAVOIR, Alfred
General Br: 596

SAVORY, Teo
General Po: 3766

SAVOY, Willard
General BAF: 249

Alien Land BAF: 249-250

SAWYER, Michael
Best Friend ADC: 334

Naomi Court ADC: 334

SAWYER, Ruth
General ASF: 513

SAYAL, Parvin
General BALE: 385

SAYERS, Dorothy Leigh
General Po: 3766; Sch: 266

Busman's Honeymoon ENES2: 209

Clouds of Witness ENES2: 209

The Documents in the Case ENES2: 209

The Five Red Herrings ENES2: 210

Gaudy Night ENES2: 210

Have His Carcase ENES2: 210

The Man Born to Be King Br: 596

Murder Must Advertise ENES1: 194; ENES2: 210

The Nine Tailors ENES2: 210

Strong Poison ENES2: 210
Unnatural Death ENES2: 210
The Unpleasantness at the Bellona Club ENES2: 210
Whose Body? ENES2: 210
The Zeal of Thy House Br: 596
SCARRON, Paul
L'Adultère innocent Ke: 161
Le Chatiment de l'avarice Ke: 161
Les Hypocrites Ke: 161
Jodelet Duelliste DC2: 303
Nouvelles tragicomiques Fi: 161
La Précaution inutile Ke: 161
Le Roman comique Fi: 161-162; Ke: 161
SCHACHNER, Nat
"Sterile Planet" ASF: 514
SCHACK, Hans Egede
Phantasterne Fi: 411; Ke: 363
SCHÄEFER, Jack
General AN: 217; ASF: 514
SCHAFER, Wilhelm
"Anckemann Tristan" Wa: 674
"An der Passhöhe" Wa: 674
"Die Bearnaise" Wa: 674
"Der Brief des Dichters und das Rezept des Landammanns" Wa: 674
"Das fremde Fräulein" Wa: 674
"Im letzte D-Zug-Wagen" Wa: 674
"Die Missgeschickten" Wa: 674
"Der Pflegling" Wa: 674
"The Shepherd Boy" Wa: 674
"Tabu" Wa: 674
SCHALLÜCK, Paul
Engelbert Reineke Fi: 387; Po: 3767
Wenn Man Aufhoren Konnte zu Lugen Fi: 387
SCHAPER, Edzard Hellmuth
General Po: 3767
SCHARY, Dore
Brightower ADC: 334
The Devil's Advocate ADC: 334
The Highest Tree ADC: 334
Sunrise at Campobello ADC: 334-335
_____ and Amos ELON
Herzl ADC: 335
SCHECHNER, Richard
Commune! ADC: 335
Dionysus in 69 ADC: 335
Makbeth ADC: 335
SCHEHADE, Georges
General Br: 597; LCAB: 155; MD: 262; Po: 3767-3768
Chagrin d'amour DC2: 303
L'Emigré de Brisbane Br: 597
The History of Vasco [Vasco; L'Histoire de Vasco] Br: 597; DC2: 303; Po: 3768
Monsieur Bob'le Br: 597; DC2: 303; MD: 262
La Soirée des proverbes Br: 598; DC2: 303
Les Violettes Br: 598; DC2: 304
The Voyage [Le Voyage] Br: 598; DC2: 304; MD: 262
SCHELANDRE, Jean de
Tyr et Sidon DC2: 304
Schelling, F.W.J. see BONAVENTURA [pseud.]
SCHERBERG, Dietrich
Spiel von Frau Jutten DC2: 304
SCHERR, Johannes
Eine Deutsch Geschichte Fi: 387
SCHEVILL, James Erwin
General MDAE: 442
Lovecraft's Follies ADC: 335
SCHICKELE, René
General Br: 598; Po: 3768-3769
SCHILDT, Runar
"Aapo" WaS1: 192
SCHILLER, Johann Christoph Friedrich von
The Bride of Messina [Die Braut von Messina] DC2: 304-305; EDC: 463; Ma: 1814
Don Carlos, Infante of Spain DC2: 305-306; EDC: 463-464; Ma: 1814-1815
Fiesco; or, The Conspiracy of Genoa [Die Verschworung

des Fiesco zu Genua]
DC2: 309-310; EDC: 464

Love and Intrigue [Kabale
und Liebe] DC2: 307-
308; EDC: 464-465; Ma:
1815-1816

The Maid of Orleans [Die
Jungfrau von Orleans]
DC2: 306-307; EDC:
465-466; Ma: 1816

Maria Stuart DC2: 308;
EDC: 466; Ma: 1817

Die Piccolomini DC2: 309

The Robbers [Die Räuber]
DC2: 309; EDC: 466-
467; Ma: 1817-1818

Turandot, Princess of China
EDC: 467

Die Verschworung des Fiesco
zu Genua see Fiesco...

Wallenstein DC2: 310-311;
EDC: 467-468; Ma: 1818-
1819

William Tell [Wilhelm Tell]
DC2: 311; EDC: 468-470;
Ma: 1819-1820

_____ and Wilhelm HEINITZ
Demetrius DC2: 305; EDC:
463

SCHISGAL, Murray
General Br: 598-599; LCAB:
155; MDAE: 444; Po:
3769

All Over Town ADC: 336

An American Millionaire
ADC: 336

Chinese ADC: 336

Dr. Fish ADC: 336

Ducks and Lovers ADC:
336

Fragments ADC: 336

Jimmy Shine ADC: 336

Luv ADC: 336-337; Br:
599; MDAE: 444

Schrecks: An Evening of
Hysteria ADC: 337

The Tiger ADC: 337; Br:
599

The Typists ADC: 337;
Br: 599

SCHLEGEL, Dorothea
Florentin Fi: 387; Ke:
330

SCHLEGEL, Friedrich von
Alarcos DC2: 312

Lucinde Fi: 387

SCHLEGEL, Johann
Hermann DC2: 312

SCHLUMBERGER, Jean
General Po: 3769-3771

Plaisir à Corneille Po: 3771-
3772

Les Yeux de dix-huit ans Po:
3772

SCHLUNCKE, Eric Otto
General MAP: 282; Po: 3772

SCHMITT, Gladys
General Po: 3772

SCHNABEL, Johann Gottfried
Insel Felsenburg Fi: 387

SCHNEIDER, Leonard A.
General Br: 599

SCHNEIDER, Marcel
General Po: 3772-3773

SCHNEIDER, Reinhold
"Las Casas vor Karl V." Wa:
675

SCHNEIDER, Rolf
Journey to Jaroslav Fi: 387

SCHNEOUR, Zalman
"The Girl" WaS1: 192

SCHNITZLER, Arthur
General Br: 599-601; MD:
262-263; Po: 3773-3781

"Aegidius" Po: 3781

Anatol [The Affairs of Anatole]
Br: 601; DC2: 312; EDC:
470; MD: 263; Po: 3781-
3782

Andreas Thameyers Letzter
Brief Fi: 387-388

Das Bacchusfest see The
Festival of Bacchus

Der Blinde Geronimo und Sein
Bruder Fi: 388

Blumen Fi: 388; WaS1: 193

Buch der Sprüche und Beden-
ken Po: 3782

The Call of Life [Der Ruf des
Lebens] Br: 601; EDC:
470; MD: 264

Casanova's Homecoming Ke:
330; Wa: 675

The Comedy of Seduction
[Komödie der Verführung]
EDC: 470; Ke: 331; MD:
263

Countess Mizzi; or, The Family
Reunion [Komtesse Mizzi;
oder, Der Familientag]
EDC: 470

Doktor Gräsler, Badearzt Fi:

388; Po: 3782

The Eccentric One [Die Uberspannte Person] EDC:
471

Der Einsame Weg see The
Lonely Way

Fair Game [Freiwild] Br:
602; EDC: 471

The Fairy Tale [Das Märchen]
Br: 603; EDC: 471

The Festival of Bacchus [Das
Bacchusfest] EDC: 471

Fink and Fliederbusch DC2:
312; EDC: 471; Po: 3783

Flirtation see Light of Love

Flucht in die Finsternis
[Flight into Darkness]
Fi: 388; Po: 3783; Wa:
675

"Frau Beate" Wa: 675

Frau Berta Garlan Fi: 388;
Wa: 675

Die Frau des Richters Fi:
388; Po: 3783

Fräulein Else Fi: 388;
Ke: 330-331; Po: 3783-
3784; Wa: 675; WaS1:
193

Freiwild see Fair Game

"Die Fremde" Wa: 675

Der Gang zum Weiher see
The Walk to the Pond

Die Gefährtin see His Helpmate

The Great Show [Zum Grossen
Wurstel] EDC: 471

The Green Cockatoo [Der
Grüne Kakadu] Br: 602;
DC2: 312; EDC: 471;
MD: 263; Po: 3784-3785

Die Griechische Tänzerin
Fi: 388

Halbzwei see One Thirty

Hands Around [Round Dance;
Reigen; La Ronde] Br:
602; DC2: 313; EDC:
471-472; MD: 264

Die Hirtenflöte Fi: 388; Ke:
331

His Helpmate [Die Gefährtin]
Br: 602; EDC: 472

Hour of Recognition [Stunde
des Erkennens] EDC:
472

Intermezzo [Zwischenspiel]
MD: 264

Jugend in Wien: An Auto-
biographie Po: 3785

Der Junge Medarus see The
Young Medarus

Komödie der Verfuhrung see
The Comedy of Seduction

Komtesse Mizzi... see Countess Mizzi...

The Last Letter of a Litterateur
[Der Letzte Brief eines Lit-
eraten] Fi: 388; WaS1:
193

Last Masks [Die Letzten Masken]
EDC: 472

The Legacy [Das Vermachtnis]
Br: 603; EDC: 472

Leutnant Gustl Fi: 388-389;
Po: 3785-3786; Wa: 675-676

Light of Love [Flirtation; Playing with Love; The Reckoning; Liebelei] Br: 601;
EDC: 472; MD: 263; Po:
3786

Literature [The Literary Sense;
Literatur] Br: 602; EDC:
472

The Lonely Way [Der Einsame
Weg] Br: 603; EDC: 472;
MD: 263

Das Märchen see The Fairy
Tale

The Murderer Fi: 389

New Year's Night [Sylvester-
nacht] EDC: 472

One Thirty [Halbzwei] EDC:
473

Paracelsus EDC: 473; Po:
3786

Pierette's Veil [Der Schleier der
Pierrette] EDC: 473

Playing with Love see Light
of Love

Professor Bernardi Br: 603;
DC2: 312; EDC: 473; MD:
263-264; Po: 3786

The Prophecy Ke: 331

The Reckoning see Light of
Love

Redegonda's Diary [Das Tagebuch der Redegonda] Ke:
331; Po: 3787

The Road to the Open [Der
Weg ins Freie] DC2: 313;
Fi: 389; Ke: 331; Po:
3788

Round Dance [La Ronde; Reig-

en] see Hands Around
Der Ruf des Lebens see
  The Call of Life
Der Schleier der Beatrice
  see The Veil of Beatrice
Der Schleier der Pierrette
  see Pierette's Veil
The Sisters; or, Casanova
  in Spa [Die Schwestern;
  oder, Casanova in Spa]
  EDC: 473
Spiel im Morgengrauen Fi:
  389; Wa: 676
Sterben Fi: 389
Stunde des Erkennens see
  Hour of Recognition
Sylvesternacht see New
  Year's Night
Das Tagebuch der Redegonda
  see Redegonda's Diary
Theresa Ke: 331
Der Tod des Junggesellen
  Po: 3787
Die Toten schweigen Fi:
  389; Wa: 676
The Transformation of Pierrot
  [Die Verwandlungen des
  Pierrot] EDC: 473
Traumnovelle Fi: 389; Po:
  3788; Wa: 676
Die Uberspannte Person see
  The Eccentric One
The Vast Domain see The
  Wide Country
The Veil of Beatrice [Der
  Schleier der Beatrice]
  DC2: 313; MD: 264
Das Vermachtnis see The
  Legacy
Die Verwandlungen des Pier-
  rot see The Transforma-
  tion of Pierrot
The Walk to the Pond [Der
  Gang zum Weiher] EDC:
  473; Fi: 388
Der Weg ins Freie see The
  Road to the Open
"Die Weissagung" Wa: 676
The Wide Country [The Vast
  Domain; Das Weite Land]
  Br: 603; EDC: 474; MD:
  264
The Young Medarus [Der
  Junge Medarus] Br: 602;
  EDC: 474
Der Zug der Schatten Br:

603; DC2: 313
Zum Grossen Wurstel see The
  Great Show
Zwischenspiel see Intermezzo
SCHNURRE, Wolfdietrich
  General Po: 3788-3789
  "Eine Rechnung die nicht Auf-
    geht" Wa: 676
  "Ein Versäumnis" Wa: 676
SCHOENBERG, Arnold
  Expectation [Erwartung] DC2:
    313
SCHOLZ, Wilhelm von
  General Po: 3789
  "Der Kopf im Fenster" Wa:
    676
SCHOOLCRAFT, Henry Rowe
  General ASF: 514
SCHORER, Mark
  "Boy in the Summer Sun" Wa:
    676
  "The Face Within the Face"
    ASF: 514; SFC: 183; Wa:
    677
  Sinclair Lewis: An American
    Life LCAB: 155
  "What We Don't Know Hurts Us"
    ASF: 514; Po: 3789; SFC:
    184; Wa: 677
SCHREINER, Olive Emilie Albertina
  [Ralph IRON]
  General TA: 261
  "The Buddhist Priest's Wife"
    Wa: 677
  "The Dream of the Wild Bees"
    Wa: 677
  From Man to Man ENES2: 210
  The Story of an African Farm
    ENES2: 210
  Trooper Peter Halket ENES2:
    210
  Undine ENES2: 210
SCHREYER, Wolfgang
  General Po: 3789
SCHULBERG, Budd Wilson
  General AN: 218; CN: 459
  The Disenchanted AN: 217-
    218; CN: 460; Po: 3789-
    3790
  What Makes Sammy Run? CN:
    460
SCHULMAN, Arnold
  A Hole in the Head ADC:
    337-338
SCHULZ, Bruno
  General Po: 3790

The Street of Crocodiles Fi:
465-466
SCHUYLER, George Samuel
General AAW: 71; BAF:
250-251; BAW: 649; HR:
133-134; LCAB: 155
Black and Conservative HR:
134
Black No More BAF: 250-
251; HR: 133
SCHWARTZ, Delmore
General ASF: 515; JW:
124; Po: 3790-3792
"America! America!" ASF:
514; SFC: 184; Wa: 677
"A Bitter Farce" SFC: 184;
Wa: 677
"The Child Is the Meaning of
This Life" ASF: 514;
Wa: 677
"Cupid's Chant" ICBAP:
108
"A Dog Named Ego" PE:
378; Po: 3792
"Father and Son" ICBAP:
109
"Genesis: Book One"
ICBAP: 109
"The Heavy Bear Who Goes
with Me" ICBAP: 109;
PE: 378; Po: 3793
"In Dreams Begin Respon-
sibilities" ASF: 514-515;
SFC: 184; Wa: 677
"In the Naked Bed, in
Plato's Cave" ICBAP:
109
"The Masters of the Heart
Touched the Unknown"
ICBAP: 109
"New Year's Eve" ASF:
515; Wa: 677
"Starlight Life Intuition
Pierced the Twelve"
ICBAP: 109
"Successful Love" ASF:
515; Wa: 677
Summer Knowledge Po: 3793
"Tired and Unhappy" PE:
378
Vaudeville for a Princess
Po: 3793
"The World Is a Wedding"
ASF: 515; SFC: 184;
Wa: 677; WaS1: 193
SCHWITTERS, Kurt

General Po: 3793-3794
"Gedicht 25" Po: 3794
"Die Zwiebel" Wa: 678
SCHWOB, Marcel
General Po: 3794-3795
SCOGGIN, John
Scoggin's Jests ERP: 399
SCOT, Sir John
General Ai: 47-48
SCOTT, Alexander [1525?-1584]
General Ai: 41
SCOTT, Alexander [1920-]
General Ai: 319
Cantrips Ai: 319
SCOTT, Dennis
General WIL: 154-155
Seven Jamaican Poets WIL:
155
Uncle Time WIL: 155
SCOTT, Duncan Campbell
General ECL: 95-97; Po:
3795-3796
SCOTT, Evelyn
General AN: 218
"Turnstile" SFC: 184; Wa:
678
"The Winter Alone" PE: 378
SCOTT, Francis Reginald
General Po: 3796
"Last Rites" PE: 378
"Mural" PE: 378
"Surfaces" PE: 378
"Trans Canada" PE: 378
SCOTT, Frederick George
General ECL: 196-197
SCOTT, Jimmie
Money BAP: 177
SCOTT, John
Ride a Black Horse ADC:
338; BAP: 178; MBA: 174
SCOTT, John Dick
General Ai: 308
SCOTT, Johnie
General BAW: 650
SCOTT, Lady John [Alicia Ann
SPOTTISWOODE]
General Ai: 139
SCOTT, Michael [1789-1835]
General Ai: 128
SCOTT, Michael [1175?-1234?]
Certayne Conceyts & Jeasts
see B., W. [translator]
SCOTT, Nathan A.
General BAW: 655-656
SCOTT, Paul
The Day of the Scorpion

ENES2: 211
The Jewel in the Crown
ENES2: 211
The Raj Quartet ENES2:
211
The Towers of Silence
ENES2: 211
SCOTT, Sarah and Lady Bar-
bara MONTAGU
A Description of Millenium
Hall ENES2: 211
SCOTT, Seret
General BAP: 178
SCOTT, Sir Walter
General Ai: 106-111; BN:
90-92; Du: 133-136; Fog:
51-53; LCAB: 156-157;
Re: 222-224
The Abbot ENES1: 194;
ENES2: 211
Anne of Geierstein ENES1:
194
The Antiquary ENES1: 194;
ENES2: 211
The Betrothed ENES1: 195
The Black Dwarf Du: 131;
ENES1: 195
"Breathes There the Man"
[from The Lay of the
Last Minstrel, Canto VI]
PE: 378
"Bridal of Triermain" Re:
224
The Bride of Lammermoor
BN: 92; Du: 131; EN:
110; ENE: 231; ENES1:
195; ENES2: 211; Ma:
1821-1822
Castle Dangerous ENES1:
195
Count Robert of Paris
ENES1: 195; ENES2: 212
"County Guy" PE: 378
The Fair Maid of Perth Du:
131; ENE: 231; ENES1:
195
The Fortunes of Nigel ENE:
232; ENES1: 195-196;
ENES2: 212; Ma: 1822
Guy Mannering Du: 131;
EN: 111; ENES1: 196;
ENES2: 212; Ma: 1822-
1823
The Heart of Mid-Lothian
BN: 92; Du: 131-132;
EN: 111; ENE: 232;

ENES1: 196; ENES2: 212;
Fog: 52; Ma: 1823-1824
"The Highland Widow" Wa: 678
Ivanhoe BN: 93; Du: 132;
EN: 111; ENE: 232; ENES1:
196; ENES2: 212; Ma: 1824-
1825
Kenilworth ENES1: 197; Ma:
1825
"The Lady of the Lake" Re:
224
A Legend of Montrose Du:
132; ENES1: 197
The Monastery Du: 132;
ENES1: 197; ENES2: 212
Old Mortality BN: 93; Du:
132; EN: 111; ENES1: 197;
ENES2: 212; LCAB: 156
Peveril of the Peak ENES1:
197
The Pirate ENES1: 197
"Proud Maisie" PE: 378
Quentin Durward ENES1: 197-
198
Redgauntlet; A Tale of the
Eighteenth Century Ai:
108; BN: 92; Du: 132;
ENE: 232; ENES1: 198;
ENES2: 213; Ma: 1826-1827
Rob Roy BN: 93; Du: 132-
133; ENE: 232-233; ENES1:
198; ENES2: 213; Ma: 1827
St. Ronan's Well BN: 93; Du:
133; ENE: 233; ENES1:
198
The Siege of Malta Ai: 110;
ENES2: 213
The Surgeon's Daughter
ENES1: 198
The Talisman ENES1: 198-199;
ENES2: 213
The Two Drovers ENES1: 199;
ENES2: 213; WaS1: 193
Waverley Ai: 110; BN: 93;
Du: 133; EN: 111; ENES1:
199; ENES2: 213; LCAB:
156; Ma: 1828-1829
Waverley Novels Ai: 107-108;
BN: 90-92; ENE: 233;
ENES1: 199; ENES2: 214;
Fog: 51-53
Woodstock ENES1: 199;
ENES2: 214
SCOTT, Tom
General Ai: 313
The Tree Ai: 313

SCOTT, Winfield Townley
  "Green and Red and Dark-
    ness" PE: 378
  "The U.S. Sailor with the
    Japanese Skull" PE: 379
SCOTT-HERON, Gil
  General BAF: 251
SCOTT-MONCRIEFF, George
  Fotheringhay Po: 3796
SCRIBE, Augustin-Eugène
  Bertrand et Raton DC2: 314
  The Glass of Water; or,
    Causes and Effects [Le
    Verre d'eau; ou Les Effets
    et les causes] DC2: 314;
    EDC: 474
  Marriage for Money [Le
    Mariage d'argent] EDC:
    474
  Slander [La Calomnie] EDC:
    474
  _____ and Ernest LEGOUVE
  Adrienne Lecouvreur DC2:
    313-314; EDC: 474
  A Queen's Gambit; or, A
    Duel of Love [Bataille de
    dames; ou Un Duel en
    amour] DC2: 314; EDC:
    474; MBD: 52
SCRIBLERIANS
  "The Lamentation of Glumdal-
    clitch for the Loss of
    Grildig. A Pastoral"
    PE: 379
SCUDERY, Madeleine de
  Clélie Fi: 162; Ke: 161
  Le Grand Cyrus Fi: 162;
    Ke: 161
  Ibrahim Fi: 162; Ke: 161
  Le Prince deguise Ke: 161
SCULLY, Anthony
  Little Black Sheep ADC:
    338
SCULLY, William Charles
  "Afar in the Desert" WaS1:
    193
  "The Battle of Ezinyoseni"
    WaS1: 193
  "By the Waters of Marah"
    WaS1: 193
  "Chicken Wings" WaS1: 193
  "Ghamba" WaS1: 193
  "The Gratitude of a Savage"
    WaS1: 193
  "The Imishologu" WaS1: 193
  "Noquala's Cattle" WaS1:

194
  "On Picket, an Episode of the
    South African War" WaS1:
    194
  "The Quest of the Copper"
    WaS1: 194
  "Rainmaking" WaS1: 194
  "Ukushwama" WaS1: 194
  "The Vengeance of Dogolwana"
    WaS1: 194
  "The White Hecatomb" WaS1:
    194
  "The Wisdom of the Serpent"
    WaS1: 194
  "The Writing on the Rock"
    WaS1: 194
SEAGER, Allan
  General ASF: 515; CN: 460;
    Po: 3797-3798
  Amos Berry CN: 460
  "The Bang on the Head" ASF:
    515
  "The Conqueror" SFC: 184;
    Wa: 678
  Death of Anger CN: 460
  Equinox CN: 461
  Hilda Manning CN: 461
  The Inheritance CN: 461
  "The Old Man of the Mountain"
    ASF: 515; Wa: 678
  "Pommery 1921" ASF: 515
  "This Town and Salamanca"
    Wa: 678
SEALEY, Clifford
  General WIL: 155
SEALEY, Karl
  General WIL: 155
SEALSFIELD, Charles
  The Cabin Log Ke: 331
  Pflanzerleben und die Farbigen
    Ke: 331
  Der Virey und die Aristokraten,
    oder Mexiko im Jahre 1812
    Fi: 389
SEAMAN, Owen
  General TA: 262
SEAMUS DE BRUCE
  General Br: 604
SEAY, James
  "It All Comes Together Outside
    the Restroom in Hogans-
    ville" PE: 379
SEBREE, Charles
  General BAW: 657; MBA:
    174
  Dry August BAP: 178

Mrs. Patterson BAP: 178-179

SECCHI, Nicolo
Gl'inganni DC2: 314
L'Intresse DC2: 314

SECHE, Alphonse
General Po: 3798

Sédar Senghor, Léopold see
SENGHOR, Léopold Sédar

SEDGWICK, Ann Douglas
General AN: 218

SEDGWICK, Catherine Maria
General AN: 218

SEDLEY, Sir Charles
General Li: 280
"Child and Maiden" PE: 379
"To Phyllis" PE: 379

SEFERIS, George
General Po: 3798-3800

SEFORIM, Mendele Mocher
[Shalom Ya'akov ABRAMO-VITSH]
"In the Days of Tumult"
WaS1: 194
"In the Heavenly and Earthly
Assemblies" WaS1: 194
"The Old Story" ["There Is
No God in Jacob"] WaS1:
194

SEGAL, Yakov Yitzhok
General Po: 3801

SEGALEN, Victor
General Po: 3801
Steles et Peintures Po: 3801

SEGALL, Harry
The Odds on Mrs. Oakley
ADC: 339
Wonderful Journey ADC:
339

SEGHERS, Anna
General Po: 3802
Auf dem Wege zur Ameri-
kanischen Botschaft Ke:
331-332; Wa: 678
"Aufstand der Fischer von
St. Barbara" Wa: 678
"Der Ausflug der toten
Mädchen" Po: 3802-3803
The Decision [Die Ent-
scheidung] Ke: 332; Po:
3803
"The End" WaS1: 194
Post ins Gelobte Land Fi:
389
Revolt of the Fishermen
Ke: 332

Transit Fi: 390; Po: 3803
Trial of Joan of Arc at Rouen,
1431 DC2: 314
Überfahrt Fi: 390

SEGUR, Comtesse de
Les Petites Filles modeles Fi:
162

SEGURA, Juan de
Processo do cartas de amores
Ke: 230

SEIDEL, Ina
Bromsehof Ke: 332
Das Haus zum Monde Ke: 332
Das Labyrinth Ke: 332
Renee and Rainer Ke: 332
Der Weg Ohne Wahl Ke: 332
The Wish Child Ke: 332

SEILER, Conrad
Sweet Land MBA: 175

SEJOUR, Victor [Juan Victor
Séjour MARCON-FERRAND]
General BAP: 180; BAW:
658-659; LCAB: 156
The Brown Overcoat BAP:
180

SEKHON, Sant Singh
"The Whirlwind" Wa: 678

SEKYI, Kobina
The Blinkards BALE: 386

SELBOURNE, David
General MDAE: 445

SELBY, Hubert, Jr.
General ASF: 516; Po: 3803
"And Baby Makes Three" Wa:
679
"Another Day Another Dollar"
ASF: 516
Last Exit to Brooklyn Po:
3804
"The Queen Is Back" ASF:
516
"Tralala" ASF: 516

SELDES, Gilbert
General APC: 42; LCAB: 156

SELLASSIE, Sahle Berhane Mariam
General BALE: 386

SELIMOVIC, Meša
The Dervish and Death Fi:
466

SELORMEY, Francis
General BALE: 386

Seltzer, Chester see MURO,
Amado

SELVINSKY, Ilya
Knight John DC2: 314

SELVON, Samuel

General WIL: 155-157
A Brighter Sun WIL: 157-
158
The Housing Lark WIL:
160-161
I Hear Thunder WIL: 160
An Island Is a World WIL:
158
The Lonely Londoners WIL:
158-159
Moses Ascending WIL: 161-
162
The Plains of Caroni WIL:
161
Those Who Eat the Cascasura
WIL: 161
Turn Again Tiger WIL: 159-
160
Ways of Sunlight WIL: 159
SEMENOV, S.
Natal'ja Tarpova Ke: 435
SEMPILL, Robert
General Ai: 48
SEMPRUN, Jorge
Le Grand voyage Fi: 162
SENANU, K.E.
General BALE: 387
SENARENS, Luis Philip
General LCAB: 156
SENCHENKO, Ivan
His Generation Ke: 435
SENDER, Ramón José
General Po: 3804-3806
Las criaturas saturnianas
Fi: 248
Crónica del alba Fi: 248
En la vida de Ignacio Morel
Po: 3807
Epitalamio del prieto Trinidad
Fi: 248-249
La esfera see The Sphere
El fruitre Po: 3807
El fugitivo Fi: 249
Imán Fi: 249; Ke: 230;
Po: 3808
Los laureles de Anselmo Fi:
249
El lugar del hombre Fi: 249;
Ke: 230; Po: 3808
Mr. Witt Among the Rebels
Fi: 249; Ke: 230
Mosén Millán Fi: 249; Po:
3808
Réquiem por un campesino
español Fi: 249
El rey y la reina Fi: 249

The Sphere [La esfera] Fi:
249; Ke: 230; Po: 3807
El verdugo afable Ke: 230
SENECA, Lucius Annaeus
General Ma: 1830-1831
Agamemnon DC2: 314-315;
EDC: 474
Hercules [Heracles] Furens
DC2: 315-316; EDC: 474-
475
Hercules [Heracles] Oetaeus
DC2: 316; EDC: 475
Hippolytus DC2: 316
Medea [Médée] DC2: 316-317;
EDC: 475
Octavia DC2: 317; EDC: 475
Oedipus DC2: 318; EDC: 475
Phaedra [Phèdre] DC2: 318;
EDC: 475
Phoenissae DC2: 318
Thebais DC2: 318
Thyestes DC2: 318-319; EDC:
475-476
Troades DC2: 319
The Workes see LODGE,
Thomas [translator]
SENGHOR, Léopold Sédar
General Po: 3809-3811
SENNA, Carl
General BAF: 252
SENTONGO, Nuwa
General BALE: 387
SEPAMLA, Sydney Sipho
General BALE: 387
SEPPANEN, Unto
Sun and Storm Ke: 363-364
SERAFIMOVICH, A.S.
City in the Steppe Fi: 466
SERAO, Matilde
La conquista di Roma Fi:
275; Ke: 250
Cuore infermo Fi: 275
Fantasia Fi: 275
Il paese di Cuccagna Fi: 275
Vita e avventure di Riccardo
Joanna Fi: 275; Ke: 250
SERENI, Vittorio
General Po: 3811
SERGE, Victor
General Po: 3811
Birth of Our Power Fi: 162
The Case of Comrade Tulayev
Ke: 435
SERGEYEV-TZENSKY, O.G.
The Oblique Helena Ke: 435
The Sadness of the Fields Ke:

435
SEROTE, Mongane Wally
General BALE: 387
SERUMAGA, Robert
General BALE: 388
The Elephants BALE: 388
Return to the Shadows BALE:
388
SETON, Ernest Thompson
General ECL: 102; Po:
3811-3812
"Lobo, the King of the Cur-
rumpaw" WaS1: 194
SETTLE, Elkanah
General Bon: 45-46; Li:
281-282
The Empress of Morocco Bon:
45-46; Li: 281
The Fairy Queen Li: 281-282
Ibrahim Bon: 46; DC2:
319; Li: 282
Pastor Fido Li: 282
SEWALL, Samuel
General AP: 482-484; Da:
39
Diary Da: 39
Phaenomena Quaedam Apoca-
lyptica AP: 483
SEWARD, Anna
General EC: 123
SEXTON, Anne
General ICBAP: 109; Ma:
1832; MP: 86; Po: 3812-
3813
"The Division of Parts" PE:
379
"For God While Sleeping"
PE: 379
"For My Lover, Returning
to His Wife" PE: 379
"For the Year of the Insane"
PE: 379
"In Celebration of My Uterus"
PE: 379
"Little Girly, My String
Bean, My Lovely Woman"
PE: 379
"The Lost Ingredient" PE:
379
Mercy Street ADC: 339
"The Operation" ICBAP:
109; PE: 379
"Some Foreign Letters" PE:
379
"To a Friend Whose Work Has
Come to Triumph" PE:

379
"The Truth the Dead Know" PE:
380
"With Mercy for the Greedy"
ICBAP: 109
"You, Dr. Martin" PE: 380
SEYMOUR, Alan
General MAP: 389
The First Day of the Year DC1:
185
SEYMOUR, Arthur James
General WIL: 162
The Guiana Book WIL: 162
Selected Poems WIL: 162
SHACKLEFORD, Otis M.
General BAF: 252-253; BAW:
660
SHACKLEFORD, Theodore Henry
General BAW: 660
SHADBOLT, Maurice
"Homecoming" Wa: 679
SHADWELL, Thomas
General Bon: 46; Li: 284-
287
Amorous Bigot Li: 285
Bury Fair DC1: 185
Epsom-Wells DC1: 185; Li:
285
The Lancashire Witches Li:
285
The Miser DC1: 185; Li: 285
The Squire of Alsatia DC1:
185; Li: 285
Sullen Lovers Li: 285-286
Timon of Athens Bon: 46;
DC1: 185; Li: 285-286
A True Widow DC1: 186; Li:
286
The Virtuoso DC1: 186; Li:
286
SHAFFER, Anthony
General MDAE: 446; TMBP:
194-195
Sleuth TMBP: 194-195
SHAFFER, Peter
General Br: 604; MBD: 75;
MD: 264; MDAE: 448;
TMBP: 201-204
The Battle of Shrivings TMBP:
202-204
Black Comedy Br: 604; EDC:
476; TMBP: 171, 202-204
Equus EDC: 476; MBD: 75;
TMBP: 194, 201-205
Five Finger Exercise Br: 604;
DC1: 186; EDC: 476-477;

MD: 264; TMBP: 202-203, 205

The Private Ear and the Public Eye EDC: 477; TMBP: 194, 202-203, 205

The Royal Hunt of the Sun Br: 604; EDC: 477-478; MBD: 75; MD: 264; TMBP: 194-195, 201-205

White Liars EDC: 478; TMBP: 194

White Lies EDC: 478; TMBP: 194, 203, 205

SHAFTESBURY, Anthony Ashley Cooper, 3rd Earl of
General EC: 124-125

SHAIRP, Mordaunt
The Green Bay Tree Br: 605

SHAKESPEARE, William
General LCAB: 157

All's Well That Ends Well DC1: 236-238; Ma: 1833-1834

Antony and Cleopatra DC1: 238-244; Ma: 1834-1835

As You Like It DC1: 244-246; LCAB: 157; Ma: 1835-1837

"But When I Came Alas to Wive" [Twelfth Night] PE: 380

The Comedy of Errors DC1: 246-247; Ma: 1837

Coriolanus DC1: 247-251; Ma: 1838-1839

Cymbeline DC1: 251-253; ED: 211; Ma: 1839

"Doubt Thou the Stars Are Five" [Hamlet, II, ii, 116-119] PE: 380

"Fear No More the Heat o' the Sun" [Cymbeline] PE: 380

Hamlet DC1: 253-279; ED: 297; LCAB: 157-158; Ma: 1839-1841; Po: 55, 522; TMBP: 222, 226

Henry IV Ma: 1844-1845; TMBP: 8

Henry IV, Part I DC1: 279-285; LCAB: 158

Henry IV, Part II DC1: 285-289

Henry V DC1: 289-293; Ma: 1842-1843; TMBP: 148; TSD: 74, 76

Henry VI Ma: 1845-1846

Henry VI, Part I DC1: 293-294

Henry VI, Part II DC1: 294-295

Henry VI, Part III DC1: 295-297

Henry VIII Ma: 1841-1842

Julius Caesar DC1: 298-302; ED: 202, 299; Ma: 1846-1847

King John DC1: 302-303; Ma: 1847-1848

King Lear DC1: 303-317; LCAB: 158; Lon: 38; Ma: 1848-1849; MBD: 38; MDAE: 101; Po: 55, 522; TMAP: 189; TMBP: 154

Love's Labour's Lost DC1: 317-319; Ma: 1849-1850

Macbeth DC1: 319-331; ED: 297; LCAB: 158; Ma: 1850-1852; Po: 522

Measure for Measure DC1: 331-336; Ma: 1852-1854

The Merchant of Venice DC1: 336-341; Ma: 1854-1855

Merry Wives of Windsor DC1: 341-342; Ma: 1855-1856

A Midsummer Night's Dream DC1: 342-345; Ma: 1857-1858

Much Ado About Nothing DC1: 345-348; Ma: 1858-1859

Othello DC1: 348-359; Ma: 1859-1861; Po: 522

Pericles, Prince of Tyre DC1: 359-360; ED: 200-201; Ma: 1861-1862

"The Phoenix and the Turtle" ICBAP: 109; LCAB: 158; Ma: 1862-1863; PE: 380

"The Rape of Lucrece" ICBAP: 109; Ma: 1863-1864

Richard II DC1: 360-363; Ma: 1864-1865; MDAE: 218; Po: 507

Richard III DC1: 363-365; LCAB: 158; Ma: 1865-1866; TMBP: 148

Romeo and Juliet DC1: 366-370; Ma: 1866-1868; Po: 55, 1524; TMBP: 49-50; TSD: 46

Sonnets--General ICBAP: 109;

Ma: 1868-1870

Sonnet 1, "From Fairest Creatures We Desire Increase" PE: 381

Sonnet 2, "When Forty Winters Shall Besiege Thy Brow" PE: 381

Sonnet 3, "Look in Thy Glass, and Tell the Face Thou Viewest" PE: 381

Sonnet 5, "Those Hours, That with Gentle Work Did Frame" PE: 381

Sonnet 7, "Lo, in the Orient When the Gracious Light" PE: 381

Sonnet 8, "Music to Hear, Why Hear'st Thou Music Sadly?" PE: 381

Sonnet 12, "When I Do Count the Clock That Tells the Time" ICBAP: 109; PE: 381

Sonnet 15, "When I Consider Everything That Grows" PE: 381

Sonnet 16, "But Wherefore Do Not You a Mightier Way" PE: 381

Sonnet 18, "Shall I Compare Thee to a Summer's Day?" PE: 381

Sonnet 19, "Devouring Time, Blunt Thou the Lion's Paws" ICBAP: 110; PE: 381

Sonnet 20, "A Woman's Face with Nature's Own Hand Painted" PE: 381

Sonnet 29, "When in Disgrace with Fortune and Men's Eyes" ICBAP: 110; PE: 382

Sonnet 30, "When to the Sessions of Sweet Silent Thought" ICBAP: 110; PE: 382

Sonnet 31, "Thy Bosom Is Endeared with All Hearts" PE: 382

Sonnet 33, "Full Many a Glorious Morning Have I Seen" ICBAP: 110; PE: 382

Sonnet 34, "Why Didst Thou Promise Such a Beauteous Day" ICBAP: 110; PE: 382

Sonnet 35, "No More Be Grieved at That Which Thou Hast Done" PE: 382

Sonnet 36, "Let Me Confess That We Two Must Be Twain" PE: 383

Sonnet 46, "Mine Eye and Heart Are at a Mortal War" PE: 383

Sonnet 49, "Against That Time, If Ever That Time Come" ICBAP: 110

Sonnet 51, "Thus Can My Love Excuse the Slow Offence" PE: 383

Sonnet 54, "Oh, How Much More Doth Beauty Beauteous Seem" PE: 383

Sonnet 55, "Not Marble, nor the Gilded Monuments" PE: 383

Sonnet 60, "Like as the Waves Make Towards the Pebbled Shore" ICBAP: 110; PE: 383

Sonnet 61, "Is It Thy Will Thy Image Should Keep Open" PE: 383

Sonnet 64, "When I Have Seen by Time's Fell Hand Defaced" ICBAP: 110; PE: 383

Sonnet 65, "Since Brass, nor Stone, nor Earth, nor Boundless Sea" PE: 383

Sonnet 66, "Tir'd with All These, for Restful Death I Cry" ICBAP: 110; PE: 383

Sonnet 71, "No Longer Mourn for Me When I Am Dead" ICBAP: 110; PE: 384

Sonnet 73, "That Time of Year Thou May'st in Me Behold" ICBAP: 110-111; PE: 384

Sonnet 74, "But Be Contented When That Fell Arrest" PE: 385

Sonnet 77, "Thy Glass Will Show Thee How Thy Beauties Wear" ICBAP: 111; PE: 385

Sonnet 80, "O, How I Faint When I of You Do Write" ICBAP: 111

Sonnet 81, "Or I Shall Live

Your Epitaph to Make"
PE: 385

Sonnet 83, "I Never Saw That
You Did Painting Need"
PE: 385

Sonnet 86, "Was It the Proud
Full Sail of His Great
Verse" PE: 385

Sonnet 87, "Farewell! Thou
Art Too Dear for My
Possessing" PE: 385

Sonnet 90, "Then Hate Me
When Thou Wilt! If Ever,
Now" PE: 385

Sonnet 92, "But Do Thy
Worst to Steal Thyself
Away" PE: 385

Sonnet 93, "So Shall I Live
Supposing Thou Art True"
PE: 385

Sonnet 94, "They That Have
Pow'r to Hurt and Will Do
None" PE: 385

Sonnet 95, "How Sweet and
Lovely Dost Thou Make
the Shame" PE: 385

Sonnet 97, "How Like a Winter Hath My Absence
Been" ICBAP: 111; PE:
385

Sonnet 100, "Where Art Thou,
Muse, That Thou For-
get'st So Long" PE: 386

Sonnet 101, "O Truant Muse,
What Shall Be Thy Amends"
PE: 386

Sonnet 104, "To Me, Fair
Friend, You Never Can
Be Old" PE: 386

Sonnet 106, "When in the
Chronicle of Wasted Time"
PE: 386

Sonnet 107, "Not Mine Own
Fears, nor the Prophetic
Soul" ICBAP: 111; PE:
386

Sonnet 108, "What's in the
Brain That Ink May Char-
acter" PE: 386

Sonnet 110, "Alas, 'Tis True
I Have Gone Here and
There" PE: 386

Sonnet 113, "Since I Left You,
Mine Eye Is in My Mind"
PE: 386

Sonnet 116, "Let Me Not to

the Marriage of True Minds"
ICBAP: 111; PE: 386-387

Sonnet 120, "That You Were
Once Unkind Befriends Me
Now" PE: 387

Sonnet 121, "Tis Better to Be
Vile Than Vile Esteemed"
PE: 387

Sonnet 122, "Thy Gift, Thy
Tables, Are Within My Brain"
PE: 387

Sonnet 123, "No, Time, Thou
Shalt Not Boast That I Do
Change" PE: 387

Sonnet 124, "If My Dear Love
Were but the Child of State"
ICBAP: 111; PE: 387

Sonnet 125, "Were't Aught to
Me I Bore the Canopy" PE:
387

Sonnet 126, "O Thou, My Lovely Boy, Who in Thy Power"
PE: 387

Sonnet 128, "How Oft When
Thou, My Music Play'st"
ICBAP: 111; PE: 387

Sonnet 129, "The Expense of
Spirit in a Waste of Shame"
PE: 387-388

Sonnet 130, "My Mistress' Eyes
Are Nothing Like the Sun"
ICBAP: 111; PE: 388

Sonnet 131, "Thou Art as
Tyrranous, So as Thou Art"
PE: 388

Sonnet 132, "Thine Eyes I
Love, and They as Pitying
Me" PE: 388

Sonnet 137, "Thou Blind Fool,
Love, What Dost Thou to
Mine Eyes" PE: 388

Sonnet 138, "When My Love
Swears That She Is Made of
Truth" ICBAP: 111; PE:
388

Sonnet 142, "Love Is My Sin,
and Thy Dear Virtue Hate"
PE: 388

Sonnet 144, "Two Loves I Have
of Comfort and Despair"
PE: 388

Sonnet 145, "Those Lips That
Love's Own Hand Did Make"
PE: 388

Sonnet 146, "Poor Soul, the
Center of My Sinful Earth"

ICBAP: 111; PE: 388-389
Sonnet 147, "My Love Is as
a Fever, Longing Still"
PE: 389
Sonnet 153, "Cupid Laid by
His Brand and Fell Asleep"
PE: 389
Sonnet 154, "The Little Love-
God Lying Once Asleep"
PE: 389
"Take Oh Take Those Lips
Away" [Measure for Meas-
ure] PE: 389
The Taming of a Shrew see
ANONYMOUS
The Taming of the Shrew
DC1: 370-372; Ma: 1870-
1871; TMAP: 23
The Tempest DC1: 372-378;
ED: 211; LCAB: 158;
Ma: 1871-1873
Timon of Athens DC1: 378-
380; LCAB: 158; Ma:
1873-1874
Titus Andronicus DC1:
380-381; ED: 272-273,
290; Ma: 1874-1875
Troilus and Cressida DC1:
381-386; ED: 297; LCAB:
159; Ma: 1875-1876;
MDAE: 418; TMBP: 168
Twelfth Night DC1: 386-
389; LCAB: 159; Ma:
1876-1877
The Two Gentlemen of Verona
DC1: 389-390; Ma: 1878
The Two Noble Kinsmen see
FLETCHER, John and
William SHAKESPEARE and
BEAUMONT, Francis and
John FLETCHER
"Venus and Adonis" ICBAP:
111-112; Ma: 1878-1879
"What Shall He Have That
Kill'd the Deer?" [As You
Like it] PE: 389
"When Daisies Pied and
Violets Blue" [Love's
Labour's Lost] PE: 389
"When Icicles Hang by the
Wall" [Love's Labour's
Lost] PE: 389
"Who Is Sylvia? What Is
She?" [Two Gentlemen of
Verona] PE: 389-390
The Winter's Tale DC1:

390-392; ED: 211; Ma: 1880-
1881
_____ and John FLETCHER
King Henry VIII DC1: 297-
298; ED: 201
SHALLÜCK, Paul
Don Quichotte in Köln Fi:
390
Engelbert Reineke Fi: 390
SHANGE, Ntozake [Paulette WIL-
LIAMS]
General MBA: 175
For Colored Girls Who Have
Considered Suicide/When the
Rainbow Is Enuf ADC: 339;
MBA: 175-177
SHAPCOTT, Thomas W.
General Po: 3813
SHAPIRO, Harvey
General JW: 125
Battle Report JW: 125
SHAPIRO, Karl Jay
General ICBAP: 112; JW:
129; LCAB: 159; Ma: 1882;
Po: 3813-3815
"Adam and Eve" Po: 3815
"Auto Wreck" ICBAP: 112;
PE: 390; Po: 3815
"The Bourgeois Poet" ICBAP:
112; LCAB: 159; Po: 3815
"Christmas Eve: Australia"
PE: 390
"The Dome of Sunday" PE:
390
"Drug Store" PE: 390
"Elegy for a Dead Soldier" Ma:
1882; PE: 390
In Defense of Ignorance Po:
3816
"The Leg" PE: 390
Poems of a Jew Po: 3816
"Poet" PE: 390
"The Progress of Faust" PE:
390
"The Retreat of W.H. Auden"
Po: 3816
A Telescope for the Emperor
DC1: 186
SHAPIRO, Stanley
Engagement Baby ADC: 339
SHAPLI, Omar
A Great Hoss Pistol ADC: 340
SHARKEY, Joe
Rhythms in Light Blue ADC:
340
SHARP, Alan

General Ai: 334
SHARP, Margery
General LCAB: 159; Po:
3817
SHARP, Saundra
The Sistuhs MBA: 178
SHARP, William [Fiona MACLEOD]
General Ai: 163; Po: 3817;
TA: 264
The House of Usna Po: 3817
SHARPE, Charles Kirkpatrick
General Ai: 119
SHARPHAM, Edward
General NI: 338-339
SHAW, David, Lee POCKRISS,
and Anne CROSSWELL
Tovarich ADC: 340
SHAW, G. Tito
He's Got a Jones MBA: 178
SHAW, George Bernard
General Br: 605-623; LCAB:
159-160; MBD: 76-87;
MD: 264-275; Mi: 273-
275; Po: 3817-3880; TA:
266-267
The Admirable Bashville, or
Constancy Rewarded Br:
623; EDC: 478
Androcles and the Lion Br:
623; DC1: 186; EDC:
478; MBD: 78, 83; MD:
275-276; Po: 3880-3881
Annajanska, the Bolshevik
Empress Br: 623-624
The Apple Cart Br: 624;
DC1: 186; EDC: 478-479;
MBD: 81, 85; MD: 276;
Po: 3881
Arms and the Man Br: 625-
626; DC1: 186-187; EDC:
479-480; Ma: 1883; MBD:
84-85; MD: 276; Po: 3882
As Far as Thought Can Reach
Br: 626
Augustus Does His Bit Br:
626; EDC: 480; MD:
276-277
Back to Methuselah Br:
626-627; DC1: 187-188;
EDC: 480-481; Ma: 1883-
1884; MBD: 78-82, 85;
MD: 277; Po: 3882-3884
"The Black Girl in Her
Search for God" Po:
3880; Wa: 679
Buoyant Billions Br: 627-

628; DC1: 188; EDC: 481;
MBD: 81-82; MD: 277; Po:
3884
Caesar and Cleopatra Br:
628-629; DC1: 188; EDC:
481-482; Ma: 1884-1885;
MBD: 76, 78, 81, 84; MD:
277-278; Po: 3884-3886
Candida Br: 629-631; DC1:
188-189; EDC: 482-483; Ma:
1885-1886; MBD: 76-77,
85; MD: 278-279; Po: 3886
Captain Bluntschli Br: 631
Captain Brassbound's Conver-
sion Br: 631; DC1: 189;
EDC: 483-484; MBD: 83;
MD: 279; Po: 3887
Cashel Byron's Profession
ENE: 233; ENES1: 200;
ENES2: 214; Po: 3887
Cymbeline Refinished Br: 632
The Dark Lady of the Sonnets
Br: 632; DC1: 189; EDC:
484; MD: 279
The Devil's Disciple Br: 632-
633; DC1: 189; EDC: 484;
MD: 279-280; Po: 3887-3888
The Doctor's Dilemma Br: 633-
634; DC1: 189; EDC: 484-
485; MBD: 85; MD: 280;
Po: 3888-3889
Everybody's Political What's
What Po: 3889
Fanny's First Play Br: 634;
EDC: 485; MBD: 77; MD:
280; Po: 3889
Far Fetched Fables Br: 634-
635
The Fascinating Foundling Br:
635
Geneva, Another Political Ex-
travaganza Br: 635; DC1:
189; EDC: 485-486; MBD:
84; MD: 280; Po: 3890
Getting Married Br: 635-636;
DC1: 190; EDC: 486; MBD:
78, 84-85; MD: 280-281;
Po: 3890-3891
The Glimpse of Reality Br:
636
Great Catherine Br: 636
Heartbreak House Br: 636-
638; DC1: 190; EDC: 486-
488; Ma: 1886-1887; MBD:
77-87; MD: 281; Po: 3891-
3893

How He Lied to Her Husband
Br: 638; MD: 281; Po:
3894
Immaturity ENES1: 200;
ENES2: 214; Po: 3894
In Good King Charles' Golden
Days Br: 638; DC1:
191; EDC: 488; MD: 281;
Po: 3894
The Inca of Perusalem Br:
638
The Interlude at the Play-
house Br: 638-639; MD:
281; Po: 3894
The Irrational Knot ENE:
233; ENES1: 200; Po:
3895
Jitta's Atonement Br: 639
John Bull's Other Island Br:
639; DC1: 191; EDC:
488; MBD: 81; MD: 282;
Po: 3895-3896
Love Among the Artists
ENE: 234; ENES1: 200;
ENES2: 214; Po: 3896
Major Barbara Br: 639-641;
DC1: 191-192; EDC: 488-
490; LCAB: 160; Ma:
1887-1888; MBD: 76, 78-
81, 83, 85-87; MD: 282;
Po: 3896-3900; TMIP: 17
Man and Superman Br: 641-
643; DC1: 192; EDC:
490-492; Ma: 1888-1889;
MBD: 76, 78-85; MD:
282-283; Po: 3900-3904
The Man of Destiny Br:
644; EDC: 492; MD: 283
The Millionairess Br: 644;
EDC: 492; MD: 283
Misalliance Br: 644-645;
DC1: 193; EDC: 492-493;
MBD: 52, 78-79, 84-85;
MD: 283-284; Po: 3904
Mrs. Warren's Profession
Br: 645-646; DC1: 193;
EDC: 493-494; Ma:
1889-1890; MBD: 77, 79-
80, 82; MD: 284; Po:
3905-3907
The Music Cure Br: 646
My Fair Lady see Pygmalion
O'Flaherty, V.C. Br: 646
On the Rocks Br: 646-
647; DC1: 193; EDC:
494; MBD: 81; MD: 284;

Po: 3907
Over-Ruled Br: 647; EDC:
494; MD: 284
Passion, Poison, and Petrifac-
tion, or The Fatal Gazogene
Br: 647; Po: 3908
The Philanderer Br: 647-648;
DC1: 193; EDC: 494; MD:
284-285; Po: 3908
Plays, Pleasant and Unpleasant
MD: 285
Press Cuttings Br: 648
Pygmalion Br: 648-649; DC1:
193; EDC: 494-496; Ma:
1890-1891; MBD: 78, 83,
85-86; MD: 285; Po: 3908-
3912
Saint Joan Br: 649-652; DC1:
193-194; EDC: 496-498;
LCAB: 160; Ma: 1891-1892;
MBD: 78-80, 82, 84-87; MD:
285-287; Po: 3912-3916
Shakes Versus Shav Br: 652;
MD: 287
The Shewing Up of Blanco Pos-
net Br: 652-653; DC1:
195; EDC: 498; MD: 287
The Simpleton of the Unexpected
Isles Br: 653; DC1: 195;
EDC: 498-499; MBD: 81,
85; MD: 287; Po: 3916-3917
The Six of Calais Br: 654
Three Plays for Puritans MD:
288
Too True to Be Good Br:
654; DC1: 195; EDC: 499;
MBD: 80-81, 85; MD: 288;
Po: 3917
An Unsocial Socialist ENES1:
200; ENES2: 214
Village Wooing Br: 654; EDC:
499
Why She Would Not Br: 654;
MD: 288; Po: 3917-3918
Widowers' Houses Br: 655;
DC1: 195; EDC: 499-500;
MBD: 78, 84; MD: 288; Po:
3918-3919
You Never Can Tell Br: 655-
656; DC1: 195; EDC: 500;
MBD: 78; MD: 288; Po:
3919
Shaw, Henry Wheeler see
BILLINGS, Josh
SHAW, Irwin
General AN: 219; Br: 656;

CFAE: 332; CN: 461;
LCAB: 160; MD: 289;
Po: 3919
"An Act of Faith" Wa: 679
The Assassin ADC: 340;
MD: 289
Bury the Dead ADC: 340;
Br: 656
Children from Their Games
ADC: 341
Choice of Wars ADC: 341
"The Dry Rock" Wa: 679
"The Eighty-Yard Run" SFC:
184; Wa: 679
The Gentle People ADC:
341; Br: 656; DC1: 195;
MD: 289
"The Girls in Their Summer
Dresses" ASF: 517; Po:
3920; SFC: 184; Wa: 679;
WaS1: 195
Lucy Crown CN: 461; Ma:
1893
"Main Currents in American
Thought" Wa: 679
"Mixed Doubles" Wa: 680
"The Passion of Lance Cor-
poral Hawkins" Wa: 680
"Residents of Other Cities"
Wa: 680
Retreat to Pleasure ADC:
341; DC1: 195
"Sailor Off the Bremen"
SFC: 185; Wa: 680
Sons and Soldiers ADC:
341; MD: 289
"Strawberry Ice Cream Soda"
ASF: 517
The Troubled Air CN: 462;
Ma: 1893
Two Weeks in Another Town
CN: 462; Ma: 1893-1894
The Young Lions AN: 218;
CN: 462; Ma: 1894
_____ and Peter VIERTEL
Survivors MD: 289
SHAW, O'Wendell
General BAF: 253; BAW:
662
SHAW, Robert
General CFAE: 333; MDAE:
450
The Man in the Glass Booth
EDC: 500; MDAE: 450;
Po: 3920
SHAW, Samuel

Words Made Visible DC1: 195
SHAWN, Wallace
Our Late Night ADC: 341
SHCHEGLOV, Mark Aleksandrovich
General Po: 3921
SHEA, Steven
Zero Sum ADC: 341
SHECKLEY, Robert
"The Academy" ASF: 517
"The Cruel Equations" Wa:
680
"A Ticket to Tranai" ASF:
517; Wa: 680
SHEEHAN, Patrick Augustine
General Po: 3921
SHELDON, Charles M.
In His Steps AN: 219
SHELDON, Edward
General Lon: 63
The Boss ADC: 342
The Garden of Paradise ADC:
342
The High Road ADC: 342
The Jest ADC: 342
Romance ADC: 342-343
Salvation Nell ADC: 343; Br:
656; DC1: 195-196; Po:
3921
Song of Songs ADC: 343
_____ and Margaret Ayer
BARNES
Dishonored Lady ADC: 343
Jenny ADC: 343
_____ and Sidney HOWARD
Bewitched ADC: 343
_____ and Charles MacARTHUR
Lulu Belle ADC: 343
SHELLEY, Elsa
Foxhole in the Parlor ADC:
344
Pick-Up Girl ADC: 344
With a Silk Thread ADC: 344
SHELLEY, Mary Wollstonecraft
General BN: 94; Du: 138;
LCAB: 160
Frankenstein BN: 94; Du:
137-138; EN: 112; ENE:
234; ENES1: 200-201;
ENES2: 214-216; Ma:
1895-1896
The Last Man BN: 94; EN:
112; ENES1: 201; ENES2:
216
"The Parvenue" Wa: 680
Perkin Warbeck ENES2: 216
Valperga ENES1: 201;

ENES2: 216
SHELLEY, Percy Bysshe
General EDT: 274-281; Fog:
55-59; ICBAP: 112;
LCAB: 160; Ma: 1901-
1902; Re: 156-166
"Adonais" Fog: 59; ICBAP:
112; LCAB: 160; Ma:
1897-1898; PE: 390-391;
Re: 163-165
"Alastor" Fog: 59-60;
ICBAP: 112; PE: 391-
392; Re: 163, 165
"The Boat on the Serchio"
ICBAP: 112
The Cenci DC1: 196; EDT:
274-281; Fog: 60; Ma:
1898; MBD: 80; Re:
159, 164
Charles the First DC1: 196;
EDT: 275-277, 280
"The Cloud" ICBAP: 112;
Ma: 1898-1899; PE: 392
A Defence of Poetry LCAB:
160; Ma: 1899
"Drinking" ICBAP: 112
"Epipsychidion" Fog: 60;
PE: 392; Re: 161, 163
"Fragment Supposed to Be an
Epithalamium of Francis
Ravaillac and Charlotte
Corday" PE: 392
"Ginevra" PE: 392
Hellas EDT: 275, 277, 280-
281; Fog: 60; Re: 160
"Hymn to Intellectual Beauty"
PE: 392; Re: 162
"Hymn to Venus" ICBAP:
113
"Indian Serenade" Fog: 60;
ICBAP: 113; PE: 393
"Invocation to Misery"
ICBAP: 113
"Julian and Maddalo" Fog:
60-61; PE: 393; Re:
162
"Lamia" PE: 393
"Lines: When the Lamp Is
Shattered" Fog: 64;
PE: 393
"Lines Written Among the
Euganean Hills" Fog:
61; ICBAP: 113; PE:
393
"Lines Written in the Bay of
Lerici" ICBAP: 113

"Lines Written on Hearing the
News of the Death of Napo-
leon" ICBAP: 113
"The Mask of Anarchy" ICBAP:
113
"Mont Blanc" Fog: 61;
ICBAP: 113; PE: 394; Re:
162, 165
"Music, When Soft Voices Die"
ICBAP: 113
"Ode to Heaven" PE: 394
"Ode to Liberty" PE: 394
"Ode to the West Wind" Fog:
61; ICBAP: 113; Ma: 1899-
1901; PE: 394-395
Oedipus Tyrannus; or, Swell-
foot the Tyrant EDT: 275-
276; Fog: 61
"On the Medusa of Leonardo da
Vinci on the Florentine Gal-
lery" PE: 395
"Ozymandias" Fog: 61; PE:
395-396
Peter Bell the Third Fog: 61
"Prince Arthanase" PE: 396
Prometheus Unbound DC1:
196-197; EDT: 275-281;
Fog: 61-63; Ma: 1902-1903;
Re: 160-161, 163, 165-166
"Queen Mab" Fog: 63
"The Revolt of Islam" [Laon and
Cythna] Fog: 63; ICBAP:
113
St. Irvyne ENES2: 216
"The Sensitive Plant" Fog:
63; ICBAP: 113; PE: 396;
Re: 159, 165
"Stanzas Written in Dejection:
Near Naples" ICBAP: 113;
PE: 396
"To a Skylark" Fog: 63;
ICBAP: 113; Ma: 1903-
1904; PE: 397
"To Ianthe" PE: 396
"To Jane, the Recollection"
PE: 396
"To Music, When Soft Voices
Die" PE: 396-397
"To Night" PE: 397
"To the Cicada" ICBAP: 114
"The Triumph of Life" Fog:
63-64; ICBAP: 114; LCAB:
161; PE: 397-398; Re:
161-165
"The Two Spirits: An Alle-
gory" PE: 398

"When the Lamp Is Shattered"
Fog: 64; PE: 393
"The Witch of Atlas" Fog:
64; PE: 398; Re: 160,
164
"The World's Great Age Be-
gins Anew" [from Hellas]
PE: 398
Zastrozzi ENES1: 201;
ENES2: 211
SHELTON, Thomas [translator]
Don Quixote by CERVANTES
ERP: 404, 407-408
SHEN TS'UNG-wen
"Hsiao-hsiao" WaS1: 195
"Hui Ming" WaS1: 195
"Living" WaS1: 195
"Quiet" WaS1: 195
SHENSTONE, William
General EC: 125-126; Me:
356-358
"The Schoolmistress" Me:
358
The Snuff-Box Me: 357
SHEPARD, Sam
General MDAE: 452; TMAP:
203-208
Action ADC: 344; TMAP:
208
Angel City ADC: 344;
TMAP: 203-206
Back Bog Beast Bait TMAP:
208
Buried Child TMAP: 206-
209
Chicago ADC: 344; TMAP:
203, 209
Cowboys #2 TMAP: 204
Curse of the Starving Class
TMAP: 209
Florence Nightingale Sings
TMAP: 207
Forensic and the Navigators
ADC: 344; TMAP: 203,
210
4-H Club TMAP: 206
Geography of a Horse Dream-
er ADC: 344-345; TMAP:
210
The Holy Ghostly ADC:
345
Icarus's Mother TMAP: 206,
210
Inacoma TMAP: 210
Killer's Head ADC: 345;
TMAP: 210

Mad Dog Blues ADC: 345;
TMAP: 204, 206-207, 211
Melodrama Play TMAP: 211
Nightwalk TMAP: 211
Oh! Calcutta! TMAP: 211-212
Operation Sidewinder ADC:
345; MDAE: 452; TMAP:
212
Red Cross ADC: 345; TMAP:
207, 212
Savage Love TMAP: 205, 212
Seduced TMAP: 207, 212-213
Suicide in B-Flat ADC: 345;
TMAP: 204, 213
Tongues TMAP: 205
The Tooth of Crime ADC:
345; TMAP: 203-204, 206,
213
True West TMAP: 203
La Turista ADC: 346; MDAE:
452; TMAP: 204, 207, 211
The Unseen Hand ADC: 346;
TMAP: 213
Up to Thursday ADC: 346;
TMAP: 213
_____ and Patti SMITH
Cowboy Mouth ADC: 346;
TMAP: 203, 209
SHEPARD, Thomas
General AP: 486-487; Da:
46
The Parable of the Ten Virgins
AP: 486-487
SHEPHERD, Jean
General ASF: 517
"Hairy Gertz and the Forty-
Seven Crappies" ASF: 517
SHEPP, Archie
General AAPD: 404; BAP:
180-181; BAW: 662
June Bug Graduates Tonight!
ADC: 346; BAP: 181; Br:
656; MBA: 178
SHEPPARD, Samuel
The Loves of Amandus and
Sophronia ERP: 408
SHERIDAN, Richard Brinsley
General EC: 126-127; Li:
288-292
The Camp Li: 288, 290
The Critic; or, A Tragedy Re-
hearsed DC1: 197; EDC:
501; Li: 288, 290; Ma:
1905
The Duenna EDC: 501; Li:
288; Ma: 1905-1906

Pizarro EDC: 501; Li: 291
The Rivals DC1: 197-198;
    EC: 127; EDC: 501-502;
    Li: 288, 291; Ma: 1906-
    1907
The School for Scandal DC1:
    198; EC: 126-127; EDC:
    502-503; Li: 288, 291-
    292; LCAB: 161; Ma:
    1907-1909
The Stranger EDC: 503; Li:
    292
A Trip to Scarborough DC1:
    198
SHERLOCK, Sir Philip M.
    General WIL: 163-164
    Anansi and the Alligator Eggs
    WIL: 164
SHERMAN, Francis Joseph
    General ECL: 200
SHERMAN, Jimmie
    General BAP: 181; BAW:
    662
    A Ballad for Watts MBA:
    178
SHERMAN, Martin
    Cracks ADC: 346
    Passing By ADC: 346
SHERMAN, Stuart Pratt
    General Po: 3921
SHERRIFF, Robert Cedric
    General MDAE: 454; Mi:
    275-276
    Badger's Green EDC: 503
    Home at Seven EDC: 503
    Journey's End Br: 657;
    EDC: 503-504; MD: 289
    Long Sunset EDC: 504;
    MDAE: 454
    Miss Mabel EDC: 504
    Shred of Evidence EDC:
    504
    The White Carnation EDC:
    504; MD: 289
    Windfall EDC: 504
    _____ and Jeanne DECASALIS
    St. Helena EDC: 504
SHERWOOD, Mary Martha
    General BN: 94-95
    The History of Henry Milner
    ENES2: 216
SHERWOOD, Robert Emmet
    General Br: 657-658; LCAB:
    161; Lon: 49-50; MD:
    289-290; MDAE: 455-456;
    Po: 3922-3923

Abe Lincoln in Illinois ADC:
    346-347; Br: 658; DC1:
    198; Ma: 1910; MD: 290
Acropolis ADC: 347; Br:
    658
Idiot's Delight ADC: 347; Br:
    658-659; DC1: 198; MD:
    290
Love Nest ADC: 348
The Petrified Forest ADC:
    348; Br: 659; DC1: 198;
    Ma: 1911; MD: 290; Po:
    3923
The Queen's Husband ADC:
    348; Br: 659; MD: 291
Reunion in Vienna ADC: 348;
    Br: 659-660; Ma: 1911-
    1912; MD: 291
The Road to Rome ADC: 348-
    349; Br: 660; MD: 291;
    Po: 3923
The Rugged Path ADC: 349;
    Br: 660; MD: 291
Small War on Murray Hill ADC:
    349; Br: 660; MD: 291;
    MDAE: 456; Po: 3923
There Shall Be No Night ADC:
    349; Br: 660-661; DC1:
    199; Ma: 1912; MD: 291
This Is New York ADC: 349-
    350; Br: 661; MD: 291
Tovarich ADC: 350; Br: 661
The Virtuous Knight Br: 661
Waterloo Bridge ADC: 350;
    Br: 661; MD: 291
SHERWOOD, Samuel
    "The Church's Flight into the
    Wilderness: An Address on
    the Times" AP: 587
SHESTOV, Lev Isaakovich
    General Po: 3923-3924
SHEVELOVE, Burt
    Too Much Johnson ADC: 350;
    Br: 661
SHEVTSOV, Ivan
    Plant Louse Fi: 466
Shidraka, King see SUDRAKA,
    King
SHIEL, Matthew Phipps
    General LCAB: 161; Po:
    3924
SHIELS, George [George MOR-
    SHIEL]
    General Br: 661; Mi: 276
    Paul Twying Br: 661
    Professor Tim Br: 661

The Rugged Path Br: 662
The Summit Br: 662
SHIGA NAOYA
  "The Apprentice's God" Wa:
    680
  "At Kinosaki" Wa: 680
  "Blind Passion" Wa: 680
  "A Certain Man and the Death
    of His Sister" Wa: 680
  "Claudius's Journal" ["The
    Diary of Claudius"] Wa:
    680; WaS1: 195
  "Confused Head" Wa: 680
  "For Grandmother" Wa: 680
  "The Good-Natured Couple"
    Wa: 681
  "Han's Crime" Wa: 681
  "An Incident" Wa: 681
  "The Just Ones" Wa: 681
  "The Kidnapping" Wa: 681
  "Kuniko" Wa: 681
  "The Old Man" Wa: 681
  "One Morning" Wa: 681
  "Otus Junkichi" Wa: 681
  "The Razor" Wa: 681
  "Seibei's Gourds" Wa: 681
  "Tree Frogs" Wa: 681
SHILLABER, Benjamin Penhallow
  General ASF: 517
SHINE, Ted
  Contribution ADC: 350;
    BAP: 182
  Contributions [three plays:
    Shoes; Plantation; and
    Contribution] ADC: 350;
    MBA: 179
  Morning, Noon and Night
    BAP: 182
SHINHAR, Isaac [orig. SHOEN-
    BERG]
  "The Soul of Esther Maadani"
    Wa: 681
SHIPP, J.A.
  General MBA: 179
SHIRLEY, Henry
  General LJCD: 255
SHIRLEY, James
  General ED: 321-322; LJCD:
    153-155, 161, 168-170;
    TSD: 97-98
  The Ball LJCD: 159
  The Cardinal DC1: 199;
    LJCD: 156-157, 170; TSD:
    97
  Changes, or Love in a Maze
    DC1: 199

The Constant Maid LJCD: 160
The Contention of Ajax and
  Ulysses LJCD: 160
Cupid and Death LJCD: 160
"Death the Leveller" PE: 398
The Duke's Mistress LJCD:
  160
The Example DC1: 199
The Gamester DC1: 199;
  LJCD: 160
"The Glories of Our Blood and
  State" [The Contention of
  Ajax and Ulysses for the Ar-
  mor of Achilles] PE: 398
Hyde Park DC1: 199; LJCD:
  156; TSD: 98
The Lady of Pleasure LJCD:
  155; TSD: 98
Love Tricks; or, The School
  of Compliment LJCD: 160
The Maid's Revenge DC1: 199
Saint Patrick of Ireland DC1:
  199; LJCD: 159; TSD: 97
The Sisters LJCD: 161
The Traitor [The Traytor]
  DC1: 199; ED: 322; LJCD:
  158-159, 170; TSD: 98
The Triumph of Beauty LJCD:
  161
The Triumph of Peace LJCD:
  157-158
The Wedding LJCD: 161
The Witty Fair One DC1: 199
SHKLOVSKII, Viktor Borisovich
  General Po: 3925
  Third Factory Fi: 466
  Zoo Fi: 466; Po: 3925
SHOAR, Abraham
  "Benjamin Pickles" Wa: 681
  "The Wine of Elijah" Wa: 681
SHOFFMAN, Gershon
  "The Barrier" Wa: 682
  "No" Wa: 682
  "The Ticket" Wa: 682
SHOHAM, Mattiyahu
  Jericho DC2: 319
SHOLOKHOV, Mikhail Aleksandro-
    vich
  General LCAB: 161; Po:
    3925-3926
  "Alien Blood" Wa: 682
  And Quiet Flows the Don
    [Quiet Flows the Don; The
    Silent Don; Tikhii Don]
    Fi: 466-467; Ke: 435-436;
    Ma: 1913; Po: 3928

"The Birthmark" Wa: 682
Destiny of a Man Fi: 466
Harvest on the Don [Podnjataja celina; Virgin Soil Upturned; Seeds of Tomorrow] Fi: 466-468; Ke: 436; Ma: 1914; Po: 3927
"The Insult" Wa: 682
"A Man's Fate" Wa: 682
Podnjataja celina see Harvest on the Don
Seeds of Tomorrow see Harvest on the Don
The Silent Don [Quiet Flows the Don] see And Quiet Flows the Don
They Fought for Their Country Fi: 467-468
Tikhii Don see And Quiet Flows the Don
Virgin Soil Upturned see Harvest on the Don
SHORTHOUSE, Joseph Henry
General BN: 95; TA: 268
Blanche, Lady Falaise ENES2: 217
The Countess Eve ENES2: 217
John Inglesant BN: 95; ENES2: 217
The Little Schoolmaster Mark ENES2: 217
Sir Percival ENES2: 217
SHPANOV, Nikolai
Conspirators Ke: 436-437
Incendiaries Ke: 437
SHUMLIN, Herman
Spofford ADC: 350
SHUMWAY, Naomi
"Ike and Us Moons" SFC: 185; Wa: 682
SHUTE, Nevil
General MAP: 284-285
Beyond the Black Stump ENES2: 217
The Chequer Board ENES2: 217
The Far Country ENES2: 217
In the Wet ENES2: 217
Landfall ENES2: 217
Lonely Road ENES2: 217
Marazan ENES2: 217
Most Secret ENES2: 217; Po: 3929
No Highway ENES2: 217

An Old Captivity ENES2: 217
On the Beach ENES2: 218; MAP: 284; Po: 3929-3930
Pastoral ENES2: 218
Pied Piper ENES2: 218
The Rainbow and the Rose ENES2: 218
Requiem for a Wren ENES2: 218
Round the Bend ENES2: 218
Ruined City ENES2: 218
So Disdained ENES2: 218
A Town Like Alice ENES2: 218
Trustee from the Toolroom ENES2: 218
What Happened to the Corbetts ENES2: 218
SHYRE, Paul
Blasts and Bravos: An Evening with H.L. Mencken ADC: 351
The Child Buyer ADC: 351
An Unpleasant Evening with H.L. Mencken ADC: 351
SICKINGER, Robert
22 Years ADC: 351
Sidney, Edward W. see TUCKER, Nathaniel Beverly
SIDNEY, Sir Philip
General Hen: 163-166; LCAB: 161; SC: 83-86
"And Have I Heard Her Say? O Cruel Pain!" ICBAP: 114
Arcadia EN: 112; ENE: 234-236; ENES1: 201-202; ENES2: 218-219; ERP: 411-478; Hen: 163-166; ICBAP: 114; Ma: 1915-1916; SC: 83-86; TSD: 38
Astrophel and Stella ICBAP: 114; Ma: 1916-1917; SC: 83-86
"Astrophel and Stella, Fourth Song: Onely Joy, Now Here You Are" PE: 398
"Astrophel and Stella, Eighth Song: In a Grove Most Rich of Shade" PE: 398
"Astrophel and Stella, Tenth Song: O Deare Life, Where Shall It Be" PE: 398
"Astrophel and Stella, Sonnet 1" ICBAP: 114; PE: 398-399

"Certaine Sonnets, 32" PE:
404-405
Defence of Poesie Hen: 179-
180; LCAB: 161; Ma:
1917-1919; SC: 85-86
"Desire" LCAB: 161
"Leave Me, O Love Which
Reachest but to Dust"
ICBAP: 115
"A Litany" PE: 405
"Loving in Truth" LCAB:
161
"Psalm 8" PE: 405
"Psalm 45" PE: 405
"Psalm 81" PE: 405
"What Toong Can Her Perfec-
tions Tell" PE: 405
"With How Sad Steps, O
Moon" ICBAP: 115
"Ye Goatherd Gods" PE:
405
SIEGEL, Eli
General Po: 3930
"Hot Afternoons Have Been
in Montana" Po: 3930
SIENKIEWICZ, Henryk
"After Bread" Wa: 682
"The Angel" Wa: 682
"Bartek the Conqueror" Wa:
682
"The Charcoal Sketches" Wa:
682
Children of the Soil Ke:
437
"A Circus Hercules" see
"Orso"
"A Comedy of Errors" WaS1:
195
The Deluge see also Trilogy
Ke: 437
"From the Memoirs of a Poz-
nan Tutor" Wa: 682
Hania Ke: 437
"In the Mist" Wa: 683
"Jamiol" Wa: 683
"Latarnik" ["The Lighthouse
Keeper"] Wa: 683
The Little Knight Ke: 437
"Lux in Tenebris Lucet" Wa:
683
"Orso" Wa: 683
Pan Michael see also Trilogy
Ke: 437
Quo Vadis Ke: 437-438
"Sachem" Wa: 683
The Teutonic Knights Ke:

438
"The Third One" Wa: 683
Trilogy Ke: 438
With Fire and Sword see also
Trilogy Ke: 438-439
Without Dogma Ke: 439
"Yanko the Musician" Wa: 683
SIEROSZEWSKI, Waclaw
The Dancer Coreenne Ke: 439
The Flight Ke: 439
"The Stolen Lady" Wa: 683
"To Be or Not to Be" Wa:
683
"The Wanderers" Wa: 683
Sierra, Gregorio Martínez see
MARTINEZ SIERRA, Gregorio
SIEVEKING, Alejandro
General Br: 662
SIFTON, Paul
General Br: 662
The Belt Br: 662
_____ and Claire SIFTON
1931 (Or Son of God) Br:
662; DC1: 200
SIGOURNEY, Lydia Howard [Hunt-
ley]
General LCAB: 161
"The Father" Wa: 683; WaS1:
195
"The Patriarch" WaS1: 195
SIGURJONSSON, Johann
Eyvindur of the Mountains
[Fjalla-Eyvindur] DC2:
320
Wish DC2: 320
SIKAKANE, Joyce N.
General BALE: 388
SIKELIANOS, Angelos
Aesculapius DC2: 320
Christ in Rome DC2: 320
Daedalus DC2: 320
Dithyramb of the Rose DC2:
320
Sibyl DC2: 320-321
SILKIN, Jon
"Amana Grass" PE: 405
"Carved" PE: 405
"Concerning Strength" PE:
405
"Death of a Son (Who Died in
a Mental Hospital Aged
One)" PE: 405
"A Death to Us" PE: 405
"From the Road I Saw a Small
Rounded Bluff" PE: 405
"Small Hills Among the Fells

Come Apart from the
Large" PE: 406
"The Two Freedoms" PE:
406
SILL, Edward Rowland
General LCAB: 161-162
"The Dead President" LCAB:
162
"Field Notes" ICBAP: 115
SILLANPÄÄ, Frans Eemil
The Maid Silja Ke: 364;
Ma: 1920
SILLITOE, Alan
General CFAE: 337-339;
CN: 462-463; LCAB:
162; Po: 3930-3932; Sch:
267
"The Bike" Wa: 683
"Canals" Wa: 684
The Death of William Posters
CFAE: 338; CN: 463;
ENES1: 202; ENES2: 219;
Po: 3931-3932; Sch: 268
"The Decline and Fall of
Frankie Buller" Wa: 684
"The Disgrace of Jim Scarf-
dale" Wa: 684
"The Firebug" Wa: 684
"The Fishing-boat Picture"
Wa: 684
The Flame of Life ENES2:
219
The General CFAE: 338;
CN: 463; ENE: 236;
ENES1: 202; ENES2:
219; Po: 3932
"The Good Woman" Wa: 684
"Guzman, Go Home" Wa:
684
Guzman Go Home and Other
Stories CFAE: 339
Key to the Door CFAE:
338; CN: 463; ENE:
236; ENES1: 202; ENES2:
219; Ma: 1921; Po: 3932;
Sch: 268
The Loneliness of the Long-
Distance Runner CFAE:
338; ENE: 236; Po:
3932-3933; Sch: 268; Wa:
684; WaS1: 195
"The Match" Wa: 684
"Noah's Ark" Po: 3933;
Wa: 684
"On Saturday Afternoon"
Po: 3933; Wa: 684

"The Other John Peel" Wa:
684
"The Ragman's Daughter" Wa:
684
"The Revenge" Wa: 685
Saturday Night and Sunday
Morning CFAE: 338; CN:
463-464; ENE: 236-237;
ENES1: 202; ENES2: 219;
Ma: 1921-1922; Po: 3933-
3934; Sch: 268
A Start in Life ENES1: 202;
ENES2: 219; Sch: 268
"To Be Collected" Wa: 685
Travels in Nihilon ENES2:
219
A Tree on Fire CFAE: 338;
CN: 464; ENES1: 202;
ENES2: 220; Ma: 1922-
1923; Po: 3931-3932
The Widower's Son ENES2:
220
SILLS, Paul
Story Theatre ADC: 351
_____ and Arnold WEINSTEIN
American Revolution: Part One
ADC: 351
SILONE, Ignazio
General Po: 3934-3935
L'avventura di un povero
cristiano Fi: 275-276; Po:
3935-3936
Bread and Wine [Pane e vino]
Fi: 276; Ke: 250-251; Ma:
1924; Po: 3936
Fontamara Ke: 251; Ma:
1924-1925
The Fox and the Camellias Ke:
251; WaS1: 196
A Handful of Blackberries Ke:
252
The School for Dictators Po:
3936
The Secret of Luca Ke: 252
The Seed Beneath the Snow
Ke: 252; Ma: 1925
SILVA, José Asunción
General Po: 3937
"Lázaro" Po: 3937
"Los maderos de San Juan"
Po: 3937
"Pataguya" WaS1: 196
SILVA CASTRO, Raúl
General Po: 3938
SILVERA, Edward S.
General BAW: 665

SILVERA, Frank
    General BAP: 183; BAW:
        665; MBA: 179
SILVERA, John
    General BAP: 183
    _____ and Abram HILL
    Liberty Deferred BAP: 183;
        Br: 662
    On Striver's Row see also
        HILL, Abram and John
        SILVERA Br: 662
SILVERBERG, Robert
    "After the Myths Went Home"
        ASF: 518; WaS1: 196
    "Woman's World" WaS1: 196
SIMAK, Clifford D.
    General LCAB: 162
    "The Big Front Yard" WaS1:
        196
    "Hunger Death" WaS1: 196
    "Shotgun Cure" WaS1: 196
    "The World of the Red Sun"
        ASF: 518
    _____ and Carl JACOBI
    "The Street That Wasn't
        There" WaS1: 196
SIMCKES, L. Seymour
    Seven Days of Mourning
        ADC: 352
SIMENON, Georges
    General Po: 3938-3941
    The Bottom of the Bottle
        Ke: 161
    The Lost Mare Ranch Ke:
        161
    Les Memoires de Maigret
        Po: 3941
SIMIC, Charles
    "The Variant" PE: 406
SIMMI, Chima
    General BALE: 388
SIMMONS, Herbert Alfred
    General BAF: 255
    Man Walking on Egg Shells
        BAF: 255
SIMMS, William Gilmore
    General AF: 228-231; ALL:
        241-242; AN: 219-220;
        ASF: 519; Cla: 120-
        121; Ho: 123-126, 155;
        LCAB: 162
    "Confessions of a Murderer"
        ASF: 518
    "How Sharp Snaffles Got His
        Capital and Wife" ASF:
        518

    Katherine Walton Ma: 1926
    "Major Rocket" ASF: 518
    Martin Faber AN: 219; Ho:
        124-125
    Mellichampe Ma: 1926
    Michael Bonham, or The Fall of
        Bexar ADC: 352
    Norman Maurice, or The Man of
        the People ADC: 352
    "Oaktibbe" ASF: 518
    The Partisan AF: 228-229;
        AN: 219; Ho: 124; Ma:
        1926-1927
    "The Plank" ASF: 518
    "Ponce de Leon" ASF: 518
    "Revolutionary Romances" Ho:
        124-125
    "Sweet William" ASF: 518
    "The Two Camps" ASF: 519;
        WaS1: 196
    Vasconselos Ho: 125
    The Wigwam and the Cabin
        Ma: 1927
    Woodcraft AF: 231; Cla:
        120; Ho: 125
    The Yemassee AN: 219; Ho:
        124-126; Ma: 1927
SIMON, Claude
    General Po: 3942
    La Bataille de Pharsale Fi:
        162-163
    Les Corps conducteurs Fi:
        163
    The Flanders Road [La Route
        des Flandres] Fi: 163; Po:
        3943
    The Grass [L'Herbe] Fi:
        163-164; Po: 3943
    Histoire Fi: 164
    Leçon de choses Fi: 164
    The Palace Fi: 164-165
    La Route des Flandres see
        The Flanders Road
    Triptyque Fi: 165
    The Wind Fi: 165; Ke: 161-
        162
SIMON, Mayo
    Happiness ADC: 352
    Walking to Waldheim ADC:
        352
SIMON, Neil
    General MDAE: 458-459;
        TMAP: 223-225
    Barefoot in the Park ADC:
        352; TMAP: 225
    California Suite ADC: 352;

TMAP: 225-226
Chapter Two ADC: 353;
TMAP: 224, 226
Come Blow Your Horn ADC:
353; TMAP: 226-227
Fools TMAP: 227
The Gingerbread Lady ADC:
353; TMAP: 227-228
God's Favorite ADC: 353;
TMAP: 228
The Good Doctor ADC: 353-
354; TMAP: 228
The Goodbye Girl TMAP:
224
I Ought to Be in Pictures
TMAP: 228-229
Last of the Red Hot Lovers
ADC: 354; TMAP: 229
Little Me TMAP: 229
No, No, Nanette TMAP: 230
The Odd Couple ADC: 354;
TMAP: 230
Plaza Suite ADC: 354;
TMAP: 230-231
The Prisoner of Second
Avenue ADC: 354-355;
TMAP: 223, 231
Promises, Promises TMAP:
232
The Star-Spangled Girl
ADC: 355; TMAP: 232
The Sunshine Boys ADC:
355; TMAP: 232-233
Sweet Charity TMAP: 233
They're Playing Our Song
TMAP: 233
SIMON, Peter
In Case of Accident ADC:
355
SIMONOV, Konstantin Mikhailo-
vich
The Fourth DC2: 321
A Good Name MD: 291
The Living and the Dead
Ke: 439; Po: 3943
The Russian People MD:
291
Wait for Me Br: 662
The World Over (And So It
Will Be) MD: 291
SIMONS, Beverly
General JW: 433; Po:
3944
SIMPSON, Helen
General MAP: 286
SIMPSON, Joshua McCarter

General AAPD: 76
SIMPSON, Louis
General ICBAP: 115; MP:
87-88; Po: 3944
The Arrivistes: Poems 1940-49
WIL: 165
"Carentan, O Carentan"
ICBAP: 115
"The Deserted Boy" MP: 88
"A Farm in Minnesota" ICBAP:
115
"The Green Shepherd" PE:
406
"The Heroes" Po: 3945
"Moving the Walls" ICBAP:
115
"My Father in the Night Com-
manding No" ICBAP: 115
"Walt Whitman at Bear Moun-
tain" PE: 406; Po: 3945
SIMPSON, Norman Frederick
General Br: 663; MBD: 87;
MD: 291; MDAE: 461;
TMBP: 210-214
The Cresta Run Br: 663;
EDC: 504; TMBP: 212, 214
The Form TMBP: 214
The Hole Br: 663; EDC:
505; MD: 291; TMBP:
210-214
On the Avenue TMBP: 214
One Over the Eight TMBP:
214
One to Another TMBP: 214
One Way Pendulum Br: 663;
DC1: 200; EDC: 505; MBD:
87; MD: 291-292; MDAE:
461; Po: 3945; TMBP: 210-
214
Playback 625 TMBP: 214
A Resounding Tinkle Br:
663-664; DC1: 200; MBD:
87; MD: 292; MDAE: 461;
Po: 3945; TMBP: 210-213,
215
Was He Anyone? TMBP: 215
SINCLAIR, Andrew
Gog ENES1: 203
SINCLAIR, May
General LCAB: 162; Po:
3946; Sch: 269-270; TA:
269-270
The Allinghams ENES1: 203
Anne Severn and the Fieldings
ENES1: 203; ENES2: 220
Arnold Waterlow ENES1: 203

Audrey Craven ENES1: 203;
ENES2: 220
"Between the Lines" WaS1:
196
The Combined Maze ENES1:
203; ENES2: 220
The Cosmopolitan ENES2:
220
The Creators ENES1: 203;
ENES2: 220
A Cure of Souls ENES1:
203; ENES2: 220
The Divine Fire ENES1:
203; ENES2: 220
Far End ENES1: 203;
ENES2: 220
"The Fault" Wa: 685
"The Finding of the Absolute"
WaS1: 197
The Flaw in the Crystal
ENES1: 203
"The Gift" Wa: 685; WaS1:
197
The Helpmate ENES1: 203;
ENES2: 220
"The Hero of Fiction" Wa:
685
History of Anthony Waring
ENES1: 203
"The Intercessor" WaS1:
197
The Judgment of Eve ENES2:
220
Kitty Tailleur ENES1: 203;
ENES2: 220
Life and Death of Harriett
Frean ENES1: 204;
ENES2: 220
Mary Olivier EN: 113;
ENES1: 204; ENES2: 220
Mr. and Mrs. Nevill Tyson
ENES1: 204; ENES2: 221
Mr. Waddington of Wyck
ENES1: 204; ENES2:
221
The Rector of Wyck ENES1:
204
"The Return" Wa: 685
"The Return of the Prodigal"
Wa: 685
The Romantic ENES1: 204;
ENES2: 221
Superseded ENES2: 221
Tasker Jevons ENES1: 204;
ENES2: 221
The Three Sisters EN: 113;

ENES1: 204; ENES2: 221
The Tree of Heaven ENES1:
204; ENES2: 221
SINCLAIR, Upton Beall
General ALL: 242-243; AN:
221; CN: 464; Ho: 139;
LCAB: 162; Po: 3946-3947;
Wo: 175
Boston ALL: 242
The Brass Check Ho: 139
Dragon Harvest AN: 220
The Jungle ALL: 242; AN:
220; CN: 465; Ma: 1928;
Po: 3948
King Coal ALL: 242; AN:
220; CN: 465
Mammonart: An Essay in Eco-
nomic Interpretation LCAB:
163
Oil! ALL: 242; AN: 220;
CN: 465; Ma: 1929;
Presidential Agent AN: 220
The Return of Lanny Budd
AN: 221; Wo: 175
Singing Jailbirds Br: 664
World's End Series [Lanny Budd
Series] CN: 465
SINGER, Isaac Bashevis
General ASF: 521-522; CN:
465-468; JW: 298-299; LCAB:
163; Ma: 1933-1934; Po:
3948-3952
"Alone" ASF: 519; Wa: 685
"The Black Wedding" ASF:
519; Wa: 685; WaS1: 197
"Blood" ASF: 520; Wa: 685
"The Cabalist of East Broadway"
Wa: 685
"The Cafeteria" ASF: 520
"The Captive" ASF: 520;
WaS1: 197
"Caricature" ASF: 520; Wa:
685
"Cockadoodledoo" ASF: 520;
Wa: 685
"The Dead Fiddler" Wa: 686
"The Destruction of Kreshev"
Wa: 686
The Family Moskat CN: 468;
Ma: 1930
"The Fast" Wa: 686
"Fool's Paradise" ASF: 520
"The Gentleman from Cracow"
ASF: 520; Wa: 686
"Getzel the Monkey" Wa: 686
"Gimpel the Fool" ASF: 520;

Ma: 1930-1931; Wa: 686;
WaS1: 197
In My Father's Court Ma:
1931
"Joy" Wa: 686
"The Last Demon" ASF:
520; Wa: 686
"The Little Shoemakers"
ASF: 520; Wa: 686;
WaS1: 197
The Magician of Lublin CN:
468-469; Ma: 1931-1932
"The Man Who Came Back"
ASF: 520; Wa: 686
The Manor CN: 469; Ma:
1932
"The Mirror" ASF: 520;
Po: 3952; Wa: 686-687
"Powers" ASF: 521; WaS1:
197
Satan in Goray CN: 469-
470; Ma: 1932-1933; Po:
3952
"The Séance" ASF: 521;
Wa: 687
"The Shadow of a Crib" Wa:
687
"Shiddah and Kuziba" ASF:
521; Wa: 687
"Short Friday" Wa: 687
"The Slaughterer" ASF:
521; Wa: 687
The Slave CN: 470-471;
Ma: 1934-1935
"The Spinoza of Market
Street" ASF: 521; Ma:
1935; Wa: 687; WaS1:
197
"Taibele and Her Demon"
Wa: 687
"The Third One" ASF: 521;
Wa: 687
"Two Corpses Go Dancing"
Wa: 687
"The Unseen" Wa: 687
"Yentl the Yeshiva Boy"
Wa: 687
"Zeitl and Rickel" Wa: 687
"Zlateh the Goat" ASF:
521
SINGER, Israel Joshua
The Brothers Ashkenazi
Ma: 1936
SINGER, James Burns
General Ai: 325
SINGH, Jagjit

General BALE: 388
SINGH, Khushwant
"Abroad and Not-So-Innocent"
Wa: 688
"A Bride for the Sahib" Wa:
688
"The Butterfly" Wa: 688
"The Constipated Frenchman"
Wa: 688
"Death Comes to Daulat Ram"
Wa: 688
"The Fawn" Wa: 688
"The Great Difference" Wa:
688
"India Is a Strange Country"
Wa: 688
"The Insurance Agent" Wa:
688
"Karma" Wa: 688
"Kusum" Wa: 688
"Little Man, You've Had a Busy
Day" ["Man, How the Gov-
ernment of India Run"]
Wa: 688
"A Love Affair in London" Wa:
688
"Maiden Voyage of the Jal
Hindia" Wa: 688
"The Man with a Clear Con-
science" Wa: 688
"The Mark of Vishnu" Wa:
688
"The Memsahib of Mandla" Wa:
688
"Mr. Kanjoos and the Great
Miracle" Wa: 689
"Mr. Singh and the Color Bar"
Wa: 689
"The Morning After the Night
Before" Wa: 689
"My Own, My Native Land"
Wa: 689
"The Portrait of a Lady" Wa:
689
"Posthumous" Wa: 689
"A Punjab Pastoral" Wa: 689
"The Rape" Wa: 689
"Rats and Cats in the House of
Culture" Wa: 689
"The Red Tie" Wa: 689
"The Riot" Wa: 689
"A Town Called Alice" Wa:
689
"The Voice of God" Wa: 689
"When Sikh Meets Sikh" Wa:
689

SINGMASTER, Elsie
  General LCAB: 163
Sinyavskii, Andrei see TERTZ,
  Abram
SION, George
  Charles le Téméraire Br:
    664
SIRIN, Vladimir [Vladimir
  NABOKOV]
  King, Queen, Knave Ke:
    439
  Luzhin's Defence Ke: 439
  Mashenka Ke: 439
SISSLE, Noble
  General BAP: 183-184;
    BAW: 670; MBA: 179
  Harlem Cavalcade BAP: 184
SISSON, Charles Hubert
  General Po: 3952
SITWELL, Edith
  General EP: 221-231; LCAB:
    163; Ma: 1937-1938; MP:
    88-89; Po: 3953-3957
  "Aubade" EP: 223, 230;
    PE: 406
  "The Canticle of the Rose"
    EP: 229; PE: 406
  "Dirge for the New Sunrise"
    EP: 229; PE: 406
  "Fantasia for Mouth Organ"
    PE: 406
  "Gold Coast Customs" PE:
    406
  "Green Song" EP: 221
  "Metamorphosis" EP: 224;
    ICBAP: 115; MP: 89;
    Po: 3957
  "O Bitter Love, O Death"
    EP: 224
  "The Shadow of Cain" EP:
    229; PE: 406
  "The Sleeping Beauty" PE:
    406
  "Spring Morning" PE: 406
  "Still Falls the Rain" ICBAP:
    115; PE: 406; Po: 3957-
    3958
  "When Sir Beelzebub" PE:
    406
  "The Winds Bastinado Whipt
    on the Calico" PE: 407
  "A Young Girl" EP: 224
SITWELL, Osbert
  General Po: 3958
  "Alive--Alive, Oh!" Wa:
    689

The Man Who Lost Himself
  ENES1: 204
SITWELL, Sacheverell
  General Po: 3958
  "Doctor Donne and Gargantua:
    The First of Six Cantos" PE:
    407
  "The Lady and the Rooks" PE:
    407
  "New Water Music" PE: 407
SIVACHOV, Mikhail
  Yellow Devil Ke: 439
SIWERTZ, Sigfrid
  The Flame Ke: 364
  The Selambs Ke: 364
SJÖGREN, Peder
  "Tears in Your Sleep" Wa:
    689
SJÖSTRAND, Östen
  I vattumannens tecken Po:
    3958
SKEETER, Sharyn Jeanne
  General BAF: 255
SKELTON, John
  General ED: 323-325; SC: 87
  "The Bowge of Courte" ICBAP:
    116
  "Magnificence" ICBAP: 116;
    DC1: 200; ED: 323-324
  "Manerly Margery Mylk and Ale"
    ICBAP: 116; PE: 407
  "Philip Sparrow" ICBAP: 116
  "Speke, Parrot" PE: 407; SC:
    87
  "The Tunning of Elinour Rum-
    ming" ICBAP: 116
  "Uppon a Deedmans Head" SC:
    87
  "With Lullay, Lullay, Like a
    Child" PE: 407
SKELTON, Robin
  "The Shell" PE: 407
  "Temple Flower" PE: 407
SKINN, Anne
  The Old Maid ENES2: 221
SKINNER, Burrhus Frederick
  Walden Two Po: 3959
SKLAR, George and Albert MALTZ
  Life and Death of an American
    Br: 664
  Peace on Earth see also
    MALTZ, Albert and George
    SKLAR Br: 664
SKULLY, James
  "Midsummer" PE: 379
SLADE, Bernard

Same Time, Next Year ADC: 356

SLAUERHOFF, Jan Jacob
General Po: 3959

SLEPCOV, Vasilij
Hard Times Fi: 468

SLESINGER, Tess
General ASF: 523
"A Life in the Day of a Writer" WaS1: 197
The Unpossessed Po: 3959

SLESSOR, Kenneth
General Po: 3959-3960
"Five Visions of Captain Cook" Po: 3960-3961

SLOAN, Anthony [Gene FEIST]
Oedipus ADC: 356

SLOAN, James Park
General LCAB: 163

SLONIMSKIJ, Mikhail
Foma Klesnev Ke: 440
The Lavrovs Ke: 440

SLOWACKI, Julius
Beatrix Cenci DC2: 321
Lilla Weneda DC2: 321

SMALL, Adam
General BALE: 389

SMART, Christopher
General EC: 127-128; Me: 363-370
"The Author Apologizes to a Lady for His Being a Little Man" PE: 407
"The Circumcision" PE: 407
"For I Will Consider My Cat Jeoffry" EC: 128; Me: 367-369; PE: 407
"The Hop-Garden" PE: 407
Hymn VI: "The Presentation of Christ in the Temple" PE: 407
Hymn XI: "Easter Day" PE: 407
Hymn XIII: "St. Philip and St. James" PE: 407
Hymns for the Amusement of Children Me: 365
Jubilate Agno EC: 127-128; ICBAP: 116; LCAB: 163; Me: 364-369; PE: 408
Magnificat Me: 366
"A Noon Piece, or, The Mowers at Dinner" PE: 408
"Pillars of the Lord" EC: 128; Me: 368

A Song to David EC: 128; ICBAP: 116; LCAB: 163; Me: 363-369; PE: 408

SMILES, Samuel
General Ai: 139

SMITH, Adam
General Ai: 71; EC: 129-130

SMITH, Alexander
General Ai: 148

SMITH, Art and Elia KAZAN
Dimitroff Br: 664

SMITH, Arthur James Marshall
General Po: 3961

SMITH, Augustus J.
Voodooism BAP: 185

SMITH, Bernard
General LCAB: 163

SMITH, Betty
A Tree Grows in Brooklyn AN: 222

Smith, Charles Henry see ARP, Bill

SMITH, Charlotte
General Be: 221-222
The Banished Man ENES1: 204
Emmeline, the Orphan of the Castle Be: 221
The Old Manor House Be: 221; ENES1: 204

SMITH, Cordwainer
"The Dead Lady of Clown Town" ASF: 523
"The Game of Rat and Dragon" ASF: 523-524; WaS1: 197
"Scanners Live in Vain" WaS1: 197

SMITH, Dodie [Dorothy Gladys SMITH]
General Mi: 276-277
Bonnet Over the Windmill Br: 664

SMITH, Edmund
Phaedra and Hippolytus DC1: 200

SMITH, Elihu Hubbard
General AP: 489; Da: 114-115

SMITH, F. Hopkinson
General AN: 222
Colonel Carter of Cartersville AN: 222

SMITH, Glen Allen
Home Away From ADC: 356

SMITH, Henry
General Hen: 30; SC: 87

SMITH, Harry Allen
  Mister Zip Po: 3961-3962
SMITH, Iain Crichton
  General Ai: 328-329
  "On a Summer's Day" PE:
    408
SMITH, J. Augustus
  Turpentine BAP: 184-185;
    MBA: 183
  _____ and Peter MORRELL
  Turpentine Br: 664
SMITH, Jean
  "Frankie Mae" ASF: 524
SMITH, John
  General AP: 492-498; Da:
    40-41
  The Generall Historie of Vir-
    ginia, New England, and
    the Summer Isles AP:
    494, 496-497; Da: 41
  The True Travels, Adven-
    tures, and Observations
    of Captaine John Smith
    AP: 495-497; Da: 41
SMITH, Lillian
  Strange Fruit AN: 222; Br:
    665; Po: 3962
SMITH, Logan Pearsall
  General LCAB: 164
SMITH, M.G.
  General WIL: 165-166
  Testament WIL: 166
SMITH, Michael Townsend
  General MDAE: 462
  I Like It Br: 665
SMITH, Milburn
  Sensations of the Bitten
    Partner ADC: 356
SMITH, Pauline
  General Po: 3962-3963
  "Anna's Marriage" Wa: 690
  "The Cart" Wa: 690
  "Desolation" Wa: 690
  "The Father" Wa: 690
  "Ludovitje" Wa: 690
  "The Miller" Wa: 690
  "The Pain" Wa: 690
  "The Pastor's Daughter" Wa:
    690
  "The Schoolmaster" Wa:
    690
  "The Sinner" Wa: 690
  "The Sisters" Wa: 690
SMITH, Ray
  "Cape Breton Is the Thought-
    Control Centre of Canada"

  Wa: 690
SMITH, Richard Penn
  General AD: 187
  Caius Marius AD: 187
SMITH, Samuel Stanhope
  General AP: 587
SMITH, Seba
  General ASF: 524
SMITH, Stevie
  "The Frog Prince" ICBAP:
    116
SMITH, Sydney Goodsir
  General Ai: 305-306
  Under the Eildon Tree Ai:
    305
SMITH, Vern E.
  The Jones Men BAF: 257
SMITH, W.H.
  The Drunkard, or The Fallen
    Saved ADC: 356
SMITH, Welton
  General BAW: 674
SMITH, William, Jr.
  The History of the Province of
    New York AP: 587
SMITH, William Gardner
  General AAW: 72; BAF: 258;
    BAW: 674
  Last of the Conquerors BAF:
    258; LCAB: 164
SMITH, William Jay
  General Po: 3963-3964
  "American Primitive" ICBAP:
    116; PE: 408; Po: 3964
SMITH, Winchell
  Only Son ADC: 357
  _____ and Frank BACON
  Lightnin' ADC: 357
  _____ and Victor MAPES
  The Boomerang ADC: 357
  _____ and Byron ONGLEY
  Brewster's Millions ADC: 357
SMITHYMAN, Kendrick
  General Po: 3964
SMOLLETT, Tobias
  General Ai: 67-68; Be: 229-
    236; Du: 141-143; LCAB:
    164
  Ferdinand, Count Fathom [The
    Adventures of Ferdinand,
    Count Fathom] Be: 234,
    236; Du: 138; EN: 114;
    ENE: 237; ENES1: 205;
    ENES2: 221
  The History and Adventures of
    an Atom Be: 231; ENES1:

204; ENES2: 221-222

Humphry Clinker [The Expedition of Humphry Clinker]
Be: 131, 229-233, 235-236; Du: 139-140; EN: 114; ENE: 237-238; ENES1: 205-206; ENES2: 222; LCAB: 164; Ma: 1939-1940

Peregrine Pickle [Adventures of Peregrine Pickle] Be: 230, 232-235; Du: 140; EN: 113-114; ENE: 239; ENES1: 206; ENES2: 222-223; Ma: 1940-1941

Roderick Random [Adventures of Roderick Random] Be: 230, 232-234, 236; Du: 140-141; EN: 114; ENE: 239; ENES1: 206; ENES2: 223; LCAB: 164; Ma: 1941-1943

Sir Launcelot Greaves [The Adventures of Sir Launcelot Greaves] EN: 114; ENE: 239; ENES1: 207; ENES2: 223-224

SMUUL, Juhan
General Po: 3964

SMYRL, David Langston
On the Lock-In MBA: 184

SNELLING, William Joseph
General ASF: 524
"The Bois Brulé" ASF: 524; Wa: 690; WaS1: 198

SNODGRASS, William DeWitt
General ICBAP: 116; LCAB: 164; Po: 3964-3965
"April Inventory" LCAB: 164; PE: 408
"A Cardinal" PE: 408
"Heart's Needle" ICBAP: 116; PE: 408
"The Operation" PE: 408
"Powwow" PE: 408

SNORRI STURLUSON
The Heimskringla Ma: 1944

SNOW, Charles Percy
General BN2: 102-103; CFAE: 341-345; CN: 471-473; LCAB: 164-165; Po: 3965-3969; Sch: 270-273

The Affair see also Strangers and Brothers CN: 473; ENE: 239-240; ENES1: 207; Ma: 1945

The Conscience of the Rich see also Strangers and Brothers CN: 473; ENES1: 207; ENES2: 224; Ma: 1945-1946

Corridors of Power CN: 473; ENE: 240; ENES1: 207; ENES2: 224

Death Under Sail ENE: 240; ENES1: 207; ENES2: 224

Homecoming see also Strangers and Brothers CN: 474; ENES1: 207; Ma: 1946

In Their Wisdom ENES2: 224

Last Things ENES1: 207

The Light and the Dark see also Strangers and Brothers CN: 474; ENES1: 207; ENES2: 224; Ma: 1946

The Malcontents ENES2: 224

The Masters see also Strangers and Brothers BN2: 102; CN: 474; ENE: 240; ENES1: 207; ENES2: 224; Ma: 1947

New Lives for Old CN: 474; ENES1: 207; ENES2: 224

The New Men see also Strangers and Brothers CFAE: 345; CN: 475; ENE: 240; ENES1: 208; ENES2: 224; Ma: 1947-1948; Po: 3969

The Search CN: 475; ENES1: 208; ENES2: 224

The Sleep of Reason see also Strangers and Brothers CN: 475; ENE: 240; ENES1: 208; ENES2: 224

Strangers and Brothers CN: 475-476; ENE: 240-241; ENES1: 208; ENES2: 224; LCAB: 165; Ma: 1948-1949; Po: 3970-3972

Time of Hope see also Strangers and Brothers CN: 476; ENES1: 208

The Two Cultures and the Scientific Revolution Po: 3972-3978

The Two Cultures: And a Second Look Po: 3978

SNYDER, Gary
General ICBAP: 117; MP: 90; Po: 3978-3979

"After Work" PE: 408
"For George Leigh-Mallory"
    Po: 3979
"I Went Into the Maverick
    Bar" PE: 408
"Marin-An" PE: 408
"Mid August at Sourdough
    Mountain Lookout" PE:
    408
"Nooksack Valley" PE: 409
"Prayer for the Great Family"
    PE: 409
"Riprap" PE: 409
"A Stone Garden" ICBAP:
    117
"Straight-Creek-Great Burn"
    PE: 409
SOANE, George
    General EDT: 285
SÖDERBERG, Hjalmar
    Doctor Glas Fi: 411
SOFFICI, Ardengo
    General Po: 3980
SOGLIANI, Giovani
    L'Uccellatoio DC2: 321
SOKOLOV, Sasha
    A School for Fools Fi: 468
SOLA, Jaime
    El alma de la aldea Ke:
    231
SOLANA, Rafael
    General Br: 665
SOLARIN, Tai
    General BALE: 389-390
SOLDATI, Mario
    "The Window" SFC: 185;
    Wa: 690
SOLDIAS, Jose Antonio
    General Br: 665
SOLER, Bartolome
    General Po: 3980
SOLIS, Dionisio
    La Segunda Celestina [El
        Encanto es la Hermosura]
        DC2: 321
SOLLERS, Philippe
    General Po: 3980
    Nombres Fi: 165
SOLLOGUB, Vladimir Aleksand-
        rovich
    "A History of Two Galoshes"
        Wa: 691
SOLOGUB, Fyodor [Fyodor Kuzmich
        TETERNIKOV]
    Bad Dreams Fi: 468
    The Created Legend Ke: 440;

    Po: 4206
    The Petty Demon [The Little
        Devil] Fi: 468; Ke: 440;
        LCAB: 176; Po: 4206
    Tvorimaja Legenda Fi: 468
SOLOMON, Carl
    "Report from the Asylum"
        Po: 3980
SOLON
    General LCAB: 165
SOLORZANO, Carlos
    General Br: 665; Po: 3981
    Doña Beatriz Po: 3981
    Los fantoches Br: 665
    El hechicero Po: 3981
    Las manos de Dios Po: 3981
SOLZHENITSYN, Alexander I.
    General LCAB: 165; Po:
        3981-3984
    August 1914 Fi: 469-471; Ma:
        1950-1951
    The Cancer Ward [Rakovyi Kor-
        pus] Fi: 471-473; Ma:
        1951; Po: 3985-3986
    A Candle in the Wind Ma:
        1951-1952
    "The Easter Procession" Wa:
        691; WaS1: 198
    The First Circle [V Kruge Per-
        vom] Fi: 473-475; Ma:
        1952; Po: 3986
    "For the Good of the Cause"
        Ke: 440; Wa: 691; WaS1:
        198
    The Gulag Archipelago Fi: 475-
        477; Ma: 1953
    "An Incident at Krechetovka
        Station" Ke: 440; Wa: 691;
        WaS1: 198
    Lenin in Zurich Fi: 477-478
    The Love-Girl and the Innocent
        Ma: 1953
    "Matryona's House" ["Matrionin
        Dvor"] Fi: 478; Ke: 440;
        Po: 3984; Wa: 691; WaS1:
        198
    One Day in the Life of Ivan
        Denisovich Fi: 478-479;
        Ke: 440; LCAB: 165; Ma:
        1953-1954; Po: 3985; Wa:
        691
    "The Right Hand" Wa: 691;
        WaS1: 198
    "Zakhar Kalita" Wa: 691;
        WaS1: 198
SOMERVILLE, Edith Oenone

General TA: 271
_____ and Martin ROSS
General Po: 3986; TA: 217
The Big House of Inver
ENES1: 208
Dan Russel the Fox ENES1:
208
An Enthusiast ENES1: 208
An Irish Cousin ENES1:
208; ENES2: 225
Mount Music ENES1: 208
Naboth's Vineyard ENES1:
209
The Real Charlotte ENES1:
209; ENES2: 225; Po:
3987; TA: 217
The Silver Fox ENES1: 209
SOMMER, Richard
"The First Planet After Her
Death" PE: 409
SONDHI, Kuldip
General BALE: 390
SONGA, Peter
General BALE: 390
SONTAG, Susan
General CFAE: 347; LCAB:
165; Po: 3987
Against Interpretation Ma:
1955; Po: 3988
The Benefactor CN: 477;
Ma: 1955
Death Kit CN: 477; LCAB:
165; Ma: 1956
Styles of Radical Will Ma:
1956
Trip to Hanoi LCAB: 165
SONTANI, Utuy
Awal Dan Mira DC2: 321
Bunga Rumah Makan DC2:
321
SOPHOCLES
General LCAB: 165
Ajax DC2: 321-323; EDC:
505-506; Ma: 1957
Antigone DC2: 323-327;
EDC: 506-508; LCAB:
165-166; Ma: 1957-1959
Electra DC2: 327-329;
EDC: 509-510; LCAB:
166; Ma: 1959
Inachus DC2: 329
Oedipus at Colonus DC2:
329-331; EDC: 510; Ma:
1960
Oedipus Rex [Oedipus the
King; Oedipus Tyrannus]

DC2: 331-339; EDC: 510-
514; LCAB: 166; Ma: 1960-
1962
Philoctetes DC2: 339-341;
EDC: 514-515; Ma: 1962-
1963
Polyxena DC2: 341
The Women of Trachis [Trach-
iniae] DC2: 341-342; EDC:
515; Ma: 1963
SOREL, Charles
Le Berger extravagant Fi:
165
Histoire comique de Francion
Fi: 165-166
SORGE, Reinhard Johannes
General Br: 665
The Beggar [Der Bettler] Br:
665
Güntwar Br: 665
SORIANO, Elena
General Po: 3988
Espejismos Ke: 231
Medea Ke: 231
La playa de los locos Ke: 231
SORLEY, Charles Hamilton
General Po: 3988
"All the Hills and Vales Along"
ICBAP: 117
SORRENTINO, Gilbert
General LCAB: 166
"The Moon in Its Flight" Wa:
691
SOTELO, Joaquin
La muralla DC2: 342
SOTHEBY, William
Orestes DC1: 200
SOTO, Juan
Alang Dios DC2: 342
SOUPAULT, Philippe
General Po: 3989
Les Champs magnétiques Po:
3989
SOUSTER, Raymond
General Po: 3989
SOUTAR, William
General Ai: 260-261; Po:
3989
SOUTHERN, Terry
General ASF: 524; CFAE:
349; CN: 477; Po: 3990
Candy CFAE: 349; CN: 477;
Po: 3990
The Magic Christian CN: 477
"The Road Out of Axotle"
LCAB: 166

SOUTHERNE, Thomas
General Bon: 46-47; Li:
294-295
The Disappointment Li: 294-
295
The Fatal Marriage Li: 295
Money the Mistress Li: 295
Oroonoko Li: 295
Sir Anthony Love Li: 295
The Wives' Excuse Li: 295
SOUTHEY, Robert
General EDT: 287; Fog:
65-66; LCAB: 166; Ma:
1966-1967; Re: 227-228
The Curse of Kehama Ma:
1964
"The Devil's Thoughts" Re:
228
"His Books" PE: 409
Joan of Arc Ma: 1964-1965;
Re: 227
Life of Nelson Ma: 1965-
1966
Roderick, the Last of the
Goths Ma: 1967
Thalaba the Destroyer Ma:
1967-1968; Re: 227
Wat Tyler EDT: 287
SOUTHON, A.E.H.
"The Leopard Men" Wa: 691
SOUTHWELL, Robert
General ICBAP: 117; SC:
88
"At Home in Heaven" PE:
409
"A Fancy Turned to a Sin-
ner's Complaint" PE:
409
"I Die Alive" PE: 409
"Mary Magdalen's Complaint
at Christ's Death" PE:
409
"New Heaven, New Warre"
ICBAP: 117
"Saint Peter's Complaint"
PE: 409
"A Vale of Tears" PE: 409
"The Visitation" ICBAP:
117; PE: 409
SOUTHWORTH, Emma Dorothy
Eliza Neville
General AN: 222-223
SOUZA, Madame de
La Duchesse de Guise DC2:
342
SOWERBY, Getha

General Br: 666
SOYFER, Jura
General Po: 3990
SOYINKA, Wole [Akinwande OLU-
WOLE]
General BALE: 393-404; Br:
666; Po: 3990-3991
A Dance of the Forests BALE:
394-396, 403-404; Br: 666
Idanre BALE: 396, 403
The Interpreters BALE: 393,
397-398, 403; LCAB: 166;
Po: 3991
The Invention BALE: 398
Kongi's Harvest BALE: 394,
396, 400-401, 403; Br: 666
The Lion and the Jewel BALE:
395, 398-403; Br: 666; Po:
3991
Madmen and Specialists BALE:
394, 397, 399, 403
The Man Died BALE: 396,
400-401, 404
Ogun Abibiman BALE: 400-401
The Road BALE: 393, 397,
400-403; Br: 666
A Shuttle in the Crypt BALE:
403
The Strong Breed Br: 666
The Swamp-Dwellers BALE:
397, 399; Br: 666; DC2:
342-343
The Trials of Brother Jero
BALE: 401-402; Br: 666
SPAFFORD, Horatio
General AP: 588
SPARK, Muriel
General Ai: 315; CFAE:
352-353; CN: 477-478;
LCAB: 166-167; Po: 3992-
3994; Sch: 274-275
The Abbess of Crewe ENES2:
225
The Bachelors CN: 478-479;
ENE: 241; ENES1: 209;
ENES2: 225; Ma: 1969
The Ballad of Peckham Rye
CFAE: 352; CN: 479;
ENES1: 209; ENES2: 225;
LCAB: 166; Ma: 1969; Po:
3994-3995; Sch: 275
"Bang, Bang--You're Dead"
Wa: 691
"Come Along, Marjorie" Wa:
691
The Comforters CN: 479;

ENE: 241; ENES1: 209;
ENES2: 225; Ma: 1969-
1970; Ri2: 462
The Driver's Seat ENES1:
209; ENES2: 225
The Girls of Slender Means
CFAE: 352; CN: 479;
ENE: 241; ENES1: 209;
ENES2: 225; Ma: 1970
"The Go-Away Bird" Wa:
692; WaS1: 198
The Hothouse by the East
River ENES1: 209;
ENES2: 225
The Mandelbaum Gate CFAE:
353; CN: 480; ENE:
242; ENES1: 209-210;
ENES2: 225; LCAB:
167; Sch: 276
Memento Mori CN: 480;
ENES1: 210; ENES2: 225;
LCAB: 167; Ma: 1970;
WaS1: 198
Not to Disturb ENES1: 210;
ENES2: 226
"The Pawnbroker's Wife" Wa:
692
"The Portobello Road" Wa:
692
The Prime of Miss Jean
Brodie Ai: 315; CFAE:
352-353; CN: 480; ENE:
242; ENES1: 210; ENES2:
226; LCAB: 167; Ma:
1970-1971; Po: 3995;
Sch: 276
The Public Image CN: 480;
ENES1: 210; ENES2:
226
Robinson CFAE: 353; CN:
480-481; ENE: 242;
ENES1: 210; ENES2: 226;
LCAB: 166; Po: 3995
"The Seraph and the Zam-
besi" Wa: 692
"The Twins" Wa: 692
SPEIGHT, Johnny
The Knacker's Yard MDAE:
463
SPEISER, Frank
The World of Lenny Bruce
ADC: 358
SPENCE, Catherine Helen
General AL: 324-325
SPENCE, Eulalie
General BAP: 186; BAW:

678; MBA: 184
Being Forty BAP: 186
The Fool's Errand MBA: 184
The Whipping BAP: 186
SPENCE, Joseph
General EC: 130
SPENCE, Lewis
General Ai: 207
SPENCER, Anne
General BAW: 679; HR: 134-
135
SPENCER, Colin
General MDAE: 464
Spitting Image MDAE: 464
SPENCER, Elizabeth
General ASF: 524; CFAE:
355; CN: 481; Po: 3996
Fire in the Morning CN: 481
"First Dark" ASF: 524
Knights and Dragons CN:
481
Light in the Piazza CN: 481
This Crooked Way CN: 481
The Voice at the Back Door
CN: 481
SPENCER, Mary Etta
General BAF: 259; BAW:
679
SPENCER, Theodore
"The Circus: Or One View of
It" PE: 409
SPENDER, Stephen
General EP: 234-237; ICBAP:
117; LCAB: 167; Ma:
1973; MP: 91; Po: 3996-
3998
"Abrupt and Charming Mover"
PE: 409
"Awakening" EP: 235; PE:
409; Po: 3998
"An Elementary School Class
Room in a Slum" PE: 410
"The Exiles" PE: 410
"The Express" EP: 235;
ICBAP: 117; Ma: 1972;
PE: 410; Po: 3998-3999
"The Funeral" Ma: 1972; PE:
410
"He Will Watch the Hawk with
an Indifferent Eye" EP:
234; ICBAP: 117; PE:
410; Po: 3999
"I Think Continually of Those"
EP: 235-236; Ma: 1972;
PE: 410
"Judas Iscariot" EP: 236;

Po: 3999
"The Juggler" ICBAP: 117
"The Landscape Near an
   Aerodrome" EP: 236;
   Ma: 1972; PE: 410
"Not Palaces" PE: 410
"Oh What Is the Use Now of
   Our Meeting and Speak-
   ing" PE: 410
"Oh Young Men Oh Young
   Comrades" PE: 410
"The Pylons" PE: 410
"Rolled Over on Europe"
   PE: 410
"Seascape" PE: 411
"There Are Some Days the
   Happy Ocean Lies" PE:
   411
"Tom's A-Cold" PE: 411
Trial of a Judge Br: 667
"Vienna" PE: 411
SPENSER, Edmund
   General LCAB: 167; Ma:
   1975-1976; SC: 91-98
   Amoretti ICBAP: 117;
   LCAB: 167; SC: 91, 94-
   95
"Amoretti, Sonnet 1" PE:
   411
"Amoretti, Sonnet 2" PE:
   411
"Amoretti, Sonnet 6" PE:
   411
"Amoretti, Sonnet 10" PE:
   411
"Amoretti, Sonnet 15" PE:
   411
"Amoretti, Sonnet 22" PE:
   411
"Amoretti, Sonnet 34" PE:
   411
"Amoretti, Sonnet 35" PE:
   411
"Amoretti, Sonnet 41" PE:
   411
"Amoretti, Sonnet 46" PE:
   411
"Amoretti, Sonnet 54" PE:
   411
"Amoretti, Sonnet 56" PE:
   412
"Amoretti, Sonnet 59" PE:
   412
"Amoretti, Sonnet 61" PE:
   412
"Amoretti, Sonnet 62" PE:

412
"Amoretti, Sonnet 64" PE: 412
"Amoretti, Sonnet 65" PE: 412
"Amoretti, Sonnet 66" PE: 412
"Amoretti, Sonnet 67" ICBAP:
   119; PE: 412
"Amoretti, Sonnet 68" PE: 412
"Amoretti, Sonnet 71" PE: 412
"Amoretti, Sonnet 72" PE: 412
"Amoretti, Sonnet 78" PE: 412
"Amoretti, Sonnet 79" PE: 412
"Amoretti, Sonnet 81" PE: 412
"Amoretti, Sonnet 85" PE: 413
"Aprill" [from The Shepherd's
   Calendar] ICBAP: 117-118;
   PE: 414
"Astrophel" PE: 413
"Colin Clouts Come Home
   Againe" ICBAP: 118
"Epithalamion" ICBAP: 118;
   LCAB: 167; PE: 413
The Faerie Queene ICBAP:
   118; LCAB: 167; Ma: 1974-
   1975; SC: 91-98
The Faerie Queene--Book I
   ICBAP: 118
The Faerie Queene--Book II
   ICBAP: 119
The Faerie Queene--Book III
   ICBAP: 119
The Faerie Queene--Book IV
   ICBAP: 119
The Faerie Queene--Book V
   ICBAP: 119
The Faerie Queene--Book VI
   ICBAP: 119
"Four Hymns" LCAB: 167;
   PE: 413
"Hymn in Honor of Beautie"
   PE: 411
"Hymn in Honor of Love" PE:
   413
"Hymn of Heavenly Beautie"
   PE: 413
"Hymn of Heavenly Love" PE:
   414
"A Hymn to Venus" [from The
   Faerie Queene] PE: 414
"January" [from The Shep-
   herd's Calendar] PE: 414
"Lyke as a Huntsman" [Sonnet
   67] ICBAP: 119; PE: 412
"Mother Hubbard's Tale"
   ICBAP: 119
"Muiopotmos, or the Fate of
   the Butterflie" ICBAP:

119; PE: 414

"November" [from The Shepherd's Calendar] PE: 414

"October" [from The Shepherd's Calendar] PE: 414

"Prothalamion" ICBAP: 119; PE: 414; SC: 91, 93-94, 97

The Shepheardes Calendar ICBAP: 119; Ma: 1977; SC: 93-94, 96

The Shepheardes Calendar-- The March Eclogue ICBAP: 119

The Shepheardes Calendar-- The April Eclogue ICBAP: 120

The Shepheardes Calendar-- The May Eclogue ICBAP: 120

The Shepheardes Calendar-- The June Eclogue ICBAP: 120

The Shepheardes Calendar-- The July Eclogue ICBAP: 120

"The Teares of the Muses" PE: 415

"To the Right Honourable the Earle of Cumberland" PE: 415

SPEWACK, Bella and Samuel SPEWACK
General Br: 667; MD: 292
Boy Meets Girl ADC: 358; Br: 667; MD: 292
Clear All Wires! ADC: 358
Festival ADC: 358
My Three Angels ADC: 358
Spring Song ADC: 359
Woman Bites Dog ADC: 359; MD: 292
_____, Samuel SPEWACK, and Cole PORTER
Leave It to Me! ADC: 359; MD: 292

SPEWACK, Samuel
The Golden State ADC: 359
Two Blind Mice ADC: 359
Under the Sycamore Tree ADC: 360

SPICER, Jack
"Billy the Kid" PE: 415

SPIELHAGEN, F.
The Hohensteins Ke: 332
In Rank and File Ke: 332

SPIGELGASS, Leonard
A Majority of One ADC: 360

SPILLANE, Mickey
General AN: 223; Po: 4000

SPITTELER, Carl
General Po: 4000
Conrad the Lieutenant Ke: 332; Po: 4001
Imago Fi: 390
Prometheus and Epimetheus Ke: 333

SPITZ, Jacques
General Po: 4001

SPITZER, Leo
General Po: 4001

Spottiswoode, Alicia Ann see SCOTT, Lady John

SPRING, Howard
Fame Is the Spur ENES2: 226
My Son, My Son ENES2: 226

SPRINGS, Elliott White
General AN: 223; Po: 4001

SPURLING, John
Macrune's Guevara MDAE: 465

SQUARZINA, Luigi
General Br: 667

SQUIRE, John Collings [Solomon EAGLE]
General LCAB: 167; TA: 272

SSEMUWANGA, John
General BALE: 404

STAATS
"Spring Thaw" PE: 415

STACTON, David Derek
General CFAE: 358

STADLER, Ernst
General LCAB: 168; Po: 4002-4003

STAËL, Madame de
General Ma: 1978-1979
Corinne Fi: 166; Ke: 162
Delphine Fi: 166; Ke: 162
Mirza Fi: 166

STAFFELDT, Shack
General Po: 4003

STAFFORD, Jean
General AN: 223; ASF: 525; CFAE: 359; CN: 482; LCAB: 168; Po: 4003-4004
Boston Adventure CN: 482

The Catherine Wheel CN:
482
"Children Are Bored on Sun-
day" SFC: 185; Wa:
692
"A Country Love Story"
ASF: 525; Wa: 692
"In the Zoo" ASF: 525;
WaS1: 198
"The Interior Castle" Po:
4004; SFC: 185; Wa:
692
The Mountain Lion CFAE:
359; CN: 482; Po: 4004
"A Reunion" SFC: 185;
Wa: 692
"A Summer Day" Wa: 692
STAFFORD, William
General ICBAP: 120; MP:
92-93; Po: 4004-4005
"Connections" PE: 415
"A Cove on the Crooked
River" PE: 415
"The Farm on the Great
Plains" PE: 415
"Fifteen" PE: 415
"In California" PE: 415
"One Home" PE: 415
"Our People" PE: 415
"The Rescued Year" ICBAP:
120
"Returned to Say" MP: 93
"Shadows" PE: 415
"Summer Will Rise" PE:
415
"Traveling Through the
Dark" PE: 415-416; Po:
4005
STAIGER, Emil
General Po: 4005
STALLINGS, Laurence
A Farewell to Arms ADC:
360
The Streets Are Guarded
ADC: 360
Stanhope, Philip Dormer see
CHESTERFIELD, Lord
STANLEY, Thomas
General ERP: 479
STANTON
"Dandelion" PE: 416
STAPLEDON, William Olaf
General LCAB: 168
Last and First Men ENES2:
226-227
Odd John ENES2: 227

Sirius ENES2: 227
The Star Maker ENES2: 227
STARKES, Jaison
J.D.'s Revenge MBA: 185
STARKWEATHER, David
General MDAE: 466
The Love Affair Br: 667
STATIUS, Publius Papinius
Silvae Ma: 1980
Thebais Ma: 1980-1981
STAUFFER, Donald
"The Lemmings" PE: 416
STAVIS, Barrie
General MDAE: 467
Lamp at Midnight ADC: 361
The Man Who Never Died
ADC: 361; BAP: 187; Br:
667
_____ and Leona STAVIS
The Sun and I ADC: 361;
BAP: 187; Br: 667
STEAD, Christina
General CN: 483; MAP:
291-295; Po: 4006-4007
The Beauties and the Furies
CN: 483
Cotters' England [American ti-
tle: Dark Places of the
Heart] CN: 483; MAP:
294
For Love Alone CN: 483-484;
MAP: 293
House of All Nations CN: 484
Letty Fox: Her Luck CN:
484; MAP: 293
The Little Hotel MAP: 292
The Man Who Loved Children
CN: 484; ENE: 242;
LCAB: 168; MAP: 291-294;
Po: 4007
Miss Herbert MAP: 292
The People with Dogs CN:
484
The Salzburg Tales MAP: 293
Seven Poor Men of Sydney
CN: 484-485; MAP: 292-
294; Po: 4007
STEAD, Robert James Campbell
General Po: 4008
STEDMAN, Edmund Clarence
General Cla: 121; LCAB:
168
STEEL, Flora Annie
General TA: 273
STEELE, Sir Richard
General EC: 131-132; Li:

296-298

The Conscious Lovers DC1: 200-201; EC: 131-132; Li: 297; Ma: 1982-1983

The Funeral DC1: 201; Li: 297; Ma: 1983

The Lying Lover DC1: 201; Li: 297-298

School for Action DC1: 201

The Spectator Ma: 1983-1985

The Tatler EC: 131-132; Ma: 1985-1986

The Tender Husband DC1: 201; Li: 298

STEELE, Wilbur Daniel

General ASF: 525

"Always Summer" Wa: 692

"An American Comedy" Wa: 692

"The Anglo-Saxon" Wa: 692

"'Arab Stuff'" Wa: 693

"At Two-in-the-Bush" Wa: 693

"Autumn Bloom" Wa: 693

"A Bath in the Sea" Wa: 693

"The Black Road" Wa: 693

"Blue Murder" Wa: 693

"The Body of the Crime" Wa: 693

"Both Judge and Jury" Wa: 693

"Brother's Keeper" Wa: 693

"Bubbles" Wa: 693

"By Appointment" Wa: 693

"Can't Cross Jordan by Myself" Wa: 693

"Ching, Ching, Chinaman" Wa: 693

"Conjuh" Wa: 693

"Crocuses" Wa: 693

"The Dark Hour" Wa: 693

"A Devil of a Fellow" Wa: 693

"Down on Their Knees" Wa: 693

"A Drink of Water" Wa: 694

"Due North" Wa: 694

"Fe-Fi-Fo-Fum" Wa: 694

"Footfalls" Wa: 694

"For They Know Not What They Do" Wa: 694

"For Where Is Your Fortune Now?" Wa: 694

"From the Other Side of the South" Wa: 694

"The Gray Goose" Wa: 694

"The Guiabless" Wa: 694

"'He That Hideth His Secret'" Wa: 694

"How Beautiful with Shoes" ASF: 525; Po: 4008; Wa: 694; WaS1: 199

"In the Shade of the Tree" Wa: 694

"Isles of Spices and Lilies" Wa: 694

"Ked's Hand" Wa: 694

"The Killer's Son" Wa: 695

"Land's End" Wa: 695

"A Life" Wa: 695

"'Lost at Sea'" Wa: 695

"Luck" Wa: 695

"The Mad" Wa: 695

"Man and Boy" ["Man Without a God"] Wa: 695

"The Man Who Sat" Wa: 695

"The Man Who Saw Through Heaven" Wa: 695

"A Man's a Fool" Wa: 695

"The Marriage Kairwan" Wa: 695

"Mary Drake and Will Todd" Wa: 695

"Never Anything That Fades..." Wa: 695

"Out of Exile" Wa: 695

"Out of the Wind" Wa: 695

"Renegade" Wa: 695

"'Romance'" Wa: 695

"Sailor! Sailor!" Wa: 695

"The Shame Dance" Wa: 696

"Six Dollars" Wa: 696

"Sooth" Wa: 696

"Survivor" Wa: 696

"The Thinker" Wa: 696

"Tower of Sand" Wa: 696

"Two Seconds" Wa: 696

"The Wages of Sin" Wa: 696

"A Way with Women" Wa: 696

"What Do You Mean--American?" Wa: 696

"When Hell Froze" Wa: 696

"White Hands" Wa: 696

"White Horse Winter" Wa: 696

"The White Man" Wa: 696

"The Woman at Seven Brothers" Wa: 696

"The Yellow Cat" Wa: 696

STEFANSSON, David

General Po: 4008
Golden Gate DC2: 343
STEFFENS, Lincoln
General APC: 77-78
Autobiography LCAB: 168
STEGNER, Wallace Earle
General ASF: 527; CFAE:
362; CN: 485; Po: 4008
All the Little Live Things
Ma: 1987
Angle of Repose Ma: 1987
"Beyond the Glass Mountain"
Wa: 697
The Big Rock Candy Mountain
CN: 485; Ma: 1987-1988
"The Blue-Winged Teal" ASF:
526; SFC: 185; Wa: 697;
WaS1: 199
"Butcher Bird" ASF: 526
"Carrion Spring" ASF: 526;
WaS1: 199
"The Chink" ASF: 526;
WaS1: 199
"Chip Off the Old Block"
Wa: 697
"The City of the Living"
SFC: 185; Wa: 697
"The Double Corner" Wa:
697
"Field Guide to the Western
Birds" ASF: 526; Wa:
697; WaS1: 199
"Genesis" ASF: 526
"Goin' to Town" ASF: 526;
WaS1: 199
"Maiden in a Tower" ASF:
526
The Preacher and the Slave
CN: 485
Remembering Laughter Po:
4009; Wa: 697
"Saw Gang" ASF: 526;
WaS1: 199
A Shooting Star CN: 485;
Ma: 1988
"The Traveler" ASF: 526;
WaS1: 199
"Two Rivers" ASF: 526;
SFC: 185; Wa: 697
"The View from the Balcony"
ASF: 526; SFC: 185;
Wa: 697
"The Women on the Wall"
ASF: 526; SFC: 186;
Wa: 697; WaS1: 199
STEHR, Hermann

The Buried God Ke: 333
Damian Ke: 333
Heiligenhof Farm Ke: 333
Three Nights Ke: 333
STEIN, David Lewis
General JW: 352
STEIN, Gertrude
General ALL: 243-246; AN:
223-224; ASF: 528; LCAB:
168; MD: 292; Ne: 86-87;
Po: 4009-4013; Wo: 179-181
The Autobiography of Alice B.
Toklas ALL: 245; Ma:
1989
"A Box" PE: 416
Counting Her Dresses DC1:
201
Doctor Faustus Lights the
Lights ALL: 245
Everybody's Autobiography
ALL: 245
"The Gentle Lena" ASF: 527;
Wa: 697; WaS1: 199
"The Good Anna" ASF: 527;
SFC: 186; Wa: 698; WaS1:
199
"Lipschitz" PE: 416; Po:
4013
"A Long Dress" PE: 416
The Making of Americans Ma:
1990-1991; Ne: 87; Wo:
179-180
"Melanctha" ASF: 527-528;
Ne: 86; Po: 4013; SFC:
186; Wa: 698; WaS1: 199
"Miss Furr and Miss Skeene"
Wa: 698
Paris France ALL: 245; Po:
4014
Tender Buttons Ma: 1991
"Things as They Are" Ma:
1991-1992; SFC: 186; Wa:
698
Three Lives Ma: 1992
Wars I Have Seen ALL: 245
Yes Is for a Very Young Man
ADC: 361
_____ and Al CARMINES
Listen to Me ADC: 361
What Happened ADC: 361;
DC1: 201
_____ and Virgil THOMSON
Four Saints in Three Acts
ADC: 361-362; Br: 668;
DC1: 201; Ma: 1989-1990;
MD: 292; Po: 4013

STEIN, Joseph
 Enter Laughing ADC: 362;
 Br: 668
 _____, Jerry BOCK, and
 Sheldon HARNICK
 Fiddler on the Roof ADC:
 362-363
 _____, Robert RUSSELL, and
 Robert MERRILL
 Take Me Along! ADC: 363
STEINBECK, John
 General ALL: 246-250; AN:
 227-230; ASF: 533-534;
 CN: 485-489; LCAB:
 168-169; MD: 292; MDAE:
 469; Ne: 87-90; Po:
 4014-4023; Wo: 185-188
 Un Américain à New York et
 à Paris Po: 4023
 "Breakfast" ASF: 529; SFC:
 186; Wa: 698
 Burning Bright ADC: 363;
 ALL: 246; CN: 489-490;
 MD: 293; MDAE: 468;
 Ne: 89; Po: 4017
 Cannery Row ALL: 246;
 AN: 225; CN: 490; Ma:
 1993-1994; Po: 4014,
 4020, 4023
 "The Chrysanthemums" ASF:
 529; Ma: 1994; Po: 4024;
 SFC: 186; Wa: 698-699;
 WaS1: 200
 Cup of Gold AN: 225; CN:
 490
 East of Eden AN: 225; CN:
 491; Ma: 1995; Ne: 89;
 Po: 4017, 4024-4025
 "Flight" ASF: 529-530;
 Ma: 1995-1996; Po: 4025-
 4026; SFC: 187; Wa: 699
 "The Gift" ASF: 530; Wa:
 700; WaS1: 200
 The Grapes of Wrath ALL:
 246-247; AN: 225-226;
 CN: 491-495; LCAB:
 169; Ma: 1996-1998; Ne:
 87-89; Po: 4016, 4020,
 4026-4032; Wo: 186-187
 "The Great Mountains" ASF:
 530; Wa: 700; WaS1: 200
 "The Harness" ASF: 530;
 Wa: 700
 "How Edith McGillcuddy Met
 R.L. Stevenson" ASF:
 530

 "How Mr. Hogan Robbed a
 Bank" ASF: 530; Wa: 700
 In Dubious Battle ALL: 246;
 AN: 226-227; CN: 495-496;
 Ma: 1998-1999; Po: 4016,
 4032; Wo: 186
 "Johnny Bear" ASF: 530;
 SFC: 187; Wa: 700; WaS1:
 200
 "The Leader of the People"
 ASF: 531; Ma: 1999; Po:
 4018, 4020, 4032; SFC: 187;
 Wa: 700-701; WaS1: 200
 The Moon Is Down ADC: 363;
 ALL: 246; Br: 668; CN:
 496; MD: 293; Po: 4020,
 4033
 "The Murder" ASF: 531; Wa:
 701; WaS1: 200
 "Murder at Full Moon" ASF:
 531
 Of Mice and Men ADC: 364;
 AN: 227; Br: 668; CN:
 496-497; Ma: 1999-2000;
 MD: 293; Ne: 89; Po:
 4033
 The Pastures of Heaven AN:
 227; CN: 497
 The Pearl AN: 227; CN:
 497-498; Ma: 2000-2001; Ne:
 89; Po: 4014, 4033-4035
 "The Promise" ASF: 531; Wa:
 701; WaS1: 200
 "The Raid" ASF: 532; Wa:
 701
 The Red Pony ASF: 532; Ma:
 2001-2002; Po: 4035; SFC:
 187; Wa: 701
 "Saint Katy, the Virgin" ASF:
 532; Wa: 701-702; WaS1:
 200
 The Short Reign of Pippin IV
 CN: 498; Ma: 2002; SFC:
 187
 "The Short Story of Mankind"
 ASF: 532
 "The Snake" ASF: 532; Po:
 4035; Wa: 702; WaS1: 200
 Sweet Thursday ALL: 246;
 AN: 227; CN: 498; Ma:
 2002; Ne: 89; Po: 4020,
 4036
 "The Time the Wolves Ate the
 Vice-Principal" ASF: 533
 To a God Unknown AN: 227;
 CN: 498-499

Tortilla Flat AN: 227; CN:
    499; Ma: 2003-2004; Po:
    4036-4037
"The Vigilante" ASF: 533;
    SFC: 187; Wa: 702
The Wayward Bus AN: 227;
    CN: 499-500; Ma: 2004;
    Po: 4014
"The White Quail" ASF: 533;
    SFC: 187; Wa: 702;
    WaS1: 200
The Winter of Our Discontent
    CN: 500; Ma: 2004-2005;
    Po: 4020, 4037
STEINER, Franz Baermann
    Unruh ohne Uhr Po: 4037
STEINER, George
    Language and Silence
    LCAB: 169
STENDHAL [Marie Henri BEYLE]
    General LCAB: 18
    L'Abbesse de Castro Ke:
        162; Wa: 702
    Armance Fi: 166-167; Ke:
        162-163
    Les Cenci Ke: 163; Wa:
        702
    The Charterhouse of Parma
        Fi: 167-169; Ke: 163-
        164; LCAB: 18; Ma:
        2006-2007
    Le Coffre et le revenant Ke:
        164; Wa: 702
    "De l'amour" LCAB: 18
    "The Duchess of Palliano"
        Wa: 702
    "Ernestine" Wa: 702
    Lamiel Fi: 169; Ke: 165
    Lucien Leuwen Fi: 169-170;
        Ke: 165; Ma: 2007-2008
    "Le Philtre" Wa: 702
    The Red and the Black [Le
        Rouge et le noir] Fi:
        170-172; Ke: 165-167;
        Ma: 2008-2009; Po: 391-
        392
    "Souvenirs d'un gentilhomme
        italien" Wa: 702
    "Vanina Vanini" Wa: 702
    Vie de Henry Brulard Fi:
        172
STEPHEN, Felix
    General BALE: 405
STEPHEN, James Kenneth
    General TA: 274
STEPHENS, Alan

"The Dragon of Things" PE:
    416
"First Twenty-four Hours" PE:
    416
"The Green Cape" PE: 416
"Homily" PE: 416
"Little Things" PE: 416
"The Main Deep" PE: 416
"The Open World" PE: 416
"Prologue: Moments in a Glade"
    PE: 416
"The Rivals" PE: 416
"The Three Sisters" PE: 416
"Tree Meditation" PE: 417
"A Walk in the Void" PE: 417
STEPHENS, Alfred George
    General AL: 330-332; Po:
        4038-4039
STEPHENS, James
    General Po: 4039-4041
    The Charwoman's Daughter
        ENES2: 227
    The Crock of Gold ENE: 242;
        ENES2: 227; Po: 4041
    Deirdre ENE: 242; ENES1:
        210; Po: 4041
    "Desire" Wa: 703; WaS1: 201
    "Etched in Moonlight" Wa:
        703; WaS1: 201
    "Hunger" WaS1: 201
    "Mongan's Frenzy" WaS1: 201
STEPHENS, James Brunton
    General AL: 334-335
    "Convict Once" AL: 335
STEPHENS, Michael
    General ASF: 536
STERLING, George
    General Po: 4041-4042
STERLING, James
    General Da: 57
STERN, David [Marie D'AGOULT]
    Valentia Fi: 172
STERN, Richard Gustave
    General CFAE: 363; CN: 501;
        Po: 4042
STERNE, Laurence
    General Be: 241-251; Du:
        148-150
    A Sentimental Journey Be:
        243, 245, 249; Du: 143-144;
        EN: 115; ENE: 243;
        ENES1: 210-211; ENES2:
        227-228; LCAB: 169; Ma:
        2010-2011
    Sermons of Mr. Yorick Be:
        244-245

Tristram Shandy [The Life
and Opinions of Tristram
Shandy, Gentleman] Be:
118, 171, 241-251, 260;
Du: 144-148; EN: 115-
116; ENE: 243-246; ENES1:
211-213; ENES2: 228-230;
LCAB: 169-170; Ma: 2011-
2012; Po: 2038, 4489-
4490
STERNHEIM, Carl
General Br: 669; MD: 293;
Po: 4042
The Bloomers [The Under-
pants; Die Hose] Br:
669; DC2: 343; MD: 293
Citizen Schippel [Burger
Schippel] Br: 669; DC2:
343
The Mask of Virtue [Die
Marquise von Arcis] Br:
669; MD: 293
1913 Br: 669; MD: 293
The Snob [Der Snob] Br:
669; DC2: 343; MD:
293
Tabula Rasa Br: 669
The Underpants see The
Bloomers
STEVENS, George Alexander
General Li: 299
STEVENS, James Floyd
General Po: 4042-4043
STEVENS, Leslie
Bullfight ADC: 364
Champagne Complex ADC:
365
Lovers ADC: 365
Marriage-Go-Round ADC:
365
STEVENS, Wallace
General ALL: 250-256;
ICBAP: 120; LCAB:
170; Ma: 2018-2020; MP:
94-96; Po: 4043-4066
"Academic Discourse at
Havana" PE: 417
"Adagia" Po: 4066-4067
"Anecdote of Men by the
Thousand" PE: 417
"Anecdote of the Jar"
ICBAP: 120; PE: 417;
Po: 4067
"The Apostrophe to Vin-
centine" PE: 417
"Arcades of Philadelphia the

Past" ICBAP: 120; PE:
418; Po: 4067
"Arrival at the Waldorf" PE:
418
"Asides on the Oboe" PE:
418; Po: 4066, 4068
"The Auroras of Autumn"
ICBAP: 120; Ma: 2013;
PE: 418; Po: 4068
"The Auroras of Autumn--II"
ICBAP: 120
"The Auroras of Autumn--VIII"
ICBAP: 120
"Autumn Refrain" PE: 418
"Banal Sojourn" PE: 418
"Bantams in Pine-Woods"
ICBAP: 121; PE: 418-419;
Po: 4068
"The Bird with the Coppery,
Keen Claws" ICBAP: 121;
PE: 419; Po: 4069
"Blanche McCarthy" PE:
419
"The Bouquet" PE: 419
"Bouquet of Roses in Moon-
light" PE: 419
Bowl, Cat and Broomstick Po:
4069
"Certain Phenomena of Sound"
PE: 419
"Chocorua to Its Neighbor"
PE: 419
"A Clear Day and No Memories"
PE: 419
"The Comedian as the Letter
C" ICBAP: 121; Ma:
2013-2014; MP: 94, 96; PE:
419-421; Po: 4062, 4069-
4070
"Connoisseur of Chaos" PE:
421
"Cortége for Rosenbloom" PE:
421
"The Course of a Particular"
PE: 421; Po: 4071
"Credences of Summer"
ICBAP: 121; MP: 95; PE:
421; Po: 4071
"The Death of a Soldier" PE:
421
"Depression Before Spring"
PE: 421·
"Description Without Place"
PE: 422
"Disillusionment of Ten
O'Clock" PE: 422

"Domination of Black" PE: 422; Po: 4071-4072

"The Dwarf" PE: 422

"Earthy Anecdote" ICBAP: 121; PE: 422; Po: 4072

"Emperor of Ice-Cream" ICBAP: 121; Ma: 2014-2015; PE: 422-423; Po: 4066, 4072-4073

"Esthétique du Mal" ICBAP: 121; PE: 423-424; Po: 4062, 4066, 4073-4074

"Evening Without Angels" PE: 424

"The Examination of the Hero in Time of War" PE: 424

"Farewell to Florida" PE: 424

"Final Soliloquy of the Interior Paramour" PE: 424

"Flyer's Fall" ICBAP: 121; PE: 424

"Frogs Eat Butterflies" PE: 424

"The Glass of Water" ICBAP: 121; PE: 424; Po: 4074

"God Is Good. It Is a Beautiful Night" PE: 425

"The Good Man Has No Shape" PE: 425; Po: 4074

"The Green Plant" ICBAP: 121; PE: 425

"Harmonium" ALL: 251; MP: 94-95; Po: 4075

"The Hermitage at the Center" ICBAP: 121; PE: 425

"A High-Toned Old Christian Woman" PE: 425; Po: 4075

"Holiday in Reality" ICBAP: 121; PE: 425

"Homunculus et La Belle Etoile" PE: 425; Po: 4075

"The House Was Quiet and the World Was Calm" PE: 425

"How to Live. What to Do" PE: 425

"The Idea of Order at Key West" ICBAP: 121; PE: 425-426

Ideas of Order Po: 4066

"In a Bad Time" PE: 426

"Infanta Marina" PE: 426

"The Irish Cliffs of Moher" PE: 426

"It Must Change" Po: 4076

"July Mountain" PE: 426

"Landscape with Boat" PE: 426

"Large Red Man Reading" PE: 426

"Last Looks at the Lilacs" PE: 426

"Lebensweisheitspielerei" PE: 426

"Less and Less Human, O Savage Spirit" PE: 427

"Life Is Motion" ICBAP: 121; PE: 427; Po: 4076

"Life on a Battleship" PE: 427

"Like Decorations in a Nigger Cemetery" ICBAP: 122; PE: 427; Po: 4076

"Lions in Sweden" ICBAP: 122; PE: 427; Po: 4077

"The Load of Sugar-Cane" PE: 427

"Loneliness in Jersey City" PE: 428

"Long and Sluggish Lines" PE: 428

"Looking Across the Fields and Watching the Birds Fly" ICBAP: 122; PE: 428

"Madame La Fleurie" PE: 428

"Man and Bottle" PE: 428

"The Man on the Dump" PE: 428

"The Man Whose Pharynx Was Bad" PE: 428

"The Man with the Blue Guitar" ICBAP: 122; Ma: 2015-2016; PE: 428; Po: 4077

"Martial Cadenza" ICBAP: 122

"Memorandum" PE: 428

"The Men That Are Falling" ICBAP: 122; PE: 429; Po: 4077

"Metamorphosis" PE: 429

"Metaphors of a Magnifico" ICBAP: 122; PE: 429; Po: 4077-4078

"Mr. Burnshaw and the Statue" Po: 4078

"Le Monocle de Mon Oncle" Ma: 2016-2017; PE: 426-427; Po: 4078

"The Motive for Metaphor" PE: 429

"Mrs. Alfred Uruguay" PE: 429

"The Necessary Angel" Po: 4079

"New England Verses" PE: 429

"No Possum, No Sop, No Taters" ICBAP: 122; PE: 429; Po: 4066

"Not Ideas About the Thing but the Thing Itself" ICBAP: 122; PE: 430

"Note on Moonlight" PE: 429

"Notes Toward a Supreme Fiction" ICBAP: 122; Ma: 2017-2018; PE: 429-430; Po: 4079-4080

"Nuances of a Theme by Williams" PE: 430

"O Florida, Venereal Soil" PE: 431

"Oak Leaves Are Hands" PE: 430

"Of Hartford in a Purple Light" PE: 430; Po: 4080

"Of Ideal Time and Choice" PE: 430

"Of Mere Being" PE: 431

"Of Modern Poetry" PE: 431

"Of the Manner of Addressing Clouds" PE: 431

"On Poetic Truth" Po: 4080

"On the Road Home" ICBAP: 122

"One of the Inhabitants of the West" ICBAP: 122; PE: 431

"An Ordinary Evening in New Haven" ICBAP: 122; Ma: 2018; PE: 431; Po: 4080

"The Ordinary Women" PE: 431

"The Owl in the Sarcophagus" ICBAP: 123; PE: 431-432; Po: 4081

"Owl's Clover" PE: 432; Po: 4081

"The Paltry Nude Starts on a Spring Voyage" PE: 432; Po: 4081

"Peter Quince at the Clavier" ICBAP: 123; PE: 432-433; Po: 4081-4083

"The Plain Sense of Things" PE: 433

"The Plot Against the Giant" PE: 433; Po: 4058

"The Poem as Icon" PE: 433

"Poem Written at Morning" PE: 433

"The Poems of Our Climate" PE: 433

"Poetry Is a Destructive Force" PE: 433

"A Postcard from the Volcano" PE: 433

"A Primitive Like an Orb" PE: 433

"Prologues to What Is Possible" ICBAP: 123; PE: 433-434

"Reality" PE: 434

"The Red Fern" PE: 434

"Repetition of a Young Captain" PE: 434

"Restatement of Romance" PE: 434

"The Rock" Ma: 2020; PE: 434; Po: 4083

"Sad Strains of a Gay Waltz" PE: 434

"Sailing After Lunch" PE: 434

"Sea Surface Full of Clouds" ICBAP: 123; PE: 434-435; Po: 4058, 4084

"The Sense of the Sleight-of-Hand Man" ICBAP: 123; PE: 435

"Six Significant Landscapes" PE: 435; Po: 4058, 4084

"The Snow Man" ICBAP: 123; PE: 435; Po: 4085

"So-and-So Reclining on Her Couch" PE: 436

"Some Friends from Pascagoula" PE: 436

"Someone Puts a Pineapple Together" PE: 436

"Somnambulisma" PE: 436

"Sonatina to Hans Christian" PE: 436

"Study of Images" PE: 436

"Study of Two Pears" PE: 436

"Sunday Morning" ICBAP: 123; LCAB: 170; Ma: 2021; PE: 436-437; Po: 4085

"Tattoo" PE: 437

"Tea at the Palaz of Hoon" PE: 437

"That Which Cannot Be Fixed" PE: 437

"Theory" ICBAP: 123; Po: 4085

"Things of August" PE: 437

"Thirteen Ways of Looking at a Blackbird" ICBAP: 123; Ma: 2021-2022; PE: 438; Po: 4058, 4086

"A Thought Revolved" PE: 438

Three Travelers Watch a Sunrise ADC: 365; Br: 670; Po: 4087

"To the One of Fictive Music" PE: 438

"To the Roaring Wind" PE: 438

"Two Figures in Dense Violet Night" ICBAP: 123; PE: 438

"Two Illustrations That the World Is What You Make of It" ICBAP: 123; PE: 438

"Two Tales of Liadoff" PE: 438

"The Ultimate Poem Is Abstract" PE: 438

"Variations on a Summer Day" PE: 439

"The Virgin Carrying a Lantern" PE: 439

"Visibility of Thought" ICBAP: 123

"The Weeping Burgher" PE: 439

"The Well Dressed Man with a Beard" ICBAP: 123; PE: 439

"What We See Is What We Think" PE: 439

"The Woman in Sunshine" PE: 439

"Woman Looking at a Vase of Flowers" ICBAP: 124; PE: 439; Po: 4087

"World as Meditation" ICBAP: 124; PE: 439

STEVENSON, Robert Louis

General Ai: 158-159; BN: 96-97; Du: 151-152; EDT: 291-292; LCAB: 170-171; TA: 276; VP: 71

"The Beach of Falesá" Ma: 2023; SFC: 187; Wa: 703

The Black Arrow ENE: 246; ENES1: 213

"The Body-Snatcher" Wa: 703

"The Bottle Imp" SFC: 187; Wa: 703

Catriona ENES1: 213

David Balfour EN: 117

Dr. Jekyll and Mr. Hyde see The Strange Case of Dr. Jekyll and Mr. Hyde

The Ebb-Tide ENES1: 213

"The House of Eld" Wa: 703

Kidnapped EN: 117; ENE: 246; ENES1: 213; ENES2: 230; Ma: 2023

"A Lodging for the Night" SFC: 187; Wa: 703

"Markheim" SFC: 188; Wa: 703-704

The Master of Ballantrae BN: 96-97; Du: 151; EN: 117; ENE: 246-247; ENES1: 213; Ma: 2023-2024

"The Merry Men" SFC: 188; Wa: 704

"The Misadventures of John Nicholson" Wa: 704

"Olalla" SFC: 188; Wa: 704; WaS1: 201

Prince Otto ENES1: 213; ENES2: 230

"Providence and the Guitar" Wa: 704

St. Ives EN: 117

The Silverado Squatters Ma: 2024

"The Sire de Malétroit's Door" SFC: 188; Wa: 704

The Strange Case of Dr. Jekyll and Mr. Hyde BN: 97; Du: 151; ENE: 247; ENES2: 230; Ma: 2025-2026; SFC: 188; Wa: 704-705; WaS1: 201

"Thrawn Janet" SFC: 188;

Wa: 705
Travels with a Donkey in the
Cévennes Ma: 2026-2027
Treasure Island EN: 117;
ENE: 247; ENES1: 214;
ENES2: 231; LCAB: 171;
Ma: 2027
"The Treasure of Franchard"
Wa: 705
"The Waif Woman" SFC:
188; Wa: 705
Weir of Hermiston EN: 117;
ENES1: 214; ENES2: 231
"Will o' the Mill" SFC: 188;
Wa: 705
The Wrecker ENES1: 214
The Wrong Box ENES1: 214
STEVENSON, William
Gammer Gurton's Needle
ED: 120; EDC: 515-516
STEWART, Desmond
Vi Connolly's Spring Song
Po: 4087
STEWART, Douglas
General MAP: 388; Po:
4087-4088
"Carnival" Wa: 705
The Fire on the Snow DC1:
201; Po: 4087-4088
"A Girl with Red Hair" Wa:
705
"Give Us This Day" Wa:
705
The Golden Lover DC1:
201-202; Po: 4088
Ned Kelly DC1: 202; Po:
4088
Shipwreck DC1: 202; Po:
4087-4088
"The Three Jolly Foxes" Wa:
705
"The Whare" Wa: 705
STEWART, Harold
General Po: 4089
STEWART, John [1540-1600]
General Ai: 42
STEWART, John [1933-]
Curving Road WIL: 166
Last Cool Days WIL: 166
STEWART, John Innes Mackin-
tosh [Michael INNES]
General Ai: 281
From London Far ENES2:
231
STEWART, Mary
General LCAB: 171

The Crystal Cave ENES2: 231
The Hollow Hills ENES2: 231
STEWART, Michael and Jerry HER-
MAN
Hello, Dolly! ADC: 365-366
STEWART, Ramona
"The Promise" Wa: 705
STEWART, Ron
Sambo BAP: 187; MBA: 185
STICKNEY, Joseph Trumbull
General ICBAP: 124; LCAB:
171; Po: 4089
"In Ampezzo" ICBAP: 124;
PE: 439
"Lakeward" PE: 439
"Oneiropolos" ICBAP: 124
Prometheus Pyrphoros DC1:
202
STIFTER, Adalbert
Abdias Fi: 390; Ke: 333;
Wa: 706; WaS1: 201
The Ancient Seal [The Old
Seal] Ke: 333; Wa: 707
"Aragonite" Wa: 706
Argentine Mica [Mica] Ke:
333; Wa: 708
Bergkristall [The Rock Crystal]
Fi: 390; Ke: 334; Wa: 708
Brigitta Fi: 390; Ke: 333;
Wa: 706; WaS1: 201
"Chips Off the Old Block" Wa:
706; WaS1: 201
"The Condor" Wa: 706; WaS1:
201
The Elderly Bachelor [Der
Hagestolz] Ke: 333; Wa:
706; WaS1: 201
Fools' Castle [Die Narrenburg]
Ke: 334; Wa: 707
"The Forest Path" Wa: 707
The Forester Ke: 333
"The Fountain in the Woods"
Wa: 707; WaS1: 201
"Der fromme Spruch" Wa: 707
"Granite" Wa: 707; WaS1:
202
Der Hagestolz see The Elder-
ly Bachelor
Der Hochwald see The
Primeval Forest
Indian Summer [Der Nach-
sommer] Fi: 390-391; Ke:
334
The Inscribed Fir Tree Fi:
390; Wa: 707
"The Kiss of Sentze" Wa: 707

"Limestone" Wa: 707-708
Die Mappe Meines Urgross-
vaters Ke: 334
Mica see Argentine Mica
Der Nachsommer see Indian
Summer
Die Narrenburg see Fools'
Castle
The Old Seal see The An-
cient Seal
"The Pitch-Burner" Wa: 708
The Primeval Forest [The
Tall Forest; Der Hochwald]
Fi: 390; Ke: 334; Wa:
708
Prokopus Fi: 391; Ke:
334; Wa: 708
The Rock Crystal see Berg-
kristall
"The Sisters" ["Two Sisters"]
Wa: 708
The Tall Forest see The
Primeval Forest
Turmaline [Turmalin] Fi:
391; Wa: 708; WaS1: 202
"Two Widows" Wa: 708
"The Village on the Heath"
Wa: 709
"The Wanderer in the Forest"
Wa: 709; WaS1: 202
Wien und die Wiener Ke:
334
"Wild Flowers" Wa: 709
Witiko Fi: 391; Ke: 334-
335
STILES, Ezra
General AP: 499-500
STILES, Thelma Jackson
General BAF: 261
STILL, James [1812-?]
General BAW: 682-683
STILL, James [1906-]
General AN: 230; Po:
4089
STILL, William
General BAW: 683
STIMAC, Anthony, Don PIPPIN,
and Steve BROWN
Fashion ADC: 366
STIMSON, Frederic J.
"Dr. Materialismus" Wa:
709
STITT, Milan
The Runner Stumbles ADC:
366
STIVENS, Dal

General MAP: 297
STOCKING, Robert
Grand Hotel ADC: 366
STOCKTON, Frank R.
General AN: 230
"The Buller-Podington Compact"
Wa: 709
"The Governor-General" Wa:
709
"The Great Staircase at Land-
over Hall" Wa: 709
"The Griffin and the Minor
Canon" Wa: 709
"The Lady, or the Tiger?" Wa:
709
"Old Pipes and the Dryad" Wa:
709
"The Reformed Pirate" Wa:
709
"The Slight Mistake" Wa: 710
"A Story of Champaigne" Wa:
710
"The Transferred Ghost" Wa:
710
STOKER, Bram
General TA: 277-278
Dracula ENE: 247; ENES1:
214; ENES2: 231; Ma: 2028;
TA: 277-278
The Lair of the White Worm
ENES2: 231
STOKES, Adrian Durham
General Po: 4090
STOKES, Herbert
General MBA: 185
The Man Who Trusted the Devil
Twice MBA: 185
The Uncle Toms MBA: 185-
186
STOKES, Jack
The Incredible Jungle Journey
of Fenda Maria MBA: 186
STOLPE, Sven
General Po: 4090
Night Music Ke: 364
Sound of a Distant Horn Ke:
364
STONE, Alma
"I'm Waving Tomorrow" ASF:
536
STONE, Elizabeth
William Langshaw ENES1: 214;
ENES2: 232
STONE, Irving
General LCAB: 171; Po:
4090

STONE, Isidor
General LCAB: 171
STONE, John Augustus
General AD: 189-190
The Ancient Briton AD:
189
Metamora; or The Last of the
Wampanoags AD: 189-
190; DC1: 202
STONE, Louis
General MAP: 299; Po:
4090
Jonah MAP: 299; Po: 4091
STONE, Peter
Full Circle ADC: 366
_____, Richard RODGERS,
and Martin CHARNIN
Two by Two ADC: 366-367
STONE, Robert
A Hall of Mirrors Po: 4091
STONE, William Leete
"The Grave of the Indian
King" ASF: 536
"Lake St. Sacrament" ASF:
536
"Mercy Disborough" ASF:
536
"The Skeleton Hand" ASF:
536
"The Spectre Fire-Ship"
ASF: 536
STOPPARD, Tom
General MBD: 88; MDAE:
471-472; Po: 4091;
TMBP: 222-227
After Magritte TMBP: 226-
227
Albert's Bridge TMBP: 227
Dirty Linen TMBP: 227
Doggs Our Pet TMBP: 227
Enter a Free Man EDC:
516; TMBP: 227
The House of Bernarda Alba
TMBP: 228
If You're Glad, I'll Be Frank
TMBP: 228
Jumpers EDC: 516; Ma:
2029; TMBP: 223, 226,
228
The Real Inspector Hound
Br: 670; EDC: 516;
Po: 4091; TMBP: 225,
228-229
Rosencrantz and Guilden-
stern Are Dead Br: 670;
EDC: 516-517; Ma: 2029-

2030; MBD: 88; MDAE:
471-472; Po: 4091-4092.
TMBP: 222-226, 229
Travesties EDC: 517; Ma:
2030; TMBP: 79, 229-230
STOREY, David
General CFAE: 365; CN:
501; MBD: 88-89; MDAE:
474; Po: 4092; Sch: 276;
TMBP: 235-238
The Changing Room MDAE:
474; TMBP: 235-236, 238
The Contractor MDAE: 474;
TMBP: 235, 237-239
Cromwell TMBP: 239
Flight into Camden CN: 501-
502; Po: 4092; TMBP: 239
Home TMBP: 237, 239-240
In Celebration MDAE: 474;
TMBP: 235-237, 240
Pasmore ENES2: 232; TMBP:
236
Radcliffe CN: 502; ENES2:
232; MDAE: 474; Po: 4092;
TMBP: 236
The Restoration of Arthur Mid-
dleton TMBP: 237-238
Saville ENES2: 232
A Temporary Life ENES2:
232; TMBP: 236
This Sporting Life CN: 502;
ENES1: 215; Po: 4092-
4093
STORM, G.
The Tale of Bolotnikov Ke:
440
STORM, Theodor
"Abseits" Wa: 710
Am Kamin Ke: 335; Wa: 710
"Another Lembeck" see "A
Festival at Haderslevhuus"
Aquis Submersus Fi: 391; Ke:
335; Wa: 710; WaS1: 202
Auf dem Staatshof see On
the Staatshof
"Auf der Universität" Wa:
710
"Beim Vetter Christian" Wa:
711
"Ein Bekenntnis" Wa: 711
"Bötjer Basch" Wa: 711
"Carsten Curator" Wa: 711
"A Chapter in the History of
Grieshuus" Wa: 711
Ein Doppelgänger Fi: 391;
Ke: 335; Wa: 711

Draussen im Heidedorf Fi: 391-392; Wa: 711

"Drüben am Markt" Wa: 711

Ekenhof Fi: 392; Wa: 711

"A Festival at Haderslevhuus" Wa: 711

From Beyond the Seas Ke: 335

"Ein grünes Blatt" Wa: 711

Eine Halligfahrt Ke: 335; Wa: 712

"Hans und Heinz Kirch" Wa: 712

"Der Herr Etatsrad" Wa: 712

Hinzelmeier Ke: 335; Wa: 712

"Im Brauerhause" Wa: 712

Im Nachbarhaus Links Ke: 335; Wa: 712

"Im Schloss" Wa: 712

"Im Sonnenschein" Wa: 712

Immensee Fi: 392; Ke: 335-336; Wa: 712

In St. Jürgen Ke: 336; Wa: 712

"John Riew" Wa: 712

"Eine Malerarbeit" Wa: 712

"Marthe and Her Clock" Wa: 712

On the Staatshof [Auf dem Staatshof] Ke: 336; Wa: 710

"Pole Poppenspäler" Wa: 712; WaS1: 202

"Posthuma" Wa: 713

Psyche Ke: 336; Wa: 713

"Regentrude" Wa: 713

"Renate" Wa: 713

The Rider of the White Horse [Der Schimmelreiter] Fi: 392; Ke: 336; Wa: 713; WaS1: 202

"Schweigen" Wa: 713

"Die Söhne des Senators" Wa: 713

"Späte Rosen" Wa: 713

Veronika Ke: 336; Wa: 714

"Viola tricolor" Wa: 714

"Von jenseit des Meeres" Wa: 714

"Waldwinkel" Wa: 714

"Zur Wald- und Wasserfreude" Wa: 714

STORNI, Alfonsina

General Po: 4093

STOUT, Rex

General ASF: 537; LCAB: 171; Po: 4093

STOW, Randolph

General CN: 502-503; MAP: 301-304; Po: 4093-4095

The Bystander CN: 503; Po: 4094

A Counterfeit Silence Po: 4094

A Haunted Land CN: 503; Po: 4094

"Magic" Wa: 714

The Merry-Go-Round in the Sea CN: 503; MAP: 302-304; Po: 4095

To the Islands CN: 503; MAP: 302-303; Po: 4094

Tourmaline CN: 504; MAP: 302-304; Po: 4094

STOWE, Harriet Beecher

General AF: 234-238; ALL: 256-258; AN: 232; ASF: 537; Ho: 127-128, 155-156; LCAB: 171

Dred: A Tale of the Great Dismal Swamp AF: 235; ALL: 257; AN: 231; Ma: 2031-2032

"Love Versus Law" ASF: 537

"The Minister's Housekeeping" Wa: 714

The Minister's Wooing AF: 235

My Wife and I AF: 238; AN: 231

Oldtown Folks AF: 234, 238; AN: 231; Ma: 2032

The Pearl of Orr's Island AN: 231

Uncle Tom's Cabin AF: 235-238; ALL: 256-258; AN: 231-232; Ho: 127-128, 155-156; LCAB: 171-172; Ma: 2032-2034

STOWERS, Walter H.

General BAF: 261

STRACHEY, Giles Lytton

General LCAB: 172; Po: 4095-4097; TA: 278-279

Elizabeth and Essex Ma: 2035-2036

Eminent Victorians Ma: 2036-2037; Po: 4098

STRACHEY, William

General Da: 58

STRAIGHT, Michael
  Caravaggio ADC: 367
STRAMM, August
  General Po: 4098
STRAND, Mark
  General ICBAP: 124; LCAB:
    172
  "The Man in the Mirror" PE:
    439
STRAUSS, Emil
  "Frau Kampe" Wa: 714
  "Der Laufen" Wa: 714
  "Der Schleier" Wa: 714
  "Der Skorpion" Wa: 714
  "Unterwegs" Wa: 715
STREET, James
  General AN: 233
STRIBLING, Tomas Sigismund
  General AN: 233; Po:
    4098
STRINDBERG, August
  General Br: 670-672; LCAB:
    172; MD: 293-299; Po:
    4099-4106
  Advent EDC: 517; MD:
    299
  Alone [Ensam] Fi: 411;
    Ke: 364; Po: 4106, 4108
  Bandet see The Bond
  Before Death [Inför Döden]
    MD: 299
  Bjalbojarlen see Earl Birger
    of Bjalbo
  Black Banners Fi: 412; Ke:
    364
  "The Boarders" WaS1: 202
  The Bond [Bandet] Br:
    673; DC2: 343; EDC:
    517; MD: 299; Po: 4106
  The Bridal Crown [Crown
    Bride; Kronbruden]
    EDC: 517, 518; MD: 299
  Brott och Brott see There
    Are Crimes and Crimes
  The Burnt House [Brända
    Tomten] EDC: 517; MD:
    299
  By the Open Sea Fi: 412
  Charles XII [Carl XII] Br:
    673; MD: 299
  Christ, or The Lamb and
    the Wild Beast [Lammet
    och Vilddjuret] MD: 299
  Comrades [Kamraterna] Br:
    673; EDC: 518; MD: 299
  The Confession of a Fool

  Ke: 364
  The Creditors [Fordringsägare]
    Br: 673; DC2: 343; EDC:
    518; Ma: 2038; MD: 299;
    Po: 4109
  Crime and Crime see There
    Are Crimes and Crimes
  Crown Bride see The Bridal
    Crown
  The Dance of Death [Danse
    Macabre; Dödsdansen] Br:
    673-674; DC2: 343-344; EDC:
    518-519; Ma: 2038-2039;
    MD: 299-300; MDAE: 61;
    Po: 4105, 4107-4108; TMAP:
    41, 72
  Debit and Credit [Debet och
    Kredit] Br: 674; MD: 300
  A Dream Play [Ett Drömpsel]
    Br: 674-675; DC2: 344;
    EDC: 519-520; LCAB: 172;
    Ma: 2039-2040; MD: 300;
    Po: 4099, 4108
  The Dutchman [The Hollander;
    Holländarn] MD: 302; Po:
    4110
  The Dwellers of Hemso Ke:
    364
  Earl Birger of Bjalbo [Bjalbo-
    jarlen] Br: 675; MD: 300
  Easter [Päsk] Br: 675; DC2:
    344; EDC: 520; MD: 300
  Englebrekt Br: 675; MD: 300
  Ensam see Alone
  Erik XIV Br: 675; MD: 300
  The Father [Fadren] Br: 676-
    677; DC2: 344-345; EDC:
    520-521; Ma: 2040-2041;
    MD: 300-301; Po: 4105,
    4109
  Folkungasagan see The Saga
    of the Folkungs
  Fordringsägare see The
    Creditors
  Den Fredlöse see The Outlaw
  Fröken Julie see Miss Julie
  Genom Öknar till Arfland see
    Moses, or Through the Wild-
    erness to the Promised Land
  The Ghost Sonata [The Spook
    Sonata; Spöksonaten] Br:
    677, 682; DC2: 346; EDC:
    521-522; LCAB: 172; Ma:
    2041-2042; MD: 301; Po:
    4099, 4110-4111
  Gillets Hemlighet see The

Secret of the Guild

The Gothic Rooms Ke: 365

The Great Highway [The
Highway; Vid Stora Lands-
vagen] Br: 678; DC2:
346; EDC: 522; MD: 301;
Po: 4105, 4112

Gustav Adolf Br: 677; DC2:
346; EDC: 522; MD: 301;
Po: 4110

Gustav III Br: 678; EDC:
522; MD: 301

Gustav Vasa Br: 378; DC2:
346; MD: 301-302

Hermione MD: 302

Herr Bengts Hustru see
Lord Bengt's Wife

Himmelrikets Nycklar... see
The Keys of the Kingdom
of Heaven...

The Hollander [Holländarn]
see The Dutchman

In Rome Br: 678

In the Outer Skerries Ke:
365

Inferno Fi: 412; Ke: 365;
Po: 4110

Inför Döden see Before
Death

The Island of Paradise Ke:
365

Isle of the Dead [Toten-
Insel] Br: 678; DC2:
347; EDC: 522; MD: 302;
Po: 4112

The Journey of Lucky Peter
[Lucky Per's Journey;
Lycko-Pers Resa] Br:
678; EDC: 522; MD: 302

Kamraterna see Comrades

The Keys of the Kingdom of
Heaven; or, St. Peter
Wanders on Earth [Himmel-
rikets Nycklar, Eller
Sankte Per Vandrar Pa
Jorden] EDC: 522; MD:
302

Kristina see Queen Christina

Kronbruden see The Bridal
Crown

Lammet och Vilddjuret see
Christ, or The Lamb and
the Wild Beast

The Last of the Knights
[Siste Riddaren] Br:

678; MD: 302

Legender Ke: 365

Leka Med Elden see Playing
with Fire

The Link Br: 678

Lord Bengt's Wife [Herr Bengts
Hustru] Br: 678-679; MD:
302

Lucky Per's Journey [Lucky
Pehr; Lycko-Pers Resa] see
The Journey of Lucky Peter

A Madman's Defense Fi: 412

Marauders [Marodörer] EDC:
523

Married MD: 302

Master Olaf [Mäster Olaf] Br:
679; EDC: 523; MD: 302

Midsummer EDC: 523

Miss Julie [Fröken Julie] Br:
679-680; DC2: 347-348;
EDC: 523-524; LCAB: 172;
Ma: 2042-2043; MD: 303;
Po: 4105

Moses, or Through the Wilder-
ness to the Promised Land
[Genom Öknar till Arfland]
MD: 303

Moses, Socrates, and Christ
Br: 680

Mother Love [Moderskärlek]
MD: 303

The Nightingale of Wittenberg
[Die Nachtigall von Witten-
berg] Br: 680; DC2: 348;
MD: 303

The Outlaw [Den Fredlöse]
Br: 680; MD: 303

Pariah [Paria] Br: 680; EDC:
524; MD: 303

Päsk see Easter

The Pelican MD: 303-304

The People of Hemso Fi: 412-
413; Ke: 365

Playing with Fire [Leka Med
Elden] MD: 304

Progress Fi: 413

Queen Christina [Kristina]
Br: 680; MD: 304

The Red Room Fi: 413; Ke:
365-366; Ma: 2043-2044

The Regent [Riksförestandaren]
Br: 680; MD: 304

The Road to Damascus [To
Damascus; Till Damaskus]
Br: 680-681; DC2: 348;
EDC: 524-525; Ma: 2044;

MD: 304-305; Po: 4099, 4111-4112

The Romantic Organist on Rano Fi: 413; Ke: 366

The Roofing Feast [The Roof-Raising Feast] Fi: 413; Ke: 366

The Saga of the Folkungs [Folkungasagan] Br: 681; DC2: 345; MD: 304

The Scapegoat Fi: 413; Ke: 366

The Secret of the Guild [Gillets Hemlighet] Br: 681; MD: 304

Simoom [Samum] Br: 681; MD: 304

Siste Riddaren see The Last of the Knights

Socrates, or Hellas MD: 304

The Son of a Servant Fi: 413

The Spook Sonata [Spök-sonaten] see The Ghost Sonata

Vid Stora Landsvagen see The Great Highway

The Storm MD: 304

The Stronger [Den Starkare] Br: 682; DC2: 349; EDC: 524; MD: 304; Po: 4111

Swanwhite [Svanevit] Br: 682; EDC: 524

There Are Crimes and Crimes [Crime and Crime: Brott-och Brott] Br: 682; DC2: 349; EDC: 518; Ma: 2038; MD: 304; Po: 4105, 4107

Tjanstekvinnans Son Ke: 366

To Damascus [Till Damaskus] see The Road to Damascus

Toten-Insel see Isle of the Dead

Tschandala Fi: 414; Ke: 366

A Witch Fi: 414

STRINGER, David
"High Eight" WaS1: 202

STRITTMATTER, Erwin
Tinko Ke: 336; Po: 4112-4113

STROZZI, Lorenzo di
La Nutrice DC2: 349

STRUG, Andrzej
"From a Friend" Wa: 715
"An Idyll" Wa: 715
"Nightmare" Wa: 715
"Prologue" Wa: 715
"The Soldier from St. Beat" Wa: 715

STUART, Francis
Black List, Section H ENES1: 215; ENES2: 232
The Coloured Dome ENES1: 215; ENES2: 232
The Flowering Cross ENES2: 232
Memorial ENES2: 232
Pigeon Irish ENES1: 215; ENES2: 233
Pillar of Cloud ENES1: 215; ENES2: 233
Redemption ENES1: 215; ENES2: 233
Try the Sky ENES2: 233
Victors and Vanquished ENES2: 233

STUART, Jesse
General AN: 233; ASF: 540; Po: 4113; Wo: 190-191
Album of Destiny Po: 4113-4114
"Angel in the Pasture" ASF: 537; Wa: 715
"Another April" ASF: 537; SFC: 188; Wa: 715; WaS1: 203
"Another Hanging" ASF: 538; Wa: 715; WaS1: 203
"'As Ye Sow, So Shall Ye Reap'" ASF: 538
"Battle Keaton Dies" ASF: 538; Wa: 715
"Battle with the Bees" ASF: 538
"The Bellin' of the Bride" Wa: 715
"Betwixt Life and Death" Wa: 715; WaS1: 203
"The Blue Tick Pig" Wa: 715
"Clearing in the Sky" ASF: 538; Wa: 715
"Corbie" Wa: 715
"Dark Winter" ASF: 538; Wa: 715
"Ezra Alcorn and April" ASF: 538

"Fight Number Twenty-Five"
ASF: 538
"Frog Trouncin' Contest"
ASF: 538; Wa: 716; WaS1:
203
"The Great Cherokee Bill"
ASF: 538
"Hair" ASF: 538; Wa: 716
"Huey, the Engineer" ASF:
538; Wa: 716
"Men of the Mountains" Wa:
716
"Miss Anna's Asleep" ASF:
538
"Nest Egg" ASF: 538; Wa:
716
"No Hero" ASF: 538
"No Petty Thief" ASF: 539
"Old Op and the Devil" ASF:
539
"One of God's Oddlings"
ASF: 539; Wa: 716
"Rain on Tanyard Hollow"
ASF: 539; WaS1: 203
"The Reaper and the Flowers"
ASF: 539
"A Ribbon for Baldy" ASF:
539
"The Slipover Sweater" Wa:
716
"A Stall for Uncle Jeff"
WaS1: 203
"The Storm" Wa: 716
"Sylvania Is Dead" ASF:
539; Wa: 716; WaS1:
203
"Testimony of Trees" WaS1:
203
"The Thing You Love" ASF:
539
"This Farm for Sale" ASF:
539; WaS1: 203
"Tim" Wa: 716
"Tradelast" ASF: 539
Trees of Heaven Po: 4114
"Uncle Casper" ASF: 539
"Uncle Jeff" ASF: 539; Wa:
716
"Walk in the Moon Shadows"
ASF: 539
"Wild Palms" ASF: 539
"Word and Flesh" WaS1:
203
"Zeke Hammertight" ASF:
539; Wa: 716
STUART, Morna

Traitor's Gate Br: 682
STUART, Ruth McEnery
"Uncle Mingo's 'Speculations'"
ASF: 541; Wa: 716
STUBBES, Philip
The Anatomie of Abuses Hen:
103; SC: 98
STURGEON, Theodore [Edward
Hamilton WALDO]
General ASF: 541; LCAB:
184
"Bulkhead" ASF: 541; WaS1:
203
"Extrapolation" WaS1: 203
"Rule of Three" WaS1: 204
"Slow Sculpture" ASF: 541
"The Touch of Your Hand"
WaS1: 204
"Thunder and Roses" Wa: 716
"Twink" WaS1: 204
"The World Well Lost" ASF:
541
STURGES, Preston
Child of Manhattan ADC: 367
Make a Wish ADC: 367
Strictly Dishonorable ADC:
367
STURGIS, Howard Overing
General Po: 4114
"The China Pot" Po: 4114
Tim ENES2: 233
STURT, George
General Po: 4115
The Bettesworth Book Po:
4115
STYRON, William
General ALL: 259-260; AN:
233; ASF: 542; CFAE:
367-370; CN: 504-505;
LCAB: 172-173; Ne: 90-91;
Po: 4115-4120
The Confessions of Nat Turner
ALL: 259; CFAE: 367-370;
CN: 505-507; LCAB: 173;
Ma: 2045-2046; Po: 4119-
4124
"The Enormous Window" ["Au-
tumn"] ASF: 541; Wa:
717
Lie Down in Darkness ALL:
259; AN: 233; CFAE: 370;
CN: 507-509; LCAB: 173;
Ma: 2046-2048; Ne: 90;
Po: 4115, 4117-4118, 4124-
4125
"The Long Dark Road" ASF:

541
The Long March ALL: 259;
    CFAE: 369; CN: 509;
    LCAB: 173; Ma: 2048-
    2049; Ne: 90-91; Po:
    4117-4118, 4125-4126; Wa:
    717
Set This House on Fire ALL:
    259; CFAE: 368, 370;
    CN: 509-511; Ma: 2049-
    2050; Ne: 90-91; Po:
    4115, 4117-4119, 4126-4129
"Sun on the River" ASF:
    542
SU MAN-SHU [English name:
    Pev MANDJU]
"Tale of Crimson Silk" Wa:
    717
SUARES, André
General Po: 4129-4131
SUASSUNA, Ariano
Auto da Compadecida Br:
    682; Po: 4131
SUBLETTE, Walter
General BAF: 262
SUCKLING, Sir John
General Ba: 102-103; LJCD:
    255-257; Ma: 2051
Aglaura DC1: 202
"A Ballad Upon a Wedding"
    PE: 439
"Out Upon It" PE: 440
"A Session of the Poets" Ba:
    102-103
"Song: Why So Pale and
    Wan, Fond Lover?"
    ICBAP: 124; PE: 440
"There Never Yet Was Woman
    Made" PE: 440
"'Tis Now, Since I Sate Down
    Before" PE: 440
"Why So Pale and Wan"
    ICBAP: 124; PE: 440
SUCKOW, Ruth
General AN: 233; ASF:
    543; Po: 4131
"Auntie Bissel" ASF: 542;
    Wa: 718
Country People LCAB: 173
"The Daughter" Wa: 718
"Elegy for Alma's Aunt Amy"
    ASF: 542
"Eltha" ASF: 542; Wa:
    718
"Eminence" ASF: 543; Wa:
    718

The Folks AN: 233
"Four Generations" ASF: 543;
    SFC: 189; Wa: 718
"Golden Wedding' ASF: 543;
    SFC: 189; Wa: 718
"Good Pals" ASF: 543; Wa:
    718
"A Homecoming" ASF: 543;
    Wa: 718
The John Wood Case Po: 4131
"A Little Girl's World" Wa:
    718
"Mame" ASF: 543; Wa: 718
"The Man of the Family" Wa:
    718
"Midwestern Primitive" Wa:
    718
"Mrs. Kemper" Wa: 718
"Mrs. Vogel and Ollie" ASF:
    543; Wa: 718
"A Pilgrim and a Stranger" Wa:
    719
"Renters" Wa: 719
"A Rural Community" ASF:
    543; Wa: 719
"Spinster and Cat" ASF: 543
"A Start in Life" ASF: 543;
    SFC: 189; Wa: 719
"Uprooted" ASF: 543; Wa:
    719
"The Valentine Box" Wa: 719
"What Have I" ASF: 543; Wa:
    719
SUDERMANN, Hermann
General Br: 683; MD: 305-
    306; Po: 4132
The Battle of the Butterflies
    [Die Schmetterlingsschlacht]
    Br: 683
Dame Care Ke: 336-337
The Destruction of Sodom
    [Sodoms Ende] Br: 683
Die Drei Reiherfedern see The
    Three Heron Plumes
Die Ehre see Honor
Das Ewig-Mannliche see It's
    a Man's World
Fritzchen Br: 683
Der Gute Ruf MD: 306
Happiness in a Nook [The Vale
    of Content; Das Gluck im
    Winkel] Br: 683
Home [Heimat; Magda] Br:
    683-684; DC2: 349; MD:
    306
Honor [Die Ehre] Br: 684

It's a Man's World [Das Ewig-
Mannliche] Br: 684
Johannes Br: 684
Johannisfeuer see St. John's
Fire
The Joy of Living [Es Lebe
das Leben] Br: 684;
MD: 306
Magda see Home
Regina Ke: 337
"Die Reise nach Tilsit" Wa:
719
St. John's Fire [Johannis-
feuer] Br: 684
Die Schmetterlingsschlacht
see The Battle of the
Butterflies
Sodoms Ende see The De-
struction of Sodom
Song of Songs Ke: 337
Der Sturmgeselle Sokrates
Br: 684; DC2: 349
Teja Br: 684
The Three Heron Plumes
[The Three Herons'
Feathers; Die Drei Reiher-
federn] Br: 684-685;
DC2: 349; MD: 306; Po:
4132
The Undying Past Ke: 337
The Vale of Content see
Happiness in a Nook
The Witches Ride Br: 685
SUDRAKA, King
Little Clay Cart DC2: 349-
350
SUE, Eugène
Mathilde Fi: 172
Les Mystères de Paris Fi:
172-173
SUEIRO, Daniel
General Po: 4132
SUELDO GUEVARA, Rubén
"El fugitivo" Wa: 719
SUKENICK, Ronald
General ASF: 544; LCAB:
173
"The Birds" WaS1: 204
"The Death of the Novel"
ASF: 544; Wa: 719
"Momentum" ASF: 544; Wa:
719
"One Every Minute" Wa:
719
"The Permanent Crisis" Wa:
720

"Roast Beef--A Slice of Life"
Wa: 720
"The Sleeping Gypsy" Wa: 720
"What's Your Story?" Wa: 720
SUKHOVO-KOBYLIN, Alexander
Vasilealexander Vasileivich
The Death of Tarelkin [Smert
Tarelkin] EDC: 525
SUMARKOV, Alexander
Hamlet DC2: 350
SUNDGAARD, Arnold
The First Crocus ADC: 368
The Great Campaign ADC:
368
Of Love Remembered ADC:
368
_____ and Marc CONNELLY
Everywhere I Roam ADC: 368
SUNDMAN, Per Olof
General Po: 4133
Expeditionen Po: 4133
SUPERVIELLE, Jules
General Po: 4133-4139
"L'Adolescente" Wa: 720
"Antoine-du-Desert" Wa: 720
La Belle au bois dormant Br:
685
"Le Boeuf et l'Ane de la
crêche" Wa: 720
Bolivar Br: 685
"L'Enfant de la haute mer"
WaS1: 204
La Fable du monde Po: 4139
"La Femme retrouvée" Wa:
720
"Le Heron Garde-Boeuf" Wa:
720
"L'Inconnue de Seine" Wa:
720
Robinson Br: 685
Shéhérazade Br: 685
Songe d'un, nuit d'été Po:
4139
"Vacances" Wa: 720
Le Voleur d'enfants Br: 685
SUROV, A.
Mad Haberdasher DC2: 350
Surrey, Earl of see HOWARD,
Henry, Earl of Surrey
SURTEES, Robert Smith
General BN: 97-98; LCAB:
173
Ask Mama ENES2: 233
Handley Cross ENES2: 233;
Ma: 2052
Hawbuck Grange ENES2: 233

Hillingdon Hall ENES2: 233
Jorrocks' Jaunts and Jollities
    BN: 97-98; ENES2: 233;
    Ma: 2052
Mr. Facey Romford's Hounds
    ENES2: 233
Mr. Sponge's Sporting Tour
    ENES2: 233
Plain or Ringlets ENES2:
    233
Young Tom Hall ENES2: 233
SUSANN, Jacqueline
    General Po: 4140
SUTHERLAND, Efua Theodora
    [Morgue]
    General BALE: 405
SUTHERLAND, John
    General Po: 4140
SUTHERLAND, Robert Garioch
    [Robert GARIOCH]
    General Ai: 287
SUTRO, Alfred
    General Mi: 277
SUTTNER, Bertha von
    Die Waffen Nieder! Fi: 395
SUTTON, Dolores
    The Web and the Rock ADC:
    368
SVEVO, Italo
    General Po: 4140-4143
    "Argo and His Master" Wa:
    720
    As a Man Grows Older
    [Senilità] Fi: 276; Ke:
    252-253; Po: 4144
    The Confessions of Zeno [La
    Coscienza di Zeno] Fi:
    276-278; Ke: 252; Po:
    4143-4144
    "Generous Wine" WaS1: 204
    "The Hoax" Wa: 720; WaS1:
    204
    A Life Fi: 279; Ke: 252
    "The Mother" Wa: 721;
    WaS1: 204
    Senilità see As a Man
    Grows Older
    "Short Sentimental Journey"
    WaS1: 204
    "The Story of the Nice Old
    Man and the Pretty Girl"
    Wa: 721; WaS1: 204
    "This Indolence of Mine"
    Wa: 721
SWADOS, Harvey
    General ASF: 544; CFAE:

371; CN: 511; JW: 302;
    LCAB: 173; Po: 4145
False Coin CN: 511-512; Po:
    4145
"Just One of the Boys" Wa:
    721
Out Went the Candle CN: 512
The Will CN: 512
SWALLOW, Alan
    General Po: 4145-4146
SWAN, Annie S.
    General Ai: 172
SWAN, Jon
    "The Magpie" PE: 441
SWEET, Alexander E.
    General ASF: 544
SWENSON, May
    General ICBAP: 124; Po:
    4146-4147
    "Cat and the Weather" Po:
    4147
    "Lion" PE: 441
SWIFT, Allen
    Checking Out ADC: 368
SWIFT, Jonathan
    General Be: 258-267; EC:
    134-136; ICBAP: 124;
    LCAB: 173-174; Ma: 2055-
    2056; Me: 374-399
    The Battle of the Books Be:
    262; EC: 136
    "Bancis and Philemon" EC:
    140; Me: 388, 391; PE:
    441
    "A Beautiful Young Nymph Go-
    ing to Bed" PE: 441
    "Bickerstaff Pamphlets" EC:
    137
    "Cadenus and Vanessa" EC:
    140-141; ICBAP: 125; Me:
    380, 386, 388, 391, 393, 395
    "Cassinus and Peter" ICBAP:
    125; PE: 441
    The Conduct of the Allies EC:
    141
    "The Day of Judgment" EC:
    140; ICBAP: 125; Me: 381,
    386; PE: 441
    "Death and Daphne" Me: 385
    "Description of a City Shower"
    EC: 140; Me: 381, 388;
    PE: 441-442
    "Description of a Salamander"
    Me: 380; PE: 442
    "Description of the Morning"
    Me: 392, 396-397; PE: 442

"Drapier's Letters" EC: 138

"Epistle to a Lady" EC: 140

"The Fable of Midas" Me: 380; PE: 442

Gulliver's Travels Be: 259-263, 265-267; EC: 138-139; EN: 117-120; ENE: 247-252; ENES1: 215-218; ENES2: 234-235; LCAB: 174; Ma: 2053-2054; Po: 2112

"The Journal" or "The Country Life" PE: 442

Journal to Stella EC: 137; Ma: 2054-2055

"The Lady's Dressing Room" EC: 139; ICBAP: 125; Me: 379, 383-384, 394; PE: 442

"The Legion Club" EC: 141; PE: 442

A Modest Proposal EC: 141-142

"Ode to Sancroft" Me: 391; PE: 442

"On Poetry: A Rapsody" EC: 140; Me: 382, 395; PE: 442

"On the Burning of Whitehall in 1697" EC: 140

"Panegyric on the Reverend D--n S---t" Me: 398-399

"A Panegyrick on the D--n, in the Person of a Lady in the North" PE: 442

Polite Conversation EC: 141

"The Progress of Beauty" PE: 443

Project for the Advancement of Religion EC: 141

"Satirical Elegy on a Late Famous General" EC: 140; Me: 389; PE: 443

"A Serious Poem upon William Wood" PE: 443

"Stella's Birth-Day, 1726/27" Me: 382; PE: 443

"Strephon and Chloe" ICBAP: 125; Me: 383; PE: 443

A Tale of a Tub Be: 243, 247, 259, 261-265; EC: 136-137, 141; Ma: 2057-2058; Ri2: 315

"To Stella, Who Collected and Transcribed His Poems" Me: 394

"Verses on the Death of Dr. Swift" EC: 140-141; ICBAP: 125; LCAB: 174; Me: 381-382, 387, 392-393, 396-397, 399; PE: 443

"Verses Wrote in a Lady's Ivory Table-Book" ICBAP: 125; PE: 443

"The Virtues of Sid Hamet the Magician's Rod" Me: 380; PE: 443

"The Windsor Prophecy" ICBAP: 125

SWIGGETT, Howard

General Po: 4147

The Power and the Prize Po: 4147

SWINBURNE, Algernon Charles

General BN: 98-99; EDT: 296-301; LCAB: 174; Ma: 2059-2060; VP: 73-74

"Anactoria" PE: 444

Atalanta in Calydon DC1: 202; EDT: 297-300; Ma: 2059; VP: 74

"Autumn in Cornwall" PE: 444

"Ave Atque Vale" PE: 444

"A Ballad of Death" PE: 444

"A Ballad of Dreamland" PE: 444

"Before the Mirror" PE: 444

"Between the Sunset and the Sea" PE: 444

Bothwell EDT: 298

"By the North Sea" PE: 444

"A Cameo" PE: 444

Chastelard EDT: 298-299

Erechtheus EDT: 298-299; VP: 74

"Faustine" PE: 444

"The Garden of Proserpine" PE: 444

"Hertha" ICBAP: 125; PE: 444

"The Hounds of Spring" PE: 445

"Hymn to Proserpine" PE: 445

"The Lake of Gaube" PE: 445

"Lancelot and Elaine" ICBAP: 125

"Laus Veneris" PE: 445

Lesbia Brandon BN: 99; ENES1: 218; ENES2: 235

Love's Cross Currents BN: 99; ENES1: 218; ENES2: 235

Mary Stuart EDT: 298

"Nephelidia" PE: 445

"A New-Year Ode: To Victor Hugo" ICBAP: 125

"A Nympholept" PE: 445

"On the Cliffs" ICBAP: 125; PE: 445

"Prelude" to Songs Before Sunrise PE: 445

La Soeur de la Reine EDT: 300-301

"A Solitude" PE: 445

"The Sundew" PE: 445

"Thalassius" ICBAP: 125; PE: 445-446; VP: 73

"Tristram of Lyonesse" ICBAP: 125; VP: 74

"The Triumph of Time" ICBAP: 125; PE: 446

SWINNERTON, Frank
General TA: 280

SYLVANUS, Erwin
Dr. Korczak and the Children [Korczak und Seine Kinder] Br: 685

SYMONDS, John Addington
General ICBAP: 126; TA: 282

SYMONENKO, Vasyl
General Po: 4147-4148

SYMONS, Arthur
General Po: 4148-4151; TA: 283

"Liber Amoris" PE: 446

"La Mélinite: Moulin Rouge" PE: 446

"Nova on the Pavement" PE: 446

"Prologue" to London Nights PE: 446

"Rosa Mundi" PE: 446

Spiritual Adventures Po: 4151

"Stella Maris" PE: 446

"Studies in Strange Sins: After the Designs of Aubrey Beardsley" ICBAP: 126; Po: 4151

"To a Dancer" PE: 446

Synge, Don [pseud.] see EDELSTEIN, Hyman

SYNGE, John Millington
General Br: 685-687;

LCAB: 174; MBD: 89-93; MD: 306-308; Mi: 277-279; Po: 4152-4156; TA: 285

The Aran Islands DC1: 202; Po: 4156

Deirdre of the Sorrows Br: 687-688; DC1: 202-203; EDC: 525-526; Ma: 2061; MBD: 90-92; MD: 308; Po: 4156-4157

In the Shadow of the Glen see The Shadow of the Glen

The Playboy of the Western World Br: 689-690; DC1: 203-204; EDC: 526-528; LCAB: 174; Ma: 2062-2063; MBD: 90-93; MD: 308; Po: 4157-4161

Riders to the Sea Br: 690-691; DC1: 204; EDC: 528-529; LCAB: 174-175; Ma: 2063-2064; MBD: 89-93; MD: 308-309; Po: 4161-4162

The Shadow of the Glen [In the Shadow of the Glen] Br: 688-689, 691-692; DC1: 203-204; EDC: 526; Ma: 2064-2065; MBD: 89-91; MD: 309; Po: 4157

The Tinker's Wedding Br: 692; DC1: 205; EDC: 529-530; Ma: 2065; MBD: 90-91; MD: 309

The Well of the Saints Br: 692-693; DC1: 205; EDC: 530; Ma: 2065-2066; MBD: 90, 93; MD: 309

SZABO, Dezso
The Lost Village Ke: 440-441

SZANIAWSKI, Jerzy
General Po: 4162

T

TABORI, George
The Emperor's Clothes MDAE: 475

TACITUS, Cornelius
The Histories Ma: 2067-2068

TAFT, Robert W.
"Attack on Barbados at Sandy Point" ICBAP: 126; PE: 446; Po: 4163

TAGGARD, Genevieve

General LCAB: 175
"The Four Songs" PE: 446
Tagger, Theodore see BRUCK-
NER, Ferdinand
TAGGERT, Brian
When Last I Saw the Lem-
mings ADC: 369
TAGORE, Rabindranath
General MD: 309-310; Po:
4163-4176
"The Atonement" WaS1: 204
Chandalika MD: 310
Char Adhyaya Po: 4177
Chitrangada [Chitra] MD:
310
"Cloud and Sun" WaS1: 204
The Curse at Farewell [Viday
Abhisap] MD: 310
"The Devotee" WaS1: 204
"The Dream" Po: 4177
"The Editor" WaS1: 205
"The Girl Between" WaS1:
205
Gitanjali Po: 4177
The King and the Queen
[Raja o Rani] MD: 310
King of the Dark Chamber
[Raja] Br: 693; DC2:
350
"A Lapse of Judgment" Po:
4169; Wa: 721
Malini MD: 310
Mukta Dhara see The Water-
fall
Natir Puja see Worship of
the Dancing Girl
Nature's Revenge [Prakritir
Pratishodh] MD: 310
"One Night" WaS1: 205
"The Postmaster" WaS1:
205
Prakritir Pratishodh see
Nature's Revenge
"Punishment" Po: 4169;
Wa: 721
Raja see King of the Dark
Chamber
Raja o Rani see The King
and the Queen
"Rashmoni's Son" WaS1: 205
Red Oleanders [Rakta-
Karabi] MD: 310
"The Return of Khokababu"
WaS1: 205
"The Troublemaker" WaS1:
205

Viday Abhisap see The Curse
at Farewell
The Waterfall [Mukta Dhara]
MD: 310
"We Crown Thee King" WaS1:
205
"A Wife's Letter" WaS1: 205
Worship of the Dancing Girl
[Natir Puja] MD: 310
Tailhède, Raymond de la see
LA TAILHEDE, Raymond de
TAILLEVENT, Michault
Moralite de Povre Commun DC2:
350
TAILOR, Robert
General NI: 339
TALCOVE, Rick
Ping Pong ADC: 369
TALFOURD, Sir Thomas Noon
General EDT: 302
Ion DC1: 205
TALIAFERRO, Harden E.
General ASF: 544
TALIB, Mohammed
General BALE: 406
TALICE, Roberto A.
General Br: 693
TALLEMANT, Paul
Voyage to the Isle of Love Ke:
167
TALLY, Ted
Terra Nova ADC: 369
TAMASI, Aron
Abel Ke: 441
Matthias, the Ice-Breaker Ke:
441
Prince of the Virgin Mary Ke:
441
A Star Is Shining Ke: 441
TAMAYO Y BAUS, Manuel
Un drama nuevo DC2: 350
Lances de honor DC2: 350
TAMMSAARE, Anton H.
Truth and Justice Ke: 441
TAMMUZ, Benjamin
"A Roll of Canvas" Wa: 721
TANIZAKI, Jun'ichirō
General Po: 4178
The Makioka Sisters Po: 4178
"Tattoo" WaS1: 205
TANNAHILL, Robert
General Ai: 112
TAPIA, Eugenio de
El viage de un curioso por
Madrid Ke: 231
TARDIEU, Jean

General Br: 693; MD: 310;
Po: 4178-4179
The A B C of Our Life
[L'A.B.C. de notre vie]
Br: 693; DC2: 351; Po:
4178
Les Amants du Metro see
The Lovers of the Metro
The Apollo Society [Le Soci-
été Apollon] Br: 693;
MD: 310
Conversation--Sinfonietta
Br: 694
Dismembered Voices DC2:
351
Un Geste pour un autre see
One Way for Another
The Information Bureau [In-
formation Window; Le
Guichet] Br: 694; DC2:
351; MD: 310
The Keyhole [La Serrure]
Br: 694
The Lovers of the Metro
[Les Amants du Metro]
Br: 694; DC2: 351; Po:
4178
One Way for Another [Un
Geste pour un autre] Br:
694
La Politesse inutile see
Useless Courtesy
Qui est la? see Who Is
There?
The Rite of Night [Le Sacre
de la nuit] Br: 694
La Serrure see The Key-
hole
Le Société Apollon see The
Apollo Society
Useless Courtesy [La Poli-
tesse inutile] Br: 694
Verb Tenses DC2: 351
Who Is There? [Qui est la?]
Br: 694
TARKINGTON, Booth
General AN: 234; LCAB:
175; MD: 310; Ne:
91-92; Po: 4179-4181;
Wo: 195
Alice Adams AN: 234; Ma:
2069; Po: 1289-1290; Wo:
195
Clarence ADC: 369; MD:
310
Colonel Satan ADC: 369

The Gentleman from Indiana Ma:
2070; Po: 4181
The Heritage of Hatcher Ide
AN: 234
The Magnificent Ambersons AN:
234; Ma: 2070-2071
The Midlander AN: 234
Monsieur Beaucaire Ma: 2071
Penrod AN: 234; Ma: 2071-
2072; Po: 4181; Wo: 195
The Plutocrat AN: 234
Seventeen ADC: 369; Ma:
2072; Po: 4182
The Turmoil AN: 234
_____ and Harry Leon WILSON
How's Your Health? ADC: 369
Tweedles ADC: 369; MD:
310
TARKOVSKII, Arsenii Aleksandro-
vich
General Po: 4182
TARLTON, Richard
Tarlton's Jests ERP: 483
TARN, Nathaniel
General Po: 4182
TARSIS, Valeriy
The Tale of the Bluebottle
Ke: 441
TASCA, Jules
The Mind with the Dirty Man
ADC: 369
TASSO, Torquato
Aminta DC2: 351
Jerusalem Delivered Ma: 2073
TATE, Allen
General ALL: 260-261; APC:
186-188; LCAB: 175; MP:
97-98; Po: 4182-4191
"Again the Native Hour" PE:
446
"Breathing" PE: 450
"The Buried Lake" ICBAP:
126; PE: 446; Po: 4188
"Causerie" PE: 446
"The Cross" PE: 447; Po:
4191
"The Crow" MP: 98
"Death of Little Boys"
ICBAP: 126; PE: 447; Po:
4191-4192
The Fathers AN: 235; Po:
4192-4193
"Fragment of a Meditation"
PE: 447
"The Immortal Woman" Wa:
721

"Last Days of Alice" MP:
98; PE: 447
"The Maimed Man" ICBAP:
126; PE: 447; Po: 4188
"The Meaning of Death" PE:
447-448
"The Meaning of Life"
ICBAP: 126; PE: 448;
Po: 4193
"The Mediterranean" ICBAP:
126; MP: 98; PE: 448;
Po: 4194
"Men get down on their
knees" PE: 450
"Message from Abroad" PE:
448
"The Migration" Wa: 721
"Mr. Pope" PE: 448; Po:
4194
"More Sonnets at Christmas,
I" PE: 448
"More Sonnets at Christmas,
IV" PE: 448
"Mother and Son" PE: 448
"The Oath" PE: 449
"Ode to Our Young Pro-
Consuls of the Air" PE:
449; Po: 4194
"Ode to the Confederate
Dead" LCAB: 175; PE:
449
"Retroduction to American
History" PE: 449
"Seasons of the Soul" ICBAP:
126; PE: 449; Po: 4194
"Shadow and Shade" PE:
450
"Sonnet at Christmas"--"This
Is the Day His Hour of
Life Draws Near" PE:
450
"The Subway" PE: 450
"The Swimmers" ICBAP:
126; PE: 450; Po: 4188
"To the Lacedemonians" Po:
4195
"Winter Mask" PE: 450
"The Wolves" PE: 450
TATE, Nahum
General Bon: 30; Li: 301-
302
A Duke and No Duke DC1:
205; Li: 302
Injured Love Li: 302
King Lear DC1: 205; Li:
302

TATHAM, John
General LJCD: 257-258
The Distracted State DC1: 205
The Rump DC1: 205
TAVEL, Ronald
General MDAE: 477; Po: 4195
Boy on the Straight-Back Chair
ADC: 370
Gorilla Queen MDAE: 477
The Last Days of British Hon-
duras ADC: 370
_____ and Al CARMINES
Gorilla Queen ADC: 370
TAYLOR, Bayard
General ALL: 261-262; AN:
235; ASF: 545
John Godfrey's Fortunes Po:
1714
TAYLOR, Cecil P.
General MDAE: 479
TAYLOR, Douglas
Horse Johnson ADC: 370
Oh, Pioneers ADC: 370
TAYLOR, Edward
General ALL: 262; AP: 503-
511; Da: 42-44; ICBAP:
126; Ma: 2074-2075
"The Accusation of the Inward
Man" [from God's Determin-
ations] PE: 450
"An Address to the Soul Occa-
sioned by a Rain" PE: 450
"The Appeale Tried" Da: 43
"Artificiall Man" Da: 43
"The Ebb and Flow" Da: 43;
ICBAP: 126; PE: 450
"An Ecstacy of Joy Let in by
This Reply Return'd in Ad-
miration" ICBAP: 127
"The Experience" PE: 451
"The Glory of and Grace in the
Church Set Out" PE: 451
God's Determinations AP:
504, 509-510; Da: 44;
ICBAP: 127; PE: 451
"Huswifery" ICBAP: 127;
Ma: 2074; PE: 451
Preparatory Meditations [Gen-
eral] AP: 504, 508-509;
ICBAP: 127
"Meditation 1.1" Da: 43;
ICBAP: 127; PE: 451
"Meditation 1.3" PE: 451
"Meditation 1.6" Da: 43;
ICBAP: 127; PE: 451
"Meditation 1.8" Da: 42;

ICBAP: 127; PE: 451-452

"Meditation 1.28" PE: 452

"Meditation 1.29" ICBAP: 127; PE: 452

"Meditation 1.30" ICBAP: 127; PE: 452

"Meditation 1.32" PE: 452

"Meditation 1.33" ICBAP: 127; PE: 452

"Meditation 1.34" PE: 452

"Meditation 1.39" PE: 452

"Meditation 1.40" PE: 452

"Meditation 1.42" PE: 452

"Meditation 2.1" PE: 452

"Meditation 2.3" PE: 452

"Meditation 2.7" PE: 452

"Meditaiton 2.10" PE: 453

"Meditation 2.23" PE: 453

"Meditation 2.26" PE: 453

"Meditation 2.27" ICBAP: 127; PE: 453

"Meditation 2.43" ICBAP: 127; PE: 453

"Meditation 2.47" PE: 453

"Meditation 2.56" PE: 453

"Meditation 2.62" Da: 43; ICBAP: 128; PE: 453

"Meditation 2.78" PE: 453

"Meditation 2.103" PE: 453

"Meditation 2.106" PE: 453

"Meditation 2.108" PE: 453

"Meditation 2.110" ICBAP: 128

"Meditation 2.112" PE: 453

"Meditation 2.138" PE: 454

"Meditation 2.149" PE: 454

"Prologue" to God's Determinations PE: 454

"The Reflexion" Da: 43; ICBAP: 128; PE: 454

"The Soul's Admiration Hereupon" ICBAP: 128

Treatise Concerning the Lord's Supper Da: 43

"Upon a Spider Catching a Fly" ICBAP: 128; PE: 454

"Upon the Sweeping Flood" PE: 454

"Upon Wedlock, and Death of Children" ICBAP: 128; Ma; 2075-2076; PE: 454

TAYLOR, Elizabeth
General CFAE: 374; CN: 512; Po: 4195; Sch: 276-277

At Mrs. Lippincote's CFAE: 374; CN: 512

TAYLOR, George E. and George M. SAVAGE
The Phoenix and the Dwarfs DC1: 206

TAYLOR, Jackie
General MBA: 187

The Other Cinderella BAP: 189-190; MBA: 187

TAYLOR, Jeanne
General BAW: 690

TAYLOR, Jeremy
General Ba: 103-104; Hen: 37

TAYLOR, John [of Caroline]
General AP: 513-514; Da: 101

TAYLOR, Peter Hillsman
General ASF: 547-548; CFAE: 375-376; LCAB: 175; Ma: 2077; MD: 311; Po: 4195-4197

"Allegiance" ASF: 545; SFC: 189; Wa: 722

"At the Drugstore" ASF: 545; Wa: 722

"Bad Dreams" ASF: 545; SFC: 189; Wa: 722

"The Captain's Son" ASF: 545

"A Cheerful Disposition" Wa: 722

"Cookie" Wa: 722

"The Dark Walk" ASF: 545; Wa: 722

"Dean of Men" ASF: 545; WaS1: 205

The Death of a Kinsman DC1: 206

"The End of the Play" ASF: 545; Wa: 722

"The Fancy Woman" ASF: 545; Wa: 722

"Friend and Protector" ASF: 545; Wa: 722

"Guests" ASF: 545; Wa: 722

Happy Families Are All Alike Ma: 2077-2078

"Heads of Houses" ASF: 545; Wa: 722

"In the Miro District" ASF: 546

"Je Suis Perdu" ASF: 546;

Wa: 722

"The Lady Is Civilized" Wa: 722

"The Little Cousin" ASF: 546; Wa: 723

"A Long Fourth" ASF: 546; SFC: 189; Wa: 723

"Miss Leonora When Last Seen" ASF: 546; Ma: 2078; Wa: 723

"Mrs. Billingsby's Wine" Wa: 723

"Nerves" ASF: 546; Wa: 723

"1939" ASF: 546; Wa: 723

"The Other Times" ASF: 546; Wa: 723

"An Overwhelming Question" ASF: 546; Wa: 723

"The Party" Wa: 723

"Porte-Cochère" Wa: 723

"Promise of Rain" ASF: 546; Wa: 723

"Rain in the Heart" ASF: 546; Wa: 723

"Reservations" ASF: 546; Wa: 723

"The School Girl" Wa: 723

"The Scoutmaster" ASF: 546; Wa: 723

"Skyline" ASF: 546; Wa: 724

"A Spinster's Tale" ASF: 547; Wa: 724

"A Strange Story" ASF: 547; Wa: 724

Tennessee Days in St. Louis DC1: 206

"Their Losses" ASF: 547; Wa: 724

"There" ASF: 547; Wa: 724

"The Throughway" ASF: 547; Wa: 724

"Two Ladies in Retirement" ASF: 547; SFC: 189; Wa: 724

"Two Pilgrims" ASF: 547; Wa: 724

"Uncles" Wa: 724

"Venus, Cupid, Folly and Time" ASF: 547; Wa: 724

"A Walled Garden" ASF: 547; Wa: 724

"What You Hear from 'Em?"

ASF: 547; Wa: 724

The Widows of Thornton Ma: 2078-2079

"A Wife of Nashville" ASF: 547; Wa: 724; WaS1: 205

A Woman of Means CFAE: 376; CN: 512; Po: 4197; SFC: 189; Wa: 724-725

TAYLOR, Philip Meadows
General BN: 99
Tara ENES1: 218

TAYLOR, Rachel Annand
General Ai: 213

TAYLOR, Renée and Joseph BOLOGNA
Lovers and Other Strangers ADC: 370

TAYLOR, Robert Lewis
General LCAB: 175

TAYLOR, Samuel Albert
Avanti! ADC: 370
Beekman Place ADC: 371
First Love ADC: 371
The Happy Time ADC: 371; Br: 694
Legend ADC: 371
Nina ADC: 371
Sabrina Fair ADC: 371-372
_____ and Richard RODGERS
No Strings ADC: 372
_____ and Cornelia Otis SKINNER
The Pleasure of His Company ADC: 372
_____ and Matt TAYLOR
Stop-Over ADC: 372

TAYLOR, Timothy and Adrian HALL
Son of Man and the Family ADC: 372

TAYLOR, Tom
General EDT: 306

TAYLOR, William Robert
Cavalier and Yankee LCAB: 175

TEASDALE, Sara
General ALL: 263; Po: 4197
"The Net" PE: 454

TEBELAK, John-Michael and Stephen SCHWARTZ
Godspell ADC: 373

TECER, Ahmet Kutsi
The Neighborhood [Kösebasi] Br: 694; DC2: 351

TEER, Barbara Ann
General BAP: 190; MBA:

187-188
Revival BAP: 190
Rituals MBA: 188
Soljourney into Truth MBA:
188
TEICHMANN, Howard
A Rainy Day in Newark ADC:
373
TEILHARD DE CHARDIN,
Pierre
General Po: 4197-4203
The Divine Milieu Po: 4203
The Phenomenon of Man Po:
4203
TEIRLINCK, Herman
General Br: 694
TEITEL, Nathan
Figures in the Sand [two
plays: Duet and Trio]
ADC: 373
TEJANI, Bahadur
General BALE: 406
TELEMAQUE, Harold M.
General WIL: 166-167
_____ and A.M. CLARKE
Burnt Bush WIL: 166-167
Téllez, Gabriel see MOLINA,
Tirso de
TEMPLE, Sir William
General Bon: 78-79
Tena, Juan Ignacio Luca de
see LUCA de TENA,
Juan Ignacio
TENDRIAKOV, Vladimir
General Po: 4204
An Extraordinary Story Ke:
441
On the Heels of Time Ke:
441
Three, Seven, Ace Ke: 441-
442; Po: 4204
The Trial Ke: 442
TENN, William
"The Liberation of Earth"
Wa: 725
"Null-P" Wa: 725
TENNANT, Kylie
General MAP: 307-308; Po:
4204
The Battlers MAP: 308
TENNYSON, Alfred, Lord
General ICBAP: 128;
EDT: 308-312; LCAB:
175; Ma: 2084-2085; VP:
76-81
"The Ancient Sage" ICBAP:

128; PE: 454
"Armageddon" PE: 454
"Ask Me No More: The Moon
May Draw the Sea" PE: 454
"Aylmer's Field" PE: 455
Becket DC1: 206; EDT:
309, 311-312
"Break, Break, Break" ICBAP:
128; PE: 455; VP: 76
"Bugle Song" PE: 455
"Cambridge" ICBAP: 128
"The Coming of Arthur"
ICBAP: 128; PE: 455; VP:
78
"Courage, Poor Heart of Stone"
[from "Maud," sect. III, Pt.
II] PE: 455
"Crossing the Bar" ICBAP:
128; PE: 455-456; VP: 76
The Cup EDT: 312
"The Defense of Lucknow" PE:
456
"Demeter and Persephone"
LCAB: 176; PE: 456
"A Dream of Fair Women" PE:
456
"The Dreamer" ICBAP: 129
"The Eagle" PE: 456
"Eleanore" PE: 456
Enoch Arden Ma: 2080; VP:
76, 80
"The Epic" PE: 456
The Falcon EDT: 312
"A Farewell" PE: 456
The Foresters EDT: 311
"Geraint and Enid" ICBAP:
129
"The Grandmother" PE: 456
Harold EDT: 310-311
"The Hesperides" PE: 456-
457; VP: 81
The Idylls of the King ICBAP:
129; Ma: 2080-2081; VP:
77-81
"In Memoriam" ICBAP: 129;
LCAB: 176; Ma: 2082-2083;
PE: 457; Po: 4198; VP:
76-81
"In Memoriam--Prologue"
ICBAP: 129; PE: 457
"In Memoriam, 7" PE: 457
"In Memoriam, 9" PE: 457
"In Memoriam, 11" PE: 457
"In Memoriam, 12" PE: 457
"In Memoriam, 14" PE: 457
"In Memoriam, 15" PE: 457

"In Memoriam, 18" PE: 458
"In Memoriam, 41 [XLI]"
  ICBAP: 129; PE: 458
"In Memoriam, 43" PE: 458
"In Memoriam, 55" PE: 458
"In Memoriam, 56" PE: 458
"In Memoriam, 67" PE: 458
"In Memoriam, 95 [XCV]"
  ICBAP: 129; PE: 458
"In Memoriam, 103" PE: 458
"In Memoriam, 114" PE: 458
"In Memoriam, 118" PE: 458
"In Memoriam, 121" PE: 459
"In Memoriam, 122" PE: 459
"In Memoriam, 123" PE: 459
"In Memoriam, 130" PE: 459
"In Memoriam, 131" PE: 459
"In the Valley of Cauteretz"
  PE: 459
"The Kraken" ICBAP: 129;
  PE: 459
"Lady Clara Vere de Vere"
  ICBAP: 129; PE: 459
"The Lady of Shalott"
  ICBAP: 130; PE: 459-
  460; VP: 76, 79
"The Last Tournament"
  ICBAP: 130; VP: 79
"Locksley Hall" ICBAP: 130;
  PE: 460; VP: 77
"Locksley Hall Sixty Years
  After" PE: 460; VP:
  80
"The Lotos-Eaters" ICBAP:
  130; PE: 460; VP: 77-78
"Lucretius" PE: 460
"The Making of Man" ICBAP:
  130
"Mariana" PE: 460
"Mariana in the South" PE:
  460
"Maud" ICBAP: 130; Ma:
  2083-2084; VP: 79-81
"Mechanophilus" ICBAP: 130
"Merlin and the Gleam" PE:
  460
"Merlin and Vivien" ICBAP:
  130
"The Mermaid" ICBAP: 130
"Morte d'Arthur" ICBAP:
  130
"Move Eastward, Happy
  Earth, and Leave" PE:
  460
"Northern Farmer: New
  Style" PE: 461

"Now Sleeps the Crimson Petal,
  Now the White" PE: 461
"Ode: O Basky Brook" PE:
  461
"Ode on the Death of the Duke
  of Wellington" PE: 461
"Ode to Memory" PE: 461
"Oenone" ICBAP: 130; PE:
  461; VP: 81
"On a Mourner" PE: 461
"The Palace of Art" ICBAP:
  131; PE: 461-462; VP:
  76-77, 80
"Pelleas and Ettarre" ICBAP:
  131
"The Poet" ICBAP: 131; PE:
  462
"The Poet's Mind" PE: 462
"The Poet's Song" PE: 462
"The Princess" ICBAP: 131;
  Ma: 2085-2087; VP: 76-78
"The Progress of Spring" PE:
  462
The Promise of May EDT: 312
Queen Mary DC1: 206; EDT:
  308-311
"Recollections of the Arabian
  Nights" ICBAP: 131; PE:
  462
"Saint Agnes' Eve" ICBAP:
  131
"St. Simeon Stylites" PE: 462
"Sea Dreams" ICBAP: 131;
  PE: 462
"The Sea-Fairies" PE: 462
"Sir Galahad" PE: 462
"A Spirit Haunts the Year's
  Last Hours" PE: 462
"The Splendor Falls on Castle
  Walls" PE: 462
"Sweet and Low" PE: 462
"Tears, Idle Tears" ICBAP:
  131; LCAB: 176; Ma: 2087;
  PE: 463; VP: 76
"Timbuctoo" PE: 463
"Time: An Ode" PE: 463
"Tiresias" PE: 463
"Tithonus" PE: 463-464; VP:
  80
"To E.L., on His Travels in
  Greece" PE: 464
"The Two Voices" ICBAP:
  131; LCAB: 176; PE: 464;
  VP: 80-81
"Ulysses" ICBAP: 131; Ma:
  2087-2088; PE: 464-465;

VP: 79-80
"Vastness" PE: 465
Terbay, Andres see SARAH,
    Roberto
TERENCE
    Andria see Maid of Andros
    The Brothers [Adelphi;
        Adelphoe; Adelphoi] DC2:
        352; EDC: 530; Ma:
        2089-2090
    The Eunuch [Eunuchus]
        DC2: 353; EDC: 531
    Heautontimorumenos see
        The Self-Tormentor
    Hecyra see Mother-in-Law
    Maid of Andros [Andria]
        DC2: 352-353; EDC: 531
    Mother-in-Law [Hecyra]
        DC2: 354; EDC: 531
    Phormio DC2: 354; EDC:
        531; LCAB: 176; Ma:
        2090-2091
    The Self-Tormentor [Heauton-
        timorumenos] DC2: 353-
        354; EDC: 531
TERESA, Saint, of Avila
    The Interior Castle Po:
        2105-2106
TERRILL, Vincent
    From These Shores ...
        Crispus Attacks MBA:
        188
TERRON, Carlos
    General Br: 695
TERRUGGI, Ugo
    Luisa e il presidente Fi:
        279
TERRY, Lucy Ann
    General AAPD: 77; BAW:
        692-693; LCAB: 4
TERRY, Megan
    General MDAE: 481
    Approaching Simone ADC:
        373
    Massachusetts Trust ADC:
        373
    Viet Rock ADC: 373
    _____ and Tom SANKEY
    The People vs. Ranchman
        ADC: 374
TERSANSZKY, J. Jeno
    Kakuk Marci Ke: 442
TERSON, Peter
    General MDAE: 483
    The Apprentices MDAE: 483
TERTZ, Abram [Andrei

SINYAVSKI]
    General LCAB: 163; Po:
        4204-4205
    "At the Circus" Fi: 479
    "Graphomaniacs" Fi: 480; Wa:
        725
    The Icicle Fi: 480
    Liubimov Fi: 480
    Pkhents Fi: 480
    The Tenants Fi: 480
    The Trial Begins Fi: 480; Ke:
        442
    You and I Fi: 480
TERZAKES, Angelos
    General LCAB: 176
TESICH, Steven
    Baba Goya ADC: 374
    The Carpenters ADC: 374
    Lake of the Woods ADC: 374
    Nourish the Beast ADC: 374
    Passing Game ADC: 374
Teternikov, Fyodor Kuzmich see
    SOLOGUB, Fyodor
TETMAJER, Kazimierz
    "To Heaven" Wa: 725
Tey, Josephine see MACKIN-
    TOSH, Elizabeth
TEYSSEDRE, Bernard
    Romans-Eclairs Po: 4206
THACKERAY, Anne Isabella [Lady
    RITCHIE]
    General BN: 99-100
THACKERAY, William Makepeace
    General BN: 101-102; Du:
        157-159; LCAB: 176
    Amelia EN: 120
    Barry Lyndon [The Luck of
        Barry Lyndon] BN: 103;
        Du: 153; EN: 120-121;
        ENES1: 219; ENES2: 237;
        Ma: 2092
    Catherine BN: 101; Du: 153;
        ENE: 252; ENES1: 218;
        ENES2: 236
    Denis Duval ENES1: 218;
        ENES2: 236
    Dennis Haggarty's Wife
        ENES2: 236; Wa: 725
    Henry Esmond BN: 103; Du:
        153-154; EN: 121; ENE:
        252; ENES1: 218-219;
        ENES2: 236; LCAB: 176;
        Ma: 2092-2094; Ri2: 466
    The History of Samuel Titmarsh
        and the Great Hoggarty
        Diamond ENES2: 236

Lovel the Widower ENES1:
219; ENES2: 236
The Luck of Barry Lyndon
see Barry Lyndon
The Newcomes BN: 103; Du:
154; EN: 121-122; ENE:
252; ENES1: 219; ENES2:
237; Ma: 2094
Pendennis BN: 103; Du:
154-155; EN: 122; ENE:
253; ENES1: 219-220;
ENES2: 237-238; LCAB:
176; Ma: 2094-2095
Philip Du: 155; EN: 122;
ENE: 253; ENES1: 220;
ENES2: 238
The Ravenswing ENES2:
238
Rebecca and Rowena ENES1:
220; ENES2: 238
The Rose and the Ring
ENES2: 238
Vanity Fair BN: 103-105;
Du: 155-157; EN: 122-
124; ENE: 253-256;
ENES1: 220-221; ENES2:
238-239; LCAB: 176-177;
Ma: 2096-2097
The Virginians; A Tale of
the Last Century BN:
105; EN: 124; ENE: 253;
ENES1: 221; ENES2:
239-240; Ma: 2097-2098
THANET, Octave
General ASF: 549
"The Bishop's Vagabond"
Wa: 725
THARAUD, Jérôme and Jean
THARAUD
General Po: 4206
THATCHER, Charles
General AL: 338
THEMBA, Daniel Canadoise
Dorsay
General BALE: 407
THEOBALD, Lewis
General Li: 304-306
Double Falsehood Li: 304-306
The Happy Captive Li: 306
King Richard the Second Li:
306
THEOCRITUS
General Ma: 2099
THEOGNIS
General LCAB: 177
THEOTOKAS, George

"The Daemon" Wa: 725
"Euripides Pendozalis" Wa:
725
"Everything's in Order"
Wa: 726
"Leonis" Wa: 726
THERIAULT, Yves
"La fleur qui faisant un
son" WaS1: 205
THEURIET, M. André
Le Fils Maugars Ke: 167
Sauvageonne Ke: 167
THIBAUDET, Albert
General Po: 4207-4208
Dépêche de Toulouse Po: 4208
Thibault, Anatole see FRANCE,
Anatole
THIBODEAUX, Richard
General BAP: 191
THIELEN, Benedict
The Lost Men AN: 235; Po:
4208
THIERRY, Camille
General BAW: 693-694
THIRKELL, Angela
General CN: 513; Po: 4208-
4209
THIRY, Marcel
General Po: 4209
THOMA, Ludwig
General Po: 4209
Brifwexel eines bayerischen
Landtagsabgeordneten Po:
4209-4210
THOMAS OF HALES
"Love Ron" PE: 472
THOMAS, Augustus
General AD: 192-195; Lon:
63; MD: 311
Alabama AD: 193-194; ADC:
374
Arizona AD: 192, 194
As a Man Thinks ADC: 374
Capital ADC: 374
Copperhead AD: 194; ADC:
375
Harvest Moon ADC: 375
The Hoosier Doctor ADC: 375
Indian Summer AD: 193
The Jew AD: 195
The Meddler ADC: 375
Nemesis ADC: 375; MD: 311
New Blood ADC: 375
The Ranger AD: 193
Rio Grande ADC: 375
Still Waters ADC: 375

The Witching Hour AD:
193-195; MD: 311
THOMAS, Caitlin
Leftover Life to Kill LCAB:
177
THOMAS, Dylan Marlais
General EP: 242-258;
ICBAP: 131; LCAB: 177;
Ma: 2104-2105; MBD:
93-94; MD: 311; MDAE:
486; MP: 99-100; Po:
4210-4229
"An Adventure from a Work
in Progress" Wa: 726
Adventures in the Skin
Trade ENES1: 221; Ma:
2100; Po: 4229; SFC:
189-190; Wa: 726
"After the Fair" Wa: 726
"After the Funeral (In Mem-
ory of Ann Jones)" EP:
256; PE: 465-466; Po:
4229
"All All and All the Dry
Worlds Lever" PE: 466
"Altarwise by Owl-Light"
EP: 243; ICBAP: 132;
LCAB: 177; Ma: 2100-
2101; PE: 466; Po: 4213,
4230-4231
"Among Those Killed in the
Dawn Raid Was a Man
Aged a Hundred" PE:
466; Po: 4231
"Anagram" Wa: 726
"And Death Shall Have No
Dominion" Ma: 2101;
PE: 467; Po: 4231
"Author's Prologue" PE:
466
"The Ballad of the Long-
Legged Bait" EP: 244,
250; ICBAP: 132; PE:
466; Po: 4232-4233; Wa:
726
"Because the Pleasure-Bird
Whistles" PE: 467
"The Burning Baby" SFC:
190; Wa: 726
"Ceremony After a Fire
Raid" PE: 467
"A Child's Christmas in
Wales" Wa: 726
"The Conversation of Prayer"
EP: 254; ICBAP: 132;
PE: 467; Po: 4213, 4233

"Death Is All Metaphors, Shape
in One History" PE: 467
"Do Not Go Gentle Into That
Good Night" ICBAP: 132;
Ma: 2101-2102; PE: 467;
Po: 4233
The Doctor and the Devils MD:
311; MDAE: 485
"The Dress" SFC: 190; Wa:
726
Eighteen Poems Po: 4233-4234
"The Empty Purse" PE: 467
"The Enemies" SFC: 190; Wa:
726
"Especially When the October
Wind" EP: 254; ICBAP:
132; PE: 467; Po: 4234
"Fern Hill" EP: 244, 246, 248,
253; ICBAP: 132; LCAB:
177; Ma: 2102; MP: 100;
PE: 467; Po: 4213, 4234-
4235
"First There Was the Lamb of
Knocking Knees" PE: 468
"The Followers" Po: 4235;
SFC: 190; Wa: 726-727
"The Force That Through the
Green Fuse Drives the
Flower" EP: 253; Ma:
2103; PE: 468; Po: 4235
"From Love's First Fever to
Her Plague" EP: 248; PE:
468
"Gaspar, Melchior, Balthasar"
Wa: 727
"The Hand That Signed the
Paper Felled a City" Po:
4235-4236
"Hold Hard, These Ancient
Minutes in the Cuckoo's
Month" PE: 468
"The Holy Six" Wa: 727
"The Horse's Ha" Wa: 727
"How Shall My Animal" ICBAP:
132; Po: 4236
"How Soon the Servant Sun"
EP: 247; ICBAP: 132; PE:
468; Po: 4236
"How to Be a Poet" Wa: 727
"The Hunchback in the Park"
PE: 468; Po: 4236
"I in My Intricate Image" or
"A Poem in Three Parts"
ICBAP: 132; PE: 469
"I See the Boys of Summer"
EP: 248, 253; PE: 469;

Po: 4220

"If I Were Tickled by the Rub of Love" ICBAP: 132; PE: 468; Po: 4236

"If My Head Hurt a Hair's Foot" Po: 4237

"In Country Heaven" PE: 469

"In Country Sleep" ICBAP: 132; PE: 469; Po: 4237

"In My Craft or Sullen Art" EP: 248; PE: 469; Po: 4237

"In the Beginning Was the Three-Pointed Star" PE: 469

"In the Direction of the Beginning" Wa: 727

"In the White Giant's Thigh" EP: 243, 253; ICBAP: 132; PE: 469; Po: 4238

"It Rains" ICBAP: 132

"Just Like Little Dogs" Wa: 727

"Lament" Po: 4238

"The Lemon" Wa: 727

"Light Breaks Where No Sun Shines" ICBAP: 132; EP: 249, 253; PE: 469-470; Po: 4238

"Love in the Asylum" ICBAP: 133; PE: 470; Po: 4239

"The Map of Love" SFC: 190; Wa: 727

"The Map of Love: No. 4" PE: 470

"Mr. Tritas on the Rocks" see "Anagram"

"The Mouse and the Woman" SFC: 190; Wa: 727

"O Make Me a Mask" EP: 246; ICBAP: 133; PE: 470; Po: 4239

"On the Marriage of a Virgin" EP: 249; ICBAP: 133; PE: 470; Po: 4239

"One Warm Saturday" Po: 4239; SFC: 190; Wa: 727

"The Orchards" Wa: 727

"Our Eunuch Dreams" ICBAP: 133; PE: 470; Po: 4240

"Out of the Sighs" PE: 470

"Over Sir John's Hill" EP: 243-244; ICBAP: 133;

PE: 470; Po: 4240

"Patricia, Edith, and Arnold" SFC: 190; Wa: 727-728

"The Peaches" Po: 4241; Wa: 728; WaS1: 206

"Poem 40: Twenty-Four Years Remind the Tears of My Eyes" PE: 470

"Poem in October" ICBAP: 133; Ma: 2103-2104; PE: 471; Po: 4241

Portrait of the Artist as a Young Dog Ma: 2105-2106; Po: 4241

"Prologue to an Adventure" Po: 4242; Wa: 728

"A Prospect of the Sea" Wa: 728

"A Refusal to Mourn the Death, by Fire, of a Child in London" EP: 244; ICBAP: 133; LCAB: 177; Ma: 2106-2107; PE: 471; Po: 4220, 4242

"The School for Witches" Wa: 728

"Sonnet II" EP: 249

"Sonnet III" EP: 249; ICBAP: 133

"A Story" Wa: 728; WaS1: 206

"There Was a Saviour" EP: 244

"This Bread I Break" PE: 471; Po: 4242-4243

"This Was the Crucifixion on the Mountain" PE: 471

"Today, This Insect" ICBAP: 133; PE: 471; Po: 4243

"The Tombstone Told When She Died" EP: 246; PE: 472; Po: 4243

"The Tree" SFC: 190; Wa: 728

"The True Story" Wa: 728

"Twenty-Four Years" ICBAP: 133; PE: 472; Po: 4213, 4243

Under Milk Wood Br: 695; DC1: 206-207; EDC: 531-532; LCAB: 177; Ma: 2107; MBD: 93-94; MD: 311-312; MDAE: 485-486; PE: 472; Po: 4244-4246; TMIP: 10

"Unluckily for a Death" ICBAP: 133; PE: 472

"The Vest" Wa: 728
"Vision and Prayer" ICBAP:
133; PE: 472
"A Visit to Grandpa's" Wa:
728
"The Visitor" Wa: 728
"We Lying by Seasand" PE:
472
"When All My Five and Coun-
try Senses See" EP:
258; ICBAP: 133; PE:
472; Po: 4246
"When Like a Running Grave"
PE: 472
"A Winter's Tale" EP: 246,
257; ICBAP: 133; MD:
100; PE: 472; Po: 4220,
4246-4247
THOMAS, Edward [Edward
EASTAWAY]
General EP: 262-266; Po:
4247-4249; TA: 286-287
"Cock-Crow" PE: 472
"The Gypsy" PE: 473
The Happy-Go-Lucky Morgans
ENES2: 240
"Home" PE: 473
"If I Should Ever by Chance"
PE: 473
"Liberty" ICBAP: 134
"Manor Farm" ICBAP: 134
"October" PE: 473
"Old Man" ICBAP: 134;
PE: 473
"The Other" EP: 264; PE:
473
"Over the Hills" PE: 473
"The Owl" EP: 265;
ICBAP: 134
"The Sign-Post" EP: 264;
ICBAP: 134; Po: 4249
"Tears" EP: 265; PE: 473
"The Watchers" EP: 263;
PE: 473; Po: 4250
"Wind and Mist" PE: 473
THOMAS, G.C.
Ruler in Hiroona WIL: 167-
168
THOMAS, Gwyn
General MDAE: 487
THOMAS, Henri
General Po: 4250-4251
THOMAS, Hugh
The World's Game CN: 513
THOMAS, Joyce Carol
Look! What a Wonder!

MBA: 188
THOMAS, Odette
Rain Falling Sun Shining WIL:
168
THOMAS, Ronald Stuart
General ICBAP: 134; Po:
4251-4252
"The Labourer" PE: 474
THOMAS, Rosemary
"The Big Nosed Adolescent
Boys" PE: 473
"St. Francis of Assisi" PE:
474
THOMAS, Will
General BAF: 263; BAW:
697
God Is for White Folks BAF:
263
THOMASON, John W., Jr.
General ASF: 548
THOMPSON, Aaron Belford
General BAW: 698
THOMPSON, Daniel Pierce
General AN: 235
The Green Mountain Boys AN:
235; LCAB: 177
Locke Amsden AN: 235
THOMPSON, Denman
General AD: 196-199
The Old Homestead AD: 197-
199; Lon: 43
THOMPSON, Edward
General Li: 307
THOMPSON, Eloise Bibb
A Reply to the Clansman
MBA: 188
THOMPSON, Flora
General Po: 4252
THOMPSON, Francis
General Ma: 2108; Po: 4252-
4254; TA: 288
"Grace of the Way" PE: 474
"The Hound of Heaven"
ICBAP: 134; LCAB: 178;
PE: 474; Po: 4254
"New Year's Chimes" PE: 474
"The Nineteenth Century" PE:
474
"Sad Semele" PE: 474; Po:
4254
"To the Dead Cardinal of
Westminster" Po: 4254
THOMPSON, John
General Po: 4255
THOMPSON, Maurice
General AF: 239-240; ASF:

548
Hoosier Mosaics AF: 240
THOMPSON, Priscilla Jane
General BAW: 700
THOMPSON, Ron S.
Cotton Club Revue MBA:
189
THOMPSON, Sam
General Br: 695
THOMPSON, Thomas
"A Shore for the Sinking"
SFC: 190; Wa: 729
THOMPSON, William C.
The Man Who Washed His
Hands ADC: 375
THOMSON, Edward William
General ECL: 202
THOMSON, James [1700-1748]
General Ai: 62-63; EC:
142-144; Li: 308-309; Me:
402-407
Agamemnon DC1: 207; Li:
308
"Autumn" Me: 406
The Castle of Indolence
EC: 143; ICBAP: 134;
Me: 402, 404
Coriolanus Li: 309
Edward and Eleanora DC1:
207; Li: 308-309
Liberty EC: 143; Me: 405
"Ode on the Winter Solstice"
EC: 144
The Seasons EC: 142-143;
Me: 402-407
Sophonisba DC1: 207; Li:
309
"Spring" ICBAP: 134; Me:
407
"Summer" Me: 406
Tancred and Sigismunda
DC1: 207; Li: 309
"The Vine" PE: 474
"Winter" Me: 407
THOMSON, James [1834-1892]
General Ai: 150; VP: 82
"City of Dreadful Night"
Ai: 150; PE: 474; VP:
82
THORDARSON, Thórbergur
General Po: 4255
THOREAU, Henry David
General ALL: 263-269;
Cla: 85-88; LCAB:
178; Ma: 2110
"All Things Are Current

Found" PE: 474
"Baker Farm" Wa: 729
"Civil Disobedience" Ma: 2109
"The Cliffs & Springs" PE:
474
"I Was Born Upon Thy Bank"
PE: 474
"It Is No Dream of Mine" PE:
474
The Journal of Thoreau Ma:
2109
"Light-winged Smoke" PE:
475
The Maine Woods ALL: 265,
267; Cla: 87; Ma: 2110
"May Morning" PE: 475
"My Boots" PE: 475
"Poem No. 189" PE: 475
"The Sluggish Smoke" PE:
475
"Smoke" PE: 475
"Smoke in the Winter" PE:
475
Walden; or, Life in the Woods
ALL: 263-265, 267-268;
Cla: 85-88; LCAB: 178;
Ma: 2110-2113
"Walking" ALL: 265
A Week on the Concord and
Merrimack Rivers ALL:
265, 267; Ma: 2114-2115
THORNHILL, Lionel L.
General BAF: 264
THORPE, Thomas Bangs
General ASF: 549
"The Big Bear of Arkansas"
ASF: 548-549; SFC: 191;
Wa: 729
"The Devil's Summer Retreat
in Arkansas" ASF: 549
"The Disgraced Scalp-Lock"
ASF: 549
"Tom Owen, the Bee Hunter"
ASF: 549
THORTHARSON, Agnar
Atoms and Madams DC2: 354
THROSSELL, Ric
Dr. Homer Speaks MAP: 385
THUCYDIDES
General LCAB: 178
History of the Peloponnesian
War Ma: 2116-2117
THUNA, Lee
The Natural Look ADC: 375;
BAP: 192
THURBER, James Grover

General APC: 29-32; ASF: 553; Br: 696; LCAB: 178; Po: 4255-4258

"Am Not I Your Rosalind?" ASF: 549; Wa: 729

"Aunt Ida" ASF: 549

"Back to the Grades" ASF: 549; Wa: 729

"The Beast in the Dingle" ASF: 549; Wa: 729

"A Box to Hide In" ASF: 549; Wa: 729

"The Breaking Up of the Winships" ASF: 549; Wa: 730

"The Cane in the Corridor" ASF: 549; Wa: 730

"The Car We Had to Push" ASF: 549; Wa: 730

"The Case for the Daydreamer" ASF: 549; Wa: 730

"The Case of Blue Ploermell" Wa: 730

"The Cat in the Lifeboat" ASF: 550

"The Catbird Seat" ASF: 550; Po: 4258; Wa: 730; WaS1: 206

"A Couple of Hamburgers" Wa: 730

"Do You Want to Make Something Out of It?" ASF: 550

"Doc Marlowe" ASF: 550; Wa: 730

"Draft Board Nights" Wa: 730

"Everything Is Wild" Wa: 730

"File and Forget" ASF: 550; Wa: 731

"A Final Note on Chanda Bell" Wa: 731

"A Friend of the Earth" Wa: 731

"A Friend to Alexander" ASF: 550; Wa: 731

Further Fables Po: 4258

"The Gentleman Is Cold" ASF: 550

"The Greatest Man in the World" ASF: 550; Wa: 731; WaS1: 206

"Here Come the Tigers" Wa: 731

"The Interview" Wa: 731

"Josephine Has Her Day" ASF: 550; Wa: 731

"The Ladies' and Gentlemen's Guide to Modern English Usage" ASF: 550

"The Last Clock" ASF: 550; Wa: 731

"The Little Girl and the Wolf" Wa: 731

"The Lover and His Lass" ASF: 550-551

"The Luck of Jad Peters" ASF: 551; Wa: 731

"The Macbeth Murder Mystery" ASF: 551; Wa: 731

"Menaces in May" ASF: 551; Wa: 731

"Mr. and Mrs. Monroe" ASF: 551

"Mr. Preble Gets Rid of His Wife" ASF: 551; Wa: 731

"More Alarms at Night" ASF: 551; Wa: 732

My Life and Hard Times Ma: 2118

"The Night the Bed Fell" Wa: 732

"The Night the Ghost Got In" ASF: 551; Wa: 732

"One Is a Wanderer" ASF: 551; Wa: 732

"The Ordeal of Mr. Matthews" ASF: 552; Wa: 732

"The Other Room" ASF: 552; Wa: 732

"The Pet Department" ASF: 552

"A Portrait of Aunt Ida" Wa: 732

"The Private Life of Mr. Bidwell" Wa: 732

"The Remarkable Case of Mr. Bruhl" ASF: 552; Wa: 732

"The Secret Life of Walter Mitty" ASF: 552; Ma: 2118-2119; Po: 4259; SFC: 191; Wa: 732-733

"Smashup" Wa: 733

"Something to Say" ASF: 552; Wa: 733

"Teacher's Pet" ASF: 552; Wa: 733

"The Unicorn in the Garden" ASF: 552; Wa: 733

"The Waters of the Moon"

ASF: 552

"The Whip-poor-will" ASF: 552; Wa: 733

"The Wood Duck" ASF: 552; Wa: 733

"You Could Look It Up" ASF: 553; Wa: 733; WaS1: 206

_____ and Elliott NUGENT

The Male Animal see also NUGENT, Elliott and James THURBER Br: 696; DC1: 207; Ma: 2118

THURMAN, Wallace

General AAW: 72; BAF: 265-266; BAP: 192; BAW: 702; HR: 137-138; LCAB: 178-179

The Blacker the Berry BAF: 266-267; Po: 4260

Infants of the Spring BAF: 267

The Interne BAF: 267

_____ and William Jourdan RAPP

Harlem BAP: 192-193; Br: 696; MBA: 189

TIBULLUS

Corpus Tibullianum Ma: 2120

TIECK, Johann Ludwig

Abdallah Fi: 392; Ke: 337

"Die Ahnenprobe" Wa: 733

Der Blonde Eckbert Fi: 392-393; Ke: 337

"Death of the Poet" Wa: 733

The Elves [Die Elfen] Fi: 393; Wa: 733

"The Enchanted Castle" Wa: 734

Franz Sternbalds Wanderungen Fi: 393; Ke: 337

"Der fünfzehnte November" Wa: 734

"Die Gemälde" Wa: 734

"Die Gesellschaft auf dem Lande" Wa: 734

Der Gestiefelte Kater DC2: 355

"Die Klausenburg" Wa: 734

Life's Overflow [Des Lebens Überfluss] Fi: 393; Ke: 337; Wa: 734

The Love-Charm [Love Magic; Liebeszauber]

Fi: 393; Ke: 337; Wa: 734

"The Moon-Possessed" Wa: 734

The Mysterious Cup Ke: 337-338

Phantasus Ke: 338

Prinz Zerbino DC2: 355

Puss in Boots DC2: 355

The Rebellion in the Cevennes Ke: 338

"Die Reisenden" Wa: 734

Der Runenberg Fi: 394; Wa: 734

Eine Sommerreise Ke: 338

Die Verkehrte Welt DC2: 355

"Die Verlobung" Wa: 734

Vittoria Accorombona Fi: 394

William Lovell Fi: 394-395

"The Witch's Sabbath" Wa: 734

Tiempo, Cesar see ZEITLIN, Israel

T'IEN HAN

General Po: 4260

TILLINGER, John

The House of Mirth ADC: 375

TILLOTSON, John

General Bon: 65-66

TILNEY, Edmund

Flower of Friendship ERP: 489

TILTMAN, Hessell

Common Clay ENES2: 240

TIMROD, Henry

General Cla: 122

"Memorial Ode" Cla: 122

TIPTOFT, John

General Hen: 209

TIREBUCK, William Edwards

Miss Grace of All Souls ENES1: 221

TIRSO DE MOLINA [Gabriel TELLEZ]

El amor y la amistad DC2: 355

Antona García DC2: 355

El aquiles DC2: 355

El bandolero Ke: 231

El burlador de Sevilla DC2: 356-357

Es camientos para el cuerdo DC2: 357

El castigo del penseque DC2: 357

La celosa de si misma DC2: 357

El celoso prudente DC2: 357

El condenado por desconfiado
DC2: 358

Don Alvaro [La próspera y
adversa fortuna de Don
Alvaro de Luna] DC2:
358

Don Gil des las calzas verdes
DC2: 358

La fingida ancadia DC2: 358

Infanzon de Illescas DC2:
359

Mari-Hernandez DC2: 359

El mayor desengano DC2:
359

El melancólico DC2: 359

El mujer que manda en casa
DC2: 359

No es amor se pinta DC2:
359

No hay Peor Sordo DC2:
359

Por el sotano el torno DC2:
359

Privar contra su gusto DC2:
359

La prospera y adversa fortuna de Don Alvaro de
Luna see Don Alvaro

La prudencia en la mujer
DC2: 360

Quien calla, otorga DC2:
360

Las quinas de Portugal DC2:
360

Tan lago me lo fiais DC2:
360

La venganza de Tamar DC2:
360

Ventura te de Dios, hijo
DC2: 360

El vergonzoso en palacio
DC2: 360

La vida de Herodes DC2:
361

TIWONI, Habib
General BAW: 703

TOBAR GARCIA, Francisco
General Br: 696

TODD, Ruthven
General Ai: 303
Over the Mountain ENES2:
240
"Rivers: On Living in
Brooklyn" PE: 475

TOLKIEN, John Ronald Reuel
General BN2: 104; CFAE:

379-385; CN: 513-514;
LCAB: 179; Po: 4261; Sch:
277-279

Farmer Giles of Ham Ma: 2121;
Sch: 279

The Fellowship of the Ring see
also The Lord of the Rings
CN: 514-515; ENES1: 221;
ENES2: 240; Ma: 2121-2122;
Sch: 280-284

The Hobbit BN2: 104; CFAE:
380-385; CN: 514; ENES1:
221; ENES2: 240; Ma: 2122-
2123; Sch: 280

The Lord of the Rings BN2:
104; CFAE: 379-384; CN:
515-518; ENE: 256-257;
ENES1: 222-223; ENES2:
240-241; LCAB: 179; Po:
4261-4267; Sch: 280-284

"On Fairy Stories" Po: 4267

The Return of the King see
also The Lord of the Rings
CN: 518; ENES1: 223; Ma:
2123-2124; Sch: 280-284

The Road Goes Ever On CFAE:
380

Silmarillion ENES2: 242; Ma:
2124-2125

The Two Towers see also
The Lord of the Rings CN:
518; Ma: 2125; Sch: 280-
284

TOLLER, Ernst
General Br: 696-697; MD:
312; Po: 4267-4268

The Blind Goddess Br: 697

Bloody Laughter [The Red
Laugh; Hinkemann; Der
Deutscher Hinkemann; Brok-
enbrow] Br: 697; EDC:
532; MD: 312

Draw the Fires [Feuer aus den
Kesseln] Br: 697

Hoopla!... see Such Is Life

The Machine Wreckers [Die
Maschinenstürmer] Br:
697; DC2: 361; EDC: 532;
MD: 313

Man and the Masses [Masses
and Man; Masse-Mensch] Br:
697-698; DC2: 361; EDC:
533; MD: 313; Po: 4269

No More Peace [Nie Wieder
Friede!] Br: 698; DC2:
361

The Red Laugh see Bloody
Laughter
Die Schwalbenbuch Br: 698
Such Is Life [Hoopla! Such
Is Life!; Hoopla! Wir
Leben] Br: 698; DC2:
361; EDC: 532; MD: 313
Transfiguration [Transforma-
tion; Die Wandlung] Br:
698; DC2: 361; EDC:
533; MD: 313
TOLSON, Melvin B.
General AAPD: 237; AAW:
73; BAP: 193; BAW:
705-706; MBA: 189; Po:
4270
Black No More MBA: 189
Fire in the Flint MBA: 189
Libretto for the Republic of
Liberia AAL: 245; AAW:
73; Po: 4270
The Moses of Beale Street
MBA: 189
Southern Front MBA: 189
TOLSTOY, Alexei Konstantino-
vich
Aelita Ke: 442
"Amena" Wa: 735
"Artemy Semyonovich Ber-
venkovsky" Wa: 735
Engineer Garin's Hyperboloid
Ke: 442
"La Famille du Vourdalak"
Wa: 735
Peter the First Ke: 442
"Le Rendezvous dans trois
cents ans" Wa: 735
The Road of Torments Fi:
481
The Road to Calvary Ke:
442
"The Vampire" Wa: 735
TOLSTOY, Aleksei Nikolaevich
General Br: 699; Po: 4269
1918 Fi: 480-481; Po:
4269-4270
The Revolt of the Machines
[Bunt mashin] DC2:
361; Po: 4269
TOLSTOY, Leo Nikolayevitch
General Br: 699; LCAB:
179; MD: 313
"Albert" SFC: 191; Wa:
735
Anna Karenina Fi: 481-483;
Ke: 442-445; LCAB:

179; Ma: 2126-2127
"The Candle" Wa: 735
"A Captive in the Caucasus"
Wa: 735
Childhood, Boyhood and Youth
Fi: 483-484; Ke: 445; Ma:
2127-2128
The Cossacks Fi: 484; Ke:
446; Ma: 2128
The Death of Ivan Ilych Fi:
484-485; Ke: 446; Ma:
2128-2129; Po: 1810-1811;
SFC: 191; Wa: 735-736;
WaS1: 206
"The Devil" SFC: 191; Wa:
736
Family Happiness [Domestic
Happiness] Fi: 485; Ke:
446; SFC: 191; Wa: 736;
WaS1: 206
The Fruits of Enlightenment
[Plody Prosveshcheniya]
Br: 699; EDC: 533
"God Sees the Truth, but
Waits" Fi: 485-486; Wa:
736; WaS1: 206
Hadji Murad Fi: 486; Wa:
736-737; WaS1: 206-207
"How Much Land Does a Man
Need?" see "Three
Arshins of Land"
The Kreutzer Sonata Fi: 486-
487; Ke: 446-447; Ma:
2129-2130; SFC: 192; Wa:
737; WaS1: 207
"A Landowner's Morning"
WaS1: 207
Light Shines in Darkness Br:
699
The Living Corpse [Redemp-
tion; Zhivoy Trup] Br:
699; DC2: 362; EDC: 533;
MD: 313
"Lucerne" SFC: 192; Wa:
737
Master and Man Fi: 487; Ke:
447
Plody Prosveshcheniya see
The Fruits of Enlightenment
"Polikushka" WaS1: 207
The Power of Darkness; or,
"If a Claw Is Caught, the
Bird Is Lost" [Vlast Tmy]
Br: 699; DC2: 362; EDC:
533-534; Ma: 2130-2131;
MD: 314

Redemption see The Living Corpse

Resurrection Fi: 487; Ke: 447-448; Ma: 2131

The Root of All Evil Br: 700; DC2: 362

"Sevastopol in August" Wa: 737

"Sevastopol in December, 1854" SFC: 192; Wa: 737; Ke: 448

"Sevastopol in May" Wa: 737

"Three Arshins of Land" ["How Much Land Does a Man Need?"] Ke: 448; SFC: 192; Wa: 737; WaS1: 207

"Three Deaths" SFC: 192; Wa: 737; WaS1: 207

"The Three Hermits" SFC: 192; Wa: 737

"The Two Hussars" SFC: 192; Wa: 737

Vlast Tmy see The Power of Darkness...

Vojna i Mir Fi: 487

War and Peace Fi: 487-491; Ke: 448-450; LCAB: 179; Ma: 2131-2133

"Where Love Is, There Is God Also" SFC: 192

"The Wood-felling" Wa: 737

Zhivoy Trup see The Living Corpse

Tomasi di Lampedusa, Giuseppe see LAMPEDUSA, Giuseppe Tomasi di

TOMELTY, Joseph
General Br: 700

Is the Priest at Home? Br: 700

Red Is the Port Light ENES2: 242

TOMKIS, Thomas
General NI: 339-340

Albumazar DC1: 207

TOMLINSON, Charles
General ICBAP: 134; LCAB: 179; MP: 101-102; Po: 4274

"After a Death" PE: 475

"Antecedents" ICBAP: 134

"At Holwell Farm" PE: 475

"Cezanne at Aix" ICBAP: 134

"The Dream" PE: 475

"Foxes Moon" PE: 475

"In the Fullness of Time" PE: 475

"Prometheus" PE: 475

"Reflections" PE: 475

Seeing Is Believing Po: 4274

"Under the Moon's Reign" PE: 476

TOMLINSON, Gordon
General LCAB: 179-180

TOMPSON, Benjamin
General Da: 58

TOMPSON, Charles
General AL: 339

TONNA, Browne Phelan
Helen Fleetwood ENES1: 223; ENES2: 242

TOOMER, Jean
General AAF: 60-62; AAPD: 135-137, 333; AAW: 73-74; ASF: 558; BAF: 268-273; BAP: 194; BAW: 708-711; Br: 700; HR: 140-158; LCAB: 180; MBA: 190; Po: 4275

"Avey" ASF: 554; Wa: 738

Balo AAPD: 333; BAP: 194; BAW: 710; HR: 149, 155; MBA: 190

"Becky" ASF: 554; Wa: 738

"Blood-Burning Moon" ASF: 554; HR: 142, 151; Po: 4275; Wa: 738; WaS1: 207

"Blue Meridian" HR: 140, 143

"Bona and Paul" ASF: 554; BAF: 269; HR: 143, 152; Wa: 738

"Box Seat" ASF: 554; HR: 153; Wa: 738-739; WaS1: 207

"Calling Jesus" HR: 148; Wa: 739

Cane AAF: 60-61; AAPD: 135-137; AAW: 74; ASF: 554-557; BAF: 268-274; BAW: 708-711; HR: 140-158; Po: 4275-4277

"Carma" ASF: 557; HR: 152; Wa: 739

"Cotton Song" PE: 476

"Drackman" Wa: 739

A Drama of the Southwest HR: 155; MBA: 190

"Esther" AAPD: 137; ASF:

557; BAW: 711; HR: 157;
Wa: 739; WaS1: 207
"Fern" AAPD: 137; ASF:
557; BAF: 273; BAW:
711; HR: 144, 148, 154,
158; Wa: 739; WaS1:
207-208
The Gallonwerps HR: 155;
MBA: 190
"Kabnis" AAPD: 333; ASF:
558; BAP: 194; HR:
144-146, 152, 154; MBA:
190; Wa: 739-740; WaS1:
208
"Karintha" ASF: 558; Wa:
740; WaS1: 208
"Love on a Train" Wa: 740
"Mr. Costyve Duditch" ASF:
558; Wa: 740
Natalie Mann MBA: 190
"Prayer" PE: 476
"Reapers" PE: 476
"Rhobert" ASF: 558; HR:
152
The Sacred Factory HR:
155; MBA: 190
"Song of the Son" ICBAP:
135; PE: 476
"Theater" ASF: 558; BAF:
271; HR: 148, 152; Wa:
740; WaS1: 208
"Winter on Earth" Wa: 740
TOPLADY, Augustus M.
"Rock of Ages" PE: 476
TOPOL, Josef
The Carnival Br: 700
The Cat on the Rails Br:
700
TORBERG, Friedrich
Die Mannschaft Fi: 395
Der 94. Psalm Fi: 395
TORELLI, Giacomo
'On Nico Ssi Piecoro DC2:
362
TORGA, Miguel
General Po: 4277
TORRE, Guillermo de
General Po: 4277
Las metamorfosis de Proteo
Po: 4277-4278
TORRENCE, Ridgely
Plays for a Negro Theatre
Po: 4278
TORRENTE BALLESTER, Gon-
zalo
General Po: 4278

Don Juan Ke: 231
Los gozos y las sombras Ke:
231
TORRES BODET, Jaime
General Po: 4278-4279
Canción de cuna Po: 4279
Obras Escogidas Po: 4279
"Páramo" Po: 4280
"Sueño" ["Buzo"] Po: 4280
TORRES RIOSECO, Arturo
General Po: 4280
Torsvan, Berick Traven see
TRAVEN, B.
TORTEL, Jean
General Po: 4281
TOTHEROH, Dan
Moor Born Br: 700
TOULET, Paul-Jean
General Po: 4281
Tour du Pin, Patrice de la see
LA TOUR DU PIN, Patrice
de
TOURE, Askia Muhammad
General AAPD: 238
TOURGEE, Albion Winegar
General AF: 242; AN: 235-
236; ASF: 558; Ho: 139-
140
Bricks Without Straw AF: 242;
Ho: 140
A Fool's Errand AN: 235; Ho:
140
TOURNELLE, Henri la
Oedipe DC2: 362
TOURNEUR, Cyril
General ED: 332; NI: 249-
257, 267, 277-279; TSD: 99-
101
The Atheist's Tragedy; or The
Honest Man's Revenge DC1:
208; ED: 332; EDC: 534;
NI: 263-267, 279; TSD:
99-100
The Revenger's Tragedy DC1:
208-210; ED: 332; EDC:
534-536; Log: 81; NI:
257-263, 279; TSD: 91, 95,
99-101
The Transformed Metamorphosis
ED: 332
TOURNIER, Michel
General Po: 4281
Vendredi ou les limbes de
Pacifique [Friday] Po:
4282
TOWNELEY

Harrowing of Hell DC1: 210
Noah DC1: 210
Peregrini DC1: 210
Prima Pastorum DC1: 210
Secunda Pastorum DC1:
210-211
TOWNSHEND, Aurelian
General LJCD: 258-259
TOYNBEE, Philip
General Po: 4282
TOZZI, Federigo
Con gli occhi chiusi Fi: 279
The Farm Fi: 279
Journal of a Clerk Fi: 279
Three Crosses Fi: 279
TRACY, Honor
General CN: 519
The First Day of Friday Ma:
2134
The Prospects Are Pleasing
Ma: 2134
The Straight and Narrow
Path Ma: 2134
TRAHERNE, Thomas
General Ba: 105-108;
ICBAP: 135
Centuries Ba: 106-107
"An Infant - Ey" ICBAP:
135; PE: 476
"My Spirit" PE: 476
"The Preparative" Ba: 106;
ICBAP: 135; PE: 476
"Thanksgivings" Ba: 107
"Thoughts I" Ba: 107;
PE: 476
"The Vision" PE: 476
TRAHEY, Jane
Ring Round the Bathtub
ADC: 376
TRAILL, Catherine Parr
General ECL: 204-205
TRAKL, Georg
General Po: 4282-4287
"Afra" Po: 4287-4288
"De Profundis" Po: 4288
"Früling der Seele" Po:
4288
"Gesang des Abgeschiedenen"
Po: 4288
"Helian" Po: 4289
"Kaspar-Hauser-Lied" Po:
4289
"Passion" Po: 4289-4290
"Die Sonne" Po: 4290
"Der Spaziergang" Po: 4290
"Die Stufen des Wahnsinns"

Po: 4290
TRAMBLEY, Estela Portillo
"Rain of Scorpions" WaS1:
208
TRANSTRÖMER, Tomas
General Po: 4291
TRANTER, Nigel
General Ai: 289
TRAVEN, B. [Berick Traven
TORSVAN]
General ASF: 559; Po: 4291-
4293; Wo: 198-199
"Der Busch" see "The Night
Visitor"
Death Ship [Das Totenschiff]
Ke: 338; Po: 4291, 4294;
Wo: 199
"Effective Medicine" Wa: 740
"Godfather Death" Wa: 740
Macario ASF: 559; Wa: 740
"Midnight Call" ASF: 559; Wa:
740
"The Night Visitor" ["Der
Busch"] ASF: 559; Wa:
741; WaS1: 208; Wo: 199
The Rebellion of the Hanged
Po: 4294
Das Totenschiff see Death
Ship
Treasure of the Sierra Madre
Ke: 338; Po: 4291
TRAVERS, Ben
General MDAE: 488
TREADWELL, Sophie
Hope for a Harvest ADC:
376; Br: 700
Ladies Leave ADC: 376
Machinal ADC: 376; Br:
700-701
Plumes in the Dust ADC: 376
TREECE, Henry
"Bardic Poem" PE: 476
TREJO, Mario
General Po: 4294-4295
TREMAINE, F. Orlin
"The Escape" Wa: 741
TREMAYNE, Sydney
General Ai: 298
TREMBLAY, Michel
Hossana ADC: 376
TRENCH, Herbert
General TA: 290
TRESSELL, Robert
General Po: 4295
The Ragged Trousered Phil-
anthropists ENES2: 242;

Po: 4295
TRETIAKOV, Sergei Mikhailovich
    Roar China Br: 701
TREVELYAN, George
    "Ladies in Parliament" ICBAP:
        135
TREVELYAN, Robert Calverley
    General Po: 4296
TREVISA, John [translator]
    General Hen: 204
TREVOR, William
    The Boarding House ENES2:
        242
    Elizabeth Alone ENES2: 242
    Miss Gomez and the Brethren
        ENES2: 242
    Mrs. Eckdorf in O'Neill's
        Hotel ENES2: 242
    The Old Boys ENES2: 242
TRIANA, José
    General Po: 4296
    The Criminals ADC: 376
TRIFONOV, Iurii
    Studenty Ke: 450
    Utolenie Zhazhdy Fi: 491
TRIGO, Felipe
    General Po: 4296
    Los abismos Ke: 231
    Alma en los labios Ke: 231
    La altísima Ke: 231
    La bruta Ke: 231
    La clave Ke: 231-232
    Del frío al fuego Ke: 232
    En la carrera Ke: 232
    Las Evas del paraiso Ke:
        232
    Las ingenuas Ke: 232
    Jarrapellejos Ke: 232
    El médico rural Ke: 232
    Murio de un beso Ke: 232
    La sed de amar Ke: 232
    Si si porque Ke: 232
    Sor Demonio Ke: 232
TRILLING, Diana
    General LCAB: 180
TRILLING, Lionel
    General APC: 190-192;
        CN: 519; LCAB: 180; Po:
        4296-4300
    The Middle of the Journey
        AN: 236; CN: 519;
        LCAB: 180; Po: 4300-
        4301
    "Of This Time, of That
        Place" ASF: 560; Po:
        4301; SFC: 192; Wa:

741
"The Other Margaret" ASF:
    560; Po: 4301; SFC: 192;
    Wa: 741
TRIOLET, Elsa
    General Po: 4302
    Le Cheval blanc Fi: 173
TRIPATHI, Suryakant [Nirala]
    General Po: 4302
TRISTAN L'HERMITE
    Mariane DC2: 362-363
    La Mort de Seneque DC2: 363
TRISTAN, Flora
    Mephis Fi: 173
TROLLOPE, Anthony
    General AL: 342-343; BN:
        107-110; Du: 164-166;
        LCAB: 180
    "Aaron Trow" WaS1: 208
    The American Senator BN:
        110; Du: 163; EN: 124;
        ENE: 257; ENES1: 223;
        ENES2: 243
    Ayala's Angel ENES2: 243
    Barchester Novels [General]
        Du: 161
    Barchester Towers BN: 110;
        Du: 159-160; ENE: 257-
        258; ENES1: 223; ENES2:
        243; Ma: 2135-2136
    The Barsetshire Novels BN:
        108-109; Ma: 2136
    The Belton Estate ENES1:
        223; ENES2: 243
    The Bertrams ENES1: 223;
        ENES2: 243
    Can You Forgive Her? BN:
        110; Du: 161-162; EN:
        124; ENE: 258; ENES1:
        223-224; ENES2: 243; Ma:
        2136-2137
    Castle Richmond ENES1: 224;
        ENES2: 243
    The Claverings ENES1: 224;
        ENES2: 243-244
    Cousin Henry BN: 110; Du:
        163; ENE: 258; ENES1:
        224; ENES2: 244
    Doctor Thorne BN: 110; Du:
        160; ENE: 258; ENES1:
        224; ENES2: 244; Ma:
        2137-2138
    Dr. Wortle's School EN: 124-
        125; ENE: 258; ENES1:
        224; ENES2: 244
    The Duke's Children BN:

110; Du: 162; ENE: 258; ENES1: 224; ENES2: 244; Ma: 2138

The Eustace Diamonds BN: 111; Du: 162; EN: 125; ENE: 258; ENES1: 224; ENES2: 244; Ma: 2138-2139

An Eye for an Eye EN: 125; ENES1: 224; ENES2: 245

The Fixed Period ENES1: 224; ENES2: 245

Framley Parsonage Du: 160; ENE: 258; ENES1: 225; ENES2: 245; Ma: 2139-2140

The Golden Lion of Granpere ENES2: 245

Harry Heathcote of Gangoil AL: 342-343; ENES2: 245

He Knew He Was Right ENES1: 225; ENES2: 245

Is He Popenjoy? ENES1: 225; ENES2: 245

John Caldigate AL: 342-343; ENES1: 225; ENES2: 245

The Kellys and the O'Kellys BN: 111; ENES1: 225; ENES2: 245

Kept in the Dark EN: 125; ENES1: 225; ENES2: 246

Lady Anna ENES1: 225; ENES2: 246

The Landleaguers ENES1: 225; ENES2: 246

The Last Chronicle of Barset BN: 111; Du: 160; ENE: 259; ENES1: 225; ENES2: 246; Ma: 2140-2141

Linda Tressel ENES1: 225; ENES2: 246

The Macdermotts of Bally-cloran ENES1: 226; ENES2: 246

"Malachi's Cove" WaS1: 208

Marion Fay ENES2: 246

Miss Mackenzie ENES1: 226; ENES2: 246

Mr. Scarborough's Family EN: 125; ENES1: 226; ENES2: 246-247

Nina Balatka ENES1: 226;

ENES2: 247

An Old Man's Love ENES1: 226; ENES2: 247

Orley Farm BN: 111; Du: 163; EN: 125; ENE: 259; ENES1: 226; ENES2: 247; Ma: 2141-2142

Palliser Novels [General] BN: 108-109; Du: 162-163; Ma: 2142-2143

Phineas Farm, the Irish Member ENE: 259

Phineas Finn BN: 111; Du: 162; EN: 125; ENES1: 226; ENES2: 247; Ma: 2143

Phineas Redux ENES1: 226; ENES2: 247; Ma: 2143-2144

The Prime Minister ENE: 259; ENES1: 226-227; ENES2: 247-248; Ma: 2144-2145

Rachel Ray ENES1: 227; ENES2: 248

Ralph the Heir ENES1: 227; ENES2: 248

Sir Harry Hotspur ENES2: 248

The Small House at Allington Du: 160-161; ENES1: 227; ENES2: 248; Ma: 2145

"The Spitted Dog" WaS1: 209

The Struggles of Brown, Jones, and Robinson ENES2: 248

The Three Clerks ENES1: 227; ENES2: 248

La Vendée ENES1: 227; ENES2: 248

The Vicar of Bullhampton Du: 163; ENE: 259; ENES2: 248; Ma: 2145-2146

The Warden BN: 111; Du: 161; EN: 125-126; ENE: 259; ENES1: 227; ENES2: 248-249; Ma: 2146-2147

The Way We Live Now BN: 109; Du: 163; EN: 126; ENE: 259-260; ENES1: 227; ENES2: 249; Ma: 2147-2148

TROLLOPE, Frances
General BN: 112
Michael Armstrong ENES1: 228; ENES2: 249
The Vicar of Wrexhill ENES2: 249

TROTT, Nicholas
General AP: 588

TROY, Hector
  Where's My Little Gloria?
    ADC: 377
TROY, William
  General Po: 4302
TROYAT, Henri
  L'Araigne Fi: 173; Po:
    4303
  La Neige en deuil Fi: 173
TRUESDALE, Tod
  Godsong MBA: 191
TRUMBO, Dalton
  General ASF: 560
TRUMBULL, John
  General AP: 515-516; Da:
    77
TS'AO YÜ
  General Po: 4303
  The Peking Man [Pei-Ching,
    Jen] Po: 4304
  Sunrise [Jih Ch'u] Po:
    4303
  Thunderstorm [Lei Yü] Po:
    4303-4304
  The Wild [Yüan Yeh] Po:
    4304-4305
TSHABANGU, Mango
  General BALE: 407
TUCHOLSKY, Kurt
  General Po: 4305
  "Die Laternenanzünder" Wa:
    741
TUCKER, James [Giacomo di
    ROSENBERG]
  Ralph Rashleigh AL: 346-
    347
TUCKER, St. George
  General AP: 517-518; Da:
    102
TUCKERMAN, Frederick Goddard
  General LCAB: 180
  "As Eponina Brought, to
    Move the King" PE: 476
  "The Cricket" PE: 476
  "An Upper Chamber in a
    Darkened House" PE:
    477
TUCKERMAN, Henry Theodore
  General LCAB: 180
TUGLAS, Friedebert
  Felix Ormusson Ke: 451
TUKE, Sir Samuel
  The Adventures of Five
    Hours Li: 313
TULYA-MUHIKA, Sam
  General BALE: 407

TUMANIAN, Ovanes
  General Po: 4306
TUMLER, Franz
  "The Coat" WaS1: 209
TUOTTI, Joseph Dolan
  Big Time Buck White ADC:
    377
TURBERVILLE, George
  General ICBAP: 135; SC: 99
  Tragical Tales SC: 99
TURCO, Lewis
  General Po: 4306
TURGENEV, Ivan
  General Br: 701; LCAB:
    180-181
  The Bachelor Br: 701
  "Bezhin Meadow" ["Byezhin
    Prairie"] SFC: 193; Wa:
    742; WaS1: 209
  "Biryuk" SFC: 193; Wa: 742
  "Brigadier" Wa: 742; WaS1:
    209
  "A Correspondence" SFC:
    193; Wa: 742
  A Country Doctor Fi: 491;
    Wa: 742
  The Diary of a Superfluous
    Man Fi: 491; Ke: 451;
    SFC: 193; Wa: 742
  Dvorjanskoe Gnezdo Fi: 491
  Fathers and Sons Fi: 491-
    492; Ke: 451-452; LCAB:
    181; Ma: 2149-2150
  First Love Fi: 492; Ke: 452;
    SFC: 193; Wa: 742; WaS1:
    209
  "The History of Lieutenant
    Ergunov" SFC: 193; Wa:
    742
  House of Gentlefolk see Nest
    of Gentlefolk
  "Khor and Kalinitch" Wa:
    742
  "A Lear of the Steppes"
    LCAB: 181; Wa: 742;
    WaS1: 209
  A Month in the Country [Mes-
    yats v Derevne] Br: 701;
    DC2: 363; EDC: 536-537;
    Ma: 2151-2152
  Nest of Gentlefolk [House of
    Gentlefolk] Fi: 492-493;
    Ke: 452-453; Ma: 2150-
    2151
  "Old Portraits" Wa: 742
  On the Eve Fi: 493; Ke:

453-454; Ma: 2152-2153
"Punin and Baburin" Wa: 742
Rudin Fi: 493; Ke: 454-455; Ma: 2153-2154
"The Singers" SFC: 193; Wa: 742; WaS1: 209
Smoke Fi: 493; Ke: 455-456; Ma: 2154-2155
Sportsman's Sketches [Sportsman's Notebook] Fi: 493; Ke: 456
Spring Torrents [The Torrents of Spring] Fi: 493; Ke: 456; Ma: 2155; Wa: 743
"The Story of Lieutenant Erguynov" WaS1: 209
"Three Meetings" Wa: 743
"A Tour of the Forest" SFC: 193; Wa: 743
Virgin Soil Fi: 493-494; Ke: 456-457; Ma: 2156-2157; Po: 1812
"The Watch" Wa: 743
"Yermolai and the Miller's Wife" Wa: 743; WaS1: 209

TURNEBE, Odet de
Contens DC2: 363

TURNER, David
General MDAE: 489
Semi-Detached MDAE: 489; Po: 4306

TURNER, Dennis
Charlie Was Here and Now He's Gone ADC: 377; BAP: 194-195

TURNER, George Reginald
General MAP: 310; Po: 4306
Young Man of Talent MAP: 310

TURNER, Lucy Mae
General BAW: 719

TURNER, Nat
General LCAB: 181

TURNER, Walter James Redfern
General Po: 4307
The Man Who Ate Popmack DC1: 211
Smaragda's Lover DC1: 211

TURNEY, Robert
Daughters of Atreus Br: 701

TURPIN, Waters Edward
General AAW: 74; BAF: 274; BAW: 720
O Canaan! BAF: 274-275
These Low Grounds BAF: 275

TUSSMAN, Malka Haifetz
General Po: 4307

TUTT, Homer J.
Gospel Train MBA: 191

TUTUOLA, Amos
General BALE: 408-412; Po: 4308
Ajaiyi and His Inherited Poverty BALE: 412
"The Complete Gentleman" Wa: 743
The Palm-Wine Drinkard BALE: 408-411; LCAB: 181; Po: 4309

TUWIM, Julian
General Po: 4309

TWAIN, Mark [Samuel Langhorne CLEMENS]
General AD: 106-107; AF: 62-70; ALL: 56-62; AN: 243-250; ASF: 567-570; Cla: 14-18; Ho: 23-31, 143-144; LCAB: 36-37; Po: 496-498
"Autobiography of a Damned Fool" ASF: 560
"The Autobiography of Belshazzar" ASF: 560
"Baker's Blue-Jay Yarn" AF: 68; Wa: 743; WaS1: 209
"The Boy's Manuscript" ASF: 560
"The Californian's Tale" ASF: 560
"The Campaign That Failed" Cla: 17
"Captain Stormfield's Visit to Heaven" ASF: 562; SFC: 193; Wa: 743; WaS1: 209
"A Cat Tale" ASF: 560
"The Celebrated Jumping Frog of Calaveras County" ASF: 561; LCAB: 37; SFC: 193; Wa: 743-744; WaS1: 210
A Connecticut Yankee in King Arthur's Court AF: 69; AN: 236; Cla: 14-18; Ho: 25-29, 31, 144; Ma: 2158-2159
"A Cure for the Blues" ASF: 561
"The Curious Republic of Gon-

dour" ASF: 561

"The Dandy Frightening the Squatter" ASF: 561; SFC: 193; Wa: 744

"The Death Disk" ASF: 561

"A Dog's Tale" ASF: 561

"A Double-Barrelled Detective Story" ASF: 561; SFC: 194; Wa: 744

"Down the Rhône" ASF: 562

"The Enchanted Sea-Wilderness" ASF: 562

"The Enemy Conquered, or Love Triumphant" ASF: 562

"Eve's Diary" ASF: 562

"Extracts from Adam's Diary" ASF: 562

"A Fable" ASF: 562; WaS1: 209

"The Facts Concerning the Recent Carnival of Crime in Connecticut" ASF: 562

The Gilded Age AF: 69; ALL: 58; AN: 236-237; Ho: 27-29

The Golden Arm" ASF: 562

"Goldsmith's Friend Abroad Again" ASF: 562

"Grandfather's Ram Story" see "The Story of the Old Ram"

"The Great Dark" ASF: 562; Wa: 744

"The Great Revolution in Pitcairn" ASF: 562

"Hellfire Hotchkiss" ASF: 562-563

"A Horse's Tale" ASF: 563

Huckleberry Finn, The Adventures of AF: 62-70; ALL: 56; AN: 237-240; Cla: 14-17; Ho: 23, 26-31, 143-144; LCAB: 37; Ma: 2159-2161; Po: 498-501, 1845

"Indiantown" ASF: 563

The Innocents Abroad Ho: 28; LCAB: 37; Ma: 2161-2162; Po: 1837

"The International Lightning Trust" ASF: 563

"The Invalid's Story" ASF: 563; Wa: 744

"Jim Baker's Blue-Jay Yarn" ASF: 563

"Jim Wolf and the Tom-Cats" ASF: 563

Joan of Arc AN: 240-241; Ho: 144

"The Latest Sensation" ASF: 563

"Letters from the Earth" ASF: 563

Life on the Mississippi Cla: 16; Ma: 2162-2163

"The Loves of Alonzo Fitz Clarence and Rosannah Ethelton" ASF: 563

"The Man That Corrupted Hadleyburg" AF: 63; ASF: 564; Ma: 2163-2164; Po: 501; SFC: 194; Wa: 744-745; WaS1: 209-210

Mark Twain's Autobiography Ma: 2164-2165

"A Medieval Romance" ASF: 565

"Methuselah's Diary" ASF: 565

"Mock Marriage" ASF: 565

"My Bloody Massacre" ASF: 565

"My Platonic Sweetheart" ASF: 565

The Mysterious Stranger AF: 63-65, 69; ALL: 61; AN: 241; Cla: 17-18; Ho: 25, 28; Ma: 2165-2166; Po: 501-502; SFC: 194-195; Wa: 745-746; WaS1: 210

"The Notorious Jumping Frog of Calaveras County" see "The Celebrated Jumping Frog of Calaveras County"

Old Times on the Mississippi Cla: 17

"The £1,000,000 Bank-Note" ASF: 565

"1002d Arabian Night" ASF: 565

"Papers of the Adam Family" ASF: 565

The Prince and the Pauper AN: 241; Ho: 31; Ma: 2166-2167

"The Private History of a Campaign That Failed" ASF: 565

"The Professor's Yarn" ASF: 566

Pudd'nhead Wilson AN: 241;
Cla: 15, 17-18; Ho: 26-
31, 144; Po: 502
"The Refuge of the Dere-
licts" ASF: 566
Roughing It Cla: 17; Ma:
2167-2168
"Sabbath Reflections" ASF:
566
"Schoolhouse Hill" ASF: 566
"The Secret History of Eddy-
pus, the World-Empire"
ASF: 566
"Sold to Satan" ASF: 567
"Some Learned Fables for
Good Old Boys and Girls"
ASF: 566
"Some Rambling Notes of an
Idle Excursion" ASF:
566
"The Stolen White Elephant"
ASF: 566
"The Story of Mamie Grant,
the Child-Missionary"
ASF: 566
"The Story of the Good Little
Boy" Wa: 746
"The Story of the Old Ram"
SFC: 195; Wa: 746
"That Day in Eden" ASF:
566
"The $30,000 Bequest" ASF:
566
Those Extraordinary Twins
AN: 241; ASF: 566;
Cla: 18; Po: 502
Tom Sawyer, the Adventures
of AF: 64-65, 67; AN:
242; Cla: 16; Ho: 23,
30-31, 144; Ma: 2168-
2169; Po: 501
Tom Sawyer Abroad AN:
242
"Tom Sawyer's Conspiracy"
ASF: 567
The Tragedy of Pudd'nhead
Wilson see Pudd'nhead
Wilson
"Traveling with a Reformer"
ASF: 567
"A True Story, Repeated
Word for Word as I Heard
It" ASF: 567; WaS1:
210
"The Turning Point of My
Life" Cla: 17

"Wapping Alice" ASF: 567
"The War Prayer" ASF: 567
"What Stumped the Bluejays"
see "Jim Baker's Blue-Jay
Yarn"
"Which Was It?" ASF: 567
"'You've Been a Damn Fool,
Mary. You Always Was!'"
ASF: 567
_____ and Charles Dudley
WARNER
The Gilded Age Ma: 2172-
2173
_____ and William Dean HOWELLS
Colonel Sellers as a Scientist
see also HOWELLS, William
Dean AD: 107
TWEEDALE, Violet
The Mammonist ENES2: 249
TWINE, Laurence
The Pattern of Painful Adven-
tures ERP: 492-493
TYLER, Margaret [translator]
The Mirror of Knighthood
ERP: 493-494
TYLER, Parker
"The Granite Butterfly" PE:
477
TYLER, Royall
General AD: 201-204; ALL:
269; AP: 519-520; Da:
102; Lon: 64
The Algerine Captive Ma:
2174
The Contrast AD: 201-204;
ADC: 377-378; ALL: 269;
DC1: 211; Lon: 64
TYNAN, Katherine
The Way of a Maid ENES2:
249
TYNDALE [or TINDALE], William
General Hen: 25; SC: 100
_____ [translator]
New Testament Hen: 220
TYNYANOV, Yuri
Death of the Vazir-Mukhtar
Ke: 457-458
TZARA, Tristan
General Po: 4309-4311

U

UDALL, Nicholas
General ED: 334; TSD: 101
Jacob and Esau EDC: 537

Ralph Roister Doister [Roister
Doister] DC1: 211-212;
ED: 334; EDC: 537;
TSD: 101
UDECHUKWU, Obiora
General BALE: 412
UDOEYOP, Nyong J.
General BALE: 413
UDOFF, Yale
Gun Play ADC: 378
UHDE, Milan
King Vavra [Král Vávra]
Br: 701
UKA, Kalu
General BALE: 413
UKRAINKA, Lesya
In the Wilderness Po: 4313
The Stone Master DC2:
363; Po: 4313
ULASI, Adaora Lily
General BALE: 413
ULLMAN, James Ramsey
The White Tower AN: 250
UNAMUNO Y JUGO, Miguel de
General Br: 701; MD: 314;
Po: 4313-4340
"El abejorro--" Wa: 746
Abel Sánchez Fi: 250; Ke:
232-233; Po: 4340; SFC:
195; Wa: 746-747; WaS1:
210
La agonía del cristianismo
Fi: 250
"Al correr los años" Wa:
747
Amor y pedagogía [Love and
Pedagogy] Fi: 250-251;
Ke: 233; Po: 4324, 4341;
SFC: 195
"Artemio, heautontimorou-
menos" Wa: 747
"As the Years Go By" Wa:
747
Aunt Tula [La tía Tula]
Fi: 253; Ke: 235; Po:
4351-4352; SFC: 195; Wa:
747; WaS1: 210
"La Beca" Wa: 747
"Bonifacio" Wa: 747
Cancionero Po: 4341-4342
El canto de las aguas eternas
Ke: 233; Wa: 747
"Caridad bien ordenada"
Wa: 747
"Un caso de longevidad"
Wa: 747

"Children of the Mind" Wa: 747
¿Cómo se hace una novela? Fi:
251; Ke: 233; Po: 4342-4343
El Cristo de Velázquez Po:
4343-4344
Del sentimiento trágico de la
vida en los hombres y en los
pueblos Po: 4326, 4344
"El dioa Pavor" Wa: 747
"Don Bernardino y Dona Etel-
vina" Wa: 747
"Don Catalino, hombre sabio"
Wa: 747
"Don Martín, o de la gloria"
Wa: 747
"Don Sivestre Carrasco, hombre
efectivo" Wa: 748
"Elegía en la muerte de un
perro" Po: 4344
"En manos de una cocinera"
Wa: 748
Fedra Po: 4335
"Fe-Razón" Po: 4345
El hermano Juan o el mundo es
teatro DC2: 364
Una historia de amor Po:
4324
"Juan Manso, cuento de muer-
tos" Wa: 748
"El lego Juan" Wa: 748
"La locura del doctor Montarco"
Wa: 748
Love and Pedagogy see Amor
y pedagogía
"La manchita de la uña" Wa:
748
The Marquis of Lumbria SFC:
195; Wa: 748
"El misterio de la iniquidad"
Wa: 748
Niebla Fi: 251-252; Ke: 233-
234; Po: 4316, 4338, 4345-
4347
Nothing Less Than a Man [Nada
menos que todo un hombre]
Fi: 251; Ke: 233; Po:
4338, 4345; SFC: 195; Wa:
748
La novela de Don Sandalio,
jugador de ajadrez Fi:
252; Ke: 233; Po: 4348
"El padrino Antonio" Wa: 748
Paz en la guerra Fi: 252;
Ke: 234; Po: 4324, 4337,
4348
"El poema vivo de amor" Wa:

748
Por tierras de Portugal y de
España Po: 4349
"¿Qué es tu viva...?" Po:
4349
"El que se enterro" Wa:
748
Raquel encadenada Po: 4335
"Robleda, el actor" Wa:
748
"Romancero del destierro"
Po: 4349
Rosario de sonetos líricos
Po: 4326
Saint Manuel the Good,
Martyr [San Manuel
Bueno, mártir] Fi: 252-
253; Ke: 234-235; Po:
2139-2140, 4337-4338,
4349-4351; SFC: 195;
Wa: 748-749; WaS1: 210
"El semejante" Wa: 749
"El sencillo don Rafael" Wa:
749
"Soledad" Po: 4335; Wa:
749
"Solitaña" Wa: 749
La tía Tula see Aunt Tula
Tres novelas ejemplares Po:
4316
Two Mothers SFC: 195;
Wa: 749
"La venda" DC2: 364; Po:
4352; SFC: 196; Wa: 749
"Ver con los ojos" Wa: 749
Vida de Don Quijote y
Sancho Po: 4352-4353
"Una visita al viejo poeta"
Wa: 749
UNDER, Marie
General Po: 4353-4354
UNDERDOWNE, Thomas [trans-
lator]
An Aethiopian History by
HELIODORUS ERP: 496
UNDERHILL, Evelyn
General WIL: 168
UNDERHILL, Irvin W.
General BAW: 721
UNDSET, Sigrid
General LCAB: 181
The Axe Ma: 2175
The Bridal Wreath Fi: 414
The Burning Bush Fi:
414; Ke: 366
The Cross Fi: 414

The Faithful Wife Fi: 414; Ke:
366
Fru Hjelde Ke: 366
Fru Martha Oulie see Mrs.
Marta Oulie
Fru Waage Ke: 366
Ida Elisabeth Fi: 414
In the Wilderness Ma: 2175
Jenny Fi: 414; Ke: 366-367;
Ma: 2175-2176
Kristin Lavransdatter Fi: 414;
Ke: 367; Ma: 2176; Po:
4354
The Longest Years Ke: 367
Madame Dorothea Fi: 414;
Ke: 367
The Master of Hestviken Fi:
414; Ke: 367; Po: 4354-
4355
The Mistress of Husaby Fi:
414
Mrs. Marta Oulie [Fru Martha
Oulie] Fi: 414; Ke: 366
The Snake Pit Ma: 2176-2177
The Son Avenger Ma: 2177
Spring Fi: 414; Ke: 367-368
The Wild Orchid Fi: 414; Ke:
368
UNGARETTI, Giuseppe
General Po: 4355-4359
L'Allegria Po: 4360
Il dolore Po: 4360
"I fiumi" Po: 4360
L'Isola Po: 4360
"Memoria di Ofelia D'Alba" Po:
4360-4361
La terra promessa Po: 4361
Tu ti spezzasti Po: 4361
"Variazioni su nulla" Po: 4361
UNRUH, Friedrich Franz von
"Die jüngste Nacht" Wa: 749
UNRUH, Fritz von
General Br: 702
The End Is Not Yet Ke: 338
A Race [Ein Geschlecht] Br:
702; DC2: 364; Po: 4362
Square [Platz] Br: 702
The Way of Sacrifice Ke: 338
UPDIKE, John
General ALL: 270-271; ASF:
574-575; CFAE: 390-392;
CN: 520; LCAB: 181; Ne:
92-93; Po: 4362-4367
"A & P" ASF: 571; Wa: 749-
750; WaS1: 210
"Ace in the Hole" ASF: 571;

Wa: 750

"The Archangel" Wa: 750

"The Astronomer" ASF: 571; Wa: 750; WaS1: 210

Bech: A Book ALL: 270; Ma: 2194

"Bech Panics" ASF: 571

"Bech Swings?" ASF: 571

"The Blessed Man of Boston, My Grandmother's Thimble, and Fanning Island" ASF: 571; Wa: 750

"The Bulgarian Poetess" ASF: 571; Wa: 750

The Centaur ALL: 271; CFAE: 390-392; CN: 521-522; LCAB: 181; Ma: 2194-2196; Po: 4362-4367

"The Christian Roommates" ASF: 572

"Churchgoing" Wa: 750

The Coup ALL: 271

Couples ALL: 270-271; CFAE: 390; CN: 522; Ma: 2196-2197; Po: 4364, 4367

"The Crow in the Woods" ASF: 572; Wa: 750

"The Dark" ASF: 572; Wa: 750

"The Day of the Dying Rabbit" Wa: 750

"Dear Alexandros" Wa: 750

"Dentistry and Doubt" ASF: 572; Wa: 750

"The Doctor's Wife" Wa: 750; WaS1: 210

"A Dying Cat" Wa: 750

"Eros Rampant" ASF: 572; Wa: 751

"Ex-Basketball Player" PE: 477

"The Family Meadow" Wa: 751

"Flight" ASF: 572; Wa: 751; WaS1: 211

"Four Sides of One Story" WaS1: 211

"Friends from Philadelphia" ASF: 572; Wa: 751

"A Gift from the City" ASF: 572; Wa: 751

"Giving Blood" ASF: 572; Wa: 751

"The Happiest I've Been"

ASF: 572; Wa: 751

"Harv Is Plowing Now" ASF: 572; Wa: 751

"The Hermit" ASF: 572; Wa: 751

"His Finest Hour" Wa: 751

"Home" Wa: 751

"In Football Season" ASF: 572; Wa: 751

"Leaves" LCAB: 181; Wa: 751

"Lifeguard" ASF: 572; Wa: 752

"Marching Through Boston" ASF: 573; Wa: 752

"Midpoint" Po: 4368

Midpoint and Other Poems CFAE: 391; Ma: 2197

"Mobile of Birds" ASF: 573

A Month of Sundays ALL: 271

"The Morning" Wa: 752

"Museums and Women" ASF: 573; Wa: 752

Museums and Women and Other Stories Ma: 2197-2198

"The Music School" ASF: 573; Ma: 2198; Wa: 752

"My Lover Has Dirty Fingernails" ASF: 573; Wa: 752

Of the Farm ALL: 271; CN: 522-523; Ma: 2199-2200; Po: 4362-4363, 4365-4366

"On the Way to School" Wa: 752

"Packed Dirt, Churchgoing, a Dying Cat, a Traded Car" ASF: 573; Wa: 752

"The Persistence of Desire" ASF: 573; Wa: 752

"The Peruvian in the Heart of Lake Winnipesaukee" ASF: 573; Wa: 752

"Pigeon Feathers" ASF: 573; Ma: 2200-2201; Po: 4364-4365; Wa: 752; WaS1: 211

The Poorhouse Fair ALL: 271; CN: 523; Ma: 2201-2202; Po: 4363-4365

Rabbit Redux ALL: 270-271; Ma: 2202

Rabbit, Run ALL: 270-271; CFAE: 390-392; CN: 523-524; LCAB: 181; Ma: 2203-2204; Ne: 92; Po: 4363-4366, 4368-4369

"The Rescue" ASF: 573;
  Wa: 753
"The Sea's Green Sameness"
  Wa: 753
"A Sense of Shelter" ASF:
  573; Po: 4369-4370; Wa:
  753
"Shillington" PE: 477
"Should Wizard Hit Mommy?"
  ASF: 574; Wa: 753
"Snowing in Greenwich Vil-
  lage" ASF: 574; Wa:
  753
"Spring Comes to Cambridge"
  Wa: 753
"Still Life" Wa: 753
"The Sunshine Poet" Wa:
  753
"The Taste of Metal" ASF:
  574; Wa: 753
Telephone Poles Ma: 2204
"Tomorrow and Tomorrow
  and So Forth" ASF: 574;
  Wa: 753; WaS1: 211
"Toward Evening" ASF:
  574; Wa: 753-754
"Twin Beds in Rome" ASF:
  574; Wa: 754
"Unstuck" Po: 4370
"The Wait" ASF: 574
"Walter Briggs" Wa: 754
"When Everyone Was Preg-
  nant" Wa: 754
"Who Made Yellow Roses
  Yellow?" ASF: 574; Wa:
  754
"Wife-Wooing" ASF: 574;
  Wa: 754
"The Witness" Wa: 754
"You'll Never Know, Dear,
  How Much I Love You"
  ASF: 574; Po: 4370;
  Wa: 754
"Your Lover Just Called"
  ASF: 574; Wa: 754
UPWARD, Edward
  General Po: 4370
  "The Railway Accident"
    WaS1: 211
  "Sunday" SFC: 196; Wa:
    754
URFE, Honoré d'
  L'Astrée Fi: 173
URIS, Leon
  Battle Cry AN: 250
  Trinity JW: 303

URQUHART, Fred
  General Ai: 299
URQUHART, Sir Thomas
  Genral Ai: 49-50; LCAB: 182
  _____ [translator]
  The Works of Rabelais ERP:
    500-504
URQUIA, Carlos Enrique
  General Po: 4370-4371
URUETA, Margarita
  General Po: 4371
USIGLI, Rodolfo
  General Br: 702; Po: 4371-
    4372
  The Impersonator [El Gesticu-
    lador] Br: 702
USK, Thomas
  The Testament of Love Hen:
    20
USTINOV, Peter Alexander
  General Br: 702; MDAE:
    491
  Banbury Nose EDC: 537
  Blow Your Own Trumpet EDC:
    537
  Halfway Up the Tree EDC:
    537
  High Balcony EDC: 537
  House of Regrets EDC: 537
  Life in My Hands EDC: 538
  The Love of Four Colonels
    Br: 702; EDC: 538; MD:
    314; MDAE: 491
  Man in the Raincoat EDC:
    538
  The Moment of Truth Br:
    703; DC1: 212; EDC: 538
  No Sign of the Dove EDC:
    538
  Paris Not So Gay EDC: 538
  Photo Finish Br: 703; EDC:
    538
  Romanoff and Juliet EDC:
    538-539; MD: 314
  The Unknown Soldier and His
    Wife EDC: 539
  Who's Who in Hell EDC: 539
UZODINMA, Edmund Chukuemeka
  Chieke
  General BALE: 414

V

VACAREZZA, Alberto
  General Br: 703

San Antonio de los Cobres
  Br: 703
VACHE, Jacques
  General Po: 4373
VACLAV, Havel
  General Po: 4373
VAILLAND, Jean
  General Po: 4373-4374
  La Loi Po: 4373
VAILLAND, Roger
  Monsieur Jean Po: 4373
  325.000 francs Fi: 173
VALDELOMAR, Abraham
  General Po: 4374
  "El caballero Carmelo" Wa:
    754
  "El vuelo de cóndores" Wa:
    754
VALENCIA, Guillermo
  General Po: 4374
VALENTIN, Thomas
  Die Unberatenen Fi: 395
VALERA, Juan
  Commander Mendoza Fi:
    253; Ke: 235
  Don Braulio Fi: 253
  Doña Luz Fi: 253-254; Ke:
    235
  "The Double Sacrifice" Wa:
    754
  "The Elf-Kiss" Wa: 754
  Formidable Juanita Fi: 254
  "Garuda or the White Stork"
    Wa: 755
  "Good Reputation" Wa: 755
  "The Green Bird" Wa: 755
  The Illusions of Doctor Faus-
    tino Fi: 254
  "The Knight of the Falcon"
    Wa: 755
  "Let Him Who Does Not Know
    You Buy You" Wa: 755
  "The Little Doll" Wa: 755
  "The Magician" Wa: 755
  Morsamor Fi: 254; Wa: 755
  "Parsondes" Wa: 755
  Pepita Jiménez Fi: 254;
    Ke: 235
  "The Prehistoric Bermejino
    or the Blue Salamander"
    Wa: 755
  "The Prisoner of Doña Men-
    cia" Wa: 755
  Rafaela Fi: 254
VALERY, Paul
  General LCAB: 182; MD:

314; Po: 4375-4401
L'Ame et la danse Po: 4401-
  4402
The Art of Poetry Po: 4378
"Au platane" Po: 4376, 4402
"Aurore" Po: 4382
Cahiers Po: 4382, 4388, 4402-
  4404
"Calypso" Po: 4404
"Cantique des colonnes" Po:
  4404
"La Ceinture" Po: 4405
Charmes Po: 4380, 4400-4401
Le Cimetière marin Po: 4381,
  4401, 4405-4407
"La Dormeuse" Po: 4407
"Ebauche d'un serpent" Po:
  4379, 4407
Eupalinos, ou l'Architecte Po:
  4408
"La Fausse morte" Po: 4408
"Féerie" Po: 4408-4409
"La Fileuse" Po: 4409
"Fragments du Narcisse" Po:
  4409
"Les Grenades" Po: 4410
Introduction à la méthode de
  Léonardo de Vinci Po:
  4410
La Jeune Parque Po: 4376,
  4379, 4400-4401, 4411-4412
Monsieur Teste Fi: 173-174;
  Ke: 167-168; Po: 4413-
  4415
My Faust [Mon Faust; Luste;
  Only One] DC2: 364; MD:
  314; Po: 4393, 4412-4413
"Ode secrète" Po: 4378, 4415
"Orphée" Po: 4415
"Palme" Po: 4382, 4416
"Les Pas" Po: 4416
Pièces sur l'art Po: 4375
"Poésie" Po: 4382
Pour votre Hêtre--"Suprême"
  Po: 4376
"Profusion du soir" Po: 4401,
  4416-4417
"La Pythie" Po: 4378-4379,
  4382
"Le Rameur" Po: 4417
Rhumbs Po: 4375
"Sinistre" Po: 4417
Stratonice Po: 4418
"Le Vin perdu" Po: 4418-4419
VALL, Seymour
  How to Be a Jewish Mother

ADC: 378

VALLE-INCLAN, Ramón María del

General Br: 703; Po: 4419-4433

Aromas de leyenda Po: 4424

Baza de espadas Fi: 254

"Beatriz" Wa: 755

La cabeza del Bautista Po: 4419

La cara de Dios Fi: 254; Po: 4433

Cara de Plata Po: 4433

Cenizas Po: 4433-4434

Comedias bárbaras Ke: 235; Po: 4434

La corte de Estella Po: 4434

La corte de los milagros Fi: 254; Po: 4434-4435

Cuento de abril Po: 4435

Los cuernos de Don Friolera DC2: 364; Po: 4435-4436

Divine Words [Divinas palabras] Br: 703; Po: 4436

El embrujado Po: 4436

La enamorada del rey Po: 4419

Esperpento de la hija del capitán Po: 4436-4437

Flor de santidad Ke: 235

El imparcial Po: 4437

Jardin Umbrio Fi: 255

Lights of Bohemia [Luces de Bohemia] DC2: 365; Fi: 255; Po: 4437-4439

Martes de Carnaval Po: 4439

Memorias del Marqués de Bradomín Po: 4439-4440

Mi hermana Antonia Po: 4440

El pasajero Po: 4424

La pipa de Kif Po: 4420, 4424, 4440

La reina castiza Br: 704; DC2: 365; Po: 4440-4441

La rosa de papel Po: 4419-4420

Rosarito Fi: 255; Wa: 755

El ruedo ibérico Fi: 255; Ke: 235; Po: 4431, 4441-4442

Sacrilegio Po: 4442

Sonata de estió Ke: 236;
Po: 4420, 4442

Sonata de otoño Ke: 236; Po: 4442-4443

Sonata de primavera Fi: 255; Ke: 236; Po: 4443

Sonatas Po: 4431, 4443-4444

Tirano Banderas Fi: 255; Po: 4420, 4429, 4444-4445

Viva mi dueño Fi: 255-256

Voces de gesta Po: 4445

VALLEJO, Antonio Buero

General Br: 136; Po: 328-330

Almost a Fairy Tale [Casi in cuento de hadas] DC2: 365

Aventura en los gris DC2: 365

Cartas boca DC2: 365

El concierto de San Ovido DC2: 365

Dawn [Madrugada] DC2: 366

The Double Story of Doctor Valmy [La doble historia del Doctor Valmy] Br: 136

Historia de una esclera see A Stairway's History

Hoy es fiesta see Today Is Holiday

In the Burning Darkness [En la ardiente oscuridad] DC2: 365; Po: 330

Irene or the Treasure [Irene o el tesoro] DC2: 366

Ladies in Waiting [Las meninas] DC2: 366

Madrugada see Dawn

Palabras en la arena see Words in the Sand

La senal que se espera see Waiting for a Sign

Un soñador para un pueblo DC2: 366; Po: 331

A Stairway's History [Historia de una escalera] DC2: 365-366; Po: 330

Today Is Holiday [Hoy es fiesta] DC2: 366

Waiting for a Sign [La senal que se espera] DC2: 366

Weaver of Dreams [La tejedora de suenos] DC2: 367

Words in the Sand [Palabras en la arena] DC2: 366

VALLEJO, César Abraham

General LCAB: 182; Po: 4445-4449

Los heraldos negros Po:

4449
Hoy me gusta la vida mucho menos Po: 4449
Poemas humanos Po: 4449-4450
Trilce Po: 4450-4451
Vallejo, Manuel Mejía see MEJIA VALLEJO, Manuel
VALLES, Jules
L'Enfant Fi: 174
Jacques Vingtras Fi: 174
VALMIKI
The Ramayana Ma: 2205
VANBRUGH, Sir John
General Bon: 47; Li: 315-316
The Mistake DC1: 212
The Provok'd Husband see also CIBBER, Colley DC1: 212
The Provoked Wife DC1: 212; Li: 315-316
The Relapse DC1: 212; Li: 315-316
VAN DEN BOS
Roode en Witte Roos DC2: 367
Vandera, Alonso Carrio de la see CARRIO DE LA VANDERA, Alonso
VAN DER POST, Laurens
General LCAB: 182; Po: 4452
VAN DE VELDE, Anton
General Br: 704
Van Dine, S.S. see WRIGHT, Willard Huntingdon
VAN DOREN, Mark
General LCAB: 182
"January Choice" PE: 477
VAN DRUTEN, John William
General MD: 314; Mi: 279
After All ADC: 378
Behold We Live ADC: 378
Bell, Book and Candle ADC: 378-379; MD: 314-315
The Distaff Side ADC: 379
Diversion ADC: 379
The Druid Circle ADC: 379; MD: 315
Flowers of the Forest ADC: 379
Gertie Maude ADC: 380
I Am a Camera ADC: 380; MD: 315
I Remember Mama ADC:

380; MD: 315
I've Got Sixpence ADC: 380-381
Leave Her to Heaven ADC: 381
London Wall ADC: 381
Make Way for Lucia ADC: 381
The Mermaids Singing ADC: 381
Most of the Game ADC: 381
Old Acquaintance ADC: 381
The Return of the Soldier ADC: 381
Solitaire ADC: 382
Somebody Knows ADC: 382
There's Always Juliet ADC: 382
The Voice of the Turtle ADC: 382; Br: 704
Young Woodley ADC: 382; Br: 704
_____ and Lloyd MORRIS
The Damask Cheek ADC: 382-383
VAN DUYN, Mona
"The Bell" SFC: 196; Wa: 755
VAN DYKE, Henry
Blood of Strawberries BAF: 275
Dead Piano BAF: 275-276
Ladies of the Rachmaninoff Eyes BAF: 276
The Story of the Other Wise Man Po: 4452-4453
VANDYNE, William J.
General BAW: 723
VANE, Sutton
General Mi: 280
Outward Bound Br: 704; DC1: 212; EDC: 539
Overture EDC: 539-540
VAN EEDEN, Frederick
General Po: 4453
VAN ITALLIE, Jean-Claude
General LCAB: 96; MDAE: 493-494
America Hurrah [three plays: Interview; TV; and Motel] ADC: 383; Br: 704; MDAE: 494
A Fable ADC: 383
Mystery Play ADC: 383
The Seagull ADC: 383
War ADC: 383

_____ and Joseph CHAIKIN
The Serpent: A Ceremony
ADC: 383-384; MDAE:
494
VAN LERBERGHE, Charles
General Po: 4453
VAN PEEBLES, Melvin
General AAPD: 407; BAF:
276-277; BAP: 196; BAW:
723-724; MBA: 192
Ain't Supposed to Die a Na-
tural Death BAP: 196-
197; MBA: 192-193
A Bear for the FBI BAF:
276-277
Don't Play Us Cheap BAP:
196-198; MBA: 192-193
Just an Old Sweet Song
MBA: 193-194
The Story of a Three Day
Pass BAP: 197; MBA:
193
Sweet Sweetback's Baadasssss
Song AAPD: 408; BAP:
197; MBA: 193
The True American BAF:
277
Watermelon Man BAP: 197;
MBA: 193
VANSITTART, Peter
General Po: 4454
VAN VECHTEN, Carl
General AN: 250-251; ASF:
576; LCAB: 182; Wo:
202-203
Nigger Heaven Po: 4453-
4454; Wo: 202
VAN VOGT, Alfred Eaton
General LCAB: 182
"Black Destroyer" WaS1:
211
"Fulfillment" Wa: 756
VAN ZANDT, Roland
Wilson in the Promise Land
ADC: 384
VARGAS LLOSA, Mario
General LCAB: 182; Po:
4454-4455
Los cachorros Po: 4454
La casa verde Po: 4454-
4455
La ciudad y los perros Po:
4455-4456
VASCONCELOS, José
General Po: 4456-4457
"The Boar Hunt" Wa: 756

VASHON, George Boyer
General AAPD: 78; BAW:
724
VAUGHAN, Henry
General Ba: 109-112; ICBAP:
135; Ma: 2206-2207
"The Book" Ba: 111
"The Character, to Etesia"
PE: 477
"Christ's Nativity" PE: 477
"Cock-Crowing" Ba: 109;
ICBAP: 135; PE: 477
"Corruption" Ba: 112; PE:
477
"Day of Judgement" Ba: 112
"The Day-spring" PE: 477
"Disorder and Frailty" PE:
477
"The Dwelling-Place" PE: 477
"L'Envoy" PE: 478
"Etesia Absent" PE: 478
"FIDA: Or the Country-
beauty" PE: 478
"I Walked the Other Day (to
Spend My Hour)" PE: 478
"In Amicum Foeneratorem" PE:
478
"Isaacs Marriage" PE: 478
"The Lamp" PE: 478
"Man" PE: 478
"Man's Fall and Recovery" PE:
478
"The Morning-Watch" Ba:
110; ICBAP: 135; PE: 478
"The Nativity Written in the
Year 1656" PE: 479
"The Night" Ba: 109-112;
ICBAP: 135; PE: 479
"The Passion" PE: 479
"Peace" PE: 479
"The Proffer" Ba: 109; PE:
479
"The Pursuite" PE: 479
"The Queer" PE: 479
"Quickness" PE: 480
"Regeneration" Ba: 110; PE:
480
"Religion" PE: 480
"The Retreat" Ba: 110; PE:
480
"The Sap" PE: 480
"The Search" PE: 480
"Silence, and stealth of dayes!"
PE: 480
Silex Scintillans Ba: 110-
112

"Song to Amoret" PE: 480
"The Starre" PE: 481
"Sure, there's a type of
Bodyes" PE: 481
"The Tempest" PE: 481
"To Amoret of the difference"
PE: 481
"To Estesia parted from him,
and looking back" PE:
481
"To His Books" PE: 481
"To His Learned Friend and
Loyal Fellow-Prisoner"
ICBAP: 135
"To I. Morgan ... upon his
sudden journey and suc-
ceeding Marriage" PE:
481
"To the River Isca" PE: 481
"Vanity of Spirit" PE: 481
"The Waterfall" Ba: 110;
ICBAP: 135; PE: 481
"The World" Ba: 109, 111-
112; ICBAP: 136; LCAB:
182; PE: 481-482
VAUGHN, H.A.
General WIL: 168
VAUTHIER, Jean
General Br: 704-705; MD:
315; Po: 4457
Captain Bada [Le capitaine
Bada] Br: 705; DC2:
367; Po: 4457
The Character Against Him-
self [Le Personnage com-
battant; Fortissima] Br:
705; DC2: 367; Po: 4457
The Dreamer [Le Rêveur]
Br: 705; Po: 4457
The Prodigies [Les Prodiges]
Po: 4457
VAZOFF, Ivan
Under the Yoke Ke: 458
VEBLEN, Thorstein
General APC: 78; LCAB:
183
VEDRES, Nicole
General Po: 4457
Vega Carpio, Lope Felix de
see LOPE [de Vega]
VEGAS SEMINARIO, Francisco
"El primogénito de los
Godos" Wa: 756
VEIRAS, Denis
History of the Sevarites
Ke: 168

Velarde, Ramón López see LOPEZ
VELARDE, Ramón
VELEZ DE GUEVARA, Luis
El diablo cojuelo Fi: 256
VELODIN, A.
General Br: 705
The Appointment [Naznacenie]
Br: 705
VENEZIS, Elias [E. MELLOS]
"Akif" Wa: 756
"The Bandit Pancho Villa" Wa:
756
"The Broken Branch" Wa: 75
"The Caique of the Theseion"
Wa: 756
"Death" Wa: 756
"The Final Hour" Wa: 756
"A Finn in Algiers" Wa: 756
"The Home of the Lost Angels"
Wa: 756
"The Immigrant of Grand Can-
yon" Wa: 756
"The Knight of Bataan and the
Verses" Wa: 756
"Lios" Wa: 756
"Moment on the Saroniko" Wa:
757
"Mycenae" Wa: 757
"Night of Asklepios" Wa: 757
"No Passage" Wa: 757
"The Old Woman of Lamia" Wa:
757
"On the Kimindeia" Wa: 757
"The Roar" Wa: 757
"The Seagulls" Wa: 757
"The State of Virginia" Wa:
757
"Tale of the Aegean" Wa: 757
"Theonichos and Mnisarete"
Wa: 757
"Tourkolimano" Wa: 757
"The Two Women and the Tow-
er" Wa: 757
VENTURA AGUDIEZ, Juan
Las tardes de Thereze Lamarck
Fi: 256
VERA, Pedro Jorge
General Br: 705
VERCORS [Jean BRULLER]
Les Animaux, dénaturés Po:
4458
Zoo Po: 4458
VERDI, Giuseppe
Aida DC2: 367
La Forza del Destino DC2:
367

Otello DC2: 367
VERESAEV, Vikent'ii Vikent'evich
General Po: 4458
The Deadlock [V tupike] Po:
4458
In a Blind Alley Ke: 458
The Sisters Ke: 458
VERGA, Giovanni
General Br: 705; Po: 4458-
4462
"Black Bread" WaS1: 211
"The Canary of No. 15"
WaS1: 211
"Cavalleria rusticana" Po:
4462; WaS1: 211
"Consolation" Wa: 757
Don candeloro e campagni
Po: 4461
La Duchessa di Leyra Fi:
279
Eros Fi: 279-280
Eva Fi: 280
"The Ghosts of Trazza
Castle" WaS1: 211
"Gramigna's Lover" WaS1:
211
Helena's Husband [Il marito
di Elena] Ke: 253; Fi:
280
The House by the Medlar
Tree [I Malavoglia] Fi:
280; Ke: 253-254; Ma:
2210; Po: 4459, 4462
"The How, the When and the
Wherefore" WaS1: 211
"Ieli the Shepherd" WaS1:
212
"Images" WaS1: 212
"In Piazza della Scala" Wa:
757
"The Last Day" ["L'ultima
giornata"] Po: 4463; Wa:
757
"Liberty" Wa: 758; WaS1:
211
La lupa see The She-Wolf
"Malaria" WaS1: 212
I Malavoglia see The House
by the Medlar Tree
Il marito di Elena see
Helena's Husband
Mastro-don Gesualdo Fi:
281; Ke: 254; Ma: 2210;
Po: 4459, 4461
"Nanni Volpe" WaS1: 212
Nedda Ke: 254; WaS1:

212
Novelle rusticane Fi: 281
Una peccatrice Fi: 281; Po:
4461-4462
"Property" WaS1: 212
"Rosso Malpelo" WaS1: 212
"The She-Wolf" [La lupa] Fi:
280; WaS1: 212
"A Simple Tale" WaS1: 212
"Stinkpot" WaS1: 212
Storia di una capinera Fi:
281
Le storie del Castello di Trezza
Fi: 281
"Story of the Saint Joseph
Donkey" WaS1: 212
"Temptation" Wa: 758
Tigre reale Fi: 281
"L'ultima giornata" see "The
Last Day"
"Via Crucis" Wa: 758
Vita dei campi Fi: 281; Po:
4463
"The Wolf Hunt" WaS1: 212
VERGILIUS MARO, Publius [VIR-
GIL]
General LCAB: 183
The Aeneid LCAB: 183; Ma:
2211-2212
Eclogues Ma: 2212-2213
Georgics LCAB: 183; Ma:
2213-2214
VERHAEREN, Emile
General MD: 315; Po: 4463-
4465
Les Débâcles Po: 4466
VERISSIMO, Erico
General Po: 4466
Noite Po: 4467
O senhor embaixador Po: 4467
O tempo e o vento Po: 4466-
4467
VERLAINE, Paul
General LCAB: 183; Ma:
2216-2217
Amour Ma: 2215
La bonne chanson Ma: 2215
Fêtes galantes Ma: 2215-2216
Poèmes saturniens Ma: 2216
Romances sans paroles Ma:
2217
Sagesse Ma: 2217-2218
VERMOREL, Claude
Jeanne Avec Nous DC2: 368
VERNE, Jules
General LCAB: 183

Around the Moon Ke: 168
Around the World in Eighty
    Days Fi: 174; Ke: 168
Castle in the Carpathians
    Fi: 174; Ke: 168
Child of the Cavern Ke:
    168
The Children of Captain
    Grant Fi: 174; Ke: 168
Clipper of the Clouds Ke:
    168
From the Earth to the Moon
    Ke: 168; Ma: 2219
Journey to the Center of the
    Earth Fi: 174; Ke:
    168-169
A Livonian Tragedy Fi:
    174
Twenty Thousand Leagues
    Under the Sea Fi: 174;
    Ke: 169; Ma: 2219
Voyages extraordinaires Fi:
    174
VERNEUIL, Louis
    General Br: 706; Po: 4467
    Affairs of State DC2: 368;
        MD: 315; Po: 4468
    Obsession MD: 315
VERPLANCK, Gulian Crommelin
    General AP: 588; Da: 115
VERWEY, Albert
    General Po: 4468
VERY, Jones
    General ALL: 272
    "The Baker's Island Lights"
        PE: 482
    "The Columbine" PE: 482
    "The Hand and Foot" PE:
        482
    "The Lost" PE: 482
    "Man in Harmony with Nature"
        PE: 482
    "The New Birth" PE: 482
    "The Revelation of the Spirit
        Through the Material
        World" PE: 482
    "To the Canary Bird" PE:
        482
    "The Tree" (p. 70 of Poems
        and Essays, 1886) PE:
        482
    "The Tree" (p. 121 of
        Poems and Essays, 1886)
        PE: 482
    "The True Light" PE: 482
VESAAS, Tarjei

"The Adventure" Wa: 758
The Bleaching Place Ke: 368
"Blue Button Lost" Wa: 758
"Bread" Wa: 758
"A Daring Ant" Wa: 758
"The Gingerbread Man" Wa:
    758
"Grain Across the Sea" Wa:
    758
"The Half-wit" Wa: 758
"The Horse from Hogget" Wa:
    758
The House in the Dark Ke:
    368
The Ice Palace Ke: 368
"In the Fish's Golden Youth"
    Wa: 758
"Last Man Home" Wa: 758
"The Little Tyke" Wa: 758
"Mist Rain" Wa: 758
"Naked" Wa: 758
The Seed Ke: 368
"Signe Tone" Wa: 758
"Snow" Wa: 759
"The Stunted Spruce" see
    "The Half-wit"
"Three Quiet Men" Wa: 759
"Twenty-One" Wa: 759
"The Vision" Wa: 759
VESTDIJK, Simon
    General Po: 4468
VEZINOV, Pavel
    With the White Horses at Night
        Fi: 494
VIALAR, Paul
    Les Hommes Br: 706
VIAN, Boris
    General Br: 706; MD: 316;
        Po: 4469
    L'Arrache-coeur Fi: 175
    The Empire Builders [Les
        Batisseurs d'empire] Br:
        706; MD: 316
    "Les Fourmis" Wa: 759;
        WaS1: 212
    The Generals' Tea Party Br:
        706
    "Le Rappel" Wa: 759; WaS1:
        212
VIDAL, Gore
    General AN: 251; ASF: 576;
        Br: 706; CFAE: 394; CN:
        525; LCAB: 183; MDAE:
        496; Po: 4469-4470
    The Best Man ADC: 384; Br:
        706; Ma: 2220; MDAE: 496

Burr: A Novel Ma: 2220
The City and the Pillar
  CN: 525; LCAB: 184;
  Ma: 2220-2221; Po: 4470
Dark Green, Bright Red
  CN: 525
"Erlinda and Mrs. Coffin"
  Wa: 759
An Evening with Richard
  Nixon... ADC: 384
In a Yellow Wood CN: 525
The Judgment of Paris CN:
  525
Julian CN: 525-526; Ma:
  2221
"The Ladies in the Library"
  Wa: 759
Messiah CN: 526
"A Moment of Green Laurel"
  Wa: 759
Myra Breckenridge Po:
  4470
On the March to the Sea
  Br: 706
"Pages from an Abandoned
  Journal" Wa: 759
"The Robin" Wa: 759
Romulus ADC: 384-385;
  Br: 707; TMAP: 171
A Search for the King CN:
  526
A Season of Comfort CN:
  526
Visit to a Small Planet ADC:
  385; Br: 707
Washington, D.C. CN: 526
Weekend ADC: 385
Williwaw CN: 526
"The Zenner Trophy" Wa:
  759
VIELE-GRIFFIN, Francis
  General Po: 4470-4471
VIERECK, Peter
  General Po: 4471-4472
  "Better Come Quietly" PE:
    483
  "Blindman's Buff" PE: 483
  "Crass Times Redeemed by
    Dignity of Souls" PE:
    483
  "Don't Look Now but Mary Is
    Everybody" ICBAP: 136;
    PE: 483; Po: 4472
  "Game Called on Account of
    Darkness" PE: 483
  "Like a Sitting Breeze" PE:

483
  "Six Theological Cradle Songs"
    PE: 483
  "Some Lines in Three Parts"
    PE: 483
  "Vale from Carthage (Spring,
    1944)" PE: 483
VIGANO, Renata
  L'Agnese va a morire Fi: 281
VIGNY, Alfred de
  "La Canne de jonc" Wa: 759
  Chatterton Br: 707; DC2:
    368
  Cinq Mars Fi: 175; Ke: 169
  Daphné Ke: 169
  Laurette ou le cachet rouge
    Ke: 169; Wa: 759
  Servitude et grandeur mili-
    taires Fi: 175; Ke: 169
  Stello Fi: 175; Ke: 169
  "La Veillée de Vincennes" Wa:
    760
VIK, Bjørg
  "They Came in Small Groups"
    WaS1: 212
VILAKAZI, Benedict Wallet
  General BALE: 414
VILALLONGA, José
  L'homme de sang Ke: 236
VILAR, Jean
  General Br: 707
  Oppenheimer Case Br: 707
VILDRAC, Charles
  General Br: 707
  L'Air du temps Br: 707
  La Brouille Br: 708
  Madame Beliard Br: 708
  Michel Auclair Br: 708
  Le Pelerin Br: 708
  The Steamer Tenacity [Le
    Paquebot Tenacity] Br:
    708
VILLALONGA, Llorenc
  Bearn o la sala de las munecas
    Ke: 236
  Desenlace en montlleo Ke: 236
  Mort de dama Ke: 236
  La novella de Palmira Ke: 236
VILLAROEL, Giuseppe
  General Po: 4473
VILLARROEL, Dinka
  General Br: 708
VILLAURRUTIA, Xavier
  General Br: 708; Po: 4473-
    4474
  Décima Muerte Po: 4475

La hiedra Po: 4474
Juego peligroso Po: 4474
La mujer legítima Po: 4474
El yerro candente Po: 4474
VILLEGAS, Antonio de
El Abencerraje Ke: 236
VILLIERS DE L'ISLE-ADAM,
    Count [Jean Marie Matthias
    Philippe AUGUSTE]
"A s'y méprendre" Wa: 760
Axel DC2: 368
L'Eve future Fi: 175
VILLIERS, George
General Li: 107
The Rehearsal DC1: 212;
    Li: 107
VILLON, François
General LCAB: 184; Ma:
    2222
VINCENT, Theophilus
General BALE: 414
VINCENTE, Gil
Don Duardos DC2: 368-369
La Sibila Casandra DC2:
    369
Virgil see VERGILIUS MARO,
    Publius
VIRJEE, Mohamed
General BALE: 414
VIRK, Kulwant Singh
"The Bull Beneath the Earth"
    Wa: 760
VIRTUE, Vivian
General WIL: 168-169
VIRUES, Christobal de
La Infelice Marcela DC2:
    369
VISCHER, Friedrich Theodor
Auch Einer Fi: 395
VITRAC, Roger
General Po: 4475
Le Camelot Br: 709
Le Coup de Trafalgar Br:
    709
Les Demoiselles du Large
    Br: 709
Victor, or All Power to the
    Children Br: 709
VITTORINI, Elio
General Po: 4475-4476
Città del mondo Fi: 281
Conversation in Sicily Fi:
    282; Ke: 254; Po:
    4476-4477
Diario in pubblico Po: 4476
Erica Fi: 282-283

La Garibaldina Fi: 283
Il garofano rosso see The Red
    Carnation
"The Lady of the Station" Wa:
    760
Men and Non-Men [Uomini e No]
    Fi: 283; Po: 4477
"My War" Wa: 760
The Red Carnation [Il garofano
    rosso] Fi: 283; Ke: 254-
    255; Po: 4476-4477
Il Sempione strizza l'occhio al
    Fréjus Po: 4476
The Twilight of the Elephant
    Fi: 283; Ke: 255
Uomini e No see Men and Non-
    Men
The Woman of Rome Fi: 283
The Women of Messina Fi:
    283-284
VIZYINOS, George
"My Mother" Wa: 760
VLAYKOV, Todor
General Po: 4478
VOINOVA, A.I.
Semi-Precious Stones Ke: 458
VOINOVICH, Vladimir
The Life and Extraordinary Ad-
    ventures of Private Ivan
    Chonkin Fi: 494
VOLEN, Iliya
"Groundka" Wa: 760
VOLODIN, Aleksandr
General Po: 4478
Factory Girl DC2: 369
Five Nights DC2: 369
VOLPONI, Paolo
Corporale Fi: 284
Memoriale Ke: 255
VOLTAIRE, François-Marie Arouet
    de
General LCAB: 184
Alzire DC2: 369
Brutus DC2: 369-370
Candide Be: 234, 248; Fi:
    175-178; Ke: 169-171;
    LCAB: 184; Ma: 2223-2224
Clizia DC2: 370
Histoire de Jenni Fi: 178
L'Ingénu Fi: 178-179; Ke:
    171
Irene DC2: 370
Mahomet DC2: 370
Mariamne DC2: 370
Merope DC2: 370
Micromegas Fi: 179; Ke: 171

Le Monde comme il va Fi:
179
La Princesse de Babylone
Fi: 179
Le Taureau blanc Fi: 179
Zadig Fi: 179-180; Ke:
171; Ma: 2224-2225
Zaïre DC2: 370; Fi: 180;
Ma: 2225
Zulime DC2: 370
VONDEL, Joost van den
Brothers [Gebroeders] DC2:
370-371
Gysbreght Van Aemstel DC2:
371
Jeptha DC2: 371
Leeuwendalers DC2: 371
Lucifer DC2: 371-372
VONNEGUT, Kurt, Jr.
General ASF: 577-578;
CFAE: 395-396; CN:
526; LCAB: 184; MDAE:
497-498; Po: 4478-4480
"All the King's Horses" WaS1:
213
"The Ambitious Sophomore"
WaS1: 213
Breakfast of Champions Ma:
2226
Cat's Cradle CN: 527; Ma:
2226-2227; Po: 4479
"EPICAC" ASF: 577; Wa:
760; WaS1: 213
"The Foster Portfolio" WaS1:
213
God Bless You, Mr. Rose-
water CN: 527; Ma:
2227; Po: 4479-4480
Happy Birthday, Wanda June
ADC: 385; Ma: 2227;
MDAE: 498
"The Manned Missiles" ASF:
577; WaS1: 213
Mother Night CN: 527; Ma:
, 2227-2228; Po: 4479
"My Name Is Everyone" see
"Who Am I This Time?"
"Next Door" WaS1: 213
Player Piano CN: 527;
Ma: 2228-2229
"The Powder Blue Dragon"
WaS1: 213
"Report on the Barnhouse
Effect" ASF: 577; WaS1:
213
"Runaways" WaS1: 213

The Sirens of Titan Ma: 2229
Slapstick: Or, Lonesome No
More! Ma: 2229
Slaughterhouse Five Ma: 2229-
2230; Po: 4479
"Thanasphere" ASF: 577
"Tomorrow and Tomorrow and
Tomorrow" ASF: 577; WaS1:
213
"Unready to Wear" WaS1: 213
"Welcome to the Monkey House"
ASF: 577; WaS1: 213
"Who Am I This Time?" WaS1:
213
VORAGINE, Jacobus de
The Golden Legend see CAX-
TON, William [translator]
VOTEUR, Ferdinand
A Right Angle Triangle MBA:
194
VOYNICH, Ethel Lillian Boôle
General Po: 4480-4481
The Gadfly EN: 126; Po:
4480-4481
VOZNESENSKY, Andrey Andree-
vich
General Po: 4481
VRIGNY, Roger
General Po: 4481
VROMAN, Mary Elizabeth
General BAF: 277-278; BAP:
198; BAW: 726
VVEDENSKY, Aleksandr
Elegy Po: 4481
VYNNYCHENKO, V.K.
The Sun Machine Ke: 458

W

WACHIRA, Godwin
General BALE: 415
WACIUMA, Charity
General BALE: 415
WADDELL, Martin
A Little Bit British ENES2:
249
WADDINGTON, Miriam
General JW: 168
WADE, John Donald
General ASF: 579; Po: 4483
"The Duggone Bust" ASF:
579
"The Life and Death of Cousin
Lucius" ASF: 579
WADESON, Antony

General Log: 269-270
WADSWORTH, Olive
"A Woman" ASF: 579
WAERNEWICK, Pierre-Henri de
Le Duc de Monmouth DC2:
372
WAGER, Lewis
Life and Repentance of Mary
Magdalene DC1: 213
WAGER, William
Enough Is as Good as a
Feast DC1: 213
The Longer Thou Livest the
More Fool Thou Art DC1:
213
The Trial of Treasure DC1:
213
WAGGERL, Karl Heinrich
General Po: 4483
WAGNER, Elin
Liberated Love Ke: 368
WAGNER, Richard
"An End in Paris" WaS1:
213
Götterdämmerung DC2: 372;
MBD: 57
"A Happy Evening" WaS1:
214
Lohengrin DC2: 372
Die Meistersinger DC2: 372
"A Pilgrimage to Beethoven"
WaS1: 214
Das Rheingold DC2: 372
Tannhäuser DC2: 373; Ri2:
46
Tristan und Isolde DC2:
373; Ri2: 46
WAGONER, David
General CFAE: 397; CN:
527; ICBAP: 136; Po:
4483
The Escape Artist CN: 528
The Man in the Middle CN:
528
Money Money Money CN:
528
Rock CN: 528
"The Spinning Ladies" ASF:
579; Wa: 761
WAIN, John
General CFAE: 399-400;
CN: 528; Po: 4483-4486;
Sch: 284-285
The Contenders CN: 528-
529; Ma: 2231
Hurry on Down [American

title: Born in Captivity]
CN: 529; ENE: 260; ENES1:
228; Ma: 2231-2232
Living in the Present CN:
529; Ma: 2232
"A Message from the Pig-Man"
Wa: 761
The Smaller Sky ENES1: 228
Strike the Father Dead CN:
529; ENE: 260; ENES1:
228; Ma: 2232
A Travelling Woman CN: 529-
530; Ma: 2232-2233
WAIYAKI, Edwin
General BALE: 415
WAKEFIELD MASTER, The
Crucifixtion DC1: 213
WALCOTT, Derek
General MBA: 194; WIL:
169-174
Another Life WIL: 176-177
The Castaway WIL: 175
The Charlatan ADC: 386;
WIL: 179
Dream on Monkey Mountain
ADC: 386; BAP: 198-199;
MBA: 194-195; WIL: 178-
179
Drums and Colours WIL: 178
The Dying Gods WIL: 177
Epitaph for the Young WIL:
174
Franklin, a Tale of the Islands
WIL: 179
The Gulf WIL: 176
Harry Dernier WIL: 177
Henri Christophe WIL: 177
In a Fine Castle WIL: 179
In a Green Night WIL: 174-175
Ione WIL: 178
The Joker of Seville WIL:
179-180
Malcochon BAP: 199; MBA:
195
Poems WIL: 174
The Sea at Dauphin WIL: 177
Sea Grapes WIL: 177
Selected Poems WIL: 175
Ti-Jean and His Brothers ADC:
386; WIL: 178
25 Poems WIL: 174
The Wedding MBA: 195
The Wine of the Country WIL:
177-178
WALDEN, Alfred Islay
General AAPD: 79; BAW:

727
WALDINGER, Ernst
General Po: 4486
Waldo, Edward Hamilton see
STURGEON, Theodore
WALI, Obiajunwa
General BALE: 415
WALKER, Alice
General AAPD: 239; ASF:
580; BAF: 278-279; BAW:
729
In Love and Trouble BAF:
279
Meridian BAF: 279-280
"Revenge" ASF: 580
"Strong Horse Tea" ASF:
580
The Third Life of Grange
Copland BAF: 279-280
WALKER, David
General BAW: 729-730;
LCAB: 184
WALKER, Drake
General BAF: 280
WALKER, George
General BAW: 731; MBA:
195
The Vagabond ENES2: 250
WALKER, Joseph A.
General BAP: 200; MBA:
196
The Believers MBA: 197
The Harangues ADC: 386;
BAP: 200; MBA: 196-197
Ododo AAPD: 409; BAP:
200; MBA: 196
The River Niger ADC: 386;
BAP: 200-201; MBA:
196-198
Yin Yang MBA: 196
WALKER, Margaret
General AAPD: 240; BAF:
281; BAW: 733-734
Jubilee BAF: 281-282
WALKER, Saunders
Roots in the South MBA:
198
WALKER, Ted
General ICBAP: 136; Po:
4486
WALL, Mervyn
General Po: 4486
WALLACE, E.G.
"Big Ancestor" Wa: 761
WALLACE, Edgar
Mr. Justice Maxwell ENE:

260
WALLACE, George B.
Ineffable Moments WIL: 180
WALLACE, Horace Binney
General ASF: 580
WALLACE, Joe
General Po: 4487
WALLACE, Rudy
The Dark Tower BAP: 201;
MBA: 198
The Moonlight Arms BAP:
201; MBA: 198
WALLACE-CRABBE, Chris
General Po: 4487
In Light and Darkness Po:
4487
WALLANT, Edward Lewis
General CN: 530; JW: 305-
306; LCAB: 184; Po:
4487-4489
The Children at the Gate CN:
530; Po: 4489
The Human Season CN: 530
The Pawnbroker CN: 531;
LCAB: 184; Po: 4489-4490
The Tenants of Moonbloom
CN: 531
WALLER, Edmund
General Ba: 113; Ma: 2234
"An Apologie for Having Loved
Before" Ba: 113; PE: 483
"At Pens-hurst" PE: 483
"Go, Lovely Rose" PE: 483
"Of a Fair Lady Playing with a
Snake" PE: 483
"On a Girdle" PE: 483
"On St. James Park as Lately
Improved by His Majesty"
PE: 483
"Panegyric to My Lord Pro-
tector" ICBAP: 136; PE:
484
"The Story of Phoebus and
Daphne Applied" PE: 484
"Upon Her Majesty's New Build-
ings at Somerset House"
PE: 484
WALPOLE, Horace
General Be: 271-273; Du:
167; EC: 144-145
The Castle of Otranto Be:
62, 200, 272-273; Du: 167;
EN: 126; ENE: 260;
ENES1: 228; ENES2: 250;
Ma: 2235-2236
Letters LCAB: 184-185

WALPOLE, Hugh
General Po: 4490; Sch:
    286; TA: 292
Above the Dark Circus
    ENES1: 228
The Blind Man's House
    ENES1: 228
The Bright Pavilions ENES1:
    228
Captain Nicholas ENES1:
    228
The Captives ENES1: 229
The Cathedral EN: 126;
    ENES1: 229
"The Clock" Wa: 761
The Dark Forest ENES1:
    229
The Duchess of Wrexe
    ENES1: 229
Farthing Hall ENES1: 229
Fortitude ENES1: 229; Ma:
    2237
The Fortress ENES1: 229
The Green Mirror ENES1:
    229
Hans Frost ENES1: 229
Harmer John ENES1: 229
The Inquisitor ENES1: 229
John Cornelius ENES1: 229
The Joyful Delaneys ENES1:
    229
Judith Paris ENES1: 229
Katherine Christian ENES1:
    229
The Killer and the Slain
    ENES1: 230
Maradick at Forty ENES1:
    230
Mr. Perrin and Mr. Traill
    ENES1: 230
The Old Ladies ENES1: 230
Portrait of a Man with Red
    Hair ENES1: 230
A Prayer for My Son ENES1:
    230
The Prelude to Adventure
    ENES1: 230
Rogue Herries ENES1: 230
The Sea Tower ENES1: 230
The Secret City ENES1:
    230
Vanessa ENES1: 230
Wintersmoon ENES1: 230
The Wooden Horse EN: 126;
    ENES1: 230
The Young Enchanted ENES1:
    230
WALROND, Eric
General BAF: 283; BAW: 735;
    HR: 159-160
"The Black Pin" ASF: 580;
    Wa: 761
"A Cholo Romance" Wa: 761
"City Love" ASF: 580; Wa:
    761
"Drought" Wa: 761
"Miss Kenny's Marriage" ASF:
    580; Wa: 761
"Tropic Death" ASF: 580; Wa:
    761
Tropic Death (Collection) BAF:
    283; WIL: 180
"The Voodoo's Revenge" Wa:
    761
"The White Snake" ASF: 581;
    Wa: 761
"The Yellow One" ASF: 581;
    Wa: 762
WALSCHAP, Gerald
General Po: 4490
WALSER, Martin
General Br: 709; Po: 4490
The Black Swan [Der Schwarze
    Schwan] Br: 709
The Detour Br: 709
Die Ehen in Philippsburg Fi:
    395
Eiche und Angora see Oaktree
    and Angora
Das Einhorn Fi: 395
Ein Fliehendes Pferd Fi: 395-
    396
Halbzeit Fi: 396; Po: 4491
Oaktree and Angora [The Rab-
    bit Race; Eiche und Angora]
    Br: 710
Der Schwarze Schwan see The
    Black Swan
WALSER, Robert
General Br: 710; Po: 4491-
    4492
"The Battle of Sempach" Wa:
    762
Der Gehülfe Fi: 396; Ke: 338
Die Geschwister Tanner Fi:
    396; Ke: 338
Jakob von Gunten Fi: 396;
    Ke: 338
Der Spaziergang Ke: 338
"Tobold" Wa: 762
"A Young Girl from Berlin"
    Wa: 762

WALSH, Robert
General AP: 521; Da: 115
WALSH, William
General Bon: 30-31
WALTARI, Mika Toimi
General Po: 4492
WALTER, Eugene
General Lon: 64
The Easiest Way ADC: 386;
Br: 710
Paid in Full ADC: 386
WALTER, Otto F.
Herr Tourel Fi: 396
WALTON, Isaak
General Ba: 114-115; Hen:
55
The Compleat Angler Ba:
115; Hen: 139
Life of Donne Ba: 114
Life of Herbert Ba: 115
The Lives Ba: 114-115
WANGUSA, Timothy
General BALE: 416
WANSHEL, Jeff
The Disintegration of James
Cherry ADC: 387
Isadora Duncan Sleeps with
the Russian Navy ADC:
387
WAPULL, George
The Tide Tarrieth for No
Man DC1: 213
WARBURTON, William
General EC: 145
WARD, Artemus
General ASF: 581
WARD, Arthur Sarsfield [Sax
ROHMER]
General Po: 4492
WARD, Douglas Turner
General AAPD: 410; BAP:
202; BAW: 737; Br:
710; MBA: 199
Brotherhood ADC: 387;
BAP: 203-204; MBA:
199-200
Day of Absence ADC: 387;
BAP: 202-204; BAW:
737; Br: 710; MBA:
199-200
Happy Ending ADC: 387;
BAP: 203-204; Br: 710;
MBA: 200
Reckoning AAPD: 410; ADC:
387; BAP: 204; MBA:
200

WARD, Edward
General EC: 146
WARD, Elizabeth Stuart Phelps
General AN: 251
WARD, Mrs. Humphrey [Mary Au-
gusta WARD]
General BN: 112; TA: 293
David Grieve ENES1: 231;
ENES2: 250
Helbeck of Bannisdale ENES1:
231
Lady Connie BN: 112; Po:
4492
Marcella ENES1: 231; ENES2:
250
Miss Bretherton ENES2: 250
Robert Elsmere BN: 112;
ENES1: 231; ENES2: 250;
Po: 4493
Sir George Tressady ENES1:
231; ENES2: 250
WARD, Nathaniel
General AP: 523-525; Da: 59
The Simple Cobler of Aggawam
in America AP: 523-524
WARD, Theodore
General AAPD: 335; BAP:
205; BAW: 738; MBA: 201
Big White Fog BAP: 205-206;
Br: 710; MBA: 201
The Daubers MBA: 201
Falcon of Adowa MBA: 201
John Brown BAP: 206
Our Lan' BAP: 206; Br:
710-711; MBA: 202
WARE, William
General AN: 251
WARHOL, Andy
Pork ADC: 387
WARING, Robert L.
General BAF: 284; BAW:
739
WARNER, Charles Dudley
General AN: 251
WARNER, Rex
General BN2: 105; CFAE:
401-402; CN: 531-532;
LCAB: 185; Po: 4493;
Sch: 287-288
The Aerodrome CN: 532;
ENES2: 251; Po: 4493
Escapade: A Tale of Average
CN: 532
Men of Stones: A Melodrama
CN: 533
The Professor CN: 533;

ENES2: 251
Return of the Traveller [Eng-
lish title: Why Was I
Killed?: A Dramatic Dia-
logue] CN: 533
The Wild Goose Chase CN:
533; Po: 4493
WARNER, Susan
General AN: 251
WARNER, Sylvia Townsend
Lolly Willowes ENES2: 251
WARNER, William
Albion's England SC: 100
Pan His Syrinx ERP: 506
WARREN, Austin
Theory of Literature LCAB:
185
WARREN, Mercy Otis
General AD: 206-207; AP:
527
The Adulateur AD: 207
The Blockheads; or The Af-
frighted Officers AD: 207
The Group AD: 207
The Motley Assembly AD:
207
WARREN, Robert Penn
General ALL: 272-274; AN:
253-254; ASF: 582; CFAE:
404-409; CN: 534-537;
ICBAP: 136; LCAB: 185;
MP: 103; Ne: 93-96; Po:
4494-4503
"Aged Man Surveys the Past
Time" PE: 484
All the King's Men ALL:
273; AN: 252; Br: 711;
CFAE: 404-409; CN:
537-541; LCAB: 185; Ma:
2238-2239; Ne: 93-96;
Po: 4495-4499, 4501, 4503-
4510
At Heaven's Gate ALL: 273;
AN: 252; CFAE: 405;
CN: 541-543; Ma: 2239-
2240; Ne: 94-95; Po:
4495-4496, 4499, 4510
"The Ballad of Billie Potts"
PE: 484; Po: 4511
Band of Angels ALL: 273;
AN: 252; CFAE: 407,
409; CN: 543; Ma: 2240-
2241; Ne: 94-95; Po:
4497, 4511-4512
"Bearded Oaks" PE: 484
"Blackberry Winter" ASF:

581; LCAB: 185; Po: 4512;
SFC: 196; Wa: 762; WaS1:
214
"Blow West Wind, Blow" PE:
484
Brother to Dragons ALL: 273;
Po: 4512-4513
The Cave ALL: 273; AN:
253; CFAE: 405, 407; CN:
543-544; Ma: 2241-2242; Ne:
94-95; Po: 4497, 4513-4514
"The Child Next Door" PE:
484
"A Christian Education" Wa:
762
"The Circus in the Attic" ASF:
581; SFC: 196; Wa: 762-
763
The Circus in the Attic and
Other Stories Po: 4514
"Composition in Red and Gold"
PE: 484
"Crime" PE: 484
"Dragon Country: To Jacob
Boehme" PE: 485
Flood ALL: 273; CFAE: 408;
CN: 544; Ne: 95; Po:
4515
"The Garden" PE: 485
"Gold Glade" PE: 485
"Her Own People" Wa: 763
"History" PE: 485
"History Among the Rocks" PE:
485
The Legacy of the Civil War
Po: 4515-4516
"Letter from a Coward to a
Hero" PE: 485
"The Life and Work of Professor
Roy Millen" Wa: 763
"Love's Parable" PE: 485
"Man Coming of Age" PE: 485
"The Mango on the Mango
Tree" PE: 485
Meet Me in the Green Glen
ALL: 273
"Mexico Is a Foreign Country"
PE: 485
"Monologue at Midnight" PE:
485
"Mortmain" Po: 4516
Night Rider ALL: 273; AN:
253; CFAE: 405, 408-409;
CN: 545-546; Ma: 2242-
2243; Ne: 96; Po: 4499,
4502, 4516

"Original Sin: A Short
Story" PE: 485
"The Patented Gate and the
Mean Hamburger" ASF:
581; SFC: 196; Wa: 763
"Pondy Woods" PE: 485
"Prime Leaf" ASF: 581;
Po: 4502; SFC: 196;
Wa: 763
Promises Po: 4517
Proud Flesh Po: 4495, 4501
"Pursuit" PE: 485-486
"The Return: An Elegy"
PE: 486
"Revelation" PE: 486
Selected Poems, New and
Old, 1923-1966 Po: 4496
"Sunset Walk in Thaw-Time
in Vermont" PE: 486
"Terror" PE: 486
"The Unvexed Isles" ASF:
581; Wa: 763
"Variation: Ode to Fear"
PE: 486
"When the Light Gets Green"
ASF: 582; Wa: 763;
WaS1: 214
Wilderness ALL: 273; CN:
546; Po: 4517
Willie Stark: His Rise and
Fall Po: 4501
World Enough and Time
ALL: 273; AN: 253;
CFAE: 405, 407; CN:
546-548; Ma: 2243-2245;
Po: 4497, 4517-4518
You, Emperors and Others
Po: 4497-4498
WARTON, Joseph
General EC: 146-147; Me:
411-416
"The Enthusiast" EC: 147;
Me: 413-415; PE: 486
"Essay on Pope" EC: 147;
Me: 416
WARTON, Thomas the Elder
General EC: 146; Me:
411-416
Poems on Several Occasions
Me: 411-412
"Retirement: An Ode" Me:
412
WARTON, Thomas the Younger
General EC: 146-148;
Me: 411-416
History of English Poetry

EC: 147
"The Progress of Discontent"
Me: 413
"To the River Lodon" Me: 411
WARUNG, Price [William ASTLEY]
"The Bullet of the Fated Ten"
WaS1: 214
"Captain Maconochie's 'Bounty
for Crime'" WaS1: 214
"The Consequences of Cun-
liffe's Crime" WaS1: 214
"Dictionary Ned" WaS1: 214
"Parson Ford's Confession"
WaS1: 214
"The Pure Merinoes' Ball"
WaS1: 214
WASHBURN, Deric
The Love Nest ADC: 388;
Br: 711
WASHINGTON, Booker T.
General APC: 78-79; BAW:
741-742; LCAB: 185
WASHINGTON, George
General AP: 530-531; Da:
84
WASSERMAN, Dale
One Flew Over the Cuckoo's
Nest ADC: 388
_____, Mitch LEIGH, and Joe
DARION
Man of La Mancha ADC: 388
WASSERMANN, Jakob
General Po: 4518-4519
Alexander in Babylon Ke:
339
The Amulet Ke: 339
Caspar Hauser Ke: 339
Clarissa Mirabel Ke: 339
Diary in a Nook Ke: 339
Doctor Kerkhoven Ke: 339
Erwin Reiner Ke: 339
Faber, or the Lost Years Ke:
339
Der Fall Maurizius see The
Maurizius Case
Gold Ke: 339
The Golden Mirror Ke: 339
The Goose Man Ke: 339
The Housekeeper Ke: 339
The Jews of Zirndorf Ke:
339
Joseph Kerkhovens Dritte
Existenz Ke: 340
Lukardis Ke: 340
The Man of Forty Ke: 340
The Maurizius Case [Der Fall

Maurizius] Ke: 340; Po: 4518-4519

Melusine Ke: 340

The Moloch Ke: 340

Oberlin's Three Stages Ke: 340

Olivia Ke: 340

The Rebellion for Young Squire Ernst Ke: 340

The Sisters Ke: 340

The Spirit of the Pilgrim Ke: 341

The Story of Young Renate Fuchs Ke: 341

Sturreganz Ke: 341

The Triumph of Youth Ke: 341

Unkissed Lips Ke: 341

Wedlock Ke: 341

World's End Ke: 341

The World's Illusion Ke: 341

WASSERSTEIN, Wendy

Uncommon Women and Others ADC: 388

WASSON, George S.

General ASF: 582; Po: 4519

WATEN, Judah

General MAP: 312-313; Po: 4519

Alien Son MAP: 312

The Unbending MAP: 312

WATENE, Kenneth

General BALE: 416

WATERHOUSE, Keith Spencer

General Br: 711; CFAE: 411; CN: 548; Ma: 2246; Sch: 288

Billy Liar CN: 548-549; ENES1: 231; ENES2: 251; Po: 4520

Jubb CN: 549; Po: 4520

WATERS, Frank

General AN: 254; Po: 4520-4521

Below Grass Roots Po: 4520-4521

The Dust Within the Rock Po: 4520-4521

"Easy Meat" Wa: 763

The Wild Earth's Nobility Po: 4520-4521

WATKINS, Lucien Bottow

General BAW: 744

WATKINS, Vernon

General EP: 268-273; Po: 4521-4522

"Arakhova and the Daemon" PE: 486

"Ballad of the Mari Lwyd" EP: 270-271; PE: 486

"The Music of Colours: The Blossom Scattered" PE: 486

"Niobe" Po: 4522

"Ode at the Spring Equinox" EP: 272

WATLING, Peter

Indian Summer Br: 711; DC1: 213

WATSON, E.L. Grant

General MAP: 174

WATSON, Henry

Valentine and Orson ERP: 507

WATSON, John [Ian MACLAREN]

General Ai: 160-161; TA: 294

WATSON, John William [William WATSON]

General TA: 295

WATSON, Roberta Bruce

General BAF: 285

WATSON, Sheila

The Double Hook Po: 4522-4523

WATSON, Thomas

General SC: 101

Absalom DC1: 214

WATSON, Wilfred

General Po: 4523

Cockcrow and the Gulls Po: 4523

WATTS, Isaac

General EC: 148

"Come, Holy Spirit, Heavenly Dove" PE: 486

WATTS-DUNTON, Theodore

General BN: 112

WAUGH, Evelyn

General BN2: 106-108; CN: 549-552; LCAB: 185-186; Po: 4523-4534; Ri2: 442-455, 466-468; Sch: 289-293

"Bella Fleace Gave a Party" Ri2: 456; WaS1: 214

Black Mischief CN: 552; ENE: 260-261; ENES1: 231; ENES2: 251: Ma: 2247; Po: 4524; Ri2: 449, 456

"Compassion" Wa: 763

Brideshead Revisited BN2:
107; CN: 553-554; EN:
126-127; ENE: 261-262;
ENES1: 231-232; ENES2:
251-252; Ma: 2247-2249;
Ri2: 443-445, 454, 456-
458; Po: 4524, 4534-4536;
Sch: 293-294
Decline and Fall CN: 554-
555; ENE: 262; ENES1:
232; ENES2: 252; Ma:
2249-2250; Po: 4524,
4530, 4533, 4536; Ri2:
445, 449, 451, 458-459;
Sch: 294-295
End of the Battle see Un-
conditional Surrender
A Handful of Dust CN: 555;
ENE: 262; ENES1: 232;
ENES2: 252; Ma: 2250-
2251; Po: 4524, 4536-
4537; Ri2: 445, 449,
459-461; Sch: 295
Helena CN: 555-556; ENE:
263; ENES1: 232; ENES2:
252; Ri2: 443, 461
Labels Ri2: 466
The Life of the Right Reverend Ronald Knox Ri2:
467-468
Love Among the Ruins CN:
556; ENES2: 252; Ri2:
445, 461
The Loved One CN: 556;
EN: 127; ENES1: 232-
233; ENES2: 252; Ma:
2251-2252; Po: 4537; Ri2:
458, 461-462; Sch: 295
Men at Arms see also Sword
of Honour CN: 557; ENE:
263; ENES1: 233; ENES2:
252; Po: 4539-4540; Ri2:
444; Sch: 296
Men at Arms Trilogy see
Sword of Honour
"Mr. Loveday's Little Outing"
Wa: 763
Officers and Gentlemen see
also Sword of Honour
CN: 558; ENE: 263;
ENES1: 233; ENES2:
252; Po: 4531, 4539-4540;
Ri2: 445; Sch: 296
The Ordeal of Gilbert Pinfold
CN: 558; ENE: 263;
ENES1: 233; ENES2:

253; Ma: 2252-2253; Ri2:
462-463; Sch: 295
Put Out More Flags CN: 558;
ENES1: 233; ENES2: 253;
Ri2: 463
Rossetti: His Life and Works
Ri2: 443, 466
Scoop CN: 558; ENES1: 233;
ENES2: 253; Po: 4538;
Ri2: 463; Sch: 295
Scott-King's Modern Europe
CN: 558: ENES1: 233; Ri2:
458
Sword of Honour [Trilogy:
Men at Arms; Officers and
Gentlemen; Unconditional
Surrender] CN: 557-558;
ENE: 263; ENES1: 233;
ENES2: 253; Ri2: 443, 445,
451-453, 464-465; Po: 4538-
4540; Sch: 296
Unconditional Surrender [Amer.
Title: End of the Battle;
see also Sword of Honour]
CN: 559; ENE: 262-263;
ENES1: 234; ENES2: 253;
Po: 4524, 4539; Ri2: 464;
Sch: 296
Vile Bodies CN: 559; ENE:
263-264; ENES1: 234;
ENES2: 253; Ma: 2253-2254;
Po: 4524, 4530, 4533, 4540-
4541; Ri2: 327, 449, 465-
466; Sch: 297
The War Trilogy see Sword
of Honour
Work Suspended CN: 559;
ENES2: 253; Ri2: 466
WAYMAN, Tom
General JW: 170
WAZYK, Adam
General Po: 4541
"Poem for Adults" Po: 4541
WEAMYS, Anna
A Continuation of Sir Philip
Sidney's Arcadia ERP: 508
WEBB, Beatrice Potter
"Pages from a Work-Girl's
Diary" WaS1: 214
WEBB, Charles Lewis
General BAF: 285
WEBB, Francis
General Po: 4542
WEBB, Frank J.
General AAW: 75; BAF:
285-286; BAW: 747

The Garies and Their Friends
BAF: 285; BAW: 747
WEBB, Mary
General Po: 4542-4543; Sch:
297-298; TA: 297
The Golden Arrow ENES2:
253; Po: 4543
Gone to Earth ENES2: 254;
Po: 4543
The House in Dormer Forest
ENES2: 254
Precious Bane EN: 127;
ENE: 264; ENES1: 234;
ENES2: 254; Po: 4544
WEBB, Phyllis
General Po: 4544
Naked Poems Po: 4544
WEBBER, Charles Wilkins
"Jack Long; or, The Shot in
the Eye" ASF: 583
WEBER, Carl Maria von
Tonkünstlers Leben, Eine
Arabeske Fi: 396
WEBER, Ephraim
General Po: 4544
WEBSTER, Bill
General BAF: 286
One by One BAF: 286
WEBSTER, Daniel
General AP: 533-534; Da:
103
WEBSTER, Henry Kitchell
General Po: 4545
WEBSTER, John
General ED: 336-339; Log:
85-89, 93, 98-101; TSD:
102-105
Appius and Virginia DC1:
214; ED: 336; Log: 104;
Ma: 2255
A Cure for a Cuckold
DC1: 214; Log: 104
The Devil's Lawcase; or,
When Women Go to Law,
the Devil Is Full of Busi-
ness DC1: 214; ED:
338; EDC: 546-547; Log:
104; Ma: 2255-2256; TSD:
104
The Duchess of Malfi see
also AUDEN, Wystan
Hugh DC1: 214-216; ED:
336, 338; EDC: 547-549;
Log: 89-91, 102-104; Ma:
2256-2257; TSD: 102-105
Sir Thomas Wyatt see

DEKKER, Thomas
The White Devil DC1: 216-218;
ED: 336-338; EDC: 549-
551; Log: 91-93, 101-102;
Ma: 2257-2259; TSD: 102-
105
WEBSTER, Noah
General AP: 536-537; Da:
104-105
WEDEKIND, Frank
General Br: 711-712; MD:
316; Po: 4545-4547
The Awakening of Spring
[Spring's Awakening; Früh-
lings Erwachen] Br: 712;
DC2: 373; MD: 316
Bismarck Br: 712
"The Burning of Egliswyl" Wa:
764
Die Büsche der Pandora see
Pandora's Box
Censorship [Die Zensur] Br:
712
Death and the Devil Br: 712
Earth Spirit [Erdgeist--Part I
of Lulu; see also Lulu
Tragedies] Br: 713; MD:
316; Po: 4546-4547
Franziska Br: 713; MD: 316
Frühlings Erwachen see The
Awakening of Spring
Die Gutgeschnittene Ecke Br:
713
Hidalla, or Karl Hetmann, the
Dwarf Giant [Karl Hetmann,
der Zwergriese] Br: 713
"The Hoary Suitor" Wa: 764
Das Höhere Leben Br: 714
Die Junge Welt Br: 714
Die Kammersänger see The
Tenor
Karl Hetmann... see Hidalla...
King Nicolo, or Such Is Life
[König Nicolo, oder So ist
das Leben] Br: 714; Po:
4547
Lulu Tragedies [see also
Earth Spirit and Pandora's
Box] DC2: 373; MD: 317
The Marquis of Keith [Der
Marquis von Keith] Br:
714; DC2: 373; MD: 317;
Po: 4547-4548
Music Br: 714
Oaha Br: 714
Pandora's Box [Die Büsche

der Pandora--Part II of
Lulu; see also Lulu
Tragedies] Br: 714;
MD: 316; Po: 4546-4547
"Princess Russalka" Wa:
764
The Quick Painter Br: 714
"The Scapegoat" Wa: 764
Simpson Br: 715
Spring's Awakening see
The Awakening of Spring
The Tenor [Die Kammer-
sänger] Br: 715
Wetterstein Castle Br: 715
The Young World Br: 715
Die Zensur see Censorship
WEDMORE, Frederick
Renunciations Po: 4548
WEEMS, Mason Locke
General AP: 539-541; Da:
84-85
WEERTH, Georg
Fragment Eines Romans Fi:
397
WEIDMAN, Jerome
General CFAE: 414; LCAB:
186; MDAE: 500
The Enemy Camp CN: 560
"The Horse That Could
Whistle Dixie" Wa: 764
I Can Get It for You Whole-
sale CN: 560
WEIL, Jiri
Life with the Star Ke: 458
WEIL, Simone
Waiting for God MDAE: 102
WEILL, Gus
Geese ADC: 389
WEINBAUM, Stanley Grauman
General LCAB: 186
WEINER, Leslie
An Evening with the Poet
Senator ADC: 389
In the Counting House ADC:
389
WEINHEBER, Josef
General Po: 4548
"Variationen auf eine Hölder-
linische Ode" Po: 4548
WEINSTEIN, Arnold
General LCAB: 186; MDAE:
501-502
The Red Eye of Love ADC:
389
_____ and William BOLCOM
Dynamite Tonite ADC:

390
_____ and Kenneth CAVENDER
Metamorphoses ADC: 390
Weinstein, Nathan Wallenstein see
WEST, Nathanael
WEINSTOCK, Jack and Willie GIL-
BERT
Catch Me If You Can ADC:
390
WEISE, Christian
Masaniello DC2: 374
WEISENBORN, Günther
General Br: 715
Die Illegalen DC2: 374
"Two Men" Wa: 764
WEISS, Peter
General Br: 715; LCAB:
186; Po: 4549-4550
Gesang vom Lusitanischen
Papang see The Song of
the Lusitanian Bogey
Hölderlin EDC: 552
The Investigation [Die Ermitt-
lung] Br: 715-716; DC2:
374; EDC: 552-553; Po:
4550-4551
Marat/Sade [The Persecution
and Assassination of Jean-
Paul Marat...; Die Verfol-
gung und Ermordung Jean
Paul Marats...] Br: 716-
717; DC2: 374; EDC: 553-
556; LCAB: 186; Ma:
2260-2261; Po: 4549, 4552-
4555; TMBP: 201
Der Schatten des Körpers des
Kutschers Fi: 397; Po:
4552
The Song of the Lusitanian
Bogey [Gesang vom Lusi-
tanischen Papang] EDC:
556
Trotzky in Exile EDC: 556
The Tower [Der Turm] Br:
717; EDC: 556-557
Vietnam Discourse EDC: 557
WEISS, Theodore
General ICBAP: 136; Po:
4555
WELBURN, Ron
General BAF: 286
WELCH, Denton
General Po: 4556
"At Sea" Wa: 764
"The Barn" Wa: 764
"Brave and Cruel" Wa: 764

Brave and Cruel [Collection]
Po: 4556-4557
"The Coffin on the Hill" Wa:
764
"The Diamond Badge" Wa:
764
"The Earth's Crust" Wa:
764
"Evergreen Seaton-Leverett"
Wa: 765
"The Fire in the Wood" Wa:
765
"A Fragment of a Life Story"
Wa: 765
"The Hateful Word" Wa:
765
In Youth Is Pleasure ENES1:
234
"The Judas Tree" Wa: 765
"Leaves from a Young Per-
son's Notebook" Wa: 765
Maiden Voyage ENES1: 234
"Memories of a Vanished
Period" Wa: 765
"Narcissus Bay" Wa: 765
"A Party" Wa: 765
"A Picture in the Snow" Wa:
765
"Sickert at St. Peter's" Wa:
765
"The Trout Stream" Wa:
765
A Voice Through a Cloud
ENES1: 234
"When I Was Thirteen" Wa:
765
WELDON, Fay
Down Among the Women
ENES2: 254
The Fat Woman's Joke
ENES2: 254
Female Friends ENES2: 254
Remember Me ENES2: 254
WELLEK, René
History of Modern Criticism
Po: 4557
Theory of Literature LCAB:
186
WELLER, George
The Crack in the Column
AN: 255
WELLER, Michael
General MDAE: 503
And Now There's Just the
Three of Us ADC: 390
The Body Builders ADC:

390
Cancer ADC: 390
Fishing ADC: 391
Moonchildren ADC: 391
WELLES, Orson
Macbeth ADC: 391
Moby Dick ADC: 391
WELLESLEY, Dorothy
"Poem" PE: 486
WELLS, Herbert George
General BN2: 110-111; LCAB:
186-187; Po: 4557-4568;
Ri2: 493-521, 537-542; Sch:
298-305; TA: 299-300
The Anatomy of Frustration
Ri2: 541-542
Ann Veronica; A Modern Love
Story ENE: 264; ENES1:
234; ENES2: 254; Ri2:
495, 504, 521
Apropos of Dolores ENES2:
254; Ri2: 495, 522
Babes in the Darkling Wood
ENES2: 254; Ri2: 495
"The Beautiful Suit" Wa: 765
Boon ENES1: 234; ENES2:
254; Ri2: 513
Brynhild ENES2: 254; Ri2:
495, 522
The Bulpington of Blup
ENES2: 254; Ri2: 495
Christina Alberta's Father
ENES2: 255; Ri2: 522
"Chronic Argonauts" Wa: 766
"The Country of the Blind"
Ri2: 522; SFC: 197; Wa:
766
The Croquet Player ENES2:
255
Crux Ansata Ri2: 538
"The Desert Daisy" Wa: 766
"The Door in the Wall" SFC:
197; Wa: 766
"The Empire of the Ants" Wa:
766
Experiment in Autobiography
Ri2: 540
"The Extinction of Mankind"
Po: 4569
"First and Last Things" Ri2:
538
The First Men in the Moon
ENE: 264; ENES1: 235;
ENES2: 255; Ri2: 130,
504, 508-509, 514, 522-523
"The Flowering of the Strange

Orchid" Wa: 766
The Food of the Gods
ENES1: 235; Ri2: 495,
523
The Future of America Po:
4569; Ri2: 540
God the Invisible King
Ri2: 539
The Happy Turning Po:
4564
The History of Mr. Polly
ENE: 264; ENES1: 235;
ENES2: 255; LCAB: 187;
Po: 4559, 4567; Ri2:
495, 499, 502, 506, 515,
523-524; Sch: 305-306
The Holy Terror Ri2: 495
In the Days of the Comet
ENE: 264; ENES1: 235;
ENES2: 255; Po: 4564;
Ri2: 502, 510, 516, 524
The Invisible Man ENE: 264-
265; ENES1: 235; ENES2:
255; Ma: 2262; Ri2: 514,
524
The Island of Dr. Moreau
ENE: 265; ENES1: 235;
ENES2: 255; Po: 4569;
Ri2: 514, 524-525
Joan and Peter; The Story
of an Education ENE:
265; ENES2: 255; Ri2:
525
Kipps; The Story of a Simple
Soul ENE: 265; ENES1:
235-236; ENES2: 256;
Po: 4559; Ri2: 499, 502,
506, 515, 525; Sch: 306;
TMBP: 102
"The Lord of the Dynamos"
Wa: 766
Love and Mr. Lewisham ENE:
265; ENES1: 236; Po:
4559; Ri2: 495, 499, 506,
515, 526
"The Man Who Could Work
Miracles" Wa: 766
Mankind in the Making Ri2:
539
Marriage EN: 127; ENES1:
236; ENES2: 256; Ri2:
526
Meanwhile ENES2: 256
Men Like Gods ENE: 265;
ENES1: 236; ENES2:
256; Ri2: 526; Sch: 306

Mind at the End of Its Tether
Po: 4564
Mr. Blettsworthy on Rampole
Island ENE: 265; ENES2:
256; Ri2: 527
Mr. Britling Sees It Through
EN: 127; ENES1: 236;
ENES2: 256; Ri2: 507, 528
A Modern Utopia ENES1: 236;
ENES2: 256; Ri2: 509,
526-527; Sch: 306
The New Machiavelli EN: 127;
ENES1: 236; ENES2: 256;
Po: 4564, 4570; Ri2: 503,
516, 528
Outline of History Po: 4570;
Ri2: 538-541
The Passionate Friends ENE:
265; Ri2: 513
"The Plattner Story" Wa: 766
"The Remarkable Case of David-
son's Eyes" Wa: 766
The Research Magnificent EN:
127; ENES2: 256; Ri2:
513
The Sea Lady ENES1: 236
The Secret Places of the Heart
ENES2: 256
The Shape of Things to Come
Ri2: 528-529
"A Slip Under the Microscope"
Wa: 766
The Soul of a Bishop EN:
128; ENES2: 256; Ri2: 508
"The Star" Ri2: 529; Wa:
766; WaS1: 215
"The Stolen Bacillus" Wa: 767
"The Stolen Body" Wa: 767
"A Story of the Days to Come"
Wa: 767
"Story of the Stone Age" Wa:
767
Things to Come Ri2: 529
The Time Machine ENE: 266;
ENES1: 236; ENES2: 256-
257; Ma: 2262-2263; Po:
4570-4571; Ri2: 495, 508-
509, 514, 518, 529-531; Sch:
306; SFC: 197; Wa: 767;
WaS1: 215
Tono-Bungay BN2: 111; EN:
128; ENE: 266; ENES1:
237; ENES2: 257; Po:
4559, 4564, 4571-4572; Ri2:
495, 499, 502, 506, 508,
515-516, 531-534; Sch: 307

"The Triumph of a Taxidermist" Wa: 767
"Under the Knife" Wa: 767
The Undying Fire ENES2: 257; Ri2: 534
The War in the Air ENES1: 237; Ri2: 504
The War of the Worlds ENE: 266; ENES1: 237; ENES2: 257; Ma: 2263-2264; Po: 4572-4573; Ri2: 495, 514, 534-536; Sch: 307
When the Sleeper Wakes ENE: 267; ENES1: 237; ENES2: 257; Po: 4573; Ri2: 536-537
The Wife of Sir Isaac Harman ENES2: 257
The Wonderful Visit ENE: 267; ENES1: 237; Po: 4573; Ri2: 537
The Work, Wealth and Happiness of Mankind Ri2: 540
The World of William Clissold ENES2: 257; Ri2: 495, 499, 537; Sch: 307
The World Set Free ENES1: 237; ENES2: 257; Ri2: 537
You Can't Be Too Careful Ri2: 495
WELLS, Linton
"Fauntleroy Fights" ASF: 583
WELTY, Eudora
General ALL: 274-276; AN: 255; ASF: 590-592; CFAE: 416-420; CN: 560-561; LCAB: 187; Ne: 96-97; Po: 4573-4578
"Asphodel" ASF: 583; Po: 4578; SFC: 197; Wa: 767
"At the Landing" ASF: 583; SFC: 197; Wa: 767-768
"The Bride of the Innisfallen" ALL: 274, 276; ASF: 583-584; Po: 4575, 4579; SFC: 197; Wa: 768
"The Burning" ASF: 584; CFAE: 419; Po: 4579; SFC: 197; Wa: 768
"Circe" ASF: 584; Wa: 768; WaS1: 215

"Clytie" ASF: 584; Po: 4579; SFC: 197; Wa: 768-769; WaS1: 215
"A Curtain of Green" ASF: 584; Ne: 97; Wa: 769; WaS1: 215
"Death of a Traveling Salesman" ASF: 584; CFAE: 417-419; LCAB: 187; Po: 4580; SFC: 197; Wa: 769; WaS1: 215
Delta Wedding AN: 255; CFAE: 417; CN: 561; Ma: 2265; Ne: 97; Po: 4576
"The Demonstrators" ASF: 584-585; Po: 4576; Wa: 769
"First Love" ASF: 585; SFC: 197; Wa: 769-770; WaS1: 215
"Flowers for Marjorie" ASF: 585; Wa: 770
"Going to Naples" ASF: 585; Po: 4575; Wa: 770
The Golden Apples CFAE: 416-417; Ma: 2265-2266; Ne: 97; Po: 4580-4581
"The Hitch-Hikers" ASF: 585; SFC: 198; Wa: 770
"Ida M'Toy" Wa: 770
"It's All Because I Love You" Po: 4574
"June Recital" ASF: 585; SFC: 198; Wa: 770; WaS1: 215
"Keela, the Outcast Indian Maiden" ASF: 585; Po: 4581; Wa: 770-771; WaS1: 215
"The Key" ASF: 585; CFAE: 417; Wa: 771; WaS1: 215
"Kin" ASF: 585; SFC: 198; Wa: 771
"Ladies in Spring" ASF: 586; Wa: 771
"Lily Daw and the Three Ladies" ASF: 586; Wa: 771
"Livvie" ASF: 586; CFAE: 418; Po: 4581-4582; Wa: 771; WaS1: 216
Losing Battles ALL: 275-276
"A Memory" ASF: 586; Po: 4582; SFC: 198; Wa: 772; WaS1: 216
"Moon Lake" ASF: 586; Wa: 772; WaS1: 216

"Music from Spain" ASF: 586; SFC: 198; Wa: 772; WaS1: 216

"No Place for You, My Love" ASF: 586; Po: 4575; SFC: 198; Wa: 772

"Old Mr. Marblehall" ASF: 586-587; Po: 4582; SFC: 198; Wa: 772; WaS1: 216

The Optimist's Daughter ALL: 275; Po: 4582-4583

"Pageant of Birds" ASF: 587

"Petrified Man" ASF: 587; CFAE: 416, 418-419; Po: 4583; SFC: 198; Wa: 773; WaS1: 216

"A Piece of News" ASF: 587; Po: 4583; SFC: 198; Wa: 773; WaS1: 216

The Ponder Heart ALL: 276; AN: 255; CFAE: 417-418; CN: 561-562; Ma: 2266; MDAE: 525; Ne: 96-97; Po: 4583-4584; SFC: 199

"Powerhouse" ASF: 587-588; Po: 4584-4585; SFC: 199; Wa: 773-774; WaS1: 216

"The Purple Hat" ASF: 588; Wa: 774

The Robber Bridegroom CN: 562; Po: 4585; SFC: 199

"Shower of Gold" ASF: 588; SFC: 199; Wa: 774; WaS1: 216

"Sir Rabbit" ASF: 588; Wa: 774; WaS1: 216

"A Southern Landscape" ASF: 588

"A Still Moment" ASF: 588; Po: 4585; SFC: 200; Wa: 774-775

"A Visit of Charity" ASF: 588; CFAE: 416, 419; Po: 4586; SFC: 200; Wa: 775

"The Wanderers" ASF: 588; Wa: 775; WaS1: 216

"Where Is the Voice Coming From?" ASF: 588; Wa: 775

"The Whistle" ASF: 589; Po: 4587; Wa: 775

"The Whole World Knows" ASF: 589; Wa; 775; WaS1: 217

"Why I Live at the P.O." ASF: 589; Po: 4574, 4587; Wa: 775-776; WaS1: 217

"The Wide Net" ASF: 589; SFC: 200; Wa: 776; WaS1: 217

"The Winds" ASF: 589; Wa: 776

"A Worn Path" ASF: 589-590; CFAE: 416, 418-419; Po: 4587-4588; SFC: 200; Wa: 776-777; WaS1: 217

WENTWORTH, William Charles
General AL: 350

WERFEL, Franz
General Br: 717-718; MD: 317; Po: 4588-4590

"Als mich dein Wandeln an den Tod verzückte" Po: 4590

Eine Blass Blaue Frauenschrift MD: 317

Bocksgesang see Goat Song

Cella oder die Überwinder: Versuch eines Romans Po: 4591

The Class Reunion Ke: 341

Embezzled Heaven Ke: 341

The Eternal Road [Der Weg der Verheissung] Br: 718; DC2: 375; MD: 318

The Forty Days of Musa Dagh Ke: 341

Goat Song [Bocksgesang] Br: 718; DC2: 375; MD: 317; Po: 4591

In Einer Nacht DC2: 375; MD: 317

Jacobowsky and the Colonel [Jacobowsky und der Oberst] Br: 718; DC2: 375; MD: 317

Juarez and Maximilian Br: 718

Mirror Man [Spiegelmensch] Br: 718; DC2: 375; MD: 318

Not the Murderer but the Murdered Is Guilty [Nicht der Mörder, Der Ermordete ist schuldig] Ke: 341; Po: 4591; Wa: 777

Das Opfer in Arcadia Br: 719; DC2: 375; MD: 317-318

The Pure in Heart Ke: 341-
    342
Schweiger Br: 719; MD:
    318
The Song of Bernadette Ke:
    342
Spiegelmensch see Mirror
    Man
Star of the Unborn Ke:
    342
Temptation [Versuchung]
    Br: 719
Die Troerinnen Br: 719;
    DC2: 375
Verdi: A Novel of the Opera
    Ke: 342
Der Weg der Verheissung
    see The Eternal Road
WERNER, Bruno E.
The Slaveship [Die Galeere]
    Ke: 342; Po: 4591
WERNER, Zacharias
Attila, Konig der Hunnen
    DC2: 375
Der Vierundzwanzigste
    Februar [24th of Febru-
    ary] DC2: 375
Wanda, Konig in der Sar-
    maten DC2: 376
WESCOTT, Glenway
General AN: 255; ASF:
    593-594; LCAB: 187;
    Ne: 98; Po: 4592
"Adolescence" Wa: 777
The Babe's Bed Wa: 777;
    Ne: 98
"The Dove Came Down" Wa:
    777
"The Dream of Audubon"
    ASF: 593; Wa: 777
"The Frenchman Six Feet
    Three" Wa: 777
Goodbye, Wisconsin Po:
    4592
The Grandmothers AN:
    255; Ne: 98; Po: 4592-
    4593
"A Guilty Woman" Wa: 777
"Hurt Feelings" ASF: 593;
    Wa: 777
"In a Thicket" Wa: 777
"Like a Lover" ASF: 593;
    Wa: 777
The Pilgrim Hawk Ne: 98;
    Po: 4593; SFC: 200;
    Wa: 778

"Prohibition" Wa: 778
"The Rescuer" ASF: 593; Wa:
    778
"The Runaway" Wa: 778
"The Sailor" Wa: 778
"The Sight of a Dead Body"
    ASF: 593; Wa: 778
"The Wedding March" Wa: 778
"The Whistling Swan" Wa: 778
WESKER, Arnold
General Br: 719-720; MBD:
    94-95; MD: 318; MDAE:
    506-508; Po: 4593-4596;
    TMBP: 248-267
Billy Liar Br: 720
Chicken Soup with Barley see
    also The Wesker Trilogy
    Br: 720-721; DC1: 218;
    EDC: 557; MD: 318; MDAE:
    507; Po: 4594; TMBP: 250-
    251, 254-255, 260-261, 267
Chips with Everything Br:
    721-723; DC1: 218; EDC:
    557; MBD: 94; MD: 318;
    TMBP: 248-252, 254, 258-
    260, 262, 265-267
Fears of Fragmentation TMBP:
    257
The Four Seasons Br: 723;
    EDC: 557; MDAE: 507;
    TMBP: 249-250, 254, 258,
    260-261, 267
The Friends EDC: 557; MBD:
    95; MDAE: 508; TMBP:
    254, 257-260, 267-268
I'm Talking About Jerusalem
    see also The Wesker Trilogy
    Br: 723; DC1: 218; EDC:
    557; MD: 319; MDAE: 507;
    Po: 4594; TMBP: 250, 252,
    268
The Journalists EDC: 557;
    TMBP: 254
The Kitchen Br: 723-724;
    DC1: 218-219; EDC: 558;
    MBD: 94-95; MD: 318;
    MDAE: 507; Po: 4596;
    TMBP: 249-253, 255, 257-
    258, 261-262, 264-266, 268
Menace Br: 724; TMBP:
    261, 268
The Old Ones EDC: 558;
    TMBP: 254, 268
"Pools" TMBP: 261
Roots see also The Wesker
    Trilogy Br: 724-725;

EDC: 558; MBD: 94-95;
MD: 319; MDAE: 506-
508; Po: 4594, 4596;
TMBP: 250, 252-257,
259, 268

Their Very Own and Golden
City Br: 725; EDC:
558; TMBP: 248-250, 254,
260, 265-266, 268

The Wesker Trilogy [Chicken
Soup with Barley; Roots;
I'm Talking About Jeru-
salem] MBD: 95; MDAE:
507; Po: 4594

WESLEY, John
General EC: 149
"Christ, Whose Glory Fills
the Skies" PE: 486

WESLEY, Richard
General BAW: 751; MBA:
203
Ace Boon Coon BAP: 208
The Black Terror AAPD:
412; ADC: 391; BAP:
208; MBA: 203-205
Cotillion MBA: 204, 206
Gettin' It Together ADC:
391; MBA: 204
Going Thru Changes ADC:
391; MBA: 204-205
Knock, Knock--Who's Dat?
MBA: 205
The Last Street Play ADC:
392; MBA: 205
The Past Is the Past ADC:
392; BAP: 209; MBA:
204-206
The Sirens ADC: 392; BAP:
209; MBA: 204, 206
The Street Corner BAP:
209
Uptown Saturday Night
MBA: 204, 206

WEST, Anthony C.
As Towns with Fire ENES2:
257
The Ferret Fancier ENES2:
258

WEST, Dorothy
General AAW: 75; BAF:
287; BAW: 752
The Living Is Easy BAF:
287-288; LCAB: 187
"The Typewriter" ASF: 594

WEST, Jane
The Advantages of Educa-
tion ENES2: 258
A Gossip's Story ENES2: 258
A Tale of the Times ENES2:
258

WEST, Jessamyn
General ASF: 594; CN: 563;
LCAB: 187; Po: 4596
Cress Delahanty CN: 563;
Po: 4597
"Horace Chooney, M.D." SFC:
201; Wa: 778
"The Lesson" ASF: 594
"Love, Death, and the Ladies'
Drill Team" ASF: 594;
Po: 4597; SFC: 201; Wa:
778
"Mr. Cornelius, I Love You"
Wa: 779
"Shivaree Before Breakfast"
SFC: 201; Wa: 779
"Sixteen" Wa: 779
The Witch Diggers AN: 255;
CN: 563; Po: 4596

WEST, Morris L.
General LCAB: 187; Po:
4597-4598
The Devil's Advocate Po:
4598

WEST, Nathanael
General ALL: 276-278; AN:
256; JW: 308-309; LCAB:
187; Ne: 99-100; Po:
4598; Wo: 206-208
"The Adventurer" ASF: 594
"A Barefaced Lie" Po: 4603
"Business Deal" ASF: 594;
Wa: 779
A Cool Million Ma: 2267; Ne:
99; Po: 4600-4601, 4603-
4604; SFC: 201; Wa: 779-
780; WaS1: 217
The Day of the Locust ALL:
277; AN: 256; Ma: 2268-
2269; Ne: 99; Po: 4599,
4603-4605; Wo: 208
The Dream Life of Balso Snell
AN: 256; Ma: 2269; Ne:
99-100; Po: 4600, 4606;
SFC: 201; Wa: 780; WaS1:
217
Miss Lonelyhearts ALL: 276-
277; AN: 256; LCAB: 187;
Ma: 2269-2271; Ne: 99-100;
Po: 4599, 4601-4603, 4606-
4609; SFC: 201-202; Wa:
781-782; WaS1: 217; Wo:

206-208
"Mr. Potts of Pottstown"
  ASF: 595
WEST, Rebecca [Cicily Isabel
  FAIRFIELD]
  General CN: 563; Po:
    4610; Ri2: 551-555; Sch:
    307-308
  The Birds Fall Down CN:
    563; ENES1: 238; Ma:
    2272; Po: 4610; Ri2: 552
  Black Lamb and Grey Falcon
    Ma: 2272; Ri2: 551, 553
  The Court and the Castle
    Ri2: 551, 554
  The Fountain Overflows
    ENES1: 238; Ma: 2272-
    2273; Ri2: 552
  Harriet Hume ENES1: 238;
    Ri2: 551-552
  The Judge ENES1: 238;
    Ri2: 552-553
  The Return of the Soldier
    ENES1: 238; Ri2: 553,
    555
  St. Augustine Ri2: 553
  The Thinking Reed ENES1:
    238; Ri2: 554
  A Train of Powder Ma: 2273;
    Ri2: 554
WEST, Wallace
  "The Last Man" WaS1: 217
  "The Phantom Dictator" WaS1:
    217
WESTHEIMER, David
  My Sweet Charlie ADC: 392
WEVER, R.
  Lusty Juventus DC1: 219
WEXLEY, John
  They Shall Not Die Br: 725
WEYMAN, Stanley John
  General TA: 301
WEYSSENHOFF, Jozef
  "Under the Thunderbolts"
    Wa: 782
WHARTON, Edith
  General ALL: 278-281; AN:
    257-260; ASF: 598-599;
    Ho: 129-132, 156; LCAB:
    187-188; Po: 4610-4616;
    Wo: 211-213
  "After Holbein" ASF: 595;
    SFC: 202; Wa: 783;
    WaS1: 218
  The Age of Innocence AN:
    257; Ho: 130-131, 156;

LCAB: 188; Ma: 2274-2275;
  Po: 4611-4613, 4616-4618
"All Souls" Wa: 783
"Autres Temps" ASF: 595;
  SFC: 202; Wa: 783; WaS1:
  218
"Beatrice Palmato" ASF: 595;
  WaS1: 218
"Bewitched" ASF: 596; Wa:
  783; WaS1: 218
"The Blond Beast" ASF: 596;
  Wa: 783; WaS1: 218
"Bunner Sisters" ASF: 596;
  SFC: 202; Wa: 783; WaS1:
  218
"The Children" ASF: 596;
  Po: 4619
"The Choice" WaS1: 218
"Cold Greenhouse" WaS1: 218
The Cruise of the Fleetwing
  Po: 4613
The Custom of the Country
  AN: 257; Ho: 156; Ma:
  2275-2276
"The Day of the Funeral" ASF:
  596
"Diagnosis" ASF: 596
"The Duchess at Prayer" ASF:
  596
Ethan Frome AN: 257; Br:
  725; Ho: 130-131; LCAB:
  188; Ma: 2276-2278; Po:
  4619-4620; SFC: 202-203;
  Wa: 783-784; WaS1: 218
"The Eyes" ASF: 596; SFC:
  203; Wa: 784; WaS1: 218
"False Dawn" Wa: 784
Fast and Loose ASF: 596;
  Ho: 132; Po: 4620
The Fruit of the Tree Ma:
  2278; Po: 4613
"The Fullness of Life" ASF:
  596; SFC: 203; Wa: 784;
  WaS1: 218
The Gods Arrive Po: 4615
"Her Son" ASF: 596; Wa:
  784
"The Hermit and the Wild Wom-
  an" ASF: 596
"His Father's Son" ASF: 597;
  Wa: 784; WaS1: 218
The House of Mirth AN: 257;
  Ho: 130-132, 156; LCAB:
  188; Ma: 2278-2280; Po:
  4612-4613, 4621-4622
Hudson River Bracketed Po:

4615, 4622
"A Journey" ASF: 597
"A Joy in the House" ASF:
597
"Kerfol" ASF: 597; Wa:
784
"The Last Asset" ASF:
597; WaS1: 219
"The Legend" WaS1: 219
"The Letters" ASF: 597;
Wa: 785; WaS1: 219
"Life and I" Wa: 785
"The Long Run" ASF: 597;
Wa: 785
"Madame de Treymes" ASF:
597; WaS1: 219
The Marne Po: 4615
"Miss Mary Pask" Wa: 785
"The Mission of Jane" SFC:
203; Wa: 785
Mother Earth Po: 4613
"Mrs. Manstey's View" ASF:
597; Wa: 785
"The Muse's Tragedy" ASF:
597; WaS1: 219
New England Po: 4613
"Old Maid" ASF: 597
"The Other Two" ASF: 597;
Wa: 785; WaS1: 219
"The Pelican" ASF: 597
"Permanent Wave" ASF: 597
"Pomegranate Seed" ASF:
597; Wa: 785
"The Pot-Boiler" Wa: 785
"The Pretext" Po: 4622-
4623; SFC: 203; Wa: 785
"The Reckoning" ASF: 598;
Wa: 785
"The Recovery" Wa: 785
The Reef Po: 4611
"Roman Fever" ASF: 598;
SFC: 203; Wa: 785
A Son at the Front Po:
4615, 4623
Summer Po: 4623; SFC:
203; Wa: 786; WaS1: 219
"The Touchstone" ASF:
598
"The Triumph of Night"
ASF: 598; Wa: 786
"The Valley of Childish
Things, and Other Em-
blems" ASF: 598; WaS1:
219
The Valley of Decision Po:
4623

"Xingu" ASF: 598; Wa: 786;
WaS1: 219
WHEATCROFT, John
Prodigal Son Po: 4624
WHEATLEY, Dennis
The Devil Rides Out ENES2:
258
The Haunting of Toby Jugg
ENES2: 258
WHEATLEY, Phillis
General AAPD: 82-84; AAW:
75-76; BAW: 754-757; Da:
85; ICBAP: 136; LCAB:
188
WHEELER, Hugh, Leonard BERN-
STEIN, and Richard WILBUR
Candide ADC: 392-393
WHEELER, Thomas Martin
Sunshine and Shadow ENES1:
237
WHEELOCK, John Hall
General Po: 4624
WHEELWRIGHT, John
General Po: 4624
WHEELWRIGHT, John Brooks
"Father" PE: 486
WHELPLEY, J.D.
"The Atoms of Chladni" Wa:
786
WHETSTONE, George
General ERP: 510-512; SC:
101
Heptameron ERP: 510-511;
Hen: 155
Promos and Cassandra DC1:
219
"Rinaldo and Giletta" ERP:
511-512; Hen: 155; SC:
101
The Rock of Regard ERP:
512
WHIPPER, Leigh
General BAP: 209; MBA: 206
WHITCHER, Frances
General ASF: 599
WHITE, Edgar
General MBA: 207
The Crucificado MBA: 207
Defense ADC: 393; MBA:
207
Les Femmes Noires ADC: 393;
BAP: 209; MBA: 207
The Life and Times of J.
Walter Smitheus ADC: 393;
BAP: 209-210; MBA: 207
WHITE, Elwyn Brooks

General APC: 34-36; ASF:
599; LCAB: 188; Po:
4625
"The Decline of Sport" Wa:
786
"The Door" ASF: 599; Po:
2625; Wa: 786
"The Hotel of the Total
Stranger" Wa: 786
"The Morning of the Day
They Did It" Wa: 786
One Man's Meat APC: 34;
Po: 4625
The Points of My Compass
APC: 35
"The Second Tree from the
Corner" Wa: 786; WaS1:
219
WHITE, Gilbert
General EC: 149
WHITE, John
General MDAE: 510
Bananas ADC: 393
Bugs ADC: 393
Veronica ADC: 393
WHITE, John Blake
General AD: 208-209
The Forgers ADC: 393
Foscari ADC: 393
Modern Honor ADC: 393
The Mysteries of the Castle
ADC: 393
The Triumph of Liberty, or
Louisiana Preserved
ADC: 394
WHITE, Joseph
General BAW: 760
The Hustle MBA: 207
The Leader MBA: 207
Old Judge Mose Is Dead
BAP: 210
WHITE, Kenneth
General ICBAP: 136; Po:
4625
WHITE, Patrick
General CN: 563-564; MAP:
318-341, 385-387; Po:
4626-4631
The Aunt's Story CN:
565; MAP: 319-321, 323,
328-329, 337-338; Po:
4629-4630, 4632
"Being Kind to Titina" Wa:
786; WaS1: 219
The Burnt Ones MAP:
329, 331-332, 338; Po:

4632
A Cheery Soul Br: 725; DC1:
219; MAP: 388; Po: 4632;
Wa: 787; WaS1: 219
"Clay" Wa: 787; WaS1: 219
The Cockatoos MAP: 321, 327;
Wa: 787
"Cocotte" WaS1: 220
"Dead Roses" Wa: 787; WaS1:
220
"Down at the Dump" MAP:
341; Wa: 787; WaS1: 220
"The Evening at Sissy Kamara's"
Wa: 787; WaS1: 220
The Eye of the Storm MAP:
319, 324-326, 332, 334, 336,
341
"Five-Twenty" Wa: 787
A Fringe of Leaves MAP: 322,
331, 339
"A Full Belly" Wa: 787
"A Glass of Tea" WaS1: 220
The Ham Funeral Br: 725;
DC1: 219; MAP: 385-386,
389; Po: 4633
Happy Valley CN: 565; MAP:
320
"The Letters" Wa: 787; WaS1:
220
The Living and the Dead CN:
565-566; MAP: 334, 340
"Miss Slattery and Her Demon
Lover" Wa: 787; WaS1:
220
Night on Bald Mountain Br:
726; DC1: 219; MAP: 387
"The Night Prowler" Wa: 787
Return to Abyssinia MAP:
386-388
Riders in the Chariot CN:
566-567; MAP: 318-319, 321,
323, 325-327, 329-330, 332-
333, 336, 341; Po: 4628-
4630, 4633-4634
The Season at Sarsaparilla Br:
726; DC1: 219; MAP: 385;
Po: 4634
"Sicilian Vespers" Wa: 787
The Solid Mandala CN: 567;
MAP: 320, 328, 332, 335,
337, 340; Po: 4630, 4634-
4635
The Tree of Man CN: 567-
568; MAP: 318, 320-324;
328-329, 331-334, 336-338,
340-341; Po: 4630, 4636-

4637
"The Twitching Colonel"
WaS1: 220
The Vivisector MAP: 320,
323-325, 328, 334, 336,
338-339
Voss CN: 568-569; MAP:
318-327, 331-334, 336-341;
Po: 4628-4630, 4637-4638
"Willy Wagtails by Moonlight"
Wa: 788; WaS1: 220
"The Woman Who Wasn't Al-
lowed to Keep Cats"
Wa: 788; WaS1: 220
"A Woman's Hand" Wa: 788
WHITE, Stanley
Beyond Human Understanding
MBA: 207-208
WHITE, Stewart Edward
General ASF: 600; AN:
260
WHITE, Terence Hanbury
General Sch: 308
The Candle in the Wind
ENES1: 238
Darkness at Pemberley
ENES1: 238
Dead Mr. Nixon ENES1: 238
Earth Stopped ENES1: 238
The Elephant and the
Kangaroo ENES1: 239
Farewell Victoria ENES1:
239
First Lesson ENES1: 239
Gone to Ground ENES1:
239
The Ill-Made Knight ENES1:
239
The Master ENES1: 239
Mistress Masham's Repose
ENES1: 239; Po: 4639
The Once and Future King
ENES1: 239; ENES2:
258; Ma: 2281; Po:
4639-4640; Ri2: 571
The Sword in the Stone
ENES1: 239
They Winter Abroad ENES1:
239
The Witch in the Wood
ENES1: 239
WHITE, Terence de Vere
The Distance and the Dark
ENES2: 258
WHITE, Walter Francis
General AAW: 76; BAF:

289-290; BAW: 762-763; HR:
161-162; LCAB: 189
Fire in the Flint BAF: 290
Flight BAF: 290
WHITE, William Allen
General AN: 260; ASF: 600;
Po: 4640
"The Gods Arrive" ASF: 600
"The Real Issue" WaS1: 220
"The Regeneration of Colonel
Hucks" ASF: 600
"The Story of Aqua Pura"
WaS1: 220
"The Story of the Highlands"
WaS1: 220
White, William Anthony Parker
see BOUCHER, Anthony
White, William Hale see RUTHER-
FORD, Mark
WHITEHAND, Robert
"American Nocturne" Wa: 788
WHITEHEAD, William
General Li: 318
WHITEING, Richard
General TA: 303
No. 5 John Street ENES1:
240
WHITFIELD, James Monroe
General AAPD: 85; BAW:
764; LCAB: 189
WHITING, John Robert
General Br: 726; MBD: 96;
MD: 319; MDAE: 512-514;
Po: 4641-4642
The Devils Br: 726-727;
DC1: 220; EDC: 558-559;
MDAE: 513; TMBP: 41,
106-107
Gates of Summer Br: 727
Marching Song Br: 727; DC1:
220; EDC: 559; MDAE:
513; TMBP: 41
A Penny for a Song DC1:
220; EDC: 559; MDAE: 513;
TMBP: 41, 262
Saint's Day Br: 727-728;
DC1: 220; EDC: 559; MBD:
96; MD: 319; MDAE: 76,
416-417, 512-514; Po: 4642;
TMBP: 16, 41, 158, 167
WHITLOCK, Brand
General AN: 261; ASF: 600;
Po: 4643-4645
Forty Years of It Po: 4645
J. Hardin and Son Po: 4645
"The Pardon of Thomas Whalen"

ASF: 600
WHITMAN, Albery Allson
General AAPD: 85-86;
AAW: 76; BAW: 765-766;
LCAB: 189
WHITMAN, Walt
General ALL: 281-292; Cla:
90-97; ICBAP: 137;
LCAB: 189-190
"Aboard at a Ship's Helm"
PE: 486
"Antoinette the Courtesan"
ASF: 600-601
"As I Ebb'd with the Ocean
of Life" ICBAP: 137;
PE: 487
"The Base of All Metaphysics"
PE: 487
"A Boston Ballad (1854)" PE:
487
"A Broadway Pageant" PE:
487
"By Blue Ontario's Shore"
["Poem of Many in One"]
PE: 487
"Calamus" Cla: 93; ICBAP:
137; PE: 487
"Calamus," No. 9 PE: 487
"Cavalry Crossing a Ford"
PE: 487
"Chanting the Square Deific"
Cla: 96; PE: 488
"Chants Democratic" ICBAP:
137
"Children of Adam" ICBAP:
137
"A Child's Reminiscence"
see "Out of the Cradle
Endlessly Rocking"
"Clef Poem" PE: 488
"Crossing Brooklyn Ferry"
Cla: 93; ICBAP: 137;
PE: 488
"Death in the School-Room"
ASF: 601
"Democratic Vistas" Cla:
92; Ma: 2282
"The Dismantled Ship" PE:
488
"Eidólons" PE: 488
"Ethiopia Saluting the Colors"
PE: 488
"Excelsior" PE: 488
"Faces" PE: 488
Franklin Evans AN: 261
"From Paumanok Starting"

ICBAP: 137
"Give Me the Splendid Silent
Sun" PE: 488
"Good-bye My Fancy!" PE:
489
"Hush'd Be the Camps Today"
LCAB: 190
"I Hear It Was Charged Against
Me" PE: 489
"I Sing the Body Electric"
LCAB: 190; PE: 489
Leaves of Grass ALL: 281-
282, 285-290; Cla: 95-97;
ICBAP: 137; LCAB: 190;
Ma: 2282-2284
"Lingering Last Drops" PE:
489
"A March in the Ranks Hard-
Prest, and the Road Un-
known" PE: 489
"Memories of President Lincoln"
ALL: 285; LCAB: 190
"The Mystic Trumpeter" PE:
489
"A Noiseless, Patient Spider"
ICBAP: 137; PE: 489
"Of the Terrible Doubt of Ap-
pearances" ICBAP: 137
"On Journeys Through the
States" PE: 489
"On the Beach at Night" PE:
489
"Our Old Feuillage" PE: 489
"Out of the Cradle Endlessly
Rocking" Cla: 96-97;
ICBAP: 137; PE: 489-490
"Passage to India" Cla: 92-
94; ICBAP: 137; PE: 490-
491
"Patroling Barnegat" PE: 491
"Pictures" PE: 491
"Pioneers! O Pioneers!" PE:
491
"Proud Music of the Storm"
Cla: 94; ICBAP: 138; PE:
491
"Revenge and Requital: A
Tale of Murder Escaped"
ASF: 601
"A Riddle Song" PE: 491
"Sail Out for Good, Eidólon
Yacht!" PE: 491
"Salut au Monde" PE: 491
"Scented Herbage of My
Breast" ICBAP: 138; PE:
492

"A Sight in Camp in the
Daybreak Gray and Dim"
PE: 492
"The Sleepers" ALL: 288;
PE: 492
"Song for Occupations" PE:
492
"Song of Myself" ALL: 284,
289; Cla: 96; ICBAP:
138; Ma: 2284-2285; PE:
492-494
"Song of Myself--Section 50"
ICBAP: 138
"Song of the Broad-Axe" PE:
494
"A Song of the Rolling Earth"
ICBAP: 138; PE: 495
Specimen Days Ma: 2285
"Spirit That Form'd This
Scene" ICBAP: 138; PE:
495
"Spontaneous Me" Cla: 97;
PE: 495
"Starting from Poumanok"
PE: 495
"There Was a Child Went
Forth" ICBAP: 138; PE:
495
"This Compost" ICBAP:
138; PE: 495
"To a Locomotive in Winter"
ICBAP: 138; PE: 495
"To the Sunset Breeze" PE:
495
"To Thee Old Cause" ICBAP:
138
"To Think of Time" PE:
495
"Transpositions" PE: 496
"Twenty-eight Young Men"
PE: 496
"Two Rivulets" PE: 496
"Unfolded Out of the Folds"
PE: 496
"A Voice from Death" PE:
496
"When I Heard the Learn'd
Astronomer" PE: 496
"When Lilacs Last in the
Dooryard Bloom'd" Cla:
91; ICBAP: 138; LCAB:
190; PE: 496-497
"Whispers of Heavenly
Death" PE: 497
"Whoever You Are Holding
Me Now in Hand" ICBAP:

138; PE: 497
"The World Below the Brine"
ICBAP: 139; PE: 497
"The Wound-Dresser" PE: 497
WHITNEY, Arthur
A Tribute to Lili Lamont ADC:
394
WHITTEMORE, Reed
General Po: 4645-4646
"A Closet Drama" PE: 497
"The Primitives" PE: 497
WHITTIER, John Greenleaf
General ALL: 292-296; Cla:
98-99; LCAB: 190
"Barbara Frietchie" PE: 497
"Birchbrook Mill" PE: 497
"The Emancipation Group"
LCAB: 190
"Ichabod" ICBAP: 139; PE:
497
"Maud Muller" PE: 498
"The Pennsylvania Pilgrim"
PE: 498
"The Pipes at Lucknow: An
Incident of the Sepoy Mutiny"
PE: 498
"Skipper Ireson's Ride" PE:
498
"Snow-Bound" ICBAP: 139;
PE: 498
"Telling the Bees" PE: 498
"To J.P." PE: 498
WHYTE, Ron
Welcome to Andromeda ADC:
394
_____, Bob SATULOFF, and
Mel MARVIN
Variety Obit ADC: 394
WHYTE-MELVILLE, George John
General BN: 113
WICKHAM, John
Casuarina Row WIL: 180
WIDEMAN, John E.
General BAF: 291; BAW:
767
A Glance Away AAL: 246;
BAF: 291
Hurry Home AAL: 246; BAF:
291
The Lynchers AAL: 246;
BAF: 291-292
WIECHERT, Ernst Emil
General Po: 4646-4648
Alti der Bestmann Ke: 342
Andreas Nyland Ke: 342
The Baroness Ke: 343

Die Blauen Schwingen Ke: 343
Die Flucht ins Ewige Ke: 343
Die Furchen der Armen Po: 4646
Gesichte des Todes Ke: 343
"Der Hauptmann von Kapernaum" Wa: 788
Hirtennovelle Ke: 343; Po: 4646
Jedermann Fi: 397; Ke: 343
The Jeromins Ke: 343; Po: 4646-4647
Die Magd des Jurgen Doskocil Ke: 343
Missa sine Nomine Po: 4646-4647
Tobias Ke: 343
"Der Todeskandidat" Wa: 788
Totenwolf Ke: 343
Der Wald Ke: 343

WIED, Gustave
General MD: 317

WIELAND, Christoph
The Abderites Ke: 343-344
Agathodämon Fi: 397; Ke: 344
Agathon Fi: 397; Ke: 344
Alkestis DC2: 376
Aristipp und Einige Seiner Zeitgenossen Fi: 397; Ke: 344
Die Dialogen des Diogenes Fi: 397
Don Sylvio of Rosalva Fi: 397-398; Ke: 344-345
The Golden Mirror Ke: 345
Peregrinus Proteus Fi: 398; Ke: 345
Die Wahl des Herkules DC2: 376

WIENERS, John
General Po: 4648

WIERZYNSKI, Kazimierz
"Patrol" Wa: 788
"World Frontiers" Wa: 788

WIESEL, Elie
General JW: 313-314

WIESSE, María
"El forastero" Wa: 788

WIGGLESWORTH, Michael
General AP: 544; Da: 45

WILBUR, Richard
General ICBAP: 139; LCAB: 190; Ma: 2286-2287; MP: 104-105; Po: 4648-4650
"Advice to a Prophet" Ma: 2286; PE: 498
Advice to a Prophet [Collection] Po: 4651
"Altitudes" ICBAP: 139
"The Aspen and the Stream" PE: 498
"Ballade for the Duke of Orleans" PE: 498; Po: 4651
"A Baroque Wall-Fountain in the Villa Sciarra" ICBAP: 139; PE: 498
"The Beacon" ICBAP: 139
"Boy at the Window" PE: 498
"Castles and Distances" PE: 498
"Ceremony" PE: 498
"The Death of a Toad" PE: 499
"Driftwood" PE: 499
"Epistemology" PE: 499
"Exeunt" PE: 499
"For the New Railway Station in Rome" ICBAP: 139; PE: 499
"A Game of Catch" WaS1: 220
"Grasse: The Olive Trees" PE: 499
"The Juggler" Po: 4651
"Junk" PE: 499; Po: 4651
"Looking into History" PE: 499
"Love Calls Us to the Things of This World" ICBAP: 139; LCAB: 190; PE: 499
"The Mill" PE: 499
"Objects" ICBAP: 139
"A Plain Song for Comadre" PE: 499
"Poplar, Sycamore" PE: 499
"The Puritans" ICBAP: 139; PE: 499; Po: 4652
"A Simile for Her Smile" PE: 499
"Statues" ICBAP: 139; PE: 499
"Still, Citizen Sparrow" PE: 499
Things of This World Ma: 2287-2288
"To an American Poet Just Dead" PE: 500; Po: 4652
"Walking to Sleep" Ma: 2288;

MP: 105; Po: 4652
"Water Walker" ICBAP: 139
"A Wood" PE: 500
"Year's-End" PE: 500
WILCOX, Ella Wheeler
"After the Fierce Midsummer
    All Ablaze" PE: 500
"The Arrival" Po: 4653
WILD, Robert
"An Epitaph for a Godly
    Man's Tomb" PE: 500;
    Po: 4653
WILDE, Oscar [Sebastian MEL-
    MOTH]
    General Br: 728-729; Du:
    170; EDT: 324-334;
    LCAB: 191; MBD: 97-99;
    MD: 319-320; TA: 305-
    306; VP: 84
"Ballad of Reading Gaol"
    PE: 500; VP: 84
"The Birthday of the Infanta"
    WaS1: 220-221
"The Canterville Ghost" Wa:
    788; WaS1: 221
De Profundis Ma: 2289; VP:
    84
"The Devoted Friend" Wa:
    788; WaS1: 221
The Duchess of Padua Br:
    729; EDC: 559
"The Fisherman and His
    Soul" Wa: 788; WaS1:
    221
The Florentine Tragedy Br:
    729; EDT: 334
For Love of the King EDT:
    325
"The Happy Prince" Wa:
    789; WaS1: 221
"A House of Pomegranates"
    WaS1: 221
An Ideal Husband Br: 729;
    DC1: 220; EDC: 559-
    560; EDT: 332; MBD:
    98; MD: 320
The Importance of Being
    Earnest Br: 729-730;
    DC1: 220-221; EDC:
    560-561; EDT: 327-334;
    LCAB: 191; Ma: 2289-
    2290; MBD: 97-99; MD:
    320-321; VP: 84
"Lady Alroy" see "The
    Sphinx Without a Secret"
Lady Windemere's Fan Br:

730-731; DC1: 221-222;
    EDC: 561; EDT: 328, 331;
    LCAB: 191; Ma: 2290-2291;
    MBD: 97-98; MD: 321
"Lord Arthur Savile's Crime"
    Wa: 789; WaS1: 221
"The Model Millionaire" WaS1:
    221
"The Nightingale and the Rose"
    Wa: 789; WaS1: 221
The Picture of Dorian Gray
    Du: 169; EN: 129; ENE:
    267-268; ENES1: 240;
    ENES2: 259; LCAB: 191;
    Ma: 2291
"The Portrait of Mr. W.H."
    Wa: 789; WaS1: 221
"The Remarkable Rocket" WaS1:
    221-222
"Requiescat" PE: 500
La Sainte Courtisane Br: 731
Salomé Br: 731; DC1: 222;
    EDC: 561-562; EDT: 327-
    331, 333-334; Ma: 2292;
    MBD: 98; MD: 321
"The Selfish Giant" Wa: 789;
    WaS1: 222
"The Sphinx Without a Secret"
    WaS1: 222
"The Star-Child" Wa: 789;
    WaS1: 222
Vera; or, The Nihilists DC1:
    222; EDC: 562
A Woman of No Importance Br:
    731; DC1: 222; EDC: 562;
    EDT: 331; MD: 321
"The Young King" Wa: 789;
    WaS1: 222
WILDENBRUCH, Ernst von
Der Mennonit DC2: 376
WILDER, Amos
    General Po: 4653
WILDER, Thornton Niven
    General ALL: 296-297; AN:
    261-262; Br: 731-733; CN:
    569-570; LCAB: 191; Lon:
    50-52; MD: 321-323; MDAE:
    516; Ne: 100-101; Po:
    4654-4660; Wo: 216-217
The Alcestiad ADC: 394; Br:
    733; MD: 323
The Angel That Troubled the
    Waters Br: 733; MD: 323
The Bridge of San Luis Rey
    AN: 261; CN: 570-571;
    Ma: 2293; Po: 4660; Wo:

217

The Cabala CN: 571; Ma:
2293

The Eighth Day CN: 571;
Ma: 2293-2294; Wo: 217

The Flight into Egypt ADC:
394

A Happy Journey to Trenton
and Camden ADC: 394;
Br: 733; DC1: 222

Heaven's My Destination
CN: 571-572; LCAB:
191; Ma: 2294; Po: 4655,
4661; Wo: 217

The Ides of March AN: 261;
CN: 572; LCAB: 191;
Ma: 2294

A Life in the Sun ADC: 394-
395; Br: 734; MDAE:
516

The Long Christmas Dinner
ADC: 395; Br: 734; DC1:
222; MD: 323

The Matchmaker ADC: 395;
Br: 734; DC1: 222; MD:
323; MDAE: 516; Po:
4655, 4659, 4661

The Merchant of Yonkers
ADC: 395-396; Br: 734

Nascunter poetae Po: 4661

Our Town ADC: 396-397;
Br: 734-736; DC1: 223;
Lon: 50-52; Ma: 2294-
2295; MD: 323; MDAE:
516; Po: 4659, 4662;
TMBP: 148

Plays for Bleeker Street
[three plays: Infancy;
Childhood; and Someone
from Assissi] ADC: 397-
398; Br: 736

Pullman Car Hiawatha ADC:
398; Br: 736

Queens of France ADC:
398; Br: 736

The Skin of Our Teeth
ADC: 398-399; Br: 736-
737; DC1: 223-224; Lon:
50; Ma: 2295; MD: 324;
Po: 4655, 4658-4659, 4662

Sloth Br: 737

Such Things Only Happen
in Books Br: 737

The Trumpet Shall Sound
Br: 737

The Woman of Andros AN:

261; CN: 572; Ma: 2295-
2296

WILDING, Michael
"The Sybarites" WaS1: 222

WILKES, John
General EC: 149-150

WILKINS, George
General ERP: 513-518; Log:
270-274
The Miseries of Enforced Mar-
riage DC1: 224
Pericles ERP: 513-518

Wilkins, Mary E. see FREEMAN,
Mary E. Wilkins

WILKINSON, Anne
General Po: 4663

WILKINSON, Brenda Scott
General BAF: 292

WILKINSON, Ellen C.
Clash ENES2: 259

WILLARD, John
The Cat and the Canary ADC:
399

WILLARD, Samuel
General AP: 588-589

WILLIAM OF SHOREHAM
"Marye, Mayde Mylde and Fre"
PE: 500

WILLIAMS, Adisa O.
General BALE: 416

WILLIAMS, Ben Ames
General ASF: 601; Po: 4663
"Thrifty Stock" ASF: 601

Williams, Bert see WILLIAMS,
Egbert Austin

WILLIAMS, Charles
General BN2: 112-113; Br:
738; MBD: 99; Po: 4664-
4667; Ri2: 561-568, 570-573;
Sch: 308-311
All Hallows' Eve ENES1: 241;
ENES2: 259-260; Po: 4668;
Ri2: 564, 567-569; Sch:
311
The Death of Good Fortune
Br: 738
Descent into Hell BN2: 112;
ENES1: 241; ENES2: 260;
LCAB: 191; Po: 4668; Ri2:
567, 569; Sch: 311
Grab and Grace Br: 738
The Greater Trumps ENES2:
260; Po: 4669; Ri2: 570;
Sch: 311
He Came Down from Heaven
Ri2: 562

The House by the Stable
  Br: 738
The House of the Octopus
  Br: 738; Ri2: 573
Judgment at Chelmsford Br:
  738; DC1: 224; Po: 4669;
  Ri2: 573
Many Dimensions ENES1:
  241; ENES2: 260; Ri2:
  570
The Place of the Lion
  ENES2: 260; Ri2: 564
Seed of Adam Br: 738;
  MBD: 99; Po: 4669;
  Ri2: 573
Shadows of Ecstasy ENES2:
  260
Thomas Cranmer of Canter-
  bury Br: 738; Po: 4669-
  4670; Ri2: 570, 573
War in Heaven ENES2: 260;
  LCAB: 191-192; Ri2:
  564, 570
WILLIAMS, Clarence
  "Ugly Chile" PE: 500
WILLIAMS, Daniel
  General WIL: 180
WILLIAMS, Denis
  General WIL: 181
  Other Leopards WIL: 181-
  182
  The Third Temptation WIL:
  182
WILLIAMS, Egbert Austin [Bert
  WILLIAMS]
  General BAP: 211; BAW:
  771; MBA: 208
WILLIAMS, Emlyn
  General Br: 738; LCAB:
  192; MD: 324; MDAE:
  517; Mi: 280-281
  Accolade DC1: 224; EDC:
  562
  The Corn Is Green Br:
  738-739; DC1: 224; EDC:
  562-563; MD: 324
  Druid's Rest EDC: 563
  He Was Born Gay EDC: 563
  He Was Born King Br: 739
  The Late Christopher Bean
  Br: 739
  The Light of Heart Br:
  739; EDC: 563
  Morning Star EDC: 563;
  MD: 324
A Murder Has Been Arranged

  EDC: 563
Night Must Fall Br: 739;
  EDC: 563
Someone Waiting EDC: 563
Spring 1600 EDC: 563
Trespass Br: 739; EDC: 563
Vessels Departing EDC: 564
Wind of Heaven EDC: 564
Yesterday's Magic EDC: 564
WILLIAMS, Espy
  Dante and Beatrice DC1: 224
  Parrhasius DC1: 224
WILLIAMS, George Washington
  General BAW: 772
WILLIAMS, Gordon Maclean
  General Ai: 335
WILLIAMS, Heathcote
  General MDAE: 518; TMBP:
  270
  AC/DC TMBP: 270-271
  The Local Stigmatic TMBP:
  270-271
  The Speakers TMBP: 270
WILLIAMS, Helen Maria
  "The History of Perourou; or,
  The Bellows-Maker" WaS1:
  222
WILLIAMS, J. Ellis
  The Aftermath DC1: 224
WILLIAMS, Jesse Lynch
  And So They Were Married
  ADC: 400
  Why Marry? ADC: 400
WILLIAMS, John
  Butcher's Crossing AAL:
  247; Po: 4670
WILLIAMS, John Ajala
  General MBA: 208-209
  Ghetto 1999 MBA: 209
WILLIAMS, John Alfred
  General AAF: 79-80; AAW:
  77; BAF: 293-295; BAW:
  775-776
  The Angry Ones AAL: 248
  Captain Blackman AAF: 80;
  AAL: 247; BAF: 295
  The Junior Bachelor Society
  BAF: 295
  The Man Who Cried I Am AAF:
  79-80; AAL: 247-248;
  AAW: 77; BAF: 294-296;
  BAW: 775-776; Ma: 2297
  Mothersill and the Foxes BAF:
  296
  "Navy Black" ASF: 601
  Night Song AAL: 248; BAF:

296; Ma: 2297-2298
Sissie AAL: 248; BAF:
    296-297; Po: 4670
"Son in the Afternoon" ASF:
    602; WaS1: 222
Sons of Darkness, Sons of
    Light BAF: 297; Ma:
    2298
WILLIAMS, John B.
    General ASF: 602
WILLIAMS, Joy
    "Taking Care" WaS1: 222
WILLIAMS, Oscar
    General Po: 4670
    "The Leg in the Subway"
        ICBAP: 140; PE: 500;
        Po: 4671
    "The Praying Mantis Visits a
        Penthouse" PE: 500
Williams, Paulette see SHANGE,
    Ntozake
WILLIAMS, Roger
    General AP: 548-554; Da:
        45-46
    A Key into the Language of
        America AP: 551-552,
        554
WILLIAMS, Samm
    Welcome to Black River MBA:
        209
WILLIAMS, Tennessee [Thomas
    Lanier WILLIAMS]
    General ALL: 297-299; ASF:
        603-604; Br: 739-744;
        LCAB: 192; Lon: 52-55;
        MD: 324-327; MDAE:
        524-529; Po: 4671-4684
    "The Angel in the Alcove"
        ASF: 602; Wa: 789
    At Liberty ADC: 400; Br:
        745; MDAE: 529; Po:
        4684
    Baby Doll Br: 745; MD:
        327; MDAE: 525; Po:
        4678, 4684
    Battle of Angels ADC:
        400; Br: 745; DC1:
        224-225; MD: 327; MDAE:
        528; Po: 4684
    Camino Real ADC: 400-401;
        Br: 745-747; DC1: 225;
        Ma: 2299; MD: 327-
        328; MDAE: 524, 526,
        528-529; Po: 4684-4685;
        TMAP: 54
    Cat on a Hot Tin Roof ADC:

401-403; Br: 747-748; DC1:
    225; Lon: 54; Ma: 2299-
    2300; MD: 328; MDAE:
    527-529; Po: 4677, 4679-80,
    4685-87
"Desire and the Black Masseur"
    ASF: 602; Ma: 2300-2301;
    Po: 4687; SFC: 203; Wa:
    789; WaS1: 223
The Eccentricities of a Nightin-
    gale ADC: 403
"The Field of Blue Children"
    ASF: 602; Wa: 789
The Garden District [two plays:
    Suddenly Last Summer and
    Something Unspoken] see
    also Something Unspoken;
    Suddenly Last Summer
    ADC: 403; Br: 748; MD:
    328
The Glass Menagerie ADC:
    403-405; Br: 748-749; DC1:
    225-226; Lon: 52; Ma:
    2301-2302; MD: 328-329;
    Po: 4673, 4687-4688
The Gnädiges Fräulein see also
    Slapstick Tragedy MDAE:
    524; Po: 4689
"Hard Candy" ASF: 602
Hello from Bertha MD: 329
I Can't Imagine Tomorrow
    ADC: 406
I Rise in Flame, Cried the
    Phoenix ADC: 406; Br:
    749; MD: 329; MDAE: 527;
    Po: 4689
"The Important Thing" Wa:
    789
In the Bar of a Tokyo Hotel
    ADC: 406; MDAE: 527
Kingdom of Earth ADC: 406;
    ASF: 602; Wa: 790
"Knightly Quest" ASF: 602;
    Wa: 790
The Lady of Larkspur Lotion
    DC1: 226; Po: 4683
"The Malediction" Wa: 790
"Man Bring This Up Road"
    ASF: 603; Wa: 790
The Milk Train Doesn't Stop
    Here Anymore ADC: 406-
    407; Br: 749; Po: 4680
"The Mysteries of Joy Rio"
    ASF: 603; Wa: 790
The Night of the Iguana ADC:
    407-408; ASF: 603; Br:

750; DC1: 226; LCAB: 192; Ma: 2302-2303; MD: 329; MDAE: 527; Po: 4680, 4689-90; TMAP: 171; Wa: 790

"One Arm" ASF: 603; Po: 4690; SFC: 203; Wa: 790

Orpheus Descending ADC: 408-409; Br: 750-751; DC1: 226; LCAB: 192; Ma: 2303-2304; MD: 329; MDAE: 525, 528; Po: 4678, 4690-4691

Period of Adjustment ADC: 409-410; Br: 751; DC1: 226; MD: 329; MDAE: 526; Po: 4691

"Portrait of a Girl in Glass" Wa: 790

Portrait of a Madonna ADC: 410

The Purification ADC: 410

The Red Devil Battery Sign ADC: 410

"The Resemblance Between a Violin Case and a Coffin" ASF: 603; Wa: 790

The Roman Spring of Mrs. Stone AN: 262; CN: 573; MDAE: 526; Po: 4691

The Rose Tattoo ADC: 410-411; Br: 751-752; DC1: 226-227; Lon: 53; Ma: 2304; MD: 329-330; MDAE: 528; Po: 4673, 4691; TMAP: 175

"Rubio y Morena" Wa: 790

Slapstick Tragedy [two plays: The Mutilated and The Gnädiges Fräulein] see also The Gnädiges Fräulein ADC: 411; MDAE: 524

Small Craft Warnings ADC: 411-412

Something Unspoken see also The Garden District Br: 752; MD: 330

Stairs to the Roof Br: 752; MD: 330

A Streetcar Named Desire ADC: 412-414; ALL: 299; Br: 752-755; DC1: 227-228; LCAB: 192; Lon:

53-54; Ma: 2305-2306; MD: 330-331; MDAE: 527; Po: 4673, 4677, 4683, 4692-4693; TMBP: 93, 99

Suddenly Last Summer see also The Garden District ADC: 414-415; Br: 755; DC1: 228; Lon: 53; Ma: 2306; MD: 331; MDAE: 526; Po: 4678, 4694; TMAP: 173, 175

Summer and Smoke ADC: 415-416; Br: 755-756; DC1: 228; Lon: 52; Ma: 2306-2307; MD: 331; Po: 4673, 4694

Sweet Bird of Youth ADC: 416; Br: 756-757; DC1: 228; LCAB: 192; Lon: 52-53; Ma: 2307-2308; MD: 331-332; MDAE: 526-527; Po: 4695-4696

This Is (an Entertainment) ADC: 417

This Property Is Condemned ADC: 417; Br: 757; DC1: 228; Po: 4683

"Three Players of a Summer Game" ASF: 603; Po: 4696; Wa: 790

27 Wagons Full of Cotton ADC: 417; Br: 757; MD: 332

The Two-Character Play ADC: 417

"Two on a Party" ASF: 603; Wa: 790

Vieux Carré ADC: 417

"The Vine" ASF: 603; Wa: 790

"The Yellow Bird" ASF: 603; Wa: 790-791

_____ and Donald WINDHAM
You Touched Me! ADC: 417-418; Br: 757-758; DC1: 229; MD: 332; Po: 4696

WILLIAMS, Thomas
"Goose Pond" ASF: 604; LCAB: 192; Wa: 791

WILLIAMS, Vinnie
Walk Egypt Po: 4697

WILLIAMS, William Carlos
General ALL: 300-304; AN: 262; ASF: 605-606; ICBAP: 140; LCAB: 192; MDAE: 530; MP: 107-109; Po: 4697-4711
"The Accident" ASF: 604;

Wa: 791
"Address" PE: 500
"The Agonized Spires" PE: 500
"Another Year" PE: 500
"Asphodel, That Greeny Flower" ALL: 301; ICBAP: 140; Ma: 2309; MP: 107-108; PE: 500-501
"The Attic Which Is Desire" ICBAP: 140; PE: 501; Po: 4712
"Between Walls" ICBAP: 140; PE: 501; Po: 4712
"Blizzard" PE: 501
"The Botticellian Trees" PE: 501
"The Burden of Loveliness" SFC: 204; Wa: 791
"Burning the Christmas Greens" PE: 501
"By the Road to the Contagious Hospital" PE: 501
"Catastrophic Birth" PE: 501
"Choral: The Pink Church" ICBAP: 140; PE: 503; Po: 4712
"Classic Scene" PE: 501
"The Clouds" PE: 501
"The Cold Night" PE: 501
"The Cold World" SFC: 204; Wa: 791
"Comedy Entombed: 1930" Wa: 791
"A Coronal" PE: 502
"Danse Pseudomacabre" Wa: 791
"The Dawn of Another Day" SFC: 204; Wa: 791
"Death the Barber" PE: 502
"The Descendant of Kings" SFC: 204; Wa: 791
"The Descent" [from Paterson] PE: 502
"The Desert Music" ALL: 301-302; ICBAP: 140; Ma: 2309-2310; MP: 108; PE: 502; Po: 4712
A Dream of Love Br: 758
"Elaine" PE: 502
"An Elegy for D.H. Lawrence" PE: 502
"A Face of Stone" ASF: 604; SFC: 204; Wa: 791
"The Farmer's Daughters" ASF: 605; Po: 4712-4713; Wa: 791
"Flowers by the Sea" PE: 502
"A Flowing River" PE: 502
"Four Bottles of Beer" ASF: 605
"Full Moon" PE: 502
"The Gift" PE: 502
"The Girl with a Pimply Face" Wa: 792
"The Great American Novel" Po: 4713; SFC: 204; Wa: 792
"The Great Figure" PE: 502
"Great Mullen" ICBAP: 140; PE: 502; Po: 4713
"El Hombre" PE: 502
"The Horse Show" PE: 502
"The Hunter" PE: 502
"The Hunters in the Snow" PE: 503
Imaginations Po: 4713
In the American Grain Ma: 2310-2311; Po: 4714
"Jean Beicke" ASF: 605; SFC: 204; Wa: 792
"The Knife of the Times" Wa: 792
Kora in Hell MP: 107-108; Po: 4715
"Lear" PE: 503
"Life Along the Passaic River" ALL: 300; Wa: 792
"Lines: Leaves Are Greygreen" PE: 503
"The Locust Tree in Flower" ICBAP: 140; PE: 503; Po: 4715
"Love Song" PE: 503
Many Loves ADC: 418; Br: 758; Po: 4715
"Mind and Body" SFC: 204; Wa: 792
"The Monstrous Marriage" PE: 503
"Nantucket" PE: 503
"A Night in June" Wa: 792
"Old Doc Rivers" ASF: 605; SFC: 204; Wa: 792
"The Orchestra" ICBAP: 140; PE: 503
Paterson ALL: 300-303; ICBAP: 140-141; Ma: 2311-2313; MP: 107-109; Po: 4715-4722

"Philomena Andronico" PE:
503
"Pictures from Brueghel"
ALL: 301; Po: 4722
"Pink and Blue" Wa: 792
"Portrait of a Lady" PE:
503
"Portrait of a Woman at Her
Bath" PE: 503
"The Pot of Flowers" PE:
503
"Queen-Ann's Lace" PE:
503
"The Red Wheelbarrow"
ICBAP: 141; Ma: 2313-
2314; PE: 503-504
"The Revelation" PE: 504
"The Right of Way" PE:
504
"The Rose" PE: 504
"St. Francis Einstein of the
Daffodils" PE: 504
"Sea-Trout and Butterfish"
PE: 504
"Song" ICBAP: 141; PE:
504
"A Sort of a Song" PE:
504
Spring and All Po: 4722-
4723
"Struggle of Wings" PE:
504
"The Term" ICBAP: 141;
PE: 504; Po: 4723
"This Is Just to Say" PE:
504
"The Three Graces" PE:
504
"The Three Letters" Wa:
792
Tituba's Children Br: 758
"To a Dog Injured in the
Street" PE: 505
"To a Poor Old Woman" PE:
505; Po: 4723
"To a Solitary Disciple"
ICBAP: 141; PE: 505
"To Be Recited to Flossie on
Her Birthday" PE: 505
"To Waken an Old Lady"
ICBAP: 141; PE: 505;
Po: 4723
"Tract" PE: 505; Po: 4723
"The Use of Force" ASF:
605; Ma: 2314-2315; Po:
4724; SFC: 204; Wa:

792-793; WaS1: 223
"The Venus" SFC: 204; Wa:
793
A Voyage to Pagany Po: 4724
"The Well-Disciplined Bargeman"
PE: 505
"The Widow's Lament in Spring-
time" PE: 505
"Without Invention Nothing Is
Well Spaced" ICBAP: 141;
PE: 505
"The World Contracted to a
Recognizable Image" PE:
505
"The Yachts" ICBAP: 141;
LCAB: 192; Ma: 2315-2316;
PE: 505; Po: 4724
"The Yellow Chimney" PE:
506
"The Young Housewife"
ICBAP: 141; PE: 506; Po:
4725
"Young Sycamore" PE: 506
WILLIAMSON, Harvey M.
General BAF: 298
WILLIAMSON, Henry
The Dream of Fair Women
ENES2: 260
The Flax of Dream ENES2:
260; Po: 4725
The Pathway ENES2: 260
The Patriot's Progress ENES2:
260
WILLIAMSON, Jack
General ASF: 607; LCAB:
192
"Breakdown" ASF: 606; WaS1:
223
"Non-Stop to Mars" WaS1:
223
"Star Bright" WaS1: 223
"With Folded Hands..." ASF:
606
WILLINGHAM, Calder
General Po: 4725
End as a Man ADC: 418
Eternal Fire CN: 573
WILLIS, Harold
A Sound of Silence ADC: 418
WILLIS, Nathaniel Parker
General AD: 211-212; AN:
262; ASF: 607; LCAB: 193
Bianca Visconti AD: 211-212
Tortesa the Usurer AD: 211-
212
WILLOUGHBY [or WILLOBY],

Henry
Avisa SC: 102
WILLS, William
General EDT: 337
WILMOT, John, Earl of Roches-
ter
General Bon: 28-29; LCAB:
149; Me: 343-351
"Against Constancy" PE:
506
"Allusion to Horace" PE:
506; Me: 349-350
"By All Love's Soft, Yet
Mighty Powers" PE: 506
"Epitaph on Charles II" PE:
506
"Fair Chloris in a Pigsty
Lay" PE: 506
"The Fall" PE: 506
"The Imperfect Enjoyment"
PE: 506; Me: 344, 347,
350
"A Letter from Artemisia to
Chloe" PE: 506-507; Me:
345, 348-350
"Love and Life" PE: 507
"The Maim'd Debauchee"
PE: 507; Me: 348
"A Ramble in St. James's"
PE: 507
"Rodomontade on His Cruel
Mistress" Me: 343
"Satire Against Reason and
Mankind" Bon: 28;
LCAB: 149; Me: 344-349;
PE: 507
Sodom: Or the Quintessence
of Debauchery DC1: 229
"Song of a Young Lady to
Her Ancient Lover" PE:
507
"Timon" PE: 507
"Tunbridge Wells" ICBAP:
105; PE: 507
"Upon Nothing" PE: 508;
Me: 348
Valentinian Bon: 28-29;
Me: 351
WILMOT, Robert
Gismond of Salerne [Tancred
and Gismund] DC1: 229
WILNER, Herbert
"Dovisch in the Wilderness"
ASF: 607
WILSON, Alexander
General Ai: 85

WILSON, Angus
General BN2: 113-114; CFAE:
425-427; CN: 573-574;
LCAB: 193; Po: 4725-4728;
Sch: 312
Anglo-Saxon Attitudes CN:
574; ENE: 268; ENES1:
241; ENES2: 260; Ma: 2317
"Et Dona Ferentes" SFC: 204;
Wa: 793
"Fresh Air Fiend" Wa: 793
Hemlock and After CFAE:
426; CN: 574-575; ENE:
268; ENES1: 241; ENES2:
260; Ma: 2317-2318; Po:
4726, 4728
Late Call CFAE: 427; CN:
575; ENE: 268-269; ENES1:
241; ENES2: 261; Ma:
2318; Po: 4726-4727
The Middle Age of Mrs. Eliot
CFAE: 427; CN: 575; ENE:
269; ENES1: 241; ENES2:
261; Ma: 2318-2319; Po:
4726-4727; Sch: 313
No Laughing Matter CFAE:
427; CN: 576; ENE: 269;
ENES1: 241-242; ENES2:
261; Ma: 2319; Po: 4728-
4729; Sch: 313
The Old Men at the Zoo CFAE:
426; CN: 576; ENE: 269;
ENES1: 242; ENES2: 261;
Ma: 2319-2320; Po: 4729;
Sch: 313
"Raspberry Jam" Wa: 793
"Realpolitik" Wa: 793
WILSON, Charles P.
General BAW: 779
WILSON, Colin
General CFAE: 429-430; CN:
576; Po: 4729-4730; Sch:
313-314
Adrift in Soho CN: 576;
ENES2: 261
The Black Room ENES2: 261
The Glass Cage ENES2: 261
The God of the Labyrinth
ENES2: 261
Lingard ENES2: 261
The Mind Parasites ENES2:
261; Po: 4729
Necessary Doubt ENES2: 261
The Outsider Po: 4730
The Philosopher's Stone ENES2:
261

Religion and the Rebel Po: 4730

Ritual in the Dark CN: 576; ENES1: 242; ENES2: 261

The Schoolgirl Murder Case ENES2: 262

The Sex Diary of Gerard Sorme ENES2: 262

The Violent World of Hugh Greene [The World of Violence] CN: 577; ENES2: 262

WILSON, Doric

Now She Dances! ADC: 418

The West Street Gang ADC: 418

WILSON, Edmund

General ALL: 304-305; APC: 194-197; LCAB: 193; Ma: 2322-2324; MDAE: 533; Po: 4730-4734

"After the Game" Wa: 793

The Age of Defeat LCAB: 193

The American Earthquake ALL: 304

Axel's Castle Ma: 2321; Po: 4734

Beppo and Beth Br: 758

Classics and Commercials Ma: 2321-2322; Po: 4731-4732

The Cold War and the Income Tax LCAB: 193

The Crime in the Whistler Room Br: 758

Cyprian's Prayer Br: 758

The Dead Sea Scrolls Po: 4734

"The Death of a Soldier" Wa: 793

"Ellen Terhune" SFC: 204; Wa: 794

"Emily in Hades" Wa: 794

"Galahad" Wa: 794

"Glimpses of Wilbur Flick" Wa: 794

I Thought of Daisy ALL: 304; Ma: 2322

"Lieutenant Franklin" Wa: 794

The Little Blue Light ADC: 419; Br: 758; DC1: 229

"The Man in the Mirror" Wa: 794

"The Man Who Shot Snapping Turtles" Wa: 794

Memoirs of Hecate County ALL: 304; AN: 263; Ma: 2324

"The Men from Rumpelmayer's" Wa: 794

"The Messiah at the Seder" Wa: 794

"The Millhollands and Their Damned Soul" Wa: 794

"Mr. and Mrs. Blackburn at Home" SFC: 205; Wa: 794

O Canada Po: 4735

"The Oppressor" Wa: 794

Patriotic Gore ALL: 304; LCAB: 193; Ma: 2324-2325; Po: 4735-4737

"The Princess with the Golden Hair" SFC: 205; Wa: 794

"Reunion" Wa: 794

The Shores of Light Ma: 2325; Po: 4731-4732

This Room and This Gin and These Sandwiches Br: 758

"Through the Abruzzi with Mattie and Harriet" Wa: 794

To the Finland Station ALL: 304; Ma: 2325-2326

The Triple Thinkers Ma: 2326

The Wound and the Bow Ma: 2326

WILSON, Ethel

General Po: 4737

"God Helps the Young Fisherman" Wa: 795

Hetty Dorval Po: 4737

"Hurry, Hurry" Wa: 795

The Innocent Po: 4738

"Mrs. Golightly and the First Convention" Wa: 795

"One Nimpish Lake" Wa: 795

WILSON, Frank

General AAPD: 335

Brother Mose [Meek Mose] BAP: 212-213; Br: 758; MBA: 209

Sugar Cane BAP: 212; MBA: 209

Walk Together, Chillun BAP: 212-213; MBA: 209-210

WILSON, Harry Leon

General LCAB: 193

WILSON, Jack
  Dark Eden ENES2: 262
  The Tomorrow Country
    ENES2: 262
WILSON, James
  General AP: 589
WILSON, John [1627?-1696]
  General Li: 320
  The Cheats Li: 320
Wilson, John [1785-1854] see
  NORTH, Christopher
WILSON, Lanford
  General MDAE: 535; TMAP:
    238-239
  Brontosaurus ADC: 419
  The Family Continues TMAP:
    239
  Fifth of July TMAP: 239-
    240
  The Gingham Dog ADC:
    419; TMAP: 240
  The Great Nebula in Orion
    TMAP: 240
  Him TMAP: 240
  Home Free! ADC: 419;
    TMAP: 240
  The Hot l Baltimore ADC:
    419; TMAP: 239-240
  Ikke, Ikke, Nye, Nye, Nye
    TMAP: 241
  Lemon Sky ADC: 419;
    TMAP: 239, 241
  Ludlow Fair ADC: 419;
    TMAP: 241
  The Madness of Lady Bright
    ADC: 420; TMAP: 239,
    241
  The Mound Builders ADC:
    420; TMAP: 241
  The Rimers of Eldritch ADC:
    420; TMAP: 239, 241-242
  The Sand Castle TMAP:
    239
  Serenading Louie ADC:
    420; TMAP: 242
  A Tale Told TMAP: 242
  Talley's Folly TMAP: 238,
    242-243
  This Is the Rill Speaking
    ADC: 420; Br: 759;
    TMAP: 243
  Wandering ADC: 420;
    TMAP: 243
WILSON, Phillip
  "One World" Wa: 795
WILSON, Robert

  The Cobbler's Prophecy DC1:
    229
  Deafman Glance ADC: 420
  I Was Sitting on My Patio This
    Guy Appeared I Thought I
    Was Hallucinating ADC: 420
  A Letter for Queen Victoria
    ADC: 420
  The Life and Times of Joseph
    Stalin ADC: 421
  The Life and Times of Sigmund
    Freud ADC: 421
  A Mad Man a Mad Giant a Mad
    Dog a Mad Urge a Mad Face
    ADC: 421
  Overture ADC: 421
  The Three Ladies of London
    DC1: 229
  _____ and Christopher KNOWLES
  The $ Value of Man ADC: 421
WILSON, Robley
  "The Apple" Wa: 795
WILSON, Sloan
  "A Letter of Admonition" SFC:
    205; Wa: 795
  The Man in the Gray Flannel
    Suit Po: 4738
WILSON, Thomas
  General SC: 102
WILTSE, David
  Suggs ADC: 421
WINCHILSEA, Anne Finch, Count-
    ess of
  General EC: 150; Me: 418-
    420
  "Adam Pos'd" Me: 419
  "An Affliction" PE: 185, 508
  "An Invocation to Sleep" PE:
    508
  "Nightingale" Me: 419
  "A Nocturnal Revery" Me:
    419-420; PE: 508
  "The Spleen" Me: 419-420;
    PE: 508
  "Tree" Me: 419
WINKLER, Eugen Gottlob
  General Po: 4738
WINSLOW, Anne Goodwin
  General ASF: 607; Po:
    4739
  "Allan Percy's Son" Wa: 795
  "Count Robert's Folly" Wa:
    795
  "A Winter in Geneva" Wa:
    795
WINTER, John Keith

The Shining Hour DC1: 229
_____ and Hattie May PAVLO
The Passionate Men ADC:
422
WINTERS, Shelly
One Night Stands of a Noisy
Passenger [three plays:
The Noisy Passenger, Un
Passage, and Last Stand]
ADC: 422
WINTERS, Yvor
General APC: 200-201;
ICBAP: 141; LCAB: 193;
Po: 4739-4743
"At the San Francisco Air-
port" ICBAP: 141
"Before Disaster" PE: 508
"The Brink of Darkness"
Wa: 796
"The California Oaks"
ICBAP: 141
"The Invaders" PE: 508
"Midas" PE: 508
"The Old Age of Theseus"
PE: 508
"Orpheus" PE: 508
"Sir Gawaine and the Green
Knight" ICBAP: 141
"The Slow Pacific Swell"
PE: 508
"A Spring Serpent" PE:
508
"A Summer Commentary"
ICBAP: 141; PE: 508
WINTHROP, John
General AP: 556-558; Da:
47
WINTHROP, Theodore
General ASF: 607
"Love and Skates" ASF:
607
"Saccharissa Mellasys" ASF:
607; Wa: 796
WIRT, William
General AP: 559-560; Da:
105
WISE, Isaac Mayer
General JW: 316
WISE, John
General AP: 562-563; Da:
47-48
WISEMAN, Adele
General JW: 354
The Sacrifice JW: 354
WISEMAN, Nicholas
Fabiola ENES2: 262

WISHENGRAD, Morton
The Rope Dancers Br: 759
WISTER, Owen
General AN: 263; ASF: 608;
LCAB: 194; Po: 4743-4745;
Wo: 220-221
"The Gift Horse" ASF: 608;
Wa: 796
Hank's Woman ASF: 608; Po:
4745; Wa: 796; Wo: 220
"How Lin McLean Went East"
ASF: 608
"Padre Ignazio" ASF: 608
"Philosophy Four" Wa: 796
"The Right Honorable the
Strawberries" ASF: 608
The Virginian AN: 263; Ma:
2327; Po: 4745-4746; Wo:
220-221
"The Winning of the Biscuit
Shooter" ASF: 608
WITHER, George
General Ba: 116
"A Christmas Carol" ICBAP:
142; PE: 508
WITKIEWICZ, Stanislaw Ignacy
General Br: 759; Po: 4747-
4748
Anonymous Work [Bezimienne
Dzieto] EDC: 564
Beelzebub Sonata; or What
Really Happened at Mor-
dowar [Sonata Belzebuba,
Czyli Prawdziwe Zdarzenie
w Mordowarze] EDC: 564
Insatiability Fi: 494
The Madman and the Nun; or,
There Is Nothing Bad Which
Could Not Turn into Some-
thing Worse [Wariat i Zakon-
nica, Czyli Nie ma Ztego,
Co By Na Jeszcze Gorsze
nie Wyszto] EDC: 564
The Shoemakers [Szewcy]
EDC: 564
They [Oni] EDC: 564
The Water Hen [Kurka Wodna]
EDC: 565; Po: 4748
WITTIG, Monique
Les Guerilleres Fi: 180
The Opoponax LCAB: 194
WITTLINGER, Karl
Do You Know the Milky Way?
[Kennen Sie die Milch-
strasse?] Br: 759
WIZENAIKE, Punyakante

"My Daughter's Wedding"
WaS1: 223
WODEHOUSE, Pelham Grenville
General Po: 4749-4750
Laughing Gas ENES2: 262
Leave It to Psmith ENES2:
262
Love Among the Chickens
ENES1: 242
Mike ENES1: 242
Old Reliable ENES2: 262
Piccadilly Jim ENES2: 262
Psmith in the City ENES1:
242; ENES2: 262
Psmith Journalist ENES2:
262
Something Fresh ENES1:
242; ENES2: 262
Thank You, Jeeves ENES1:
242; ENES2: 262-263
Uneasy Money ENES1: 242
The White Feather ENES1:
242
WOHMANN, Gabriele
"The Boxing Match" WaS1:
223
"Hamster, Hamster!" WaS1:
223
"Internal Excuse" WaS1:
223
"The Sailing Regatta" WaS1:
224
"A Scandal for the Park"
WaS1: 224
"Seaway" WaS1: 224
"Sunday at the Kreisands"
WaS1: 224
"The Truth About Us" WaS1:
224
WOLCOT, John [Peter PINDAR]
"Ode Upon Ode" ICBAP:
142
WOLF, Christa
Der geteilte Himmel Fi:
398; Po: 4750
Kindheitsmuster Fi: 398
The Quest for Christa T.
Fi: 398
WOLF, Friedrich
General Br: 759
Patrioten DC2: 376
Professor Mamlock Br: 760
Sailors of Cattaro [Die Mat-
rosen von Cattaro] Br:
760
WOLFE, Bernard

General Po: 4750
WOLFE, Thomas
General ALL: 305-309; AN:
264-268; ASF: 610-611;
LCAB: 194-195; MD: 332;
Ne: 102-106; Po: 4750-4766;
Wo: 225-227
"Boom Town" Po: 4766; SFC:
205; Wa: 796
"Chickamauga" ASF: 608; SFC:
205; Wa: 796
"Child by Tiger" ASF: 609;
SFC: 205; Wa: 796; WaS1:
224
"Circus at Dawn" SFC: 205;
Wa: 796
"The Company" Wa: 796
Concerning Honest Bob Br:
760
"Death the Proud Brother"
ASF: 609; Po: 4766
Deferred Payment Br: 760
"God's Lonely Man" Po: 4756;
SFC: 205; Wa: 796-797
"The Hills Beyond" ASF: 609;
Po: 4766
"'I Have a Thing to Tell You'"
ASF: 609
"In the Park" ASF: 609; Wa:
797
"The Lion at Morning" ASF:
609; SFC: 205; Wa: 797
Look Homeward, Angel ALL:
308; AN: 263-264; LCAB:
195; Ma: 2328-2330; Ne:
105-106; Po: 4750, 4752,
4763, 4765-4770
"The Lost Boy" ASF: 609; Ma:
2330; Po: 4756; SFC: 205;
Wa: 797
Mannerhouse Br: 760; DC1:
230; MD: 332; Po: 4770
"No Cure for It" SFC: 205;
Wa: 797
"No Door" ASF: 609; Po:
4770; Wa: 797
"A Note on Experts" ASF:
609; Wa: 797
Of Time and the River AN:
264; Ma: 2330-2331; Po:
4759, 4763, 4765, 4771; Wo:
226
"Oktoberfest" ASF: 609
"Old Man Rivers" ASF: 610
"Only the Dead Know Brooklyn"
Wa: 797

"The Party at Jack's" ASF:
610
"A Portrait of Bascom Hawke"
ASF: 610; Wa: 797
The Return of Buck Gavin
Br: 760
"The Return of the Prodigal"
SFC: 206; Wa: 797
The Third Night Br: 760
The Web and the Rock AN:
264; Ma: 2331-2332; Ne:
105; Po: 4763, 4771
"The Web of Earth" ASF:
610; SFC: 206; Wa: 797-
798; WaS1: 224
Welcome to Our City Br:
760; MD: 332
You Can't Go Home Again
AN: 264; Ma: 2332-2333;
Ne: 104; Po: 4750, 4763,
4772
WOLFENSTEIN, Alfred
Fahrt Po: 4772
WOLFERT, Ira
General AN: 268; CN: 577
Married Men CN: 577
Tucker's People CN: 577
WOLFF, Egon Raul
General Br: 760; Po: 4772
A Touch of Blue [La niña
madre; La polla] Br: 761
WOLFRAM VON ESCHENBACH
Parzival Ma: 2334-2335
WOLFSKEHL, Karl
General Po: 4773
WOLFSON, Victor
American Gothic ADC: 422
Bitter Stream ADC: 422
Excursion ADC: 422
Pride's Crossing ADC: 422
WOLLSTONECRAFT, Mary
General EC: 150-151
WONODI, Okogbule
General BALE: 416-417
"Why Are We Here" BALE:
416-417
WOOD, Anthony
General Bon: 79
WOOD, Charles
General LCAB: 195; MDAE:
537; TMBP: 276-277
A Bit of Family Feeling
TMBP: 277
A Bit of a Holiday TMBP:
276
Dingo MDAE: 537

H: Being Monologues in Front
of Burning Cities MDAE:
537; TMBP: 277
Meals on Wheels TMBP: 277
Veterans TMBP: 276-277
WOOD, Maxine
On Whitman Avenue Br: 761
WOOD, Mrs. Henry
General BN: 113
East Lynne ENES2: 263
Johnny Ludlow ENES2: 263
Mrs. Halliburton's Troubles
ENES1: 243
WOOD, Odella Phelps
General BAF: 299; BAW:
781
WOODE, Nathaniel
The Conflict of Conscience
DC1: 230
WOODS, John
"Best in the Orchard" PE:
509
WOODWORTH, Samuel
General AD: 214-215
The Cannibals, or Massacre Is-
land ADC: 423
The Deed of Gift ADC: 423
The Forest Rose, or American
Farmers AD: 214-215;
ADC: 423
La Fayette, or The Castle of
Olmutz ADC: 423
The Widow's Son, or Which Is
the Traitor? ADC: 423
WOOLF, Leonard Sidney
General Po: 4773
"Pearls and Swine" WaS1: 224
"A Tale Told by Moonlight"
WaS1: 224
"Three Jews" WaS1: 224
"The Two Brahmans" WaS1:
224
The Village in the Jungle
ENES1: 243; ENES2: 263;
Po: 4774
The Wise Virgins ENES1: 243
WOOLF, Virginia
General BN2: 115-118; LCAB:
195; Po: 4774-4784; Ri2:
581-588, 596-597; Sch: 314-
322
Between the Acts EN: 129-
130; ENE: 270; ENES1:
243-244; ENES2: 263-264;
Ma: 2336-2337; Po: 4784-
4785; Ri2: 589-590; Sch:

322
The Common Reader Po: 4785
"The Duchess and the Jeweller" SFC: 206; Wa: 798
Flush Ma: 2337-2338
"A Haunted House" Po: 4786; SFC: 206; Wa: 798
Jacob's Room BN2: 118; EN: 130-131; ENE: 270; ENES1: 244; ENES2: 264; Ma: 2338-2339; Po: 4776, 4783; Ri2: 590; Sch: 322-323
"Kew Gardens" SFC: 206; Wa: 798; WaS1: 224
"The Lady in the Looking Glass" Wa: 798
"Lappin and Lapinova" Wa: 798
"The Legacy" Wa: 798
"Lives of the Obscure" Po: 4786
"The Man Who Loved His Kind" Wa: 798
"The Mark on the Wall" SFC: 206-207; Wa: 799
Mr. Bennett and Mrs. Brown Po: 4786
"Moments of Being" Po: 4791; SFC: 207; Wa: 799
"Monday or Tuesday" SFC: 207; Wa: 799
Mrs. Dalloway BN2: 116-118; EN: 131-134; ENE: 270-272; ENES1: 244-245; ENES2: 264-266; LCAB: 195; Ma: 2339-2340; Po: 4774, 4776, 4782-4783, 4786-4791; Ri2: 591-592; Sch: 323-325
"Mrs. Dalloway in Bond Street" WaS1: 224
"The New Dress" SFC: 207; Wa: 799; WaS1: 224
Night and Day EN: 134-135; ENE: 272; ENES1: 246; ENES2: 266; Ma: 2340-2342; Ri2: 592; Sch: 325
Orlando EN: 135-136; ENE: 272-273; ENES1: 246;

ENES2: 266; Ma: 2342-2343; Po: 4792-4794; Ri2: 592-593; Sch: 325-326
A Room of One's Own ENE: 273; Ma: 2343-2344
"The Shooting Party" Wa: 799
"A Society" SFC: 207; Wa: 799
"Solid Objects" SFC: 207; Wa: 799-800
"The String Quartet" SFC: 207; Wa: 800
"A Summing Up" Wa: 800
Three Guineas ENE: 273; Ma: 2344
To the Lighthouse BN2: 115-116, 118; EN: 136-138; ENE: 273-274; ENES1: 246-248; ENES2: 267-268; LCAB: 195; Ma: 2344-2346; Po: 4774-4775, 4782-4783, 4794-4797; Ri2: 593-595; Sch: 326-327
"An Unwritten Novel" SFC: 207; Wa: 800
The Voyage Out EN: 138-139; ENE: 274; ENES1: 248; ENES2: 268; Ma: 2346-2347; Po: 4782; Ri2: 595; Sch: 327-328
The Waves BN2: 117; EN: 139-140; ENE: 274-275; ENES1: 248-249; ENES2: 268-269; Ma: 2347-2349; Po: 4775, 4778, 4782, 4797-4799; Ri2: 595-596; Sch: 328-329
The Years EN: 140-141; ENE: 275; ENES1: 249; ENES2: 269-270; Ma: 2349-2350; Po: 4799-4800; Ri2: 596; Sch: 329
WOOLLCOTT, Alexander
General Po: 4800
WOOLMAN, John
General AP: 567-570; Da: 48
WOOLRICH, Cornell
General ASF: 612
"The Loophole" ASF: 612
WOOLSON, Constance Fenimore
General AF: 244-245; AN: 268-269; ASF: 612; Cla: 122-123; Ho: 140; LCAB: 195
"At the Chateau of Corinne" Wa: 800
"Bro" Wa: 800

"Castle Nowhere" Wa: 800
"A Christmas Party" Wa: 800
"Dorothy" Wa: 800
East Angels AF: 244
"Felipa" Wa: 800
"A Florentine Experiment" Wa: 800
"For the Major" ASF: 612
"The Front Yard" ASF: 612; Wa: 800
"In Venice" ASF: 612; Wa: 800
"Jeannette" Wa: 800
"King David" ASF: 612; Wa: 801
"The Lady of Little Fishing" Wa: 801
"Misery Landing" Wa: 801
"Miss Elizabetha" Wa: 801
"'Miss Grief'" ASF: 612
"Neptune's Shore" Wa: 801
"The Old Agency" Wa: 801
"Old Gardiston" ASF: 612; Wa: 801
"Peter the Parson" Wa: 801
"The Pink Villa" Wa: 801
"Rodman the Keeper" Wa: 801
"St. Clair's Flats" Wa: 801
"Sister St. Luke" Wa: 801
"The South Devil" Wa: 801
"The Street of the Hyacinth" Wa: 801
"A Transplanted Boy" Wa: 801
"Up in the Blue Ridge" Wa: 801
"A Waitress" Wa: 801
Wooton, Sir Henry see WOTTON, Sir Henry
WORBOISE, Emma Jane
The House of Bondage ENES2: 270
Overdale ENES2: 270
Thornycroft Hall ENES2: 270
WORDSWORTH, William
General EDT: 338-340; Fog: 67-72; ICBAP: 142; LCAB: 195; Re: 85-98
"Anecdote for Fathers" ICBAP: 142
"Animal Tranquility and Decay" PE: 509
"Anticipation. October, 1803" PE: 509
"The Barberry-Tree" ICBAP: 142
The Borderers DC1: 230; EDT: 338-340; Fog: 72
"The Brothers" PE: 509
"The Childless Father" PE: 509
"Composed Among the Ruins of a Castle in North Wales" PE: 509
"Composed Upon Westminster Bridge" PE: 509-510
"The Daffodils" Fog: 72; ICBAP: 142
"The Danish Boy" PE: 510
"Descriptive Sketches" Fog: 72; ICBAP: 142
"Elegiac Stanzas" ["Peele Castle"] ICBAP: 142; PE: 510
"An Evening Walk" PE: 510; Re: 94
The Excursion Fog: 72; ICBAP: 142; Re: 88, 91, 92, 94
"The Fountain" PE: 510
"Goody Blake and Harry Gill" PE: 510
"Hart-Leap Well" PE: 510
"Home at Grasmere" Re: 89, 91
"I Grieved for Buonaparte" PE: 511
"I Thought of Thee, My Partner and My Guide" PE: 511
"I Travelled Among Unknown Men" PE: 511
"I Wandered Lonely as a Cloud" ICBAP: 142; LCAB: 195-196; PE: 511-512
"I Watch and Long Have Watched with Calm Regret" PE: 512
"The Idiot Boy" ICBAP: 142; PE: 510-511
"Inscription for the House (an Outhouse) on the Island of Grasmere" ICBAP: 142
"It Is a Beauteous Evening" PE: 511
"It Is Not to Be Thought Of" PE: 511
"Laodamia" PE: 512
"Lines Composed a Few Miles

Above Tintern Abbey"
  Fog: 75; ICBAP: 144;
  LCAB: 196; Ma: 2351-
  2352; PE: 512-513
"Lines Written in Early
  Spring" PE: 513
"London, 1802" PE: 513
"Lucy Gray, or Solitude"
  PE: 513; Re: 94
"Lyrical Ballads" Fog:
  72; Ma: 2352; Re: 90-
  91, 94
"The Mad Mother" PE: 513
"Matthew" PE: 513
"Michael" Fog: 73; PE:
  513-514; Re: 89
"Mutability" PE: 514
"My Heart Leaps Up When I
  Behold" PE: 514
"A Night-Piece" PE: 514
"Nutting" Fog: 72; ICBAP:
  143; PE: 514
"October, 1803" ["When
  Looking on the Present
  Face of Things"] ICBAP:
  143; PE: 514
"Ode: Intimations of Immor-
  tality" Fog: 72-73;
  ICBAP: 143; LCAB: 196;
  Ma: 2353-2354; PE: 514-
  515; Re: 90, 94, 96
"Ode to Duty" PE: 515
"The Old Cumberland Beg-
  gar" PE: 516
"On the Extinction of the
  Venetian Republic" PE:
  516
"On the Power of Sound"
  ICBAP: 143; PE: 516
"Peele Castle" see "Elegiac
  Stanzas"
"Personal Talk" ICBAP:
  143
Peter Bell Fog: 73; ICBAP:
  143; Re: 87, 94
"A POET!--He Hath Put His
  Heart to School" Fog:
  73; PE: 516
"A Poet's Epitaph" PE:
  516
"Power of Music" PE: 516
The Prelude Fog: 73-74;
  ICBAP: 143; LCAB:
  196; Ma: 2354-2355; Re:
  88-90, 92-94, 96
"The Recluse" Fog: 74

"Resolution and Independence"
  Fog: 74; ICBAP: 143;
  LCAB: 196; PE: 516-517;
  Re: 90
"The Ruined Cottage" ICBAP:
  143; PE: 517; Re: 88, 96
"Salisbury Plain" PE: 517;
  Re: 96
"The Sea Was Laughing at a
  Distance, All" PE: 517
"She Dwelt Among Untrodden
  Ways" ICBAP: 143; PE:
  517
"She Was a Phantom of Delight"
  PE: 517
"Simon Lee" PE: 517
"Simplon Pass" ICBAP: 144
"A Slumber Did My Spirit Seal"
  ICBAP: 144; PE: 517-518
"Sole Listener, Duddon! To
  the Breeze That Played"
  PE: 518
"Solitary Reaper" Fog: 75;
  ICBAP: 144; PE: 518-519
"Stanzas Written in My Pocket-
  Copy of Thomson's 'Castle
  of Indolence'" PE: 519
"Stepping Westward" PE: 519
"Strange Fits of Passion Have
  I Known" PE: 519
"Surprised by Joy--Impatient
  as the Wind" PE: 519
"The Tables Turned" ICBAP:
  144
"The Thorn" Fog: 75; PE:
  519-520; Re: 87
"Three Years She Grew in Sun
  and Shower" PE: 520
"Tintern Abbey" see "Lines
  Composed a Few Miles Above
  Tintern Abbey"
"To Lucy" ICBAP: 144
"To My Sister" PE: 520
"To the Cuckoo" PE: 520
"The Tuft of Primroses" PE:
  520
"The Two April Mornings"
  PE: 520
"Vernal Ode" PE: 521
"We Are Seven" PE: 521
"The White Doe of Rylstone"
  Re: 89-90
"The Winds Come to Me from
  the Fields of Sleep" PE:
  521
"The World Is Too Much with

Us" Fog: 75; PE: 521
"Written in Very Early Youth"
PE: 521
"Yarrow Revisited" PE: 521
"Yarrow Unvisited" PE: 521
"Yarrow Visited" PE: 521
"Yew-Trees" PE: 521
WORKMAN, James
Liberty in Louisiana ADC:
423
WORKU, Daniachew
General BALE: 417
The Thirteenth Sun BALE:
417
WORREL, Patricia
General WIL: 183
WOTTON, Sir Henry
General Ba: 116-117
"A Hymn to My God..." PE:
521
WOTTON, Sir Henry [trans-
lator]
A Courtlie Controversie of
Cupids Cautels by Jacques
YVER ERP: 519-520
WOUK, Herman
General AN: 269-270; CFAE:
431-432; CN: 577; JW:
318; Po: 4800-4801
The Caine Mutiny AN: 269;
CFAE: 431-432; CN:
577-578; JW: 318; Po:
4800-4802
The Caine Mutiny Court-Mar-
tial ADC: 423-424; Br:
761
The City Boy AN: 269
Marjorie Morningstar An:
269; CN: 578-579; JW:
318; LCAB: 196; Po:
4800-4802
Nature's Way ADC: 424
This Is My God Po: 4802
The Traitor ADC: 424
The Winds of War JW: 318
Youngblood Hawke CN: 579
WRATISLAW, Theodore William
Graf
General TA: 307
WRIGHT, Austin Tappan
Islandia Po: 4802
WRIGHT, Charles Stevenson
General BAF: 300-301;
BAW: 785
The Messenger BAF: 301
The Wig BAF: 301; Po:

4803
WRIGHT, Harold Bell
General AN: 270
The Eyes of the World Po:
4803
WRIGHT, James
General ICBAP: 144; MP:
110; Po: 4803-4804
"The Accusation" PE: 521
"Ars Poetica: Some Recent
Criticism" PE: 522
"As I Step Over a Puddle at
the End of Winter, I Think
of an Ancient Chinese Gov-
ernor" LCAB: 196; MP:
110; PE: 522
"At the Slackening of the Tide"
ICBAP: 144; PE: 522;
Po: 4804
"Autumn Begins in Martin's
Ferry, Ohio" PE: 522
The Branch Will Not Break
Po: 4803-4804
"A Centenary Ode: Inscribed to
Little Crow, Leader of the
Sioux" PE: 522
"A Dream of Burial" PE: 522
"Gambling in Stateline, Nevada"
PE: 522
The Green Wall Po: 4803-4804
"The Idea of the Good" PE:
522
"I Try to Waken and Greet the
World Once Again" PE: 522
"Lying in a Hammock at William
Duffy's Farm in Pine Island,
Minnesota" PE: 522
"Many of Our Waters: Varia-
tions on a Poem by a Black
Child" PE: 522
"The Morality of Poetry" PE:
522
"The Old WPA Swimming Pool
in Martins Ferry, Ohio" PE:
522
"On the Skeleton of a Hound:
PE: 523
Saint Judas Po: 4803-4804
"To the Ghost of a Kite" PE:
523
WRIGHT, Judith
General Po: 4804-4806
"Dark Gift" Po: 4806
Five Senses Po: 4806-4807
WRIGHT, Margaret
"Happy New Year" Wa: 802

WRIGHT, Richard

General AAF: 64-68; AAL:
252-256; AAPD: 336-337;
AAW: 78-80; ALL: 309-
311; AN: 270-271; ASF:
614-616; BAF: 303-314;
BAP: 213, 215; BAW:
789-790; Br: 761; CN:
579-580; ICBAP: 144;
LCAB: 196; MBA: 210;
Ne: 107-108; Po: 4807-
4812; Wo: 231-233

"Almos' a Man" see "The
Man Who Was Almost a
Man"

"Between the World and Me"
PE: 523

"Big Black Good Man" ASF:
613; Wa: 802

"Big Boy Leaves Home"
ASF: 613; Wa: 802;
WaS1: 225

Black Boy AAL: 254-255;
BAF: 313; BAW: 789;
Ma: 2356; Ne: 107-108;
Wo: 232

"Bright and Morning Star"
ASF: 613; Ma: 2356-2357;
SFC: 208; Wa: 802;
WaS1: 225

Daddy Goodness AAPD:
336-337

"Down by the Riverside"
ASF: 613; Wa: 802-803;
WaS1: 225

Eight Men BAF: 314; Po:
4812

"Fire and Cloud" ASF: 613;
Wa: 803; WaS1: 225

"The Juggler" BAW: 790

Lawd Today AAL: 255;
BAF: 307, 314-315; CN:
581

"Long Black Song" ASF:
613; Ma: 2357; SFC:
208; Wa: 803; WaS1:
225

The Long Dream BAF: 315;
Br: 761; CN: 581

"Man, God Ain't Like That"
ASF: 613; Wa: 803

"Man of All Work" ASF:
613; Wa: 803

"The Man Who Killed a
Shadow" Wa: 803

"The Man Who Lived Under-
ground" AAF: 65-66; ASF:
614; BAF: 311; LCAB: 196;
Po: 4813; Wa: 803-804;
WaS1: 225

"The Man Who Saw the Flood"
ASF: 614

"The Man Who Was Almost a
Man" ASF: 614; MBA:
210; Wa: 804; WaS1: 225

"The Man Who Was Almost a
Shadow" ASF: 614

Native Son AAF: 64-66; AAL:
254; AAW: 78-79; ALL:
309-310; AN: 270; BAF:
303-315; BAW: 789-790;
CN: 581-583; LCAB: 196;
Ma: 2357-2359; Ne: 107-
108; Po: 4812-4816; Wo:
231-233

The Outsider AAF: 68; AAL:
254-255; AAW: 78-80; BAF:
305, 307, 312-313, 315-316;
BAW: 789-790; CN: 583;
LCAB: 196; Ma: 2359-2360;
Ne: 107-108; Po: 4812,
4816-4817; Wo: 232

Savage Holiday CN: 584

"Silt" Wa: 804

"Superstition" ASF: 614

Uncle Tom's Children ALL:
310; BAF: 307, 316; BAW:
789; Wo: 232

"The Voodoo of Hell's Half-
Acre" ASF: 614

——————— and Louis SAPIN

Daddy Goodness ADC: 424;
BAP: 213-214; Br: 761;
MBA: 210

WRIGHT, Sarah E.

General BAF: 316; BAW:
792

This Child's Gonna Live BAF:
317

WRIGHT, Willard Huntingdon [S.S.
VAN DINE]

General Po: 4817

WROTH, Lady Mary

Urania ENES2: 270; ERP:
520-521

WU TSU-HSIANG

"Fan Village" WaS1: 225

WULFSTAN

Homilies Hen: 15

WYATT, Sir Thomas

General ICBAP: 144; LCAB:
196; SC: 102-104

"At Last Withdraw Your Cruelty" PE: 523

"Avysing the Bright Beams of These Fair Eyes" PE: 523

"Behold Love, Thy Power How She Despiseth" PE: 523

"Desire, Alas, My Master and My Foe" PE: 523

"Disdain Me Not" PE: 523

"Divers Doth Use as I Have Heard and Know" PE: 523

"Forget Not Yet the Tried Intent" PE: 523

"Hate Whome Ye List" PE: 523

"Heaven and Earth" PE: 523

"If Fancy Would Favor" PE: 523

"In Dowtfull Brest..." SC: 103

"In Eternum" PE: 523

"It May Be Good Like It Who List" PE: 524

"It Was My Choice, It Was No Chance" PE: 524

"The Long Love That in My Thought Doth Harbor" ICBAP: 144

"The Lover Compareth His State to a Ship in a Perilous Storm Tossed on the Sea" PE: 524

"Madame, withouten many wordes" SC: 103

"My Galy Charged with Forgetfulness" ICBAP: 145; PE: 524

"My Lute Awake!" ICBAP: 145; PE: 524

"My Poynz, I Cannot Frame Me Tune to Fayne" ICBAP: 145

"Ons as Me Thought Fortune Me Kyst" PE: 524

"Patience, Though I Have Not" PE: 524

"Penitential Psalms" ICBAP: 145

"Processe of Tyme Worketh Suche Wounder" PE: 524

"Psalm 6" PE: 524

"Psalm 32" PE: 525

"Psalm 38" PE: 525

"Psalm 51" PE: 525

"Psalm 102" PE: 525

"Psalm 143" PE: 525

"Resound My Voyse; Ye Wodes That Here Me Plain" PE: 525

"There Was Never Nothing More Me Payned" PE: 525

"They Flee from Me" ICBAP: 145; LCAB: 197; PE: 525-526; SC: 102-103

"Tho I Cannot Your Crueltie Constrain" PE: 526

"To Wisshe and Want and Not Obtain" PE: 526

"Unstable Dream, According to the Place" PE: 526

"What Menythe Thys?" PE: 526

"What Word Is That" PE: 526

"Who So List to Hunt" PE: 526

"Ys Yt Possyble" PE: 524

WYCHERLEY, William

General Bon: 48-49; Li: 322-328

The Country Wife Bon: 48-49; DC1: 230-231; EDC: 565-566; Li: 323, 325-327; Ma: 2361-2362; MDAE: 69, 86, 398

The Gentleman Dancing Master DC1: 231; EDC: 567; Li: 325; Ma: 2362-2363

Love in a Wood; or St. James Park DC1: 231; EDC: 567; Li: 325; Ma: 2363-2364

The Man of Mode see ETHEREGE, George

The Plain Dealer Bon: 48-49; DC1: 232; EDC: 567-568; Li: 323, 327-328; Ma: 2364-2365

WYCLIF, John

[Sermons, Homilies, Polemical Tracts] Hen: 19

WYLIE, Elinor

General ALL: 311; AN: 271; LCAB: 197; Po: 4817-4818

"Castilian" PE: 526

"Cold-Blooded Creatures" PE: 526

"The Eagle and the Mole" Po:

4819
"Hymn to Earth" PE: 527;
Po: 4819
"Into the Poet's Shoes" Po:
4819-4820
"Puritan Sonnet" PE: 527
"Sanctuary" PE: 527
"This Corruptible" PE: 527
"The Tortoise in Eternity"
PE: 527
"Velvet Shoes" PE: 527;
Po: 4820
"Venetian Glass Nephew"
Wa: 804
WYLIE, Philip
General APC: 80; ASF:
616; LCAB: 197
WYMARK, Owen
General MDAE: 538
WYNDHAM, John
General LCAB: 82
"Consider Her Ways" WaS1:
225
The Day of the Triffids
ENES2: 270
Re-Birth ENES2: 271
Trouble with Lichen ENES2:
271
WYNTER, Sylvia
General WIL: 182
The Hills of Hebron WIL:
182-183
Shh ... It's a Wedding WIL:
183
WYSS, Johann Rudolf
The Swiss Family Robinson
LCAB: 197; Ma: 2366
WYZEWA, Teodor de
General Po: 4820

Y

YAARI, Yehudah
"Between the Dog and the
Shepherd" Wa: 804
YACINE, Kateb
General Po: 4821
Nedjma Po: 4821
YAKUBOVICH, Pyotr Filipovich
In the World of Castaways
Ke: 458
YAÑEZ, Augustín
General Po: 4822
Al filo del agua Po: 4823-
4824

Divina floración Po: 4822
Llama de amor viva Po: 4822
La tierra pródiga Po: 4824
Las tierras flacas Po: 4824
YANKOWITZ, Susan
General MDAE: 539
Still Life ADC: 424
_____ and Joseph CHAIKIN
Terminal ADC: 424-425
YANOVSKY, Yury
Living Water Ke: 458
YARINGTON, Robert
General Log: 274
Two Lamentable Tragedies
DC1: 232
YATES, Richard
"A Really Good Jazz Piano"
LCAB: 197; WaS1: 225
YEATS, Jack Butler
General Po: 4825
In Sand Br: 762
La La Noo Br: 762
The Scourge of the Gulph Br:
762
YEATS, William Butler
General Br: 762-766; ICBAP:
145; LCAB: 197; Ma:
2370-2371; MBD: 100-106;
MD: 332-336; Mi: 281-283;
MP: 112-115; Po: 4825-
4902; TA: 309-310
"An Acre of Grass" ICBAP:
145; PE: 529; Po: 4902-
4903
"Adam's Curse" PE: 527; Po:
4903
"After Long Silence" PE: 527;
Po: 4903
"All Soul's Night" PE: 527
"Among School Children"
ICBAP: 145; Ma: 2367-
2368; PE: 528-529; Po:
4904
"Among School Children--V"
ICBAP: 145
"The Apparitions" PE: 529
"At Algeciras--A Meditation
Upon Death" PE: 529
At the Hawk's Well Br: 766;
DC1: 232-233; EDC: 568-
569; MBD: 101, 105-106;
MD: 336; Po: 4905
Autobiographies Po: 4905-
4906
"Baile and Aillinn" Po: 4842
"The Ballad of Father Gilligan"

PE: 529
"Before the World Was Made"
    PE: 529
"Beggar to Beggar Cried"
    PE: 529
"The Black Tower" ICBAP:
    145; PE: 529-530; Po:
    4906
"Blood and the Moon" PE:
    530
"A Bronze Head" ICBAP:
    146; PE: 530; Po: 4906
"Byzantium" ICBAP: 146;
    Ma: 2368-2369; PE: 530-
    531; Po: 4897, 4899, 4906-
    4908
Calvary Br: 766-767; DC1:
    233; EDC: 569; MBD:
    100, 102; MD: 336; Po:
    4896, 4908
"The Cap and Bells" ICBAP:
    146; PE: 531; Po: 4908
"Cast a Cold Eye" PE: 532
The Cat and the Moon Br:
    767; EDC: 569; MD: 336;
    PE: 532
Cathleen ni Houlihan Br:
    767; DC1: 233; EDC:
    569; Po: 4909
The Celtic Twilight Po:
    4865
"The Chambermaid's First
    Song" ICBAP: 146; PE:
    532
"The Chambermaid's Second
    Song" ICBAP: 146; PE:
    532
"The Choice" PE: 532
"The Circus Animals' Deser-
    tion" PE: 532
"A Coat" Po: 4909
"The Cold Heaven" PE: 532
"The Collar-Bone of a Hare"
    PE: 532
"Come Gather Round Me
    Parnellites" PE: 532
"The Coming of Wisdom with
    Time" PE: 532
"Coole Park" PE: 532
"Coole Park and Ballylee,
    1931" ICBAP: 146; PE:
    532; Po: 4909
The Countess Cathleen Br:
    767-768; DC1: 233; EDC:
    569-570; MBD: 101, 105;
    MD: 336-337; Po: 4909-

4910
Country of the Young Po:
    4910
"Crazy Jane and Jack the Jour-
    neyman" PE: 533
"Crazy Jane and the Bishop"
    PE: 533
"Crazy Jane Grown Old Looks
    at the Dancers" ICBAP:
    146; PE: 533
"Crazy Jane on God" PE: 533
"Crazy Jane on the Day of
    Judgment" PE: 533
"Crazy Jane" Poems Po: 4829,
    4841, 4868
"Crazy Jane Reproved" Po:
    4910-4911
"Crazy Jane Talks with the
    Bishop" ICBAP: 146; PE:
    533; Po: 4911
"The Crucifixion of the Outcast"
    Po: 4911
"Cuchulain Comforted" PE:
    533
"The Curse of Cromwell" PE:
    533
"Death" PE: 533
The Death of Cuchulain Br:
    768; DC1: 233; EDC: 570-
    571; MBD: 103, 105; MD:
    337; Po: 4911-4912
"The Death of the Hare" PE:
    533
"A Deep-Sworn Vow" PE: 533
Deirdre Po: 4912-4913
"The Delphic Oracle upon
    Plotinus" PE: 534; Po:
    4913
"Demon and Beast" PE: 534
"Dhoya" Po: 4914
"A Dialogue of Self and Soul"
    ICBAP: 146; LCAB: 197;
    PE: 534
Diarmuid and Grania Br: 769;
    MBD: 61; Po: 4914
Discoveries Po: 4914
"The Dolls" PE: 534; Po:
    4915
"The Double Vision of Michael
    Robartes" PE: 534
"Down by the Salley Gardens"
    Po: 4915
The Dreaming of the Bones
    Br: 769; DC1: 233; EDC:
    571; MBD: 101; MD: 337;
    Po: 4897, 4915

"Easter 1916" ICBAP: 146;
MP: 113; PE: 534; Po:
4915-4916
"Ego Dominus Tuus" PE:
535; Po: 4858
"The Empty Cup" PE: 535;
Po: 4929
"Father and Child" PE: 535
Fighting the Waves Br:
769; MD: 337
"First Love" PE: 535
"The Fisherman" PE: 535
"The Folly of Being Com-
forted" PE: 535; Po:
4916-4917
"For Anne Gregory" PE:
535
Four Plays for Dancers Br:
769; EDC: 571; MBD:
105; Po: 4883, 4917
"Friends" PE: 535
"A Friend's Illness" Po:
4917
"The Friends of His Youth"
PE: 535
A Full Moon in March Br:
770; EDC: 571; MBD:
101, 104-105; MD: 337-
338; Po: 4917-4918
"A General Introduction to
My Work" Po: 4918
The Green Helmet Br: 770;
EDC: 571-572; MBD:
102, 106; Po: 4841, 4918-
4919
"The Gyres" ICBAP: 146;
PE: 535-536; Po: 4919
"The Happy Townland" PE:
536
"The Hawk" PE: 536
"He Bids His Beloved Be at
Peace" PE: 536
"He Thinks of His Past
Greatness When a Part
of the Constellation of
Heaven" PE: 536
"Her Vision in the Wood"
ICBAP: 146; PE: 536;
Po: 4919
The Herne's Egg Br: 770;
DC1: 234; EDC: 572;
MD: 338; Po: 4920
"The Hero, the Girl, and
the Fool" Po: 4920-
4921
"High Talk" ICBAP: 146;

PE: 536; Po: 4921
"His Confidence" ICBAP: 146
"His Dream" PE: 536
"His Memories" PE: 536
"The Hosting of the Sidhe" PE:
536
The Hour Glass Br: 770-771;
DC1: 234; EDC: 572; MBD:
101, 104; MD: 338; PE:
537; Po: 4921-4922
"Human Dignity" PE: 537
"I Am of Ireland" PE: 537;
Po: 4922
"I Wander by the Edge" PE:
537
"In Memory of Eva Gore-Booth
and Con Markiewicz" PE:
537; Po: 4876
"In Memory of Major Robert
Gregory" PE: 537; Po:
4922-4923
"In the Seven Woods" PE:
537; Po: 4923
"The Indian to His Love" PE:
537
"Into the Twilight" PE: 537
"An Irish Airman Foresees His
Death" PE: 537; Po: 4923
The Island of Statues Br:
771
"John Kinsella's Lament for
Mrs. Mary Moore" PE: 537
"King and No King" ICBAP:
147
The King of the Great Clock
Tower Br: 771; EDC: 572;
MBD: 104; MD: 338
The King's Threshold Po:
4835, 4923-4924
"The Lady's First Song"
ICBAP: 147; PE: 538
"The Lady's Second Song"
ICBAP: 147; PE: 538
"The Lady's Third Song"
ICBAP: 147; PE: 538
"The Lake Isle of Innisfree"
ICBAP: 147; PE: 538; Po:
4873, 4924-4925
"The Lamentation of the Old
Pensioner" PE: 538
The Land of Heart's Desire
Br: 772; EDC: 572; MD:
338
"Lapis Lazuli" ICBAP: 147;
PE: 538; Po: 4866, 4925
Last Poems and Two Plays

Po: 4925-4926

"Leda and the Swan" ICBAP:
147; Ma: 2369; MP: 115;
PE: 538-539; Po: 4838,
4926-4927

"Line Written in Dejection"
PE: 539

"The Living Beauty" PE:
539

"Long-Legged Fly" ICBAP:
147; PE: 539-540; Po:
4866, 4889, 4927-4928

"The Lover Asks Forgive-
ness Because of His Many
Moods" ICBAP: 147

"The Lover Mourns for the
Change That Has Come
upon Him and His Beloved
and Longs for the End of
the World" PE: 540

"The Lover's Song" ICBAP:
147; PE: 540

"The Magi" ICBAP: 147;
PE: 540; Po: 4838, 4928-
4929

"The Man and the Echo" PE:
540

"The Man Who Dreamed of
Faeryland" PE: 540

"The Mask" PE: 540

"Meditations in Time of Civil
War" PE: 540; Po:
4839, 4929-4930

"Memory" PE: 541

"Men Improve with Years"
PE: 541

"The Mermaid" PE: 541

"Meru" PE: 541

"Michael Robartes and the
Dancer" PE: 541; Po:
4834, 4930

"Michael Robartes Asks For-
giveness Because of His
Many Moods" see "The
Lover Asks Forgive-
ness..."

"Mohini Chatterjee" PE: 541

"The Moods" PE: 541

"Mother of God" PE: 541;
Po: 4839

"The Municipal Gallery Revisited" ICBAP: 147;
PE: 541; Po: 4930

"The New Faces" PE: 541

"News for the Delphic Oracle"
ICBAP: 147; PE: 541-

542; Po: 4931

"Nineteen Hundred and Nineteen" ICBAP: 147; LCAB:
198; PE: 542; Po: 4931

"Old Tom Again" PE: 542

"On a Picture of a Black
Centaur by Edmund Dulac"
PE: 542; Po: 4931

"On a Political Prisoner" PE:
542; Po: 4876

On Baile's Strand Po: 4835;
Po: 4932

The Only Jealousy of Emer
Br: 772-773; DC1: 234;
EDC: 572-573; MBD: 105;
MD: 338-339; Po: 4932

"Parnell's Funeral" ICBAP:
148; PE: 542; Po: 4932

"The Phases of the Moon" PE:
542

The Player Queen Br: 773;
DC1: 234; EDC: 573;
MBD: 100, 102; MD: 339;
Po: 4933

The Pot of Broth Br: 773

"A Prayer for My Daughter"
ICBAP: 148; LCAB: 198;
PE: 542-543; Po: 4834,
4933

Purgatory Br: 773-774; DC1:
234-235; EDC: 573-574;
MBD: 100-106; MD: 339;
Po: 4897, 4934-4935

"Red Hanrahan's Song About
Ireland" PE: 543; Po:
4935

Responsibilities Po: 4841, 4935

"The Results of Thought" PE:
543

The Resurrection Br: 774;
DC1: 235; EDC: 574;
MBD: 100-101; MD: 339;
Po: 4896, 4935-4936

"Ribh at the Tomb of Baile and
Aillinn" PE: 543; Po: 4842

"Ribh Denounces Patrick" PE:
543

"Ribh in Ecstasy" PE: 543

"The Rose" PE: 543

"The Rose of Battle" PE: 543

"The Rose Tree" ICBAP: 148;
PE: 543

"Running to Paradise" PE:
543

"The Sad Shepherd" PE: 543;
Po: 4826

"Sailing to Byzantium"
ICBAP: 148; LCAB: 198;
Ma: 2371-2372; MP: 115;
PE: 543-546; Po: 4897,
4899, 4936-4939
"The Second Coming" ICBAP:
148; LCAB: 198; Ma:
2372-2373; PE: 546-547;
Po: 4940-4941
"The Secret Rose" PE: 547;
Po: 4865
"September 1913" PE: 547
The Shadowy Waters Br:
775; DC1: 235; EDC:
574; MBD: 105; MD:
339-340; Po: 4941
"The Song of the Happy
Shepherd" PE: 547; Po:
4826, 4941
"The Song of Wandering
Aengus" ICBAP: 148;
PE: 547; Po: 4942
Sophocles' King Oedipus Br:
775
"The Sorrow of Love" PE:
547
"The Spur" PE: 547; Po:
4942
"The Statues" PE: 547-548;
Po: 4889
"The Stolen Child" ICBAP:
148; PE: 548; Po: 4942
"Summer and Spring" PE:
548
"Symbols" PE: 548
"That the Night Come"
ICBAP: 148; PE: 548;
Po: 4943
"There" PE: 548
"The Three Bushes" ICBAP:
148; PE: 548; Po: 4943
"The Three Hermits" PE:
548
"Three Things" PE: 548
"A Thought from Propertius"
PE: 548
"To a Friend Whose Work
Has Come to Nothing"
PE: 548
"To a Shade" PE: 548
"To a Young Beauty" PE:
548
"To D.W." PE: 549
"To His Heart, Bidding It
Have No Fear" PE: 549
"Towards Break of Day"

Po: 4884, 4943
"The Tower" ICBAP: 148; Ma:
2373-2374; MP: 112, 114;
PE: 549; Po: 4825, 4839,
4944
"Two Songs from a Play" PE:
549
"The Two Trees" PE: 549; Po:
4944
"Under Ben Bulben" ICBAP:
148; PE: 549-550; Po: 4945
"Under the Moon" PE: 550
"Under the Round Tower" PE:
550
"Vacillation" PE: 550
"The Valley of the Black Pig"
PE: 550
A Vision MP: 113; PE: 550;
Po: 4889, 4946
"The Wanderings of Oisin" PE:
550; Po: 4947
"The Way of Wisdom" Po:
4947
"What Magic Drum?" PE: 550
"What Then?" PE: 550
"The Wheel" Po: 4884, 4947
"When You Are Old" PE: 550;
Po: 4947
"The White Birds" PE: 551
"Who Goes with Fergus?" PE:
551; Po: 4947
"The Wild Old Wicked Man" Po:
4948
"The Wild Swans at Coole"
ICBAP: 148; MP: 114; PE:
551; Po: 4840-4841, 4948-
4949
"The Winding Stair" MP: 113;
Po: 4825, 4949
"The Withering of the Boughs"
PE: 551
"A Woman Young and Old"
Po: 4949
The Words Upon the Window-
Pane Br: 776; DC1: 235;
EDC: 574-575; MBD: 100-
101; MD: 340; Po: 4897,
4949-4950
_____ and Lady GREGORY
Deirdre Br: 768-769; DC1:
233; EDC: 575; MBD:
100-101, 104; MD: 337; Po:
4912-4913
King Oedipus EDC: 575; MBD:
102
The King's Threshold Br:

771; DC1: 234; EDC:
575; MBD: 100-102; MD:
338
On Baile's Strand Br: 772;
DC1: 234; EDC: 576;
MBD: 101, 103; MD: 338
The Unicorn from the Stars
Br: 775; DC1: 235;
EDC: 576; MBD: 102-103;
MD: 340; Po: 4945
_____, Lady GREGORY, and
Douglas HYDE
Where There Is Nothing Br:
775-776; EDC: 576; MBD:
103, 106; MD: 340
YEH SHAO-CHÜN [YEH SHENG-
T'AO]
"Autumn" WaS1: 226
"The English Professor"
WaS1: 226
"Rice" WaS1: 226
YEHOSHUA, Abraham B.
"Continuing Silence of the
Poet" Wa 804
"Facing the Forest" Wa:
804
"A Long Summer's Day" Wa:
804
"Three Days and a Child"
Wa: 804
YELLEN, Samuel
"The Passionate Shepherd"
ASF: 617
YERBY, Frank
General AAW: 81; BAF:
318-319; BAW: 795; Po:
4950
Benton's Row BAF: 320
Bride of Liberty BAF: 320
Captain Rebel BAF: 320
The Dahomean BAF: 320
The Devil's Laughter BAF:
320
Fairoaks BAF: 320
Floodtide BAF: 320-321
The Foxes of Harrow BAF:
321
The Garfield Honor BAF:
321
The Girl from Storyville
BAF: 321
Goat Song BAF: 319, 321
The Golden Hawk BAF:
321
Griffin's Way BAF: 321-
322

"Health Card" ASF: 617
Judas, My Brother BAF: 322
An Odor of Sanctity BAF: 322
Pride's Castle BAF: 322
Saracen Blade BAF: 322
The Serpent and the Staff
BAF: 322
Speaks Now BAF: 322-323
Tobias and the Angel BAF:
323
The Vixens BAF: 323
"Wisdom" PE: 551
A Woman Called Fancy BAF:
323
YERBY, Lorees
The Last Minstrel ADC: 425
Save Me a Place at Forest Lawr
ADC: 425
YEROVI, Leonidas
General Br: 776
Yevtushenko, Evgeny see
EVTUSHENKO, Evgenii
Aleksandrovich
YEZIERSKA, Anzia
General ASF: 617; JW: 320
"Lost Beauty" Wa: 804
"Wings and Hunger" Wa: 804
YIZHAR, S.
"Before Leaving" Wa: 805
"Ephraim Returns to the Lu-
cerne" Wa: 805
"Ha-Shabui" Wa: 805
"The Prisoner" Wa: 805
"The Runaway" Wa: 805
YONGE, Charlotte Mary
General BN: 113-114
The Clever Woman of the Family
ENES1: 250
The Daisy Chain ENES1: 250;
ENES2: 271
The Heir of Redclyffe ENES1:
250; ENES2: 271
Hopes and Fears ENES1: 250
YORDAN, Philip
Anna Lucasta ADC: 425; Br:
776
Yorke, Henry Vincent see
GREEN, Henry
YOUD, Samuel
Pendulum ENES2: 271
YOUNG, Al
General BAF: 324; BAW:
797
Sitting Pretty BAF: 324
Snakes BAF: 324
Who Is Angelina? BAF: 324-

325
YOUNG, Andrew
  General Ai: 228
  The Adventures of Miss Lucy
    Watson ENES2: 271
YOUNG, Clarence, III
  Perry's Mission ADC: 425;
    BAP: 215; MBA: 211
YOUNG, Douglas
  General Ai: 301
YOUNG, E.H.
  The Curate's Wife ENES2:
    271
  Miss Mole ENES2: 271
  The Misses Mallett ENES2:
    271
YOUNG, Edward
  General EC: 151-152; Li:
    329; Me 423-425
  Night Thoughts EC: 151-
    152; ICBAP: 148; Me:
    423-425
  Universal Passion Me: 424
YOUNG, Ella
  General Po: 4950
YOUNG, Francis Brett
  General TA: 312
  The Black Diamond ENES1:
    250; ENES2: 271
  The City of Gold ENES1:
    250; ENES2: 271
  Dr. Bradley Remembers
    ENES1: 250
  Jim Redlake ENES1: 250
  My Brother Jonathan
    ENES1: 250
  Portrait of Clare ENES2:
    271
  This Little World ENES1:
    250
  Wistanlow ENES1: 251
YOUNG, Marguerite
  Miss MacIntosh, My Darling
    Po: 4951
YOUNG, Stanley
  Ask My Friend Sandy ADC:
    425
  Bright Rebel ADC: 426
  Mr. Pickwick ADC: 426
  Robin Landing ADC: 426
YOUNG, Stark
  General Po: 4951-4952
  The Saint ADC: 426; Br:
    776; DC1: 235; Po: 4952
  So Red the Rose AN: 271;
    Po: 4952

YOUNG, Thomas
  General AP: 589
YOUNG, Tommy Scott
  Southern Fried MBA: 211
YOURCENAR, Marguerite
  General Po: 4953
  Alexis, ou Le Traité du vain
    combat Po: 4954
  The Memoirs of Hadrian
    [Mémoires d'Hadrien] Ke:
    171; Po: 4954
  L'Oeuvre au noir Fi: 180
  Presentation critique de Con-
    stantin Cavafy Po: 4955
YOVKOV, Yordan
  "Shibil" Wa: 805
YU DAFU [YÜ TA-FU]
  "Late Blooming Osmanthus"
    WaS1: 226
  "The Past" WaS1: 226
  "Sinking" WaS1: 226
  "Ts'ia Shih Chi" WaS1: 226
YU, Ts'ao
  Sunrise DC2: 376
  Thunderstorm [Lei-yu] DC2:
    376
YUSHKEVICH, Semyon Solomono-
    vich
  The Jews Ke: 458-459
YVER, Jacques
  A Courtlie Controversie of
    Cupids Cautels see WOT-
    TON, Henry [translator]

Z

ZABOLOTSKII, Nikolay Alekseevich
  General Po: 4957
Zagal, Oscar Castro see CASTRO
    ZAGAL, Oscar
ZAIKA, Nikolai
  My Love Ke: 459
ZALDUMBIDE, Gonzalo
  General Po: 4958
ZAMACOIS, Eduardo
  General Po: 4958
ZAMYATIN, Eugeny
  General Po: 4958
  "The Cave" WaS1: 226
  Sever Fi: 494
  Uezdnoe Fi: 494
  We [My] Fi: 494-496; Ke:
    459; Po: 4959-4961
ZANGWILL, Israel
  General Br: 776; Po: 4961;

TA: 313-314
"Anglicization" Wa: 805
"The Bearer of Burdens" Wa: 805
"The Big Bow Mystery" Wa: 805
"Chad Gadya" Wa: 805
"Cheating the Gallows" Wa: 805
Children of the Ghetto ENES1: 251; ENES2: 272
"The Converts" Wa: 805
"The Diary of a Meshummad" Wa: 805
"A Double-Barrelled Ghost" Wa: 805
"Elijah's Goblet" Wa: 805
"The Gray Wig" Wa: 806
"The Hirelings" Wa: 806
"Holy Wedlock" Wa: 806
"I Become a Sorter" Wa: 806
"The Jewish Trinity" Wa: 806
Jimmy the Carrier ENES1: 251; ENES2: 272
"The Keeper of Conscience" Wa: 806
The King of Schnorrers ENES1: 251; ENES2: 272; Wa: 806
"The Land of Promise" Wa: 806
The Mantle of Elijah ENES1: 251; ENES2: 272
The Master ENES1: 251; ENES2: 272
"The Memory Clearing House" Wa: 806
"Merely Mary Ann" Wa: 806
"Messiah and Miracle" Wa: 806
"The Model of Sorrow" Wa: 806
"Noah's Ark" Wa: 806
"An Odd Life" Wa: 806
The Premier and the Painter ENES1: 251; ENES2: 272
"The Red Mark" Wa: 807
"The Sabbath Question in Sudminster" Wa: 807
"Samooborona" Wa: 807
"Satan Mekatrig" Wa: 807
"The Serio-Comic Governess"

Wa: 807
"They That Walk in Darkness" Wa: 807
"To Die in Jerusalem" Wa: 807
"Transitional" Wa: 807
"A Yiddish 'Hamlet'" Wa: 807
ZAPOLSKA, Gabriela
"The Cuckoo" Wa: 807
"Little Kitten" Wa: 807
"The Victim" Wa: 807
ZARDI, Federico
General Br: 776
ZARDOYA, Concha
Corral de vivos y muertos Po: 4961-4962
ZAYAS, María de
El castigo de la miseria Fi: 256
ZAYTSEV, Boris
Anna Ke: 459
Gleb's Journey Ke: 459
ZEITLIN, Israel [Cesar TIEMPO]
General Br: 777
Pan Criollo Br: 777
ZELAZNY, Roger
"The Graveyard Heart" Wa: 807
"A Rose for Ecclesiastes" Wa: 807
ZEMAN, Jack
Past Tense ADC: 426
ZENO GANDIA, Manuel
Cuentos Po: 4962
ZEPEDA, Eraclio
"Benzulu" WaS1: 226
"El Caguamo" WaS1: 226
ZEROMSKI, Stefan
Ashes Fi: 496; Ke: 459
"The Crows" Wa: 808
"Doctor Piotr" Wa: 808
"Dusk" Wa: 808
The Faithful River Ke: 459
The Homeless Ke: 459
Labours of Sisyphus Ke: 459
A Story of a Sin Ke: 460
"The Strong One" Wa: 808
"Whatever Happens, May It Strike Me" Wa: 808
ZETTLER, Michael
Please Hang Up and Dial Again ADC: 426
ZEVACO, Michel
General Po: 4962
ZEWI, Meki
General BALE: 417
ZIEGLERUS, Hieronymous

Samson DC2: 376
ZILAHY, L.
  The Angry Angel Ke: 460
  The Deserter Ke: 460
  The Dukays Ke: 460
  Two Prisoners Ke: 460
ZILLICH, Heinrich
  "Der baltische Graf" Wa:
    808
ZIMMER, Bernard
  General Br: 777
  Bava l'Africain Br: 777
  Pauvre Napoleon Br: 777
  Le Veau Gras Br: 777
  Les Zouaves Br: 777
ZINDEL, Paul
  And Miss Reardon Drinks a
    Little ADC: 426-427
  The Effect of Gamma Rays
    on Man-in-the-Moon Mari-
    golds ADC: 427
  Ladies at the Alamo ADC:
    427
  The Secret Affairs of Mildred
    Wild ADC: 427
ZIRIMU, Elvania N.
  General BALE: 417
ZIRIMU, Pio
  General BALE: 417
ZOE-OLDENBOURG, Madame
  Destiny of Fire Ke: 172
ZOFFER, G.
  The End of All Natural
    Things ADC: 427
ZOLA, Emile
  General LCAB: 198
  L'Argent Ke: 172
  L'Assommoir Fi: 180-181;
    Ke: 172
  Attack on the Mill Ke: 172
  Au bonheur des dames Fi:
    181; Ke: 172
  La Bête humaine Fi: 181;
    Ke: 172
  La Confession de Claude Ke:
    173
  The Conquest of Plassans
    Fi: 181; Ke: 173
  "Les coquillages de M.
    Chabre" Wa: 808
  La Curée Fi: 181-182; Ke:
    173
  La Débâcle Fi: 182; Ke:
    173
  Doctor Pascal [Le Docteur
    Pascal] Fi: 182; Ke:

    173; Ma: 2376
  The Downfall Ma: 2376
  Earth Ma: 2376-2377
  La Faute de l'abbé Mouret Fi:
    182-183; Ke: 173-174
  Fécondité Fi: 183; Ke: 174
  La Fortune des Rougon Fi:
    183-184; Ke: 174
  Germinal Fi: 184-185; Ke:
    174-175; Ma: 2377-2378
  The Joy of Life [La Joie de
    vivre] DC2: 377; Fi: 185;
    Ke: 175; Ma: 2378
  Labor Ma: 2378-2379
  Lourdes Ke: 175-176
  Madeleine Férat Ke: 176
  Nana Fi: 185; Ke: 176; Ma:
    2379
  L'Oeuvre Fi: 185-186; Ke:
    176-177
  Une Page d'amour Fi: 186
  Paris Fi: 186; Ke: 177
  Pot-Bouille Fi: 186; Ke: 177
  Le Rêve Ke: 177
  Rome Ke: 177
  Rougon-Macquart Fi: 186-187;
    Ke: 177; Ma: 2379-2380
  Son Excellence Eugène Rougon
    Fi: 187; Ke: 177
  La Terre Fi: 182; Ke: 177-
    178
  Thérèse Raquin DC2: 377; Fi:
    187; Ke: 178
  Travail Ke: 178
  Le Ventre de Paris Fi: 187-
    188; Ke: 178
  Vérité Fi: 188; Ke: 178
ZORILLA, Francisco Rojas y
  Apoteosis de don Pedro Calderon
    [Don Pedro Calderon] DC2:
    377
  Los Aspides de Cleopatra DC2:
    377
  Del Rey Abajo, Ninguno DC2:
    378
  Don Juan Tenorio DC2: 377-
    378
  Donde Hay Agravios no Hay
    Celos DC2: 377
  Lucrecia y Tarquino DC2: 378
  Morir Pensando Matar DC2:
    378
  Numancia cercada DC2: 378
  Numancia destruída DC2: 378
ZORIN, Leonid
  The Deck [Paluba] Br: 777

ZOSHCHENKO, Mikhail M.
   "Adventures of a Monkey"
      Po: 4962; Wa: 808
   "An Amusing Adventure"
      Wa: 808
   Before Sunrise [Pered Vosk-
      hodom Solntza] Fi: 496;
      Ke: 460; Po: 4962-4963
   "Healing and Psychics" Wa:
      808
   "Kocherga" Wa: 808
   Youth Restored Fi: 496;
      Ke: 460
ZSCHOKKE, Heinrich
   "Das Abenteuer der Neu-
      jahrsnacht" Wa: 808
   "The Dead Guest" Wa: 809
   "Jonathan Frock" Wa: 809
   Prinzessin von Wolfenbuttel
      Ke: 345
ZUBLY, John Joachim
   General AP: 571
ZUCKMAYER, Carl
   General Br: 778; MD:
      340-341; Po: 4963-4965
   The Captain from Kopenick
      [Der Hauptmann von
      Köpenick] Br: 778; DC2:
      379; Po: 4964-4965
   The Cold Light [Das Kalte
      Licht] Br: 778; DC2:
      379; MD: 341; Po: 4966
   The Devil's General [Des
      Teufels General] Br:
      778-779; DC2: 378-379;
      Po: 4964, 4966
   Des Gesang im Feuerofen
      Br: 779; DC2: 379
   Der Hauptmann von Köpenick
      see The Captain from
      Kopenick
   Herbert Engelmann Br:
      779; Po: 4965
   Das Kalte Licht see The
      Cold Light
   Kreutzweg Po: 4966
   Rivalen DC2: 379; Lon:
      25
   Schinderhannes DC2: 379;
      Po: 4964
   Des Teufels General see
      The Devil's General
   Ulla Winblad DC2: 379;
      MD: 341; Po: 4966-4967
ZUKOFSKY, Louis
   General JW: 134; MP: 117;

      Po: 4967
   "A" 1-12 MP: 117
   "Anew" PE: 551
   "For You I Have Emptied the
      Meaning" PE: 551
   "Glad They Were There" PE:
      551
   "Has the Sum" PE: 551
   "A Last Cigarette" PE: 552
   "Mantis" and "'Mantis' an In-
      terpretation" PE: 552
   "Poem Beginning 'The'" PE:
      552
ZUNZUNEGUI, Juan Antonio de
   General Po: 4967-4968
   Esta oscura desbandada Fi:
      256
   La vida como es Ke: 236; Po:
      4969
ZWEIG, Arnold
   General Po: 4969-4970
   "The Beast" Wa: 809
   Das Beil von Wandshek Fi:
      398
   The Case of Sergeant Grischa
      Fi: 398-399; Ke: 345
   "Coffee" Wa: 809
   "The Crow" Wa: 809
   The Crowning of a King [Ein-
      setzung eines Königs] Fi:
      399; Ke: 345
   "Departure" Wa: 809
   "Early Spring" Wa: 809
   Education Before Verdun [Er-
      ziehung vor Verdun] Fi:
      399; Ke: 345
   Einsetzung eines Königs see
      The Crowning of a King
   "The Enemy" Wa: 809
   "Episode" Wa: 809
   Erziehung vor Verdun see
      Education Before Verdun
   Die Feuerpause Fi: 399
   "The Firing Range" Wa: 809
   "Glance at Germany" Wa: 809
   "Helbret Friedenbringer" Wa:
      809
   Junge Frau von 1914 see
      Young Woman of 1914
   "Little Hero" Wa: 809
   "The Louse" Wa: 809
   "Man of Peace" see "Helbret
      Friedenbringer"
   "Notes About a Family Named
      Klopfer" Wa: 809
   Die Novellen um Claudia Fi:

399
"The Receipt" Wa: 809
"Revenge" Wa: 809
"Schönberg Quartet" Wa:
   810
"A Spot in the Eye" Wa:
   810
Versunkene Tage Fi: 399
"Wasps" Wa: 810
Young Woman of 1914 [Junge
   Frau von 1914] Fi: 399;
   Ke: 345
ZWEIG, Stefan
   General Po: 4970-4971
   Die Augen des ewigen
      Bruders see The Eyes
      of the Undying Brother
   "Brief einer Unbekannten"
      see "Letter from an Un-
      known Woman"
   "Brennendes Geheimnis" Wa:
      810
   Buch Mendel Fi: 399
   The Buried Candelabrum
      Ke: 345
   The Chess Game [The Royal

Game; Schachnovelle]
   Fi: 399; Po: 4971; Wa:
   810; WaS1: 226
The Eyes of the Undying
   Brother [Die Augen des
   ewigen Bruders] Wa:
   810; Ke: 345
Fantastic Night Ke: 345
Jeremiah Br: 779
"Leporella" Wa: 810; WaS1:
   226
"Letter from an Unknown
   Woman" ["Brief einer
   Unbekannten"] Wa: 810;
   WaS1: 226
The Royal Game see The
   Chess Game
Schachnovelle see The
   Chess Game
"Twenty-Four Hours in a
   Woman's Life" SFC: 208;
   Wa: 810
"Verwirrung des Gefühle"
   Wa: 810
ZWELONKE, D.M.
   General BALE: 417

Professor Alan Weiner is Chief, Reference Division, Baruch College Library. He holds an M.L.S. degree from Pratt Institute Graduate School of Library and Information Science and an M.P.A. degree from John Jay College. He has more than twenty years experience as a reference librarian in academic and public libraries and is actively engaged in the work of college-wide and professional organizations.

Professor Spencer Means, Assistant Chief, Reference Division, Baruch College Library, received his M.S.L.S. degree from the University of North Carolina at Chapel Hill and holds an M.A. degree in English from Duke University. He is the compiler of an annual bibliography of dissertations in comparative literature published by the American Comparative Literature Association.